Investigating Deviance

An Anthology

Bruce A. Jacobs
University of Missouri, St. Louis

Foreword by

Barry Glassner
University of Southern California

Roxbury Publishing Company
Los Angeles, California

Library of Congress Cataloging-in-Publication Data
  Jacobs, Bruce A. (Bruce Abel), 1968-
Investigating deviance : an anthology / Bruce A. Jacobs.
p. cm.
Includes bibliographical references and index
ISBN 1-891487-56-6
1. Deviant Behavior. I. Title
  HM811 .J33 2002
  302.5'42—dc21   2001019794
                                             CIP

Publisher: Claude Teweles
Managing Editor: Dawn VanDercreek
Production Editor: Joshua H. R. Levine
Production Assistants: Kathryn Croom, Todd Kingsley, and Carla Max-Ryan
Typography: Synergistic Data Systems
Cover Design: Marnie Kenney

Printed on acid-free paper in the United States of America. This book meets the standards for recycling of the Environmental Protection Agency.

ISBN 1-891487-56-6

ROXBURY PUBLISHING COMPANY
P.O. Box 491044
Los Angeles, California 90049-9044
Voice: (310) 473-3312 • Fax: (310) 473-4490
E-mail: roxbury@roxbury.net
Website: www.roxbury.net

Contents

Part I: Constructing Deviance

Howard S. Becker
Becker contends that deviant behavior is whatever is labeled as such by those with the power to do so.

Barry Glassner
An account of the media's role in generating fear to shape perceptions of deviance and social problems.

Kai T. Erikson
A discussion of basic issues in the construction of deviant behavior and the role that deviance plays in properly functioning societies.

Daniel Patrick Moynihan
Borrowing from the classic statements of Emile Durkheim and Kai Erikson, Moynihan suggests that societies can tolerate only so much deviance and, when overloaded, will redefine egregious behavior as tolerable conduct.

Part II: Explaining Deviance

Michael Gottfredson and *Travis Hirschi*
Gottfredson and Hirschi's general theory of deviance begins with the rather controversial assumption that human nature, if not evil, is inherently antisocial.

Part III: Researching Deviance

Part IV: Drugs

Part V: Violence

Part VI: Sexual Deviance: Prostitution, Rape, and Homosexuality

Part VIII: Mental Illness

Part IX: Stigma and Identity Management

The fixation on being thin has had profound and disturbing effects, marginalizing people who, in some form or fashion, cannot or do not measure up. More troubling, it has created entirely new standards of physical attractiveness that many find unattainable. Eating disorders are one consequence.

Shoplifting is a solitary offense but one rife with social and transactional overtones; without the possibility of getting caught, there would be no motivation to steal. Katz explores these "seductions of crime" and their role in deviant identity formation.

Athletic participation allows disabled men to transform a discrediting attribute into a positive source of valuation, resulting in positive reinforcement, enhanced self-esteem, the respect of others, and a reaffirmed sense of masculinity.

Sport is supposedly not the "proper" domain for "ladies"; it violates standards of appropriate gender-role conduct. When female athletes are labeled lesbians, they must respond accordingly. The authors examine these responses.

The fraternity is the quintessential heterosexual institution. It stands for everything that is macho—from homophobia and athletic prowess to alcohol abuse and the subjugation of women. Some gay men, however, have "borrowed" the institution and use it for the collective expression of gay identity.

Part X: Deviance and Social Control

Acknowledgments

Portions of the section and article introductions for this book were adapted with permission from *Dealing Crack: The Social World of Streetcorner Selling* (Bruce A. Jacobs, Northeastern University Press, 1999, Boston) and *Robbing Drug Dealers: Violence Beyond the Law* (Bruce A. Jacobs, Aldine de Gruyter, 2000, New York).

I would like to thank Bob Bursik, Scott Decker, Joy Jacobs, Dennis Mares, Jody Miller, Rick Rosenfeld, and Richard Wright for their advice, counsel, and assistance at various stages of this project. Thanks as always go to my parents Lynn and Frank, and brother and sister David and Joy. Special thanks go to Jennifer and Noah Jacobs for their support and editorial insights. This book would not have been possible without them.

I also wish to thank the reviewers of this book, whose names are as follows: Frank Scarpitti of the University of Delaware, Richard A. Wright of Arkansas State University, Theresa A. Martinez of the University of Utah, Cheryl Rae Tieman of Radford University, Craig Forsyth of the University of Louisiana, Jacqueline Boles of Georgia State University, and Susan Tiano of the University of New Mexico. ✦

Foreword

Barry Glassner
University of Southern California

Bruce Jacobs has assembled an outstanding anthology of readings in the sociological study of deviance. In this compact volume, students will find an excellent and informative selection of the most important theoretical and empirical works in the field. Each section includes classic and contemporary works, and the volume as a whole presents a balanced picture of the field.

From the outset, Jacobs makes clear that deviance is partly, but not entirely, in the eye of the beholder. From a sociological point of view, deviance consists in the interplay of behaviors and responses to behavior—in what people do, and in how others respond to what they do.

Theories and explanations of deviancy abound, not only within sociology, but in numerous other academic and professional fields and among the general public. Those theories themselves influence what deviancy is and what behaviors are identified as deviant. Herein lies a difference between the study of the social world and study of the physical world. The earth does not become flat because some group says it is flat, but a person may become a prostitute (or alcohol abuser or violent criminal) in response to others telling them that this is their destiny.

It becomes important, therefore, to understand a range of theories and explanations for deviance—a task that this collection facilitates by excerpting many of the key theories and making them accessible and engaging for the student reader.

Equally important, this anthology introduces students to a variety of research tools that social scientists employ in the study of deviance. Essays look at a range of qualitative and quantitative approaches and discuss some of the most enduring controversies in the field—for example, whether to trust official statistics and reports by criminals.

The greater part of the book consists, however, not of theoretical and methodological essays, but empirical studies of deviant behavior. Provocative and well documented, these works examine the full range of behaviors that are considered deviant in modern and postmodern societies. The sections on drug use, violence, sexual deviance, white collar deviance, and mental illness present many of the most important studies.

Significantly, in the final sections of the book, students are presented with research on how persons and social institutions deal with deviancy. The penultimate section examines how individuals manage the stigma and spoiled identities that come from being labeled deviant. The final group of studies looks at the flip side of that same coin: how major social institutions process and control people who engage in behavior judged deviant.

Easy to follow but never simplistic, the essays in this volume provide a good grounding in the sociological study of deviance. ✦

Topical Matrix

Under each topic heading below are listed the articles in this anthology that apply.

Deviance and Social Construction
- Chapter 2: "Fear, the Media, and the Construction of Deviance" by Barry Glassner
- Chapter 18: "The Social Construction of Drugs and Drug Use" by Robert F. Meier and Gilbert Geis

Deviance, Labeling, and Social Typing
- Chapter 1: "Outsiders" by Howard S. Becker
- Chapter 53: "Driving While Black" by Elijah Anderson
- Chapter 56: "Surveillance and Reputation in America" by Steven L. Nock

The Functions of Deviance
- Chapter 3: "On the Sociology of Deviance" by Kai T. Erikson
- Chapter 4: "Defining Deviancy Down" by Daniel Patrick Moynihan

Studying Deviance and Deviants
- Chapter 15: "Studying Sex: An American Survey" by Edward O. Laumann, Robert T. Michael, John H. Gagnon, and Stuart Michaels
- Chapter 16: "Researching Crack Dealers" by Bruce A. Jacobs

Theories of Deviance
- Chapter 5: "Deviance and Low Self-Control" by Michael Gottfredson and Travis Hirschi (**Control Theory**)
- Chapter 6: "Deviance, the American Dream, and Social Institutions" by Steven F. Messner and Richard Rosenfeld (**Institutional Anomie Theory**)
- Chapter 7: "Deviance and Oppositional Culture: The Code of the Streets" by Elijah Anderson (**Cultural Deviance Theory**)
- Chapter 8: "The Theory of Differential Association" by Edwin H. Sutherland and Donald R. Cressey (**Differential Association Theory**)
- Chapter 9: "A General Strain Theory of Crime and Delinquency" by Robert Agnew (**General Strain Theory**)
- Chapter 10: "Crime and Deviance in the Life Course" by Robert J. Sampson and John H. Laub (**Life-Course Theory**)
- Chapter 11: "Techniques of Neutralization" by Gresham Sykes and David Matza (**Neutralization Theory**)
- Chapter 12: "A Radical Conception of Crime and Deviance" by Michael J. Lynch and W. Byron Groves (**Marxist Theory**)
- Chapter 13: "Gender, Crime, and Deviance" by Kathleen Daly (**Feminist Theory**)
- Chapter 14: "Deviance, Labeling, and Reintegrative Shaming" by John Braithwaite (**Reintegrative Shaming Theory**)

Deviant Identity Development
- Chapter 23: "American Women and Smoking: 22 Million Just Don't Get It" by Ann Colston Wentz
- Chapter 46: "Anorexia Nervosa and Builimia: The Development of Deviant Identities" by Penelope A. McLorg and Diane E. Taub
- Chapter 47: "Becoming a Shoplifter: The Seductions of Deviance" by Jack Katz

Subcultures and Deviant Social Organization
- Chapter 17: "Gender and Research With the Police" by Jennifer Hunt
- Chapter 29: "The Social Organization of Prostitution" by Robert F. Meier and Gilbert Geis

Introduction

The editor intends this anthology to be comprehensive and logically composed. To this end, its structure is simple and straightforward, applying a back-to-basics approach that captures the essence of deviant behavior—its construction, explanation, commission, and control. I have supplied background material specific to each section *and to each article*. That material both connects the book's component parts and yet lets sections stand on their own. Its organization also allows the text to build sequentially.

The book's theoretical coverage is comprehensive yet measured, drawing from classic as well as recent approaches (although the emphasis is on the latter).

The selections chosen to represent forms of deviant behavior are incisive, engaging, ethnographic, timely, and highly readable—articles that students will genuinely enjoy and learn from. Deviance on the edge, as well as more mundane forms that resonate directly with students' everyday experiences, is incorporated within an overarching scheme of drugs, sex, violence, white-collar crime, and mental illness—the meat and potatoes of rule-breaking.

There is a special section on identity management with an emphasis on the acquisition and management of stigma. Within these primary sections, all major analytic categories relevant to deviance and its commission have been incorporated as independent variables. These include structural, institutional, and situational contexts; subjective foreground conditions; careers and subcultures; socialization into norms; deviant styles and motives; and deviant social organization.

A section on researching deviance is provided early to expose readers to the process by which scholars conduct deviance research (both ethnographic and survey): how they identify and infiltrate difficult-to-penetrate settings, negotiate emergent dilemmas and contradictions, and secure valid data.

A section on deviance and social control concludes the book, concentrating on four broad themes of major contemporary—and student—interest: profiling, prison life, judicial discretion, and surveillance.

Gender is incorporated throughout the book as a crucial mediating variable. Feminist perspectives, as well as approaches that focus on masculinity and deviance, are included. ✦

Part I

Constructing Deviance

Deviance intrigues. Deviance shocks and titillates. Deviance harms, sometimes seriously. Yet deviance is essential to any properly functioning society; no healthy civilization can exist without it. Deviant behavior defines boundaries between acceptable and unacceptable conduct. It generates symbolic distinctions between insiders and outsiders, which is essential for the construction and maintenance of solidarity (Durkheim 1938). Deviance permits some individuals to release pent-up tensions and frustrations (people who might otherwise not have an outlet in the face of strict regulation; Marx 1981). Deviance facilitates social change by encouraging people to question norms, attitudes, and values that are counterproductive or anachronistic (see, e.g., Tittle and Paternoster 2000). By triggering penalties, deviance affirms the power of formal institutions to sanction. Vast resources and substantial economic activity revolve directly or indirectly around the detection, punishment, and control of deviance.

Definitions of deviance vary widely. Some suggest it is conduct labeled as such by those with the social, economic, or political power to do so. Others claim it is rare and infrequent behavior, a departure from the normal or "average." Many insist that it is an absolute phenomenon—that certain behaviors, regardless of time, place, or era, lie outside the bounds of acceptability.

The absolutist perspective is a popular one. Most members of the general public justifiably view murder, rape, robbery, assault, and property destruction to be morally wrong across time and space. Yet such offenses can be functional, and even necessary, for the survival of a given social system. In some cultures, these "crimes" actually double as social control devices geared to punish some act that the culture considers an affront, although the sanctions are administered on a *private* basis:

The Eskimos of the American Arctic . . .kill people in response to various offenses, including adultery, insult, or simply being a nuisance. . . .[Among native tribes in Venezuela and Brazil], women are routinely subjected to corporal punishment by their husbands. . . .In parts of East Africa, husbands often assault their wives, sometimes with a slap, sometimes with a fist, a foot, or a stick (Edgerton 1972, 164). . . .Property destruction may also be a mode of social control. An extreme form is house burning, a practice quite frequent . . .in parts of East Africa. . . .Among the Cheyenne of the American Plains, a man's horse might be killed (Llewellyn and Hoebel 1941, 117), and in Northern Albania, a dog might be killed [as punishment for something its owner has done] (Hasluck 1954, 76–78). . . .Where women are regarded as the property of their fathers or husbands, rape may provide a means of retaliation against a man, . . .even a widow might be attacked by a

1

group of men as an act of revenge against her deceased husband (Hanawalt 1979, 109, 153). (Quoted in Black 1983, 35)

Scholars are hard-pressed to come up with a single behavior that is considered deviant regardless of context or historical era. Incest, child molestation, and homosexual rape have all, at some point in time, been acceptable activities. Homicide, arguably the most heinous and serious of all forms of deviance, is justifiable even today under a number of different circumstances—from self-defense to war to relieving someone with incurable pain (euthanasia). Though lying is thought to be universally bad, how many of us prevaricate on a daily basis to prevent others from feeling hurt or embarrassed or uncomfortable? Some commentators suggest that social order would crumble in the absence of such "white lies." Treason—the ultimate expression of disloyalty—is at first glance universally worthy of condemnation, but disloyalty is in the eye of the beholder. One side's traitor is the other side's savior.

To say that deviance is rare and infrequent behavior—conduct that departs from the average—is probably not correct either. Many behaviors are rare and infrequent but are not "deviant," at least in the negative sense that term generally connotes. Refusing to watch television, being a vegetarian, or practicing celibacy are three examples (see Tittle and Paternoster 2000). Many behaviors are neither rare nor infrequent but are deviant nonetheless (e.g., nose-picking, cutting into line at the store, violating the speed limit). The question of how rare an activity has to be before it is considered deviant is perplexing. Very rare or somewhat rare? Is it a percentage, a certain number of standard deviations from the mean (average), or something else? Tittle and Paternoster (2000, 5) suggest that the answer is as arbitrary as it is elusive:

One might decide that any behavior falling within two standard deviations of the mean (or one or three) is conforming, while any behavior outside that range is deviant. Or alternatively we might say that any behavior is as deviant as the magnitude of its standard score (meaning that the more it exceeds the mean in either direction, the greater its deviance).

The main problem with such applications is that hard empirical evidence of the frequency or prevalence of a behavior can rarely be obtained.

Another unsettling definition says that a behavior is not deviant as long as enough people engage in it: rape, incest, child molestation, robbery, and homicide would all be acceptable if sufficient numbers of people engaged in them (Tittle and Paternoster 2000). Widespread malfeasance does indeed happen on occasion, as instances of mob violence and ethnic cleansing attest, but such behavior is still deviant by most objective standards. Immunity for people caught up in such movements is short-lived, and when the dust clears and investigations proceed, steep punishments are often invoked. Less egregious forms of rule-breaking (tax-cheating, speeding, fighting, underage drinking) are widely committed on a daily basis, but, according to the statistical model, they are not considered deviant. Indeed, national surveys suggest that someone who has never violated the law in these ways is *extremely deviant*. Criminality, paradoxically, is conformity.

The most effective definitions of deviance assert simply that deviance is behavior in violation of norms, the situation-specific expectations of conduct that permeate all spheres of social life. The normative model suggests that deviance does not reside in the actor or in the context but in the interface between the two. Because this interface is in a constant state of flux—expectations of conduct are always changing—the normative model explains how one behavior can be deviant or conformist depending on the time and place of its commission. Eating with one's hands, for example, is deviant at a five-star restaurant but not at McDonald's (or if the food in question is a dinner roll). Screaming and jumping up and down is deviant for a college lecturer but not if she or he has just won the Powerball lottery prize. Drinking alcohol is deviant for a 13-year-old boy but generally not if the beverage is wine and if it is imbibed during a religious ceremony. Throwing money away is deviant for a person tossing hundred-dollar bills into the trash dumpster but not for the same person casting coins into the local wishing well. In every case, it is not the behavior itself but the situational and interactional context surrounding it that counts most. The *relativity of deviance* lies at the core of the normative model (Goode 1997).

Norms typically are taken for granted. Everybody "knows" what is and what is not acceptable behavior. Only when norms are violated do they actually become visible. Harold Garfinkel, a sociologist at UCLA, has illustrated this simple but powerful line of reasoning through his use of "breach experiments," in which he directs his students to purposely break norms to establish that they exist. In some experiments, the students treated store customers as if they were employees; in others, they stood too close to someone in a public setting or faced the wrong direction in elevators; some students acted like tenants in their own homes. The typical reaction is that the norm violators are ill in some way; surely no people in their right minds would make such a fundamental lapse in judgment. Befuddlement is only to be expected: breach experiments question social order itself, obliterating taken-for-granted realities and undermining the assumptions that allow social life to flow smoothly.

Deviance, whether the everyday variety perpetrated in breach experiments or the more extreme versions that capture the public eye, invariably elicits *sanctions*. Sanctions are merely *reactions* to behavior and can be either positive or negative. A smile, for example, is a sanction (obviously a positive one). So is a job promotion, a medal, and a certificate of accomplishment. Social deviance, however, usually elicits strong negative sanctions, because the sanctions are meted out by powerful institutional bodies; such sanctions can incapacitate affected parties for long periods of time. For serious rule-breakers, sanctions serve as both retribution and deterrence; they punish those who have strayed from society's rules and inform others what is in store if they do the same.

If not all sanctions are negative, neither is all deviance. The notion that deviance is limited to offensive or disvalued behavior is mistaken and may be attributed to the tendency for people to equate deviance with crime, even though the two are fundamentally distinct. Nose-pickers, cross-dressers, and bungee-jumpers generally are in violation of norms, but nothing they are doing is against the law (in most places). For deviance to be crime, it must first meet the legality requirement. Criminologists call this the *nullum crimen sine lege* principle: "there can be no crime without law." Laws are norms that have been formally codified. Norms become laws only after the concerted actions of well-placed and influential moral entrepreneurs, who generate broad-based popular support for their positions. Laws, thus, are political in nature and are typically put in place for political reasons. [1]

Because norms are historically specific and situationally contingent, laws are always changing. It was once illegal, for example, to engage in homosexual sex, marry out of one's race, or masturbate. Just the same, many behaviors that used to be completely legal (though perhaps deviant) have now been criminalized. Underage sex, heroin use, and underage alcohol consumption come to mind first.

Harm has also been suggested to be a necessary and sufficient criterion for defining crime and deviance, but this also is inaccurate. There are plenty of harmful acts that are neither deviant nor criminal (e.g., killing enemies during wartime). There are also many harmful acts that are criminal but not necessarily deviant (marijuana smoking, drinking alcohol at a high school party). Moreover, behaviors that involve putatively little harm to oneself or others are often treated as if they are extremely criminal. The draconian penalties meted out for small-time drug possession are examples, especially for substances illicit only because people with power say they are. Equating deviance with harm also ignores the fact that some deviance is prosocial, or "positive" in nature. Workaholics, body builders, philanthropists, and geniuses are prototypical positive deviants.

Note

1. Thanks to an anonymous reviewer for pointing this out. ✦

1
Outsiders

Howard S. Becker

Rules about acceptable and unacceptable conduct are created. Through a process of claims-making and moral entrepreneurship, offensive conduct is singled out for negative sanctions. Labels are created and then applied, after which rule-breakers internalize the "master status" of offender and commit even more deviance (Hughes 1945). Eminent sociologist Edwin Lemert (1967) characterizes this secondary deviation as self-fulfilling prophecy, behavior that occurs when people act in accordance with the expectations of others.

Labeling theory depicts a vicious cycle in which social groups define deviance, deviance leads to labels, and labels lead to chronic offending. The blame really lies in the system for creating "evil" and then dramatizing it (Tannenbaum 1938). But the labeling perspective has been roundly and justly criticized for, among other things, its "underdog ideology"—implying that without labels, deviance would not exist. Clearly, this implication is ludicrous. There is widespread agreement about the wrongfulness of a whole spectrum of deviant behaviors (e.g., rape, robbery, and murder); such acts are judged to be wrong in and of themselves rather than because some label says they are wrong. Nonetheless, the labeling perspective is very useful for understanding the process by which deviant behavior is socially constructed and for suggesting that all deviance (even heinous forms) is inevitably in the eye of the beholder.

All social groups make rules and attempt, at some times and under some circumstances, to enforce them. Social rules define situations and the kinds of behavior appropriate to them, specifying some actions as "right" and forbidding others as "wrong."

When a rule is enforced, the person who is supposed to have broken it may be seen as a special kind of person, one who cannot be trusted to live by the rules agreed on by the group. He is regarded as an *outsider*.

But the person who is thus labeled an outsider may have a different view of the matter. He may not accept the rule by which he is being judged and may not regard those who judge him as either competent or legitimately entitled to do so. Hence, a second meaning of the term emerges: the rule-breaker may feel his judges are *outsiders*.

In what follows, I will try to clarify the situation and process pointed to by this double-barreled term: the situations of rule-breaking and rule-enforcement and the processes by which some people come to break rules and others to enforce them.

Some preliminary distinctions are in order. Rules may be of a great many kinds. They may be formally enacted into law, and in this case the police power of the state may be used in enforcing them. In other cases, they represent informal agreements, newly arrived at or encrusted with the sanction of age and tradition; rules of this kind are enforced by informal sanctions of various kinds.

Similarly, whether a rule has the force of law or tradition or is simply the result of consensus, it may be the task of some specialized body, such as the police or the committee on ethics of a professional association, to enforce it; enforcement, on the other hand, may be everyone's job or, at least, the job of everyone in the group to which the rule is meant to apply.

Many rules are not enforced and are not, in any except the most formal sense, the kind of rules with which I am concerned. Blue laws, which remain on the statute books though they have not been enforced for a hundred years, are examples. (It is important to remember, however, that an unenforced law may be reactivated for various reasons and regain all its original force, as recently occurred with respect to the laws governing the opening of commercial establishments on Sunday in Missouri.) Informal rules may similarly die from lack of enforcement. I shall mainly be concerned with what we can call the actual operating rules of groups, those kept alive through attempts at enforcement.

Finally, just how far "outside" one is, in either of the senses I have mentioned, varies from case to case. We think of the person who commits a traffic violation or gets a little too drunk at a party as being, after all, not very different from the rest of us and treat his infraction tolerantly. We regard the thief as less like us and punish him severely. Crimes such as murder, rape, or treason lead us to view the violator as a true outsider.

In the same way, some rule-breakers do not think they have been unjustly judged. The traffic violator usually subscribes to the very rules he has broken. Alcoholics are often ambivalent, sometimes feeling that those who judge them do not understand them and at other times agreeing that compulsive drinking is a bad thing. At the extreme, some deviants (homosexuals and drug addicts are good examples) develop full-blown ideologies explaining why they are right and why those who disapprove of and punish them are wrong.

Definitions of Deviance

The outsider—the deviant from group rules—has been the subject of much speculation, theorizing, and scientific study. What laymen want to know about deviants is: why do they do it? How can we account for their rule-breaking? What is there about them that leads them to do forbidden things? Scientific research has tried to find answers to these questions. In doing so it has accepted the common-sense premise that there is something inherently deviant (qualitatively distinct) about acts that break (or seem to break) social rules. It has also accepted the common-sense assumption that the deviant act occurs because some characteristic of the person who commits it makes it necessary or inevitable that he should. Scientists do not ordinarily question the label "deviant" when it is applied to particular acts or people but rather take it as given. In so doing, they accept the values of the group making the judgment.

It is easily observable that different groups judge different things to be deviant. This should alert us to the possibility that the person making the judgment of deviance, the process by which that judgment is arrived at, and the situation in which it is made may all be intimately involved in the phenomenon of deviance. To the degree that the common-sense view of deviance and the scientific theories that begin with its premises assume that acts that break rules are inherently deviant and thus take for granted the situations and processes of judgment, they may leave out an important variable. If scientists ignore the variable character of the process of judgment, they may by that omission limit the kinds of theories that can be developed and the kind of understanding that can be achieved.[1]

Our first problem, then, is to construct a definition of deviance. Before doing this, let us consider some of the definitions scientists now use, seeing what is left out if we take them as a point of departure for the study of outsiders.

The simplest view of deviance is essentially statistical, defining as deviant anything that varies too widely from the average. When a statistician analyzes the results of an agricultural experiment, he describes the stalk of corn that is exceptionally tall and the stalk that is exceptionally short as deviations from the mean or average. Similarly, one can describe anything that differs from what is most common as a deviation. In this view, to be left-handed or redheaded is deviant, because most people are right-handed and brunette.

So stated, the statistical view seems simple-minded, even trivial. Yet it simplifies the problem by doing away with many questions of value that ordinarily arise in discussions of the nature of deviance. In assessing any particular case, all one need do is calculate the distance of the behavior involved from the average. But it is too simple a solution. Hunting with such a definition, we return with a mixed bag—people who are excessively fat or thin, murderers, redheads, homosexuals, and frame violators. The mixture contains some ordinarily thought of as deviants and others who have broken no rule at

The statistical definition of deviance, in short, is too far removed from the concern with rule-breaking which prompts scientific study of outsiders.

A less simple but much more common view of deviance identifies it as something essentially pathological, revealing the presence of a "disease." This view rests, obviously, on a medical analogy. The human organism, when it is working efficiently and experiencing no discomfort, is said to be "healthy." When it does not work efficiently, a disease is present. The organ or function that has become deranged is said to be pathological. Of course, there is little disagreement about what constitutes a healthy state of the organism. But there is much less agreement when one uses the notion of pathology analogically, to describe kinds of behavior that are regarded as deviant. For people do not agree on what constitutes healthy behavior. It is difficult to find a definition that will satisfy even such a select and limited group as psychiatrists; it is impossible to find one that people generally accept as they accept criteria of health for the organism.[2]

Sometimes people mean the analogy more strictly, because they think of deviance as the product of mental disease. The behavior of a homosexual or drug addict is regarded as the symptom of a mental disease just as the diabetic's difficulty in getting bruises to heal is regarded as a symptom of his disease. But mental disease resembles physical disease only in metaphor:

Starting with such things as syphilis, tuberculosis, typhoid fever, and carcinomas and fractures, we have created the class "illness." At first, this class was composed of only a few items, all of which shared the common feature of reference to a state of disordered structure or function of the human body as a physiochemical machine. As time went on, additional items were added to this class. They were not added, however, because they were newly discovered bodily disorders. The physician's attention had been deflected from this criterion and had become focused instead on disability and suffering as new criteria for selection. Thus, at first slowly, such things as hysteria, hypochondriasis, obsessive-compulsive neurosis, and depression were added to the category of illness. Then, with increasing zeal, physicians and especially psychiatrists began to call "illness" (that is, of course, "mental illness") anything and everything in which they could detect any sign of malfunctioning, based on no matter what norm. Hence, agoraphobia is illness because one should not be afraid of open spaces. Homosexuality is illness because heterosexuality is the social norm. Divorce is illness because it signals failure of marriage. Crime, art, undesired political leadership, participation in social affairs, or withdrawal from such participation—all these and many more have been said to be signs of mental illness.[3]

The medical metaphor limits what we can see much as the statistical view does. It accepts the lay judgment of something as deviant and, by use of analogy, locates its source within the individual, thus preventing us from seeing the judgment itself as a crucial part of the phenomenon.

Some sociologists also use a model of deviance based essentially on the medical notions of health and disease. They look at a society, or some part of a society, and ask whether there are any processes going on in it that tend to reduce its stability, thus lessening its chance of survival. They label such processes deviant or identify them as symptoms of social disorganization. They discriminate between those features of society which promote stability (and thus are "functional") and those which disrupt stability (and thus are "dysfunctional"). Such a view has the great virtue of pointing to areas of possible trouble in a society of which people may not be aware.[4]

But it is harder in practice than it appears to be in theory to specify what is functional and what dysfunctional for a society or social group. The question of what the purpose or goal (function) of a group is and, consequently, what things will help or hinder the achievement of that purpose, is very often a political question. Factions within the group disagree and maneuver to have their own definition of the group's function accepted. The function of the group or organization, then, is decided in political conflict, not given in the nature of the organization. If this is true, then it is likewise true that the questions of what rules are to be enforced, what behavior regarded as deviant, and which people labeled as outsiders must also be regarded as political.[5] The functional view of deviance, by ignoring the political aspect of the phenomenon, limits our understanding.

Another sociological view is more relativistic. It identifies deviance as the failure to obey group rules. Once we have described the rules a group enforces on its members, we can say with some precision whether or not a person has violated them and is thus, on this view, deviant.

This view is closest to my own, but it fails to give sufficient weight to the ambiguities that arise in deciding which rules are to be taken as the yardstick against which behavior is measured and judged deviant. A society has many groups, each with its own set of rules, and people belong to many groups simultaneously. A person may break the rules of one group by the very act of abiding by the rules of another group. Is he, then, deviant? Proponents of this definition may object that while ambiguity may arise with respect to the rules peculiar to one or another group in society, there are some rules that are very generally agreed to by everyone, in which case the difficulty does not arise. This, of course, is a question of fact, to be settled by empirical research. I doubt there are many such areas of consensus and think it wiser to use a definition that allows us to deal with both ambiguous, and unambiguous situations.

Deviance and the Responses of Others

The sociological view I have just discussed defines deviance as the infraction of some agreed-upon rule. It then goes on to ask who breaks rules, and to search for the factors in their personalities and life situations that might account for the infractions. This assumes that those who have broken a rule constitute a homogeneous category, because they have committed the same deviant act.

Such an assumption seems to me to ignore the central fact about deviance: it is created by society. I do not mean this in the way it is ordinarily understood, in which the causes of deviance are located in the social situation of the deviant or in "social factors" which prompt his action. I mean, rather, that *social groups create deviance by making the rules whose infraction constitutes deviance,* and by applying those rules to particular people and labeling them as outsiders. From this point of view, deviance is *not* a quality of the act the person commits, but rather a consequence of the application by others of rules and sanctions to an "offender." The deviant is one to whom that label has successfully been applied; deviant behavior is behavior that people so label.[6]

Since deviance is, among other things, a consequence of the responses of others to a person's act, students of deviance cannot assume that they are dealing with a homogeneous category when they study people who have been labeled deviant. That is, they cannot assume that these people have actually committed a deviant act or broken some rule, because the process of labeling may not be infallible; some people may be labeled deviant who in fact have not broken a rule. Furthermore, they cannot assume that the category of those labeled deviant will contain all those who actually have broken a rule, for many offenders may escape apprehension and thus fail to be included in the population of "deviants" they study. Insofar as the category lacks homogeneity and fails to include all the cases that belong in it, one cannot reasonably expect to find common factors of personality or life situation that will account for the supposed deviance.

What, then, do people who have been labeled deviant have in common? At the least, they share the label and the experience of being labeled as outsiders.

Notes

1. Cf. Donald R. Cressey, "Criminological Research and the Definition of Crimes," *American Journal of Sociology,* LVI (May, 1951), 546–551.

2. See the discussion in C. Wright Mills, "The Professional Ideology of Social Pathologists,"

American Journal of Sociology, XLIX (September, 1942), 165–180.

3. Thomas Szasz, *The Myth of Mental Illness* (New York: Paul B. Hoeber, Inc., 1961), pp. 44–45; see also Erving Goffman, "The Medical Model and Mental Hospitalization," in *Asylums: Essays on the Social Situation of Mental Patients and Other Inmates* (Garden City: Anchor Books, 1961), pp. 321–386.

4. See Robert K. Merton, "Social Problems and Sociological Theory," in Robert K. Merton and Robert A. Nisbet, editors, *Contemporary Social Problems* (New York: Harcourt, Brace and World, Inc., 1961), pp. 697–737; and Talcott Parsons, *The Social System* (New York: The Free Press of Glencoe, 1951), pp. 249–325.

5. Howard Brotz similarly identifies the question of what phenomena are "functional" or "dysfunctional" as a political one in "Functionalism and Dynamic Analysis," *European Journal of Sociology,* II (1961), 170–179.

6. The most important earlier statements of this view can be found in Frank Tannenbaum, *Crime and the Community* (New York; McGraw-Hill Book Co., Inc., 1951), and E. M. Lemert, *Social Pathology* (New York: McGraw-Hill Book Co., Inc., 1951). A recent article stating a position very similar to mine is John Kitsuse, "Societal Reaction to Deviance: Problems of Theory and Method," *Social Problems,* 9 (Winter, 1962), 247–256.

2
Fear, the Media, and the Construction of Deviance

Barry Glassner

Fear is one of the most powerful of human emotions. Fear is blinding. Fear invades the psyche and overwhelms it. Fear arises from perception, so if people believe something is dangerous or risky or threatening, then that fear is real to them. But things that people often fear the most actually pose little or no objective danger. When fear mediates the construction of deviance, the consequences are anything but good.

Few institutions are better at generating misplaced fears than the ratings-obsessed news media, who routinely elevate the rare and sensational to the "everyday." Isolated events are magnified into full-blown social catastrophes. Anomalies become representative of larger, more ominous patterns. Exceptions to the rule become the rule itself. With "no danger . . .too small to magnify into a national nightmare" (Glassner 1999, xxi), citizens believe that gloom and doom are always just around the corner.

In the past, most people thought that bad things would never happen to them—a phenomenon social psychologists call the "illusion of control" (Langer 1975). Now it seems that control itself is illusory, and a cultural paranoia seems to grow stronger with each passing news cycle. Although fear has always played a part in the construction of deviance, in the age of video and sound bites, its influence seems to have become greatly magnified.

Deviance, we know, is that which is so labeled by the people with the power to make and attach the labels. Howard Becker suggests that "moral entrepreneurs" are the principal actors in this drama, persons who translate their values and concerns into norms by virtue of political, social, and economic influence. Traditionally, the media are thought to be mere mouthpieces in this process, listening to policymakers and reporting what they tell them, but increasingly, they seem to be exerting a primary influence in their own right. Fear mongering is done first and foremost for ratings: the news business is a business; ratings attract advertisers, and advertisers mean profit. The consequences, however,—intended or unintended—are troubling. When the media's "dubious statistics" and stilted representations make us fear the wrong things, serious forms of rule-breaking will be trivialized and too many resources will be dedicated to the wrong kinds of causes. Policymakers, in turn, feel the need to sanction rule-breaking that does not need to be sanctioned—resulting in what some suggest to be an ever-intruding state, in which the most minute forms of deviance are singled out for social control while far more serious problems are ignored.

Why are so many fears in the air, and so many of them unfounded? Why, as crime rates plunged throughout the 1990s, did two-thirds of Americans believe they were soaring? How did it come about that by mid-decade 62 percent of us described ourselves as "truly desperate" about crime—almost twice as many as in the late 1980s, when crime rates were higher? Why, on a survey in 1997, when the crime rate had already fallen for a half dozen consecutive years, did more than half of us disagree with the statement "This country is finally beginning to make some progress in solving the crime problem"?[1] . . . .

Give us a happy ending and we write a new disaster story. In the late 1990s the unemployment rate was below 5 percent for the first time in a quarter century. People who had been pounding the pavement for years could finally get work. Yet pundits warned of imminent economic disaster. They predicted inflation would take off, just as they had a years earlier—also erroneously—when the unemployment rate dipped below 6 percent.[2]

We compound our worries beyond all reason. . . .

We had better learn to doubt our inflated fears before they destroy us. Valid fears have their place; they cue us to danger. False and overdrawn fears only cause hardship. . . .

We all pay one of the costs of panics: huge sums of money go to waste. Hysteria over the ritual abuse of children cost billions of dollars in police investigations, trials, and imprisonments. Men and women went to jail for years "on the basis of some of the most fantastic claims ever presented to an American jury," as Dorothy Rabinowitz of the *Wall Street Journal* demonstrated in a series of investigative articles for which she became a Pulitzer Prize finalist in 1996. Across the nation expensive surveillance programs were implemented to protect children from fiends who reside primarily in the imaginations of adults.[3]

The price tag for our panic about overall crime has grown so monumental that even law-and-order zealots find it hard to defend. The criminal justice system costs Americans close to $100 billion a year, most of which goes to police and prisons. In California we spend more on jails than on higher education. Yet increases in the number of police and prison cells do not correlate consistently with reductions in the number of serious crimes committed. Criminologists who study reductions in homicide rates, for instance, find little difference between cities that substantially expand their police forces and prison capacity and others that do not.[4]

The turnabout in domestic public spending over the past quarter century, from child welfare and antipoverty programs to incarceration, did not even produce reductions in *fear* of crime. Increasing the number of cops and jails arguably has the opposite effect: it suggests that the crime problem is all the more out of control.[5]

Panic-driven public spending generates over the long term a pathology akin to one found in drug addicts. The more money and attention we fritter away on our compulsions, the less we have available for our real

needs, which consequently grow larger. While fortunes are being spent to protect children from dangers that few ever encounter, approximately 11 million children lack health insurance, 12 million are malnourished, and rates of illiteracy are increasing.[6]

I do not contend, as did President Roosevelt in 1933, that "the only thing we have to fear is fear itself." My point is that we often fear the wrong things. . . .

One of the paradoxes of a culture of fear is that serious problems remain widely ignored even though they give rise to precisely the dangers that the populace most abhors. Poverty, for example, correlates strongly with child abuse, crime, and drug abuse. Income inequality is also associated with adverse outcomes for society as a whole. The larger the gap between rich and poor in a society, the higher its overall death rates from heart disease, cancer, and murder. . . .

Two Easy Explanations

In the following discussion, I will try to answer two questions: Why are Americans so fearful lately, and why are our fears so often misplaced?

. . .[One] popular explanation blames the news media. We have so many fears, many of them off-base, the argument goes, because the media bombard us with sensationalistic stories designed to increase ratings. . . .

Disproportionate coverage in the news media plainly has effects on readers and viewers. When Esther Madriz, a professor at Hunter College, interviewed women in New York City about their fears of crime they frequently responded with the phrase "I saw it in the news." The interviewees identified the news media as both the source of their fears and the reason they believed those fears were valid. Asked in a national poll why they believe the country has a serious crime problem, 76 percent of people cited stories they had seen in the media. Only 22 percent cited personal experience.[7]

When professors Robert Blendon and John Young of Harvard analyzed forty-seven surveys about drug abuse conducted between 1978 and 1997, they too discovered that the news media, rather than personal experience, provide Americans with their predominant fears. Eight out of ten adults say that drug abuse has never caused problems in their family, and the vast majority report relatively little direct experience with problems related to drug abuse. Widespread concern about drug problems emanates, Blendon and Young determined, from scares in the news media, television in particular.[8]

Television news programs survive on scares. On local newscasts, where producers live by the dictum "if it bleeds, it leads," drug, crime, and disaster stories make up most of the news portion of the broadcasts. Evening newscasts on the major networks are somewhat less bloody, but between 1990 and 1998, when the nation's murder rate declined by 20 percent, the number of murder stories on network newscasts increased 600 percent (*not* counting stories about O. J. Simpson).[9]

After the dinnertime newscasts the networks broadcast newsmagazines, whose guiding principle seems to be that no danger is too small to magnify into a national nightmare. Some of the risks reported by such programs would be merely laughable were they not hyped with so much fanfare: "Don't miss *Dateline* tonight or YOU could be the next victim!" Competing for ratings with drama programs and movies during prime-time evening hours, newsmagazines feature story lines that would make a writer for *Homicide* or *ER* wince.[10]

"It can happen in a flash. Fire breaks out on the operating table. The patient is surrounded by flames," Barbara Walters exclaimed on ABC's *20/20* in 1998. The problem—oxygen from a face mask ignited by a surgical instrument—occurs "more often than you might think," she cautioned in her introduction, even though reporter Arnold Diaz would note later, during the actual report, that out of 27 million surgeries each year the situation arises only about a hundred times. No matter, Diaz effectively nullified the reassuring numbers as soon as they left his mouth. To those who "may say it's too small a risk to worry about" he presented distraught victims: a woman with permanent scars on her face and a man whose son had died.[11]

The gambit is common. Producers of TV newsmagazines routinely let emotional accounts trump objective information. In 1994 medical authorities attempted to cut short the brouhaha over flesh-eating bacteria by publicizing the fact that an American is fifty-five times more likely to be struck by lightning than die of the suddenly celebrated microbe. Yet TV journalists brushed this fact aside with remarks like, "whatever the statistics, it's devastating to the victims" (Catherine Crier on *20/20*), accompanied by stomach-turning videos of disfigured patients.[12]

Sheryl Stolberg, then a medical writer for the *Los Angeles Times*, put her finger on what makes the TV newsmagazines so cavalier: "Killer germs are perfect for prime time," she wrote. "They are invisible, uncontrollable, and, in the case of Group A strep, can invade the body in an unnervingly simple manner, through a cut or scrape." Whereas print journalists only described in words the actions of "billions of bacteria" spreading "like underground fires" throughout a person's body, TV newsmagazines made use of special effects to depict graphically how these "merciless killers" do their damage.[13] . . .

Morality and Marketing

To blame the media is to oversimplify the complex role that journalists play as both proponents and doubters of popular fears. It is also to beg the same key issue that the millennium hypothesis evades: why particular anxieties take hold when they do. Why do news organizations and their audiences find themselves drawn to one hazard rather than another?

Mary Douglas, the eminent anthropologist who devoted much of her career to studying how people interpret risk, pointed out that every society has an almost infinite quantity of potential dangers from which to choose. Societies differ both in the types of dangers they select and the number. Dangers get selected for special emphasis, Douglas showed, either because they offend the basic moral principles of the society or because they enable criticism of disliked groups and institutions. In *Risk and Culture*, a book she wrote with Aaron Wildavsky, the authors give an example from fourteenth-century Europe. Impure water had been a health danger long before that time, but only after it became convenient to accuse Jews of poisoning the wells did people become preoccupied with it. . . .

From a psychological point of view extreme fear and outrage are often projections. Consider, for example, the panic over violence against children. By failing to provide adequate education, nutrition, housing, parenting, medical services, and child care over the past couple of decades we have done the nation's children immense harm. Yet we project our guilt onto a cavalcade of bogeypeople—pedophile preschool teachers, preteen mass murderers, and homicidal au pairs, to name only a few.[14]

When Debbie Nathan, a journalist, and Michael Snedeker, an attorney, researched the evidence behind publicized reports in the 1980s and early 1990s of children being ritually raped and tortured they learned that although seven out of ten Americans believed that satanic cults were committing these atrocities, few of the incidents had actually occurred. At the outset of each ritual-abuse case the children involved claimed they had not been molested. They later changed their tunes at the urging of parents and law enforcement authorities. The ghastly tales of abuse, it turns out, typically came from the parents themselves, usually the mothers, who had convinced themselves they were true. Nathan and Snedeker suggest that some of the mothers had been abused themselves and projected those horrors, which they had trouble facing directly, onto their children. Other mothers, who had not been victimized in those ways, used the figure of ritually abused children as a medium of protest against male dominance more generally. Allegations of children being raped allowed conventional wives and mothers to speak out against men and masculinity without having to fear they would seem unfeminine. "The larger culture," Nathan and Snedeker note, "still required that women's complaints about inequality and sexual violence be communicated through the innocent, mortified voice of the child." . . .[15]

Within public discourse fears proliferate through a process of exchange. It is from crosscurrents of scares and counterscares that the culture of fear swells ever larger. . . .

The short answer to why Americans harbor so many misbegotten fears is that immense power and money await those who tap into our moral insecurities and supply us with symbolic substitutes. . . .

Start with silly scares, the kind that would be laughable were they not advanced with utter seriousness by influential organizations, politicians, and news media. Promoted by the same means as other fears—and often to the same ends—they afford a comfortable entry point into fear mongers' bag of tricks. . . .

"There is no terror in the bang, only in the anticipation of it," said the ultimate master of terror, Alfred Hitchcock.[16] Fear mongers regularly put his wisdom to use by depicting would-be perils as imminent disasters. . . .

Notes

1. Crime data here and throughout are from reports of the *Bureau of Justice Statistics* unless otherwise noted. Fear of crime: Esther Madriz, *Nothing Bad Happens to Good Girls* (Berkeley: University of California Press, 1997), ch. 1; Richard Morin, "As Crime Rate Falls, Fears Persist," *Washington Post* National Edition, 16 June 1997, p. 35; David Whitman, "Believing the Good News," *U.S. News & World Report*, 5 January 1998, pp. 45–46.

2. Bob Herbert, "Bogeyman Economics," *New York Times*, 4 April 1997, p. A15; Doug Henwood, "Alarming Drop in Unemployment," *Extra*, September 1994, pp. 16–17; Christopher Shea, "Low Inflation and Low Unemployment Spur Economists to Debate 'Natural Rate' Theory," *Chronicle of Higher Education*, 24 October 1997, p. A13.

3. Dorothy Rabinowitz, "A Darkness in Massachusetts," *Wall Street Journal*, 30 January 1995, p. A20 (contains quote); "Back in Wenatchee" (unsigned editorial), *Wall Street Journal*, 20 June 1996, p. A18; Dorothy Rabinowitz, "Justice in Massachusetts," *Wall Street Journal*, 13 May 1997, p. A19. See also Nathan and Snedeker, *Satan's Silence*, James Beaver, "The Myth of Repressed Memory," *Journal of Criminal Law and Criminology* 86 (1996): 596–607; Kathryn Lyon, *Witch Hunt*

(New York: Avon, 1998); Pam Belluck, "'Memory' Therapy Leads to a Lawsuit and Big Settlement," *New York Times*, 6 November 1997, pp. A1, 10.

4. Elliott Currie, *Crime and Punishment in America* (New York: Metropolitan, 1998); Tony Pate et al., *Reducing Fear of Crime in Houston and Newark* (Washington, DC: Police Foundation, 1986); Steven Donziger, *The Real War on Crime* (New York: Harper Collins, 1996); Christina Johns, *Power, Ideology and the War on Drugs* (New York: Praeger, 1992); John Irwin et al., "Fanning the Flames of Fear," *Crime and Delinquency* 44 (1998): 32–48.

5. Steven Donziger, "Fear, Crime and Punishment in the U.S.," *Tikkun* 12 (1996): 24–27, 77.

6. Peter Budetti, "Health Insurance for Children," *New England Journal of Medicine* 338 (1998): 541–42; Eileen Smith, "Drugs Top Adult Fears for Kids' Well-being," *USA Today*, 9 December 1997, p. D1. Literacy statistic: Adult Literacy Service.

7. Madriz, *Nothing Bad Happens to Good Girls*, see esp. pp. 111–14; David Whitman and Margaret Loftus, "Things are Getting Better? Who Knew," *U.S. News and World Report*, 16 December 1996, pp. 30–32.

8. Robert Blendon and John Young, "War on Illicit Drugs." See also Ted Chiricos et al., "Crime, News, and Fear of Crime," *Social Problems* 44 (1997): 342–57.

9. Steven Stark, "Local News: The Biggest Scandal on TV," *Washington Monthly* (June 1997): 38–41; Barbara Bliss Osborn, "If It Bleeds, It Leads," *Extra*, September-October 1994, p.15; Jenkins, *Pedophiles and Priests*, pp. 68–71; "It's Murder," *USA Today*, 20 April 1998, p. D2; Lawrence Grossman, "Does Local TV News Need a National Nanny?" *Columbia Journalism Review* (May 1998): 33.

10. Regarding fearmongering by newsmagazines, see also Elizabeth Jensen et al., "Consumer Alert," *Brill's Content* (October 1998): 130–47.

11. ABC, *20/20*, 16 March 1998.

12. Thomas Maugh, "Killer Bacteria a Rarity," *Los Angeles Times*, 3 December 1994, p. A29; Ed Siegel, "Roll Over, Ed Murrow," *Boston Globe*, 21 August 1994, p. 14; Crier quote from ABC's *20/20*, 24 June 1994.

13. Sheryl Stolberg, "'Killer Bug' Perfect for Prime Time," *Los Angeles Times*, 15 June 1994; pp. A1, 30–31; Quotes from Brown, "Flesh-eating Bug"; and Michael Limonick and Leon Jaroff, "The Killers All Around," *Time*, 12 September 1994; pp. 62–69.

14. See Maria Warner, "Peroxide Mug-Shot," *London Review of Books*, 1 January 1998; pp. 10–11.

15. Nathan and Snedeker, *Satan's Silence* (quote from p. 240).

16. Hitchcock quoted in Leslie Halliwell, *Halliwell's Film Companion* (New York: Harper Collins, 1995).

3
On the Sociology of Deviance

Kai T. Erikson

Arguably the most important function of social control is to mark boundaries for acceptable and unacceptable behavior. Defining what is acceptable or unacceptable is often difficult because societies are made up of competing interest groups. Family, community, and culture often conflict with one another and muddle definitions of normative behavior. The point to keep in mind is that the appropriateness of conduct is never taken for granted; it varies as widely as there are situations to generate norms. For any social system, the challenge is to articulate enough norms with sufficient generalizability to make social order possible.

Even in functional societies—or perhaps especially in them—order depends on some level of deviance. Deviance identifies limits of acceptable conduct. Deviance generates distinctions between "insiders" and "outsiders." Deviance triggers sanctions, and sanctions permit punishment. Punishment affirms the executive power of the state, is cathartic for citizens, and enhances internal cohesion. Punishment used to be quite a spectacle—with all the atmosphere, violence, and entertainment value of a gladiator fight. Although humanitarian and political concerns have since caused it be sanitized, its underlying purpose remains unchanged.

Deviance cannot and should not be punished away. Policies geared to do this are as misguided as they are doomed to fail. New forms of deviance inevitably emerge in the vacuum created by the forcible disappearance of old ones; behavior that used to be considered acceptable is redefined as offensive; lesser forms of rule-breaking mutate into serious transgressions. Deviance and social order exist symbiotically, the vitality of each dependent on the permanence of the other. Indeed, Erikson implies that some of the greatest social damage caused by deviant behavior is caused less by the actual behavior and more by the Draconian attempts to control it. Today's punishment-obsessed society frequently makes this all too clear.

Human actors are sorted into various kinds of collectivity, ranging from relatively small units such as the nuclear family to relatively large ones such as a nation or culture. One of the most stubborn difficulties in the study of deviation is that the problem is defined differently at each one of these levels: behavior that is considered unseemly within the context of a single family may be entirely acceptable to the community in general, while behavior that attracts severe censure from the members of the community may go altogether unnoticed elsewhere in the culture. People in society, then, must learn to deal separately with deviance at each one of these levels and to distinguish among them in his own daily activity. A man may disinherit his son for conduct that violates old family traditions or ostracize a neighbor for conduct that violates some local custom, but he is not expected to employ either of these standards when he serves as a juror in a court of law. In each of the three situations he is required to use a different set of criteria to decide whether or not the behavior in question exceeds tolerable limits.

In the next few pages we shall be talking about deviant behavior in social units called "communities," but the use of this term does not mean that the argument applies only at that level of organization. In theory, at least, the argument being made here should fit all kinds of human collectivity—families as well as whole cultures, small groups as well as nations—and the term "community" is only being used in this context because it seems particularly convenient.[1]

The people of a community spend most of their lives in close contact with one another, sharing a common sphere of experience which makes them feel that they belong to a special "kind" and live in a special "place." In the formal language of sociology, this means that communities are boundary maintaining: each has a specific territory in the world as a whole, not only in the sense that it occupies a defined region of geographical space but also in the sense that it takes over a particular niche in what might be called cultural space and develops its own "ethos" or "way" within that compass. Both of these dimensions of group space, the geographical and the cultural, set the community apart as a special place and provide an important point of reference for its members.

When one describes any system as boundary maintaining, one is saying that it controls the fluctuation of its consistent parts so that the whole retains a limited range of activity, a given pattern of constancy and stability, within the larger environment. A human community can be said to maintain boundaries, then, in the sense that its members tend to confine themselves to a particular radius of activity and to regard any conduct which drifts outside that radius as somehow inappropriate or immoral. Thus the group retains a kind of cultural integrity, a voluntary restriction on its own potential for expansion, beyond that which is strictly required for accommodation to the environment. Human behavior can vary over an enormous range, but each community draws a symbolic set of parentheses around a certain segment of that range and limits its own activities within that narrower zone. These parentheses, so to speak, are the community's boundaries.

Now people who live together in communities cannot relate to one another in any coherent way or even acquire a sense of their own stature as group members unless they learn something about the boundaries of the territory they occupy in social space, if only because they need to sense what lies beyond the margins of the group before they can appreciate the special quality of the experience which takes place within it. Yet how do people learn about the boundaries of their community? And how do they convey this information to the generations which replace them? . . .

. . .[T]he only material found in a society for marking boundaries is the behavior of its members—or rather, the networks of interaction which link these members together in regular social relations. And the interactions which do the most effective job of locating and publicizing the group's outer edges would seem to be those which take place between deviant persons on the one side and official agents of the community on the other. The deviant is a person whose activities have moved outside the margins of the group, and when the community calls him to account for that vagrancy it is making a statement about the nature and placement of its boundaries. It is declaring how much variability and diversity can be tolerated within the group before it begins to lose its distinctive shape, its unique identity. Now there may be other moments in the life of the group which perform a similar service: wars, for instance, can publicize a group's boundaries by drawing attention to the line separating the group from an adversary, and certain kinds of religious ritual, dance ceremony, and other traditional pageantry can dramatize the difference between "we" and "they" by portraying a symbolic encounter between the two. But on the whole, members of a community inform one another about the placement of their boundaries by participating in the confrontations which occur when persons who venture out to the edges of the group are met by policing agents whose special business it is to guard the cultural integrity of the community. Whether these confrontations take the form of criminal trials, excommunication hearings, courts-martial, or even psychiatric case conferences, they act as boundary-maintaining devices in the sense that they demonstrate to whatever audience is concerned where the line is drawn between behavior that belongs in the special universe of the group and behavior that does not. In general, this kind of information is not easily relayed by the straightforward use of language. Most readers of this paragraph, for instance, have a fairly clear idea of the line separating theft from more legitimate forms of commerce, but few of them have ever seen a published statute describing these differences. More likely than not, our information on the subject has been drawn from publicized instances in which the relevant laws were applied—and for that matter, the law itself is largely a collection of past cases and decisions, a synthesis of the various confrontations which have occurred in the life of the legal order.

It may be important to note in this connection that confrontations between deviant offenders and the agents of control have always attracted a good deal of public attention. In our own past, the trial and punishment of offenders were staged in the market place and afforded the crowd a chance to participate in a direct, active way. Today, of course, we no longer parade deviants in the town square or expose them to the carnival atmosphere of a Tyburn, but it is interesting that the "reform" which brought about this change in penal practice coincided almost exactly with the development of newspapers as a medium of mass information. Perhaps this is no more than an accident of history, but it is nonetheless true that newspapers (and now radio and television) offer much the same kind of entertainment as public hangings or a Sunday visit to the local gaol. A considerable portion of what we call "news" is devoted to reports about deviant behavior and its consequences, and it is no simple matter to explain why these items should be considered newsworthy or why they should command the extraordinary attention they do. Perhaps they appeal to a number of psychological perversities among the mass audience, as commentators have suggested, but at the same time they constitute one of our main sources of information about the normative outlines of society. In a figurative sense, at least, morality and immorality meet at the public scaffold, and it is during this meeting that the line between them is drawn.

Boundaries are never a fixed property of any community. They are always shifting as the people of the group find new ways to define the outer limits of their universe, new ways to position themselves on the larger cultural map. Sometimes changes occur within the structure of the group which require its members to make a new survey of their territory—a change of leadership, a shift of mood. Sometimes changes occur in the surrounding environment, altering the background against which the people of the group have measured their own uniqueness. And always, new generations are moving in to take their turn guarding old institutions and need to be informed about the contours of the world they are inheriting. Thus single encounters between the deviant and his community are only fragments of an ongoing social process. Like an article of common law, boundaries remain a meaningful point of reference only so long as they are repeatedly tested by persons on the fringes of the group and repeatedly defended by persons chosen to represent the group's inner morality.

Each time the community moves to censure some act of deviation, then, and convenes a formal ceremony to deal with the responsible offender, it sharpens the authority of the violated norm and restates where the boundaries of the group are located.

For these reasons, deviant behavior is not a simple kind of leakage which occurs when the machinery of society is in poor working order, but may be, in controlled quantities, an important condition for preserving the stability of social life. Deviant forms of behavior, by marking the outer edges of group life, give the inner structure its special character and thus supply the framework within which the people of the group develop an orderly sense of their own cultural identity. Perhaps this is what Aldous Huxley had in mind when he wrote:

> Now tidiness is undeniably good—but a good of which it is easily possible to have too much and at too high a price. . . .The good life can only be lived in a society in which tidiness is preached and practiced, but not too fanatically, and where efficiency is always haloed, as it were, by a tolerated margin of mess.[2]

This raises a delicate theoretical issue. If we grant that human groups often derive benefit from deviant behavior, can we then assume that they are organized in such a way as to promote this resource? Can we assume, in other words, that forces operate in the social structure to recruit offenders and to commit them to long periods of service in the deviant ranks? This is not a question which can be answered with our present store of empirical data, but one observation can be made which gives the question an interesting perspective—namely, that deviant forms of conduct often seem to derive nourishment from the very agencies devised to inhibit them. Indeed, the agencies built by society for preventing deviance are often so poorly equipped for the task that we might well ask why this is regarded as their "real" function in the first place.

It is by now a thoroughly familiar argument that many of the institutions designed to discourage deviant behavior actually operate in such a way as to perpetuate it. For one thing, prisons, hospitals, and other similar agencies provide aid and shelter to large numbers of deviant persons, sometimes giving them a certain advantage in the competition for social resources. But beyond this, such institutions gather marginal people into tightly segregated groups, give them an opportunity to teach one another the skills and attitudes of a deviant career, and even provoke them into using these skills by reinforcing their sense of alienation from the rest of society.[3] Nor is this observation a modern one:

> The misery suffered in gaols is not half their evil; they are filled with every sort of corruption that poverty and wickedness can generate; with all the shameless and profligate enormities that can be produced by the impudence of ignomiry, the range of want, and the malignity of despair. In a prison the check of the public eye is removed; and the power of the law is spent. There are few fears, there are no blushes. The lewd inflame the more modest; the audacious harden the timid. Everyone fortifies himself as he can against his own remaining sensibility; endeavoring to practice on others the arts that are practiced on himself; and to gain the applause of his worst associates by imitating their manners.[4]

These lines, written almost two centuries ago, are a harsh indictment of prisons, but many of the conditions they describe continue to be reported in even the most modern studies of prison life. Looking at the matter from a long-range historical perspective, it is fair to conclude that prisons have done a conspicuously poor job of reforming the convicts placed in their custody; but the very consistency of this failure may have a peculiar logic of its own. Perhaps we find it difficult to change the worst of our penal practices because we *expect* the prison to harden the inmate's commitment to deviant forms of behavior and draw him more deeply into the deviant ranks. On the whole, we are a people who do not really expect deviants to change very much as they are processed through the control agencies we provide for them, and we are often reluctant to devote much of the community's resources to the job of rehabilitation. In this sense, the prison which graduates long rows of accomplished criminals (or, for that matter, the state asylum which stores its most severe cases away in some back ward) may do serious violence to the aims of its founders; but it does very little violence to the expectations of the population it serves.

These expectations, moreover, are found in every corner of society and constitute an important part of the climate in which we deal with deviant forms of behavior.

To begin with, the community's decision to bring deviant sanctions against one of its members is not a simple act of censure. It is an intricate rite of transition, at once moving the individual out of his ordinary place in society and transferring him into a special deviant position.[5] The ceremonies which mark this change of status, generally, have a number of related phases. They supply a formal stage on which the deviant and his community can confront one another (as in the criminal trial); they make an announcement about the nature of his deviancy (a verdict or diagnosis, for example); and they place him in a particular role which is thought to neutralize the harmful effects of his misconduct (like the role of prisoner or patient). These commitment ceremonies tend to be occasions of wide public interest and ordinarily take place in a highly dramatic setting.[6] Perhaps the most obvious example of a commitment ceremony is the criminal trial, with its elaborate formality and exaggerated ritual, but more modest equivalents can be found wherever procedures are set up to judge whether or not someone is legitimately deviant.

Now an important feature of these ceremonies in our own culture is that they are almost irreversible. Most provisional roles conferred by society—those of the student or conscripted soldier, for example—include some kind of terminal ceremony to mark the individual's movement back out of the role once its temporary advantages have been exhausted. But the roles allotted the deviant seldom make allowance for this type of passage. He is ushered into the deviant position by a decisive and often dramatic ceremony, yet is retired from it with scarcely a word of public notice. And as a result, the deviant often returns home with no proper license to resume a normal life in the community. Nothing has happened to cancel out the stigmas imposed upon him by earlier commitment ceremonies; nothing has happened to revoke the verdict or diagnosis pronounced upon him at that time. It should not be surprising, then, that the people of the community are apt to greet the returning deviant with a considerable degree of apprehension and distrust, for in a very real sense they are not at all sure who he is.

A circularity is thus set into motion which has all the earmarks of a "self-fulfilling prophesy" to use Merton's fine phrase. On the one hand, it seems quite obvious that the community's apprehensions help reduce whatever chances the deviant might otherwise have had for a successful return home. Yet at the same time, everyday experience seems to show that these suspicions are wholly reasonable, for it is a well-known and highly publicized fact that many if not most ex-convicts return to crime after leaving prison and that large numbers of mental patients require further treatment after an initial hospitalization. The common feeling that deviant persons never really change, then, may derive from a faulty premise; but the feeling is expressed so frequently and with such conviction that it eventually creates the facts which later "prove" it to be correct. If the returning deviant encounters this circularity often enough, it is quite understandable that he, too, may begin to wonder whether he has fully graduated from the deviant role, and he may respond to the uncertainty by resuming some kind of deviant activity. In many respects, this may be the only way for the individual and his community to agree what kind of person he is.

Moreover this prophesy is found in the official policies of even the most responsible agencies of control. Police departments could not operate with any real effectiveness if they did not regard ex-convicts as a ready pool of suspects to be tapped in the event of trouble, and psychiatric clinics could not do a successful job in the community if they were not always alert to the possibility of former patients suffering relapses. Thus the prophesy gains currency at many levels within the social order, not only in the poorly informed attitudes of the community at large, but in the best informed theories of most control agencies as well.

In one form or another this problem has been recognized in the West for many hundreds of years, and this simple fact has a curious implication. For if our culture has supported a steady flow of deviation throughout long periods of historical change, the rules which apply to any kind of evolutionary thinking would suggest that strong forces must be at work to keep the flow intact—and this because it contributes in some important way to the survival of the culture as a whole. This does not furnish us with sufficient warrant to declare that deviance is "functional" (in any of the many senses of that term), but it should certainly make us wary of the assumption so often made in sociological circles that any well-structured society is somehow designed to prevent deviant behavior from occurring.[7] . . .

. . . [T]he amount of deviation a community encounters is apt to remain fairly constant over time. To start at the beginning, it is a simple logistic fact that the number of deviancies which come to a community's attention are limited by the kinds of equipment it uses to detect and handle them, and to that extent the rate of deviation found in a community is at least in part a function of the size and complexity of its social control apparatus. A community's capacity for handling deviance, let us say, can be roughly estimated by counting its prison cells and hospital beds, its policemen and psychiatrists, its courts and clinics—and while this total cannot tell us anything important about the underlying psychological motives involved, it does say something about the manner in which the community views the problem. Most communities, it would seem, operate with the expectation that a relatively constant number of control agents is necessary to cope with a relatively constant number of offenders. The amount of men, money, and material assigned by society to "do something" about deviant behavior does not vary appreciably over time, and the implicit logic which governs the community's efforts to man a police force or maintain suitable facilities for the mentally ill seems to be that there is a fairly stable quota of trouble which should be anticipated.

In this sense, the agencies of control often seem to define their job as that of keeping deviance *within bounds* rather than that of obliterating it altogether. Many judges, for example, assume that severe punishments are a greater deterrent to crime than moderate ones, and so it is important to note that many of them are apt to impose harder penalties when crime seems to be on the increase and more lenient ones when it does not, almost as if the power of the bench were being used to keep the crime rate from getting out of hand.

Generally speaking, we invoke emergency measures when the volume of deviance threatens to grow beyond some level we have learned to consider "normal," but we do not react with the same alarm when the volume of deviance stays within those limits. As George Bernard Shaw once pointed out, a society completely intent on suppressing crime would punish every offender with all the severity it could manage—for the present system, with its careful attention to the formula that punishment should vary with the circumstances of the crime, only seems to suggest that society can afford certain kinds of crime more readily than others. From this point of view, every society acts on the assumption that it possesses the machinery for curbing crime—the power to impose inhibiting punishments—yet that power is ordinarily used in such a way as to stabilize rather than eliminate the amount of crime in the social order. . . .

Notes

1. In fact, the first statement of the general notion presented here was concerned with the study of small groups. See Robert A. Dentler and Kai T. Erikson, "The Functions of Deviance in Groups," *Social Problems*, VII (Fall 1959), pp. 98–107.

2. Aldous Huxley, *Prisons: The "Carceri" Etchings by Piranesi* (London: The Trianon Press, 1949), p. 13.

3. For a good description of this process in the modern prison, see Gresham Sykes, *The Society of Captives* (Princeton, N.J.: Princeton University Press, 1958). For discussions of similar problems in two different kinds of mental hospital, see Erving Goffman, *Asylums* (New York: Bobbs-Merrill, 1962) and Kai T. Erikson, "Patient Role and Social Uncertainty: A Dilemma of the Mentally Ill," *Psychiatry*, XX (August 1957), pp. 263–274.

4. Written by "a celebrated" but not otherwise identified author (perhaps Henry Fielding) and quoted in John Howard, *The State of the Prisons*, London, 1777 (London: J. M. Dent and Sons, 1929), p. 10.

5. The classic description of this process as it applies to the medical patient is found in Talcott Parsons, *The Social System* (Glencoe, Ill.: The Free Press, 1951).

6. See Harold Garfinkel, "Successful Degradation Ceremonies," *American Journal of Sociology*, LXI (January 1956), pp. 420–424.

7. Albert K. Cohen, for example, speaking for a dominant strain in sociological thinking, takes the question quite for granted: "It would seem that the control of deviant behavior is, by definition, a culture goal." See "The Study of Social Disorganization and Deviant Behavior" in Merton et al., *Sociology Today* (New York: Basic Books, 1959), p. 465.

4
Defining Deviancy Down

Daniel Patrick Moynihan

Fifty years ago, a child who brought a gun to school and fired it into the air during recess might have made national headlines. The same story today would barely make the local news. Perceptions of the seriousness of deviance mutate over time. Conduct that used to be judged heinous is reinterpreted to be something far less severe. Deviance is "not fixed but elastic—it 'stretches' or contracts with the passage of time. What was once taken as completely unacceptable conduct begins to be taken for granted.... [There is still evil but] the things regarded as evil are far more heinous than before" (Tittle and Paternoster 2000, 202).

This is precisely the point Moynihan makes here. Borrowing from the classic statements of Emile Durkheim and Kai Erikson, Moynihan suggests that societies can tolerate only so much deviance, and when they deem themselves overloaded, they will redefine formerly egregious behavior as tolerable conduct. Social deviance must be kept within certain limits, lest society implode in its attempt to regulate it. Redefinition permits a society's social control capacity to be enhanced, ensuring its smooth operation.

One of the most interesting aspects of Moynihan's argument is what he downplays. American society has become more punitive than ever before, increasing the depth and breadth of social control in ways intended to capture ever-expanding numbers and types of deviants. Some scholars suggest that we have entered a "culture of surveillance," where monitoring and detection have diffused outward from criminal justice and into society at large. Fear has in large measure driven this expansion, fear fueled by sensationalistic media implying that bad things can happen to any-

body at any time. Fear breeds the need for control, and the need for control makes surveillance more palatable, even if it means everyone (including the "innocent") will be scrutinized. How such patterns interface with, and contradict, some of the dynamics discussed by Moynihan promises to be of considerable interest.

In one of the founding texts of sociology, *The Rules of Sociological Method* (1895), Emile Durkheim set it down that "crime is normal." "It is," he wrote, "completely impossible for any society entirely free of it to exist." By defining what is deviant, we are enabled to know what is not; and hence to live by shared standards. This aperçu appears in the chapter entitled "Rules for the Distinction of the Normal from the Pathological." Durkheim writes:

> From this viewpoint the fundamental facts of criminology appear to us in an entirely new light.... [T]he criminal no longer appears as an utterly unsociable creature, a sort of parasitic element, a foreign, inassimilable body introduced into the bosom of society. He plays a normal role in social life. For its part, crime must no longer be conceived of as an evil which cannot be circumscribed closely enough. Far from there being cause for congratulation when it drops too noticeably below the normal level, this apparent progress assuredly coincides with and is linked to some social disturbance.

Durkheim suggests, for example, that "in times of scarcity" crimes of assault drop off. He does not imply that we ought to approve of crime—"[p]ain has likewise nothing desirable about it"—but we need to understand its function. He saw religion, in the sociologist Randall Collins's terms, as "fundamentally a set of ceremonial actions, assembling the group, heightening its emotions, and focusing its members on symbols of their common belongingness." In this context "a punishment ceremony creates social solidarity."

The matter was pretty much left at that until seventy years later when, in 1965, Kai T. Erikson published *Wayward Puritans*, a study of "crime rates" in the Massachusetts Bay Colony. The plan behind the book, as Erikson put it, was "to test [Durkheim's] notion that the number of deviant offenders a community can afford to recognize is likely to remain stable over time." The notion proved out very well indeed.

Despite occasional crime waves, as when itinerant Quakers refused to take off their hats in the presence of magistrates, the amount of deviance in this corner of seventeenth-century New England fitted nicely with the supply of stocks and whipping posts. Erikson remarks:

> It is one of the arguments of the . . . study that the amount of deviation a community encounters is apt to remain fairly constant over time. To start at the beginning, it is a simple logistic fact that the number of deviancies which come to a community's attention are limited by the kinds of equipment it uses to detect and handle them, and to that extent the rate of deviation found in a community is at least in part a function of the size and complexity of its social control apparatus. A community's capacity for handling deviance, let us say, can be roughly estimated by counting its prison cells and hospital beds, its policemen and psychiatrists, its courts and clinics. Most communities, it would seem, operate with the expectation that a relatively constant number of control agents is necessary to cope with a relatively constant number of offenders. The amount of men, money, and material assigned by society to "do something" about deviant behavior does not vary appreciably over time, and the implicit logic which governs the community's efforts to man a police force or maintain suitable facilities for the mentally ill seems to be that there is a fairly stable quota of trouble which should be anticipated.

In this sense, the agencies of control often seem to define their job as that of keeping deviance within bounds rather than that of obliterating it altogether. Many judges, for example, assume that severe punishments are a greater deterrent to crime than moderate ones, and so it is important to note that many of them are apt to impose harder penalties when crime seems to be on the increase and more lenient ones when it does not, almost as if the power of the bench were being used to keep the crime rate from getting out of hand.

Erikson was taking issue with what he described as "a dominant strain in sociological thinking" that took for granted that a well-structured society "is somehow designed to prevent deviant behavior from occurring." In both authors, Durkheim and Erikson, there is an undertone that suggests that, with deviancy, as with most social goods, there is the continuing problem of demand exceeding supply. Durkheim invites us to

> imagine a society of saints, a perfect cloister of exemplary individuals. Crimes properly so called, will there be unknown; but faults which appear venial to the layman will create there the same scandal that the ordinary offense does in ordinary consciousness. If, then, this society has the power to judge and punish, it will define these acts as criminal and will treat them as such.

Recall Durkheim's comment that there need be no cause for congratulations should the amount of crime drop "too noticeably below the normal level." It would not appear that Durkheim anywhere contemplates the possibility of too much crime. Clearly his theory would have required him to deplore such a development, but the possibility seems never to have occurred to him.

Erikson, writing much later in the twentieth century, contemplates both possibilities. "Deviant persons can be said to supply needed services to society." There is no doubt a tendency for the supply of any needed thing to run short. But he is consistent. There can, he believes, be *too much* of a good thing. Hence "the number of deviant offenders a community *can afford* to recognize is likely to remain stable over time." [My emphasis]

Social scientists are said to be on the lookout for poor fellows getting a bum rap. But here is a theory that clearly implies that there are circumstances in which society will choose *not* to notice behavior that would be otherwise controlled, or disapproved, or even punished.

It appears to me that this is in fact what we in the United States have been doing of late. I proffer the thesis that, over the past generation, since the time Erikson wrote, the amount of deviant behavior in American society has increased beyond the levels the community can "afford to recognize" and that, accordingly, we have been re-defining deviancy so as to exempt much conduct previously stigmatized, and also quietly raising the "normal" level in categories where behavior is now abnormal by any earlier standard. This redefining has evoked fierce resistance from defenders of "old" standards, and accounts for much of the present "cultural war" such as proclaimed by many at the 1992 Republican National Convention.

Let me, then, offer three categories of re-definition in these regards: the *altruistic*, the *opportunistic*, and the *normalizing*.

The first category, the *altruistic*, may be illustrated by the deinstitutionalization movement within the mental health profession that appeared in the 1950s. . . .

Our second, or *opportunistic* mode of re-definition, reveals at most a nominal intent to do good. The true object is to do well, a long-established motivation among mortals. In this pattern, a growth in deviancy makes possible a transfer of resources, including prestige, to those who control the deviant population. This control would be jeopardized if any serious effort were made to reduce the deviancy in question. This leads to assorted strategies for re-defining the behavior in question as not all that deviant, really. . . .

Our *normalizing* category most directly corresponds to Erikson's proposition that "the number of deviant offenders a community can afford to recognize is likely to remain stable over time." Here we are dealing with the popular psychological notion of "denial." In 1965, having reached the conclusion that there would be a dramatic increase in single-parent families, I reached the further conclusion that this would in turn lead to a dramatic increase in crime. In an article in *America,* I wrote:

From the wild Irish slums of the 19th century Eastern seaboard to the riot-torn suburbs of Los Angeles, there is one unmistakable lesson in American history: a community that allows a large number of young men to grow up in broken families, dominated by women, never acquiring any stable relationship to male authority, never acquiring any set of rational expectations about the future—that community asks for and gets chaos. Crime, violence, unrest, unrestrained lashing out at the whole social structure—that is not only to be expected; it is very near to inevitable.

The inevitable, as we now know, has come to pass, but here again our response is curiously passive. Crime is a more or less continuous subject of political pronouncement, and from time to time it will be at or near the top of opinion polls as a matter of public concern. But it never gets much further than that. In the words spoken from the bench, Judge Edwin Torres of the New York State Supreme Court, Twelfth Judicial District, described how "the slaughter of the innocent marches unabated: subway riders, bodega owners, cab drivers, babies; in laundromats, at cash machines, on elevators, in hallways." In personal communication, he writes: "This numbness, this near narcoleptic state can diminish the human condition to the level of combat infantrymen, who, in protracted campaigns, can eat their battlefield rations seated on the bodies of the fallen, friend and foe alike. A society that loses its sense of outrage is doomed to extinction." There is no expectation that this will change, nor any efficacious public insistence that it do so. The crime level has been *normalized.*

Consider the St. Valentine's Day Massacre. In 1929 in Chicago during Prohibition, four gangsters killed seven gangsters on February 14. The nation was shocked. The event became legend. It merits not one but two entries in the *World Book Encyclopedia.* I leave it to others to judge, but it would appear that the society in the 1920s was simply not willing to put up with this degree of deviancy. In the end, the Constitution was amended, and Prohibition, which lay behind so much gangster violence, ended.

In recent years, again in the context of illegal traffic in controlled substances, this form of murder has returned. But it has done so at a level that induces denial. James Q. Wilson comments that Los Angeles has the equivalent of a St. Valentine's Day Massacre every weekend. Even the most ghastly re-enactments of such human slaughter produce only moderate responses. On the morning after the close of the Democratic National Convention in New York City in July, there was such an account in the second section of the *New York Times*. It was not a big story; bottom of the page, but with a headline that got your attention: "3 Slain in Bronx Apartment, but a Baby is Saved." A subhead continued: "A mother's last act was to hide her little girl under the bed." The article described a drug execution; the now-routine blindfolds made from duct tape; a man and a woman and a teenager involved. "Each had been shot once in the head." The police had found them a day later. They also found, under a bed, a three-month-old baby, dehydrated but alive. A lieutenant remarked of the mother, "In her last dying act she protected her baby. She probably knew she was going to die, so she stuffed the baby where she knew it would be safe." But the matter was left there. The police would do their best. But the event passed quickly; forgotten by the next day, it will never make *World Book*.

Nor is it likely that any great heed will be paid to an uncanny reenactment of the Prohibition drama a few months later, also in the Bronx. The *Times* story, page B3, reported:

9 Men Posing as Police Are Indicted in 3 Murders

Drug Dealers Were Kidnapped for Ransom

The *Daily News* story, same day, page 17, made it *four* murders, adding nice details about torture techniques. The gang members posed as federal Drug Enforcement Administration agents, real badges and all. The victims were drug dealers, whose families were uneasy about calling the police. Ransom seems generally to have been set in the $650,000 range. Some paid. Some got it in the back of the head. So it goes.

Yet, violent killings, often random, go on unabated. Peaks continue to attract some notice. But these are peaks above "average" levels that thirty years ago would have been thought epidemic. . . .

A Kai Erikson of the future will surely need to know that the Department of Justice in 1990 found that Americans reported only about 38 percent of all crimes and 48 percent of violent crimes. This, too, can be seen as a means of *normalizing* crime. In much the same way, the vocabulary of crime reporting can be seen to move toward the normal-seeming. A teacher is shot on her way to class. The *Times* subhead reads: "Struck in the Shoulder in the Year's First Shooting Inside a School." First of the season. . . .

The hope—if there be such—of this essay has been twofold. It is, first, to suggest that the Durkheim constant, as I put it, is maintained by a dynamic process which adjusts upwards and *downwards*. Liberals have traditionally been alert for upward redefining that does injustice to individuals. Conservatives have been correspondingly sensitive to downward redefining that weakens societal standards. Might it not help if we could all agree that there is a dynamic at work here? It is not revealed truth, nor yet a scientifically derived formula. It is simply a pattern we observe in ourselves. Nor is it rigid. There may once have been an unchanging supply of jail cells which more or less determined the number of prisoners. No longer. We are building new prisons at a prodigious rate. Similarly, the executioner is back. There is something of a competition in Congress to think up new offenses for which the death penalty is seemed the only available deterrent. Possibly also modes of execution, as in "fry the kingpins." Even so, we are getting used to a lot of behavior that is not good for us.

As noted earlier, Durkheim states that there is "nothing desirable" about pain. Surely what he meant was that there is nothing pleasurable. Pain, even so, is an indispensable warning signal. But societies under stress, much like individuals, will turn to pain killers of various kinds that end up concealing real damage. There is surely nothing desirable about this. If our analysis wins general acceptance, if, for example, more of us came to share Judge Torres's genuine alarm at "the trivialization of the lunatic crime rate" in his city (and mine), we might surprise ourselves how well we respond to the manifest decline of the American civic order. Might.

Part II

Explaining Deviance

The goal of any theory is to explain, predict, and understand. Theory is cumulative, building on prior insights and incorporating new ones to approximate "the truth" about the phenomenon being studied. The process relies heavily on hypothesis formation, observation, and testing—strategies undertaken to figure out if the topic of inquiry is being explained in the simplest, most accurate, and most efficient way possible. Theory has a reputation for being abstract, "in the clouds," and unrelated to real-life concerns, but these attributions are not true (Neuman 1999). Theorists want to explain the most with the least and to do it in the most uncomplicated way possible.

At the heart of any theory is causation, and theories of deviance are no different. Ascertaining the root causes of deviance has become something of a Holy Grail, consuming scholarly attention for the better part of five centuries. Philosophers, religious figures, academicians, and social commentators have grappled with etiological factors for as long as rules have existed to be broken. Only recently, however, has the enterprise become systematic and rigorous. Admittedly, not all such efforts have been objective or value-free. Researchers early in the twentieth century produced "evidence" that deviants were a biologically inferior class of humans, a species that had failed to fully evolve and whose behavior was crude, lewd, and habitually out-of-bounds. These scholars suggested that rule-breakers were "degenerates [who] lacked the natural sentiments of probity and pity [consideration, sympathy, empathy] . . .normally present in their civilized brethren" (Garofolo quoted in Pfohl 1985, 96). Because deviance was hereditary, it also was uncorrectable. Draconian measures followed, and tens of thousands were involuntarily sterilized, jailed, or exterminated on the basis of genetic "defects" that were often nothing more than physical characteristics that the wider society disliked or deemed suspicious. Many such policies lasted well into the twentieth century, as Pfohl (1985, 109) notes:

> As late as 1976 . . .eleven . . .states allowed the sterilization of "hereditary criminals." Seven others permitted such procedures to be involuntarily used to control sex offenders, degenerates, and "moral degenerates." The vague terminology of such laws is troubling. Consider an Oregon statute allowing sterilization for "all persons who are feebleminded, insane, epileptic, habitual criminals, incurable syphilitics, moral degenerates or perverts, and who are . . .or will likely become, a menace to society."

Psychological approaches came into vogue shortly thereafter. They enjoy perhaps the broadest popular following today, in part because of the general public's fixation with the deviant mind and in part because of the widespread belief that deviance is indicative of underlying mental illness. Psychological perspectives vary in level of sophistication—from the armchair theorizing of pseudo-intellectuals and media pundits to the complex cognitive models offered by renowned academics at the nation's leading universities. All, however, share the notion that deviance is rooted in some defect of the individual psyche.

Sigmund Freud, father of modern psychoanalysis, suggests that unresolved childhood traumas are to blame. Traumas, he claims, produce (among other things) an overdeveloped superego, which, in turn, triggers an abiding sense of guilt that cries out for punishment. Deviant behavior emerges to secure that punishment and cleanse that guilt (Freud 1943). Contemporary psychologists argue that deviance is a product of personality traits; low self-control, rebelliousness, risk-taking, impulsivity, and poor self-esteem are principally implicated. Since such traits tend to be stable in individuals over time, deviance persists unless or until there is some cognitive intervention to mitigate them.

Few interventions, however, are of much value for deviance triggered by mental pathology—a host of maladies that includes everything from neuroses (chronic difficulty coping with everyday life) to psychoses (lack of contact with reality, delusions of persecution) to sociopathy (asocial, amoral, impulsive, aggressive, and chronically deceptive behavior). That deviance is a manifestation of mental illness makes a seductive argument, especially when the behavior involved is truly heinous. Surely, the woman (Susan Smith) who locked her two toddlers in a car and pushed it into the lake; the man who homosexually raped, killed, and then ate his victims (Jeffrey Dahmer); the commuter (Colin Ferguson) who shot a passenger train full of innocent people for no apparent reason; or the Florida couple who allegedly dropped 12-pound sledgehammers on their retarded child's feet, locked him in a darkened bathroom, gagged, with hands tied behind his back and a bucket placed over his head to reinforce his sense of isolation (Harris 2000) must be "whacko." Why else would someone do such horrible things? Such explanations, however, are notoriously circular: people are sick when they do such terrible things, and because these acts are so terrible, the people who commit them must be sick.

Sociological explanations currently dominate the field of deviance theory, and for good reason. Sociological approaches focus on processes and on the structural and interactional forces that transform deviant propensities (tendencies or predispositions to behavior) into hard-and-fast conduct. Propensities to deviate inhere in everyone to varying degrees but are meaningless unless or until they are brought out in real-life circumstances. How they emerge and what they look like is in large part subjective. Two people with identical sets of "risk factors," for example, will not deviate at the same level or the same frequency. Identical risk factors can lead to very different kinds of deviance in different situations; someone determined to deviate one moment may not be the next (Jacobs and Wright 1999; Katz 1988). The situationally contingent nature of sociological approaches helps account for this variation by addressing the institutional, subcultural, and interactional conditions that mediate all social action.

Sociologists prefer studying the influence of structures and institutions on behavior, so it is not surprising that the lion's share of scholarly attention has been devoted to the concept of anomie. Anomie refers to the state of "normlessness" that occurs when social structures are unable to meet the expectations of the individuals who are part of the structure. Anomie is especially acute during periods of rapid social change, since people tend to be more weakly tied to social structures at these times than at any others. Many triggers have been implicated, but economic ones are primary: Sudden bursts of prosperity, severe depressions, and major shifts in the mode of economic production are foremost (Durkheim 1951).

Some analysts contend that anomie is a relatively permanent feature of social life, and American life in particular, where chronic discrepancies between cultural goals (especially those pertaining to material success) and institutional means generate strain (strain, in turn, leads to anomie). In materialistic societies, deviance is a mirror image of opportunity, so those on the lowest rungs of the socioeconomic hierarchy will be most at risk. A great deal of deviance by such persons is "innovative"—illegal activity committed for material gain (e.g., robbery, burglary, shoplifting, drug dealing). Innovation, however, is by no means limited to the less affluent. In materialistic societies, no amount of money is ever enough, and white-collar and middle-class deviance is common. Nor is innovation the only possible adaptation. Some people "retreat," consuming drugs and alcohol in chronic fits of escapism. Others eschew material goals and lash out at everything that mainstream society deems important and worthwhile; their lives become filled with resistance, rage, and re-action-formation. Still others replace the society's dominant goals and means with something completely different (participation in religious cults is one such response; see Merton 1938). How a person will react to a given set of circumstances is in large measure unknowable, since situational contexts are in a constant state of flux. The point to remember is that structural conditions (like anomie) provide a backdrop against which all decisions, be they deviant or conformist, are rendered.

Institutions provide a background for behavior but situations provide the foreground; sociological theories that focus on the dynamic contribution of situations are generally referred to as "process theories." Process theories redress errors that emerge when structural theories are applied crudely and without proper sensitivity at the individual level (Brown et al. 1996, 281). Many people, for example, will experience a great deal of structural strain yet never deviate. Others will experience minimal strain yet become habitual offenders. Criminologist Edwin Sutherland (1937) says the answer lies in differential association; association with and exposure to other deviants in small-group settings causes deviant attitudes, rationalizations, and values to be learned. The more frequently and the longer a person interacts with norm violators, Sutherland suggests, the more importance a person vests in those

interactions, and the more impressionable one is when those interactions take place, the more likely the exposed person will stray. The theory is classless because it applies to everyone in the socioeconomic structure, regardless of position. Indeed, Sutherland does not put much credence in theories that claim people break rules for money, status, or prestige (as many of the structural theories do) because law-abiding people pursue conformist activities (like a regular job) for the very same reasons.

Process approaches that focus on the *cultural* contribution to rule-breaking are related to theories like differential association insofar as the focus remains on the "normative content of [groups] and how members of groups are trained [to deviate] through a learning process" (Brown et al. 1996, 294). Cultural theories, however, focus more explicitly on the social and interpersonal forces that generate, transmit, and prize deviant norms over conventional ones. Paradoxically, these theories suggest that deviance actually is conformity—conformity to norms of groups that run in opposition to those of the mainstream. The notion that deviance is relative must be reiterated here; deviance is part and parcel of an alternative normative structure that makes rule-breaking normal, justified, and accepted. Indeed, failure to act in prescribed but deviant ways would itself be deviant. Circumscribed (deviant) social worlds require the enactment of prevailing conduct norms, lest one be labeled an outsider and face attendant exploitation. Theories that apply this approach include Wolfgang and Ferracuti's (1967) subculture of violence thesis, Sellin's (1938) culture conflict approach, and Miller's (1958) lower-class culture theory.

Some process theories focus on the opposite side of the deviance coin, asking not so much why people stray but why they conform. Travis Hirschi's (1969) control theory is preeminent. In it, he points out that everyone has strong, innate urges to act on their impulses—to want things without working for them, to seek physical pleasure without regard for social convention, to release pent-up aggressions through reflexive rather than reflective action. Some people have less self-control than others, and these individuals represent the greatest threat to social order. Low self-control, however, can be enhanced in decidedly sociological ways, notably through the establishment of strong social bonds with key caregivers. Hirschi argues that the more attached an individual is to loving parents and other central authority figures, the less prone he or she will be to act on his or her impulses. The social bond acts as a protective shield, enticing would-be deviants to conform because they realize there is too much to lose if they do not. Strong social bonds lead to involvement in conventional pursuits, belief in moral authority, and a stake in conformity, all of which function to direct deviant energies in socially acceptable ways. Parents are the key component in this equation, and control theorists go so far as to suggest that chronic deviation is more a function of bad parenting than anything else. Holding parents responsible for the deviant acts of their children is a popular position among policymakers who subscribe to this perspective and, in fact, many states mandate criminal penalties—fines, probation, and even jail time—for adults who fail to parent adequately.

Finally, there are process theories that place blame squarely on society for individual deviance. Foremost among them is the labeling perspective, which suggests that deviants are not born out of anomie, culture, learning, biology, psychology, or anything else but by a capricious system of legislation and enforcement that functions to stigmatize some behaviors and ignore others. The "system" makes otherwise good people bad. The process is fairly straightforward: People engage in conduct that violates some arbitrary social rule; they are caught and labeled; they internalize the identity of "offender," which triggers a self-fulfilling prophecy that results in yet more deviance (Becker 1963). This is Cooley's (1902) principle of the looking-glass self at its best (or worst), where one's self-image is a direct function of others' perceptions: "You think I am a certain kind of person, you expect a certain kind of behavior from me, and, in keeping with those expectations, I'm going to act in precisely the

way you expect me to." Labeling theory articulates a feedback loop in which initial acts of deviance lead to a deviant label, which lead to more rule-breaking (secondary deviance), which leads to yet more attention from social control agents and reinforcement of the deviant label, as the internalized status of offender takes on a powerful logic all its own.

Wittingly or unwittingly, policymakers reinforce this cycle by insisting that deviants be stigmatized through severe punishment (e.g., jail), which results in a permanent record and extreme difficulty in reintegrating into the mainstream. The intention is to make an example out of those who violate rules, with the hope of deterring them and others from doing the same, but the process often backfires badly. It also has little or no effect on would-be deviants, who typically think that they will never get caught—or may not care if they do. The prospect of getting caught may even entice some to perform deviate acts where they would not have previously: by making something against the rules, it often becomes more attractive, as anyone who has ever been drawn to forbidden fruit can attest.

By no means is this an exhaustive discussion of deviance theories. Nor is it intended to suggest that any one of them is superior to, or more comprehensive than, any of the others. Rather, it is intended to provide a convenient framework with which to conceptualize and organize key principles and to set the stage for the more detailed discussions that follow. Though each approach focuses on particular levels and units of analysis, each attempts to explain essentially the same things: why people deviate, under what conditions, and why rates of deviance vary across time and space. Structural theories are concerned with large-scale social forces; process theories implicate culture, groups, and interactions; "bridging" theories blame a little bit of everything. At the heart of each approach is a concern with causality—the factor or factors responsible for creating a climate conducive to rule-breaking and for making deviance seem logical and acceptable. ✦

5
Deviance and Low Self-Control

Michael Gottfredson
Travis Hirschi

Gottfredson and Hirschi's general theory of deviance begins with the rather controversial assumption that human nature, if not evil, is inherently antisocial. People, they suggest, are born with the innate disposition to seek pleasure without regard for social convention, to live hedonistically for the here and now, to pursue solutions that are easy and available rather than moral, to exploit others for instrumental ends. Some people are more naturally predisposed to act in these ways than others—that is, they have less self-control—but self-control has a strong learned component. It is cultivated through a process of socialization with key caregivers. Parents are modally responsible in this role, so those who fail to monitor and sanction their offspring appropriately set them up for habitual rule-breaking later on.

As opposed to differential association and culture conflict theories—which suggest that deviance is a product of socialization— Gottfredson and Hirschi suggest that deviance is actually a product of failed socialization. The contemporary trend toward single-parent families and "high-velocity" lifestyles is likely to make matters worse (by undermining an already weakened system of regulation). Some control theorists go so far as to suggest that schools and other institutions may have to become parental substitutes (that among other things, should provide formal religious instruction and courses in child-rearing and should administer corporal punishment for rule violators). Holding parents responsible for the sins of their unsupervised children is another option, a policy that has been gaining increasing popularity in the wake of serious criminal violence perpetrated by young children.

. . . [I]ndividual differences in the tendency to commit criminal acts . . . *remain reasonably stable with change in the social location of individuals and change in their knowledge of the operation of sanction systems*. This is the problem of self-control, the differential tendency of people to avoid criminal acts whatever the circumstances in which they find themselves. Since this difference among people has attracted a variety of names, we begin by arguing the merits of the concept of self-control. . . .

The Elements of Self-Control

Criminal acts provide *immediate* gratification of desires. A major characteristic of people with low self-control is therefore a tendency to respond to tangible stimuli in the immediate environment, to have a concrete "here and now" orientation. People with high self-control, in contrast, tend to defer gratification.

Criminal acts provide *easy or simple* gratification of desires. They provide money without work, sex without courtship, revenge without court delays. People lacking self-control also tend to lack diligence, tenacity, or persistence in a course of action.

Criminal acts are *exciting, risky, or thrilling*. They involve stealth, danger, speed, agility, deception, or power. People lacking self-control therefore tend to be adventuresome, active, and physical. Those with high levels of self-control tend to be cautious, cognitive, and verbal.

Crimes provide *few or meager long-term benefits*. They are not equivalent to a job or a career. On the contrary, crimes interfere with long-term commitments to jobs, marriages, family, or friends. People with low self-control thus tend to have unstable marriages, friendships, and job profiles. They tend to be little interested in and unprepared for long-term occupational pursuits.

Crimes require *little skill or planning*. The cognitive requirements for most crimes are minimal. It follows that people lacking self-control need not possess or value cognitive or academic skills. The manual skills required for most crimes are minimal. It follows that people lacking self-control need not possess manual skills that require training or apprenticeship.

Crimes often result in *pain or discomfort for the victim*. Property is lost, bodies are injured, privacy is violated, trust is broken. It follows that people with low self-control tend to be self-centered, indifferent, or insensitive to the suffering and needs of others. It does not follow, however, that people with low self-control are routinely unkind or antisocial. On the contrary, they may discover the immediate and easy rewards of charm and generosity.

Recall that crime involves the pursuit of immediate pleasure. It follows that people lacking self-control will also tend to pursue immediate pleasures that are *not* criminal: they will tend to smoke, drink, use drugs, gamble, have children out of wedlock, and engage in illicit sex.

Crimes require the interaction of an offender with people or their property. It does not follow that people lacking self-control will tend to be gregarious or social. However, it does follow that, other things being equal, gregarious or social people are more likely to be involved in criminal acts.

The major benefit of many crimes is not pleasure but relief from momentary irritation. The irritation caused by a crying child is often the stimulus for physical abuse. That caused by a taunting stranger in a bar is often the stimulus for aggravated assault. It follows that people with low self-control tend to have minimal tolerance for frustration and little ability to respond to conflict through verbal rather than physical means.

Crimes involve the risk of violence and physical injury, of pain and suffering on the part of the offender. It does not follow that people with low self-control will tend to be tolerant of physical pain or to be indifferent to physical discomfort. It does follow that people tolerant of physical pain or indifferent to physical discomfort will be more likely to engage in criminal acts whatever their level of self-control.

The risk of criminal penalty for any given criminal act is small, but this depends in part on the circumstances of the offense. Thus, for example, not all joyrides by teenagers are equally likely to result in arrest. A car stolen from a neighbor and returned unharmed before he notices its absence is less likely to result in official notice than is a car stolen from a shopping center parking lot and abandoned at the convenience of the offender. Drinking alcohol stolen from parents and consumed in the family garage is less likely to receive official notice than drinking in the parking lot outside a concert hall. It follows that offenses differ in their validity as measures of self-control: those offenses with large risk of public awareness are better measures than those with little risk.

In sum, people who lack self-control will tend to be impulsive, insensitive, physical (as opposed to mental), risk-taking, short-sighted, and nonverbal, and they will tend therefore to engage in criminal and analogous acts. Since these traits can be identified prior to the age of responsibility for crime, since there is considerable tendency for these traits to come together in the same people, and since the traits tend to persist through life, it seems reasonable to consider them as comprising a stable construct useful in the explanation of crime.

The Many Manifestations of Low Self-Control

Our image of the "offender" suggests that crime is not an automatic or necessary consequence of low self-control. It suggests that many noncriminal acts analogous to crime (such as accidents, smoking, and alcohol use) are also manifestations of low self-control. Our image therefore implies that no specific act, type of crime, or form of deviance is uniquely required by the absence of self-control.

Because both crime and analogous behaviors stem from low self-control (that is, both are manifestations of low self-control) they will all be engaged in at a relatively high rate by people with low self-control. Within the domain of crime, then, there will be much versatility among offenders in the criminal acts in which they engage.

Research on versatility of deviant acts supports these predictions in the strongest possible way. The variety of manifestations of low self-control is immense. In spite of years of tireless research motivated by belief in specialization, no credible evidence of specialization has been reported. In fact, the evidence of offender versatility is overwhelming (Hirschi 1969; Hindelang 1971; Wolfgang, Figlio, and Sellin 1972; Petersilia 1980; Hindelang, Hirschi, and Weis 1981; Rojeck and Erickson 1982; Klein 1984).

By versatility we mean that offenders commit a wide variety of criminal acts, with no strong inclination to pursue a specific criminal act or pattern of criminal acts to the exclusion of others. Most theories suggest that offenders tend to specialize, whereby such terms as robber, burglar, drug dealer, rapist, and murderer have predictive or descriptive import. In fact, some theories create offender specialization as part of their explanation of crime. For example, Cloward and Ohlin (1960) create distinctive subcultures of delinquency around particular forms of criminal behavior, identifying subcultures specializing in theft, violence, or drugs. In a related way, books are written about white-collar crime as though it were a clearly distinct specialty requiring a unique explanation. Research projects are undertaken for the study of drug use, or vandalism, or teen pregnancy (as though every study of delinquency were not a study of drug use and vandalism and teenage sexual behavior). Entire schools of criminology emerge to pursue patterning, sequencing, progression, escalation, onset, persistence, and desistance in the career of offenses or offenders. These efforts survive largely because their proponents fail to consider or acknowledge the clear evidence to the contrary. Other reasons for survival of such ideas may be found in the interest of politicians and members of the law enforcement community who see policy potential in criminal careers or "career criminals" (see, e.g., Blumstein et al. 1986).

Occasional reports of specialization seem to contradict this point, as do everyday observations of repetitive misbehavior by particular offenders. Some offenders rob the same store repeatedly over a period of years, or an offender commits several rapes over a (brief) period of time. Such offenders may be called "robbers" or "rapists." However, it

should be noted that such labels are retrospective rather than predictive and that they typically ignore a large amount of delinquent or criminal behavior by the same offenders that is inconsistent with their alleged specialty. Thus, for example, the "rapist" will tend also to use drugs, to commit robberies and burglaries (often in concert with the rape), and to have a record for violent offenses other than rape. There is a perhaps natural tendency on the part of observers (and in official accounts) to focus on the most serious crimes in a series of events, but this tendency should not be confused with a tendency on the part of the offender to specialize in one kind of crime.

Recall that one of the defining features of crime is that it is simple and easy. Some apparent specialization will therefore occur because obvious opportunities for an easy score will tend to repeat themselves. An offender who lives next to a shopping area that is approached by pedestrians will have repeat opportunities for purse snatching, and this may show in his arrest record. But even here the specific "criminal career" will tend to quickly run its course and to be followed by offenses whose content and character is likewise determined by convenience and opportunity (which is the reason why some form of theft is always the best bet about what a person is likely to do next).

The evidence that offenders are likely to engage in noncriminal acts psychologically or theoretically equivalent to crime is, because of the relatively high rates of these "noncriminal" acts, even easier to document. Thieves are likely to smoke, drink, and skip school at considerably higher rates than nonthieves. Offenders are considerably more likely than nonoffenders to be involved in most types of accidents, including household fires, auto crashes, and unwanted pregnancies. They are also considerably more likely to die at an early age (see, e.g., Robins 1966; Eysenck 1977; Gottfredson 1984). . . .

Note that these outcomes are consistent with four general elements of our notion of self-control: basic stability of individual differences over a long period of time; great variability in the kinds of criminal acts engaged in; conceptual or casual equivalence of criminal and noncriminal acts; and inability to predict the specific forms of deviance engaged in, whether criminal or noncriminal. In our view, the idea of an antisocial personality defined by certain behavioral consequences is too positivistic or deterministic, suggesting that the offender must do certain things given his antisocial personality. Thus we would say only that the subjects in question are *more likely* to commit criminal acts as [the data indicate they are]. We do not make commission of criminal acts as part of the definition of the individual with low self-control. . . .

The Causes of Self-Control

We know better what deficiencies in self-control lead to than where they come from. One thing is, however, clear: low self-control is not produced by training, tutelage, or socialization. As a matter of fact, all of the characteristics associated with low self-control tend to show themselves in the absence of nurturance, discipline, or training. Given the classical appreciation of the causes of human behavior, the implications of this fact are straightforward: the causes of low self-control are negative rather than positive; self-control is unlikely in the absence of effort, intended or unintended, to create it. . . .

The major "cause" of low self-control thus appears to be ineffective child-rearing. Put in positive terms, several conditions appear necessary to produce a socialized child. . . .

. . .[T]he minimum conditions seem to be these: in order to teach the child self-control, someone must (1) monitor the child's behavior; (2) recognize deviant behavior when it occurs; and (3) punish such behavior. This seems simple and obvious enough. All that is required to activate the system is affection for or investment in the child. The person who cares for the child will watch his behavior, see him doing things he should not do, and correct him. The result may be a child more capable of delaying gratification, more sensitive to the interests and desires of others, more independent, more willing to accept restraints on his activity, and more unlikely to use force or violence to attain his ends. . . .

References

Blumstein, Alfred, Jacqueline Cohen, Jeffrey Roth, and Christy Visher. 1986. *Criminal Careers and "Career Criminals."* Washington, D.C.: National Academy Press.

Cloward, Richard, and Lloyd Ohlin. 1960. *Delinquency and Opportunity.* New York: The Free Press.

Eysenck, Hans. 1977. *Crime and Personality.* Rev. ed. London: Paladin.

Glueck, Sheldon, and Eleanor Glueck. 1950. *Unraveling Juvenile Delinquency.* Cambridge, Mass.: Harvard University Press.

Gottfredson, Michael. 1984. *Victims of Crime: The Dimensions of Risk.* London: HMSO.

Hindelang, Michael J. 1971. "Age, Sex, and the Versatility of Delinquent Involvements." *Social Problems,* 18:522–535.

Hindelang, Michael J., Travis Hirschi, and Joseph Weis. 1981. *Measuring Delinquency.* Beverly Hills, CA: Sage.

Hirschi, Travis. 1969. *Causes of Delinquency.* Berkeley: University of California Press.

Klein, Malcolm. 1984. "Offense Specialization and Versatility Among Juveniles." *British Journal of Criminology,* 24:185–194.

McCord, William, and Joan McCord. 1959. *Origins of Crime: A New Evaluation of the Cambridge-Somerville Study.* New York: Columbia University Press.

Petersilia, Joan. 1980. "Criminal Career Research: A Review of Recent Evidence." In *Crime and Justice: An Annual Review of Research,* vol. 2, edited by M. Tonry and N. Morris (pp. 321–379). Chicago: University of Chicago Press.

Robins, Lee. 1966. *Deviant Children Grown Up.* Baltimore: Williams and Wilkins.

Rojeck, Dean, and Maynard Erickson. 1982. "Delinquent Careers." *Criminology,* 20:5–28.

Rutter, Michael, and Henri Giller. 1984. *Juvenile Delinquency: Trends and Perspectives.* New York: Guilford.

West, Donald, and David Farrington. 1973. *Who Becomes Delinquent?* London: Heinmann.

Wolfgang, Marvin, Robert Figlio, and Thorsten Sellin. 1972. *Delinquency in a Birth Cohort.* Chicago: University of Chicago Press.

6
Deviance, the American Dream, and Social Institutions

Steven F. Messner

Richard Rosenfeld

Dreams are often as vividly experienced as they are difficult to recall. The American Dream has this elusive quality. It is less a dream and more an aspiration—for a lifestyle that many Americans find difficult to attain, particularly those on the lowest rungs of the socioeconomic ladder. The Dream revolves centrally around achieving material success in all its glory—the two-story house, sport utility vehicle, trendy clothes, and expensive accessory items. Those who cannot measure up will do everything in their power to adapt. For many, deviance becomes a functional adaptation, that is, behavior geared to make up for perceived scarcities.

American deviance, if not exclusively economic, revolves ultimately, or at least implicitly, around the accomplishment of economic goals. Even deviance that appears to be noneconomic may, at heart, be economically motivated. Materialistic societies promote an "ends justifies the means" mentality, and behavior gets reduced to its core economic utility. "Tasks that are primarily noneconomic in nature tend to receive meager cultural support, and the skillful performance of these tasks elicits little public recognition" (Messner and Rosenfeld 1994, 8). Good grades, for example, are only important insofar as they lead to better-paying or more prestigious jobs. Learning for learning's sake, to expand one's intellectual horizons, is a joke; the "piece of paper" (college degree) is all that matters. Institutions charged with shaping behavior, from the family to the school to the media, all play second fiddle to "the market" and exist only to reinforce the message that one's life is meaningless in the absence of material success.

Messner and Rosenfeld build on Robert Merton's classic thesis. Like Merton, they contend that the disjuncture between culturally approved goals and institutionally available means is a relatively permanent feature of American life. Like Merton, they observe that some people will have more connections, capital, and resources than others and that deviance is often a mirror image of opportunity. Like Merton, they suggest that deviance is rooted strongly in economic factors. But Messner and Rosenfeld go beyond Merton by focusing on the larger institutional arena and its influence in weakening social controls. The fixation on goals relative to means creates an "anything goes" mind-set, where deviance becomes not only justified, but necessary. Such a mind-set leads to moral decay, disrespect for other people and social institutions (including the legal system), and widespread deviance not just in the United States but in all societies that extol the virtues of material success above all else.

Crime in Sociological Perspective

The sociological approach to the study of crime and deviance has a long and venerable tradition. The pioneers of quantitative criminology—Quetelet and Guerry—highlighted the importance of social factors in their studies of official crime statistics in France in the early nineteenth century. Using maps shaded to reflect the varying levels of crime in the provinces of France, these scholars documented the striking regularity in the spatial distributions of crime and related these distributions to other social and economic factors. Quetelet in particular was impressed by the connection between crime rates and features of the larger social environment. In a famous (and somewhat hyperbolic) statement, Quetelet wrote:

The crimes which are annually committed seem to be a necessary result of our social organization. . . .Society prepares the crime, and the guilty are only the instruments by which it is executed.[1]

Karl Marx, a founding figure in sociology writing later in the nineteenth century, also drew attention to the link between crime and the basic features of the organization of society. As part of his more general critique of the inherent flaws of capitalism, Marx (1859) argued that "there must be something rotten in the very core of a social system which increases its wealth without diminishing its misery, and increases in crimes even more rapidly than in numbers." Whereas Marx directed attention to the economic foundations of society, another of the classic figures in sociology, Emile Durkheim, emphasized the importance of the moral order for understanding deviant behavior. Durkheim explained how the rapid social changes associated with modernization could lead to *anomie*, a weakening of the social norms that restrain individual impulses. Anomie, Durkheim (1966) argued, is conducive to two lethal forms of deviant behavior: suicide and homicide (see especially 346–360).

The sociological approach to the study of crime and deviance continued to develop in the early and middle years of the twentieth century. Following in the footsteps of Quetelet and Guerry, researchers at the University of Chicago used maps to plot rates of juvenile delinquency and other "social pathologies" across different neighborhoods of the city (Liska and Messner 1999). The so-called Chicago School of urban sociology held that high rates of crime and deviance reflect *social disorganization*, a condition wherein the informal social controls in the neighborhood (rooted in relations with family members, neighbors, shopkeepers, and others) have ceased to be effective. Taking a somewhat more macro-level approach, the sociologist Robert K. Merton (1938) linked high crime and deviance to disorganization at the societal level in his famous essay "Social Structure and Anomie." Merton claimed that American culture and social structure are incompatible in a fundamental sense. The culture encourages everyone to succeed

(understood largely in monetary terms), while the social structure distributes opportunities for success unequally. This "disconnect" between cultural orientations and structural realities pressures some people to abandon the legitimate means for success and to substitute alternative, sometimes criminal, means.

In short, criminologists have long recognized that a full understanding of criminal behavior requires consideration of the larger social context. The purpose of this chapter is to explicate a contemporary perspective on crime that places primary emphasis on the social context: institutional-anomie theory. This theory is predicated upon the core principle of earlier sociological approaches that crime is to some extent a product of the basic social organization of a society. The theory explains how crime results from the nature and relationships among a society's major institutions, such as the family, economy, education, and political system, and from prevailing cultural orientations. In the pages that follow, we introduce the general concepts used in institutional-anomie theory, present the main substantive arguments of the theory, review relevant evidence, identify key issues for future research, and consider briefly the implications of our arguments for creating a society with relatively low levels of crime.

The General Conceptual Framework

Institutional-anomie theory links crime to the basic features of social organization—*culture* and *social structure*. Culture consists of the values, goals, beliefs, and norms shared by the members of a society. Culture defines "the rules of the game" that distinguish one society from another. Examples of cultural elements within American society include the value placed on individual freedom, equal opportunity for success, and the use of monetary standards for measuring social standing and achievement. These examples point to a core value complex in American culture, the "American Dream," which specifies that economic success is attainable by anyone who works hard, plays by the rules, and is willing to engage in competition with others for jobs, income, and status. We have argued that the American Dream has special relevance for understanding the high crime rates in the United States compared with other developed societies (Messner and Rosenfeld 1997a).

The other dimension of social organization, social structure, refers to the social positions that people occupy and the roles accompanying these positions. For example, the position of "parent" carries with it the role obligation of caring for children; the position of "student" is accompanied by the obligation to attend classes; and so on. Social positions are knit together by their accompanying roles, which specify the legitimate expectations people have of one another and their obligation to fulfill those expectations. The full range of interconnected positions and roles defines the social structure of a society.

The two dimensions of social organization, culture and social structure, are united through a society's major *social institutions*. It is useful to think of institutions as complexes of positions, roles, values, and norms that constitute the pillars of a society, anchored in the social structure and supporting the culture. The function of an institution is to channel social behavior within the grooves specified by the social structure according to the rules that comprise the culture. All societies of any complexity contain economic, political, educational, religious, and kinship institutions.

Each of the multiple institutions comprising a social structure cannot function properly in isolation from the others. If the family system, for example, is to successfully perform the function of preparing a society's "new recruits" for the demands and opportunities of membership, it must depend on the effective functioning of the economy (to provide sustenance and employment), the political system (to mobilize the resources necessary to achieve collective goals), and in complex societies, the education system (to provide advanced or technical training required for the performance of occupational roles). And, of course, the operation of economic, political, and educational systems depends upon the "raw material" of individ-ual persons who have been more or less effectively socialized in the family.

The interdependence of social institutions is central to the explanation of crime offered by institutional-anomie theory. It is useful to think about this interdependence as constituting an *institutional balance of power*, which refers to the relations of mutual dependence among social institutions. Societies differ, however, in the particular form the institutional balance of power assumes. In some societies, certain institutions assume dominant positions in the balance of power; in other societies, the same institutions are subordinate and are dominant. In summary, if in all societies institutions necessarily depend on one another, the relations of mutual dependence need not be, and in fact rarely are, perfectly balanced or equal.

The central proposition of institutional anomie theory is that a society's distinctive level and form of crime are products of its institutional balance of power. In market capitalist societies, the particular institutional configuration of greatest relevance to crime is that in which the economy dominates the balance of power. Such societies, for reasons explained below, have a strong tendency toward *anomie*, which refers to an overall weakening of the regulatory force of basic values and norms. However, anomic societies are not the only societies with high rates of crime. Societies with differing institutional configurations, for example, those in which political or religious institutions are dominant, also may exhibit high levels of criminal activity, even if the type of crime differs from that observed in anomic societies. We describe the anomic form of the institutional balance of power in greater detail in the following pages and contrast it with other crime-producing institutional forms. Before elaborating on the specifics of institutional-anomie theory, however, we should make a final general observation about our portrait of social organization.

The picture we have drawn of culture, social structure, and institutions is an ideal-typical depiction. Actual societies are hardly as tidy and coherent as the picture implies. In reality, culture and social structure are never perfectly matched: Not all social positions and roles are culturally scripted, and some cultural values and norms are not fully institutionalized. In the United States, for example, the persistence of race and sex discrimination serves as a reminder that the value placed on equal opportunity for all is often honored in the breach.

Our intention in presenting the image of a perfectly organized society is to make a fundamental point about the sociology of crime and deviance, the intellectual home of institutional-anomie theory. Crime and other forms of non-normative behavior are normal and inevitable features of societies, even those in which institutions function smoothly.[2] Neither defective individuals nor malfunctioning social systems are required for crime to occur. The normal pressures and opportunities associated with the nature of social organization itself will always produce some amount and type of deviant conduct, and in those societies with developed legal systems, some of that conduct will be defined as criminal. Institutional-anomie theory seeks to explain the elevated levels and differing types of criminal activity that result from particular forms of institutional imbalance. As a sociological theory of crime, it recognizes that perfectly organized societies are imaginary, if useful, constructs and that crime rates cannot fall to zero. However, by specifying with some precision the institutional sources of crime, it encourages us to imagine the social changes required to move a little closer to perfection.

Social Organization and Crime

Institutional-anomie theory stipulates that an important cultural condition that promotes high levels of crime is *anomie*. The concept of anomie has been used in many different ways in the sociological literature, and scholars continue to debate its various meanings (see, for example, Orru 1987). For our purposes, the distinctive feature of anomie is the *deregulation* of both the goals that people are encouraged to aspire to, and the means that are regarded as acceptable in the pursuit of these goals.

The regulation of goals is particularly challenging in market capitalist societies. That is because a primary feature of everyday life in such societies—the production and exchange of the goods and services required for subsistence—is organized around the principles of profit and loss. Indeed, the pursuit of profit or monetary gain is the driving motivational force underlying a capitalist economy. If people were not motivated to accumulate monetary rewards, the capitalist economy would grind to a halt.

Note, however, that the economic goals of profit and gain are elusive; they have no clear stopping points. No matter how much money one accumulates, there is always more that could in theory be attained. In a real sense, the "sky's the limit" in the pursuit of profit, which means of course that there is no limit at all. The primary goals associated with the market economy, therefore, have an inherently unregulated, anomic quality.

The establishment of restraints on the selection of the means for pursuing goals is also a challenging task in capitalist societies. The capitalist economy is predicated upon competition. Consumers try to purchase items at the lowest price; sellers try to obtain the highest price. Employees fight for high wages; employers maneuver to minimize labor costs. In this ongoing economic struggle, all participants in the market are encouraged to develop a highly calculating orientation to the means that they use to realize their goals. How likely is it that a given course of action will yield maximum gain at minimal cost? From a purely economic standpoint, in other words, what matters is what works. The norms guiding economic action are in this sense what the sociologist Robert Merton (1938) referred to as *efficiency norms*. When behavior is governed exclusively by such standards, the means for pursuing goals lack any *moral regulation;* they are selected on the basis of purely techical considerations without regard for what is right or wrong. Under these conditions, goals are achieved by any means necessary.

Anomie, in the sense of deregulated goals and means, is a natural tendency in market capitalist societies. Not all capitalist societies, however, are anomic. Recall that the economy is only one social institution among many, including the family, the schools, and the political system. These other, noneconomic institutions typically have different operating principles, or *moral codes* (see Wolfe 1989). They provide alternative social goals to those of profit and gain. They employ alternative standards for earning admiration and respect. To the extent, then, that these noneconomic institutions play a vital role in society, they will temper the anomic tendencies inherent in the economic realm of a capitalist society.

Anomie is particularly likely in market capitalist societies, we are suggesting, when the economy assumes dominance in the institutional balance of power. Such economic dominance manifests itself in three important ways (see Messner and Rosenfeld 1997a, Chapter 4). First, the roles of other institutions are *devalued* in comparison with those of the dominant institution. For example, the homeowner accrues more status than the homemaker; the economically successful alumni stand out as the "stars" at the twentieth high school reunion. Second, noneconomic institutional roles must *accommodate* to economic needs and requirements when role demands conflict. To illustrate, parents often worry about finding time for their families, but few workers agonize about finding time for their jobs. Finally, under conditions of economic dominance, noneconomic institutions are *penetrated* by the language and logic of the economy. The market becomes the model for social relationships, and people are thought of as "calculating maximizers" in all their dealings with others; and to some extent, they become so (Schwartz 1994).

Economic dominance and anomie are thus mutually reinforcing social structural and cultural conditions in market capitalist societies. When non-economic institutions lose their vitality, people orient their behavior towards the anomic imperatives of the market economy. And, as anomic cultural orientations permeate a society, the economy assumes ever greater importance as the institutional domain governing behavior.

Institutional-anomie theory holds that a society characterized by an anomic culture and economic dominance in the institutional balance of power is likely to exhibit high rates of crime. The lack of effective regulation of goals and means implies that the culture pressures people to strive relentlessly for success, understood with reference to the elusive goal of monetary gain, and to do so with the most technically expedient means at hand. That these means are often criminal in nature should not be surprising because the basic idea of much (if not all) crime is to get things the easy way (Gottfredson and Hirschi 1990; Felson 1997). As a result, some elements of the culture (the pursuit of profit by any means necessary) ironically promote behavior at odds with other elements of the culture (social prohibitions formally codified in the laws).

At the same time, economic dominance in the institutional balance of power implies that noneconomic institutions will have difficulty fulfilling their distinctive functions. These functions include socializing people into the shared moral beliefs of the culture, and regulating behavior by dispensing rewards and punishments in accord with the performance of institutional roles. In short, a society with an anomic culture and an imbalanced institutional structure tilted toward the economy will simultaneously generate cultural pressures for crime while at the same time eroding the cultural and social restraints against crime. High levels of crime are likely to be observed in such a society, reflecting the core features of its social organization.

Institutional-anomie theory not only predicts high *levels* of crime under conditions of anomie and economic dominance, but particular *types* of crime as well. Anomic societies tend to produce distinctively high rates of what can be viewed as "anomic crime." These are crimes with a highly *instrumental* motive, that is, the crime functions as an instrument to secure a specific goal, which usually involves taking something of value from someone. In addition, anomic crimes are likely to involve force or the threat of force. Predatory street crimes such as robbery are a good example of these kinds of offenses, which combine the goal of economic gain with the technically most proficient means of securing the goal, including if necessary the use of violence. Because firearms are highly effective instruments for securing compliance from victims, we should also expect to find high levels of gun-related crime in anomic societies. We draw just such a connection in our study of U.S. crime rates, which attributes high rates of robbery, homicide, and gun-related violence in the United States to the anomic tendencies of the "American Dream" and the dominance of the economy in the American institutional structure (Messner and Rosenfeld 1997a).

High levels of anomic crime are produced when the economy dominates the institutional structure of market capitalist societies. Given the spread of free-market arrangements throughout the world since the demise of the former Soviet Union and Eastern bloc socialist states, from the perspective of institutional-anomie theory, we would expect to observe increasing rates of predatory street crime in societies where such crimes once were relatively rare. In fact, a particularly anomic form of market dominance seems to have taken hold in Russia. A minor journalistic industry has emerged documenting Russia's so-called "dog-eat-dog capitalism" and attendant social dislocations including rising crime rates (Bohlen 1992; Erlanger 1994; Handelman 1995; Gordon 1996; Holmes 1997).

Although economic dominance in societies undergoing rapid social change is an important global development, it is not the only form of institutional imbalance that leads to high levels of crime. The principal claim of institutional-anomie theory is that institutional imbalance *per se*, and not simply dominance of the economy, produces high rates of criminal activity. We should expect, therefore, to find elevated levels and distinctive forms of criminality in societies in which the institutional balance of power is dominated by the political system and in those where so-called "civil" institutions, such as the family and religion, are dominant.

Consider, first, the situation of political dominance. As the state assumes an ever expanding role in regulating everyday life, the opportunities for the exercise of personal agency are diminished. A sense of direct responsibility for the well-being of others accordingly atrophies, and people develop a cynical orientation towards personal responsibility and accountability. This type of moral climate, we suggest, invites corruption on the part of both the powerful and powerless alike (for examples, see Wolfe's [1989, 168–177] discussion of tax avoidance and underground economic activity in Scandinavia).

By contrast, consider the dominance of the institutional balance of power by civil institutions, such as the kinship system or religion. Whereas economic dominance is associated with the cultural condition of anomie, and state dominance with moral cynicism and withdrawal, civic dominance leads to a kind of extreme moral vigilance or *hypermoralism*. People develop a strong sense of interpersonal obligations, but these obligations are restricted to those with whom they share particular social statuses or identities, often based on kin, ethnic, or religious affiliations. In the absence of any universalistic rules of conduct, a sense of obligation to others who are outside of the relevant social groups is virtually nonexistent.

This type of moral code encourages crimes in the defense of the moral order itself, albeit understood in narrow and highly particularistic terms. Such offenses include vigilanteeism, hate crimes, and violations of human rights that might not be crimes in a legalistic sense but are widely regarded as crime-equivalents (cf. Michalowski and Kramer 1987). Because perceived disturbances in the traditional sex-role system are viewed as striking at the heart of civil society, women have been disproportionately victimized by such violations of human rights and crimes of social control (for examples, see Borger 1997; Herbert 1997; *New York Times* 1997).

The common element cutting across the different moral orders associated with the three forms of institutional imbalance discussed above is that they are each "incomplete" in an important sense. They fail to incorporate elements of the moral codes associated with other institutions. A market economy tends to foster respect for individual rights and for voluntary personal choices. Markets also are "universalizing" institutions; they encourage people to venture beyond the confines of local social settings and ties in search of more customers, higher incomes, and lower costs.

These moral orientations associated with markets do not in themselves produce crime. To the contrary, when properly joined with sentiments of mutual obligation, they bolster the norm of "reciprocity" that joins the expectations of some roles to the obligations of others (borrower to lender, landlord to tenant, student to teacher) and thus serve to inhibit criminal victimization. The institutions of civil society and the state foster such sentiments of mutual obligation, the former promoting a sense of interpersonal obligation and the latter sentiments of collective solidarity. However, the institutions of civil society do not embody the universalism of the market, nor does the state manifest values of individual autonomy.

A full understanding of the social and cultural sources of crime, in summary, must consider not only the values and beliefs that are favored when a particular institution dominates the institutional balance of power but also the consequences for crime when alternative cultural prescriptions are renounced or insufficiently developed. The market promotes crime when the freedom of action that it encourages is left unchecked by considerations of collective order and mutual obligation. These political and social values, likewise, assume degraded forms in the absence of attention to individual rights and liberties, which typically accompany market arrangements. It follows that crime is likely to be minimized when the respective cultural orientations of the three institutional complexes are balanced such that each serves as a continuous reminder of the indispensability of the others.

Evidence in Support of Institutional-Anomie Theory

Our intention in developing institutional-anomie theory has been to stimulate debate and research about the broad cultural and social sources of crime in modern societies. The examples we have offered of different patterns of crime in societies under alternative institutional configurations are just that, examples; and the implied causal relationships require much more systematic attention by researchers. Nevertheless, a body of research has begun to emerge on crime and market dominance that lends some support to the theory. In a study of property crime rates across the United States, Chamlin and Cochran (1995) found that levels of property crime were lower in states with stronger families (measured by the ratio of marriages to divorces), high levels of religious participation (measured by church membership), and high levels of political involvement (measured by voter turnout rates). In other words, consistent with the predictions of institutional-anomie theory, the strength of noneconomic institutions (family, church, and state) appears to be associated with lower levels of criminal involvement in the United States.

These investigators then tested a more subtle implication of the theory, which is that the strength of noneconomic institutions *conditions* the impact of economic deprivation on crime rates. Strong families, churches, and political institutions should, in essence, "soften the blow" of economic hardship, resulting in a weaker association between indicators of deprivation and property crime rates in states where the strength of the noneconomic institutions is greater. The researchers found support for this hypothesis. In states with strong noneconomic institutions, property crime rates are less closely associated with the rate of poverty than in states with weak noneconomic institutions. This test was repeated with different measures of economic deprivation, and the results generally confirmed those produced when the state poverty rate was used to measure deprivation.[3]

Another study, one we conducted, assessed the effect on homicide rates of the strength of the political system (the *polity*) in relation to the market economy for a sample of about forty nations (Messner and Rosenfeld 1997b). The relative strength of the polity was measured by scoring each nation according to its "decommodification of labor" as reflected in the extensiveness of policies that insulate personal well-being from pure market forces (e.g., family support, social security, unemployment insurance).[4] We hypothesized that, other things equal, nations with highly decommodified policies, in the form of broad and generous social welfare and insurance programs, would have lower rates of homicide than those with more restrictive policies. In such societies, we reasoned, the institutional balance of power was less likely to be dominated by the market economy and more likely to reflect the norms of collective support and mutual obligation associated with the state. We found that, controlling for other influences, the level of decommodification is in fact related to the homicide rate: In societies with greater decommodification—and, by extension, stronger political institutions—homicide rates are lower than in those where persons are afforded less protection from market forces.

A final line of research that we have been engaged in links anomie and the strength of political and civic institutions to the concepts of social trust and social capital. *Social capital* refers to the capacity of groups to cooperate in the attainment of collective goals and is typically measured with indicators of social trust and civic engagement (Coleman 1990; Brehm and Rahn 1997; Jackman and Miller 1998). In environments with depleted social capital, people are likely to perceive others as untrustworthy and as "out for themselves." Under such conditions, the level of anomie is likely to be very high, because the absence of regulatory standards— the essence of anomie—leaves little basis for trust in others. The other component of social capital, civic engagement, is usually assessed in terms of the extensiveness of organizational membership and political involvement, both indicators of the strength of civic and political institutions.

In an investigation of a national sample of U.S. geographic areas, we found an inverse relationship between an area's homicide rate and a measure of social trust derived from responses to national surveys (Rosenfeld

and Messner 1998). In a subsequent analysis based on the same sample, we combined our measure of social trust with indicators of organizational membership and political involvement to assess the level of social capital across communities. We found that areas with high levels of social capital tend to have low homicide rates, controlling for other determinants of homicide. Because it is reasonable to assume that high rates of criminal violence will reduce trust in others and promote withdrawal from the community, we evaluated the *reciprocal* (two-way) relationship between homicide and social capital. That analysis confirmed our earlier finding that the level of social capital in an area influences its homicide rate, even controlling for the presumed effect of homicide on social capital (Messner, Rosenfeld, and Baumer 1999).

Future Research

Institutional-anomie theory has thus received some support in the empirical literature. However, research remains in the beginning stages. Subsequent analysis will almost certainly lead to refinements and modifications in the explanatory framework. In addition, a critical task for future research is to move beyond the situation of market dominance to assess the relationship between crime and institutional imbalance more broadly. It would seem of special importance to analyze critically the zero-sum assumption in our assessment of the institutional balance of power, the idea that a society's institutional structure is "imbalanced" by the domination of a single institution.

Our argument presumes that the institutional balance of power does not function effectively and a specific form of criminality is activated when a single institution is dominant. Yet, the case could be made that two of the major institutions may dominate a society without significant tension between them. Consider a society, such as Singapore, where an authoritarian and seemingly stable national government coexists with an equally strong market economy. China could well emerge into a similar configuration with the continued development of market arrangements. Such instances call attention to the possibility of alternative, complex forms of institutional dominance under differing cultural circumstances. They also serve as a reminder that markets are not universal guarantors of individual freedom or, more precisely, that the relationship between economic and political freedom will vary according to different understandings of the meaning and scope of individual rights.

Another promising avenue for further inquiry is the presumed opposition, in our discussion and elsewhere, between civil society and the state. We have proposed, following Wolfe (1989), that an expansive regulatory state runs the risk of eroding the informal controls and sources of moral vitality of civil institutions. While suggestive, this conception of the antagonistic relationship between the state and civil society fails to reflect the complex historical interconnections between the two institutional sectors. Skocpol (1996, 22) argues, for example, that in the United States the welfare state and community-based voluntary associations historically "have operated in close symbiosis," each responsible for the continued growth and effectiveness of the other. In a similar vein, Robert D. Putnam has pointed out that his recent research on the decline in voluntary associations and civic involvement in the United States (Putnam 1995) should not be construed as support for a retreat from activist government. "Social capital," he writes, "is not a substitute for effective public policy but rather a prerequisite for it and, in part, a consequence of it" (Putnam 1996, 28). As an example, Putnam (1996) mentions neighborhood crime watch groups, which sprang from government funded anticrime programs during the 1970s.

While we believe that the ideas presented in this essay require careful empirical scrutiny and conceptual refinement, we hope that the requisite scholarly research is carried out with due regard for the policy implications of our arguments. A major task with respect to crime control confronting both the developed and developing societies is to promote a proper balance among the three major institutional realms of society—market, state, and civil society. We suspect that the most pressing danger for most societies in this era of the "triumph of capitalism" (Teeple 1995) is market dominance. Accordingly, crime control will require concerted efforts to tame the imperatives of an increasingly globalized market, thereby reducing the spread of anomic predatory crime, which is of growing concern throughout the world. However, as indicated in our discussion of the crimes committed in the name of traditional moral codes, the challenge is to strengthen the institutions of the state and civil society without sacrificing the respect for individual rights and the protections against absolutism and fanaticism that socially embedded markets provide.

Notes

1. Quoted in Vold, Bernard, and Snipes (1998, 310). See this source for a general discussion of Quetelet's and Guerry's contributions to criminology.

2. The classic statement of the "normality" of crime is Durkheim's (1964).

3. When the unemployment rate was substituted for the poverty rate, the family indicator did not have the expected effect of reducing the association between deprivation and crime rates. For a discussion of the sensitivity of tests of institutional-anomie theory to differing measures of key theoretical constructs, see Piquero and Piquero (1998).

4. The concept of the *decommodification of labor* is based on Gosta Esping-Andersen's (1990) analysis of national social welfare policies.

References

Bohlen, Celestine. (1992). "The Russians' new code: If it pays, anything goes." *New York Times*, August, 30, 1, 6.

Borger, Julian. (1997). "Women are killed for family honor." *St. Louis Post-Dispatch*, November, 6:A11.

Brehm, John and Wendy Rahn. (1997). "Individual-level evidence for the causes and consequences of social capital." *American Journal of Political Science*, 41:999–1023.

Chamlin, Mitchell B. and John K. Cochran. (1995). "Assessing Messner and Rosenfeld's institutional-anomie theory: A partial test." *Criminology*, 33:411–429.

Coleman, James S. (1990). *Foundations of Social Theory*. Cambridge, MA: Harvard University Press.

Durkheim, Emile. [1895] (1964). *The Rules of Sociological Method*. Reprint. New York: Free.

——. [1897] (1966). *Suicide: A Study in Sociology* Reprint. New York: Free.

Erlanger, Steven. (1994). "Russia's new dictatorship of crime." *New York Times,* May 15.

Esping-Andersen, Gosta. (1990). *The Three Worlds of Welfare Capitalism*. Princeton, NJ: Princeton University Press.

Felson, Marcus. (1997). *Crime and Everyday Life,* Second Edition. Thousand Oaks, CA: Pine Forge.

Gordon, Michael R. (1996). "Slaying tells of Russia's deadly capitalism." *New York Times,* November, 5:A3.

Gottfredson, Michael R. and Travis Hirschi. (1990). *A General Theory of Crime*. Stanford, CA: Stanford University Press.

Handelman, Stephen. (1995). *Comrade Criminal: Russia's New Mafia*. New Haven, CT: Yale University Press.

Herbert, Bob. (1997). "Algerian Terror." *New York Times,* November, 9(4):15.

Holmes, Stephen. (1997). "What Russia teaches us now." *The American Prospect,* July–August, 30–39.

Jackman, Robert W. and Ross A. Miller. (1998). "Social capital and politics." *Annual Review of Political Science,* 47–73.

Liska, Allen E. and Steven F. Messner. (1999). *Perspectives on Crime and Deviance,* Third Edition. Upper Saddle River, NJ: Prentice Hall.

Marx, Karl. (1859). "Europe: Population, crime and pauperism." *New York Daily Tribune,* September 16.

Merton, Robert K. (1938). "Social structure and anomie." *American Sociological Review,* 3:672–682.

Messner, Steven F. and Richard Rosenfeld. (1997a). *Crime and the American Dream,* Second Edition. Belmont, CA: Wadsworth.

——. (1997b). "Political restraint of the market and levels of criminal homicide: A cross-national application of institutional-anomie theory." *Social Forces,* 75:1393–1416.

Messner, Steven F., Richard Rosenfeld, and Eric Baumer. (1999). "Estimating the reciprocal effects of social capital and homicide rates." Paper presented at the meeting of the American Society of Criminology, Toronto, Ontario Canada, November 17–20.

Michalowski, Raymond J. and Ronald C. Kramer. (1987). "The space between laws: The problem of corporate crime in a transnational context." *Social Problems,* 34:34–53.

New York Times. (1997). "The Taliban's war on women," November, 5:A26.

Orru, Marco. (1987). *Anomie: History and Meanings*. Boston: Allen and Unwin.

Piquero, Alex and Nicole Leeper Piquero. (1998). "On testing institutional-anomie theory with varying specifications." *Studies on Crime and Crime Prevention,* 7:61–84.

Putnam, Robert D. (1995). "Tuning in, tuning out: The strange disappearance of social capital in America." *PS: Political Science and Politics,* December, 64:683.

——. (1996). "Robert Putnam responds." *The American Prospect,* March–April:26–28.

Rosenfeld, Richard and Steven F. Messner. (1998). "Beyond the criminal justice system: Anomie, institutional vitality, and crime in the United States." Paper presented at the meeting of the American Sociological Association, San Francisco, CA, August 21–25.

Schwartz, Barry. (1994). *The Costs of Living: How Market Freedom Erodes the Best Things in Life*. New York: W. W. Norton.

Skocpol, Theda. (1996). "Unravelling from above." *The American Prospect,* March–April:20–25.

Teeple, Gary. (1995). *Globalization and the Decline of Social Reform*. Atlantic Highlands, NJ: Humanities.

Vold, George B. (1998). *Theoretical Criminology,* Fourth Edition. New York: Oxford University Press.

Wolfe, Alan. (1989). *Whose Keeper? Social Science and Moral Obligation*. Berkeley: University of California Press.

7
Deviance and Oppositional Culture

The Code of the Streets

Elijah Anderson

Cultural theories of deviance suggest that rule-breaking is part and parcel of normative codes that make deviance not only expected but justified. Deviance is relative, so within deviant subcultures, rule-breaking actually is conformity, merely to a different set of normative expectations. Deviance ranges from the serious to the mundane, the instrumental to the expressive, the conflictual to the cooperative. Regardless of form, subcultures provide the resources and connections necessary for it to thrive, and be reinforced.

Sociologists have long focused on the role that structural disadvantage plays in subculture formation; the theme goes back to the work of Albert Cohen, Richard Cloward and Lloyd Ohlin, and Walter Miller. Dramatic changes in the post-World War II economy—deindustrialization, the widespread loss of high-paying manufacturing jobs, and the disappearance of social capital—left many citizens behind, with little opportunity and even less hope (see also Jacobs 1999; 2000). Alienation and frustration became pervasive. Traditional methods for securing material success—the basis of respect in a capitalist world—ceased to exist. Against this backdrop, respect becomes an almost external entity that must be seized, protected, and maintained at all costs. Respect rises by putting others down, so everyone's "public bearing must send the unmistakable, if sometimes subtle, message that one is capable of violence, and possibly mayhem, when the situation requires it . . ." (Anderson 1999, 72).

In street life, the image one projects is everything. The streets are a caricature of the larger cinematic society, which endorses style over substance (see Denzin 1995). Every encounter is loaded with reputational meaning. Demeanor and comportment are crucial indicators of one's essential character, and conflicts are the ultimate proving ground. How a person reacts under fire provides unobstructed insight into his essential self. As Anderson (1999) suggests, those who pass muster need not worry about future encroachments, nor need they campaign for regard. They gain it rather by the "force of their manner." True badasses occupy the apex of street social hierarchies, feared for their exploitive capabilities yet envied for their insularity from exploitation (for these points, see Jacobs 2000, 130–131).

Street culture is rife with aggression and one-upmanship. It is an unstable world where contagions of violence can be ignited at any moment. On the streets, it is not only better to be feared than loved, it is essential. The widespread enactment of the street code has the net effect of making already downtrodden urban communities even more difficult places to live. Urban neighborhoods become a "stark tableau of pathology and vice" that citizens traverse in fear (Stansell 1982, 321). As deterioration takes on a logic of its own, street life—and the informal justice it promotes—becomes the only realistic alternative.

Of all the problems besetting the poor inner-city black community, none is more pressing than that of interpersonal violence and aggression. It wreaks havoc daily with the lives of community residents and increasingly spills over into downtown and residential middle-class areas. Muggings, burglaries, carjackings, and drug-related shootings, all of which may leave their victims or innocent bystanders dead, are now common enough to concern all urban and many suburban residents. The inclination to violence springs from the circumstances of life among the ghetto poor—the lack of jobs that pay a living wage, the stigma of race, the fallout from rampant drug use and drug trafficking, and the resulting alienation and lack of hope for the future.

Simply living in such an environment places young people at special risk of falling victim to aggressive behavior. Although there are often forces in the community which can counteract the negative influences, by far the most powerful being a strong, loving, "decent" (as inner-city residents put it) family committed to middle-class values, the despair is pervasive enough to have spawned an oppositional culture, that of "the streets," whose norms are often consciously opposed to those of mainstream society. These two orientations—decent and street—socially organize the community, and their coexistence has important consequences for residents, particularly children growing up in the inner city. Above all, this environment means that even youngsters whose home lives reflect mainstream values—and the majority of homes in the community do—must be able to handle themselves in a street-oriented environment.

This is because the street culture has evolved what may be called a code of the streets, which amounts to a set of informal rules governing interpersonal public behavior, including violence. The rules prescribe both a proper comportment and a proper way to respond if challenged. They regulate the use of violence and so allow those who are inclined to aggression to precipitate violent encounters in an approved way. The rules have been established and are enforced mainly by the street-oriented, but on the streets the distinction between street and decent is often irrelevant; everybody knows that if the rules are violated, there are penalties. Knowledge of the code is thus largely defensive; it is literally necessary for operating in public. Therefore, even though families with a decency orientation are usually opposed to the values of the code, they often reluctantly encourage their children's familiarity with it to enable them to negotiate the inner-city environment.

At the heart of the code is the issue of respect—loosely defined as being treated "right," or granted the deference one deserves. However, in the troublesome public environment of the inner city, as people in-

creasingly feel buffeted by forces beyond their control, what one deserves in the way of respect becomes more and more problematic and uncertain. This, in turn, further opens the issue of respect to sometimes intense interpersonal negotiation. In the street culture, especially among young people, respect is viewed as almost an external entity that is hard-won but easily lost, and so must constantly be guarded. The rules of the code in fact provide a framework for negotiating respect. The person whose very appearance—including his clothing, demeanor, and way of moving—deters transgressions feels that he possesses, and may be considered by others to possess, a measure of respect. With the right amount of respect, for instance, he can avoid "being bothered" in public. If he is bothered, not only may he be in physical danger but he has been disgraced or "dissed" (disrespected). Many of the forms that dissing can take might seem petty to middle-class people (maintaining eye contact for too long, for example), but to those invested in the street code, these actions become serious indications of the other person's intentions. Consequently, such people become very sensitive to advances and slights, which could well serve as warnings of imminent physical confrontation.

This hard reality can be traced to the profound sense of alienation from mainstream society and its institutions felt by many poor inner-city black people, particularly the young. The code of the streets is actually a cultural adaptation to a profound lack of faith in the police and the judicial system. The police are most often seen as representing the dominant white society and not caring to protect inner-city residents. When called, they may not respond, which is one reason many residents feel they must be prepared to take extraordinary measures to defend themselves and their loved ones against those who are inclined to aggression. Lack of police accountability has in fact been incorporated into the status system: the person who is believed capable of "taking care of himself" is accorded a certain deference, which translates into a sense of physical and psychological control. Thus, the street code emerges where the influence of the police ends and personal responsibility for one's safety is felt to begin. Exacerbated by the proliferation of drugs and easy access to guns, this volatile situation results in the ability of the street-oriented minority (or those who effectively "go for bad") to dominate the public spaces.

Decent and Street Families

Although almost everyone in poor inner-city neighborhoods is struggling financially and therefore feels a certain distance from the rest of America, the decent and the street family in a real sense represent two poles of value orientation, two contrasting conceptual categories. The labels "decent" and "street," which the residents themselves use, amount to evaluative judgments that confer status on local residents. The labeling is often the result of a social contest among individuals and families of the neighborhood. Individuals of the two orientations often co-exist in the same extended family. Decent residents judge themselves to be so while judging others to be of the street, and street individuals often present themselves as decent, drawing distinctions between themselves and other people. In addition, there is quite a bit of circumstantial behavior—that is, one person may at different times exhibit both decent and street orientations, depending on the circumstances. Although these designations result from so much social jockeying, there do exist concrete features that define each conceptual category.

Generally, so-called decent families tend to accept mainstream values more fully and attempt to instill them in their children. Whether married couples with children or single-parent (usually female) households, they are generally "working poor" and so tend to be better off financially than their street-oriented neighbors. They value hard work and self-reliance and are willing to sacrifice for their children. Because they have a certain amount of faith in mainstream society, they harbor hopes for a better future for their children, if not for themselves. Many of them go to church and take a strong interest in their children's schooling. Rather than dwelling on the real hardships and inequities

facing them, many such decent people, particularly the increasing number of grandmothers raising grandchildren, see their difficult situation as a test from God and derive great support from their faith and from the church community.

Extremely aware of the problematic and often dangerous environment in which they reside, decent parents tend to be strict in their child-rearing practices, encouraging children to respect authority and walk a straight moral line. They have an almost obsessive concern about trouble of any kind and remind their children to be on the lookout for people and situations that might lead to it. At the same time, they are themselves polite and considerate of others, and teach their children to be the same way. At home, at work, and in church, they strive hard to maintain a positive mental attitude and a spirit of cooperation.

So-called street parents, in contrast, often show a lack of consideration for other people and have a rather superficial sense of family and community. Though they may love their children, many of them are unable to cope with the physical and emotional demands of parenthood, and find it difficult to reconcile their needs with those of their children. These families, who are more fully invested in the code of the streets than the decent people are, may aggressively socialize their children into it in a normative way. They believe in the code and judge themselves and others according to its values.

In fact the overwhelming majority of families in the inner-city community try to approximate the decent-family model, but there are many others who clearly represent the worst fears of the decent family. Not only are their financial resources extremely limited, but what little they have may easily be misused. The lives of the street-oriented are often marked by disorganization. In the most desperate circumstances people frequently have a limited understanding of priorities and consequences, and so frustrations mount over bills, food, and, at times, drink, cigarettes, and drugs. Some tend toward self-destructive behavior; many street-oriented women are crack-addicted ("on the pipe"), alcoholic, or involved in complicated relationships with men who abuse them. In addition, the seeming intractability of their situation, caused in large part by the lack of well-paying jobs and the persistence of racial discrimination, has engendered deep-seated bitterness and anger in many of the most desperate and poorest blacks, especially young people. The need both to exercise a measure of control and to lash out at somebody is often reflected in the adults' relations with their children. At the least, the frustrations of persistent poverty shorten the fuse in such people—contributing to a lack of patience with anyone, child or adult, who irritates them.

In these circumstances a woman—or a man, although men are less consistently present in children's lives—can be quite aggressive with children, yelling at and striking them for the least little infraction of the rules she has set down. Often little if any serious explanation follows the verbal and physical punishment. This response teaches children a particular lesson. They learn that to solve any kind of interpersonal problem one must quickly resort to hitting or other violent behavior. Actual peace and quiet, and also the appearance of calm, respectful children conveyed to her neighbors and friends, are often what the young mother most desires, but at times she will be very aggressive in trying to get them. Thus she may be quick to beat her children, especially if they defy her law, not because she hates them but because this is the way she knows to control them. In fact, many street-oriented women love their children dearly. Many mothers in the community subscribe to the notion that there is a "devil in the boy" that must be beaten out of him or that socially "fast girls need to be whupped." Thus much of what borders on child abuse in the view of social authorities is acceptable parental punishment in the view of these mothers.

Many street-oriented women are sporadic mothers whose children learn to fend for themselves when necessary, foraging for food and money any way they can get it. The children are sometimes employed by drug dealers or become addicted themselves. These children of the street, growing up with little supervision, are said to "come up hard."

They often learn to fight at an early age, sometimes using short-tempered adults around them as role models. The street-oriented home may be fraught with anger, verbal disputes, physical aggression, and even mayhem. The children observe these goings-on, learning the lesson that might makes right. They quickly learn to hit those who cross them, and the dog-eat-dog mentality prevails. In order to survive, to protect oneself, it is necessary to marshal inner resources and be ready to deal with adversity in a hands-on way. In these circumstances physical prowess takes on great significance.

In some of the most desperate cases, a street-oriented mother may simply leave her young children alone and unattended while she goes out. The most irresponsible women can be found at local bars and crack houses, getting high and socializing with other adults. Sometimes a troubled woman will leave very young children alone for days at a time. Reports of crack addicts abandoning their children have become common in drug-infested inner-city communities. Neighbors or relatives discover the abandoned children, often hungry and distraught over the absence of their mother. After repeated absences, a friend or relative, particularly a grandmother, will often step in to care for the young children, sometimes petitioning the authorities to send her, as guardian of the children, the mother's welfare check, if the mother gets one. By this time, however, the children may well have learned the first lesson of the streets: survival itself, let alone respect, cannot be taken for granted; you have to fight for your place in the world.

Campaigning for Respect

These realities of inner-city life are largely absorbed on the streets. At an early age, often even before they start school, children from street-oriented homes gravitate to the streets, where they "hang"—socialize with their peers. Children from these generally permissive homes have a great deal of latitude and are allowed to "rip and run" up and down the street. They often come home from school, put their books down, and go right back out the door. On school nights eight-

and nine-year-olds remain out until nine or ten o'clock (and teenagers typically come in whenever they want to). On the streets they play in groups that often become the source of their primary social bonds. Children from decent homes tend to be more carefully supervised and are thus likely to have curfews and to be taught how to stay out of trouble.

When decent and street kids come together, a kind of social shuffle occurs in which children have a chance to go either way. Tension builds as a child comes to realize that he must choose an orientation. The kind of home he comes from influences but does not determine the way he will ultimately turn out—although it is unlikely that a child from a thoroughly street-oriented family will easily absorb decent values on the streets. Youths who emerge from street-oriented families but develop a decency orientation almost always learn those values in another setting—in school, in a youth group, in church. Often it is the result of their involvement with a caring "old head" (adult role model).

In the street, through their play, children pour their individual life experiences into a common knowledge pool, affirming, confirming, and elaborating on what they have observed in the home and matching their skills against those of others. And they learn to fight. Even small children test one another, pushing and shoving, and are ready to hit other children over circumstances not to their liking. In turn, they are readily hit by other children, and the child who is toughest prevails. Thus, the violent resolution of disputes, the hitting and cursing, gains social reinforcement. The child, in effect, is initiated into a system that is really a way of campaigning for respect.

In addition, younger children witness the disputes of older children, which are often resolved through cursing and abusive talk, if not aggression or outright violence. They see that one child succumbs to the greater physical and mental abilities of the other. They are also alert and attentive witnesses to the verbal and physical fights of adults, after which they compare notes and share their interpretations of the event. In almost every case the victor is the person who physically won the altercation, and this person often enjoys the esteem and respect of onlookers. These experiences reinforce the lessons the children have learned at home: might makes right, and toughness is a virtue, while humility is not. In effect they learn the social meaning of fighting. When it is left virtually unchallenged, this understanding becomes an ever more important part of the child's working conception of the world. Over time the code of the streets becomes refined.

Those street-oriented adults with whom children come in contact—including mothers, fathers, brothers, sisters, boyfriends, cousins, neighbors, and friends—help them along in forming this understanding by verbalizing the messages they are getting through experience: "Watch your back." "Protect yourself." "Don't punk out." "If somebody messes with you, you got to pay them back." "If someone disses you, you got to straighten them out." Many parents actually impose sanctions if a child is not sufficiently aggressive. For example, if a child loses a fight and comes home upset, the parent might respond, "Don't you come in here crying that somebody beat you up; you better get back out there and whup his ass. I didn't raise no punks. Get back out there and whup his ass. If you don't whup his ass, I'll whup your ass when you come home." Thus, the child obtains reinforcement for being tough and showing nerve.

While fighting, some children cry as though they are doing something they are ambivalent about. The fight may be against their wishes, yet they may feel constrained to fight or face the consequences—not just from peers but also from caretakers or parents, who may administer another beating if they back down. Some adults recall receiving such lessons from their own parents and justify repeating them to their children as a way to toughen them up. Looking capable of taking care of oneself as a form of self-defense is a dominant theme among both street-oriented and decent adults who worry about the safety of their children. There is, thus, at times a convergence in their child-rearing practices, although the rationales behind them may differ.

Self-Image Based on 'Juice'

By the time they are teenagers, most youths have either internalized the code of the streets or at least learned the need to comport themselves in accordance with its rules, which chiefly have to do with interpersonal communication. The code revolves around the presentation of self. Its basic requirement is the display of a certain predisposition to violence. Accordingly, one's bearing must send the unmistakable if sometimes subtle message to "the next person" in public that one is capable of violence and mayhem when the situation requires it, that one can take care of oneself. The nature of this communication is largely determined by the demands of the circumstances but can include facial expressions, gait, and verbal expressions—all of which are geared mainly to deterring aggression. Physical appearance, including clothes, jewelry, and grooming, also plays an important part in how a person is viewed; to be respected, it is important to have the right look.

Even so, there are no guarantees against challenges, because there are always people around looking for a fight to increase their share of respect—or "juice," as it is sometimes called on the street. Moreover, if a person is assaulted, it is important, not only in the eyes of his opponent but also in the eyes of his "running buddies," for him to avenge himself. Otherwise he risks being "tried" (challenged) or "moved on" by any number of others. To maintain his honor he must show he is not someone to be "messed with" or "dissed." In general, the person must "keep himself straight" by managing his position of respect among others; this involves in part his self-image, which is shaped by what he thinks others are thinking of him in relation to his peers.

Objects play an important and complicated role in establishing self-image. Jackets, sneakers, gold jewelry, reflect not just a person's taste, which tends to be tightly regulated among adolescents of all social classes, but also a willingness to possess things that may require defending. A boy wearing a fashionable, expensive jacket, for example, is vulnerable to attack by another who covets the jacket and either cannot afford to buy one or wants the added satisfaction of depriving someone else of his. However, if the boy forgoes the desirable jacket and wears one that isn't "hip," he runs the risk of being teased and possibly even assaulted as an unworthy person. To be allowed to hang with certain prestigious crowds, a boy must wear a different set of expensive clothes—sneakers and athletic suit—every day. Not to be able to do so might make him appear socially deficient. The youth comes to covet such items—especially when he sees easy prey wearing them.

In acquiring valued things, therefore, a person shores up his identity—but since it is an identity based on having things, it is highly precarious. This very precariousness gives a heightened sense of urgency to staying even with peers, with whom the person is actually competing. Young men and women who are able to command respect through their presentation of self—by allowing their possessions and their body language to speak for them—may not have to campaign for regard but may, rather, gain it by the force of their manner. Those who are unable to command respect in this way must actively campaign for it—and are thus particularly alive to slights.

One way of campaigning for status is by taking the possessions of others. In this context, seemingly ordinary objects can become trophies imbued with symbolic value that far exceeds their monetary worth. Possession of the trophy can symbolize the ability to violate somebody—to "get in his face," to take something of value from him, to "dis" him, and thus to enhance one's own worth by stealing someone else's. The trophy does not have to be something material. It can be another person's sense of honor, snatched away with a derogatory remark. It can be the outcome of a fight. It can be the imposition of a certain standard, such as a girl's getting herself recognized as the most beautiful. Material things, however, fit easily into the pattern. Sneakers, a pistol, even somebody else's girlfriend, can become a trophy. When a person can take something from another and then flaunt it, he gains a certain regard by being the owner, or the controller, of that thing. But this display of ownership can then provoke other people to challenge him. This game of who controls what is thus constantly being played out on inner-city streets, and the trophy—extrinsic or intrinsic, tangible or intangible—identifies the current winner.

An important aspect of this often violent give-and-take is its zero-sum quality. That is, the extent to which one person can raise himself up depends on his ability to put another person down. This underscores the alienation that permeates the inner-city ghetto community. There is a generalized sense that very little respect is to be had, and therefore everyone competes to get what affirmation he can of the little that is available. The craving for respect that results gives people thin skins. Shows of deference by others can be highly soothing, contributing to a sense of security, comfort, self-confidence, and self-respect. Transgressions by others which go unanswered diminish these feelings and are believed to encourage further transgressions. Hence one must be ever vigilant against the transgressions of others or even *appearing* as if transgressions will be tolerated. Among young people, whose sense of self-esteem is particularly vulnerable, there is an especially heightened concern with being disrespected. Many inner-city young men in particular crave respect to such a degree that they will risk their lives to attain and maintain it.

The issue of respect is thus closely tied to whether a person has an inclination to be violent, even as a victim. In the wider society people may not feel required to retaliate physically after an attack, even though they are aware that they have been degraded or taken advantage of. They may feel a great need to defend themselves *during* an attack, or to behave in such a way as to deter aggression (middle-class people certainly can and do become victims of street-oriented youths), but they are much more likely than street-oriented people to feel that they can walk away from a possible altercation with their self-esteem intact. Some people may even have the strength of character to flee, without any thought that their self-respect or esteem will be diminished.

In impoverished inner-city black communities, however, particularly among young males and perhaps increasingly among females, such flight would be extremely difficult. To run away would likely leave one's self-esteem in tatters. Hence people often feel constrained not only to stand up and at least attempt to resist during an assault but also to "pay back"—to seek revenge—after a successful assault on their person. This may include going to get a weapon or even getting relatives involved. Their very identity and self-respect, their honor, is often intricately tied up with the way they perform on the streets during and after such encounters. This outlook reflects the circumscribed opportunities of the inner-city poor. Generally people outside the ghetto have other ways of gaining status and regard, and thus do not feel so dependent on such physical displays.

By Trial of Manhood

On the street, among males these concerns about things and identity have come to be expressed in the concept of "manhood." Manhood in the inner city means taking the prerogatives of men with respect to strangers, other men, and women—being distinguished as a man. It implies physicality and a certain ruthlessness. Regard and respect are associated with this concept in large part because of its practical application: if others have little or no regard for a person's manhood, his very life and those of his loved ones could be in jeopardy. But there is a chicken-and-egg aspect to this situation: one's physical safety is more likely to be jeopardized in public *because* manhood is associated with respect. In other words, an existential link has been created between the idea of manhood and one's self-esteem, so that it has become hard to say which is primary. For many inner-city youths, manhood and respect are flip sides of the same coin; physical and psychological well-being are inseparable, and both require a sense of control, of being in charge.

The operating assumption is that a man, especially a real man, knows what other men know—the code of the streets. And if one is not a real man, one is somehow diminished as a person, and there are certain valued things one simply does not deserve. There is thus believed to be a certain justice to the code, since it is considered that everyone has the opportunity to know it. Implicit in this is that everybody is held responsible for being familiar with the code. If the victim of a mugging, for example, does not know the code and so responds "wrong," the perpetrator may feel justified even in killing him and may feel no remorse. He may think, "Too bad, but it's his fault. He should have known better."

So when a person ventures outside, he must adopt the code—a kind of shield, really—to prevent others from "messing with" him. In these circumstances it is easy for people to think they are being tried or tested by others even when this is not the case. For it is sensed that something extremely valuable is at stake in every interaction, and people are encouraged to rise to the occasion, particularly with strangers. For people who are unfamiliar with the code—generally people who live outside the inner city—the concern with respect in the most ordinary interactions can be frightening and incomprehensible. But for those who are invested in the code, the clear object of their demeanor is to discourage strangers from even thinking about testing their manhood. And the sense of power that attends the ability to deter others can be alluring even to those who know the code without being heavily invested in it—the decent inner-city youths. Thus a boy who has been leading a basically decent life can, in trying circumstances, suddenly resort to deadly force.

Central to the issue of manhood is the widespread belief that one of the most effective ways of gaining respect is to manifest "nerve." Nerve is shown when one takes another person's possessions (the more valuable the better), "messes with" someone's woman, throws the first punch, "gets in someone's face," or pulls a trigger. Its proper display helps on the spot to check others who would violate one's person and also helps to build a reputation that works to prevent future challenges. But since such a show of nerve is a forceful expression of disrespect toward the person on the receiving end, the

victim may be greatly offended and seek to retaliate with equal or greater force. A display of nerve, therefore, can easily provoke a life-threatening response, and the background knowledge of that possibility has often been incorporated into the concept of nerve.

True nerve exposes a lack of fear of dying. Many feel that it is acceptable to risk dying over the principle of respect. In fact, among the hard-core street-oriented, the clear risk of violent death may be preferable to being "dissed" by another. The youths who have internalized this attitude and convincingly display it in their public bearing are among the most threatening people of all, for it is commonly assumed that they fear no man. As the people of the community say, "They are the baddest dudes on the street." They often lead an existential life that may acquire meaning only when they are faced with the possibility of imminent death. Not to be afraid to die is by implication to have few compunctions about taking another's life. Not to be afraid to die is the quid pro quo of being able to take somebody else's life—for the right reasons, if the situation demands it. When others believe this is one's position, it gives one a real sense of power on the streets. Such credibility is what many inner-city youths strive to achieve, whether they are decent or street-oriented, both because of its practical defensive value and because of the positive way it makes them feel about themselves. The difference between the decent and the street-oriented youth is often that the decent youth makes a conscious decision to appear tough and manly; in another setting—with teachers, say, or at his part-time job—he can be polite and deferential. The street-oriented youth, on the other hand, has made the concept of manhood a part of his very identity; he has difficulty manipulating it—it often controls him.

Girls and Boys

Increasingly, teenage girls are mimicking the boys and trying to have their own version of "manhood." Their goal is the same—to get respect, to be recognized as capable of setting or maintaining a certain standard. They try to achieve this end in the ways that have been established by the boys, including posturing, abusive language, and the use of violence to resolve disputes, but the issues for the girls are different. Although conflicts over turf and status exist among the girls, the majority of disputes seem rooted in assessments of beauty (which girl in a group is "the cutest"), competition over boyfriends, and attempts to regulate other people's knowledge of and opinions about a girl's behavior or that of someone close to her, especially her mother.

A major cause of conflicts among girls is "he say, she say." This practice begins in the early school years and continues through high school. It occurs when "people," particularly girls, talk about others, thus putting their "business in the streets." Usually one girl will say something negative about another in the group, most often behind the person's back. The remark will then get back to the person talked about. She may retaliate or her friends may feel required to "take up for" her. In essence this is a form of group gossiping in which individuals are negatively assessed and evaluated. As with much gossip, the things said may or may not be true, but the point is that such imputations can cast aspersions on a person's good name. The accused is required to defend herself against the slander, which can result in arguments and fights, often over little of real substance. Here again is the problem of low self-esteem, which encourages youngsters to be highly sensitive to slights and to be vulnerable to feeling easily "dissed." To avenge the dissing, a fight is usually necessary.

Because boys are believed to control violence, girls tend to defer to them in situations of conflict. Often if a girl is attacked or feels slighted, she will get a brother, uncle, or cousin to do her fighting for her. Increasingly, however, girls are doing their own fighting and are even asking their male relatives to teach them how to fight. Some girls form groups that attack other girls or take things from them. A hard-core segment of inner-city girls inclined toward violence seems to be developing. As one thirteen-year-old girl in a detention center for youths who have committed violent acts told me, "To get

people to leave you alone, you gotta fight. Talking don't always get you out of stuff." One major difference between girls and boys: girls rarely use guns. Their fights are therefore not life-or-death struggles. Girls are not often willing to put their lives on the line for "manhood." The ultimate form of respect on the male-dominated inner-city street is thus reserved for men.

'Going for Bad'

In the most fearsome youths such a cavalier attitude toward death grows out of a very limited view of life. Many are uncertain about how long they are going to live and believe they could die violently at any time. They accept this fate; they live on the edge. Their manner conveys the message that nothing intimidates them; whatever turn the encounter takes, they maintain their attack—rather like a pit bull, whose spirit many such boys admire. The demonstration of such tenacity "shows heart" and earns their respect.

This fearlessness has implications for law enforcement. Many street-oriented boys are much more concerned about the threat of "justice" at the hands of a peer than at the hands of the police. Moreover, many feel not only that they have little to lose by going to prison but that they have something to gain. The toughening-up one experiences in prison can actually enhance one's reputation on the streets. Hence the system loses influence over the hard core who are without jobs, with little perceptible stake in the system. If mainstream society has done nothing *for* them, they counter by making sure it can do nothing *to* them.

At the same time, however, a competing view maintains that true nerve consists in backing down, walking away from a fight, and going on with one's business. One fights only in self-defense. This view emerges from the decent philosophy that life is precious, and it is an important part of the socialization process common in decent homes. It discourages violence as the primary means of resolving disputes and encourages youngsters to accept nonviolence and talk as confrontational strategies. But "if the deal goes down," self-defense is greatly encouraged. When there is enough positive support for this orientation, either in the home or among one's peers, then nonviolence has a chance to prevail. But it prevails at the cost of relinquishing a claim to being bad and tough, and therefore sets a young person up as at the very least alienated from street-oriented peers and quite possibly a target of derision or even violence.

Although the nonviolent orientation rarely overcomes the impulse to strike back in an encounter, it does introduce a certain confusion and so can prompt a measure of soul-searching, or even profound ambivalence. Did the person back down with his respect intact or did he back down only to be judged a "punk"—a person lacking manhood? Should he or she have acted? Should he or she have hit the other person in the mouth? These questions beset many young men and women during public confrontations. What is the "right" thing to do? In the quest for honor, respect, and local status—which few young people are uninterested in—common sense most often prevails, which leads many to opt for the tough approach, enacting their own particular versions of the display of nerve. The presentation of oneself as rough and tough is very often quite acceptable until one is tested. And then that presentation may help the person pass the test, because it will cause fewer questions to be asked about what he did and why. It is hard for a person to explain why he lost the fight or why he backed down. Hence many will strive to appear to "go for bad," while hoping they will never be tested. But when they are tested, the outcome of the situation may quickly be out of their hands, as they become wrapped up in the circumstances of the moment.

An Oppositional Culture

The attitudes of the wider society are deeply implicated in the code of the streets. Most people in inner-city communities are not totally invested in the code, but the significant minority of hard-core street youths who are have to maintain the code in order to establish reputations, because they

have—or feel they have—few other ways to assert themselves. For these young people the standards of the street code are the only game in town. The extent to which some children—particularly those who through upbringing have become most alienated and those lacking in strong and conventional social support—experience, feel, and internalize racist rejection and contempt from mainstream society may strongly encourage them to express contempt for the more conventional society in turn. In dealing with this contempt and rejection, some youngsters will consciously invest themselves and their considerable mental resources in what amounts to an oppositional culture to preserve themselves and their self-respect. Once they do, any respect they might be able to garner in the wider system pales in comparison with the respect available in the local system; thus they often lose interest in even attempting to negotiate the mainstream system.

At the same time, many less alienated young blacks have assumed a street-oriented demeanor as a way of expressing their blackness while really embracing a much more moderate way of life; they, too, want a nonviolent setting in which to live and raise a family. These decent people are trying hard to be part of the mainstream culture, but the racism, real and perceived, that they encounter helps to legitimate the oppositional culture. And so on occasion they adopt street behavior. In fact, depending on the demands of the situation, many people in the community slip back and forth between decent and street behavior.

A vicious cycle has thus been formed. The hopelessness and alienation many young inner-city black men and women feel, largely as a result of endemic joblessness and persistent racism, fuels the violence they engage in. This violence serves to confirm the negative feelings many whites and some middle-class blacks harbor toward the ghetto poor, further legitimating the oppositional culture and the code of the streets in the eyes of many poor young blacks. Unless this cycle is broken, attitudes on both sides will become increasingly entrenched, and the violence, which claims victims black and white, poor and affluent, will only escalate.

Reprinted by permission of Elijah Anderson, from "The Code of the Streets" (May 1994, *Atlantic Monthly*, pp. 81–94). For editorial reasons, the title of this selection has been modified from the original. ✦

8
The Theory of Differential Association

Edwin H. Sutherland

Donald R. Cressey

Differential association begins with the assumption that human nature is not inherently evil or antisocial but is corruptible by external forces. Sutherland and Cressey dismiss biological and psychological approaches, insisting rather that deviant behavior is learned. It is learned in a process of communication with other deviants, typically in small groups, where norms, attitudes, and rationalizations in support of rule-breaking are acquired. Such "differential associations," as the authors call them, vary in frequency, intensity, duration, and priority; the likelihood of doing deviance increases as exposure to definitions favorable to norm violation increases. Knowing how to commit a deviant act is not enough. Knowledge is a necessary but not a sufficient condition for rule-breaking, since even those with vast amounts of deviant know-how often insist that rule-breaking is wrong—morally, socially, politically, or otherwise.

Research suggests that the overwhelming majority of norm violations are committed by offenders who operate in collectivities, however loosely defined. It is rare for people to deviate spontaneously—to decide that rule-breaking is cool, rewarding, or worthwhile without having received some outside reinforcement. The earlier such reinforcement takes place and the more respected its source, the more likely a person will stray.

Differential association theory redresses errors that plague structural approaches like strain and anomie by focusing on the immediate situational context of offending. It explains, for example, why so many people exposed to strained and anomic conditions never deviate, as well as why those who find themselves facing perfectly manageable conditions become habitual rule-breakers. The answer lies in group relationships and how these relationships affect individual values and decisions.

The following statement refers to the process by which a particular person comes to engage in criminal behavior.

1. *Criminal behavior is learned.* Negatively, this means that criminal behavior is not inherited, as such; also, the person who is not already trained in crime does not invent criminal behavior, just as a person does not make mechanical inventions unless he has had training in mechanics.

2. *Criminal behavior is learned in interaction with other persons in a process of communication.* This communication is verbal in many respects but includes also "the communication of gestures."

3. *The principal part of the learning of criminal behavior occurs within intimate personal groups.* Negatively, this means that the impersonal agencies of communication, such as movies and newspapers, play a relatively unimportant part in the genesis of criminal behavior.

4. *When criminal behavior is learned, the learning includes (a) techniques of committing the crime, which are sometimes very complicated, sometimes very simple; (b) the specific direction of motives, drives, rationalizations, and attitudes.*

5. *The specific direction of motives and drives is learned from definitions of the legal codes as favorable or unfavorable.* In some societies an individual is surrounded by persons who invariably define the legal codes as rules to be observed, while in others he is surrounded by persons whose definitions are favorable to the violation of the legal codes. In our American society these defini-

tions are almost always mixed, with the consequence that we have culture conflict in relation to the legal codes.

6. *A person becomes delinquent because of an excess of definitions favorable to violation of law over definitions unfavorable to violation of law.* This is the principle of differential association. It refers to both criminal and anti-criminal associations and has to do with counteracting forces. When persons become criminal, they do so because of contacts with criminal patterns and also because of isolation from anti-criminal patterns. Any person inevitably assimilates the surrounding culture unless other patterns are in conflict; a Southerner does not pronounce "r" because other Southerners do not pronounce "r." Negatively, this proposition of differential association means that associations which are neutral so far as crime is concerned have little or no effect on the genesis of criminal behavior. Much of the experience of a person is neutral in this sense, e.g., learning to brush one's teeth. This behavior has no negative or positive effect on criminal behavior except as it may be related to associations which are concerned with the legal codes. This neutral behavior is important especially as an occupier of the time of a child so that he is not in contact with criminal behavior during the time he is so engaged in the neutral behavior.

7. *Differential associations may vary in frequency, duration, priority, and intensity.* This means that associations with criminal behavior and also associations with anti-criminal behavior vary in those respects. "Frequency" and "duration" as modalities of associations are obvious and need no explanation. "Priority" is assumed to be important in the sense that lawful behavior developed in early childhood may persist throughout life, and also that delinquent behavior developed in early childhood may persist throughout life. This tendency, however, has not been adequately demonstrated, and priority seems to be impor-

tant principally through its selective influence. "Intensity" is not precisely defined but it has to do with such things as the prestige of the source of a criminal or anti-criminal pattern and with emotional reactions related to the associations. In a precise description of the criminal behavior of a person these modalities would be stated in quantitative form and a mathematical ratio be reached. A formula in this sense has not been developed, and the development of such a formula would be extremely difficult.

8. *The process of learning criminal behavior by association with criminal and anti-criminal patterns involves all of the mechanisms that are involved in any other learning.* Negatively, this means that the learning of criminal behavior is not restricted to the process of imitation. A person who is seduced, for instance, learns criminal behavior by association, but this process would not ordinarily be described as imitation.

9. *While criminal behavior is an expression of general needs and values, it is not explained by those general needs and values since non-criminal behavior is an expression of the same needs and values.* Thieves generally steal in order to secure money, but likewise honest laborers work in order to secure money. The attempts by many scholars to explain criminal behavior by general drives and values, such as the happiness principle, striving for social status, the money motive, or frustration, have been and must continue to be futile since they explain lawful behavior as completely as they explain criminal behavior. They are similar to respiration, which is necessary for any behavior but which does not differentiate criminal from non-criminal behavior.

It is not necessary, at this level of explanation, to explain why a person has the associations which he has; this certainly involves a complex of many things. In an area where the delinquency rate is high, a boy who is sociable, gregarious, active, and athletic is very likely to come in contact with the other boys in the neighborhood, learn delinquent behavior from them, and become a gangster; in the same neighborhood the psychopathic boy who is isolated, introverted, and inert may remain at home, not become acquainted with the other boys in the neighborhood, and not become delinquent. In another situation, the sociable, athletic, aggressive boy may become a member of a scout troop and not become involved in delinquent behavior. The person's associations are determined in a general context of social organization. A child is ordinarily reared in a family; the place of residence of the family is determined largely by family income; and the delinquency rate is in many respects related to the rental value of the houses. Many other aspects of social organization affect the kinds of associations a person has.

The preceding explanation of criminal behavior purports to explain the criminal and non-criminal behavior of individual persons. As indicated earlier, it is possible to state sociological theories of criminal behavior which explain the criminality of a community, nation, or other group. The problem, when thus stated, is to account for variations in crime rates and involves a comparison of the crime: rates of various groups or the crime rates of a particular group at different times. The explanation of a crime rate must be consistent with the explanation of the criminal behavior of the person, since the crime rate is a summary statement of the number of persons in the group who commit crimes and the frequency with which they commit crimes. One of the best explanations of crime rates from this point of view is that a high crime rate is due to social disorganization. The term "social disorganization" is not entirely satisfactory and it seems preferable to substitute for it the term "differential social organization." The postulate on which this theory is based, regardless of the name, is that crime is rooted in the social organization and is an expression of that social organization. A group may be organized for criminal behavior or organized against criminal behavior. Most communities are organized both for criminal and anti-criminal behavior and in that sense the crime rate is an expression of the differential group organization. Differential group organization as an explanation of variations in crime rates is consistent with the differential association theory of the processes by which persons become criminals.

9
A General Strain Theory of Crime and Delinquency

Robert Agnew

Strain theory rests on the assumption that deviance results from fundamental disjunctures (gaps) between culturally promoted goals and institutionally available means. When such goals are economic in origin (and in materialistic societies, economic goals are primary), strain results; strain affects those on the lowest rungs of the socioeconomic hierarchy most. Deviance becomes a mirror image of opportunity.

Yet, Robert Agnew asks in this selection, why do so may individuals from strained parts of the social structure never deviate, or never deviate in significant ways? And why do so many from "unstrained" backgrounds embark on a path of persistent rule-breaking? Agnew contends that the answer does lie in strain but in a broader version, one that accounts for sources that are not necessarily economic. Borrowing from the psychology of aggression, equity, and reinforcement, Agnew suggests that strain has a number of more general sources: (1) discrepancies between outcomes that are fair or just and those that actually occur (which can create cognitive dissonance and frustration); (2) the removal of positively valued stimuli (e.g., being "ditched" by one's friends or significant others); and (3) the presentation of negatively valued stimuli (e.g., abuse, neglect, trauma). In everyday life, different sources of strain can overlap at any given point in time and can have an additive or perhaps multiplicative effect on conduct. Deviance emerges as a stress-relieving mechanism (e.g., drinking, drug use, and violent retaliation).

Of course, not all adaptations need be deviant. A variety of management techniques are available to reduce negative affect. People can ignore or downgrade stress; they can focus on positive events to the exclusion of negative ones; they can use frustrating incidents as learning devices to improve their character. The strength of Agnew's approach lies in its ability to account for a range of disjunctures that have less to do with the dictates of a distant and impersonal economy and more to do with the vicissitudes of everyday life. And it is these vicissitudes that all of us must confront and manage on a day-to-day basis.

Strain Theory as Distinguished From Control and Differential Association/Social Learning Theory

Strain, social control, and differential association theory are all sociological theories: They explain delinquency in terms of the individual's social relationships. Strain theory is distinguished from social control and social learning theory in its specification of (1) the type of social relationship that leads to delinquency and (2) the motivation for delinquency. First, strain theory focuses explicitly on *negative relationships with others*: relationships in which the individual is not treated as he or she wants to be treated. Strain theory has typically focused on relationships in which others prevent the individual from achieving positively valued goals. Agnew (1985a), however, broadened the focus of strain theory to include relationships in which others present the individual with noxious or negative stimuli. Social control theory, by contrast, focuses on the *absence of significant relationships with conventional others and institutions*. In particular, delinquency is most likely when (1) the adolescent is not attached to parents, school, or other institutions; (2) parents and others fail to monitor and effectively sanction deviance; (3) the adolescent's actual or anticipated investment in conventional society is minimal; and (4) the adolescent has not internalized conventional beliefs. Social learning theory is distinguished from strain and control theory by its focus on *positive relationships with deviant others*. In particular, delinquency results from association with others who (1) differentially reinforce the adolescent's delinquency, (2) model delinquent behavior, and/or (3) transmit delinquent values.

Second, strain theory argues that adolescents are *pressured into delinquency by the negative affective states—most notably anger and related emotions—that often result from negative relationships* (see Kemper, 1978, and Morgan and Heise, 1988, for typologies of negative affective states). This negative affect creates pressure for corrective action and *may* lead adolescents to (1) make use of illegitimate channels of goal achievement, (2) attack or escape from the source of their adversity, and/or (3) manage their negative affect through the use of illicit drugs. . . .

Strain theory, then, is distinguished by its focus on negative relationships with others and its insistence that such relationships lead to delinquency through the negative affect—especially anger—they sometimes engender. . . .

Strain as the Disjunction Between Aspirations and Expectations/Actual Achievements

The classic strain theories of Merton, A. Cohen, and Cloward and Ohlin argue that the cultural system encourages everyone to pursue the ideal goals of monetary success and/or middle-class status. Lower-class individuals, however, are often prevented from achieving such goals through legitimate channels. In line with such theories, adolescent strain is typically measured in terms of the disjunction between *aspirations* (or ideal goals) and *expectations* (or expected levels of goal achievement). These theories, however, have been criticized for several reasons (see Agnew, 1986, 1991b; Clinard, 1964; Hirschi, 1969; Kornhauser, 1978; Liska, 1987; also see Bernard, 1984; Farnworth and Leiber, 1989). Among other things, it has been charged that these theories (1) are unable to explain the extensive nature of middle-class delinquency, (2) neglect goals other than monetary success/middle-class status, (3) neglect barriers to goal achievement other

than social class, and (4) do not fully specify why only *some* strained individuals turn to delinquency. The most damaging criticism, however, stems from the limited empirical support provided by studies focusing on the disjunction between aspirations and expectations (see Kornhauser, 1978, as well the arguments of Bernard, 1984; Elliott et al., 1985; and Jensen, 1986). . . .

Strain as the Disjunction Between Expectations and Actual Achievements

As indicated above, strain theories in criminology focus on the inability to achieve *ideal* goals derived from the cultural system. This approach stands in contrast to certain of the research on justice in social psychology. Here the focus is on the disjunction between *expectations* and *actual achievements* (rewards), and it is commonly argued that such expectations are existentially based. . . . The justice literature argues that the failure to achieve such expectations may lead to such emotions as anger, resentment, rage, dissatisfaction, disappointment, and unhappiness—that is, all the emotions customarily associated with strain in criminology. Further, it is argued that individuals will be strongly motivated to reduce the gap between expectations and achievements—with deviance being commonly mentioned as one possible option. . . .

Strain as the Disjunction Between Just/Fair Outcomes and Actual Outcomes

The above models of strain assume that individual goals focus on the achievement of specific outcomes. Individual goals, for example, focus on the achievement of a certain amount of money or a certain grade-point average. A third conception of strain, also derived from the justice/equity literature, makes a rather different argument. It claims that individuals do not necessarily enter interactions with specific outcomes in mind. Rather, they enter interactions expecting that certain distributive justice rules will be followed, rules specifying how resources should be allocated. The rule that has received the most attention in the literature is that of equity. (An equitable relationship is one in which the outcome/input ratios of the actors involved in an exchange/allocation relationship are equivalent; see Adams, 1963, 1965; Cook and Hegtvedt, 1983; Walster et al., 1978. . . .

Summary: Strain as the Failure to Achieve Positively Valued Goals

Three types of strain in this category have been listed: strain as the disjunction between (1) aspirations and expectations/actual achievements, (2) expectations and actual achievements, and (3) just/fair outcomes and actual outcomes. Strain theory in criminology has focused on the first type of strain, arguing that it is most responsible for the delinquency in our society. Major research traditions in the justice/equity field, however, argue that anger and frustration derive primarily from the second two types of strain. . . .

Strain as the Removal of Positively Valued Stimuli From the Individual

The psychological literature on aggression and the stress literature suggest that strain may involve more than the pursuit of positively valued goals. Certain of the aggression literature, in fact, has come to de-emphasize the pursuit of positively valued goals, pointing out that the blockage of goal-seeking behavior is a relatively weak predictor of aggression, particularly when the goal has never been experienced before (Bandura, 1973; Zillman, 1979). The stress literature has largely neglected the pursuit of positively valued goals as a source of stress. Rather, if one looks at the stressful life events examined in this literature, one finds a focus on (1) events involving the loss of positively valued stimuli and (2) events involving the presentation of noxious or negative stimuli (see Pearlin, 1981, for other typologies of stressful life events/conditions).[1] So, for example, one recent study of adolescent stress employs a life-events list that focuses on such items as the loss of a boyfriend/girlfriend, the death or serious illness of a friend, moving to a new school district, the

divorce/separation of one's parents, suspension from school, and the presence of a variety of adverse conditions at work. . . .

Strain as the Presentation of Negative Stimuli

. . . .A wide range of noxious stimuli have been examined in the literature, and experimental, survey, and participant observation studies have linked such stimuli to both general and specific measures of delinquency—with the experimental studies focusing on aggression. Delinquency/aggression, in particular, has been linked to such noxious stimuli as child abuse and neglect (Rivera and Widom, 1990), criminal victimization (Lauritsen et al., 1991), physical punishment (Straus, 1991), negative relations with parents (Healy and Bonner, 1969), negative relations with peers (Short and Strodtbeck, 1965), adverse or negative school experiences (Hawkins and Lishner, 1987), a wide range of stressful life events (Gersten et al., 1974; Kaplan et al., 1983; Linsky and Straus, 1986; Mawson, 1987; Novy and Donohue, 1985; Vaux and Ruggiero, 1983), verbal threats and insults, physical pain, unpleasant odors, disgusting scenes, noise, heat, air pollution, personal space violations, and high density (see Anderson and Anderson, 1984; Bandura, 1973, 1983; Berkowitz, 1982, 1986; Mueller, 1983). . . .

The Links Between Strain and Delinquency

Three sources of strain have been presented: strain as the actual or anticipated failure to achieve positively valued goals, strain as the actual or anticipated removal of positively valued stimuli, and strain as the actual or anticipated presentation of negative stimuli. While these types are theoretically distinct from one another, they may sometimes overlap in practice. So, for example, the insults of a teacher may be experienced as adverse because they (1) interfere with the adolescent's aspirations for academic success, (2) result in the violation of a distributive justice rule such as equity, and (3) are conditioned negative stimuli and so are experienced as noxious in and of themselves. Other examples of overlap can be given, and it may sometimes be difficult to disentangle the different types of strain in practice. Once again, however, these categories are ideal types and are presented only to ensure that all events with the potential for creating strain are considered in empirical research.

Each type of strain increases the likelihood that individuals will experience one or more of a range of negative emotions. Those emotions include disappointment, depression, and fear. Anger, however, is the most critical emotional reaction for the purposes of the general strain theory. Anger results when individuals blame their adversity on others, and anger is a key emotion because it increases the individual's level of felt injury, creates a desire for retaliation/revenge, energizes the individual for action, and lowers inhibitions, in part because individuals believe that others will feel their aggression is justified (see Averill, 1982; Berkowitz, 1982; Kemper, 1978; Kluegel and Smith, 1986: Ch. 10; Zillman, 1979). Anger, then, affects the individual in several ways that are conducive to delinquency. Anger is distinct from many of the other types of negative affect in this respect, and this is the reason that anger occupies a special place in the general strain theory.[2] It is important to note, however, that delinquency may still occur in response to other types of negative affect—such as despair, although delinquency is less likely in such cases.[3] The experience of negative affect, especially anger, typically creates a desire to take corrective steps, with delinquency being one possible response. Delinquency may be a method for alleviating strain, that is, for achieving positively valued goals, for protecting or retrieving positive stimuli, or for terminating or escaping from negative stimuli. Delinquency may be used to seek revenge; data suggest that vengeful behavior often occurs even when there is no possibility of eliminating the adversity that stimulated it (Berkowitz, 1982). And delinquency may occur as adolescents try to manage their negative affect through illicit drug use (see Newcomb and Harlow, 1986). The general strain theory, then, has the potential to explain a broad range of delinquency, including theft, aggression, and drug use. . . .

Conclusion

Much of the recent theoretical work in criminology has focused on the integration of different delinquency theories. This paper has taken an alternative track and, following Hirschi's (1979) advice, has focused on the refinement of a single theory. The general strain theory builds upon traditional strain theory in criminology in several ways. . . .[T]he general strain theory points to several new sources of strain. In particular, it focuses on three categories of strain or negative relationships with others: (1) the actual or anticipated failure to achieve positively valued goals, (2) the actual or anticipated removal of positively valued stimuli, and (3) the actual or anticipated presentation of negative stimuli. Most current strain theories in criminology only focus on strain as the failure to achieve positively valued goals, and even then the focus is only on the disjunction between aspirations and expectations/ actual achievements. The disjunctions between expectations and achievements and just/fair outcomes and achievements are ignored. The general strain theory, then, significantly expands the focus of strain theory to include all types of negative relations between the individual and others. . . .

Notes

1. The stress literature has also focused on positive events, based on the assumption that such events might lead to stress by overloading the individual. Accumulating evidence, however, suggests that it is only undesirable events that lead to negative outcomes such as depression (e.g., Gersten et al., 1974; Kaplan et al., 1983; Pearlin et al., 1981; Thoits, 1983).

2. The focus on blame/anger represents a major distinction between the general strain theory and the stress literature. The stress literature simply focuses on adversity, regardless of whether it is blamed on another. This is perhaps appropriate because the major outcome variables of the stress literature are inner-directed states, like depression and poor health. When the focus shifts to outer-directed be-

havior, like much delinquency, a concern with blame/anger becomes important.

3. Delinquency may still occur in the absence of blame and anger (see Berkowitz, 1986; Zillman, 1979). Individuals who accept responsibility for their adversity are still subject to negative affect, such as depression, despair, and disappointment (see Kemper, 1978; Kluegel and Smith, 1986). As a result, such individuals will still feel pressure to take corrective action, although the absence of anger places them under less pressure and makes vengeful behavior much less likely. Such individuals, however, may engage in innerdirected delinquency, such as drug use, and if suitably disposed, they may turn to other forms of delinquency as well. Since these individuals lack the strong motivation for revenge and the lowered inhibitions that anger provides, it is assumed that they must have some minimal disposition for deviance before they respond to their adversity with outerdirected delinquency (see the discussion of the disposition to delinquency).

References

Agnew, Robert. 1985a. A revised strain theory of delinquency. *Social Forces*, 4:151–167.

——. 1986. Challenging strain theory: An examination of goals and goal-blockage. Paper presented at the annual meeting of the American Society of Criminology, Atlanta.

——. 1991b. Strain and subcultural crime theory. In Joseph Sheley (ed.), *Criminology: A Contemporary Handbook*. Belmont, CA: Wadsworth.

Anderson, Craig A. and Dona C. Anderson. 1984. Ambient temperature and violent crime: Tests of the linear and curvilinear hypotheses. *Journal of Personality and Social Psychology*, 46:91–97.

Averill, James R. 1982. *Anger and Aggression*. New York: Springer-Verlag.

Bandura, Albert. 1973. *Aggression: A Social Learning Analysis*. Englewood Cliffs, NJ: Prentice Hall.

——. 1983. Psychological mechanisms of aggression. In Russell G. Geen and Edward Donnerstein (eds.), *Aggression: Theoretical and Empirical Reviews*. New York: Academic Press.

Berkowitz, Leonard. 1982. Aversive conditions as stimuli to aggression. In Leonard Berkowitz (ed.), *Advances in Experimental Social Psychology*. Vol 15. New York: Academic Press.

——. 1986. *A Survey of Social Psychology*. New York: Holt, Rinehart, and Winston.

Bernard, Thomas J. 1984. Control criticisms of stain theories: An assessment of theoretical and empirical adequacy. *Journal of Research in Crime and Delinquency*, 21:353–372.

Clinard, Marshall B. 1964. *Anomie and Deviant Behavior*. New York: Free Press.

Elliott, Delbert, David Huizinga, and Suzanne Ageton. 1985. *Explaining Delinquency and Drug Use*. Beverly Hills, CA: Sage.

Farnworth, Margaret and Michael J. Leiber. 1989. Strain theory revisited: Economic goals, educational means, and delinquency. *American Sociological Review*, 54:263–274.

Gersten, Joanne C., Thomas S. Langer, Jeanne G. Eisenberg, and Lida Ozek. 1974. Child behavior and life events: Undesirable change or change per se. In Barbara Snell Dohrenwend and Bruce P. Dohrenwend (eds.), *Stressful Life Events: Their Nature and Effects*. New York: John Wiley & Sons.

Hawkins, J. David and Denise M. Lishner. 1987. Schooling and delinquency. In Elmer H. Johnson (ed.), *Handbook on Crime and Delinquency Prevention*. New York: Greenwood.

Healy, William and Augusta F. Bonner. 1969. *New Light on Delinquency and Its Treatment*. New Haven, Conn.: Yale University Press.

Hirschi, Travis. 1969. *Causes of Delinquency*. Berkeley: University of California Press.

Jensen, Gary. 1986. Dis-integrating integrated theory: A critical analysis of attempts to save strain theory. Paper presented at the annual meeting of the American Society of Criminology, Atlanta.

Kaplan, Howard B., Cynthia Robbins, and Steven S. Martin. 1983. Toward the testing of a general theory of deviant behavior in longitudinal perspective: Patterns of psychopathology. In James R. Greenley and Roberta G. Simmons (eds.), *Research in Community and Mental Health*. Greenwich, Conn.: Jai Press.

Kemper, Theodore D. 1978. *A Social Interactional Theory of Emotions*. New York: John Wiley & Sons.

Kluegel, James R. and Eliot R. Smith. 1986. *Beliefs about Inequality*. New York: Aldine De Gruyter.

Kornhauser, Ruth Rosner. 1978. *Social Sources of Delinquency*. Chicago: University of Chicago Press.

Lauritsen, Janet L., Robert J. Sampson, and John Laub. 1991. The link between offending and victimization among adolescents. *Criminology*, 29:265–292.

Linsky, Arnold S. and Murray A. Straus. 1986. *Social Stress in the United States.* Dover, Mass.: Auburn House.

Liska, Allen E. 1987. *Perspectives on Deviance.* Englewood Cliffs, NJ: Prentice Hall.

Mawson, Anthony R. 1987. *Criminality: A Model of Stress-Induced Crime.* New York: Praeger.

Morgan, Rick L. and David Heise. 1988. Structure of emotions. *Social Psychology Quarterly,* 51:19–31.

Mueller, Charles W. 1983. Environmental stressors and aggressive behavior. In Russell G. Geen and Edward I. Donnerstein (eds.), *Aggression: Theoretical and Empirical Reviews.* Vol. 2. New York: Academic Press.

Newcomb, Michael D. and L. L. Harlow. 1986. Life events and substance use among adolescents: Mediating effects of perceived loss of control and meaninglessness in life. *Journal of Personality and Social Psychology,* 51:564–577.

Novy, Diane M. and Stephen Donohue. 1985. The relationship between adolescent life stress events and delinquent conduct including conduct indicating a need for supervision. *Adolescence,* 78:313–321.

Pearlin, Leonard I., Elizabeth G. Menaghan, Morton A. Lieberman, and Joseph T. Mullan. 1981. The stress process. *Journal of Health and Social Behavior,* 22:337–356.

Rivera, Beverly and Cathy Spatz Widom. 1990. Childhood victimization and violent offending. *Violence and Victims,* 5:19–35.

Short, James F. and Fred L. Strodtbeck. 1965. *Group Process and Gang Delinquency.* Chicago: University of Chicago Press.

Straus, Murray. 1991. Discipline and deviance: Physical punishment of children and violence and other crimes in adulthood. *Social Problems,* 38:133–154.

Thoits, Peggy. 1983. Multiple identities and psychological well-being: A reformulation and test of the social isolation hypothesis. *Journal of Community Psychology,* 10:341–362.

Vaux, Allan and Mary Ruggiero. 1983. Stressful life change and delinquent behavior. *American Journal of Community Psychology,* 11:169–183.

Zillman, Dolf. 1979. *Hostility and Aggression.* Hillsdale, N.J.: Lawrence Erlbaum.

Adapted from *Criminology,* vol. 30:47–87 with permission of the American Society of Criminology. Copyright © 1992. ✦

10
Crime and Deviance in the Life Course

Robert J. Sampson

John H. Laub

are neither permanent nor linear. Even individuals whose prospects seem particularly bleak can be redeemed if the right social and microstructural transitions are made. But deviant careers wax and wane, so transitions out of deviance are never fully complete. Emergent situations can reignite deviant inclinations in even the most insulated of individuals, affecting their career trajectories in difficult-to-predict ways. The key to long-term desistance is a stake in conformity powerful enough to protect at-risk individuals from the pushes and pulls that might otherwise trigger fits of rule-breaking.

Accounting for the onset, persistence, and desistence of deviant careers may be the most important undertaking of contemporary deviance research. Most theoretical models are static, focusing on a discrete number of variables and their contribution to rule-breaking at a fixed point in time. More nuanced models are developmental in nature, exploring the dynamic interchange between social, economic, and interpersonal forces and their life-course-specific effect on deviant behavior over time.

Life course models such as the one proposed by Sampson and Laub are grounded in social control theory, a theory that looks at the role that weakened social bonds play in rule-breaking. The social bonding process is dynamic, changing, and constantly emergent—a function of circumstances that people confront as they move from childhood to adolescence to young adulthood to mature adulthood. At each point in the life course, different social forces (socioeconomic, familial, occupational, interpersonal) determine whether and when a person will break rules, which kind, and for how long. Sampson and Laub's model effectively explains why some people begin deviant careers late in life, why others terminate involvement early, and why still others vacillate between conformity and rule-breaking throughout the life course.

Contrary to deterministic approaches suggesting that bad temperaments, parental neglect and abuse, economic strain, and deviant peer relations result in "life-course-persistent offending," it is clear that most deviant careers

. . .[A]lthough criminal behavior does peak in the teenage years, evidence reviewed below indicates an early onset of delinquency as well as continuity of criminal behavior over the life course. By concentrating on the teenage years, sociological perspectives on crime have thus failed to address the life-span implications of childhood behavior. . . .

. . .[T]he life-course perspective highlights continuities and discontinuities in behavior over time and the social influences of age-graded transitions and life events. Hence, the life course is concerned not only with early childhood experiences but also with salient events and socialization in adulthood. To the extent that the adult life course does explain variation in adult crime unaccounted for by childhood development, change must be considered part of the explanatory framework in criminology, along with the stability of early individual differences. . . .

The Life Course Perspective

The life course has been defined as "pathways through the age differentiated life span," where age differentiation "is manifested in expectations and options that impinge on decision processes and the course of events that give shape to life stages, transitions, and turning points" (Elder 1985). Similarly, Caspi et al (1990: 15) conceive of the life course as a "sequence of culturally defined age-graded roles and social transitions that are enacted over time." Age-graded transitions are embedded in social institutions and are subject to historical change (Elder 1975, 1991).

Two central concepts underlie the analysis of life-course dynamics. A trajectory is a pathway or line of development over the life span such as worklife, marriage, parenthood, self-esteem, and criminal behavior. Trajectories refer to long-term patterns and sequences of behavior. Transitions are marked by specific life events (e.g. first job or first marriage) that are embedded in trajectories and evolve over shorter time spans— "changes in state that are more or less abrupt" (Elder 1985: 31–32). Some transitions are age-graded and some are not; hence, what is often assumed to be important is the normative timing and sequencing of changes in roles, statuses, or other socially defined positions along some consensual dimension (Jessor et al 1991). For example, Hogan (1980) emphasizes the duration of time (spells) between a change in state and the ordering of events, such as first job or first marriage, on occupational status and earnings in adulthood. Caspi et al (1990: 25) argue that delays in social transitions (e.g. being "off-time") produce conflicting obligations that enhance later difficulties (see also Rindfuss et al 1987). As a result, life-course analyses are often characterized by a focus on the duration, timing, and ordering of major life events and their consequences for later social development.

The interlocking nature of trajectories and transitions may generate turning points or a change in the life course (Elder 1985: 32). Adaptation to life events is crucial because the same event or transition followed by different adaptations can lead to different trajectories (Elder 1985: 35). The long-term view embodied by the life-course focus on trajectories implies a strong connection between childhood events and experiences in adulthood. However, the simultaneous shorter-term view also implies that transitions or turning points can modify life trajectories—they can "redirect paths." Social institutions and triggering life events that may

modify trajectories include school, work, the military, marriage, and parenthood (see e.g. Elder 1986, Rutter et al 1990, Sampson & Laub 1990).

In addition to the study of trajectories of change and the continuity between childhood behavior and later adulthood outcomes, the life-course framework encompasses at least three other themes: (i) a concern with the social meanings of age throughout the life course, (ii) intergenerational transmission of social patterns, and (iii) the effects of macrolevel events (e.g. Great Depression, World War II) and structural location (e.g. class and gender) on individual life histories (see Elder 1974, 1985). As Elder (1991) notes, a major objective of the study of the life course is to link social history and social structure to the unfolding of human lives. To address these themes individual lives are studied through time, with particular attention devoted to aging, cohort effects, historical context, and the social influence of age-graded transitions. . . .

Stability of Crime and Deviance

. . .[T]he linkage between childhood misbehavior and adult outcomes is found across life domains that go well beyond the legal concept of crime. This phenomenon is usually defined as heterotypic continuity—continuity of an inferred genotypic attribute presumed to underlie diverse phenotypic behaviors (Caspi & Bem 1990: 553). For instance, a specific behavior in childhood might not be predictive of the exact same behavior in later adulthood but might still be associated with behaviors that are conceptually consistent with that earlier behavior (Caspi & Moffitt 1991: 4). Although not always criminal per se, adult behaviors falling in this category might include excessive drinking, traffic violations, marital conflict or abuse, and harsh discipline of children. Gottfredson & Hirschi (1990: 91) invoke a similar idea when they refer to adult behaviors "analogous" to crime such as accidents, smoking, and sexual promiscuity. . . .

Implications for Social Theories of Crime

There is ample evidence that antisocial behavior is relatively stable across stages of the life course, regardless of traditional sociological variables like stratification. As Caspi & Moffitt (1991: 2) conclude, robust continuities in antisocial behavior have been revealed over the past 50 years in different nations (e.g. Canada, England, Finland, New Zealand, Sweden, and the United States) and with multiple methods of assessment (e.g. official records, teacher ratings, parent reports, and peer nominations of aggressive behavior). These replications across time and space yield an impressive generalization that is rare in the social sciences.

Antisocial behavior in childhood also predicts a wide range of troublesome adult outcomes, supporting Hagan & Palloni's (1988) observation that delinquent and criminal events "are linked into life trajectories of broader significance, whether those trajectories are criminal or noncriminal in form" (1988: 90, see also Hagan 1991). Because most research by criminologists has focused either on the teenage years or adult behavior limited to crime, this idea has not been well integrated into the criminological literature. . . .

Change and the Adult Life Course

. . .[W]e begin to answer this question with a seeming paradox—while studies reviewed earlier do show that antisocial behavior in children is one of the best predictors of antisocial behavior in adults, "most antisocial children do not become antisocial as adults" (Gove 1985: 123). Robins (1978) found identical results in her review of four longitudinal studies, stating that most antisocial children do not become antisocial adults (1978: 611). A follow-up of the Cambridge-Somerville Youth study found that "a majority of adult criminals had no history as juvenile delinquents" (McCord 1980: 158). Cline (1980: 665) states that although there is "more constancy than change . . .there is sufficient change in all the data to preclude simple conclusions concerning criminal career progressions." He concludes that there is far more heterogeneity in criminal behavior than previous work has suggested, and that many juvenile offenders do not become career offenders (Cline 1980: 669–70). Loeber

& LeBlanc make a similar point: "Against the backdrop of continuity, studies also show large within-individual changes in offending, a point understressed by Gottfredson & Hirschi" (1990: 390). . . .

. . .[S]ocial factors may work to modify childhood trajectories for the majority of youth who are not "life course persistent" [Moffitt 1991]. In support of this idea recent criminological research suggests that salient life events influence behavior and modify trajectories—a key thesis of the life course model. A follow-up of 200 Borstal boys found that marriage led to "increasing social stability" (Gibbens 1984: 61). Knight et al (1977) discovered that while marriage did not reduce criminality, it reduced antisocial behavior such as drinking and drug use (see also Osborn & West 1979, West 1982, Rand 1987). . . .

. . .[T]his is an important methodological point that applies to the stability of crime. Looking back over the careers of adult criminals exaggerates the prevalence of stability. Looking forward from youth reveals the successes and failures, including antisocial adolescents who go on to be normal functioning adults. This is the paradox noted earlier—adult criminality seems to be always preceded by childhood misconduct, but most conduct-disordered children do not become antisocial or criminal adults (Robins 1978). . . .

. . .Sampson & Laub (1990) theorized that social ties to the adult institutions of informal social control (e.g. family, community, work) influence criminal behavior over the life course despite delinquent and antisocial background. Their organizing principle derived from the central idea of social control theory—crime and deviance result when an individual's bond to society is weak or broken. Their theoretical model focused on the transition to adulthood and, in turn, the new role demands from higher education, full-time employment, military service, and marriage. Unlike much life-course research, however, Sampson & Laub (1990) emphasized the quality or strength of social ties more than the occurrence or timing of discrete life events (cf. Hogan 1978, Loeber & LeBlanc 1990: 430–32). For example, while

Gottfredson & Hirschi (1990: 140–41) argue that marriage per se does not increase social control, a strong attachment to one's spouse and close emotional ties increase the social bond between individuals and, all else equal, should lead to a reduction in criminal behavior (cf. Shover 1985: 94). Similarly, employment alone does not increase social control. It is employment coupled with job stability, job commitment, and ties to work that should increase social control and, all else equal, lead to a reduction in criminal behavior. It was thus the social capital in the institutional relationship that was hypothesized to dictate the salience of informal social control at the individual level. . . .

Rethinking Stability and Change

Taken as a whole, the foregoing review suggests that conclusions about the inevitability of antisocial continuities have either been overstated or misinterpreted. . . .

Assessing Individual Change

A promising direction for future research is the analysis of individual pathways of crime and deviance. That is, rather than relying on stability coefficients or aggregate age-crime curves, an alternative conception of change is to map individual trajectories embedded in the life course. . . .

. . .As one example, it is quite common to study whether unemployed persons have higher crime rates than the employed. It is rare that we investigate whether an individual moving from employment to a state of unemployment increases criminal activities, a methodology where each person acts as his or her own control (Farrington 1988: 180). Only by studying both individual change trajectories and between-individual differences in stability are we likely to resolve some of the current controversies on age and crime. . . .

Further Research Needs

Advances in knowledge on crime and delinquency over the life course require not only rethinking what we mean by stability and change, but a fresh infusion of data we

can use to address key limitations of past research. . . .

. . .[L]ongitudinal studies of crime have often failed to measure the timing and sequencing of changes in salient life events over the life course. In fact, longitudinal data sets in criminology frequently focus on unchanging demographic characteristics that have little bearing on theories of the life course (see Tonry et al 1991, Blumstein et al 1986). To establish influences on individual development one must account not only for background factors but the changing nature of important life events (e.g. work, family, and military ties), especially during the late adolescence to young adulthood transition. . . .

Conclusion

The traditional hostility among sociologists toward research establishing early childhood differences in delinquency and antisocial behavior that remain stable over time is unwarranted. Not only can stability be studied sociologically, its flip side is change, and the latter appears to be systematically structured by adult bonds to social institutions. The unique advantage of a sociological perspective on the life course is that it brings the formative period of childhood back into the picture yet recognizes that individuals can change through interaction with key social institutions as they age. With improvements in measurement and conceptualization, the prospects appear bright for future research to uncover the interlocking trajectories of crime, deviance, and human development.

References

Abbot, A., Hrycak, A. 1990. Measuring resemblance in sequence data: An optimal matching analysis of musicians' careers. *Am J. Sociol.* 96:144–85.

Baltes, P., Nesselroade, J. 1984. Paradigm lost and paradigm regained: Critique of Dannefer's portrayal of life-span developmental psychology. *Am Sociol. Rev.* 49:841–46.

Blumstein, A., Cohen, J. 1979. Estimation of individual crime rates from arrest records. *J. Crim. Law Criminol.* 70:561–85.

Blumstein, A., Cohen, J., Roth, J., Visher, C., eds. 1986. *Criminal Careers and "Career Criminals."* Washington, DC: Natl. Acad. Sci.

Blumstein, A., Cohen, J., Farrington, D. 1988. Criminal career research: Its value for criminology. *Criminology* 26:1–35.

Bonderson, U. 1989. *Prisoners in Prison Societies.* New Brunswick: Transaction.

Braithwaite, J. 1989. *Crime, Shame, and Reintegration.* Cambridge: Cambridge Univ. Press.

Brim, O., Kagan, J. 1980a. Constancy and change: A view of the issues. See Brim & Kagan 1980b, pp. 1–25.

Brim, Kagan, J., eds. 1980b. *Constancy and Change in Human Development.* Cambridge: Harvard Univ. Press.

Cairns, R. B. 1986. Phenomena lost: Issues in the study of development. In *The Individual Subject and Scientific Psychology*, ed. J. Valsiner, pp. 97–111. New York: Plenum.

Caspi, A. 1987. Personality in the life course. *J. Pers. Soc. Psychol.* 53:1203–13.

Caspi, A., Elder, G. H. Jr., Bem, D. 1987. Moving against the world: Life-course patterns of explosive children. *Dev. Psychol.* 22:308–13.

Caspi, A., Bem, D. 1990. Personality continuity and change across the life course. In *Handbook of Personality: Theory and Research*, ed. L. A. Pervin, pp. 549–75. New York: Guilford

Caspi, A., Elder, G. H. Jr., Herbener, E. 1990. Childhood personality and the predictions of life-course patterns. See Robins & Rutter 1990, pp. 13–35.

Caspi, A., Moffitt, T. 1991. The continuity of maladaptive behavior: From description to understanding in the study of antisocial behavior. In *Manual of Developmental Psychopathology*, eds. D. Cicchetti, D. Cohen. New York: Wiley. In press.

Cline, H. F. 1980. Criminal behavior over the life span. See Brim & Kagan 1980b, pp. 641–74.

Elder, G. H. Jr. 1974. *Children of the Great Depression.* Chicago: Univ. Chicago Press.

Elder, G. H. Jr. 1975. Age differentiation and the life course. *Annu. Rev. Sociol.* 1:165–90.

Elder, G. H. Jr. 1985. Perspective on the life course. In *Life Course Dynamics*, eds. G. H. Elder, Jr., pp. 23–49. Ithaca: Cornell Univ. Press

Elder, G. H. Jr. 1986. Military times and turning points in men's lives. *Dev. Psychol.* 22:233–45.

Elder, G. H. Jr. 1991. The life course. In *The Encyclopedia of Sociology*, eds. E. F. Borgatta, M. L. Borgatta. In press.

Farrington, D. 1988. Studying changes within individuals: The causes of offending. See Rutter 1988b, pp. 158–83.

Gibbens, T. C. N. 1984. Borstal boys after 25 years. *Br. J. Criminol.* 24:49–62.

Gottfredson, M., Hirschi, T. 1990. *A General Theory of Crime.* Stanford: Stanford Univ. Press.

Gove, W. R. 1985. The effect of age and gender on deviant behavior: A biopsychosocial perspective. In *Gender and the Life Course*, ed. A. S. Rossi, pp. 115–44. New York: Aldine.

Hagan, J. 1991. Destiny and drift: Subcultural preferences, status attainments, and the risks and rewards of youth. *Am. Sociol. Rev.* 56:567–82.

Hagan, J., Palloni, A. 1988. Crimes as social events in the life course: Reconceiving a criminological controversy. *Criminology* 26:87–100.

Hogan, D. P. 1978. The variable order of events in the life course. *Am. Sociol. Rev.* 43:573–86.

Hogan, D. P. 1980. The transition to adulthood as a career contingency. *Am. Sociol. Rev.* 45:261–76.

Jessor, R., Donovan, J., Costa, F. 1991. *Beyond Adolescence: Problem Behavior and Young Adult Development.* Cambridge: Cambridge Univ. Press.

Knight, B. J., Osborn, S. G., West, D. 1977. Early marriage and criminal tendency in males. *Br. J. Criminol.* 17:348–60.

Loeber, R., LeBlanc, M. 1990. Toward a developmental criminology. In *Crime and Justice*, eds. M. Tonry, N. Morris, 12:375–437. Chicago: Univ. Chicago Press.

McCord, J. 1980. Patterns of deviance. In *Human Functioning in Longitudinal Perspective*, eds. S. B. Sells, R. Crandall, M. Roff, J. S. Strauss, W. Pollin, pp. 157–65. Baltimore: Williams & Wilkins.

Moffitt, T. E. 1991. *Life-Course Persistent and Adolescence Limited to Antisocial Behavior: A Developmental Taxonomy.* Univ. Wisc., Madison. Unpublished manuscript.

Osborn, S. G., West, D. 1979. Marriage and delinquency: A postscript. *Br. J. Criminol.* 18:254–56.

Rand, A. 1987. Transitional life events and desistance from delinquency and crime. See Wolfgang et al 1987, pp. 134–62.

Rindfuss, R., Swicegood, C. G., Rosenfeld, R. 1987. Disorder in the life course: How common and does it matter? *Am. Sociol. Rev.* 52:785–801.

Robins, L. 1978. Sturdy childhood predictors of adult antisocial behavior: Replications from longitudinal studies. *Psychol. Med.* 8:611–22.

Rutter, M., Quinton, D., Hill, J. 1990. Adult outcomes of institution-reared children: Males and females compared. See Robins & Rutter 1990, pp. 135–57.

Sampson, R. J., Laub, J. H. 1990. Crime and deviance over the life course: The salience of adult social bonds. *Am. Sociol. Rev.* 55:609–27.

Shover, N. 1985. *Aging Criminals*. Beverly Hills: Sage.

Tonry, M., Ohlin, L. E., Farrington, D. P. 1991. *Human Development and Criminal Behavior: New Ways of Advancing Knowledge*. New York: Springer-Verlag

West, D. 1982. *Delinquency: Its Roots, Careers, and Prospects*. London: Heinemann.

Wolfgang, M., Thornberry, T., Figlio, R., eds. 1987. *From Boy to Man: From Delinquency to Crime*. Chicago: Univ. Chicago Press.

We would like to thank Avshalom Caspi, John Hagan, Richard Jessor, and Terri Moffitt for their helpful comments on an earlier draft.

11
Techniques of Neutralization

Gresham Sykes

David Matza

The notion that subcultures are responsible for individual *deviance is a popular one. It has been offered to account for everything from gang membership to chronic drug use to homosexuality. It says that subcultural membership transmits deviant values, and deviant values, in turn, inspire habitual rule-breaking. In this selection, Sykes and Matza question this assumption, arguing that the notion of a deviant subculture is both deterministic and imprecise. Why do so many offenders, they ask, deviate infrequently, episodically, or not at all, even when exposed to substantial and sustained prodeviance messages?*

The authors suggest that offenders are not nearly as committed to deviant values as many subcultural theorists believe. Offenders drift in and out of deviant worlds, responding to emergent circumstances flexibly and unpredictably, as the mood strikes them. Most deviants, argue Sykes and Matza, are deeply concerned about how others perceive them and will do everything in their power to deflect negative attributions. Neutralization tactics—linguistic devices that explain and justify untoward behavior—help deviants do precisely this.

Though such tactics are retrospectively voiced (they excuse and justify past *behavior), they are* prospectively *available. This distinction is crucial since the ability to neutralize may facilitate the decision to break social rules in the first place: If would-be offenders know that future rule-breaking can be explained away, deviance becomes far easier to commit. Sykes and Matza conclude that deviants and conformists are not that much different from one another. Some simply "drift"*

more than others, and these differences can often be traced to the immediate circumstances surrounding some contemplated deviant act.

In attempting to uncover the roots of juvenile delinquency, the social scientist has long since ceased to search for devils in the mind or stigma of the body. It is now largely agreed that delinquent behavior, like most social behavior, is learned and that it is learned in the process of social interaction.

The classic statement of this position is found in Sutherland's theory of differential association, which asserts that criminal or delinquent behavior involves the learning of (a) techniques of committing crimes and (b) motives, drives, rationalizations, and attitudes favorable to the violation of law.[1] Unfortunately, the specific content of what is learned—as opposed to the process by which it is learned—has received relatively little attention in either theory or research. Perhaps the single strongest school of thought on the nature of this content has centered on the idea of a delinquent subculture. The basic characteristic of the delinquent subculture, it is argued, is a system of values that represents an inversion of the values held by respectable, law-abiding society. The world of the delinquent is the world of the law-abiding turned upside down and its norms constitute a countervailing force directed against the conforming social order. Cohen[2] sees the process of developing a delinquent subculture as a matter of building, maintaining, and reinforcing a code for behavior which exists by opposition, which stands in point by point contradiction to dominant values, particularly those of the middle class. Cohen's portrayal of delinquency is executed with a good deal of sophistication, and he carefully avoids overly simple explanations such as those based on the principle of "follow the leader" or easy generalizations about "emotional disturbances." Furthermore, he does not accept the delinquent subculture as something given, but instead systematically examines the function of delinquent values as a viable solution to the lower-class, male child's problems in the area of social status. Yet in spite of its virtues, this image of juvenile delinquency as a form of behavior based on competing or countervailing values and norms appears to suffer from a number of serious defects. It is the nature of these defects and a possible alternative or modified explanation for a large portion of juvenile delinquency with which this paper is concerned.

The difficulties in viewing delinquent behavior as springing from a set of deviant values and norms—as arising, that is to say, from a situation in which the delinquent defines his delinquency as "right"—are both empirical and theoretical. In the first place, if there existed in fact a delinquent subculture such that the delinquent viewed his illegal behavior as morally correct, we could reasonably suppose that he would exhibit no feelings of guilt or shame at detection or confinement. Instead, the major reaction would tend in the direction of indignation or a sense of martyrdom.[3] It is true that some delinquents do react in the latter fashion, although the sense of martyrdom often seems to be based on the fact that others "get away with it" and indignation appears to be directed against the chance events or lack of skill that led to apprehension. More important, however, is the fact that there is a good deal of evidence suggesting that many delinquents *do* experience a sense of guilt or shame, and its outward expression is not to be dismissed as a purely manipulative gesture to appease those in authority. Much of this evidence is, to be sure, of a clinical nature or in the form of impressionistic judgments of those who must deal firsthand with the youthful offender. Assigning a weight to such evidence calls for caution, but it cannot be ignored if we are to avoid the gross stereotype of the juvenile delinquent as a hardened gangster in miniature.

In the second place, observers have noted that the juvenile delinquent frequently accords admiration and respect to law-abiding persons. The "really honest" person is often revered, and if the delinquent is sometimes overly keen to detect hypocrisy in those who conform, unquestioned probity is likely to win his approval. A fierce attachment to a humble, pious mother or a forgiving, upright priest (the former, according to many observers, is often encountered in both juvenile delinquents and adult criminals) might be dismissed as rank sentimentality, but at least it is clear that the delinquent does not necessarily regard those who abide by the legal rules as immoral. In a similar vein, it can be noted that the juvenile delinquent may exhibit great resentment if illegal behavior is imputed to "significant others" in his immediate social environment or to heroes in the world of sport and entertainment. In other words, if the delinquent does hold to a set of values and norms that stand in complete opposition to those of respectable society, his norm-holding is of a peculiar sort. While supposedly thoroughly committed to the deviant system of the delinquent subculture, he would appear to recognize the moral validity of the dominant normative system in many instances.[4]

In the third place, there is much evidence that juvenile delinquents often draw a sharp line between those who can be victimized and those who cannot. Certain social groups are not to be viewed as "fair game" in the performance of supposedly approved delinquent acts while others warrant a variety of attacks. In general, the potentiality for victimization would seem to be a function of the social distance between the juvenile delinquent and others and thus we find implicit maxims in the world of the delinquent such as "don't steal from friends" or "don't commit vandalism against a church of your own faith."[5] This is all rather obvious, but the implications have not received sufficient attention. The fact that supposedly valued behavior tends to be directed against disvalued social groups hints that the "wrongfulness" of such delinquent behavior is more widely recognized by delinquents than the literature has indicated. When the pool of victims is limited by considerations of kinship, friendship, ethnic group, social class, age, sex, etc., we have reason to suspect that the virtue of delinquency is far from unquestioned.

In the fourth place, it is doubtful if many juvenile delinquents are totally immune from the demands for conformity made by the dominant social order. There is a strong likelihood that the family of the delinquent will agree with respectable society that delinquency is wrong, even though the family may be engaged in a variety of illegal activities. That is, the parental posture conducive to delinquency is not apt to be a positive prodding. Whatever may be the influence of parental example, what might be called the "Fagin" pattern of socialization into delinquency is probably rare. Furthermore, as Redl has indicated, the idea that certain neighborhoods are completely delinquent, offering the child a model for delinquent behavior without reservations, is simply not supported by the data.[6]

The fact that a child is punished by parents, school officials, and agencies of the legal system for his delinquency may, as a number of observers have cynically noted, suggest to the child that he should be more careful not to get caught. There is an equal or greater probability, however, that the child will internalize the demands for conformity. This is not to say that demands for conformity cannot be counteracted. In fact, as we shall see shortly, an understanding of how internal and external demands for conformity are neutralized may be crucial for understanding delinquent behavior. But it is to say that a complete denial of the validity of demands for conformity and the substitution of a new normative system is improbable, in light of the child's or adolescent's dependency on adults and encirclement by adults inherent in his status in the social structure. No matter how deeply enmeshed in patterns of delinquency he may be and no matter how much this involvement may outweigh his associations with the law-abiding, he cannot escape the condemnation of his deviance. Somehow the demands for conformity must be met and answered; they cannot be ignored as part of an alien system of values and norms.

In short, the theoretical viewpoint that sees juvenile delinquency as a form of behavior based on the values and norms of a deviant subculture in precisely the same way as law-abiding behavior is based on the values and norms of the larger society is open to serious doubt. The fact that the world of the delinquent is embedded in the larger world of those who conform cannot be overlooked nor can the delinquent be equated with an adult thoroughly socialized into an alternative way of life. Instead, the juvenile delinquent would appear to be at least partially committed to the dominant social order in that he frequently exhibits guilt or shame when he violates its proscriptions, accords approval to certain conforming figures, and distinguishes between appropriate and inappropriate targets for his deviance. It is to an explanation for the apparently paradoxical fact of his delinquency that we now turn.

As Morris Cohen once said, "one of the most fascinating problems about human behavior is why men violate the laws in which they believe." This is the problem that confronts us when we attempt to explain why delinquency occurs despite a greater or lesser commitment to the usages of conformity. A basic clue is offered by the fact that social rules or norms calling for valued behavior seldom if ever take the form of categorical imperatives. Rather, values or norms appear as *qualified* guides for action limited in their applicability in terms of time, place, persons, and social circumstances; the moral injunction against killing, for example, does not apply to the enemy during combat in time of war, although a captured enemy comes once again under the prohibition. Similarly, the taking and distributing of scarce goods in a time of acute social need is felt by many to be right; although under other circumstances private property is held inviolable. The normative system of a society, then, is marked by what Williams has termed *flexibility*; it does not consist of a body of rules held to be binding under all conditions.[7]

This flexibility is, in fact, an integral part of the criminal law in that measures for "defenses to crimes" are provided in pleas such as nonage, necessity, insanity, drunkenness, compulsion, self-defense, and so on. The individual can avoid moral culpability for his criminal action—and thus avoid the negative sanctions of society—if he can prove that criminal intent was lacking. *It is our argument that much delinquency is based on what is essentially an unrecognized extension of defenses to crimes, in the form of justifica-*

tions for deviance that are seen as valid by the delinquent but not by the legal system or society at large.

These justifications are commonly described as rationalizations. They are viewed as following deviant behavior and as protecting the individual from self-blame and the blame of others after the act. But there is also reason to believe that they precede deviant behavior and make deviant behavior possible. It is this possibility that Sutherland mentioned only in passing and that other writers have failed to exploit from the viewpoint of sociological theory. Disapproval flowing from internalized norms and conforming others in the social environment is neutralized, turned back, or deflected in advance. Social controls that serve to check or inhibit deviant motivational patterns are rendered inoperative, and the individual is freed to engage in delinquency without serious damage to his self image. In this sense, the delinquent both has his cake and eats it too, for he remains committed to the dominant normative system and yet so qualifies its imperatives that violations are "acceptable" if not "right." Thus the delinquent represents not a radical opposition to law-abiding society but something more like an apologetic failure, often more sinned against than sinning in his own eyes. We call these justifications of deviant behavior techniques of neutralization; and we believe these techniques make up a crucial component of Sutherland's "definitions favorable to the violation of law." It is by learning these techniques that the juvenile becomes delinquent, rather than by learning moral imperatives, values or attitudes standing in direct contradiction to those of the dominant society. In analyzing these techniques, we have found it convenient to divide them into five major types.

The Denial of Responsibility

In so far as the delinquent can define himself as lacking responsibility for his deviant actions, the disapproval of self or others is sharply reduced in effectiveness as a restraining influence As Justice Holmes has said, even a dog distinguishes between being stumbled over and being kicked, and modern society is no less careful to draw a line between injuries that are unintentional, i.e., where responsibility is lacking, and those that are intentional. As a technique of neutralization, however, the denial of responsibility extends much further than the claim that deviant acts are an "accident" or some similar negation of personal accountability. It may also be asserted that delinquent acts are due to forces outside of the individual and beyond his control such as unloving parents, bad companions, or a slum neighborhood. In effect, the delinquent approaches a "billiard ball" conception of himself in which he sees himself as helplessly propelled into new situations. From a psychodynamic viewpoint, this orientation toward one's own actions may represent a profound alienation from self, but it is important to stress the fact that interpretations of responsibility are cultural constructs and not merely idiosyncratic beliefs. The similarity between this mode of justifying illegal behavior assumed by the delinquent and the implications of a "sociological" frame of reference or a "humane" jurisprudence is readily apparent.[8] It is not the validity of this orientation that concerns us here, but its function of deflecting blame attached to violations of social norms and its relative independence of a particular personality structure.[9] By learning to view himself as more acted upon than acting, the delinquent prepares the way for deviance from the dominant normative system without the necessity of a frontal assault on the norms themselves.

The Denial of Injury

A second major technique of neutralization centers on the injury or harm involved in the delinquent act. The criminal law has long made a distinction between crimes which are *mala in se* and *mala prohibita*— that is between acts that are wrong in themselves and acts that are illegal but not immoral—and the delinquent can make the same kind of distinction in evaluating the wrongfulness of his behavior. For the delinquent, however, wrongfulness may turn on the question of whether or not anyone has clearly been hurt by his deviance, and this matter is open to a variety of interpretations. Vandalism, for example, may be defined by the delinquent simply as "mischief"—after all, it may be claimed, the persons whose property has been destroyed can well afford it. Similarly, auto theft may be viewed as "borrowing," and gang fighting may be seen as a private quarrel, an agreed upon duel between two willing parties, and thus of no concern to the community at large. We are not suggesting that this technique of neutralization, labelled the denial of injury, involves an explicit dialectic. Rather, we are arguing that the delinquent frequently, and in a hazy fashion, feels that his behavior does not really cause any great harm despite the fact that it runs counter to law. Just as the link between the individual and his acts may be broken by the denial of responsibility, so may the link between acts and their consequences be broken by the denial of injury. Since society sometimes agrees with the delinquent, e.g., in matters such as truancy, "pranks," and so on, it merely reaffirms the idea that the delinquent's neutralization of social controls by means of qualifying the norms is an extension of common practice rather than a gesture of complete opposition.

The Denial of the Victim

Even if the delinquent accepts the responsibility for his deviant actions and is willing to admit that his deviant actions involve an injury or hurt, the moral indignation of self and others may be neutralized by an insistence that the injury is not wrong in light of the circumstances. The injury, it may be claimed, is not really an injury; rather, it is a form of rightful retaliation or punishment. By a subtle alchemy the delinquent moves himself into the position of an avenger and the victim is transformed into a wrong-doer. Assaults on homosexuals or suspected homosexuals, attacks on members of minority groups who are said to have gotten "out of place," vandalism as revenge on an unfair teacher or school official, thefts from a "crooked" store owner—all may be hurts inflicted on a transgressor, in the eyes of the de-

linquent. As Orwell has pointed out, the type of criminal admired by the general public has probably changed over the course of years and Raffles no longer serves as a hero;[10] but Robin Hood, and his latter day derivatives such as the tough detective seeking justice outside the law, still capture the popular imagination, and the delinquent may view his acts as part of a similar role.

To deny the existence of the victim, then, by transforming him into a person deserving injury is an extreme form of a phenomenon we have mentioned before, namely, the delinquent's recognition of appropriate and inappropriate targets for his delinquent acts. In addition, however, the existence of victim may be denied for the delinquent, in a somewhat different sense, by the circumstances of the delinquent act itself. Insofar as the victim is physically absent, unknown, or a vague abstraction (as is often the case in delinquent acts committed against property), the awareness of the victim's existence is weakened. Internalized norms and anticipations of the reactions of others must somehow be activated, if they are to serve as guides for behavior; and it is possible that a diminished awareness of the victim plays an important part in determining whether or not this process is set in motion.

The Condemnation of the Condemners

A fourth technique of neutralization would appear to involve a condemnation of the condemners or, as McCorkle and Korn have phrased it, a rejection of the rejectors.[11] The delinquent shifts the focus of attention from his own deviant acts to the motives and behavior of those who disapprove of his violations. His condemners, he may claim, are hypocrites, deviants in disguise, or impelled by personal spite. This orientation toward the conforming world may be of particular importance when it hardens into a bitter cynicism directed against those assigned the task of enforcing or expressing the norms of the dominant society. Police, it may be said, are corrupt, stupid, and brutal. Teachers always show favoritism and parents always "take it out" on their children. By a slight extension, the rewards of conformity—such as material success—become a matter of pull or luck, thus decreasing still further the stature of those who stand on the side of the law-abiding. The validity of this jaundiced viewpoint is not so important as its function in turning back or deflecting the negative sanctions attached to violations of the norms. The delinquent, in effect, has changed the subject of the conversation in the dialogue between his own deviant impulses and the reactions of others; and by attacking others, the wrongfulness of his own behavior is more easily repressed or lost to view.

The Appeal to Higher Loyalties

Fifth, and last, internal and external social controls may be neutralized by sacrificing the demands of the larger society for the demands of the smaller social groups to which the delinquent belongs such as the sibling pair, the gang, or the friendship clique. It is important to note that the delinquent does not necessarily repudiate the imperatives of the dominant normative system, despite his failure to follow them. Rather, the delinquent may see himself as caught up in a dilemma that must be resolved, unfortunately, at the cost of violating the law. One aspect of this situation has been studied by Stouffer and Toby in their research on the conflict between particularistic and universalistic demands, between the claims of friendship and general social obligations, and their results suggest that "it is possible to classify people according to a predisposition to select one or the other horn of a dilemma in role conflict."[12] For our purposes, however, the most important point is that deviation from certain norms may occur not because the norms are rejected but because other norms, held to be more pressing or involving a higher loyalty, are accorded precedence. Indeed, it is the fact that both sets of norms are believed in that gives meaning to our concepts of dilemma and role conflict.

The conflict between the claims of friendship and the claims of law, or a similar dilemma, has of course long been recognized by the social scientist (and the novelist) as a common human problem. If the juvenile de-

linquent frequently resolves his dilemma by insisting that he must "always help a buddy" or "never squeal on a friend," even when it throws him into serious difficulties with the dominant social order, his choice remains familiar to the supposedly law-abiding. The delinquent is unusual, perhaps, in the extent to which he is able to see the fact that he acts in behalf of the smaller social groups to which he belongs as a justification for violations of society's norms, but it is a matter of degree rather than of kind.

"I didn't mean it." "I didn't really hurt anybody." "They had it coming to them." "Everybody's picking on me." "I didn't do it for myself." These slogans or their variants, we hypothesize, prepare the juvenile for delinquent acts. These "definitions of the situation" represent tangential or glancing blows at the dominant normative system rather than the creation of an opposing ideology; and they are extensions of patterns of thought prevalent in society rather than something created *de novo*.

Techniques of neutralization may not be powerful enough to fully shield the individual from the force of his own internalized values and the reactions of conforming others, for as we have pointed out, juvenile delinquents often appear to suffer from feelings of guilt and shame when called into account for their deviant behavior. And some delinquents may be so isolated from the world of conformity that techniques of neutralization need not be called into play. Nonetheless, we would argue that techniques of neutralization are critical in lessening the effectiveness of social controls and that they lie behind a large share of delinquent behavior. Empirical research in this area is scattered and fragmentary at the present time, but the work of Redl,[13] Cressey,[14] and others has supplied a body of significant data that has done much to clarify the theoretical issues and enlarge the fund of supporting evidence. Two lines of investigation seem to be critical at this stage. First, there is need for more knowledge concerning the differential distribution of techniques of neutralization, as operative patterns of thought, by age, sex, social class, ethnic group, etc. On *a priori* grounds it might be assumed that these justifications for deviance will be more readily seized by segments of society for whom a discrepancy between common social ideals and social practice is most apparent. It is also possible however, that the habit of "bending" the dominant normative system—if not "breaking" it—cuts across our cruder social categories and is to be traced primarily to patterns of social interaction within the familial circle. Second, there is need for a greater understanding of the internal structure of techniques of neutralization, as a system of beliefs and attitudes, and its relationship to various types of delinquent behavior. Certain techniques of neutralization would appear to be better adapted to particular deviant acts than to others, as we have suggested, for example, in the case of offenses against property and the denial of the victim. But the issue remains far from clear and stands in need of more information.

In any case, techniques of neutralization appear to offer a promising line of research in enlarging and systematizing the theoretical grasp of juvenile delinquency. As more information is uncovered concerning techniques of neutralization, their origins, and their consequences, both juvenile delinquency in particular, and deviation from normative systems in general may be illuminated.

Notes

1. E. H. Sutherland, *Principles of Criminology*, revised by D. R. Cressey. Chicago: Lippincott, 1955, pp. 77–80.

2. Albert K. Cohen, *Delinquent Boys*. Glencoe, Ill.: The Free Press, 1955.

3. This form of reaction among the adherents of a deviant subculture who fully believe in the "rightfulness" of their behavior and who are captured and punished by the agencies of the dominant social order can be illustrated, perhaps, by groups such as Jehovah's Witnesses, early Christian sects, nationalist movements in colonial areas, and conscientious objectors during World Wars I and II.

4. As Weber has pointed out, a thief may recognize the legitimacy of legal rules without accepting their moral validity. Cf. Max Weber, *The Theory of Social and Economic Organization* (translated by A. M. Henderson and Talcott Parsons), New York: Oxford University Press, 1947, p. 125. We are arguing here, however, that the juvenile delinquent frequently recognizes *both* the legitimacy of the dominant social order and its moral "rightness."

5. Thrasher's account of the "Itschkies"—a juvenile gang composed of Jewish boys—and the immunity from "rolling" enjoyed by Jewish drunkards is a good illustration. Cf. F. Thrasher, *The Gang,* Chicago: The University of Chicago Press, 1947, p. 315.

6. Cf. Solomon Kobrin, "The Conflict of Values in Delinquency Areas," *American Sociological Review,* 16 (October, 1951), pp. 653–661.

7. Cf. Robin Williams, Jr., *American Society,* New York: Knopf, 1951, p. 28.

8. A number of observers have wryly noted that many delinquents seem to show a surprising awareness of sociological and psychological explanations for their behavior and are quick to point out the causal role of their poor environment.

9. It is possible, of course, that certain personality structures can accept some techniques of neutralization more readily than others, but this question remains largely unexplored.

10. George Orwell, *Dickens, Dali, and Others,* New York: Reynal, 1946.

11. Lloyd W. McCorkle and Richard Korn, "Resocialization Within Walls," *The Annals of the American Academy of Political and Social Science,* 293, (May, 1954), pp. 88–98.

12. See Samuel A. Stouffer and Jackson Toby, "Role Conflict and Personality," in *Toward a General Theory of Action,* edited by Talcott Parsons and Edward A. Shils, Cambridge: Harvard University Press, 1951, p. 494.

13. See Fritz Redl and David Wineman, *Children Who Hate,* Glencoe: The Free Press, 1956.

14. See D. R. Cressey, *Other People's Money,* Glencoe: The Free Press, 1953.

12
A Radical Conception of Crime and Deviance

Michael J. Lynch

W. Byron Groves

Talk of a fair and impartial system is just talk, and immunity from social control is restricted to those who can afford it. Social rules are stilted to benefit the rich and the powerful, and capitalism is geared to promote, maintain, and perpetuate class differences. Radical theorists suggest that this picture will not change unless or until there is upheaval in the system itself. Revolution requires collectivization and consciousness-raising on a grand scale, a daunting task for anyone, but especially so for those who are least empowered. In the interim, deviance emerges as a form of resistance. Ironically, deviance only provides the state greater justification to increase the intensity of social control.

The notion of power is central to radical theory. Power lies at the core of judgments about acceptable and unacceptable behavior. Radical theorists contend that there is no such thing as a deviant act. Deviance is a social construction, and deviant acts are defined as such by those with the power to do so. Power comes in a variety of forms—social, political, religious, and the like—but its principal source is economic. In any society, control over resources translates into control over policy. Nowhere is this more true than in capitalistic societies, where resources and political influence go hand-in-glove.

The theory says that deviant behavior is behavior deemed threatening, disvalued, or offensive to the interests of the ruling class. Rule-breaking perpetrated by members of the subordinate classes is given particular legislative and enforcement scrutiny. The police and the courts are geared primarily to enforce the infractions of the subordinate classes. Deviance that actually brings more harm to society (both monetarily and interpersonally) than lower-class rule-breaking is either ignored or defined as harmless because it is perpetrated by the powerful and because it typically occurs during the course of normal business. Noted criminologist Edwin Sutherland calls this "white-collar crime"; it is explored in greater detail later in this book.

Critiques of early radical theories of crime causation offer the following observations: first, radicals, like conflict and labelling theorists, have seen crime simply as the mirror image of control, thus ruling out questions of causation, or succumbing to tautological reasoning where the only cause of crime is law (Spitzer 1980, 180; Akers 1980; Quinney 1970, 123). A second criticism is that radicals have limited themselves to an oversimplified, "uni-causal" approach where the only source of crime is capitalism (Shichor 1980). And third, many have argued that avoiding the issue of causation has resulted in a neglect of empirical research among radicals (Sparks 1980; Shichor 1980; Taylor et al. 1975).

In recent years radicals have addressed each of these criticisms. Specifically, they have added to the insights drawn from conflict and labelling theories (Greenberg 1981); have qualified the depiction of capitalism as the "source of all evil" without deemphasizing the structuring power of capitalism's political economy (Mankoff, 1978); and have undertaken a number of important empirical studies (Hagan and Bernstein 1979; Hagan and Albonetti 1982; Hagan and Leon 1977; Lizotte 1975; Lizotte et al. 1982; Humphries and Wallace 1980; Jacobs 1979; Liska et al. 1981; Greenberg 1981; Groves and Corrado 1983 Hagan et al. 1987, 1985, 1979; Box and Hale 1983a,

1983b; Lynch 1988a; Lynch et al. 1988). Thus, the criticisms listed above may have been legitimate in 1975. They no longer apply today.

When discussing Marx we referred to his views on class conflict, materialism, and the dialectic. The following four propositions relate those materials to the issue of causation:

1. The capitalist system has at its core a conflict between labor and capital, which means that capitalism is one in a long sequence of historical systems based on inequalities between those who own and those who work.

2. Through this fundamental structural inequality between labor and capital, society becomes stratified into social classes characterized by tremendous differences in wealth, status, power, and authority.

3. Taken together, these differences constitute variable material conditions of life which offer persons in different social classes vastly different opportunities in terms of life chances and life choices.

4. Among these opportunities are the chance or choice of becoming criminal.

Class, as we argued in chapter two, is an important category for radicals. Social stratification accounts for the unequal distribution of chances and choices available to persons at different locations in the class structure. It also accounts for the differential allocation of incentives and motivations for both criminal and non-criminal behavior. To support these claims radicals emphasize the causal connection between political economy, inequality, and crime.

Social Class, Stratification, and Inequality

As noted in chapter one, Marx defined social classes in terms of their relation to the means of production, and since then social theorists (e.g. Max Weber) have expanded Marx's conception to include unequal distributions of socially valued items such as power, prestige, wealth, or income. By focusing on how class position affects life chances, political power, and socialization patterns, radicals reaffirm the causal influence of economic factors on social life.

The most dramatic and decisive factor in social stratification is wealth which "is extraordinarily concentrated in the United States" (Gilbert and Kahn 1982, 105). Federal Reserve Board figures indicate that the top 20 percent of consumers own over 76 percent of the total wealth, while the bottom 20 percent hold only 0.2 percent (Gilbert and Kahn 1982, 106). More dramatically, the top 1 percent of the wealthy in the U.S. own 42 percent of all wealth (Perlow 1988, 52).

Income is also unequally distributed. The U.S. Bureau of the Census reports that nearly half of all income is received by 20 percent of families and individuals, while the bottom 20 percent receive only 4 percent of the total income. Putting aside political rhetoric concerning progress and equality, the fact is that distributions of income and wealth have remained fairly constant in the U.S. over the past 50 years (Currie and Skolnick 1984, 100–107). Contrary to the you-can-make-it-if-you-try ideology, this suggests that there is little chance that a significant number of lower class persons will advance in the American class structure.

In addition, recent data on occupational stratification point to a decline in both the quality and rewards associated with white collar work, a drop in blue collar employment, an increase in menial labor, and permanent levels of unemployment. These trends suggest "an increased hardening of class lines" (Gilbert and Kahn 1982, 83), which particularly affect women and blacks in terms of wealth, income and occupation. For example, women on average earn only 66 percent of what men take home in wages (Currie and Skolnick 1984), and many households below the official poverty level established by the U.S. government are female headed households. Blacks are also at a disadvantage. In 1981 the median family income for whites was $23,517, while the median family income for blacks was only $13,266 (Currie and Skolnick 1984, 147). Unemployment rates for black males are twice those of white males (U.S. Commission on Civil Rights), and blacks who have jobs are paid less on average for the same work, or are restricted to minimum wage and poorly paid service sector employment (Currie and Skolnick 1984, 162–181).

To supplement our discussion of inequality, we present a few "quality of life" indicators for persons in disadvantaged socioeconomic positions. Though many such indicators exist (e.g., pertaining to illness, mental health, housing, perceived deficiencies in self-concept and happiness, etc.), we limit discussion to those which help us understand ways in which stratification and inequality bear on criminal behavior patterns.

Compared with the middle and upper classes, the American have far less access to quality education and, as a consequence, have lower educational levels. They are also more likely to be unemployed, or employed in secondary labor markets which offer undesirable work and inferior wages. Their families are more likely to be large, and they are less likely to remain cohesive. And last but not least, poor persons are more likely to be victims of violent crime (Van Fossen 1979; Bradburn and Caplovitz 1965; Gurin et al. 1960; Gilbert and Kahn 1982; Kohn and Schoolert 1969).

Turning to the top of the class structure, it comes as no surprise that those holding positions of relative advantage are able to gain additional leverage by translating economic strength into political power. As Mills (1956) demonstrates in his *Power Elite*, wealthy people are able to lobby for their interests, purchase political power with campaign contributions, secure important positions in both the public and private sectors, involve themselves in corporate and government decisions at the highest levels, and generally use their political and economic power to shape national policy in accordance with their interests.

All of this helps explain why radicals see political economy and inequality as such important contributors to crime causation. From a radical perspective, stratification and inequality are in large part due to political and economic factors as these relate to the antagonism between capital and labor—itself a defining characteristic of capitalism.

If Marx was right, if productive relationships condition social relationships, and if the relations of production vary such that different social classes relate to the system of production in different ways, then class standing should have a significant impact on social relationships, i.e., familial and educational relationships. As we shall see, many social relationships are directly related to criminal behavior. Thus, the extent to which capitalism adversely influences these relationships is the extent to which it shares responsibility for generating crime.

Political Economy, Inequality, and Crime

We begin with a question: What do social class, menstruation, broken homes, race, unemployment, and lunar cycles have in common? The answer: each has been specified as a cause of crime. This tells us two things: first, criminologists have traveled far and wide in their quest to discover the causes of crime (even to the moon!). And second, that causation is no simple matter. But where does this leave the student? What allows one to choose between causes as dissimilar as I.Q. and capitalism?

To answer these questions let us review an issue raised [earlier]. That chapter introduced the dialectic. It argued that dialectical thinking broadened causal inquiry to include the effects of political and economic institutions as these bear on the crime problem. In practical terms this means that radical criminologists attempt to make sense of causation by placing micro-causal explanations in a wider socio-political context. By broadening the scope of criminological inquiry to include significant social, political, and economic institutions, radical criminologists simultaneously expanded the arena in which we search for causes. The goal of radical inquiry is to expand and integrate causal levels, to try and see how micro-level variables such as broken homes or defective educational institutions are "shaped by larger social structures" (Greenberg 1981, 86. . . .

With this strategy in mind three British criminologists (Taylor, Walton, and Young 1973) wrote a now famous book entitled *The*

New Criminology, in which they argued that models of crime causation must include a macro-level analysis which incorporates a *political economy of crime*. Central to their argument are ways in which crime is affected by "the overall social context of inequalities of power, wealth and authority in the developed industrial society" (Taylor et al. 1973, 270). In addition to their emphasis on political economy, which they see as constituting the "wider origins" of the deviant act, Taylor, Walton, and Young argue that radical criminology must also explain the "immediate origins" of criminal behavior (Taylor et al. 1973, 271). Reduced to its simplest terms, Taylor et al. (1973) suggest that the wider arena of political economy will condition more immediate social milieus, and that these two levels together cause crime. What follows is a review of several studies which emphasize political economy and inequality as these bear on both the wider and immediate origins of criminal behavior.

Political Economy, Inequality, and Crime: The Evidence

In specifying ways in which economic institutions and structures cause crime, Blau and Blau (1982) published an empirical study that relies explicitly on Marxian predictions. After demonstrating that socioeconomic inequalities increase rates of violence, they conclude that inequality is the root cause of both social disorganization and crime. In their view inequality increases alienation and undermines social cohesion

> by creating multiple parallel social differences which widen the separations between ethnic groups and between social classes, and it creates a situation characterized by much social disorganization and prevalent latent animosities. (Blau and Blau 1982, 119)

Michalowski (1985, 410) makes this same point in simpler terms when he notes that "inequality tends to increase crime by weakening the social bond." Both the Blaus and Michalowski argue that it is inequality rather than simple poverty which produces

crime (see Michalowski 1985, 406–409 for further discussion).

The emphasis on inequality may put some of the recent controversy regarding social class and crime into perspective. Recent statistical studies suggest a weak direct effect of social class on crime (Tittle et al. 1978; Messner 1982). But this does not mean that social class is unimportant. On the contrary, radical theory suggests that inequality affects other processes which in turn impact directly on crime. Thus, for instance, Blau and Blau (1982) suggest that family disorganization (e.g., percent divorced, percent female headed families) mediates the effect of inequality. Indeed, they found that percent divorced was positively related to inequality, and that percent divorced had the strongest direct effects on crime.

Lee Rainwater has also offered a causal framework which combines wider and immediate origins by relating crime and family disorganization to inequality and racial oppression. Adding race to his discussion of social class, Rainwater (1970) argues that the economic marginality of black men leads to tense and conflicting role relationships, which increases marital instability and ultimately leads to a pattern of female-based households and matrifocal family structure. Like Blau and Blau, he concludes that inequality, low economic status, and race interact to produce crime through social disorganization. Simply put, both studies suggest that those who are economically disadvantaged are more likely to suffer disorganized or "segregated" family structures, and that strains experienced in these types of families provide a fertile precondition for increased rates of crime and delinquency.

Inequality, Family Disorganization, and Crime

Family measures such as percent divorced and percent headed by women have long been powerful correlates of delinquency, and many have suggested that family disorganization is an important cause of crime (Nye 1958; Hirschi 1983). However, in line with their preference for contextual explanations, radicals view family structure as an intervening rather than an independent variable. This is the strategy adopted by both Blau and Blau (1982) and Rainwater (1970). Others have suggested that inconsistent family socialization patterns can be traced to experiences in the workplace (see Hagan et al. 1979, 1985, 1987; Hill and Atkinson 1989). Inconsistent socialization patterns have been firmly established as a cause of delinquency (Glueck and Glueck 1950; McCord, McCord, and Zola 1959; Hirschi 1969).

Drawing on the works of Kohn (1969, 1976, 1977), Edwards (1979), and Etzioni (1970), Colvin and Pauly (1983) argue that socialization experiences in the workplace spill into socialization experiences in the home, and that negative experiences in either setting increase the likelihood that children will "engage in serious, patterned delinquency" (Colvin and Pauly 1983, 515).

In pursuing this claim Colvin and Pauly conclude that stable socialization experiences in desirable white-collar professions promote internalized moral commitments to the workplace. Parents in these occupations encourage family socialization experiences which rely on *internalized control structures*, a type of control which promotes a child's attachment to the socialization sequence. As a result, socialization experiences are "positive" in that children have "initial bonds of high intensity" to the family unit.

Blue collar employees, on the other hand, work under *utilitarian control structures*, which means that their bond to the organization depends on a calculation of extrinsic material rewards (e.g., pay increases, seniority, job security). Workers socialized in this way tend to reproduce that structure in the family, producing "calculative bonds of intermediate intensity in their children" (Colvin and Pauly 1983, 536).

And finally, parents holding low skill, low pay, dead-end jobs are exposed to *inconsistent coercive control structures* that are externally enforced. Such parents are likely to impose inconsistent controls on their children, oscillating between punitiveness to permissiveness. In this section of the working class we can expect "more alienated initial bonds to be produced in children who experience such arbitrary, inconsistent, and coercive

family control structures" (Colvin and Pauly 1983, 536). One drawback in Colvin and Pauly's model is that it does not examine unemployed families. Parents in these families are not exposed to consistent socialization patterns that can be replicated within the home, and the controls employed in this type of family (especially the chronically unemployed) are likely to be very unstable, differing from one family to the next, and within the same family over time. Given Colvin and Pauly's other assertions, it follows that chronically unemployed parents are least able to employ social control methods which minimize criminal behavior among their children. As a result, those children are more likely to violate the law and to be arrested for those violations.

In sum, Colvin and Pauly (1983, 535–536) suggest that persons socialized under coercive control structures at work will employ similar socialization methods in the home or, more generally, that different parental attitudes toward child rearing will be produced in different work-related contexts. By combining sound sociological research with secure empirical findings in criminology concerning the relationship between inconsistent socialization patterns and delinquency, Colvin and Pauly broaden causal inquiry and conclude that (1) socialization patterns in both workplace and family settings are distributed along class lines, (2) that these patterns are defined by the relations of production underlying capitalism, and (3) that these differential socialization sequences determine "the patterned processes of development of both delinquent and non-delinquent behavior" (Colvin and Pauly 1983, 525). Their consistent Marxist approach breathes new life into the traditional emphasis on family structure as an "independent" variable. Again, this is the strategy preferred by radicals, who always try to place micro-level variables within a more encompassing causal context.

Economic Conditions and Criminal Behavior

The emphasis on linking crime with the economic structure of society is logically appealing given empirical distributions of criminal behavior. For example, 93 percent of Index Crimes involve property offenses (Sourcebook 1986, 319—we include robbery in this estimate since it is performed for economic gain). And surely the primary motivation behind white-collar and corporate crime is economic. Thus, both crimes of the powerful and powerless are closely linked with economic motivations.

There are a number of ways to establish an empirical connection between the economic system and criminal behavior. For example, radical theorists have examined how perceived and real economic inequality causes crime (e.g., Blau and Blau 1982). Others have suggested that capitalist class structures limit the ability of certain individuals to make non-criminal choices (Groves and Frank 1987). In terms of street crime, the concern with social class gives rise to the observation that those in marginal economic positions are most likely to become involved in street crime, or to be labelled as street criminals (Spitzer 1975; Quinney 1980; Platt 1978). To test this assertion, let us review the connection between unemployment and crime.

Unemployment and Criminal Behavior

A number of radical theorists claim to have established a relationship between crime and unemployment (Quinney 1980, 1979; Reiman 1984; Box 1981, 1984, 1987; Box and Hale 1983a, 1983b; Greenberg 1977a; Chiricos 1987; Platt 1978; Currie 1985; Bohm 1985; Gordon 1973, 1971). While traditional criminologists are also concerned with this issue, their approach fails to address the economic sources of unemployment. Radicals, by contrast, are concerned with the structural sources of unemployment, how increases or decreases in the rate of unemployment affect rates of criminal activity, and how the economy can be restructured to reduce unemployment.

Unemployment is a consequence of the normal operation of capitalist economies. To increase profit and produce more value (especially surplus value), capitalists are forced to pursue technological innovations which increase productivity. When more technology is employed in the production process, there is a high probability that human labor will be replaced. As a result, many technological innovations (e.g., machines that perform work formerly done by wage workers) remove workers from the production process. Thus, in its normal development, capitalism's increasing reliance on machine technology creates a surplus or economically marginal population, and this includes both unemployed and under-employed workers (Marx 1974, 631–648).

While unemployment is a fact of life associated with American capitalism, it can be controlled to a certain extent. But using the Phillips Curve, economists have demonstrated that inflation is the price for maintaining low levels of unemployment (Dolan 1977, 258–262). Further, there is general agreement that this trade-off between inflation and unemployment cannot be solved within the structural confines of capitalism (Applebaum 1979). This is an example of what Marx meant when he accused capitalism of harboring internal and irreconcilable contradictions.

Whether one uses radical or traditional economic approaches, it is agreed that unemployment is an intractable feature of capitalism. Having established this, we turn to the connection between unemployment and crime. Addressing this issue Greenberg (1977a, 648) notes that:

> persons who are unemployed can be assumed to have a greater incentive to steal than those who are not. In addition, they may risk less when they engage in crime, for they cannot lose their jobs if caught. If this reasoning is correct, crime rates will increase during periods of unemployment.

In this view crime becomes a rational response to a structural constraint (in this case, unemployment) associated with capitalism (Quinney, 1980; Gordon 1971, 1973). Unemployed individuals have fewer choices available to them (Groves and Frank 1987; Box 1987, 29). As a result of the limited choices, crime may become an attractive alternative. In addition, given the pressure to succeed—which in the U.S. is measured by material possessions—even those who are not absolutely impoverished feel that they have failed if they cannot purchase more than food and shelter. Crime is one way both the absolutely and relatively impoverished can obtain material evidence of "success."

In a recent review of the literature on unemployment and crime, Chiricos (1987) concluded that there was a non-spurious correlation between the rate of unemployment and levels of property crime. Given that capitalism is unable to avoid generating unemployment, and the logical and empirical connections between unemployment and crime, there is ample justification for the claim that capitalism sets causal parameters for crime production. This contention will be addressed later in this chapter. First, we examine arguments which go beyond the unemployment-crime connection.

Beyond Unemployment and Crime

It certainly makes sense to suggest that unemployment causes crime. The empirical relation between crime and unemployment, however, is not overwhelmingly strong, and unemployment cannot explain the general upward trend in crime over the past thirty years (Freeman 1983). Furthermore, there is scant evidence linking unemployment with violent crime. This latter finding is not at all surprising to a number of traditional criminologists, who claim that unemployment should have little if any effect on the crime rate (Wilson and Herrnstein 1985; Wilson and Cook 1985; Fox 1978). This finding would, however, appear to contradict the expectations of a radical model of crime.

But radical criminologists seem unconcerned by the modest empirical relationship between crime and unemployment. Bohm, for example, using a broader contextual model, has argued that radical theorists should assume that "the relationship between unemployment and most criminal behavior in the United States is spurious and is due to the influence . . .[of] the social relations peculiar to a capitalist mode of production" (1985, 213). Bohm suggests that radicals should not link crime to unemployment,

but should examine the broader social relationships which might cause both crime and unemployment. Capitalism, for instance, fosters competition, self-interest, and subordination of the working class. In this view crime is not simply the result of unemployment, it is the result of competition over scarce resources (including jobs) and the promotion of self-interest. In Bonger's (1916) terms, capitalism promotes egoism, which in turn generates crime in all classes.

This approach is more consistent with observable crime trends. The white-collar or corporate criminal, for example, is employed, yet still commits crime. Competitive pressures to cut the costs of production often merge with an egoistic pursuit of capital accumulation, and these concerns supply ample motivation for violating the law. In Bohm's view, self-interest and competition influence all members of a capitalist society, and this sets up conditions conducive to criminal behavior among all classes (see also Engels, 1981, 1978, for a similar argument).

While Bohm's approach downplays the significance of unemployment as a primary cause of crime, he remains sensitive to the idea that unemployment creates additional strains which may lead individuals to criminality. Unemployment is particularly high among young minority males, who constitute a large at risk crime population (1985, 215). Bohm acknowledges the idea that unemployment is caused by the natural progression of capitalism, yet sensitizes us to forces beyond unemployment which affect all classes and also act as causes of crime.

Addressing the issue of social policy, Bohm argues that we must transcend capitalism in order to solve the crime problem. In his view creating jobs will not reduce crime, since the overall experience of capitalism still leaves the majority of the population alienated and vulnerable to criminal incentives. Other radicals have argued that if there is a connection between unemployment and crime, creating more jobs will reduce the property crime rate here and now (Currie 1985; Quinney 1980; Chiricos 1987). Thus, there is tension in the policy recommendations suggested by radical theorists. Short term policies which can be instituted under the current system clash with the long-term policies for altering the social order. . . .

Box (1987) has also suggested that radicals downplay the significance of unemployment, and focus instead on broader economic conditions that affect all social classes. Like Bohm, Box argues that the unemployment explanation fails to account for crimes of the powerful. He suggests that radicals examine the connection between recession and crime.

In Box's view, recessions create conditions conducive to crime which affect both the powerless and the powerful. The powerful are under additional pressure to maintain or increase profits during recessions. Faced with a recession, white-collar workers confront a constellation of organizational motivations and incentives which can easily lead to violations of law. On the other hand recessions drive the lower class further into poverty, block legitimate means to success, and reduce commitment to the conventional social order. All of this makes increases in crime more likely among the lower class.

Recessions also affect the way powerful persons view the powerless. Recessions bring with them unemployment and an enlarged surplus population. This surplus population is "viewed more suspiciously by the governing elite, not because it actually does become disruptive and rebellious, but because it might" (Box 1987, 62). This increased fear results in increased state coercion of the powerless in the form of rising arrest and incarceration rates (Box 1987, 62–63). Recessionary trends also affect the way police enforce the law, and Box claims that recessions can be linked to an increased number of police crimes, including fabricating evidence, police brutality, and the killing of offenders perceived as threats to the social order (Box 1987, 63–65).

Surplus Value and Crime

A recent trend in radical theory has been to examine the relationship between crime rates and the rate of surplus value (Lynch 1988a; Lynch, Groves, and Lizotte 1988). This research attempts to link the driving productive forces of capitalism to the production of criminal behavior.

Marx's clearest illustration of surplus value describes it as the ratio of paid to unpaid labor, which implies that workers produce value far in excess of what they receive in wages. This excess is appropriated by the capitalist, who uses it for capital expansion and profit. There are two primary ways to increase the rate of surplus value. First, the working day may be extended with no commensurate increase in wages (absolute surplus value). And second, more efficient machines may replace people in the production process (relative surplus value). Either of these strategies allows owners to achieve their desired goal, which is to squeeze more production from the labor process. Given that capitalists derive profit from high rates of surplus value, it is in their interest to keep that rate as high as possible.

Marx went on to argue that increases in the rate of surplus value were directly related to the economic marginalization of the labor force. For its part the extraction of absolute surplus value means that employed laborers receive a smaller share of the surplus they produce. The extraction of relative surplus value, on the other hand, creates unemployment and underemployment as a result of workers being technologically displaced. In effect, a rising rate of surplus value affects both employed and unemployed laborers (Perlow 1988).

As the rate of surplus value rises, more and more people become economically marginal. This decreases commitment to the conventional order, and increases the probability that persons will engage in crime. Lynch (1988a) and Lynch, Groves, and Lizotte (1988) have uncovered a statistically significant relationship between the rate of surplus value and property crime arrest rates in the U.S. from 1950–1975. This research demonstrates that Marx's key economic concept—the extraction of surplus value—is useful for explaining how capitalist economic systems generate conditions conducive to street crime—especially property crime, the most prevalent type of crime in our society.

Does Capitalism Cause Crime?

Several theorists use Marxist arguments to suggest that capitalism stimulates a significant proportion of all criminal behavior. They are indebted, though in different ways, to theorists such as Engels (1973, 1978, 1981, 1983) and Bonger (1916), who argued that criminal behavior is a direct reflection of the strains associated with life under capitalism.

Engels' point is twofold. First, he points out that many technological advances associated with capitalism expel workers from production, generate unemployed populations, and result in "want, wretchedness, and crime" (1973, 173). This theme reappears in the contemporary writings of Quinney (1979, 1980) and Gordon (1971, 1973), who suggest that crime is a rational response to systems of inequitable distribution characteristic of capitalism. Spitzer (1975) also argues that capitalism excludes certain groups from meaningful attachment to economic and social institutions. For Spitzer, those with a reduced stake in conformity—which includes those who are economically marginal—are more likely to engage in criminal behavior.

Engels' second point is that capitalism generates competitive structural and psychological orientations which are both beneficial and harmful to society. Competition benefits capitalists when it functions to keep wages low and productivity high. On the other hand, Marx noted that in their competitive scramble to control and monopolize markets, it is often the case that "one capitalist kills many." Similarly, competition can benefit the working class when labor is scarce and owners must pay high wages to attract workers. But competition can also injure the working class; not only must they compete with owners for better working conditions, they are often forced to compete with one another for a limited number of jobs and resources. Consequently, Engels views crime as the result of competition over scarce resources, and sees competition engendered by capitalism as the cause of crime by the masses (1964, 224; 1973, 168–173), the businessman (1964, 201–202, 209), and

middle classes (1981, 49). Further, he sees a collective psychological component to competition, which he describes as follows (1964, 224):

> Competition has penetrated all the relationships of our life and completed the reciprocal bondage in which men now hold themselves. Competition is the great mainspring which jerks into activity our aging and withering social order, or rather disorder. . . .Competition governs the numerical advances of mankind; it likewise governs its moral advance . . .[S]tatistics of crime . . .[show] the peculiar regularity with which crime advances year by year. The extension of the factory system is followed everywhere by an increase in crime. This regularity proves that crime, too, is governed by competition; that society creates a demand for crime which is met by a corresponding supply. . . .

In *Criminality and Economic Conditions* (1916), Bonger makes a similar argument. For Bonger, however, the competitiveness created by capitalism manifests itself as egoism in individuals—and it is egoism which generates crime among all classes. While Bonger believed egoism was evenly distributed throughout the class structure, he noted that the political strength of the ruling class enabled it to perform exploitative acts without having those acts defined as crimes. This explains why more lower class persons are processed by the criminal justice system.

Engels (1964, 224) and Marx (1981, 52–53) also claim that capitalism "creates a demand for crime which is met by a corresponding supply" (Engels 1964, 224). Expanding on this theme, Colvin and Pauly (1983) and the Schwendingers (1976) suggest that the inequality and stratification which accompany capitalism affect educational opportunities, which in turn structure an individual's propensity to crime. Greenberg (1985) explains variations in delinquency rates in terms of the structural demands of capitalism; Barnett (1981a) has analyzed criminal opportunity as it relates to capital accumulation; and Wallace and Humphries (1981) have reinterpreted the criminogenic effects of urbanization and industrialization by placing these processes within a broader Marxist perspective on investment and capital accumulation. Each of these studies employs a broad contextual approach to crime, and each is a solid contribution to the radical perspective on crime causation.

References

Akers, R. L. 1980. "Further Critical Thoughts on Marxist Criminology: Comments on Turk, Toby, and Klockars." In J. Inciardi, ed. *Radical Criminology: The Coming Crisis.* Beverly Hills: Sage.

Applebaum, E. 1979. "The Labor Market." In A. S. Eichner, ed. *A Guide to Post-Keynesian Economics.* White Plains, NY: M. E. Sharpe.

Barnett, H. 1981a. "Wealth, Crime and Capital Accumulation." In D. Greenberg, ed. *Crime and Capitalism.* Palo Alto, CA: Mayfield.

Blau, J. and P. Blau. 1982. "The Cost of Inequality: Metropolitan Structure and Violent Crime." *American Sociological Review* 47: 114–129.

Bohm, R. 1985. "Beyond Unemployment: Toward a Radical Solution to the Crime Problem." *Crime and Social Justice* 21–22: 213–222.

Bonger, W. 1916. *Criminality and Economic Conditions.* Boston: Little, Brown, and Company.

Box, S. 1981. *Deviance, Reality, and Society.* New York: Holt, Rinehart, and Winston.

——. 1984. *Power, Crime, and Mystification.* London: Tavistock.

——. 1987. *Recession, Crime and Punishment.* Totowa, NJ: Barnes and Noble.

Box, S. and C. Hale. 1983a. "Liberation and Female Criminality in England and Wales Revisited." *British Journal of Criminology* 22: 35–49.

Box, S. and C. Hale. 1983b. "Liberation or Economic Marginalization: The Relevance of Two Theoretical Arguments to Female Crime Patterns in England and Wales, 1951–1980." *Criminology* 22, 4: 473–497.

Bradburn, N. M. and B. Caplovitz. 1965. *Reports on Happiness.* Chicago: Aldine.

Chiricos, T. G. 1987. "Rates of Crime and Unemployment: An Analysis of Aggregate Research Evidence." *Social Problems* 34, 2: 187–212.

Colvin, M. and J. Pauly. 1983. "A Critique of Criminology: Toward an Integrated Structural-Marxist Theory of Delinquency Production." *American Journal of Sociology* 90, 3: 513–551.

Currie, E. 1985. *Confronting Crime.* New York: Pantheon.

Currie, E. and J. Skolnick. 1984. *America's Problems.* Boston: Little, Brown and Company.

Dolan, E. 1977. *Basic Economics.* Hindsdale, IL: Dryden Press.

Edwards, R. 1979. *Contested Terrain: The Transformation of the Workplace in the Twentieth Century.* New York: Anchor Books.

Engels, F. 1983. "Crisis, Joint-Stock Companies, and State Intervention." In T. Bottomore and P. Goode, eds. *Readings in Marxist Sociology.* Oxford: Clarendon Press.

Engels, F. 1981. "Demoralization of the English Working Class." In D. Greenberg, ed. *Crime and Capitalism.* Palo Alto, CA: Mayfield.

Engels F. 1978 (1894). *Anti-Durhing.* Moscow: Progress Publishers.

Engels, F. 1973. *The Conditions of the Working Class in England.* Moscow: Progress Publishers.

Engels, F. 1964. "Outlines of a Critique of Political Economy." In D. Struik, ed. *The Economic and Philosophic Manuscripts of 1844.* New York: International Publishers.

Etzioni, A. 1970. "Compliance Theory." In O. Grusky and G. Miller, eds. *The Sociology of Organizations.* New York: The Free Press.

Fox, J. A. 1978. *Forecasting Crime.* Lexington, MA: Lexington Books.

Freeman, R. B. 1983. "Crime and Unemployment." In J.Q. Wilson, ed. *Crime and Public Policy.* San Francisco: ICS Press.

Gilbert, D. and J. A. Kahn. 1982. *The American Class Structure: A New Synthesis.* Homewood, IL: Dorsey Press.

Glueck, S. and E. Glueck. 1950. *Five Hundred Delinquent Women.* New York: Knopf.

Gordon, D. M. 1973. "Capitalism, Class, and Crime in America." *Crime and Delinquency* 19: 163–186.

Gordon, D. M. 1971. "Class and the Economics of Crime." *The Review of Radical Political Economy* 3: 51–72.

Greenberg, D. F. 1977a. "The Dynamics of Oscillatory Punishment Process." *Journal of Criminal Law and Criminology"* 68, 4: 643–651.

Greenberg, D. F. 1981. *Crime and Capitalism.* Palo Alto, CA: Mayfield.

Groves, W. B. and C. Corrado. 1983. "Culture as Metaphysics: An Appraisal of Cultural Models." *Crime and Social Justice* 20: 99–120.

Groves, W. B. and N. Frank. 1987. "Punishment, Privilege and the Sociology of Structured Choice." In W. B. Groves and G. R. Newman, eds. *Punishment and Privilege*. New York: Harrow and Heston.

Gurin, G., J. Veroff, and S. Feld. 1960. *Americans View Their Mental Health*. New York: Basic Books.

Hagan , J. and J. Leon. 1977. "Rediscovering Delinquency: Social History, Political Ideology, and the Sociology of Law." *American Sociological Review* 42, 4: 457–598.

Hagan, J. and I. Bernstein. 1979. "Conflict in Context: The Sanctioning of Draft Resisters." *Social Problems* 27: 109–122.

Hagan, J., A. R. Gillis and J. Simpson. 1987. "Class in the Household: A Power-Control Theory of Gender and Delinquency." *American Journal of Sociology* 92: 788–816.

Hagan, J., A. R. Gillis and J. Simpson. 1985. "The Class Structure of Gender and Delinquency: Toward a Power-Control Theory of Common Delinquent Behavior." *American Journal of Sociology* 90, 6: 1151–1178.

Hagan, J., A. R. Gillis and J. Simpson. 1979. "The Sexual Stratification of Social Control: A Gender Based Perspective on Crime and Delinquency." *British Journal of Criminology* 30: 25–38.

Hill, G. D. and M. P. Atkinson. 1989. "Gender, Family Control and Delinquency." *Criminology* 26, 1: 127–147.

Hirschi, T. 1983. "Crime and the Family." In J. Q. Wilson, ed. *Crime and Public Policy*. San Francisco: ICS Press.

Hirschi, T. 1969. *The Causes of Delinquency*. Berkeley: University of California Press.

Humphries, D. and D. Wallace. 1980. "Capitalist Accumulation and Urban Crime: 1950–1971." *Social Problems* 28, 2: 180–193.

Jacobs, D. 1980. "Marxism and the Critique of Empiricism: A Comment on Bierne." *Social Problems* 27, 4: 467–470.

Jacobs, D. 1979. "Inequality and Police Strength." *American Sociological Review* 44: 913–924.

Kohn, M. 1977. *Class and Conformity*. Chicago: University of Chicago Press.

Kohn, M. 1976. "Social Class and Parental Values: Another Confirmation of the Relationship." *American Sociological Review* 34: 659–678.

Kohn, M. and C. Schoolert. 1969. "Class, Occupation and Orientation." *American Sociological Review* 41: 538–545.

Liska, A., J. Lawrence, and M. Benson. 1981. "Perspectives on the Legal Order: The Capacity for Social Control." *American Journal of Sociology* 87: 413–426.

Lizotte, A. 1978. "Extra-Legal Factors in Chicago's Criminal Courts: Testing the Conflict Model of Criminal Justice." *Social Problems* 25: 564–580.

Lizotte, A., J. Mercy, and E. Monkkennon. 1982. "Crime and Police Strength in an Urban Setting: Chicago, 1947–1970." In J. Hagan, ed. *Quantitative Criminology*. Beverly Hills: Sage.

Lynch, M. J. 1988a. "Surplus Value, Crime and Punishment: A Preliminary Examination." *Contemporary Crises* 12: 329–344.

Lynch, M. J., W. B. Groves, and A. Lizotte. 1988. "The Extraction of Surplus Value and Property Crime Rates in the U.S., 1950–1974: A Preliminary Examination." Paper presented at the meetings of the American Society of Criminology, Nov., Montreal, Canada.

Mankoff, M. 1978. "On the Responsibility of Marxist Criminologists: A Reply to Quinney." *Contemporary Crises* 2, 3: 293–301.

Marx, K. 1981. "Crime and Capital Accumulation." In D. Greenberg, ed. *Crime and Capitalism*. Palo Alto, CA: Mayfield.

Marx, K. 1976 (1867). *Das Capital*. 1st of 3 Volumes. New York: International Publishers.

Messner, S. 1982. "Poverty, Inequality and Urban Homicide Rates." *Criminology* 20: 103–114.

Michalowski, R. J. 1985. *Order, Law, and Crime: An Introduction to Criminology*. New York: Random House.

Mills, C. W. 1956. *The Power Elite*. New York: Oxford University Press.

Nye, F. I. 1958. *Family Relationships and Delinquent Behavior*. New York: Wiley.

Perlow, V. 1988. *Super Profits and Crises: Modern U.S. Capitalism*. New York: International.

Platt, A. 1978. "Street Crime—A View From the Left." *Crime and Social Justice* 9: 26–34.

Quinney, R. 1970. *The Social Reality of Crime*. Boston: Little Brown and Company.

Quinney, R. 1979. *Criminology*. Boston: Little Brown and Company.

Quinney, R. 1980. *Class, State and Crime*. New York: Longman.

Rainwater, L. 1970. *Behind Ghetto Walls: Black Families in a Federal Slum*. Chicago: Aldine.

Reiman, J. 1984. *The Rich Get Richer and the Poor Get Prison*. New York: Wiley.

Schwendinger, J. R. and H. Schwendinger. 1976. "Rape Victims and the False Sense of Guilt." *Crime and Social Justice* 6: 4–17.

Shichor, D. 1980. "The New Criminology: Some Critical Issues." *British Journal of Criminology* 20, 1: 1–19.

Sourcebook. 1980–1987. *The Sourcebook of Criminal Justice Statistics*. Albany, NY: Michael J. Hindelang Research Center.

Sparks, R. F. 1980. "A Critique of Marxist Criminology." In N. Morris and M. Tonry, eds. *Crime and Justice: An Annual Review of Research*. Chicago: University of Chicago Press.

Spitzer, S. 1980. "Left-Wing Criminology—an Infantile Disorder?" In J. Inciardi, ed. *Radical Criminology: The Coming Crisis*. Beverly Hills: Sage.

Taylor, I., P. Walton, and J. Young. 1973. *The New Criminology: For a Social Theory of Deviance*. New York: Harper and Row.

Taylor, I., P. Walton, and J. Young. 1975. *Critical Criminology*. London: Routledge and Kegan Paul.

Tittle, C. R. and W. J. Villemez. 1978. "The Myth of Social Class and Criminality: An Empirical Assessment of the Empirical Evidence." *American Sociological Review* 43: 643–656.

Van Fossen, B. 1979. *The Structure of Social Inequality*. Boston: Little, Brown, and Company.

Wallace, D. and D. Humphries. 1981. "Urban Crime and Capitalist Accumulation: 1950–1971." In D. Greenberg, ed. *Crime and Capitalism*. Palo Alto, CA: Mayfield.

Wilson, J. Q. and P. Cook. 1985. "Unemployment and Crime—What Is the Connection?" *The Public Interest* 79: 3–8.

Wilson, J. Q. and R. Herrnstein. 1985. *Crime and Human Nature*. New York: Simon and Schuster.

13
Gender, Crime, and Deviance

Kathleen Daly

There is no one single feminist theory of deviance, but all such theories focus on gender and its relationship to rule-making and rule-breaking. Feminist scholars seek to redress the weaknesses of male-centered theories of deviance, which ignore women and girls, treat them as (sexualized) adjuncts to male rule-breakers, or explain their deviance in exclusively male or exclusively "female" terms. Feminists insist on more nuanced explanations that "explicitly [take] into account the effects of gender and, more significantly, gender stratification, on women's lives and development" (Curran and Renzetti 1994, 272).

The traditional focus of feminism is on power—specifically, power differences and their role in perpetuating inequality. Male-dominated social, political, and economic institutions systematically exclude and trivialize women, placing them in a chronic state of disadvantage. The root of the problem lies in patriarchy, a "sex/gender system in which men dominate women, and that which is considered masculine is typically more highly valued than that which is considered feminine" (Curran and Renzetti 1994, 272). In patriarchal societies, gender stratification is as important a structural influence on behavior as social class, race, or ethnicity, but one would scarcely know this from existing theoretical models (see also Chesney-Lind and Sheldon 1992).

The consequences of patriarchy are often most pernicious during the social control process. Since deviance is not proper "feminine" behavior, women who commit it are often treated worse than men. Harsh sentences are reserved for female rule-violators, even for relatively minor offenses; males who commit similar offenses often go comparatively un-sanctioned. Differential treatment is particularly sinister when the rule-breaking that triggers the sanctions is itself inspired by patriarchal abuse. Young girls, for example, are frequent targets of sexual trauma, especially by older male relatives (usually fathers or uncles), who invoke the right of access and claim them as property. Girls who try to escape typically are returned to the very conditions from which they tried to run, and if they refuse, they are incarcerated—thus, ostensible survival strategies are criminalized (admittedly, not all feminists share this view). If the rule-breakers avoid incarceration, they are forced to navigate the dog-eat-dog world of the streets—begging, shoplifting, and engaging in occasional prostitution to survive. Even more victimization at the hands of predatory males is likely to follow, placing many in a predicament from which they cannot escape.

Explaining Patterns of Lawbreaking

A decade ago, Meda Chesney-Lind and I identified two related, though distinct, theoretical problems for criminology in the study of women, gender, and crime. They are the gender ratio problem (why are men more likely involved in or arrested for crime than women?) and the generalizability problem (do theories of crime based on boys' or men's lives apply to girls or women?; Daly and Chesney-Lind 1988). For most nonfeminist scholars, interest remains in addressing the gender ratio problem, with the working assumption that a "gender-neutral" theory is preferable. Here we see a clash in theoretical objectives.

On the one hand, Darrell Steffensmeier and Emilie Allan suggest that "the traditional gender-neutral theories [derived from male samples] provide reasonable explanations of less serious forms of [crime]" for men and women (1996, p. 473). Such thinking is common in nonfeminist and liberal feminist[1] analyses of gender and crime (e.g., Smith and Paternoster 1987; Simon and Landis 1991). On the other hand, feminist scholars, including myself, find it illogical to say that traditional theories derived from male samples are gender-neutral. Traditional theories are more appropriately labeled *male-specific*, not gender-neutral. Such theories may, of course, be relevant to girls and women: we would expect that elements of social control, learning, labeling, and opportunity would be applicable in a general sense. However, even if particular elements are applicable, they may not be applicable in the same ways or to the same degree. Likewise, elements from theories developed from all-female samples may be applicable to boys and men, but not necessarily in the same ways or to the same degree.

We should abandon the concept of, and the quest for, gender-neutral criminological theories. Instead, we should use terms that better describe the theoretical enterprise to identify variables, factors, or conceptual elements that have similar and different influences on lawbreaking for boys/men and girls/women. This is just one potential focus of theoretical work; there are others, as follows.

Gender Ratio of Crime. What is the nature of, and what explains the "gender gap" in, lawbreaking and arrests for crime? What is the nature of, and what explains variation in, the kinds of offenses that girls/women and boys/men get involved with (or arrested for), in terms of both prevalence and incidence? What is the nature of, and what explains gender based variation in, arrest rates across nations, including developed and developing countries?

Gendered Crime. What are the contexts and qualities of boys'/men's and girls'/women's illegal acts? What is the social organization of specific offenses (e.g., drug dealing, prostitution, and credit frauds)?

Gendered Pathways to Lawbreaking. What is the nature of, and what explains the character of, girls'/women's and boys'/men's pathways to lawbreaking? What brings people to the street, to use illegal drugs, to become involved in workplace crime, or to be arrested and prosecuted for crime? How do boys/men and girls/women move in and out of foster homes, conventional work, jails and prisons, hospitals, and halfway houses?

Gendered Lives. How does gender organize the ways in which men and women survive, take care of themselves and their children, and find shelter and food? How does gender structure thinkable courses of action and identities?

Researchers may address these thematics with a focus on class, racial, ethnic, age, regional, or other sources of variability. Or they may decide to analyze one particular group, such as black women. Using Don Gibbons's (1994) categories, the gender ratio of crime and gendered crime address "the rates question," gendered crime and gendered pathways attend to questions of "why they did it," and gendered lives examines general life course trajectories that may or may not include lawbreaking. These thematics can also be linked to the sources of field expansion discussed earlier. Nonfeminist inquiries on gender and crime are principally focused on the gender ratio and gendered crime problems; they attempt to measure rates of involvement in crime/delinquency and to explain "gaps" in such involvement. Scholars in this tradition may draw from a nascent understanding of feminist theories, but their guiding metaphors and concepts come largely from criminology. By comparison, feminist inquiries on gender and crime are principally focused on demonstrating the ways in which the social organization of gender shapes women's and men's lives on the streets and in neighborhoods, workplaces, and households. Research tends to focus on gendered crime, gendered pathways, and gendered lives, although not exclusively.

All four thematics are relevant to research on boys and men. Specifically, boys' and men's lawbreaking, pathways to crime, and lives are no less gendered than girls' or women's. Yet with the exception of emergent research on masculinities and crime, gendered and racialized analyses of boys and men have largely been unexplored by mainstream criminology.

Gender Ratio of Crime

For two reasons, this is the largest and most heavily populated research area: it accords with a sociological preference to examine patterns and variability across aggregates, and the requisite large data sets (self-report, victimization, arrests) are available for descriptive and predictive numerical analyses, which have been the preferred data source for developing theory in mainstream criminology. Scholars focus on gender differences in rates of crime involvement or variable rates of involvement for particular crime categories, such as violent, property, or public order offenses. The most popular explanations for the gender ratio of crime have been versions of control, opportunity, and social learning theories (e.g., Adler 1975; Hagan, Gillis, and Simpson 1987, 1990; Heidensohn 1985; Morris 1987; Simon 1975). Recent contributions by Broidy and Agnew (1997), Heimer (1995), and Jensen (1996) identify variables that reduce gender gaps in lawbreaking. They include measures of machismo, risk taking, self-esteem, and respect for the law.

One problem that can emerge in statistical analyses of the gender ratio of crime is that scholars may assume (wrongly) that women's arrest rates should always be lower than men's. For example, Sommers and Baskin, based on their analysis of arrest rates for men and women, disaggregated by race and ethnicity, conclude that "the claim of a clear and consistent gender-ratio relationship is spurious" (1992, p. 197). One wonders why the authors thought it necessary to set up this "straw-man" sort of argument. To posit an invariant relationship would necessitate an assumption of some essential gender difference that stands outside history and culture, an untenable assumption in light of the past three decades of feminist scholarship. Gender-ratio claims can be made, but they must be keyed to roughly similar groups, and they must take social, economic, and cultural organization seriously.

Gendered Crime

Gendered crime may be used in conjunction with the gender ratio of crime, as scholars aim to interweave gender ratios with analyses of the gendered social organization of crime. For example, Steffensmeier and Allan present a "gendered model of female offending and gender differences in crime" (1996, p. 475) that centers largely, although not exclusively, on the gender ratio of crime

and gendered crime.[2] I use the term *gendered crime* to refer to (1) the ways in which street life, drug and sex markets, informal economies, crime opportunities, and crime groups are ordered by gender and other social relations; and (2) variation in the sequencing and contexts of men's and women's lawbreaking, including their offense roles, accounts of themselves, and how their acts are translated into official crime categories. Ethnographic research and some interview studies may capture both of these aspects of gendered crime.

There are several ways to conduct research on gendered crime. One can count the frequency of offense elements, such as the size of the crime group, the role played (e.g., Alarid et al. 1996; Daly 1989; Decker et al. 1993), even as we know that these elements may not be sufficiently nuanced to reveal the gestalt of crime (Daly 1994, pp. 165–167). Another approach is to link gender (and race, class, age) identities to crime as a gendered line of action and as situationally accomplished (Messerschmidt 1993). Recent research on boys and men reveals the ways in which masculine identities and privileges enable certain types of risk-taking behavior in boys (Canaan 1991) more so than in girls (Bottcher 1995), encourage certain forms of violence (Polk 1994), and solidify male group identities in the workplace (Messerschmidt 1993). In fact, the more one becomes familiar with the literature on gendered crime, the more one sees the limits of "gender gap" explanations. The latter lack a sense of place (e.g., neighborhood, workplace, the street); group contexts (e.g., peer groups, families, sports, schools, gangs, clubs, detention centers); and the performance and consolidation of gender identities and reproduction of gender hierarchies.

Gendered Pathways

The idea of gendered pathways emphasizes biographical elements, lifecourse trajectories, and developmental sequences. There are nonfeminist and feminist versions of the pathways idea. The former draws on the notion of "career" to chart deepening commitments to deviant identities and activities, as well as pathways to desistance (e.g.,

Rosenbaum 1981; the life-course analyses of Sampson and Laub 1993; the criminal career orientation of Blumstein, Cohen, and Farrington 1988). Feminist versions may draw on the concept of "blurred boundaries" of victimization/criminalization to describe linkages between girls' experiences of victimization and their subsequent involvement in crime (e.g., Arnold 1990; Chesney-Lind 1989; Gilfus 1992; Joe and Chesney-Lind 1995). Gendered pathways can be linked to gendered crime in charting sequences of girls' routes to the street, likely forms of income generation, and relationships with other women, men, and children (Carlein 1988; Maher 1997; Miller 1986). These feminist versions of the pathways idea are compatible with the longitudinal tradition in criminology, although that tradition has not, until recently, been mindful of sex/gender divisions.

Here I briefly consider feminist work on the blurred boundaries of victimization and criminalization. During the 1980s, it became apparent to some feminist activists and academics that a portion of imprisoned women, especially those convicted of homicide-related offenses, were confined because they were fighting back against abusive mates. Although activists gave the impression that *most* imprisoned women were sexually or physically abused while growing up (see Daly 1992, p. 49), surveys of convicted and imprisoned women put the figure at about 30 percent (Bureau of Justice Statistics 1992, p. 10; Daly 1994, p. 293). Something of a causal nexus began to emerge in explaining a portion of women's crime as arising from their having been victimized, whether in the immediate or distance past. Moreover, there was evidence from Cathy Widom's (1989) research that children who were adjudicated abused or neglected were more likely than a control group to be arrested for crimes as adults.[3] This kind of explanation, which focused on women's experiences of victimization as one precipitant of their lawbreaking, contrasted sharply with 1970s explanations, which centered on women's freedom from constraints and new opportunities for crime (Adler 1975; Simon 1975).

Prior victimization (and socioeconomic marginality, more generally) can render male and female lawbreakers less blameworthy for their acts (Daly 1994). At the same time, such explanations may obscure actors' agency and responsibility for crime (Allen 1987). Recent feminist analyses are now challenging both 1970s and 1980s explanations of women's crime. Whereas a major 1970s explanation (focusing on women's liberation from constraints) accorded "too much" volition and freedom in depicting girls' and women's lawbreaking, a major 1980s explanation (focusing on women's victimization as a precipitant of crime) accorded too little (Maher 1997). Pat Carlein suggests a way out of this conceptual problem: "[W]omen's own vivid accounts [show us] how they set about making their lives within conditions . . . not . . . of their own choosing." Acting or "choosing" to act is constrained within "certain [material] conditions, political discourses, and gender ideologies" (1988, pp. 14, 108). Working with gendered pathways and gendered lives, feminist scholars are now showing the ways in which female lawbreakers move within overlapping spheres of volition and constraint. We are depicting women's behavior and actions in context, along with women's understandings of themselves and others, which have long featured in studies of men.

Gendered Lives

Martha Fineman (1990), a feminist legal scholar, coined the term *women's gendered lives* to refer to significant differences in the ways that "women experience society" compared with men. "The concept of a gendered life," Fineman (1995, p. 45) suggests,[4] begins with the observation that women's existences are constituted by a variety of experiences—material, psychological, physical, social, and cultural—some of which may be described as biologically based, while others seem more rooted in culture and custom. For some time, Fineman has been challenging gender neutral legal theories, especially in family law and policy, for their "neutering" of gender difference and effacement of women's life worlds, experiences, and contributions. Her critique of gender-neutral legal theory is applicable to gender-neutral criminological theory.

There are several ways to develop the idea of women's (or men's) gendered lives in criminological research. One is to show how the "gender related conditions of life" (Bottcher 1995) structure delinquent (and nondelinquent) actions and identities. Jean Bottcher's interviews of "high risk" adolescents (those whose brothers had been incarcerated) suggest that the social organization of gender acts as social control: compared with the boys, girls were "insulated . . . from delinquent interest and activity" (p. 37). This approach reverses the dependent and independent variables in traditional criminological theories: rather than analyze gender as a correlate of crime, one would analyze crime as a correlate of gender. In taking such an approach, one needs to draw from research on "how gender actually plays out in personal lives, especially among adolescents" (p. 35). Unfortunately, research on "personal lives" is typically absent in theories of gender and crime (see, e.g., Hagan, Gillis, and Simpson 1987, 1990; Heimer 1995), leading to the predictable consequence of generating critiques of terms and assumptions used (e.g., Morash and Chesney-Lind's 1991 critique of power-control theory). We may do better by starting with concrete studies of boys'/men's and girls'/women's lives, rather than with ungrounded, commonsensical assumptions in the professional rush to devise grand theory.[5]

Another approach to gendered lives, which can be used with gendered pathways, is to document how varied methods of income generation over time relate to turning points in women's lives (such as pregnancy and care of children) and to state supports for housing or welfare. Regina Austin (1992, pp. 1801–1811) shows what can be learned by studying "hustling" as women (and men) move between "street and straight" worlds, and Maher (1997) documents the connections between neighborhood conditions, drug markets, and the declining value of sex work for women in New York City neighborhoods. It is rare to find criminologists using "gender-related conditions of life" as a starting point in describing and explaining girls'

or women's lawbreaking. Such an approach is more common in anthropological research on lawbreaking (e.g., Sullivan 1989; Valentine 1978) and feminist research on victimization (e.g., Hester, Kelly, and Radford 1996; Kelly 1988; Stanko 1990).

Future Directions

Different sources of field expansion, one beginning with theories of crime and the other beginning with theories of gender, have created several types of knowledge about women, gender, and crime. The field of criminology is more complex than my dichotomy would suggest, but this scheme helps to clarify the directions the field is taking today.

The first source of field expansion, which begins with theories of crime, is following in the footsteps of traditional criminology by aiming to develop a grand or "comprehensive" theory of gender and crime (or gender and delinquency) that explains gender gaps in lawbreaking. A sense that nearly all the important variables have been discovered can be gleaned from statements such as "The model completely accounts for the gender gap in school deviance, theft, drug use, and violence. There is no significant gender difference in *any* form of delinquency once differences in means and slopes of predictor variables are taken into account" (Heimer 1995, p. 164).

To translate, this means that several key variables in the model, risk taking and self-esteem, had different influences on male and female delinquency. Heimer's (1995) study is astonishing in that she argues for developing an "interactionist" model of delinquency that attends to how "the *meaning* of behavior . . . varies across gender" (p. 167), but her empirical referent is derived solely from multivariate analyses of survey data. She cites no research on the life worlds of adolescents or on how meanings are constructed in interaction.

The second source of field expansion comes from feminist scholars, who are interested to begin with theories of gender and with studies of women's lives, and to apply this body of knowledge to crime. This group is less interested in devising a grand theory of gender and crime, and more inclined to identify the ways in which gender structures men's and women's life worlds, identities, and thinkable courses of action.

Whereas one source of knowledge seeks to explain away gender gaps, the other seeks to reveal the tenacity of gender (and other social divisions) in social life. Whereas one wishes to identify a gender-neutral theory of crime, the other sees no meaning in devising such a theory in a social world ordered by gender divisions. Steffensmeier and Allan (1996), who attempt to put these disparate sources of knowledge together, say they want to develop a "gendered" approach that is "gender neutral" (p. 474). They argue that there is "no need for gender-specific theories," but they acknowledge that "qualitative studies reveal major gender differences in the context and nature of offending" (p. 482). They propose taking a "middle road" position, which "acknowledges the utility of traditional theory and . . .the organization of gender" (p. 482).

Although one may appreciate Steffensmeier and Allan's (1996) desire to have it both ways, I would argue that the theoretical road they wish to travel is a muddled one. Taking a cue from Fineman (1994, drawing from Merton), we may do better by developing theories of the middle range, rather than of the middle ground. Middle-range theories of gender and crime would not endeavor to synthesize the gender ratio of crime, gendered crime, gendered pathways, and gendered lives, as Steffensmeier and Allan (1996) aim to do. The approach instead would be to take one, or perhaps several, of these thematics, and to provide a partial window of understanding on gender and crime. And most crucially, rather than explaining away gender gaps, we should aim to bring gender into view by analyzing how it affects the life worlds of men and women (as crime victims, offenders, or criminologists), as well as the production of knowledge about crime.

Intellectual work does not occur in a vacuum. A recent generation of feminist scholars is interpreting women's lawbreaking somewhat differently than a decade ago (see

also Campbell 1990). This development reflects a shift in theoretical stance and may also reflect differences in the age cohorts and the circumstances of the women studied. An older cohort of women and those who have been imprisoned may more often give victimization-based accounts of themselves (see, e.g., Daly 1994; Gilfus 1992), although studies by Carlein (1988) and Maher (1997) of women in this cohort depict a more volitional actor. We might expect that research on a younger cohort of women by a younger cohort of scholars would reflect actors invested with "more agency," even as they are constrained by structures of male domination. Studies by Miller (1996) and Ogilvie (1996) are indicative of this tendency. Miller (1996) challenges previous research for depicting gang girls merely as "victims of male gang members' sexism," for using victimization as the primary explanation for girls' involvement in crime, or for characterizing young women as "street feminists." She argues for a more layered understanding of victimization and agency, which recognizes that girls "actively participate in gender oppression," even as they say they are the equals of the boys. Emma Ogilvie (1996) critiques Judith Allen's (1989) emphasis on "the masculinity of criminality," arguing that it forecloses an ability to register female lawbreaking and denies women agency, responsibility, and pleasure in lawbreaking. The theoretical stance of a researcher matters, of course: some studies of younger cohorts of women may continue to focus on girls' experiences with victimization (Joe and Chesney-Lind 1995).

While acknowledging these complexities, my impression is that arguments explaining girls' or women's crime as spawned, in part, from women's victimization are not as popular with a younger cohort of feminist scholars in the 1990s as they were in the 1980s. Nor, as importantly, may such victimization explanations be popular with the female subjects of feminist research. It is not possible to disentangle major themes in academic and pop feminism today (more interested in female "agency"; not wanting to be "victims") from how girls and women construct themselves in interviews with researchers.

As Heidensohn suggests, modern feminism may have had an indirect effect on "how deviant women perceive themselves, act on those perceptions, and address their problems" (1994a, p. 32). Perhaps women's deviance in the 1990s is considered less deviant, both to researchers and to women lawbreakers themselves, than it was twenty or thirty years ago. Or perhaps little has changed, but today we pay greater attention to the words, experiences, and life worlds of girls and women, and are interpreting them differently. Theoretical wisdom would suggest the need to contemplate these interpretive problems: they feature in any commentary on gender in a gendered social order.

Notes

1. While there are differences between nonfeminist and liberal feminist analyses, I term this group *nonfeminist*. I want to distinguish it from feminist analyses that utilize a more critical, sophisticated approach in describing and explaining women's (and men's) life worlds and circumstances, gender differences, and linkages with other social divisions such as class, race, ethnicity, and age. Nonfeminist analyses use commonsensical understandings of gender, in the same way that members of the general population use commonsensical understandings of class rather than the more sophisticated analyses of class by sociologists.

2. The authors also touch on gendered pathways and the social organization of gender. Ultimately, however, all the arrows in their model point toward an explanation of the gender ratio of crime (Steffensmeier and Allan 1996, p. 475).

3. In Widom's model, with an expected arrest rate of 20 percent, having been abused or neglected as a child increased that rate to 25 to 36 percent. Variable risk factors based on gender, race, and age explain the range, with the highest risk category being those who were older, black, and male.

4. Fineman also addresses differences among women, which I do not discuss here.

5. Howard Becker's (1973, pp. 180–194) critique of sociologists making "common events and experiences mysterious" is applicable to criminology: "Sociologists have generally been reluctant to take a close look at what sits in front of their noses" (p. 194), even though "common sense and science enjoin us to look at things closely before we start theorizing about them" (p. 192). One consequence is that "we may find ourselves theorizing about activities which never occur in the way we imagine" (p. 192).

References

Adler, Freda. 1975. *Sisters in Crime: The Rise of the New Female Criminal*. New York: McGraw-Hill.

Akers, Ronald L. 1997. *Criminological Theories: Introduction and Evaluation*. 2nd ed. Los Angeles: Roxbury.

Alarid, Leanne Fiftal, James W. Marquart, Velmer S. Burston Jr., Francis T. Cullen, and Steven J. Cuvelier. 1996. "Women's Roles in Serious Offenses: A Study of Adult Felons." *Justice Quarterly* 13:431–54.

Allen, Hilary. 1987. *Justice Unbalanced*. Philadelphia: Open University Press

Allen, Judith. 1989. "Men, Crime and Criminology: Recasting the Questions." *International Journal of the Sociology of Law* 17:19–39.

Arnold, Regina. 1990. "Processes of Victimization and Criminalization of Black Women." *Social Justice* 17:153–66.

Austin, Regina. 1992. "'The Black Community,' Its Lawbreakers, and a Politics of Identification." *Southern California Law Review* 65:1769–1817.

Baskin, Deborah, and Ira Sommers. 1993. "Females' Initiation into Violent Street Crime." *Justice Quarterly* 10:559–583.

Becker, Howard S. 1973. *Outsiders*. New York: Free Press.

Beirne, Piers, and James W. Messerschmidt. 1995. *Criminology*. 2nd ed. San Diego: Harcourt Brace Jovanovich.

Belknap, Joanne. 1996. *Invisible Woman: Gender, Crime, and Justice*. Belmont, CA: Wadsworth.

Blumstein, Alfred, Jacqueline Cohen, and David Farrington. 1988. "Criminal Career Research: Its Value for Criminology." *Criminology* 26:1–35.

Bottcher, Jean. 1995. "Gender as Social Control." *Justice Quarterly* 12:33–57.

Broidy, Lisa, and Robert Agnew. 1997. "Gender and Crime: A General Strain Theory Perspective." Unpublished manuscript, Department of Sociology, Washington State University.

Bureau of Justice Statistics. 1992. *Women in Jail, 1989*. Washington, D.C.: U.S. Department of Justice, Bureau of Justice Statistics.

Cain, Maureen, ed. 1989. *Growing Up Good*. Newbury Park, CA: Sage.

Campbell, Anne. 1990. "On the Invisibility of the Female Delinquent Peer Group." *Women and Criminal Justice* 2:41–62.

——. 1991. *The Girls in the Gang*. 2nd ed. New York: Basil Blackwell.

Canaan, Joyce E. 1991. "Is 'Doing Nothing' Just Boys Play? Integrating Feminist and Cultural Studies Perspectives on Working-Class Young Men's Masculinity." In *Off-Centre: Feminism and Cultural Studies*, edited by Jackie Stacey, Sarah Franklin, and Celia Lury. New York: Harper Collins Academic.

Carlein, Pat. 1988. *Women, Crime and Poverty*. Philadelphia: Open University Press.

Chesney-Lind, Meda. 1989. "Girls' Crime and Woman's Place: Toward a Feminist Model of Female Delinquency." *Crime and Delinquency* 35:5–29.

Chesney-Lind, Meda, and Randall G. Shelden. 1992. *Girls, Delinquency and Juvenile Justice*. Pacific Grove, CA: Brooks/Cole.

Daly, Kathleen. 1989. "Gender and Varieties of White-Collar Crime." *Criminology* 27:769–794.

——. 1992. "Women's Pathways to Felony Court: Feminist Theories of Lawbreaking and Problems of Representation." *Southern California Review of Law and Women's Studies* 2:11–52.

——. 1994. *Gender, Crime, and Punishment*. New Haven, CT: Yale University Press.

Daly, Kathleen, and Meda Chesney-Lind. 1988. "Feminism and Criminology." *Justice Quarterly* 5:497–538.

Daly, Kathleen, and Michael Tonry. 1997. "Race, Gender, and Sentencing." In *Crime and Justice: A Review of Research*, vol. 22, edited by Michael Tonry. Chicago: University of Chicago Press.

Decker, Scott, Richard Wright, Alison Redfern, and Dietrich Smith. 1993. "A Woman's Place Is in the Home: Females and Residential Burglary." *Justice Quarterly* 10:143–162.

Denno, Deborah W. 1994. "Gender, Crime, and the Criminal Law Defenses." *Journal of Criminal Law and Criminology* 85:80–180.

Einstadter, Werner, and Stuart Henry. 1995. *Criminological Theory: An Analysis of Its Underlying Assumptions*. New York: McGraw-Hill.

Esbensen, Finn-Aage, and David Huizinga. 1993. "Gangs, Drugs, and Delinquency in a Survey of Urban Youth." *Criminology* 31:565–587.

Fineman, Martha. 1990. "Challenging Law, Establishing Differences: The Future of Feminist Legal Scholarship." *Florida Law Review* 42:25–43.

——. 1994. "Feminist Legal Scholarship and Women's Gendered Lives." In *Lawyers in a Postmodern World*, edited by Maureen Cain and Christine B. Harrington. Buckingham, England: Open University Press.

——. 1995. *The Neutered Mother, the Sexual Family, and Other Twentieth Century Tragedies*. New York: Routledge.

Gibbons, Don C. 1994. *Talking About Crime and Criminals: Problems and Issues in Theory Development in Criminology*. Englewood Cliffs, NJ: Prentice-Hall.

Gilfus, Mary E. 1992. "From Victims to Survivors to Offenders: Women's Routes of Entry and Immersion into Street Crime." *Women and Criminal Justice* 4:63–89.

Hagan, John, A. R. Gillis, and John Simpson. 1987. "Class in the Household: A Power-Control Theory of Gender and Delinquency." *American Journal of Sociology* 90: 1151–1178.

——. 1990. "Clarifying and Extending Power-Control Theory." *American Journal of Sociology* 95:1024–1037.

Hagedorn, John M. 1994. "Homeboys, Dope Fiends, Legits, and New Jacks." *Criminology* 32:197–219.

Harding, Sandra. 1986. *The Science Question in Feminism*. Ithaca, NY: Cornell University Press.

Heidensohn, Frances M. 1985. *Women and Crime*. New York: New York University Press.

——. 1992. *Women in Control? The Role of Women in Law Enforcement*. Oxford: Oxford University Press.

——. 1994a. "From Being to Knowing: Some Issues in the Study of Gender in Contemporary Society." *Women and Criminal Justice* 6:13–37.

——. 1994b. "Gender and Crime." In *The Oxford Handbook of Criminology*, edited by Mike Maguire, Rod Morgan, and Robert Reinder. Oxford: Oxford University Press.

——. 1996. *Women and Crime*. 2nd ed. London: Macmillan.

Heimer, Karen. 1995. "Gender, Race, and the Pathways to Delinquency." In *Crime and Inequality*, edited by John Hagan and Ruth Peterson. Palo Alto, CA: Stanford University Press.

Hester, Marianne, Liz Kelly, and Jill Radford, eds. 1996. *Women, Violence and Male Power*. Philadelphia: Open University Press.

Hill, Gary D., and Elizabeth M. Crawford. 1990. "Women, Race and Crime." *Criminology* 28:601–626.

Jefferson, Tony. 1996. "Introduction" to special issue on "Masculinities, Social Relations, and Crime." *British Journal of Criminology* 36:337–347.

Jensen, Gary. 1996. "Gender Variation in Juvenile Crime: New Findings on Persistent Issues." Paper presented at the annual meeting of the American Society of Criminology, Chicago.

Joe, Karen, and Meda Chesney-Lind. 1995. "'Just Every Mother's Angel': An Analysis of Gender and Ethnic Variations in Youth Gang Membership." *Gender and Society* 9:408–430.

Kelly, Liz. 1988. *Surviving Sexual Violence.* Minneapolis: University of Minnesota Press.

Kruttschnitt, Candace. 1994. "Gender and Interpersonal Violence." In *Understanding and Preventing Violence*, vol. 3, *Social Influences*, edited by Albert J. Reiss and Jeffrey Roth. Washington, D.C.: National Academy Press.

——. 1996. "Contributions of Quantitative Methods to the Study of Gender and Crime, or Bootstrapping Our Way into the Theoretical Thicket." *Journal of Quantitative Criminology* 12:135–161.

Kruttschnitt, Candace, and Rosemary Gartner. 1993. "Introduction to the Special Issue on Gender, Crime, and Criminal Justice." *Journal of Quantitative Criminology* 9:323–327.

Laub, John H., and Joan M. McDermott. 1985. "An Analysis of Serious Crime by Young Black Women." *Criminology* 23:81–98.

Maguire, Kathleen, Ann L. Pastore, and Timothy J. Flanagan, eds. 1993. *Sourcebook of Criminal Justice Statistics, 1992.* Washington, D.C.: U.S. Government Printing Office.

Maher, Lisa. 1995a. "Dope Girls: Gender, Race, and Class in the Drug Economy." Ph.D. diss., School of Criminal Justice, Rutgers University.

——. 1995b. "In the Name of Love: Women and Initiation to Illicit Drugs." In *Gender and Crime*, edited by R. Emerson Dobash, Russell R. Dobash, and Lesley Noakes. Cardiff: University of Wales Press.

——. 1997. *Sexed Work: Gender, Race, and Resistance in a Brooklyn Drug Market.* Oxford: Clarendon Press.

——. Maher, Lisa, and Richard Curtis. 1992. "Women on the Edge of Crime: Crack Cocaine and the Changing Contexts of Street-Level Sex Work in New York City." *Crime, Law, and Social Change* 18:221–258.

Maher, Lisa, and Kathleen Daly. 1996. "Women in the Street-Level Drug Economy: Continuity or Change?" *Criminology* 34:465–491.

Mann, Kenneth, Stanton Wheeler, and Austin Sarat. 1980. "Sentencing the White-Collar Offender." *American Criminal Law Review* 17:479–500.

Martin, Susan E., and Nancy C. Jurik. 1996. *Doing Justice, Doing Gender.* Newbury Park, CA: Sage.

Messerschmidt, James W. 1993. *Masculinities and Crime: Critique and Reconceptualization of Theory.* Lanham, MD: Rowman and Littlefield.

Miller, Eleanor. 1986. *Street Woman.* Philadelphia: Temple University Press.

Miller, Jody. 1995. "Gender and Power on the Streets." *Journal of Contemporary Ethnography* 23:427–452.

——. 1996. "Female Gang Involvement in a Midwestern City: Correlates, Nature, and Meanings." Ph.D. diss., University of Southern California, Department of Sociology.

Moore, Joan. 1991. *Going Down to the Barrio: Homeboys and Homegirls in Change.* Philadelphia: Temple University Press.

Morash, Merry, and Meda Chesney-Lind. 1991. "A Reformulation and Partial Test of Power-Control Theory." *Justice Quarterly* 8:347–377.

Morris, Allison. 1987. *Women, Crime and Criminal Justice.* New York: Basil Blackwell.

Ogilvie, Emma. 1996. "Masculine Obsessions: An Examination of Criminology, Criminality and Gender." *Australian and New Zealand Journal of Criminology* 29:205–226.

Ogle, Robbin, Daniel Maier-Katkin, and Thomas J. Bernard. 1995. "A Theory of Homicidal Behavior Among Women." *Criminology* 33:173–193.

Polk, Kenneth. 1994. "Masculinity, Honour, and Confrontational Homicide." In *Just Boys Doing Business?* edited by Tim Newburn and Elizabeth A. Stanko. New York: Routledge.

Pollock-Byrne, Jocelyn M. 1990. *Women, Prison, and Crime.* Pacific Grove, CA: Brooks/Cole.

Ptacek, James. 1988. "Why Do Men Batter Their Wives?" In *Feminist Perspectives on Wife Abuse*, edited by Kersti Yllo and Michele P. Bogard. Newbury Park, CA: Sage.

Rosenbaum, Marsha. 1981. *Women on Heroin.* New Brunswick, NJ: Rutgers University Press.

Sampson, Robert J., and John Laub. 1993. *Crime in the Making: Pathways and Turning Points Through Life.* Cambridge, MA: Harvard University Press.

Sanchez, Lisa. 1996. "Agency and Resistance in a Local Sexual Economy." Unpublished manuscript, Department of Criminology, Law and Society, University of California, Irvine.

Schulhofer, Stephen J. 1995. "The Feminist Challenge in Criminal Law." *University of Pennsylvania Law Review* 143:2151–2207.

Simon, Rita. 1975. *Women and Crime.* Lexington, MA: Lexington Books.

Simon, Rita, and Jean Landis. 1991. *The Crimes Women Commit, the Punishments They Receive.* Lexington, MA: Lexington Books.

Simpson, Sally S. 1991. "Caste, Class, and Violent Crime: Explaining Difference in Female Offending." *Criminology* 29:115–135.

Smith, Douglas A., and Raymond Paternoster. 1987. "The Gender Gap in Theories of Deviance: Issues and Evidence." *Journal of Research in Crime and Delinquency* 24:140–172.

Sommers, Ira, and Deborah Baskin. 1992. "Sex, Race, Age, and Violent Offending." *Violence and Victims* 7:191–201

———. 1993. "The Situational Context of Violent Female Offending." *Journal of Research in Crime and Delinquency* 30:136–162.

Stanko, Elizabeth A. 1990. *Everyday Violence: How Women and Men Experience Male Violence.* New York: Routledge.

Steffensmeier, Darrell. 1983. "Organization Properties and Sex-Segregation in the Underworld: Building a Sociological Theory of Sex Differences in Crime." *Social Forces* 61:1010–1032.

———. 1993. "National Trends in Female Arrests, 1960–1990: Assessment and Recommendations for Research." *Journal of Quantitative Criminology* 9:411–441.

Steffensmeier, Darrell, and Emilie Allan. 1996. "Gender and Crime: Toward a Gendered Theory of Female Offending." *Annual Review of Sociology* 22:459–487.

Sullivan, Mercer L. 1989. *"Getting Paid": Youth Crime and Work in the Inner City.* Ithaca, NY: Cornell University Press.

Sutherland, Edwin H. [1949] 1983. *White Collar Crime: The Uncut Version.* New Haven, CT: Yale University Press.

Taylor, Carl S. 1993. *Girls, Gangs, Women and Drugs.* East Lansing: Michigan State University Press.

Tripplet, Ruth, and Laura B. Myers. 1995. "Evaluating Contextual Patterns of Delinquency: Gender-Based Differences." *Justice Quarterly* 12:59–84.

Valentine, Bettylou. 1978. *Hustling and Other Hard Work: Lifestyles in the Ghetto.* New York: Free Press.

Widom, Cathy Spatz. 1989. "Child Abuse, Neglect, and Violent Criminal Behavior." *Criminology* 27:251–271.

Wilson, Margo, and Martin Daly. 1992. "Who Kills Whom in Spouse Killings? On the Exceptional Sex Ratio of Spousal Homicides in the United States." *Criminology* 30:189–215.

Wonders, Nancy A., and Susan L. Caulfield. 1993. "Women's Work? The Contradictory Implications of Courses on Women and the Criminal Justice System." *Journal of Criminal Justice Education* 4:79–100.

My thanks to Tamara Burrows, Martha Fineman, Hennessey Hayes, Lisa Maher, Jody Miller, Emma Ogilvie, and Michael Tonry for comments on an earlier draft.

From *Handbook of Crime and Punishment,* edited by Michael Tonry. Copyright © 1998 by Oxford University Press. Used by permission of Oxford University Press, Inc. For editorial reasons, the title of this selection has been modified from the original. ✦

14
Deviance, Labeling, and Reintegrative Shaming

John Braithwaite

Deviant behavior elicits sanctions, and sanctions are designed to punish. Conventional wisdom holds that the more swift, certain, and severe the sanction, the greater its deterrent power: Would-be offenders will contemplate the costs of their anticipated act and refrain for fear of consequences. If the American criminal justice system is any indication, however, such an approach does not appear to be working. With nearly two million persons incarcerated in federal, state, and local facilities—the highest per capita incarceration rate of any Western industrialized nation—would-be offenders still believe they will not be caught. And, even if they accept the possibility, they often put it out of mind long enough to commit the crime in question.

When punishment actually is delivered, the picture does not necessarily become better. Punishment often carries unintended consequences that reverberate well into the future. With punishment comes stigmatization, and with stigmatization comes shame. Rule-breakers become pariahs and outcasts, which bolsters their deviant self-image, enhances their likely future participation in deviant subcultures, and promotes recidivism (repeat offending). Societies with low rates of deviance, by contrast, tend to shame people "potently and judiciously," as Braithwaite puts it. They punish offenders but then reintegrate them. They affirm that offenders are moral people who have simply made a mistake.

Braithwaite calls this "reintegrative shaming." His theory, of the same name, is a direct response to the dilemma first proposed by labeling theory—how to punish people without putting them on a course of lifetime deviance. Recall that labeling theory suggests that the treatment for deviance is the problem; punishment and deviant labels spark a chain of events in which future rule-breaking becomes a self-fulfilling prophecy. Reintegrative punishment, Braithwaite suggests, can break this cycle by using the power of informal social control (i.e., family and community) to redirect deviant energies into conventional ways. Whether retribution-minded, punishment-obsessed societies such as the United States can do this remains to be seen. Criminal justice is a growth industry that depends on ever-increasing numbers of clients for survival; strict punishment ensures a captive market.

. . . [T]he crucial distinction is between shaming that is reintegrative and shaming that is disintegrative (stigmatization). Reintegrative shaming means that expressions of community disapproval, which may range from mild rebuke to degradation ceremonies, are followed by gestures of reacceptance into the community of lawabiding citizens. These gestures of reacceptance will vary from a simple smile expressing forgiveness and love to quite formal ceremonies to decertify the offender as deviant. Disintegrative shaming (stigmatization), in contrast, divides the community by creating a class of outcasts. Much effort is directed at labeling deviance, while little attention is paid to de-labeling, to signifying forgiveness and reintegration, to ensuring that the deviance label is applied to the behavior rather than the person, and that this is done under the assumption that the disapproved behavior is transient, performed by an essentially good person. Quoting Suchar, Page (1984: 10) sees the defining characteristic of stigmatization as assignment of a deviant characteristic to the person as a master status.

> The individual . . . is assigned a 'master status trait': homosexual, drug addict, prostitute, juvenile delinquent, or others . . . this label will dominate all other 'char-

acteristics' of the individual; 'good athlete,' 'good conversationalist,' 'good dancer,' and the like are subordinated to or negated by this trait which is immediately felt to be more central to the 'actual' identity of the individual.

One might think that, notwithstanding the criminogenic consequences of assignment to a deviant master status, stigmatization might still be more useful for crime control than reintegrative shaming because being made an outcast is a more terrible sanction than being shamed and then forgiven. The theory will come to reject this view because the nub of deterrence is not the severity of the sanction but its social embeddedness; shame is more deterring when administered by persons who continue to be of importance to us; when we become outcasts we can reject our rejectors and the shame no longer matters to us. We will see . . .that the deterrence literature supports the view that the severity of sanctions is a poor predictor of the effectiveness of social control, while the social embeddedness of sanctions is an important predictor.

The Family Model

The best place to see reintegrative shaming at work is in loving families. Griffiths has described a 'family model' of the criminal process as one in which, instead of punishment being administered within the traditional framework of disharmony and fundamentally irreconcilable interests, it is imposed within a framework of reconcilable, even mutually supportive interests:

Offenses, in a family, are normal, expected occurrences. Punishment is not something a child receives in isolation from the rest of his relationship to the family; nor is it something which presupposes or carries with it a change of status from 'child' to 'criminal child.' When a parent punishes his child, both parent and child know that afterward they will go on living together as before. The child gets his punishment, as a matter of course, within a continuum of love, after his dinner and during his toilet training and before bed-time story and in the middle of general family play, and he is pun-

ished in his own unchanged capacity as a child with failings (like all other children) rather than as some kind of distinct and dangerous outsider. (Griffiths, 1970: 376)

Family life teaches us that shaming and punishment are possible while maintaining bonds of respect. Two hypotheses are suggested: first, families are the most effective agents of social control in most societies partly because of this characteristic; second, those families that are disintegrative rather than reintegrative in their punishment processes, that have not learnt the trick of punishing within a continuum of love, are the families that fail at socializing their children.

The second hypothesis is consistent with the child development literature (consider, e.g., Berkowitz, 1973; Patterson, 1982). Perhaps the classic studies in this genre are those of Baumrind (1971, 1978). She found an 'authoritative' child rearing style which combined firm control (setting clear standards and insisting on compliance with them) with nurture and encouragement more likely to secure superior control of undesirable behavior such as aggression than 'authoritarian' (close control by parents who were cold and detached) or 'permissive' (loose control by nurturant parents) child rearing styles.

For social learning theory reasons alone, families in which disapproval rather than approval is the normal state of affairs are incapable of socializing children by withdrawal of approval. Trasler explains why the effectiveness of shaming depends on continued social integration in a relationship sustained by social approval:

The contrast between the ordinary enjoyment of [parents'] approval and the distress of being temporarily out of favour is essential, if the child is constantly fearful and insecure in his relationship with his parents, the withdrawal-of-approval technique will not succeed in establishing a specific avoidance response. (Trasler, 1972: 144)

Our theory predicts that cultures in which the 'family model' is applied to crime control both within and beyond the family will be cultures with low crime rates. The family analogy forces us to think more clearly about what we mean by shaming, however.

What Is Shaming?

Developmental psychologists sometimes like to make distinctions between socialization by shaming and by guilt-induction (Dienstbier et al., 1975; see also French, 1985). Shaming, according to this distinction, follows transgressions with expressions of the lower esteem the offense has produced in the eyes of external referents like parents and neighbors; guilt-induction responds to transgressions with admonitions concerning how remorseful the child should feel within herself for perpetrating such an evil act. The distinction is rather too fine for our theoretical purposes because 'guilt-induction' always implies shaming by the person(s) inducing the guilt and because, as we will argue later, in broader societal terms guilt is only made possible by cultural processes of shaming. For our purposes, to induce guilt and to shame are inextricably part of the same social process. This is not to deny the distinction which Benedict (1946) and others make between guilt as a failure to live up to the standards of one's own conscience and shame as a reaction to criticism by other people. But you cannot induce guilt without implying criticism by others. In other words, from the perspective of the offender, guilt and shame may be distinguishable, but guilt *induction* and *shaming* are both criticism by others. Equally, the old distinction between shame and guilt cultures has no place in my theoretical framework because the consciences which cause us guilt are, according to the theory, formed by shaming in the culture.

Of what, then, does shaming consist? It can be subtle: a frown a tut-tut, a snide comment, a turning of the back, a slight shaking of the head, a laugh; it can be a direct verbal confrontation in which the offender is admonished about how guilty she should feel or how shocked her relatives and friends are over her conduct; it can be indirect confrontation by gossip which gets back to the offender; it can be broadcast via the mass media or by a private medium (as when the feminist paints a slogan on the front fence of a rapist); it can be officially pronounced by a judge from the bench or by a government which names a wrongdoer in an official report or in the chamber of the legislature; it can be popularized in mass culture by a film which moralizes about a certain act of wrongdoing.

The modalities of shaming are often culturally specific: in republican Rome criminals had the doors of their house burned, and persons who had been wronged followed their offenders about dressed in mourning clothes and with disheveled hair, sometimes chanting against the person at home or in public places (Lintott, 1968; cited in Bayley, 1985: 22). In Cuban or Chinese Peoples' Courts, ordinary citizens verbally denounce wrongdoing as part of the trial process. Freidson and Rhea (1972) showed that the almost universal sanction applied to clinic doctors who engaged in professional deviance was for colleagues and administrators to 'talk to them,' first 'man to man,' then if this did not work, by enlisting the aid of other talkers, up to the ultimate sanction of a talking-to by a formal committee of colleagues. Under the time-honored naval tradition of 'Captain's mast,' a seaman who fell asleep on watch, for example, could be denounced by the captain in the presence of members of the ship's company assembled on deck for the purpose of shaming him. In Crow Indian culture, shaming is effected by a polite mocking of another's inappropriate behavior called 'buying-of-the-ways.'

> One Indian recalled a childhood occasion when he became angry and reacted by laying on the ground and pouting, not in and of itself unusual. However, another playmate laid on the ground next to him and imitated his pouting, thereby 'buying his ways.' Through such mimicry, the first pouting child sees his own action and is reminded of his inappropriate behavior. . . .
>
> On occasion, and particularly among adults, the correcting scenario of ridicule is accentuated by the 'buyer-of-the-ways' actually approaching the rule violator and offering a small token of money (i.e., several dollars) which is supposed to be

graciously accepted, even if with embarrassment. The buyer then announces to onlookers what has taken place and what is about to take place, at which time the buyer rather dramatically repeats the inappropriate behavior. (Austin, 1984: 36)

Though shaming is often associated with a formal punishment, it does not have to be, as in this Crow example where shaming (informal punishment) is actually associated with a tangible reward.

The Uncoupling of Shame and Punishment

Western theorizing on deterrence often refers to the greater importance of the shame associated with punishment than of the punishment itself. Andenaes (1974: 78) put it this way:

That the offender is subjected to the rejection and contempt of society serves as a deterrent; the thought of the shame of being caught and of the subsequent conviction is for many stronger than the thought of the punishment itself.

Andenaes continued that the ducking stool, the stocks and the pillory were 'not only instruments of corporal punishment but were used to reduce the status of the offender as well.' (Andenaes, 1974: 78–79)

Yet the recent history of Western punishment practices has amounted to a systematic uncoupling of punishment and public shaming. The public visibility of the pillory and the chain-gang were replaced by penal practices to warehouse offenders away from public view. Public executions and flogging became private executions and floggings.

Viewed in a narrow historical context, this uncoupling was a good thing. Public exhibitions of state acts of brutality against other human beings perhaps did as much to legitimate brutality as it did to delegitmate crime. In differential association terms, they involved the state in communicating definitions favorable to violence. More critically to the present analysis, most of the shaming was stigmatizing rather than reintegrative, as von Hippel concluded on continental punishment during the Middle Ages:

Public executions of capital, mutilating, corporal and dishonoring punishments, often aggravated by horrible methods of inflicting them, dulled the aim of deterrence and harmed general deterrence by brutalizing the conscience of people. Equally disastrous was the effect of this penal law from the point of view of individual prevention. The outlawed, the banished, the mutilated, the branded, the shamed, the bereft of honor or stripped of power it expelled from the community of decent people and thus drove them out on the highway. Therefore the penal law itself recruited the habitual and professional criminals, who flourished in those days. (von Hippel, 1925: 158)

Branding on the cheek of offenders was abandoned in eighteenth century England because it had 'not had its desired effect by deterring offenders from the further committing of crimes and offences, but, on the contrary, such offenders, being rendered thereby unfit to be entrusted in any service or employment to get their livelihood in any honest and lawful way, become the more desperate' (Pike, 1876: 280–1).

While compassionate people must applaud the demise of these practices, the revulsion from them has produced a pervasive uncoupling of punishment and shaming in some Western societies. In my home state of Queensland, it used to be common for pubs which sold watered-down beer to be ordered by the court to display signs prominently indicating that the proprietor had recently been convicted of selling adulterated beer. The practice was stopped because it was regarded as 'Dickensian,' and because adverse publicity was regarded as having uncertain impacts that undermined the proportionality of sentences determined by the courts. Shoham (1970: 12–13) has described a number of shame-based or 'poetic punishments' that have now disappeared, such as a baker being required to walk in the public square with underweight loaves hung around his neck.

Shearing and Stenning have shown that one of the most important trends in contemporary criminal justice is its privatization. Private security officers are fast becoming more pervasive agents of social control than public police. A characteristic of this private enforcement is its total rejection of a moral conception of order and the control process:

> Within private control, order is conceived primarily in instrumental rather than moral terms. Order is simply the set of conditions most conducive to achieving fundamental community objectives. Thus in a business corporation, for instance, order is usually whatever maximizes profit. (Shearing and Stenning, 1984: 339)

The corporate security division will typically respond to a detected embezzler by getting the money back and sacking the employee. No thought is given to the fact that the non-public nature of this enforcement, free of any moral content, might mean that the embezzler will be thrown back on to the labor market only to be picked up by, and to victimize, another private actor.

One contention of this book is that the uncoupling of shame and punishment manifested in a wide variety of ways in many Western countries is an important factor in explaining the rising crime rates in those countries. Equally, if we look at the only clear case of a society which has experienced a downward trend in crime rates since World War II, Japan, it might be argued that this was a result of the re-establishment of cultural traditions of shaming wrongdoers, including effective coupling of shame and punishment. The decline was not simply an immediate post-war phenomenon: between 1976 and 1980 the number of murders in Japan fell 26 percent; during the same period in the United States, murders increased by 23 percent (Fenwick, 1983: 83). The Japanese crime rate is probably the lowest of any developed country (Ames, 1981).

Reintegrative Shaming in Japan

Following World War II, the Japanese suffered from anomie, in the Durkheimian sense of a general breakdown of norms governing group and individual behavior: 'The more weakened the groups to which [the individual] belongs, the less he depends on them, the more he consequently depends only on himself and recognizes no other

rules of conduct than what are founded on his private interests' (Durkheim 1951: 209). According to Dahrendorf (1985), a similar anomie characterized Germany in the immediate aftermath of the humiliation of defeat in World War II. But Japan did not meekly follow the blueprint for Westernization of their criminal justice system which the occupying Americans attempted to impose following the war. In this the Japanese may have been fortunate, if one is to heed Bayley's conclusion from his comparative study of Japanese and United States police:

> Searching for an explanation of the remarkably different crime rates in Japan and the United States, it is a mistake to write off as fortuitous the fact that Japanese, compared with Americans, are less combative in confrontation with authority; that offenders against the law are expected to accept the community's terms for resocialization rather than insisting on legal innocence and bargaining for the mitigation of punishment; that individual character is thought to be mutable, responsive to informal sanctions of proximate groups; that government intervention in social life is more acceptable and that individuals feel a moral obligation to assist actively in preserving moral consensus in the community. (Bayley, 1976: 1)

Japan might be expected to have a high crime rate according to its demographics. It modernized at an extraordinarily rapid rate; it is highly urbanized in densely packed cities. The proportion of Japanese employed in agriculture declined from 30 percent in 1960 to 10 percent in 1980. On the other hand, it has enjoyed lower unemployment rates than other countries and it is culturally homogeneous. Its criminal justice system is efficient (in the sense of apprehending a high proportion of offenders) but extremely lenient (it sends very few of them to prison). George (1984: 52) reports that in 1978 Japanese police cleared 53 percent of known cases of theft, but only 15 percent of the 231,403 offenders involved were arrested. Prosecution only proceeds in major cases or more minor cases where the normal process of apology, compensation and forgiveness by the victim breaks down. Fewer than 10 percent of those offenders who are convicted receive prison sentences, and for two-thirds of these, prison sentences are suspended. Whereas 45 percent of those convicted of a crime serve a jail sentence in the US, in Japan the percentage is under two (Haley, 1982: 273). Even 27 percent of murder cases result in suspended sentences of imprisonment in Japan. Moreover, the average length of sentence has reduced over the years (Bayley, 1976: 141; Adler, 1983: 102). Recalling World War II and the modern-day exploits of the 'Red Army' and other protest groups, it is difficult to argue that the Japanese have a genetic or cultural legacy of non-violence.

The conclusions of the leading scholars who have studied the social context of Japan's low and declining crime rate (Clifford, 1976; Bayley, 1976; Adler, 1983; Fenwick, 1985) can be read as support for the notion of high interdependency in Japanese society (with employers and neighbors as well as families), highly developed communitarianism, and these two characteristics fostering a shaming of offenders which is reintegrative. Consider this further conclusion from Bayley:

> The feeling that security consists in acceptance is transferred from the family to other groups, allowing them to discipline members through the fear of exclusion. This accounts for the ability of the police to discipline their own members so effectively. By enwrapping the officer in family-like solicitude, the organization raises the psychological costs of expulsion. Similarly a Japanese accepts the authority of law as he would the customs of his family. The policeman is analogous to an elder brother who cautions against offending the family. . . .

> In psychological terms, the system relies on positive rather than negative reinforcement, emphasizing loving acceptance in exchange for genuine repentance. An analogue of what the Japanese policeman wants the offender to feel is the tearful relief of a child when confession of wrongdoing to his parents results in a gentle laugh and a warm hug. In relation to American policemen, Japanese officers want to be known for the warmth of

their care rather than the strictness of their enforcement. (Bayley, 1976: 156)

Here is the family model writ large. Shaming as a feature of Japanese culture is well known to even the most casual observers of Japan. What is not so widely known is the reintegrative nature of this shaming. The fact that convicted American offenders are more than twenty times as likely to be incarcerated as convicted Japanese offenders says something about the respective commitments of these societies to outcasting versus reintegration.

When an individual is shamed in Japan, the shame is often born by the collectivity to which the individual belongs as well—the family, the company, the school—particularly by the titular head of the collectivity.

> When a young constable raped a woman in Tokyo several years ago, his station chief resigned. In this way, junior and senior ranks express a shared commitment to blameless performance. This view of responsibility is part of Japanese culture more largely. When a fighter aircraft struck a commercial airliner, causing it to crash, the minister of defense resigned. Parents occasionally commit suicide when their children are arrested for heinous crimes. . . .

> Japanese policeman are accountable, then, because they fear to bring shame on their police 'family,' and thus run the risk of losing the regard of colleagues they think of as brothers and fathers. (Bayley, 1983: 156)

Families are of course the key social units which take responsibility for reintegrating the convicted offender. Beyond the family, however, are a staggering proliferation of community volunteers. Japan is covered by 540,000 local liaison units of Crime Prevention Associations and 10,725 Vocational Unions for Crime Prevention, 126,000 volunteer cooperators for Juvenile Guidance (doing street work with juveniles), 8,000 Big Brothers and Sisters for delinquents, 320,000 volunteers in the Women's Association for Rehabilitation, 80,000 members of the Voluntary Probation Officers Association, 1,640 voluntary prison visitors, 1,500 'Cooperative Employers' willing to provide jobs for probationers and parolees, 2,028 Police School Liaison Councils, plus many others (see references cited in Adler, 1983: 104–105; and Clifford, 1976). The national commitment to reintegration is even written into Article I of the Offenders' Rehabilitation Law:

> The objective of this law is to protect socially and promote individual and public welfare by aiding the reformation and rehabilitation of offenders . . .and facilitating the activities of crime prevention. All the people are required to render help according to their position and ability, to accomplish the objective mentioned in the previous paragraph.

The crime prevention associations and other voluntary groups are linked with a system of informal local government that extends into every household, and with a neighborhood-based form of policing. Even popular culture underlines the notion of shame followed by reintegration:

> Betty Latham [1967], an American anthropologist, has shown that Japanese folktales stress repentance and reform whereas Western folktales stress punishment and often death. Western societies seem to give up more quickly on people than Eastern ones. In a Japanese translation of 'Little Red Riding Hood,' for example, the wicked wolf falls on his knees and tearfully promises to mend his ways. In the Western version, the wolf is simply killed. (Bayley, 1985: 105)

Apology has a central place in the aftermath of Japanese legal conflicts (Wagatsuma and Rosett, 1986; Haley, 1986). Ceremonies of restoration to signify the reestablishment of harmony between conflicting parties are culturally pivotal; the best way for this reconciliation to occur is by mutual apology, where even a party who is relatively unblameworthy will find some way in which he contributed to the conflict to form the basis of his apology.

There are a multitude of cultural bases for Japanese aversion to outcasting and commitment to reintegration. According to Wagatsuma and Rosett (1986) apology in Japan amounts to dissociation from that evil part of oneself that committed an unaccept-

able act. Japanese idiom frequently accounts for wrongdoing with possession by a 'mushi' (worm or bug). Criminals are therefore not acting according to their true selves; they are victims of a 'mushi' which can be 'sealed off,' 'thus permitting people to be restored to the community without guilt' (Wagatsuma and Rosett, 1986: 476). The cultural assumption of basic goodness and belief in each individual's capacity for eventual self-correction means that 'nurturant acceptance' ('amayakashi') is the appropriate response to deviance once shame has been projected to and accepted by the deviant. Thus, Bayley explains the distinctive pattern of police-offender encounters in Japan:

> An American accused by a policeman is very likely to respond 'Why me?' A Japanese more often says 'I'm sorry.' The American shows anger, the Japanese shame. An American contests the accusation and tries to humble the policeman; a Japanese accepts the accusation and tries to kindle benevolence. In response, the American policeman is implacable and impersonal; the Japanese policeman is sympathetic and succoring. (Bayley, 1976: 150)

Japan's crime control achievements may of course be purchased at a cost (see, e.g., Fataba, 1984). The interdependency, the shaming, the communitarian mobilization to resocialize wrongdoers, are ingredients of a culture in which duties to the community more often than in the West overwhelm the rights of individuals. . . .Critics also sometimes suggest that Japan's high suicide rate shows that the effective suppression of crime simply means that personal problems manifest themselves in other ways. However, the evidence of an inverse relationship between the intra-punitiveness and extra-punitiveness of societies is weak (Cohen and Fishman, 1985), and Clifford (1976: 141) has shown that while the Japanese suicide rate may seem high compared to the crime rate, it is fairly average in international terms. This is in spite of the fact that Japanese culture grants a degree of approval to suicide that other cultures do not. Expanding the theory . . .to other forms of deviance beyond crime would lead to the prediction that forms of deviance which are most socially approved (least subject to reintegrative shaming), like suicide in Japan, will be most common. Or, if there is less shame for women entering the mentally ill role and more shame for women in entering the criminal role, the theory could be used to predict a higher ratio of mental illness to crime for women than for men—a finding that occurs in Japan and all other societies. . . .

References

Adler, F. 1983. *Nations Not Obsessed With Crime.* Littleton, CO: F. B. Rothman.

Ames, W. L. 1981. *Police and Community in Japan.* Berkeley: University of California Press.

Andenaes, J. 1974. *Punishment and Deterrence.* Ann Arbor: University of Michigan Press.

Austin, W. T. 1984. 'Crow Indian Justice: Strategies of Informal Social Control,' *Deviant Behavior* 5, 31–46.

Baumrind, D. 1971. 'Current Patterns of Parental Authority,' *Developmental Psychology Monograph* 4, 1 Pt. 2.

Baumrind, D. 1978. 'Parental Disciplinary Patterns and Social Competence in Children,' *Youth and Society* 9, 239–276.

Bayley, D. H. 1976. *Forces of Order: Police Behavior in Japan and the United States.* Berkeley: University of California Press.

Bayley, D. H. 1983. 'Accountability and Control of the Police: Some Lessons for Britain,' in T. Bennett (ed.), *The Future of Policing.* Cambridge: Institute of Criminology.

Bayley, D. H. 1985. *Social Control and Political Change.* Research Monograph No. 49. Woodrow Wilson School of Public and International Affairs, Princeton University.

Benedict, R. 1946. *The Chrysanthemum and the Sword: Patterns of Japanese Culture.* Boston: Houghton Mifflin.

Berkowitz, L. 1973. 'Control of Aggression,' in B. M. Caldwell and R. Riecute (eds.), *Review of Child Development Research.* Chicago: University of Chicago Press.

Clifford, W. 1976. *Crime Control in Japan.* Lexington, MA: Lexington Books.

Cohen, B. and Fishman, G. 1985. 'Homicide and Suicide Rates: A Macroanalysis,' Paper presented to American Society of Criminology Meeting, San Diego.

Dahrendorf, R. 1985. *Law and Order: The Hamlyn Lectures.* London: Stevens and Sons.

Dienstbier, R. A., Hillman, D., Lehnkoff, J., Hillman, J., and Valkenaar, M. F. 1975. 'An Emotion-Attribution Approach to Moral Behavior: Interfacing Cognitive and Avoidance Theories of Moral Development,' *Psychological Review* 82, 1299–1315.

Durkheim, E. 1951. *Suicide,* translated by J. A. Spaulding and G. Simpson. New York: Free Press.

Fataba, I. 1984. 'Crime, Confession and Control in Contemporary Japan,' *Law in Context* 2, 1–30.

Fenwick, C. R. 1983. 'Culture, Philosophy and Crime: The Japanese Experience.' *International Journal of Comparative and Applied Criminal Justice,* 9, 67–81.

Freidson, E. and Rhea, B. 1972. 'Processes of Control in a Company of Equals,' in E. Freidson and J. Lorber (eds.), *Medical Men and Their Work,* Chicago: Aldine-Atherton.

French, P. A. 1985. 'Publicity and Control of Corporate Conduct: Hester Prynne's New Image,' in B. Fisse and P. A. French (eds.), *Corrigible Corporations and Unruly Law,* San Antonio: Trinity University Press.

George, B. J. 1984. 'Discretionary Authority of Public Prosecutors in Japan,' *Law in Japan,* 17, 42–72.

Griffiths, J. 1970. 'Ideology in Criminal Procedure or a Third "Model" of the Criminal Process,' *Yale Law Journal,* 79, 359–417.

Haley, J. O. 1982. 'Sheathing the Sword of Justice in Japan: An Essay on Law Without Sanctions,' *Journal of Japanese Studies,* 8, 265–281.

Haley, J. O. 1986. 'Comment: The Implications of Apology,' *Law and Society Review,* 20, 499–507.

Lintott, A. W. 1968. *Violence in Republican Rome,* Oxford: Clarendon Press.

Page, R. M. 1984. *Stigma,* London: Routledge and Kegan Paul.

Patterson, G. R. 1982. *Coercive Family Process,* Eugene, OR: Castalia Publishing Co.

Pike, L. O. 1876. *A History of Crime in England,* Vol. II, London: Smith Elder and Co.

Shearing, C. D. and Stenning, P. C. 1984. 'From the Panopticon to Disney World: The Development of Discipline,' in A. N. Doob and E. L. Greenspoon (eds.), *Perspectives in Criminal Law: Essays in Honor of John L. J. Edwards,* Aurora, Ontario: Canada Law Book Inc.

Shoham, S. 1970. *The Mask of Cain,* Jerusalem: Israel University Press.

Trasler, G. 1972. 'The Context of Social Learning,' in J. B. Mays (ed.), *Juvenile Delinquency: The Family and the Social Group,* Longman.

von Hippel, R. 1925. *Deutsches Strafrecht,* Berlin.

Wagatsuma, H. and Rosett, A. 1986. 'The Implications of Apology: Law and Culture in Japan and the United States,' *Law and Society Review,* 20, 461–498.

Part III

Researching Deviance[1]

Good theory cannot be obtained in the absence of good data. And good data often cannot be obtained without going into the field and investigating what it is that deviants do and how they do it. Some forms of deviance will be more amenable to investigation than others, because they are more common, visible, or accessible to observation. Certain types of rule-breaking are so blatant as to make studying them a simple matter of looking around—as anyone who has ever witnessed someone picking his nose, drinking excessive amounts of alcohol, or violating the speed limit can tell you. Though intriguing, such behaviors are not particularly compelling to study precisely because they occur so frequently and are so out in the open. This is not the case with serious rule-breaking—norm violations so serious that offenders must keep them hidden from outside view.

Studying deviance "on the edge" (that is, among serious offenders) can teach us a great deal about deviance at the core, and for that reason alone, the enterprise is a vitally important one. Important, but not easy. Serious rule-breakers typically are members of "hidden populations," persons who participate in heavily stigmatized or illegal behavior that carries severe sanctions—formal, informal, or both. Members of hidden populations frequently find it necessary to lead secret lives. This makes them hard to locate. Once located, they usually are reluctant to provide valid and reliable information about what it is they do (Irwin 1972, 117).

Such reluctance is only to be expected. There are real consequences for indiscretion. Exposure could mean jail time; the more damaging the information, the more offenders have to lose if found out. Unremarkably, those who study serious rule-breakers often are perceived to be undercover agents seeking to obtain damning evidence for legal purposes. One of the most common suspicions that deviants have about researchers is that they are covert operatives of some sort. As Sluka (1990, 115) notes, "It is difficult to find [a researcher] who has done fieldwork who has not encountered this suspicion" (for these and other points, see Jacobs 1999).

Some investigators try to overcome this obstacle by engendering trust in those they wish to study, which may take a good deal of time; it may also require the researcher to act in risky ways. With some deviant populations, for example, access is not possible unless or until the researcher becomes a member of the subculture under study. If becoming a member requires participation in the same activities as his or her research subjects (to prove him- or herself, as it were), real problems will be in the offing. The sociological and anthropological literatures are filled with cases of researchers going "too far"—breaking the law, losing their objectivity, and even going native (leaving the research role completely to become a member of the investigated group). There is a fine balance between trust and distance, familiarity and objectivity, and it must be achieved if

107

richly detailed "thick description" is to be obtained.

Collecting "thick description" relies principally, though by no means exclusively, on the use of qualitative methods—interviewing, observation, and the like. Qualitative methods permit investigators to decode the manner in which respondents (in this case, active deviants) think and act in real-life settings and circumstances. They permit researchers to document the full range of conduct norms, beliefs, and interaction patterns relevant to some deviant population and to describe a body of knowledge not easily understood by the general public (Adler 1985; Agar 1973; Johnson et al. 1997). Qualitative methods provide insight into the ways in which deviants interpret, assess, organize, perceive, and classify their social worlds (see Lex 1990, 393). They give a richer understanding of causal relationships pertaining to all facets of experience (Fleisher 1995, 21, 104). Qualitative methods, finally, document emergent processes—especially vital when the processes being explored lie at the "forefront of broader trends" that require real-time identification for effective social policy (see Golub and Johnson 1999, 1737; for these and other points, see Jacobs 2000).

Valid descriptive information about rule-breakers typically cannot be obtained from "official sources." Interviews with deviants in prison, for example, might be easier, safer, and more convenient than interviews secured "on the streets," but the data are likely to be skewed in fundamental ways. Institutionalized deviants represent a certain kind of rule-breaker and are different from their uncaught counterparts in some central and systematic way. Because these offenders are institutionalized, they obviously are unsuccessful at avoiding apprehension; samples that draw from them are thus really drawing from *failed* deviants. Within the institution itself, there are powerful forces at work that influence the substance of respondents' comments. If an interviewee believes, for example, that answering questions in a particular way is likely to result in specific institutional benefits (e.g., more free time, additional privileges, early release), then she or he will respond in accordance with those

expectations. (How many of us have a told a parent, teacher, or another authority figure something less than the truth to secure a valued benefit or advantage? We may not be imprisoned but the principle is the same.) Sutherland and Cressey (1970, 68) justifiably assert that those who have had "intimate contacts with [deviants] 'in the open' know that [deviants] are not 'natural' in police stations, courts, and prisons and that they must be studied in their everyday life outside of institutions if they are to be understood." Polsky (1967, 123) is even more emphatic, warning that, "we can [not] afford the convenient fiction that in studying [deviants] in their natural habitat, we . . .discover nothing really important that [cannot] be discovered from [deviants] behind bars. What is true for studying the gorilla of zoology is likely to be even truer for studying the gorilla of criminology" (see also Jacobs 1999).

As another possible "official" source of information, arrest records are similarly inadequate. Every year, the Uniform Crime Reports (UCR) is published by the FBI, providing a nationwide portrait of serious deviance—the number of offenses of particular types committed, sorted by the offender's race, gender, age, and ethnicity, area of the country, and size of city (among other things). UCR figures are derived primarily from victim reports of crime and from "officers who discover infractions," but mostly from the latter. This process is enormously subjective and relies on police reporting practices that are themselves fraught with bias. As Jerome Miller (1996, 27, 58) observes, "Arrest patterns are highly susceptible to local police tactics, prosecutorial policies, media interest, and politics. The UCR statistics routinely [mask] police overcharging and [omit] such crucial narrative information as arrest summaries, victim statements, and other observational indicators that might place these data in context." What emerges are "truncated and highly distorted versions of reality," so much so that "apparently objective data . . .cannot be taken at face value."

The vast majority of serious deviations never reach the attention of police anyway.

Most disputes and conflicts that would otherwise lead to formal police action "are withdrawn or abandoned before coming to a formal resolution" (Horwitz 1990, 99). A significant percentage of deviations of all types goes undetected or ignored. Some suggest, for example, that the risk of arrest may be as low as one in 11,000, although, clearly, the likelihood varies by type of offense (see Maher and Dixon 1999). What is clear is that being arrested is largely a function of being at the wrong place at the wrong time. Since the police react to infractions, they are rarely around when offenses occur. Also, their response time is slow enough so that meaningful action is not possible when they do arrive. And offenders engage in a wide array of tactics to inhibit the ability of authorities to detect them. The more experienced the offender, the more skilled she or he is at evading capture (for these points, see Jacobs 2000).

For police to be effective, they also must be called; social control agents typically do not generate their own cases (Horwitz 1990, 99). Yet victims often remain silent. Vast amounts of deviance, even the very serious "index crimes" that attract so much public and media attention (e.g., murder, rape, robbery), go unreported for any number of reasons. Some offenses may be so angering or humiliating that nothing short of personal vengeance will do. Other deviant acts do not present enough evidence or are too insignificant to justify calling the authorities (see Laub 1997). Still others trigger an intense need for formal intervention that rapidly dissipates. Yet more transpire between people who know one another (see Wolfgang 1958), and it is "a general principle of social life . . .that one should not introduce exterior power into private domains" (Horwitz 1990, 104; for these and other points, see Jacobs 2000). For all of these reasons, a better strategy for research may involve going to the offenders themselves and actually asking them what it is they do, how they do it, and why. The following selections seek to capture precisely how this is done.

Note

1. Parts of this section were adapted with permission from *Dealing Crack: The Social World of Streetcorner Selling*, Bruce A. Jacobs, Boston: Northeastern University Press, 1999. ✦

15
Studying Sex

An American Survey

Edward O. Laumann

Robert T. Michael

John H. Gagnon

Stuart Michaels

The *"sex drive"* is one of the most powerful of human impulses—for good reason, since the survival of the human race would otherwise not be possible. Sex preoccupies as well as fascinates. Some studies suggest that people (especially men) think about it dozens, if not hundreds, of times a day. Strong norms, however, regulate all aspects of sexuality—when to have it, with whom, how, and under what conditions. Such norms, of course, are not always followed. For some people, the only worthwhile sex is that which is taboo; the physical pleasure is enhanced by its rebellious or adventuresome quality.

Nationwide surveys tell us, however, that adventuresome sex is more the exception than the rule. The overwhelming majority of Americans are sexual "squares," exhibiting low rates of homosexuality and promiscuity and high rates of marital fidelity. In any given year, most people have only one sex partner. For women, the median number of lifetime partners is two; for men it is six. On average, people have sex only twice a week and when they do, it is over quickly. Americans of all social classes report high rates of sexual satisfaction (Boxer 2000).

The major challenge of any social survey is to collect valid data, and in sex surveys this challenge is especially daunting. Sex is deeply personal, eminently private, and for many, quite embarrassing. Conventional wisdom holds that people will hide, change, or lie about their behavior for fear of "looking bad." Who, for instance, is willing to identify the number of times they masturbate each week, list sexually transmitted diseases with which they have been diagnosed, or discuss the content and frequency of their deviant sexual thoughts (all to a total stranger)? If nothing else, fear of ridicule causes many to refuse to answer or to lie.

Despite the difficulties, obtaining sexual information is profoundly important. Effective social policy is not possible without valid data, and public health depends on the kind of information revealed in real-time surveys. For sex researchers, the challenge is to construct instruments that maximize response rates and reliability and minimize fear of exposure. In this selection, Laumann and his colleagues explore precisely how this is done. They discuss how sex surveys are conceptualized, how sensitive questions are generated and worded, how reliability checks are woven into the interview schedule, how different methods are used to cross-check and "triangulate" responses, and how populations are identified and ultimately sampled. What emerges is a bird's eye view of survey research in action, capturing how researchers quantify carnal behavior (see also Boxer 2000).

Most people with whom we talked when we first broached the idea of a national survey of sexual behavior were skeptical that it could be done. Scientists and laypeople alike had similar reactions: "Nobody will agree to participate in such a study." "Nobody will answer questions like these, and, even if they do, they won't tell the truth." "People don't know enough about sexual practices as they relate to disease transmission or even to pleasure or physical and emotional satisfaction to be able to answer questions accurately." It would be dishonest to say that we did not share these and other concerns. But our experiences over the past seven years, rooted in extensive pilot work, focus-group discussions, and the fielding of the survey itself, resolved these doubts. . . .

The society in which we live treats sex and everything related to sex in a most ambiguous and ambivalent fashion. Sex is at once highly fascinating, attractive, and, for many at certain stages in their lives, preoccupying, but it can also be frightening, disturbing, or guilt inducing. For many, sex is considered to be an extremely private matter, to be discussed only with one's closest friends or intimates, if at all. And, certainly for most if not all of us, there are elements of our sexual lives never acknowledged to others, reserved for our own personal fantasies and self-contemplation. It is thus hardly surprising that the proposal to study sex scientifically, or any other way for that matter, elicits confounding and confusing reactions. Mass advertising, for example, unremittingly inundates the public with explicit and implicit sexual messages, eroticizing products and using sex to sell. At the same time, participants in political discourse are incredibly squeamish when handling sexual themes, as exemplified in the curious combination of horror and fascination displayed in the public discourse about Long Dong Silver and pubic hairs on pop cans during the Senate hearings in September 1991 on the appointment of Clarence Thomas to the Supreme Court. We suspect, in fact, that with respect to discourse on sexuality there is a major discontinuity between the sensibilities of politicians and other self-appointed guardians of the moral order and those of the public at large, who, on the whole, display few hang-ups in discussing sexual issues in appropriately structured circumstances. . . .

. . .[U]ntil quite recently, scientific research on sexuality has been taboo and therefore to be avoided or at best marginalized. While there is a visible tradition of (in)famous sex research, what is, in fact, most striking is how little prior research exists on sexuality in the general population. Aside from the research on adolescence, premarital sex, and problems attendant to sex such as fertility, most research attention seems to have been directed toward those believed to be abnormal, deviant, criminal, perverted, rare, or unusual, toward sexual pathology, dysfunction, and sexually transmitted disease—the label used typically reflecting the way in which the behavior or condition in question is to be regarded. "Normal sex" was somehow off limits, perhaps because it was considered too ordinary,

trivial, and self-evident to deserve attention. . . .

. . .[T]o understand the results of our survey, the National Health and Social Life Survey (NHSLS), one must understand how these results were generated. To construct a questionnaire and field a large-scale survey, many research design decisions must be made. To understand the decisions made, one needs to understand the multiple purposes that underlie this research project. Research design is never just a theoretical exercise. It is a set of practical solutions to a multitude of problems and considerations that are chosen under the constraints of limited resources of money, time, and prior knowledge. . . .

Major Issues in Designing a Study of Sexuality in the Age of AIDS

Turning to the research design of the NHSLS itself, we divide the discussion into three parts: the sample design, the selection and training of the interviewers, and the interview itself. . . .

Sample Design. The sample design for the NHSLS is the most straightforward element of our methodology because nothing about probability sampling is specific to or changes in a survey of sexual behavior. . . .

Probability sampling, that is, sampling where every member of a clearly specified population has a known probability of selection—what lay commentators often somewhat inaccurately call random sampling—is the sine qua non of modern survey research (see Kish 1965, the classic text on the subject). There is no other scientifically acceptable way to construct a representative sample and thereby to be able to generalize from the actual sample on which data are collected to the population that that sample is designed to represent. Probability sampling as practiced in survey research is a highly developed practical application of statistical theory to the problem of selecting a sample. Not only does this type of sampling avoid the problems of bias introduced by the researcher or by subject self-selection bias that come from more casual techniques, but it also allows one to quantify the variability in the estimates derived from the sample.

There seems to be greater confusion around this issue in sex research than in other fields. Several reasons may account for this. First, sex research is closely associated with and often derives from medical and psychological research, in which sampling issues are deemphasized or ignored. While neglect of sampling in medical research can occasionally have negative consequences, it is not nearly so problematic as in areas like demography and other kinds of research oriented toward large populations where systematic variability in traits and behaviors of interest is an essential feature of the population being studied. As long as members of a population are identical or very similar in terms of the features of research interest, then it is appropriate to study only a small number of population members . . .because there is no relevant variability across the population at large. In effect, looking at a few members tells you all you need to know about all members of that population. . . .

Sample Size

How large should the sample be? There is real confusion about the importance of sample size. In general, for the case of a probability sample, the bigger the sample, the higher the precision of its estimates.[1] This precision is usually measured in terms of the amount of sampling error accruing to the statistics calculated from the sample. The most common version of this is the statement that estimated proportions (e.g., the proportion of likely voters planning to vote for a particular candidate) in national political polls are estimated as being within plus or minus 2 or 3 percent of the overall population figure. The amount of this discrepancy is inversely related to the size of the sample: the larger the sample, the smaller the likely error in the estimates. This is not, however, a simple linear relation. Instead, in general, as the sample size increases, the precision of the estimates derived from the sample increases by the square root of the sample size. For example, if we quadruple the sample size, we improve the estimate only by a factor of two. That is, if the original sample has a sampling error of

plus or minus 10 percent, then the quadrupled sample size will have an error of plus or minus 5 percent. . . .

In order to determine how large a sample size for a given study should be, one must first decide how precise the estimates to be derived need to be. To illustrate this reasoning process, let us take one of the simplest and most commonly used statistics in survey research, the proportion. Many of the most important results reported in this book are proportions. For example, what proportion of the population had more than five sex partners in the last year? What proportion engaged in anal intercourse? With condoms? Estimates based on our sample will differ from the true proportion in the population because of sampling error (i.e., the random fluctuations in our estimates that are due to the fact that they are based on samples rather than on complete enumerations or censuses). If one drew repeated samples using the same methodology, each would produce a slightly different estimate. If one looks at the distribution of these *estimates*, it turns out that they will be normally distributed (i.e., will follow the famous bell-shaped curve known as the Gaussian or normal distribution) and centered around the true proportion in the population. The larger the sample size, the tighter the distribution of estimates will be. . . .

. . .[I]n deciding the sample size needed for a study, one must consider the subpopulations for which one will want to construct estimates. For example, one almost always wants to know not just a single parameter for the whole population but parameters for subpopulations such as men and women, whites, blacks, and Hispanics, and younger people and older people. Furthermore, one is usually interested in the intersections of these various breakdowns of the population, for example, young black women. The size of the interval estimate for a proportion based on a subpopulation depends on the size of that group in the sample (sometimes called the *base "N,"* i.e., the number in the sample on which the estimate is based. It is actually this kind of number that one needs to consider in determining the sample size for a study.

....[W]e applied just these sorts of considerations to come to the conclusion that we needed a sample size of about 20,000 people. . . .

First, let us consider the cooperation or response rate. No survey of any size and complexity is able to get every sampling-designated respondent to complete an interview. Individuals can have many perfectly valid reasons why they cannot participate in the survey: being too ill, too busy, or always absent when an effort to schedule an interview is made or simply being unwilling to grant an interview. While the face-to-face or in-person survey is considerably more expensive than other techniques, such as mail or telephone surveys, it usually gets the highest response rate. Even so, a face-to-face, household-based survey such as the General Social Survey successfully interviews, on the average, only about 75 percent of the target sample (Davis and Smith 1991). The missing 25 percent pose a serious problem for the reliability and validity of a survey: is there some systematic (i.e., nonrandom) process at work that distinguishes respondents from nonrespondents? That is, if the people who refuse to participate or who can never be reached to be interviewed differ systematically in terms of the issues being researched from those who are interviewed, then one will not have a representative sample of the population from which the sample was drawn. . . .Unfortunately, one usually has no (or only minimal) information about nonrespondents. It is thus a challenge to devise ways of evaluating the extent of bias in the selection of respondents and nonrespondents. Experience tells us that, in most well-studied fields in which survey research has been applied, such moderately high response rates as 75 percent do not lead to biased results. And it is difficult and expensive to push response rates much higher than that. . . .

Because of our subject matter and the widespread skepticism that survey methods would be effective, we set a completion rate of 75 percent as the survey organization's goal. In fact, we did much better than this; our final completion rate was close to 80 percent. . . .We have compared our sample and our results with other surveys of various sorts and have been unable to detect systematic biases of any substantive significance that would lead us to qualify our findings at least with respect to bias due to sampling.

One might well ask what the secret was of our remarkably high response rate, by far the highest of any national sexual behavior survey conducted so far. There is no secret. Working closely with the NORC senior survey and field management team, we proceeded in the same way as one would in any other national area probability survey. We did not scrimp on interviewer training or on securing a highly mobilized field staff that was determined to get respondent participation in a professional and respectful manner. It was an expensive operation: the average cost of a completed interview was approximately $450.

We began with an area probability sample, which is a sample of households, that is, of addresses, not names. Rather than approach a household by knocking on the door without advance warning, we followed NORC's standard practice of sending an advance letter, hand addressed by the interviewer, about a week before the interviewer expected to visit the address. In this case, the letter was signed by the principal investigator, Robert Michael, who was identified as the dean of the Irving B. Harris Graduate School of Public Policy Studies of the University of Chicago. The letter briefly explained the purpose of the survey as helping "doctors, teachers, and counselors better understand and prevent the spread of diseases like AIDS and better understand the nature and extent of harmful and of healthy sexual behavior in our country." The intent was to convince the potential respondent that this was a legitimate scientific study addressing personal and potentially sensitive topics for a socially useful purpose. AIDS was the original impetus for the research, and it certainly seemed to provide a timely justification for the study. . . .

Gaining respondents' cooperation requires mastery of a broad spectrum of techniques that successful interviewers develop with experience, guidance from the research team, and careful field supervision. This project required extensive training before entering the field. While interviewers are generally trained to be neutral toward topics covered in the interview, this was especially important when discussing sex, a topic that seems particularly likely to elicit emotionally freighted sensitivities both in the respondents and in the interviewers. Interviewers needed to be fully persuaded about the legitimacy and importance of the research. Toward this end, almost a full day of training was devoted to presentations and discussions with the principal investigators in addition to the extensive advance study materials to read and comprehend. . . .A set of endorsement letters from prominent local and national notables and refusal conversion letters were also provided to interviewers. A hotline to the research office at the University of Chicago was set up to allow potential respondents to call in with their concerns. Concerns ranged from those about the legitimacy of the survey, most fearing that it was a commercial ploy to sell them something, to fears that the interviewers were interested in robbing them. Ironically, the fact that the interviewer initially did not know the name of the respondent (all he or she knew was the address) often led to behavior by the interviewer that appeared suspicious to the respondent. For example, asking neighbors for the name of the family in the selected household and/or questions about when the potential respondent was likely to be home induced worries that had to be assuaged. Another major concern was confidentiality—respondents wanted to know how they had come to be selected and how their answers were going to be kept anonymous. . . .

Mode of Administration: Face-to-Face, Telephone, or Self-Administered

Perhaps the most fundamental design decision, one that distinguishes this study from many others, concerned how the interview itself was to be conducted. In survey research, this is usually called the *mode* of interviewing or of questionnaire administration. We chose face-to-face interviewing, the

most costly mode, as the primary vehicle for data collection in the NHSLS. . . .

A number of recent sex surveys have been conducted over the telephone. . . .The principal advantage of the telephone survey is its much lower cost. Its major disadvantages are the length and complexity of a questionnaire that can be realistically administered. . . .[T]he NHSLS, cut to its absolute minimum length, averaged about ninety minutes. Extensive field experience suggests an upper limit of about forty-five minutes for phone interviews of a cross-sectional survey of the population at large. . . .Another disadvantage of phone surveys is that it is more difficult to find people at home by phone and, even once contact has been made, to get them to participate. . . .[And] are people more likely to answer questions honestly and candidly or to dissemble on the telephone as opposed to face to face? Nobody knows for sure.

The other major mode of interviewing is through self-administered forms distributed either face to face or through the mail.[2] When the survey is conducted by mail, the questions must be self-explanatory, and much prodding is typically required to obtain an acceptable response rate. . . .This procedure has been shown to produce somewhat higher rates of reporting socially undesirable behaviors, such as engaging in criminal acts and substance abuse. We adopted the mixed-mode strategy to a limited extent by using four short, self-administered forms. . . .When filled out, these forms were placed in a "privacy envelope" by the respondent so that the interviewer never saw the answers that were given. . . .

The fundamental disadvantage of self-administered forms is that the questions must be much simpler in form and language than those that an interviewer can ask. . . .One has much less control over whether (and therefore much less confidence that) respondents have read and understood the questions on a self-administered form. The NHSLS questionnaire (discussed below) was based on the idea that questions about sexual behavior must be framed as much as possible in the specific contexts of particular patterns and occasions. We found that it is impossible to do this using self-administered questions that are easily and fully comprehensible to people of modest educational attainments.

To summarize, we decided to use face-to-face interviewing as our primary mode of administration of the NHSLS for two principal reasons: it was most likely to yield a substantially higher response rate for a more inclusive cross section of the population at large, and it would permit more complex and detailed questions to be asked. . . . The main unresolved question is whether another mode has an edge over face-to-face interviewing when highly sensitive questions likely to be upsetting or threatening to the respondent are being asked. As a partial control and test of this question, we have asked a number of sensitive questions in both formats so that an individual's responses can be systematically compared. . . .[and the responses are consistent between formats].

Gender Matching of Interviewers and Respondents

. . .[T]he question of gender matching in a survey on sex looms especially large. . . . There is no question that women have an easier time gaining access to a household because they are regarded as less threatening and viewed with less suspicion as to their motives. . . .But the question does arise as to what effect the gender of the interviewer has on the interaction with the respondent during the actual interview. . . .Although many laypeople have worried that women interviewers might be viewed as mother figures to whom respondents would be less likely to admit socially disapproved sexual behavior, it seems just as plausible that they might be seen as a generalized version of the sympathetic, nurturant professional, such as a nurse or social worker, to whom one may unburden all of one's problems.

Race Matching of Interviewers and Respondents

Similar considerations apply to race. Slightly more evidence may exist for race effects in interviewing, although most of this research has been on topics specifically related to racial themes. . . .Again, there are arguments on both sides of the issue.

Recruiting and Training Interviewers

We firmly believed that it was very important to recruit and train interviewers for this study very carefully. In particular, we worried that interviewers who were in any way uncomfortable with the topic of sexuality would not do a good job and would adversely affect the quality of the interview. We thus took special steps in recruiting interviewers to make it clear what the survey was about, even showing them especially sensitive sample questions. We also assured potential recruits that there would be no repercussions should they not want to work on this study; that is, refusal to participate would not affect their future employment with NORC. None of these steps seemed to hinder the recruitment effort. In general, interviewers like challenging studies. Any survey that is not run of the mill and promises to be of current public relevance is regarded as a good and exciting assignment—one to pursue enthusiastically. In short, we had plenty of interviewers eager to work on this study. Of course, a few interviewers did decline to participate because of the subject matter. . . .

The Questionnaire. The questionnaire itself is probably the most important element of the study design. It determines the content and quality of the information gathered for analysis. Unlike issues related to sample design, the construction of a questionnaire is driven less by technical precepts and more by the concepts and ideas motivating the research. . . .

. . .[T]he essence of survey research is to ask a large sample of people from a defined population the *same set of questions*. To do this in a relatively short period of time, many interviewers are needed. In our case, about 220 interviewers from all over the country collected the NHSLS data. The field period, beginning on 14 February 1992 and ending in September, was a time in which over 7,800 households were contacted (many of which turned out to be ineligible for the study) and 3,432 interviews were completed. Central to this effort was gathering comparable information on the same attributes from each and every one of these respondents. The attributes measured by the questionnaire become the variables used in the data analysis. They range from demographic characteristics (e.g., gender, age, and race/ethnicity) to sexual experience measures (e.g., numbers of sex partners in given time periods, frequency of particular practices, and timing of various sexual events) to measures of mental states (e.g., attitudes toward premarital sex, the appeal of particular techniques like oral sex, and levels of satisfaction with particular sexual relationships).

The basic problem in writing a questionnaire thus becomes the construction of a formal protocol that combines the specific wording of questions as well as instructions and skip patterns that allow the interviewer to take all the respondents over the same material. As much as possible, each respondent should be asked the same questions in the same words and in the same order since variations in wording and order are known to affect the responses that one gets (cf. Bradburn, Sudman, et al. 1979; Groves 1989). There are two ways to approach this problem. One approach is to make the questionnaire very simple, treating each question as a separate summary statement that can be answered independently of all other questions. This is what one must do in a self-administered questionnaire. It is also almost always the practice in questionnaires that focus on attitudes. . . .

Very early in the design of a national sexual behavior survey, . . .we faced the issue of where to draw the boundaries in defining the behavioral domain that would be encompassed by the concept of sex. This was particularly crucial in defining sexual activity that would lead to the enumeration of a set of sex partners. There are a number of activities that commonly serve as markers for sex and the status of sex partner, especially intercourse and orgasm. While we certainly wanted to include these events and their extent in given relationships and events, we also felt that using them to define and ask about sexual activity might exclude transactions or partners that should be included. Since the common meaning and uses of the term *intercourse* involve the idea of the intromission of a penis, intercourse in that sense as a defining act would at the very least exclude a sexual relationship between two

women. There are also many events that we would call sexual that may not involve orgasm on the part of either or both partners. . . .

Another major issue is what sort of language is appropriate in asking questions about sex. It seemed obvious that one should avoid highly technical language because it is unlikely to be understood by many people. One tempting alternative is to use colloquial language and even slang since that is the only language that some people ever use in discussing sexual matters. There is even some evidence that one can improve reporting somewhat by allowing respondents to select their own preferred terminology (Blair et al. 1977; Bradburn et al. 1978; Bradburn and Sudman 1983). Slang and other forms of colloquial speech, however, are likely to be problematic in several ways. First, the use of slang can produce a tone in the interview that is counterproductive because it downplays the distinctiveness of the interviewing situation itself. An essential goal in survey interviewing, especially on sensitive topics like sex, is to create a neutral, nonjudgmental, and confiding atmosphere and to maintain a certain professional distance between the interviewer and the respondent. A key advantage that the interviewer has in initiating a topic for discussion is being a stranger or an outsider who is highly unlikely to come in contact with the respondent again. It is not intended that a longer-term bond between the interviewer and the respondent be formed, whether as an advice giver or a counselor or as a potential sex partner.[3]

The second major shortcoming of slang is that it is highly variable across class and education levels, ages, regions, and other social groupings. It changes meanings rapidly and is often imprecise. Our solution was to seek the simplest possible language—standard English—that was neither colloquial nor highly technical. For example, we chose to use the term *oral sex* rather than the slang *blow job* and *eating pussy* or the precise technical but unfamiliar terms *fellatio* and *cunnilingus*. Whenever possible, we provided definitions when terms were first introduced in a questionnaire—that is, we tried to train our respondents to speak about sex in our terms. Many terms that seemed clear to us may not, of course, be universally understood; for example, terms like *vaginal* or *heterosexual* are not understood very well by substantial portions of the population. Coming up with simple and direct speech was quite a challenge because most of the people working on the questionnaire were highly educated, with strong inclinations toward the circumlocutions and indirections of middle-class discourse on sexual themes. Detailed reactions from field interviewers and managers and extensive pilot testing with a broad cross section of recruited subjects helped minimize these language problems. . . .

On Privacy, Confidentiality, and Security

. . .[I]ssues of respondent confidentiality are at the very heart of survey research. The willingness of respondents to report their views and experiences fully and honestly depends on the rationale offered for why the study is important and on the assurance that the information provided will be treated as confidential. . . .The subject matter of the NHSLS makes the issues of confidentiality especially salient and problematic because there are so many easily imagined ways in which information voluntarily disclosed in an interview might be useful to interested parties in civil and criminal cases involving wrongful harm, divorce proceedings, criminal behavior, or similar matters. . . .

Security

Any survey on the scale of the NHSLS requires large numbers of people in the survey organization to be involved in physically handling interview records, and this poses considerable scope for intentional or inadvertent disclosure of an individual's answers. Special procedures were imposed to minimize the number of people who could, in principle, know the personal identity of respondents. . . .

Notes

1. This proposition, however, is not true when speaking of nonrandom samples. The original Kinsey research was based on large samples. As noted earlier, surveys reported in magazines are often based on very large numbers of returned questionnaires. But, since these were not representative probability samples, there is no necessary relation between the increase in the sample size and how well the sample estimates population parameters. In general, nonprobability samples describe only the sample drawn and cannot be generalized to any larger population.

2. We ruled out the idea of a mail survey because its response rate is likely to be very much lower than any other mode of interviewing (see Bradburn, Sudman, et al. 1979).

3. Interviewers are not there to give information or to correct misinformation. But such information is often requested in the course of an interview. Interviewers are given training in how to avoid answering such questions (other than clarification of the meaning of particular questions). They are not themselves experts on the topics raised and often do not know the correct answers to questions. For this reason, and also in case emotionally freighted issues for the respondent were raised during the interview process, we provided interviewers with a list of toll-free phone numbers for a variety of professional sex and health-related referral services (e.g., the National AIDS Hotline, an STD hotline, the National Child Abuse Hotline, a domestic violence hotline, and the phone number of a national rape and sexual assault organization able to provide local referrals).

References

Blair, Ellen, Seymour Sudman, Norman M. Bradburn, and Carol Stacking. 1977. "How to ask questions about drinking and sex: Response effects in measuring consumer behavior." *Journal of Marketing Research*, 14:316–321.

Bradburn, Norman M., and Seymour Sudman. 1983. *Asking Questions: A Practical Guide to Questionnaire Design.* San Francisco: Jossey-Bass.

Bradburn, Norman M., Seymour Sudman, Ed Blair, and Carol Stacking. 1979. "Question threat and response bias." *Public Opinion Quarterly*, 42:221–234.

Davis, James Allan, and Tom W. Smith. 1991. *General Social Surveys, 1972–1991: Cumulative Codebook*. Chicago: National Opinion Research Center.

Groves, Robert M. 1989. *Survey Errors and Survey Costs*. New York: Wiley.

Kish, Leslie. 1965. *Survey Sampling*. New York: Wiley.

16
Researching Crack Dealers

Bruce A. Jacobs

interrogated by authorities who mistook him for a drug dealer or buyer. Dealers witnessed these incidents and took them as proof that Jacobs was not undercover, solidifying his legitimacy for the remainder of the project. The methodological significance of these incidents and others for the study of serious deviant populations are addressed.

Although some analysts dismiss ethnography as "the poor sociologist's substitute for the novel" (Bell and Newby 1972, 1), the importance of qualitative methods for the study of deviant behavior cannot be overstated. Such methods provide a thorough understanding of the daily behaviors and careers of hidden or hard-to-reach rule-breakers. They allow researchers to decipher the manner in which these persons and groups interact. They describe a world not easily grasped by the general public.

Streetcorner crack dealers are one of many hidden populations. Some researchers view the notion of "hiddenness" in terms of the group's reachability (its size relative to the broader population, the ease or difficulty in selecting members to interview, and the extent to which reliable responses can be obtained), but a more useful characterization would refer first to the group's low social visibility. Visibility is a function of the offensive behaviors the group's members engage in and which they must actively conceal (or attempt to) from outsiders (for these issues, see Spreen 1992; Watters and Biernacki 1989). Streetcorner crack sellers are therefore a paradox of sorts. There is perhaps no other openly observable and publicly accessible behavior that is as negatively sanctioned by law and society as streetcorner crack selling. Dealers must be available to their customers (for these points, see Jacobs 1999).

In the following selection, Jacobs explores the methods he used to gain entry, develop rapport, and earn the trust of these crack sellers. Notably, Jacobs documents the paradoxical role that social control agents played in generating access to offenders. On a number of occasions, Jacobs was stopped, searched, and

"Yo, Bruce, come on down the set [neighborhood]. Meet where we usually do," Luther said, and hung up the phone.[1] A trusted contact for an ongoing study of street-level crack dealers and a crack dealer himself, I had no reason to question him. "Just another interview," I thought. Notebooks and file folders in hand, I went to the bank, withdrew fifty dollars for subject payments, and drove fifteen minutes to the dope set I was coming to know so well.

Luther flagged me down as I turned the corner. The seventeen-year-old high school drop-out opened the door and jumped in. "Swerve over there." He pointed to a parking space behind the dilapidated three-story apartment building he called home. "Stop the car—turn it off." Nothing out of the ordinary; over the previous three months, we often would sit and talk for a while before actually going to an interview. This time, though, there was an urgency in his voice I should have detected but did not. He produced a pistol from under a baggy white T-shirt. "Gimme all your fuckin' money or I'll blow your motherfuckin' head off!"

"What the fuck's your problem?" I said, astonished that someone I trusted had suddenly turned on me. The gun was large, a six-shooter, probably a long-barrel .45. It was ugly and old looking. Most of its chrome had been scratched off. Its black handle was pockmarked from years of abuse. Why was he doing this? How did I get myself into this situation? It was the kind of thing you hear about on the evening news but don't expect to confront, even though I knew studying active offenders risked such a possibility.

I frantically pondered a course of action as Luther's tone became more and more hostile. He was sweating. "Just calm down, Luther, just calm down—everything's cool," I trembled. "Don't shoot—I'll give you what you want." "Gimme all your fucking money!" he repeated. "I ain't fuckin' around—I'll waste you right here!" I reached in my left-hand pocket for the fifty dollars and handed it over. As I did so, I cupped my right hand precariously an inch from the muzzle of his gun, which was pointing directly into my abdomen. I can survive a gunshot, I thought to myself, as long as I slow the bullet down.

He snatched the five, crisp ten-dollar bills and made a quick search of the vehicle's storage areas to see if I was holding out. "OK," he said, satisfied there were no more funds. "Now turn your head around." I gazed at him inquisitively. "Turn your motherfuckin' head around!" For all I knew, he was going to shoot and run; his right hand was poised on the door handle, his left on the trigger. "Just take your money, man, I'm not gonna do anything." "Turn the fuck around!" he snapped. "OK," I implored, "I won't look, just lemme put my hand over my eyes." I left small openings between my fingers to see what he was really going to do. If he were truly going to fire, which he appeared to be intent on doing—the gun was being raised from the down-low position in which it had been during the entire encounter to right below head level—I would smack the gun upward, jump out of the car, and run a half block to the relative safety of a commercial street.

As I pondered escape routes, he jammed the gun into his pants as quickly as he had drawn it, flung open the door, and disappeared behind the tenements. I hit the ignition and drove slowly and methodically from the scene, grateful to have escaped injury, but awestruck by his brazen violation of trust. All I could do was look back and wonder why.

If this were the end of the story, things would have normalized, I would have learned a lesson about field research, and I would have gone about my business. But Luther was not through. Over the next six weeks, he called my apartment five to ten times a day, five days a week, harassing, taunting, irritating, baiting me. Perhaps twice over that six-week period, I actually

picked up the phone—only to find out it was he and hang up. Luther would call right back and let the phone ring incessantly, knowing I was there and letting the answering machine do the dirty work. On several occasions, it became so bad that I had to disconnect the line and leave the apartment for several hours.

I'd arrive home to see the answering machine lit up with messages. "I can smell the mousse in your hair—huh, huh, huh," his sinister laugh echoing through the apartment. "I know you're there, pick it up." More often than not, I would hear annoying dial tones. One message, however, caught my undivided attention: "897 Longacre—huh, huh, huh," he laughed as I heard him flipping through the phone book pages and identifying my address. "We'll [he and his homeboys] be over tomorrow." I didn't sleep well that night or for the next six weeks.

What was I to do—report the robbery, and go to court and testify to stop what had become tele-stalking? Some researchers contend that when crimes against fieldworkers occur, staff are to "report them to the police to indicate that such violations will have consequences."[2] I did not feel I had this option. Calling the authorities, no matter how much I wanted to, would not only have endangered future research with Luther's set and those connected to it, but would also have risked retaliation—since Luther's homies knew where I lived and worked.

So I called the phone company and got caller ID, call return, and call block. These devices succeeded in providing his phone number and residence name, which I used to trace his actual address, but I could still do nothing to stop him. Changing my number was the last thing I wanted to do, because those who smell fear often attack. As other researchers have noted, concern about "violence may cause ethnographers to appear afraid or react inappropriately to common street situations and dangers. . . .Fearful behavior is easily inferred by violent persons" and may often lead to violence itself.[3] Thus, Berk and Adams stress the importance of maintaining one's cool when threatened: "The investigator will be constantly watched and tested by the very people he is studying.

This is especially true [with] delinquents who . . .value poise in the face of danger."[4] Danger, it must be remembered, is "inherent" in fieldwork with active offenders, "if for no other reason than there is always the possibility of dangerous cultural misunderstandings arising between researchers and subjects."[5] This is especially true of research among active streetcorner crack sellers, who routinely use violence or threats of violence to gain complicity.[6]

After enduring six weeks of this post-robbery harassment, and with no end in sight, I had to do something. I called the police and told them the story. An officer came out and listened to messages I had saved. As he listened, the telephone rang, and Luther's number displayed on the caller ID. "Do you want me to talk to him?" the officer asked sternly. "No," I replied, feeling more confident with a cop three feet away. "Lemme see if I can work things out." I picked up the phone and started talking.

"What do you want?"

"Why do you keep hangin' up on me? All I want is to talk."

"What do you expect me to do, *like* you? [sardonically, on the verge of losing it]. You fuckin' robbed me and I trusted you and now you call me and leave these fuckin' messages and you want me to *talk* to you? [incredulous]"

"I only did that 'cause you fucked me over. I only ganked [robbed] you 'cause *you fucked me.*"

"What are you talking about?"

He proceeded to explain that without him, none of the forty interviews I obtained would have been possible. True, Luther was the first field contact to believe that I was a researcher, not a cop. He was my first respondent, and he was responsible for starting a snowball of referrals on his word that I was "cool."[7] But after he could no longer provide referrals, I moved on, using his contacts to find new ones and eliminating him from the chain. My newfound independence was inexplicable to him and a slap in the face. He wanted vengeance; the robbery and taunting were exactly that.[8]

Ethnography and Social Distance

Such are the risks ethnographers take when studying dangerous, unstable offenders. Although "robbery, burglary, and theft from field staff are uncommon, [they] do occur. In fact, many crack distributors are frequent and proficient robbers, burglars, and thieves."[9] Not so ironically, someone I had trusted and considered a "protector"[10] had become someone to be protected from. Such flip-flops are entirely possible in the world of active offenders, who themselves often admit an inability to control or understand their behavior.

All of this merely underscores the changeable, unpredictable nature of fieldwork relations, especially with active offenders. Johnson notes that "[i]t is incumbent on the investigator to assess the influences of these changes."[11] The important point is for researchers to put themselves in a position where they can do this. Unfortunately, the very nature of criminological fieldwork may work against this.

Much of the problem revolves around the dilemma between social distance and immersion in fieldwork, and the difficulty researchers have in resolving it. The notion of "social distance" is thought to be in some ways foreign to the ethnographic enterprise. Wolff, for example, contends that successful fieldwork inevitably requires surrender—psychological, social, and otherwise—to the setting, culture, and respondents one is studying. It requires "total involvement, suspension of received notions, pertinence of everything, identification, and risk of being hurt."[12] Ethnographers are advised to immerse themselves in the native scene,[13] to become a member of what they are studying.[14] They are told to become an actual physical and moral part of the setting.[15] As Berk and Adams put it, "The greater the social distance between the participant observer and the subjects, the greater the difficulty in establishing and maintaining rapport."[16]

Building rapport with active offenders typically becomes more difficult, though, as the "deviantness" of the population one studies increases.[17] With any offender population, trying to become "one of them" too quickly can be downright harmful. Some contend that the most egregious error a fieldworker can make is to assume that the fieldworker can gain the immediate favor of his or her hosts by telling them that he or she wants to "'become one of them' or by implying, by word or act, that the fact that they tolerate his [or her] presence means that he [or she] is one of them."[18] Similarly, Polsky warns that "you damned well better not pretend to be 'one of them,' because they will test this claim out and one of two things will happen. Either the researcher will get drawn into participating in actions one would otherwise not engage in, or the researcher could be exposed as a result of not doing so, the latter having perhaps even greater negative repercussions."[19] The more attached the researcher gets too early in the process, the more vulnerable she or he may be to exploitation. The researcher is still a researcher, no matter how close the researcher thinks she or he is getting. Subjects know this and may also know there will be few if any serious repercussions if they try to pull something, especially at the beginning of research when the fieldworker tends to be the most desperate for acceptance. Problems are only compounded by the fact that researchers tend to be far more streetwise by the end of fieldwork than they are at the beginning. Perhaps the least important time to be streetwise is at the end; both the number and seriousness of threats tend to decline with time. Where threats are often highest—at the beginning, when the researcher may be labeled a narc, a spy, or simply a suspicious character—the researcher may also be least capable of handling them. This only makes the threats that do materialize more threatening.

Researchers who are victimized at this early stage may often be barred from reporting it; doing so threatens to breach promises of confidentiality and anonymity made to subjects. The practical matter of being labeled a narc who "sold someone out" is a separate issue and potentially more problematic: snitching violates a sacred norm of street etiquette, even if the person being snitched on is in the wrong. At best, snitching will terminate future chains of respondents. At worst, it will label the researcher a "rat" and subject him or her to street justice. Both outcomes are of course undesirable and will likely bring an end to one's research.

Being immersed while remaining to some degree objective is the key. Some researchers stress the importance of using "interactional devices and strategies that allow the fieldworker to stay on the edges of unfolding social scenes rather than being drawn into their midst as a central actor."[20] Others recommend engaging in a paradoxical and "peculiar combination of engrossment and distance."[21] Like the Simmelian stranger, researchers are told to be familiar yet not too familiar, involved yet not too involved, all the while making the balance seem natural.[22] Some modicum of social distance is thus critical to the ethnographic enterprise—"as a corrective to bias and overrapport brought on by too strong an identification with those studied."[23]

In some sense, then, social distance between the researcher and the active offenders she or he studies *can* be beneficial. As Wright and Decker observe, "[T]he secrecy inherent in criminal work means that offenders have few opportunities to discuss their activities with anyone besides associates, a matter which many find frustrating."[24] By definition, criminal respondents will often have "certain knowledge and skills that the researcher does not have."[25] This asymmetry may empower them to open up or to open up sooner than they otherwise would. Offenders may enjoy speaking about their criminal experiences with someone who is "straight." Perhaps it is a satisfaction gained from teaching someone supposedly smarter than they, at least in terms of academic degrees. The fact that respondents may see something in the research that benefits them, or an opportunity to correct faulty impressions of what it is they actually do,[26] only facilitates these dynamics.

All of it may come down to dramaturgy. Yet, the very nature of criminological fieldwork dictates that the researcher either can't or won't "act" in certain ways at certain times. Acting inappropriately can compromise the research itself, the fieldworker's ability to remain in the setting, or the ability to remain there safely. The moral and practical conundrum between social distance, immersion, and "participant" observation in criminological fieldwork may, in many ways, be unresolvable.

My failure to manage the distance/immersion dialectic with Luther appeared to have more to do with a practical shortfall in managing informant relations—a myopia if you will—than with going native. Clearly, I had lost objectivity in the process of "handling" Luther. Whether this was a function of over immersion is open to question, but it undoubtedly played some role. Whether it was avoidable is also open to question, particularly when one considers the practical and methodological paradoxes involved in fieldwork with active offenders. Although myopic (mis)management led to my exploitation by Luther, without putting myself in such a position, I would never have been able to collect the data I did. In many ways, the "shortfall" was necessary and, at some level, advantageous.

The bottom line is that no matter how deft the fieldworker is at managing relations, he or she ultimately never gains total control. Criminological fieldworkers exist in a dependent relationship with their subjects.[27] This makes one wonder who is indeed the "subject" and what he or she can be "subject to" at any given moment. Some contend that the hierarchical relationship between interviewer and subject in social research is "morally indefensible"[28] and should be thrown out. Perhaps the hierarchy may be jettisoned as a matter of course, by the very nature of the fieldworker-active offender relationship. Luther's actions toward me stand as an exemplary case.[29]

Studying Active Offenders

Studying active drug dealers is problematic precisely because their activity is criminal. Active offenders are generally "hard to locate because they find it necessary to lead clandestine lives. Once located, they are reluctant, for similar reasons, to give accurate and truthful information about themselves."[30] "Outsiders" are often perceived as narcs seeking to obtain damaging evidence for juridical purposes.[31] Indeed, the most common suspicion that subjects have about fieldworkers is that they are spies of some sort. As Sluka notes, "It is difficult to find an [ethnographer] who has done fieldwork who has not encountered this suspicion."[32]

Collecting data from drug dealers, particularly from active ones, is likely to be difficult and dangerous unless one can construct friendships within a dealing community.[33] Because of this difficulty, some researchers target institutional settings.[34] Such settings afford the chance of obtaining data without the risk of physical harm associated with "street" interviews.[35] Unfortunately, collecting valid and reliable data in such settings may not be entirely possible, as criminologists have "long suspected that offenders do not behave naturally" in them.[36] Sutherland and Cressey argue that "[t]hose who have had intimate contacts with criminals 'in the open' know that criminals are not 'natural' in police stations, courts, and prisons and that they must be studied in their everyday life outside of institutions if they are to be understood."[37] Polsky is more emphatic, commenting that "we can no longer afford the convenient fiction that in studying criminals in their natural habitat, we . . . discover nothing really important that [cannot] be discovered from criminals behind bars. What is true for studying the gorilla of zoology is likely to be even truer for studying the gorilla of criminology."[38] There are fundamental qualitative differences between the two types of offenders. Institutionalized drug dealers, for example, may represent those not sophisticated or skilled enough to prevent apprehension, or those who simply do not care about getting caught and who sell to anyone with money. Studies of incarcerated offenders are thus open to the charge of being based on "unsuccessful criminals, on the supposition that successful criminals are not apprehended or are at least able to avoid incarceration." This weakness is "the most central bogeyman in the criminologist's demonology."[39]

Knowing this, I entered the field and began frequenting a district near a major university that is both prestigious and expensive, yet which borders a dilapidated neighborhood with a concentrated African

American population and heavy crack sales. A lively commercial district, with restaurants, quaint cafes, bars, theaters, and stores, splits the two. The area is known for racial and ethnic diversity, making it relatively easy for most anyone to blend in. Over a nine-month period, I frequented the area and made myself familiar to the regular crowd of hangers-out in the dividing commercial district. Some of these individuals were marginally homeless and spent entire days in the district smoking, drinking, playing music, and begging. Though not crack dealers themselves, they knew who the dealers were and where they worked. After gaining their trust, I was shown the dealers' congregation spots and quickly took to the area.

At first, I would simply walk by, not explicitly acknowledging that anything was going on. Sometimes I would be escorted by one of the "vagabonds," but most of the time I went alone. My objective was simply to let dealers see me. Over the days and weeks, I walked or drove through slowly to gain recognition, trying to capitalize on what Goffman has called second seeings: "[U]nder some circumstances if he and they see each other seeing each other, they can use this fact as an excuse for an acquaintanceship greeting upon next seeing. . . ."[40] Unfortunately, this did not go as easily as Goffman suggests, as dealers openly yelled "SCAT!"—a term for the police undercover unit—at me.[41] Jump-starting participation was clearly the toughest part of the research because dealers suspected I was the police. Ironically, it was the police who gave me my biggest credibility boost.

Police and Credibility

In . . ."Criminological *Verstehen*: Inside the Immediacy of Crime," Ferrell notes that "a researcher's strict conformity to legal codes can be reconceptualized as less a sign of professional success than a possible portent of methodological failure . . .a willingness to break the law," by contrast, "[opens] a variety of methodological possibilities."

Hanging with offenders on street corners, driving them around in my car, and visiting their homes must have been a curious sight. My appearance is somewhat akin to that of a college student. Shorts, T-shirts, crosstrainers, and ball caps with rounded brims, "just like SCAT wear 'em" (as one respondent put it), make up my typical attire. Further, I am white, clean-cut, and affect a middle-class appearance, traits the relatively poor, African American respondents associated with the police. These traits appeared to make them even more leery that I was SCAT, or that I worked for SCAT in some capacity.

To offenders who hadn't gotten to know me well, or to those waiting to pass judgment, I was on a deep-cover assignment designed to unearth their secrets and put them in jail. To cops on the beat, I was just another college boy driving down to crackville with a user in tow to buy for me. Such relations are commonplace in the street-level drug scene and have generalized subcultural currency: users serve as go-betweens and funnel unfamiliar customers to dealers for a finder's fee, usually in drugs and without the customer's consent, but generally with his or her tacit permission. When cops see a relatively nicely dressed, clean-shaven white boy driving a late-model car (with out-of-state plates, I might add) and a black street person in the passenger seat, they lick their chops.

Several police stops of me in a one-month period lent some credibility to this proposition. I had not obtained, as Wright and Decker had, a "prior agreement with the police"[42] whereby the police knew what I was doing and pledged not to interfere. I chose not to; the last thing I wanted was to let police know what I was doing. As Polsky explains, "Most of the danger for the fieldworker comes not from the cannibals and headhunters but from the colonial officials. The criminologist studying uncaught criminals in the open finds sooner or later that law enforcers try to put him on the spot—because, unless he is a complete fool, he uncovers information that law enforcers would like to know. . . ."[43] Because my grant was not a federal one, I could not protect the identity of my respondents with a certificate of confidentiality (which theoretically bars police from obtaining data as it pertains to one's subjects). My work was undercover in a sense and eminently discreditable. However, contrary to admonitions by some to avoid contact with the police while doing research with dangerous populations,[44] my run-ins with police turned out to be the most essential tool for establishing my credibility.

My first run-in came two weeks after making initial contact with offenders. I was driving Luther through a crack-filled neighborhood—a neighborhood which also happened to have the highest murder rate in a city which itself had the fourth-highest murder rate in the nation.[45] We were approaching a group of ten mid-teen youths and were about to stop when a St. Louis city patrol car pulled behind. Should I stop, as I planned on doing, and get out and talk with these youths (some of whom Luther marginally knew), or would that place them in imminent danger of arrest? Or should I continue on as if nothing was really going on, even though I had been driving stop and go, under ten miles an hour, prior to and during the now slow-speed pursuit? I opted for the latter, accelerating slowly in a vain attempt to reassert a "normal appearance."[46]

Sirens went on. I pulled over and reassured Luther there was nothing to worry about since neither of us had contraband (I hoped). As officers approached, I thought about what to tell them. Should I say I was a university professor doing field research on crack dealers (a part I clearly didn't look), lie, or say nothing at all? "Whatcha doin' down here?" one of the officers snapped. "Exit the vehicle, intertwine your fingers behind your heads, and kneel with your ankles crossed," he commanded. The searing June sidewalk was not conducive to clear thinking, but I rattled something off: "We used to work together at _____. I waited tables, he bussed, and we been friends since. I'm a sociology major up at _____ and he said he'd show me around the neighborhood sometime. Here I am." "Yeah right," the cop snapped again while searching for the crack he thought we already had purchased. Three other police cars arrived, as the cop baited Luther and me as to how we really knew each other, what each other's real names were (which neither of us knew at the time), and what we were doing here. Dissatisfied with my answers, a sergeant took over, lecturing me on the evils of crack and how it would destroy a life oth-

ers in this very neighborhood wished they had. I found no fault with the argument, listened attentively, and said nothing. After a final strip search in the late afternoon sun revealed nothing, they said I was lucky, vowed to take me in if I ever showed my face again, and let us go.

On a second occasion, Luther and his homie Frisco were in my car when we pulled up to a local liquor store. The two became nervous upon seeing two suits in a "tec" (detective) car parked at the phone booth. I told Luther and Frisco to wait, and I went into the store. As I exited, the two men approached and showed their badges. "What you doin' with these guys—do you know 'em?" "Yes," I said, deciding to tell them who I *really* was and what I was doing. "Mind if we search your car?" one asked. "No problem," I replied. "Go right ahead." As one searched my car (for crack, guns, or whatever else he thought he'd find), his partner cuffed both Luther and Frisco and ran warrants. As I soon learned, both detectives knew the two as repeat violent offenders with long rap sheets. They took Frisco in on an outstanding warrant and let Luther go with me. "I respect what you're doing," the searching officer said as he finished and approached, "but you don't know who you're dealing with. These guys are no good." I told him thanks and promptly left with Luther, feeling remorseful about Frisco being taken in only because he was with me.

On a third occasion, I was sitting on my car making small talk with four or five dealers when a patrol car rolled by. The officers inside gave a stern look and told us to break it up. "All right," I said, not going anywhere. We continued to talk for a few minutes when the officers, clearly agitated, rolled by again and demanded in no uncertain terms, "Break it up and we mean now." I hopped in my car, drove four or five blocks, made a left, and heard sirens. "Here we go again." This time, I was not nearly as nervous as I had been on the other occasions, ready to dispense my professor line, show my consent forms and faculty ID, and see their shocked reaction. "Get out of the car and put your hands on the trunk," the driver predictably ordered as I began my explanation. They searched me anyway, perhaps thinking it was just another mendacious story, but I kept conversing in a relaxed, erudite tone. Cops are known to have perceptual shorthands to render quick and accurate typifications of those with whom they're interacting,[47] and I could tell my conversational style was creating a good impression. I told them that I was doing interviews, that I was paying respondents for their time, and that the research was part of a university grant designed to better understand the everyday lives of urban youth. This was, of course, specious. The study's true purpose was to identify how crack dealers avoid arrest, something I dared not admit, for obvious reasons. "You can do what you want," one of them said, satisfied after a thorough search revealed no contraband, "but if I were you, I'd be real careful. You don't want to mess around with these punks." His words rang all too true several weeks later when Luther pointed the gun at my abdomen.

I did not realize it at the time, but my treatment by police was absolutely essential to my research. Police provided the "vital test"[48] I desperately needed to pass if my study were to be successful. The differential enforcement practices of these police officers (and many others around the country)—in which young, minority males are singled out as "symbolic assailants" and "suspicious characters" deserving of attention[49]—benefited *me* immensely. Police detained *me* because I was with "them." Driving alone in these same areas at the same time, though suspicious, would not likely have attracted nearly as much attention. I was "guilty by association" and "deserving" of the scrutiny young black males in many urban locales receive consistently. For my research, at least, this differential enforcement was anything but negative.

As Douglas notes, it is often necessary for researchers to convince offenders they are studying that the researchers do not represent the authorities.[50] Sluka adds that subjects "are going to define whose side they think you are on. They will act towards you on the basis of this definition, regardless of your professions."[51] Words may be futile in convincing offenders who or what one really

is. Ultimately, "actions speak louder than words. . . .[T]he researcher will have to demonstrate by . . .actions that he is on the side of the deviants, or at least, not on the side of the officials."[52] The police had treated me like just another user, and had done so with offenders present. This treatment provided the "actions" for me, the picture that spoke a thousand words.

Offenders' accounts of my treatment spread rapidly through the grapevine, solidifying my credibility for the remainder of the project and setting up the snowball sampling procedure I would use to recruit additional respondents. Without the actions of *police* I may not have been accepted by *offenders* as readily as I was or, perhaps, never accepted at all. A skillful researcher can use the police—indirectly and without their knowledge or, as in my case, without even the researcher's own intent—to demonstrate to offenders that the researcher is indeed legitimate and not an undercover police officer. Often thought to be a critical barrier to entry, the police may be the key to access. Of course, undercover officers themselves can manipulate this very dynamic to gain credibility with those they target—something savvy law enforcement administrators may exploit by setting up fake arrests in plain view. Such tactics may make a researcher's identity even more precarious; in my case, though, this did not occur.

Why police never attempted to confiscate my notes during these pull-overs I'll never know. Perhaps it was because the notes appeared to be chicken scratch and were indecipherable by anyone but me. Perhaps it was because my notes didn't reveal anything the cops did not already know, or at least thought they knew. Regardless, the law is clearly against ethnographers, who can be held in contempt and sent to jail for protecting sources and withholding information.[53] As Carey points out, "There is no privileged relationship between the . . .researcher and his subject similar to that enjoyed by the lawyer and client or psychiatrist and patient."[54] This, of course, says nothing about issues of guilty knowledge or guilty observation.[55] Being aware of dealing operations and watching transactions take place makes one an accessory to their commission, a felony whether one participates or not. Fieldworkers are co-conspirators by definition, no matter their motive or intent. As Polsky concludes, "If one is effectively to study adult criminals in their natural settings, he must make the moral decision that in some ways he will break the law himself."[56]

Researching Active Crack Sellers: In Perspective

By definition, criminological fieldworkers regularly intrude into the lives of individuals engaged in felonies—felonies for which these individuals can receive hard time. The more illegal the behavior, the more offenders as research subjects have to lose if found out. Obviously, this makes it tougher—and more risky—for researchers to gain access.

Street-level crack selling is thus a paradox of sorts: there is perhaps no other behavior so openly visible and so negatively sanctioned by law as crack selling. It must be this way for sellers to be available to their customers. This is particularly true in a declining drug market such as St. Louis,[57] where demand is finite and dwindling, while the number of sellers has remained constant or increased. To compete in such conditions, sellers will often stand out longer and in more difficult conditions than they previously would, in greater numbers, and in greater numbers together. Individual sellers also may rush to customers to steal sales from competitors, drawing even more attention. This situation creates ideal conditions for police—or researchers—to identify open-air sellers and infiltrate them.

Access notwithstanding, the importance of a strong indigenous tie to the research setting at the beginning of field relations—as a way of vouching for the researcher—cannot be overstated. Access and safe access are two wholly different notions. In my case, this tie was Luther—or at least so I thought. More generally, it is an indigenous offender or ex-offender turned fieldworker who acts as gatekeeper and protector. Yet, in a twist of sorts, field research with active offenders often requires strong ties in order to generate weak ones—that is, to initiate the methodological snowball. Micro-structurally and methodologically, this is unique; multiple weak ties rather than one or two strong ones are thought to be indispensable for social-network creation.[58] Indeed, one or two strong ties may actually cut off an actor from an entire social network.

In field research, developing strong ties with the wrong person or persons can, at a minimum, bias the sample or, worse, generate no sample at all.[59] Researchers may gain entry, but it may be with the wrong person. As my encounter with Luther attests, the outcome can be far more threatening than obtaining a biased sample or no sample. Perhaps the larger point here is that, no matter how strong or safe one's ties, danger is inherent in fieldwork with active offenders. Nowhere is this more true than among streetcorner crack sellers. Although many dangers can be addressed through planning and preparation, more often than not, danger management hinges on a creative process of "trial and blunder"[60] and results from a combination of skill and luck.[61] As Sluka notes, "[G]ood luck can sometimes help overcome a lack of skill, and well-developed skills can go far to help overcome the effects of bad luck. But sometimes no amount of skill will save one from a gross portion of bad luck."[62] Inevitably, criminological fieldwork is unpredictable and less subject to rational planning than we want it to be. How researchers handle this problem ultimately is a personal choice.

Researching active offenders requires one to balance conflicting agendas. Such agendas emanate from specific audiences—whether police or criminals—each with their own biases toward the ethnographic enterprise. Simply taking sides or currying favor with one audience over the other is not the issue, though this may be done at some point. Research strategies must be weighed carefully because their consequences are inevitably dialectical: police can get you "in" with offenders, but offenders can get you "in trouble" with police. Personal security is dependent on offender acceptance, yet security can be compromised by dependency. Police can be researchers' last bastion of hope against volatile offenders, but reliance on authorities may undermine the very purpose for being in the field. Caught among these contradictions stands the researcher, a true one-person "island in the street."[63] In this lonely position, the researcher must decide when to shade the truth and when to be forthright, when to offer and when to omit, when to induce and when to lie back. Such judgments are subjective and context specific, as any ethnographer will tell you. They must be made with the audience in mind, whether that audience is legal or illegal, academic or social. Each choice affects the kinds of data obtained and revealed. And how far an ethnographer is willing to go to get such data intertwines with the results that ethnographer hopes ultimately to obtain—as my encounter with Luther attests.

Notes

1. All names are pseudonyms to protect identities.

2. Terry Williams, Eloise Dunlap, Bruce D. Johnson, and Ansley Hamid, "Personal Safety in Dangerous Places," *Journal of Contemporary Ethnography* 21 (1992): 365.

3. Williams et al., "Personal Safety," 350.

4. Richard A. Berk and Joseph M. Adams, "Establishing Rapport with Deviant Groups," *Social Problems* 18 (1970): 110.

5. Jeffrey A. Sluka, "Participant Observation in Violent Social Contexts," *Human Organization* 49 (1990): 114.

6. Williams et al., "Personal Safety," 347.

7. Patrick Biernacki and Dan Waldorf, "Snowball Sampling," *Sociological Methods and Research* 10 (1981): 141–63.

8. See Harold Garfinkel, "Conditions of Successful Degradation Ceremonies," *American Journal of Sociology* 61 (1956): 420–24.

9. Williams et al., "Personal Safety," 364.

10. Williams et al., "Personal Safety," 350.

11. John M. Johnson, "Trust and Personal Involvements in Fieldwork," in *Contemporary Field Research*, ed. Robert M. Emerson (Prospect Heights, Ill.: Waveland, 1983), 205.

12. Kurt H. Wolff, "Surrender and Community Study: The Study of Loma," in *Reflections on Community Studies*, eds. Arthur J. Vidich, Jo-

seph Bensman, and Maurice R. Stein (New York: Wiley, 1964), 237.

13. Robert H. Lowie, *The History of Ethnological Theory* (New York: Farrar and Rinehart, 1937), 232.

14. Hortense Powdermaker, *Stranger and Friend: The Way of an Anthropologist* (New York: Norton, 1966), 19.

15. E. E. Evans-Pritchard, *Social Anthropology and Other Essays* (New York: Free Press, 1964), 77–79.

16. Berk and Adams, "Establishing Rapport," 103.

17. Berk and Adams, "Establishing Rapport."

18. Rosalie H. Wax, "The Ambiguities of Fieldwork," in *Contemporary Field Research*, ed. Robert M. Emerson (Prospect Heights, Ill.: Waveland, 1983), 195.

19. Ned Polsky, *Hustlers, Beats, and Others* (Chicago: Aldine, 1967), 124.

20. Robert M. Emerson, ed., *Contemporary Field Research* (Prospect Heights, Ill.: Waveland, 1983), 179.

21. Ivan Karp and Martha B. Kendall, "Reflexivity in Field Work," in *Explaining Human Behavior: Consciousness, Human Action, and Social Structure*, ed. Paul R. Secord (Beverly Hills, Calif.: Sage, 1982), 261.

22. Georg Simmel, "The Stranger," in *Georg Simmel*, ed. Donald Levine (Chicago: University of Chicago Press, 1908), 143–49.

23. Emerson, *Contemporary*, 179.

24. Richard T. Wright and Scott H. Decker, *Burglars on the Job: Streetlife and Residential Break-Ins* (Boston: Northeastern University Press, 1994), 26.

25. Berk and Adams, "Establishing Rapport," 107.

26. See Polsky, *Hustlers*.

27. Peter K. Manning, "Observing the Police: Deviance, Respectables, and the Law," in *Research on Deviance*, ed. Jack D. Douglas (New York: Random House, 1972), 213–68.

28. Annie Oakley, "Interviewing Women: A Contradiction in Terms," in *Doing Feminist Research*, ed. Helen Roberts (London: Routledge and Kegan Paul, 1981), 41.

29. Luther's stalking came to an end only because police picked him up on two unrelated counts of armed robbery and armed criminal action. He is now serving ten years in a Missouri state penitentiary. With the help of colleagues, I moved. My phone number is now unlisted and unpublished, something I recommend to

other ethnographers researching active offenders.

30. John Irwin, "Participant Observation of Criminals," in *Research on Deviance*, ed. Jack D. Douglas (New York: Random House, 1972), 117.

31. See Erich Goode, *The Marijuana Smokers* (New York: Basic, 1970).

32. Sluka, "Participant Observation," 115.

33. See Patricia Adler, *Wheeling and Dealing: An Ethnography of an Upper-Level Drug Dealing and Smuggling Community* (New York: Columbia University Press, 1985).

34. Diana Scully, *Understanding Sexual Violence* (Boston: Unwin Inman, 1990).

35. Michael Agar, *Ripping and Running: A Formal Ethnography of Urban Heroin Addicts* (New York: Seminar Press, 1973).

36. Wright and Decker, *Burglars*, 5.

37. Edwin Sutherland and Donald Cressey, *Criminology*, 8th ed. (Philadelphia: Lippincott, 1970), 68.

38. Polsky, *Hustlers*, 123.

39. George McCall, *Observing the Law* (New York: Free Press, 1978), 27.

40. Erving Goffman, *Relations in Public: Micro Studies of the Public Order* (New York: Basic Books, 1971), 323.

41. SCAT is an acronym for "street corner apprehension team." This fifteen-man undercover team is charged with curbing street-level drug sales by apprehending dealers immediately after sales to one of their "buy" officers. Hiding nearby in unmarked cars, personnel "swoop" down on offenders in an attempt to catch them with marked money just given them by buy officers. This money either has traceable dye or serial numbers previously recorded that link dealers to undercover transactions. SCAT units were highly feared because they were reportedly merciless in their arrest procedures (i.e., they conducted strip searches).

42. Wright and Decker, *Burglars*, 28.

43. Polsky, *Hustlers*, 147.

44. See Sluka, "Participant Observation."

45. Federal Bureau of Investigation, *Crime in the United States* (Washington, D.C.: Government Printing Office, 1995).

46. See Erving Goffman, *Stigma: Notes on the Management of Spoiled Identity* (Englewood Cliffs, N.J.: Prentice Hall, 1963).

47. See John Van Maanen, "The Asshole," in *Policing: A View from the Streets*, eds. Peter K. Manning and John Van Maanen (Santa Monica: Goodyear, 1978), 221–38.

48. Erving Goffman, *Frame Analysis: An Essay on the Organization of Experience* (Cambridge, Mass.: Harvard University Press, 1974).

49. See Jerome Skolnick, "A Sketch of the Policeman's 'Working Personality,'" in *Criminal Justice: Law and Politics*, ed. George F. Cole (North Scituate, Mass.: Duxbury Press, 1980).

50. Jack D. Douglas, "Observing Deviance," in *Research on Deviance*, ed. Jack D. Douglas (New York: Random House, 1972), 3–34.

51. Sluka, "Participant Observation," 123.

52. Douglas, "Observing Deviance," 12.

53. Irving Soloway and James Walters, "Workin' the Corner: The Ethics and Legality of Fieldwork among Active Heroin Addicts," in *Street Ethnography*, ed. Robert S. Weppner (Beverly Hills, Calif.: Sage, 1977), 175–76.

54. James T. Carey, "Problems of Access and Risk in Observing Drug Scenes," in *Research on Deviance*, ed. Jack D. Douglas (New York: Random House, 1972), 77.

55. See Adler, *Wheeling*, 24.

56. Polsky, *Hustlers*, 133–34.

57. Andrew Gollub, Farrukh Hakeem, and Bruce D. Johnson, "Monitoring the Decline in the Crack Epidemic with Data from the Drug Use Forecasting Program," Unpublished manuscript, 1996.

58. Mark Granovetter, "The Strength of Weak Ties," *American Journal of Sociology* 78 (1973): 1360–80.

59. Douglas's research on nudist beach goers, for example, was jeopardized because of his early bond with a marginal and generally disliked participant (something Douglas did not know until later)—a participant with whom he was able to bond precisely because of that person's marginality; see Douglas, "Observing Deviance."

60. See Karp and Kendall, "Reflexivity."

61. Robert F. Ellen, *Ethnographic Research: A Guide to General Conduct* (London: Academic Press, 1984), 97.

62. Sluka, "Participant Observation," 124.

63. Martin Sanchez-Jankowski, *Islands in the Street: Gangs in American Urban Society* (Berkeley: University of California Press, 1991).

The research on which this chapter is based was funded by Grant No. S–3–40453 from the

University of Missouri Research Board. Points of view or opinions expressed in this document are those of the author and do not necessarily represent those of the UMRB. I would like to thank Jeff Ferrell and Richard Wright for their helpful comments and criticisms on an earlier version of this chapter.

17
Gender and Research With the Police

Jennifer Hunt

Before modern times, people settled grievances and resolved conflicts on their own. "Law" was largely informal, and rule-breakers were sanctioned by way of family and community. People who "got out of line" were identified and punished and then quickly brought back into the fold. The efficiency of social control deterred would-be rule-breakers; social control was woven into the very fabric of daily life. Increases in population size, density, mobility, and industrialization changed all this, creating anonymous and diffuse living arrangements in need of formal social control. The emergence of the modern police force was one consequence.

Urban police are paramilitary groups vested with the full power of the state to resolve conflicts and maintain social stability. Their principal responsibility is to uphold order; they are empowered to use force to do so if necessary. Police often define their work in very dramatic terms, so as to emphasize its putative dangerousness. In truth, most police work is extraordinarily routine. It also is safe. Force is rarely used; the vast majority of officers will never take their weapons out of their holsters over the course of their careers, much less fire them. Paperwork fills their days and daily obligations center around providing advice, counsel, and general assistance. Some analysts justifiably assert that police work is closer to social work than anything else.

The perception of threat, however, continues to be an orienting perspective, a perspective that shapes police culture in important ways. The police distrust anyone who is not like them. They believe that others are out to discredit and expose them. Outsiders seeking to gain entry—academic researchers, in particular—therefore find it extraordinarily difficult. Entry is especially arduous for female researchers: in police culture, there is no tolerance for anything weak, and weakness and femininity are perceived to go hand-in-hand.

In this selection, Jennifer Hunt provides a glimpse of how she was able to overcome her "double deviant" status. What emerges is a picture of Hunt skillfully drawing from gender stereotypes to co-opt them and, in the process, establishing that she is both competent *and* trustworthy. Her savvy, sensitivity, and responsiveness to challenges proves her to be not only an acceptable outsider but an acceptable *female* outsider. Hunt provides a model for how to confront and defeat gender barriers in all manner of sex-segregated settings, whether they involve social control subcultures or deviant ones.

In reading this selection, readers should keep in mind that the social context of rule-breaking cannot be understood in the absence of a focus on the culture in which rule enforcers operate. Deviance and social control exist interdependently, and how deviants think and act is in large measure contingent on the behaviors and policies of those who control them.

Sociological field workers of varied theoretical persuasions share a common methodological problem. They desire a sharing relationship with research subjects who do not volunteer their presence and who have little in common with the researcher. In order to facilitate the construction of this relationship, the researcher must develop rapport, "that mysterious necessity of anthropological fieldwork" (Geertz 1973:419). Classical ethnographers have defined rapport as the amount of trust between researcher and subjects necessary to facilitate the acquisition of valid and reliable data (Miller 1952; Pelto and Pelto 1973:197; Shaffir et al. 1980:180–189). Once sufficient rapport is built, the researcher gains access to the hidden dimensions of the subjects' world. Implicit in classical discussions is the assumption that a separation between researcher and members is an essential aspect of field relations. Thus the researcher must sustain a delicate balance between involvement and detachment in order to maintain the necessary amount of rapport to do adequate field work. If he is too detached and experiences "under-rapport," subjects will be hostile and uncooperative. If he is too involved and identifies intimately with a particular group, "over-rapport" will impede research by undermining scientific objectivity. . . .

Researcher as Spy

When a field-worker first enters a police setting, he is commonly viewed as a "stranger whose loyalty and trustworthiness are suspect" (Manning 1972:248; Ericson 1981a:31). At best the researcher is perceived as a "social critic" (Van Maanen 1978:316) who seeks to discredit the police by publicizing compromising details of their occupational life. At worst, he is seen as a "spy" for some external or internal agency involved in a formal investigation of police misconduct (see Manin 1980:225).

In my case, the policemen's suspicion that I was an undercover agent for the Internal Affairs Bureau or the FBI was intensified by the political dynamics of the field situation. The Justice Department and a policewoman plaintiff had sued the police department charging discrimination in the hiring and promotion of female officers. As a result, 100 woman officers were hired and the city contracted an outside firm to compare the patrol performance of male and female rookies. I was one of six consultants employed by the firm to administer the study and conduct field observations. As it turned out, the city planned to use the evaluation to bolster its case against the women in court, a use the researchers felt might compromise the study. I believed that the police elite intended to and actually did manipulate the results to prove female incompetence. Because of this, I took steps to minimize that possibility. Two other consultants and I eventually hired an attorney who threatened legal action if the city

and the firm interfered with the administration of the study.

In order to limit my access to information that could compromise its case in court, the department tried to sabotage my relations with the police. They instituted formal rules to ensure my isolation and fostered the view that I was a spy. The word was spread that I would report illegal activity and rank-and-file officers were warned to avoid me.

Even if the department had affirmed my status as an independent researcher, I still would have been suspect, in part because the role of spy was consistent with my gender identity. As a civilian and a moral woman I represented the formal order of law and the inside world of the academy. As both FBI and police internal security also represented the formal order, it was logical to assume I was allied with them. In addition, no policeman believed a woman was politically capable of fighting the department to promote honest research; instead, the dominant elite would use me for their own purposes. Given my gender and formal orientation, many policemen assumed that I would naively report their activities to the department out of a sense of moral responsibility.

My identity as researcher and woman presented a physical as well as a political threat to the police. Thus, the skills and personality attributes associated with the good cop contradict those associated with both academic researcher and woman. The crime-fighting cop is aggressive, suspicious and cynical. He is skilled in the use of weapons and the manipulation of physical means to maintain order. In contrast, the domestic woman and intellectual are both perceived as passive and trusting. They display competence in reading, writing and the manipulation of verbal means to accomplish goals. Because I was a woman and a researcher, the police assumed that I would not act rationally in an emergency nor back up my partners in a dangerous situation, both of which are minimally necessary to establish credibility as a participant observer doing research among police. This is particularly important when the researcher is working as a second person in a "one-man" car.

As long as I was perceived as an anti-police spy, there was little hope that I could develop a dialogue with police and expand my understanding of their everyday life. Consequently, I had to counteract the department's attempt to sabotage my relations with the rank and file by constructing an alternative social identity that would pass in the informal world of the street.

The available categories of women who inhabit the informal realm were problematic. Thus both "dyke" and "whore" exhibit some characteristics associated with competent police work. They are aggressive, tough and street wise. In addition, the "whore" does share the policeman's political world and is unlikely to expose him from a naive commitment to the formal order. At the same time, both "dyke" and "whore" are too "dirty" to be trustworthy. Both participate in illicit activity and are therefore subject to departmental blackmail to ensure cooperation. In addition, the wealth and generosity of her clientele determine the hooker's status. Thus, a successful prostitute would most likely sell herself to the elite rather than the rank and file. Although she would not expose them from a commitment to the formal order, she would betray them if it was good business. Finally, the "dyke" is also viewed as dangerous because she harbors a deep hatred for men and would like to do them harm.

In summary, neither "dyke" nor "whore" nor moral woman provided a trustworthy gender identity. Consequently, I had to negotiate a new category of "street-woman-researcher" which would neutralize the dangers and maximize the assets of the three known categories in order to establish sufficient trust to do adequate fieldwork.

Constructing Masculinity: Field-worker as 'Dyke'

Spatial Orientation

In order to overcome my natural association with the low status inside world of women and management, it was important to display a preference for the high status outside domains associated with the crime-fighting activities of the "real cop" of the rank and file. This spatial re-orientation inevitably implied masculinization because there was no known category of feminine woman who inhabits the informal world of men.

During the summer training at the police academy I avoided the main building where classes in traffic laws and report writing were taught. I also avoided unnecessary contact with high-ranking "inside administrators" who maintained offices in the main building. Instead, I participated in classes including "Mechanics of Arrest," "Physical Training" and "Self Defense" which were concerned with the physical and perceptual skills associated with "real police work." Consequently, I associated largely with persons perceived as "outside men" and "real cops."

I also spent time at the pistol range, a most police-like location where men learned the skills of violence associated with crime-fighting and rescue work. Although I was an incompetent marksman, I loved to shoot and was determined to master the art of deadly force. As the range was associated with guns and guns symbolized both masculinity and "real police work," my constant presence on the range signaled a profound rejection of the feminine inside domain.

When I left the academy and went on patrol I continued to construct manhood in environmental terms. In particular, I displayed a preference for high-crime sectors which did not produce calls to disperse the disorderly crowds of children who "hung out" in low-crime neighborhoods. Although I enjoyed "family disputes" and "demented persons" more than many policemen, I showed an obvious preference for the exciting jobs involving possible crimes in progress, weapons and fights.

Combat Personality

While at the academy and on patrol, I displayed skills and personality attributes which complemented my masculine spatial orientation. Some police, for example, were impressed with my knowledge of judo techniques (gained independently) which they associated with hand-to-hand combat. Once several "PT" instructors requested a demonstration. One officer sat on the ground with his back to me and I applied a choke. For a few seconds, I forgot to tell him how a judo player indicates submission. Consequently, the officer was almost unconscious when he "tapped out" and I released him. Surprised that a small woman could subdue a man, he demanded another demonstration in order to develop a counter-technique. Several weeks later, he asked me to show the choke to recruits.

Pistol practice provided the perfect opportunity to display the esteemed characteristics of masculine aggression and heart. One day I was practicing combat shooting and as usual, my score was abominable. Ashamed, I left the range with my target hidden so no one could see it. However, a pistol instructor and several unknown off-duty officers approached and asked how I did. I responded, "Not so good today, but tomorrow I'll blow the mother's guts out." Astonished, one officer commented, "Did you hear what she said?!" They both smiled and nodded their heads approvingly. I had shown that I was not a passive woman but a competent "man" who could feel just as violent as they.

On the street, I continued to display the combat personality associated with the "crime-fighting cop." One evening I was patrolling with a male officer when we observed people pouring out of a bar. A man then yelled, "You better get in here quick. There's a helluva fight going on!" The officer ran out of the car while I grabbed the radio and requested a backup. As I threw down the transmitter and started to run towards the bar, I heard radio acknowledge, "5420 (car number), use caution. There's a report of a stabbing at that location."

When I opened the door, I looked to my left and noticed a man sitting at the bar. He looked relatively harmless: one hand was on the table and the other was holding a drink. Most of the action was occurring at the far end of the room. People were yelling and crying. Three wounded suspects were all armed with knives. The police officer seemed to be pointing his gun in three different directions. When I approached the rookie officer, I grabbed an hysterical waitress reaching for a knife that she had apparently dropped on a

stool. Meanwhile the rookie disarmed one man while the other voluntarily discarded his weapon.

After the backups arrived, the wounded taken to the hospital and a crime scene established, the rookie and I returned to the car and waited for the lieutenant. We both felt exhilarated from the action. I turned to my partner and said, "If he (the stab victim) dies, it'll be a really good pinch!" The officer grinned and shook his head in agreement. The lieutenant overheard my comment and responded, "You're just like the rest of them."

The bar incident provided additional evidence that I was a "good man" whose skills and personality conformed with "street cop" rather than "management cop" culture.[1] First I could back up my partner in a dangerous situation. I was also as "hard" and "pinch hungry" as the rest of the police. I cared more about making a felony arrest than saving a drunk man's life. Most important, I showed them that I could attain the state of "combat high" which facilitates rational action in a stressful situation.

Acting Crazy

A brave police officer may also be labeled "crazy" because he takes unusual risks. The risks may involve a physical or social confrontation with superior power. They may also represent a symbolic challenge to the cultural system's dominant classificatory order. The risk-taking behavior of the crazy person is often viewed as unpredictable and dangerous because it contradicts rules that order experience, or violates the routine ways that members utilize social rules. As social disorder is often viewed in physical terms, the crazy person is sometimes seen as potentially violent. Consequently, he may often do what he pleases because people fear him.

Although I was neither exceptionally brave nor violent, I earned the reputation for being crazy because I acted in an unpredictable manner which violated expected adult behavior of someone of my status. For example, some officers thought I was crazy when I acted as bait during the training of the police attack dogs by hiding in a locker during a mock building search.

On other occasions my efforts to reduce the boredom of patrol resulted in demonstrations of "crazy" behavior. One evening, for example, I walked into a district and announced to the officer from the mounted patrol unit that I was going to "liberate" his horse. Surprised, he responded, "Oh no you don't" and proceeded to take me with him for a ride around the district. After another officer allowed me to ride his horse while he talked to some friends, he explained that the horse was assigned to him for retraining because he had become difficult to handle. When I asked the officer why he let me ride a "wild" horse, he responded, "Well, I already heard you were crazy."

I also produced craziness by symbolically reversing the sexual order of classification. One afternoon, two veteran officers urged me out of my patrol car because they wanted to show me the prisoner they had in the wagon. Laughing hysterically, both officers warned me, "You better be careful. We've gotta bulldyke in the wagon and she might want to eat your pussy." When they opened the door, I observed a woman huddled in the back of the wagon who kept repeating the words, "I want to eat your pussy." When the "turnkey" approached the wagon to see what all the commotion was about, I turned around and told him with a serious expression on my face, "You'd better be careful. They've got a bulldyke in the wagon and she might want to eat your pussy." As the officer walked away he commented, "How can someone as crazy as a cop evaluate cops?"

In summary, my reputation for crazy behavior complemented my masculine combat identity. In contrast to feminine irrationality which implied loss of control and weakness, my display of police-like craziness suggested both courage and strength. From their perspective, I had "balls" enough to challenge the social order of things. Thus, craziness had implications for my status as well as gender identification. In particular, it confirmed my alienation from management because I was viewed as a possible rebel who might challenge the social order.

Producing Resistance

The challenge to power implicit in my crazy behavior also took direct political form. In particular, I gained the street cops' trust by demonstrating a defiant attitude towards the elite and a "masculine" identification with the interests of the rank and file.

One day the Chief Inspector of the Training Division requested that I come into his office for a meeting. The meeting appeared to be less a functional, getting-something-done meeting than a power display. The Chief kept me waiting for a long period while he talked on the phone about irrelevant matters. Rank-and-file police officers called in to attend to small errands were also kept waiting. Although I never took public notes about the activity of rank-and-file officers, I did take notes during this meeting even when the Chief was on the telephone. Gradually, however, I became impatient and left the room to purchase a box of candy. When I returned I furtively offered some to the police officer sitting next to me. He refused and whispered, "You're not supposed to eat 'Dots' in front of the Chief!" to which I responded, "The whole scene's like a circus and you always eat candy at the circus." He agreed. Later that day the officer took me aside and commented smiling, "You must be scaring the hell out of them by taking notes in the meeting like that."

My actions at the meeting presented clear evidence of my political affiliation. The Chief displayed his superiority by keeping me waiting while he attended to irrelevant matters and spoke on the phone. In defiance, I countered his power by eating "Dots" in his presence. My actions revealed my contempt for him as well as my refusal to submit to his authority. At the same time, I showed the Chief and the rank and file that I was an intelligent politician. I took notes on the Chief "to get something on him." I thus became a subversive in the eyes of the rank and file as well as the elite.

A similar opportunity to produce dissidence arose when I first went out on patrol. After a 4 x 12 shift, several rookies invited me to attend a police hockey game. Although attendance violated the departmental rule forbidding fraternization, I decided to go.

While I was watching the game a sergeant approached and explained that he wasn't supposed to talk to me, but then began to discuss the department's attitude towards the new female officers. Suddenly a hockey puck flew over a metal fence, hit the sergeant in the head and knocked him unconscious. After he opened his eyes and it was clear that his injuries were minor, I began to laugh. I told him, "This is what happens when you talk to me, they get you with a flying hockey puck!"

The next day I bought the sergeant a card which depicted a lot of cartoon creatures looking up at the sky with open mouths. Extended from the creatures' mouths I typed, "Don't puck with me." Thus, the flying hockey puck became the symbol of coercion that the informal system employed to demand obedience of the men. The words represented resistance. The sergeant loved the card and showed it to everyone.

In these encounters I revealed unequivocally that I was an ally in the policemen's struggle against the patronage elite. In contrast to "asskissers" and "inside men," I would not sell myself to gain favors and upward mobility. In recognition of my status as a subversive one officer affectionately nicknamed me "the sneak."

Constructing Masculinity: Field-worker as 'Whore'

Although my displays of toughness appeared predominantly "butch" in character, at times I was also viewed as a "whore."[2] Thus one officer explained, "Well, you curse, so they think you fool around." As cursing could have confirmed the lesbian identity of a woman who doesn't sleep with men, their assessment was also based on my reaction to other gender tests.

On one occasion I met an off-duty officer while shooting at the range. He was curious about the study and offered me a ride to the train station as an excuse for a personality test. After we had a drink at a local pub, he took me to a topless bar. He adjusted the seating so I was directly facing the dancer. After an hour in which I hid in my discomfort and managed a normal conversation,

the officer took me to the train. Several weeks later I encountered the same policeman discussing some informal features of police work with colleagues. As I approached, they all stopped talking but resumed their conversation when the officer introduced me and commented, "She's O.K. I took her to a topless place and she didn't mind."

A similar incident occurred on my first night on patrol when my veteran partner proceeded to show me a copy of *Hustler* magazine. He asked me to read an article which obscenely portrayed a supervisor who catered to superiors by harassing the powerless rank and file. He compared the man to his sergeant. Ignoring the pornographic pictures and the style of the piece, I remarked on its content and empathized with the worker's plight. For the next few hours, the officer continued to test me by displaying other glimpses of the policeman's informal world. I was handed a loaded non-regulation 9mm automatic pistol which I admired and returned. We drank free coffee for an hour in a restaurant while I composed cover stories to account for our absence from the street. When we returned to the district at the end of the shift, a colleague asked loudly, "Well, did she learn anything?" My partner responded, "I think she knows it already." He then introduced me to his friends and invited me back for another tour.

In summary, in these two initiation rites the policemen directly tested my status and gender by exposing me to their informal world of illicit sex. As neither officer would have taken his wife to a topless bar nor shown her *Hustler* magazine, they treated me like a "whore." I confirmed my separateness from the domestic domain by acting like one. Thus, in contrast to the wife I expressed no moral outrage. Instead, I ignored the sex and "didn't mind." In contrast to the "dyke," I displayed no contempt for the policeman's illicit expressions of masculinity. Instead, I admired his secret gun.

The transformation of identity implicit in my exposure to the policeman's sexual life was complemented by my participation in symbolic corruption. Such illicit activity was inevitably accompanied by demonstrations of police-like skill in rule negotiation. In particular, I showed I could construct cover stories to account for my own and others' indiscretions.

One day another female observer and I left a mango for a particular range instructor who had never tasted one. Two other instructors stole it and ate it. The next day one of the perpetrators approached and asked if it was spiked. He had mistaken the turpentine flavor of the mango for gin. I responded, "Do you really want to know?"—a comment which illustrated my understanding of the informal rule that "what you don't know about, hear about or remember, can't get you or anyone else into trouble." The instructor then suggested, "Next time try rum." My friend and I obtained some rum and a hypodermic needle and spent the next day in the police academy bathroom stalls trying to inject the mango with rum. We gave the spiked fruit to the instructor who apparently spread the word of our activity throughout the department. For weeks after the incident, strange policemen would approach me and inquire about mangoes. I would always respond, "I don't know nothing about mangoes" and thus reinforce their sense that I knew how to lie to cover up my illicit behavior as well as theirs.

My participation in the policeman's illicit moral world not only confirmed my gender identity as a "whore." It also directly affirmed my status identification with the rank and file. Like the "real street cop" I, too, engaged in acts of rebellion against management, including illicit sexual pleasures, drinking on duty and otherwise stealing departmental time.

In serious incidents I continued to display my allegiance to the rank and file by taking action to protect the men from possible contradictory testimony in court. For example, if I witnessed an incident involving the use of weapons or illegal force by police, I would disappear and avoid interrogation by internal investigating units. If circumstances made disappearance impossible, I would try other tactics to resist making statements. After a prisoner in a district detention cell had stuffed toilet paper in his clothing and set himself on fire, the police officers with

whom I was riding were called to transport him to the hospital. A departmental investigation was necessary to determine if there was any police responsibility in the attempted suicide. When the homicide detectives questioned me about the incident, I told them that I hadn't seen any more than the police officers had already described. Later, when they again asked me if I was sure I had nothing to add, I responded, "I don't recall nothing." They smiled and said I would have to ride with them sometime.

Constructing Femininity: Field-worker as Woman

In my fieldwork I negotiated a street identity by displaying personality attributes which contradicted those associated with the domestic woman. As the street woman's illicit activity usually takes a sexual form, the police assumed I would sleep with them. Initial inquiries into my gender orientation were therefore followed by overt attempts to seduce me.

In the context of the policeman's world, sexual conquest has many meanings.[3] If I slept with the police, it would confirm my identity as a "whore." I would therefore fit a known category of female who belonged on the street, my gender ambiguity would diminish and the symbolic order would be restored. If I participated in the policemen's sexual exploits, they could also control me through the accumulation of "dirty knowledge." In contrast to the feminine woman, I would be unlikely to betray the police without risk to myself.

Although my identity as "whore" might restore the classificatory order and subject me to internal control, it would not necessarily make me trustworthy. In fact, in view of the current political situation, my sexual submission could also be dangerous. If I became a "whore" and allowed the police to know about my illicit activities, I would be subject to blackmail by the elite. They could use me to manipulate the study results or gain information about the subversive activities of rank-and-file members. In a less conflictual context, an identity as "whore" might be reassuring in part because the interests of elite and rank and file would overlap. In a conflict situation, in contrast, it was imperative that I retain my independence from informal control by maintaining relative purity.[4] Only then could the rank and file trust me to conduct an honest study without compromising their political interests.

In fact, my reaction to the policemen's sexual overtures generally confirmed the ambiguity of my gender. On the one hand, I sometimes acted like a moral woman and politely refused. Thus, when an attractive man tempted me with a friendly conversation followed by an invitation to go out after a "four to twelve," I would invoke the formal rule prohibiting fraternization with police.

On the other hand, if the policeman's request seemed impolite I would respond with "masculine" anger and even the threat of physical violence. One night, for example, I was at the Fraternal Order of Police (FOP) bar with a squad of male and female officers. As the FOP was known as a "meat market" for policemen "on the make," an approach was inevitable. I was crossing the crowded room to talk to the sergeant with my police companion not far behind. Suddenly a drunk cop put his hand underneath my shirt and up my back. Surprised, I turned around and threatened, "Do you wanta get kicked in the balls?" He looked shocked, laughed nervously, and left. My companion also started laughing and patted me on the shoulder approvingly.

After some time on the street, most invitations ceased because I gained the reputation for being unavailable. Thus, when I inquired why no one asked me out anymore, a policeman responded, "Everyone knows you won't go out with cops." I therefore appeared part moral woman as well as "dyke" and "whore."

The ambiguity of my sexual identity was heightened by other displays of femininity. I could, for example, show empathy in a womanly way. When a female recruit failed her pistol qualification test she broke down crying in front of her platoon. Although many men undoubtedly sympathized, they were embarrassed by her tears and did not know what to do. I approached the woman and tried to comfort her. At the same time I en-

couraged her not to give up but to try again on the re-test.

At times I also displayed a feminine vulnerability which allowed the men to experience masculine concern and protectiveness. Once, for example, I left a catastrophic political meeting almost in tears. Before I could escape to the bathroom, an officer interrupted and asked, "Was it that bad?" I responded, "Yes, it was worse. I feel like I'm gonna cry." He looked at my face and commented tenderly, "Cops aren't supposed to cry."

The feminine aspects of my gender identity were ritually restored in a game played with an academy instructor. When I felt extremely bored I occasionally behaved in a peculiar manner. In particular, I would pace the halls of the academy practicing judo "foot sweeps." One "PT" instructor would then sneak up behind and grab me around the neck. A brief struggle would ensue in which I would try to throw him. He would then jab his knee into the back of my leg, a move that would have sent me flying across the room had I not been forcibly restrained. When I would finally admit defeat, he would let me go. In this ritual, the sexual order of power was restored: the tough judo player was transformed into a weak and helpless woman.

Field-worker as a Liminal Figure

In summary, my fieldwork involved the construction of a new category of female who combined elements of masculinity and femininity. I was aggressive, tough, hard and corrupt like a "dyke" or a "whore." I was also sexually aloof empathetic and vulnerable like a moral woman. As part man, I could be trusted to back up my partner and lie for the police. As part moral woman, I could perform an honest study because I was not involved in a system of favors that demands ethical compromise from its members. Therefore, in contrast to my old identity as moral woman and spy, my new identity as "street-woman-researcher" constituted a trustworthy category of person in the policemen's eyes. My displays of masculinity, craziness and resistance were also important to the development of trust because they defined my opposition to the elite and identification with the rank and file. In fact, liminal gender identity itself represented a form of subversion which helped to cement relationships with a politically rebellious rank and file. . . .

Notes

1. In the bar incident, I also displayed good judgment. I did not run blindly into a dangerous situation but instead called a backup before proceeding. Policemen also remarked on other displays of caution and police defensiveness. For example, one officer noted that I "stood by the side of the door" when he answered a routine call. He nodded approvingly when I responded, "I don't want to get my head blown off for nothing." Other officers commented on my ability to perceive "incongruity" (Sacks 1978) and danger. These skills did not come naturally. The mistakes I made while doing fieldwork in New York and the lessons in police work received from New York police greatly facilitated my field work in Metro City.

2. The three female observers who participated in the study seemed to represent the three different categories of female. Mary represented the "moral woman." Susan represented the "whore" and I represented the "dyke." One police officer compared the three women in the following manner: "I couldn't take Mary home for dinner because my mother wouldn't let her out of the house until I promised to marry her. I couldn't take Susan home for dinner because my father'd try to seduce her. I couldn't take (the author) home for dinner because she'd slip and say, 'Pass the fuckin' butter.'"

3. The defeminization and reclassification of the "moral woman" into subordinate categories of female also served to neutralize the pollution inherent in the mingling of sexual intercourse and war (blood), two "concrete expressions of creation and destruction" (see Friedrich 1978:35–36).

4. Many researchers assume that the fieldworker's formal status as a non-member decreases trust because he is not subject to organizational controls (see Ericson 1981a:33; Van Maanen 1978:318). In contrast, I suggest that his independence may, under certain circumstances, increase his trustworthiness.

References

Berger, Peter, and Thomas Luckmann. 1967. *The Social Construction of Reality.* Garden City, NY: Anchor.

Berk, Richard A., and Joseph M. Adams. 1970. Establishing Rapport with Deviant Groups. *Social Problems* 18:102–117.

Bittner, Egon. 1973. Objectivity and Realism in Sociology. In *Phenomenological Sociology: Issues and Applications.* George Psathas, ed. Pp. 109–125. New York: Wiley.

Blum, Alan, and Peter McHugh. 1971. The Social Ascription of Motives. *American Sociological Review* 36:98–109.

Bogdan, R., and S. J. Taylor. 1975. *Introduction to Qualitative Research Methods: A Phenomenological Approach to the Social Sciences.* New York: Wiley.

Bologh, Roslyn Wallach. 1979. *Dialectical Phenomenology: Marx's Method.* London: Routledge & Kegan Paul.

Buckner, Taylor H. 1978. Transformations of Reality in the Legal Process. In *Phenomenology and Sociology.* Thomas Luckmann, ed. Pp. 311–323. Middlesex: Penguin.

Crapanzano, Vincent. 1980. *Tuhami: Portrait of a Moroccan.* Chicago: University of Chicago.

Demos, John. 1982. The Changing Faces of Fatherhood: A New Exploration in American Family History. In *Father and Child: Developmental and Clinical Perspectives.* Stanley H. Cath, Alan R. Gurwitt and John Munder Ross, eds. Pp. 425–445. Boston: Little Brown.

Dwyer, Kevin. 1979. The Dialogic of Ethnology. *Dialectical Anthropology* 4:205–224.

Easterday, Lois, Diana Papademas, Laura Schorr, and Catherine Valentine. 1977. The Making of a Female Researcher: Role Problems in Field Work. *Urban Life* 6:333–348.

Emerson, Robert M. 1983. *Contemporary Field Research.* Boston: Little Brown.

Epstein, Cynthia Fuchs. 1970. *Woman's Place: Options and Limits in Professional Careers.* Berkeley: University of California.

Ericson, Richard V. 1981a. *Making Crime: A Study of Detective Work.* Toronto: Butterworth

——. 1981b. Rules for Police Deviance. In *Organizational Police Deviance: Its Structure and Control.* Clifford D. Shearing, ed. Pp. 83–110. Toronto: Butterworth.

——. 1982. *Reproducing Order: A Study of Police Patrol Work.* Toronto: University of Toronto.

Friedrich, Paul. 1978. *The Meaning of Aphrodite.* Chicago: University of Chicago.

Frielich, Morris. 1970. *Marginal Natives: Anthropologists at Work.* New York: Harper & Row.

Garfinkel, Harold. 1967a. *Studies in Ethnomethodology.* Englewood Cliffs: Prentice Hall.

——. 1967b. Passing and the Managed Achievement of Sex Status in an Intersexed Person. In *Studies in Ethnomethodology.* Pp. 116–185. Englewood Cliffs: Prentice Hall.

Geertz, Clifford. 1973. Deep Play: Notes on the Balinese Cockfight. In *The Interpretation of Cultures.* Pp. 412–453. New York: Basic Books.

Goffman, Erving. 1959. *The Presentation of Self in Everyday Life.* Garden City: Doubleday.

Golde, Peggy. 1970. Introduction. In *Women in the Field.* Peggy Golde, ed. Chicago: Aldine.

Gouldner, Alvin. 1970. *The Coming Crisis of Western Sociology.* New York: Avon.

Haas, Jack, and William Shaffir. 1980. Fieldworkers' Mistakes at Work: Problems in Maintaining Research and Researcher Bargains. In *Fieldwork Experience: Qualitative Approaches to Social Research.* William B. Shaffir, Robert A. Stebbins and Allan Turowetz, eds. Pp. 244–256. New York: St. Martin's.

Heap, James L., and Phillip A. Roth. 1973. On Phenomenological Sociology. *American Sociological Review* 38:354–367.

Johnson, John. 1975. *Doing Field Research.* New York: Free Press.

Kanter, Rosabeth Moss. 1977. *Men and Women of the Corporation.* New York: Basic Books.

Kotarba, Joseph A. 1980. Discovering Amorphous Social Experience: The Case of Chronic Pain. In *Fieldwork Experience: Qualitative Approaches to Social Research.* William B. Shaffir, Roben A. Stebbins, and Allan Turowetz, eds. Pp. 57–67. New York: St. Martin's.

Manning, Peter K. 1972. Observing the Police: Deviants, Respectables, and the Law. In *Research on Deviance.* Jack D. Douglas, ed. Pp. 213–268. New York: Random House.

——. 1977. *Police Work: The Social Organization of Policing.* Cambridge: MIT.

——. 1979. Metaphors of the Field: Varieties of Organizational Discourse. *Administrative Science Quarterly* 24:660–671.

Manin, Susan. 1980. *Breaking and Entering, Policewomen on Patrol.* Berkeley: University of California.

Miller, S. M. 1952. The Participant Observer and "Over-Rapport." *American Sociological Review* 17:97–99.

Morgan, David. 1981. Men, Masculinity and the Process of Sociological Inquiry. In *Doing Feminist Research.* Helen Roberts, ed. Pp. 83–113. London: Routledge & Kegan Paul.

Pastner, Carroll McC. 1982. Rethinking the Role of the Woman Field Worker in Purdah Societies. *Human Organization* 41:262–264.

Pelto, Pertti J., and Gretel H. Pelto. 1973. Ethnography: The Fieldwork Enterprise. In *Handbook of Social and Cultural Anthropology.* John J. Honigman, ed. Pp. 241–288. Chicago: Rand McNally.

Pettigrew, Joyce. 1981. Reminiscences of Fieldwork Among the Sikhs. In *Doing Feminist Research.* Helen Roberts, ed. Pp. 62–82. London: Routledge & Kegan Paul.

Pollner, Melvin, and Robert M. Emerson. 1983. The Dynamics of Inclusion and Distance in Fieldwork Relations. In *Contemporary Field Research.* Robert M. Emerson, ed. Pp. 235–252. Boston: Little Brown.

Psathas, George. 1973. Introduction. In *Phenomenological Sociology: Issues and Applications.* George Psathas, ed. Pp. 1–21. New York: John Wiley.

Rabinow, Paul. 1977. *Reflections on Fieldwork in Morocco.* Berkeley: University of California.

Reiss, Albert J., Jr. 1971. *The Police and the Public.* New Haven: Yale University.

Reuss-Ianni, Elizabeth, and Francis A. J. Ianni. 1983. Street Cops and Management Cops: The Two Cultures of Policing. In *Control in the Police Organization.* Maurice Punch, ed. Pp. 251–274. Cambridge: MIT.

Rosaldo, Michelle Zimbalist. 1974. Woman, Culture and Society: A Theoretical Overview. In *Woman, Culture and Society.* Michelle Zimbalist Rosaldo and Louise Lamphere, eds. Pp. 17–42. Stanford: Stanford University.

Rustad, Michael L. 1982. *Women in Khaki: The American Enlisted Woman.* New York: Praeger.

Sacks, Harvey. 1978. Notes on Police Assessment of Moral Character. In *Policing: A View from the Street.* Peter K. Manning and John Van Maanen, eds. Pp. 187–201. Santa Monica, CA: Goodyear.

Sahlins, Marshall D. 1965. On the Sociology of Primitive Exchange. In *The Relevance of Models for Social Anthropology.* Michael Banton, ed. Pp. 139–236. London: Tavistock.

Sanday, Peggy Reeves. 1981. *Female Power and Male Dominance: On the Origins of Sexual Inequality.* Cambridge: Cambridge University Press.

Schreiber, Carol Tropp. 1981. *Changing Places: Men and Women in Transitional Occupations.* Cambridge: MIT.

Shaffir, William B., Robert A. Stebbins, and Allan Turowetz. 1980. *Fieldwork Experience: Qualitative Approaches to Social Research.* New York: St. Martin's.

Skolnick, Jerome H. 1975. *Justice Without Trial.* New York: Wiley.

Sudnow, David. 1967. *Passing On: The Social Organization of Dying.* Englewood Cliffs: Prentice Hall.

Turner, Victor. 1969. *The Ritual Process: Structure and Anti-Structure.* Ithaca: Cornell University Press.

Van Maanen, John. 1978. Epilogue: On Watching the Watchers. In *Policing: A View from the Street.* Peter K. Manning and John Van Maanen, eds. Pp. 292–318. Santa Monica: Goodyear.

——. 1979. The Fact of Fiction in Organizational Ethnography. *Administrative Science Quarterly* 24:539–549.

——. 1983. The Moral Fix: On the Ethics of Fieldwork. In *Contemporary Field Research.* Robert M. Emerson, ed. Pp. 269–287. Boston: Little Brown.

Warren, Carol A. B., and Paul K. Rasmussen. 1977. Sex and Gender in Field Research. *Urban Life* 6:349–369.

Wax, Rosalie H. 1952. Field Methods and Techniques: Reciprocity as a Field Technique. *Human Organization* 11:34–37.

——. 1979. Gender and Age in Fieldwork and Fieldwork Education. No Good Thing Is Done by Any Man Alone. *Social Problems* 26:509–522.

——. 1983. The Ambiguities of Fieldwork. In *Contemporary Field Research.* Robert M. Emerson, ed. Pp. 191–202. Boston: Little Brown.

Adapted with permission from The Society for Applied Anthropology. Copyright © 1984, *Human Organization*, 43:283–296. For editorial reasons, the title of this selection has been modified from the original. ✦

Part IV

Drugs

People have used mind-altering substances since the dawn of time—partly for escape, partly for experimentation, partly for relief of symptoms, mostly for pleasure. Thousands of psychoactive compounds exist in the natural world. Still others are products of human ingenuity. Whatever their type, effects, or method of use, the process by which certain substances are defined as legal and acceptable while others are deemed to be death-producing contraband is of vital sociological interest. The difference between illegal and legal drugs is largely an arbitrary one—very much like the difference between water and holy water: both come from the tap—it comes down to how the two substances are *socially constructed* (Szasz 1985).

Some readers may not be aware that heroin, cocaine, and marijuana used to be completely legal in this country. In the late 1800s, opiates could be purchased cheaply and easily in the form of patent medicines at general stores and pharmacies across the nation. A host of maladies—headaches, stomach aches, coughs, inflamed sinuses, among others—would quickly disappear after sufferers consumed these elixirs. In truth, heroin cures nothing, but its analgesic (pain numbing) properties are so potent that all symptoms of illness are eliminated. Cocaine (a stimulant processed from the leaves of the coca bush) was similarly touted as a medical miracle—*the answer* for everything from fatigue to depression to sexual frigidity. It was a common ingredient in wine, cigarettes,

and, yes, Coca-Cola. Sigmund Freud, world famous psychoanalyst, dispensed it to some of his patients and was sufficiently enthusiastic about its properties to snort a considerable amount himself. Marijuana once grew as wild as dandelions (hence the moniker "weed") and was smoked by thousands for its calming euphoria, particularly in the American Southwest; no significant negative health consequences were reported.

All of this changed, thanks to a volatile mixture of racism, economics, demagoguery, and moral panic. Take, for example, heroin. By 1875, Chinese immigrants by the thousands had settled into the American West to build the transcontinental railroad. A virulent economic depression hit the nation at around the same time the railroads were completed, leaving a sizable pool of Chinese laborers in direct competition with white workers for an increasingly limited supply of jobs. The Chinese were perceived to work harder, longer, and cheaper than their white counterparts, making their labor market presence a threat. The best way to neutralize that threat was to criminalize something the Chinese and only the Chinese did. This behavior happened to be smoking opium, a cultural and recreational activity not unlike drinking beer was to white working-class Americans at around the same time. A moral panic was cleverly created, in which the Chinese were depicted as evil "dope fiends," who lured unsuspecting white boys and girls into vile opium dens, making them addicts and sex slaves for life. These were lies, but the American public came to believe them, thanks to a concerted public relations effort by persons in positions of power and influence. The criminalization of all forms of opium (e.g., heroin, morphine) soon followed.

This pattern, in which illicit drugs get associated with particular population groups deemed threatening, and are then criminalized to control the groups that use them, is one that has been replicated time and again in American drug policy. Cocaine use was tied to African-American males, who, on "drug-crazed missions," allegedly raped white women and were impervious to police bullets (law enforcement reportedly switched from .32 to .38 caliber weapons for precisely this reason). Marijuana was associated with Mexican immigrants in the American Southwest, who, like their Chinese counterparts a half-century earlier, represented an economic threat to white labor. LSD, a hallucinogenic, was linked to insurgents and malcontents out to promote social upheaval in the 1960s. When a government-funded study revealed an association between LSD use and chromosomal damage (albeit a false one), the substance quickly found itself on the DEA's list of banned substances. Popular contemporary drugs—designer drugs, in particular, like Ecstasy, Roofies, and GHB—have faced the same fate in recent years.

Drugs are criminalized not because of their objective harm but because of the perceived harmfulness of the population who uses them. There is no compelling medical justification, for example, to outlaw heroin. It is addictive but no more so than nicotine, caffeine, or alcohol—all of which can be purchased legally at millions of outlets across the country. Heroin's primary negative side effect is constipation, not a particularly pernicious one, and one shared by chocolate, dark soda, and bananas. Some analysts contend that the real harm from drugs comes only *after* they are criminalized. Stiff legal sanctions result in: (1) purer, more concentrated forms of the substance (traffickers must limit their risk by reducing the volume of the substance they smuggle into the coun-

try and sell on the streets, thereby maximizing the "bang for the purchaser's buck"); (2) an absence of quality control (leading to overdoses and deaths); (3) extraordinarily high prices (risk must be factored into the cost equation to make it worth a seller's while); (4) prolific amounts of income-generating crime by users in order to pay for their habit; (5) violence as a principal means of resolving grievances; and (6) the widespread corruption of police.

The federal government spends over $20 billion a year on drug control, with not much to show for it. Drugs are cheaper, purer, and more widely available than ever before. Thousands upon thousands of drug market participants have been arrested and jailed, only to be replaced by thousands more.[1] Scores of high-intensity drug-trafficking areas have been squashed, only to be supplanted by new ones. Drug markets, as Dorn and Murji (1992, 170) note, are very much like a "squishy balloon: apply pressure to them in one place and there will be some diminution of the problem, yet it is likely that the market will balloon out in another place or an adjacent site, involving new and possibly more cautious or sophisticated dealers and perhaps a different range of drugs." Displacement and its consequences are not unlike "throwing water on an oil fire" (Rengert 1996, 8). And when markets are sufficiently large, they can absorb formal social control initiatives without suffering any damage: the risk of getting caught in completing any one transaction falls when police resources are spread across numerous sites (Rengert 1996, 87, 124). Strategies such as going after "Mr. Big"—trying to behead large-scale dealing operations by going after their leaders—do not work either. They result in new, more complex, and more insular leadership structures, which are even more resistant to interdiction (see Hamid 1998; see also Drug Enforcement Agency 1997; Rengert 1996; for these and other points, see Jacobs 2000). All attempts on the part of law enforcement to clamp down on illegal drugs bring responses on the part of those targeted to thwart any curtailment of the traffic. As Ryan (1994, 226) observes, the "interaction of law enforcers and deviants produces a dialectical process of change, each side responding to the moves of the other by altering its social organization and personnel."

The point is that people have wanted, and always will want, to use drugs. Attempting to stifle this drive by threatening harsh punishments is not likely to do much good. Policies that work through informal norms are inevitably better, as they persuade users from *within deviant subcultures* to consume fewer drugs, consume them less frequently, and consume safer forms of them. For policymakers, the challenge becomes one of adjusting the social control mix so as to push these subcultures in the "least undesired direction" (Dorn and South 1990, 186). Such moderating of policy is easier said than done, particularly in the punishment-crazed era of the "Drug War," where citizens and government officials both widely believe that the only way to eradicate the drug "scourge" is to incarcerate it away. With nearly two million people in prison, a large percentage of whom are incarcerated for drug-related offenses (and with drug markets still thriving), nothing could be further from the truth.

Experience has shown that drug use, drug markets, and their attendant social ills decline first and foremost from within; order finally emerges not from external pressure but from an equilibrium that comes about internally (Gasset in McWilliams 1996). Crack, whose growing stigma has whisked demand right away from it, has proved this convincingly. Recent and significant declines in consumption and consumption-related violence have occurred, in large measure, independent of government policies and interference; crack is no longer "cool" to use, and people who consume it have been effectively ostracized. Yet rather than capitalizing on these self-moderating tendencies, policymakers continue to institute draconian measures, "beefing up drug squads and incarcerating people at unprecedented rates for increasingly petty . . .charges" (Curtis 1999, 20). Although such measures may accelerate the process of decline in the short term, in the long run they entrench the culture of opposition that allows drug markets and drug use to thrive in the first place (for these and other points, see Jacobs, 2000).

Note

1. The following paragraphs have been adapted with permission from *Robbing Drug Dealers: Violence Beyond the Law* (Aldine De Gruyter, 2000). ✦

18
The Social Construction of Drugs and Drug Use

Robert F. Meier

Gilbert Geis

Everybody knows, or thinks they know, what a drug is. Heroin, cocaine, marijuana, speed, and a host of other substances come to mind first. They are drugs because they have strong psychoactive (mood-altering) properties, limited medical utility, high addiction potential, and, most important, because they have been defined by the legal system as drugs. Of course, there are plenty of psychoactive, addictive substances with limited medical utility that are completely legal—alcohol, nicotine, and caffeine, to name just a few. How substances are defined and perceived is, like everything else, a social construction. Scholars who study drugs from a historical perspective seek to identify the social, economic, and political forces that have led some substances to be banned and others to be embraced. In this selection, Meier and Geis explore these important issues, examining contemporary drug policy and its historical antecedents.

Drug-taking has occurred for thousands of years. Some analysts suggest that the desire to get high is a fundamental human drive, not unlike hunger, thirst, or sex (Siegel 1989). Many of us seek to alter our moods on a daily basis, often through activities that have nothing to do with "taking drugs." Skydiving, listening to music, and vigorous exercise are three prominent examples. Many commentators suggest that there is nothing inherently wrong with altering one's consciousness, as

long as it does not interfere with the welfare of others. This is the classic libertarian argument voiced by John Stuart Mill some two hundred years ago: As long as an activity does not injure anyone else in the process of performing it, governments have no right to tell us we cannot do it—even if it brings harm to us. Government exists only to prevent the transfer of harm, not its self-infliction.

Such a position gets tricky when it comes to substance abuse. Drugs are addicting. They ruin lives. They undermine families and communities. They are costly, spawn predatory crime, and inspire violent drug markets. Their use, some suggest, leads to moral bankruptcy and ultimately the destruction of society itself. Such beliefs have fueled a multibillion-dollar drug war stretching over two decades. Yet, despite a massive influx of resources and manpower aimed at curtailing their use, drugs are cheaper, purer, and more available than ever before. Perhaps it would be better to treat drug markets and their attendant ills as a medical problem, where the primary goal is to reduce the harm associated with their use and distribution.

What Is a Drug?

To say that drug taking is an everyday experience for many Americans fails to give meaning and scope to the importance of drugs in the United States. The word "drug" is used in a number of different contexts and the meaning often changes with the speaker. To some, drugs are substances that cause addiction; to others, they are healing chemicals when prescribed by a medical specialist; to others, they are recreational substances to be used only in social situations; to others, they are sources of high income and substantial prestige; and to still others, they are nothing more than perfectly legal foods, such as coffee, cola drinks, and cigarettes. Who is right? They all are.

Erich Goode (1993:37) says that a drug is anything we *call* a drug. This simple statement reflects the current confusion regarding drugs. What is a drug? A chemical? Something that alters one's mood, alters one's body, or creates a habit? Drugs are not

146

just chemicals; everything is made up of chemicals. Drugs may alter one's moods, but there are plenty of things that alter our moods that are not commonly perceived as drugs, such as the effect a woman wearing a perfume has on some men, or the way a man walking in a certain way affects some women. In the same respect, drugs may alter one's body, but then so does a disease, fatty foods, or a bullet in the heart, for that matter. Some drugs can be habit-forming, but so can everything from a popular television show to a particular breakfast cereal to a favorite chair. Likewise, some drugs can be addicting, but not everything that is addicting is a drug; a husband and wife in a codependent relationship can be just as addicted to each other. The properties that are said to belong to drugs clearly belong to countless other things, some of which are more emotional than chemical. Consequently, the overall confusion regarding the nature of drugs and the meaning of the word "addiction" makes the very notion of "drugs" a broad subject impregnated with many different meanings.

So, Goode reasons, drugs are simply things we call drugs. The important question is why some things are called drugs while others are not. We commonly consider heroin a drug but often fail to give that same label to nicotine, even though both produce physical dependency with prolonged use. We usually consider marijuana to be a drug but do not always apply the same label to cola soft drinks, even though both are used recreationally and share a number of common properties. In some respects, the definition of "drug" is not nearly as important as its connotation. The social connotation of a term refers to how it is used in society, thus its context and meaning beyond the word's formal definition. The term "drug" contains two morally opposing connotations, each of which relates to how the drug is used: (1) a substance used in medicine, under controlled circumstances, to help people with a medical problem; or (2) a substance used illegally, under clandestine circumstances, with the effect of harm either to the user and/ or to others. The former connotation refers to a "normal" circumstance, the latter implies deviant drug use.

These connotations—one socially approved, the other disapproved—can be used for the very same drug, depending on the circumstances. Opiates are "good" if used under medically approved circumstances to help relieve pain in a patient. However, they are "bad" if used illegally outside a medical context and/or for physical self-gratification. To make matters even more confusing, the same individual can use drugs legally at one time and illegally at another. The medical profession has a high number of addicts compared to other professions. Medical professionals can administer a legal drug appropriately at one time, such as to a patient, and administer that same legal drug inappropriately at another time, such as to themselves to get high.

The connotations for some drugs are so powerful that they are considered deviant regardless of the medical context. Heroin, for example, is an extremely powerful painkiller that has not been approved for medical use in the United States despite that it is more effective than morphine, its medical cousin.

Contemporary concern over drugs is widespread and has often reached the level of public hysteria. The present "War on Drugs" has failed to take into account two points having to do with the overall context in which drug taking is found. First, public concern over drugs is extremely faddish. For instance, some drugs are considered to be "in" at certain times; at other times they are "out." That is, public concern about drugs focuses for a short time on a particular drug and then moves on to another, independent of any characteristic of the drug or the result of the public attention. In the 1960s, marijuana was of great concern. In the 1970s, there was much national discussion about methaqualone or "Quaaludes" and "Angel Dust." Heroin is always in vogue in drug discussions, but it appeared to be an epidemic in the 1970s. Through the mid-1980s, cocaine and heroin were the most talked about drugs. In the 1990s, it is crack cocaine, though there is some evidence that heroin is again surfacing as a drug of choice among many users. In each instance, the law has been perceived as not only the preferred method of intervention but the most effective as well—as long as, that is, the penalties are high enough.

Second, drug-taking behavior in general is so much a part of the behavioral patterns of people in the United States that it is inconceivable that all segments of the American public will abstain from all drug use. Legal drug use is so common that it is virtually unrecognized as drug use at all. Many people do not consider coffee, cigarettes, or soft drinks as drugs or substances containing drugs.

Drug taking is learned initially by most persons in the context of using legally available drugs. Taking such drugs is the first time most of us experience the association between chemical substances and desired end-results, such as reducing headaches, increasing bowel regularity, suppressing appetite, clearing stuffed noses, or keeping us awake at night. This connection is crucial because some of the desired end results involve certain moods that can be produced only by certain drugs, some of which are illegal.

Most of our concern with drugs has been focused on relatively few substances, most of which are against the law to use. These substances, including marijuana, heroin, cocaine, and methamphetamines, share two important characteristics: (1) we have defined them as a "problem," and (2) we believe the law is the best means to solve this problem. Both of these characteristics have been questioned, especially in recent years, and one source of that doubt is the role of all drugs in our daily lives and the ways in which illegal drugs are used.

Patterns of Drug Use

Many Americans wake up in the morning with one drug on their mind: coffee (in effect, caffeine). At work, they may feel the need for a mid-morning drug (aspirin) as pressures build, then another drug (alcohol) at lunch. A mid-afternoon break may involve a cigarette (nicotine) and a cola (more caffeine). Then cocktails (alcohol) before supper, with wine (more alcohol) perhaps during the meal. Then an after-dinner drink, followed by another cigarette (how many drugs is that for the day?). At bedtime, some people need pills to stay awake, others want pills to sleep. At different times during the day, we might have consumed a prescription medicine for an illness or taken some over-the-counter cold remedy to relieve congestion. The next day, the cycle starts all over again.

Drugs are connected to several features of American life (especially television commercials) that promote their use. First, as previously suggested, there is a close connection in the minds of most people between drugs and physical well-being. For example, we come to learn that various physical discomforts can be alleviated with drugs. So if you have a headache, take aspirin. Upset stomach? Take Alka-Seltzer. Menstrual cramps? Athletes foot? Pains of any kind? The solution to all these problems is the same: drugs.

Second, the use of a drug like alcohol is often associated with certain social and life events and just as often dissociated with any discussion of drugs, particularly among lay people. Even the oft used phrase "drugs and alcohol" suggests that alcohol is not a drug. Yet alcohol is a widely recognized drug, one that is frequently used in the United States. Although most people do not drink heavily, some people consume large amounts of alcohol with considerable regularity—as clearly evidenced by countless Alcoholics Anonymous meetings across the country. For many, though certainly not everyone, drinking is closely associated with particular social or religious occasions. The following are among those occasions that commonly require alcohol consumption:

- Birthdays
- New Year's Eve celebration
- Parties
- Celebrating a job or promotion
- Getting fired or demoted
- Birth of a baby
- Wake or funeral
- Sporting events
- Dates
- Religious ceremonies
- Graduations
- Weddings
- Meals

- Hospitalization
- Recovery
- Meetings with friends
- "Night-caps"
- Saturday nights

There are as many occasions for drinking as there are for greeting cards. And of course, some people don't need any occasion at all to drink.

Third, drug taking is also closely associated with the attainment of desired moods or psychological well-being. If we happen to have a mood that we do not like, we can alter it with drugs. Sometimes, we can generate a new mood (e.g., euphoria) or alter an existing one (e.g., depression) with the same drug. It is the mood-altering property of some drugs that has both attracted and repelled many potential users, thus adding to the ambivalence many people experience about drugs. An example of this ambivalence is reflected in a *Time* magazine cover story a few years before cocaine grabbed national headlines. The cover illustrated a martini glass filled with white powder with the caption, "Cocaine: A Drug with Status—and Menace." In the story, cocaine was described as "no more harmful than equally moderate doses of alcohol and marijuana, and infinitely less so than heroin" (Baum, 1996:142).

In these ways, drugs are seen by many as being very versatile as well as functional. Yet, regardless of specific pharmacological properties, some of the drugs that help create physical and mental well-being and contribute to the meaning of social and religious events are illegal. They are either closely regulated by law, to be dispensed only by a physician and pharmacist, or they are illegal under all circumstances. Yet, patterns of the use of illegal drugs do not differ in many respects from the use of legal drugs. In fact, there are many similarities between the consumption patterns we see with alcohol and those associated with such illegal drugs as marijuana, heroin, and cocaine.

Current Drug Policies and How We Got There

The overall policy in the United States with respect to drugs is one of legal repres-

sion. That is, the United States relies primarily on the criminal law. . . .

Drugs, Race, and Ethnicity

American awareness of drug taking, and the subsequent rise of a legal response to this behavior, began in the 1800s, at a time when many patent medicines contained what would later be considered illegal drugs, particularly opiate derivatives (Inciardi,1986: Chapter 1). These drugs, as well as raw opium, were widely used in the nineteenth century in the United States, particularly by women who took them for "female disorders." At that time, many of the drugs could be easily and legally purchased. Two important drugs are derived from opium—morphine, a potent drug that was isolated initially in 1804, and heroin, which is about three times more powerful than morphine, first isolated in 1898. In fact, heroin was originally manufactured by pharmaceutical chemists to be sold over drugstore counters as a cough remedy. Cocaine was first isolated in the late 1850s, but it did not become popular in the United States until the 1880s, when it was proclaimed a wonder drug and sold in wine products as a stimulant (Morgan, 1981:16).

Even the intravenous ingestion of morphine was not uncommon at the time. The 1897 edition of the Sears Roebuck catalog, for example, contained hypodermic kits that included a syringe, two needles, two vials, and a carrying case. The cost: $1.50. Extra needles were available for 25 cents or $2.75 per dozen (Inciardi, 1986:5–6).

As shocking as this may seem by today's anti-drug standards, it was not this kind of drug taking that was of major public concern. That concern was later motivated not by the drugs themselves but by the kinds of people who used them. Some of the initial laws against drugs were directed at particular groups of opiate users, such as the Chinese and Mexicans. Patterns of opiate use were quite different around the turn of the century than they are in present-day cities.

One of the earliest laws on opiates was passed in 1875 in the city of San Francisco. It prohibited the smoking of opium in then-popular opium dens (Brecher, 1972). The law was fueled by the public fear that Chinese men were luring white women into these dens for sexual purposes. Few Americans understood that opium dens occupied roughly the same position in Chinese culture as that of the saloon in white American culture. Although there were some opium addicts, most Chinese used opium infrequently and mainly on social occasions.

This first law displayed a number of characteristics that would be found in many of its successors: It prohibited the use of a particular drug associated with a particular group, without apparent regard to the physiological properties of the drug. In other words, it was not the physical effects of the opium or opiate derivatives that concerned lawmakers, but—in this case—the use of the drug by the Chinese.

The racial nature of the law was reflected in a number of its ingredients. The law ignored opium and other products made from opium that were used by whites in over-the-counter substances and in different forms (i.e., liquid, powder, or pill form). Instead, it focused on the smoking of opium in specially designated areas (i.e., opium dens). In other words, one could consume opium, but not by smoking and not in dens.

Federal drug legislation followed this city ordinance in 1888. As with the San Francisco city law, the federal legislation attempted to restrict opium trading and smoking. As with the city ordinance, the federal law did not prohibit the use of opium itself, only how it was consumed; nor did it prohibit the sale and use of opium in the form that involved most whites nor restrict the actions of whites engaged in opium trade.

There was apparently little concern with drug addiction in the late 1800s, at least no more than with drunkenness. But social awareness of addiction increased in the first quarter of the twentieth century. That concern eventually generated legislation, such as the Pure Food and Drug Act of 1906 and the Harrison Act of 1914. The intent of the Pure Food and Drug Act was to regulate the manufacture of patent medicines and over-the-counter drugs that contained heroin and cocaine, but the effect was to make such substances illegal. The Harrison Act was initially a revenue measure designed to make drug transactions a matter of public record so that taxes could be paid on them. But it became a major piece of legislation that defined narcotic drug taking as illegal (which included cocaine as a narcotic, although it is not a narcotic) and defined as criminals all those who took those drugs.

One might think that the intent of the legislation was to control addiction, but it was not merely the fear of addiction that fueled this legislation. Samuel Gompers, president of the American Federation of Labor from 1886 to 1924, reportedly used racist imagery to accelerate drug legislation. Herbert Hill writes:

> Gompers conjures up a terrible picture of how the Chinese entice little white boys and girls into becoming "opium fiends." Condemned to spend their days in the back of laundry rooms, these tiny lost souls would yield up their virgin bodies to their maniacal yellow captors. "What other crimes were committed in those dark fetid places," Gompers writes, "when these little innocent victims of the Chinamen's wiles were under the influence of the drug, are almost too horrible to imagine. . . .There are hundreds, aye, thousands, of our American girls and boys who have acquired this deathly habit and are doomed, hopelessly doomed, beyond the shadow of redemption." (Hill, 1973:51)

Subsequent legislation broadened the definition of illegal drugs to include marijuana and hashish. Because it does not dissolve in water, marijuana cannot be injected; it must be taken orally by smoking and eating, and its effects are variable and slow. As a result, research on the medical use of marijuana never materialized to the degree of research on the opiate drugs and cocaine. Even today, although there is reason to believe that marijuana might be useful in some limited medical situations, it does not have the cloak of medical legitimization worn by many other drugs. Noteworthy, though, was the passage of referendums in 1996 in both Arizona and California to allow marijuana use on a doctor's order to ease pain, such as that associated with cancer. Early in 1997, Attorney General Janet Reno announced that federal agents would withdraw drug-prescribing privileges and perhaps prosecute criminally physicians who "pushed" marijuana for their patients on the basis of the new California and Arizona statutes. Reno maintains that the referendums represented illegal intrusion by the states into a matter controlled by federal law.

As with other drugs that were subsequently made illegal, marijuana use was associated initially with marginal social groups. Large-scale use around the turn of the century was reported among migrant workers in the U.S. Southwest. Eventually, as marijuana users migrated to urban areas, its use spread to other urban immigrant groups, such as African Americans. Some occupational groups were closely associated with marijuana; jazz musicians, for example, reportedly had especially high rates of marijuana use through the 1920s and 1930s. Spurred by the vigorous campaign of Harry Anslinger, Commissioner of the Treasury Department's Bureau of Narcotics, marijuana legislation was not long in coming. The use of marijuana outside the mainstream of white, middle-class society, and the lobbying efforts of the Bureau of Narcotics resulted in the Marijuana Tax Act of 1937.

The racist motivation of this early legislation is unmistakable, as is the fear generated by certain drugs. Throughout the twentieth century, it has been the characteristics of users, not those of the drugs, that have been the better predictors of drug laws. . . .

References

Baum, Dan. 1996. *Smoke and Mirrors: The War on Drugs and the Politics of Failure.* Boston: Little Brown.

Brecher, Edward M. 1972. *Licit and Illicit Drugs.* Boston: Little Brown.

Goode, Erich. 1993. *Drugs in American Society,* 4th edition. New York: Knopf.

Hill, Herbert. 1973. "Anti-Oriental Agitation," *Society,* 10:43–54.

Inciardi, James. 1986. *The War on Drugs.* Palo Alto, CA: Mayfield.

Morgan, H. Wayne. 1981. *Drugs in America: A Social History, 1800–1980.* Syracuse, NY: Syracuse University Press.

19
Marijuana and Lifestyle

Exploring Tolerable Deviance

Andrew Hathaway

O*f all illicit drugs, marijuana is arguably the "least deviant." Recent surveys suggest that record numbers of people of all ages report using the substance. Recent Drug Use Forecasting data indicate that for the first time in several reporting cycles, the percentage of urban arrestees testing positive for marijuana is equal to or greater than those testing positive for cocaine, which was once the drug of choice for most. Marijuana is perceived to be safe, nonaddicting, and a fun way to pass the time. Previously associated with the 1960s counterculture of hippies and rebellion, marijuana has become as mainstream as alcohol or tobacco. Indeed, we seem to be approaching an era where tobacco and marijuana are undergoing something of a role reversal: Marijuana was recently legalized by several states for medicinal use, even as many of those same states were suing cigarette companies for hundreds of billions of dollars in health care compensation.*

Make no mistake, marijuana is not likely to be wholly decriminalized any time soon. Drug war rhetoric continues to be sufficiently powerful to maintain its "enemy" status. But it may not matter. "Weed" has been fully integrated into conventional lifestyles and has gained widespread acceptance from all manner of racial, ethnic, and socioeconomic groups. The adult middle-class users interviewed by Hathaway in this selection suggest that marijuana use has emerged as an important form of "tolerable deviance," rule-breaking committed not for shock value, rebellion, or escapism but for pragmatic reasons related to the successful accomplishment of a moral, upstanding life. The drug, Hathaway suggests,

complements a conventional lifestyle and is conducive to harmonious living with others. It permits relaxation, tranquility, enhanced clarity, expanded consciousness, release from worry, euphoria, opportunity for camaraderie, tolerance, more intimate personal relationships, pain relief, and heightened energy. None of these effects interfere with users' daily obligations. Quite the contrary, marijuana enhances their ability to manage them.

Attempts to sanction, punish, or otherwise deter such persons from smoking weed are likely to result in volatile adaptations that create significant instability, forcing users underground or inspiring them to switch to "harder" drugs. Hathaway concludes that the best way to "control" such "deviance" is to do nothing at all. Fighting tolerable deviance is counterproductive and destabilizes a situation that already is well under control.

. . . [W]hat does increasing social tolerance mean for today's marijuana consumers? Put otherwise, how does the drug fit into their everyday lives? And why do they use it? Regular use of such an illegal substance is bound to generate a distinctive lifestyle centered on the ways it is acquired, consumed, and kept secret. Accordingly, the majority of research on marijuana use—following Becker's (1955) thesis that such behavior is contingent on the failure of controls to prevent it—has been couched in a deviance framework that locates marijuana users within "a subculture organized around the particular deviant activity" (Becker 1963:31). . . .

The User's Outlook

In this study, I found that moving from a pattern of use that is dependent on one's level of participation with other users to one that is independently regulated marks a crucial transition in the marijuana user's relationship to the drug. Participation with other users remains a prominent feature of social life for many users. Unlike the rationalizations of certain other delinquent groups (see

Sykes and Matza 1957), however, their reasons for using the drug reflect their own personal lifestyles. Such justifications for deviance may be considered equally invalid by the legal system and by society at large, but they too originate in the flexibility of the normative system of society, to which, despite using marijuana, people are otherwise committed.

Today's middle-class marijuana users clearly do not advocate "a general repudiation of the entire conventional world" (Becker 1963:39). This does not mean that they share none of the same contempt for dominant values (which dictate the legitimate ways of altering consciousness while suppressing other ways) expressed by the subterranean cultures of the 1960s, for anticonformist values are often associated with social movements led by the educated youth of society. Brown et al. (1974) referred to this phenomenon as the *expressive student subculture*.

Following their school years and consequent immersion in this subculture, Brown et al. (1974) argued, young adults will stop using marijuana as a result of their commitment to nonstudent roles and becoming socially isolated from other users. Although it is plausible that many users have indeed emerged from this type of subculture, their continuing use of the drug does not necessarily suggest an inability to commit to conventional adult roles. Instead, adapting one's marijuana use to suit an otherwise conventional way of life appears to make the practice significant on a more personal level than that previously fostered through affiliation with marijuana using groups.

Despite this shift toward distinctly personal rationalizations for using the drug, it is apparent that for many people marijuana use still holds a measure of its former symbolic value; that is, it represents certain liberal ideals or attitudes that continue to shape their social outlooks. To illustrate, more than one half (57%) of those interviewed attributed to those who use marijuana a combination of qualities subsumed here under the concept of open-mindedness, or greater tolerance of the lifestyles and opinions of others. Further distinctions between users and nonusers centered on somewhat related concepts. Twenty percent of respondents, for example, stating fundamental differences between free-thinking individuals who question lawful authority and those who simply accept the limitations that are placed on their freedom, considered their marijuana use an expression of nonconformity and social rebellion. As one interviewee stated,

> Users have a real incentive to think about why the law is structured the way it is and where the law comes from; it is created by people, and there are reasons for people creating it. Motivation to look at the law differently can make people quite different; it dictates a different outlook on how the world is structured and why you can do some things and not others. The law-abiding citizen becomes something to be much more skeptical about.

Another 20% of those interviewed, noting the cross-cultural and cross-class proliferation of marijuana use, held a rather more vague conception of users sharing a universal experience. Some users expressed a clear preference for the company of other users. The majority (80%), however, reported being just as comfortable in the presence of nonusers, providing the latter are reciprocally accepting of a lifestyle that is different from their own. Whereas the preponderance of fellow users in their social networks certainly could be argued to possess a certain "narcissism of similarity" (Bellah et al. 1985:72), the differences among users made them less different from nonusers than subcultural theories of deviance tend to suggest. Although respondents often saw other users as the kind of people they could relate to with ease, this view had become somewhat modified over time.

Having come into contact with increasingly different types of marijuana users, more than one third (37%) reported that they were no longer sure of the differences that distinguish users from non-users. One woman responded, "I used to see differences, but not anymore—now the redneck kids smoke as much as anyone else. It's not just the hippie/bohemian thing anymore; people from all walks of life and all age groups use it." Another said, "Some smokers, I have lots in common with; others, I'm a complete world apart—smoking doesn't make us share anything." Thus, the ideological cohesion of marijuana users seems to have diminished with the diffusion of the practice to broader segments of society. The drug's symbolic value for users, having become relatively ambiguous over time, has been displaced by rather more pragmatic strategies for coping with everyday life. Accordingly, its connection with certain ideals is of less relevance to users today; the motivation to use marijuana is more likely a function of its applicability as part of an otherwise conventional lifestyle.

Data from this study indicate that people use marijuana because they consider its effects both pleasant and useful; the drug is an amenity that is believed to enhance their overall quality of life. Although respondents reported that, if they had to, they would be able to adjust to life without marijuana with little difficulty, many of them also suspected that they would feel somewhat deprived and would likely seek a substitute. A number of different activities, from physical exercise to meditation, were offered as possible alternatives for producing marijuana's desired effects. Such activities, however, were believed to approximate only certain aspects of the marijuana experience. Furthermore, the alternatives were considered to be largely inexpedient in relation to using the drug. According to one woman, for example,

> Real deep meditation is very much the same but it's a lot of work to get there and it doesn't last very long. . . . Through meditation, you have to take each step to build that up naturally; with marijuana, you jump to a similar level much faster.

Several of those interviewed also noted the expedience of using marijuana as opposed to alcohol and other drugs. One man said, "Having been a heavy drinker, I know that pot is a much more manageable drug." Another stated, "I haven't found anything else you can do on a regular basis and still maintain any semblance of normal." Consequently, 22 (73%) of the respondents considered marijuana unique in the benefits it provided. In the following sections, I examine these aspects of the marijuana experience, with special emphasis on how different people put these effects to use in meeting their own specific needs.

The Marijuana Experience

Although it is often classified as a depressant, there are important differences between cannabis (the Latin term for preparations made from the hemp plant, such as marijuana and hashish) and other narcotic drugs, such as cocaine and morphine, or sedatives, including alcohol and the barbiturates. Most important, tolerance or physiological dependence on cannabis is held to be rare; that is, a person discontinuing its use does not undergo symptoms of withdrawal (Ebin 1961). Burroughs defined cannabis as a consciousness-expanding drug that, unlike narcotic or sedative drugs, actually "increases awareness of surroundings and bodily processes" and further, "serves as a guide to psychic areas which can then be re-entered without it" (see Solomon 1966:443, 446). Noting a universal and biological motive, beginning in childhood, for people to periodically seek to alter "normal" waking consciousness, Weil (1972) discussed positive aspects of "stoned" thinking that have little to do with the use of mind-altering drugs. As mentioned above, the people in this study were generally aware that such experiences are achievable in other ways but, for the time being at least, considered marijuana use the most pragmatic and enjoyable means at their disposal.

Respondents' marijuana experiences largely corroborated the findings of past studies (e.g., Ames 1958); a sense of euphoria or well-being was almost invariable, with some reports of altered awareness and time perception. Nineteen (63%) of them described the experience as relaxing, or peaceful. In the words of one man, it was "like any dampening or calming of the synapses in the brain—you feel gentler." Conversely, however, nearly one half (47%) of them considered marijuana a stimulant for the mind, or body, or both. According to one woman, "I feel a little like a maple might feel in the spring when its sap starts to rise; more mentally and physically aware, sort of tingly and invigorated—a general feeling of wellbeing."

Marijuana's euphoric properties are thus experienced in ways that appear somewhat paradoxical. Accordingly, reasons for using the drug reflected a duality of purpose that was largely contingent on situational factors. Not only did different people use the drug for different reasons, but it was also used for different purposes at different times, thus taking on more than one specific role for the same individual. More than one quarter (27%) of the interviewees, citing psychological and environmental factors that altered individual experiences, had difficulty providing a single coherent description of its effects. In addition to the potency and amount of the drug consumed, variables reported to alter the nature of marijuana experiences included the following: one's prior mood or state of mind, one's personal knowledge or self-awareness regarding the drug's effects on the mind and body, and the social and physical setting in which the drug is used.

Overall, the user's stage of life, and the way of life this entailed, were found to be the primary forces determining how marijuana's effects were experienced and used. With experience people learn that, whether alone or with others, there is a right time and a wrong time for them to use the drug. These situations are largely contingent on lifestyle, with highly specified patterns of use tending to emerge through the demarcation of appropriate times and places. Such distinctions do not necessarily correspond with the separation between work and leisure in recreational drug use once noted by Veblen (1899). Marijuana is used as an accompaniment to work as well as leisure. The format of the following discussion reflects this functional duality, addressing in particular the perceived benefits and drawbacks of using the drug in both realms of everyday life.

Marijuana and Leisure

In a recent study (Erickson 1989), it was found that "for nearly all respondents, cannabis use was predominantly a social activity, engaged in with friends and partners during evenings, weekends, and other leisure time" (p. 179). In this study, people also reported using the drug primarily for leisure. Most of them, however, had patterns of consumption that were largely independent of other users. Although they often used marijuana in the company of others, social use of the drug was only one facet of their leisure time consumption. Only 11 (37%) of the interviewees found using marijuana especially conducive to social interactions, which suggests that its function as a social lubricant is largely taken for granted, and thus subsidiary to its more personal applications.

Marijuana's role in shaping social relations was clearly more important to some users than it was to others. For the latter, its social uses were hardly distinguishable from those of alcohol; both drugs provide a shared experience and relaxed atmosphere, granting participants greater freedom of expression with others. For some respondents, however, marijuana's influence extended well beyond transitory social gatherings, for it was believed to foster a unique kind of openness and mutual understanding in their personal, and most intimate, relationships. As one woman said,

> It allows me to be more honest with people I feel I can be honest with. This has helped me to build a really strong relationship with my husband; it has given us some really interesting space to bond in and be together. . . .Time and work can do the same thing, but dope seems to give you a secret back door to the human condition that gives you access to something fundamentally human and guides you so that you get to know yourself and other people in different ways.

This kind of understanding rarely carries over into users' relationships with nonusers, however, especially when the latter are outwardly opposed to the practice. Respondents commonly reported having to divide their social lives between nonusers and users—with whom they could truly be themselves—marijuana use constituting an immediate barrier to the depth of friendship possible with the former. Thus, whereas users often view the drug as having a positive influence on both social and intimate relationships, they also recognize its potential to disrupt, or prevent, any ongoing relationships with intolerant nonusers. Although these are generally not the kind of people users tend to associate with anyway, the mere existence of such a boundary imposes certain limitations on the range of social settings or outlets available to them. In view of the predominantly nonsocial use patterns found in this sample, in the rest of this section on leisure I look at ways of using marijuana that take place outside the social context.

Seventy percent of interviewees reported using marijuana mainly for relaxation, ordinarily at the end of the workday as a way to relieve stress and ultimately induce sleep. Although they generally agreed that there were numerous other ways to relax, using marijuana was preferred for its ability to immediately take one's focus off work-related concerns. As one person commented,

> It enables me to unwind before bed after a long day of work and helps me sleep without needing a couple of hours to do it—I don't have a couple of hours to unwind because I have to be up in 8 hours. I enjoy being able to come home and immediately relax in the 5 to 10 minutes it takes to roll a joint. The moment I smoke a joint my brain and all the worries of the day are turned off, and it's just the basic functions left behind; whatever I'm doing can become the primary focus for me.

As with alcohol, moderation in one's nighttime consumption is often recommended to avoid a morning hangover. This is a reportedly rare occurrence, however, that is noticeably less severe than that associated with a night of drinking. According to one respondent, "Dope will never prevent me from getting up in the morning and going to work; alcohol will."

Another source of concern was the possibility of having to cope in a situation where a certain amount of "straight" composure may be necessary, such as operating a motor vehicle or interacting in public. In general, as there were no reports of situations arising in which they had been unable to cope, it appears that the ability to maintain normal standards of composure while high is closely related to experience, that is, the range of different situations that one has experienced, or allowed oneself to experience, while under the influence of the drug. The next goal of this work is to clarify the concept of euphoria in describing certain aspects of the marijuana experience.

In most cases, euphoria is experienced as a stimulation of the senses. A stimulant by definition rouses one to activity, and this is precisely what the drug appears to do in certain circumstances. Notwithstanding the paradoxical implications of this claim, the experience may also be described as a heightened awareness, or consciousness, of one's surroundings. As this can occur on both a mental and a physical level, I discuss each of these. Almost one half (43%) of the respondents described marijuana's effects as heightened mental awareness, which was considered useful for leisure because it made activities more interesting and thus more enjoyable. Moreover, they reported feeling better about the world and their immediate surroundings, approaching things with a fascination that seemed almost childlike. One person commented,

> It brightens my mood; I have a great time and see the fun stuff in the world. It helps me remember to appreciate food, colors, beautiful things. . . .You get so blase to things in the real world. It's like a reeducation; dope says, "Whoa, wait a minute—this is delicious!"

This quote reveals some of the difficulty encountered in attempting to distinguish between marijuana's various effects on the mind and body; discussion of one invariably leads into discussion of the other. It is sufficient here to note that the drug is commonly credited with enhancing the full spectrum of sensory pleasures. As marijuana's work-related uses will provide more concrete examples of how people make use of its influence on their mental capacities, further discussion of this topic is reserved for the final section.

Returning to marijuana's effect on the body, nearly one half (43%) of interviewees reported increased levels of physical awareness when using the drug. This effect not only made different forms of sensory stimulation more pleasurable, but some also reported prolonged bursts of energy, enabling them to pursue physically demanding leisure activities with greater vigor than they would otherwise. Others extolled marijuana's analgesic properties, which gave them relief from a wide range of physical complaints. One sufferer of chronic back pain reported using marijuana as an integral part of her daily regimen of self-directed therapy. She said,

My body holds a lot of tension and trying to live with less body tension is pretty important to me right now. . . .It's helpful in getting my body to remember how to relax. In giving me deep, involved relaxation for stretching. . . .I get a specific sense of how my hips are constructed and can tell where the misalignment occurs at various parts of my body. I can really push the limits of my awareness of how my body is put together—what affects what, where my problems are, and what I need to do to change it.

Once again, people learned to make practical use of marijuana's effects as a result of their cumulative experiences with the drug. When used as a tool to enhance one's leisure time, marijuana's range of applications is limited mainly by situational constraints stemming from perceptions of social propriety and the user's ability to cope in a given situation. The right and wrong times to use the drug clearly differ from one individual to the next. Whereas a few respondents indicated that marijuana consumption often limited their physical capabilities, making them more reclusive and less motivated to do different things; just the opposite effect was reported by most. According to one young man,

To sit in one spot and get stoned is a complete waste. I need to do something, to see and feed my brain and suck up as much as I can. I feel very confined when I have to stay in one spot; I always try to do something outside where I'm free to move.

The final topic of this section deals with another of marijuana's commonly reported effects on the mind. In some ways, it closely resembles the aforementioned property of enhanced mental awareness of one's self or one's surroundings. In other ways it differs, however, in that it centers more directly on the possibility of gaining a whole new outlook, or perspective, while under the drug's influence. Furthermore, this effect constitutes one of marijuana's more versatile attributes, for the influence is often claimed to carry over beyond the drug-induced state, providing the user with a different way of viewing the world that can be useful in many different areas of his or her life.

One half of those interviewed reported that they gained a different outlook on life as a result of using marijuana. For some, the change in perspective provided little more than escape from mundane reality. Accordingly, two people commented, "It opens windows that aren't open all the time. . . .It's just a different way of looking at things, especially as you get older; being inside your brain for that long gets boring" and

It allows me to step back a little bit and look at the world in a little more colorful light, or warped perspective, instead of taking it so seriously. It lets my sense of humor come out instead of getting intense and overwrought about things.

Others, stressing the drug's value for their work as well as their leisure, seemed to take this influence far more seriously. Consequently, others said,

It's like a different part of my personality or mental thought, which doesn't seem to have boundaries, opens up and I'm able to see things in abstract, or from a different dimension. It has made me a stronger person and far clearer in how I deal with situations and work. I'm able to look at points from a different, abstract point of view, not just top to bottom.

It opens a space in my head to think about things outside of the way I would normally think about them; it gives new significance and a new angle to things. These observations tend to be borne out when I'm not stoned; they tend to be right. It has allowed me to think about things that are important to my career.

Thus, for many users, the term *escapism* poorly describes the role of marijuana in their lives. It may give them a different slant on reality, but the insights it provides are perceived as being closely linked to the real world and hence useful for solving everyday kinds of problems. The following section explores the ways people use marijuana for work, and some of the situations and types of work in which they tend to abstain from using the drug.

Marijuana and Work

Forty percent of the sample reported using marijuana at least occasionally while actually performing their jobs. Not surprisingly, these were all freelance and after-hours workers who are not required to observe the norms of the conventional work world, which ordinarily prohibit the use of illicit drugs both on and off the job. Before examining marijuana's work-related benefits for those whose consumption is necessarily restricted to their hours of leisure, I look at some of the ways these on-the-job users use the drug in carrying out their daily work.

Their responses indicated that they used marijuana frequently, albeit selectively, for a wide range of occupational tasks. As noted with leisure, the drug's different uses, taken together, present a paradox. In the words of one respondent, using the drug gave her "a strange ability to focus and not focus at the same time; you can focus but it's on your own terms." Whereas marijuana was commonly used to take the user's mind off work so as to enhance his or her enjoyment of leisure time, it was also used at work for jobs demanding prolonged concentration, or attention to meticulous details. Whether tasks were highly specialized, or just plain monotonous, a number of respondents reported that marijuana provided them with the patience and precision they required to reach their utmost working potential. According to one person, "It allows me to attain perfection in detailed computer work, to take the extra time in the tedious processing of final details to get exactly what I want."

Not everybody is willing and able to use the drug in this way, however. Respondents varied widely in the extent to which they found marijuana applicable to their daily work. Whereas some users regularly use the drug as a way to enhance job performance and productivity, for others, as one man put it, "grass and responsibility never enter the same realm." Some people, having found that marijuana often took their focus away from the task at hand, preferred not to use it during the more technical stages of their work. Others seemed to have developed a greater sense of control over the drug. An interior designer and art consultant suggested that she had learned to create the conditions necessary for isolating and exploiting the properties she found useful. She said,

> I like to have my day figured out and be focused first. . . .Once I have my day figured out, I can have a toke, go out to the studio and focus on exactly what I have to do for hours and hours. Everything has a flow. If it doesn't, I'll stop, have a coffee and a toke and go back to work, [asking myself] now do you have the flow—now is the perspective better?

As stated earlier, it is the user's application of a perspective seen to be outside his or her usual point of view that seems particularly useful. Being able to look at things differently reportedly gave users a better understanding of how they fit together, allowing them to see nuances they might otherwise miss, or home in on certain things while disregarding those of lesser importance. Marijuana was used quite selectively for highly interpretive types of work as part of the process of "getting an outline down" or for facilitating the transition between projects or different stages of a project. Two interviewees (one a writer, the other an academic researcher) said, "I often get stoned the day before I write a story. It helps me figure out what's important and interesting in the story; things that hadn't seemed important can become crucial to the whole story" and

> My first time going over the data, it allows me to juggle more data and consider more aspects of the data. I take notes and chase them down later when I'm straight. . . .I may not smoke for 2 weeks

during the technical phase of a project, but the first thing I do when the project ends is smoke a joint. It helps me to reset the registers to zero, clear my mind, and get on with the interpretation.

For the majority of those interviewed, however, the drug was still further removed from working life. Its perceived benefits had more to do with how the user's leisure-time consumption affected his or her temperament in general and how this was seen as useful in dealing with other people and the difficult situations commonly encountered while at work. Respondents typically reported that using marijuana made them calmer, more tolerant people. For one physiotherapist and rehabilitation practitioner, it granted the special patience and empathy he required for effectively tending to the needs of his clients. He stated,

For the most part, when I'm putting people through physical routines, I'm motivating them. If I was all tense and motivated, I would be too pushy and it would become resistive. It gives me a place in myself where I can sit back and watch what I'm doing and not take everything personally, which makes me realize that people aren't really resisting. I get a lot better results from my ability to relax and let go of those frustrations at the end of the day.

In various terms, the sample described the drug as providing "the extra trimming in life," a sense of humor, or serenity of mind, transcending all commonly accepted boundaries between work and leisure. As the following responses suggest, people often feel the need to get away from their usual way of looking at things; their way of accomplishing this, using marijuana, just seemed better suited to their lifestyles than other possible ways: "Drugs, as something that gets you out of it, are not necessarily ingested. Everybody needs something that gets them out of their normal world, be it television, sports, whatever" and

There are other activities that will allow me to balance my aggressive reactions to this world with what I need to do to survive and live in it. Most of them require so much time, though. . . .Rather than hav-

ing to go out and do insane things on a regular basis, marijuana allows me to do it in a very gentle, small way every day.

Summary

Exploring marijuana's different uses showed its range of applications to be highly diversified, varying from one user to the next and largely contingent on the extent to which use of the drug was considered amenable to the user's particular way of life. In more general terms, the motivations behind people's patterns of use were found to originate in their common and basic need to effectively meet and manage the challenges of daily living. Viewed as noncompulsive, adaptable behavior, the recreational use of marijuana takes on new meaning as a viable, indeed positive, element of lifestyle. Accordingly, the primary aim of this article was to elucidate the role of the drug in the everyday lives of users, focusing in particular on people's reported patterns of marijuana use and the ways they explain and justify them. . . .

References

Ames, F. 1958. "A Clinical and Metabolic Study of Acute Intoxication With Cannabis Sativa and Its Role in the Model Psychoses." *Journal of Mental Science* 104:972.

Becker, H. S. 1955. "Marijuana Use and Social Control." *Social Problems* 3:35–44.

———. 1963. *Outsiders: Studies in the Sociology of Deviance.* New York: Free Press.

———. 1967. "History, Culture and Subjective Experiences: An Exploration of the Social Basis of Drug-Induced Experiences." *Journal of Health and Social Behavior* 8(September):163–176.

Bellah, R. N., R. Madsen, W. A. Sullivan, A. Swidler, and S. M. Tipton. 1985. *Habits of the Heart: Individualism and Commitment in American Life.* Berkeley: University of California Press.

Brown, J. W., D. Glaser, E. Waxer, and G. Geis. 1974. "Turning Off: Cessation of Marijuana Use After College." *Social Problems* 21:527–538.

Ebin, D., ed. 1961. *The Drug Experience.* New York: Orion Press.

Erickson, P. G. 1989. "Living With Prohibition: Regular Cannabis Users, Legal Sanctions, and Informal Controls." *The International Journal of the Addictions* 24(3):175–188.

Solomon, D. 1966. *The Marijuana Papers*. New York: New American Library.

Sykes, G. M. and D. Matza. 1957. "Techniques of Neutralization: A Theory of Delinquency." *American Sociological Review* 6(December):664–670.

Veblen, T. 1899. *The Theory of the Leisure Class*. New York: B. W. Heubsch.

Weil, A. 1972. *The Natural Mind: A New Way of Looking at Drugs and the Higher Consciousness*. Boston: Houghton Mifflin.

I acknowledge the assistance of the editors of *Deviant Behavior* and Bob Stebbins for his comments on drafts of this article.

20

'I Take Care of My Kids'

Mothering Practices of Substance-Abusing Women

Phyllis L. Baker

Amy Carson

There are few worse villains in contemporary America than the drug-abusing mother. Popular perception—fueled by inflammatory media images of children physically ignored and emotionally neglected, children whose Christmas toys are sold for drugs, children forced into prostitution to feed their mother's voracious drug habit—have convinced the public that drug-using moms are the worst of the worst. Such images fuel a punitive discourse in which politicians and citizens alike call for the harshest possible treatment; incarceration and the forceful removal of children from their homes figure prominently.

Yet if one were to go to the women themselves, and ask them what it is they do and why they do it, an altogether different story might emerge. Indeed, drug-using mothers insist that they are good moms who fulfill their children's basic needs, protect them from the evils of the streets, and maintain a functional household. Drugs, these women contend, don't interfere with mothering but complement it. Their children, they claim, are as well-adjusted as any child growing up in an affluent, suburban home.

Critics justifiably respond that such claims are bogus, the appeals of desperate addicts in chronic denial who seek to absolve themselves of responsibility for reprehensible conduct. In the absence of actually seeing these mothers do what it is they talk about, we will never know. What does become clear from this selection, however, is that the picture may not be as

lopsided as so many of us are led to believe; even women caught in the throes of chronic addiction can be caring, committed, capable, and compassionate. Policies geared to protect children from their substance-abusing mothers might be better if focused less on harsh punishment and more on the cultivation of skills that permit drug use and mothering to coexist peacefully.

Research on substance abuse indicates that there are a number of characteristics unique to women. Women have a different path to addiction that requires smaller quantities of alcohol and drugs but rapidly progresses to addiction and other related health problems (Grella 1996). Women who abuse substances also report a higher incidence of anxiety, depression, and other psychiatric disorders than do men (Benishek et al. 1992). Rape and other sexual assault characterize the history of many substance-abusing women (Hanke and Faupel 1993). Women also report feelings of guilt and shame related to their drug abuse and the impact of their addiction on their families (Rosenbaum 1979). Serious, life-threatening illnesses and diseases can compromise the health status of substance-abusing women.[1] In short, substance-abusing women live in a complex social and psychological environment. What does it mean to be a substance-abusing woman and a mother?

Substance-abusing women, who also take on the responsibilities of motherhood, experience increased problems because of the demands placed on them by the contemporary ideology of mothering. Notions about mothering in the United States are based on a white, middle-class, heterosexual standard that places the biological mother as the sole parent to deliver constant care and attention to her children (Hays 1996; Hill Collins 1994; McMahon 1995; Nakano Glenn, Chang, and Forcey 1994). Although this ideology tells us that mothering is constituted by women's biological role in reproduction, a sociological perspective dictates that mothering should be seen as a social construct (Hays 1996;

Nakano Glenn, Chang, and Forcey 1994). It was not until late modernity that motherhood evolved as a legal institution, became normalized, and brought with it notions of "good" and "bad" mothering as cultural boundaries for women (Smart 1996). Hays noted that

> the model of the white, native-born middle class has long been, and continues to be, the most powerful, visible, and self-consciously articulated, while the child-rearing ideas of new immigrant groups, slaves, American Indians, and the poor and working classes have received relatively little positive press. (1996, 21)

Critics of this contemporary ideology of mothering agree that the boundaries of "appropriate" mothering practices are demanding, conflicting, and unattainable. Hays argued that the contemporary ideology of mothering dictates that mothers follow the principles of "intensive mothering," a process that is "child centered, expert guided, emotionally absorbing, labor intensive, and financially expensive" (1996, 8). The socially constructed definition of mothering requires limitless amounts of the mother's monetary and emotional resources to be directed toward the fulfillment of all the child's needs and desires, making her own needs secondary to those of her children (Hays 1996; McMahon 1995; Smart 1996).

The conventional ideology of mothering continues to be based on a model of white families, who enjoy a relatively greater degree of economic security and racial privilege (Hill Collins 1994); it fails to represent or recognize other ways of mothering that coexist with the dominant model. Blum and Deussen observed "alternative" practices in which Black mothers resisted assumptions that a deserving mother must be singularly and exclusively present and that legal marriage is required for good mothering (1996, 208). Latina immigrant domestic workers who leave their children to come to the United States for work build alternate constructions of motherhood that contradict that of the United States' white and middle class model (Hondagneu-Sotelo and Avila 1997). Lewin showed how lesbian mothers resist the cultural opposition between "les-

bian" and "mother" but experience these two dimensions of their identity as competing and interfering (1994, 343). Thus, any woman who is not white, middle-class, married, and heterosexual is a bad mother.

Substance-abusing mothers have been stigmatized, labeled as unfit, and targeted for disapproval due to their failure to meet cultural standards for mothering. Condemnation of substance-abusing mothering is common in most of the studies about them that research the effects of alcohol and illegal drug use on the fetus and the children (Chazotte, Youchah, and Comerford Freda 1995; Lawton Hawley et al. 1995), the effects of treatment on continued use (Smith et al. 1992), the predictive factors for continued use (Richman, Rospenda, and Kelley 1995), and/or drug taking behaviors and lifestyles (Grant Higgins, Hendel Clough, and Wallerstedt 1995). Regardless of topic, these traditional studies reinforce the notion that substance-abusing women are bad mothers because they accept the dominant discourse on mothering. Recent disapproval is particularly evident in the construction of crack mothers, particularly African American and Latina mothers, as the epitome of maternal villains who actively and permanently damage their offspring (McNeil and Litt 1992, 31). These constructions of substance-abusing mothers have led to the development of a "bio-underclass" (McNeil and Litt 1992) who become victims of a cultural captivation with the "criminalization of pregnancy." There is such reproach for substance-abusing mothers that a platform for fetal rights has resulted in punitive policies and legislation enhancing the ability of prosecutors to charge substance-abusing, pregnant women (mostly minority and low-income women) with offenses ranging from drug trafficking to homicide (Albertson Fineman 1995; Litt and McNeil 1997; Young 1994). These mothers are incarcerated, separated from their newborns, and lose custody of their children. Within a very punitive social, political, and economic climate, any substance abusing woman is invariably a "bad" mother, for it is assumed that the search for, and the use of, substances makes her inattentive, self-indulgent, and negligent rather than exclusively mindful of her children's needs (Ettorre 1992).

Missing from the extant literature is research in which substance-abusing mothers speak for themselves, explaining their visions of a "good" mother, and how they believe they fit into that vision. Seventeen substance-abusing mothers in residence at a substance-abuse treatment facility were directly and intimately interviewed about their lives and children to explore their cultural knowledge about mothering and their observations of their own mothering practices. The data presented in this article are unique in providing the participants' detailed perceptions of their mothering practices. Contrary to the conclusions of most of the literature on substance abusing mothers, these women describe themselves as caring and committed moms.

Methodology

An interpretive and qualitative methodology aims to acquire the member's perspective and to report it without imposing an outsider's point of view (Neuman 1994; Sands and McClelland 1994). This differs from the vast majority of research on substance abuse that has been largely acquired through studies dominated by male researchers and male participants (Ettorre 1992), typically using quantitative methods such as cross-sectional surveys, institutionally based surveys, and rigorous experimental models. Although large-scale, quantitative research generates useful data, it fails to take into account the feelings, strengths, behaviors, and experiences of the participant. The interpretive and qualitative study reported here transgresses the boundaries of traditional methodologies by focusing on what substance-abusing women had to say about their lives.

To collect substance-abusing mother's voices, I engaged in participant observation and gave semistructured interviews at "A Place to Be,"[2] a comprehensive residential substance-abuse treatment program for pregnant women and women with children. The program design attempts to meet the special needs of pregnant women and women with child care responsibilities who might otherwise be denied admission into a traditional treatment program. During participant observation at several treatment groups, I made appointments with women willing to be interviewed. Once we agreed upon a suitable date and time, 17 on-site semistructured interviews were recorded. Only 15 of the interviews were later transcribed because the tape recorder malfunctioned during 2 interviews.

The interviewing environment allowed for participants to raise topics and elaborate on issues that they deemed pertinent, creating a situation for discovery of new categories of meaning. The one- to two-hour interviews focused on the residents' biographical experiences as organized around a single moment in their lives—residency in the residential treatment program. The final interview guide I developed contained 11 general topics: demographic (age, race, children, drug of choice, stage of treatment, clean date), substance-abuse story, history of previous treatment programs, mothering, drug experiences, relapse, comparison of life stages, involvement in welfare, criminal justice, child protective services, and view of future. Although mothering was not included as a topic on the initial interview guide, it soon emerged as central to the participants' lives and, therefore, became central to the data collection and analysis. Experience with, and evaluation of, treatment modes; conditions present during the etiology of use; and lifestyle changes resulting from use also emerged as important themes during the interviews. To determine patterns in the data regarding the participants' views of their mothering, I undertook a systematic content analysis of the interview transcripts and participant observation field notes. Essential to the interviewing environment was my commitment to place the women's accounts at the center of analysis.

In addition to the uniqueness of the research design, the participants were also unique. Of the study sample, 15 of the women were white and 2 were African American. The women ranged in age from 20 years to 41 years. I came to consider most of them poor or working-class because subsistence concerns dominated their lives and they were often at the mercy of the criminal justice, welfare, and human service bureaucracies. Women from more privileged classes are not as vulnerable to state intervention. Crack-cocaine and crystal methamphetamine were the drugs of choice for 14 women, alcohol was the drug of choice for 2 women, and painkillers were drugs of choice for 1 woman. The mothers addicted to crack or crystal looked sickly and had far worse problems with child protective services and the criminal justice system.

"A Place to Be" was an uncommon type of substance-abuse treatment center because residents were allowed to have their children with them while in treatment and because the center mandated attendance at parenting classes. Consequently, I assume some social desirability effects in how the respondents talked about and viewed their mothering practices. Furthermore, the sample is unique because the women self-selected for the interviews. Because of the self-selection factor and the qualitative nature of the research design, the findings are not representative of all substance-abusing women whether they be street addicts, middle-class housewives, or even working-class women in treatment at "A Place to Be." Nevertheless, the data offer us insight into a social reality about which social scientists, policy makers, and laypeople have made assumptions without much depth and understanding. Important to note before turning to the findings is that this study focuses on women's stories about their mothering practices and not on their actual practices.

Findings

Regardless of variation among the respondents, motherhood emerged as a fundamental part of their lives. As they told stories about themselves as mothers, the women revealed a picture of a complex existence embroiled in contradictions about the quality of their mothering practices. When their drug-using lifestyle exposed their children to danger; when they were physically, financially, and emotionally unavailable for their children; and when they did not keep their children's behavior under control, they viewed themselves as bad mothers. In contrast, they viewed themselves as good mothers when they protected their children from a harmful lifestyle, fulfilled what they saw as their children's practical needs, and were able to cope with everyday life stresses without losing their tempers. Partner relationships and physical punishments were notably absent as themes in the interviews. This is surprising because the extant literature often cites violence as an outcome of stimulant use and partner relationships as creating and facilitating women's drug use. My guess is that they did not mention these topics in any depth because their treatment program focused on the inappropriateness of physical punishment and on the importance of self-determination rather than dependency in intimate relationships.[3] The working-class mothers in this study defined good and bad mothering practices similarly to those McMahon described in *Engendering Motherhood* (1995); that is, they defined good and bad mothering in the same ways as "typical" working-class women. These women's commitments to their children, their desires to be "intensive" mothers, and their ambivalence about the quality of their mothering were consistent throughout the interviews.

Bad Mothering Practices

A number of studies have documented the presence of parenting problems among substance-abusing parents and the risks to children posed by parental substance use. These include findings that parents who have used drugs may have difficulty providing a safe environment for their children (Bijur et al. 1992); families of drug users may lack bonding and attachment (Kumpfer and Turner 1990–1991); the parent's need to acquire drugs or alcohol may at times supersede the child's need for love, attention, supervision, food, and clothing (Inciardi, Lockwood, and Pottieger 1993). In the same way, the mothers in this study sometimes characterized themselves as victimizing their children. The women recognized and felt guilty about the times in which they failed to be good mothers. These descriptions reveal ways substance-abusing mothers accepted the constraints of the dominant ideology of good mothering and recognized themselves as bad mothers.

Exposing to Danger. The women often talked about exposing their children to a dangerous lifestyle, including perinatal abuse of illegal substances. Vicki described her perinatal substance abuse:

> I smoked a lot of pot when I was pregnant with my daughter, and I did cocaine very excessively . . .I mean, I did it every day, and then would sleep for three or four days. My daughter was born addicted. When I was going to the hospital to have my daughter, I was so high, so high. I kept snorting, doing lines all day thinking the pain would go away.

Vicki was in the minority. Most of the women attempted to reduce or eliminate use during pregnancy. Lola, a 29-year-old white mother of one, started drinking alcohol in third grade and taking illegal substances in seventh grade. "A Place to Be" was her first treatment attempt. She reduced her use while pregnant and explained, "I didn't know I was pregnant for five months. So when I found out, I tried to quit using. I still did use, just not as much. Seth [my son] was born positive anyway." Naomi, a 41-year-old white mother of three used methamphetamine and cocaine since she was 15 years old and had been through six treatment programs. Like Lola, she attempted to quit using while pregnant and stayed clean for five months. But she said that she eventually "went on a five-day roll and used an ounce and a half of cocaine." Lola and Naomi, like most of the mothers I interviewed, attempted to reduce their substance abuse while pregnant and clearly demonstrated through those efforts that they believed perinatal use of harmful substances was a sign of a bad mom.

More generally, these women recognized their drug-abusing lifestyle as dangerous to their children. For instance, Natasha, a 23-year-old white mother of three children, who starting using at age 13 and had been through two other treatment programs, spoke of her lifestyle in which "we did a lot of drinking beer and fighting and more fights and it was just terrible. It was a very bad life-style for Tia [her daughter] to be in. We always had fights and big parties." Similarly, Carol reported that her children saw her husband run her over with a car. At other times they "watched him kick me up and down the hallways of our house. It was real abusive." Carol was a 31-year-old white mother of five children who had used illegal substances since she was 18 years old. Her drug of choice was methamphetamine, and she had been through three other treatment programs.

In addition to viewing violence in the drug lifestyle, some of the children were direct victims of it. Carol discussed being unaware or unable to do anything about sexual and physical abuse of her children as a characteristic of a bad mother. Her second husband sexually and physically abused all her children. He was sentenced to 61 years in prison for the assaults. He passed on genital herpes to Carol's daughter. Carol wished she could have prevented this abuse from happening to her children.

Besides violence, the substance-abusing mothers acknowledged other problems associated with their lifestyle. Nettie, a 30-year-old white mother of three children was addicted to methamphetamine for 14 years and now in her first treatment program said that there would be "dirty needles and broken needles in the garbage, and my kids seen that." Linda spoke about using with her daughter: "My daughter [11 years old] wanted to experiment with it [marijuana] one night when I was drinking and using, and I let her be in the room while it was going on, and I shouldn't have." She was a 28-year-old white mother of three children, a polydrug user, and had been in seven treatment programs. Linda told a story about a time when she was drunk and had an accident in which she hit five cars, a telephone pole, and injured someone while her baby daughter was in the car.

Being Physically, Financially, and Emotionally Unavailable. Another theme in the women's talk about their bad parenting practices centered on their inability to be available physically, financially, or emotionally. While abusing substances, many women left their children with relatives, baby-sitters, or alone. Several women also spoke about spending money on drugs, which left their children without any luxuries and, sometimes, without necessities. Finally, some women acknowledged that their substance use left them emotionally inaccessible for their children. Ultimately, then, the residents' unavailability to their children while using substances was seen as another bad mothering practice.

Ullie is a good example of someone who described behavior consistent with much of the extant literature on crack-cocaine users (Inciardi, Lockwood, and Pottieger 1993; Mahan 1996; Taylor 1993). Ullie was a 24-year-old African American pregnant mother of five children who started smoking crack-cocaine when she was 17 years old. She had been through five treatment programs for substance abuse. In the following quote, Ullie describes ways in which she was physically unavailable for her children:

> It was sick behavior. Staying out all night leaving kids with my mom when I know she has to go to work, taking her car, taking my kids on drug runs, leaving them in the car while I went into a dope house to smoke.

Vicki reported behaviors that she perceived as bad for her children, saying,

> I was never, never responsible because I could leave my kids with my grandma and take off for three days or four days or whenever I felt the need to. I would just skip on, and I knew they would be taken care of.

A 25-year-old white mother of three children, a poly-substance abuser since she was 12 years old and in her third treatment program, Greta described how she would leave her kids when she abused illegal substances.

> I ended up getting into it so much at work that I left my children at the baby-sitter, and I left for the weekend. My husband had to go pick them up. And after that I just, I left the house. It controlled my life. I forgot about my kids. I forgot about my husband. I forgot about everything. I quit my job. We [my friends and I] went on road trips; we slept in cars, slept at parks;

we slept on the side of the road on the freeway.

Greta left her children for months while she immersed herself into a crack-abusing lifestyle. Each of these women described a lifestyle that was so compelling and addicting that they were willing to leave their children in order to pursue it.

A majority of the residents also spoke about their inability to financially take care of their children. Quinne said that

> Margaret [my daughter] was the one that suffered from me using because she didn't get anything extra. She didn't get anything that every little girl needs. She's 10 years old. She didn't get to go to the mall with me on Saturdays and spend money on the movies or games or little pink dresses because I was spending all that money on myself and that was not fair to her.

Quinne was a 30-year-old white mother of one who had been smoking crack cocaine since she was 20 years old. "A Place to Be" was her first treatment program. Ullie said that she would take the welfare check meant for her children and spend it on herself. She commented, "I was spending and getting so high. I would wake up the next day knowing I spent $400. That can be really frustrating, knowing that I had to go through the whole month with nothing." Micah was a 29-year-old white mother of two children. Her drug of choice was methamphetamine, which she had been using since she was 15 years old. Micah was in her fourth treatment program. Like Ullie and Quinne, she also felt guilty because she took a lot of things away from her children. Micah mentioned that she did not buy her children things very often but that when she did, she would often take them back and get money to buy drugs.

Finally, the women described themselves as emotionally unavailable for their children. The words "I was not there for them" were spoken often by the residents during the interviews. For instance, Carol said, "They did not have me there a lot of the times." Vicki claimed that her children were emotionally abused because she was gone so much of the time. Candie, a 24 year-old white pregnant mother of three children, who had used methamphetamine since she was 16 years old and was in her second treatment program, admitted that she was inaccessible for her baby from the time she got home from giving birth at the hospital. Candie disclosed,

I started [using] the day I got out of the hospital. It got way crazy. I was up for four or five days, and then I would sleep for a couple. I also had postpartum depression really bad; so, from the beginning I was just out of my mind. I did not know what was going on.

Similarly, Naomi explained,

There was a lot of expanses of time that I cannot remember my son's childhood. I know that I was *there*. I know I did not physically abuse him, but I'm sure that I neglected him a lot. I did not go to his Little League games or his school programs. I could not because I was high. I *thought* I was taking care of his emotional needs, but I'm sure I wasn't.

These women attested to their emotional unavailability for their children and considered their emotional, financial, and physical unavailability as bad mothering practices.

Lacking Control Over Children. As a final example of a bad mothering practice, the women frequently talked about discipline problems with their children as a primary characteristic of a problematic parenting style. Ullie described her lack of control: "I tend to let my children play the parenting role. Sometimes I tend to do what they want instead of taking control, instead of letting them know that I'm the mother." Katie, a 22-year-old white mother of two children, a methamphetamine user for 14 years, and in her second treatment program, responded to a question about her mothering by saying that she was a young mom and that "we're [my son and I] more like friends than mother and son. I let him walk on me a lot. He gets away with a lot." In another case, Quinne reported that her daughter "took big advantage of me when she knew that I was high, and she knew my attitude change, so she knew that all I wanted to do was be alone." At these times, Quinne's daughter

would ask for things and to go places because she knew her mom would say yes.

Part of the reason that these women lacked control over their children, some mothers would tell me, is because they would send their children away from them when they did not want to be bothered with child rearing while they were high. Linda revealed as much when she said,

I used to let them [my children] get away with a lot, like go out, just so they would get away from me. And I would let them go out and play all night until dark, and I shouldn't have. They should have been in doing their chores and getting ready for bed.

Micah also felt that she failed to keep her children's behavior under control and that her children took advantage of her. She stated,

I'm not a very strict mother, and my oldest one kinda picked up on that real quick, and I just got shoved out of the way, but I let that happen. I let them run all over me. I was *not* a very good disciplinarian at all. I let them pretty much do *what* they wanted *when* they wanted so I didn't have to *deal* with them.

Linda and Micah, like the other mothers, believed they were bad moms when they lacked control over their children because they were high and wanted their children to leave them alone. These women believed that not supervising one's children was a sign of bad mothering.

Documentation of parenting problems among substance-abusing parents confirms the existence of these forms of child-rearing practices and similarly argues that parental substance use had a negative effect on children. Rosenbaum (1981) found that heroin-using women experience difficulty managing their children along with their habit. More recently, Inciardi, Lockwood, and Pottieger (1993) graphically described the particular case of crack-addicted women. Involved in a cycle of prostitution, drug dealing, and constant drug use, cocaine-abusing women resist socially acceptable employment opportunities because they cannot financially support their drug habit and their children.

The stories told by the women in this study expand what is known about substance-abusing mothers' behaviors by illustrating, from the women's perspectives, their sense of the trouble they had integrating their substance abuse with good parenting. The residents at "A Place to Be" perceived themselves as failing to fulfill their roles as socially acceptable mothers when they put their children in danger, when they were unavailable for their children, and when they lacked control over them. The guilt these women felt indicates that they accepted, at least in part, the parameters of the dominant ideology of intensive mothering.

Good Mothering Practices

The substance-abusing women interviewed for this project avoided the cultural claim that they were bad mothers. They did this by asserting that they cared for, and were deeply committed to, their children even though they were addicts. Not much literature has been written from the substance-abusing mothers' perspectives, and even more notably absent is research on the times when substance-abusing women follow mothering practices that fall within the boundaries of the dominant ideology. Rosenbaum (1979) noted that many studies fail to recognize how these women really care about their children and try hard to balance their use and that care. As a result, these women's voices have not been heard and the depiction of their mothering practices may be inaccurate and more negative than appropriate or valid. One of the few exceptions is Colten's (1982) comparison of heroin-addicted and nonaddicted mothers. Although the heroin-addicted mothers were more apt to express doubts about their adequacy as mothers, both groups shared many of the same experiences with their children, had similar relationships with their children, and expressed similar feelings and attitudes regarding their children.

All of the residents interviewed for this project perceived themselves as good moms, in some aspect or another, even when they were using. According to the women, a sub-

stance-abusing mother can be a good mom as long as she takes care of her child(ren)'s practical needs, protects her children from harm, and copes with everyday life struggles without losing her temper. The assertion by these women that they were good mothers reveals how they avoided and manipulated the contemporary ideology of motherhood.

Fulfilling Practical Needs. The most pervasive theme in the residents' talk about their good mothering focused on fulfilling their child(ren)'s practical needs for food, cleanliness (clothes and house), and education. Micah acknowledged that she thought she was doing a good job as a mom because "I was still cooking my daughters' meals on time. I was getting my kids to school on time. I was keeping my house clean." Quinne said, "I was functional. Margaret [her daughter] went to bed; I read her bedtime stories. I gave her baths; I did everything with her that I was supposed to do." Nettie noted that her substance abuse did not interfere with her family life: "I was there for the kids. I made sure my bills were paid and my rent was paid." Like Nettie, Naomi asserted that "I always took care of them. I knew that they were dressed right. No matter how high I got, my kids were always tended to, *always*. I cannot ever remember my kids being cold, hungry, abandoned, left unattended."

Vicki summed up these women's understandings of themselves as substance abusing moms by saying of her children, "They're clean, they're always well-groomed, and they're well dressed." To these women, fulfilling their children's needs for food, shelter, clothing, and education was the most important role they played as mothers.

Protecting From Harm. Protecting children comprises a second set of mothering practices about which the women in this study felt proud. The ways they protected their children included not abusing substances while pregnant and not doing drugs around children. Being good moms, even though they used illegal substances, meant that the women protected their children from harm.

Katie did not do methamphetamine or alcohol while pregnant because she believed the use of such substances was bad for the woman and the fetus. Despite this belief, Katie smoked marijuana to relax and to keep from going into premature labor because a doctor in California prescribed marijuana for her. Quinne also asserted that she stayed clean during her pregnancy. She said, "I didn't abuse during either pregnancy. I was able to stop using when I was pregnant." Similarly, Naomi reported,

My son was born on December 2nd. When I found out I was pregnant, I quit using everything. I thought, "While I'm pregnant, I don't need to use." I smoked cigarettes, and that was the only thing that I didn't give up. So I quit using. I stayed clean for seven months.

Katie, Quinne, and Naomi stayed clean because they cared about the health of their fetuses and babies. Staying clean while pregnant indicated to the women in this study that they were good mothers.

Besides not using drugs while pregnant, many women protected their children by not using drugs in front of them. Ullie stated that even though her son's hair sample came back positive for crack-cocaine, she never smoked in front of him. Quinne described how she would tell her boyfriend and daughter that she had some housework to do upstairs. She would then go upstairs, smoke crack-cocaine, get rid of the smell, get herself together, and go back downstairs. Linda tried not to do drugs around her children. She said that her children did not know very much about drugs but "they do know anyway. They can usually tell when I'm high, but I don't smoke pot in front of them. But I do drink in front of them." When Candie had her intravenous use of methamphetamine under "control," she would wait until her children went to school to do her first "hit" of the day.

I'd get up and feed my kids and get them off to school. I wouldn't do any drugs until they were gone. Then I would justify it, after they left. It was OK to do it when they weren't there.

She controlled her drug use thereby fulfilling her role as a good mother. Naomi said that her son was aware of her use but that she "never used in front of him. I never left

needles or anything around where he could see it." To these women, not doing drugs in front of their children or while they were pregnant meant they were being good mothers.

Coping With Stress. A third mothering practice that indicated to these substance-abusing women that they were good mothers was when they used drugs as a means to cope with everyday life pressures. The drugs were not used to "party" but to maintain emotional and physical well-being to effectively function for their children. This sort of coping happened in two ways: The women would control the amount and timing of their substance use, and they used the drugs to relieve stress they felt from their husband, children, and social service agencies.

Nettie is an example of someone who talked about her coping experiences. She said, "I could keep it under control. I mean, I didn't let it interfere with my family life. I was there for my kids; I didn't push my kids off." Candie reported that when she started using again after her fourth treatment, she had control over methamphetamine. She explained,

I had everything under control. I didn't totally go out of control like before. I could keep my job, and I had my kids, and I could still use. I thought I was doing pretty good, even though I was still firing [intravenous drug use].

Controlling the amount of her use allowed her to maintain a relatively functional lifestyle. Similarly, Quinne said, "I wouldn't do all the things that somebody else on crack-cocaine would do. I could manage my mood swings. I could, unless I had a large amount, manage it." Each of these women coped with substance abuse by controlling the amount and time of their use to practice good mothering.

The use of drugs to relieve stress was the other way of coping. For example, Edith was a 34-year-old mother of two children who was addicted to prescription pain pills for six years and was in treatment for the first time. She described her substance-abuse experiences and reasoned that she abused pain pills because they helped her manage her children, stating,

> As far as how it made me feel, I got every-thing done, the housecleaning. It [pain pills] made me feel great. I managed with the kids. A lot of reason I used was to deal with my kids. Single parenting is like the hardest job in the world. It made me feel good. I was more alert. I baked. I cooked. I cleaned. I dealt with the kids better. We played; we did all kinds of things.

Edith concluded that her use made her a better mom. Likewise, Micah contended that she would "go to the bathroom and get high to chill out" when she was angry with her children. Linda acknowledged,

> I used to get so stressed out with having so many kids at once that I just tried to drink to get out of parenting or some-thing. I think it [my use] was just to cope with three kids. I thought if I was drunk it would be easier.

Substance use, these women argued, helped them to cope with their children.

Some of the moms contended that using helped them to deal with their partners and with social service agencies. Carol said, "That's another reason why I started using again [after treatment] because it just be-came too overwhelming for me. I blamed myself [for the sexual abuse of my children by my second husband]." Naomi asserted that living with her husband, who was a "big-time" marijuana dealer who strictly con-trolled her life, was very stressful. She said,

> I was still smoking pot *all* day, *every* day. It was my only way of coping, or so I thought at the time, because I wanted to kill this man. I would lay there at night, and I would think of ways to kill him. "Should I cut his throat? Get it over with. How can I kill him without getting caught? Make it look like an accident."

Naomi and Carol were in abusive relation-ships and used drugs as a way to cope with their partners.

Other women asserted that they used drugs to cope with social service and legal systems, which were placing too many de-mands on them. For example, Carol said that she ended up using again after treatment be-cause

> they [Department of Human Services] were putting me under so much pressure that I said, "To hell with it. They're threat-ening to put me in prison. Why not use?" They were telling me I was an unfit mother. But I knew I took care of my kids.

In short, these moms asserted that sub-stance use helped them to calm down, to deal with everyday life situations, and to be better mothers. These findings of women coping with stress support some researchers' claims that addicts use substances to self-medicate, thereby receiving relief from distressing feel-ings, events, and symptoms (see Abrams and Nisura 1987; Cooper et al. 1992; Lisansky Gomberg 1993; Weiss, Griffin, and Mirin 1992).

The residents of "A Place to Be" contended that they were good moms, at least part of the time. Good mothering practices in-cluded protecting children from harm, ful-filling children's practical needs, and coping with everyday life stresses while maintain-ing their composure. Although there is not much research to support the notion that an addict can, in some ways, be a good mother, addicted women who participated in this study described themselves as caring and committed mothers, thereby defying the dominant cultural stereotype of substance-abusing women as mothers who have little or no parenting skills, are out of control, and do not care for their children. Reports of pos-itive mothering practices were uniform across respondents regardless of differences among them.

Conclusion

There is little dispute that parental sub-stance abuse can have negative effects on children, physically, socially, and psycholog-ically. What can be disputed is that drug-ad-dicted mothers are always bad parents. Al-though the women in residential treatment interviewed for this study realized that their substance-abusing lifestyles had, at times, a negative impact on their children, they also insisted that they exhibited behaviors associ-ated with socially acceptable, intensive parenting. Ambivalent about the quality of their parenting and yet cognizant of the negative impact it had on their children, the women did not see themselves as bad or unfit mothers, nor were they willing to admit that they were always incapable or less competent than other mothers. Rather, they clearly and uniformly evoked images of themselves and detailed practices that illustrated their capabilities as parents.

The women in this study described their mothering practices primarily in relation to the "needs" of the children. Missing from their talk is an explicit consideration of their parenting experiences in terms of class, gender, or race. Sometimes respondents articulated feelings of powerlessness and recognized the public assistance systems as intrusive and victimizing, noticing that they were not protected or privileged in the same way as middle-class women. The participants did not, however, claim that their class position had an impact on their parenting experiences. Similarly, an analysis of gender was also absent in their talk about mothering. This is most clear in the participants' lack of discussion of their partners during the interviews. An absence of talk about their partners is, in part, due to resocialization away from dependence on men taking place during treatment, although it also attests to an assumption that the primary care of children should be in the mothers' hands, a classic patriarchal notion. Finally, the white women in this study (15 out of 17 respondents) did not verbally locate themselves in the race hierarchy with race privilege. None of them mentioned their race in any meaningful way, exemplifying Frankenberg's (1993) idea that white women's race privilege is invisible to them. Missing from these women's talk is a socially based analysis of their "problems" and therefore no direct challenge to class, gender, and race arrangements.

Just as surely, though, their voices contained active avoidance and manipulation of the white middle-class heterosexual mothering model. Claiming to be and viewing themselves as "great" mothers illustrates that these women reject a portrayal of them as bad mothers and instead create for themselves more inclusive boundaries for acceptable mothering practices. In this way, the substance-abusing mothers in this study act similarly to other groups of marginalized women such as Hispanic, African American, lesbian, and working-class mothers, who resist the dominant discourse about mothering. In the participants' understandings of their mothering practices, we see the potency of ideology and the omnipresence of agency come alive.

This article gives substance-abusing women a voice by analyzing their visions of a "good" mother and how they think they fit into that vision. These women add one further and complicating critique to the dominant ideology of mothering. Because substance-abusing women do not fit the model of a "good woman" or of the "ideal mom" does not mean that they were not committed or were uncaring. Similar to other marginalized women, the substance-abusing women in this project reported loving their children and caring for them in many ways even when this love and caring conflicted with the women's own personal needs while using drugs.

Notes

1. For a thorough discussion of health-related problems, including sexually transmitted diseases and the human immunodeficiency virus (HIV) refer to the following sources: (1) clinical aspects: Lowinson et al. (1994), (2) practical approaches in the treatment of women who abuse alcohol and other drugs: Des Jarlais, Hagan, and Friedman (1997).

2. I used pseudonyms for all personal names, treatment centers, and locations mentioned during the interviews to ensure confidentiality.

3. Because I developed the interview guide with topics raised by the participants and because the participants did not raise partner relationships and physical punishment as topics, they were not on the interview guide. In retrospect, I should have included them. Nonetheless, it is notable that they were absent. Sometimes what the interviewees do not say is as interesting as what they do say.

References

Abrams, D., and R. S. Nisura. 1987. Social learning theory. In *Psychological theories of drinking and alcoholism*, edited by H. T. Blane and K. E. Leonard. New York: Guilford.

Benishek, L., K. Bieschke, B. Stoffelmayr, B. Mavis, and K. Humphreys. 1992. Gender differences in depression and anxiety among alcoholics. *Journal of Substance Abuse* 4:235–245.

Bijur, R., M. Kurzon, M. Overpeck, and R. Scheidt. 1992. Parental alcohol use, problem drinking, and children's injuries. *Journal of the American Medical Association* 267:3166–3171.

Blum, L. M., and T. Deussen. 1996. Negotiating independent motherhood: Working-class African American women talk about marriage and motherhood. *Gender & Society* 10:199–211.

Chazotte, C., J. Youchah, and M. Comerford Freda. 1995. Cocaine use during pregnancy and low birth weight: The impact of prenatal care and drug treatment. *Seminars in Perinatology* 19:293–300.

Collins, R. Hill. 1994. Shifting the center: Race, class, and feminist theorizing about motherhood. In *Representations of Motherhood*, edited by D. Bassin, M. Honey, and M. M. Kaplan. New Haven, CT: Yale University Press.

Colten, M. E. 1982. Attitudes, experiences, and self-perceptions of heroin addicted mothers. *Journal of Social Issues* 38:77–92.

Cooper, M., M. Russell, J. Skinner, M. Frone, and R. Mundar. 1992. Stress and alcohol use: Moderating effects of gender, coping, and alcohol expectancies. *Journal of Abnormal Psychology* 101:139–152.

Des Jarlais, D. C., H. Hagan, and S. R. Friedman. 1997. Practical approaches in the treatment of women who abuse alcohol and other drugs. Contract no. CSAT–93–0006, pp. 25–31. Rockville, MD: Department of Health and Human Services, Public Health Service.

Ettorre, E. M. 1992. *Women and substance use*. New Brunswick, NJ: Rutgers University Press.

Fineman, M. Albertson. 1995. *The neutered mother, the sexual family and other twentieth century tragedies*. New York: Routledge.

Frankenberg, Ruth. 1993. *White women, race matters: The social construction of whiteness*. Minneapolis: University of Minnesota Press.

Glenn, E. Nakano, G. Chang, and L. R. Forcey. 1994. *Mothering: Ideology, experience, and agency*. New York: Routledge.

Gomberg, E. S. Lisansky. 1993. Women and alcohol: Use and abuse. *Journal of Nervous and Mental Diseases* 181:211–219.

Grella, C. E. 1996. Background and overview of mental health and substance abuse treatment systems: Meeting the needs of women who are pregnant or parenting. *Journal of Psychoactive Drugs* 28 (4):319–343.

Hanke, R. J., and C. E. Faupel. 1993. Women opiate users' perceptions of treatment services in New York City. *Journal of Substance Abuse Treatment* 10:513–522.

Hawley, T. Lawton, T. Halle, R. Drasin, and N. Thomas. 1995. Children of addicted mothers: Effects of the "Crack Epidemic" on the caregiving environment and the development of preschoolers. *American Journal of Orthopsychiatry* 65:364–379.

Hays, S. 1996. *The cultural contradictions of motherhood*. New Haven, CT: Yale University Press.

Higgins, R. Grant, D. Hendel Clough, and C. Wallerstedt. 1995. Drug-taking behaviours of pregnant substance abusers in treatment. *Journal of Advanced Nursing* 22:425–432.

Hondagneu-Sotelo, R., and E. Avila. 1997. "I'm here, but I'm there." The meaning of Latina transnational motherhood. *Gender & Society* 11:548–571.

Inciardi, J., D. Lockwood, and A. Pottieger. 1993. *Women and crack cocaine*. New York: Macmillan.

Kumpfer, K., and C. W. Turner. 1990–91. The social ecology model of adolescent substance abuse: Implications for prevention. *International Journal of Addictions* 25 (4A):435–464.

Lewin, E. 1994. Negotiating lesbian motherhood: The dialectics of resistance and accommodation. In *Mothering: Ideology, experience, and agency*, edited by E. N. Glenn, G. Chang, and L. R. Forcey. New York: Routledge.

Litt, J., and M. McNeil. 1997. Biological markers and social differentiation: "Crack Babies" and the construction of the dangerous mother. *Health Care for Women International* 18:31–41.

Lowinson, J. H., R. Ruiz, R. B. Millman, and J. G. Langrod, eds. 1994. *Substance abuse: A comprehensive textbook*. 3d ed. Baltimore: Williams & Wilkins; Center for Substance Abuse Treatment.

Mahan, S. 1996. *Crack cocaine, crime, and women: Legal, social, and treatment issues*. Vol. 4, Drugs, Health, and Social Policy Series. Thousand Oaks, CA: Sage.

McMahon, M. 1995. *Engendering motherhood: Identity and self-transformation in women's lives*. New York: Guilford.

McNeil, M., and J. Litt. 1992. More medicalizing of mothers: Fetal alcohol syndrome in the USA and related developments. In *Private risks and public dangers*, edited by S. Scott, G. Williams, S. Platt, and H. Thomas. Ashgate, VT: Ashgate.

Neuman, W. L. 1994. *Social research methods: Qualitative and quantitative approaches*. 2d ed. Needham Heights, MA: Allyn & Bacon.

Richman, J. A., K. M. Rospenda, and M. A. Kelley. 1995. Gender roles and alcohol abuse across the transition to parenthood. *Journal of Studies on Alcohol* 56:553–557.

Rosenbaum, M. 1979. Difficulties in taking care of business: Women addicts as mothers. *American Journal of Drug and Alcohol Abuse* 6:431–446.

——. 1981. Women addicts' experience of the heroin world: Risk, chaos, and inundation. *Urban Life* 10 (1):65–81.

Sands, R. G., and M. McClelland. 1994. Emic and etic perspectives in ethnographic research on the interdisciplinary team. In *Qualitative research in social work*, edited by E. Sherman, and W. J. Reid. New York: Columbia University Press.

Smart, C. 1996. Deconstructing motherhood. In *Good enough mothering? Feminist perspectives on lone motherhood*, edited by E. B. Silva. New York: Routledge.

Smith, I. E., D. Z. Dent, C. D. Coles, and A. Falek. 1992. A comparison study of treated and untreated pregnant and postpartum cocaine-abusing women. *Journal of Substance Abuse Treatment* 9:343–348.

Taylor, C. S. 1993. *Girls, gangs, women and drugs*. East Lansing: Michigan State University Press.

Tutty, L., M. Rothery, and R. Grinnell Jr. 1996. *Qualitative research for social workers: Phases, steps, tasks*. Needham Heights, MA: Allyn & Bacon.

Weiss, R. D., M. L. Griffin, and S. M. Mirin. 1992. Drug abuse as self-medication for depression: An empirical study. *American Journal of Drug and Alcohol Abuse* 18 (2):121–129.

Young, I. M. 1994. Punishment, treatment, empowerment: Three approaches to policy for pregnant addicts. *Feminist Studies* 20:33–57.

Authors' Note

The authors thank the University of Northern Iowa for research support through project grants and a 1997 summer fellowship. A version of this article was presented at the 1997 meeting of the Midwest Sociological Society. We also thank graduate assistants Leslie Lanning and Lori Wiebold for their administrative, bibliographic, and editorial help. William Downs, Sharon Hays, and Michael Ueber made helpful comments on previous drafts.

21
The Ethic of 'Responsible Drinking'

Earl Rubington

Alcohol and college life have a long and notorious relationship. Binge drinking has become something of a rite of passage on many campuses, where getting drunk and having a good time go hand-in-hand. Contests have emerged, especially on the fraternity scene, where members see who can drink the most in the shortest period of time. Thousands of overdoses are reported each year, and excessive alcohol consumption has been implicated in everything from assault to theft to rape. Stories of drunk students falling from balconies or choking on their own vomit have become as common as they are tragic.

All this occurs despite the fact that minimum drinking ages exist and that most college students fall well below them. Universities, state legislatures, and police departments have tried to "up the ante" by beefing up enforcement, but college students are wily and they adapt. Fake IDs, unsupervised "keg parties," and unscrupulous merchants continue to make liquor inexpensive and easy to obtain. Universities nevertheless know they must try hard to monitor student drinking.

RAs (residential assistants in dormitories) constitute a primary line of defense against underage drinking. RAs are informal agents of social control; they are students, usually older, charged with policing the behavior of other students, usually younger. Because RAs are also students, they often relate to the other residents on a peer level. But because they are vested with university authority, they must also act in a quasi-formal capacity. This dual relationship affects their enforcement styles in intriguing ways.

Such styles are undeniably influenced by the fact that RAs live and work in the same place as the rule-breakers they are charged with monitoring. This proximity creates dilemmas: being too strict, for example, can create significant tensions; being too lenient can result in attributions of "softness." Neither bodes well for the efficient management of a residence hall, so an appropriate balance must be struck. Control must be even more nuanced when targets of enforcement have moved in from different residence halls where wholly different expectations of social control exist. The potential for conflict is ever present.

Above anything else, RAs wish to cultivate an ethic of "responsible drinking." Their use of discretion is geared to this end and changes to account for situation-specific factors. The process can be tortuous for all parties involved but especially for the RAs who, by enforcing an unpopular rule, can become equally unpopular themselves. The relationship between deviants and control agents is inevitably tense but necessarily flexible. Nowhere is this flexibility more important than in the implementation of college alcohol policy, where RAs attempt to push drinking in the least undesired direction.

... [D]espite laws enjoining sales, purchase, possession, or consumption of alcoholic beverages by minors, more underaged youth drink today, and more of them are "binge drinkers." The law causes youth to drink, and the lack of enforcement only makes underage drinkers indifferent to or contemptuous of the law (Mosher 1980; Engs and Hanson 1989a). Since 1987, when all 50 states raised the drinking age to 21, although teenage drinking and driving has declined, teenage drinking remains at high levels.

Whether alcohol problems on campus are more prevalent than a generation ago, college administrators seem more concerned (Engs 1977). They seek to eliminate underage drinking on campus through formulating more detailed alcohol policies, more stringent sanctions, or a combination of both. As a consequence, freshman residence halls have become (the focal point for the kinds of problems that contradiction between law and its enforcement can create. The vast majority of entering 1st-year students not only are already drinking but are also quite well accustomed to obtaining alcoholic beverages with impunity (O'Hare 1990). Thus, when they enter residence halls in the fall, they experience culture shock when they learn that the college forbids them to drink on campus. Most 1st year students believe that they have been denied their "right to drink" (Engs and Hanson 1989b) and face a conflict between how they define drinking and how their college does.

It falls to residential assistants (RAs) to enforce the policies administrators have formulated. Documenting and reporting infractions of residence hall rules are an important part of RAs' duties (Blimling and Miltenberger 1990; Upcraft 1982). Unlike other agents of control such as police officers, prison guards, mental hospital attendants, and elementary school teachers, RAs live, work, and associate with the people whom they may have to report for infractions of residence hall rules (Becker 1952; Reiss 1971; Perrucci 1974; Zimmer 1986; Lombardo 1989). Thus, the complexity of RAs' social situation makes study of their enforcement role theoretically significant. . . .

Setting and Method

These studies took place in South, East, and West Halls, three CU freshman residence halls. (Names of the persons and places, including "City University," are fictitious.) The three residence halls housed men and women on alternate floors. An upperclass student of the same gender had a single room on each floor and served as the RA. Data for the three studies came from tabulation and analysis of all infractions RAs recorded on discipline cards, examination of residence hall staff logs, some participant observation, and interviews with resident directors (RDs), graduate assistants (GAs), and RAs in each of the three study years. The analysis and interpretation in this paper is based primarily on interviews with RAs. In the interview quotes that follow, R = residential assistant, D = residence director, and G = graduate assistant.

Becoming a Residential Assistant

RAs constitute the first line of defense of college alcohol policy. In the course of making rounds, RAs confront residents in situations that may require action on their part. In time, they develop their own style, a term RAs use when discussing their work as prohibition agents. Stages in RA careers and development of their styles follow below.

RAs as Residents

CU requires that RAs have some prior experience as residents in a college residence hall. Most had been residents in one of CU's freshman residence halls. RAs who drank as freshmen reported a variety of experiences with their floor RAs. Most reported that their RAs were quite lax in enforcement of the no-drinking rule. Some reported RAs' collusion in alcohol violations.

A few recalled being "written up" for alcohol violations when they were freshmen, but most reported that they drank in the residence hall with impunity. One male said he got drunk once a week throughout the year without ever being written up. Others recalled their RAs inviting them into their room for a drink, or joining in a drinking party already going on in the informant's room. Still others noted that when the RA on rounds came upon them drinking in their rooms, he or she simply closed the door. One informant noted that the RA simply had them "dump" the beer (pour contents in sink or toilet bowl). And one female said that her RA used to call up on the phone to warn them when the RA on duty was making rounds. Thus RAs as freshmen were socialized to a number of ideas about drinking in the residence halls. Their freshman experiences showed them that drinking was ubiquitous, its enforcement lax.

Formal and Informal Training

Both in the week before freshmen arrive and then later throughout the academic year, RAs attend training sessions, mainly lectures on a variety of subjects. The closest thing to "hands-on" experience that participants recalled was role-playing, which took place the week before classes started. It involved new RAs getting some idea of what went on behind closed doors. They had to knock on a resident's door, identify themselves as the RA, and request permission to enter. Once inside, they confronted veteran RAs acting as residents of the room and simulating one of the many kinds of situations they could expect to deal with once the fall quarter started. Underage drinking, domestic disputes, insubordination, suicidal residents, and the smell of marijuana were but a few of the surprises veteran RAs had in store for them. After the new RA responded to the situation, the veterans suggested other ways he or she could have handled the situation or commended the new RA for what he or she did.

In the early weeks of the quarter, veteran RAs sometimes accompany 1st-year RAs when they are making rounds. One source of informal training comes from observing how veterans manage confrontations with residents. Discussion with them after the fact also provides information for novice RAs on how to act should they come upon similar situations. In time, RAs fashion their own particular style by blending or avoiding techniques veteran RAs employ. Being matter-of-fact or strictly business, using humor to defuse situations, and taking charge more quickly are only some of the points made in interviews. Some noted that with experience they managed confrontations with less time and effort.

The First Floor Meeting

In the first week of the fall quarter, RDs meet with all residents of the building and orient them to Big Town, CU, and residence hall rules. They point out that underage students cannot have alcohol in their rooms and cannot drink; and they tell them that anyone who breaks the rules will be subject to sanctions. Later, RAs hold their own first floor meetings. After mutual introductions, they also inform their residents about CU's alcohol policy.

At these meetings, RAs present their views about alcohol policy in one of four ways: tacit, proscriptive, conditional, or prescriptive. The few RAs who take the tacit route say nothing at all about the subject. Presumably, they believe that the RD has said all that

needs to be said on the subject. A somewhat larger number of RAs are proscriptive. On the subject of alcohol and other drugs, they are both succinct and specific: They simply say: "Don't do it here." Most RAs, however, are conditional in their alcohol policy orientations. The way R-4 stated alcohol policy to her floor was typical. She said: "I don't see it, smell it, or hear it. [Hear it?] Quarters [a drinking game played with quarters], opening cans. The implied message is if I don't see it, smell it, or hear it, there's nothing I can do about it." First-year RAs were more apt to be prescriptive. Some wondered if they had sent mixed messages to their residents. For example, R-2 said: "I know you're gonna be drinking. It's gonna happen. Be quiet. Be in control. Don't let it get out of hand. Some may have thought that validated drinking. Some took it that way."

RAs have notions on how to present themselves as rule enforcers at the start of the fall quarter. At the outset, some present themselves as sticklers. R-7 pointed out: "I decided to tell them that I was going to be strict, sort of scare them. Common sense says it's easier to go from hard to soft than from soft to hard. It's harder to get tough. . . .I'm majoring in marketing. It's only common sense to start with a higher price, then mark it down."

But, on the whole, RAs have a different relationship with the residents of their own floors than with residents of the other floors in the building. For one thing, they live on their own floors. They do not make scheduled rounds on their floor except when on duty. Although they do write up residents of their own floor, they are more lenient when disciplining them; they are more apt to use informal rather than formal means of social control. But, at the same time, they have to be somewhat concerned about the behavior of their own residents. For instance, RAs are subject to periodic performance reviews and evaluation by their RDs. "Problem floors" as well as "troublemakers" get labeled quickly after just a few rounds. Disorder, vandalism, noise, trash in the hallways, and numerous write-ups, reflect on the floor RA's competence and affect his or her performance evaluation as well as reputation with fellow RAs.

A "wild floor" makes for considerable work for all the other RAs when they have to make rounds. These RAs sometimes let the RA who has made extra work for them know how they feel; through direct comments or indirectly, in the staff log.

Making Rounds

RAs are most likely to come upon alcohol violations when making rounds. If they see people drinking in hallways or in their rooms, or if they hear loud voices or stereos coming from a room, they confront residents. Confrontation requires them to knock on the door, identify themselves as the RA, and request permission to enter. Once inside, if they see open cans of beer, people holding cans, or people drinking from containers, they ask all present for their IDs. After restoring order, they go downstairs to fill out discipline cards. They enter all names from the IDs on the cards along with the violations, and they enter the same information in the staff log.

The first time RAs make rounds, they experience some anxiety; but in a very short time it becomes, as one of them described it, "second nature." Confrontations with residents, of course, are not always matters of routine. RAs are expected to remain cool, assertive, and in control of the situation rather than become angry or excited. However, numerous contingencies attend RA-resident confrontations. As G-1 said: "You never know what you'll find once they open the door." A number of RAs have pointed out that residents become upset simply because RAs have intervened in their activities. These enforcement encounters generate understanding on not only how residents feel about being written up, but also how RAs themselves feel about writing up residents.

Thus, enforcement can be problematic for RAs. It soon becomes incumbent on them to fashion their own personal solutions to problems of their identity as RAs, situation control, and exercise of authority.

RAs expressed dislike about having to write up residents, having to document violations in accordance with Housing Office requirements. In addition to disliking the idea in general, some said they really didn't enjoy "getting people in trouble." Many residents, for example, took being written up quite personally and claimed that the RA was "out to get them." RAs reported that they often went out of their way the following morning to say hello to residents they had written up the night before. Greeting them as if nothing had happened, they sought to communicate that they had been "only doing their job." Whereas some residents came to understand, others did not. They showed their animosity by refusing to return the greeting.

Development of a Style

Over time, RAs solve problems of confrontation by developing what they call their "style." As experience with enforcing rules becomes routine, RAs opt for one of three styles: strict ("by-the-book"), moderate ("in between"), or lenient ("laid-back").

RAs who are "by-the-book" approach all encounters as if the matter were "cut and dried." They have a no-nonsense, matter-of-fact approach; take command of a situation immediately; collect IDs rapidly; are strictly business, quick, and cool. For the most part, they are rule-oriented. RAs who are "laid-back" are more apt to give residents the benefit of the doubt. More often situation oriented, they will find a way to restore order without having to write residents up if possible. RAs who are "in between" are more often person-oriented. If residents are cooperative in a confrontation and do not give them a "hard time," they may manage a situation without necessarily documenting a violation of residence hall rules. But, as is generally the case with police—citizen contacts, disrespect guarantees being written up (Westley 1970; Reiss 1971; Black 1978). D-1 summarized the three types of RA styles when she said that "there are RAs who write up everything they see, RAs who will give a person a chance, and RAs who ignore everything."

RAs evolve their own styles out of a combination of observation, experience, and discussion with other RAs. R-2, for example, blended the styles of the two other veteran RAs, becoming an "in between." He said: "I hang around more with R-10 and R-11. R-11 gives more leeway, he deals personally, he's a humanist, he's friends with his residents, he's a fun guy. R-11, he's by-the-book: This is the policy, that's it. I learned from them. I relied on them. I found a middle ground." But here R-2 was talking about developing a style for dealing with his own floor.

Making rounds, however, brings RAs into more fleeting contacts with residents of a whole building on the dozen or more times they make rounds in the course of a quarter. These contacts necessarily turn on whether there has been a violation of the rules, which requires RAs to assert their authority, take charge, and alter the situation. Breaking up drinking parties, getting people in a room to leave, quieting residents, and getting them to dump the beer are just some examples. What is quite clear is that most RAs handle residents of their own floors differently. As R-12 said: "You use your discretion. I treat guys on my floor different from the rest of the building."

As previously noted, what makes RAs different from other control agents is that they live and work in the same place with people they may have to report for violating rules. During the course of an academic year they can make contact with residents of the whole building, but they are much more likely to come into frequent contact with residents of their own floor. The more frequent the contact between people, the more likely that something like friendship may develop (Homans 1951). Some RAs commented, for example, that visiting residents in their room and accepting a slice of pizza may set up expectations for special consideration at some later time. R-14 dropped in to visit a friend on her floor. Her friend's boyfriend was present, drinking a beer. R-14 had the boyfriend dump the beer, which upset her friend. Some RAs are aware of the need, as they put it, to "walk the line" between being a friend and being an RA. The friend—RA or cop—counselor conflict has been a problem for RAs ever since the establishment of the position (Upcraft 1982).

But if all RAs work in the same building, particularly when they are "on duty," they live on their home floors. As R-24 said: "I have to live with these guys for the rest of the year." And so variation in violation sites can

make for variations in enforcement styles. RAs enforce rules on their home floors as well as on all floors and locations within the building, but once home floor versus all other floors is taken into account the site of enforcement makes for variations in styles of enforcement.

First, there are RAs who are "by-the-book" on all floors, their own as well as others. They know the rules, and when in the presence of a violation they write up the violator no matter who he or she is or where the violation took place. These sticklers can be generalists or specialists. R-15 considered making noise a more serious violation than drinking in one's room; he specialized in writing up residents for noise violations. Most violators he cited were residents of his floor. R-3 and R-16, both former problem drinkers, on the other hand, were specialists in writing up residents for alcohol violations whether on their home floors or on any of the others. But whether generalists or specialists, pure "by-the-book" RAs are paragons of consistency in the enforcement of residence hall rules. Most pure "by-the-book" RAs in this study were either seniors or veteran RAs, and more of them were women.

Next are those RAs who are "laid-back" with respect to their home floors but "by-the-book" when dealing with residents of any of the other floors. D-2 said: "R-17 is most lax enforcing rules on his floor. He loves his floor; they can do no wrong: But he's very consistent when enforcing rules off his floor." Other residence hall staff agreed that RAs are less strict with residents of their own floor. R-18 exemplified reluctance to document infractions on one's own floor. She acknowledged that when making "double-duty" rounds, she always stayed in the background when they got to her floor and let the other RA write up any of her residents. Being "laid-back" with one's own floor and "by-the-book" with all other floors is probably the typical enforcement style.

RAs who are "laid-back" on all floors are least frequent but most notorious. There are three degrees of "laid-backness": lenient, lax, and absent. Generally, the overly lenient lean more in the direction of friend rather than RA when it comes to confrontations with residents, irrespective of floors. This means that most of the time such an RA gives the resident the benefit of the doubt. Walking by an open door and seeing a student drinking, the RA may just close the door. Coming upon a student standing or walking in the corridor with an open beer in his or her hand, the RA may suggest that the person go to his or her room and close the door. On occasion, such an RA may ask the resident to dump a beer without later recording the incident on a discipline card and noting it on the staff log. The distinction between the lenient and the lax is that lenient RAs see the violation but do not treat it as such, whereas lax RAs go out of their way not to see any violations that require documenting. G-1 once accompanied R-5 on rounds. He was amazed at R-5's selective inattention. R-5 was a master at "looking the other way."

Laxity on the home floor can also come about when RAs have "lost control" of their floor. Overidentification with residents, coupled with an inability to accept identity as an RA and to exercise the authority that goes with the position, produces loss of control. D-1 pointed out R-19 as a good example of an RA who had lost control of his floor. Residents of his floor were written up for numerous trash, vandalism, noise, and alcohol violations. When I interviewed R-19 later, he said that his first two alcohol write-ups had made him most uncomfortable. He went on to say: "I was a freshman once. How do I get off getting them in trouble when I did the same things?" And later in that same interview he acknowledged that "I am more lax on my own floor."

Absence produces the third degree of "laid-backness." Occasionally RAs are off their floors for extended periods if they are holding another job, or are spending much of their time with a boyfriend or girlfriend. Extended absence produces the situation of "when the cat's away, the mice will play," as R-20 put it. A classic example of absence was R-21: Although he served as RA for an entire academic year, he wrote only one violation for that year. In turn, his floor was known as the wildest. The other seven RAs all wrote up a considerable number of violations whenever they made rounds on R-21's floor.

The last category consisted of RAs who were "in betweens." RAs who called themselves "in betweens" were most conscious of what they called "gray areas." They said that all RAs varied in their personal tolerances for alcohol and for noise. And some "in betweens" acknowledged that their mood sometimes influenced whether they wrote up a resident for a violation. The few "in betweens" were most apt to be women who made fine distinctions about incidents that came to their attention. These few were usually seniors and/or veteran RAs.

After a while, both residents and RAs become aware of these varied styles of enforcement among RAs. Consistency in rule enforcement can well become an issue, as it was in East Hall in the 1989–1990 academic year, when the "by-the-books" lined up against the "laid-backs" and the "in-betweens."

'Lightening Up'

During interviews, RAs either volunteered information or answered questions on how they as well as residents may have changed over the course of the academic year. On changes in residents' drinking, RAs gave one of four answers: Most drinking took place during the fall quarter (the "rite of passage" argument), during winter quarter (the "cabin fever" argument), during spring quarter (the "spring fever" argument), or at the beginning and end of each quarter (the "tension release" argument).

RAs said their own behavior changed with the quarters for one of three reasons: They "lightened up," they became apathetic, or they "burned out." Typically, they complained of "living in a fishbowl," of lacking privacy. Although part of their job was surveillance, they deplored the fact that they "were always being watched." Informants often said that, whereas they had lightened up, it was usually the other RAs who had become apathetic or were burnouts. Over time, costs of rule enforcement began to outweigh its benefits. Yet despite variations in enforcement styles as well as lightening up as the year went on, in serving their own particular enforcement interests, RAs managed to collaborate in fashioning a common understanding of what the term "responsible drinking" came to mean in residence hall life.

The Ethic of 'Responsible Drinking'

Keeping the peace in CU residence halls depends on the ethic of "responsible drinking." For alcohol educators, responsible drinking means persons understand the action of alcohol, know their limits, make informed choices when they drink, and are prepared to take the consequences of their drinking, whatever they may be (Weisheit 1990). Responsible drinking means something entirely different to residence hall staff.

They take it as inevitable that freshmen are going to drink, that there is no stopping them. They claim that most freshmen drink, that many of them have fake IDs. They see empty cans and bottles in the trash cans. Many residents tell them about their drinking experiences. They overhear conversations in the building about parties, escapades, incidents, and hangovers. They see or hear residents vomiting in the bathroom at night or early in the morning. They come to know those rare residents who do not get out of bed until midafternoon. They know of vandalism, verbal or physical assaults that sometimes follow drinking, and occasions when they or other RAs have had to call campus police to deal with unruly, insubordinate residents. They know of cases of alcohol poisoning.

For RAs, drinking is a problem only if it makes trouble for them. Thus, those residents who drink behind closed doors, with few people in the room and voices or stereos lowered, have learned how to "drink responsibly." They are not, in D-1's words, "calling attention to themselves." G-4 said that when having an administrative meeting with residents she sometimes asked them why they hadn't considered "closing the door and turning it down."

At the beginning of the fall quarter, RAs are "gung ho," eager, enthusiastic. In line with Housing Office's suggestion that they start out tough as top sergeants, they come on in early confrontations as "hard-asses."

They employ more aggressive tactics on rounds. They intimidate residents who try to sneak alcohol into the building. Since the development of the student rights movement, staff are not permitted to examine gym, duffel, or hockey bags, or to open the refrigerators that many students have in their rooms, or to enter rooms without residents' permission. Nevertheless, in the beginning of the year, they ask students if they may see what's in their bags or in their refrigerators. They always catch naive 1st-year students who are unaware of their rights. Once caught with unopened bottles or cans, residents must either remove them from the building or dump them while RAs watch.

The aggressive drive in the early weeks of the fall quarter probably discourages some residents from drinking in the residence halls. These early weeks also constitute a mutual testing period; residents and RAs alike negotiate over the definition and enforcement of the no-drinking rule. Over time, RAs spell out their definition of the rule. Agreement with their terms constitutes the ethic of "responsible drinking." "Responsible drinking" means drinking that goes on behind closed doors and makes no public trouble. Drinking that is not disorderly, disruptive, or destructive is considered responsible. For example, although the Housing Handbook lists public drunkenness as a violation, RAs don't write up residents who return to the residence hall intoxicated after a night's drinking if they can make it to their rooms without making a disturbance.

RAs interviewed attributed the marked decline in alcohol violations to the workings of the agreement. RAs said residents learned what they could and could not get away with. If for many this meant not drinking in the building, for others it meant learning the best times and places for sneaking alcohol in, adjusting their drinking to the RAs' cycle of rounds, finding out which RAs were hard on alcohol violations and which were not, becoming aware that they did not have to say what was in bags or refrigerators, and opening doors slowly when RAs knocked so as to conceal open containers. For most, it meant becoming more discreet when they did drink in the residence hall. And the reciprocal of the exercise of residents' discretion was the gradual relaxation of strict enforcement of the no-drinking rule by the RAs.

The ratio of actual to reported alcohol violations, of course, can never be known. Some RAs exaggerate the frequency of clandestine drinking. R-23 estimated that "we only catch about 30 percent of them." R-24 said that if she were to write up all the violations that came to her attention, they would probably total around 30 after all of her three rounds. Exaggerated or not, these estimates suggest that RAs' compliance with the terms of the unwritten agreement, that is, the ethic of "responsible drinking," keeps the peace in CU's freshman residence halls.

Discussion

RAs face a particular role problem. On the one hand, the university asks them to enforce a rule inside the residence hall that is violated regularly outside. On the other hand, RAs live, work, and study among the very people who are subject to the rule they are required to enforce. Central to their dilemma is the social fact that those who enforce an unpopular rule can become as unpopular as, if not more so than, the rule itself. . . .

References

Becker, Howard S. 1952. "The Career of the Chicago Public School Teacher." *American Journal of Sociology* 57:470–477.

Black, Donald J. 1978. "The Social Organization of Arrest." Pp. 154–160 in *Deviance: The Interactionist Perspective*, 2nd ed., edited by Earl Rubington and Martin S. Weinberg. New York: Macmillan.

Blimling, Gregory S., and Lawrence J. Miltenberger. 1990. *The Resident Assistant*. Dubuque, IA: Kendall/Hunt.

Homans, George C. 1951. *The Human Group*. New York: Harcourt Brace.

Lombardo, Lucien X. 1989. *Guards Imprisoned: Correctional Officers at Work*. Cincinnati: Anderson.

Mosher, James F. 1980. "The History of Youthful-Drinking Laws: Implications for Current Policy." Pp. 11–38 in *Minimum Drinking-Age Laws*, edited by Henry Wechsler. Lexington, MA: Lexington Books.

O'Hare, T. M. 1990. "Drinking in College: Consumption Patterns, Problems, Sex Differences and Legal Drinking Age." *Journal of Studies on Alcohol* 51:536—541.

Perrucci, Robert. 1974. *Circle of Madness*. Englewood Cliffs, NJ: Prentice Hall.

Reiss, Albert J. 1971. *The Police and the Public*. Chicago: University of Chicago Press.

Upcraft, Lee. 1982. *Residence Hall Assistants in College*. San Francisco: Jossey-Bass.

Weisheit, Richard A. 1990. "Contemporary Issues in the Prevention of Adolescent Alcohol Abuse." Pp. 194–207 in *Alcoholism: Introduction to Theory and Treatment*, edited by David A. Ward. Dubuque, IA: Kendall/Hunt.

Westley, William. 1970. *Violence and the Police*. Cambridge, MA: MIT Press.

Zimmer, Lynn. 1986. *Women Guarding Men*. Chicago: University of Chicago Press.

22
Ritalin Ascendant

Lawrence H. Diller

Some analysts contend that attention deficit disorder is the single most pressing problem affecting children today. Recent reports suggest that hundreds of thousands are diagnosed with it every year, and a large percentage of these children are given the drug Ritalin to regulate their behavior. Indeed, as many as 1 million children take this drug daily in the United States, a figure that has quadrupled in the last 15 years (Glassner 1999). Critics ask whether such treatment is necessary. Kids have been, and will always be unruly, especially in a classroom setting where impulsive tendencies must be channeled into productive and disciplined energy. But is disruptive behavior indicative of organic pathology? Is it worthy of a medical diagnosis, let alone a powerful psychoactive drug? These are the questions Diller sets out to answer.

Hyperactivity subsumes a complex of behaviors, from the inability to sit still to disrespect for teachers to aggression toward other children to the willful destruction of school property. Historically, such conduct was labeled disorderly, rebellious, and even antisocial but not pathological. With the rise of the medical model in the mid- to late twentieth century, however, came the belief that deviance was indicative of disease that could be controlled through physiologically based interventions. Behavioral disorders, it was announced, were no different from organic ones and required the same approach to cure them. Attention deficit was transformed from conduct to disease in precisely this fashion.

In this selection, Diller asserts that the diagnosis of attention deficit disorder is, in some cases, grounded less in medical reality and more in the institutional necessity to generate maximum conformity among the greatest number of children with the minimum amount of effort and cost. In the era of the quick fix, Ritalin has become precisely what the doctor—and the teacher—ordered. A pharmacological solution is being applied to what is essentially a management problem—how to create an attentive classroom atmosphere conducive to learning as quickly, effortlessly, and as cheaply as possible.

Such an approach, however, may perform a much greater disservice to children in the long run. If children come to believe that problems can be solved by popping a pill, they may not work through the underlying forces that give rise to their behavior. They also may be more inclined to use harder, illegal drugs when they get older (marijuana and cocaine in particular). Also, treating the issue of deviance in class as a medical disorder ignores the larger-scale social problems (e.g., poverty, blocked opportunities, underresourced and overcrowded schools) that are likely to be partly responsible for the problem.

The important thing to remember is that Ritalin is a drug just like cocaine, heroin, or marijuana, except, of course, that it is legal, administered by conventional institutions, and used to engender compliance. Hence, drug-taking and social control are ironically intertwined; one is not possible without the other.

> Something is awry, all right, but something not entirely medical in nature.
>
> —Robert Coles, M.D.,
> *The Mind's Fate*

It's midday at an elementary school in a comfortable American suburb. The lunch bell has just rung, and kids are noisily pouring out of classrooms to enjoy a brief recess in the schoolyard before mealtime.

Inside, next door to the principal's office, the school secretary is arranging bottles of medication on a tray. Scotch-taped to the tray are little photos of fourteen children, labeled with their names and keyed to the bottles. Though by now she pretty much knows who gets what, at the beginning of the school year this system helped make sure she didn't make mistakes—that each of the children taking Ritalin at school received the right pill and dose.

At least a dozen more youngsters among the 350 attending this school took the same medication at home before school but aren't required to take a midday dose. At a nearby school of similar size, the kids getting Ritalin are organized in ten-minute shifts because their number exceeds thirty. And this weekday ritual is carried out—with variations in the number of kids and the personnel responsible for handing out the pills—at schools across the United States.

Attention deficit disorder, or ADD—the condition for which the medication Ritalin is most commonly prescribed—was formerly called hyperactivity, as reflected in its alternative acronym: ADD/HD (attention deficit/ hyperactivity disorder). Its diagnosis is based on problems with attention, focus, impulsivity, or overactivity at school or at home. Since 1990 the number of children and adults diagnosed with ADD has risen from about 900,000 to almost 5 million as we near the end of the decade. This figure—derived from the amount of medication prescribed for ADD—suggests a problem of epidemic proportions.

The sharp rise in ADD diagnosis is directly tied to another startling statistic—a 700 percent increase in the amount of Ritalin produced in the United States during the same time period.[1] An increase of this magnitude in the use of a single medication is unprecedented for a drug that is treated as a controlled substance. Ritalin belongs to the class of drugs known as stimulants, and it is closely related to amphetamine. Although Ritalin has been around for a long time, some people are still surprised to learn that it is essentially a form of speed. Others do know this but believe that the drug has a paradoxical "calming" effect on children, an effect different from the one it produces in adults.

Sorting out myth from fact about Ritalin isn't easy, but the remarkable rise in its use makes it imperative that we try. Perhaps even more important is to explain why the demand for it—and the pressure on parents and physicians to provide it—has become so intense. The phenomena of Ritalin use and soaring ADD diagnoses are related more than statistically. They are deeply intertwined, so that to examine one issue is to examine both. . . .

The statistics about ADD and Ritalin are embodied as real families and their children in my practice of behavioral pediatrics. At my office in a suburb twenty-five miles east of San Francisco, I evaluate and treat a wide variety of developmental, learning, and behavior problems of children and adolescents. I see children, teenagers, and their families, some of whom bring children as young as two years old for treatment of suspected ADD. Increasingly, adults are among my patients—most of them parents of children diagnosed with ADD who believe they themselves share its symptoms, or people who have heard that I do assessments for ADD.

The families are mostly white, middle- and upper-middle-class. In nearly all cases, at least one parent has a job; in most families, both parents are working. The children are experiencing problems at home, at school, or in multiple settings. Some don't respond to requests; some have unusual or exaggerated fears; some lag behind in school. Some young patients display frequent temper tantrums, language delay, or autism. But more and more often these days, the reason kids are in my office is that their parents, teachers, or primary-care doctors think they might "have" ADD. And more and more, those parents and caretakers are expecting me to supply Ritalin.

'Doctor, do you test for ADD?'

My first phone conversation with Sheila Gordon, the mother of six-year-old Steven, began with this question. (The names of all patients mentioned in this book have been changed unless otherwise specifically stated. Nearly all of the personal stories are from my medical practice. I have also changed some of the other details such as their occupations or the number of children in the family to further protect my patients' privacy while attempting to maintain the essence of their problem or situation.) It is a question I first heard only a few years ago, but today hardly a day goes by without a concerned parent raising it. Her voice uneven with distress, Sheila went on to tell me that Steven, her only child, was struggling in the first grade and that the teacher advised having him tested for ADD. She wanted to find out if her son had attention deficit disorder. And she wanted to find out if he needed Ritalin to control it.

Confronted with a familiar dilemma, I shifted uneasily in my chair. How could I tell Sheila over the telephone that, to my knowledge, there *was* no real test for ADD? Perhaps she would think I wasn't well informed about the condition—after all, the teacher had told her to get Steven tested. I wanted to tell her that an ADD diagnosis is complicated, and that the condition now described as ADD can have many causes and many symptoms. In order to help Steven, I would have to evaluate his basic personality, his emotions, his learning abilities, and the demands and responses of his family and school. There was no simple, definitive biological or psychological marker or test I could call on. But I suspected this was not the answer she was looking for.

When someone speaks of "having" ADD (as in having asthma or diabetes), they are implying the condition is biologically based, and that the behavior is neurological in origin. Sheila seemed to accept that Steven's problems might be caused by his brain chemistry. This is a belief widely held today about children with ADD-related symptoms, but one with which I am not entirely comfortable. I believe that brain chemistry expresses itself as personality, that this is inherent and exerts a powerful influence on behavior, but that environment—especially for children—also plays a critical role. I wanted to convey to Sheila that I was uneasy with her perception of ADD—but how to say it without making her uneasy? It would be better to wait until I met the whole family, including Steven himself, to explain the complex realities of ADD and how they might apply to this child. For the moment, I asked Sheila for more detail about the problems Steven was having in school. He was doing well academically, she said, but the teacher had called home several times to report that

he was having trouble "staying on task" when he worked alone, and staying with the group during class activities. He would habitually play with pencils or wander off to the window, for example, when a story was being read. On the playground, he wasn't "keeping his hands to himself," doing an excessive amount of grabbing and some hitting. The teacher had "seen other children like Steven" and suggested he get a medical evaluation. Specifically, she suspected ADD.

Sheila paused briefly and then added: "I know that one kid in Steve's class is taking Ritalin. His parents say it's made a big difference." Again she hesitated, then spoke in a rush: "I *hate* the idea of putting Steve on a drug, but I'm really worried about him not getting along with the other kids. Do you think it might help him? Would it change his personality?"

I understood Sheila's anxiety about her son. I had heard the same note of distress over the phone from many parents, and I've seen the pain and havoc that a seriously unhappy, acting-out child can cause in families. I told her I could evaluate Steven—a process that would take several meetings with him and both parents—and provide an opinion on what was going on and what to do about it. Medication might be part of the eventual treatment, I said—but I would never recommend it as an option before seeing the child.

Sheila seemed relieved, and we set up a first appointment for her and her husband. I'd see Steven later. . . .

I vividly recall the first time I witnessed the change that some children exhibit when they start taking Ritalin. One of our patients at the Child Study Unit was a little boy who had never been able to play with a toy for more than a minute without throwing it aside and racing off. After Ritalin, he sat and played quietly for twenty minutes, while his parents and I marveled at the transformation.

Since then I have evaluated hundreds of children and adolescents for the diagnosis of ADD and treatment with Ritalin. Each individual and family has had a unique background, circumstances, and problems—but patterns have emerged. The most obvious pattern has been a distinct shift in the number and kinds of patients referred for an ADD evaluation. Over the first fifteen years of my practice, perhaps two dozen kids each year emerged from my office with an ADD diagnosis. Most of them fit the typical profile long associated with the condition: boys from six to twelve years old, extremely hyperactive and impulsive, functioning poorly (if at all) in a normal school situation. Many of these kids were quite out of control, and intervention with medication (usually Ritalin) was often needed to give other treatments a chance to work.

The parents of these earlier patients were beleaguered and confused: They didn't know what was going on with their kids, were typically accused of bad parenting, and only rarely were aware of the condition called ADD. They may have heard about Ritalin's ability to "calm down" overactive children, but most were fearful of giving stimulant medication to their own son or daughter—I practically had to go on bended knee to get their consent. Some parents were relieved to learn that the problem might spring partly from the child's inherent personality (rather than from their own failure as parents). Others—especially some fathers—didn't buy the concept of ADD at all. Rather than admitting that something might be "mentally" wrong with their child, they preferred to think he just needed more discipline (typically, they thought the child's mother was too "soft" with him).

As of the early 1990s, however, my experience with families and ADD was clearly changing. The sheer volume of my cases went up dramatically, from two dozen a year to more than a hundred at present. I was evaluating more and more children under the age of five for the condition, as well as more children, teenagers, and adults with no signs of hyperactivity—people whose main problem was an inability to pay attention and get their work done. Many of this newer group of patients I judged to be less severely affected by ADD symptoms, and some I thought were doing fairly well. Far more often than in the past, a first-time visit would be prefaced by a phone call like Sheila Gordon's, indicating that someone (usually a parent or teacher) already suspected that ADD was responsible for a child's troubles. Indeed, as ADD became a familiar term, families almost seemed to welcome the diagnosis: Here at least was a clear answer to the behavior puzzles that plagued them.

And though some parents remained uncomfortable with giving medication for behavior problems, in general I encountered far less resistance to Ritalin. I found myself prescribing a lot more of the drug. The difference was simple to measure: California (like many states) requires a distinctive prescription form for Ritalin and other potentially addictive drugs. (In my practice they're used only for Ritalin.) Before 1990 I needed perhaps one pad of a hundred forms every nine months; by 1997 I realized it was one every three months.

What was going on with ADD and Ritalin, and why? I don't remember exactly when I started to feel deeply concerned about the trend I was witnessing and my own part in it. Perhaps it was the fourth or fifth time I saw a young patient who was struggling a bit in school but otherwise seemed to be functioning well enough—a child whom I didn't see as a clear candidate for medication, and yet who had been prescribed Ritalin even before I met him. Or perhaps it was when I realized that only medical solutions were being proposed to behavior problems that I saw as having many possible sources: in overscheduled families or in crowded classrooms, for example. But once I realized what was happening, the questions couldn't be tuned out. Were other doctors worrying about this? Was it unique to our area? Was anyone in the professional literature raising these issues? Was the rise in ADD cases and Ritalin demand a benign phenomenon, or was it time to start looking critically at the matter? . . .

Lately, American society—in particular, American psychiatry—has moved strongly toward accepting yet another explanation for problems of behavior, motivation, and performance: that they are caused by some dysfunction of the brain. The roots of this movement go deep, and this book will trace them. The message that follows from this model has been unequivocal and powerful:

If a problem is neurologically based, it should be treated with a drug.

In many cases, medication is surely called for. In many others, I have doubts. Offering Ritalin can help people who don't fit well into the here and now, I've assured myself. Inarguably, it can help certain kids adapt to an ever more challenging school environment. But I've wondered: Is there still a place for childhood in the anxious, downsizing America of the late 1990s? What if Tom Sawyer or Huckleberry Finn were to walk into my office tomorrow? Tom's indifference to schooling and Huck's "oppositional" behavior would surely have been cause for concern. Would I prescribe Ritalin for them, too?

The surge in Ritalin use tells us volumes about how we explain—and deal with—the problems many children and adults are having in coping with their world today. And the controversy over its use reflects the divide between two competing theories about behavior and performance problems. In one camp are those who believe such problems are chiefly attributable to a child's inherent brain chemistry. According to this view, medication is the best (sometimes the only) treatment. The other side posits that problem behaviors are the result of how children have been and are being treated. According to this view, children develop problems because they are subject to inappropriate or misguided expectations and responses. In other words, there is nothing inherently wrong with the child; what is needed are improvements in parenting, teaching, or the social environment. . . .

Is America ready to have 10 percent of its children taking Ritalin? Because boys are disproportionately represented in the total population of kids diagnosed with ADD, *this would mean giving the drug to one in six boys between the ages of five and twelve.*[2] This prospect seems not to faze some researchers. In their view, if a medication "works" on a certain condition, then we ought to use it.

There's no question that Ritalin can in most cases bring about short term improvements in behavior. I and many others, however, find that enthusiasm about the drug's efficacy has obscured a larger, murkier picture. The prospect of Ritalin being given to so many children raises many questions. Among them: How safe is the drug for children and for adults, and what are its possible side effects? Does it help patients overcome their ADD symptoms over the long term? Is there a chance that Ritalin, by addressing symptoms, may mask some of the true causes of behavior problems? And what does the greatly expanded use of such a drug say about the institutions traditionally charged with the "nurture" of children: our homes and families, our schools, our health care system?. . . .

Policy makers, law enforcement officials, and the courts are concerned with Ritalin as a potential drug of abuse. Has there been a rise in the abuse of Ritalin along with its sanctioned use for ADD? Should we maintain current restrictions on its use, including special prescriptions regulated by the government? Or since most patients won't abuse Ritalin, should the restrictions be relaxed? Policymakers must ask other questions, too: How should disability be legally defined for ADD? What are the consequences for our educational system and workplaces of numerous people receiving special allowances because of such a disability? What are the cost/benefit choices of dealing with ADD as a society?

Another powerful group with a huge investment in ADD and Ritalin is the pharmaceutical industry, which has profited enormously from the jump in Ritalin use and would surely benefit from a less restrictive policy on its use. The DEA estimates that pharmaceutical companies earn approximately $450 million a year with stimulants (nearly all legal use of stimulants in the United States is for ADD treatment.)[3] What if the number of American children affected by the disorder really is 10 percent? How would it affect revenues if all those children were receiving medication? How many families will turn instead to the growing number of special diets, food supplements, homeopathic preparations, exercise regimens, and hands-on treatments promising to ameliorate or eliminate ADD-related behaviors?

And, finally, there is nearly everyone else—all the citizens of our hardworking, stress-fueled society. Can low doses of stimulants help anyone—children or adults, ADD diagnosis or not—concentrate better on boring tasks? If it does work this way, why shouldn't anyone try Ritalin? Can it help a person improve his or her performance when some career-related circumstance has raised the bar dramatically?

The ADD-Ritalin issue reveals something about the kind of society we are at the turn of the millennium—for no country besides America is experiencing such a rise in Ritalin use. . . . Is there a message in this pill? If so, what is the Ritalin boom telling us? Ritalin seems to have become the drug for our day. As competition on every level intensifies, our preoccupations as a culture increasingly center on performance. And our children, whether we realize it or not, have been serving as a proving ground for the premise of medicating to enhance perfor-

mance. Are we likely to see a time in the not-so-distant future when a large part of America will be running on Ritalin?

Notes

1. Based upon data from the Drug Enforcement Administration (DEA), U.S. Department of Justice. Ritalin production and use are presented in great detail [later].

2. Based upon about a 4:1 or 5:I ratio of boys to girls currently diagnosed with ADD.

3. Based upon statements from Gene R. Haislip, deputy assistant administrator, Drug Enforcement Administration, Office of Diversion Control. The pharmaceutical industry is discussed in more detail [later].

23
American Women and Smoking

22 Million Just Don't Get It

Ann Colston Wentz

Each day in the United States, 3,000 people light up for the first time. Many are girls and young women, and the preponderance will become addicted. In a culture that venerates physical attractiveness, cigarette smoking is perceived to be an effective way to lose weight and maintain a slender figure. Many women report that they would rather take the chance of contracting lung cancer and emphysema than face the reality of being "fat." Cigarette smoking is reinforcing in a number of ways. There is a mild high and a tingly sensation as nicotine—the psychoactive agent in tobacco— is absorbed by the capillary-rich lungs to cross the blood-brain barrier, typically within five seconds of inhalation. Coupled with its hip, cool, and trendy status—at least in many circles of teenagers and young adults—its allure becomes almost irresistible.

Within the last five years, however, the institutional environment has become considerably more hostile to smokers. State legislatures across the country have made it illegal to light up in movie theaters, restaurants, government buildings, and even bars. A punitive judgment of 146 billion dollars was recently reached against several cigarette manufacturers for concealing evidence about tobacco's deleterious health effects. The product's destructive impact on the nation's public health is significant. Every year, some 400,000 people die from diseases of the heart and lung caused directly or indirectly by cigarette smoke; an estimated 50,000 people die annually from second-hand smoke exposure; one-quarter of all deaths from accidental fires are caused by improperly extinguished cigarettes (chemicals are commonly added to cigarette paper to keep the cigarettes burning, which makes smokers buy more of them).

Negative consequences are not a deterrent for those who believe that bad things will not happen to them. This belief is especially strong among the young, and cigarettes' popularity among young women is not likely to wane any time soon. Some feminist researchers suggest that tobacco consumption is just one more way in which the mandates of modern American patriarchy victimize those who can least afford to be victimized. Already exploited by an oppressive social system, women buy into idealized cultural images of physical attractiveness (often unattainable) and addict themselves to a lethal substance in the process.

Over 20 million women in the United States smoke cigarettes. Of all females 18 years of age and older in this country, 23.5 percent were smokers in 1991.[1] Of those, 25 percent were pregnant.[2] These numbers do not even include younger women and girls, who make up the fastest growing group of new smokers. That they will continue to smoke is part of the tobacco industry's strategy, since 90 percent of current smokers began their habit while teenagers and half began to smoke under the age of 14 years. Although most adults who smoke say they would like to quit, only about 2.5 percent per year manage to do so.[3] That means that a hooked teenager can be counted on to buy cigarettes for the next 50 years. These rough numbers are staggering: A pack or so a day, 20–30 cigarettes, translates to 200 a week, 10,400 a year, half a million a lifetime. All this occurs in a setting where it is estimated that the profit margin in cigarette sales ranks among the highest in American industry, garnering for tobacco companies profits three to five times that of average corporations.[4] So, no wonder 22.2 million American women don't get it; business interests count on them as being close to 30 percent of the market and conspire to keep them puffing away their health.

The explanations for this rising tide of women smokers, perhaps more acceptable to our ears, include misguided vanity, mimicry, and other myths. For example, many female teenagers begin to smoke to control their weight and are certain they will gain weight if they stop. Earlier studies did indeed document a five-pound average weight gain over time in quitters, compared with about a pound of gain in continuing smokers for the duration of the study. Recent evidence, however, suggests that the gain may not be permanent and that body mass index and body weight actually decrease in female ex-smokers with increasing years.[5] Other explanations include a lack of educational programs enrolling those likely to initiate smoking, inadequate funding and resources directed toward smoking control, and society's inability both to perceive the magnitude of the problem and to personalize it. However, the success of educational programs that are implemented can be documented to provide cost effective tobacco-related behavior modification.[6] Thus, it seems that the best explanation for our unacceptably high smoking rates among women lies in the persuasive power of the large, organized, well-funded, and very determined tobacco lobbying effort.

For example, when the state of California in 1989 passed Proposition 99, which raised the cigarette tax by 25 cents and directed the additional revenues to smoking prevention and cessation programs, particularly in the schools, the tobacco industry increased its political expenditures tenfold and effectively prevented full implementation of the mandate. Begay et al.[7] report that only 14.7 percent of revenues was spent on education and prevention, not the 20 percent passed by law, resulting in 174.7 million dollars of underfunding.

Other recent studies also point out indirectly the enormous power of the tobacco industry. Passive smoking, airline smoke, and tar and nicotine levels are issues that have brought out the tobacco lobbyists. The finding that tar and nicotine levels do not predict smokers' exposure to carbon monoxide or the metabolite of tobacco, cotinine, is simply interpreted that low-tar and low-nicotine cigarette brands are not safer. However, 45 percent of smokers believe that smoking cigarettes low in nicotine and tar somehow is less dangerous, according to the 1989 Surgeon General's report. Marketing has been the major influence in the spread of this message. Why do tobacco companies advertise the tar and nicotine content of their low-yield brands if not to market the message that low numbers mean safe?

Nevertheless, everyone knows cigarette smoking is bad for one's health. After all, each pack of cigarettes contains a warning. What more people need to understand and take to heart is that cigarette smoking is the most preventable cause of premature death in this country. Statistics released by the Centers for Disease Control (CDC) attribute 1,198,887 years of potential life lost in 1988 due to smoking.[8] An impact study, the Smoking-Attributable Mortality, Morbidity, and Economic Cost (SAMMEC) report, estimates the number of deaths from neoplastic, cardiovascular diseases associated with cigarette smoking and reports 5,048,740 years of life expectancy lost.[9] Those figures do not approach the impact of smoking-induced morbidity, just mortality

Two thoughts. First, why doesn't the Food and Drug Administration (FDA) get involved? The two things required of drugs and medications released for use in this country are efficacy and safety. Tobacco is a deadly product. Why not place the tobacco industry under the same requirement as the pharmaceutical industry? Second, those of us who are for a smoke-free America by the year 2000 ought to mount a personal, educational, one-on-one, informative, and supportive antismoking campaign with our patients. Ironically, many of us in medicine ourselves smoke—we need first to heal ourselves. Beyond that, 22.2 million American women need our help. Women's health depends on us.

Notes

1. Centers for Disease Control. "Cigarette Smoking Among Adults—United States, 1991." *MMWR* 1993; 42:230.

2. Windsor, R. A., Li, C. Q., Lowe, J. B., Perkins, L. L., Ershoff, D., Glynn, T. "The dissemination of smoking cessation methods for pregnant women: Achieving the year 2000 objec-

tives." *American Journal of Public Health* 1993; 83:173.

3. *The health benefits of smoking cessation: A report of the Surgeon General.* Washington, DC: U.S. Dept. of Health and Human Services, 1990 [DHHS publ. CDC 90–8416].

4. Kale, W. "Philip Morris' war cry called dangerous move." Richmond (VA) *Times-Dispatch* April 6, 1993 :B7, B12.

5. Chen, Y., Horne, S. L., Dosman, J. A. "The influence of smoking cessation on body weigh may be temporary." *American Journal of Public Health* 1993; 83:1330.

6. Elder, J. R., Wildey, M., de Moor, C., et al. "The long-term prevention of tobacco use among junior high school students: Classroom and telephone intervention." *American Journal of Public Health* 1993; 83:1239.

7. Begay, M. E., Traynor, M., Glantz, S. A. "The tobacco industry, state politics, and tobacco education in California." *American Journal of Public Health* 1993; 83:1214.

8. Centers for Disease Control. "Cigarette smoking-attributable mortality and years of potential life lost—United States, 1988." *MMWR* 1991; 40:62, 69.

9. Centers for Disease Control, "Cigarette smoking-attributable mortality and years of potential life lost—United States, 1990." *MMWR* 1993; 42:645.

Part V

Violence

Few types of deviance elicit more fear than interpersonal violence. Murder, rape, robbery, and assault are consistently ranked near the top of lists of behaviors that alarm the most people. Such fears are particularly pronounced in the United States, and for good reason. The United States typically reports the highest rates of violence of any country in the Western industrialized world. Roughly 23,000 homicides, 600,000 robberies, 100,000 rapes, and a million assaults are reported to the police every year. Self-report and victimization surveys suggest there actually may be many more.

Fear of being a victim of violence is pervasive, and it fundamentally influences how people conduct their daily lives. How many readers have avoided certain areas, stayed inside, glanced furtively over their shoulders, refused to open a door for a stranger, or suspected an otherwise innocent party of wrongdoing out of fear? How many have beefed up security in their homes—installed deadbolts, burglar bars, or elaborate alarm systems—for fear of being victimized by some predatory other? How many have taken self-defense courses or armed themselves with mace, pepper spray, and a host of other anticrime devices to make themselves feel safe? Real or imagined, fear drives actions geared to make people more immune from victimization.

The media, from which many citizens get their information about violence, only amplify such fears. There is a common expression in the news business that "if it bleeds, it leads." Blood, guts, and gore generate attention and attention generates ratings, so stories about violent crime are regularly and prominently featured. The local and national airwaves are literally saturated with images of school shootings, bank robberies, gang warfare, assault rapes, and various other nefarious acts that people commit against one another. Such coverage almost always suggests, or at least implies, that anybody can be a victim. Violence, we are told, is random, senseless, unprovoked, and ubiquitous, potentially affecting anyone who finds himself or herself at the wrong place at the wrong time. Focusing on a few sensational events and portraying them as representative, the media actively promote a siege mentality.

America is a violent society, but not nearly as violent as TV and newspapers would have us believe. Modern civilization is extraordinarily safe, safer than at any time in the history of humankind. Most of us will go through our daily lives without ever being victimized by a predatory aggressor. When violence does happen, it tends *not* to involve random attacks by psychopathic strangers but, rather, violations by persons who know the victim, often intimately. Many of these attacks are triggered by something done by the victim (Polk 1993). Homicide victims (for example) are routinely the first to brandish a deadly weapon, to threaten force, or to actually strike the eventual perpetrator. Offensive measures lead to escalation; the object of aggression responds in kind, the interaction becomes more and more violent, and death is the end result (Wolfgang 1958; see also Brown et al. 1996, 397).

Robbery, the taking of something of value through force or threat of force, has been called the most feared violent crime because it couples property loss with the *possibility* of homicide. The possibility is real; 2,000 people die every year in the United States during robberies or attempted robberies. The loot seized from a typical robbery is not very large, about $840 according to the FBI (see also Brown et al. 1996). The high-stakes bank robberies and armored car heists that receive so much media attention (and are depicted in popular films such as *Heat* and *Dead Presidents*) actually are quite rare. Most offenders prefer not to rob hard targets; surveillance cameras, security guards, locked vaults, and witnesses increase the difficulty of escape, and, for many, the risk of detection is simply not worth the rewards. Less lucrative, though more vulnerable, targets, like gas stations, mini-marts, taxicabs, and other small businesses, tend to be chosen first.

Some offenders, disappointed with the perceptibly low take of street robberies and deterred by the prospect of arrest, prefer fleecing victims who are themselves involved in crime. Drug sellers represent one such target; in many ways, they represent the ideal robbery mark. They are visible, accessible, and plentiful. They deal only in cash. Many are targets of their own making—showing off, bragging, or otherwise calling attention to themselves. Others are identified through gossip or inside information. The urban topography provides numerous staging areas from which to attack them. Robberies can be melded with drug purchases, allowing perpetrators to capitalize on the element of surprise. Compliance is secured rapidly and at acceptable risk. Bystanders are reluctant to intervene; on the streets, no one wants to get involved in someone else's troubles. The threat of retaliation is real but can be reduced to tolerable levels. Obviously, drug sellers cannot call the police to report their victimization (for these points, see Jacobs 2000, 141).

Domestic violence—aggression that occurs in the home between husbands and wives, girlfriends and boyfriends, parents and children, and siblings—has only recently begun to attract the kind of media and scholarly attention previously reserved for offenses like robbery. This change has been fueled by a number of sources—women's newfound economic power (which has translated into political influence), increasing sensitivity to the plight of children, the widespread diffusion of mental health and social workers into the home, and, perhaps most importantly, a few sensational events that galvanized public attention (see, e.g., Brown et al. 1996). In the mid-1990s, Americans were transfixed by the stories of Nicole Simpson and Lorena Bobbitt, two women who reportedly suffered substantial physical and mental trauma at the hands of their abusive husbands. Mrs. Simpson was ultimately killed; many, if not most, believe the killer was her famous husband O. J., although this was never proved in criminal court (a civil judgment, however, found Mr. Simpson liable). Lorena Bobbitt was reportedly beaten and raped by her husband multiple times over a period of months and years, prompting her, at one fateful moment, to wake up, secure a knife from the kitchen, sever her husband's sexual organ, and throw it in a ditch some distance from her house. (The organ was eventually recovered and reattached successfully.) Mrs. Bobbitt was acquitted by reason of temporary insanity, inspiring other victims of chronic battering to justify their own acts of retaliation against abusive men. Some of these pleas were successful; some were not.

It is important to remember that the "violence" in domestic violence is meted out by both men and women—"the percentage of wives having used physical violence often exceeds that of the husbands" (Steinmetz 1977–1978, 500)—but aggression dispensed by men tends to be more forceful and to do more damage (because of sheer physical differences between the sexes). These differences are amplified when alcohol is involved, and alcohol is involved much of the time. Common to all forms of domestic violence, however, is the notion that victims and offenders are around each other a lot, living in quarters that produce stress, envy, anger, and petty jealousies. These conditions inspire frustration, and frustration, in turn, sparks disputes that culminate in physical and sometimes lethal aggression.

By no means is domestic violence a new phenomenon; more powerful family members have assaulted less powerful ones since the family-as-institution came into existence thousands of years ago: "Infanticide—the ultimate form of child abuse—was common in ancient Egypt and throughout the middle ages and into the early modern period (sixteenth and seventeenth centuries) of Anglo-American history" (Brown et al. 1996, 418). In early-modern Scotland, some women opted to murder their illegitimate offspring (and risk capital punishment in the process) rather than face the extreme public humiliation that accompanied having a child out of wedlock (Taylor 1954; see also Brown et al. 1996). In many societies, men were once legally allowed to beat and abuse their wives, as long as the method and extent of punishment remained within specified limits:

> In eighteenth century France the law restricted violence against wives to "blows, thumps, kicks, or punches on the back if they leave no traces." Moreover, the law did not allow for the use of "sharp-edged or crushing instruments" (Andersen 1988, 170). The phrase "rule of thumb" is derived from English common law, which specified that a man could beat his wife—for disciplinary reasons—as long as he used a stick no thicker than his thumb (*ibid.*). An ordinance, still in effect

in Pennsylvania in the 1970s, prohibited a husband from beating his wife after ten o'clock in the evening and on Sundays. (Martin 1982, 266 quoted in Beirne and Messerschmidt 1991, 81)

Violence is not only or primarily interpersonal in nature. In actuality, the obverse is true. The most horrendous acts of aggression have been perpetrated by corporations, organizations, and nation-states against other institutions and people during the pursuit of various instrumental and expressive goals. War, which many contend is nothing more than politically sanctioned murder, is responsible for tens of millions of lives lost over hundreds of years. Thousands of people have been executed by governments across the centuries as retribution for serious criminal behavior; some commentators suggest that the death penalty represents nothing more than state-sanctioned murder. Shoddily produced consumer goods are responsible for 30,000 deaths and 20 million serious injuries every year. As many as 100,000 people are killed and 10 million disabled simply trying to make a living (Beirne and Messerschmidt 1991, 185; Cullen et al. 1987, 67). Importantly, "much of this harm may be considered a product of violence rather than accidental forces because the risk was unreasonable, avoidable, or associated with violation of existing civil or criminal law" (Brown et al. 1996, 425). These and other instances of institutional crime and violence are explored in greater detail later in this book. This section focuses on the various interpersonal manifestations of violence. ✦

24
Next Time She'll Be Dead

What Is 'Domestic Violence'?

Ann Jones

It might seem counterintuitive to suggest that the greatest physical and emotional threat many women face comes from precisely the persons who are supposed to love them the most: their husbands. The fact that "battered woman syndrome" has become an accepted and widely recognized part of the public discourse is as telling as it is troublesome. Thousands of women are abused by violent, out-of-control spouses on a daily basis. Many observers understandably ask, why not leave? Why stay in a relationship riddled with trauma and abuse? Why not escape the violence to pursue a life of peace and security?

For most battered women, leaving is easier said than done. Powerful emotional and economic forces are at work to give women few realistic alternatives beyond staying. Abandoning one's family is a traumatic event for anyone, but especially for women whose social value hinges on their "feminine loyalty" as wives and mothers. Breaking up the family is deeply stigmatizing and may undermine any perceived benefits of liberation. Paradoxically, it also is the case that many battered women deeply love their husbands and fear a profound emotional void by leaving. As a group, women lack the kind of economic power that makes independence practical; many rely on their husbands for key resources, a dependency amplified when children are involved (although these circumstances are changing).

Many women resolve their predicament by rationalizing it. Some assert, for example, that they are not really being hurt, that their men are loving people who are sick and cannot control their outbursts, that they themselves

caused the attacks (so their men should not be held responsible), or that tolerating the abuse of one's husband is the "right thing to do." Battered women effectively prolong their exposure to violence by intellectualizing it.

Some women may never escape. Others may go only after the violence gets so bad that they can no longer take it. Whatever the case, escape cannot happen unless or until powerful catalysts for change emerge—either in resources, options, or in the very nature of the relationship itself. Jones makes it clear that the experience of violent victimization goes through a definable "emotional career," and only those with the right mix of sensitivity, awareness, support, and luck will emerge successfully in the end. Even then, the larger social forces that contribute to domestic violence will likely continue.

"Domestic violence" is one of those gray phrases, beloved of bureaucracy, designed to give people a way of talking about a topic without seeing what's really going on.[1] Like "repatriation" or "ethnic cleansing," it's a euphemistic abstraction that keeps us at a dispassionate distance, far removed from the repugnant spectacle of human beings in pain. We used to speak of "wife beating"—words that brought to mind a picture of terrifying action, a big, heavy-handed man with a malicious eye, and a slight woman, dazed and bent, raising her arms against the blows, and crying out, "No!" Or we called it "wife torture," the words of Frances Power Cobbe that conjure the scenes *between* beatings: the sullen husband, withdrawn and sulking, or angry and intimidating, dumping dinner on the floor, throwing the cat against the wall, screaming, twisting a child's arm, needling, nagging, manipulating, criticizing the bitch, the slut, the cunt who never does anything right, who's ugly and stupid, who should keep her mouth shut, who should spread her legs now, who should be dead, who will be if she's not careful. Dickens drew such scenes, and Hardy and D. H. Lawrence, Dostoevsky and Zola, Doris Lessing, Toni Morrison, Margaret Atwood, Alice Munro, Alice

Walker, Joyce Carol Oates. But we prefer to speak of "domestic violence."

I suspect that some academic researcher coined the term, dismayed by the fact that all those beaten wives are *women*, and reaching for some pretentious and gender-neutral "objective" term. During the Carter administration, when women's issues enjoyed a heady moment of legitimacy in the nation's capital, professionals in mental health and justice, equipped with professional vocabularies, took up the problems of "spouse abuse," "conjugal violence," and "marital aggression"—and a great renaming took place, a renaming that veiled once again the sexism a grass-roots women's movement had worked to uncover.[2] Even feminist advocates for women, who called their cause "the battered women's movement," eventually succumbed; they adopted "domestic violence" in their fund raising proposals, so as not to offend men controlling the purse strings by suggesting that men were in any way to blame for this "social problem." So well does the phrase "domestic violence" obscure the real events behind it that when a Domestic Violence Act (to provide money for battered women's services) was first proposed to Congress in 1978, many thought it was a bill to combat political terrorism within the United States.

It's difficult to face up to the sexism behind the "social problem," for the public mind, like the individual, is apt to minimize, deny, repress, and forget the bad news.[3] Women in particular may have trouble facing the facts of sexist violence against women. Psychiatry professor Judith Lewis Herman observes: "Most women do not in fact recognize the degree of male hostility toward them, preferring to view the relations of the sexes as more benign than they are in fact. Similarly, women like to believe that they have greater freedom and higher status than they do in reality."[4] Nevertheless, it's absolutely necessary to keep that sexism in sight if we hope to make sense of battery, for the immensity and viciousness of male violence aimed specifically at women are otherwise incomprehensible.

Any battered woman, who has surely been called a lot of bad names, can tell you that words have the power of blows; but the words we commonly use to discuss battering aren't up to the task. Male violence disappears in euphemism. The old term "wife beating" named only one piece of male violence and only one relationship—marriage—between assailant and victim; and it focused attention on the victim, not the perpetrator. But at least it suggested what goes on. Current terms like "domestic violence" and its academic progeny "partner abuse," "familial dysfunction," and "spousal dissonance" obscure its nature altogether.

On the other hand, the term "battered woman"—adopted by the battered women's movement from nineteenth century feminist campaigns against "wife beating"—suggests a graphic picture, but one that may also mislead: the picture of a woman more or less constantly subjected to serious physical assault, a helpless victim. It alludes to only one form of male violence against women in the home, and it seemingly excludes so many others that most "battered women," sizing up their own circumstances, don't see themselves as "battered." Again, in emphasizing physical damage, the term "battered" masks the real nature and purpose of the "batterer's" behavior.

The terms "battered woman," "domestic violence victim," and "abused woman," which emphasize a woman's situation as the victimized object of another's actions, also obscure her subjectivity and actions. They suggest that "battered" woman is *all* she is, that "victim" is her identity. Yet women who have lived through such violence, who know the immense daily expenditure of strength and attention and self-discipline it takes to survive, rarely identify themselves as "victims." They think of themselves as strong women who can somehow "cope." Many who escape speak of themselves as "formerly battered women" or "survivors" or "veterans" of violence, but these terms suggest a status achieved after the fact; they do not describe the active woman in the day by day process of coping with, combating, and escaping her "partner's" violence. . . .

The term "battered woman," which puts the focus on her, also encourages us to overlook her children; but there can be no doubt that male violence inflicts terrible damage upon them. Uncounted millions of children live in households dominated by violent men. Millions of children see and hear their mothers beaten repeatedly, a traumatic experience that many experts regard as in itself a form of child abuse. Some studies suggest that children who witness battering may suffer long-term consequences; both as children and as adults they may be particularly anxious, depressed, or aggressive.[5] And one major review of psychological studies of batterers found only one point of common history: many batterers witnessed the battery of their mothers when they were boys.[6] Millions of children become targets of violence as well, for the man who batters a woman is likely to abuse the kids, too. Two studies found that between 53 and 70 percent of men who battered a wife or girlfriend also abused a child; and in households with four or more children, 92 percent of the batterers abused the children.[7] Two other studies of children who received hospital treatment for abuse found that between 45 and 59 percent of their mothers were battered women.[8] Such children, too, are likely to become depressed, anxious, or aggressive; and the physical and emotional damage that will freight their adult lives is beyond calculation and repair.

The term "battered woman" also sets apart women who are victims of one form of male violence, as though there is something peculiar about *them*, and obscures the universal pattern of male dominance. (This is another reason why battered women themselves resist the label.) Labeling separate categories of male violence—battering, rape, incest, pimping, murder, and so on—makes each "problem" seem smaller than it is, a local condition, or a personal one. . . .

The actual physical damage to women is real. "Domestic violence" is the leading cause of injury to women in the United States. According to the National Clearinghouse on Domestic Violence, men batter three or four million women a year.[9] According to the National Centers for Disease Control, more women are treated in emergency rooms for battering injuries than for (nonmarital) rapes, muggings, and traffic

accidents *combined*.[10] Untold numbers of women suffer permanent injuries—brain damage, blindness, deafness, speech loss through laryngeal damage, disfigurement and mutilation, damage to or loss of internal organs, paralysis, sterility, and so on. Countless pregnant women miscarry as a result of beatings, and countless birth defects and abnormalities can be attributed to battery of the mother during pregnancy. So many battered women have been infected with HIV by batterers who force them into unprotected sex, in some cases deliberately to prevent their having sex with other men, that the National Centers for Disease Control have identified a direct link between battering and the spread of HIV and AIDS among women.[11] And every day at least four women die violently at the hands of men who profess to love them.[12] . . .

It's vital to understand that battering is not a series of isolated blow-ups. It is a *process of deliberate intimidation intended to coerce the victim to do the will of the victimizer.* The batterer is not just losing his temper, not just suffering from stress, not just manifesting "insecurity" or a spontaneous reaction "provoked" by something the victim did or (as psychologists put it) "a deficit of interpersonal skills" or an "inhibition in anger control mechanisms." These are *excuses* for violence, popular even among therapists who work with batterers; yet we all know aggrieved, insecure, stressed out people with meager interpersonal skills who lose their temper *without* becoming violent. We assume, then, that the grievances of the violent man must be worse, and that under extreme stress he has spun out of control. He looks it, and that's what he says: "I wasn't myself." "I was drunk." "I went bananas." "I lost it." "I went out of my mind." It's lines like these that provide a public excuse and deceive a battered woman into giving one more chance to the so-called *real*, nonviolent man underneath. But in fact that violence *is* himself, perfectly *in* control and *exercising* control. . . .

It's doubtful any living woman could meet the rigid specifications of the batterer. Marriage counselors observe that even when batterers purport to be "working" on their "relationship," they are intent upon *devaluing* their partner rather than *understanding* her. Typically, they denigrate what women say with comments like "She went on and on about nothing" or "She was in a bitchy mood," but when pressed by counselors, David Adams says, "men cannot recall their wives' actual words or specific complaints."[13] Many counselors observe that what a batterer calls "nagging" is a woman's repetition of what she *knows* he hasn't heard. Counseling batterers in Duluth, Minnesota, Ellen Pence noticed that men rarely call the women they abuse by *name*, presumably because they don't see women as persons in their own right. In one men's group session, she counted ninety-seven references to wives and girlfriends, many of them obscene, before a man mentioned his wife by name. When Pence insisted they use names, many men "could hardly spit it out." Pence points out that many women still lose their last name at marriage; marry a controlling man, she says, and "Your front name goes too."[14] Then the batterer tries to pummel this "nonentity" into the "person" he wants: the perfect wife. . . .

It is equally vital to understand that women are battered *because they will not give in*. One survivor who now counsels abused women put it this way: "Most of the battered women I meet are really strong women, and that's why they get beat—because they don't take no shit. And that's why I got beat—because I wouldn't act like he wanted me to act, talk like he wanted me to talk, be who he wanted me to be."[15] As I've said, the FBI reports that a woman is beaten in the United States every ten seconds or so, but we can better understand what's going on by thinking of it this way: every ten seconds a woman *resists*.

Her concerns are complex. Like most women, battered or not, she probably places a higher value on human connections and the compromises necessary to preserve them than do most men; and despite her shock and anger, there is no one who has greater compassion for the batterer, at least at first, than the battered woman herself. But she also values herself. Under threat of violence, a woman may give up bits and pieces of herself: her preferences, her opinions, her voice, her friends, her job, her freedom of movement, her sexual autonomy. She may learn to lie, or at least to keep the truth to herself. She may learn to say the sex was good when it wasn't, or that she's sorry when she's not. Unable ever to give the "right" answer, she may retreat into silence. It's often easy to mistake her apparent passivity for submission, masochism, complicity. But she does not give in. Uncle Remus and Br'er Rabbit, experts on outwitting violent oppression, called it "laying low." A battered woman lies low while she tries first to make sense of her situation, then to change it, and finally to get out.

In the long run, battering a woman to control her is almost certain to fail, for battered women *leave*. It is not too much to say that from the first moment a man abuses her, a woman begins, in some sense, to leave—emotionally, spiritually, physically. Shocked at first, she may try to stop the violence by trying to become "a better person," but she ends by trying to be in another place. She may embezzle from the grocery money for months, placating the batterer all the while she squirrels away the price of a ticket to freedom. Abused women describe this process of going underground within themselves, hiding out inside, lying low until they can emerge, like some moth shedding caterpillar skin, becoming themselves. Escapees say: "Now I'm *myself* again."

When it comes to getting out, women are enormously ingenious, resourceful, and brave. They have to be because it's at this point—when "his woman" escapes—that the abuser is most dangerous. Absolutely dependent upon her submission for his own sense of power and control, he can not bear to lose her. In many cases, that false sense of power is the only identity a man has; to lose "his woman" is to lose himself. Thus, he is far more likely to kill her (and perhaps himself as well) as she tries to leave or *after she has left*, than if she stays with him. ("If I can't have you, nobody can," he says.)

Battered women know this, and they leave anyway. One formerly battered woman explained to talk show host Sally Jesse Raphael: "It takes a lot of maneuvering, a lot of mental exercise, to get out." At a speak-out for formerly battered women in Seattle, a woman who had been afraid for her life described her escape into hiding: she booked an early morning flight to a distant city, then asked her husband for permission to go regularly to early mass to pray for God's guidance in "being a better wife." "On Monday I went to mass," she said. "On Tuesday I went to mass. On Wednesday I went to mass. On Thursday I went to the airport." Another woman told me how she ejected a battering husband who refused to leave *her* house. "He's a boxer," she explained, "and he had closed in my garage as a workout room. What I did, while he was at work one day, was cut this giant hole in the garage door with a huge power saw, and I backed a truck up to the hole, and I took all his boxing training things and all his clothes and personal stuff and anything I thought he might want, and I put it on the truck, took it to his mother's house, dumped it in the yard, and said, 'Enough is enough.' Since then I'm on my third restraining order."[16]

In the short run though, battering *works*. It may be mean and cowardly and cruel and criminal and an evolutionary throwback, but for the batterer's immediate gratification, it works fine. Just as many parents use physical force, or the threat of it, to make children "behave," many men know that there's nothing like a good pow in the kisser, or the threat of it, to keep the little lady in line. Individual men beat individual women to make those women do what they want. And the widespread practice of wife beating intimidates all women and reinforces our society's habitual pattern of male dominance. A little muscle gets a guy a little sex, a little peace and quiet, a little attention, another drink, and in the great cosmic scheme of things, it helps keep a man's world a man's world. What could be more efficient?. . .

I recall a conversation with the son of a woman who was on trial for shooting her battering husband. After enduring years of abuse for the sake of keeping the family together, she finally shot her husband when he started to abuse the children, including the boy I was talking to. The boy said he loved his mother, but "none of this" would have happened if she had "acted right"—which

meant, as her husband had wanted her to. As his own bride, the boy intended to find "a girl who does everything right"; he had recently broken up with his girlfriend because she took a sip from his can of beer, and he considered girls who drink "immoral. I asked him if he ever had any doubts about *his* ability to do "everything right," and it was clear from his bafflement that the question had never crossed his mind. Living up to another's impossible expectations was not *his* job, but *hers*. He was fourteen years old.[17] . . .

. . . [Men] learn from the instruction manuals of popular culture—from films and rock videos and pornography and beer commercials—more up-to-the-minute manliness scripts, conflating violence and sex. No one claims these days that battering is part of man's essential nature, for there are lots of men—probably more than half the male population—who never have done it and never will. But no one claims that battering is "abnormal" behavior for men either. Rather, it is "an extreme form of normality, an exaggeration of how society expects men to behave."[18] Great numbers of men, in every segment of the population, still swagger through "relationships" with all the finesse of Rambo. And many young men—the MTV fans who are fast making date rape and fraternity gang rape campus traditions—seem to regard the use of violence against women as, if not part of man's nature, certainly man's *right*.

Given the structure of this "man's world," men can scarcely think otherwise. And violence against women is so sturdily buttressed by cultural supports that it can almost be mistaken for the national pastime, as indeed it is by groups of men who gang rape women just for the fun of it, or murder women just for the thrilling rush of power it brings. After more than a decade of talking to wife beaters and beaten wives, Ellen Pence, founder of the Duluth Domestic Abuse Intervention Project, describes the cultural context that supports and encourages battering. Every part of life, she says, is affected by hierarchical structures—the school, the church, the military, the government—so it seems "natural" to us always that someone be "in charge" and others be subordinate. In the family, that someone in charge is the man. (Female-headed households, though they are rapidly coming to outnumber male-headed households, still don't count as *real* families; and couples who try to share authority equally will find that the world's representatives—the banker, for example, or the car salesman—see the man as *really* in charge.) "Every abuser," Pence says, "operates out of the belief that there is a natural order to things, and that by virtue of his sex, he should be at the top of the family system." Secondly, the culture objectifies women in pornography, videos, ads, adult "entertainment," TV shows, beauty contests, and the like, encouraging the abuser to think of women, especially *his* women, as available and intended for his use. Thirdly, the culture compels women to submit through a combination of psychological conditioning that trains them to "understand" and take care of men, economic arrangements that plunge female-headed households into poverty, and legal license that permits men to coerce *their* women by threats and violence.[19]

Notes

1. To see what "domestic violence" looks like, see Donna Ferrato, *Living with the Enemy* (New York: Aperture, 1991).
2. Susan Schechter, *Women and Male Violence: The Visions and Struggles of the Battered Women's Movement* (Boston: South End Press, 1982), p. 201.
3. Judith Lewis Herman, *Trauma and Recovery* (New York: Basic, 1992), p. 9.
4. Ibid., p. 69.
5. Telephone interview with Susan Schechter, Program Coordinator of AWAKE (Advocacy for Women and Kids in Emergencies), Children's Hospital, Boston, Mass., Jan. 22, 1993.
6. Gerald T. Hotaling and David B. Sugarman, "An Analysis of Risk Factors in Husband to Wife Violence: The Current State of Knowledge," *Violence and Victims* 1, no. 2 (1986): 101–124.
7. Lenore E. Walker, *The Battered Woman Syndrome* (New York: Springer, 1984), p. 59; Lee

H. Bowker, Michelle Arbitell, and J. Richard McFerron, "On the Relationship Between Wife Beating and Child Abuse," in *Feminist Perspectives on Wife Abuse*, ed. Kersti Yllo and Michelle Bograd (Newbury Park, CA: Sage, 1988), pp. 162–163.
8. Evan Stark and Anne Flitcraft, "Women and Children at Risk: A Feminist Perspective on Child Abuse," *International Journal of Health Services*, 18, no. 1 (1988); Linda McKibben et al., "Victimization of Mothers of Abused Children: A Controlled Study," *Pediatrics* 84 no. 3 (1989).
9. Laura S. Harper, "Battered Women Suing Police for Failure to Intervene: Viable Legal Avenues After *DeShaney v. Winnebago County Department of Social Services*," 75 *Cornell Law Review* 1393, 1426, n 216 (1990).
10. Surgeon General Antonia C. Novello, quoted in "Physicians Begin a Program to Combat Family Violence," *New York Times*, Oct. 17, 1991, p. 15.
11. Sally Jacobs, in "Hub and Beyond, HIV Seen as Latest Whip for Batterers," *Boston Globe*, Jan. 24, 1993, pp. 21, 24.
12. Marilyn French, *The War Against Women* (New York: Summit, 1992), p. 187.
13. David Adams, "Treatment Models of Men Who Batter: A Profeminist Analysis," in Yllo and Bograd, eds., *Feminist Perspectives*, p. 191.
14. Ellen Pence, "How Society Gives Men Permission to Batter," *In Our Best Interest*, part 2, a videotape produced by the Women's Coalition, Duluth, Minn., n.d.
15. Interview with a survivor of battery who requested anonymity, in Minnesota, Sept. 2, 1987.
16. Interview with a survivor of battery who requested anonymity, in Hawaii, Nov. 28, 1987.
17. Interview in Indiana, May 5, 1979. Name withheld.
18. Elizabeth Wilson, *What Is to Be Done About Violence Against Women?* (London: Penguin, 1983), p. 95.
19. Pence, "How Society Gives Men Permission to Batter," *In Our Best Interest*, part 2.

25
Gang Violence

Scott H. Decker

Barrik Van Winkle

Colors, graffiti, turf, automatic weapons, drive-by shootings—these are the things for which street gangs are most known. Violence perpetrated by gang members in the 1980s and 1990s at times reached epidemic proportions, fueled by involvement in the crack trade and the widespread diffusion of firearms. Urban communities were woefully unprepared for the crisis. Many neighborhoods came to resemble something out of the vigilante Wild West—settings where street justice supplanted the rule of law.

Embroiled in a culture of violence, many gang members learn early on that respect can come to them only by their seizing it (Anderson 1999). Encroachments on their person or territory (physical) or on their character (verbal) warrant swift, certain, and severe reactions. The importance of "badness" puts a premium on offensive aggression. Failure to act is to punk out, and to punk out risks the ultimate stigma. Cowards will find their personal safety in serious jeopardy. In the violent world of street gangs there is no place, or mercy, for the weak (see also Jacobs 2000, 2).

Gang violence has both instrumental and expressive purposes; the two orientations are not mutually exclusive, and they actually dovetail nicely on many occasions. Why are gangs so violent? Decker and Van Winkle suggest that street gangs are not only organized for violence, they select people who have propensities for violence and then amplify these propensities by weakening members' ties to mainstream social institutions that might otherwise have a restraining influence (e.g., job, family, church, school). When a critical mass of gangs and gang members concentrates in a particular geographic area, conflict spirals and contagions of aggression often ensue. Attempts to settle grievances generate countergrievances, spawning lethal retaliatory cycles (Blumstein 1995). Few deviant subcultures embroil, or threaten to embroil, mainstream society in so pernicious a way. Understanding why gangs form and how they operate is crucial for developing policies geared to control them.

'Piling on Crabs and Shooting Slobs': Violence and Gangs

Beating Crabs. If it wasn't for Beating Crabs I don't think that I would be in a gang right now. (Male #057, "Smith & Wesson," fifteen-year-old Neighborhood Posse Blood)

[Our] group is the Rolling 60's. Basically we're just a fighting crew. What we do is to fight and make money. We rough ourselves up. Get ourselves tougher cause we feel we better than all the rest. So like if a Hoover comes up and he talks shit then we have to whup his ass because Hoovers think they crazier than us but we the craziest but we know what we doing. We like Al Capone back in his days, suited up and know what he doing. We just not normally kick ass. (Male #092, "Derone," twenty-one-year-old Rolling 60's Crip)

Violence and violent crime is a central part of our subjects' lives in manifold ways. The "violence of everyday life,"[1] for example, is excessively high in their neighborhoods and families. City rates of child abuse, forcible theft, rape, assaults, and homicide are well above those for the St. Louis metropolitan area and the nation. Although we did not systematically explore the level of family and neighborhood violence in our interviews, enough background information allows us to infer its existence at high levels. Eight of our subjects mentioned having a relative who died from gunshot wounds or some other form of homicide; *more than half knew another gang member who had been shot.* Eleven of our subjects are now dead. Further evidence is apparent . . .by the importance of threat and the need for protection in generating gangs and membership.

A second arena in which violence and conflict are central is in the nature and characteristics of gangs and gang membership. Frederick Thrasher, writing nearly seventy years ago, observed that what boys receive from membership in gangs is

> the thrill and zest of participation in common interest, more especially in corporate action, in hunting, capture, conflict, flight and escape. *Conflict with other gangs and the world about them* furnishes the occasion for many of their exciting group activities. (1927, 37, emphasis added).

This finding is just as true today and, in fact, it is echoed in our subjects' own words. Conflict, especially the use of lethal violence, not only differentiates these gangs and their members from other delinquent groups (and nondelinquent groups), it also epitomizes both the nature of St. Louis youth gangs and their appeal for our subjects.

> That's what it originated from, a clique. Say we all together one day walking down the street and someone says such and such jumped me one day. Let's go find him. They came back with a whole bunch of people and got to fighting each other. Eventually those two sides decided they didn't like each other. [Our gang] originated when a person got killed out there. Before that we was just all friends hanging out. One night everybody drinking and a car rolled back and some Slobs got out and started shooting. The person who got shot is dead. When he got killed, that's when it all originated. From that one incident. (Female #046, "Lady Tee," sixteen-year-old 74 Hoover Crip)

> Because we get together and everybody drinks and then we want to holler at some girls. Some girls don't want to talk so we disrespect them or call them a name. After that they go get they brothers or whatever and they be the opposite from us and they hurt one of us and we go hurt one of them. (Male #056, "Tony," seventeen-year-old 19th Street Hoover Crip)[2]

The observation by Thrasher that conflict with other groups often was combined with the pursuit of "thrills" is echoed in the following quote.

> Somebody was playing around in the car but we knew them. They cut they lights off and started driving down. We started shooting at they car and then they came out. We seen them duck down and then they got back up and we knew them and they was just playing around. (Male #074, "Shon," sixteen-year-old Crenshaw Mob Gangster)

Every act of violence by gang members embodies a salient characteristic of St. Louis gangs—protection from real and apparent threats of physical violence and revenge or retaliation for real or perceived injuries and insults. "Jumping in" an initiate not only replicates a real event often committed against gang members; it also experientially shows the new member what he will be protected from and what he will be revenged for. This ritual also reassures old members that the initiate has the courage and ability to defend or revenge them if it is ever necessary. Other violent acts by gang members—drive-bys, drug turf protection, beating up welshing customers—serve as deterrents and warnings. These acts advertise to all that the gang intends to protect its own and how far its members will go in standing up for each other.

Finally, violence is endemic in a third arena, their individual status and role behaviors as gang members. Members are expected to always be ready to commit violence, to participate in violent acts, and to have engaged in some sort of violence in their initiation. Several measures support this assertion. Fewer than five subjects (all female) had never been in a gang related fight of some sort. Thirteen subjects, at the time of our interviews, volunteered that they had been shot.[3] Three subjects, in fact, had each been shot twice in their lives to that point. Even more startling, eleven of the ninety-nine active members we interviewed are no longer alive—victims of homicide. Eleven dead out of ninety-nine yields a homicide rate of more than 11,000 homicides per 100,000 population—a rate more than *1,000* times greater than the U.S. rate. Even annualizing that rate over the five years since we started interviewing (2,222 per 100,000), this is a startling statistic. By comparison, the 1992 Uniform Crime Reports show a national homicide rate of 9.3 per 100,000, a rate of 15.7 for the St. Louis Metropolitan area, and a rate of 57 per 100,000 for St. Louis City. The most relevant comparison group would be the national population of gang members, unavailable for obvious reasons. The best available comparison to our subjects is young black males of similar ages. In 1990 the homicide rate for black males aged fifteen to nineteen was 116 per 100,000 and for black males aged twenty to twenty-four it was 162 per 100,000. The rate of violent death for our subjects is thus thirteen times greater than the rate for twenty to twenty-four-year-old black males if we annualize, and *sixty eight times higher* as an annual rate. A grim statistic indeed.

In the remainder of this chapter we discuss the violence and violent criminality engaged in by our subjects. We start with a statistical overview of what interviews tell us about the kinds and frequency of violence and the possession and use of weapons. We then provide a qualitative discussion of kinds, causes and circumstances of violent acts committed by our subjects followed by an examination of levels and frequency. We conclude with our subjects' views on violence, responses that convey a sense of fear, fatalism, and enjoyment.

'We Just Grew Up Fightin'

Violence is an ordinary part of most of our subjects lives, although it obviously intensifies once they joined a gang and became more involved in gang activities. One subject described why he joined the gang in this way.

> We just grew up like that. We grew up fightin, if, I don't know, we just grew up fightin and everybody hangin around so they decided to call they self somethin since we hung around like that went out doin things and stuff. (Male #002, "Eric," sixteen-year-old Thundercat)

Violence in and by the gang starts early for our subjects: seventy subjects said they were "jumped in" for their initiation.

> Well, first we talk to them about what we do all that type of stuff. The next day he's gotta wear all blue and stand in a circle and everybody just rush him all at one time and then back off of him and see if

he still standing. If he drop he got to get back up and take it again. That's how you initiate a man. I say about nine people around and just rush him with heads and if he fall he's got to get back up. If he want out he want out, let go of the circle and walk out. (Male #003, "Jerry," eighteen-year-old Thundercat)

> A group of niggers, you in the middle of a circle, then all the sudden they rush you and you have to fight back. They have to beat you until you bleed. If you survive, you win. Then they give you hugs and stuff and call you Cuz. (Male #044, "Paincuzz," sixteen-year-old Rolling 60's Crip)

"Beating in" has different levels of intensity and often may only be the start of internal gang violence.

> No, see we got older people. They tied them down to a telephone pole and beat the hell out of them. Fuck that. Yeah, tied to a telephone pole. There be about six niggers, sometimes more than six. The younger ones just take a little beat down, not like what they go through. At least we didn't get tied down. [To become a full fledged member] you got to get a tattoo on your arm and then you got to get your Blood name carved in your left arm. Sometimes they get the end of a hangar, the hook, and they put it up under the fire for real long time and then they carve that shit in your arm. Yeah, I got one. (Male #068, "CK," sixteen-year-old Piru 104 Blood)

Eight subjects said they had to shoot someone for their initiation.

> I met these Bloods and they said do you want to get in? I had to get these Crabs and that type of stuff. I ran and got my .38, I ran by, I'm a Blood so I said what's up Fuz and they said no Cuz, I started shooting, pow, pow and we drove off. And that's how I became one. I don't know if I hit them or not. (Male #057, "Smith & Wesson," fifteen-year-old Neighborhood Posse Blood)

> His name was Eliminator. He was 13. We asked him how he wanted to get in and he said he wanted to do a ride-by and shoot the person who killed his brother. So he did a ride-by shooting and killed him.

(Male #069, "X-Men," fourteen-year-old Inglewood Family Gangster)

Pop somebody. Not no ride-bys, you walk up to them and you pop them. You got to do it, just get it over with no hesitation. (Male #086, "Gunn," nineteen-year-old Rolling 60's Crip)

And several subjects mentioned other kinds of violence involved in joining a gang.

To be a Crip you have to put your blue rag on your head and wear all blue and go in a Blood neighborhood that is the hardest of all of them and walk through the Blood neighborhood and fight Bloods. If you come out without getting killed that's the way you get initiated. Another set say you got to swim across some river or something like that. If you make it back you in there or you got to smoke somebody in your family or something like that. (Male #084, "Rolo," fifteen-year-old Rolling 60's Crip)

These acts at initiation serve to legitimate and normalize violence within the gang.

Not every gang member we interviewed was excessively violent.

I had to rob somebody but I didn't do it. I just told them a lie. (Male #052, "Jonathan," fifteen-year-old 107 Hoover Crip)

Well first somebody had to pick a fight and get in trouble with a teacher but I didn't get in trouble with the teacher because it was a sub and they don't do nothing to us really. Just picking a fight with somebody and getting in trouble with a teacher and stuff. (Female #078, "Tina," fifteen-year-old Treetop Blood)

Eighty-four subjects mentioned "fighting" as "something they did with their gang," while nineteen said it was what they did the most with their fellow members. Seventy-six subjects said that a good reason to belong was to "defend their neighborhood," and eighty-four said that they belonged for "protection." And if their neighborhoods are unsafe and in need of protection, the supervised confines of educational establishments were not much better. Seventy-eight subjects said there were gang fights at their schools, eighty-three said that weapons (usually guns) were brought to school, and

thirty-eight said that weapons were used at school.

Gun possession and use is another window into our subjects' violent propensities and opportunities. Guns were the overwhelming weapon of choice for gang-motivated and gang-related violence. Eighty subjects said they owned guns (two subjects reported they owned over one hundred guns), and the mean number of guns reported was four and a half (the mode was one). Only 192 guns were specifically identified by our subjects, and 75 percent of those were handguns of one sort or another. Subjects also mentioned owning other kinds of weapons besides firearms.

Hand grenades? I got about fifty of them. (Male #001, "Mike-Mike," twenty-year-old Thundercat)

Sixty-six subjects said they had used their guns at least once. When we asked what caused them to use their gun most recently, forty-seven gave no answer. Of the fifty-two subjects who answered, three gave the relatively innocuous answer of "celebrating the New Year." Twenty-six subjects had last used their guns in a gang fight, four in a drive-by shooting; four because a drug customer tried to rob them; four because they were attacked by a stranger; and eleven subjects gave a variety of miscellaneous answers (e.g., robberies, shooting at gang rivals who were passing by, etc.).

Other weapons besides guns were mentioned, though infrequently. Eighty-eight subjects (97 percent of those who answered this question) said that gang violence involved weapons, and the same number said that "guns" were the weapons used in violence (only two subjects mentioned knives, and one mentioned bats or sticks). Nevertheless, one subject mentioned rather unusual weapons involved in gang conflicts:

Guns, knives, we even had a boy that had arrows. I ain't bullshiting you. He come up there with motherfucking arrows, thought he was Rambo. Sat in a motherfuckin' tree started shooting at us. Hit one of my boys dead in his leg, went right through it. The last fight that broke out was the time that cat was sitting up in the tree. He was sittin' in a distant tree. He had a three string bow, real powerful. He sat up there and had a scope on it and everything. I don't know who he was tryin' to tag. The first time we heard it I said I could have sworn I heard something. It missed us. The second time it hit my boy dead in his leg and went right through it. It was like the end with the feathers was sittin' right at the top and the rest was sticking way out. He ran and he broke it then he fell. I said damn, somebody's shootin' arrows at our ass. So then my boy got up and he started looking around, looking everywhere, looked up in the tree and saw him shooting arrows. He climbed in the tree, swung that nigger down and beat him with his own bow and shit. (Male #092, "Derone," twenty-one-year-old Rolling 60's Crip)

The only time that we have killed this one boy named Kevin. He was a Treetop and he was runnin' through the woods and my boy had a machete and he hit him, he cut him all up in his rear. (Male #092, "Derone," twenty one-year-old Rolling 60's Crip)

Our subjects most recent arrests also show how commonplace violence is: Seventeen were for assault, six for peace disturbances, three for weapons violations, two for obstructing police, and one was for homicide. Nine subjects had an assault conviction; six had weapons violations convictions; one had a manslaughter conviction. Ten subjects had done time for assault, four for weapons violations, and one for manslaughter.

'We Be Fighting All the Time': Causes and Kinds of Violence

While we would like to report that our subjects sharply differentiate their use of lethal versus nonlethal violence according to targets, too many subjects' descriptions invalidate the distinction. It is our impression that violence that lacks a gang motive or is unrelated to the gang is less likely to be lethal.

Yeah. I, uh close as I shot somebody was on the forty-one Lee, cause an old man got on the bus, no the man wasn't old, but he was drunk, and he kept on playing wit me, and I told 'em he better get away from me, then he kept on hittin on me, I say hey

man, you better go on man, and I kept tellin' the bus driver and the bus driver wouldn't do nothin, and then so he grabbed me like this but he was standing up and I was sittin down and he grabbed me and had me in a hold, and I pulled out the gun, a .32 and popped him in his stomach. Naw. I jumped off the bus. The bus driver wouldn't let me off the bus, so I said you don't let me off the bus you gonna get shot, so he opened up the bus. (Male #002, "Eric," sixteen-year-old Thundercat)

We were at the White Castle one day and one of my partners stepped on this guy's foot. He said excuse me and he had his friend with him and my partner said I said excuse me, I'm sorry just like that. He punched my partner in the face and we just got to fighting. I didn't know my partner had this pistol in his pocket and shot him in his leg, paralyzed him. (Male #040, "Knowledge," twenty-one-year-old Compton Gangsters)

Violence by and towards gang members seems to lurk around every corner. Sometimes it is a sudden unexpected eruption, sometimes the result of long simmering feuds or disagreements that are not seemingly gang motivated or related.

I was down in the projects, Vaughn, this girl was [performing oral sex]. She was doing this to everybody. The next day my brother came and got me and we went on the south side. She was there. I got out of the car, I asked her could I have it. She got to swinging on me. I hit her a couple of times, my brother hit her a couple of times. I got tired of whupping her. I got tired of hitting her so I shot her. I didn't kill her though. She still live around the corner. [I shot her] in the side. (Male #034, "Lil Gene Mack," eighteen-year-old 19th Street Rolling 60's Crip)

[The last fist fight] that was yesterday at the community center. It was just talk about one of the guys in the neighborhood. The crazy thing about it was it was amongst us. One of the guys said that he had fucked this guy's sister and he heard it and they got to fighting. It was harmless. He was just defending his sister's name. He can't keep her pants up. (Male

#040, "Knowledge," twenty-one-year-old Compton Gangster)

Just hanging around with gang members can lead to violence:

INT: How old were you when you first started hanging out with them?

MALE #053, "Jimmy," eighteen-year-old 107 Hoover Crip: About 14.

INT: How old were you when you first became a member?

053: Not too long ago, when I turned 18.

INT: They let you escape that long without really joining up?

053: Yeah. When I used to hang with them about four years ago some dude threw some gasoline on me and set me on fire.

INT: That's how you started hanging out with them?

053: Yeah, been shot twice.

INT: So they threw gasoline on you and shot you a couple of times and that's one of the reasons you started hanging out with the 107s?

053: Yeah.

Gang membership—claiming or perpetrating—increases the potential and actuality of violence. Initiations are violent. Colors make a person a target, a victim, and a victimizer.

MALE #050, "John," nineteen-year-old Rolling 60's Crip: One day I was on the Kingshighway bus and I was going to go get my Social Security card. I was walking down Kingshighway. I wasn't into no gang and these dudes walked up to me. They was Bloods, we call them Slobs. They walked up to me like what's up Blood. You in the wrong hustle. I ain't with that gang stuff Cuz. So they was gonna fight me. So I say fuck that. Went back on the north side, got drunk and then got up with the Crips. Just like that.

INT: Because the Bloods wanted to beat you up?

050: Yeah. I wear blue so I'm going to get beat up anyways so I say I just deal with the Crips.

Even going out to meet interviewers can be dangerous.

I got shot by a guy two weeks ago. I was walking out the door to meet Dietrich on the corner and I got shot. I was out front of the door and some of my boys was behind me. I don't know who it was. It had to be somebody outside of the neighborhood. Over in the city, the city is about three blocks from us, no North Side Bloods. It must have been somebody from over there. We was meeting Dietrich on the corner, we was walking out the door. I heard a gun shot and I got hit and I knew it. I had walked back in the house like I forgot something and raised my shirt up and it was bloody and I said I got shot. So my brother called an ambulance and I went back on outside and put my head down. I thought I was going to faint. [I got shot] at the bottom of my heart. It went through my liver and my stomach and my diaphragm. Someone from the city. I figure whoever walked out the door first was going to be shot. There's Bloods in the city, it had to be Bloods. (Male #024, "Hamilton," sixteen-year-old 107 Hoover Gangster Crip)

Disrespect has to be corrected and answered—physically. And drug turfs are defended; customers who cheat you are violently punished.

A guy came in, he had the wrong colors on, he got to move out. He got his head split open with a sledgehammer, he got two ribs broken, he got his face torn up. We dropped him off on the other side of town. If he did die, it was on the other side of town. (Male #013, "Darryl," twenty-nine-year-old Blood)

I had to pistol whip a guy, I shot him in the knee. Since then he never came back. (Male #017, "Billy," twenty-one-year-old North Side Crip)

If a member becomes a victim, revenge is necessary. And this revenge is schismogenic, resulting in an increasing cycle of retaliation and revenge.

INT: What happened yesterday?

MALE #039, "Kaons BIC," seventeen-year-old Compton Gangster: This dude had beat up one of our friends. He was cool with one of my friends but he had beat up another one of my friends before. They came back and busted one of my friend's head. We was going to get him.

I was standing on Sarah somewhere and three Bloods walked up to me. I knew I was on Blood territory but that's the route I have to go to get to my aunt's house. I was standing outside and on the corner and then they approached me. They didn't say not one word. They just hit me. I went back like this and then they ran. I just went pow, pow and shot it three times. I hit one of them in the leg. He fell down so I just ran on up to my auntie's house and called the fellas. Then they came on down and had it out. (Male #020, "Lil Thug," sixteen-year-old Gangster Disciple)

About two weeks, ago some group called _____ but they Crips too, they had it out with one of our boys and stuff. We had a little argument and they came and got us. There was about ten of us walking around seeing what was up. We got to shooting at them and stuff. Some of them got to fighting and stuff and threw my friend down. He got shot in the chest twice. My boy got shot yesterday, TJ, he got shot yesterday. Some dudes drove up on him. (Male #053, "Jimmy," eighteen-year-old 107 Hoover Crip)

Getting out of this violent cycle is not easy. One subject told this story of how his brother left a gang.

My big brother. He was in the 38s. They say to get out of the 38s you got to kill your parents, kill one of your parents. My brother was making good grades, got him a scholarship and everything and he was like I'm leaving this alone. They tried to make him kill my mother. He was like, you must be crazy and I was on his side. So the leader, _____, big husky dude, him and my brother got into it. They was fighting and he pulled a gun out so, I stabbed him in the back. I thought he was going to shoot my brother, which he was so, I stabbed him in the back. He paralyzed now. (Male #037, "Big Money," twenty-two-year-old Compton Gangster)

Cowardice is highly disapproved, since standing up for your friends and fellow members is almost a sacred duty (and a raison d'etre for being in a gang).

One time I had a fight, this dude was supposed to be down with me, dude named Steve. We went around the corner on Becker, that's the next street up from Genevieve. I was up there, I had beat up four Bloods up there on Lillian and everybody seen it. So the next day I went around the corner. I was standing right there and a Blood came and I said what's up man. Me and him got to banging and stuff and after that he ran and brought a whole bunch of dudes with him. The dude that was supposed to be with me, Steve, I said you down with me man? He said yeah man. So I'm up there fighting and I turned around looking for him and he was gone. Then I was fighting all by myself. I was messed up. I had six stitches right here, my two ribs is broken right here, I got cracked in the face with a 40-ounce bottle. There's still a piece of glass in my eye right, it's just stuck up in there. When I seen him [Steve] I beat him down. Male #053 "Jimmy," eighteen-year-old 107 Hoover Crip)

Gang members also get involved in gang violence through serendipity (or stupidity) as this story of the death of Hit Man T—a Blood leader—illustrates:

Somebody disagrees and then they wind up fighting each other. That's how Hit Man T got killed. It was a disagreement with the Crips. They was gonna fight and Hit Man T came between them. It was two sets, Rolling Sixties and 19th. A 60 came to a party and a 19 was on this side of St. Louis Avenue. Our side had all the pistols, they ain't have none and Hit Man T drove up to the light and he had on all red, his boys in the back seat had on red, they had they hats turned to the left. A dude shot the car up. Hit Man T pulled off to the side, why you all shooting, man? They got to hitting on him. The police came and couple of young dudes shot him in his face. Everybody was out there fighting and the police was coming up to them and dudes was popping and the police was ducking by they cars and had they thing out telling everybody freeze. Everybody run. They couldn't shoot the crowd. Him and his boy got shot but his boy never did make it to the hospital. He went and they say he had his old lady take the bullet out. Hit Man T was still alive, he got shot with a .380 in his face. He was still alive and telling the police to fuck his leg. The police was telling him he had to wait till the paramedics came cause he got shot in the leg first but he was fighting back. He shouldn't have did what he did. . . . If somebody shot you car up and you ain't got no weapon it's no sense in getting out for real. He was in his car, the car was running, the light was green and there was about 100 people on that side and about 300 people on our side, gang people and people that wasn't in no gang. People on phones, getting gas, just walking around cause it's hot outside. He should have kept going. (Male #056, "Tony," seventeen-year-old 19th Street Hoover Crip)

Another similar example of misdirected behavior illustrates further stupidities.

There was some cats from Illinois. Vice Lords. They came to us, what's up, you all some Bloods? Fuck no, I ain't no Slob. What you all Crips? No, I ain't no Crips. You all Disciples? No. Then they pulled out they little .22s and shot at us. So we went and got guns and rolled down on them. We seen them at the bus stop so we went and parked in the alley. Come out and shot them, whupped they ass. All of them got shot. That was dumb what they done. They went and tried to catch the bus. They just shot at us and then go catch the bus right down the street from where we hang out. (Male #036, "NA," eighteen-year-old Compton Gangster BIC)

Unfortunately, gang members are not the only victims of gang-related violence. Several subjects mentioned having their houses shot up.

My bedroom window, man, they shot through the wall. I was up there with one of my little gals, my baby's mamma. My son was up in there. I said get down and pushed her on the bed and rolled him out of the bed. I reached under the bed. I was so mad, my son was up there. I reached under my mattress, dude, I was so mad I went on the south side and smoked like three niggers up in the projects. You can jack with me, mess with me I don't care what you do to me, don't mess with my kid. (Male #033, "Larry," eighteen year-old Thundercat)

Others mentioned fights and/or killings with police and security guards, and with guns around there are bound to be accidents.

I had a uh little cousin got shot in the chest. Everybody was in the house playin wit a gun and uh my cousin Kenny had shot her in the uh chest. Hey man she was thirteen, yeah uh, pulled the gun back but he didn't know it was no bullet or nothing when he shot her, shot her in her chest. We was all cryin and stuff but she didn't have no funeral or nothin and then we all went to jail but they knew it was an accident so they just let em go and stuff. (Male #002, "Eric," sixteen-year-old Thundercat)

'We Don't Go Looking for It; If It Happens, It Happens': Attitudes Towards Violence

Although we began this chapter with a statement reflecting a "love" of violence, most of our subjects do not revel in confrontation to quite the degree that subject boasted of (to be fair, he was probably bragging and exaggerating both his love of violence and his involvement in it). The most common attitude toward the possibility of violence and actually initiating it was more fatalistic and commonplace.

INT: When do members of your gang use violence?

MALE #092, "Derone," twenty-one-year-old Rolling 60's Crip: Only when violence is necessary. Like at a confrontation or somebody talk crap or if somebody throw up the wrong sign then we fuck they ass up.

If a Blood would shoot me and I happen to get hit, I get hit. Then I be dead. (Male #025, "Tony," seventeen-year-old Hoover Gangster Crip)

There is, in fact, something of "a man's gotta do what a man's gotta do" about our subjects' responses to violence, perhaps because it is a normal and expected part of their lives. At times there was also a rather chilling, matter-of-fact attitude in our subjects' descriptions of violence and killing.

Oh man, you shoot somebody and they don't die they shoot you and you be feuding until one of you all dead. A dude named Scotty and Kevin. Every time they see each other. They done shot a pregnant girl at Saints a few months ago. Kevin was trying to hit him. They will go on with it. (Male #012, "Lance," twenty-year-old West Side Mob member)

INT: What's good about being in your gang?

MALE #028, "Killa 4 Ren," fifteen-year-old 187 Crip: People are killed, that's good.

INT: People are actually dead now?

028: Yeah. Paralyzed one dude two weeks ago.

INT: Tell me about the last drive-by shooting. That was two weeks ago right?

028: Yeah. We shot that guy.

INT: When was the last time that somebody was killed?

028: Last month. I tore that dude up, had to shoot him.

INT: What was it about?

028: He was a Blood so we shot him. No that wasn't last month, that was on a Sunday.

INT: So he was a Blood and that was the reason he got shot. He was killed right?

028: His brother was in the paper talking about how we killed him.

INT: He's dead though right?

028: Yeah, he dead. Yeah. The only reason we shot him was cause he threatened him in Union Station. Called him a little Crab and stuff like that. Had to shoot him. They was talking about who going to shoot him. I said I'll do it.

Other subjects seem also bored with violence, or talking about violence, and some gave the impression of being tired with that whole scene.

MALE #034, "Lil Gene Mack," eighteen-year-old 19th Street Rolling 60's Crip: We haven't had any problems for awhile now but it's been hot. It's going to come. There's going to be a lot of deaths.

INT: How come?

034: Colors.

INT: What kinds of things have you done to defend your turf?

034: I did a lot. I have did a lot. I shot people, I've been shot, I've gang banged. It's getting old, man, it's getting old. You do it so much it don't faze you no more. Every time I go out now I'm killing me somebody. It don't hurt, it don't faze me no more.

Several subjects also tried to point out that what they do is not all that terrible and that there are, after all, far worse gangs in the world (Los Angeles gangs are especially favored in this regard).

We never killed nobody that I know of. We have put people in a coma, paralyzed them stuff like that but we ain't never killed nobody. Gave them brain damage. (Male #036, "NA," eighteen-year-old Compton Gangster BIC)

INT: How are gangs on the east side different from over here?

MALE #044, "Paincuzz," sixteen-year-old Rolling 60's Crip: Worser.

INT: Worse in what ways?

044: Over here we kill Bloods and Crips but over there they will kill your mother, your father, and your little baby sister.

And a sufficient number of subjects mentioned fear or the psychological effects of being on the receiving or giving end of violence.

I've had dreams about it. It scares me sometimes. I used to walk by myself all sagging and all blue on. My girlfriend say aren't you scared some Bloods gonna drive past and start shooting? I didn't trip off of it, just walked. (Male #050, "John," nineteen-year-old Rolling 60's Crip)

When, when you shoot a person it seem like everybody watching you. I always thought somebody was after me. Every time I'd hear a police car I'd jump. Every time my mother call me I say WHAT! cause the cops was bothering me but it was an accident. I shot him though. (Male #003, "Jerry," eighteen-year-old Thundercat)

This evidence leads to an important question, "Why is the level of violence so high among gang members, higher even than their race/age/sex cohort?" Three answers have been proposed. On the one hand, it can be argued that gangs are organized for violence. Like the military, they provide the training, weaponry, ideology, motive, discipline, and leadership for engaging in violence. From this perspective, gang violence can be viewed as the outcome of a group whose formal purpose is to organize violence for instrumental purposes. An alternative perspective argues that gangs amplify violence; that is, gangs provide a collective process that weakens ties to social institutions and increases interactions with and attachments to individuals already involved in crime.

A third explanation is that gang membership is selected for violence. Individuals who are already prone to violent behaviors, and who have such a history, select each other as compatriots, and since violence is the initial bond of their relationship, they continue these behaviors as their group coalesces and grows. Although we did not systematically probe for information on pregang levels of violence, we assume that it was at very high levels for our subjects. The neighborhood rates of assaultive violence discussed in this chapter . . .are just the tip of the iceberg and point to an endemic culture of violence in our subjects' neighborhoods. Many of them had witnessed or been affected by lethal assaultive violence (not to mention that all had probably been witnesses to or been involved in nonlethal violence) by their early teens. By the time they joined the gang, most of our subjects were veterans of playground and street fights—which did not usually involve weapons or lethal consequences. But we assume that individuals with violent proclivities select themselves (and are selected by others) for gang membership. They both create and attract threats within their social circle and neighborhood and thus are more likely to be in need of protection. They both seek out like-inclined individuals (existing gang members and other violence-prone adolescents) and are sought out by the same.

The last two views (contagion and selection) are far more consistent with the data reviewed here, data that shows gangs lack ideology, discipline, and formal structure, and that gang violence is primarily expressive and retaliatory (or situationally spontaneous), hardly the product of a formal organization employing rational means-ends chains.

'It Don't Hurt, It Don't Faze Me No More'

Not all subjects, of course, are as blase as "Lil Gene Mack" tried to be in our interview. Eight subjects, after all, could not say when their gang used violence and eleven subjects said that violence did not involve the use of weapons. Nevertheless, violence is the force that creates and holds St. Louis gangs together. Starting with threats inside and outside the neighborhood creating the need for protection and culminating in endless repetitions of revenge and retaliation, violence permeates the lives of our subjects. And it appears to be getting worse. Our subjects recognize the pervasiveness of violence in a variety of ways. Fifty-eight subjects said that the gang scene had become more violent in the year prior to their interview, and seven said there was more use of guns (only twelve said that the gang scene was less violent).

Violence comes in many forms for these gang members and their neighbors and friends. Some of what gang members do serves "functional purposes"—protection of home turf and favored hangouts, protection of drug turfs and disciplining customers, defending members and neighbors from "outsiders." But much of the violence we have recorded in our interviews seems "expressive." Gang members proving their manhood, their toughness, their hardness through initiations, trespassing on rival territories, and beating or shooting the opposition's colors. Though it contains elements of self-protection, the expressive character is evident in efforts to establish dominance or identity. Viewed in this light, violence that erupts over what appear to be petty acts—disrespecting a color, stepping in front of another person, flashing hand signs, driving through a rival neighborhood—takes on a deeper and more serious meaning. These "petty" acts represent symbolic threats to the existence of the gang and its members, as they challenge its prime values.

Some of this violence also arises from the routine interactions of our subjects as they carry out their daily activities. The inevitable frictions of daily life, especially when individuals are pursuing criminal careers, can quickly get out of hand and lead to escalating confrontations. And since our subjects are often armed, violently prone, and structurally less powerful than many of their interlocutors, their reactions are just as likely to be violent and potentially deadly (Tedeschi and Felson 1994). Fundamental personal identity is also involved. Most of the gang members portrayed in our study are proud, insecure, tough teenagers and young adults whose self-esteem, self-worth, and identity appear to be constantly at risk. Toughness, manliness, not backing down, are important values of their world and their psyches—to be upheld even at the cost of their own or others' lives.

Whatever the "purpose" of violence, it often leads to retaliation and revenge creating feedback loops where each killing requires a new killing. And too often the targets of such attacks are not even the perpetrators of the previous action—just some generalized Slob or Crab or an innocent bystander. In 1993, for example, the Fairgrounds Park neighborhood, in the middle of our subject recruitment area, had a population of 3,026. From 1991 through 1993, the Fairgrounds neighborhood averaged just under 9 homicides per year, or an annual rate of 286 per 100,000 citizens, four times higher than the city rate and thirty times the national homicide rate. Rates for serious assault in this neighborhood are also astronomical; for the same three year period, Fairgrounds Park averaged nearly 6,000 assaults per 100,000 residents, five times higher than the city of St. Louis and thirteen times higher than that for the United States.

Gangs do not really resemble the stereotype presented at the beginning of the chapter. Most of our subjects do not revel in assaultive and lethal violence against each other, innocent bystanders, and any who attempt to thwart them. Nor is gang violence as common as the public may think. Yet it is far too common and far too lethal to be dismissed easily or waved away. Eleven homicides out of ninety-nine interview subjects represents a high level of mortality, both for social science research and in the lives of most Americans.

But gang members live in a culture apart from most of us, a world in which violence is endemic and ever present. Gang members are radically separated from both public and private institutions of society. . . .Nevertheless, because of their involvement in criminality and violence, gang members still remain intimately connected to one American institution—the criminal justice system.

Notes

1. We borrow this phrase from the title of Nancy Scheper Hughes' book about Brazilian favelas.

2. This is a rather old trope. Aristophanes—parodying the opening paragraph of Herodotus—wrote on the causes of the Peloponnesian War that "and thus for the sake of three whores the whole of Greece was set aflame."

3. To be honest, one subject admitted that he had accidentally shot himself.

References

Federal Bureau of Investigation. *Uniform Crime Reports*. Washington, DC: USGPO.

Tedeschi, James T. and Richard B. Felson 1994. *Violence, Aggression, and Coercive Actions.* Washington, DC: American Psychological Association.

Thrasher, Frederick. 1927. *The Gang.* Chicago: University of Chicago Press.

26
Hate Crimes

The Rising Tide of Bigotry and Bloodshed

Jack Levin

Jack McDevitt

Constructions of deviance are mutable. Conduct once considered highly deviant can become quite conventional (e.g., homosexuality, interracial marriage). Conduct once considered normal can become powerfully stigmatized (e.g., cigarette smoking, driving under the influence). Constructions of deviance are elastic, adjusting to the political, social, and cultural climate of the time (Tittle and Paternoster 2000). Strategically positioned "moral entrepreneurs" mobilize support and galvanize dissension in keeping with the policies they wish to see codified into new rules.

Hate violence, the infliction of harm by one or more persons onto one or more others because of gender, race, religion, ethnicity, or sexual orientation, is illustrative. Hate violence has only recently emerged in the public consciousness as a serious social problem, but it has existed for centuries. A few isolated but sensational recent cases may be responsible— the dragging death of a black Texas man by white racists, the torture killing of a Wyoming homosexual, and the mass shooting of Jewish children at a Los Angeles day care center, among others. Hate violence is really no different from any other form of violence, but it is perceived to be different because it is senseless, excessively brutal, and unprovoked. People are victimized not on the basis of what they have done but because of who they are.

Levin and McDevitt explore the etiology, social organization, and enactment of hate violence. They contend that hate violence emerges from a noxious combination of economic hardship and social diversification, which, in the presence of incendiary social messages

(from, for example, music and television), triggers aggression as the best solution. Focusing on one discrediting aspect of their victims' identities, hate criminals use violence to subjugate everyone in that same category, and realize their own (twisted) political objectives in the process. The power of hate crime lies in its symbolism, and hate offenders seize on that symbolism for both motivation and justification—labeling theory in reverse, but with a vigilante bent.

Levin and McDdevitt conclude that the only realistic policy solution is more severe punishment, a somewhat dubious proposition given that the deterrent value of legal sanctions is already so weak. The most effective kind of social control is inevitably informal, so hate crime will continue unless or until there are fundamental changes in the fabric of society itself. Greater social integration, for example, typically encourages people to focus on one another as people rather than as categories, cultivating the kind of understanding that leads to tolerance.

Reign of Terror

It was June 18, 1984. Outspoken radio personality Alan Berg had spent another routine morning behind the microphone at superstation KOA in Denver, exchanging verbal barbs on the air with assorted lunatics, activists, survivalists, racists, and shut-ins. Later in the day, the bearded and graying talk show host picked up his ex-wife Judith Lee who had flown in from Chicago to spend the weekend visiting her parents and Alan. The couple passed the afternoon together, catching up on the details of one another's lives. They drove to Alan's fashionable apartment, dined together at a popular restaurant in a western suburb nearby, and then stopped at a 7-Eleven store to buy dog food for Alan's shaggy Airedale.

Just before 9:00 p.m., Berg dropped Judith at the Cherry Creek shopping center, where she had parked her car for the afternoon. He then drove alone toward his modern, three-story townhouse on Adams Street.

Denver was unusually warm on this late-spring evening. The moon was hidden behind a thick layer of clouds, and more clouds were predicted for the following day.

Berg maneuvered his black Volkswagen beetle into the lighted driveway in front of his apartment, turned off the engine, and pulled up the emergency brake. Taking a last drag from his cigarette, he opened the door. The street was dark and quiet as he picked up the 7-Eleven bag from the seat next to him and began to step to the pavement. He was suddenly distracted by the headlights of an approaching car, then an explosion of gunshots. Before he could have known what hit him, Berg's six-foot-two, 150 pound body lay face up in a pool of blood, killed by thirteen bullets from an automatic MAC-10 pistol.

When the police arrived on the scene, Berg's right leg was inside his VW, and his hand still gripped the paper bag he had carried. Several cans of dog food had rolled into the street.[1]

It didn't take a multimillion-dollar task force to discover that Berg had been murdered or why. His assailants turned out to be members of a neo-Nazi hate group that awarded points to its "Aryan Warriors" for killing Jews, blacks, government officials, and reporters. One of the Nazis at the scene of the crime later bragged that "Berg went down so fast it was like someone pulled the rug out from under him."[2]

Berg's controversial show on Denver's KOA radio had been the talk of the town, but not all of the talk was complimentary. The fifty-year-old ex-criminal lawyer routinely berated racists, urging them to phone and express their venomous points of view. "Any Nazis out there?" the chain-smoking, coffee-addicted talk show host would ask on the air. "I'm a Jew and I'd like to talk to you."

Nazis frequently obliged him. So did Klansmen and members of the Aryan Nations. Over the airwaves, they blamed the hard economic times on "Jew Rothschild bankers," claiming that the "Zionist Occupation Government" (ZOG) exercised total control over the economic resources of the United States. They challenged the authenticity of the Holocaust, suggesting instead that the atrocities committed by the Nazis had been fabricated by Jewish organizations in a bid to arouse the sympathy of the world. Some decried the "mongrelization" of the white race and expressed disdain for civil rights legislation. Others predicted that God would soon eliminate both Jews and blacks from the face of the earth . . .the sooner the better, they said.

And Berg challenged every one of his bigoted callers. He belittled them, debated with them, poked fun at them, and then usually hung up on them. Berg was both popular and despised, but he was always provocative. As a rival talk show host recalled after his death, Berg "made a living making enemies on the air."[3] Earlier in his career, his "enemies" had gotten him suspended and fired, had mailed indignant letters to the Federal Communications Commission, and had sent bomb threats to Berg's office at the station. The subject of the program Berg was scheduled to discuss the morning *after* his murder was gun control.

Investigators were convinced that Berg had been ambushed by five members of a neo-Nazi hit squad, but they were also sure that the evidence was lacking to obtain murder convictions at the state level. The alleged ringleader of the group, thirty-one-year-old Robert Jay Mathews, was the founder and leader of an organized hate group calling itself *Bruder Schweigen*, the Silent Brotherhood. His primary objective was, by means of murder, armed robbery, and counterfeiting, to fund the racist activities of the white supremacist movement. Mathews was later killed in a gun battle with federal agents. The other four alleged perpetrators—David Lane, Bruce Pierce, Richard Scutari, and Jean Craig—were already serving time on charges of federal racketeering by the time the investigation had gotten underway. Whatever proof prosecutors had against the four racists was strictly circumstantial, based mainly on the testimony of members of hate groups who were willing to turn state's evidence in return for reduced sentences on other charges. Witnesses claimed that Berg had in fact infuriated racists in his audience by ridiculing them, and that he had been singled out for execution by the Silent Brotherhood.

Several months after Berg was assassinated, FBI agents located the murder weapon at the home of an Aryan Nations director near Hayden Lake, Idaho. Bullets from the gun matched slugs taken from Berg's body and other bullets found at a house near Troy, Montana—the home of one of the defendants, Bruce Pierce.[4]

Lacking evidence to convince a jury "beyond a reasonable doubt," the district attorney in Denver dropped the idea of obtaining murder indictments. But federal prosecutors, relying instead on an often-used tactic, charged the three men and one woman in federal court with having conspired to violate Berg's civil rights by killing him. (It is generally easier to prove a conspiracy to murder than the murder itself.) After thirteen days of proceedings involving more than thirty-one witnesses, Lane and Pierce were found guilty by a federal jury. Scutari and Craig were acquitted.

One thing was clear about Berg's execution: It was a "hate crime"—a legally prohibited activity motivated by Berg's being "different." Thus, hate offenses are directed against members of a particular group simply because of their membership in that group.[5] The basis for an attack may be a victim's race, ethnicity, religion, sexual orientation, or gender—indeed, any physical or cultural characteristic which, in the mind of offenders, separates the victim from themselves. The victim's individual characteristics are, from the attacker's point of view, all but irrelevant. The killers of Alan Berg could have cared less that their victim was tall and thin, liked baseball, lived originally in Chicago, or had a family. All that seemed to count was the fact that Berg was "a loud-mouthed Jew."

Unlike Berg's murder, most hate crimes do not involve organized hate groups, whose members are dedicated to the goal of achieving racial purity. Perpetrators usually are not card-carrying members of any racist organizations; they do not wear uniforms, armbands, or sheets; most have never even heard of the Aryan Nations or the Silent Brotherhood.

Hate crimes are more often committed under ordinary circumstances by otherwise unremarkable types—neighbors, a coworker at the next desk, or groups of youngsters looking for a thrill. . . .

In assaultive hate crimes, the attack is often excessively violent. In Bangor, Maine, for example, three teenage boys beat senseless a twenty-three-year-old man whom they believed to be gay. Then, they threw him off a bridge to his death on the rocks below. The three youths later boasted to their friends that they had "jumped a fag and kicked the shit out of him and threw him in the stream."[6] Some hatemongers make a career of attacking people who are different. On the night of August 20, 1980, Joseph Paul Franklin, a thirty-nine-year-old former member of the KICIC and American Nazi Party, gunned down two young black men as they jogged alongside two white women in a Salt Lake City park. Ten years later, when asked from his prison cell to explain why he had committed the murders, Franklin replied, "I'll say that it was just because they were race mixing." Franklin was later connected to thirteen killings across the United States. In 1984, he was convicted of bombing a synagogue in Chattanooga, Tennessee, and in 1986 was sentenced to two more life terms for killing an interracial couple in Madison, Wisconsin.[7]

Alan Berg was slain by members of an organized group whose raison d'etre was to rid the world of "subhuman" blacks, "mongrels," and Jews. In Michael Griffith's death, teenagers translated their racism into brutal violence. The incident would in all likelihood never have happened had the three "intruders" been white. But hate crimes aren't always so easily labeled as such. When violence is perpetrated by youngsters in the neighborhood, it can become difficult to determine motivation. Was it a bias crime—an act of hate-inspired violence? Or, was it an indiscriminate attack that could have been directed against anyone, regardless of race, religion, or gender? . . .

Recent research strongly suggests that hate crimes reported to the police have certain characteristics that distinguish them from other types of offenses. First, hate crimes tend to be *excessively brutal*. A study of 452 hate crimes reported to the Boston police[8] found that fully half of them were assaults. . . .The remaining 50 percent consisted of acts of vandalism or destruction of property (for example, painting a swastika on a synagogue or throwing a rock through a window). Thus, one of every two hate crimes reported to the Boston police was a personal attack. This statistic is surprising when compared with the national figure on the nature of crimes: nationally, only 7 percent of all crimes reported to the police are assaults.[9] Hate offenses are much more likely to entail personal violence.

The *hatred* in such crimes gets expressed when force is exercised beyond what may be necessary to subdue victims, make them comply, disarm them, or take their worldly goods. Almost three-quarters of all assaultive hate crimes—unlawful personal attacks, even if only with threatening words—result in at least some physical injury to the victim. The relative viciousness of these attacks can be seen by comparing them to the national figures for all crimes, in which only 29 percent of assault victims generally receive some physical injury. By contrast, many victims of hate crime assaults—fully 30 percent—wind up requiring treatment at a hospital because of the severity of their injuries. For assaults of all kinds, this figure is only 7 percent. Once again, it appears that hate crimes are particularly violent. . . .

A second characteristic of hate crimes reported to the police is that they are often apparently senseless or irrational crimes *perpetrated at random on total strangers*. As a society, we fear random violence against strangers even more than violence that has a logical basis. For example, if it is reported on the evening news that a drug deal "went bad" and one of the participants killed the other, we react with very little fear or even concern. After all, criminals are killing criminals over territorial disputes. And because *we* are not criminals, and therefore not competing with them in business, *we* feel perfectly safe and secure.

In sharp contrast, a story about random violence, such as unexplained attacks against innocent bystanders in a public place (for example, a public park or a post office), engenders widespread fear and anxiety. The reason

for this is complex, but one element is that the violence is committed by a stranger against someone he has never met before. This makes all of us feel vulnerable as potential victims. Any one of us could be next. . . .

The fact that hate crime victims are interchangeable may help to focus the debate. With respect to race, *any* black family that moves into certain neighborhoods will likely be attacked. With respect to sexual orientation, *any* man thought to be gay who happens to walk down a particular street will in all likelihood be assaulted. Similarly, gender-motivated hate crimes should include those attacks in which the offender is looking for *any* woman. By this criterion, acquaintance rape and acts of domestic violence, no matter how despicable, would be excluded from consideration as hate offenses. Only random attacks against women would be included. . . .

Another characteristic of hate crimes is that they are usually *perpetrated by multiple offenders*. This is a group crime frequently carried out by youthful perpetrators operating together for the purpose of attacking the members of another group. . . .

. . .[C]learly, there is safety in numbers. The hatemongers who instigate an altercation believe that they are less likely to be hurt in a group because they have their friends to protect them. The group also grants a certain degree of anonymity. If everyone participated, then no one person can easily be singled out as bearing primary responsibility for the attack. Because they share it, the blame is diluted. Finally, the group gives its members a dose of psychological support for their blatant bigotry. Feeding initially on the hatred of one or a few peers, escalation becomes a game in which members of the group incite one another toward ever-increasing levels of violence. To do his part and "prove himself," therefore, each offender feels that he must surpass the previous atrocity. . . .

Nasty Pictures in Our Heads

Learning to hate is almost as inescapable as breathing. Like almost everyone else, the hate crime offender grows up in a culture that defines certain people as righteous, upstanding citizens; while designating others as sleazy, immoral characters who deserve to be mistreated. As a child, the perpetrator may never have had a firsthand experience with members of the groups he will later come to despise and then victimize. But, early on, merely by conversing with his family, friends, and teachers or by watching his favorite television programs, he learns the characteristics of disparaging stereotypes. . . .

To some extent, the tendency to generalize about other people is probably universal. Almost everybody, based on personal experience that may or may not be limited, makes at least some generalizations about what other groups of people are like. The beliefs that we call stereotypes are, however, of a different order. First, every member of a stereotyped group is seen as a rubber stamp of everyone else in that group. Individual differences are totally obscured. Second, stereotypes usually cannot be modified by contradictory evidence. No argument or evidence is compelling enough to change the hatemonger's mind. He is emotionally invested in believing the worst about the members of a stigmatized group. And, third, the person who accepts the validity of a nasty stereotype isn't simply trying to make sense of his world. More likely, he is looking for a convenient excuse to express hostility, to attack and brutalize the people he despises. . . .

Throughout history, many groups have been *infantilized*. So long as they "stayed in their place" and played the inferior role to which they were assigned, they were stereotyped as children or infants.[10] For example, women have traditionally been regarded as "girls" who should remain at home—in the kitchen and bedroom—where they "belong," or so it was said. The particular image varied from generation to generation, but the intent was always the same—to keep women in a subservient position in their relations with men. To be in style, women of the 1920s were asked to look like children. Some wore their dresses cut to look like the shirts worn by little boys some ten years earlier. Others bobbed their hair like a baby's, hoping to give their face the appearance of "a small child: round and soft, with a turned-up nose, sau-

cer eyes and a pouting 'bee-stung' mouth." During the 1960s, young women similarly dressed as if they were little girls. They wore very short ruffled frocks and made up their eyes to create a baby-faced look. Miniskirts, baby-doll nightgowns, and lacy baby-doll dresses all made "grown women look like toddlers with a glandular affliction, or like severely retarded nubile teenagers."[11]

Also much like children, women were viewed as diminutive or as the weaker sex and therefore in need of masculine protection, often whether they wanted it or not. Just to make sure that they remained weak enough, stylish women of the nineteenth century were expected to wear tight corsets to achieve the stylish hourglass figure. Those women who complied may have been in high fashion, but they suffered weakness, shortness of breath, and back pain, sometimes severe enough to cause disability (and therefore greater dependency on men).

Race has also served as a basis for infantilization. During slavery, the "Little Black Sambo" image depicted black American men as boys who lacked either the sophistication or the intelligence to fend for themselves—hence, the justification for what was popularly believed to be a "white man's burden": because some whites regarded blacks as inherently inferior, slavery was widely considered as absolutely essential for the survival of the black race.[12]

The members of a group are typically infantilized only as long as they conform to a docile and obliging role vis-à-vis those in positions of power. If the members of a stigmatized group get "too uppity"—perhaps even rebellious—they are no longer stereotyped as having the characteristics of children, but are instead regarded as animals or demons. In a word, they are *dehumanized*. After all, you cannot kill children, regardless of how much they misbehave; but it is perfectly acceptable—perhaps even obligatory—to slaughter an animal or to kill "the devil.". . .

The importance of the personal threat in the stereotyping process can be seen in the acceptance of vicious beliefs concerning a range of groups whose members, having challenged the status quo by their new visibility, are currently the targets of hatred. As more and more Americans have grown fearful of contracting AIDS, for example, they have also stereotyped lesbians and gays as "a pervasive, sinister, conspiratorial, and corruptive threat." The traditional view of gays as essentially laughable—"as queens, fairies, limp-wrists, and nellies"—could hardly have put them at so much risk. But to stereotype gays as the destroyers of civilization is to make life easier for potential gay-bashers everywhere, who seek some kind of justification and support for their criminal behavior.[13]

Many people have a distorted view of social reality, because they usually don't bother to validate or test their beliefs about others in any systematic way. Thus they can go through a lifetime clinging to old stereotypes that are patently false, without the slightest hint that they are essentially being inaccurate and unfair. . . .

Whatever the causal factors responsible for hate offenses, those who attack other human beings because they are different would like *validation* in doing so. To an increasing extent, hatemongers find solace, if not inspiration, in the humor, entertainment, music, and politics that we share as a people, in a growing culture of hate that is being directed wholly toward the members of our society.[14]

Notes

1. Stephen Singular, *Talked to Death: The Life and Murder of Alan Berg* (New York: William Morrow, 1987); also, Philip Lamy, "The Meek Shall Not Inherit the Earth: Survivalism and the American Millennial Myth" (Doctoral dissertation submitted to the Department of Sociology and Anthropology, Northeastern University, July 1991).

2. James Coates, "Trial Opens for 11 in Neo-Nazi Group," *Chicago Tribune*, September 13, 1985, p. 12.

3. James Coates, *Armed and Dangerous: The Rise of the Survivalist Right* (New York: The Noonday Press, 1987).

4. James Coates, "Rightist Hate Groups Put on the Defensive." *Chicago Tribune*, November 9, 1987, p. 10.

5. According to the FBI definition, hate need not be the total motivation but only a partial motivation: "A criminal offense committed against a person or property which is motivated, in whole or in part, by the offender's bias against a race, religion, ethnic/national origin group, or sexual orientation group" (U.S. Department of Justice, *Hate Crime Data Collection Guidelines*, Washington, DC: Federal Bureau of Investigation, 1990).

6. Center for Democratic Renewal, *They Don't All Wear White Sheets: A Chronology of Racist and Far Right Violence—1980–1986* (Atlanta: Center for Democratic Renewal, 1987).

7. Ibid.

8. Ibid.

9. Jack McDevitt, "The Study of the Character of Civil Rights Crimes in Massachusetts 1983–1989" (Paper presented at annual meeting of the American Society of Criminology, Reno, Nevada, November 1990).

10. Jack Levin and William C. Levin, *The Functions of Discrimination and Prejudice* (New York: Harper & Row, 1982).

11. Alison Lurie, *The Language of Clothing* (New York: Random House, 1981), p. 81.

12. Levin and Levin, *The Functions of Discrimination and Prejudice;* Jack Levin, William C. Levin, and Arnold Arluke, "Powerful Elders" (Paper presented at the annual meeting of the American Sociological Association, Pittsburgh, August 1992); Nel Noddings, *Women and Evil* (Berkeley: University of California Press, 1989); Sam Keen, *Faces of the Enemy* (San Francisco: Harper & Row, 1986).

13. Richard D. Mohr, "Anti-Gay Stereotypes," in *Gays/Justice. A Study of Ethics, Society and Law* (New York: Columbia University Press, 1988), pp. 21–27.

14. Levin and Levin, *The Functions of Discrimination and Prejudice.*

27
Robbing Drug Dealers

Violence Beyond the Law

Bruce A. Jacobs

Despite the widely held assumption that violence is something that happens only (or primarily) to law-abiding citizens, a disproportionate share of victims are themselves involved in crime. Drug dealers are a good example, offenders who, for a number of reasons, make ideal robbery targets. They are plentiful, visible, and accessible. They deal strictly in cash and tend to have lots of it; drug selling is a high-volume, repeat business. Their merchandise is valuable, portable, and flexible; it can be used, sold, or both. They often wear clothing and jewelry with considerable monetary worth and greater trophy value; on the streets, stolen property enhances the taker's status (Anderson 1999, 30, 75). They cannot rely on bystanders to come to their aid; operative norms dictate that witnesses mind their own business or suffer the consequences. They have no recourse to the police either: black market entrepreneurs cannot be "victims" and therefore lack access to official means of grievance redress. Contrary to conventional wisdom, most drug dealers are not armed, particularly those operating on the streets. Aggressive policing has made it not worth the risk; most dealers are far more afraid of being arrested than of being robbed. These conditions create the perfect target, one flush with cash and drugs, yet utterly defenseless. Drawing from interviews with active drug robbers, Jacobs explores these and other issues.

Robbery is all about material gain and few offenses rival the riches promised by drug robbery. Cash seizures can measure in the thousands of dollars, drug hauls in ounces rather than grams. Luxury accessory items (e.g., cars, jewelry) are frequently side benefits of heists. . . .

High-yield crimes are critical for those who burn money as fast as they make it. Drug robbers do precisely that. Their lifestyle is one driven by the open-ended pursuit of illicit street action. Illegal drug use figures most prominently in their "life as party" (Shover 1996). The vast majority consume mind-altering substances in significant quantities at tremendous cost. The urge to use drugs was in many ways beyond their ability to control (Wright and Decker 1994:40). The quest for intoxication was a basic drive—much like hunger, thirst, and sex are for ordinary citizens (see Siegel 1989:10). Indeed, no amount ever really seemed enough to satiate. "I got to get high, I got to get high," J Rock pronounced. "That's what I got to do. I got to get high. . . .Nothing to me but getting high, time to get high, time to get high, got to get high." June Bug claimed that $800, an amount which could buy nearly an ounce of crack (about 150, $20 rocks) "ain't no money. What is $800 . . . ? You can run through $800 in 45 minutes [using crack]." . . .

There is perhaps no better way to relieve intense, immediate, and costly pharmacological cravings than through drug robbery. Widely available, readily accessible, and possessing the precise goods respondents want most, drug sellers represent obvious targets. "I'm a dope fiend," Do-dirty explained. "They got the money and the dope. That's a high, you see what I'm saying. If you got the money and you got the dope, Do-dirty gonna get his." Curly concurred:

> You ain't got no money, you need a fix. You got a pistol. It's some dope in the street. You don't have to make your mind up, your mind already made. You need some dope and the quickest mark you can get. . . .

Loot seized from drug dealers offered the best of possible worlds. As YoYo put it, "You got your dope, you got something to smoke and then you also got some way you can make your money back and keep your stuff going on and on"—implying that she would use at least part of her drug haul to generate additional revenues. . . .

Sanction Threats

Rewards—be they financial, pharmacological, or cognitive—are only half of the equation. Crime benefits cannot be considered in the absence of crime risks. And the risks of drug robbery are appealingly small, particularly as they pertain to formal sanction threats. As noted previously, illicit contexts render law unavailable as a matter of course. Participants in blackmarket enterprise cannot be "victims" and as such, can be exploited with relative impunity. "What he [dealer] gonna do," Slim observed confidently, "call the police and tell [them] I took his drugs from him?" "You can never report a drug related robbery," Darnell declared. "You [can't] go to the police and say 'he took $1,300 from me in cash and 50 pills [of heroin, worth $500].'" "Come on," J Rock echoed, "get real, fuck that." Even if a police report is made, authorities typically write it off or officiously remark that the victim in question got what he deserved. . . .Bystanders are reticent to intervene and also reluctant to come forward as witnesses; on the streets, the ability to mind one's own business is vital (Jacobs 1999a). Disastrous consequences await those who snitch. Thus, people "see but don't see" (Anderson 1999:133; see also Liska and Warner 1991 on how the fear of crime constrains reporting).

Immunity of this nature does not accompany more ordinary offenses. Not only are structural barriers against reporting absent, there is a much higher risk of third-party intervention. "People can hear you breaking into they car," Lewis revealed, "burglar alarms go off, dogs barking, you see what I'm saying? . . .You got a better chance [with drug robbery], better chance to run off but if you breaking into a car you gonna hear the dog barking, peoples turn the lights on." The threat of official detection is commensurately higher:

Police come real quick for [burglarizing] people. . . .That's how you get caught up

. . .walking in people houses. . . .People got alarms, you all know that.—*K-red*

You rob [burglarize] a house, you caught by the police. You shoplift out of a store, you gonna wind up being caught.—*Snap*

Insulation from official consequences comes at a price, however. Resistance and retribution are part-and-parcel of many offenses, especially those perpetrated against persons who themselves are involved in crime. The threat of victim-retaliation is widely assumed in discussions of drug dealing. Vendors are depicted to be armed, dangerous, and primed to react (see, e.g., Bourgois, 1995). Conventional wisdom holds that such persons will not stay in business, or stay in business for long, if they allow themselves to be victimized (Maher and Daly 1996; Johnson et al. 1985). The message that one cannot be trifled with must be communicated with stark clarity (see also Anderson 1999).

It was somewhat surprising to learn, therefore, that "soft" dealers—those disinclined to resist or retaliate—reportedly dominated the street scene. A reflection of drug market circumstances unique to St. Louis or of the particular stereotypes of these respondents, such reports highlight an important perception that guided their actions. "[D]ope dealers out here right now today man," Ray Dog insisted, "[they] are straight up chumps. . . .They are punks. . . .They are the weakest." Do-dirty declared that dope dealers are "the most punk ass niggers in the world." Ray Ray remarked that he robbed "bitches, bitch ass fools that ain't gonna do nothing . . .dudes that's weak, that's soft . . .that's real scary that . . .ain't gonna do nothing [and there are a lot of them]."

As a general rule, streetcorner dealers were perceived to be softer than those who sold from houses. They tended to be younger and less likely to be armed—presumably to avoid the double sanction of drug *and* weapons possession (a considerable risk on the open streets). "They don't believe in carrying no guns," Do-dirty reported. "If he get caught he got possession and CCW. So he gonna . . .stash his pistol [away from his body]." Darnell concurred: "Why you have a gun out there? You already gonna catch a dope case, you know what I'm saying? So why catch a concealed weapon [case also]?" Or, as June Bug put it:

> Five out of ten, a drug dealer out there selling drugs ain't got no pistol . . .'cause he's worried about the police riding on him. See he can throw the drugs away but it's hard to throw a pistol away cause they [police] can go get that pistol. . . .

Moralistic Action?

The allure of drug robbery transcended utilitarian notions of risk and reward. A number of offenders waxed philosophical about their motivations, claiming such offenses were activated, at least in part, by moralistic concerns. The notion of "crime as social control" is nothing new (Black 1993). Since time immemorial, people have taken the law into their own hands to right perceived wrongs. . . .

. . . .In most cases, retributive motives appeared to be grounded in some need to right a perceived *personal* wrong. The nature of such wrongs varied, from blows to self-esteem, to transactional "insults," to affronts to personal dignity. . . .

As hard drug addicts, respondents were especially sensitive about how their status was perceived by others—particularly those who supplied them. Dealers were known to have "big heads," talking down to their customers and treating them in disparaging ways. "Once they start selling drugs they get a big head," Lewis illustrates. "They talk to you like you a kid, you know, and tell you how to spend your money this way and that way." On the streets, this cannot be tolerated; "esteem is so precarious that it can be taken away with just a word" (Anderson 1999:75, 95). Indeed, affronts that casual observers might consider trivial were imbued with profound meaning here. The widespread acceptance of the word "trivial" betrays the utter inability of outsiders "to interpret and make sense of the semiotic significance of opaque social events" (Campbell 1986:122). Seemingly innocuous encounters might very well result in conflicts fraught with reputational—and retributional—meaning:

> When I seen [this dealer] I said "Hey, what's up Tony, how you doing?" "All right man, just chilling and stuff like that." "Oh man you looking bad, you still on drugs and stuff like that?" "Yeah, you know." So I kind of take that personal, you know what I'm saying? Why do you look down on me when you probably doing things wrong?. . .I just sit down and think about, OK, so he got all this [money] and then he gonna talk down on me like that?. . .I was like, I'm gonna get this dude.—*Low Down*

> I robbed him cause he was talking shit, he pissed me off. Otherwise I just don't do that to people.—*Kilo*

> He didn't know how to talk to peoples . . .like he feel like that [he didn't owe nobody] shit and he could talk to you any kind of way. . . .I didn't like him. . . .We had a few words . . .so I figured that one of these days I would get him.—*Lewis*

Condescension was a sure-fire way for dealers to trigger animosity, particularly given the synergistic relationship they had with their customers.

> These cats [crack dealers] man because they think they better than the next motherfucker man. . . .Them little cats discriminate the motherfuckers that smoke crack. "Oh he just an old crackhead motherfucker," you see what I'm saying you know. But what the motherfucker fails to realize is man, you know, we make you, you don't make us. Without us your crack ain't shit cause you will still be stuck with that shit you know. So I prefer to get the crack dealers because the majority of them be cats, you know, they don't have no respect for the older dudes you know. Because you know, I'm not begging you for anything, I'm buying what I want from you but I still got to be a crackhead motherfucker to you.—*June Bug.* . . .

Often, dealer insults were transactional in nature—grounded in conduct specific to some purchase attempt. Lewis recalled trying to buy $50 worth of heroin for $45—a common tactic on the streets where users try to stretch their money as far as possible. The dealer, however, "took my money and balled it up and threw it in my face, threw it back to me. . . .He wanted to talk to [me] like [I was] a drug addict . . .and I felt he couldn't talk to me that kind of way. . . .I said to myself, 'that's ok . . .I'll be back tonight . . .I'm gonna stalk you.'" . . .

Dealers who refused to front drugs or give credit, especially to longtime customers who had proven their brand-loyalty, were perceived to be especially insolent. . . .

> Like I ask them for something and they don't give it to me. A guy on the street, he selling rock and I told him like this, "Man, look, I'm hurting, I need my motherfucking medicine and I need it right now. . . .I asked for something and you wouldn't give me nothing so now I want it all.". . .He say, "what you talking about?" "I want your motherfucking crack." "I ain't giving you shit." I upped on him, "Give it here and he give it to me. . . ."You think I'm bullshitting? . . .Give me all your dope and all your money now. . . .You think I'm bullshitting?" I'll rob his ass.—*J Rock*. . . .

Being ripped off or shorted was an equally powerful catalyst. . . .K-red, for example, reportedly revenge-robbed a dealer of $600 in cash and a gram of heroin (valued at about $250) after being sold just $10 worth of fake heroin. Bacca, trying to collect on a larger drug debt, was told by the debtor that he had "nothing" and to "get out of his face." He promptly went home, loaded his pistol, and returned to rob the seller. Likewise, Jay recounted an incident in which he helped a dealer-associate rehab a house, who tried to "get over" by paying him in crack rather than cash. Drugs are not considered payment in kind, and Jay perceived this to be demeaning of his essential character (by implying that he was a stigmatized "crackhead" whose existence revolved solely around securing the drug). He turned to drug robbery to collect what was perceived to be properly owed to him:

> I do rehabbing on houses . . .and I had did some work on one of his apartments for him, some drywall and stuff and he didn't ever finish giving me all the money 'cause me hanging around, you know, he would give me a little dope here a little dope there to compensate and I told him "I did-

n't ask you for that shit. . . .I wasn't working for crack, I was working for money, and he felt like he didn't have to give me no money cause he had gave me some crack. . . .He owed me $100 at that point. The rest of it he had paid me, but he still owed me $100. I wanted him to give me $100. He didn't want to give me $100 cause he said he gave me some crack. Then he tried to give me some more crack and I told him I wasn't working for no fucking crack. . . .I said "I want my money." He said "I don't owe you no motherfucking money." He said "man I gave you the crack." I said "Man I don't work for no fucking crack man. I said I was working for money. . . ."I want my motherfucking money." He said "I ain't gonna give you no money man cause I done gave you too much crack." I turned off like I was gonna walk off. I just went in my [pants] and pulled my gun out. Told him he was gonna give me my money. I took about $400 . . .from him that day.

Perceived insults are one thing; advances against one's very personhood or "form," as they say on the streets, were quite another. Indeed, threats to one's personal autonomy represented arguably the most serious instance of negative reciprocity. After a drug market associate snitched to the police on J Rock, he felt irresistibly compelled to take matters into his own hands. "A friend will never tell on nobody," he insisted. "He tell, he rat on me. . . .Three years of my life [in prison] and everything [all the crime] I do I ain't never get caught and that nigger get me caught. . . .That's why I did what I had to do." Lady Bug robbed a dealer for being too sexually forward with her cousin; their relationship was apparently close enough to transform the incident into a personal vendetta that would end only after vengeance (the subsequent robbery resulted in the shooting of three of the dealer's associates). Baby Doll fleeced a dealer in retaliation for her own rape a few months prior:

> . . .this guy. He had did something to me, he had raped me. . . .So I had set it in my mind that I had wanted to get him. So I set him up. I told him that somebody wanted to get kind of like an 8 ball or something like that. So . . .I took him on the set to get him robbed.

One may justifiably wonder why respondents turned to robbery as the means to exact revenge. Why not assault or burglarize victims, or deface their property? Why not seek the ultimate payback and kill them? Perhaps drug robbery represents the best combination of financial harm, physical threat, and mental intimidation. Assaults are too simple; black eyes and busted lips heal. Defaced property can be fixed or replaced. Theft without contact is not personal or humiliating enough. Murder generates bodies, and bodies bring heat (something drug robbers dearly want to avoid). Drug robbery mixes the most hurtful elements of property and violent crime, and is perhaps the best way to exact bloodless revenge. Most importantly, offenders can secure exactly what they want—and need—to keep the party going. . . .

References

Anderson, Elijah 1999. *Code of the Street*. New York: Norton.

Black, Donald. 1993. *The Social Structure of Right and Wrong*. San Diego, CA: Academic Press.

Bourgois, Philippe 1995. *In Search of Respect: Selling Crack in El Barrio*. Cambridge: Cambridge University Press.

Campbell, Anne. 1986. "The Streets and Violence." In *Violent Transactions: The Limits of Personality*. A. Campbell and J. J. Gibbs, eds. Pp. 115–132. New York: Basil Blackwell.

Jacobs, Bruce A. 1999a. *Dealing Crack: The Social World of Streetcorner Selling*. Boston: Northeastern University Press.

Johnson, Bruce D., Paul Goldstein, Edward Preble, James Schmeidler, Douglas S. Lipton, Barry Spunt, and Thomas Miller 1985. *Taking Care of Business: The Economics of Crime by Heroin Abusers*. Lexington, MA: Lexington Books.

Liska, Allen and Barbara Warner 1991. "Functions of Crime: A Paradoxical Process." *American Journal of Sociology* 96:1441–1463.

Maher, Lisa and Kathleen Daly 1996. "Women in the Street-Level Drug Economy: Continuity or Change?" *Criminology* 34:465–491.

Shover, Neal 1996. *Great Pretenders*. Boulder: Westview.

Siegel, Ronald K. 1989. *Intoxication: Life in Pursuit of Artificial Paradise*. New York: Dutton.

Wright, Richard T. and Scott H. Decker 1994. *Burglars on the Job*. Boston: Northeastern University Press.

28
The Spectrum of Child Abuse

R. Kim Oates

Few forms of violence are more disturbing than child abuse. Children are defenseless, which makes them uniquely vulnerable. They lack the social, economic, political, and physical capital necessary to deter aggressors or to fend them off after the abuse has already started. Child abuse comes in many forms, from incest and molestation to hitting and slapping to verbal intimidation and emotional battery. Neglect can also be a form of abuse; failing to provide for a child's basic wants and needs can be as bad as or worse than forcibly inflicting pain on him or her.

Statistics on the number of children abused annually in the United States are difficult to provide, primarily because the offense is so underreported. Abuse typically occurs in the privacy of a home, so it has little chance of being discovered and reported to the general public. Children, moreover, often cannot or will not go to the police, either because they do not know any better or because they are too afraid. Abusers often threaten additional harm—and even death—if victims expose them. Children who do report being abused may not even be believed; their accusations may be dismissed as flights of fancy or attempts at petty vengeance (e.g., in return for being grounded or spanked). Abusers know this and sometimes use it to their advantage.

Constructions of abuse, like other forms of deviance, are historically contingent and culturally specific. Acts that used to be considered discipline in this country, for example—whippings, mouth-washings with soap, enforced isolation, and the like—are now considered abusive. America's historical penchant for corporal punishment at times conflicts with more contemporary parenting paradigms that exclude the use of force. The tension between "old school" and "new age" methods is at times strong, resulting in something of a cultural schizophrenia about acceptable ways to discipline children.

The current political climate is extraordinarily sensitive to child abuse, so much so that sensational cases periodically crop up that are later found to be without merit. In the infamous (and nationally televised) McMartin Preschool Trial, it was alleged that school administrators engaged in ritualistic and satanic torture against children in their care, charges that were ultimately disproved (the children were apparently "coached" by therapists to recall incidents that never happened). No one is served by false accusation, especially children who really *have* been abused; their complaints may, in consequence, be unjustly discounted, making all children that much more defenseless.

Almost daily, we are confronted by newspaper reports, magazine articles or television programs describing child abuse. What is child abuse and why is there so much media attention? Is child abuse increasing? Are reports exaggerated? Can we believe what children say? What do we know about the perpetrators of abuse? What happens to abused children—will some become abusers when they grow up? How can abused children be treated? How can scarce resources be best used? How can we reduce the incidence of child abuse? These are typical of the questions that the public, as well as professionals, often ask. Unfortunately, there are no simple answers. Child abuse is a complex problem and complex problems rarely have a simple solution. . . .

The Spectrum of Child Abuse

Child abuse can be divided into four broad areas:

- Physical abuse
- Sexual abuse
- Neglect and nonorganic failure to thrive
- Emotional abuse

Historical Background

...Society sometimes pays only lip service to the concept that children are our most precious resource and that they need to be loved, nurtured, and protected. In historical terms, this is a relatively new concept for society as a whole. . . .

It is not surprising then that child abuse has been an integral part of children's fairy tails, such as *Hansel and Gretel,* and of nursery rhymes, such as this well-known example:

There was an old woman who lived in a shoe. She had so many children she did not know what to do. She gave them some broth without any bread, and whipped them all soundly and put them to bed.

Even the much-loved puppet show *Punch and Judy* tells how Judy gives Mr. Punch her baby to mind. At first Mr. Punch rocks the baby on his knee. The baby begins to cry. Mr. Punch responds by rocking the baby harder and, eventually, violently. The crying persists. Mr. Punch then loses control, hits the baby, and throws it out of the window to its death.

Various forms of child abuse have been documented and sometimes condoned in the past. Many cultures used infanticide as an acceptable method of family planning and to dispose of weak, premature, or deformed infants (Bakan, 1971). Sometimes, children were killed for superstitious reasons as it was believed that slain infants would benefit the sterile woman, kill disease, and confer health, vigor, and youthfulness. To ensure durability of important buildings, children were sometimes buried under the foundations (Radbill, 1974). In England, during the industrial revolution in the mid-eighteenth century, children from poor families provided industry with a cheap work force. Children as young as 5 years of age worked in factories for up to 14 hours each day and often suffered additional cruel treatment during this time. . . .

Infanticide was common in England as late as the nineteenth century. In London, 80 percent of illegitimate children who were sent out to wet nurses died, often because they would be killed by the wet nurses, who would continue to collect nursing fees (Fraser, 1976). Newborn children could be insured for about one English pound under a "burial club" insurance policy. If the child died, the parents could claim between three and five pounds in insurance, which meant that some parents killed their infants or had someone else kill them in order to claim the insurance (Fraser, 1976). . . .

Child physical abuse is now accepted as one of the more serious problems of childhood, although the denial of its extent and existence, which resulted in its being so slow to be recognized, still exists. Denial can be a problem for some members of the medical profession, ranging from a disbelief that parents actually can injure their children to not wanting to become involved because recognition may mean reporting and reporting may mean going to court. Some may be reluctant to do more than treat the injury because they erroneously believe that doctor-patient confidentiality may be compromised. At times, there is a tendency to identify with the parents, particularly when the abuser is of a similar professional standing and ethnic background or may not fit the professional stereotype of what a "child abuser" is like. The fact is that child physical abuse is common and should be considered when unexplained or unlikely injuries occur.

Incidence

Although we do not know the incidence of physical abuse, we do know that most abuse occurs within the privacy of the child's home and that as most abusers give a false explanation of injuries that come to medical attention, the reported incidence of physical abuse is underestimated. We also know that not all reports of abuse are genuine. Some may be malicious, while others may be reports of actual abuse that cannot to be substantiated. Thus, there is the situation of simultaneous underreporting of real cases and some degree of overreporting. . . .

Sexual Abuse

Sexual exploitation of children by adults is not new. What is new is the professional and public awareness of a problem that has been present for many centuries. . . .

It is worth asking why recognition of this problem took so long. For a long period, families and professionals had protected themselves and their feelings by pretending that sexual abuse was rare and something that only involved "other people." When sexual abuse of children was referred to, it was usually in the media and involved lurid, often violent episodes of stranger assault. The regular and persistent abuse of children in their own homes, by people on whom they were dependent and whom they should have been able to trust, was not mentioned, mainly because discussion of sexual abuse within a family can be a threat to the very structure of that family. As inadequate as some family relationships may be, they are often all the family has. In the past, when a child did tell someone of the abuse, the child was often not believed or was even punished for making such an outrageous suggestion. For those parents who listened to their children and became concerned enough to take the child to the doctor, the claim was often dismissed by the professional as the result of a vivid juvenile imagination. Professionals complied in the denial of this problem because they had no experience or training in the area and because it was often too uncomfortable for them.

Persistence by a relatively small number of professionals and by sections of the feminist movement, along with increased media awareness, has brought child sexual abuse more into the open, although the level of denial still remains high for some. Many are reluctant to believe that anyone, especially someone who appears to be normal, could abuse a child sexually. This reluctance leads to taking refuge in questioning the child's credibility, reliability, and motives, even shifting blame to the child and thus reinforcing the stereotype that a real child molester is someone who is a sinister stranger—not at all like our friends or family (Summitt, 1990). . . .

Neglect and Nonorganic Failure to Thrive

Two aspects of child abuse, neglect and nonorganic failure to thrive, have been somewhat ignored by professionals and the media (Wolock & Horowitz, 1984). Physical abuse and sexual abuse are active events that often have obvious consequences. These forms of abuse suggest an urgency to treat, protect, and prevent. Neglect is more insidious. It is not well defined, does not need sophisticated high technology to make the diagnosis, and rarely produces the outrage that may accompany reports of physical or sexual abuse. . . .

Neglect
Definition and Incidence. Children have a number of basic needs. These include the needs for love and security, opportunities, new experiences, praise, recognition, and responsibility, as well as for adequate food, housing, clothing, medical care, and education. Neglect is usually regarded as the failure of parents to provide these things, particularly the material items. . . .

Nonorganic Failure to Thrive
Definition. Some infants whose needs for adequate nutrition and emotional stimulation are neglected develop nonorganic failure to thrive. . . .

Nonorganic failure to thrive or growth failure where the problem is primarily one of caretaking is now recognized to be a complex problem in which a variety of factors can play a part to different degrees. These include environmental stresses on the family, minor medical problems in the infant that make feeding stressful or ineffective, problems of attachment, and difficulties in parenting capabilities. . . .

Emotional Abuse

Emotional abuse tends to be the hidden form of child abuse. Yet it is at the very heart of child abuse. It has been argued that, rather than emotional abuse being part of the spectrum of child abuse and neglect, it is the factor that underlies all other forms of abuse because of the psychological message of worthlessness and debasement that is received by children who are physically and sexually abused (Garbarino, 1989). . . .

. . .[E]motional abuse of children is always totally unacceptable, but cultural norms have to be remembered. Behaviors that may seem abusive in some cultures could be acceptable in others and may not be harmful if they do not involve the replacement of love with rejection and withdrawal. However, when the behavior toward the child conveys a culture-specific message of rejection or when it impairs the development of a socially relevant psychological process, such as the development of self-esteem, then it is emotional abuse, whatever the family's cultural norms (Garbarino, Guttman, & Seeley, 1986).

Because emotional abuse does not leave any physical injuries, it does not come to the attention of medical, law enforcement, or welfare authorities as frequently as the more dramatic forms of abuse. Its ongoing nature means that there is usually no crisis, such as the discovery of sexual abuse or the injuries from physical abuse, to precipitate a consultation with a person involved in child health or welfare. . . .

References

Bakan, D. 1971. *Slaughter of the Innocents: A Study of the Battered Child Phenomenon.* San Francisco: Jossey-Bass.

Fraser, B.G. 1976. The child and his parents: A delicate balance of rights. In R.E. Helfer and C.H. Kempe (eds.) *Child Abuse and Neglect: The Family and the Community.* Cambridge, MA: Ballinger.

Garbarino, J. 1989. The psychologically battered child: Towards a definition. *Pediatric Annals,* 18:502–504.

Garbarino, J., Guttman, E., and Seeley, J.W. 1986. *The Psychologically Battered Child.* San Francisco: Jossey-Bass.

Radbill, S.X. 1974. A history of child abuse and infanticide. In R.E. Helfer & C.H. Kempe (eds.), *The Battered Child* (2nd ed.). Chicago: University of Chicago Press.

Summitt, R.C. 1990. The specific vulnerability of children. In R.K. Oates (ed.). *Understanding and Managing Child Sexual Abuse.* Philadelphia: W.B. Saunders.

Wolock, I. and Horowitz, B. 1984. Child maltreatment as a social problem: The neglect of neglect. *American Journal of Orthopsychiatry* 54:530–543.

Part VI

Sexual Deviance: Prostitution, Rape, and Homosexuality

Sex, it seems, is everywhere—television, movies, magazines, and music. It is used to sell everything from mouthwash to blue jeans to automobiles. Messages, both overt and covert, permeate American culture about the importance of sex appeal. Yet sex, paradoxically, is as constrained as it is ubiquitous, governed by specific conduct norms that define appropriate sexual behavior and sanction activity deemed deviant. Sexual norms are not unique to American society. One of the most distinctive features of all human civilizations is the "variety and strength of controls that govern sexual behavior." Sex is one of the most strongly regulated of all human acts; even in permissive societies, it receives special attention. "Even those individuals who regard sex between consenting adults as natural and private have had to recognize the powerful social pressures, norms, attitudes, and taboos on sex, independent of legal restrictions" (Meier and Geis 1997, 124–125).

Taboos and restrictions give rise to all sorts of sexual deviance, prostitution being one noteworthy example. Prostitution thrives precisely because of sexual constraint. If sex were freely available, there would be no reason for people to sell it. Men (or women) could have sexual relationships with anyone they wanted, whenever they desired. Kingsley Davis perhaps puts it best (1966, 360):

> The attempt to control sexual expression, to tie it to social requirements, especially the attempt to tie it to the durable relation of marriage and the rearing of children, or attach men to a celibate order, or to base sexual expression on love, creates the opportunity for prostitution. It is analogous to the blackmarket, which is the illegal but inevitable response to an attempt to control the economy. The craving for sexual variety, for perverse gratification, for novel and provocative surroundings, for ready and cheap release, for intercourse free from entangling cares and civilized pretense—all can be demanded from the woman whose interest lies solely in the price. The sole limitation on the man's satisfactions is in this instance, not morality or convention, but his ability to pay (quoted in Meier and Geis 1997, 54–55).

Prostitution has existed for thousands of years. It has been called the world's oldest profession, though by most standards, it is not a profession at all. Its functional importance, however, cannot be denied. Some commentators suggest that it provides a sexual safety valve, siphoning off men who, facing scarcity, might otherwise commit assault. Rape rates, these analysts suggest, are kept low by virtue of the prostitution outlet, though studies to prove this are few and far between. Many feminists understandably bristle at such a conclusion, arguing that a specific class of women set aside solely for male sexual gratification does more harm than good (see Brownmiller 1975). It bolsters the perception that women are inferior and exist primarily for male sexual release. It encourages men to commodify all women as sexual objects, not just prostitutes. It fuels a misogynist discourse, providing labels that function to deride any woman who strays from prevailing sexual norms (e.g., whore, slut, tramp, etc.). It obfuscates the patriarchal and institutional forces that drive many women into prostitution in the first place and often keep them there. It glosses over the fact that prostitution is often a "dirty and dangerous enterprise," replete with beatings, "loveless copulations," unremunerated sexual services, and even rape (Meier and Geis 1997, 48).

Prostitution's illegal status may, paradoxically, make things worse. Participants in blackmarket enterprises are beyond the law and thus cannot be "victims" in the eyes of authorities. Thus, prostitutes make popular targets for assault and robbery; police routinely dismiss their complaints or officiously remark that they are getting what they deserve. To avoid arrest, (street) prostitutes must often work in darkened areas without benefit of protection from others; in some jurisdictions, two or more women congregating on a street corner constitute a brothel. Such policies create a reliance on pimps for protection. Pimps can be substantial safety risks themselves, beating, assaulting, and otherwise exploiting those under their "care." The risk of arrest compels prostitutes to forgo security measures designed to qualify potentially shady customers. Some street prostitutes, for example, will jump into cars with unknown clients as quickly as possible to minimize the possibility of police detection. Others will refuse to carry condoms, fearing such implements will be labeled "criminal tools" (for which the police can arrest and charge them). The need for speed clouds judgment and enhances the likelihood of engaging in high-risk sexual practices, particularly for women whose cognitions are already impaired by drugs and alcohol (which tends to be common). Prostitution's outlaw status means that there is no system for regulating the health and welfare of either sex workers or their clients, which makes possible the unchecked spread of sexually transmitted diseases. By arresting prostitutes and levying fines on them, the government becomes, in a sense, a pimp—forcing them to go right back on the streets to pay the fines off, which leads to yet more arrests and fines, creating a vicious cycle (see Meier and Geis 1997).

Legalizing prostitution, as has been done in 14 of 17 counties in Nevada, is fraught with problems of its own. One of the primary missions of government is to uphold and protect conventional morality. By making sex work legal, states essentially give their OK to recreational sex for money, an unseemly proposition at best. They also tacitly admit there is nothing they can do to control prostitution, which makes governing bodies look weak and ineffectual (perhaps encouraging even more disrespect for the law in unrelated spheres; Schur 1965). Then there is the disquieting notion that women and girls on the "borderline" will be "encouraged to take up prostitution by the mere fact that it is legal" (United Nations in Meier and Geis 1997, 57); even though legal taboos can make something deviant appear attractive, their removal can have the same effect.

Another factor to consider is the incidental crime likely to be generated if the sex trade were legalized, including the expansion of criminal subcultures that support prostitution (e.g., organized crime, drug markets). Still another is the rise in the community "nuisance factor." Indeed, some analysts suggest that if prostitution were decriminalized, special zones would be established for sex work, areas that would quickly dwindle into a maelstrom of vice. If it is the case that poorer, less enfranchised communities suffer first (and they almost always do), already downtrodden areas could become utterly uninhabitable (for an overview of these and other issues, see Meier and Geis 1997).

Prostitution is a significant form of sexual deviance, but it is not the only one, or the most important one. Sexual deviance subsumes a panoply of aberrant behaviors, from homosexuality and cross-dressing to exhibitionism and deviant sexual practices. The form that often receives the most media and popular concern, however—because of its heinousness, violence, and brutality—is rape, "carnal knowledge of a female forcibly and against her will" (Federal Bureau of Investigation 1996). Nearly 100,000 rapes occur in the United States every year—one of the highest per capita rates in the western industrialized world—but many scholars believe this figure is grossly underreported and may actually be as high as ten times that figure.

Part of the problem is definitional. Many sexual assaults are not categorized as rapes because they do not obviously involve force or threat of force. But coercion can be less than overt, and a preponderance of assaults involve subtle pressure or intimidation in an implied quid pro quo ("this for that"): If you don't give me what I want (sex), I'm not going to give you what you want (money, companionship, emotional commitment, etc.). Because scripts governing sexual behavior often are vague, particularly in acquaintance situations, miscommunication is common and can lead to assaultive incidents. Thus, Antioch College, a small liberal arts school in Ohio, requires that students of both sexes (but particularly males) get *formal permission* from would-be sex partners at every stage of an intimate encounter, from hand-holding and kissing, to fondling, groping, and intercourse (see also Brown et al. 1996). Although some suggest such requirements go a little too far, any policy that makes sexual expectations as unambiguous as possible is probably a good first step toward exposing, and neutralizing, the conditions that contribute to assault.

The bulk of the undercounting problem, however, can be traced to the fact that rape typically occurs between people who know one another, often intimately; intimacy militates against reporting. Victims of date/acquaintance/intimate-partner rape typically assume that the police will not believe them or that they will suffer retribution if they expose their assailant. Others may be too embarrassed to report the assault or believe that they should have been able to prevent it. Yet more want to protect the assailant's reputation or economic standing (see Bureau of Justice Statistics 1993). Until recently, the law did not even recognize intimate-partner rape as rape. Thus, wives could be sexually assaulted by their husbands without penalty of criminal sanction; they were "property," which provided men the right of sexual access any time, any place. Changes in legislation have come only because of increases in female economic power, which have translated into greater political influence.

The public mostly believes that rape is a product of a few sick individuals who simply cannot control their sexual impulses, but scholars offer more nuanced explanations. Social psychologists (some of them at least) propose a "forbidden fruit" model, suggesting that people want most what they cannot have, and when they cannot get it, they will take it forcefully, without permission. Sex is a scarce resource; rape emerges to make it less scarce. Sociobiologists contend that rape is a natural, evolutionary response on the part of males to advance their genes into successive generations. Having sex with as many women as possible, with or without their permission, puts their DNA at a competitive advantage relative to others and, on a broader scale, guarantees survival of the species itself. Sociological explanations, however, largely dominate the scholarly discourse, explanations suggesting that rape is produced and mediated by *cultural* forces.

Powerful images of women as sexual toys, as objects to be conquered, as tools existing solely for male sexual gratification are widely disseminated and internalized, providing what sociologist John Gagnon calls the sexual scripts that trigger assault. Popular discourse surrounding sexual relations, particularly among young males (the modal rape-prone category), suggests that women are not so much partners in an equal and loving enterprise as prey to be conquered and exploited in competitive, zero-sum games. Pornography amplifies this mentality, and although the vast majority of men exposed to explicit material never rape, its effects are subtle and cumulative—creating a climate in which the sexual exploitation of women becomes normative and acceptable. To many women, every man is a potential rapist, and this belief colors their thoughts and actions on a daily basis. Although rape may be, statistically speaking, a relatively rare event, fear drives perceptions, and perceptions drive actions. Some women will not venture outside alone at certain places or at certain times. Others feel safe only when accompanied by a man (even though they feel vulnerable precisely because of the actions of men). Asymmetrical gender relations are thereby reproduced, as all men benefit from rape by a few.

A culture that objectifies women and treats them as sexual prey also is one that makes men sexually fearful of one another. The existence of male-on-male homosexual sex invokes the possibility of *male rape,* tying into male's deep-seated insecurities, which may not even be recognized on a conscious level. Homophobia is one troubling response, a compensation mechanism whereby men show their disdain for everything homosexuals do and stand for. Homophobia is self-righteous, it is prejudicial, and it is grounded in exclusionary interpretations of acceptable masculinity. Some scholars suggest that homophobic reactions may be the principal means by which men with latent homosexual tendencies assert that they are heterosexual through and through. "By hating and attacking gay men, they can reassure themselves that they are not gay, but supremely masculine" (Goode 1997, 255; see also Goleman in Goode 1997).

Disdain for homosexuality, although less extreme than in the past, continues to be strong; nearly 70 percent of Americans responding to a recent poll said that it is immoral, and 88 percent from another poll asserted that is always or almost always wrong (Shapiro 1994; Klassen et al. 1989; see also Meier and Geis 1997). There is no known civilization that values homosexuality, though "some have tolerated it at different times, in different individuals, and under different circumstances" (Meier and Geis 1997, 132).

The prevalence of homosexuality is in some dispute. It is widely assumed that homosexuals comprise about 10 percent of the American adult population, but there is ample evidence to suggest that this figure may be both too high and too low. Part of the problem lies in defining who is and who is not gay. How many homosexual acts, for example, does a person have to commit before she or he earns the label? Is a person who has gay sex *once* a homosexual? Can a person who has never engaged in homosexual sex be considered gay as long as he or she is attracted to members of his or her own sex? What about a person who has heterosexual sex but fantasizes about gay partners? What about someone who participates in both heterosexual and homosexual sex but who considers himself heterosexual? What about the situational homosexual—someone who has gay sex because there are no members of the opposite sex around (e.g., in prison, boarding schools or other "one-sex societies")? Does the nature of the specific sexual act have any bearing? Many participants in homosexual sex, for instance, believe that only the passive recipient or "insertee" is gay. Does a person have to participate in a homosexual subculture to be considered gay? The list of possible contingencies is endless and speaks to the complexity and subjectivity involved in labeling someone a homosexual. The fundamental issue comes down to "act vs. identity" and, specifically, whether behavior makes (defines) the person or the person makes the behavior.

Sexual identity is a fluid concept. Despite popular perceptions, men are not "naturally" attracted to women, nor are women "naturally" attracted to men. Attraction is a social construction, mediated by a complicated and powerful process of socialization that starts early and extends throughout the lifecourse. In most cases, sex identity and gender identity are consistent, and biology is indeed destiny. But this is not always the case, and, for whatever reason, some people stray. Theories about the "causes" of homosexuality are as diverse as the inclusion criteria are difficult to nail down. Psychologists suggest that homosexuals are emotionally confused, perhaps as a consequence of unresolved childhood traumas, domineering mothers, or emotionally absent fathers. Anthropologists argue that homosexuality is a distinctly cultured construction. Some societies, war-focused tribes in primitive regions of the world, for instance, institutionalize homosexual sex to toughen up young boys and make warriors out of them (the exchange of seminal fluid is said to transfer courage and bravery from adult to child). Sociologists, meanwhile, tell us that homosexuality is learned. The same mechanisms implicated in the learning of heterosexual behavior are implicated here; the object of sexual desire just happens to be a member of one's own sex. Homosexual attraction and behavior can occur for a number of reasons, but incomplete socialization is principally implicated:

> The learning of sexuality is not a uniform experience, because sexual socialization is an imperfect process and some individuals will come to derive sexual satisfaction from objects and people outside the group's normative structure. This can be expected for at least two reasons. First, the area of eroticism is an ambiguous one for socializers. Many parents and others feel uncomfortable about offering sex education that includes sex-specific information. For most socializers, the topic of sex is embarrassing. This seems to be particularly true for parents and children, as neither seems comfortable thinking of the other as sexual beings. . . .Second, the area of sexuality covers much ground, from appropriate partners to appropriate time, objects, places, and ages. In fact, sexual norms are among the most complicated of all social norms because of the different combinations of contingencies that one must learn. . . .It is not surprising, therefore, that there are instances in which the socialization process fails to adequately prepare individuals for sexual growth and maturation within the group (Meier and Geis 1997, 120–121).

In recent years, owing to the increasingly prominent role health practitioners are playing in the deviance construction process, ho-

mosexuality has been "medicalized." That is, its causes are said to be biological—a particular gene, area of the brain, or hormonal deficit. Intriguingly, many homosexuals prefer biological explanations, partly because they legitimate "scientifically" what the homosexuals report feeling about themselves all along, that they are different in some central way and simply cannot be attracted to members of the opposite sex, no matter how hard they try. Medical models assert that homosexuality is not an illness or a perversion or the result of poor psychosexual development but a trait, just like eye color, height, or bone structure—a trait ascribed at birth. Trying to fight one's natural attractions is futile, frustrating, and counterproductive. Many homosexuals find this comforting.

If nothing else, medicalization has triggered increasing tolerance of homosexuality in the wider society. "Coming out" is not nearly the wrenching ordeal it once was. Openly gay lifestyles are becoming more and more acceptable. Popular television shows now routinely depict prominent gay characters. Homosexual organizations have gained increasing power on a variety of social, economic, and political fronts. A number of state governments have gone so far as to discuss legalizing same-sex marriages; Vermont recently enacted such a policy into law. In many urban locales across the country, being a homosexual is no longer the Scarlet Letter it once was. The stigma is not completely eradicated, however, and in the age of AIDS, homosexuals continue to be vilified by high-grounded moralists for their "unnatural" behavior. Whether gays should be permitted to serve in the military, be ordained as religious leaders, be allowed to adopt and rear children, or be granted special protections under the law all promise to be topics of major controversy for years to come (for more on this, see Meier and Geis 1997). ✦

29
The Social Organization of Prostitution

Robert F. Meier

Gilbert Geis

Prostitution typically is defined as the exchange of sexual gratification for material reward, usually money. Rewards, however, are not limited to money, nor need they be explicitly material. Many people exchange sex for drugs or for a better job or for power, however that may be defined. Others do it for companionship, attention, or emotional security. Sexual intercourse need not be part of the equation either. Sexual gratification is the issue, and gratification is a diffuse notion, meaning different things to different people.

As a form of deviance, prostitution is not unlike other forms of "victimless" crime. The offense is transactional and involves consensual participation. There is a perception of self-judged harmlessness and, generally speaking, there are no complaining witnesses (Schur 1965). Prostitution is illegal primarily, if not exclusively, because it violates current moral expectations of acceptable sexual behavior. There is nothing inherently wrong with selling or purchasing sex; it is wrong because people with the power and influence to make laws say it is wrong. In that sense, prostitution is like any other form of deviance, an inevitable product of social construction.

Meier and Geis walk us through the social and legal controversies swirling around what has been called the world's oldest profession. Included in their analysis is a short history of prostitution, its social organization, its dynamic legal status, and feminist perspectives on the occupation. There are no easy answers to the many and pressing issues the trade

churns up, and social policy needs to be sensitive to all the players involved, but especially to the women who constitute its participants.

There are any number of definitions of prostitution. It has been defined as any sexual exchange in which the reward for the prostitute is neither sexual nor affectional (James, 1977), and also as the performance of acts of nonmarital sex as a vocation (Polsky, 1967). A more elaborate definition was proposed by Paul Gebhard (1969:24):

> A female prostitute is a person who for immediate cash payment will engage in sexual activity with any person (usually male), known or unknown to her, who meets her minimal requirements as to age, sobriety, cleanliness, race, and health.

It has been argued that sexual intercourse between a married couple, particularly in the days before the feminist impact on contemporary attitudes and behavior, was much like prostitution. According to this argument, a woman typically refused sexual favors to a man until she was engaged or was married to him and assured of his financial support. Thus, sexual access was being exchanged for financial security, as if it were a commodity to be bartered. Such a stance stimulates debate but fails to acknowledge the very real difference between the commercial enterprise of prostitution and other social arrangements that are governed by far more complex conditions and rules.

Prostitutes, of course, are found in any gender. But both historically and currently the spotlight tends to be on female prostitutes for two reasons: they far outnumber their male counterparts and unlike male prostitutes, they are regarded as exemplars of gender subordination and exploitation, a matter which highlights important political and ideological issues. In any case, the clients of both male and female prostitutes are overwhelmingly male. For these reasons, we will concentrate on women and girl prostitutes (for representative studies of male prostitution see Cates and Markley, 1992; Reiss, 1961; van der Poel, 1992). . . .

Prostitution and Sexual Liberation

For a time, it seemed that prostitution would devolve into a non-issue like homosexuality as far as the law was concerned, though for very different reasons. The introduction of birth control pills, feminist efforts for equality in all spheres, and the pronounced loosening of sexual taboos have combined to create considerably greater opportunities for consensual sexual activity prior to and outside of marriage. Prostitution, it was thus presumed, would be priced out of existence because of the declining necessity to resort to pay-for-sex.

At least three major factors worked against such a development. First and undoubtedly foremost, the appearance of AIDS, a lethal immune system disorder, has checked dramatically the growing number of casual sexual encounters.

Second, prostitution continues to survive because it offers a commodity that cannot be readily found in other sexual arenas. That commodity involves the marketplace exchange of money for the unemotional provision of sexual gratification with no strings attached. Today, women, particularly those who are well-educated and informed, demand sexual satisfaction from a partner as their right—a demand that some men may not always be willing (or able) to satisfy (McCormick, 1994). Some males who try to stereotype women claim that prostitutes do not need to be wooed, flattered, or entertained, either romantically or sexually. Prostitutes will not complain the next morning that they were callously used or that their personal integrity was abused. As an example of customer satisfaction, one study indicates that almost half of the streetwalkers' clients in a New Jersey city were repeat clients, engaging in sex with a prostitute more than once a month (Freund, Lee, and Leonard, 1989). Though prostitutes do not provide romance or love, these males further contend, neither will they make any claim to continue a relationship nor interpret their sexual conduct as anything beyond a mere business transaction.

This point was emphasized in the pioneering study of male sexual behavior by Alfred Kinsey and his colleagues. "At all social levels men go to prostitutes because it is simpler to secure a sexual partner commercially than it is to secure a sexual partner by courting a girl." Kinsey et al. also observed that intercourse with a prostitute is likely to be a good deal cheaper than intercourse resulting from courtship, which could involve (in Kinsey's oddly detailed inventory) "flowers, candy, 'coke dates,' dinner engagements, parties, evening entertainments, moving pictures, theaters, night clubs, dances, picnics, weekend house parties, car rides, longer trips, and all sorts of other expensive entertainment" before the male "might or might not be able to obtain the intercourse he wanted" (Kinsey, Pomeroy, and Martin, 1948:608). Sexual etiquette has changed considerably since Kinsey's time, but the underlying accuracy of his chauvinistic position, however outdated, is probably true for at least some portion of sexual interactions.

Third, prostitutes offer a service that is not otherwise readily available to persons who find themselves beyond the pale of sexual appeal. Those too old, unattractive, or shy, or those who are unable to easily find a consenting sexual partner can turn to prostitutes as a simple solution to their problem. Prostitutes will also perform certain sexual acts (e.g., fellatio) that might be unavailable to some males in normal relationships. For the right price, all this can be accomplished in less than fifteen minutes. . . .

The Cast in the Performance of Prostitution

Prostitution involves people and institutions that play a number of different roles in the enterprise. At the core of the business of prostitution are the men and women who provide direct sexual stimulation to others in return for money. Within this group, there is a considerable distinction between streetwalkers at the bottom of the heap, prostitutes who work in massage parlors, and call girls (including outcall and escort services), who are considered the elite of the business (Bryant and Palmer, 1975). Debra Satz (1995:68) provides a vignette of members of the latter group:

Many call girls drift into prostitution after "run of the mill promiscuity," led neither by material want nor lack of alternatives. Some are young college graduates, who upon graduation earn money by prostitution, while searching for other jobs. Call girls can earn between $30,000 and $100,000 annually. These women have control over the entire amount they earn as well as an unusual degree of independence, far greater than in most other forms of work. They can also decide who they wish to have sex with and when they wish to do so. There is little resemblance between their lives and that of the streetwalker.

From interviews with working prostitutes, Wardell Pomeroy (1965:184) documented that 40 percent of these women remained in the business because of "the interesting people they meet." One call girl told him: "I have an eighth grade education and nearly every day I meet doctors, lawyers, bankers, and actors who I never would meet if I wasn't in the life." Her point was brought home in scandalous fashion when a $200-a-night call girl told a tabloid newspaper in 1996 about her assignations with 48-year-old Dick Morris, a top advisor to President Clinton and the major proponent of the administration's focus on "family values." Morris encouraged the call girl to eavesdrop on his telephone conversations with Clinton. After Morris resigned his position under pressure, it was disclosed that, although married, he had maintained a long-term relationship with a woman he had met through a Dallas escort service, had fathered a child by her, and was supporting her while she completed a university degree (Gooding, 1996; see also Morris, 1997).

In addition to the prostitutes themselves, there are others who derive income from some part of the prostitution network. Best known are pimps, who almost invariably associate only with female prostitutes. They promote the prostitute's work and take most of her earnings. Pimps, who often run a stable of prostitutes, typically offer protection, romance, and security (Milner and Milner, 1973). Then there are the cab drivers, bellhops, hotel desk men and elevator operators, the bartenders, and others whose jobs put them in a position to attract customers for a prostitute in return for a percentage of the woman's earnings (Reichert and Frey, 1985). Those who rent premises which they know are used for the purposes of prostitution also depend on the business for at least a portion of their livelihood. Finally, there are the customers of prostitutes—the "johns"—who form another set of major players. . . .

Feminism and Prostitution

The women's movement that flourished for a time in the early years of the twentieth century took a strong position against prostitution (Musheno and Seeley, 1986). Jane Addams, a social worker and one of the movement's leaders, maintained that curtailing prostitution, particularly in public places, would considerably reduce any allure that might attract perspective recruits to the business. Her reasoning is similar to the argument today that the attractive lifestyle of drug dealers in the slums—their expensive automobiles, elegant clothes, and desirable female companions—encourages youngsters there to emulate them. Addams put her case this way:

> Were the streets kept clear, many young girls would be spared familiar knowledge that such a method of earning money is open to them. . . .The legal suppression [of prostitution] would not only protect girls but would enormously minimize the risks and temptation for boys (Addams, 1912:48–49).

The more recent revival of the feminist movement, part of the social revolution that swept America in the 1960s, initially placed prostitution at the head of its agenda of the major criminal behaviors that needed to be addressed. But feminist attention to prostitution largely evaporated soon after because of an inability to convince streetwalkers and other women "in the life" that they ought to give up what they were doing and adopt a safer, more respectable, and more dignified lifestyle. As one prostitute put it, "A woman has the right to sell her sexual services just as much as she has a right to sell her brains to a law firm" (Jenness, 1990:405). Another said, "Radical feminism . . .sees all pros [prostitutes] as exploited sex slaves. I think this has left people confused, especially other feminists and the political left" (Overs, 1994:119).

After a while, the women's movement switched its criminal justice focus to rape (and later also to child and spousal abuse), though every once in a while issues regarding prostitution resurface, only to be abandoned because they produce an acrimonious internal splintering within feminist circles. The feminist debate on prostitution pits two conflicting interpretations against each other. The question is whether prostitution is an ugly and intolerable consequence of the power of men over women and the sexual exploitation of women, or a commercial enterprise like so many others that is engaged in by a seller who possesses a commodity that has a market value.

These questions have been difficult and divisive for American feminists (Reanda, 1991:202), and the schism within the women's movement on prostitution is said to be deep (Jolin, 1994:69). One arm of the feminist movement repudiates the idea that women freely choose prostitution, that prostitution is a valid job, and that it can be carried on in a humane manner. Prostitution, opponents of this position insist, is based on male domination, the treatment of women as commodities, and enforced sexual access and sexual abuse. It is said to violate women's dignity and to represent a crime against women by men (Romenesko and Miller, 1993; Weitzer, 1991).

Women who take this position regard prostitution as the product of a patriarchal society in which females are defined from an early age as sex objects. Child sexual abuse, incest, and similar female victimizations are said to lie at the core of one's entry into prostitution (Freeman, 1989–1990). This position equates prostitution with slavery and points out that few words can evoke such contempt and loathing as the word "whore" or its equivalent in any language (Reanda,1991:203). Often quoted is Simone de Beauvoir's (1953:569) observation in *The Second Sex* that "prostitution sums up all the forms of feminine slavery at once." This viewpoint has also been expressed by Laurie Shrage (1989:349):

Because of the cultural context in which prostitution operates, it epitomizes and perpetuates pernicious patriarchal beliefs and values and, therefore, is both damaging to the women who sell sex and, as an organized social practice, to all women in our society.

A milder version of Shrage's position is offered by Debra Satz who believes that prostitution is wrong "insofar as the sale of women's sexual labor reinforces basic patterns of sex discrimination." Satz (1995) writes, "I argue that contemporary prostitution contributes to, and also introduces, the perception of women as socially inferior to men." Satz's position, of course, raises questions about any social occurrence in which members of one gender do something that cannot be done, or at least not done as well, by members of the other gender. Athletic events, such as track meets, almost invariably show the men outshining the women. Should such events be eliminated because they make women appear to be inferior?

On the other side are feminists who believe that the problem is that their sisters-in-arms focus only on what they see as male sexual domination of women and that they fail to campaign for policies that would allow prostitutes and potential prostitutes to choose a more redeeming way of life. Laura Reanda (1991:203) has berated some women—"antiporn feminists and other moralists"—for not attending to the financial impoverishment of working and underclass women. "Eliminate this mammoth motivating force and much prostitution would disappear," she maintains. Those left doing "sex work" (the emerging term of preference among feminists for prostitution) would be "on the game" because they liked it; in this regard, "true sexual determination (a basic feminist demand) should include a woman's right to sell sex—if she wants to." Another woman close to the world of prostitution had made the same point:

Antiporn feminists have patronizingly told strippers and prostitutes that we should raise our consciousness and develop self-esteem (by working as toilet cleaners and factory hands). No thanks, sisters (Roberts, 1994:45).

The viewpoint being criticized has been called the "brainwash theory" which, according to Gayle Rubin, "explains erotic diversity by assuming that some sexual acts are so disgusting that no one would willingly perform them. Therefore, the reasoning goes, anyone who does so must have been forced or fooled" (Rubin, 1984:306). Others go to the furthest extreme, like Camille Paglia (1994:58–59) who insists that the prostitute is the "ultimate liberated woman, who lives on the edge and whose sexuality belongs to no one." . . .

The Prostitute

Research studies regarding prostitution indicate that in contemporary times it is almost totally an occupation entered into voluntarily. Prostitution offers a considerable range of vocational advantages, including flexible work hours, contact with diverse kinds of people, a heightened sense of activity, and the opportunity to make substantial sums of money and pay no taxes. Such consequences do not accrue to all prostitutes, nor perhaps even to very many. For those women whose involvement is the most tawdry, prostitution can be a dirty and dangerous enterprise. There can be beatings, loveless copulations, and little financial reward (Miller, 1993). The loss of self-esteem that seems to result from the practice of prostitution is, of course, a function of broader social attitudes, which themselves are at least partly a function of the legal sanctions raised against such behavior. It seems likely, at any rate, that removing the legal ban against prostitution would not harm the self-esteem of its practitioners and might help them to realize that they are employed in an acceptable occupation.

The harms that come to the individual prostitute from her work seem to be neither so extreme nor so totally unavoidable that laws should be enacted to protect her by outlawing her behavior. If society prefers women to follow what it regards as more admirable kinds of pursuits, it could provide such outlets and make them more accessible in order to counteract whatever appeal prostitution offers. . . .

Customers

In a society characterized by sexual inhibitions, it could be argued that the abatement of prostitution by whatever means would encourage chastity and sexual abstinence among those who now consort with prostitutes for the purposes of sexual outlet. America is not, however, such a society. The assumption has to be that the absence of prostitutes for sexual activity would lead men deprived of them to other means of releasing strong, compelling sexual energies. Such outlets could be masturbation, more intense courtship or seduction patterns, sex by force, or behavior patterns that psychiatrists label as inhibitions and sublimations, commonly involving the transfer of sexual energies into nonsexual pursuits, such as the drive for power or acts of aggression.

The possibility exists that the availability of sexual liaisons with prostitutes discourages marriage, which some men may find more demanding than impersonal sexual contact. But American society does not seem to be that strongly dedicated to the encouragement of marriage, and a considerable percentage of prostitutes' customers—both male and female prostitutes—are married men.

Much discussion has centered around the possibility that the absence of *prostitution* would lead men to seek sexual satisfaction by force. Acts of *forcible rape* and prostitution may indeed share some characteristics. Both are illicit, both can involve brutality beyond the sex itself, and both seem to require the humiliation of the female. In neither behavior is the woman viewed as a person requiring sexual satisfaction nor is she likely to achieve such satisfaction. In neither are demands for sophisticated sexual performance placed upon the male. Indeed, studies of rape report that to a very large degree the offender is impotent during the commission of the crime (Burgess and Holstrom, 1974).

The research of Eugene Kanin (1957; Kanin and Parcell, 1977; Kirkpatrick and Kanin, 1957) on the incidence of forced intercourse in dating situations on a college campus is particularly informative. The value of Kanin's work abides in the fact that he queried students during two widely separated times—first in 1957 and then in 1977. He found that the number of cases in which sexual force was employed by college males during a date had increased dramatically. Kanin believed that this was because at the time of the initial study, college men were much more were willing to grant their dates the moral right to say no. Following the sexual revolution, a new generation of college men more frequently assumed that their dates were sexually experienced and that their reluctance was a personal rejection. In that sense, they regarded their own aggression, despite strong signals to the contrary, as reasonable.

Information concerning the relationship between prostitution—legal or otherwise—and crimes of sexual violence is inconclusive, perhaps necessarily so, given the number of confounding variables involved. Societies probably encourage or discourage both rape and prostitution as a consequence of commitments to certain attitudes and values. It is likely that these commitments, rather than legal codes, significantly influence the rates for both behaviors.

The results of the only research study that has looked at the issue of rape and prostitution, conducted in Australia in the late 1960s, presented methodological difficulties that serve as warning signs for cautious interpretations. Between the early 1950s and the middle 1960s, the rape rate had risen steadily in the Australian state of Queensland. The increase was particularly precipitous after 1961, characterized by a sharp rise in the number of gang rapes, or "pack" rapes as they are known in Australia.

The legal position on prostitution had shifted during this period. Brothels were tolerated by Queensland police until the end of 1958. Thereafter, they were closed. Rape rates jumped 149 percent following the closing of the brothels, although other personal offenses committed by men rose only 49 percent. The Australian researcher expressed concern over his interpretation of these figures:

> This, of course, does not of itself prove that the increase in the number of convictions for rape and attempted rape was caused by the closing of the brothels, but

it does show clearly that there was a remarkable increase in the conviction rate for these two crimes after this closing (Barber, 1969).

The researcher suggests that persons who perpetrate forcible rape share to a considerable extent the socioeconomic traits of those who most often visit prostitutes. It was this group, he argues, that was most severely affected by the closing of the brothels and whose members turned to rape when denied such a sexual outlet. Interviews with the rapists to verify or disprove this assumption would seem to be essential before the interpretation could be regarded as anything more than a very tentative finding. . . .

Conclusion

A number of arguments opposed to outlawing prostitution were offered recently by an Englishwoman who told how as a youth she had been coerced into sexual behavior by a policeman who threatened to arrest her for "living off the earnings of prostitution." Her only crime was that, as a runaway, she had been supplied with food by prostitutes. She offered the following arguments that she believed supported decriminalization of prostitution:

1. The laws breed corruption.

2. The laws turn the government into the trade's biggest pimp through fines which the women have to go out and earn.

3. The laws institutionalize and reinforce the whore stigma, which encourages rape and violence against prostitutes and also against other women thought to behave like hustlers.

4. The laws are a denial of a prostitute's basic civil and human rights. They make it illegal for women to work together for safety's sake (two or more women constitute a brothel), effectively forcing women into the streets, where they must work alone and at great personal risk.

5. Much of the taxpayers' money is wasted on prosecuting and imprisoning prosti-

tutes. This would be better spent on improving women's lives, providing housing, health care, child care, and education (Roberts, 1994).

A compilation of arguments for and against decriminalized prostitution has been set out in a document issued by the United Nations (1959) that based its information on prostitution worldwide. Though the roster is now almost forty years old, the issues it raises remain as essential to the debate today as they did at the time.

The following are the major arguments offered in the UN report for defining prostitution as a criminal offense:

1. It is the responsibility of the government to regulate public morals in the interest of the public good; hence, to make prostitution a punishable offense.

2. The abolition of the legal ban against prostitution will merely replace controlled prostitution by clandestine prostitution.

3. It would be difficult to enforce regulatory provisions against prostitution, when prostitution itself is not considered a punishable offense.

4. Women and girls on the borderline will be encouraged to take up prostitution by the mere fact that it is legal.

5. The absence of laws against prostitution will be interpreted by the public as the government's support of commercialized vice as a "necessary evil," thereby admitting its inability to control it. . . .

. . .[T]o concede the inevitability of prostitution, [Elliott Abramson] argues, is a misguided and defeatist position:

> Is it any more 'unreasonably' intrusive to seek to protect people from the self-inflicted torments and privations of a life of prostitution than it is to try to protect them from perversely ingesting adulterated food which could make them seriously ill or kill them?

He thinks that psychotherapy, medical attention, job training, educational experiences, and child support are some of the services that ought to be provided to prostitutes—and mandated for them by law, if necessary—to move them from "'the life' to life" (Abramson, 1978–1979:374).

Finally, there is the strong feminist position of Susan Brownmiller (1975:392) who believes that practicing and tolerating prostitution reinforces in men a vicious attitude about the nature of women and produces attitudes that lead to rape:

> [M]y horror at the idea of legalized prostitution is not that it institutionalizes the concept that it is a man's mandatory right, if not his divine right, to gain access to the female body, and that sex is a female service that should not be denied the civilized male. Perpetuation of the concept that the "powerful male impulse" must be satisfied with immediacy by a co-operating class of woman, set aside . . .and licensed for the purpose, is part and parcel of the mass psychology of rape.

The following represent counterarguments offered by the United Nations in support of the position that prostitution should be removed from the concerns of criminal law:

1. Outlawing prostitution represents an unwarranted invasion into the private lives of persons participating in a voluntary activity.

2. Between prostitution and other sexual relations outside of marriage, there is only a difference of degree; hence, it is too arbitrary to penalize only those who meet the arbitrary criteria for crime that defines only one form of the same kind of behavior.

3. Experience teaches us that prostitution cannot be eliminated by mere legal enactments, and that making prostitution a crime often encourages clandestine operations and control by underworld organizations. As long as the demand for prostitution exists, there will always be a corresponding supply of persons to cater to that demand.

4. Illegal prostitution often leads to police behavior that is in itself detrimental to the common good.

5. Declaring prostitution against the law creates among those engaged in it an antagonistic attitude that hampers their chances of abandoning it for employment that society may regard as more desirable. . . .

References

Abramson, Elliott M. 1978–1979. "A Note on Prostitution: Victims Without Crime—Or There's No Crime but the Victim Is Ideology." *Duquesne Law Review* 17:355–379.

Addams, Jane. 1912. *A New Conscience and an Ancient Evil.* New York: Macmillan.

Albert, Alexa E., David L. Warner, Robert A. Hatcher, and James Trussell. 1995. "Condom Use Among Female Commercial Sex Workers in Nevada's Legal Brothels." *American Journal of Public Health* 85:1514–1520.

Allred, Gloria, and Lisa Bloom. 1994. "Perspective on Prostitution: Prosecution or Persecution?" *Los Angeles Times,* December 6:B7.

Aquinas, Thomas. 1273/1947. *Summa Theologica.* New York: Benziger Brothers.

Augustine of Hippo. 386/1844–1864. "De Ordine." Pp. 977–1020 in Jacques Paul Migne, ed., *Patrologiae Cursus Completus, Series Latina.* Paris: P. Geuther.

Barber, R. N. 1969. "Prostitution and the Increasing Number of Convictions for Rape in Queensland." *Australian and New Zealand Journal of Criminology* 2:169–174.

Bellis, David J. 1990. "Fear of AIDS and Risk Reduction among Heroin-Addicted Female Street Prostitutes: Personal Interviews with 72 Southern California Subjects." *Journal of Alcohol and Drug Education* 35:26–37.

Boyer, Edward J. 1995. "Official Business: Former Clients Testify as Heidi Fleiss Trial Begins." *Los Angeles Times,* June 30:B4.

Brownmiller, Susan. 1975. *Against Our Will: Men, Women and Rape.* New York: Simon and Schuster.

Bryant, Clifford D., and C. Eddie Palmer. 1975. "Massage Parlor and 'Hand Whores': Some Sociological Observations." *Journal of Sex Research* 11:227–241.

Buckley, William. 1995. "Thou Shalt Not . . .What?" *National Review,* July 31:71.

Burgess, Ann W., and Lynda Lytle Holstrom. 1974. *Rape: Victims of Crisis.* Bowie, MD: Brady.

Campbell, Carole A. 1991. "Prostitution, AIDS, and Preventive Health Behavior." *Social Science and Medicine* 32:1367–1378.

Cates, Jim A., and Jeffrey Markley. 1992. "Demographic, Clinical, and Personality Variables Associated with Male Prostitution by Choice." *Adolescence* 27:695–714.

Davis, Kingsley. 1966. "Sexual Behavior." Pp. 354–372 in Robert K. Merton and Robert Nisbet, eds., *Contemporary Social Problems,* 2nd ed. New York: Harcourt, Brace, and World.

Davis, Nanette, ed. 1993. *Prostitution: An International Handbook of Trends, Problems, and Policies.* Westport, CT: Greenwood.

de Beauvoir, Simone. 1953. *The Second Sex.* Howard M. Parshley, trans. New York: Knopf.

Decker, John F. 1979. *Prostitution: Regulation and Control.* Littleton, CO: Fred B. Rothman.

"Divine Brown's Unpromising Career." 1995. *Tampa Tribune,* August 12:14.

Edwards, Susan S. M. 1993. "England and Wales." Pp. 108–128 in Nanette J. Davis, ed., *Prostitution: An International Handbook on Trends, Problems, and Policies.* Westport, CT: Greenwood.

Ehrlich, Dan. 1995. "Take It for Granted, She Walks Out On Hugh." *Daily News* (New York), July 3:3.

Freeman, Jody. 1989–1990. "The Feminist Debate Over Prostitution Reform: Prostitutes' Rights Groups, Radical Feminists, and the Impossibility of Consent." *Berkeley Women's Law Journal* 5:75–109.

Freund, Matthew, Nancy Lee and Terri L. Leonard. 1989. "Sexual Behavior of Prostitutes with Their Clients in Camden, New Jersey." *Journal of Sex Research* 28:579–591.

Frey, James H., Loren R. Reichert, and Kenneth Y. Russell. 1981. "Prostitution, Business and Police: The Maintenance of an Illegal Economy." *Police Journal* 54:239–249.

Gebhard, Paul H. 1969. "Misconceptions about Female Prostitutes." *Medical Aspects of Human Sexuality* 8 (March):24, 28–30.

Goldstein, Paul J., Lawrence J. Ouellet, and Michael Fendrich. 1992. "From Bang Brides to Skeezers: A Historical Perspective on Sex-for-Drugs Behavior." *Journal of Psychoactive Drugs* 24:349–361.

Gooding, Richard. 1996. "Clinton Aide Kept Mistress 15 Years." *Star,* September 17:5–8, 38, 45.

Great Britain. 1957. Committee on Homosexual Offences and Prostitution, Report (Command 247). London: Her Majesty's Stationery Office.

Haskell, Molly. 1974. *From Reverence to Rape: The Treatment of Women in the Movies.* New York: Holt, Rinehart, and Winston.

Hubler, Shawn. 1996. "Court Overturns Fleiss' Conviction, Orders New Trial." *Los Angeles Times*, May 30:A1, A24.

Ibrahim, Youssef M. 1996. "In Kiosks of London, Card Games Get Dirty." *New York Times*, August 17:4.

James, Jennifer. 1977. "Prostitutes and Prostitution." Pp. 368–428 in Edward Sagarin and Fred Montanino eds., *Deviants: Voluntary Actors in a Hostile World*. Morristown, NJ: General Learning Press.

Jenness, Valerie. 1990. "From Sex as Sin to Sex as Work." *Social Problems* 37:403–420.

Jolin, Annette. 1994. "On the Backs of Working Prostitutes: Feminist Theory and Prostitution Policy." *Crime and Delinquency* 40:69–83.

Kanin, Eugene J. 1957. "Male Aggression in Dating Courtship Relations." *American Journal of Sociology* 63:197–204.

Kanin, Eugene J., and Stanley R. Parcell. 1977. "Sexual Aggression: A Second Look at the Offended Female." *Archives of Sexual Behavior* 6:67–76.

Katyal, Neal K. 1993. "Men Who Own Women: A Thirteenth Amendment Critique of Forced Prostitution." *Yale Law Journal* 103:791–826.

Kinsey, Alfred, Wardell B. Pomeroy, and Clyde E. Martin. 1948. *Sexual Behavior in the Human Male*. Philadelphia: Saunders.

Kirkpatrick, Clifford, and Eugene J. Kanin. 1957. "Male Sex Aggression on a University Campus." *American Sociological Review* 63:197–204.

Koltnow, Barry. 1996. "A Woman Scorned." *Orange County (CA) Register*, February 20:Accent 1–2.

Lowman, John. 1992. "Street Prostitution Control: Some Canadian Reflections on the Finsbury Park Experiment." *British Journal of Criminology* 32:1–17.

Maslin, Janet. 1996. "Hollywood Woman of Affairs." *New York Times*, February 9:B3.

Matthews, Roger. 1986. "Policing Prostitution: A Multi-Agency Approach." *Middlesex Polytechnic, Centre for Criminology*, Paper no. 1.

McCormick, Naomi B. 1994. *Sexual Salvation: Affirming Women's Sensual Rights and Pleasures*. Westport, CT: Praeger.

Michael, Robert T., John Gagnon, Edward O. Laumann and Gina Kolata. 1994. *Sex in America: A Definitive Survey*. Boston: Little, Brown.

Miller, Jody. 1993. "Your Life Is on the Line Every Night You're on the Streets: Victimization and Resistance Among Street Prostitutes." *Humanities and Society* 17:422–446.

Milner, Christina, and Richard Milner. 1973. *Black Players: The Secret World of Black Pimps*. Boston: Little, Brown.

Morris, Dick. 1997. *Behind the Oval Office*. New York: Random House.

Musheno, Michael, and Kathryn Seeley. 1986. "Prostitution, Policy and the Women's Movement: Historical Analysis of Feminist Thought and Organization." *Contemporary Crises* 10:237–255.

Overs, Cheryl. 1994. "Sex Work, HIV and the State." *Feminist Review* 48:110–121.

Paglia, Camille. 1994. *Vamps and Tramps*. New York: Vintage Books.

Polsky, Ned. 1967. *Hustlers, Beats and Others*. Chicago: Aldine.

Pomeroy, Wardell B. 1965. "Some Aspects of Prostitution." *Journal of Sex Research* 1:177–187.

Potterat, John J., Donald E. Woodhouse, John B. Muth, and Stephen Q. Muth. 1990. "Estimating the Prevalence and Career Longevity of Prostitute Women." *Journal of Sex Research* 27:233–243.

Primoratz, Igor. 1993. "What's Wrong with Prostitution?" *Philosophy* 68:159–182.

"Prostitution Arrest Trends." 1995. Pp. 283–286 in *Crime in the United States 1994: Uniform Crime Reports for the United States*. Washington, DC: Federal Bureau of Investigation, United States Department of Justice.

Quigley, John. 1992. "The Dilemma of Prostitution Law Reform: Lessons from the Soviet Russia Experiment." *American Criminal Law Review* 29:1197–1234.

Reanda, Laura. 1991. "Prostitution as a Human Rights Question: Problems and Prospects of United Nations Action." *Human Rights Quarterly* 13:202–228.

Reckless, Walter C. 1933. *Vice in Chicago*. Chicago: University of Chicago Press.

Reichert, Loren D., and James H. Frey. 1985. "The Organization of Bell Desk Prostitution." *Sociology and Social Research* 69:516–526.

Reiss, Albert J. 1961. "The Social Integration of Peers and Queers." *Social Problems* 9:102–120.

Remez, Lisa. 1996. "Nevada's Licensed Sex Workers Achieve Minimal Condom Breakage Rates." *Family Planning Perspectives* 28:35.

Reynolds, Helen. 1986. *The Economics of Prostitution*. Springfield, IL: Thomas.

Rio, Linda M. 1991. "Psychological and Sociological Research and the Decriminalization or Legalization of Prostitution." *Archives of Sexual Behavior* 20:205–218.

Roberts, Nickie. 1994. "The Game's Up." *New Statesman Society* 7 (July 16):44–45.

Romenesko, Kim, and Eleanor M. Miller. 1989. "The Second Step in Double Jeopardy: Appropriating the Labor of Female Street Hustlers." *Crime and Delinquency* 35:109–135.

Rubin, Gayle. 1984. "Thinking Sex: Notes for a Radical Theory of the Politics of Sexuality" Pp. 267–319 in Carole S. Vance, ed., *Pleasures and Danger: Exploring Female Sexuality.* Boston: Routledge and Kegan Paul.

Rushing, Sandra M. 1994. *The Magdalene Legacy: Exploring the Wounded Icon of Sexuality.* Westport, CT: Berin & Garvey.

Satz, Debra. 1995. "Markets in Women's Sexual Labor." *Ethics* 106:63–85.

Shah, Diane K. 1993. "The Hardest Working Girl in Show Business." *Esquire* 120 (November):66–73.

Shrage, Laurie. 1989. "Should Feminists Oppose Prostitution?" *Ethics* 99:347–361.

Siebert, Mark. 1996. "From House of Prostitution to the Halls of Congress?" *Des Moines Register,* April 2:1A, 2A.

Simons, Geoffrey L. 1972. *Pornography Without Prejudice: A Reply to Objections.* London: Abelard-Schuman.

St. James, Margo. 1987. "The Reclamation of Whores." Pp. 81–87 in Laurie Bell ed., *Good Girls/Bad Girls: Sex Trade Workers and Feminists Face to Face.* Toronto: The Women's Press.

Thomas, Kevin. 1996. "Dark Side of Hollywood Glitz in 'Madam.'" *Los Angeles Times,* February 9:F10, F12.

United Nations. 1959. *Study on Traffic in Persons and Prostitution.* New York: United Nations.

van der Poel, Sari. 1992. "Male Prostitution: A Neglected Phenomenon." *Crime, Law and Social Change* 18:259–275.

Waddell, Charles. 1996. "HIV and the Social World of Female Commercial Sex Workers." *Medical Anthropological Quarterly* 10:75–82.

Wambaugh, Joseph. 1970. *The New Centurions.* New York: Dell.

Weinraub, Bernard. 1996. "Play a Hooker and Hook an Oscar." *New York Times,* February 20:B1–B2.

Weitzer, Ronald. 1991. "Prostitutes' Rights in the United States: The Failure of a Movement." *Sociological Quarterly* 32:23–41.

Winick, Charles, and Paul M. Kinsie. 1971. *The Lively Commerce: Prostitution in the United States.* Chicago: Quadrangle.

Ybarra, Michael J. 1996. "A Graphic Lesson for Patrons in Fight Against Prostitution." *New York Times,* May 11:12.

Zeldes, Ilya. 1981. *The Problem of Crime in the USSR.* Springfield, IL: Thomas.

30
Erotic Cyberspace

The Internet and 'Logging On' to Sex

Keith F. Durkin

Clifton D. Bryant

Technology is often responsible for the creation of a deviant innovation, and sexual deviance is no exception. As Durkin and Bryant observe, automobiles were designed for transportation, but their utility for covert fornication is now storied; motion pictures evolved to provide wholesome family entertainment, but the medium has been widely adapted for pornographic purposes; telephones provided a means for two-way communication across long distances, but that communication can be decidedly graphic in nature (as any consumer of phone sex services will tell you). Arguably, however, few technological innovations have had as profound an effect on sexual deviance as the computer, a device that has revolutionized sexual interaction.

Internet-based bulletin boards permit users to send and receive graphic sexual messages—textual and pictorial—with full benefit of anonymity. The Internet is a breeding ground for fantasy and release, enticing participants to say and do things they may never have even contemplated before. Persons who previously may not have had a "voice" now have one, to which others listen and respond. Suddenly having this vast audience can be extraordinarily liberating; it can be empowering and dangerous as well. Computer correspondents sometimes assume fictitious identities to exploit others for instrumental ends, and nefarious conduct is facilitated by the very anonymity that makes the computer a desirable tool for communication. Durkin and Bryant point out how ostensibly impersonal communiques can lead to actual contact between participants

(whose curiosities are piqued), with potentially sinister consequences.

Durkin and Bryant interpret the social meaning of electronic erotica in a number of ways. They contend that erotic communiques are intellectual graffiti, an outlet for carnal thoughts that cannot be expressed anywhere else, and a means for reinforcing and fueling fantasy. They suggest the erotica are a facilitating mechanism for social change, spreading new and innovative sexual practices instantaneously and exponentially. They observe that electronic erotica bring similarly minded individuals together for a shared purpose and consolidate deviants into a critical mass, which ultimately facilitates the transmission of deviant norms. Indeed, the musings of one person can be picked up and reproduced by thousands, creating a snowball effect that culminates in the formation of elaborate deviant networks.

New forms of deviancy, including sexual deviancy, are not entirely the invention of the fertile imagination. More often, new opportunities in the pursuit of deviancy are provided by innovations in technology. Such opportunities, in turn, invite or occasionally even drive exploration and experimentation in using the technology, with the result that new, and sometimes ingenious residual functions and latent uses of the technology relevant to deviancy are discovered. Thus, novel configurations of deviant behavior, including sexual deviancy, may evolve in a kind of serendipitous fashion from technological invention.

Technology and Deviant Behavior

Behavioral scientists have long recognized that emerging technology has a powerful influence on human behavior, although frequently there is a delay or lag between the emergence of the technology and the social behavioral adaptation to it (Ogburn 1964).[1] The social response to technology often takes the form of technicways, or normative and patterned behavioral configurations (Odum 1937; Bryant 1984).[2] Whereas technicways generally assume functional dimensions, they may also mutate and take on dysfunctional or even deviant parameters. These deviant technicways often encompass sexually proscribed behavior. Furthermore, deviant sexual technicways would appear to divide and multiply in an entropic fashion.

Some examples of technology and sexually deviant adaptation include the automobile, which was intended as a means of transportation but has also proved to be a splendid platform for private assignation and fornication, as well as a major "vehicle" for a wide variety of clandestine sexual misconduct, and Edison's motion picture projector, which was intended for wholesome vicarious entertainment but has also proved to be extremely effective in affording vicarious carnal gratification in the form of pornographic films. The telephone also has served to generate a multitude of opportunities for carnal gratification. Its capacity for anonymous communication has made possible the obscene phone call.[3] It has also afforded the opportunity for the telephone masturbator to use a telephone conversation with a female as the basis for sexual fantasy and carnal stimulation, incorporating the autoerotic activity into the fantasy.[4] The effectiveness of this practice has been exploited in recent years by so-called "dial-a-porn" services,[5] which offer sexually explicit conversation for salacious purposes on a commercial basis. Undoubtedly, in time many others will grasp the deviant efficacy of the telephone and perceive additional innovative uses.

The citizens-band (CB) radio is another case in point. The CB radio initially appealed to persons who sought a convenient and efficient means for communicating in emergencies and in other inopportune circumstances. Truck drivers proved to be an enthusiastic customer group, using the CB radio to contact other truckers. Prostitutes also found truck drivers to be an enthusiastic customer group for their sexual services, and for some prostitutes, using the CB radio, which proved to be an expedient way to contact truckers, became a standard mode of soliciting customers (Klein 1981; Luxenburg and Klein 1984). Like legitimate business-

people, deviant commercial enterprises are often quick to take advantage of new technology to improve efficiency and maximize profits. For example, rather than the bordello prostitute of times past, the prostitute contacted by telephone—the "call girl"—is now the norm in some locales. Prostitutes in some resort cities, such as Las Vegas, are said to carry beepers, in order to be able to respond quickly to telephone requests for sexual services.

The near explosion of technological advances in recent decades, in such fields as electronics, photography, and communications, to mention but a few, has deluged society with a cornucopia of devices and appliances, compelling in their novelty and application, but ominous in their latent deviant capabilities. Numerous instruments and mechanisms ranging from the Polaroid camera to the camcorder have been shown to have suitable utility for the facilitation of sexual deviance. Of the most recent technological products, the computer promises to open enormous new frontiers of opportunity for the proliferation and enhancement of sexual deviance, to have an applicability for carnal behavior that is socially volatile in both its perversity and import.

The Computer, Cyberspace, and Deviant Information

The computer, although intended primarily as a mechanism for extremely rapid, extraordinarily complex, computational purposes, quickly came to be seen also as a communication device. The computer paired with modern telephone technology has come to serve as a highly efficient means of contacting persons and corporate entities all over the world. On-line bulletin board systems, known as BBSs, are essentially modern-day, high-tech, electronic "party lines," by which users can send and receive messages, engage in conversations, and upload and download files. The electronic entity or domain that encompasses bulletin boards and all of the other communicative potential of computers has become known as "cyberspace" (Gibson, 1989). By linking up with a particular, specialized BBS, one can use a computer to contact individuals with mutual interests anywhere in the world. In 1987, there were 4,000 BBSs; by 1992, there were 44,000. Periodicals such as *Boardwatch* or *Computer Shopper* list and describe the array of available BBSs (see *New York Times* 1989, p. B38). On-line services such as CompuServe, Prodigy, America Online, and Delphi offer the computer user immediate access to all sorts of information, such as news, weather, travel services, and stock market quotes, as well as access to all kinds of specialized interest bulletin boards and the means to send and receive private messages. On-line services thus permit people to contact and communicate with persons who share similar interests and avocations, which may involve such disparate topics as cooking, cats, and chess (see *U.S. News and World Report* 1985, p. 59)

Because the on-line services reach an unknown multitude of computer users (inasmuch as institutional computers are used by vast numbers of individuals for purposes not related to their work, the actual number of persons who can access BBSs cannot be accurately calculated), there is the potential for an enormous range of interests to be addressed, including deviant interests. Aware of this market, entrepreneurs of all stripes are rising to the need and offering unique BBSs to satisfy even the most exotic requirements. A relatively superficial exploration of available bulletin boards reveals a diverse array of nonsexual, deviant variants seeking subscribers, or interested persons who might like to share information. Included among this genre of BBS is one that collects and distributes all sorts of law-enforcement radio codes, including generic codes and frequencies as well as special codes for specific law enforcement agencies. While these codes are made available ostensibly to help computer users better "enjoy" and understand the radio traffic on a police scanner, it is patently obvious that this master list of police codes could easily find miscreant uses. Additionally, this bulletin board provides a compendium of information concerning plants and substances that have psychotropic properties but are technically not illegal to possess at this time. It also contains

relatively detailed information about automatic teller machine (ATM) fraud, which would no doubt be quite instructive to a would-be ATM thief. The same bulletin board gives advice on how to cause vandalistic damages, including lists of useful vandalism tools (wire cutter, BB gun, etc.) and appealing sites to be vandalized, such as the showroom windows of automobile dealerships.

In addition to bulletin boards that deliberately provide deviant information, some bulletin boards are used by individuals seeking technical advice for deviant acts. Several years ago, for example, a 10-year-old youngster in the Midwest placed an ad seeking instructions for making a time bomb on a bulletin board devoted to scientific interests. Someone with the necessary expertise did provide the information, and the boy subsequently blew up a mailbox using a bomb that he had constructed (Jackson 1989, p. 20).

The Carnal Computer and Cybersex

Sometimes the interest being catered to by a bulletin board may be sex, particularly esoteric variations of sex that frequently are deviant and sometimes illegal. This potential use of bulletin boards has not escaped the notice of relevant U.S. governmental agencies. The Attorney General's Commission on Pornography (U.S. Department of Justice 1986, p. 1437), for example, has stated:

> The personal home computer provides individuals with an extraordinary new form of communication and information access. Providers of sexually explicit materials have taken advantage of this new technology by making computer subscription services the most recent advance in "sexually explicit communications."

Although the computer can be used to communicate directly with specific individuals in other locales using e-mail and other modes of communication, initial and subsequent contacts involving "erotic entertainment" are often made through intermediate computer networks, in the form of sexually oriented bulletin boards.[6] Because it allows "two users to exchange intimacies in private" (*Time* 1984, p. 83), the computer bulletin board, particularly when used for erotic purposes, can perhaps best be likened to the Valentine box in grammar or middle school into which students could put anonymous Valentine messages to be taken out and read by those to whom they were addressed. The box could also be used to respond privately. The sexually oriented computer bulletin board permits users to trade pseudonymous messages.

The initial anonymity of these bulletin boards may give way to a more intimate and personalized (albeit guarded) form of carnal interaction. One newspaper account (Markoff 1992, p. 5), for example, describes this process:

> One recent evening, users of the America Online network had the opportunity to visit a series of "rooms," offering, for example, "Naughty Girls," "Romance Connection" and a "Gay Room." After meeting electronically in the public room—actually a window in which comments from many users scroll by—new friends adjourned to private rooms for intimate conversations, often using noms de plume or "handles."

Exchanging erotic verbal chit-chat via computer has been labeled as a new form of "erotic entertainment in which consenting computer owners exchange X-rated messages over the telephone lines" (*Time* 1984, p. 83). Allegedly, some couples who meet over the computer and exchange erotic pleasantries sometimes move on to exchange names, telephone numbers, and pictures; they may even arrange dates. Some have gotten married (*Time* 1984, p. 83). Media accounts have even reported a new formalized or institutionalized bond between computer daters that represents a step in commitment that is short of marriage but perhaps more analogous to an engagement. Some computer partners enter into a "cyber-wedding," an electronic bond that lets the individuals "pledge their love while looking ahead to a future that could include real-life marriage—if they hit it off [when they later meet in person]" (Haight 1994, p. 1).

A few years back, erotic exchange by computer was said to be "mostly lighthearted flirting" (*Time* 1984, p. 83). Recently, however, computer sex has been moving in more intimate and compelling directions. On-line socializing with a member of the opposite sex that has moved beyond lighthearted flirting has been termed "hot chatting" (Tamosaitis 1994, p. 56). The anonymity that computer interaction affords provides self-confidence, allows the individual to assume almost any identity (e.g., become any age, take on any appearance, and effect any persona), and promotes inspiration. A person can interact with a "computer pal," develop a symbolic sexual intimacy, share erotic fantasies, talk "dirty," and in the process, experience a "tonic" for his or her real-life sex. Hot chatting in cyberspace appears to help energize the libido of persons who have a jaded sex relationship with their regular partner. As one 45 year-old attorney was reported to have revealed (Tamosaitis 1994, p. 68):

> I've been married for 15 years and sex with my wife has grown routine. But after I've spent some time in erotic banter with a sensitive female online, I bring new enthusiasm and desire back into my bedroom.

Such an erotic process would seem to be functional, provided the individual does not become unduly preoccupied with his or her cyberspace "lover." Such preoccupation could conceivably lead to marital friction.

While hot chatting may be a developmental process, with the interaction moving in incremental fashion to more intense levels of salacious conversation, it appears that participants' intentions often are obvious from the outset, as evidenced by the computer names they select. One researcher (Matek 1988, pp. 120–121) has observed, for example, that

> [O]bscene content is not always a part of this chatter, but the names or "handles" chosen by many of these participants divulge a sexual implication: Honey Blonde, Priapus Rex, Wet End, Love for Tender, Bilady Jugs. At times the "conversation," too is suggestive, and occasionally the computer screens read like a pornographic novel, as two or more strangers engage in "computer sex," with each of the participants describing successive steps in their fantasy encounter.

Obviously, some individuals derive carnal enjoyment from the mutual use of sexual words with a person of the opposite sex, and the computer handily affords the opportunity with both convenience and anonymity.

The Computer and Sexual Deviancy

The computer bulletin board system can provide an enormous, and extremely rapid, contact network for persons of related interests, including those interested in sexual deviancy. Individuals can seek, identify, and communicate with fellow deviants of similar carnal persuasion across the country, and even around the world. Information from deviant subcultures can be broadly disseminated, and interested new persons can be recruited. Individuals can learn of formal meeting sites, and informal gathering places, and can even arrange a personal rendezvous.

The sexual computer network offers a high degree of anonymity, protection, and secrecy. Individuals can, through their personal computer, verbalize their sexual fantasies, and, in some instances, go on to operationalize them. The sexual bulletin boards operate at varying levels of lasciviousness. Some are hardly more than "naughty," while others are disturbingly degenerate, even to the point of being pathological. As in an onion, when each layer of carnality is peeled back, another deeper and more perverse layer is revealed. There are ominous signs in this phenomenon. There are reported to be instances in which attempts were made to solidify contacts with teenagers or children who had inadvertently discovered some of the bulletin boards while playing with a computer (*Los Angeles Times* 1989, pp. 20–21). One newspaper account (Markoff 1992, p. 5) reports:

> Last fall, a 42-year-old man in Fremont, California, using a nationwide computer conferencing system, posed as a 13-year-old homosexual boy. He said he was electronically approached by someone identifying himself as a 50-year-old New Yorker who tried to arrange a meeting. In Massachusetts in January, a man was indicted for raping a 12-year-old boy whom he befriended through a computer bulletin board.

In a case that occurred several years ago, law enforcement authorities from California arrested two men in Virginia who were trying to locate a 12-year-old child to molest and then to murder as the subject matter for a "snuff" film (Jackson 1989, pp. 20–21). The authorities discovered the plot through an ad placed by the two men on a computer bulletin board seeking other people with a sexual interest in children. In a telephone conversation with an undercover detective, one of the men indicated that he recognized the risk involved in kidnapping a youngster and then murdering him, but that "the pleasure of doin' it would be worth it." When arrested, one of the men had a supply of muriatic acid to apply to the youngster's corpse.

Apparently these are not isolated incidents. A press release from the U.S. Department of Justice issued on Tuesday, August 31, 1993, reported that "people who use computers to obtain child pornography are being arrested and charged by federal prosecutors" (p. 1). The press release went on to say that since May, six persons had been charged or indicted, and nine more cases were to be filed in September. In these cases, the Justice Department had obtained information about a child pornography bulletin board in Aalborg, Denmark, known as BAMSE. They had learned that several hundred Americans were using this bulletin board and were paying fees to download graphic images, text, and computer games dealing with child and hard-core pornography. The U.S. authorities asked the Danish police to search the home of the Danish national who operated the bulletin board. The Danish police did so and seized the computer system records and a large number of pornographic pictures of children. A few months later, at the request of U.S. authorities, Danish police raided another home and obtained the computer records of another child pornography bulletin board known as SCREWDRIVER. U.S. Customs Service officials traveled to Denmark to copy the computer records. After examining the records, they discerned that a number of Americans had been "importing" child pornography by computer. A massive federal law enforcement effort called "Operation Long Arm" served 31 search warrants in 15 states and 30 cities. The various indictments reported in the press release resulted from that operation. According to the release, the searches, arrests, and indictments were possible because, "since each purchase had to be made by electronic messaging, detailed records were obtainable" (U.S. Department of Justice, August 13, 1993, p. 2).

Agents of various law enforcement agencies, such as U.S. postal inspectors, routinely explore sexually oriented bulletin boards with the intention of catching offenders who are transmitting child pornography or looking to exploit or victimize children. In 1989, after exploring on-line services, a group of postal inspectors, Illinois state police, Chicago police, and Cook County (Illinois) deputy sheriffs arrested 90 people on charges of trafficking in child pornography and child molestation (Jackson 1989, p. 20).

Reports of children encountering the dangers of sexual deviancy as they explore cyberspace are becoming more numerous. One recent newspaper account (Schwartz 1993, p. 26), for example, relates that "an 8-year-old girl [inadvertently was] attempting computer conversations with a group of transvestites." The little girl, according to the newspaper report was "using her computer and modem to make new friends through a service called America Online" (Schwartz 1993, p. 1) and discovered an electronic discussion group called "TV chat," which stood for "transvestite chat." The little girl thought it meant "television chat." An adult who happened to be monitoring the interaction fortunately steered the youngster to a more suitable discussion group. The same newspaper account told of a mother who discovered that her "telecomputing 13-year old son [had] started getting messages full of sexual innuendo from adult women" (Schwartz 1993, p. 26). The same mother also was appalled when "her 11-year-old son was approached on line recently by a woman in her 30s who invited him to do it, perhaps not knowing his age." A Massachusetts prosecutor asserted, "Instead of hanging around the playground looking for the loneliest kid, potential child molesters merely have to log on" (Kantrowitz et al. 1994, p. 40).

The hazards of cybersex do not pertain only to children. Electronic erotica may also come to be a "rival" in a marriage. In another newspaper report (Garreau 1993, p. A10), the author reveals:

One woman wrote *The Washington Post* complaining that her husband, who had been in therapy for his sexual problems, found affirmation, acceptance and ultimately physical companionship in the bondage and discipline conference on CompuServe, one of several large switching systems on which subscribers can order merchandise, make airline reservations, check the weather and talk dirty. The pair is now divorcing.

There is yet another danger in cyberspace. Females are more sought after than men for computer talk. As a result, some users resort to "gender bending"—a person of one sex (usually a man) portraying himself as the opposite sex. According to a newspaper report, "male wallflowers have learned, however, that if they sign on as women they are instantly flocked to" (Garreau 1993, p. A10). Sometimes gender bending can become quite elaborate, and even sinister. One such instance was the case of "Joan," a gregarious computer user who used the handle "Talkin Lady" and became something of an electronic celebrity (see Van Gelder 1985, p. 94). "Joan" claimed to be a New York neuropsychologist in her late 20s who was confined to a wheelchair because of a serious automobile accident that had killed her boyfriend and left her severely disfigured and with multiple physical handicaps. "Joan" had many computer friends and fans. One of her fans, a married woman, developed such affectionate ties to her as a sexual confidant and vicarious "lover" that she almost left her husband. In reality, "Joan" was a prominent New York psychiatrist named Alex in his 50s who made a hobby out of his computer deception. On one occasion, "Joan" introduced a woman "she" met through the computer to the real-life Alex, who went on to have an affair with her. It was traumatic to many of "her" contacts when "Joan's" true identity was revealed.

This type of occurrence, coupled with the reported attempts (sometimes successful) on the part of some individuals to lure juveniles into meetings for sexual purposes, raises the possibility of "gender bending" as a device for developing a misrepresented relationship with a woman via computer and luring her into a meeting for perverse purposes.

The use of cyberspace for criminal intent with a sexual dimension sometimes assumes convoluted parameters. It has been reported, for example, that authorities have uncovered that a "violence-prone organization" called the Aryan Brotherhood Youth Movement had established electronic bulletin boards in three different states in order to compile lists of suspected homosexuals for the intended purpose of assaulting them (Jackson 1989, p. 20).

Computer Guides to Sexual Deviance

Whereas there are numerous bulletin boards that address nonsexual deviancy, a significant number also have a sexual orientation. These are available in great variety. Some are like travel guides, in that they provide information about the sexual services (and prices) available in different cities in the United States, Mexico, various countries in Europe, and so forth. Sometimes, specific establishments are mentioned, and some bulletin boards even provide an estimate of mugging risk in each city or place of business.

Some of these travel guide bulletin boards deal essentially with prostitution services; others provide details about other sexual commodities, including erotic dancing, stripping, table dancing, lap dancing, nude showering on stage, dancers having sex with each other, being able to inspect the genital areas on nude dancers ("some women will give you a view of spots only her gynecologist sees," advises one bulletin board), and being allowed to touch or fondle the performers. Given today's tolerant standards, the on-line travel guides to erotic establishments are relatively tame.

Computer Bulletin Boards and Sexual Deviancy 'Menus'

Some on-line bulletin board services make direct appeals for individuals of more perverse appetites. A lengthy exploration of the diversity of bulletin boards available in cyberspace reveals an amazing inventory of sexual interests, carnal activities, and exotic enterprises. A bulletin board can be accessed for almost any sexual appetite or persuasion. The topics discussed on these boards range from erotic enemas to zoophilia and include such singular subject matter as ritual genital mutilation, naming the penis, semen speed at ejaculation, having sex with a tiger, breast size versus IQ, pubic hair removal techniques, and a "pop-up" Kama Sutra book. In fact, there have been recent postings from *ampotemnophiles*, or persons with an "erotic obsession or fetish for amputated limbs or digits" (Money et al. 1977). One of these individuals had a leg amputated some years ago and now wished to have the other leg amputated as well (presumably for erotic reasons). This person was seeking a medical professional to perform the procedure, and also wished to contact others of similar desires.

It is also not uncommon to find individuals attempting to sell pornographic tapes, some of which deal with the most bizarre sexual practices (e.g., urolinga and coprophilia), through on-line bulletin boards. In the area of homosexual behavior, one service lists more than 400 gay and lesbian bulletin boards with highly unique names. Among the more active are those concerned with sadism and masochism (S/M). Some of the boards emphasize interest in sexual bondage, self-bondage, sexual spankings, electric shocks, and so on. There seems to be considerable personal e-mail traffic, and some of the messages involve invitations to get together for shopping or dinner when next visiting a particular city, suggesting a long-term network of individuals. Other messages have referred to a "whipping demonstration" to be held in a large East Coast city on a certain date and invited those interested to attend. The existence of elaborate S/M subcultures, complete with consciousness raising groups, sex clubs, specialized periodicals, and theatrical companies, has been reported by various researchers (e.g., Weinberg and Falk 1980), but the computer appears to expand greatly the geographical boundaries of such subcultures, and dramatically facilitate communication among members and between members and interested individuals.

Perhaps one of the most unusual of the many sexual bulletin boards are those that concern bestiality (i.e., sexual activities with animals). Some of the information offered on such bulletin boards is so outlandish that one might at first assume it is an elaborate hoax, and, if not a hoax, then perhaps the meanderings of someone's fertile fantasy life. The files from some of the bulletin boards, however, are simply too extensive and too detailed to represent a hoax; it is highly doubtful that someone would go to that much trouble to perpetrate a joke! (One bulletin board did suggest that it began as a joke but soon attracted a sincere and dedicated following of persons with a genuine interest.) Furthermore, the information appears to grow at a rate greater than an individual's fantasy could generate.

The information available on these bulletin boards includes question and answer files that provide both an introduction and an orientation to bestiality. Some provide graphics files that, according to the editor of the service, "should tell you everything you need to know." Numerous animal-related sex concerns are discussed. Also available are detailed reviews of films and videotapes allegedly portraying sexual activity between humans and animals. Clearly, the market for this type of materials is such that their production is justified. There is every reason to believe that the bestiality subculture will grow and that the number of persons involved will proliferate; the computer bulletin board supports such expansion by facilitating contact and communication among persons with such bizarre erotic interests, even when they are geographically separated by vast distances.

In fact, there is every reason to believe that many, if not most, of the deviant sexual subcultures will expand, become more elaborate, and involve more people because of the on-line bulletin boards. In the past, such subcultures were most frequently limited to particular geographical areas, such as large metropolitan areas along the East or West Coasts. Now those subcultures can readily network with individuals across the nation, or even worldwide. Even persons who reside in small towns in the heartland can more readily contact other individuals with similar sexual interests in their general vicinity and interact with them via computer. If conditions of mutual trust can be met, meetings can be arranged; and, in time, larger groupings can be formed.

There is the possibility that bulletin board users may be inspired by other users to attempt convoluted erotic gratification through, for example, sexual asphyxia (see Lowery and Wetli 1982) or other anti-social or violent sexual practices. The hazard inherent in carnal scenarios of these varieties, of course, is that they may be harmful or dangerous to self or others, especially the youthful computer user.

Some of the sexual themes featured on bulletin boards are merely the sexually exotic. Others are grotesque in their singularity. Still others are redolent of pathology. Some cross the line of illegality. Most if not all, however, would be of interest to the sexologist or the researcher of deviant behavior.

The Social Meaning of Electronic Erotica

The emergence of computer sex can be interpreted at various functional levels. First, it may be viewed as *intellectual graffiti*. Like some more conventional varieties of graffiti, computer erotica can be an outlet for a person's carnal thoughts or a manifestation of sexuality. It can be a plea for sexual advice (or an attempt to give it), or it may afford a sense of sexual self-assertion or even an expression of hostile sexuality, inasmuch as graffiti blatantly violates the social norms that circumscribe sexual expression while avoiding external social sanction (see Bryant 1982, pp. 116–117, 129). In a similar vein, cybersex may sometimes function as an *electronic aphrodisiac*, helping to energize the libido and reinvigorate a genuine sexual relationship that has been burdened by routine and ennui.

Computer erotica can also be conceptualized as *interactive externalized fantasy*. The isolated sexual deviant with an unusual sexual preference may previously have had to rely on fantasy for carnal fulfillment. Now such fantasies can be operationalized within a social context. In addition to simply facilitating contact with others who have similar inclinations, computer bulletin boards also make it easier for sexual fantasies to be reinforced and fed. A passing erotic interest of perverse stripe that might have withered previously may now be nourished by the knowledge that other persons who harbor similar erotic desires exist and that anonymous interaction through the computer is possible.

Furthermore, the computer would seem to serve as a *catalytic* or *facilitating mechanism*. In the past, technological change has often proved to be the catalyst for dramatic social change, sometimes highly functional and other times highly dysfunctional. Often, the social change has been sufficiently widespread and has had enough social support to constitute a new normative pattern—a technicway. But technological change has often also been a catalyst for new forms of deviant behavior. The computer has proved to be something of a supercatalyst for both functional social change and deviant behavior. In effect, the computer "makes it happen!"

The computer may also be viewed as a *germination* and *distribution mechanism* for sexual deviancy. It possesses the capabilities for creating, imitating, enhancing, and extending deviant sexual behavior. The computer can provide an incredibly rapid communication link with a vast number of people throughout the United States and the world. In this way, the process of diffusion, including the diffusion of criminal and deviant practices, can be expanded and facilitated in an almost exponential fashion. The Tibetan monk writes his prayers on a piece of paper, places the paper in his prayer wheel, and spins the wheel, thereby "multiplying" and "amplifying" his message to the gods. The computer seems to serve much the same function, "multiplying" and "amplifying" the deviant messages to all those who log on.

The computer operates as a *social consolidation mechanism*, inasmuch as it can aggregate large numbers of individuals of similar sexually deviant persuasion with great facil-

ity. The individual deviant can easily identify other, similar deviants and subsequently form social coalitions. In doing so, a "critical mass" of persons seeking a social context for their deviant inclinations is achieved. The computer is also a highly effective learning device, and the would-be deviant can readily locate expertise and edification.

Most important, perhaps, the computer can be conceptualized as a *mechanism of metamorphosis*, or a kind of deviant "dream machine." Deviant sexual fantasies that might well have remained simply the distorted musings of an imaginative mind may now be operationalized and implemented. Like the genie in the bottle, the computer can transform deviant sexual reverie into deviant reality by feeding and enriching the individual's fantasies, aiding him or her in identifying others with analogous sexual predilections, assisting in the coalescence of like-minded sexual deviants, and contributing to the constitution of an opportunity structure for the actualization of the fantasied behavior. . . .

Notes

1. All sorts of technological inventions and procedures have had a heavy impact on society. The steam engine, the cotton gin, the telegraph, the telephone, the automobile, the airplane, the still and movie cameras, radio, television, and the computer have all drastically altered the nature of social life. Even simple inventions such as the safety pin, the paper clip, the aerosol spray can, and the safety razor have brought about significant changes in cultural patterns and social behavior. Various behavioral scientists have spoken to the question of technology and social change. William F. Ogburn (1964), for example, advanced the notion of *cultural lag* by suggesting that nonmaterial culture change occurs more slowly than material culture change. In effect, technological change invites adaptation, but the subsequent social change may be slow in occurring.

2. Howard W. Odum (1937) also addressed social change and pointed out that, where new technology is accepted, the response or adaptation to the innovation or new technological process takes the form of *technicways*, or normative behavior patterns. A technicway encompasses more than merely the socially ha-

bituated use of a particular technique or tool, however. For Odum, the concept also referred to a more generalized value system stance or ideological posture as an adaptive response to certain technology and innovation. The cause and effect linkages may be somewhat more convoluted than simple innovation-producing behavioral response. For example, after King Gillette invented the safety razor, home shaving for men became a national grooming pattern. Beyond this, however, social values shifted to the point that the bearded male face was considered objectionable, if not uncouth, certainly among "gentlemen" (at least until the 1960s). In his discussion of Odum's concept, Bryant (1984) suggested that technicways do not always occur as a single swell of normative adaptive response to new technology, but rather, in some instances, the social response may occur in a chain-reaction fashion, assuming the form of *secondary* or even *tertiary* technicways as well as *primary*. The availability of the husband's safety razor in the home led to the grooming pattern of women shaving their legs (a secondary technicway), and, in time, the shaven legs led to the fashion of shorter skirts (a tertiary technicway).

Further reflection on the ripple effect of social adaptation to innovation and new technological processes seems to indicate that technicways may often mutate, as it were, in an aberrant fashion, becoming *deviant* technicways. Such seems to have been the case with numerous innovations, including the computer.

3. The maker of an obscene phone call, relying on anonymity, can telephone a victim and utter obscenities or sexually explicit suggestions, or simply breathe heavily into the receiver, in a real or simulated lustful fashion and derive vicarious carnal gratification in the process (Nadler 1968, pp. 521–526; Mead 1975, pp. 127–128; Matek 1988, pp. 113–130).

4. Other, more elaborative variations on telephone-related sexual deviancy include the telephone masturbator (Brockopp and Lester 1969, pp. 10–13; Lester 1973, pp. 257–260). The male deviant calls a female (often a counselor at an open-line crisis therapy agency) and, sexually stimulated by the sound of the female therapist's voice, engages in masturbation. The telephone masturbator uses the conversation with the unknown female as the basis for sexual fantasy and vicarious carnal stimulation. He can embellish the sexual drama with his own imaginative ability and masturbate as a constituent part of the fantasy, with complete anonymity, thanks to the technology of the telephone.

5. For those of less imaginative bent, the telephone has enabled the offering of "dirty" stories, obscene language, and salacious conversation from a female as part of a commercial service. Alleged to have originated in Japan (*Parade* 1976, p. 20), the so-called "dial-a-porn" services have become big business in the United States. The individual with a lascivious aural appetite can dial an advertised telephone number and be carnally entertained, either by a conversation with a paid female performer, or by listening to a prerecorded message (see Borna, Chapman, and Menezes 1993; Glascock and LaRose 1993). In either instance, the caller hears sexually explicit talk or sounds and is billed for the time on the line, on his or her monthly telephone bill (U.S. Department of Justice 1986, pp. 1428–1436). (Although primarily used by males, women do use these services.)

6. Both a computer and a modem (a telecommunicational device for computers) are a prerequisite for gaining access to these sexually orientated bulletin boards. To access these services, users dial the bulletin board's inbound phone number. Some of these numbers may be obtained from advertisements in computer or pornographic magazines, others by word-of-mouth. Moreover, once one bulletin board is accessed, information about other boards can readily be obtained from that service. When people initially call one of these bulletin boards, they typically have to complete a registration process. Users normally have to indicate that they are older than 18 or 21, and that they are not an employee of any law enforcement agency. Also, users normally have to pay a registration fee. Although this payment may be made by mail, many services allow users to make the payment on line by credit card. After this process is complete, users can readily access the sexually explicit services offered.

One notable exception to the aforementioned procedures is USENET. USENET is an international noncommercial information network used by persons at academic institutions, research facilities, and major corporations. This network is made possible by more than 1,600 mainframe computers that act as data transfer stations (Horvitz 1989). Access is free to persons at sponsoring sites. It is estimated that well over 500,000 people have access to USENET (Horvitz 1989). Information on this network is categorized into newsgroups, each of which provides postings on one or more of a multitude of topics. There are hundreds of newsgroups, a few of which are dedicated to topics of a prurient nature. For example, there are newsgroups dedicated to bestiality, sadomasochism, masturbation, and pornographic movies. Several newsgroups contain personal ads from a multitude of sexual deviants, such as, for example, sadomasochists and swingers.

References

Borna, Shaheen, Joseph Chapman, and Dennis Menezes. 1993. "Deceptive Nature of Dial-a-Porn Commercials and Public Policy Alternatives." *Journal of Business Ethics* 12:503–509.

Brockopp, Gene W., and David Lester. 1969. "The Masturbator." *Crisis Intervention* 1:10–13.

Bryant, Clifton D. 1982. *Sexual Deviancy and Social Proscription.* New York: Human Science Press.

——. 1984. "Odum's Concept of the Technicways: Some Reflections on an Under-developed Sociological Nation." *Sociological Spectrum* 4:115–142.

Forester, Tom. 1990. "Software Theft and the Problem of Intellectual Property Rights." *Computer and Society* 20:2–11.

Garreau, Joel. 1993, November 29. "Bawdy Bytes: The Growing World of Cybersex." *The Washington Post,* pp. 1, A10.

Glascock, Jack, and Robert LaRose. 1993. Dial-a-Porn Recordings: The Role of the Female Participant in Male Sexual Fantasies. *Journal of Broadcaster & Electronic Media* 39:313–324.

Haight, Kathy. 1994, March 7. "Love: Couples Are Meeting, Courting, Getting Married On-Line." *Roanoke Times and World-News* (Extra Section) pp. 1, 3.

Horvitz, Robert. 1989. "The USENET Underground." *Whole Earth Review* (Winter):111–115.

Jackson, Robert L. 1989, October 1. "Computer-Crime Sleuths Go Underground." *Los Angeles Times,* p. 20.

Kantrowitz, Barbara, Patricia King, and Debra Rosenberg. 1994, April 18. "Child Abuse in Cyberspace." *Newsweek,* p. 40.

King, Rob. 1981. "Computer Abuse and Computer Crime as Organizational Activities." *Computers and Society* 11:12–24.

Klein, Lloyd. 1981. "Sex Solicitation by Short-Wave Radio." *Creative Sociology* 9:61–68.

Lester, David. 1973. "Telephone Counseling and the Masturbator: A Dilemma." *Clinical Social Work Journal* 1:257–260.

Los Angeles Times. 1989, October 1. "Child Molesters Use Electronic Networks: Computer-Crime Sleuths Go Undercover," pp. 20–21.

Lowery, Sharon A., and Charles V. Wetli. 1982. "Sexual Asphyxia: A Neglected Area of Study." *Deviant Behavior* 4:19–40.

Luxenburg, Joan, and Lloyd Klein. 1984. "CB Radio Prostitution: Technology and the Displacement of Deviance." *Journal of Offender Counseling, Services, and Rehabilitation,* 9(Fall/Winter):71–87.

Markoff, John. 1992, March 22. "Sex by Computer: The Latest Technology Fuels the Oldest of Drives." *New York Times,* p. 5.

Matek, Ord. 1988. "Obscene Phone Callers." *Journal of Social Work and Human Sexuality* 7:113–130.

Mead, Beverly F. 1975. "Coping with Obscene Phone Calls." *Medical Aspects of Human Sexuality* 9:127–128.

Money, John, Russell Jobaris, and Gregg Furth. 1977. "Ampotemnophilia: Two Cases of Self-Demand Amputation as a Paraphilia." *Journal of Sex Research* 13:115–125.

Nadler, R. p. 1968. "Approach to Psycho-Analysis of Obscene Telephone Calls." *New York State Journal of Medicine* 68:521–526.

The New York Times. 1989, April 2. "As Computer Bulletin Boards Grow: If It's Out There It's Posted Here," p. B38.

Odum, Howard W. 1937. "Notes on the Technicways in Contemporary Society." *American Sociological Review* 2:336–346.

Ogburn, William F. 1964. *On Culture and Social Change.* Chicago: University of Chicago Press.

Parade. 1976, July 4. "Dirty-Story Time," p. 20.

Schwartz, John. 1993, November 28. "Caution: Children at Play on the Information Highway (Access to Adult Networks Holds Hazards)." *The Washington Post,* pp. 1, 26.

Tamosaitis, Nancy. 1994. "Modem Sex: Can On-line Fantasies Rev Up Your Libido?" *Longevity,* 56, 68.

Time. 1984, May 14. "X-Rated: The Joys of Compusex," p. 83.

U.S. Department of Justice. 1986. *The Attorney General's Commission on Pornography,* Final Report. Washington, DC: U.S. Government Printing Office.

——. 1993, August 31. "Feds Crack Down on Computer Importation of Child Pornography." Press release.

U.S. News and World Report. 1985, June 3. "For Every Taste a Bulletin Board," p. 59

Van Gelder, Lindsey. 1985, October. "The Strange Case of the Electronic Lover." *Ms.* pp. 94, 99, 101–104, 117, 123–124.

Weinberg, Thomas S., and Gerhard Falk. 1980. "The Social Organization of Sadism and Masochism." *Deviant Behavior* 1:379–394.

31
Men Who Have Sex With Other Men

Barry D. Adam

Alan Sears

E. Glenn Schellenberg

Unprotected homosexual sex is, needless to say, high-risk deviance. Although HIV infection is not the death sentence it once was (protease inhibitors and combination drug therapy are now available to remove symptoms and prolong life) the risk of contracting the disease is sufficiently high to make unsafe sex something like Russian roulette. Of course, awareness of risk need not translate into behavior to avoid it; rationalizations are available to permit actors to "reason away" risky conduct and make it appear less dangerous, or perhaps not dangerous at all.

Some homosexual men, for instance, believe they can tell from physical or interpersonal cues that a prospective partner is HIV-positive or negative. Others use precautions only when they believe the person or situation denotes high risk. Still others dismiss the need for precautions, especially when they are drunk or depressed or when an "opportunity too good to pass up" presents itself. Safe sex practices are especially challenging for men involved in monogamous relationships: Insisting on condom use can be equivalent to an accusation of infidelity, which functions to undermine intimacy and perhaps jeopardize the relationship.

The authors provide substantial support for the neutralization paradigm first offered by Sykes and Matza (1957). That is, deviant behavior is not nearly so bothersome when rule-violators can explain away the negative conse-quences that attend to it. By promoting a false sense of security, however, such intellectualizations merely put the rule-breaker in greater jeopardy.

Educational campaigns designed to increase awareness of AIDS and safe sex practices have made a remarkable impact.[1] National populations as a whole, and gay men in particular, are now highly knowledgeable about the ways in which HIV can be transmitted (e.g., Jadack, Hyde, & Keller, 1995; Lewis, Malow, & Ireland, 1997; Myers, Godin, Calzavara, Lambert, & Locker, 1993; O'Donnell, San Doval, Vornfett, & O'Donnell, 1994). Many gay men have managed to integrate safe sex into their everyday lives (e.g., Ekstrand & Coates, 1990; Hunt et al., 1993), yet this change remains incomplete (e.g., Gruer & Ssembatya-Lule, 1993; Hunt et al., 1993; Kelly et al., 1995; Meyer & Dean, 1995; Offir, Fisher, Williams, & Fisher, 1993; Perkins, Leserman, Murphy, & Evans, 1993; Peterson et al., 1992). Whereas some gay men occasionally relax the safety standards that usually govern their sexual activities, others have never adopted safe sex to a great degree. Because the prevalence of HIV-infection in the Western world remains higher among men who have sex with men than among any other segment of the population, unsafe male-to-male sex continues to pose a major public-health challenge.

Much of the research on safe sex education has focused on the association between knowledge about AIDS and sexual practices (see Joffe, 1996; Kippax, Connell, Dowsett, & Crawford, 1993). In the initial phase of the epidemic, primary concerns included tailoring educational programs to specific high-risk populations (e.g., gay men, injection-drug users) and identifying those who were undereducated about AIDS. A central assumption of this approach was that information would shift attitudes, which, in turn, would lead to changes in behavior. As Kippax et al. (1993) remark,

> The dominant model of health education that has been adopted by many AIDS researchers, particularly in the United

States, is a refinement of what might be called the KAP (or behavior) model—knowledge, attitudes, practices (or KAP). The KAP model is a linear one, which initially assumed that knowledge shapes or determines attitudes which, in turn, shape or determine behavior. (p. 5)

As levels of knowledge and awareness about AIDS rose rapidly in many countries throughout the 1980s, it became increasingly clear that rates of safe sex practice often failed to keep up. For example, in one study (Fisher, Fisher, Williams, & Malloy, 1994), a KAP model accounted for 35 percent of the variance in gay men's AIDS-preventive behavior. Although this association is relatively strong in social-science research, it should not go unnoticed that almost two-thirds of the variance could not be attributed to individual differences in knowledge of HIV transmission. Indeed, as people in the European Union, North America, and Australia became increasingly knowledgeable about the basic facts of how HIV is spread, the attention of researchers turned toward the gap between knowledge and behavior (e.g., Catania, Kegeles, & Coates, 1990; Waddell, 1992), which tends to be particularly large for heterosexuals (Maticka-Tyndale, 1992; Maxwell, Bastani, & Yan, 1995; Maxwell & Boyle, 1995).

Accordingly, issues of *compliance* and *relapse* in terms of conformity to safe sex norms came to dominate the agendas of many researchers, who asked why people "who know better" still have unsafe sex (e.g., Adib, Joseph, Ostrow, & James, 1991; Kelly et al., 1991; McCusker, Stoddard, McDonald, Zapka, & Mayer, 1992; see Hart, Boulton, Fitzpatrick, McLean, & Dawson, 1992, for a review and critique). This approach attempts to identify factors that compromise rationality, the assumption being that rationality would win out if these factors were eliminated (Hart et al., 1992). Perhaps the factor most commonly identified as an impediment to safe sex is substance abuse (Ekstrand & Coates, 1990; Kalichman et al., 1994; Leigh, 1990; Lewis & Ross, 1995; Meyer & Dean, 1995; Paul, Stall, & Davis, 1993; Penkower et al., 1991; Peterson et al., 1992; Siegel, Mesagno, Chen, & Christ, 1989;

Waddell, 1992). Nonetheless, results from studies conducted in the United Kingdom (Weatherburn et al., 1993), the United States (Temple & Leigh, 1992), Australia (Gold, Skinner, & Ross, 1994), Belgium (Bolton, Vincke, Mak, & Dennehy, 1992), and Canada (Myers et al., 1992) raise questions about the reliability of this finding.

The "rational man" approach also tends to equate all homosexual practices with high levels of risk, presuming that the simple intervention of the condom suffices as the technique for HIV prevention in all circumstances. Prevention strategies that advocate using a condom every time are consistent with this approach. We know, however, that many male-to-male sex practices carry no risk of transmitting HIV (e.g., mutual masturbation), whereas others have negligible (e.g., anilingus) or low (e.g., receptive fellatio) risk (McClure & Grubb, 1999). Even unprotected anal intercourse carries no risk of transmitting HIV if neither participant is infected with HIV. Traditional KAP and rational-man models also fail to provide a clear understanding of how AIDS messages interact with the meanings and reasoning that homosexually active men use in understanding and expressing their sexuality (Adam, 1992; Donovan, Mearns, McEwan, & Sugden, 1994; Dowsett, 1996; Flowers, Sheeran, Beail, & Smith, 1997; Joffe, 1996; King, 1993; Kippax et al., 1993; Parker & Carballo, 1990). In fact, such models—in combination with discourse about "gaps," "relapse," and so on—tend to gloss over the ways in which standards of practice for safe sex are often provisional and inconsistent.

In the present study, we interviewed homosexually active men about their sexuality. A primary goal was to obtain detailed accounts of recent incidents of unsafe sex. We predicted that levels of knowledge of HIV and AIDS would be uniformly high, and that unsafe sex would be associated with relatively complex issues, such as participants' sexual and affective preferences, the nature of the relationship between partners, ambiguities about what is truly safe, and the influence of dominant cultural values and discourse. In other words, we did not expect that unsafe sex would be best attributed to gaps in knowledge, or to complicating factors that block the progression from knowledge to attitudes to practices. Indeed, gay communities have often displayed a rich expertise around AIDS and HIV, and the history of AIDS has seen important clashes between competing forms of expertise (Altman, 1994). Some of the most successful safe sex campaigns have built on existing community infrastructures and know-how (see Dowsett, 1990; Watney, 1989). We hoped, then, that by obtaining a detailed account of men's understandings of unsafe sex, we could inform the development of future prevention efforts.

We assumed that men who had been sexually active with other men in the recent past would have first-hand familiarity with safe sex practices and the discourse surrounding such practices. By conducting in-depth, semi-structured interviews with a sample of these men, we hoped to uncover affective and emotional preferences that influence sexual decision making. Our qualitative approach enabled us to highlight the complexities men encounter in the real world of sexual interaction. Understanding such complexities is crucial if education campaigns are to engage with men's existing sexual knowledge and practices. Compared to standard quantitative approaches, qualitative research methods may provide a deeper understanding of perceptions of AIDS messages and the reasoning processes by which people exempt themselves from these messages (Donovan et al., 1994; Maticka-Tyndale, 1992). To anticipate the results somewhat, our findings imply that it is not simply the *absence* of information that leads men to unsafe sexual practices, but also the *presence* of particular preferences, feelings, and worldviews. Thus, our main argument is that the next generation of safe-sex education programs will need to engage with the complex considerations that guide men's sexual decision-making (see also Flowers, Sheeran, et al., 1997).

Previous empirical and theoretical studies with gay and bisexual men point to a range of understandings about sexual practices that appear to influence how men make decisions around safe sex. Studies from different countries have identified several issues that recur, including the association of safe sex with emotional and physical distance, distrust, and thoughts of death (Prieur, 1990); the demonstration of trust in couples (Connell, Davis, & Dowsett, 1993); the meaning of semen and insemination (Odets, 1994); the perceived riskiness of ejaculation in oral sex (Lowy & Ross, 1994); the transgressive value of homosexuality (Pollak, 1988); and the rhetoric of drive, lapse, and inadvertence (Boulton, McLean, Fitzpatrick, & Hart, 1995).

In one study (Gaies, Sacco, & Becker, 1995), American gay men were asked to imagine a sexual encounter with a very attractive partner. Although respondents reported thinking about the personal consequences of HIV infection, they also considered whether insisting on using condoms might ruin the "golden opportunity," whether the promise of pleasure justified some risk, and how important it was for them to have sex with the imagined partner. In an Australian study (Gold et al., 1994), HIV-positive gay men rationalized unsafe sex in the following terms: being in a negative mood state, having nothing to lose, taking advantage of a sexual opportunity, disliking condoms, resolving to withdraw without ejaculation, and demonstrating confidence in themselves and their partners. By contrast, HIV-negative men rationalized unsafe sex by believing they could infer a partner's HIV-status, being in a long-term relationship, wanting time out from having to worry about AIDS, disliking condoms, and being in a negative mood state. These findings are comparable to those from other reports (Kelly et al., 1991; Levine & Siegel, 1992; Offir et al., 1993). In each case, gay men justified unsafe sex in terms of a highly refined calculus of risk, or excused it by mentioning factors such as drunkenness, sexual passion, emotional needs, or partner coercion. Denying one's vulnerability to AIDS is not solely the province of gay men; similar factors were identified in a sample of the general population from the Netherlands (Sandfort & van Zessen, 1992).

In sum, the goals of the present study were threefold: (a) to examine the influence of sexual and affective preferences on gay and bisexual men's sexual behavior, (b) to investigate the ways these men define their own sexual activities as *safe* or *unsafe*, and (c) to improve our understanding of the reasoning processes involved when determining whether to practice safe sex.

Method

Participants

A convenience sample of 102 men who have sex with men was recruited to be as diverse as possible in terms of their cultural background, sexual identity, relationship status, age, social class, and educational level. The men lived in the Ottawa (n = 26), Toronto (n = 37), and Windsor (n = 37) areas, or in other communities in the Southern Ontario region of Canada (n = 2). Recruitment strategies were similar to those used previously to study homosexually active men (e.g., Carballo-Dieguez, Remien, Dolezal, & Wagner, 1999; Gold et al., 1994; Kalichman et al., 1994; Myers et al., 1992; Peterson et al., 1992; Waddell, 1992). These included advertising in the gay press, making appeals at meetings of gay organizations, and distributing leaflets at gay bars in the three target cities. Additional participants were recruited through the personal networks of the researchers and research assistants.

The participants ranged in age from 19 to 72 years (M = 35.2 years). Most of the men identified their sexual orientation as gay or homosexual (n = 86), with the remainder identifying as bisexual (n = 10), heterosexual (n = 2), or other (e.g., "bi-curious," n = 4). A majority of the participants had tested negative for HIV (n = 81); the remaining men were either HIV-positive (n = 11) or had not been tested (n = 10). The sample was relatively well-educated: 12 men had a graduate degree and 46 had completed college or university. Of the remaining men, 30 had some university or college education and 6 had finished high school; another 8 did not graduate from high school. Participants' incomes varied greatly: 20 of the men earned more than $50,000 per year, whereas 30 earned less than $10,000. The remaining participants had incomes ranging from $10,000 to

$20,000 (n = 21), or from $20,000 to $50,000 (n = 31). (Incomes are reported in Canadian dollars: $1 US = $1.45 Canadian.)

English was the first language of 74 men, 15 first spoke French, and 13 reported that their mother tongue was a language other than English or French. When asked which language they usually spoke, 90 spoke English, 11 spoke French, and 1 spoke Spanish. First-named responses to a question about ethnicity included British (n = 36), French (n = 17), other European (n = 18), Canadian (n = 11), African and Afro-Caribbean (n = 5), Latin American (n = 4), Asian (n = 4), aboriginal (n = 2), Middle Eastern (n = 2), and Jewish (n = 2). When asked about their relationship status, the vast majority of the sample chose one of three categories: single or not dating (n = 46), dating a man (n = 26), or living with a male partner (n = 24). Other participants reported that they were involved in a dating relationship with a woman (n = 3), living with a female partner (n = 1), living with a male partner and dating a woman (n = 1), or dating both a man and a woman (n = 1).

On average, the interview took approximately 90 minutes. Participants received token remuneration ($20 Canadian) for their time and trouble.

Procedure

After being briefed on the overall objectives of the study and providing their written consent to participate (including consent to audiotape the interview), the participants completed a short questionnaire in addition to being interviewed. The questionnaire consisted of demographic categories, a checklist of sexual activities practiced with regular and casual male partners, and a knowledge measure that required participants to rate 11 male-to-male sex acts in terms of the likelihood that each act could result in transmission of HIV. Detailed analyses of these quantitative data will be reported elsewhere. The interviews were semi-structured, with pre-established "probes" used to ensure that we obtained detailed information about recent and memorable sexual experiences, particularly those that participants considered to be unsafe. Many of the probes were designed to elicit factors that make sex particularly satisfying, based on the assumption that satisfaction of desire would exert a strong influence on decision making during sexual interactions. The present report is based primarily on responses to the probe: "Describe the last time you had unsafe sex with a man."

Most of the interviews were conducted by research assistants who were graduate students in clinical or applied psychology programs and had research interests in human sexuality. A bilingual assistant interviewed French-speaking participants. Approximately 10 percent of the interviews were conducted by the authors.

Analytic Strategy

Tapes of the interviews were transcribed and organized using qualitative research software (QSR NUD-IST), which allowed us to identify all comments related to instances of unsafe sex. The analyses involved identifying recurring themes the men used in their accounts and organizing informative quotes around these themes. We assumed that people in their everyday activities deploy rich ways of knowing that are integrally related to their behaviors (see Smith, 1987). Our intent was to highlight connections between unsafe sex on the one hand, and men's understanding of their sexuality and of HIV/AIDS discourse on the other hand.

The analyses followed a modified version of grounded-theory principles. Our analytical strategy was to capture emerging themes from the interviews rather than to code the data into a preexisting scheme. However, in contrast to the classical grounded-theory approach of Glaser and Strauss (1967), we do not claim that our initial reading of the transcripts was naive. Our own experiences as gay men and AIDS activists as well as our prior theoretical orientations (as discussed in the introduction) obviously shaped our approach to the data.

The analytic process involved six steps:

1. In a preliminary reading of the transcripts, we identified key themes emerging from participants' reflections on their self-defined unsafe sexual activities.

2. Quotes relevant to the themes were grouped together.

3. The thematic categories were refined, merged, or subdivided based on associations and overlap among quotes. For example, two quotes that seemed initially to be making the same point might seem quite different when placed side-by-side.

4. Representative quotes from each of the refined thematic groups were selected and connected according to the narrative of the paper.

5. Every interview was read in detail and categorized according to the presence or absence of a particular theme.

6. The thematic structure was further refined by the authors until a consensus was reached.

Results and Discussion

Whenever participants are quoted in the qualitative analyses that follow, demographic characteristics (sexual identity, age, HIV-status, and occupation) are reported in parentheses after each quote. These represent self-reported categories. In other words, previously married men with children are classified as "gay" rather than "bisexual" if that was the participant's choice. Similarly, men who provided nonstandard descriptions of their sexual identity (e.g., omnisexual) are classified accordingly. While cultural differences are important considerations in any social-science research (e.g., Diaz, 1998; Landrine, 1995; Myrick, 1999), no cultural group among our non-white participants was represented by more than five men. (In general, Canadian society is multicultural without having large minority categories such as African American or Latino.) Accordingly, our analyses of the interviews do not address the issue of cultural differences in safe sex practices.[2]

Overview

Most of the men reported some sort of sexual activity they defined as unsafe[3] during the last 5 years. Eleven men stated categorically that they never had unsafe sex; these claims were consistent between the interview and the checklist. Another 19 men reported no unsafe sexual acts over the past 5 years. Many of these men had to reach back to the early or mid-1980s—when widespread awareness of the AIDS epidemic was just emerging—to identify the last time they had unsafe sex. For example, one man remarked, "I had unsafe sex probably from 1968 to 1986. The idea of safe sex was not in my vocabulary or my understanding" (Gay, 41, HIV-positive, businessman). Another man noted, "Well it depends on the definition. If you mean fucking or getting fucked without a condom, then it must have been with Ted. That was more than 15 or 16 years ago" (Gay, 59, HIV-negative, retired). This leaves 72 participants who reported at least one incident of unsafe sex over the last 5 years, a number that is relatively high by epidemiological standards. The second quote ("it depends on the definition") makes it clear, however, that some participants were aware of discrepancies in various definitions of safe and unsafe. Moreover, despite a consensus in our sample that unprotected anal sex is risky, other sexual activities considered to be unsafe proved to cover a wide variety of practices.

Participants' responses indicated that they did not practice unsafe sex out of ignorance in any simple sense. Rather, they offered detailed accounts of their experiences of unsafe sex in which they assessed the safety of particular activities while explaining their preferences and choices. Five recurring themes emerged from the interviews that highlighted specific obstacles to practicing safe sex as well as the issues our participants considered in sexual encounters. First, sexual decision-making in *couple relationships* was often complicated by the men's HIV status and by issues of monogamy, trust, and intimacy. Second, unsafe sexual activity was sometimes described as being *inadvertent or involuntary*. Third, *negative self-images and moods* appeared to be predictive of a willingness to have unsafe sex. Fourth, by reading signs that a particular partner was "likely" to be HIV-negative, strategies of *intuiting safety* often led to unsafe sex. Finally, *unclear boundaries between safe and unsafe activities* complicated the decision-making

process. The remainder of the present report is organized around these five themes.

Couple Relationships

Twenty-three participants reported having unsafe sex in the context of a continuing relationship. Most of these involved some form of agreement (either tacit or verbalized) between two HIV-negative men. Twelve of the 23 had arrived at an explicit agreement with their partner about permitting unsafe sex inside the relationship. Following Kippax et al. (1993), we consider these to be instances of *negotiated safety*. Most couples agreed on a safe-sex-only policy with casual partners; a few agreed to refrain from having other sexual partners altogether. These kinds of agreement about sex with others outside the relationship allow two HIV-negative men to have unprotected yet safe sex with each other. One participant remarked:

> We chose about two years ago, I'm guessing, that sex between the two of us would be unprotected. It was something of a long agonizing decision. Especially with all the friends who told us, "You can't possibly do that." To answer your question, it came to be that way by mutual agreement and a longstanding agreement as well, the agreement being that sex between us is unprotected, but we absolutely trust each other to have protected sex with anyone else. We also know we're both HIV-negative. (Gay, 24, HIV-negative, clerk)

Others made a point of incorporating HIV-testing into these agreements. For example:

> We initiated the relationship with the feeling that we be only safe until we both got tested. And we were tested again Tuesday. . . . I got my results back and they were negative for the second time. So then we had unprotected sex for the first time on Tuesday. That was different. It was very special. (Gay, 31, HIV-negative, clerk)

Explicit discussion of outside relationships combined with knowledge of both partners' HIV status can create a situation in which unprotected sex within a relationship is completely safe. The question of trust is always an issue, however, because the mutual safety of the partners depends on consistent adherence to the terms of the arrangement (i.e., no unsafe encounters with other partners).

Negotiating safety can be particularly complex when partners do not share the same HIV status. The notion of an on-going and shared future is disrupted when one of the partners has a life-threatening disease that can be transmitted to the other partner (Adam & Sears, 1996). Nonetheless, people tend to be relatively unconcerned about contracting HIV (Pilkington, Kern, & Indest, 1994) or germs in general (Nemeroff, 1995) from a close partner. One of our HIV-positive participants described a pattern of inconsistent condom use with an HIV-negative partner:

> He is not HIV-positive despite our histories. I am, and we don't use any form of condom, protection. . . . We do discuss it from time to time because generally I guess I am more the bottom than the top in the relationship, but I like to fuck too, and every once in a while he wants to get fucked, and I do. Usually I don't cum, if I am fucking him, if I want to cum then I usually will use a condom. But the number of times that we have fucked and cum without a condom is more frequent than not. (Gay, 33, HIV-positive, unemployed)

Hence, condom use is one of a series of interconnected considerations that guide sexual practices within a relationship. The last quote also highlights a distinction many participants made between the insertive and receptive roles in anal sex, and between anal sex with and without ejaculation. Both of these issues are discussed further below.

Other men noted that unsafe sex was more likely to occur within an ongoing relationship because it was viewed as a means of expressing or maintaining a feeling of intimacy or romance. In practice, the process of negotiating safety can be complicated by underlying and often implicit presumptions about monogamy and fidelity. As Sobo (1995) noted in her study of African American women, the discourse of monogamy may work to prevent the adoption of safe sex practices. Similar findings were reported

among a sample of women over 30 years of age from the United Kingdom (Maxwell & Boyle, 1995). The monogamy script was less predominant among the men we interviewed than among these samples of women. In relationships in which it arose, however, it sometimes served as an impediment to practicing safe sex. Unsafe sex appears to be read as a primary sign of the special trust that partners in a couple have for each other (Afifi, 1999; Ames, Atchinson, & Rose, 1995; Bartos, 1994; Bartos, McLeod, & Nott, 1993; Flowers, Smith, Sheeran, & Beail, 1997; Hospers, Molenaar, & Kok, 1994; Silvestre, Lyter, Valdiserri, Huggins, & Rinaldo, 1989). Such symbolism can inhibit partners from adopting protection, which can be interpreted as an accusation of infidelity. Indeed, one participant explained the lack of condom use in his relationship this way: "No, he didn't want to. For him, if we practiced safe sex, he would be admitting to going outside [the relationship]" (Gay, 48, HIV-negative, unemployed; translated from French). Seven of the men we interviewed spoke of their relationships in these terms; an additional four spoke with some regret of having been caught up in a set of assumptions that led them to practice unprotected sex with a man who was later found to be having unsafe sex with other partners. One participant spoke directly about the trade-offs he experienced in thinking about introducing condoms into his relationship:

> Once I suspected he was being unfaithful to me, it was very difficult to say, "OK, from now on I want you to wear a condom," without undermining what was at that point a really shaky relationship. And I wanted him. There was nothing worse than being gay and gray. . . . And since I'm 54 years old, quite frankly I wanted him around. (Bisexual, 54, HIV-negative, city employee)

Negotiations about safety may be precluded when questions of trust are embedded in a romantic discourse. For example, when sexual monogamy is equated with trust, insistence on using condoms can symbolize distrust. Obviously, a great deal of trust is required in the present historical context for gay-male couples to forsake using condoms, particularly when traditional concepts of romance make no provision for the confession of sexual activity outside of a relationship. Moreover, because trust can be subject to deterioration, desire and romance can provide unwarranted reassurance about presumptions of monogamy.

In general, our participants' responses confirm that reconciling safe sex with the emotional dynamics of a relationship is too complicated to be portrayed simply as a gap in knowledge or information. Moreover, instances of negotiated safety serve as an important reminder that one cannot simply categorize all men who report having unprotected anal intercourse (on a questionnaire, in an interview, etc.) as having engaged in unsafe sex. It is noteworthy that unprotected male-female sex in the context of a committed relationship (marriage or otherwise) is rarely considered unsafe.

Inadvertent or Involuntary Unsafe Sex

Sixteen participants described instances of unintended unsafe sexual encounters, or cases in which such encounters were clearly the exception rather than the norm. In these cases, unsafe sex was understood in retrospect to be an accident. Two men attributed unsafe sex to intense passion that began during semi-conscious sleep. One of these remarked:

> We got to doing our thing, but before either one of us climaxed, we took a break and had a little snooze. . . . And I decided, I guess, in my semi-sleep state that I was going to pull off the condom that I had on. Ten or 15 minutes later, we were back to getting screwed again. We never stopped the second time to put back on the condom. . . . The second time around it was like a dog in heat. My mind was thinking it. My mind knew that I shouldn't have been having sex with this guy not wearing a condom but it was not enough to control the heat instincts. (Gay, 38, HIV-negative, musician)

Twelve men described a surprise moment of unsafe intercourse in the midst of sexual activity that involved verbal and nonverbal gestures. For example, one man said:

> I just blurted out that I'm HIV-negative and the next thing I know he's sitting on it. I mean I haven't done that for a long time. Two years. It was good. I mean, no fluids were shared between us. I mean we did have unsafe sex a little bit. . . . Then he put the condom on and we had safe sex so it wasn't totally unsafe. (Gay, 24, HIV-negative, waiter)

These incidents were described as momentary, nonorgasmic breaks in sexual encounters that also included the use of condoms.

Five participants described unsafe sex in the context of first-time sexual encounters. Initial sexual experiences are often unplanned, taking a spontaneous and covert form because of the potential dangers of discovery. Social taboos against talking about sex, particularly in the case of younger people and same-sex encounters, also mean that sexual initiations often take place in a context where there is little knowledge or access to information. One participant described his first gay encounter with a 38-year-old when he was 21:

> It was the first time I ever actually had real intercourse, where I actually had gay intercourse. It was just incredible. . . .I made good friends with one guy. . . .He took me to his place and we had unsafe sex—all the way. It was incredible. . . .There was some kind of trust between us already built up, I guess. . . .I guess he realized that I'd never been with anyone else except for a couple of females and they were OK. (Gay, 31, HIV-negative, professional)

This participant's account drew on two other narrative lines that entered repeatedly into accounts of unsafe sex: (a) a gay/straight distinction that reproduces the widely-held view that heterosexual sex is a safe practice, and (b) an interpretive process of reading a complex set of physical and character signs to determine a partner's HIV status. Both of these themes are treated more extensively below.

In some cases, men attributed their involvement in unsafe sex directly to willful acts on the part of their partners. For example, three participants cited instances of engaging in receptive anal sex believing that their partner was wearing a condom only to discover later that he was not. One of these men made the following observation: "Where the unsafe sex came in is he was originally wearing a condom and half way through the sex he took it off and continued and he was in a top position" (Gay, 39, HIV-positive, travel agent).

Two participants attributed unsafe sex to sexual assault. In one of these cases, a young man (who was a heterosexual, fundamentalist Christian at the time) had a first-time sexual experience with a man that he characterizes as a "rape"; nevertheless, he sought out this same man for his second and third experiences as well. He noted:

> I was only 16 at the time. So we went back to his apartment [from an apartment building gym] and he just started completely working my sensations, kissing me for the first time, touching me. It was the first time I had ever gotten a blow job. He pinned me down and raped me, and then after he got done and got off inside my ass—and I guess he must have hit my prostate because I got off without him actually touching me, or me touching myself. . . . And that was interesting and there were two other times while I was visiting my girlfriend during that week that I went back to the same guy. It was just the spontaneity of the thing. (Gay, 21, HIV-negative, waiter)

The other interviewee described a nonconsensual act of anal sex that occurred at a warehouse party for leather men. Only one participant described an act of accidental unsafe sex due to a condom breaking.

When reflecting upon their participation in unsafe sex, some of our participants viewed their involvement as involuntary, inadvertent, or otherwise beyond their control. Regardless of whether these encounters were "truly" accidental, in most cases the men were referring to relatively isolated incidents rather than regular practices.

Negative Self-Images and Moods

Seventeen participants explained unsafe sexual experiences in terms of a heightened orientation to risk-taking that was often associated with depression or a negative mood

state. Although risk-taking can be an important part of sexual pleasure, it can cloud or come into direct conflict with considerations of safety. Five participants noted explicitly that they were using sex as a way of escaping from negative feelings. For example, one man referred to sex as "animal" and "wild" but later talked about his need to relieve feelings of depression:

> This was the first time in my life where I, like, with somebody had really let go and we were really just animal about each other. It was just wild. . . .[Unsafe sex has happened] a couple of times in the bathhouse because I've felt very lonely and very sad, really needed affection, and allowed myself to open myself up so much so that I just went beyond my boundaries and my own limitations. (Sexual, 37, HIV-negative, artist)

This quote highlights the gulf between a sense of responsibility that is connected with safe sex practices, and feelings of abandon that can accompany sex when it is used as a means of escape. Other researchers have also identified a positive association between unsafe sex and using sex as an escape from everyday life (Pollak, 1988), and between sexual risk-taking and depression (Hospers et al., 1994).

Unsafe sex may become particularly likely when drugs and alcohol are used to heighten a sense of abandon. One participant noted:

> About that time last July when I had that [unsafe encounter] and the sensation was just incredibly much—incredibly richer and all that and—but I know at the same time that if I were not even sober, but less blitzed than I was, then I would not have given myself into that. It would have felt far too self-conscious and wrong and all of that. Apart from times when I have essentially chosen to disable my judgment (laughs). . . . I am not able in my experience to start having—to start fucking unsafely. (Gay, 31, HIV-negative, student)

It may be simplistic, however, to identify drug or alcohol use as a cause of unsafe sex. Physiological effects of drugs require interpretation, and drug vernacular provides a rhetoric of exculpation. For example, a cross-cultural study of alcohol consumption found that people become intoxicated in culturally expected ways (McAndrew & Edgerton, 1969). Indeed, the respondent quoted above was candid about having "chosen to disable [his] judgment" rather than blaming drug use for his actions. Another man made it clear that he did not think that drug use influenced his ability to behave rationally:

Any time I use drugs they just make me more friendly, happier, mellower. I get sort of a stronger surge from them to do something more aggressive, that's true, but I don't think it hinders my rational decision making. I think the only thing drugs do to me is inhibit all my inhibitions. (Gay, 33, HIV-negative, researcher)

The notion that sexual activity involves surrender to the "heat of the moment" is part of a broader understanding of sex as ecstatic (Bartos et al., 1993; Díaz, 1997). This perspective requires that sexual activity be outside of the ordinary, a break from everyday obligations and commitments. One participant (cited above) mentioned that "the heat instincts" during a particular encounter were stronger than his will to use a condom. Another participant viewed it this way: "I guess I simply enjoy sex and the pleasure and the excitement of the moment should be more important than [safety] to me" (Gay, 68, HIV-negative, professional).

Such escapes from the mundane to the ecstatic can be shaded with self-negation, representing a flight from oneself. On the basis of observations from his practice in clinical psychology, Odets (1995) reported that unsafe sex was linked to covert or overt self-destructive intent. Five of our participants discussed sexual experiences in which risk-taking was difficult to distinguish from overt self-destructiveness. One described his participation in unsafe sex as a self-destructive quest at one point, and as a fatalistic resignation to destiny at another:

I am one of those stupid, even ridiculous people who favors safe sex, who promotes safe sex, teaches safe sex to everybody, who always has a condom on himself, but who never uses it, for two reasons. . . . The first is that for quite a while I exposed myself to the dangers of

unprotected encounters in order to try to catch AIDS. It was a disguised form of suicide. The second reason was that I considered that it was one of those things that happens, an occupational hazard. If I was going to get it, I would get it. If I didn't, I didn't. (Gay, 36, HIV-negative, social services; translated from French)

The same participant stated later that he was abused as a child, that he was a recovering alcoholic and addict, and that he believed that getting drunk or high is related to unsafe sex because one loses a sense of danger. For this man, a troubled life resulting in a general state of unhappiness or depression appears to be associated with self-destructive tendencies in general, and with engaging in unsafe sex in particular.

Three respondents who described conservative religious upbringings reported difficulties adopting safe-sex practices that incorporated elements of self-destructive intent. These men were raised to think of nonmarital sexual activity as a transgression. As such, they had difficulty reconciling the idea of safety with that of transgression. Having "fallen into temptation" through expression of their homosexual desire, they found themselves caught up in the "AIDS as punishment" discourse propagated by conservative churches, which, ironically, can become a self-fulfilling prophecy by increasing risk of exposure to HIV through unsafe sex. The following participant traced a period of unsafe sex in his life to his struggle over acknowledging his homosexuality while he was a member of a fundamentalist Christian denomination:

I developed maybe a fatalistic attitude, and either I'm going to get it or I'm not. And if I get it, well, then I'm out of here. Like I'm being punished, and you have to remember too I still believed that very, very strongly that what I was doing was wrong, and well, if I got it, well, God was just punishing me and that was it. (Gay, 41, HIV-negative, nurse)

Another man drew a link between his religious upbringing and his approach to sex as an unconstrained plunge into ecstasy. He contrasted his own sexual behavior with that of his friends, whom he described as having a more self-controlled sexual style. He also drew an explicit link between his conservative religious upbringing and troubles dealing with his sexuality:

> For those individuals who grow up in a strong religious environment, they have a problem accepting their sexual lifestyle as being part of their lifestyle or their existence. They have a strong religious sense. They always want to go, "OK, God's going to punish you. He's going to punish you tomorrow for this, whatever you did last night. There's going to be major punishment. He'll be like raining brimstone and fire on you." And you have a guilty conscience in a strong way. (Gay, 33, HIV-negative, researcher)

Thus, for this man, safe sex may be irrelevant when divine retribution is impending. In some cases, HIV-positive people who have been immersed in conservative religious traditions continue to struggle with this punitive logic after their diagnosis (Adam & Sears, 1996).

In certain situations, then, depression or simply a heightened sense of sexual risk-taking can work against insistence on safe sex. Nonetheless, obstacles in the progression from knowledge to attitudes and behavior often include very rational considerations of the risks and pleasures involved.

Intuiting Safety

Twelve participants described attempts to read implicit signs of a partner's HIV status as a method of ascertaining safety, a process that has been observed among young heterosexual men and women in the U.S. (Williams et al., 1992) and Canada (Maticka-Tyndale, 1992), and among gay men in studies from several countries (Ames et al., 1995; Aveline, 1995; Gold et al., 1994). This strategy involves a shift in emphasis from the sexual *act* to the sexual *partner*—or from the universal to the particular—by evaluating a partner's HIV status from various cues. In the following excerpt, the participant reflects on the likelihood that his partner was HIV-positive and on the risk of the particular act. Specifically, he intuits a sense of trust and safety from his partner's youth and by adopting the insertive role in anal sex:

> About a month and a half ago, I fucked a guy without using a condom so that is unsafe sex by general standards. I don't feel it was unsafe because I don't feel that I am HIV-positive and I don't think he is.

How do you make that judgment?

> Not in very good ways. Just because he is young and relatively inexperienced and just in the fact that I am fucking him. (Gay, 30, HIV-negative, service industry)

At times, HIV-negative status may be inferred from connections with heterosexuality. For example, the next participant expressed a certain embarrassment in confronting his fantasy logic, although his candor allowed a glimpse into sexual decision making that was not unusual:

> The guy fit within a certain kind of fantasy of mine that made me want to, and also I felt this—stupid reason—because he fit into this certain criterion, I felt he was a safer candidate to have unsafe sex with. . . .He gave the illusion of being straight—his haircut, his body type, his attitude, what he would or wouldn't do. (Gay, 39, HIV-negative, artist)

Another participant (quoted earlier) noted that because his sexual history included only "a couple of females," his partner had intuited he was HIV-negative. Thus, the idea that heterosexuals are safe while homosexual men are not safe can be adopted by gay men as well as the heterosexual mainstream (Boulton et al., 1995). This notion sets up a self-negating dynamic, such that unsafe sex is justified simply because it is (or seems) heterosexual, which ultimately assures that it is not safe.

Each of the six participants who reported recent sexual activity with women as well as men adopted some form of this perspective. For example, one man reported that he had unsafe sex with women but not with men:

> With guys, no [unsafe sex], with women, yes. I've had unsafe sex with women like so many times. A few years ago I had no idea I could get a girl pregnant. It was really stupid at the time. (Omnisexual, 19, HIV-negative, odd jobs)

Boundaries Separating Safe From Unsafe

Safe-sex decision making becomes particularly complex when prevention messages are contradictory or when the epidemiology itself is unclear. Gay men often have a rich unofficial knowledge of HIV-associated risks, which was developed and shared through largely informal processes. Pioneering efforts in safe-sex education generally wove together this unofficial knowledge with the best scientific knowledge of the time (see Watney, 1989). Areas of ambiguity for lay people are often direct reflections of areas of contention in "official" sources (e.g., epidemiology, medicine, or public health; see Kippax et al., 1990; Myers et al., 1993). Indeed, awareness of gray areas in the demarcation of safe from unsafe may be better interpreted as a sign of sophistication rather than one of ignorance.

Boundaries between what participants considered to be safe and unsafe were particularly ambiguous in four instances: unprotected sex in couple relationships, being the insertive partner in anal sex, anal intercourse without ejaculation, and fellatio with ejaculation. The ambiguity of unprotected sex between couples who are both HIV-negative (discussed above) stems from problems over how practices inside the relationship relate to outside activities. Remarks about unprotected anal sex from two participants cited above indicate that the receptive role was viewed as considerably more risky than the insertive role. Whereas one man noted that the sex was less risky "just in the fact that I am fucking him," another noted his heightened risk because his partner "was in a top position." These lay-person observations are particularly interesting when one considers that virtually no safe-sex education program makes a distinction in risk between insertive and receptive roles. Although a recent epidemiological report (McClure & Grubb, 1999) acknowledges that more cases have been attributed to the receptive role, it also classifies both roles identically as high risk. On the one hand, homosexually active men may have greater levels of expertise than they are "supposed" to have, with some—perhaps most—being aware of fine nuances in distinctions on the basis of risk.

On the other hand, knowledge that the insertive role carries reduced levels of risk may provide little comfort when the reduction remains unspecified. In the worst case, men may place themselves at risk by judging the insertive role to be less risky than it actually is.

The practice of anal intercourse without ejaculation raised additional questions for our participants. Although they recognized that it is risky—as do the experts (McClure & Grubb, 1999)—some felt that the actual level of risk was ambiguous. The ambiguity here appeared to depend primarily on the success of the insertive partner in withdrawing before ejaculation. Five interviewees described unsafe sexual encounters that were interrupted before orgasm. One (cited above) noted that "no fluids were shared" as a way of explaining that his risk was reduced from what it would have been otherwise. Another man described his encounter with a police officer:

> We started getting into it and he fucked me but he didn't come but I mean afterwards I was completely freaked out because I thought, "Oh my god, oh my god, what did I just do?" When you get caught up in the heat of the moment and before, and before I knew he was going to come, I kind of pushed him off because I knew that was going to happen, and then he ended up coming on my chest which is safe enough. (Gay, 31, HIV-negative, professional)

Participants appeared to be using a common-sense assumption that "less semen means less risk" in order to modify their assessment of the risks of unprotected anal sex. The assumption in these instances may be providing false assurances, however, because of the "impossibility of determining how much preejaculatory fluid has been deposited in the rectum" and the "efficiency of transmission through penile-anal intercourse" (McClure & Grubb, 1999, p. 28).

Seven participants ruminated over the risks of oral sex, Kippax et al. (1990) found this to be an area of ambiguity among Australian gay men in research conducted as early as 1987. This particular ambiguity is likely exacerbated by national differences in education and prevention programs. Whereas official AIDS-education sources in the U.S. have maintained that unprotected oral sex poses risks similar to unprotected anal sex, Canadian authorities classify insertive oral sex as *negligible risk*, receptive oral sex as *low risk*, and insertive and receptive anal sex as *high risk* (McClure & Grubb, 1999). All of the men we interviewed lived in areas that are proximate to the U.S., with regular access to American media (TV, radio, magazines). Moreover, many of the men from Windsor were likely to be regular participants in Detroit gay life (only the Detroit River separates Windsor from Detroit), with frequent exposure to American safe-sex messages (e.g., pamphlets at bars).

Nonetheless, our interviews revealed a widespread consensus among Canadian gay and bisexual men that fellatio without orgasm need not be abandoned to qualify for safe sex. It is interesting to note, however, that official Canadian guidelines (McClure & Grubb, 1999) do not distinguish between fellatio with or without orgasm. For example, a recent poster from the AIDS Committee of Toronto refers to the "ABCs of oral sex and HIV: A—*It*, B—*is*, C—*low risk*," with no reference to ejaculation. The question of swallowing semen during oral sex remains fraught, however, and of concern to gay men around the world (Hospers et al., 1994). Like all of our participants who worried about oral sex, the next man expressed concern about ingestion of semen:

In a bathhouse someone ejaculated in my mouth but generally I try to avoid that, but when that happens, I spit immediately. But in that case, the position was such that he came so deeply in my mouth that I practically swallowed it all. . . . I was more angry with myself perhaps for not having taken the precaution of saying to him, "Don't come in my mouth." I should have said that to him. (Gay/formerly married, 53, HIV-negative, civil servant; translated from French)

Another man made the following observation:

So I think I ended up having oral sex with four or five guys, but I don't remember

exactly, I don't know if I swallowed or not. . . .

You would consider swallowing to be unsafe?

To an extent, yeah, it is, for me, I don't do it often. It's just when there's a lot more [semen] involved, you're sure [HIV-infection] would happen. (Gay, 33, HIV-negative, researcher)

Some men established practices that made them feel more secure about oral sex. For example, a few participants described routines that combined not swallowing with other hygienic practices. One remarked:

I didn't swallow it, if that is what you mean by safe. It was as far as I am concerned. Well, the fact that I did not swallow it, and I rinsed right after. I went over to the sink, and washed my hands and rinsed my mouth, and left. (Gay, 31, HIV-positive, cabinet maker)

Again, men appear to rely on a combination of official knowledge (oral sex is low risk, at least in Canada) and unofficial knowledge (less semen = less risk) in devising such routines, particularly when the scientific literature is ambiguous. This ambiguity is illustrated in the Canadian guidelines, which classify receptive fellatio with or without taking semen in the mouth as low risk, yet specify that the risk "can be reduced by avoiding ejaculation of semen in the mouth" (McClure & Grubb, 1999, p. 24).

A final quote from a participant who was confused about the risk of anilingus is particularly illuminating: "I don't know what the official stand is on anilingus, you know, rimming and that" (Gay, 34, HIV-negative, teacher). Canadian authorities consider anilingus to have negligible risk for transmitting HIV (McClure & Grubb, 1999). Regardless, it is the mention of an "official stand" that is interesting here. The term combines the idea of authority with a sense that expertise exists at a level distinct from practical, everyday solutions. Indeed, in at least four different sexual contexts (sex within a committed relationship, insertive anal sex, anal sex without ejaculation, and oral sex with ejaculation), participants appear to incorporate official knowledge with unofficial knowledge to arrive at a practical solution. In some cases, the resulting solution may be overly safe. In others, it may not be safe enough.

Conclusions and Implications

We interviewed homosexually active men in order to examine the factors and considerations that influence whether men engage in unsafe sexual practices. Interviewees' responses confirmed that factors other than lack of knowledge play a central role in deciding to have unsafe sex and rationalizing about it afterward. Indeed, our participants exhibited levels of AIDS knowledge that appeared to be remarkably sophisticated and to extend well beyond the information provided in most HIV-prevention campaigns. Our findings suggest that HIV-prevention programs might benefit from engaging with the rich understandings of sexual risk and safety that many men have already developed. Such an approach would need to address directly the issues at the forefront of the minds of gay and bisexual men, such as avoiding ejaculation during anal and oral sex, the distinction between the insertive and receptive roles in anal sex, and whether condoms are needed in couple relationships.

Although safe-sex campaigns often convey universal messages ("Use a condom every time"), such a straightforward and simplistic approach may not fit well with the emotional complexities that influence the sexual practices of men with regular partners. Many couples have worked out unique and creative ways to make sex safe in the context of an ongoing relationship. Such strategies may be specific to a particular couple or may remain problematic to varying degrees. Nonetheless, for prevention programs to be effective, they may need to address these individual strategies head-on, highlighting what works and what does not. In short, for gay male HIV-prevention programs to have continuing efficacy and relevance, they may be compelled to engage with the issues that are at the forefront of the population they intend to serve. In Australia (see Kippax et al., 1993; Rotello, 1995) and Canada (Maxwell, 1997), specific education campaigns have been designed around the negotiation of safety in couple relationships. These campaigns include discussion of abandoning condoms between two HIV-negative men while making explicit the need for clear communication and trust between partners.

Some of our participants attempted to make their sexual lives compatible with the desire to communicate trust in couple relationships. Such attempts met with varying degrees of success. The degree to which condom use can be equated with the message "I don't trust you" appears to be directly associated with the degree to which the abandonment of condoms is interpreted as a sign of fidelity. This logic was conveyed on billboards in the streets of Geneva during the 12th World AIDS Conference which read (roughly translating from French), "Not faithful in bed, faithful to condoms." The implicit logic of this advertisement may be self-negating because it identifies safe sex as a practice of morally dubious people. Male homosexual couples may be less susceptible to this logic than their heterosexual counterparts, however, because they are less likely to treat monogamy as an essential sign of love or trustworthiness.

Our data suggest that safe-sex education programs may benefit by addressing the ambiguous risks of particular sex acts. Several of our participants' accounts took the form of retrospective inquiries about the safety of a particular sexual interaction. In these cases, participants attempted to apply scientific knowledge of what constitutes "safety" to their own experiences and were sometimes left in doubt in the end. Other participants relied on a variety of discourses about determining safety that, at times, intersected and diverged from the discourses propounded by public-health authorities and community-based AIDS organizations. Many of these reports of unsafe sex revealed the instability and permeability of the boundaries that separate safe from unsafe. Moreover, participants' responses highlighted the limitations of prevention strategies that ignore the emotional and communicative value of sexual expression. Unsafe practices are not so much a question of a lack of knowledge or the disablement of reason, but the result of a complex consideration of scientific and nonscientific factors that will need to be addressed if HIV-transmission is to be affected.

In some cases, ill-advised prevention strategies that have little relevance to gay men may actually end up promoting unsafe sex, albeit inadvertently. For example, the "know your partner" advice propagated by public-health authorities—especially common in the early days of the epidemic—allows people to exempt themselves from the need for safe sex by "reading signs" of their partner's putative safety (Ames et al., 1995). Indeed, our data show that some homosexually-active men attempt to intuit their partner's HIV status on the basis of unreliable signs (e.g., age and heterosexuality). A related study of U.S. college students (Misovich, Fisher, & Fisher, 1996), reported that it was common for students to believe that knowing a partner well made safe sex unnecessary. Moreover, students who held this belief were significantly less likely than other students to adopt safe-sex practices. The differences between our sample and the one examined by Misovich et al. (i.e., Canadian vs. American, homosexually-active men vs. heterosexual men and women, a wide range of ages with a mean of 35 vs. a narrow range with a mean of 20), as well as the difference between methods (qualitative interviews vs. quantitative questionnaires) imply that this finding may generalize widely. In other words, "know your partner" strategies may be relatively counter-productive across populations.

The relatively sophisticated and nuanced levels of knowledge exhibited by our participants raise additional questions about the efficacy of prevention programs that appear to assume widespread ignorance among their target populations. From our perspective, health-education programs should attempt to engage with existing cultures and stocks of knowledge rather than intervening with a vacuum of "ignorance." Some American programs are particularly curious in this regard, having deviated markedly throughout the history of the epidemic from those in Canada, Australia, and Europe regarding the

risks of oral sex. For example, Gay Men's Health Crisis (the largest and oldest AIDS organization in the U.S.) currently classifies oral sex as high-risk behavior, albeit with a caveat noting that oral sex is less risky than anal sex (Gay Men's Health Crisis, 1999a). They also note that "the biggest risk from oral sex is getting cum in the mouth. The only way to be totally safe is to lick only the shaft or to use a condom" (Gay Men's Health Crisis, 1999b). When American gay men are asked about sex with casual partners, however, most endorse the use of condoms for anal sex but not for oral sex (e.g., Herek & Glunt, 1995). In other words, the behavior and attitudes of American gay and bisexual men are similar to those of our Canadian participants. Moreover, many American researchers who study the sexual behavior of gay and bisexual men classify unsafe sex simply as "unprotected anal sex" (e.g., Kelly et al., 1991, 1995; Peterson et al., 1992), which implies that any act of oral sex is relatively safe. In short, education programs that are inconsistent with the views of experts and the opinions and practices of their target audience may need to be rethought.

Participants' responses highlighted the dangers of the bedrock semiotic binary of our culture, which equates homosexuality with sexual risk and heterosexuality with safety. This equation influences gay and bisexual men in their decisions about whether to adopt or to drop safe sex. Men who are deemed to be "straight" according to superficial signs are sometimes treated as if they pose no risk for HIV infection. Thus, cultural identification of AIDS with homosexuality contributes to increasing unsafe sex among men, apart from generating mass complacency among heterosexual men and women.

For some men who have sex with men, personal crises—whether extraneous to sexuality (such as job loss or depression) or intrinsic (coming out under difficult circumstances)—appear to be associated with unsafe sex and other risky activities. In particular, the coming-out processes of married men and conservative, religious men may involve considerable personal turmoil that is associated with unsafe practices. Although conventional public-health strategies typically hold individuals responsible for preventing HIV transmission, our interviews showed the harmful effects on some men of homophobic ideologies that can lead to personal conflicts about using condoms during sex.

When describing instances of unsafe sex, none of our respondents mentioned rationales that have attracted a good deal of media attention, political debate, and research funding, namely (a) that new drug combinations have made gay men complacent about safe sex, (b) that gay men are succumbing to an ideology of "bare backing" as a result of AIDS fatigue or as a backlash against safe sex, or (c) that the unreliability of condoms jeopardizes safe sex. Some of these perceived problems may be more conjecture than fact. Although much less attention is being targeted toward the complex problems associated with the emotional aspects of sexual relationships and the sometimes ambiguous boundaries between safe and unsafe activity, our data imply that these types of problems influence the decision-making processes that surround safe sex.

Ultimately, gay and bisexual men need to have the opportunity to think carefully about the issues raised in these findings and those reported in similar studies. Such a process could be facilitated by prevention programs that deal in a straightforward manner with issues that are of greatest concern to homosexually active men. When populations are relatively well informed about HIV and AIDS, a shift in emphasis from knowledge of AIDS to the complexities of sexual practice may help people navigate through the snares and pitfalls that lead to exposure to HIV. It is particularly important to abandon the assumption that a single "correct" strategy can deal with multiple difficult issues, which are often idiosyncratic and context-specific. As it stands now, men who have sex with men sometimes exempt themselves from risk categories on the basis of moralistic or otherwise ill-advised judgements about appropriate sexual comportment. Ironically, those who exempt themselves *from* risk often engage in practices that place them *at* risk. Exposure of these discursive

tangles that organize everyday life merits a place in HIV-prevention programs.

Notes

1. We are aware of the shift in terminology from safe to safer adopted by some researchers and educators. We chose to use "safe" because we were interested in the construction of safety made by our participants, most of whom referred to "safe" sex.

2. Preliminary quantitative analyses of the sexual-behaviors and demographics questionnaires revealed that recent participation in unprotected anal sex (i.e., in the 6 months prior to the interview) was not associated with respondents' age, income, occupation, or cultural background.

3. The interviewers did not define unsafe for the participants. In fact, many participants had definitions that diverged from standards used by AIDS researchers and organizations.

References

Adam, B. D. (1992). Sociology and people living with AIDS. In J. Huber & B. E. Schneider (eds.), *The social context of AIDS* (pp. 3–18). Newbury Park, CA: Sage.

Adam, B. D., & Sears, A. (1996). *Experiencing HIV: Personal, family, and work relationships.* New York: Columbia University Press.

Adib, S. M., Joseph, J. G., Ostrow, D. G., & James, S. A. (1991). Predictors of relapse in sexual practices among homosexual men. *AIDS Education and Prevention, 3,* 293–304.

Afifi, W. A. (1999). Harming the ones we love: Relational attachment and perceived consequences as predictors of safe-sex behavior. *The Journal of Sex Research, 36,* 198–206.

Altman, D. (1994). *Power and community: Organizational and cultural responses to AIDS.* London: Taylor & Francis.

Ames, L., Atchinson, A., & Rose, D. T. (1995). Love, lust, and fear. *Journal of Homosexuality, 30,* 53–73.

Aveline, D. T. (1995). A typology of perceived HIV/AIDS risk-reduction strategies used by men who "cruise" other men for anonymous sex. *The Journal of Sex Research, 32,* 223–234.

Bartos, M. (1994). Community vs population. In P. Aggleton, P. Davies, & G. Hart (eds.), *AIDS: Foundations for the future* (pp. 81–96). London: Taylor & Francis.

Bartos, M., McLeod, J., & Nott, P. (1993). *Meanings of sex between men.* Canberra, Australia: Australian Government.

Bolton, R., Vincke, J., Mak, R., & Dennehy, E. (1992). Alcohol and risky sex: In search of an elusive connection. *Medical Anthropology, 14,* 323–363.

Boulton, M., McLean, J., Fitzpatrick, R., & Hart, G. (1995). Gay men's accounts of unsafe sex. *AIDS Care, 7,* 619–630.

Carballo-Dieguez, A., Remien, R. H., Dolezal, C., & Wagner, G. (1999). Reliability of sexual behavior self-reports in male couples of discordant HIV status. *The Journal of Sex Research, 36,* 152–158.

Catania, J. A., Kegeles, S. M., & Coates, T. J. (1990). Towards an understanding of risk behavior: An AIDS risk reduction model (ARRM). *Health Education Quarterly, 17,* 53–72.

Connell, R. W., Davis, M. D., & Dowsett, G. W. (1993). A bastard of a life. *Australian and New Zealand Journal of Sociology, 29,* 112–135.

Díaz, R. M. (1997). Latino gay men and psychocultural barriers to AIDS prevention. In M. P. Levine, P. M. Nardi, & J. M. Gagnon (eds.), *In changing times: Gay men and lesbians encounter HIV/AIDS* (pp. 222–244). Chicago: University of Chicago Press.

——. (1998). *Latino gay men and HIV: Culture, sexuality, and risk behavior.* New York: Routledge.

Donovan, C., Mearns, C., McEwan, R., & Sugden, N. (1994). A review of the HIV-related sexual behavior of gay men and men who have sex with men. *AIDS Care, 6,* 605–617.

Dowsett, G. W. (1990). Reaching men who have sex with men in Australia: An overview of AIDS education, community intervention and community attachment strategies. *Australian Journal of Social Issues, 25,* 186–198.

——. (1996). *Practicing desire: Homosexual sex in the era of AIDS.* Stanford, CA: Stanford University Press.

Ekstrand, M. L., & Coates, T. J. (1990). Maintenance of safer sexual behaviors and predictors of risky sex: The San Francisco men's health study. *American Journal of Public Health, 80,* 973–977.

Fisher, J. D., Fisher, W. A., Williams, S. S., & Malloy, T. E. (1994). Empirical tests of an information-motivation-behavioral skills model of AIDS-preventive behavior with gay men and heterosexual university students. *Health Psychology, 13,* 238–250.

Flowers, P., Sheeran, P., Beail, N., & Smith, J. A. (1997). The role of psychosocial factors in HIV risk-reduction among gay and bisexual men: A quantitative review. *Psychology and Health, 12,* 197–230.

Flowers, P., Smith, J. A., Sheeran, P., & Beail, N. (1997). Health and romance. *British Journal of Health Psychology, 2,* 73–86.

Gaies, L. A., Sacco, W. P., & Becker, J. A. (1995). Cognitions of gay and bisexual men in sexual situations: Development of the Sex and AIDS Thought Scale (SATS). *AIDS Education and Prevention, 7,* 513–522.

Gay Men's Health Crisis. (1999a). *HIV & AIDS: The basics.* Retrieved June 14, 1999 from the World Wide Web: *http://www.gmhc.org/stopping/basics.html.*

——. (1999b). *Safer sex guidelines for gay men.* Retrieved June 14, 1999 from the World Wide Web: *http://www.gmhc.org/stopping/disclaimer/gaymen.html.*

Glaser, B. G., & Strauss, A. L. (1967). *The discovery of grounded theory: Strategies for qualitative research.* Chicago: Aldine.

Gold, R. S., Skinner, M. J., & Ross, M. W. (1994). Unprotected anal intercourse in HIV-infected and non-HIV-infected gay men. *The Journal of Sex Research, 31,* 59–77.

Gruer, L. D., & Ssembatya-Lule, G. (1993). Sexual behavior and use of the condom by men attending gay bars and clubs in Glasgow and Edinburgh. *International Journal of STD & AIDS, 4,* 95–98.

Hart, G., Boulton, M., Fitzpatrick, R., McLean, J., & Dawson, J. (1992). 'Relapse' to unsafe behavior among gay men: A critique of recent behavioural HIV/AIDS research. *Sociology of Health and Illness, 14,* 216–232.

Herek, G. M., & Glunt, E. K. (1995). Identity and community among gay and bisexual men in the AIDS era: Preliminary findings from the Sacramento men's health study. In G. M. Herek & B. Greene (eds.), *AIDS, identity, and community: The HIV epidemic and lesbians and gay men* (pp. 55–84). Thousand Oaks, CA: Sage.

Hospers, H., Molenaar, S., & Kok, G. (1994). Focus group interviews with risk-taking gay men. *Patient Education and Counseling, 24,* 299–306.

Hunt, A. J., Weatherburn, P., Hickson, F. C. I., Davies, P. M., McManus, T. J., & Coxon, A. P. M. (1993). Changes in condom use by gay men. *AIDS Care, 5,* 439–448.

Jadack, R. A., Hyde, J. S., & Keller, M. L. (1995). Gender and knowledge about HIV, risky sexual behavior, and safer sex practices. *Research in Nursing & Health, 18,* 313–324.

Joffe, H. (1996). AIDS research and prevention: A social representational approach. *British Journal of Medical Psychology, 69,* 169–190.

Kalichman, S. C., Johnson, J. R., Adair, V., Rompa, D., Multhauf, K., & Kelly, J. A. (1994).

Sexual sensation seeking: Scale development and predicting AIDS-risk behavior among homosexually active men. *Journal of Personality Assessment, 62,* 385–397.

Kelly, J. A., Kalichman, S. C., Kauth, M. R., Kilgore, H. G., Hood, H. V., Campos, P. E., Rao, S. M., Brasfield, T. L., & St. Lawrence, J. S. (1991). Situational factors associated with AIDS risk behavior lapses and coping strategies used by gay men who successfully avoid lapses. *American Journal of Public Health, 81,* 1335–1338.

Kelly, J. A., Sikkema, K. J., Winett, R. A., Solomon, L. J., Roffman, R. A., Heckman, T. G., Stevenson, L. Y., Perry, M. J., Norman, A. D., & Desiderato, L. J. (1995). Factors predicting continued high-risk behavior among gay men in small cities: Psychological, behavioral, and demographic characteristics related to unsafe sex. *Journal of Consulting and Clinical Psychology, 63,* 101–107.

King, E. (1993). *Safety in numbers: Safer sex and gay men.* New York: Routledge.

Kippax, S., Connell, R. W., Dowsett, G. W., & Crawford, J. (1993). *Sustaining safe sex: Gay communities respond to AIDS.* London: Falmer.

Kippax, S., Crawford, J., Dowsett, G. W., Bond, G., Sinnott, V., Baxter, D., Berg, R., Connell, R. W., & Watson, L. (1990). Gay men's knowledge of HIV transmission and 'safe' sex: A question of accuracy. *Australian Journal of Social Issues, 25,* 199–219.

Landrine, H. (ed.) (1995). *Bringing cultural diversity to feminist psychology: Theory, research, and practice.* Washington, DC: American Psychological Association.

Leigh, B. C. (1990). The relationship of substance use during sex to high-risk sexual behavior. *The Journal of Sex Research, 27,* 199–213.

Levine, M. P., & Siegel, K. (1992). Unprotected sex: Understanding gay men's participation. In J. Huber & B. E. Schneider (eds.), *The social context of AIDS* (pp. 47–71). Newbury Park, CA: Sage.

Lewis, J. E., Malow, R. M., & Ireland, S. J. (1997). HIV/AIDS risk in heterosexual college students: A review of a decade of literature. *Journal of American College Health, 45,* 147–158.

Lewis, L. A., & Ross, M. W. (1995). *A select body: The gay dance party subculture and the HIV/AIDS pandemic.* London: Cassell.

Lowy, E., & Ross, M. (1994). It'll never happen to me. *AIDS Education and Prevention, 6,* 467–482.

Maticka-Tyndale, E. (1992). Social construction of HIV transmission and prevention among heterosexual young adults. *Social Problems, 39,* 238–252.

Maxwell, A. E., Bastani, R., & Yan, K. X. (1995). AIDS risk behaviors and correlates in teenagers attending sexually transmitted diseases clinics in Los Angeles. *Genitourinary Medicine, 71,* 82–87.

Maxwell, C., & Boyle, M. (1995). Risky heterosexual practices among women over 30: Gender, power, and long term relationships. *AIDS Care, 7,* 277–293.

Maxwell, J. (1997). *I can relate: Gay men, relationships, condoms.* Retrieved June 14, 1999 from the World Wide Web: *http://www.actoronto.org/cl/safersex.nsf.*

McAndrew, C., & Edgerton, R. B. (1969). *Drunken comportment: A social explanation.* Chicago: Aldine.

McClure, C., & Grubb, I. (1999). *HIV transmission: Guidelines for assessing risk* (3rd ed.). Ottawa, Canada: Canadian AIDS Society.

McCusker, J., Stoddard, A. M., McDonald, M., Zapka, J. G., & Mayer, K. H. (1992). Maintenance of behavioral change in a cohort of homosexually active men. *AIDS, 6,* 861–868.

Meyer, I. H., & Dean, L. (1995). Patterns of sexual behavior and risk taking among young New York City gay men. *AIDS Education and Prevention, 7* (Suppl.), 13–23.

Misovich, S. J., Fisher, J. D., & Fisher, W. A. (1996). The perceived AIDS-preventive utility of knowing one's partner well: A public health dictum and individuals' risky sexual behavior. *Canadian Journal of Human Sexuality, 5,* 83–90.

Myers, T., Godin, G., Calzavara, L., Lambert, J., & Locker, D. (1993). *The Canadian survey of gay and bisexual men and HIV infection: Men's survey.* Ottawa, Canada: Canadian AIDS Society.

Myers, T., Rowe, C. J., Tudiver, F. G., Kurtz, R. G., Jackson, E. A., Orr, K. W., & Bullock, S. L. (1992). HIV, substance use and related behavior of gay and bisexual men: An examination of the talking sex project. *British Journal of Addiction, 87,* 207–214.

Myrick, R. (1999). In the life: Culture-specific HIV communication programs designed for African American men who have sex with men. *The Journal of Sex Research, 36,* 159–170.

Nemeroff, C. J. (1995). Magical thinking about illness virulence: Conceptions of germs from "safe" and "dangerous" others. *Health Psychology, 14,* 147–151.

Odets, W. (1994). AIDS education and harm reduction for gay men. *AIDS & Public Policy Journal, 9,* 3–15.

Odets, W. (1995). *In the shadow of the epidemic: Being HIV-negative in the age of AIDS.* Durham, NC: Duke University Press.

O'Donnell, L., San Doval, A., Vornfett, R., & O'Donnell, C. R. (1994). STD prevention and challenge of gender and cultural diversity: Knowledge, attitudes, and risk behaviors among Black and Hispanic inner-city STD clinic patients. *Sexually Transmitted Diseases, 21,* 137–148.

Offir, J. T., Fisher, J. D., Williams, S. S., & Fisher, W. A. (1993). Reasons for inconsistent AIDS-preventive behaviors among gay men. *The Journal of Sex Research, 30,* 62–69.

Parker, R. G., & Carballo, M. (1990). Qualitative research on homosexual and bisexual behavior relevant to HIV/AIDS. *The Journal of Sex Research, 27,* 497–525.

Paul, J. P., Stall, R., & Davis, F. (1993). Sexual risk for HIV transmission among gay/bisexual men in substance-abuse treatment. *AIDS Education and Prevention, 5,* 11–24.

Penkower, L., Dew, M. A., Kingsley, L., Becker, J. T., Satz, P., Schaerf, F. W., & Sheridan, K. (1991). Behavioral, health and psychosocial factors and risk for HIV infection among sexually active homosexual men: The multicenter AIDS cohort study. *American Journal of Public Health, 81,* 194–196.

Perkins, D. O., Leserman, J., Murphy, C., & Evans, D. L. (1993). Psychosocial predictors of high-risk sexual behavior among HIV-negative homosexual men. *AIDS Education and Prevention, 5,* 141–152.

Peterson, J. L., Coates, T. J., Catania, J. A., Middleton, L., Hilliard, B., & Hearst, N. (1992). High-risk sexual behavior and condom use among gay and bisexual African-American men. *American Journal of Public Health, 82,* 1490–1494.

Pilkington, C. J., Kern, W., & Indest, D. (1994). Is safer sex necessary with a "safe" partner? Condom use and romantic feelings. *The Journal of Sex Research, 31,* 203–210.

Pollak, M. (1988). *Les homosexuels et le sida: Sociologie d'une epidemie* [Gay men and AIDS: Sociology of an epidemic]. Paris: Metailie.

Prieur, A. (1990). Norwegian gay men: Reasons for continued practice of unsafe sex. *AIDS Education and Prevention, 2,* 109–115.

Rotello, G. (1995, February 21). Beyond condoms. *The Advocate,* 80.

Sandfort, T. G. M., & van Zessen, G. (1992). Denial as a barrier for HIV prevention within the general population. *Journal of Psychology and Human Sexuality, 5,* 69–87.

Siegel, K., Mesagno, E. P., Chen, J.-Y., & Christ, G. (1989). Factors distinguishing homosexual males practicing risky and safer sex. *Social Science and Medicine, 28,* 561–569.

Silvestre, A., Lyter, D., Valdiserri, R., Huggins, J., & Rinaldo, C. (1989). Factors related to seroconversion among homo- and bisexual men after attending a risk-reduction educational session. *AIDS, 3,* 647–650.

Smith, D. E. (1987). *The everyday world as problematic: A feminist sociology.* Toronto, Canada: University of Toronto Press.

Sobo, E. J. (1995). *Choosing unsafe sex: AIDS-risk denial among disadvantaged women.* Philadelphia: University of Pennsylvania Press.

Temple, M. T., & Leigh, B. C. (1992). Alcohol consumption and unsafe sexual behavior in discrete events. *The Journal of Sex Research, 29,* 207–219.

Waddell, C. (1992). Social correlates of unsafe sexual intercourse. *Australian and New Zealand Journal of Sociology, 28,* 192–207.

Watney, S. (1989). Taking liberties: An introduction. In E. Carter & S. Watney (eds.), *Taking liberties: AIDS and cultural politics* (pp. 11–57). London: Serpent's Tail.

Weatherburn, P., Davies, P. M., Hickson, F. C. I., Hunt, A. J., McManus, T. J., & Coxon, A. P. M. (1993). No connection between alcohol use and unsafe sex among gay and bisexual men. *AIDS, 7,* 115–119.

Williams, S. S., Kimble, D. L., Covell, N. H., Weiss, L. H., Newton, K. J., Fisher, J. D., & Fisher, W. A. (1992). College students use implicit personality theory instead of safer sex. *Journal of Applied Social Psychology, 22,* 921–933.

32
Turn-Ons for Money

Interactional Strategies of the Table Dancer

Carol Rambo Ronai

Carolyn Ellis

In many ways, sexuality is a commodity just like any other that is bought and sold in a marketplace. It has value, it can be exchanged, and its exchange invokes distinct forms of social organization. But sexuality is unique because it is so strongly regulated as to time, place, content, and context. Paradoxically, sex also is in tremendous demand, particularly among men who are taught that an insatiable sexual appetite is culturally acceptable. Scarce resources in high demand invariably spawn markets to remove that scarcity. Table dancing, or "stripping," has emerged in part for this reason.

Women take off their clothes for money; the men who pay them—and they are almost always men—receive physical, erotic, emotional, and especially sexual gratification in return. The exchange is based on principle of "counterfeit intimacy"; dancers act as if they are sexually interested, but their interest is only as deep as the pockets of those from whom they hope to secure tips.

Ronai and Ellis explore the interactional strategies that table dancers use to cultivate counterfeit intimacy—how they develop a "perceptual shorthand" (Skolnick 1966) to distinguish good tippers from bad ones, how they identify men who might be too sexually forward or expect too much, and how they single out men who might consume too much of their attention. Indeed, Ronai and Ellis observe that some men enter such clubs more in search of a girlfriend or a wife than a striptease. Table dancers generally want no part of

such persons and will "lead them on" to secure gifts, money, and other material rewards, after which the man's advances are politely declined.

Significantly, the authors paint a picture of empowerment in a disempowering context. Stripping for money is not a high-status profession (in most cases), but it is a significant source of material rewards nonetheless, rewards realistically available in few other female vocations. Patriarchal oppression is ultimately responsible for this state of affairs, but Ronai and Ellis contend that table dancers come out ahead in the end: Gender becomes a resource with which to beat men at their own game. Dancers emerge as freewheeling entrepreneurs who carve out their own autonomous niche in an otherwise oppressive context, using expressive deviance and microstrategies of resistance to exploit men for money, goods, and services, even as they entice their male targets to believe that the men actually are in control.

She swayed from side to side above him, her hands on his shoulders, her knee brushing gently against the bulge in his pants. He looked up at the bottom of her breasts, close enough to touch, but subtly forbidden. His breath came in ever shorter gasps.

This is the world of the table dancer—a world where women exchange titillating dances for money. Our study looks at the dynamic processes of interaction that occur in the exchange. Previous studies (Carey et al., 1974; Gonos, 1976; McCaghy and Skipper, 1969, 1972; Salutin, 1971; Skipper and McCaghy, 1970, 1971) have concentrated on "burlesque" or "go-go" dancers, sometimes referring to them more generally as stripteasers. Dancers' interactions with customers were restricted, for the most part, to the stage setting where they danced and received money from customers. Because investigators in these studies occupied positions as researchers or researchers as customers, and relied to a large extent on survey and interview techniques, this work led to a static description of this occupation.

Boles and Garbin (1974) have looked at customer-stripper interaction in a setting where strippers sold drinks in addition to performing stage acts. Although they described interaction, they interpreted it in terms of norms, club motif, and customer goals. They found that the conflict between customers' goals and strippers' goals resulted in "counterfeit intimacy" (Foote, 1954), a situation in which an aura of intimacy masked mutually exploitative interactions.

Although counterfeit intimacy is a structural reality in such contexts, this description created another model of behavior that ignored the interactive, dynamic nature of the exchanges and set up in its place stiff caricatures behaving in an unbending, cardboard manner. As actors get caught up in dialogue, they exchange symbols, extract meanings, and modify expectations of what goals they can reasonably expect to reach. Interaction has a tentative quality (Blumer, 1969; Turner, 1962); goals are in a constant state of flux.

The nature of selling and performing table dances that we describe yields more opportunity for interaction between customer and dancer than in previous studies. A table dancer must be a charming and sexy companion, keep the customer interested and turned on, make him feel special, and be a good reader of character and a successful salesperson; at the same time, she must deal with her own negative feelings about the customer or herself, negotiate limits, and then keep him under control to avoid getting fired by management.

Much of the early research literature has described stripping as a deviant occupation. Later, Prus and Irini (1980) looked at stripping as conforming to the norms of a bar subculture. Demystifying this "deviant" activity even further, we show that bargaining strategies in the bar actually mirror "respectable" negotiation in mainstream culture.

We begin by discussing the methods we used to elicit indepth understanding of strategies used by table dancers. After describing the dance club setting, we turn to a description and analysis of particular tactics used on the stage, at the tables between stage acts, and then during the table dances in the pits.

Our conclusion analyzes how this exchange reflects buying and selling in service occupations as well as the negotiation of gender relationships in mainstream society.

Methods

Our study approaches stripping from the point of view of dancers and the dancer as researcher, the people with the most access to the thoughts, feelings, and strategies of exotic dancers. Dancers concentrate on manipulating men as they pursue money in exchange for a turn-on. In order for their strategies to work, they must understand and coordinate them with the games of men.

Our information comes primarily from the experiences of the first author who danced during 1984 and 1985 to pay her way through school. As a "complete-member-researcher" (Adler and Adler, 1987), she conducted opportunistic research (Riemer, 1977), that is, she studied a setting in which she was already a member. She interviewed dancers to find out how and why they began this occupation and kept a journal of events that happened while dancing. Later, she reconstructed, in chronological field notes, a retrospective account of her own dancing history, paying special attention to strategies, emotion work, and identity issues. She used "systematic sociological introspection" (Ellis, forthcoming) to put herself mentally and emotionally back into her experiences and record what she remembered (see Bulmer's, 1982, concept of "retrospective participant observation").

In May 1987, the first author danced in one strip bar for the explicit purpose of gathering data for a master's thesis, chaired by the second author. With approval of bar management, but without the knowledge of other dancers, she acted in the dual capacity of researcher and dancer. This time her primary identity was that of researcher, although as a complete member-researcher she attempted to "become the phenomenon" (Adler and Adler, 1987; Jorgensen, 1989; Mehan and Wood, 1975). When she danced, she took on the identity of a dancer, suffered identity conflicts similar to those she had experienced during earlier dancing, and shared a common set of experiences and feelings with other dancers. She kept field notes of events, which were buttressed by "interactive introspection" (Ellis, 1988), whereas the second author talked her through her experiences, probing at and recording her feelings and thoughts. She conducted informal interviews in the dressing room with dancers and on the floor with customers. Sometimes she revealed her dual role to customers as a strategy to keep them interested in spending more money and to get them to introspect about their own motives for being in the bar.

Because this article is concerned with describing dancers' subtle manipulation strategies that occurred semiprivately, we pulled much of our material from episodes engaged in by the first author, in which process was most easily observed. Because we believe that sociologists should acknowledge the role of their own introspection in their research (Ellis, forthcoming), the first author reveals which of the experiences in the article are hers. Throughout this article, we refer to the first author by her dancer name, Sabrina.

We realize the bias inherent in using introspection primarily from one source. For example, Sabrina, more than most dancers, tended to attract customers interested in mental stimulation as well as physical turn-on. Yet we could not have gained an in-depth understanding of intimate exchange, for example during table dances, in any other way. To understand this bias, we compared Sabrina's strategies and experiences with those of other dancers we observed and other bar participants with whom we talked. Later in 1987, we conducted interviews with four strippers, eight customers, four managers, three bar owners, and a law officer. This article then uses a triangulated method (Denzin, 1978; Webb et al., 1965) to present typical responses from field work and in-depth ones from current and retrospective introspection.

Setting

An exotic dance club located in the Tampa Bay area of Florida provided the setting for this study. Since liquor was served, full nudity was prohibited by state law. Appearing individually in full costume on stage, each stripper gradually removed her clothing during a dance routine. By the end of the act, the dancer wore pasties that concealed her nipples and panties that covered genitals, pubic hair, and the cheeks of her derriere. Men handed out tips to dancers during performances.

Between acts, dancers strolled around the floor, making themselves available to spend time with customers. They made money if customers bought them drinks. However, the main attraction and source of income in this bar was the table dance. A dancer "sold" dances in a complicated negotiation process through which she convinced the client that he was turned on to her and/or that she was turned on to him. At the same time, she controlled the situation so that she was not caught disobeying "house" rules, many of which corresponded to what county authorities considered illegal. For example, since "charging" for a table dance was considered soliciting, the dancer, using word games similar to those used by the masseuse studied by Rasmussen and Kuhn (1976), suggested that there was "generally a contribution of $5."

After a dancer successfully sold a dance, she led her customer to one of the two elevated corners of the bar, known generically as the "The Pit," and affectionately nicknamed by customers as "Horny Holler" and "The Passion Pit." Railings and dim lights offered an artificial boundary between this area and the rest of the bar. Clothed in a bra-like top and full panties or other revealing costume, the dancer leaned over a seated patron, her legs inside his, and swayed suggestively in rhythm to the music playing in the bar. Theoretically, customers were allowed to touch only the hips, waist, back, and outside of a dancer's legs. Many men tried and some succeeded in doing more. Disobeying rules prohibiting direct sexual stimulation or touching meant more money for dancers, but it also meant risking that management might reprimand them or that a "customer" would turn out to be an undercover officer or a representative looking for infractions on behalf of club management.

Elements of Strategy

On the Stage

A dancer used symbols that appealed to her audience. At the same time, these symbols distanced her from customers and denoted that the stage was a performance frame (Goffman, 1974; Mullen, 1985). Her appearance, eye contact, manner, and choice of music made up her main expressive equipment.

Having a "centerfold" figure was an obvious asset for dancers. But the best looking woman did not always make the most money. A dancer's presentation of self was also a crucial factor in a customer's decision to tip her. Similar to strippers described by Gonos (1976) and Robboy (1985), women often portrayed exaggerated stereotypes through their clothing style and movement. For instance, a "vamp style" dancer wore suggestive street clothing such as a leather micro-mini skirt, spike-heeled boots, and a halter-style top while strutting around the stage displaying overt sexual mannerisms such as "flushing" (opening her shirt to reveal her pasty-clad breasts). Others had a "gimmick." For example, one woman was an acrobat; another stood on her head while twirling her large breasts. In contrast, a more sensual dancer dressed in sexy bedroom clothing such as a corset and garters or a teddy, and displayed subtle sensual behavior such as slow undulation of the hips.

A dancer chose symbols that drew a certain type of customer to her. Dressing the part of the vamp, for example, reflected an extroverted attitude that attracted customers out to have a good time. Overtly sexual dancers were more likely to perform sexual favors in the bar or meet a man for sex outside the bar. The sensual presentation of self attracted customers who were interested in a "serious," private interaction. Customers interpreted each dancer's symbols as cues to what it might be like to interact with her or, specifically, to have sex with her. For example, Tim, a regular customer, discussed Samantha, a sensual dancer: "She is nothing to look at. God, she's only twenty-six, and we both know she looks like forty. But the way she moves, man! She promises the moon and stars in bed."

Most dancers used eye contact to "feel out" a patron. Managing frequent eye contact while dancing on stage usually meant a tip for the dancer and made a customer feel as if a dancer was specifically interested in him.

A dancer's first close contact with a customer often occurred while accepting a tip. During the exchange, the dancer formed impressions about how the customer was reacting to her, and the customer decided whether he was attracted to the woman. The customer stood at the side of the stage holding currency, which signaled the dancer that he wanted to tip her. The dancer greeted him while accepting the tip in her garter and said "thanks," perhaps giving him a "special" look.

At this point, a dancer might choose from several courses of action, such as "coming on" to a customer, doting on a customer, and using humor. When dancers "came on" to customers, they grinned, wiggled their breasts, spread their legs, struck their buttocks, suggestively sucked their fingers, talked dirty, or French kissed.

Others, such as the sensual dancer, doted on a customer for a few seconds. She caressed his arm, wrapped her arms around his neck, and smiled while he tipped her. If she felt confident of his interest, typical comments she might make were: "I would love a chance to get to know you," or "I look forward to sitting with you," which meant accompanying him to his table after her stage performance.

Humor was an effective and safe tool for generating a good impression while accepting a tip on stage. Customers generally construed a funny statement made by a dancer as friendly and spontaneous. Often it made a nervous client more at ease. Sabrina noted lines she used: "What's a nice guy like you doing in a dump like this?" or "I bet you'd look better up here than I do."

Familiar with the usual "acts" of dancers, such as coming on and showing phony interest, customers were pleased when they thought a woman had "dropped the routine." Often this meant only that she had staged a less frequently displayed one. A dancer had to be careful not to use the same line more than once on the same person, or let a customer overhear it being used on another man. No matter a customer's taste, he wanted a sincere performance.

Dick, a customer who was feeling jilted one evening, commented to Sabrina:

> The thing with that chick, Dana, is that she makes a big deal out of you while she is onstage, but if you watch her real close, you notice she looks at everyone who tips her that way.

Another customer reported he did not like a dancer in the bar named Tammy because she was insincere:

> She frenched me and told me to insert my dollar deeply (in her garter). Now I ain't stupid. I know a come on like that is a fake.

A dancer's music affected how a customer viewed her. This was reflected in Tim's comment about Jessica: "That girl has a great body, but every time I hear her music [heavy metal] I get the creeps thinking about what she must be like." While most women danced to top-40 music, some used other music to attract a tip from a particular kind of client. Mae, an older dancer in her late thirties, played country music and presented herself as a country woman. Bikers and blue-collar workers were loyal to Mae, expressing sentiments like: "She's the only real woman in the bar."

On the Floor

Offstage, interaction was even more complex. Between stage performances, a dancer circulated among customers and offered her company. Body language, expressions, and general appearance helped define each customer's interest in her and the difficulty of being with him. Once a dancer located an interested customer and introduced herself, or followed up on a contact made while performing on stage, she then had to convince him that he wanted to spend time with her. Ordinarily, her eventual goal was to sell a table dance.

Choosing a Customer

The ideal customer had a pleasant disposition, was good looking, had time and money to spend, and was sitting at one of the tables on the floor. Most customers did not meet all these criteria. Dancers weighed these features for each customer and also compared them against the circumstances of the evening. Sabrina often asked herself: "What do I want more right now? Money or someone nonthreatening to sit with?" Her answer was different depending upon time of night, how much money she had made already, and how she felt at the moment. Other dancers made the same calculations. For example, three hours before the bar closed one night, Naomi said, "I know this guy I'm sitting with doesn't have a lot of money, but I've made my hundred for the night so l can afford to take it easy." Another time, Vicky said,

> God! I know I should be out there hustling instead of drinking with Jim, but I just can't get into it. I guess I'll just get fucked-up and blow it off today.

Darcy displayed a more typical attitude,

> It's twelve thirty already and I haven't made shit! This guy I'm sitting with better cough it up or I'm taking off.

Negotiations with oneself and with the customer were always in process. Throughout the interaction, each participant tried to ascertain what she or he was willing to give and how much could be acquired from the other.

Attractive customers appeared, at first, more appealing. They were pleasant to look at and the dancer could pretend to be on a date while sitting with them. But these men seemed to know they were more desirable than others in the bar and were more likely to bargain with those resources. The end result was that the dancer spent most of the interaction trying to convince the customer to spend money while he tried to persuade her to go out on a date.

When Sabrina was new to the profession, she decided one evening to sit with a good looking, blonde-haired man. She reported the following:

I started talking to him and eventually led the conversation to the point where I asked, "Would you care for a table dance?"

"Later," he replied.

I continued to make small talk. "Do you come in here often?"

"I stop in once every few months," he responded.

For the next 15 minutes we covered various topics of conversation such as his job and my schooling. Then I asked him again, "Do you want a table dance?"

"Are you going to go to 'le Bistro' with me tomorrow night?"

"I'll think about it," I responded, in hopes of getting a table dance out of him before I turned him down. "Do you want that table dance?"

"Will you go out with me?" he insisted.

"I'm still considering it," I lied. We volleyed back and forth for 30 minutes. Finally, he told me, "I don't want a dance. I just want to know if you will go out with me."

This customer was aware that Sabrina would not stay with him unless she thought he might want a dance. Both used strategies and gambled time hoping one would give in to the other's goals. Each lost a bet.

Sometimes customers who were old, heavy, unattractive, or otherwise weak in social resources came into the bar. Many women avoided these men, while others, like Sabrina, realized unattractive men were eager for company and tended to treat a dancer better and spend more money than their more attractive competitors would. With the right strategies, dancers could control these men. For example, a dancer might corner a customer into treating her as he would his granddaughter by acting polite and addressing him as "sir." This insinuated that, of course, he would never act inappropriately. Some accepted the role to such an extent that they acted like grandfathers. One man told Scarlet that she was cute, tweaked her cheek, and compared her to his granddaughter.

When scanning the bar and deciding whom to approach first, a dancer tried to find the man who appeared to have the most money. Logically, the better a customer was dressed, the more likely he was to have money. However, he also had a higher probability of already being in the company of another dancer.

Making sure a customer was not spoken for by another dancer was important. It was considered dangerous (one could get into an argument) and rude to sit with another dancer's customer. Some regular customers, for instance, visited the bar to see particular dancers. These customers often turned down another dancer's offer of company by saying they were "waiting for someone." When a dancer entered the bar, she immediately scanned the room, paying particular attention to which women were seated with which customers. If she noticed later that a woman had left a table for a long period of time, she then asked her if it was okay to sit with that customer. This served the dual purpose of following tacit rules (i.e., being polite) and gave the dancer an opportunity to gather information about the customer in question.

Sabrina was warned about a customer in this manner. Upon asking Debbie if she was finished with "the old man in the corner wearing a hat," Debbie replied, "Sure, you can have him. That's 'Merv the perv.' He has lots of money, but he'll want to stick his finger up your asshole for twenty bucks a feel."

A dancer might ignore all other customers to sit with one of her "regulars." When two or more of her regulars were in the bar, she had to juggle them, first sitting with one and then the other. It was difficult to table dance for both of them and still portray "special attachment." Eventually, she had to offer an account (Scott and Lyman, 1968) to one of them. One excuse was to appeal to the principle of fairness: "I really want to be with you, but he came in first and now I have to be with him." Or she might appeal to higher loyalties (Sykes and Matza, 1957), insinuating that the decision was out of her control: "I have to go sit with another customer now. My bosses know I avoid him and they're watching me."

Time in the bar correlated with decreased spending. If a customer had been spending for a while, it was fair to assume that he would run out of money or would soon decide to leave, that is, unless he was intoxicated and freely using a credit card. Dancers in this situation risked having to deal with and control a problematic person who did not remember or pay for the correct number of dances purchased. On the other hand, a dancer might convince a drunk credit card customer to pay for more dances than he actually bought.

A customer's location in the bar indicated his attitude toward female company. In this club, sitting at the bar meant little interest in interacting with dancers. Patrons near the stage wanted to see the show. Being seated at one of the tables in the floor area was conducive to interaction with dancers and to inquiries about table dances.

At the Tables

Once a customer accepted an offer of company, a dancer sat with him and introduced herself. Her overall goal remained fairly consistent—money with no hassle. Many women also enjoyed the attention they received and got an exhibitionist thrill out of being desired and told how beautiful they were. Others believed the compliments were just part of the game. Some liked the feeling of conquering and being in control. Others felt degraded and out of control.

The customer's manifest goal was impersonal, sexual turnons for money; a close examination showed other objectives that shadowboxed with and sometimes transcended this more obvious goal. Although most customers initially focused on the pursuit of sex in or outside the bar, they also came looking for a party, to feel good about themselves, to find a friend or companion, or to develop a relationship. A dancer's strategies varied depending on her personality and her perception of the customer.

Some women said nothing. A customer who wanted passive indifference from an attractive female willing to turn him on liked this approach. Sex, not conversation, was his goal. The dancer did not have to initiate ac-

tivity nor get to know the customer. Her role was to respond as a sexual nonperson by allowing him to kiss and fondle her body. Verbal interaction potentially endangered the continuance of the exchange.

Most customers wanted a dancer to interact with them. Seduction rhetoric (Rasmussen and Kuhn, 1976) became part of the dancer's sexual foreplay before the table dance as well as a vehicle for the customer to persuade the dancer to see him outside the bar. By talking "dirty" and acting "like a whore"—for example, telling stories about kinky sex in her life outside the bar—a dancer could keep a customer "going," eager to buy the next dance, ready to believe the dancer might have sex with him later.

If a customer wanted a prostitute, he dropped hints such as, "Do you do work on the side?" or "Where does a guy go for a good time around here?" or "Do you date?" Sometimes he propositioned outright: "Will you go to bed with me for a hundred dollars?" The more blatant proposals told the dancer that the customer was not a police officer; all of the requests informed her he had money to spend and opened up the possibility of using strategies to extract it.

One strategy dancers used in this situation was to mislead a customer into thinking she might meet him later if he bought table dances from her now. From the first author:

> Ted bought dances from me two at a time. After several of these, he asked, "Are you going to see me at the Holiday Inn tonight?"
>
> "Why should I?" I responded.
>
> "Because I am new in town and have lots of money."
>
> "I don't go out with strange men," I said.
>
> "Well, why don't you get to know me then," he said. He bought two more dances, then asked, "Do you know me now?" I smiled at him. He continued, "Why don't you meet me after you're done working. What time do you get off?"
>
> In an effort to shift the focus of the conversation, I said suggestively, "When do you get off?"

"I get off on you baby!" He exclaimed. "I'm in room 207. Will you be there?"

To keep him going while not committing myself, I said, "I don't know." We talked a while, and then he asked again. I replied, "I've never turned a trick in my life. I'm not sure I ever will."

"So we won't do it for money," he said. "Come see me tonight." He buys two more dances and we sit down again. I start the conversation first this time to keep him interested yet deter him from bringing up my meeting him. "Tell me, Ted, what is the kinkiest thing you have ever done in bed." This conversation kept us busy for a while, until, sixty dollars later, he asks, "Do I go to the bank machine or not?"

"What do you mean?" I ask.

"If you are going to see me tonight, I need to go to the teller. I'm out of money."

I had a big grin on my face and asked, "Will you be back here after the teller?"

"Probably not," he replied.

"Too bad," I said.

"Would you see me if I bought more dances?" he asked. I was tempted to say maybe, but I thought at this point I was being too obvious.

"Probably not," I said.

He stood to leave. "You show up tonight at room 207 if you want. It was fun."

Similar to the strippers discussed by Prus and Irini (1980), a few women used the bar setting as a place to make contacts for their prostitution careers, while many more had sex occasionally outside the bar to augment their incomes. Before accepting an offer, a woman usually asked other dancers about the customer or spent time getting to know him. Interacting with him then gave her an opportunity to make money table dancing. Most women claimed they had sex "only for the money." A few, such as Sasha, seemed to enjoy sexual contact in and out of the bar. Sasha's enthusiasm—"I'm so horny, I want a cock tonight"—was deemed deviant by the other dancers, who ostracized her—usually

avoided her and talked behind her back—for her overt enjoyment.

The customer who wanted a date outside the bar could be handled in a similar manner to the customer looking for a prostitute. Often a dancer conveyed the impression, "if only I knew you were safe" by saying: "You could be Jack-the-Ripper," "You could be a cop," "It's not safe to date everyone you meet in here." Then she suggested interest by saying, "I need a chance to get to know you better." The logical way for a dancer to get to know the customer was for him to spend time and money buying drinks and table dances from her. Lured by the offer of expensive dinners or vacations, and sometimes attracted by a man she liked, most dancers occasionally accepted dates.

If customers were in the bar "to party" (to be entertained) in groups, such as bachelor parties, a dancer wasted no time on interaction. She asked immediately if they wanted a dance. These men interacted mostly with each other, requiring dancers to be lively and entertaining hostesses while treating them like sex objects. Often they commented on her body—her big tits, nice ass, or ugly face—as though she were not there. Party groups purchased dances with the same attitude and frequency as they bought rounds of drinks.

Most men who came to the bar seemed to want to find a friend or companion, or in some other way be treated as a special person. One of Sabrina's customers left the bar twice during an evening to change shirts, just to see if she recognized him when he returned. The best ploy in this situation was for the dancer to put on an honest front, altercasting (Weinstein and Deutschberger, 1963) her customer into the role of being special and "different" from other men.

Most successful dancers were able to hold conversations with these men. Asking his name, where he lived, occupation, and what he did with his spare time provided initial interaction. Finding common ground helped conversation run smoothly. Asking questions at a leisurely pace, making comments, and showing interest both verbally and nonverbally afforded a semblance of credibility to the conversational process. This dialogue helped the dancer to "check out" (Rasmussen and Kuhn, 1976) the customer to make sure he was not a police officer, determine how much money he had to spend and which of her interactional strategies might make him willing to part with it. Giving the customer an opportunity to talk about himself and to demonstrate whatever expertise he had made him feel good about himself. A customer pleased with his presentation of self was more apt to spend money. Sabrina told this story:

> In the field, I had a regular customer, Ray, who was a systems' analyst. I was shopping for a computer at the time, so I enlisted Ray's assistance. Ray had an opportunity to show off his expertise, and feel like he was helping. He turned-on to the contrast of seeing me as intellectual and a sex object.

The best way for a dancer to convince a customer that she found him appealing and unique was to find a likable characteristic about the customer and continually tell him how impressed she was with him and with that trait. For example, some men liked to be praised for their appearance, success, intelligence, sexual desirability, trustworthiness, or sensitivity. The dancer had to convey to him directly that she preferred his company to others in the bar, or indirectly through such statements as "You're not as vulgar as the rest of these guys in here"; "You're more intelligent than most men I meet in here"; "You're not just another one of these assholes," or "I appreciate your spending time with me. When I'm sitting with you I'm safe from those animals out there." The message was that because of his specialness, she could be "straight" with him, be who she really was, instead of putting on one of her usual acts.

This tactic worked best with customers the dancer liked and enjoyed talking to; otherwise, it was difficult to muster up and maintain the sincerity necessary for a believable performance. When this strategy worked, the dancer had close to total control of the interaction. Then the customer tried hard to meet the dancer's expectations, spending money and treating her like a date or friend to avoid disappointing her. If he stopped spending money, the dancer might say, and sometimes mean:

> I'll see you later. Don't get angry with me. I know you understand that I have to make money, although I would rather spend time with you. If I don't find anything, I'll come back and visit.

Sometimes the customer responded by spending more money to keep the dancer around. If not, he was forced to "understand" her leaving because he and the dancer had an honest relationship and she had been "straight" with him about the nature of her job. This strategy was an effective way to cultivate regular customers.

Sometimes a dancer did not have anything in common with a customer. Over time, most dancers worked up routine questions to keep conversation flowing. Sabrina frequently used lines such as: "What do you look for in a woman?" "Why do you visit strip bars?" "What is your opinion of that dancer over there?" "I try," she said, "to get the customer to share something personal with me. I like for him to feel like there is something more solid than a salesperson-customer relationship."

Some regular customers acted as if they were involved in a long-term, serious relationship with a dancer. They bought her expensive gifts such as diamonds, minks, cars, and flowers. These customers seemed to forget the businesslike nature of the bar setting. Dancers in these interactions appeared involved with the customers. However, most did not take the relationship outside the bar, since this would have cut off a source of income. But they tried to convince the men of their desire to leave the bar scene and be saved by them, even though it was impossible now. Sabrina, for example, had many offers from men who wanted to rescue her from the bar. She developed a routine to solicit this desire from men—it usually meant more money for her in the bar—but that allowed her to reject their proposals without causing anger. She explained:

> I presented myself as attractive and intelligent, but helpless, trapped by circumstances. When they asked me to leave the bar, I told them I had to work to pay for

school. When they suggested setting me up in a place of my own, I told them I was independent and wanted to do it on my own. This put them off, but kept them interested and earned their respect.

Mae, a dancer mentioned earlier, seemed to have a knack for cultivating these types of relations. Sabrina describes a discussion with Mae while sharing a ride home.

Mae had been given a mink coat that night by a customer and she had given it back to him.

Always intimidated by this woman, I took a moment to get up some nerve and finally asked, "Why did you give back the mink?" "l couldn't hock it for very much, and I won't use it here in Florida. I'd rather get money," she stated.

"How are you going to get money?" I asked. "I'll get more money from him by being the type of person who gives this stuff back than if I keep it. I have lots of customers who give me nicer stuff than that mink."

She spoke to the driver, "Hey, do you remember that necklace Tom gave me?"

The driver replied, "It's true, Mae can really get them going. That necklace was a grand, easy." "Did you keep the necklace?" I asked.

"Hell yes!" she responded.

Mae had a routine that could "really get them going." But she and other dancers, usually the older ones, who used this technique often, took some aspect of the relationship seriously. They saw these men as "options" or possibilities for a life change. On the other hand, they felt this was too good to be true, or were unsure about making the change because of other factors in their lives, such as a husband or children. Keeping the interaction going, yet not allowing it to take place outside the bar, meant they were able to have romance, feel appreciated, and, to some extent, have a relationship while they continued making money in their occupations. However, the occasional relationship that did work out in the bar kept everyone hoping. Sabrina, for example, met her husband there.

Closing the Sale

A dancer rapidly closed a sale on a table dance to a man who wanted sexual favors in the bar. But since these men often violated rules regarding touching and sexual stimulation, some dancers did not feel that they were worth the trouble. For example, one night Annette came into the dressing room and announced, "I just left this old geezer who wanted me to rub him off with my knee. I'm not into it. If someone else wants to, go for it."

The same problems existed after a quick sale to men in the bar for a party. In this situation, a dancer had to concentrate on not acting offended long enough to perform table dances and collect her money. For some dancers, the money was not worth the degradation. As a result, they avoided the bachelor parties.

The customer who wanted to be treated as special took more time. Questioning allowed time for the dancer to convince him that he wanted a table dance from her. It was important that she not appear pushy, yet she needed to determine quickly whether she could make money from this person. Would he buy table dances? Did he want to spend time getting to know a dancer or go directly to a dance? Answers to such questions guided the dancer in constructing her behavior toward the customer.

If a customer purchased a drink for a dancer, she then knew that he was interested enough to spend some time with her. Some customers, however, bought drinks for dancers but refused to purchase table dances, claiming table dances got them "worked up for nothing." If a customer acknowledged that right away, a dancer then had to make a decision about staying or leaving based on the availability of other moneymaking opportunities in the bar. If the action in the club was slow, she might stay with him since she made $1 on every drink he bought for her. Regular customers were always good for a drink: "I'll go sit with Jim today," said Sharon. "At least I know he'll buy me a drink if nothing else." Often a dancer gave the waitress a secret signal indicating that no liquor should be put in her glass. The waitress brought the drink in a special glass, placed a dollar under the dancer's napkin and the drink on top of it.

Most women closed on a dance after the first drink had arrived and it was apparent that the customer liked her. If the customer said no, most dancers left fairly quickly. But in rare cases a customer paid $50–$100 for a dancer to sit with him for a while. This guaranteed the dancer money without trouble and bought the customer companionship. Customers who saw themselves in an involved relationship with a dancer generally rejected table dances in favor of company. When these customers bought dances they treated the dancer gently, barely touching her for fear of offending her.

Even when a dancer was not paid for her company, it was not always a good idea for her to leave immediately when a man refused a table dance. As a rare and novel routine, staying made the dancer appear sincere in her interest and less concerned about making money. Sabrina occasionally used this approach:

"Why are you still sitting here?" the customer asked immediately after he had turned me down for a table dance.

"I'm finishing my drink," I replied.

"Then you are leaving?" he asked.

"Oh, sir, I had no idea you wanted me to go. You must be waiting for someone. Forgive me for being so rude," I said tongue in cheek. I stood to leave.

"Hold it, hold it. Sit back down. I don't necessarily want you to leave. The girls always leave after you say no to a dance. You must be new here. You really should leave when customers say no. You won't make any money this way." During this exchange he was clutching my arm. He loosened his grip. "Wouldn't that be rude to just up and walk off?" I asked incredulously. He stares at me a minute, and then smiles. "Lady," he says. "You are a card. I want a table dance." He bought four.

In the Pits

Once a customer agreed to a table dance, another set of complex exchanges took place. Although interaction varied with the particular dancer and customer, common routines offered promise of what was to come. Leading the customer to the pit, one acrobatic dancer followed a routine of bending from the waist and peering at her customer from between straight legs. Ascending the stairs to the pit, she performed various kicks and other gestures to demonstrate her flexibility. Another dancer sashayed gracefully in an elegant and poised, yet seductive, manner. Sabrina's style was to talk in a sexy way as she walked: "See that corner. That's my corner. I love to take my men there."

Once in the pit, a woman sat close to the man. Often she put her hand on his leg, draped an arm on his shoulder, or swung a leg over his lap. Some girls necked with their customers, French kissing with a frenzied passion. Other dancers allowed kisses only on the cheek.

If a customer tried to French kiss when a dancer did not want it, she had several "routines" to control him. Leveling a questioning look at the customer and then backing away from him was enough to stop most men. When a client voiced dissatisfaction over the limitation—"What did you do that for?" or "What's your problem? Why are you so cold?"—it usually indicated an aggressive and potentially problematic customer. Sabrina's response to this was, "Imagine if I kissed every guy in the bar like that before I kissed you. Would that be a turn-on for you?" Most customers backed off then with comments such as, "You're absolutely right. I never thought of that before." By their continuous attempts, however, it was apparent that some were being insincere, assuming, like the dancer, that if they moved more slowly, they would get more of what they wanted. But sometimes the restriction reflected positively on the customer's impression of the dancer. One customer stated to Sabrina after she used this routine: "You have a lot of respect for yourself. I like that."

While some women danced immediately, many waited one or two songs before actually starting a table dance. Sabrina noted that she rarely danced on the first available song because it gave off the impression that she was just interested in making money quickly. She preferred to sit with a customer for a while, talk, drink, and get to know him better. This created a sexual or intimate atmosphere and convinced him that she liked spending time with him. Often this cultivated customers who were likely to buy a greater number of dances, and return to visit her later.

At the beginning of a new song, a dancer might say: "Would you like that table dance now?" or "Let's go for it, baby," depending on the type of interaction in which they were involved. Sexually oriented behavior on the part of the customer called for aggressive behavior from the dancer; less sexually overt actions required more subtle requests.

Table Dances

Strategy became important during a table dance; close quarters meant a dancer's presentation could be difficult to maintain and a customer hard to control. Normally, a dancer attempted to maintain eye contact with a patron, operating on the premise that it demonstrated interest and that if he had his eyes on her, he wouldn't have his hands on her as much. Sabrina hypothesized that a customer confronting a dancer's eyes was forced to acknowledge her "personhood," and that he then was less likely to violate it. Another impression given off (Goffman, 1959) by the dancer's body language was that the intimate exchange demonstrated by this eye contact might be impinged upon by the customer's groping at her body. Sometimes eye contact was difficult if a customer caused the dancer to laugh or feel disgusted (for example, if he was ugly or panting). In this situation, a dancer could turn away from him and make an impersonal shaking of her derriere part of her dance.

Sexual activity was illegal during table dances, but it sometimes occurred. Customers and dancers acknowledged that "hand jobs," oral sex, and intercourse happened, although infrequently. Once a customer requested that Sabrina wear a long skirt during a table dance so that intercourse could take place unobserved.

More common were body-to-penis friction and masturbation. The most frequent form consisted of the customer sliding down to the end of his seat, spreading his legs, and pulling the dancer in close to him where she could then use her knees discreetly to rub his genitals while she danced. Customers sometimes wore shorts without underwear to allow their genitals to hang out the side, or they unzipped their pants to bare their genitals, or masturbated themselves by hand while watching the dancer.

If a customer insisted on violating rules—putting his fingers inside the dancer's briefs or touching her breasts—a dancer might dance much faster than normal, or sway quickly side to side, to escape the wandering hands. If he was insistent, a dancer might grab his wrists teasingly, but firmly, and say, "No, no," addressing him as if he were a misbehaving child.

These attempts to control the customer could not be too aggressive at the outset, or the customer would be turned off. A subtle game was being played: The customer attempted to get the dancer to go as far as she would, and bend the rules. without antagonizing her so much that she stopped dancing; the dancer attempted to keep him in line, but in such a way that he still wanted to buy dances from her. A particularly good strategy at this point was for the dancer to make it look as if she were interested in what he wanted to do, but, because of management, was unable to oblige him. "Look, this would be fine, but I'm going to get in trouble with management. They're going to catch us if you keep acting like this." This disclaimer (Hewitt and Stokes, 1975) shifted the focus of the patron's annoyance to management and away from her and reasserted the idea that this was a respectable occupation with rules (see Hong et al., 1975).

If a man continued to act inappropriately, the dancer most likely lost her money and the negotiation process broke down. If the customer did not pay after the dance, the dancer had no recourse. Her only power was her seductiveness or ability to persuade the customer subtly that he "owed" it to her. Fights between customers and dancers started occasionally because a man did not want to pay a woman who "didn't give him a good dance." Management quickly squelched these and fired or fined dancers who were involved.

Most dances, however, were successful. After one of these, a dancer might give the customer a reward for "being good." Sabrina reported that she kissed the customer, closed mouthed, on the cheek or on the corner of his mouth. By gently resting her fingers on his chin, tilting up his head, and delivering a kiss, she left the impression, "I'm involved with you. I like you."

After a table dance had been completed, the next goal was to keep the interaction going so that the customer would buy more dances. If a customer continued to hold onto a dancer after the song ended, it usually signaled that he wanted her to dance through the next song. If he let her go, a dancer might look inquisitively at the customer and ask, "Is that all for now? Do you want to continue?" or "Will you want a dance later?" The questions asked depended on the dancer's impression of how involved the customer was with the dance. At the least, she encouraged him to look her up the next time he returned to the bar.

Exchange From the Bottom Up

Interaction in strip bars reflects negotiation in "respectable" society. What is being exchanged—economic resources for sexual titillation, ego gratification, and submission—is viewed in our society as honorable (Lasch, 1977; Lipman-Blumen, 1984; Safilios-Rothschild, 1977). The strategies dancers use to sell their product are similar to those used by sellers in reputable service occupations (Bigus, 1972; Browne, 1973; Davis,1959; Henslin,1968; Prus,1987; Katovich and Diamond, 1986). Unlike many deviant sales (Luckenbill, 1984), dancers and customers normally are protected by a structured, bureaucratic setting with formal rules.

Interaction in a strip club represents negotiation in a buyer's market: sexual turn-on is available for the asking. Although men show some interest in being customers simply by walking through the door, they must be persuaded to "buy" from a certain dancer. To establish control, women use facilitating (Prus, 1987) or cultivating techniques (Bigus, 1972); much like those used by service workers trying to sell a product directly to a client. To acquire customers, a dancer must develop mutual trust. The most important weapon in the arsenal of interaction is to present oneself as sincere: be warm and imply realness, appear spontaneous, give out insider information to show loyalty, accentuate honesty, demonstrate that one is different from others in similar positions, or tell hard-luck stories. At the same time, a dancer must attempt to determine the trustworthiness of her customer: Will he pay for the dance, and will he hassle her later?

Once trust is established, the dancer must promote repeat patronage and customer loyalty (Prus, 1987). This is done by calling on the norm of reciprocity (Gouldner, 1960). The expectation is that the customer will repay friendship, special attention, and favors with money. Thus a hard sell often is not as productive as other more indirect techniques, such as taking personal interest in customers (Prus, 1987), nurturing pseudo friendships, or effecting obligation (Bigus, 1972). Much like any business relationship, the seller must gauge time spent in an encounter to pay-off potential.

Interaction in the bar also reflects power dynamics in mainstream society. As a subordinate group, women in general have responded to men's macromanipulation of societal institutions by using micromanipulation—interpersonal behaviors and practices—to influence the power balance (Lipman-Blumen, 1984). Women in the bar play a game that they know well; in some form, they have been forced to play it for years. They are accustomed to anticipating male behavior, pleasing and charming men, appearing to be what they want, and following their rules. At the same time, dancers are skilled at manipulating to get their own needs met. The bar is a haven for them; they are old hands.

Women who dance for a living have fewer resources or opportunities to manipulate the macrostructure than do most women. Many come from broken homes where fathers often were absent. They frequently had distant relations with parents and left home at an early age. They had sexual experience earlier than other females had. Financial crisis often served as the impetus for starting this occupation. Few have sufficient training or education to make as much money in other occupations (Carey et al., 1974; Skipper and McCaghy, 1971).

Although dancers often have few resources, they are used to taking care of themselves. The occupation of stripping demands that they be tough. It provides them with a context of control. Being the purveyors and gatekeepers of sexuality has always provided powerful control for women (Safilios-Rothschild, 1977); it served this function even more for those women who make sexual turn-on into an occupation.

In male-female relationships, sex is "shrouded in romantic mystique" (Salutin, 1971). It has been okay for women to exchange sex for financial security (Salutin, 1971), as long as they confined the exchange to the context of love and marriage (Safilios-Rothschild, 1977). On this level, the activity in the bar is deviant. There this shroud is removed, revealing the rawness of the exchange, the unequal distribution of macropower, and the often cold, calculating nature of the microstrategies. There, sexuality is carried out in public between people who are often strangers. The dancers use sex as a direct currency of exchange: turn-ons for money. They are not likely to have illusions of love. For them, this is a job. When they are tempted to redefine the situation, their histories with men or the realities of their lives remind them otherwise.

For some dancers then, there is a feeling that they have won the ultimate game in American society, which continues to judge the value of women by their attractiveness and seductiveness (Chernin, 1982). Dancers get validation, attention, and money for displaying these characteristics and argue that they are doing nothing more than most women do, not as much as some.

Yet, this world is not a haven for women. If they could make the same money and have the same freedom in another occupation, most dancers would pursue an alternative to table dancing, but they cannot (Prus and Irini, 1980; Robboy, 1985). Most also have

internalized "honorable" exchange, and, without the shroud of romance, outright trading of their bodies sometimes breaks through as degrading (Prus and Irini, 1980; Salutin, 1971; Skipper and McCaghy, 1971). They suffer identity problems as they take on the negative attitudes of mainstream society toward their occupation (Rambo [Ronai], 1987; Skipper and McCaghy, 1970, 1971). Many are disillusioned with males to the point that they characterize their audience as degenerates (McCaghy and Skipper, 1969), yet these same degenerates decide their take-home pay.

The negotiation process we have described then is a case study of exchange between those differentially empowered. As in other occupations in which a person's job requires emotion management, stripping has high emotional costs (Hochschild, 1983). Stripping, as a service occupation, pays well, but costs dearly.

References

Adler, P. A., and P. Adler. (1987). *Membership Roles in Field Research*. Newbury Park, CA: Sage.

Bigus, O. (1972). "The milkman and his customer: A cultivated relationship." *Urban Life and Culture* 1:131–165.

Blumer, H. (1969). *Symbolic Interactionism: Perspective and Method*. Englewood Cliffs, NJ: Prentice Hall.

Boles, J., and A. P. Garbin. (1974). "The strip club and customer-stripper patterns of interaction." *Sociology and Social Research* 58:136–144.

Browne, J. (1973). *The Used-Car Game: A Sociology of the Bargain*. Lexington, MA: Lexington Books.

Bulmer, M. (1982). "When is disguise justified? Alternatives to covert participant observations." *Qualitative Sociology* 5:251–264.

Carey, S. H., R. A. Peterson, and L. K. Sharpe. (1974). "A study of recruitment and socialization in two deviant female occupations." *Soc. Symposium* 11:11–24.

Chernin, K. (1982). *The Obsession: Reflections on the Tyranny of Slenderness*. New York: Harper Collophon.

Davis, F. (1959). "The cab driver and his fare: Facets of a fleeting relationship." *American Journal of Sociology* 65:158–165.

Denzin, N. K. (1978). *The Research Act*. New York: McGraw-Hill.

Ellis, C. (1988). "Keeping emotions in the sociology of emotions." University of South Florida. (unpublished).

——. (forthcoming). "Sociological introspection and emotional experience." *Symbolic Interaction* 13.1.

Foote, N. N. (1954). "Sex as play." *Social Problems* 1:159–163.

Goffman, E. (1959). *The Presentation of Self in Everyday Life*. Garden City, NY: Doubleday.

——. (1974). *Frame Analysis: An Essay on the Organization of Experience*. Cambridge, MA: Harvard Univ. Press.

Gonos, G. (1976). "Go-go dancing: A comparative frame analysis." *Urban Life* 9:189–219.

Gouldner, A. (1960). "The norm of reciprocity." *Amer. Soc. Rev.* 25:161–178.

Henslin, J. (1968). "Trust and the cab driver." In M. Truzzi. (ed.), *Sociology and Everyday Life* (pp. 138–155). Englewood Cliffs, NJ: Prentice Hall.

Hewitt, J., and R. Stokes. (1975). "Disclaimers." *Amer. Soc. Rev.* 40:1–11.

Hochschild, A. (1983). *The Managed Heart: Commercialization of Human Feeling*. Berkeley: Univ. of California Press.

Hong, L. K., W. Darrough, and R. Duff (1975). "The sensuous rip-off: Consumer fraud turns blue." *Urban Life and Culture* 3:464–470.

Jorgensen, D. L. (1989). *Participant Observation*. Newbury Park, CA: Sage.

Katovich, M. A., and R. L. Diamond. (1986). "Selling time: Situated transactions in a noninstitutional environment." *Soc. Q.* 27:253–271.

Lasch, C. (1977). *Haven in a Heartless World*. New York: Basic Books.

Lipman-Blumen, J. (1984). *Gender Roles and Power*. Englewood Cliffs, NJ: Prentice Hall.

Luckenbill, D. F. (1984). "Dynamics of the deviant sale." *Deviant Behavior* 5:337–353.

McCaghy, C. H., and J. K. Skipper. (1969). "Lesbian behavior as an adaptation to the occupation of stripping." *Social Problems* 17:262–270.

——. (1972). "Stripping: Anatomy of a deviant life style." In S. D. Feldman and G. W. Thielbar (eds.), *Life Styles: Diversity in American Society* (pp. 362–373). Boston: Little, Brown.

Mehan, H., and H. Wood. (1975). *The Reality of Ethnomethodology*. New York: John Wiley.

Mullen, K. (1985). "The impure performance frame of the public house entertainer." *Urban Life* 14:181–203.

Prus, R. (1987). "Developing loyalty: Fostering purchasing relationships in the marketplace." *Urban Life* 15:331–366.

Prus, R., and S. Irini. (1980). *Hookers, Rounders, and Desk Clerks: The Social Organization of the Hotel Community*. Salem, WI: Sheffield.

Rambo (Ronai), C. (1987). "Negotiation strategies and emotion work of the stripper." University of South Florida. (unpublished).

Rasmussen, P., and L. Kuhn. (1976). "The new masseuse: Play for pay." *Urban Life* 5:271–292.

Riemer, J. W. (1977). "Varieties of opportunistic research." *Urban Life* 5:467–477.

Robboy, H. (1985). "Emotional labor and sexual exploitation in an occupational role." Presented at the annual meetings of the Mid South Sociological Society, Little Rock, AK.

Safilios-Rothschild, C. (1977). *Love, Sex, and Sex Roles*. Englewood Cliffs, NJ: Prentice Hall.

Salutin, M. (1971). "Stripper morality." *Transaction* 8:12–22.

Scott, M. B., and S. M. Lyman. (1968). "Accounts." *Amer. Soc. Rev.* 33:46–62.

Skipper, J. K., and C. H. McCaghy. (1970). "Stripteasers: The anatomy and career contingencies of a deviant occupation." *Social Problems* 17:391–405.

——. (1971). "Stripteasing: A sex oriented occupation." In J. Henslin (ed.) *The Sociology of Sex* (pp. 275–296). New York: Appleton Century Crofts.

Sykes, G., and D. Matza. (1957). "Techniques of neutralization: A theory of delinquency." *Amer. Soc. Rev.* 22:664–670.

Turner, R. (1962). "Role-taking: Process versus conformity." In A. M. Rose (ed.), *Human Behavior and Social Process* (pp. 20–40). Boston: Houghton Mifflin.

Webb, E. J., D. T. Campbell, R. D. Schwartz, and L. Sechrest. (1965). *Unobtrusive Measures*. Chicago: Rand McNally.

Weinstein, Eugene A., and Paul Deutschberger. (1963). "Some dimensions of altercasting." *Sociometry* 26:454–466.

Authors' Note

An earlier version of this article was read at the annual meetings of the Southern Sociological Society, March 1988. We are grateful to Danny Jorgensen for his participation in this project and to Patricia Adler, Peter

Adler, Michael Flaherty, and anonymous reviewers for comments on earlier drafts.

Adapted from Carol Rambo Ronai and Carolyn Ellis, *Journal of Contemporary Ethnography*, vol. 18/1989, pp. 271–298. Copyright © 1989 by Sage Publications. Reprinted by permission of Sage Publications, Inc. ✦

33
Sex Tourism and Child Prostitution in Asia

Heather Montgomery

Childhood is supposed to be a time of inno-cence, a time to dream and play, a time to ex-periment in the blissful exuberance of youth. Children have a special place in society, shielded from the obligations of adult life and protected (to some extent) from the corrupting influences that go with it. Protection and pa-ternalism are particularly important in the realm of sexuality, where restrictions on sexual behavior are strong. Children are not supposed to talk about sex; they are not supposed to watch sexual acts on TV; they are not supposed to engage in sex (though many do all three); and, emphatically, they are not supposed to en-gage in sex for money.

In many ways, these restrictions are uniquely American. Cultural and structural conditions vary greatly throughout the world, and such conditions have an enormous influ-ence on the types of sexual activities that a so-ciety deems acceptable. In parts of the Third World, for example, child sexuality is not nearly so taboo as in the United States. In Thailand, grinding poverty (one example of a "structural condition") has made child prosti-tution something of a necessity. Profits from the trade keep entire families and communities afloat. The children are not ostracized; rather, they are embraced as entrepreneurs whose ac-tivity makes economic survival possible. Par-ticipating children reject the label of victim, claiming they are acting voluntarily and of their own free will. Their clients do not exploit them, they report, but are "friends" with whom they genuinely enjoy spending time. Sex is only one facet of the exchange, and not the most sig-nificant part. Although children and their fam-ilies may recognize that selling sex to tourists is unseemly, they intellectualize it as necessary.

Until some of the larger structural forces that promote unrelenting poverty are amelio-rated, the trade will no doubt continue. This is not to suggest, as Montgomery argues, that it should be condoned or approved. Nor is it to suggest that some children are not at times forced into the vocation against their wills. Sexual slavery is indeed a major problem in the Third World, although Montgomery in-sists that the children she interviewed did not fall into this category. She argues that the trade should be understood in context and that the people who perform it should be given a voice. Until child-savers, advocates, and other "do-gooders" from the West realize this, policies they formulate will be misguided and may even promote more harm than good.

E very few years an issue relating to chil-dren attracts the attention of the media and is quickly turned into an international cause célèbre. In the 1970s, it was malnourished and starving children in Africa. During the early 1980s, it was child labor in Asia, which was followed by street children in South America. Now it is child prostitution. It is of-ten seen as the problem of the nineties, lead-ing to new laws being passed in some coun-tries enabling that country to prosecute its own citizens for abuses committed against children abroad. . . . The increase in aware-ness about incest and child abuse in Western countries has sensitized people to abuse in other countries and the suspicion that some Western men are perpetuating this abuse has created a climate of absolute intolerance to child prostitution in all circumstances (LaFrontaine 1990; Jenkins 1992).

Child prostitution is viewed as an evil which must be eradicated by all means pos-sible. This is a perfectly understandable re-sponse and one with which few people, ex-cept possibly pedophiles or others with obvious ulterior motives, would disagree. However with all the concern about child prostitution, individual children who sell sex have been largely overlooked. . . . [C]hildren themselves are rarely allowed to speak. . . .

. . .[T]he desire for information is for stories which emphasize the degradation and abuse of children, not the mundane aspects of their lives or even the areas of their lives away from prostitution. . . .

. . .[T]here is a continuing fascination with it which is fed by the media and the NGOs and it is clearly an issue which both repels and allures. While newspaper articles often claim to be raising awareness, they can also titillate. This public interest in child sex undoubtedly exists but it is not the straightforward reflection of outrage that it claims to be. It rarely raises awareness and frequently has the effect of harnessing prurient horror for political ends which often substitute understanding for sensationalism and moral outrage. Child prostitution is cast as a clear cut case of good and evil while ignoring the wider political economy that allows child prostitution to flourish. . . .There is a stereotype of child prostitution that claims that they are tricked into leaving home, or sold by impoverished parents into a brothel where they are repeatedly raped and terrorized into servicing up to twenty clients a night. . . .The children with whom I worked were not in any of these categories however, and they present a different, but rarely acknowledged model of child prostitution. They were technically "free" in that they were not debt-bonded or kept in brothels and they lived with their parents. They were perhaps not typical of all child prostitutes in Thailand but they are an important group whose lives and identities challenge many of the expected stereotypes of child prostitution. . . .

. . .None of the children liked prostitution but they did have strategies for rationalizing it and coming to terms with it. They had found an ethical system whereby the public selling of their bodies did not affect their private sense of humanity and virtues. When I asked one thirteen-year-old about selling her body, she replied "it's only my body" but when I asked about the difference between adultery and prostitution, she would tell me that adultery was very wrong. In her eyes, adultery was a betrayal of a private relationship whereas prostitution was simply done for money. . . .

Within this community it was relatively easy to find out who had sex for money and who did not, but the children's perceptions of what they did were much more complex. . . .

The children's attitudes towards prostitution were often contradictory. They would readily say that they "had guests" or were "supported by foreigners" or they would use other phrases suggesting prostitution but that they disliked the term "prostitution" (*sopheni*). They would rather use words that conveyed an ambiguity and a conceptual distance between selling sex and working. Their reactions to the term prostitution suggest they knew of the stigma involved with it and were keen to downplay its importance for them. They continually emphasized that they did not "sell sex" but that they "went out for fun with foreigners." While some clients simply bought sex, these sorts of relationships were disliked and rarely talked about. What they preferred to discuss were the men who were "friends" and who consequently had reciprocal obligations with the children and their families. The children were more comfortable talking about love and romance than they were about commercial transactions and preferred to stress relationships above money. They consciously downplayed the importance of money to themselves. They never set a price for sexual acts: money that was given to them after sex was referred to as a gift or as a token of appreciation. Money was not the end point of the exchange but a way of expressing affection. . . .

It is easy to claim that the children are misguided or that they suffer from a form of false consciousness. Simply because a child does not recognize exploitation, it does not necessarily mean that it has not occurred. Poor Thai children are extremely vulnerable to abuse from richer, Western men and there is an obvious sense in which these children are exploited. They were also aware that prostitution was considered unacceptable by others in their society and they have good reasons to deny its importance and place in their lives. However, these children do explicitly reject the status of victims. They actively try to form reciprocal arrangements with their clients and the rejection of labels such as prostitution is not simply a denial of reality but a way of manipulating that reality. They recognize the structural power their clients have over them and do their best to direct it to their benefit. . . .

For the children that I knew, however, neither prostitution nor sexuality were the focus of their identity. Identity was so bound up in status, prestige and hierarchy that sexuality was a means to those ends rather than an end in itself. Identity was also based around belonging to a community. . . .

. . .[I]t brought in enough money to look after parents or pay for a family house, and a child could view herself as a good, dutiful daughter. Prostitution was the means to this end but it was no end in itself. It was a way of paying back debts to parents and fulfilling filial obligations. . . .It is vital to look at children's own perceptions and explanations of what they do before anyone can try to help them and that we must acknowledge the importance of children's strategies and forms of control if we are to fully understand what enables them to continue to find meaning in their own lives.

. . .[T]he conditions that the children lived in were extremely difficult. Their lack of education, their poverty and ill health all made them vulnerable to abuse and exploitation by those with more power. Yet, prostitution is always seen as the ultimate indignity and one which is far beyond all others. It is also always seen as one which they passively accept. . . .

The children that I knew did not passively accept this abuse and having a sense of control over some aspects of their lives was fundamental to them. For some, prostitution was a bad option with better pay than other bad options while others complied with their family's wishes that they become prostitutes as a way of showing their filial duty. . . .

. . .[T]he money that prostitution brought in did enable the community to function and to stay together and this was a real achievement by the children. It was their money that supported their parents and kept the families together. Even though they were socially and economically very marginal, by most definitions they were dutiful children whose

respect and difference [sic] towards their parents was honorable and admirable. For people who are poor and powerless, prostitution does not seem a unique and ultimate horror (as many outsiders view it) or something they have to be forced into but one difficult choice among many. They can be forced into many forms of work that they dislike such as scavenging or collecting garbage, neither of which pay nearly as well as prostitution. . . .They choose not to represent themselves as victims and not to align themselves with negative connotations that others have placed on prostitution. Their power and ability to change their situation are extremely constrained but their constructions of their own identities and ways of viewing the world show a clear difference between them and the passive victims that child prostitutes are constantly assumed to be. . . .

. . .[P]ersonally I felt that these children were exploited but that this exploitation came not through prostitution but through their general poverty and social exclusion. . . . If they were not prostitutes, they still would have been impoverished and probably forced into the illegal labor market in a sweatshop or as a scavenger. These children were neglected by the state and given few viable options by their society. In this situation examining prostitution in isolation from other economic and social choices is pointless and leads only to narrow moralistic arguments about whether prostitution is "right" or whether any prostitute, either adult or child "really" chooses prostitution. . . .

References

Jenkins, Philip. 1992. *Intimate Enemies: Moral Panics in Contemporary Great Britain*. New York: Aldine de Gruyter.

LaFrontaine, Jean. 1990. *Child Sexual Abuse*. Cambridge: Polity Press.

Montgomery, Heather (1998). "Children, Prostitution, and Identity" from *Global Sex Workers*, edited by Kamala Kempadoo and Joe Doezema. New York: Routledge. ✦

34
Fraternities and Rape on Campus

Patricia Yancey Martin

Robert A. Hummer

There is a widespread assumption that rapists are solitary strangers who prowl the streets looking for appropriate victims, striking randomly, suddenly, and without provocation. Such a notion is perfectly understandable. Movies and news programs bombard us with images of predatory offenders who coldly case their targets and use brute force to secure compliance. The belief among many women (and some men) is that anyone can be a victim at any time and that the only way to reduce one's chances of being assaulted is to scan one's environs, curtail one's movements, and become expert in self-defense.

Although real, the threat of being raped by a stranger pales in comparison to the risk of being raped by someone one knows. Scholars suggest that as many as 90 percent of all rapes are committed by persons with whom a victim is familiar. Rape is, of course, a person-on-person offense, but powerful cultural and organizational forces play an important mediating role in its occurrence. That said, few cultures or organizations promote a climate more conducive to rape than the college fraternity.

With their emphasis on athletic prowess, power and domination, alcohol consumption, and sexual conquest, fraternities embody aggressive masculinity at its worst. Women are seen as physical objects who exist only for the fulfillment of male sexual desire. Men who have sexual relations most frequently and with the greatest number of women have the highest status within the organization. Many men join fraternities in the first place primarily because of the promise of sexual access. Selection effects, coupled with fraternity culture

itself, combine to create an atmosphere that leads directly and indirectly to sexual assault.

Martin and Hummer explore the dynamics of brotherhood and its contributing role to this atmosphere. The emphasis on loyalty, secrecy, and group protection establishes boundaries and ensures that norm violations (whether they involve sex or not) will be kept "in-house." Heavy alcohol consumption clouds judgment and weakens sexual inhibitions. Norms that support aggression combine with those that commodify women to create a volatile mix. Brotherhood is socially constructed to venerate everything masculine and dismiss everything feminine, which justifies the abuse of females. Sex emerges as a zero-sum game; getting it without emotional commitment—or even explicit permission—becomes a goal. The important thing to remember, Martin and Hummer contend, is that fraternity culture—rather than the beliefs of individual members per se—contributes most to this climate of coercion.

Rapes are perpetrated on dates, at parties, in chance encounters, and in specially planned circumstances. That group structure and processes, rather than individual values or characteristics, are the impetus for many rape episodes was documented by Blanchard (1959) 30 years ago (also see Geis 1971), yet sociologists have failed to pursue this theme (for an exception, see Chancer 1987). A recent review of research (Muehlenhard and Linton 1987) on sexual violence, or rape, devotes only a few pages to the situational contexts of rape events, and these are conceptualized as potential risk factors for individuals rather than qualities of rape-prone social contexts.

Many rapes, far more than come to the public's attention, occur in fraternity houses on college and university campuses, yet little research has analyzed fraternities at American colleges and universities as rape-prone contexts (cf. Ehrhart and Sandler 1985). Most of the research on fraternities reports on samples of individual fraternity men. One group of studies compares the values, attitudes, perceptions, family socioeconomic status, psychological traits (aggressiveness, dependence), and so on, of fraternity and nonfraternity men (Bohrnstedt 1969; Fox, Hodge, and Ward 1987; Kanin 1967; Lemire 1979; Miller 1973). A second group attempts to identify the effects of fraternity membership over time on the values, attitudes, beliefs, or moral precepts of members (Hughes and Winston 1987; Marlowe and Auvenshine 1982; Miller 1973; Wilder, Hoyt, Doren, Hauck, and Zettle 1978; Wilder, Hoyt, Surbeck, Wilder, and Carney 1986). With minor exceptions, little research addresses the group and organizational context of fraternities or the social construction of fraternity life (for exceptions, see Letchworth 1969; Longino and Kart 1973; Smith 1964).

Gary Tash, writing as an alumnus and trial attorney in his fraternity's magazine, claims that over 90 percent of all gang rapes on college campuses involve fraternity men (1988, p. 2). Tash provides no evidence to substantiate this claim, but students of violence against women have been concerned with fraternity men's frequently reported involvement in rape episodes (Adams and Abarnael 1988). Ehrhart and Sandler (1985) identify over 50 cases of gang rapes on campus perpetrated by fraternity men, and their analysis points to many of the conditions that we discuss here. Their analysis is unique in focusing on conditions in fraternities that make gang rapes of women by fraternity men both feasible and probable. They identify excessive alcohol use, isolation from external monitoring, treatment of women as prey, use of pornography, approval of violence, and excessive concern with competition as precipitating conditions to gang rape (also see Merton 1985; Roark 1987).

The study reported here confirmed and complemented these findings by focusing on both conditions and processes. We examined dynamics associated with the social construction of fraternity life, with a focus on processes that foster the use of coercion, including rape, in fraternity men's relations with women. Our examination of men's social fraternities on college and university campuses as groups and organizations led us to conclude that fraternities are a physical and sociocultural context that encourages the sexual coercion of women. We make no claims that all fraternities are "bad" or that all fraternity men are rapists. Our observations indicated, however, that rape is especially probable in fraternities because of the kinds of organizations they are, the kinds of members they have, the practices their members engage in, and a virtual absence of university or community oversight. Analyses that lay blame for rapes by fraternity men on "peer pressure" are, we feel, overly simplistic (cf. Burkhart 1989; Walsh 1989). We suggest, rather, that fraternities create a sociocultural context in which the use of coercion in sexual relations with women is normative and in which the mechanisms to keep this pattern of behavior in check are minimal at best and absent at worst. We conclude that unless fraternities change in fundamental ways, little improvement can be expected.

Methodology

Our goal was to analyze the group and organizational practices and conditions that create in fraternities an abusive social context for women. We developed a conceptual framework from an initial case study of an alleged gang rape at Florida State University that involved four fraternity men and an 18-year-old coed. The group rape took place on the third floor of a fraternity house and ended with the "dumping" of the woman in the hallway of a neighboring fraternity house. According to newspaper accounts, the victim's blood-alcohol concentration, when she was discovered, was .349 percent, more than three times the legal limit for automobile driving and an almost lethal amount. One law enforcement officer reported that sexual intercourse occurred during the time the victim was unconscious: "She was in a life-threatening situation" (*Tallahassee Democrat*, 1988b). When the victim was found, she was comatose and had suffered multiple scratches and abrasions. Crude words and a fraternity symbol had been written on her thighs (*Tampa Tribune*, 1988). When law enforcement officials tried to investigate the case, fraternity members refused to cooperate. This led, eventually, to a five-year ban of the fraternity from campus by the university and by the fraternity's national organization.

In trying to understand how such an event could have occurred, and how a group of over 150 members (exact figures are unknown because the fraternity refused to provide a membership roster) could hold rank, deny knowledge of the event, and allegedly lie to a grand jury, we analyzed newspaper articles about the case and conducted open-ended interviews with a variety of respondents about the case and about fraternities, rapes, alcohol use, gender relations, and sexual activities on campus. Our data included over 100 newspaper articles on the initial gang rape case; open-ended interviews with Greek (social fraternity and sorority) and non-Greek (independent) students ($n = 20$); university administrators ($n = 8$, five men, three women); and alumni advisers to Greek organizations ($n = 6$). Open-ended interviews were held also with judges, public and private defense attorneys, victim advocates, and state prosecutors regarding the processing of sexual assault cases. Data were analyzed using the grounded theory method (Glaser 1978; Martin and Turner 1986). In the following analysis, concepts generated from the data analysis are integrated with the literature on men's social fraternities, sexual coercion, and related issues.

Fraternities and the Social Construction of Men and Masculinity

Our research indicated that fraternities are vitally concerned—more than with anything else—with masculinity (cf. Kanin 1967). They work hard to create a macho image and context and try to avoid any suggestion of "wimpishness," effeminacy, and homosexuality. Valued members display, or are willing to go along with, a narrow conception of masculinity that stresses competition, athleticism, dominance, winning, conflict, wealth, material possessions, willingness to drink alcohol, and sexual prowess vis-à-vis women.

Valued Qualities of Members

When fraternity members talked about the kind of pledges they prefer, a litany of stereotypical and narrowly masculine attributes and behaviors was recited and feminine or woman-associated qualities and behaviors were expressly denounced (cf. Merton 1985). Fraternities seek men who are "athletic," "big guys," good in intramural competition, "who can talk college sports." Males "who are willing to drink alcohol," "who drink socially," or "who can hold their liquor" are sought. Alcohol and activities associated with the recreational use of alcohol are cornerstones of fraternity social life. Nondrinkers are viewed with skepticism and rarely selected for membership.[1]

Fraternities try to avoid "geeks," nerds, and men said to give the fraternity a "wimpy" or "gay" reputation. Art, music, and humanities majors, majors in traditional women's fields (nursing, home economics, social work, education), men with long hair, and those whose appearance or dress violate current norms are rejected. Clean-cut, handsome men who dress well (are clean, neat, conforming, fashionable) are preferred. One sorority woman commented that "the top ranking fraternities have the best looking guys."

One fraternity man, a senior, said his fraternity recruited "some big guys, very athletic" over a two-year period to help overcome its image of wimpiness. His fraternity had won the interfraternity competition for highest grade point average several years running but was looked down on as "wimpy, dancy, even gay." With their bigger, more athletic recruits, "our reputation improved; we're a much more recognized fraternity now." Thus a fraternity's reputation and status depends on members' possession of stereotypically masculine qualities. Good grades, campus leadership, and community service are "nice" but masculinity dominance—for example, in athletic events, physical size of members, athleticism of members—counts most.

Certain social skills are valued. Men are sought who "have good personalities," are friendly, and "have the ability to relate to girls" (cf. Longino and Kart 1973). One fraternity man, a junior, said: "We watch a guy [a potential pledge] talk to women . . .we want guys who can relate to girls." Assessing a pledge's ability to talk to women is, in part, a preoccupation with homosexuality and a conscious avoidance of men who seem to have effeminate manners or qualities. If a member is suspected of being gay, he is ostracized and informally drummed out of the fraternity. A fraternity with a reputation as wimpy or tolerant of gays is ridiculed and shunned by other fraternities. Militant heterosexuality is frequently used by men as a strategy to keep each other in line (Kimmel 1987).

Financial affluence or wealth, a male-associated value in American culture, is highly valued by fraternities. In accounting for why the fraternity involved in the gang rape that precipitated our research project had been recognized recently as "the best fraternity chapter in the United States," a university official said: "They were good-looking, a big fraternity, had lots of BMWs [expensive, German-made automobiles]." After the rape, newspaper stories described the fraternity members' affluence, noting the high number of members who owned expensive cars (*St. Petersburg Times*, 1988).

The Status and Norms of Pledgeship

A pledge (sometimes called an associate member) is a new recruit who occupies a trial membership status for a specific period of time. The pledge period (typically ranging from 10 to 15 weeks) gives fraternity brothers an opportunity to assess and socialize new recruits. Pledges evaluate the fraternity also and decide if they want to become brothers. The socialization experience is structured partly through assignment of a Big Brother to each pledge. Big Brothers are expected to teach pledges how to become a brother and to support them as they progress through the trial membership period. Some pledges are repelled by the pledging experience, which can entail physical abuse; harsh discipline; and demands to be subordinate, follow orders, and engage in demeaning routines and activities, similar to those used by the military to "make men out of boys" during boot camp.

Characteristics of the pledge experience are rationalized by fraternity members as necessary to help pledges unite into a group, rely on each other, and join together against outsiders. The process is highly masculinist in execution as well as conception. A willingness to submit to authority, follow orders, and do as one is told is viewed as a sign of loyalty, togetherness, and unity. Fraternity pledges who find the pledge process offensive often drop out. Some do this by openly quitting, which can subject them to ridicule by brothers and other pledges, or they may deliberately fail to make the grades necessary for initiation or transfer schools and decline to reaffiliate with the fraternity on the new campus. One fraternity pledge who quit the fraternity he had pledged described an experience during pledgeship as follows:

> This one guy was always picking on me. No matter what I did, I was wrong. One night after dinner, he and two other guys called me and two other pledges into the chapter room. He said, "Here, X, hold this 25 pound bag of ice at arms' length 'til I tell you to stop." I did it even though my arms and hands were killing me. When I asked if I could stop, he grabbed me around the throat and lifted me off the floor. I thought he would choke me to death. He cussed me and called me all kinds of names. He took one of my fingers and twisted it until it nearly broke. . . .I stayed in the fraternity for a few more days, but then I decided to quit. I hated it. Those guys are sick. They like seeing you suffer.

Fraternities' emphasis on toughness, withstanding pain and humiliation, obedience to superiors, and using physical force to obtain compliance contributes to an interpersonal style that de-emphasizes caring and sensitivity but fosters intragroup trust and loyalty. If the least macho or most critical pledges drop out, those who remain may be more receptive to, and influenced by, masculinist values and practices that encourage the use of force in sexual relations with women and the covering up of such behavior (cf. Kanin 1967).

Norms and Dynamics of Brotherhood

Brother is the status occupied by fraternity men to indicate their relations to each other and their membership in a particular fraternity organization or group. Brother is a male-specific status; only males can become brothers, although women can become "Little Sisters," a form of pseudo-membership.

"Becoming a brother" is a rite of passage that follows the consistent and often lengthy display by pledges of appropriately masculine qualities and behaviors. Brothers have a quasi-familial relationship with each other, are normatively said to share bonds of closeness and support, and are sharply set off from nonmembers. Brotherhood is a loosely defined term used to represent the bonds that develop among fraternity members and the obligations and expectations incumbent upon them (cf. Marlowe and Auvenshine [1982] on fraternities' failure to encourage "moral development" in freshman pledges).

Some of our respondents talked about brotherhood in almost reverential terms, viewing it as the most valuable benefit of fraternity membership. One senior, a business-school major who had been affiliated with a fairly high-status fraternity throughout four years on campus, said:

> Brotherhood spurs friendship for life, which I consider its best aspect, although I didn't see it that way when I joined. Brotherhood bonds and unites. It instills values of caring about one another, caring about community, caring about ourselves. The values and bonds [of brotherhood] continually develop over the four years [in college] while normal friendships come and go.

Despite this idealization, most aspects of fraternity practice and conception are more mundane. Brotherhood often plays itself out as an overriding concern with masculinity and, by extension, femininity. As a consequence, fraternities comprise collectivities of highly masculinized men with attitudinal qualities and behavior norms that predispose them to sexual coercion of women (cf. Kanin 1967; Merton 1985; Rapport and Burkhart 1983). The norms of masculinity are complemented by conceptions of women and femininity that are equally distorted and stereotyped and that may enhance the probability of women's exploitation (cf. Ehrhart and Sandler 1985; Sanday 1981, 1986).

Practices of Brotherhood

Practices associated with fraternity brotherhood that contribute to the sexual coercion of women include a preoccupation with loyalty, group protection and secrecy, use of alcohol as a weapon, involvement in violence and physical force, and an emphasis on competition and superiority.

Loyalty, Group Protection, and Secrecy. Loyalty is a fraternity preoccupation. Members are reminded constantly to be loyal to the fraternity and to their brothers. Among other ways, loyalty is played out in the practices of group protection and secrecy. The fraternity must be shielded from criticism. Members are admonished to avoid getting the fraternity in trouble and to bring all problems "to the chapter" (local branch of a national social fraternity) rather than to outsiders. Fraternities try to protect themselves from close scrutiny and criticism by the Interfraternity Council (a quasi-governing body composed of representatives from all social fraternities on campus), their fraternity's national office, university officials, law enforcement, the media, and the public. Protection of the fraternity often takes precedence over what is procedurally, ethically, or legally correct. Numerous examples were related to us of fraternity brothers' lying to outsiders to "protect the fraternity."

Group protection was observed in the alleged gang rape case with which we began our study. Except for one brother, a rapist who turned state's evidence, the entire remaining fraternity membership was accused by university and criminal justice officials of lying to protect the fraternity. Members consistently failed to cooperate even though the alleged crimes were felonies, involved only four men (two of whom were not even members of the local chapter), and the victim of the crime nearly died. According to a grand jury's findings, fraternity officers repeatedly broke appointments with law enforcement officials, refused to provide police with a list of members, and refused to cooperate with police and prosecutors investigating the case (*Florida Flambeau*, 1988).

Secrecy is a priority value and practice in fraternities, partly because fullfledged membership is premised on it (for confirmation, see Ehrhart and Sandler 1985; Longino and Kart 1973; Roark 1987). Secrecy is also a boundary-maintaining mechanism, demarcating in-group from out-group, us from them. Secret rituals, handshakes, and mottoes are revealed to pledge brothers as they are initiated into full brotherhood. Since only brothers are supposed to know a fraternity's secrets, such knowledge affirms membership in the fraternity and separates a brother from others. Extending secrecy tactics from protection of private knowledge to protection of the fraternity from criticism is a predictable development. Our interviews indicated that individual members knew the difference between right and wrong, but fraternity norms that emphasize loyalty, group protection, and secrecy often overrode standards of ethical correctness.

Alcohol as Weapon. Alcohol use by fraternity men is normative. They use it on weekdays to relax after class and on weekends to "get drunk," "get crazy," and "get laid." The use of alcohol to obtain sex from women is pervasive—in other words, it is used as a weapon against sexual reluctance. According to several fraternity men whom we interviewed, alcohol is the major tool used to gain sexual mastery over women (cf. Adams and Abarnael 1988; Ehrhart and Sandler 1985). One fraternity man, a 21-year-old senior, described alcohol use to gain sex as follows: "There are girls that you know will fuck, then some you have to put some effort into it. . . .You have to buy them drinks or find out if she's drunk enough. . . ."

A similar strategy is used collectively. A fraternity man said that at parties with Little Sisters: "We provide them with 'hunch punch' and things get wild. We get them drunk and most of the guys end up with one." "'Hunch punch,'" he said, "is a girls' drink made up of overproof alcohol and powdered Kool-Aid, no water or anything, just ice. It's very strong. Two cups will do a number on a female." He had plans in the next academic term to surreptitiously give hunch punch to

women in a "prim and proper" sorority because "having sex with prim and proper sorority girls is definitely a goal." These women are a challenge because they "won't openly consume alcohol and won't get openly drunk as hell." Their sororities have "standards committees" that forbid heavy drinking and easy sex.

In the gang rape case, our sources said that many fraternity men on campus believed the victim had a drinking problem and was thus an "easy make." According to newspaper accounts, she had been drinking alcohol on the evening she was raped; the lead assailant is alleged to have given her a bottle of wine after she arrived at his fraternity house. Portions of the rape occurred in a shower, and the victim was reportedly so drunk that her assailants had difficulty holding her in a standing position (*Tallahassee Democrat*, 1988a). While raping her, her assailants repeatedly told her they were members of another fraternity under the apparent belief that she was too drunk to know the difference. Of course, if she was too drunk to know who they were, she was too drunk to consent to sex (cf. Allgeier 1986; Tash 1988).

One respondent told us that gang rapes are wrong and can get one expelled, but he seemed to see nothing wrong in sexual coercion one-on-one. He seemed unaware that the use of alcohol to obtain sex from a woman is grounds for a claim that a rape occurred (cf. Tash 1988). Few women on campus (who also may not know these grounds) report date rapes, however; so the odds of detection and punishment are slim for fraternity men who use alcohol for "seduction" purposes (cf. Byington and Keeter 1988; Merton 1985).

Violence and Physical Force. Fraternity men have a history of violence (Ehrhart and Sandler 1985; Roark 1987). Their record of hazing, fighting, property destruction, and rape has caused them problems with insurance companies (Bradford 1986; Pressley 1987). Two university officials told us that fraternities "are the third riskiest property to insure behind toxic waste dumps and amusement parks." Fraternities are increasingly defendants in legal actions brought by pledges subjected to hazing (Meyer 1986;

Pressley 1987) and by women who were raped by one or more members. In a recent alleged gang rape incident at another Florida university, prosecutors failed to file charges but the victim filed a civil suit against the fraternity nevertheless (*Tallahassee Democrat*, 1989).

Competition and Superiority. Interfraternity rivalry fosters in-group identification and out-group hostility. Fraternities stress pride of membership and superiority over other fraternities as major goals. Interfraternity rivalries take many forms, including competition for desirable pledges, size of pledge class, size of membership, size and appearance of fraternity house, superiority in intramural sports, highest grade point averages, giving the best parties, gaining the best or most campus leadership roles, and, of great importance, attracting and displaying "good looking women." Rivalry is particularly intense over members, intramural sports, and women (cf. Messner 1989).

Fraternities' Commodification of Women

In claiming that women are treated by fraternities as commodities, we mean that fraternities knowingly, and intentionally, use women for their benefit. Fraternities use women as bait for new members, as servers of brothers' needs, and as sexual prey.

Women as Bait. Fashionably attractive women help a fraternity attract new members. As one fraternity man, a junior, said, "They are good bait." Beautiful, sociable women are believed to impress the right kind of pledges and give the impression that the fraternity can deliver this type of woman to its members. Photographs of shapely, attractive coeds are printed in fraternity brochures and videotapes that are distributed and shown to potential pledges. The women pictured are often dressed in bikinis, at the beach, and are pictured hugging the brothers of the fraternity. One university official says such recruitment materials give the message: "Hey, they're here for you, you can have whatever you want," and, "We have the best looking women. Join us and you can

have them too." Another commented: "Something's wrong when males join an all-male organization as the best place to meet women. It's so illogical."

Fraternities compete in promising access to beautiful women. One fraternity man, a senior, commented that "the attraction of girls [i.e., a fraternity's success in attracting women] is a big status symbol for fraternities." One university official commented that the use of women as a recruiting tool is so well entrenched that fraternities that might be willing to forgo it say they cannot afford to unless other fraternities do so as well. One fraternity man said, "Look, if we don't have Little Sisters, the fraternities that do will get all the good pledges." Another said, "We won't have as good a rush [the period during which new members are assessed and selected] if we don't have these women around."

In displaying good-looking, attractive, skimpily dressed, nubile women to potential members, fraternities implicitly, and sometimes explicitly, promise sexual access to women. One fraternity man commented that "part of what being in a fraternity is all about is the sex" and explained how his fraternity uses Little Sisters to recruit new members:

> We'll tell the sweetheart [the fraternity's term for Little Sister], "You're gorgeous; you can get him." We'll tell her to fake a scam and she'll go hang all over him during a rush party, kiss him, and he thinks he's done wonderful and wants to join. The girls think it's great too. It's flattering for them.

Women as Servers. The use of women as servers is exemplified in the Little Sister program. Little Sisters are undergraduate women who are rushed and selected in a manner parallel to the recruitment of fraternity men. They are affiliated with the fraternity in a formal but unofficial way and are able, indeed required, to wear the fraternity's Greek letters. Little Sisters are not full-fledged fraternity members, however; and fraternity national offices and most universities do not register or regulate them. Each fraternity has an officer called Little Sister Chairman who oversees their organization and activities. The Little Sisters elect officers among themselves, pay monthly dues to the fraternity, and have well-defined roles. Their dues are used to pay for the fraternity's social events, and Little Sisters are expected to attend and hostess fraternity parties and hang around the house to make it a "nice place to be." One fraternity man, a senior, described Little Sisters this way: "They are very social girls, willing to join in, be affiliated with the group, devoted to the fraternity." Another member, a sophomore, said: "Their sole purpose is social—attend parties, attract new members, and 'take care' of the guys."

Our observations and interviews suggested that women selected by fraternities as Little Sisters are physically attractive, possess good social skills, and are willing to devote time and energy to the fraternity and its members. One undergraduate woman gave the following job description for Little Sisters to a campus newspaper:

It's not just making appearances at all the parties but entails many more responsibilities. You're going to be expected to go to all the intramural games to cheer the brothers on, support and encourage the pledges, and just be around to bring some extra life to the house. [As a Little Sister] you have to agree to take on a new responsibility other than studying to maintain your grades and managing to keep your checkbook from bouncing. You have to make time to be a part of the fraternity and support the brothers in all they do. (*The Tomahawk*, 1988)

The title of Little Sister reflects women's subordinate status; fraternity men in a parallel role are called Big Brothers. Big Brothers assist a sorority primarily with the physical work of sorority rushes, which, compared to fraternity rushes, are more formal, structured, and intensive. Sorority rushes take place in the daytime and fraternity rushes at night so fraternity men are free to help. According to one fraternity member, Little Sister status is a benefit to women because it gives them a social outlet and "the protection of the brothers." The gender-stereotypic conceptions and obligations of these Little Sister and Big Brother statuses indicate that fraternities and sororities promote a gender hierarchy on campus that fosters subordination and dependence in women, thus encouraging sexual exploitation and the belief that it is acceptable.

Women as Sexual Prey. Little Sisters are a sexual utility. Many Little Sisters do not belong to sororities and lack peer support for refraining from unwanted sexual relations. One fraternity man (whose fraternity has 65 members and 85 Little Sisters) told us they had recruited "wholesale" in the prior year to "get lots of new women." The structural access to women that the Little Sister program provides and the absence of normative supports for refusing fraternity members' sexual advances may make women in this program particularly susceptible to coerced sexual encounters with fraternity men.

Access to women for sexual gratification is a presumed benefit of fraternity membership, promised in recruitment materials and strategies and through brothers' conversations with new recruits. One fraternity man said: "We always tell the guys that you get sex all the time, there's always new girls. . . .After I became a Greek, I found out I could be with females at will." A university official told us that, based on his observations, "no one [i.e., fraternity men] on this campus wants to have 'relationships.' They just want to have fun [i.e., sex]." Fraternity men plan and execute strategies aimed at obtaining sexual gratification, and this occurs at both individual and collective levels.

Individual strategies include getting a woman drunk and spending a great deal of money on her. As for collective strategies, most of our undergraduate interviewees agreed that fraternity parties often culminate in sex and that this outcome is planned. One fraternity man said fraternity parties often involve sex and nudity and can "turn into orgies." Orgies may be planned in advance, such as the Bowery Ball party held by one fraternity. A former fraternity member said of this party:

The entire idea behind this is sex. Both men and women come to the party wearing little or nothing. There are pornographic pinups on the walls and usually porno movies playing on the TV. The music carries sexual overtones. . . .They just get schnockered [drunk] and, in most cases, they also get laid.

When asked about the women who come to such a party, he said: "Some Little Sisters just won't go. . . .The girls who do are looking for a good time, girls who don't know what it is, things like that."

Other respondents denied that fraternity parties are orgies but said that sex is always talked about among the brothers and they all know "who each other is doing it with." One member said that most of the time, guys have sex with their girlfriends "but with socials, girlfriends aren't allowed to come and it's their [members'] big chance [to have sex with other women]." The use of alcohol to help them get women into bed is a routine strategy at fraternity parties.

Conclusions

In general, our research indicated that the organization and membership of fraternities contribute heavily to coercive and often violent sex. Fraternity houses are occupied by same-sex (all men) and same-age (late teens, early twenties) peers whose maturity and judgment is often less than ideal. Yet fraternity houses are private dwellings that are mostly off-limits to, and away from scrutiny of, university and community representatives, with the result that fraternity house events seldom come to the attention of outsiders. Practices associated with the social construction of fraternity brotherhood emphasize a macho conception of men and masculinity, a narrow, stereotyped conception of women and femininity, and the treatment of women as commodities. Other practices contributing to coercive sexual relations and the cover-up of rapes include excessive alcohol use, competitiveness, and normative support for deviance and secrecy (cf. Bogal-Allbritten and Allbritten 1985; Kanin 1967).

Some fraternity practices exacerbate others. Brotherhood norms require "sticking together" regardless of right or wrong; thus rape episodes are unlikely to be stopped or reported to outsiders, even when witnesses disapprove. The ability to use alcohol without scrutiny by authorities and alcohol's frequent association with violence, including sexual coercion, facilitates rape in fraternity houses. Fraternity norms that emphasize the value of maleness and masculinity over femaleness and femininity and that elevate the status of men and lower the status of women in members' eyes undermine perceptions and treatment of women as persons who deserve consideration and care (cf. Ehrhart and Sandler 1985; Merton 1985).

Androgynous men and men with a broad range of interests and attributes are lost to fraternities through their recruitment practices. Masculinity of a narrow and stereotypical type helps create attitudes, norms, and practices that predispose fraternity men to coerce women sexually, both individually and collectively (Allgeier 1986; Hood 1989; Sanday 1981, 1986). Male athletes on campus may be similarly disposed for the same reasons (Kirshenbaum 1989; Telander and Sullivan 1989).

Research into the social contexts in which rape crimes occur and the social constructions associated with these contexts illumine rape dynamics on campus. Blanchard (1959) found that group rapes almost always have a leader who pushes others into the crime. He also found that the leader's latent homosexuality, desire to show off to his peers, or fear of failing to prove himself a man are frequently an impetus. Fraternity norms and practices contribute to the approval and use of sexual coercion as an accepted tactic in relations with women. Alcohol-induced compliance is normative, whereas, presumably, use of a knife, gun, or threat of bodily harm would not be because the woman who "drinks too much" is viewed as "causing her own rape" (cf. Ehrhart and Sandler 1985).

Our research led us to conclude that fraternity norms and practices influence members to view the sexual coercion of women, which is a felony crime, as sport, a contest, or a game (cf. Sato 1988). This sport is played not between men and women but between men and men. Women are the pawns or prey in the interfraternity rivalry game; they prove that a fraternity is successful or prestigious. The use of women in this way encourages fraternity men to see women as objects and sexual coercion as sport. Today's societal norms support young women's right to engage in sex at their discretion, and coercion is unnecessary in a mutually desired encounter. However, nubile young women say they prefer to be "in a relationship" to have sex while young men say they prefer to "get laid" without a commitment (Muehlenhard and Linton 1987). These differences may reflect, in part, American puritanism and men's fears of sexual intimacy or perhaps intimacy of any kind. In a fraternity context, getting sex without giving emotionally demonstrates "cool" masculinity. More important, it poses no threat to the bonding and loyalty of the fraternity brotherhood (cf. Farr 1988). Drinking large quantities of alcohol before having sex suggests that "scoring" rather than intrinsic sexual pleasure is a primary concern of fraternity men.

Unless fraternities' composition, goals, structures, and practices change in fundamental ways, women on campus will continue to be sexual prey for fraternity men. As all-male enclaves dedicated to opposing faculty and administration and to cementing in-group ties, fraternity members eschew any hint of homosexuality. Their version of masculinity transforms women, and men with womanly characteristics, into the out-group. "Womanly men" are ostracized; feminine women are used to demonstrate members' masculinity. Encouraging renewed emphasis on their founding values (Longino and Kart 1973), service orientation and activities (Lemire 1979), or members' moral development (Marlowe and Auvenshine 1982) will have little effect on fraternities' treatment of women. A case for or against fraternities cannot be made by studying individual members. The fraternity qua group and organization is at issue. Located on campus along with many vulnerable women, embedded in a sexist society, and caught up in masculinist goals, practices, and values, fraternities' violation of women—including forcible rape—should come as no surprise.

Note

1. Recent bans by some universities on open-keg parties at fraternity houses have resulted in heavy drinking before coming to a party and an increase in drunkenness among those who attend. This may aggravate, rather than

improve, the treatment of women by fraternity men at parties.

References

Adams, Aileen, and Gail Abarbanel. 1988. *Sexual Assault on Campus: What Colleges Can Do.* Santa Monica, CA: Rape Treatment Center.

Allgeier, Elizabeth. 1986. "Coercive Versus Consensual Sexual Interactions." G. Stanley Hall Lecture to American Psychological Association Annual Meeting, Washington, DC, August.

Blanchard, W. H. 1959. "The Group Process in Gang Rape." *Journal of Social Psychology* 49: 259–66.

Bogal-Allbritten, Rosemarie B., and William L. Allbritten. 1985. "The Hidden Victims: Courtship Violence Among College Students." *Journal of College Student Personnel* 43: 201–4.

Bohrnstedt, George W. 1969. "Conservatism, Authoritarianism and Religiosity of Fraternity Pledges." *Journal of College Student Personnel* 27: 36–43.

Bradford, Michael. 1986. "Tight Market Dries Up Nightlife at University." *Business Insurance* (March 2): 2, 6.

Burkhart, Barry. 1989. Comments in Seminar on Acquaintance/Date Rape Prevention: A National Video Teleconference, February 2.

Burkhart, Barry R., and Annette L. Stanton. 1985. "Sexual Aggression in Acquaintance Relationships." In *Violence in Intimate Relationships,* edited by G. Russell (pp. 43–65). Englewood Cliffs, NJ: Spectrum.

Byington, Diane B., and Karen W. Keeter. 1988. "Assessing Needs of Sexual Assault Victims on a University Campus." In *Student Services: Responding to Issues and Challenges* (pp. 23–31). Chapel Hill: University of North Carolina Press.

Chancer, Lynn S. 1987. "New Bedford, Massachusetts, March 6, 1983–March 22, 1984: The 'Before and After' of a Group Rape." *Gender & Society* 1: 239–60.

Ehrhart, Julie K., and Bernice R. Sandler. 1985. *Campus Gang Rape: Party Games?* Washington, DC: Association of American Colleges.

Farr, K. A. 1988. "Dominance Bonding Through the Good Old Boys Sociability Network." *Sex Roles* 18: 259–77.

Florida Flambeau. 1988. "Pike Members Indicted in Rape." (May 19): 1, 5.

Fox, Elaine, Charles Hodge, and Walter Ward. 1987. "A Comparison of Attitudes Held by Black and White Fraternity Members." *Journal of Negro Education* 56: 521–34.

Geis, Gilbert. 1971. "Group Sexual Assaults." *Medical Aspects of Human Sexuality* 5: 101–13.

Glaser, Barney G. 1978. *Theoretical Sensitivity: Advances in the Methodology of Grounded Theory*. Mill Valley, CA: Sociology Press.

Hood, Jane. 1989. "Why Our Society Is Rape-Prone." *New York Times*, May 16.

Hughes, Michael J., and Roger B. Winston, Jr. 1987. "Effects of Fraternity Membership on Interpersonal Values." *Journal of College Student Personnel* 45: 405–11.

Kanin, Eugene J. 1967. "Reference Groups and Sex Conduct Norm Violations." *The Sociological Quarterly* 8: 495–504.

Kimmel, Michael, ed. 1987. *Changing Men: New Directions in Research on Men and Masculinity*. Newbury Park, CA: Sage.

Kirshenbaum, Jerry. 1989. "Special Report, An American Disgrace: A Violent and Unprecedented Lawlessness Has Arisen Among College Athletes in All Parts of the Country." *Sports Illustrated* (February 27): 16–9.

Lemire, David. 1979. "One Investigation of the Stereotypes Associated with Fraternities and Sororities." *Journal of College Student Personnel* 37: 54–57.

Letchworth, G. E. 1969. "Fraternities Now and in the Future." *Journal of College Student Personnel* 10: 118–22.

Longino, Charles F., Jr., and Cary S. Kart. 1973. "The College Fraternity: An Assessment of Theory and Research." *Journal of College Student Personnel* 31: 118–25.

Marlowe, Anne F., and Dwight C. Auvenshine. 1982. "Greek Membership: Its Impact on the Moral Development of College Freshmen." *Journal of College Student Personnel* 40: 53–57

Martin, Patricia Yancey, and Barry A. Turner. 1986. "Grounded Theory and Organizational Research." *Journal of Applied Behavioral Science* 22: 141–57.

Merton, Andrew. 1985. "On Competition and Class: Return to Brotherhood." *Ms.* (September): 60–65, 121–22.

Messner, Michael. 1989. "Masculinities and Athletic Careers." *Gender & Society* 3: 71–88.

Meyer, T. J. 1986. "Fight Against Hazing Rituals Rages on Campuses." *Chronicle of Higher Education* (March 12): 34–36.

Miller, Leonard D. 1973. "Distinctive Characteristics of Fraternity Members." *Journal of College Student Personnel* 31: 126–28.

Muehlenhard, Charlene L., and Melaney A. Linton. 1987. "Date Rape and Sexual Aggression in Dating Situations: Incidence and Risk Factors." *Journal of Counseling Psychology* 34: 186–96.

Pressley, Sue Anne. 1987. "Fraternity Hell Night Still Endures." *Washington Post* (August 11): B1.

Rapport, Karen, and Barry R. Burkhart. 1983. "Personality and Attitudinal Characteristics of Sexually Coercive College Males." *Journal of Abnormal Psychology* 93: 216–21.

Roark, Mary L. 1987. "Preventing Violence on College Campuses." *Journal of Counseling and Development* 65: 367–70.

St. Petersburg Times. 1988. "A Greek Tragedy." (May 29): 1F, 6F.

Sanday, Peggy Reeves. 1981. "The SocioCultural Context of Rape: A Cross Cultural Study." *Journal of Social Issues* 37: 5–27.

——. 1986. "Rape and the Silencing of the Feminine." In *Rape*, edited by S. Tomaselli and R. Porter (pp. 84–101). Oxford: Basil Blackwell.

Sato, Ikuya. 1988. "Play Theory of Delinquency: Toward a General Theory of 'Action.'" *Symbolic Interaction* 11: 191–212.

Smith, T. 1964. "Emergence and Maintenance of Fraternal Solidarity." *Pacific Sociological Review* 7: 29–37.

Tallahassee Democrat. 1988a. "FSU Fraternity Brothers Charged." (April 27): 1A, 12A.

——. 1988b. "FSU Interviewing Students About Alleged Rape." (April 24): 1D.

——. 1989. "Woman Sues Stetson in Alleged Rape." (March 19): 3B.

Tampa Tribune. 1988. "Fraternity Brothers Charged in Sexual Assault of FSU Coed." (April 27): 6B.

Tash, Gary B. 1988. "Date Rape." *The Emerald of Sigma Pi Fraternity* 75(4): 1–2.

Telander, Rick, and Robert Sullivan. 1989. "Special Report, You Reap What You Sow." *Sports Illustrated* (February 27): 20–34.

The Tomahawk. 1988. "A Look Back at Rush, A Mixture of Hard Work and Fun" (April/May): 3D.

Walsh, Claire. 1989. Comments in Seminar on Acquaintance/Date Rape Prevention: A National Video Teleconference, February 2.

Wilder, David H., Arlyne E. Hoyt, Dennis M. Doren, William E. Hauck, and Robert D. Zettle. 1978. "The Impact of Fraternity and Sorority Membership on Values and Attitudes." *Journal of College Student Personnel* 36: 445–49.

Wilder, David H., Arlyne E. Hoyt, Beth Shuster Surbeck, Janet C. Wilder, and Patricia Imperatrice Carney. 1986 "Greek Affiliation and Attitude Change in College Students."

Journal of College Student Personnel 44: 510–19.

Adapted from Patricia Yancey Martin and Robert A. Hummer, *Gender & Society,* vol. 3/1989, pp. 457–473. Copyright © 1989 by Sage Publications. Reprinted by permission of Sage Publications, Inc. ✦

Part VII

White-Collar Deviance

Deviance is traditionally thought to be a characteristic of the marginalized. This is perfectly understandable. Norms typically reflect the imposition of behavioral codes from the powerful onto the powerless. There is a widespread assumption that the biggest threat to social order comes from "below," and norms develop to ensure that such persons are kept "in line." Sociologists reinforce this perception by focusing on street deviance and crime to the exclusion of "suite" deviance and crime, particularly in theoretical approaches, which largely drive the discipline.

Yet the biggest threat to social order, and the reciprocity required to maintain it, comes from above—from the most powerful, whose deviance not only is more harmful (in both absolute and relative terms) but also is less likely to be detected. Enforcement mechanisms, particularly in capitalistic societies, typically are not directed in any meaningful way toward the ruling classes, so "crimes of the suites" receive a low priority. When coupled with their magnitude, this lack of enforcement makes them especially insidious. The very nature of suite crimes, moreover, lends itself to the perception that they are not truly injurious. Whereas street crime is personal, direct, forceful, and one-on-one, suite crime is anonymous, impersonal, indirect, invisible, and putatively unintentional (Reiman 1990). That is, they occur during the course of normal business and can be easily rationalized as a necessary survival tactic in a cutthroat bureaucratic or capitalistic world.

Radical criminologists, however, justifiably ask whether oil companies who knowingly sell 87 octane gas in pumps labeled 93 octane are any less guilty of robbery than masked offenders wielding weapons inside the local 7-Eleven (in fact, it is probably an even more insidious form of robbery because the victims never know they've been "taken"). Multiply the thousands upon thousands of gallons of 87 gas sold at the 93 price and surely the monetary damage dwarfs that secured in the typical armed robbery. But armed robbery seems more dangerous (and harmful) precisely because it involves the forceful and direct removal of property from one individual by another. Private property lies at the essence of the capitalistic mode of production (without it, there would be no such thing as theft), so its plundering symbolizes the plundering of the system itself (Reiman 1990). This elegant form of political alchemy justifies the harsh treatment that predatory offenders receive at the hands of the criminal justice system: they are criminals whose behavior warrants strict punishment. White-collar offenders are "violators" whose behavior warrants "regulation"—regulation so weak as to be largely symbolic. The Occupational Health and Safety Administration (OSHA), for example—the government agency charged with overseeing safety violations (many of which are intentional, to save money and boost profits, but appear to be unintentional) in American workplaces—employs just 2,000 inspectors to monitor roughly 6 million workplaces (see Glassner 1999, 198).

White-collar deviance has been conceptualized in a number of ways, but the definition proposed by Reiss and Biderman is perhaps the most comprehensive. White-collar deviance, they suggest, consists of

> those violations of law in which penalties are attached that involve the use of a violator's position of economic power, influence, or trust in the legitimate economic or political institutional order for the purpose of illegal gain, or to commit an illegal act for personal or organizational gain. (Reiss and Biderman 1980, 4)

White-collar deviance has numerous manifestations, from fraud, embezzlement, bribery, and insider trading to price fixing and false advertising to industrial espionage, hazardous material dumping, the sale of defective consumer products, and the failure to maintain safe working conditions. A few poignant examples can help bring its reach and impact into greater focus.

Every year, doctors defraud the government and the American public out of hundreds of millions of dollars by overcharging, billing for services not rendered, or performing unnecessary surgeries; thousands of such surgeries result in grave injury or even death to the patient. The drinking water of communities across the country is habitually polluted by companies who, seeking to save money, intentionally fail to follow proper waste disposal procedures. Manufacturers routinely produce and sell products that kill and maim those who use them. The Ford Pinto is notorious, a car responsible for the fiery deaths of as many as 900 people, lives that could have easily been saved had Ford installed an eleven-dollar part to prevent gas tanks from rupturing during rear-end collisions. Ford knew it could prevent such deaths but, after conducting a cost-benefit analysis, decided it was cheaper to pay damages than recall and repair the vehicles (Dowie 1977). Employees entrusted with financial responsibility, low-level and high-level alike, routinely bilk organizations out of hundreds of millions of dollars a year, adding as much as 15 percent to the prices the rest of us must pay; in one case, a department store cashier stole "one nickel, dime, or quarter from every roll of change she made over a period of 20 years [and] was able to purchase a home with the money she [pilfered]" (Conklin 1977, 6; see also Beirne and Messerschmidt 1991). The fact that such offenses are so easily rationalized by those who commit them—"No one got hurt," "The company can absorb the loss," "They deserve what they had coming," "I was going to pay it back," "What I did really wasn't wrong," among others—makes them only easier to commit.

The readings chosen for this section are intended to reveal important contradictions in the construction and enforcement of "upper-class" deviance. Understanding what serious crime and deviance are and are not, and how society actively promotes these biased representations, constitutes a major objective. Occupational norms that promote and facilitate deviance are also a core concern. ✦

35 Crime in Cyberspace

Gene Stephens

*F*ew forms of deviance have grown as exponentially in scope and magnitude as computer crime. In the electronic age, computers are king, running everything from banks and Fortune 500 companies to family pharmacies and suburban homes. Justifiably, computers have been called one of the greatest of human innovations—on a par with electricity, the automobile, and the airplane. With every innovation, however, come opportunities for those gifted, motivated, and skilled enough to take advantage for their own instrumental ends. Computer crime, in this sense, becomes a logical outcome.

Stephens explores the various forms of computer crime, its monetary and interpersonal toll, and the challenges it presents for law enforcement. Computer crime is extraordinarily difficult to detect, owing largely to the anonymous, impersonal, and unobtrusive way in which it typically is committed. To catch offenders, social control agents must navigate a sophisticated electronic maze—a daunting task that requires enormous resources and skill (both of which are scarce in regulatory bodies). Not surprisingly, some of the most successful computer detectives have been computer criminals themselves; organizations spend millions of dollars a year trying to locate and recruit them, offering exorbitant salaries, plush offices, and other fringe benefits.

As participants in a deviant subculture, computer criminals may never have physical contact with one another, but this does not matter. Interaction is a point, click, or keystroke away. Technology permits boundless opportunities for network formation and provides the resources and connections deviants need to thrive. The appeal of computer-mediated deviance is unique, bridging the instrumental and the expressive, providing material rewards that motivate and emotional ones that reinforce. In the electronic age, the extent and type of information swapped will determine which particular forms of computer deviance emerge and which persist.

*B*illions of dollars in losses have already been discovered. Billions more have gone undetected. Trillions will be stolen, most without detection, by the emerging master criminal of the twenty-first century—the cyberspace offender.

Worst of all, *anyone* who is computer literate can become a cybercrook. He or she is everyman, everywoman, or even everychild. The crime itself will often be *virtual* in nature—sometimes recorded, more often not—occurring only in cyberspace, with the only record being fleeting electronic impulses.

But before discussing the infohighway crimes we can expect to see in the years ahead, let's look at the good news: The most-dreaded types of offenses—crimes such as murder, rape, assault, robbery, burglary, and vehicle theft—will be brought under control in the years ahead by a combination of technology and proactive community policing. Creation of the cashless society, for example, will eliminate most of the rewards for robbers and muggers, while computer-controlled smart houses and cars will thwart burglars and auto thieves. Implanted bodily function monitors and chemical drips (such as "sober-up" drugs and synthesized hormones) will keep most of the sexually and physically violent offenders under control.

More importantly, proactive policies—seeking out crime-breeding situations and taking steps to eliminate them before the crime occurs—may alleviate much of the burgeoning violence among young people. Tender, loving care demonstrated by informed parenting, universal health and day care, mentoring, and communal attention to children's welfare can prevent another generation of starved-for-attention juveniles from becoming criminals.

But cyberspace offenders—ranging in age from preteen to senior citizen—will have ample opportunities to violate citizens' rights for fun and profit, and stopping them will require much more effort. Currently, we have only primitive knowledge about these lawbreakers: Typically, they are seen only as nuisances or even admired as innovators or computer whizzes. But increasingly, the benign "hacker" is being replaced by the menacing "cracker"—an individual or member of a group intent on using cyberspace for illegal profit or terrorism.

Access to cyberspace has begun to expand geometrically, and technology is making the information superhighway even more friendly and affordable for millions of users. But foolproof protective systems can probably never be developed, although some high-tech entrepreneurs are certainly trying. Even if a totally secure system could ever be developed, it would likely disrupt the free flow of information—an unacceptable intrusion to most users. In fact, it is the ease of access that is driving this rapidly expanding field of crime.

What are the major cybercrimes being committed, how, and by whom? More importantly, where is cybercrime headed in the twenty-first century? Let's look at six cyberspace crime categories: communications, government, business, stalking, terrorism, and virtual.

Communications Crimes

Already, cellular theft and phone fraud have become major crimes. Low-tech thieves in airports and bus terminals use binoculars to steal calling-card access numbers as unsuspecting callers punch in their phone codes. Other thieves park vans beside busy interstate highways and use equipment obtained from shopping mall electronics stores to steal cellular phone access codes from the air. Within moments of these thefts, international calls are being made with the stolen numbers in what is becoming a multi-billion-dollar-a-year criminal industry.

Phone company employees, meanwhile, are also stealing and selling calling card numbers, resulting in more hundreds of mil-

lions of dollars in unauthorized calls. In 1994, an MCI engineer was charged with selling 60,000 calling card numbers for $3 to $5 each, resulting in more than $50 million in illegal long-distance charges. In another case, when a phone company tried to institute a call-forwarding program, crackers quickly defrauded the system of more money than the company stood to make in legal profits.

In the future, the opportunities for hacking and cracking will escalate, with telephones, computers, faxes, and televisions interconnected to provide instantaneous audiovisual communication and transmission of materials among individuals. The wide appeal of new multimedia communication systems will likely create such a huge volume of subscribers that the price will plummet and make access by all possible. But if billions of dollars of losses to thieves are compounded by billions more required to repair damages created by system terrorists, the cost might become prohibitive to all but the wealthy.

Cybercrimes Against the Government

In 1995, the U.S. Internal Revenue Service instituted stringent new regulations on electronic tax filing and returns. This move was to stop a rash of fraud that cost taxpayers millions in 1994: Returns that were processed quickly via this method turned out to be for tens of thousands of fictitious corporations and individuals. Similarly, in an attempt to stop food stamp fraud, the government issued electronic debit cards to a trial population and plans to go nationwide with the system later in the decade. However, early reports show that many recipients are selling their benefits for cash—50¢ to 60¢ on the dollar—to merchants who then receive full payment.

Cyberpunks regularly break into government computer systems, usually out of curiosity and for the thrill of the challenge. They often intercept classified data and sometimes even interrupt and change systems. One U.S. Justice Department official reported that military computers are the most vulnerable, "even less secure than university computers." This official noted that, during Operation Desert Storm, hackers were able to track both actual and planned troop movements.

James V. Christy II, director of an Air Force unit of computer-crime investigators, set up a team of hackers to test the security of military computer systems. He reported that the hackers broke into Pentagon systems "within 15 seconds" and went on to break into over 200 Air Force systems with no one reporting or even recognizing the break-ins.

Ironically, computer hackers often beat the system using the very technology intended to stop them. For example, federal law-enforcement agencies use an Escrowed Encryption Standard to protect classified information and a chip-specific key to decrypt the system. Experienced hackers can easily discover the key and use it to obtain passwords, gaining full access to encrypted systems.

Newer, more-secure encryption systems for protecting government and international business transactions require storing the "keys" in "escrow" with a specific government agency—usually the U.S. Treasury Department. Hackers and civil libertarians find this security solution unacceptable because it impedes the free flow of information and puts almost all sensitive and important data in the hands of government officials. This is seen by many as being dangerous to individual freedoms and a major step in the direction of creating a class structure based on the "information rich" and "information poor."

As more government data is stored in computers, protection will become both more vital and more difficult. When the livelihood of an individual depends on data in government computers, the temptation to "adjust" that record to increase benefits and reduce charges will be great. Many will try to do the adjusting themselves; others will be willing customers for a burgeoning black market of professional crackers. For those who have little need for government benefits but would like to eliminate their tax liability, a highly destructive method would be to plant a computer virus in government computers to destroy large numbers of records.

In this way, suspicion would not fall on an individual.

Targeting Business

Today, most banking is done by electronic impulse, surpassing checks and cash by a wide margin. In the near future, nearly all business transactions will be electronic. Thus, access to business computers equals access to money.

Recently, computer hacker John Lee, a founder of the infamous "Masters of Deception" hacker group, discussed his 10-year career, which began when he was 12 years old and included a one-year prison term in his late teens. Without admitting to any wrongdoing, Lee said that he could "commit a crime with five keystrokes" on the computer. He could: (1) change credit records and bank balances; (2) get free limousines, airplane flights, hotel rooms, and meals "without anyone being billed"; (3) change utility and rent rates; (4) distribute computer software programs free to all on the Internet; and (5) easily obtain insider trading information. Though prison was "no fun," Lee admitted that he would certainly be tempted to do it all again.

In a groundbreaking study published in *Criminal Justice Review* in the spring of 1994, Jerome E. Jackson of the California State University at Fresno reported the results of a study of a new group of criminals he called "fraud masters." These professional thieves obtain credit cards via fake applications, or by electronic theft, and pass them around among their peers internationally for profit. These young men and women want the "good life" after growing up in poverty. They are proud of their skills of deception and arrogant enough to feel they won't be caught. Indeed, none of those in the five-year case study were caught.

As seen in the $50-million-plus losses in the MCI case, a far greater threat to businesses than hackers are disgruntled and financially struggling employees. As internal theft from retail stores has always been many times greater in volume than theft from shoplifters, robbers, and burglars, theft by employees armed with inside information and computer access is and will continue to be a much larger problem than intrusion by hackers, crackers, and terrorists combined. By the turn of the century, 80% of Americans will process information as a major part of their employment, according to a United Way study.

In addition, the future portends new and brighter "for-profit" invasion of business computers. As one Justice Department official warns, "This technology in the hands of children today is technology that adults don't understand." The first generation of computer-literate citizens will reach adulthood shortly after the turn of the century and will surely open a new age in the annals of crime and crimefighting.

Cyberstalking

One frightening type of cybercriminal emerging rapidly is the cyberstalker. Possibly the most disturbing of these criminals is the pedophile who surfs computer bulletin boards, filled with bright young boys and girls, in search of victims. He develops a cyberspace relationship and then seeks to meet the child in person to pursue his sexual intentions. Already recognized as a serious problem, cyberstalking has spawned the cybercop—a police officer assigned to computer bulletin boards in search of these pedophiles. Once a suspect is spotted, the cybercop plays the role of a naive youngster and makes himself or herself available for a meeting with the suspect in hopes of gaining evidence for an arrest.

Also surfing the network, in search of pedophiles, are computer pornography sellers who offer magazine-quality color photographs of young boys and girls in a variety of sexually suggestive or actual sexual acts. Such a ring was broken up in 1994 and was found to have clients in several countries, with the pictures themselves transmitted from Denmark.

Another type of stalker expected to be seen more in the future is the emotionally disturbed loner, seeking attention and companionship through cyberspace, and who often becomes obsessed with a bulletin board "friend." If this person obtains personal information about the cyberspace acquaintance, he or she sometimes seeks a close, often smothering relationship. If spurned, the stalker launches a campaign of cyberspace harassment, moving into real-space harassment if adequate information is obtained. Cyberspace vengeance can take many forms, from ruining credit records and charging multiple purchases to the victim to creating criminal records and sending letters to employers informing them of the "shady background" of the victim.

In the twenty-first century, with access to the information superhighway available to all and information from data banks networked into dossiers reserved for "official use only" (but easily accessible to hackers and crackers), stalking will not only increase but be facilitated by a new generation of portable computers. Organic nanocomputers may one day be implanted in the human brain, making possible a new crime: mindstalking. Unauthorized intrusion and seduction will reach directly into the victim's brain, making the stalker harder to evade and even more difficult to escape.

Remote Terrorism

In London a couple of years ago, terrorists placed deadly missiles in the back of a truck and remotely sent them flying toward the home of the British prime minister. The missiles exploded on the lawn without harm to the prime minister or the house, but they could have killed him and created an international crisis—clearly the intent of the bombers.

Today, terrorists have the capacity to detonate explosives in another country by means of computers and radio signals bounced off satellites. Because the emerging information superhighway is without borders, computer viruses and other information-destroying instruments can be hurled at business or government officials and facilities from anywhere on the globe.

In the future, information will be so crucial to success in business and personal life that being cut off from it will be like being held hostage or kidnapped. Terrorists who can cut communications off to an individual, group, community, or wider society will have the power and ability to spread fear and panic.

As with stalkers, terrorists will find new opportunities when computer implants in human brains become widely available. Borrowing a twentieth-century technique from psychology—subliminal conditioning—terrorists might recruit unsuspecting accomplices via low-intensity audiovisual messages aimed directly at individuals with brain-implanted computers. Unsuspecting implantees might unconsciously begin to modify their attitudes in the direction sought by the terrorists, or worse, even begin to join in terrorist activities. Political terrorists, whose agenda often is to change the world to suit their beliefs, are the most likely candidates to embrace this new approach and other emerging technologies to gain direct access to the minds of the populace.

Virtual Crimes

Stock and bond fraud is already appearing in cyberspace—stocks and bonds that appear on the markets, are actively traded for a short time, and then disappear. The stocks and bonds are nonexistent, only the electronic impulses are real.

In a recent case, a trader was paid $9 million in commissions for what appeared to be some $100 million in sales of bonds. But investigators now feel that these bonds may never have changed hands at all, except in cyberspace. In the future, a virtual reality expert could create a hologram in the form of a respected stockbroker or real estate broker, then advise clients in cyberspace to buy certain stocks, bonds, or real estate. Unsuspecting victims acting on the advice might later find that they had enlarged the coffers of the virtual-reality expert, while buying worthless or nonexistent properties.

This is just the tip of the iceberg in what might be tagged as "virtual crime"—offenses based on a reality that only exists in cyberspace. As virtual reality becomes increasingly sophisticated, it is the young adults in the first decade of the twenty-first century who—having grown up with virtual reality—will create the software and determine the legal and criminal uses of this technology. And with virtual reality potentially reaching directly into the brains of recipients via "organic" computers, the ability to separate cyberspace reality from truth outside cyberspace will be one of the greatest challenges of the twenty-first century.

Twenty-First Century Expectations

The outlook for curtailing cyberspace crime by technology or conventional law-enforcement methods is bleak. Most agencies do not have the personnel or the skills to cope with such offenses, and to date all high-tech approaches have been met by almost immediate turnabouts by hackers or crackers.

As individuals see and talk to each other over computers in the next few years, and as nanotechnology makes computers even more portable, new technology will emerge to protect data. But simplifying systems to make them more universally acceptable and accessible will also make them more vulnerable to intruders.

Control of access by optical patterns, DNA identification, voice spectrographs, encryption, and other methods may slow down hackers, but no method is foolproof or presents much of a challenge to today's most talented cyberpunks. The trouble is that in the future many more users will have skills far beyond those of today's crackers—a process one expert termed "the democratization of computer crime."

Still, there is much to be gained by easy access to the information superhighway. The "cyberpunk imperatives," a code subscribed to many hackers, include: (1) information should be free so that the most capable can make the most of it; (2) the world will be better off if entrepreneurs can obtain any data necessary to provide needed or desired new products and services; and (3) decentralization of information protects us all from "Big Brother."

Cybercrime probably cannot be controlled by conventional methods. Technology is on the side of the cyberspace offender and motivation is high—it's fun, exciting, challenging, and profitable. The only real help is one that has not proven very successful in recent decades: conscience and personal values, the belief that theft, deception, and invasion of privacy are simply unacceptable.

Behavioral psychologists argue that all values are learned by a system of rewards and, to a lesser extent, punishment. Thus, if these values are necessary for survival, children should consciously be conditioned to live by them. If all citizens—all computer users—were taught these values and sought to live by them, cyberspace could become the wondrous and friendly place its creators have envisioned.

Ironically, the greatest possible allies to be found in this search for values in cyberspace are the adolescent hackers of the 1980s, many of whom are the software programmers of the 1990s. In his book, *Secrets of a Super-Hacker*, a hacker named "Knightmare" says that "true hackers" love to break into systems and leave proof of their skills, but do not hurt individuals by stealing tangible goods or money, or destroying files or systems.

"Hacker ethics," Knightmare writes, include informing computer managers about problems with their security and offering to teach and share knowledge about computer security when asked. Increasingly, government and business computer managers are asking. Many of the Fortune 500 companies and numerous government agencies have hired hackers to test their systems and even design new security protocols for them.

Thus, hackers are helping to protect the information superhighway from crackers and terrorists. As one hacker says, "Hackers love computers and they want the Net safe."

Originally published in the September–October 1995 issue of *The Futurist*. Used with permission from the World Future Society, 7910 Woodmont Avenue, Suite 450, Bethesda, Maryland, 20814. Telephone: 301/656-8274; Fax: 301/951-0394; http://www.wfs.org. ✦

36
Corporate Deviance

David R. Simon

*F*ew Americans realize how much risk they assume on a daily basis from products they purchase to make their lives easier, more satisfying, or more convenient. Safety and consumer product violations are typically given little attention by the corporate-controlled media and even less by executive bodies charged with regulating organizational malfeasance. Legislative efforts typically focus on the "real criminals," that is, those who commit predatory, one-on-one crime—burglars, robbers, rapists, murderers, and the like. Corporate crime is often not considered crime at all because it occurs during the course of normal business, is putatively "unintended," and inflicts harm on many anonymously rather than a few directly. The impersonal nature of corporate deviance is arguably its most insidious quality, especially when one considers that victims may never be aware that they have been victimized. Even if they do become aware, they often realize there is not much they can do about it.

Simon provides a laundry list of corporate offenses that, even when uncovered, often elicit no more than mild legal sanctions. Standard practice in the "punishment" of corporate deviance involves the use of so-called consent decrees, which are anything but punitive: The company agrees to stop whatever it has been accused of doing (e.g., illegal dumping, manufacturing unsafe products, exposing workers to known health risks, etc.), while it asserts (through the decree) that it has done nothing wrong. Monetary fines, usually small, typically are levied, after which the company can go back to conducting business as usual. Incarceration is almost never a part of the bargain. Imagine a bank robber or residential burglar being offered such a deal.

The articles in this section affirm the notion that deviance is in the eye of the beholder and that rule-breaking perpetrated by the wealthy is judged by qualitatively different standards than that committed by the poor or disenfranchised. Simon locates the root of the problem in capitalism itself, which promotes an anything-goes, profit-obsessed mentality that functions to trivialize violations that occur during the course of making money. Regulation is not the answer, we are told by capitalists, because it promotes huge, ill-conceived, and inefficient government bureaucracies. Besides, they add, the system itself depends on wealth accumulation, so too much regulation can stifle the innovation and growth that fuels it. Although often effective, such arguments are merely ploys to entice audiences to believe that the capitalist system is the only one that works and that deviance—even serious organizational deviance—must be accepted as a necessary evil.

This chapter addresses the corporate disregard for the welfare of people, involving the abuse of consumers, workers, and society itself. Our thesis is that the profit-maximizing behaviors practiced by corporations under monopoly capitalism are hazardous to our individual and collective health and therefore constitute another manifestation of elite deviance. . . .

Unsafe Products

Commonly, the concern over violence in society is directed toward murder, rape, child abuse, and riots. We do not include in the context of violence the harm inflicted on people by unsafe products. The National Commission on Product Safety has revealed that 20 million Americans are injured [annually] in the home as a result of incidents connected with consumer products. "Of the total, 110,000 are permanently disabled and 30,000 are killed. A significant number could have been spared if more attention had been paid to hazard reduction."[1] . . .

'Health' Products

There are numerous examples of corporations that have marketed products to promote health that were known to be dangerous. What follows is a representative sample of such cases.

- Item: In 1995, three "Luv'N'Care" baby pacifier marketing firms pleaded guilty to 14 violations of federal law and Consumer Product Safety Commission (CPSC) regulations. Under the August 1995 plea agreement, the companies will pay a $140,000 criminal penalty for marketing pacifiers that put defenseless children at risk of suffocating or choking to death. The CPSC claimed they had received dozens of complaints between 1990 and 1994 about the pacifiers.[2]

- Item: In 1995, three former executives of C. R. Bard, Inc., were convicted of conspiring to defraud the Food and Drug Administration (FDA) through heart catheter sales. C. R. Bard pleaded guilty to 391 counts in conjunction with the catheters and was fined $61 million in criminal and civil fines, the largest FDA-prosecution fine ever. In an effort to maximize profits, Bard had used unsuspecting patients—many of whom were elderly and infirm—as human guinea pigs, inserting heart catheter tips with inflatable balloons into coronary arteries, concealing malfunctions—which included balloon rupture and deflation problems and tip breakages. Broken tips caused heart injuries requiring emergency coronary bypass surgery to remove the tips.[3]

- Item: Eli Lilly and Company pleaded guilty in 1985 to federal charges that it had failed to report to the government deaths and toxic reactions associated with its arthritic drug Oraflex.[4] Lilly had also marketed DES (diethylstilbestrol), which has been found to cause reproductive problems in the children of mothers who used it in the 1950s. The Lilly product Darvon has been associated with 11,000 deaths and 79,000 emergency room visits.[5]

Dangerous Nutrition

The food industry is obviously big business. In this section, we examine how the food industry, in its search for more profits, often disregards the health of consumers, which constitutes deviance. We explore four areas in which human considerations are often secondary to profit: (1) the sale of adulterated products; (2) the extensive use of chemical additives; (3) the increased use of sugar and fats; and (4) enticing children.

Adulterated Products

We will use the meat industry as our illustration of blatant disregard for the health of consumers. Upton Sinclair's expose of the Chicago stockyards and meatpacking houses around 1900 showed how spoiled meat was sold, how dangerous ingredients (such as rats and dung) were used in sausage, and how rats overran piles of meat stored under leaking roofs.[6] President Theodore Roosevelt commissioned an investigation of Chicago meatpackers, and as a result, the Meat Inspection Act of 1906 required that meat sold in interstate commerce had to be inspected according to federal standards. However, meat processed and sold within a state was not subject to the law, omitting as late as 1967 nearly 15 percent of the meat slaughtered and 25 percent of all meat processed in the United States. As a result:

> Surveys of packing houses in Delaware, Virginia, and North Carolina found the following tidbits in the meat: animal hair, sawdust, flies, abscessed pork livers, and snuff spit out by the meat workers. To add even further flavoring, packing houses whose meat did not cross state lines could use 4-D meat (dead, dying, diseased, and disabled) and chemical additives that would not pass federal inspection. Such plants were not all minor operations; some were run by the giants Armour, Swift, and Wilson.[7]

In 1967, the Wholesome Meat Act was passed, specifying that state inspection standards must at least match federal standards. This was accomplished in 1971, but there have been continuing violations. One problem is "Number 2" meat—that returned by a retailer to a packer as unsatisfactory and then resold as Number 2 meat to another customer if it meets standards of wholesomeness. As an example of how this can be abused, consider the following occurrence in a Los Angeles Hormel plant:

> When the original customers returned the meat to Hormel, they used the following terms to describe it: "moldy liverloaf, sour party hams, leaking bologna, discolored bacon, off-condition hams, and slick and slimy spareribs." Hormel renewed these products with cosmetic measures (reconditioning, trimming, and washing). Spareribs returned for sliminess, discoloration, and stickiness were rejuvenated through curing and smoking, renamed Windsor Loins, and sold in ghetto stores for more than fresh pork chops.[8]

This Hormel abuse occurred because the U.S. Department of Agriculture inspector, who was paid $6,000 annually by Hormel for overtime, looked the other way.[9]

Meat packers are also deceptive about what is included in their products. The labels on packages are not always complete. Consider, for instance, the ingredients of the hot dog:

> The hot dog . . . by law can contain 69 percent water, salt, spices, corn syrup and cereal, and 15 percent chicken; that still leaves a little room for goat meat, pigs' ears, eyes, stomachs, snouts, udders, bladders and esophagus—all legally okay. There is no more all-American way to take a break at the old ball game than to have water and pigs' snouts on a bun, but you might prefer to go heavier on the mustard from now on.[10]

Upton Sinclair's lurid description of the 1900s-era Chicago slaughterhouses fits some situations even today. In 1984, Nebraska Beef Processors and its Colorado subsidiary, Cattle King Packing company—the largest supplier of ground meat to school lunch programs and also a major supplier of meat to the Department of Defense, supermarkets, and fast-food chains—was found guilty of (1) regularly bringing dead animals into its slaughterhouses and mixing rotten meat into its hamburgers, (2) labeling old meat with phony dates, and (3) deceiving U.S. Department of Agriculture inspectors

by matching diseased carcasses with the healthy heads from larger cows.[11]

The Nebraska Beef–Cattle King scandal was not an isolated case. Two additional examples make this point. In 1979, a New Jersey firm was convicted of making pork sausage with an unauthorized chemical that masks discoloration of spoiled meat. And in 1982, a California company used walkie-talkies to avoid inspectors while doctoring rotten sausage.[12]

Extensive Use of Additives

The profits from the food industry come mainly from processing farm goods through fortifying, enriching, and reformulating to produce goods that look appealing, have the right taste and aroma, and will not spoil. More than 1,500 food additives have been approved for use as flavors, colors, thickeners, preservatives, and other agents for controlling the properties of food. Let's briefly look at some of these additives.[13]

- Sodium nitrates and nitrates are added to keep meat products appearing blood red. Nitrates are also used to preserve smoked fish.

- A variety of preservatives is used to prevent the spoilage of bread, cereals, margarine, fish, confections, jellies, and soft drinks. The most commonly used are BHT, BHA, sodium benzoate, and benzoic acid.

- About 95 percent of the color in the food we eat is the result of synthetic colors added. The use of red dye No. 2 was prohibited by the government when it was found to cause cancer in mice, although it is still allowed in maraschino cherries because it is assumed that no one will eat more than one or two at a time.

- Flour, that all-purpose staple, is bleached and conditioned by a number of potent poisons—hydrogen acetone, benzyl peroxide, chlorine dioxide, nitrogen oxide, and nitrosyl chloride. Also added to flour are such strengtheners as potassium bromate and ammonium presulfate.

An indirect additive that affects the health of consumers is one that is fed to animals.

Diethylstilbestrol (DES), an artificial female sex hormone, fattens about 75 percent of the beef cattle in the United States. This hormone is added because it causes dramatic weight gain on less feed. It has been outlawed for use with poultry, although hens are fed arsenic because it makes them lay more eggs.

Sugar substitutes are another type of food additive that has questionable health consequences. Cyclamate was banned in 1970 after tests linked it to various types of cancer. And saccharin, another additive, has been shown to be dangerous but has not been banned; Congress has only decreed that food containing saccharin must carry warning labels. The latest sugar substitute, aspartame (or Nutrasweet), is also believed by some scientists to pose a health danger to some 50 million regular users. However, no ban or warning has been issued for products containing Nutrasweet. . . .

There is a great deal of controversy among scientists about the effects of additives in our diet. "Altogether, laboratory tests have produced evidence that some 1,400 substances—drugs, food additives, pesticides, industrial chemicals, cosmetics—might cause cancer. But there are only a few chemicals which all the experts see as linked to human cancer."[14] Typically, government scientists disagree with the scientists hired by industry.[15] Several considerations, though, should make us cautious about what we eat.

First, many of the additives are poisons. The quantities in food may be minute, but just what are the tolerance levels? Is any poison, in any amount, appropriate in food? Is there the possibility of residue build-up in vital organs? Second, what happens to laboratory animals fed relatively large quantities of these additives? They are poisoned; they do get cancer; and they do suffer from other maladies induced by the additives.

Finally, what happens with the interaction of these additives on humans? Scientists may be able to test the effects of a few chemicals, but what about the hundreds of thousands of possible combinations? In a slice of bread, for example, there can be as many as 93 possible different additives. The danger is that it takes years—maybe 20 or 30—of eating a particular diet for an individual to develop cancer. Since most of the additives are relatively new, we do not know what they may eventually cause. We do know that the average American has increased his or her yearly intake of food additives from three pounds in 1965 to about five pounds in 1977.[16] And cancer rates continue to rise.

Why, then, do companies insist on adding these potentially harmful chemicals to our food? One possibility is that consumers demand more variety and convenience. But more important, the food industry has found that processing synthetic foods is very profitable. As one food marketer remarked, "The profit margin on food additives is fantastically good, much better than the profit margins on basic, traditional foods."[17] Hightower has shown how this works:

> It gets down to this: Processing and packaging of food are becoming more important pricing factors than the food itself. Why would food corporations rather sell highly processed and packaged food than the much simpler matter of selling basics? Because processing and packaging spell profits.
>
> First, the more you do to a product, the more chances there are to build in profit margins—Heinz can sell tomatoes for a profit, or it can bottle the tomatoes for a bigger profit, or it can process the tomatoes into ketchup for still more profit, or it can add spices to the ketchup and sell it as barbeque sauce for a fat profit, or it can add flavors and meat tenderizer to the barbeque sauce for the fattest profit of all.
>
> Second, processing and packaging allows artificial differentiation of one company's product from that of another—in other words, selling on the basis of brand names. Potatoes can be sold in bulk, or they can be put in a sack and labeled Sun Giant, which will bring a higher price and more profit.
>
> Third, processing and packaging allow the use of additives to keep the same item on the shelf much longer and they allow for shipment over long distances, thus expanding the geographic reach of a corporation.

Fourth, processing and packaging separate consumers from the price of raw food, allowing oligopolistic middlemen to hold up the consumer price of their products even when the farm price falls. When the spinach crop is so abundant that spinach prices tumble at the farm level, the supermarket price of Stouffer's frozen spinach souffle does not go down.[18]

What's more, American corporations, in their quest for profits, have knowingly marketed defective medical devices, lethal drugs, carcinogens, toxic pesticides, and other harmful products overseas when they have been banned for sale in the United States. . . .

Enticing Children

The increased consumption of additives, sugar, and fats in food by children is a special health concern. Children are an important market, and food producers have spent multimillions of dollars in advertising aimed at them. Obviously, these corporations believe that their advertising influences the interests, needs, and demands of children. This belief is backed by research findings that show that children are susceptible to this influence. One study of youngsters in grades one to five found that 75 percent had asked their mothers to purchase the cereals they had seen on television. In another study, 80 percent of the mothers of children aged two to six expressed the conviction that television ads did cause their children to ask for certain products.[19]

The nutritional problem emanating from the television advertising blitz aimed at children is that the most advertised food products are sugar-coated cereals, candies, and other sweet snack foods. One study, for example, found that 96 percent of all food advertising on Saturday and Sunday children's TV programs was for sweets.[20] This report by the Federal Trade Commission (FTC) shows that these advertisements are effective, for several reasons:

(a) children's requests for specific, brand-name cereals and snack foods are frequently, if not usually, honored by their parents; (b) very high proportions of children are able to name specific (heavily advertised) brands as their favorites; (c) when asked to list acceptable snacks, high proportions of children mention cookies, candy, cake, and ice cream, including specific (heavily advertised) products; (d) U.S. consumption of snack desserts has increased markedly since 1962, and significant proportions of the purchases are made by children.[21]

The television directed at children is effective because the advertisers have done their research. Social science techniques have been used by motivation researchers in laboratory situations to determine how children of various ages react to different visual and auditory stimuli. Children are watched through two-way mirrors, their behavior is photographed, and their autonomic responses (e.g., eye-pupil dilation) are recorded to see what sustains their interest, their subconscious involvement, and the degree of pleasure they experience.[22] Thus, advertisers have found that, if one can associate fun, power, or a fascinating animated character with a product, then children will want that product. . . .

The Tobacco Industry

Although a number of industries have been guilty of manufacturing, advertising, and selling harmful products, we will consider only the tobacco industry. In 1979, fifteen years after the first Surgeon General's warning that smoking is linked to lung cancer and other ills, the Secretary of Health, Education, and Welfare issued the new Surgeon General's report on the health hazards of smoking cigarettes. The report summarized 30,000 previously published scientific studies and provided strong evidence that:

1. Smoking is a leading cause of lung cancer and a major factor in heart disease, bronchitis, and emphysema.

2. The babies of mothers who smoke while pregnant are born lighter and display slower rates of physical and mental growth than babies born to nonsmokers.

3. Two-pack-a-day smokers have a 100 percent greater risk of dying in any given year than nonsmokers.

4. Smoking is especially hazardous to workers in certain occupations (asbestos, rubber, textile, uranium, and chemical industries).

5. Smoking kills 400,000 Americans and costs taxpayers $18 billion annually, and passive smoke kills an additional 50,000 Americans.[23]

No medical group or scientific group in the world has disputed the conclusion that smoking is very injurious to health, yet the tobacco industry continues to push its products (buttressed, we might add, by government subsidies). In 1988, the tobacco industry spent an estimated $2.5 billion promoting its products, much of it aimed at portraying smoking as a youthful and attractive habit. . . .

- Item: Cigarettes are heavily advertised in black-oriented magazines such as *Ebony, Jet,* and *Essence.* Billboards advertising cigarettes are used in black communities four to five times more often than in white communities. Smoking rates among African Americans have increased from 26 to 29 percent in the 1990s, but smoking rates among whites have stayed constant at 25.5 percent.

- Item: African-American men are 30 percent more likely than white males to die from smoking-related diseases, and blacks who give up smoking are more likely than whites to start smoking again.[24]

- Item: Of the top ten companies advertising in Hispanic markets, two are cigarette companies. (Philip Morris was number one, and R. J. Reynolds was number ten.)

- Item: In 1989, the Canadian government charged that Imperial Tobacco Ltd. (which owns Brown and Williamson in the United States) and RJR MacDonald (owned by U.S. conglomerate RJR Nabisco) deliberately attempted to hook children ages eighteen and under through its advertising. Evidence was produced documenting tobacco firms' marketing plans for young smokers, which attempted to change youths' attitudes on smoking and health. Documents also made clear attempts at convincing French-speaking Canadian youths ages twelve to seventeen to begin smoking filtered and so-called light cigarettes.

- Item: It has been estimated by the United Nations that 500 million people in Third World nations will die within the next decade from smoking related illnesses. Cigarettes are very heavily advertised in Asia, Africa, and Latin America as a result of the lack of legal restrictions (e.g., warning labels) faced by tobacco producers in other parts of the world, such as North America and Europe.[25] Tobacco companies look to expand their market overseas, particularly in developing countries. Philip Morris, for example, sells more than 175 brands in 160 countries, and its foreign sales have grown rapidly.[26] The foreign market also provides companies with a market for the high-tar brands that are losing sales in the United States. The problem with all this, of course, is that the tobacco firms are promoting the use of a known health hazard for their own profit. . . .

Dangerous Working Conditions

. . .[T]he mining industry illustrates the two major dangers of the workplace—injuries from on-the-job accidents and exposure to toxic chemicals at work that have long-term negative effects. On-the-job accidents cause 3.3 million injuries annually requiring hospital treatment. Exposure to toxic chemicals causes at least 100,000 worker deaths each year and 390,000 new cases of occupational diseases.[27] We will focus on this latter type of workplace hazard.

The dangers today are invisible contaminants such as nuclear radiation, chemical compounds, dust, and asbestos fibers in the air. Because of increased production and use of synthetic chemicals in industry over recent decades, the level of danger from these contaminants is increasing. Just in the microelectronics industry, for example, 5,000 chemicals are used (solvents, acids, and gases), and of these, about 500 are rated as dangerous.[28] . . .

Consider the following examples of the specific risks of continued exposure in certain industries.

- Item: Workers in the dyestuffs industry (working with aromatic hydrocarbons) have about thirty times the risk of the general population of dying from bladder cancer.[29]
- Item: The wives of men who work with vinyl chloride are twice as likely as other women to have miscarriages or stillbirths.[30]
- Item: In 1978, Occidental Chemical Company workers handling the pesticide DBCP were found to be sterile as a result of the exposure, substantiating a 1961 study by Dow Chemical that indicated that DBCP caused sterility in rats.[31]
- Item: A 1976 government study determined that, if 129,000 workers were exposed to the current legal level of cotton-dust exposure, over a period of time, 23,497 would likely become byssinotics (victims of "brown lung").[32]
- Item: Starting with 632 asbestos workers in 1943, mined each of their fates after twenty years of employment. By 1973, 444 were dead, a rate 50 percent greater than for the average white male. The rate for lung cancer was 700 percent greater than expected, and the rate for all types of cancers was four times as great.[33] . . .

The lack of concern for the safety of workers in the plastics and asbestos industries is typical of other industries, as well. Safety regulations for cotton dust have been opposed by the textile industry. As usual, industry argued that it would cost billions to clean up the mills, jobs would be lost, and prices to consumers would rise dramatically. Similarly, copper refiners have resisted rigorous safety regulations. For example, a study of mortality among Tacoma smelter workers found the death rate from lung cancer to be between three and four times as high as normal and ten times as high for workers exposed to the highest toxic concentrations. Moreover, a study found that children within a half mile of the smelter had absorbed as much arsenic as the workers themselves.[34] Despite these findings, the owner of the smelter in Tacoma, ASARCO, led an industry-wide campaign against the government's new standards. Again, the company offered the familiar argument that the costs of compliance would be $100 million, adding 15 cents to the now 72 cents needed to produce a pound of copper.

This raises the critical question: At what point are profits more important than human lives? Speaking of the cotton industry, which is representative of other major industries, one observer has argued:

> In a society in which profits did not take precedence over people, . . . the finer points of byssinosis [brown lung disease] would have been considered tangential long ago and the road to its prevention would now be clear.
>
> Better air-filtration systems would have been installed and other capital expenditures made. But in the United States, where society is tuned to a different chord, the present delay over preventive measures, like the oblivion which preceded it, is rooted not in science and technology but in economics and politics—in the callous traditions of the cotton industry and in government's compromising ways.[35]

Finally, we should ask: What is a crime? Is it not when a victim is hurt (physically, emotionally, or financially) by the willful act of another? When 100,000 Americans die annually from occupationally related diseases, is that a crime?

Officially, these deaths and the human suffering induced by willful neglect for worker safety are not considered crimes. . . .

Polluting the Environment

The assault on the environment is the result of an ever larger population, higher rates of consumption, and an increasing reliance on technology. These are worldwide trends. "Not only are more societies acquiring more efficient tools wherewith to exploit the earth; nearly everywhere, there are increasing numbers to do the exploiting, and befoul the air, water, and land in the process."[36]. . .

In a capitalist system, private businesses make decisions based on making profit. This places the environment in jeopardy. Best and Connolly have shown how corporate decision makers choose alternatives that have negative impacts on the ecology.[37] They describe the logic of capitalism in the following:

> Under such circumstances [capitalism] it is quite irrational for any individual producer or consumer to accept the higher costs involved in curtailing various assaults on the environment. Thus a company that purified the water used in production before disposing it into streams would add to its own costs, fail to benefit from the purified water flowing downstream, and weaken its competitive market position with respect to those companies unwilling to institute purified procedures. Since it is reasonable to assume that other companies in a market system will not voluntarily weaken their position in this way, it is irrational for any single company to choose to do so. . . . Thus a range of practices which are desirable from the vantage point of the public are irrational from the vantage point of any particular consumer or producer. And a range of policies which are rational from the vantage point of individual consumers and producers are destructive of the collective interest in preserving nonrenewable productive resources and in maintaining the environment's capacity to assimilate wastes.[38] . . .

Pollution, as we have seen, is a direct consequence of an economic system in which the profit motive supersedes the concern for the environment. This is made clearer when corporations are unwilling to comply with government regulations and to pay damages for ecological disasters such as oil spills. Consider the following examples:

DuPont

The largest chemical company in the United States has given the world nylon, Teflon, Freon, and leaded gasoline (which it still makes for markets overseas); is the country's number-one emitter of toxins, releasing poisons at the rate of just under a million pounds a day, according to the EPA's 1989 data; is the world's largest producer of ozone-destroying chlorofluorocarbons (CFCs) and leads all other companies in domestic deep-well injection of toxic wastes (254.9 million pounds in 1989). Recently, DuPont was forced to pay $1.4 million in damages for concealing records showing that six employees had developed lung damage from asbestos exposure. Its operation of the government's Savannah River nuclear-weapons complex (1950–1989) polluted water sources for the area and has been connected to elevated levels of leukemia, lung cancer, and other diseases.

Rockwell

The EPA has identified 166 separate hazardous-waste dumps at Rockwell's Rocky Flats nuclear-weapons facility outside Denver, including Hillside 881, "thought to be the worst-polluted spot in the country and a threat to local drinking water." In 1992, Rockwell paid $18.5 million in fines for environmental violations (including five felonies) at Rocky Flats. Rockwell also is the second-largest emitter of airborne toxins in the heavily polluted Los Angeles Basin; it has admitted to ten accidental releases of radioactive materials there over the past twenty years, and has been identified by the state authorities as possibly responsible for high rates of bladder cancer.

General Motors

General Motors releases three times as much toxic pollution as its main U.S. competitor, Ford Motor Co., paid the most in OSHA penalties of any U.S. company between 1977 and 1990; has been linked with 200 Superfund sites, including a landfill in New York that will take an estimated $100 million to clean up; and is the top producer of ozone-depleting chemicals in California. A GM plant in Saginaw, Michigan, pumped toxic material into the environment at the rate of more than a thousand pounds an hour in 1989.

General Electric

Even as General Electric was giving failing actor Ronald Reagan his big break as host of a 1950s TV series, it was neglecting to warn residents near its Hanford Nuclear Reservation in Washington State about its regular releases of radioactive substances into the environment. GE plants also discharged 500,000 pounds of PCBs into the Hudson River over a thirty-year period. One of the three major manufacturers of nuclear-power plants, GE has been sued by several utility companies for supplying them with deficient nuclear-containment vessels. GE designed Mexico's only nuclear power plant, which has dumped radioactive water into the Gulf of Mexico.

Georgia Pacific

According to 1991 EPA data, Georgia Pacific has the worst air-permit compliance record in the forest-products industry, and has pulp and paper mills that were cited as out of compliance for a cumulative sixty-one quarters (fifteen-plus years!). It also has plants emitting dangerously high amounts of cancer-causing chloroform into the air of at least four states. Recently, G-P was fined $5 million for tax evasion in a scheme that would have allegedly damaged a wetlands area, and lost two court decisions concerning its release of the fiendishly toxic pollutant dioxin.

Cargill

Although Cargill is one of the world's largest grain traders, meat packers, flour millers, and seed companies, and also runs steel mills, this $49 billion company is able to operate in great secrecy because it is privately held. Nonetheless, Cargill has been cited for over 2,000 OSHA violations since 1987; spilled 40,000 gallons of toxic phosphoric solution into the Aliifia River in Florida in 1988, causing a massive fish kill; and since 1991 has had the worst air compliance record of any company in its industry. It is also one of the top two emitters of toxics in its industry, according to the EPA. In 1991, then-governor Bill Clinton criticized the company for releasing into Arkansas rivers animal waste comparable to the output of 21 million

people, or about ten times the state's population.

USX

Formerly United States Steel Corporation, USX operates a notorious steelworks in Gary, Indiana, which has been fined $34 million in penalties and cleanup costs for dumping toxin-laden wastewater, and $1.6 million more for violating the Clean Air Act. USX has also been repeatedly cited for violating air standards for toxic emissions in Pennsylvania at its Fairless and its Clairton works. Additionally, USX's Marathon subsidiary was responsible for a hydrofluoric-acid leak that led to the evacuation of 4,000 people in Texas City in 1987. USX owns Marathon and Speedway gas stations in the Midwest and Southeast.

Exxon

We have chosen here to list Exxon, the nation's largest energy company, which was responsible for one of the worst ecological disasters in history—the *Exxon Valdez* oil spill of 11.2 million gallons off Alaska in 1989. Exxon has been linked to 22 Superfund sites; three of its chemical plants alone emitted over 7.5 million pounds of toxics in 1988; and its mining subsidiary has one of the worst safety records in the country. . . .

Conclusion

This chapter has shown conclusively the fundamental flaw of capitalism. Corporations are formed to seek and maximize profits. All too often, the result is a blatant disregard for human and humane considerations. It is too simplistic to say that corporations are solely responsible for these dangers to individuals and society. In many cases, consumers insist on convenience rather than safety. They would rather smoke or drink diet cola with saccharin than have the government demand that they quit. Moreover, consumers typically would rather take an unknown risk than pay higher prices for products, which would pay for the cost of cleaning up the pollution. So, too, workers would rather work in an unsafe plant than be unemployed. But for the most part, these attitudes are shaped by corporate advertising and corporate extortion (threatened higher prices and unemployment if changes are enforced). Also, corporations are guilty of efforts to persuade us that the dangers are nonexistent or minimal when the scientific evidence is irrefutable. They also do everything possible to block efforts by the government and consumer groups to thwart their corporate policies. . . .

Notes

1. National Commission on Product Safety, "Perspectives on Product Safety," in *Consumerism for the Consumer Interest*, ed. David A. Aaker and George S. Day (New York: Free Press, 1974), 321–322. See also, Amitai Etzioni, "Mindless Capitalism, an Unyielding Elite," *Human Behavior* 4 (November 1975), 10–12; and Ralph Nader, ed., *The Consumer and Corporate Accountability* (New York: Harcourt Brace Jovanovich, 1973), 51.

2. *Multinational Monitor*, October 1995.

3. *Multinational Monitor*, October 1995.

4. John Summa, "Eli Lilly," *Multinational Monitor* 9 June 1988, 20–22.

5. Mokhiber, 334, 340.

6. Upton Sinclair, *The Jungle* (First published in 1905. Reprint, New York: New American Library, 1960).

7. Charles H. McCaghy, *Deviant Behavior: Crime, Conflict, and Interest Groups* (New York: Macmillan, 1976), 215.

8. Harrison Wellford, *Sowing and Wind: A Report from Ralph Nader's Center for Study of Responsive Law on Food Safety and the Chemical Harvest* (New York: Grossman, 1972), 69.

9. McCaghy, 216.

10. Robert Sherrill, cited in McCaghy, 216 (originally appeared in *New York Times Book Review*, 4 March 1973, 3). See also Gene Marine and Judith Van Allen, *Food Pollution: The Violation of Our Inner Ecology* (New York: Holt, Rinehart, and Winston, 1972), Chapter 2; and Jennifer Cross, *The Supermarket Trap: The Consumer and the Food Industry*, rev. ed. (Bloomington: Indiana University Press, 1976), Chapter 9.

11. Neal Karlen, "A 'Mystery Meat' Scandal," *Newsweek* 24 September 1984, 29 and Mark Thomas, "Ex-Cattle King Worker Acknowledges Fraud," *Denver Post* 31 January 1984, 1, 11.

12. Norm Brewer, "Bad School Meat Spurs Crackdown in Inspecting," *USA Today*, 21 December 1983, 8–A.

13. The following discussion of additives is taken primarily from Daniel Zwerdling, "Food Pollution," in *The Capitalist System*, 2nd ed., ed. Richard C. Edwards, Michael Reich, and Thomas E. Weisskopf (Englewood Cliffs, NJ: Prentice Hall, 1978) 19–24. See also Jacqueline Verrett and Jean Carper, *Eating May Be Hazardous to Your Health* (Garden City, NY: Doubleday Anchor Books, 1975).

14. Julie Miller, "Testing for Seeds of Destruction," *The Progressive* 39 (December 1975), 37–40. See also Richard F. Spark, "Legislating against Cancer," *The New Republic* 3 June 1978, 16–19.

15. It is even possible that financial ties to huge food corporations may shade the so-called expert testimony of nutritionists, as argued by Benjamin Rosenthal, Michael Jacobson, and Marcy Bohm, "Professors on the Take," *The Progressive* 40 (November 1976), 42–47.

16. 1965 data are from Marine and Van Allen, 38; 1977 data are from Hugh Drummond, "Add Poison for Flavor and Freshness," *Mother Jones* 2 (April 1977), 13.

17. Quoted in Zwerdling, 20.

18. From *Eat Your Heart Out: Food Profiteering in America*, by Jim Hightower. Copyright 1975 by Jim Hightower. Reprinted by permission of Crown Publishers, Inc.

19. Marilyn Elias, "How to Win Friends and Influence Kids on Television (and Incidentally Sell a Few Toys and Munchies at the Same Time)," *Human Behavior* 4 (April 1974), 20. For an extensive review of research, see National Science Foundation, *The Effects of Television* (Washington, DC: U.S. Government Printing Office, 1976).

20. Federal Trade Commission, *Staff Report on Television Advertising to Children* (Washington, DC: U.S. Government Printing Office, 1978), 57.

21. Summarized in U.S. Commission on Civil Rights, *Window Dressing on the Set: An Update* (Washington, DC: U.S. Government Printing Office, 1979), 49.

22. Elias, 16–23.

23. See "Slow Motion Suicide," *Newsweek* 22 January 1979, 83–84; United Press International, 12 January 1979; and Associated Press, 12 January 1979.

24. Darmstadter, 24.

25. These examples are taken from Larry C. White, *Merchants of Death: The American Tobacco Industry* (New York: William Morrow, 1988), 129–131. See also Morton Mintz, "Marketing Tobacco to Children," *The Progressive* 5 (May 1991), 24–29.

26. Eric Eckholm, "Four Trillion Cigarettes," *The Progressive* 42 (July 1978), 26; White, 199–200.

27. Joan Claybrook, *Retreat from Safety: Reagan's Attack on America's Health* (New York: Pantheon, 1984), 78.

28. "High Tech and Health," in *Diagnosis: Capitalism, by Dollars and Sense* (Somerville, MA: Economic Affairs Bureau, 1985), 15.

29. Philip Cole and Marlene B. Goldman, "Occupation," in *Persons at High Risk of Cancer*, ed. Joseph E. Fraumeni, Jr. (New York: Academic Press, 1975), 171.

30. Dorothy McGhee, "Workplace Hazards: No Women Need Apply," *The Progressive* 41 (October 1977), 25.

31. Daniel Ben-Horin, "The Sterility Scandal," *Mother Jones* 4 (May 1979), 51–63.

32. Jeanne Schinto, "The Breathless Cotton Workers," *The Progressive* 41 (August, 1977), 29.

33. Reported in Samuel S. Epstein, *The Politics of Cancer* (San Francisco: Sierra Club Books, 1978), 84–86. See also Lea Zeldin, "The Asbestos Menace," *The Progressive* 42 (October 1978), 12.

34. Roger M. Williams, "Arsenic and Old Factories," *Saturday Review* 20 (January 1979), 26.

35. Schinto, 28. For a description of how the government has waffled in this area, see "Brown Lung Compromise," *The Progressive* 42 (August 1978), 13.

36. Harold Sprout and Margaret Sprout, *The Context of Environmental Politics* (Lexington: University Press of Kentucky, 1978), 17.

37. The following is based primarily on Michael H. Best and William E. Connolly, "Nature and Its Largest Parasite," in *The Capitalist System*, 2nd ed., ed. Richard C. Edwards, Michael Reich, and Thomas E. Weisskopf (Englewood Cliffs, NJ: Prentice Hall, 1978), 418–425, excerpted from their book *The Politicized Economy* (Lexington, MA: D. C. Heath, 1976).

38. Best and Connolly, 419.

37
Organized Deviance

David R. Simon

Frank E. Hagan

Organized crime in America has a long history. Names like Al Capone, Pretty Boy Floyd, Bugs Moran, and Legs Diamond have become part of the public consciousness; they are reknowned for their wealth, respected for their power, and feared for the methods they used to secure that money and power. Extortion, bribery, assault, and lethal violence have long been staples of the trade, used with cool calculation and unflinching resolve to obtain desired outcomes. At one time, the Mafia and related organizations controlled virtually every vice known to humankind—from drugs to gambling to sex work and everything in between. The fact that such vices have been largely illegal ensured their profitability, an unintended consequence that permits organized crime to thrive in the first place.

The Mob no longer enjoys the monopoly control it once did. Drug and prostitution markets have become democratized; gambling is now legal almost everywhere; and police stings have taken their toll. Its influence nevertheless remains strong. Mob-directed political corruption, hazardous waste dumping, numbers-running, bookmaking, racketeering, loan-sharking, and money laundering continue to exact billions of dollars a year in direct and indirect economic costs. New criminal syndicates are emerging where old ones have tailed off. Russian and Colombian cartels are now major players, particularly on the eastern seaboard of the United States where opportunities for corruption, drug-running, and other illicit activities are plentiful. Some factions appear to exhibit all the hierarchical differentiation, role specificity, and functional interdependence of a Fortune 500 company; their na-

tional and global influence is likely to be felt for some time to come.

Organized crime bridges the legitimate and the illegitimate, comingling players from legal and illegal worlds in a diffuse web of deviant relations. Insofar as the reach of organized crime extends to the highest levels of officialdom, it can fundamentally affect how deviance itself is constructed and controlled. But organized crime is very much a shadow government unto itself, acting as judge, jury, and executioner in a world where violence and its threat are the principal regulatory mechanisms.

Criminal syndicates play a crucial role in perpetuating old forms of deviance and inspiring new ones. This role is especially relevant in today's electronic age, where technological advancement and human greed make fertile ground for criminal innovation. The authors provide an overview of these and other issues, offering poignant examples and colorful anecdotes of real-life organized criminals in action.

The Mob Is Bullish on America

The mob has always been a fan of the profits to be made in the free enterprise system; they simply have been a bit fuzzy on the approved or legitimate means of doing so. In February 1997, perhaps prematurely, the *New York Times* reported, "Officials Say Mob Is Shifting to New Industries" (Raab, 1997). With successful law enforcement crackdowns on traditional organized crime activities such as extortion and bid-rigging rackets, Mafia crime families in New York were reported as shifting their focus to frauds in health insurance, prepaid telephone cards, and small Wall Street brokerage houses.

The authorities in New Jersey said they uncovered what might be the prototype of the mob's medical care strategy in August, when they arrested 12 men accused of being members of a Genovese crew, or unit. The crew's leaders were charged with siphoning payments from Tri-Con Associates, a New Jersey company that arranged medical, dental, and optical care for more than one million patients in group plans throughout the country. Investigators said that the mobsters set up Tri-Con, investing their own money and using employees as managers, and intimidated some health plan administrators into approving excessive payments to the company. New Jersey authorities said Tri-Con in effect became a broker, linking networks of health-care providers, including physicians, hospitals and dentists with group plans for companies and unions (Raab, 1997).

Prepaid phone cards are a relatively new business, grossing about $1 billion in 1996 and offering a new target for organized crime. The Gambino crime family set up a company that stole over $50 million from companies and phone callers. According to one account, the Gambinos sold $20 cards that became worthless after only $2 or $3 in calls because they had not been programmed for the correct amount. The telephone carriers also lost money due to credit they extended to the phony company, which never paid them for the calls. John "Junior" Gotti was involved in the telephone card business but, as of this writing, appeared to be operating it as a legitimate business (Bastone, 1997).

At least three New York City crime families were involved in frauds with initial public offerings in over-the-counter stocks handled by small brokerage firms. In these swindles the mob lends money to brokers who are in debt or wish to expand their business. They then force the brokers to sell them most of the low-priced shares in a company before its stock is available as initial public offerings. The mob and brokers quickly inflate the value of the shares by fake transactions or trading among themselves. The brokers are forced to inflate prices further by pushing them on unsuspecting investors. The mobsters then sell, making huge profits before the overvalued stock plunges (Bastone, 1997).

Mob infiltration of big business can threaten the heartline of our nation's economy. Organized crime becomes such a central part of core institutions that it can compromise the government itself. . . .

Organized Crime Myths Exposed

. . .[T]he distinction between organized crime and various forms of white-collar deviance is often a very fine line. Related to this reality is another that is often overlooked in discussions of organized criminal syndicates. That is, it is usually assumed that organized crime members are part of some alien conspiracy who bully their way into various neighborhoods and businesses, guns ablaze, with no cooperation or invitation from people or organizations. This is one of the great myths about crime syndicates (Kappeler et al., 1997, 110ff).

The reality, more often than not, is just the opposite (Quinney, 1975, 145). As Lyman and Potter state,

> . . .*organized criminals, legitimate business people, and government officials are all equal players in the marketplace of corruption. Each comes to the marketplace with goods or services wanted by others, and a rather routine and institutionalized series of exchanges takes place. . . . Who initiates such a deal depends on the circumstances, and the initiator is as likely to be the legitimate actor as the criminal (1997, 359).* . . .

. . .[C]ertain legitimate business and entertainment interests have long used crime syndicates for a variety of purposes:

- Chemical firms have used the Mafia to cheaply dispose of hazardous waste.

- Businesses have long hired crime families to stop labor unions from forming, while certain unions (like the Teamsters) have allied themselves with the Mafia in order to win union recognition from employers.

- Corporations and crime syndicates have formed business partnerships in the United States and offshore islands to build gambling casinos and resorts. Syndicate members have also been used to train pit bosses and dealers in casinos (Kohn, 1976).

- Disreputable landlords have hired mob-controlled arson rings to burn down slum buildings whose insurance value has exceeded their assessed property value.

- Organized crime has also been a proven customer of legal goods and services, such as long-distance phone calls to operate illegal gambling bets, traffic in narcotics, and legally invest capital in market securities and new businesses (King, 1975).

- Organized crime families are consumers of a large variety of everyday products and services: pagers, cellular phones, chemicals for processing illegal drugs and office supplies (computers, stick-up note pads, writing implements, and the like).

- Organized crime has served as an alternative employment source in poor neighborhoods, and its drug trafficking in these areas may distract residents from political discontent (McIntosh, 1973; Spitzer, 1975; Tabor, 1971).

- Banks, wholesale jewelers, check cashing services, major investment houses, and many other businesses have been handsomely paid to launder profits from drug trafficking (see below).

- Stolen cargo (cigarettes, gasoline, and numerous other stolen products) can be bought from smugglers at prices substantially below wholesale, and sold for large profits.

- For businesses and individuals with bad credit, Mafia loan sharks have long served as a source of badly needed cash. (See also Pearce, 1976, 140.) . . .

Equally interesting, as well, are [Sammy "The Bull"] Gravano's [former underboss of New York's Gambino crime family] recollections concerning cooperation of various business executives and corrupt members of the criminal justice system. One stronghold of the New York City mob families was the construction industry. Gravano owned a cement pouring business, and one of his partners was Joe Madonia, who was not a mob member, but who owned a legitimate company, Ace Partitions. More important, concrete pouring on every major construction contract in New York City—meaning $2 mil-

lion or more—could not take place until it received the approval of four of the City's five crime families. (The Bonanno family was excluded from construction considerations due to its dispute with the other families.) Colombo family member Ralph Scopo was president and business manager of the local cement and concrete workers union.

All the New York City concrete pouring firms under mob control would take turns being low bidder on the projects. The prices of the contracts were immediately increased by the cement pouring firms, so much so that the price of a cubic yard of poured cement in Manhattan became the highest in the nation. Legitimate builders, contractors, and developers, who also worked on the projects, would follow the mob's lead by jacking up their prices as well. The legitimate firms knew full well that the Cosa Nostra was their silent partner, but went along with the mob's scam because the profits on non-mob firms also increased! After all, all costs were passed on to those who bought or leased office space or condos in these projects (Maas, 1997, 271). . . .

Contemporary Global Crime Syndicates

Unquestionably the most important contemporary organized crime phenomenon is global organized crime (Viviano, 1995, 17ff). The end of the Cold War created new opportunities for transnational organized crime. "Transparent national borders, fewer trade restrictions, and truly global financial and telecommunications systems provide significant opportunities for criminal organizations to expand operations beyond national boundaries" (Kerry, 1997b, 161). Russian organized crime has formed an unholy alliance with Sicilian, Asian, Mexican, and Colombian syndicates, and the results are devastating.

- In Russia, thousands of poorly guarded nuclear warheads and hundreds of unsafe reactors (20,000 safety violations during 1993 inspections and 78 shutdowns for safety reasons) are rusting away on the Soviet fleet, many with nuclear fuel aboard. The Russian Academy of Sciences estimated in 1995 that the Russian Mafiya now owns 50 to 80 percent of all voting stock in Russia's legitimate corporations (Kerry, 1997a, 160).

- Drug cartels from Colombia, Russia, Italy, Japan, and China instantly transfer huge sums around the world with "wire" (actually satellite) transfers, using offshore banks. The cartels manipulate accounts drawn in the names of "shell" corporations. The economies of a number of tiny sovereign nations, such as the Cayman Islands, are completely dependent on laundering transactions.

Organized crime groups from the former Soviet Union, Asia, and Italy are forming partnerships among themselves as well as with the drug barons of Latin America. All syndicates are engaging in corruption on a grand scale.

- In 1995, more than 6,000 Italian bureaucrats, corporate executives, and politicians (among them a staggering 438 deputies and senators) were under investigation or have been indicted on various corruption charges. One estimate is that the Mafia has paid $40 billion in bribes to executives and officials over the past decade. On March 2, 1995, seven-time Prime Minister Giulio Andreotti was indicted for being a "made member" of the Italian Mafia (Kerry, 1997a, 73).

- The Colombian cartels now trade cocaine to the Italian Mafia in exchange for heroin. The Colombian Cali cartel boss now earns $4 billion annually from cocaine, and has invested hundreds of millions in banks in Russia, Europe, and the United States.

- In Mexico, the former Mexican Federal Deputy Attorney General Eduardo Valle Espinosa resigned his official post in frustration in May 1996, and it is estimated that at least half of Mexico's federal police chiefs and attorney generals receive illegal payoffs from drug dealers. Some police chief candidates now pay $1 to $2 million just to get hired.

From 1988 to 1994, the brother of the former president of Mexico transferred over $80 million from a Citibank (a U.S. bank) branch in Mexico through Citibank's New York headquarters to a secret Swiss bank account. Mexico's chief drug czar had to resign in 1997 when it was learned that he had ties to Mexico's drug cartel (Kerry, 1997a, 100–153, 159–161).

- Of the approximately 1.5 million U.S. vehicles stolen each year, several hundred thousand are illegally exported out of the country to Central America and Eastern Europe. One Colombian criminal, Gabriel Taboada, testified at a U.S. Senate committee hearing that he bribed diplomats, who are exempt from paying duty on imported cars, "to import cars in their name" (Kerry, 1997a, 72).

Approximately $500 billion in currency is laundered annually utilizing various global financial institutions, making money laundering the third largest industry in the world. Federal law requires that banks report all cash deposits of $10,000 or more to the Internal Revenue Service (IRS). In 1975, there were only 3,000 such activities reported. By 1988, there were 5.5 million reported annually. It is now estimated that the total amount of drug money laundered each year is an immense $300 billion, about half of all funds connected to the worldwide drug trade. Of this amount, $100 billion is laundered in the U.S. Nine-tenths of this amount ends up overseas, often in secret Swiss accounts, where it can then be freely moved. This outflow of money contributes substantially to the nation's foreign trade deficit (Simon, 1996, 140ff).

The largest money laundering operation ever uncovered took place in 1989. U.S. banks were used to ship $1 billion a year to cocaine traffickers. The drug profits were disguised as proceeds from phony front businesses—wholesale gold and jewelry—run largely out of Los Angeles. Another money laundering investigation in 1990, Operation Polar Cap, resulted in the freezing of hundreds of accounts in 173 American banks, more than half of which were in New York and Florida. The accounts contained some $400 million in Colombian drug profits. Another source of laundered money are storefront check-cashing and money-transmitting services, most of which are unlicensed and run by newly arrived or illegal immigrants. Most of these are in states with few regulators, who are unable to keep up with the growth of such businesses. This is especially true of Florida, Texas, New York, and California. Each year, such operations take billions in cash from drug dealers and send it overseas. These storefront operations defraud honest customers by failing to send their money to requested addressees. Many customers cannot complain because they are either newly arrived immigrants ignorant of the law, or illegals (Kerry, 1997a, 157–160).

Russian Organized Crime

Mafiya groups in Russia inherited a unique survival skill in the Soviet Communist system that put them in a position to take advantage of the new, weak, and yet unorganized fledgling democracy in Russia or the more liberal democratic system to be found in Western Europe and the United States. Kenney and Finckenauer (1995, 274) note:

> All the emigres from the former Soviet Union share a common heritage—a staterun, centrally planned Soviet command economy that produced massive shortages as well as widespread bribery and thievery. No area of life in the Soviet Union was exempt from pervasive, universal corruption. Scarce goods and services unavailable through normal channels could usually be gotten through blat (connections) or na lev (on the left). An illegal second or shadow economy arose to operate in tandem with the official economy.

Konstantin Simis in *USSR, The Corrupt Society* (1982) claims that the Soviet system bred corruption on a massive scale. This did not readily decline with the demise of the Soviet Union. The young Russian democracy is now threatened by the breakdown of law enforcement, the growth of private armies, and

protection rackets that regularly resort to violence. The Russian Interior Ministry reported in 1994 that 70 to 80 percent of private businesses and banks had been forced to pay protection money (Brunker, 1997). Russian gangs in the United States have been particularly involved in health care fraud, insurance scams, antiquities swindles, forgery, and gas tax evasion. In March 1997 a Russian group (Globus) was arrested for a fraudulent stock scheme bilking investors out of millions by convincing them to invest in a fraudulent Internet company. Between 1993 and 1996, 400 business executives and politicians were killed in Russia after challenging organized crime or official corruption, and 90 percent of the businesses in St. Petersburg were paying protection money (Payton, 1997). Parallels might be drawn with America's early robber barons; the boundary between legality and illegality is blurred. . . .

References

Bastone, William. 1997. "Mob bell, they're all connected at Gotti Jr.'s telephone card company." *The Village Voice*, http://www.villagevoice.com,89/ink/bastone.html.

Brunker, Mike. 1997. "Russians shine at white-collar crime." *MSNBC*, http://www.msnbc.com,80/news/66789.as.

Kappeler, V., et al. 1997. *The mythology of crime and criminal justice*, 2nd ed. Prospect Heights, IL: Waveland.

Kenney, Dennis J., and James O. Finckenaur. 1995. *Organized crime in America*. Belmont, CA: Wadsworth.

Kerry, John 1997a. *The new war.* New York: Simon and Schuster.

Kerry, John. 1997b. "Organized crime goes global while the U.S. stays home." *Washington Post*, 11 May, C1.

King, R. 1975. "Gambling and crime." In *An economic analysis of crime*, edited by L.J. Kaplan and D. Kessler. Springfield, IL: Charles C. Thomas, 40.

Kohn, H. 1976. "The Nixon-Hughes-Lansky connection," *Rolling Stone* 20, May 41–50, 77–78.

Lyman, M.D., and G.W. Potter. 1997. *Organized crime.* Upper Saddle River, NJ: Prentice Hall.

Maas, Peter 1997. *Underboss: Sammy The Bull Gravano's story of life in the Mafia.* New York: Harper Paperbacks.

McIntosh, M. 1973. "The growth of racketeering." *Economy and Society* 2, 63–64.

Payton, Jack R. 1997. "Gangsterism plagues Russia." *St. Petersburg Times*, 11 May, A1.

Pearce, F. 1976. *Crimes of the powerful*. London: Pluto Press.

Quinney, Richard C. 1975. *Criminology, analysis and critique of crime in America*. Boston: Little, Brown.

Raab, Selwyn. 1997. "Officials say mob is shifting crime to new industries." *New York Times*, 10 February, A1.

Simis, Konstantin. 1982. *USSR, the corrupt society*. New York: Simon and Schuster.

Simon, David R. 1996. *Elite deviance*, 5th ed. Needham Heights, MA: Allyn and Bacon.

Spitzer, Stephen. 1975. "Toward a Marxian theory of deviance," *Social Problems* 22 (February), 640–653.

Tabor, M. 1971. "The plague, capitalism and dope genocide." In *The triple revolution emerging*, edited by R. Perucci and M. Pilsuk. Boston: Little, Brown, 241–249.

Viviano, Frank. 1995. "The new Mafia order." *Mother Jones*, May/June, 17–23.

38

Accounts of Professional Misdeeds

The Sexual Exploitation of Clients by Psychotherapists

Mark R. Pogrebin

Eric D. Poole

Amos D. Martinez

Those accused of sexual misconduct obviously have a strong vested interest in explaining how it happened. Their career, livelihood, and professional reputation depend on credible explanations. Pogrebin, Poole, and Martinez explore the range of explanations therapists offer to this end. Each account has as its objective to separate act from identity and thereby protect the identity from permanent damage. The authors conclude that discredited actors able to project a "normal self" in an abnormal situation can have their aberrant behavior viewed as atypical and not representative of their essential character. Deviant labels, in other words, can be explained away with the right mix of discourse and skill. Whether the therapists' accounts are heartfelt makes no matter. Deceptive accounts deflect negative attributions just as surely as their sincere counterparts.

The idea that the most meaningful sexual partnerships occur within relationships built on trust, empathy, and caring is something most people would agree with. Mutual understanding leads to emotional attachment and, in turn, to physical intimacy. This may be true in the majority of cases, but it is generally not true where power or authority imbalances exist between participating actors. Nowhere are imbalanced sexual relations more problematic than in encounters between therapists and their patients.

Persons who seek psychological treatment are, by definition, in a position of vulnerability. There is something wrong, they are hurting, and they have come for help. To root out the core of their difficulties, patients must disclose their innermost secrets. This disclosure requires normally operant defenses to be temporarily lowered, making patients susceptible to advances from those in whom they have placed their trust. Understandably, sexual relations between therapists and their patients have a long history of prohibition. If caught, therapists who transgress can expect strong sanctions from both criminal justice and regulatory bodies.

Intimate sexual relationships between mental health therapists and their clients have been increasingly reported in recent years (Akamatsu 1987). In a survey of over 1400 psychiatrists, Gartell, Herman, Olarte, Feldstein, and Localio (1987) found that 65 percent reported having treated a patient who admitted to sexual involvement with a previous therapist.[1] National self-report surveys indicate that approximately 10 percent of psychotherapists admit having had at least one sexual encounter with a client (Gartell, Herman, Olarte, Feldstein, and Localio 1986; Pope, Keith-Spiegel, and Tabachnick 1986). It is suggested that these surveys most likely underestimate the extent of actual sexual involvement with clients because some offending psychotherapists either fail to respond to the survey or fail to report their sexual indiscretions (Gartell et al. 1987). Regardless of the true prevalence rates, many mental health professional associations explicitly condemn sexual relations between a therapist and client. Such relationships represent a breach of canons of professional ethics and are subject to disciplinary action by specific licensing or regulatory bodies.

Psychological Impact on Client

Individuals who seek treatment for emotional or mental health problems assume a dependency role in a professional client relationship in which direction and control are exerted by the therapist. The client's most intimate secrets, desires, and fears are revealed to the therapist. Therapeutic communication relies on the development of trust between client and therapist. In order to be successful, therapy requires the individual in treatment to abandon the psychic defenses that shield his or her genuine self from scrutiny (Pope and Bouhoutsos 1986). The lowering of these defenses in a therapeutic relationship increases the client's emotional vulnerability. Because the potential for manipulation or exploitation of the client is heightened in such relationships, Benetin and Wilder (1989) argue that the therapist must assume a higher degree of professional responsibility to ensure that personal trust is not abused.

As Finkelhor (1984) points out, the therapeutic relationship is fundamentally asymmetrical; thus, the controlling presumption is that a client's volition under conditions of therapeutic dependency must always be considered problematic. The client cannot be considered capable of freely consenting to enter into a sexual relationship with a therapist. The therapist's sexual exploitation of a client represents an obvious violation of trust, destroying any therapeutic relationship that has been established. The client often experiences intense feelings of betrayal and anguish at having been victimized by the very person who had been trusted to help (Pope and Bouhoutsos 1986). Sexual exploitation by a therapist can result in clients' suffering emotional instability, conflicts in interpersonal relationships, and disruptions in work performance (Benetin and Wilder 1989).

The Colorado State Grievance Board

Historically in Colorado, grievances against licensed mental health providers were handled by two separate licensing boards: the Board of Psychologist Examiners and the Board of Social Work Examiners. During the past 20 years, the state witnessed a proliferation of practitioners in the unregulated field of psychotherapy. Individuals trained in traditional professional fields of psychology, counseling, and social work may call themselves psychotherapists, but anyone else with (or without) training in any field may refer to their practice as psychotherapy. In short, psychotherapists are not subject to mandatory licensing requirements in Colorado. Largely through the lobbying efforts of licensed mental health practitioners, the state legislature was persuaded to address some of the problems associated with the operation of a decentralized grievance process that failed to regulate unlicensed practitioners of psychotherapy. The result was the passage of the Mental Health Occupations Act, creating on July 1, 1988 the State Grievance Board within the Colorado Department of Regulatory Agencies.

The State Grievance Board has the responsibility to process complaints and undertake disciplinary proceedings against the four categories of licensed therapists and against unlicensed psychotherapists. Upon the filing of a complaint, the eight-member board (comprising four licensed therapists and four public members) initiates the following action:

1. The named therapist receives written notice and is given 20 days to respond in writing;

2. When deemed appropriate by the board, the complainant may review the therapist's response and is given 10 days to submit further information or explanation; and

3. The board reviews the available information and renders a decision about the complaint.

If the board determines that disciplinary action against a licensed therapist is warranted, the board is increased by an augmenting panel of three members, each of whom is a licensed practitioner in the same field as the psychotherapist subject to sanctioning. The board can issue a letter of admonition, place restrictions on the license or the practice, require the therapist to submit to a mental or physical examination, or seek an injunction in a state district court to limit or to stop the practice of psychotherapy. When the complaint involves an unlicensed practitioner, injunctive action is the board's only disciplinary remedy.

The governing state statute further mandates that psychotherapists provide their clients with a disclosure statement concerning their credentials (e.g., degrees and licenses) and specific client rights and information (e.g., second opinion and legal confidentiality, as well as therapeutic methods and techniques and fee structure, if requested). In the Model Disclosure Statement developed by the State Grievance Board, the impropriety of sexual relations is specifically noted:

> In a professional relationship (such as ours [client and therapist]), sexual intimacy between a therapist and a client is never appropriate. If sexual intimacy occurs, it should be reported to the State Grievance Board.

During 1988 the state legislature also enacted a statute making sexual contact between therapist and client a criminal offense (Colorado Revised Statutes 18-3-405.5, Supplement 1988).

Since 1988, sexual intimacy between therapists and clients has been explicitly and formally recognized as one of the most serious violations of the professional-client relationship, subject to both regulatory or administrative and criminal penalties. Yet, between August 1, 1988 and June 30, 1990, 10 percent ($n = 33$) of the 324 complaints filed with the State Grievance Board involved allegations of sexual misconduct. Given the implications that these sexual improprieties raise for both the client as victim and the therapist as offender, we wish to examine the written accounts submitted to the board by psychotherapists who have had complaints of sexual misconduct filed against them. . . .

Method

To the 33 complaints of sexual misconduct filed from August 1988 through June 1990, 30 written responses from psychotherapists were submitted to the State Grievance Board. . . . Twenty-four therapists admitted

to sexual involvement with clients; six denied the allegations. In the present study we examine the statements of the 24 therapists who provided accounts for their sexual relations with clients. . . .Twenty-one therapists are men; three are women. . . .

Findings

Accounts are "linguistic device[s] employed whenever an action is subjected to valuative inquiry" (Scott and Lyman 1968, p. 46). An important function of accounts is to mitigate blameworthiness by representing one's behavior in such a way as to reduce personal accountability. This involves offering accounts aimed at altering the prevailing conception of what the instant activity is, as well as one's role in the activity. Excuses, justifications, and apologies all display a common goal: giving a "good account" of oneself.

Excuses

Appeal of Defeasibility. In an appeal of defeasibility, one accounts for one's behavior by denying any intention to cause the admitted harm or by claiming a failure to foresee the unfortunate consequences of one's act, or both. As Lyman and Scott (1989, pp. 136–37) explain:

> The appeal of defeasibility invokes a division in the relation between action and intent, suggesting that the latter was malfunctioning with respect to knowledge, voluntariness, or state of complete consciousness.

In the following account, the therapist claims ignorance of professional rules of conduct governing relations with clients:

> I did not know that seeing clients socially outside of therapy violated hospital policy. . . .[I]f I realized it was strictly forbidden, I would have acted differently.

The next case involves a female therapist who had engaged in a long-term sexual relationship with a female client. The therapist couches her account in terms of failing to be informed by her clinical supervisors that the relationship was improper:

> Both Drs. Smith and Jones had total access to and knowledge of how I termi-

nated with her [the client] and continued our evolving relationship. Neither of them in any way inferred that I had done anything unethical or illegal. I do not understand how I can be held accountable for my actions. There were no guidelines provided by the mental health center around this issue. Both Drs. Smith and Jones knew of and approved of my relationship with her.

Other appeals of defeasibility incorporate elements of defective insight and reasoning, or just poor judgment, in an effort to deny intent. An appropriate vocabulary of motive is necessarily involved in the presentation of such appeals. For example, Scully and Marolla (1984, pp. 540–541) report that convicted rapists attempted to

. . .negotiate a non-rapist identity by painting an image of themselves as a "nice guy." Admitters projected the image of someone who had made a serious mistake but, in every other respect, was a decent person.

The deviant actor makes a bid to be seen as a person who has many of the same positive social attributes possessed by others. This individual presents the basic problem simply: "Everybody makes mistakes"; "It could happen to anyone"; or "We all do stupid things." Such fairly standard, socially approved phrases or ideas are used to sensitize others to their own mistakes, thereby reminding them of their own vulnerability and limiting their opportunity to draw lines between themselves and the individual deviant. The basic message is that the deviant act is not indicative of one's essential character (Goffman 1963). This message is supplemented by an effort to present information about the "untainted" aspects of self. In these presentational cues, deviant actors seek to bring about a softening of the moral breach in which they are involved and relieve themselves of culpability.

In the following example, a therapist admits that she simply misinterpreted her own feelings and did not consciously intend to become sexually involved with her client:

It was after a short period of time that I first experienced any sexual feelings toward her. I did excuse the feelings I had as

something which I never would act on. Unfortunately, I did not understand what was happening at the time.

Similarly, another therapist seeks to diminish culpability by attributing his sexual indiscretion to a misreading of his client's emotional needs:

I experienced her expressions of affection as caring gestures of our spiritual bond, not lust. And I had no reason to suspect otherwise from her, since I had been so clear about my aversion to romantic involvement. We had sexual intercourse only once after termination. I am not promiscuous, neither sexually abusive nor seductive.

Another variant of the appeal of defeasibility involves a claim that the inappropriate behavior was an unforeseen outcome of the therapeutic process itself. This denial of responsibility requires articulating one's position in the professional argot of psychotherapy. Such professionals are able to provide rather complex and compelling accounts of themselves, attempting to convince an audience of peers of the "real" meaning or "correct" interpretation of their behavior. As Lofland (1969, p. 179) posits,

. . .since they are likely to share in the universe of understandings and cultural ideology of expert imputors, they are more likely to be aware of what kinds of reasons or explanations such imputors will buy.

The therapist in the next account focuses on the unique problems arising in the professional-client relationship that contributed to the sexual misconduct:

The two inappropriate interactions occurred when she was a practicing psychotherapist and I was seeing her as a client, supervisee, and socially. I believe that my unresolved countertransference and her transference greatly contributed to the events.

In related accounts, therapists provide a professional assessment or opinion that the therapeutic techniques utilized in treating their clients got out of hand. This approach is shown in the following:

The initial development of a change in the relationship centered around my empathetic feelings that touched on unresolved feelings of loss in my own life. One aspect of the treatment centered around a lifetime of severe feelings of abandonment and rejection that the client felt from her family. This worked powerful feelings within me and I responded by overidentifying with the client, becoming emotionally vulnerable and feeling inappropriate responsibility to ease the client's pain.

Some of these professional accounts provide lengthy and detailed descriptions of various treatment techniques utilized because of the ineffectiveness of prior intervention attempts. These therapists stress the multifarious nature of the problems encountered in treatment that warranted the use of more complex and often more risky types of treatment. The following case shows the compromising position in which the therapist placed himself in attempting to foster the client's amenability to treatment:

Because we were at an impasse in therapy I adjusted the treatment to overcome resistance. I employed several tactics, one of which was to share more of my personal life with her; another was to see her outside the usual office setting.

A slight variation of this defeasibility claim involves what Scott and Lyman (1968, p. 48) call the "gravity disclaimer," where the actor recognizes the potential risks involved in the pursuit of a particular course of action but suggests that their probability could not be predetermined.

When she came in she was very down, to the point that she was staring at the floor. I felt she was not being reached in a cognitive way, so I tried to reach her using a sensory approach. I was trying to communicate to her: caring, love, acceptance, compassion and so on. Unfortunately, with the sensory approach there is a fine line not to be crossed, and I crossed it.

The appeal of defeasibility is a form of excuse that links knowledge and intent. Actors diminish blameworthiness by defining their acts as occurring without real awareness or intent; that is, they attempt to absolve themselves of responsibility by denying having knowingly intended to cause the untoward consequences. Had they known otherwise, they would have acted differently.

Scapegoating. Scapegoating involves an attempt to blame others for one's untoward behavior. Scapegoating is available as a form of excuse in the professional-client relationship because of the contextual opportunity for the therapist to shift personal responsibility to the client. The therapist contends that his or her actions were the product of the negative attributes or will of the client, e.g., deceit, seduction, or manipulation. The therapist in the following example recognizes the wrongfulness of his behavior but deflects responsibility by holding the client culpable for her actions:

I am not denying that this sexual activity took place, nor am I trying to excuse or justify it. It was wrong. However, the woman who complained about me is a psychologist. She was counseling me as well, on some vocational issues. So if anyone had cause for complaint under the regulations, it seems it would be me.

Another example of an account where the therapist attempts to "blame the victim" for the improper sexual activity reveals the focus on his diminished personal control of the relationship:

That I became involved in a sexual relationship with her is true. While my actions were reprehensible, both morally and professionally, I did not mislead or seduce her or intend to take advantage of her. My fault, instead, was failing to adequately safeguard myself from her seductiveness, covert and overt.

Here we have a therapist recognizing the impropriety of his actions yet denying personal responsibility because of the client's overpowering charms. The message is that the therapist may be held accountable for an inadequate "self-defense" which left him vulnerable to the client's seductive nature, but that he should not be culpable for the deviant sexual behavior since it was really he who was taken in and thus "victimized." The therapist's account for his predicament presumes a "reasonable person" theory of behavior; that is, given the same set of circumstances, any reasonable person would be expected to succumb to this persuasive client.

Justifications

Sad Tale. The sad tale presents an array of dismal experiences or conditions that are regarded—both collectively and cumulatively—as an explanation and justification for the actor's present untoward behavior. The therapists who presented sad tales invariably focused on their own history of family problems and personal tribulations that brought them to their present state of sexual affairs with clients:

> Ironically, her termination from therapy came at one of the darkest periods of my life. My father had died that year. I had met him for the first time when I was in my twenties. He was an alcoholic. Over the years we had worked hard on our relationship. At the time of his dying, we were at peace with one another. Yet, I still had my grief. At the time I had entered into individual therapy to focus on issues pertaining to my father's alcoholism and co-dependency issues. I then asked my wife to join me for marriage counseling. We were having substantial problems surrounding my powerlessness in our relationship. Therapy failed to address the balance of power. I was in the worst depression I had ever experienced in my entire life when we began our sexual involvement.

Therapists who employ sad tales admit to having sexual relations with their clients, admit that their actions were improper, and admit that ordinarily what they did would be an instance of the general category of the prohibited behavior. They claim, however, that their behavior is a special case because the power of circumstance voids the defining deviant quality of their actions. This type of account is similar to Lofland's (1969, p. 88) "special justification," where the actor views his current act as representative of some category of deviance but does not believe it to be entirely blameworthy because of extenuating circumstances. One therapist outlines the particular contextual factors that help explain his misbehavior:

The following situations are not represented as an excuse for my actions. There is no excuse for them. They are simply some of what I feel are circumstances that formed the context for what I believe is an incident that will never be repeated.

(1) Life losses: My mother-in-law who lived with us died. My oldest son and, the next fall, my daughter had left home for college.

(2) Overscheduling: I dealt with these losses and other concerns in my life by massive overscheduling.

Other therapists offer similar sad tales of tragic events that are seen to diminish their capacity, either physically or mentally, to cope with present circumstances. Two cases illustrate this accounting strategy:

> In the summer of 1988, my wife and I separated with her taking our children to live out-of-state. This was a difficult loss for me. A divorce followed. Soon after I had a bout with phlebitis which hospitalized me for ten days.

> My daughter, who lived far away with my former wife, was diagnosed with leukemia; and my mother had just died. Additional stress was caused by my ex-wife and present wife's embittered interactions.

Sad tales often incorporate a commitment to conventionality whereby one's typical behavior is depicted as conforming to generally approved rules or practices—the instant deviant act being the exception. The imputation is that "the exception proves the rule"; that is, one's normally conventional behavior is confirmed or proven by the rare untoward act.[2] The transgression may thus be viewed as an exception to the deviant classification to which it would justifiably belong if the special circumstances surrounding the enactment of the behavior in question did not exist. Given such circumstances, individuals depict themselves as more acted upon than acting. In the next case the therapist outlines the special circumstances that account for his behavior:

> I had "topped out" at my job, was being given additional responsibilities to deal with, had very little skilled staff to work with, and received virtually no support

from my supervisor. I was unconsciously looking for a challenging case to renew my interest in my work, and she fit that role. My finally giving into her seduction was an impulsive act based on my own hopelessness and depression.

Sad tales depict individuals acting abnormally in abnormal situations. In short, their instant deviance is neither typical nor characteristic of the type of person they really are, that is, how they would act under normal conditions. They are victims of circumstance, for if it were not for these dismal life events, their sexual improprieties would never have occurred.

Denial of Injury. Denial of injury is premised on a moral assessment of consequences; that is, the individual claims that his or her actions should be judged as wrong on the basis of the harm resulting from those acts. Again, the actor acknowledges that in general the behavior in which he or she has engaged is inappropriate but asserts that in this particular instance no real harm was done. This type of account was prevalent among the therapists who had engaged in sexual relations with clients following the termination of therapy.

> A good therapy termination establishes person-to-person equality between participants. Blanket condemnations of post-therapy relationships also are founded on a belief that such relationships invariably cause harm to the former patient. I defy anyone to meet Gerry, interview her, and then maintain that any harm was done to her by me.

The issue of sexual involvement with former clients represents an unresolved ethical controversy among therapists. On the one hand, the American Psychiatric Association has no official policy which categorically bans sexual relations between a psychiatrist and a former patient; instead, there is a case-by-case analysis of such relationships conducted by an ethics committee to determine their propriety. On the other hand, some states have enacted statutes that expressly prohibit any sexual relations between psychotherapists and former clients during a specified post-therapy time period. The stat-

utory period in Colorado is six months following the termination of therapy.

Despite this explicit restriction, some therapists in the present study still insist that their sexual relationships with former clients are neither in violation of professional standards of conduct nor in conflict with state law.

> Her psychotherapy with me was successfully concluded two months prior to her seeking a social relationship with me. She herself was unequivocal in her desire for a social relationship with me, which was entirely free from any therapeutic need or motivation. . . .I expressly clarified to her that in becoming socially involved I no longer could ever again function as her therapist. With the dual relationship problem laid aside, strictly speaking, such relationships are not unethical since no ethical rule of conduct has ever been formulated against them. . . .I hope that I have convincingly demonstrated that there is no generally accepted standard of psychological practice in . . .post-termination relationships, and so I cannot have violated the statute.

In denial of injury one seeks to neutralize the untoward behavior by redefining the activity in such a way as to reduce or negate its negative quality, such as injury, harm, or wrong. To some extent this involves structuring one's accounts to alter the dominant conceptions of what the activity is. Accounts thus sometimes go beyond the "linguistic forms" that Scott and Lyman have emphasized. Deviance reduction often involves manipulation of various symbols as a basis for one's behavioral account. As seen in the preceding denials of injury, therapists sought to have their sexual relations with former clients redefined according to a professional code of conduct that is subject to individual interpretation. This ethical code may be seen as symbolically governing the therapist-client relationship, establishing the grounds on which the therapist may make autonomous moral judgments of his or her own behavior.

Apology

Scott and Lyman (1968, p. 59) assert that "every account is a manifestation of the underlying negotiation of identities." In a sense, it is probably more accurate to conceive of accounts as referring to desired outcomes rather than as negotiating techniques. They indicate a sought-after definition of the situation, one in which the focus on the deviant act and the shame attached to the individual are lessened. For example, Goffman (1971) argues that the apology, as an account, combines an acknowledgment that one's prior actions were morally reprehensible with a repudiation of both the behavior and the former self that engaged in such activity.

Two consequences of an accused wrongdoer's action are guilt and shame. If wrongful behavior is based on internal standards, the transgressor feels guilty; if the behavior is judged on external normative comparisons, the person experiences shame. Shame results from being viewed as one who has behaved in a discrediting manner. In the following three cases, each therapist expresses his remorse and laments his moral failure:

> I find myself in the shameful position that I never would have thought possible for me as I violated my own standards of personal and professional conduct.

> I feel very badly for what I have done, ashamed and unprofessional. I feel unworthy of working in the noble profession of counseling.

> I entered into therapy and from the first session disclosed what I had done. I talked about my shame and the devastation I had created for my family and others.

Schlenker and Darby (1981) observe that the apology incorporates not only an expression of regret but also a claim of redemption. An apology permits a transgressor the opportunity to admit guilt while simultaneously seeking forgiveness in order that the offending behavior not be thought of as a representation of what the actor is really like. One therapist expresses concern for his actions and proposes a way to avoid such conduct in the future:

> I continue to feel worry and guilt about the damage that I caused. I have taken steps I felt necessary which has been to decide not to work with any client who could be very emotionally demanding, such as occurs with people who are borderline or dependent in their functioning.

This account seems to imply that one's remorse and affirmative effort to prevent future transgressions are sufficient remedies in themselves, preempting the need for others to impose additional sanctions. Self-abasement serves a dual purpose in the apology. First, it devalues the untoward behavior, thus reaffirming the moral superiority of conventional conduct. Second, it represents a form of punishment, reprimanding oneself consistent with the moral judgments of others. The message is that the actor shares the views of others, including their assessment of him or her, and both desires and deserves their acceptance. As Jones and Pittman (1982, pp. 255–256) contend:

> To the extent that the threatened actor sustains his counteractive behavior or to the extent that the counteractive behavior involves effort and costly commitments, social confirmation will have the restorative power sought.

Several elements of self-management combine when an apology is offered. While confessing guilt and expressing shame, the individual directs anger at himself or herself—denouncing the act and the actor. The actor then attempts to insulate his or her identity from the stigma of the deviant act, reconfirming an allegiance to consensual values and standards of conduct. As Goffman (1971, p. 113) observes, the deviant

> . . .splits himself into two parts, the part that is guilty of an offense and the part that dissociates itself from the delect and affirms a belief in the offered rule.

In the following account, the therapist accepts responsibility for his behavior but attempts to make amends by demonstrating a desire to learn from his mistakes:

> I am firmly aware that my judgment at the time was both poor and impaired. I am also aware that my thinking was grandiose and immature. One cannot hold a position of public trust and violate community standards. I have incorporated that knowledge into my thoughts and acts.

The demonstration of shared understandings may also be seen as consistent with a desire to preserve self-respect; moreover, self-initiated or proactive response to one's own deviance may serve as a mechanism to lessen the actor's feelings of shame and embarrassment, to militate against negative effect, and to foster a more favorable image of self. Goffman (1971) calls this ritual attempt to repair a disturbed situation "remedial work." In the next account the therapist reveals his effort to repair his spoiled identity:

> I have been grieving for Betty and the pain I have caused her. I am deeply distressed by my actions and am doing everything within my power for personal and professional discipline and restoration. I have tried through reading, therapy, and talking with other men who had experienced similar situations to understand why I allowed this to happen.

Such impression-management strategies involving remedial work convey to others that the actor is "solicitous for the feelings of and sensibilities of others and . . .willing to acknowledge fault and accept or even execute judgment for the untoward act" (Lyman and Scott 1989, p. 143). Hewitt and Stokes (1975, p. 1) further note that actors "gear their words and deeds to the restoration and maintenance of situated and cherished identities." The vast majority of apologies were offered by therapists who sought restoration of self by immediately entering therapy themselves. In the following case, the therapist's realization of the emotional damage resulting from her homosexual affair with a client led to her self-commitment to a mental hospital:

> I truly had no prior awareness of my vulnerability to a homosexual relationship before she became a client. In fact, it was such an ego dystonic experience for me that I soon ended up in the hospital myself and had two years of psychotherapy. From this therapy, as well as some follow-up therapy, I have come to understand the needs which led to such behavior. I regret the negative impact it has had on both of our lives.

Efforts to gain insight into their sexual transgressions appear critical to the therapists' transformation of self. By entering therapy, the individual becomes the object of the therapeutic process, whereby the "act" and the "actor" can be clinically separated. The very therapeutic context in which the initial deviance arose is now seen as the means by which the therapist can be redeemed through successful treatment. Through therapy individuals gain awareness of the causal processes involved in their deviant activity and are thus empowered to prevent such transgressions in the future. Introspective accounts convey a commitment both to understand and to change oneself. In this way, the therapist disavows his or her former discredited self and displays the new enlightened self.

Discussion

The consequences of deviant activity are problematic, often depending on a "definition of the situation." When a particular definition of a specific situation emerges, even though its dominance may be only temporary, individuals must adjust their behavior and views to it. Alternative definitions of problematic situations routinely arise and are usually subject to negotiation. Thus, it is incumbent upon the accused therapist to have his or her situation defined in ways most favorable to maintaining or advancing his or her own interests. When "transformations of identity" are at stake, such efforts become especially consequential (Strauss 1962). The imputation of a deviant identity implies ramifications that can vitally affect the individual's personal and professional life. As noted earlier, the negotiation of accounts is a negotiation of identities. The account serves as an impression-management, technique, or a "front," that minimizes the threat to identity (Goffman 1959). If the therapist can provide an acceptable account for his or her sexual impropriety—whether an excuse, justification, or apology—he or she increases the likelihood of restoring a cherished identity brought into question by the deviant behavior.

There is a close link between successfully conveying desired images to others and being able to incorporate them in one's own self-conceptions. When individuals offer accounts for their problematic actions, they are trying to ease their situation in two ways: by convincing others and by convincing themselves. An important function of accounts is to make one's transgressions not only intelligible to others but intelligible to oneself. Therapists sought to dispel the view that their deviation was a defining characteristic of who they really were; or, to put it another way, they attempted to negate the centrality or primacy of a deviant role imputation. The goal was to maintain or restore their own sense of personal and professional worth notwithstanding their sexual deviancy. In a way, laying claim to a favorable image in spite of aberrant behavior means voiding the apparent moral reality, that is, the deviance-laden definition of the situation that has been called to the attention of significant others (Grievance Board) by a victim-accuser (former client). . . .

Notes

1. Clients who suffer sexual exploitation often experience self-blame and are reluctant to disclose their victimization to others. Some are unsure what to do or to whom to report, and others simply believe it would do no good to report (Brown 1988).

2. "The exception that proves the rule" is a form of illogical reasoning that individuals use to interpret observations that contradict their preconceived views. In the present case, however, this rationalization process may be seen as an accounting scheme used by actors to explain the apparent contradiction between their typical "normal behavior" and the "deviant exception."

References

Akamatsu, J. T. 1987. "Intimate Relationships with Former Clients: National Survey of Attitudes and Behavior Among Practitioners." *Professional Psychology: Research and Practice* 18:454–458.

Benetin, J., and M. Wilder. 1989. "Sexual Exploitation and Psychotherapy." *Women's Rights Law Reporter* 11:121–135.

Brown, L. S. 1988. "Harmful Effects of Post-Termination Sexual and Romantic Relationships Between Therapists and Their Former Clients." *Psychotherapy* 25:249–255.

Finkelhor, D. 1984. *Child Sexual Abuse: New Theory and Research.* New York: Free Press.

Gartell, N., J. Herman, S. Olarte, M. Feldstein, and R. Localio. 1986. "Psychiatrist-Patient Sexual Contact: Results of a National Survey. I: Prevalence." *American Journal of Psychiatry* 143:1126–1131.

———. 1987. "Reporting Practices of Psychiatrists Who Knew of Sexual Misconduct by Colleagues." *American Journal of Orthopsychiatry* 57:287–295.

Goffman, E. 1959. *The Presentation of Self in Everyday Life.* Garden City, NY: Doubleday.

———. 1963. *Stigma: Notes on the Management of Spoiled Identity.* Englewood Cliffs, NJ: Prentice Hall.

———. 1971. *Relations in Public: Microstudies of the Public Order.* New York: Basic Books.

Hewitt, J. P., and R. Stokes. 1975. "Disclaimers." *American Sociological Review* 40:1–11.

Jones, E. E., and T. S. Pittman. 1982. "Toward a Theory of Strategic Self-Presentation." Pp. 231–262 in *Psychological Perspectives on the Self*, edited by J. M. Suls. Hillsdale, NJ: Erlbaum.

Lofland, J. 1969. *Deviance and Identity.* Englewood Cliffs, NJ: Prentice Hall.

Lyman, S. M., and M. B. Scott. 1989. *A Sociology of the Absurd* (2nd ed.). Dix Hills, NY: General Hall.

Pope, K. S., and J. Bouhoutsos. 1986. *Sexual Intimacy Between Therapists and Patients.* New York: Praeger.

Pope, K. S., P. Keith-Spiegel, and B. G. Tabachnick. 1986. "Sexual Attraction to Clients: The Human Therapist and the (Sometimes) Inhuman Training System." *American Psychologist* 41:147–158.

Schlenker, B. R., and B. W. Darby. 1981. "The Use of Apologies in Social Predicaments." *Social Psychology Quarterly* 44:271–278.

Scott, M. B., and S. M. Lyman. 1968. "Accounts." *American Sociological Review* 33:46–62.

Scully, D., and J. Marolla. 1984. "Convicted Rapists' Vocabulary of Motive: Excuses and Justifications." *Social Problems* 31:530–544.

Strauss, A. 1962. "Transformations of Identity." Pp. 63–85 in *Human Behavior and Social Processes: An Interactional Approach*, edited by A. M. Rose. Boston: Houghton Mifflin.

39
Doctor-Assisted Suicide

Bonnie Steinbock

S*hould doctors be granted the right to assist in taking someone's life? Under what circumstances? What criteria make a life no longer meaningful or manageable? Is incurable pain or terminal illness sufficient justification? Or does euthanasia violate the sacred Hippocratic Oath, in which doctors swear to do no harm?*

The issue of doctor-assisted suicide surged to the forefront of American political consciousness in the 1990s, after Dr. Jack Kevorkian used his infamous suicide machine to euthanize several patients under his care. He videotaped the proceedings, and segments of these tapes were reproduced luridly on evening newscasts—sparking a firestorm of controversy that ended in Kevorkian's imprisonment for murder. Kevorkian's aim was to make public what some doctors have been doing privately for hundreds of years but dared not reveal for fear of social, legal, and disciplinary sanctions. Kevorkian's real success, however, lay in promoting a more honest and frank discussion about the role that doctors should play in facilitating death, and under what conditions their participation is justified.

Policymakers generally are reluctant to support legalized euthanasia (for fear of the political repercussions). The issue has been placed on a number of state ballots in recent years, but it either has failed to pass (typically by slim margins) or become tied up in the courts. Surveys indicate that Americans are deeply divided on the issue. Many fear that legalizing doctor-assisted suicide would cheapen the sanctity of life and trigger a "slippery slope," where death would become a more acceptable alternative for less serious conditions. The matter may well be a private one— between patients, their families, and their physicians—but it has broad legal and ethical im-

plications. The question of whether doctors have the right to "play God" may, in many ways, be unresolvable. So is the question of whether doctors exist to prolong life or to end suffering. If both suffering and life are extended at the same time, what is the proper medical course of action, and is that course ethical?

The Controversy

That it is one thing to kill someone and quite another to let that person die is a common assumption. Precisely how to distinguish killing from letting die might be a task best left to philosophers, but the assumption that there is a distinction, and that the distinction has moral significance, is clearly reflected in our law, in religious discussions, and in contemporary medical writing.

It seems to be generally true that it is worse to kill a person than to let him or her die. When Kitty Genovese was stabbed to death on a New York street, thirty-eight people heard her screams and did nothing at all—not even call the police—to help her. Depending on their degree of awareness of the situation (that she was in danger of death) and their ability to do something about it, it seems probable that at least some of the thirty-eight could be said to have let her die. But under our legal system, they are guilty of no crime. And from a moral point of view, their behavior, while reprehensible, isn't as bad as that of her killer.

Philosophers have begun to question the moral significance of the killing/letting die distinction. They ask, first, how the distinction should be characterized, and secondly, whether the distinction provides support for our moral judgments. In general, killing someone involves actually doing something which causes his or her death. Causing death by stabbing, drowning, poisoning—these are clearcut examples of killing. Letting die usually involves *refraining* from doing something that could save a person in mortal danger: not calling the police, not throwing the lifeline, not operating. But there can be cases of killing in which the killer does nothing (e.g., killing by starving to death), and there can be cases of letting die which involve doing something (e.g., hiding the lifeline that could save the drowning person). We see, then, that even characterizing the distinction correctly is a difficult task. Even more difficult is determining its moral relevance.

Should the fact that a form of behavior is more correctly characterized as a killing or as a letting die affect our judgment of its rightness or wrongness? The answer may seem to be obviously yes. After all, it is clearly against the law to kill another person (with certain exceptions, such as self-defense); and with certain exceptions, the law is indifferent to letting die. Secondly, the Sixth Commandment explicitly prohibits killing (or wrongful killing) but is silent about letting die. And while the Hippocratic Oath explicitly enjoins doctors from giving deadly medicine to anyone, it does not provide clear guidance concerning when treatment may be omitted and a patient allowed to die. In three areas, then—law, religion, and medicine—the moral significance of the killing/ letting die distinction seems to be upheld. . . .

Often a distinction is drawn between active and passive euthanasia. Active euthanasia involves intentionally killing the patient for reasons of compassion. Passive euthanasia involves refraining from doing something that could prolong or save a human life, for reasons of compassion. Many members of the medical profession acknowledge engaging in, and supporting the idea of, passive euthanasia, while strongly rejecting the idea of active euthanasia. But why? . . .

The question . . .is not whether the distinction between killing and letting die is in itself morally significant, but what is the intentional termination of a life? Is foreseeing the death as certain sufficient to characterize a doctor's ceasing treatment as intentional termination of life? Or must doctors cease treatment *in order to* cause death for their action to be so described? This second condition is not always met. It may be that the doctor discontinues treatment in order to comply with the patient's request. Even if the patient wants to die, this does not mean that

this is the doctor's reason for terminating treatment.

A doctor may also refrain from initiating or continuing treatment because she or he thinks that the benefits of treatment do not justify the amount of suffering that will be inflicted on the patient. This is particularly so when treatment prolongs life but cannot cure or ameliorate the condition. Many doctors would want to distinguish between foreseeing that death will occur without treatment and intending that the patient die. . . .

. . .[M]embers of the medical profession generally reject the idea of euthanasia, seeing their role as healing and prolonging life rather than ending it. However, doctors cannot always cure, and there are times when the prolonging of life is of questionable value. Indeed, in some cases, prolonging life might be seen as prolonging dying. At some point, it may be appropriate for doctors to stop staving off death. But at what point?

As we noted earlier, Anglo-American law does not recognize "mercy killings." Doctors may not actively kill their patients, even with the kindest of motives. They have more discretion in the area of omissions, for what they are required to do to save or prolong life is determined in part by contemporary medical practice. What contemporary medical practice is, however, is not always clear. In addition, such practice is no doubt influenced by doctors' interpretation of the law, since doctors are not likely to do what they believe is prohibited by law. . . .

Sometimes defective newborns are neglected in order that they might die. In such cases, death is viewed as preferable to life for the infants, and this may be a reasonable attitude, considering the quality of care too often prevalent in the United States. The question is, however, why it is thought preferable to let these babies die rather than to kill them quickly and painlessly. Defective newborns have even been left to starve to death, which seems morally worse than killing them quickly. Of course, doctors and nurses are prohibited by law from directly killing defective newborns, whatever the motivation, but it should be noted that they are also prohibited from leaving them to starve. Doing so is at least criminal neglect and possibly homicide. . . .

It is apparently not uncommon for doctors to leave children with certain diseases (such as spina bifida and meningo-myeloceles) unoperated. While a certain percentage die within the first year of life, many do not die quickly, but slowly over months or years, dying of meningitis, hydrocephalus, or renal disease. Some people maintain that the decision not to operate is, in effect, a decision that the child shall die. They ask if, having made this decision, on the grounds that it is in the child's best interest, it would not be better to alleviate pain and suffering by accelerating death.

Other doctors would insist that the decision to "let nature take its course" is not a decision that the child shall die. They would distinguish between foreseeing that the child will die, if untreated, and intending that it should die. We will return to this distinction in the following sections. Does it embody a significant moral difference? Or is the distinction sophistical, a way of avoiding "dirty hands"? . . .

. . .[A]n argument against active euthanasia and infanticide is that it will have a bru-talizing effect on those who carry it out. Others deny that this will happen and argue that a quick and painless death is often in the best interests of a defective newborn. The truth of this depends on the amount of unavoidable pain the infant will be forced to suffer if left untreated. If pain can be alleviated and the infant is not neglected, it is not clear why a quick death should be thought preferable to allowing to die. Allowing a child to die can be accompanied by loving care by hospital staff and parents. This might have psychological benefits for the people involved, such as reducing feelings of guilt. Such an approach is also more in line with traditional conceptions of the role of doctors, and a change in the conception could conceivably have adverse effects on the doctor-patient relationship. . . .

Adapted from *Killing and Letting Die*, Bonnie Steinbock and Alastair Norcross (eds.). Copyright © 1994. Adapted with permission from Fordham University Press. For editorial reasons, the title of this selection has been modified from the original. ✦

Part VIII

Mental Illness

Deviance and mental illness are long-standing bedfellows. The notion that rule-breaking is rooted in some failure of the psyche is deep-seated and appeals to common sense: All actions are preceded by thoughts, so if those thoughts are, for some reason, in a state of disequilibrium, deviant behavior becomes a logical outcome. A variety of causal explanations have been offered. Psychoanalysts, and Sigmund Freud in particular, blame disequilibrium in the structure of personality, which is made up of the id, superego, and ego. The id houses everyone's instinctual drives and urges—for sexual satisfaction, hedonism, and aggressive release. The superego (also called the conscience) is a person's moral center, responsible for channeling behavior in ethical, upstanding ways. The ego mediates between the drives/urges of the id and the moral mandates of the superego, operating on what Freud calls the "reality principle." An overactive id, underdeveloped superego, or ineffectual ego can spell real trouble; each has been implicated in habitual deviance.

Failed completion of personality *development* also has been associated with chronic rule-breaking. The Freudian school suggests that three stages are germane to this process: oral, anal, and phallic. The *oral* stage spans the period from birth to about one and a half years old; in this stage conduct is oriented almost exclusively around the pursuit of pleasure by way of the mouth, tongue, and lips. Conflict arises when infants are weaned from the breast or bottle and taught to comply with prevailing social norms, a traumatic time for many. The anal stage follows and, as its name implies, relates to issues surrounding the retention/release of one's bowels. When toddlers realize they can control how and when they defecate, power struggles (with parents) ensue and can have lasting effects on behavior. The phallic stage typically spans the ages of two to five and denotes awareness of one's genitals and the recognition that boy and girl genitals are different. Initial understandings of gender and gender role identity emerge at this time (see Freud 1933).

Problems arise when persons fail to go through these stages completely, in the correct order, or in a sufficiently smooth manner. It is said, for example, that thievery represents an inadequate transition out of the anal stage, where affected individuals are unable to freely "let go of their own feces [and] become endlessly involved in the deviant acquisition and retention of property" (Pfohl 1985, 98). Sexual deviance, meanwhile, symbolizes poorly formed gender identification, a function of unresolved relations between parents and (typically) their opposite-sex offspring in the phallic stage. Alcoholism and nicotine addiction represent failed completion of the oral stage, fixations that, as we all know, are as persistent as they are difficult to break.

Sigmund Freud is a household name and many of his arguments are widely recognized, even by those with little in the way of formal education. The influence of psychoanalysis on public discourse cannot be denied, as phrases like "Freudian slip," "Oedipal complex," and "sublimated desire" clearly attest. Yet the psychoanalytic approach is plagued by methodological and conceptual problems that undermine some of its most innovative propositions. Freud's three-part structure of the mind, for one, is entirely abstract. There is no id, ego, or superego that anyone can see, feel, or touch. The theory is therefore unverifiable. Psychoanalysis also relies on case studies of individual patients for theoretical "proof," studies that ask patients (who are not representative of the general population) to recall information about events that occurred decades previously. The belief that events early in childhood have *the most important* effect on later deviant behavior—the heart of the psychoanalytic approach—also is questionable, at best. Tens of thousands of hours of life experience come after age 5, and it is hard to imagine that they will not influence behavior in equal or more significant ways.

Other psychologists focus less on developmental issues and more on particular personality traits that purportedly differentiate deviants and nondeviants. In *The Criminal Personality*, Yochelson and Samenow (1976) suggest that serious rule-breaking is a function of thought patterns peculiar to all offenders regardless of race, age, sex, or socioeconomic status. They say that fifty-two such patterns exist, but eight are principally implicated in chronic rule-violation: unrelenting optimism, fear of injury or being insulted, intense anger, manipulativeness, chronic lying, inflexibly high self-image, great energy, and the view that other people's property is one's own. A number of such traits have also been linked to antisocial personality disorder, more commonly referred to as sociopathy. Sociopaths possess a "mask of sanity" (Cleckley 1988), exuding charm and amiability on the surface but seethe with anger, hate, and bitterness just below. Sociopaths tend to be highly aggressive and lack the ability to express remorse for even the most heinous offenses; it is not uncommon for sociopaths to report a sense of total de-

tachment during the commission of brutal crimes, as if they were some third party watching things unfold from a distance. Ted Bundy was labeled a sociopath. So were John Wayne Gacy, Jeffrey Dahmer, and a host of other incorrigibles. Some studies suggest that as many as 3 percent of the adult population is sociopathic and perhaps 20 percent of the adult criminal population (see Pfohl 1985, 102).

Sociopathy and other personality disorders typically are identified by way of rigorous diagnostic tests—the Minnesota Multiphasic Personality Inventory (MMPI) and the California Psychological Inventory (CPI), in particular. Both contain hundreds of statements describing various forms of conduct to which respondents are directed to answer affirmatively or negatively. These responses, in turn, are grouped into various scales, and each of these scales measures a different aspect of personality; on both the MMPI and CPI, three scales are associated with deviant personality.

Research culled from both tests suggests that there are identifiable differences between deviants and nondeviants and that subtypes of deviants (e.g., thieves vs. violent offenders) score differently from one another. As a diagnostic tool, however, such tests are fatally flawed. Notably, they are unable to measure traits independent of behavior. The 550 statements on the MMPI, for example, ask respondents to agree or disagree with some described conduct, conduct in which respondents have often already engaged: The behavior defines the attribute, the attribute defines the behavior, and nothing is defined in the process—typical circular reasoning.

Biosocial psychologist Hans Eysenck (1977) attempted to break this tautology by incorporating the notion of "conditionability" in his model—how individuals respond to rewards and punishments and how these responses, in turn, shape personality development. Persons who condition poorly, he argues, are more inclined to be extroverted sensation-seekers and also to suffer from what Eysenck calls low cortical arousal. The cerebral cortex is the part of the brain responsible for higher-order intellectual functioning, decision making, and abstract reasoning; people whose cortical arousal is low are not stimulated easily by external prompts and thus have difficulty in responding to rewards and punishments. This, in turn, hinders their ability to learn right from wrong—the building blocks of conscience. Coupled with preexisting sensation-seeking tendencies, such persons may be "doomed" from the start. By locating the source of deviance in conditionability rather than in traits per se, Eysenck escapes the circular reasoning that plagues most personality theories of deviance and provides a deeper, more comprehensive explanation. Without a doubt, such efforts are laudable, but it must be remembered that deviant personality traits are differentially distributed throughout the population. Some people simply have more of them, or more intense forms of them, than others, and these differences are in many cases the result of situational and interactional forces.

The notion that mental illness and deviant behavior are linked is as strong today as ever. The trend toward medicalizing deviance, and mental illness in particular, has played no small role. The late twentieth century was witness to nothing short of a revolution in the construction and control of mental pathology, fueled by a burgeoning pharmaceutical industry and promises of "better living through chemistry." Research has demonstrated the role of neurotransmitters—chemical messengers in the brain that regulate mood and emotion—as a key source of many, if not most, mental disorders. Deficits in serotonin have been associated with chronic depression, acute anxiety, paranoia, irritability, excitability, impulsive fire-setting, and predatory aggression. Low levels of norepinephrine have been linked to compulsive gambling, and insufficient amounts of dopamine have been correlated with illicit drug use (for an overview, see Curran and Renzetti 1994, 78). Chemical imbalances impel affected individuals to seek stimulation and excitement from the environment to boost circulating neurotransmitters in the brain. A host of psychotropic medications—Prozac, Zoloft, Paxil, and Serzone, among others—have been developed to short-cir-

cuit this process and "fix" pharmacologically what people might otherwise attempt to fix behaviorally, fueling a multibillion-dollar business that seems to grow exponentially every year. The widespread acceptance of these medications, within the therapeutic community and beyond, attests to the prevailing belief that mental pathology (and the deviance it promotes) is organic and can be resolved through pharmacological interventions.

The drugging of deviance has a long and not so illustrious history, going back to the days of Thorazine, a powerful antipsychotic and tranquilizer, the use of which often resulted in irreversible side-effects, including central nervous system damage, involuntary tremors, and speech distortions (see Pfohl 1985, 111). Yet even Thorazine is preferable to some of the interventions once used by mental health practitioners to "cure" rule-breakers, from dunking and bloodletting to starvation and restraint to isolation and shock therapy to lobotomies with ice picks and syringes infused with hot gas (Pfohl 1985, 110). Common to all such measures (modern pharmacological ones included) is a focus on eradicating the symptoms of disorder rather than eliminating their root causes. This is perfectly understandable and consistent with the mandates of a quick fix society (the United States is one prominent example): Need money? Go to the ATM. Feeling hungry? Hit the drive-thru. Important letter? Send it by FedEx or, better yet, by fax or e-mail. Complicated and "multitiered" interpersonal problems get reduced to simplistic physiological disorders, which are governed by the "pursuit of technocratic solutions" and "biochemical formulations" (Pfohl 1985, 124). Readers should keep in mind, however, that even the most advanced of psychotropic medications will be of little value unless intensive counseling, cognitive therapy, and behavioral modification are coupled with their use. Symptoms might initially disappear but only temporarily, and new ones will likely emerge in different places and in new forms. The best and most lasting solutions take time, patience, and considerable effort—as anyone with chronic mental illness will tell you.

The idea that mental illness is a *social construction* rather than some objective pathology would clearly surprise those who subscribe to the medical model. But sociologists claim precisely this, and focus on the decisive role that social forces play in the origin and symptoms of mental disorder. Every civilization known to man has "mentals" in its midst, but who they are and how and why they are defined that way is culturally specific and time-delimited. As such, the "reality" of mental illness varies from society to society; behavior and people labeled "crazy" in one context may be perceived as entirely normal in another (Goode 1997, 399). The labeling process is indeed powerful, so powerful, in fact, that mental illness can be said to exist where it really does not. Behavior that is in every sense of the word "normal" can be defined as disordered and cause others to perceive a person as crazy, even if he or she is not. People so labeled may then internalize the label and, through a self-fulfilling prophecy, actually become "crazy."

The sociological underpinnings of mental illness beckon social scientists to study how rates of disorder are differentially distributed throughout populations. Thus, they ask whether certain "types of people" are more susceptible than others and how this susceptibility varies across social space. In America, rates of mental illness are mediated strongly by gender, but the effect of gender seems to cut both ways. Some studies suggest that women are more likely to suffer from mood disorders (depression in particular) but that men are more likely to be diagnosed with serious disturbances like schizophrenia and antisocial personality. Since these "male" disorders are associated with aggressive and violent behavior, men also are more likely to be institutionalized. Marriage seems to confer a modicum of protection on at least some men, however—providing them the emotional and social support necessary to maintain good mental health. (Some sociologists argue, however, that rates of disorder are lower among men who marry because they are naturally more competent and stable, which is demonstrated by their ability to secure mates.) Married *women*, however, do not seem to enjoy the

same protection; some studies actually show them to be at greater risk than unmarried women: "marriage is a stressful, anxiety-provoking, oppressive, [and] exploitative institution, incompatible with the mental health of women (Bernard 1982)" (Goode 1997, 410).

Socioeconomic status is also implicated in the distribution of mental illness across the population. Except for lesser forms of disorder like depression and obsessive compulsiveness, there appears to be a strong inverse relationship between mental health and socioeconomic status: that is, poor people are more susceptible than the more affluent (Goode 1997). Admittedly, this may be an artifact of class or cultural bias in the labeling/disposition process; unstable behavior of the poor is typically perceived to be more threatening. Mental stability is judged by a "middle class yardstick," so "lower class values and behavior are more likely to be regarded as disordered by the psychiatric profession, composed, as it is, of persons who are toward . . .the top of the social class ladder" (Goode 1997, 411). There are other possible hypotheses, however. One suggests that poverty itself promotes illness; the stress, anxiety, and frustration caused by chronic resource deprivation builds up and can have a cumulative impact on mental health. Since the poor, on average, tend to have inferior access to psychological and medical services, there also are fewer buffers to prevent them from going "over the edge." Another theory suggests that socioeconomic status is an effect rather than cause of mental illness: the poor drift to the bottom of the class structure precisely because there is something "wrong" with them (Goode 1997). Caught there, they only become worse, embroiled in a vicious cycle of illness, poverty, and more illness.

Whatever the distribution of mental illness across a population, the sociological task is to distinguish cause from effect and to explore the relative contribution of structural and interactional forces. Specifying precisely how this is done is beyond the scope of the present discussion, but the important thing to remember is that mental illness and social deviance are reciprocally embedded. Every society has a normative order. Every society has people who violate it by acting weird, wild, bizarre, or odd. It is the "behavioral manifestations" of mental illness and not the disorder itself, that is sociologically germane (Goode 1997, 414). Mental illness is defined that way because the behavior it produces is perceived to be disruptive—to upset the normally smooth flow of social intercourse. Because it is disruptive in so many different spheres of social life—unlike other forms of deviance, which tend to be limited to particular focal areas (e.g., drug use, sexual deviance, etc.)—it is "almost unique. . . .It is freefloating [and therefore] eminently generalizable." Someone is labeled "ill not because of having done anything in [a given] area of life, but because one has done many things in many areas that are . . .manifestations of . . .disorder, dysfunction, or disorganization. . . ." (Goode 1997, 414). As Goode concludes, "this is true of practically no other form of deviant behavior" (1997, 414). ✦

40
Nowhere to Go

Homelessness and Mental Illness

E. Fuller Torrey

We have all seen them: the people on street corners and park benches, filthy and unkempt, begging for food, their worldly possessions strewn about them like so much litter. Some of us offer money or words of encouragement. Others cross to the other side of the street, hoping to avoid a confrontation. Most of us see but do not see, secretly blaming the homeless for the condition we believe they have created.

It would be circular to say that the homeless are on the streets because there is no place else for them to go. But there used to be such a place—the mental hospital, significant since many homeless people also suffer from mental illness. With deinstitutionalization came their wholesale release into the community. Since these people had no viable safety net, and no realistic plan for treatment existed, release was a recipe for disaster. Living in squalor is not pleasant by any standards, but disabling depression and delusions of persecution make it considerably worse. Add exposure to the elements, acute hunger, and the ever-present threat of criminal victimization, and an already bad situation becomes much worse.

There are, of course, effective treatments for many mental illnesses. Powerful new psychotropic medications seem to emerge on an annual basis, and intensive counseling has proved to have an ameliorative effect. Despite claims to the contrary, state governments have abundant resources to provide both, but they choose not to. Radical sociologists point out that the economic costs of treatment are not in the best interests of the "ruling class," who can better spend resources on projects near and dear to them and from which they can directly profit—defense spending, space exploration, and prison construction, to name just a few.

With nearly two million people incarcerated nationwide, a substantial portion of whom are suffering from chronic mental illness, penitentiaries have ironically become the new insane asylum (offering, however, little in the way of treatment). These and other paradoxes, and their troubling implications for real-life "mentals" living on the streets of urban America, are explored here.

Well, we have to take our share of the illnesses of our time, and it seems afterall only right that—having lived for years in relatively good health—we should sooner or later receive our part. As for me, you must know that I shouldn't precisely have chosen madness if there had been any choice, but once such a thing has taken hold of you, you can't very well get out of it.[1]

—Vincent Van Gogh, from an 1899 letter while he was involuntarily confined in a psychiatric hospital

In the shadows of mental illness there are many faces. One is that of Thomas McGuire (not his real name), a 45-year-old human resource specialist who for 15 years had been employed by a large manufacturing firm. A college graduate, he had served with the Air Force in Vietnam, had been married for 22 years, and had a teenage son and daughter. He lived in a large city in the eastern United States and used a prestigious university teaching hospital for emergency medical care.

On March 19, 1985, Mr. McGuire went to the emergency room complaining of chest pain and shortness of breath. An electrocardiogram confirmed he was having a heart attack. He was admitted to the hospital and treated for his heart problem. During the admission process, doctors carefully explored precipitating risk factors such as hypertension, cholesterol level, smoking, and work stress. Upon discharge, Mr. McGuire was enrolled in a follow-up program to decrease his cholesterol level and thereby reduce the chances of his having another heart attack.

Ten years later, on November 14, 1995, Mr. McGuire went to the same emergency room. He had called 911 and described suicidal symptoms. According to the notes of the physicians who saw him, Mr. McGuire had lost almost 50 pounds in the previous six months; was sleeping very little; had spent thousands of dollars foolishly, including mailing a postcard with $70 in stamps on it; had written numerous letters to his congressman offering to reorganize the government and "ship icebergs to Africa and reforest the Sahara"; and claimed to be a prophet who was "ushering in the millennium." Mr. McGuire's wife told the emergency room doctors that he had been hospitalized for one previous manic episode 20 years before, and had a history of periodic episodes of hypomania (minor attacks of mania) for which he had not been treated. The resident psychiatrist diagnosed Mr. McGuire as having acute manic-depressive illness (bipolar disorder) and recommended his admission to the hospital. Mr. McGuire refused voluntary admission, so his wife and son offered to testify to support an involuntary admission. The senior psychiatrist, however, refused to admit Mr. McGuire involuntarily, writing in his hospital chart "There are no issues of danger to self [or] others. . . . Though patient is mentally impaired he does not at present show enough evidence to warrant detention." Mr. McGuire was released from the emergency room without being given any medication. A few hours later he hung himself with a rope he found in the basement of his home. His wife found him, and paramedics brought him to the emergency room from which he had just been released. He was pronounced dead there.

The contrast between the treatment Mr. McGuire was given for his heart attack and the treatment he received for his manic-depressive illness vividly illustrates what is wrong with our psychiatric health care system. Both conditions are well-established medical emergencies, one involving dysfunction of the heart, the other of the brain. Both conditions demand immediate hospitalization and the rapid administration of medication. Once stabilized, both conditions should be followed up with a plan for decreasing risk factors that might trigger recurrence and for providing education about early warning signs.

The reasons Mr. McGuire received excellent care for his heart attack but disgraceful treatment for his manic-depressive illness can be surmised from the notes of his psychiatrists and from what is known about psychiatric services in the state where he lived. It is a state that has closed over 80 percent of its public psychiatric beds in an effort to shift costs from the state government to the federal government. . . . Increasing numbers of psychiatric emergencies have been referred to that university hospital and to other general hospitals in the community, many of which are already overcrowded and unprepared to treat such severely ill patients. It is a state in which civil rights lawyers and other advocates have waged a highly publicized fight to limit the grounds for involuntary psychiatric hospitalization to danger-to-self-or others, and to have this interpreted as narrowly as possible in the courts. . . .It is also a state with a long history of promoting "mental health" issues. And some members of the staff at the university hospital at which Mr. McGuire sought treatment still adhere to a psychoanalytic, rather than a medical understanding of mental illness. It is possible that the senior psychiatrist who released Mr. McGuire without treating him did not consider manic-depressive illness to be a medical emergency but rather to be a product of intrapersonal and interpersonal conflict that should be treated with long-term psychotherapy.

Mr. McGuire's negligent treatment is not an aberration. Similar examples occur throughout the United States virtually every day. Mr. McGuire did not seek help in a rural area with no trained psychiatrists, nor in a city such as Miami, Houston, or Los Angeles, which are known to have very poor public psychiatric services, nor in a public psychiatric hospital such as Hawaii State Hospital, which has been designated as the worst public psychiatric hospital in the United States.[2] Mr. McGuire sought treatment in a prestigious university hospital in a city reputed to be a regional medical Mecca.

The mental illness crisis, then, consists of hundreds of thousands of men and women like Mr. McGuire who represent a large percentage of the estimated 2.2 million Americans with untreated severe mental illnesses. On any given day, approximately 150,000 of them are homeless, living on the streets or in public shelters. Another 159,000 are incarcerated in jails and prisons, mostly for crimes committed because they were not being treated. Some of them become violent and may terrorize their families, towns, or urban neighborhoods. A very large number have died prematurely as a result of accidents and suicide. Tragically, most of these instances of homelessness, incarcerations, episodes of violence, and premature deaths are unnecessary. We know what to do, but for economic, legal, and ideological reasons we fail to do it.

Who Are the Severely Mentally Ill and What Is Wrong With Them?

"Mental illness" is a nonspecific term that covers a broad array of brain disorders, human behaviors, and personality types. The term commonly designates one end of an amorphous mental health-mental illness spectrum. This [chapter] is concerned only with *severe mental illnesses,* defined in 1993 by the National Advisory Mental Health Council, an arm of the National Institute of Mental Health, as including "disorders with psychotic symptoms such as schizophrenia, schizoaffective disorder, manic-depressive disorder, autism, as well as severe forms of other disorders such as major depression, panic disorder, and obsessive-compulsive disorder."[3] The Council determined that over a one-year period, 2.8 percent of the adult population in the United States is affected by such severe mental illness. Additional studies estimated that 3.2 percent of children and adolescents ages 9 through 17 have a severe mental illness in any given six-month period. Based on the total 1995 U.S. population of 262 million, this means that during that year approximately 5.6 million people ages 9 or older had a severe mental illness. According to the National Advisory Mental Health Council, the cost of their care was $27 billion

for direct treatment costs and $74 billion if indirect costs such as maintenance and lost productivity are included. These numbers do not include people with a primary diagnosis of alcohol or drug addiction, although many severely mentally ill people also abuse alcohol or drugs.

Research over the past decade has clarified what is wrong with those diagnosed with severe mental illnesses. They have neurobiological disorders of their brains that affect their thinking and moods and that can be measured by changes in both brain structure and function. Figure 40.1 [not shown here] illustrates these changes as shown on MRI (magnetic resonance imaging) scans of two pairs of identical twins. In one pair, one twin has schizophrenia and his identical co-twin is well, and in the other pair, one twin has manic-depressive illness and her co-twin is well. In both cases, the affected twin has larger cerebral ventricles, the fluid-carrying spaces in the brain, suggesting that the affected twins have had some loss of brain tissue associated with their illnesses. Not everyone with schizophrenia and manic-depressive illness has enlarged cerebral ventricles, but many do.

Research on schizophrenia, schizoaffective disorder, manic-depressive disorder, autism, and severe forms of major depression, panic disorder, and obsessive-compulsive disorder has also revealed a variety of functional disease-related changes in the brains of affected individuals. These include changes in the neurochemistry, metabolism, electrical activity, neurological function, and neuropsychological function of the brain. Some of these changes may be caused by the medication being taken for the illness, but the majority are not medication-related and can be found in those who have never taken medication.

It has now been established that severe mental illnesses, as defined by the National Advisory Mental Health Council, are neurobiological disorders of the brain. These illnesses are thus in the same category as other brain disorders such as Parkinson's disease, Alzheimer's disease, and multiple sclerosis. Like severe mental illnesses, each of these disorders is associated with measurable abnormalities in brain structure and function. And, as with severe mental illnesses, it is not yet known what factors—genes, developmental effects, viruses, toxins, or metabolic defects—contribute to the biological chain of events causing these disorders.

Can They Be Treated and Are They Being Treated?

A persistent myth about severe mental illness is that it cannot be treated. In fact, according to the 1993 report of the National Advisory Mental Health Council, "The efficacy of many treatments for severe mental disorders is comparable to that in other branches of medicine, including surgery."[4] For schizophrenia and schizoaffective disorder (a mixture of schizophrenia and manic-depressive disorder) research has shown that standard antipsychotic medication will "reduce psychotic symptoms in 60 percent of patients and in 70–85 percent of those experiencing symptoms for the first time."[5] Newer antipsychotics such as clozapine are effective in an additional one-third of people who do not respond to the standard antipsychotics. For manic-depressive illness, approximately 75 percent of sufferers respond to lithium, carbemazopine, or a combination of ancillary medications. For severe depression, at least 80 percent respond to tricyclic (Elavil, Norpramin), selective serotonin reuptake inhibitor (SSRI) (Prozac, Zoloft, and others) or monoamine oxidase inhibitor, (MAOI) (e.g., Nardil, Parnate) antidepressants; some of the nonresponders can be successfully treated using electroconvulsive therapy (ECT). For severe panic disorder, between 70 and 90 percent of sufferers respond to an antidepressant or a benzodiazepine class of medication. And for severe obsessive-compulsive disorder, approximately 60 percent react at least moderately well to one or more antidepressants. Of all the severe mental illnesses, only autism has no effective medication at this time.

It should be emphasized that medications are not the only treatment for those with severe mental illnesses. Many also require re-

habilitation and supportive counseling. Excellent model programs have been developed to provide these, including the Program in Assertive Community Treatment (PACT), which originated in Madison, Wisconsin; clubhouse programs patterned after New York City's Fountain House; and employment programs such as Fairweather Lodges, transitional employment programs, and job skills training. . . .[T]he important point to remember is that we have effective treatments for the majority of people with severe mental illnesses. The medications do not cure the illnesses, but rather control the symptoms just as insulin does in diabetes. *The mental illness crisis, then, has not occurred because we do not have effective treatments. Rather, it exists because we do not use these treatments for a substantial number of those afflicted.* As we will see, the reasons for this failure say more about our national politics and ideology than about our scientific progress.

Of the 5.6 million individuals who had a severe mental illness in 1995, how many were receiving treatment? According to the National Advisory Mental Health Council, approximately 60 percent of severely mentally ill adults receive treatment in any given year.[6] For schizophrenia, the treatment rate appears to be even lower; for example, a 1981 study of people with schizophrenia living in Baltimore reported that only 50 percent were receiving treatment.[7] If we use an estimated overall treatment rate of 60 percent, then 40 percent are not receiving treatment. Based on the total of 5.6 million, that means that approximately 2.2 million severely mentally ill people are not being treated. These are the men, women, and children at the heart and core of the mental illness crisis.

Who are these people? Mr. McGuire was one of them. Among the thousands of others in the shadows are the following individuals whom I have known:

- A woman with schizophrenia who lived with her parents, and later with her unmarried brother, for 45 years until her recent death. She had originally become ill at age 16 and was hospitalized for six months, but that took place before antipsychotic medications were available. Over the years, her family periodically encouraged her to see a psychiatrist, but she refused. Her family provided for all her needs, and she lived an isolated, hermitlike existence, spending most of the time in her own room.

• A man now in his late 30s, who has suffered from periodic episodes of severe depression for almost 20 years. He also abuses alcohol and occasionally drugs, and it is these problems that he and his family focus on. His depression has never been treated.

• A woman in her 40s with manic-depressive illness who dropped out of school in the eighth grade because of severe "emotional difficulties." She lives in a rural area, and the nearest mental health center is a two-hour drive away. Her family is not well educated and does not understand why she "thinks funny" and sometimes stays in her room for weeks at a time. In one episode, when she became manic, her elderly parents locked her in the attic for several days so she would not run away.

• A 56-year-old man with paranoid schizophrenia, a graduate of an Ivy League university, who has spent the past 20 years wandering the country, often sleeping in public shelters or in the woods. He believes the FBI implanted microchips in his brain and that these broadcast voices in his head. His family has tried on several occasions to get him involuntarily committed to a hospital for treatment, but in court the man is calm, articulate, and able to convince the judge that he has the right to live his alternate lifestyle.

• A 28-year-old man with schizoaffective disorder (a mixture of schizophrenia and manic-depressive disorder) who lives beneath a bridge in a large Eastern city. He spent five years in a South Carolina prison for manslaughter, and he periodically threatens people on the street who refuse his demands for money, most of which he uses to buy marijuana and alcohol. Since he left prison, he has received no treatment.

People like these can be found in every city, town, and rural area in the United States.

In addition to the 2.2 million people who receive no treatment, there is another group who are often forgotten—those who, like Mr. McGuire, have died as a direct or indirect result of not being treated. Suicide is the most common cause of their death. The lifetime suicide rate among those with schizophrenia is 10 to 13 percent and among those with manic-depressive illness 15 to 17 percent, as opposed to about 1 percent among the general population. In addition to suicide, many people with severe mental illnesses die prematurely because of accidents and untreated physical illnesses. We don't know how many of them would be alive today if they had received adequate treatment, but almost certainly hundreds of thousands have paid with their lives for an illness that need not have been fatal.

Deinstitutionalization: A Psychiatric *'Titanic'*

Deinstitutionalization is the name given to the policy of moving severely mentally ill people out of large state institutions and then closing part or all of those institutions; it has been a major contributing factor to the mental illness crisis. (The term also describes a similar process for mentally retarded people. . . .)

Deinstitutionalization began in 1955 with the widespread introduction of chlorpromazine, commonly known as Thorazine, the first effective antipsychotic medication, and received a major impetus 10 years later with the enactment of federal Medicaid and Medicare. Deinstitutionalization has two parts the moving of the severely mentally ill out of the state institutions, and the closing of part or all of those institutions. The former affects people who are already mentally ill. The latter affects those who become ill after the policy has gone into effect and for the indefinite future because hospital beds have been permanently eliminated.

The magnitude of deinstitutionalization of the severely mentally ill qualifies it as one of the largest social experiments in American history. In 1955, there were 558,239 severely mentally ill patients in the nation's public psychiatric hospitals. In 1994, this number had been reduced by 486,620 patients, to 71,619, as seen in Figure 40.2 [not shown here]. It is important to note, however, that the census of 558,239 patients in public psychiatric hospitals in 1955 was in relationship to the nation's total population at the time, which was 164 million.

By 1994, the nation's population had increased to 260 million. If there had been the same proportion of patients per population in public mental hospitals in 1994 as there had been in 1955, the patients would have totaled 885,010. The true magnitude of deinstitutionalization, then, is the difference between 885,010 and 71,619. In effect, approximately 92 percent of the people who would have been living in public psychiatric hospitals in 1955 were not living there in 1994. Even allowing for the approximately 40,000 patients who occupied psychiatric beds in general hospitals or the approximately 10,000 patients who occupied psychiatric beds in community mental health centers (CMHCs) on any given day in 1994, that still means that approximately 763,391 severely mentally ill people (over three-quarters of a million) are living in the community today who would have been hospitalized 40 years ago. That number is more than the population of Baltimore or San Francisco.

Deinstitutionalization varied from state to state. In assessing these differences in census for public mental hospitals, it is not sufficient merely to subtract the 1994 number of patients from the 1955 number, because state populations shifted in the various states during those 40 years. In Iowa, West Virginia, and the District of Columbia, the total populations actually decreased during that period, whereas in California, Florida, and Arizona, the population increased dramatically; and in Nevada, it increased more than sevenfold, from 0.2 million to 1.5 million. The table [not shown here] in the Appendix takes these population changes into account and provides an effective deinstitutionalization rate for each state based on the number of patients hospitalized in 1994 subtracted from the number of patients that would have been expected to be hospitalized in 1994 based on that state's population. It assumes that the ratio of hospitalized patients to population would have remained constant over the 40 years.

Rhode Island, Massachusetts, New Hampshire, Vermont, West Virginia, Arkansas, Wisconsin, and California all have effective deinstitutionalization rates of over 95 percent. Rhode Island's rate is over 98 percent, meaning that for every 100 state residents in public mental hospitals in 1955, fewer than 2 patients are there today. On the other end of the curve, Nevada, Delaware, and the District of Columbia have effective deinstitutionalization rates below 80 percent.

Most of those who were deinstitutionalized from the nation's public psychiatric hospitals were severely mentally ill. Between 50 and 60 percent of them were diagnosed with schizophrenia. Another 10 to 15 percent were diagnosed with manic-depressive illness and severe depression. An additional 10 to 15 percent were diagnosed with organic brain diseases—epilepsy, strokes, Alzheimer's disease, and brain damage secondary to trauma. The remaining individuals residing in public psychiatric hospitals had conditions such as mental retardation with psychosis, autism and other psychiatric disorders of childhood, and alcoholism and drug addiction with concurrent brain damage. The fact that most deinstitutionalized people suffer from various forms of brain dysfunction was not as well understood when the policy of deinstitutionalization got under way.

Thus deinstitutionalization has helped create the mental illness crisis by discharging people from public psychiatric hospitals without ensuring that they received the medication and rehabilitation services necessary for them to live successfully in the community. Deinstitutionalization further exacerbated the situation because, once the public psychiatric beds had been closed, they were not available for people who later became mentally ill, and this situation continues up to the present. Consequently, approximately 2.2 million severely mentally ill people do not receive any psychiatric treatment.

Deinstitutionalization was based on the principle that severe mental illness should be treated in the least restrictive setting. As further defined by President Jimmy Carter's Commission on Mental Health, this ideology rested on "the objective of maintaining the greatest degree of freedom, self-determination, autonomy, dignity, and integrity of body, mind, and spirit for the individual while he or she participates in treatment or receives services."[8] This is a laudable goal and for many, perhaps for the majority of those who are deinstitutionalized, it has been at least partially realized.

For a substantial minority, however, deinstitutionalization has been a psychiatric *Titanic*. Their lives are virtually devoid of "dignity" or "integrity of body, mind, and spirit." "Self-determination" often means merely that the person has a choice of soup kitchens. The "least restrictive setting" frequently turns out to be a cardboard box, a jail cell, or a terror-filled existence plagued by both real and imaginary enemies. Even one Thomas McGuire is too many; hundreds of thousands are a disgrace.

Notes

1. Rewald, J. (1962). "Post-impressionism: From Van Gogh to Gauguin." New York: Museum of Modern Art, p. 321.

2. Torrey, E.F., Erdman, K., Wolfe, S.M. and Flynn, L.M. (1990). "Care of the seriously mentally ill: A rating of state programs" (3rd ed.). Washington, DC: Public Citizen Health Research Group and National Alliance for the Mentally Ill, pp. 175–176.

3. "Health care reform for Americans with severe mental illnesses: Report of the National Advisory Mental Health Council." (1993). *American Journal of Psychiatry*, 150, 1447–1465.

4. Ibid.

5. Ibid.

6. Ibid.

7. Von Korff, M., Nestadt, G., Romanoski, A., Anthony, J., Eaton, W., Merchant, A., Chahal, R., Kramer, M., Folstein, M., and E. Gruenberg (1985). "Prevalence of treated and untreated DSM-III schizophrenia." *Journal of Nervous and Mental Disease*, 173, 577–581.

8. Munetz, M.R. and Geller, J.L. (1993). "The least restrictive alternative in the postinstitutional era." *Hospital and Community Psychiatry*, 44, 967–973.

41

The Compulsion to Amputate One's Own Limbs

Apotemnophilia and Mental Disorder

Carl Elliott

tempted to try it. It could even become "cool," attracting a cultural chic not unlike the contemporary obsession with body piercing, tattooing, and other forms of self-mutilation. The contagion process should not be underestimated in the spread of deviant behavior, and apotemnophilia—however outlandish it may seem—is no exception. In this fascinating article, Elliott locates and identifies apotemnophiliacs, interviews them at length about their condition, dissects the disturbing thought-patterns that go into the obsession, and explores the emergent internet-based subculture where apotemnophiliacs share their thoughts, desires, and wishes.

It is hard to believe that anyone would want to voluntarily cut off a healthy arm or leg. But that is precisely what people with a condition called apotemnophilia have a compulsion to do. And it is a compulsion through and through, not unlike someone who must flick the light switch on and off fifty times before entering a room, or open every door with a paper towel to avoid contact with germs. Whether caused by childhood trauma or biochemical imbalances, those who suffer from this condition insist that they will never be "right" unless or until their gruesome mission is complete. Apotemnophiliacs feel as if they're not whole, as if they are not supposed to have all four limbs and that the only way to "cure" their condition is to remove one or more of them. Unable to find doctors to help them, some resort to crude methods for self-surgery (e.g., chain saws, shotgun blasts, tying oneself to train tracks)—with sometimes disastrous outcomes.

Telling an apotemnophiliac to renounce his or her desires, however macabre, is tantamount to telling him or her to give up everything that is meaningful and important. In this sense, mental pathology is inextricably linked to perceptions of identity and selfhood. Elliott fears, however, that publicizing the disorder—giving it a formal psychiatric diagnosis and letting everyone know it exists—might ultimately do more harm than good. People who never thought about self-amputation might be

In January of this year British newspapers began running articles about Robert Smith, a surgeon at Falkirk and District Royal Infirmary, in Scotland. Smith had amputated the legs of two patients at their request, and he was planning to carry out a third amputation when the trust that runs his hospital stopped him. These patients were not physically sick. Their legs did not need to be amputated for any medical reason. Nor were they incompetent, according to the psychiatrists who examined them. They simply wanted to have their legs cut off. In fact, both the men whose limbs Smith amputated have declared in public interviews how much happier they are, now that they have finally had their legs removed.

Healthy people seeking amputations are nowhere near as rare as one might think. In May of 1998 a seventy-nine-year-old man from New York traveled to Mexico and paid $10,000 for a black-market leg amputation; he died of gangrene in a motel. In October of 1999 a mentally competent man in Milwaukee severed his arm with a homemade guillotine, and then threatened to sever it again if surgeons reattached it. That same month a legal investigator for the California state bar, after being refused a hospital amputation, tied off her legs with tourniquets and began to pack them in ice, hoping that gangrene would set in, necessitating an amputation. She passed out and ultimately gave up. Now she says she will probably have to lie under a train, or shoot her legs off with a shotgun.

For the first time that I am aware of, we are seeing clusters of people seeking voluntary amputations of healthy limbs and performing amputations on themselves. The cases I have identified are merely those that have made the newspapers. On the Internet there are enough people interested in becoming amputees to support a minor industry. One discussion listserv has 1,400 subscribers.

"It was the most satisfying operation I have ever performed," Smith told a news conference in February. "I have no doubt that what I was doing was the correct thing for those patients." Although it took him eighteen months to work up the courage to do the first amputation, Smith eventually decided that there was no humane alternative. Psychotherapy "doesn't make a scrap of difference in these people," the psychiatrist Russell Reid, of Hillingdon Hospital, in London, said in a BBC documentary on the subject, called *Complete Obsession*, that was broadcast in Britain last winter. "You can talk till the cows come home; it doesn't make any difference. They're still going to want their amputation, and I know that for a fact." Both Smith and Reid pointed out that these people may do themselves unintended harm or even kill themselves trying to amputate their own limbs. As the retired psychiatrist Richard Fox observed in the BBC program, "Let's face it, this is a potentially fatal condition."

Yet the psychiatrists and the surgeon were all baffled by the desire for amputation. Why would anyone want an arm or a leg cut off? Where does this sort of desire come from? Smith has said that the request initially struck him as "absolutely, utterly weird." "It seemed very strange," Reid told the BBC interviewer. "To be honest, I couldn't quite understand it."

The True Self?

In 1977 the Johns Hopkins psychologist John Money published the first modern case history of what he termed "apotemnophilia"—an attraction to the idea of being an amputee. He distinguished apotemnophilia from "acrotomophilia"—a sexual attraction to amputees. The suffix *-philia* is important here. It places these conditions in the group of psychosexual disorders called paraphilias, often referred to outside medicine as perversions. Fetishes are a fairly common sort of paraphilia. In the same way that some people are turned on by, say, shoes or animals, others are turned on by amputees. Not by blood or mutilation—pain is not usually what they are looking for. The apotemnophile's desire is to be an amputee, whereas the acrotomophile's desire is turned toward those who happen to be amputees.

I found John Money's papers on amputee attraction at the University of Otago, in Dunedin, New Zealand, shortly after the Falkirk story made the news. Money is an expatriate New Zealander, and he has deposited his collected manuscripts in the Otago medical library. I had come to Dunedin to write a book at the university's Bioethics Centre, where I'd worked in the early 1990s. I have a medical degree, teach university courses in philosophy, and write a fair bit about the philosophy of psychiatry, and I was interested in the way that previously little-known psychiatric disorders spread, sometimes even reaching epidemic proportions, for reasons that nobody seems fully to understand. But I had never heard of apotemnophilia or acrotomophilia before the Falkirk story broke. I wondered: Was this a legitimate psychiatric disorder? Was there any chance that it might spread? Like Josephine Johnston, a lawyer in Dunedin who is writing a graduate thesis on the legality of these amputations (and who first brought the Falkirk case to my attention), I also wondered about the ethical and legal status of surgery as a solution. Should amputation be treated like cosmetic surgery, or like invasive psychiatric treatment, or like a risky research procedure.

Reviewing the medical literature, one might conclude that apotemnophilia and acrotomophilia are extremely rare. Fewer than half a dozen articles have been published on apotemnophilia, most of them in arcane journals. Most psychiatrists and psychologists I have spoken with—even those who specialize in paraphilias—have never heard of apotemnophilia. On the Internet, however, it is an entirely different story. Acrotomophiles are known on the Web as "devotees," and apotemnophiles are known as "wannabes." "Pretenders" are people who are not disabled but use crutches, wheelchairs, or braces, often in public, in order to feel disabled. Various Web sites sell photographs and videos of amputees; display stories and memoirs; recommend books and movies; and provide chat rooms, meeting points, and electronic bulletin boards. Much of this material caters to devotees, who seem to be far greater in number than wannabes. It is unclear just how many people out there actually want to become amputees, but there exist numerous wannabe and devotee listservs and Web sites.

Like Robert Smith, I have been struck by the way wannabes use the language of identity and selfhood in describing their desire to lose a limb. "I have always felt I should be an amputee." "I felt, this is who I was." "It is a desire to see myself, be myself, as I 'know' or 'feel' myself to be." This kind of language has persuaded many clinicians that apotemnophilia has been misnamed—that it is not a problem of sexual desire, as the *-philia* suggests, but a problem of body image. What true apotemnophiles share, Smith said in the BBC documentary, is the feeling "that their body is incomplete with their normal complement of four limbs." Smith has elsewhere speculated that apotemnophilia is not a psychiatric disorder but a neuropsychological one, with biological roots. Perhaps it has less to do with desire than with being stuck in the wrong body.

Yet what exactly does it mean to be stuck in the wrong body? For the past several years I have been working with a research group interested in problems surrounding the use of medical interventions for personal enhancement. One of the issues we have struggled with is how to understand people who use the language of self and identity to explain why they want these interventions: a man who says he is "not himself" unless he is on Prozac; a woman who gets breast-reduction surgery because she is "not the large-breasted type"; a bodybuilder who says he took anabolic steroids because he wants to look on the outside the way he feels on the inside; and—perhaps most common—transsexuals whose experience is described as "being trapped in the wrong body." The image is striking, and more than a little odd. In each case the true self is the one produced by medical science.

At first I was inclined to think of this language as a literal description. Maybe some people really did feel as if they had found their true selves on Prozac. Maybe they really did feel incomplete without cosmetic surgery. Later on, however, I came to think of the descriptions less as literal than as expressions of an ambivalent moral ideal—a struggle between the impulse toward self-improvement and the impulse to be true to oneself. Not that I can see no difference between a middle-aged man rubbing Rogaine on his head every morning and a man whose discomfort in his own body is so all-consuming that he begins to think of suicide. But we shouldn't be surprised when any of these people, healthy or sick, use phrases like "becoming myself" and "I was incomplete" and "the way I really am" to describe what they feel, because the language of identity and selfhood surrounds us. It is built into our morality, our literature, our political philosophy, our therapeutic sensibility, even our popular culture. This is the way we talk now. This is the way we think. This is even the way we sell cars and tennis shoes. We talk of self-discovery, self-realization, self-expression, self-actualization, self-invention, self-knowledge, self-betrayal, and self-absorption. It should be no great revelation that the vocabulary of the self feels like a natural way to describe our longings, our obsessions, and our psychopathologies.

This leads to larger questions about the nature of identity. What prompts people to conceptualize themselves as amputees? And at a time when identity seems so malleable, when so many people profess uncertainty about who they really are, is it possible that the desire for this particular identity might spread?

'I Knew I Didn't Want My Leg'

The question to be answered is not only why people who want to be amputees use the language of identity to describe what they feel but also what exactly they are using it to describe. One point of contention among clinicians is whether apotemnophilia is, as John Money thought, really a paraphilia. "I think that John Money confused the apotemnophiles and the acrotomophiles," Robert Smith wrote to me from Scotland. "The devotees I think are paraphilic, but not the apotemnophiles." The point here is whether we should view apotemnophilia as a problem of sexual desire—a variety of the same condition that includes pedophilia, voyeurism, and exhibitionism. Smith, in agreement with many of the wannabes I have spoken with, believes that apotemnophilia is closer to gender-identity disorder, the diagnosis given to people who wish to live as the opposite sex. Like these people, who are uncomfortable with their identities and want to change sex, apotemnophiles are uncomfortable with their identities and want to be amputees.

But just what counts as apotemnophilia is part of the problem in explaining it. Some wannabes are also devotees. Others who identify themselves as wannabes are drawn to extreme body modification. There seems to be some overlap between people who want finger and toe amputations and those who seek piercing, scarring, branding, genital mutilation, and such. Some wannabes, Robert Smith suggests, want amputation as a way to gain sympathy from others. And finally, there are "true" apotemnophiles, whose desire for amputation is less about sex than about identity. "My left foot was not part of me," says one amputee, who had wished for amputation since the age of eight. "I didn't understand why, but I knew I didn't want my leg." A woman in her early forties wrote to me, "I will never feel truly whole with legs." Her view of herself has always been as a double amputee, with stumps of five or six inches.

Many devotees and wannabes describe what Lee Nattress, an adjunct professor of social work at Loma Linda University, in Cal-

ifornia, calls a "life-changing" experience with an amputee as a child. "When I was three years old, I met a young man who was completely missing all four of his fingers on his right hand," writes a twenty-one-year-old woman who says she is planning to have both her arms amputated. "Ever since that time, I have been fascinated by all amputees, especially women amputees who were missing parts of their arms and wore hook prostheses." Hers is not an unusual story. Most wannabes trace their desire to become amputees back to before the age of six or seven, and some will say that they cannot remember a time when they didn't have the desire. Nattress, who surveyed fifty people with acrotomophilia (he prefers the term "amelotasis") for a 1996 doctoral dissertation, says that much the same is true for devotees. Three quarters of the devotees he surveyed were aware of their attraction by the age of fifteen, and about a quarter wanted to become amputees themselves.

Many of the news reports about the case at the Falkirk and District Royal Infirmary identified Smith's patients as having extreme cases of body dysmorphic disorder. Like people with anorexia nervosa, who believe themselves to be overweight even as they become emaciated, people with body dysmorphic disorder are preoccupied with what they see as a physical defect: thinning hair, nose shape, facial asymmetry, the size of their breasts or buttocks. They are often anxious and obsessive, constantly checking themselves in mirrors and shop windows, or trying to disguise or hide the defect. They are often convinced that others find them ugly. Sometimes they seek out cosmetic surgery, but frequently they are unhappy with the results and ask for more surgery. Sometimes they redirect their obsession to another part of the body. But none of this really describes most of the people who are looking for amputations—who, typically, are not convinced they are ugly, do not imagine that other people see them as defective, and are usually focused exclusively on amputation (rather than on, say, a receding hairline or bad skin). Amputee wannabes more often see their limbs as normal, but as a kind of surplus. Their desires frequently come with chillingly precise specifications: for instance, an above-the-knee amputation of the right leg.

By calling apotemnophilia a paraphilia, John Money placed it in a long and distinguished lineage of psychosexual disorders. The grand old man of psychosexual pathology, Richard von Krafft-Ebing, catalogued an astonishing range of paraphilias in his *Psychopathia Sexualis* (1886), from necrophilia and bestiality to fetishes for aprons, handkerchiefs, and kid gloves. Some of his cases involve an attraction to what he called "bodily defects." One was a twenty-eight-year-old engineer who had been excited by the sight of women's disfigured feet since the age of seventeen. Another had pretended to be lame since early childhood, limping around on two brooms instead of crutches. The philosopher René Descartes, Krafft-Ebing noted, was partial to cross-eyed women.

Yet the term "sexual fetish" could be a misleading way to describe the fantasies of wannabes and devotees, if what is on the Web is any indication (and, of course, it might well not be). Many of these fantasies seem almost presexual. I don't want to be misunderstood: there is plenty of amputee pornography on the Internet. *Penthouse* has published in its letters section many of what it terms "monopede mania" letters, purportedly from devotees, and *Hustler* has published an article on amputee fetishism. But many other amputee Web sites have an air of thoroughly wholesome middle-American hero worship, and perhaps for precisely that reason they are especially disconcerting, like a funeral parlor in a shopping mall. Some show disabled men and women attempting nearly impossible feats—running marathons, climbing mountains, creating art with prostheses. It is as if the fantasy of being an amputee is inseparable from the idea of achievement—or, as one of my correspondents put it, from an "attraction to amputees as role models." "I've summed it up this way," John Money said, a little cruelly, in a 1975 interview. "Look, Ma, no hands, no feet, and I still can do it." One woman, then a forty-two-year-old student and housewife whose history Money presented in a 1990 research paper, said one of the appeals of being an am-

putee was "coping heroically." A man told Money that his fantasy was that of "compensating or overcompensating, achieving, going out and doing things that one would say is unexpectable." One of my amputee correspondents wrote that what attracted him to being an amputee was not heroic achievement so much as "finding new ways of doing old tasks, finding new challenges in working things out and perhaps a bit of being able to do things that are not always expected of amputees."

On the Web

I am on the phone with Max Price, a graphic designer in Santa Fe, who has offered to talk to me about apotemnophilia. (He has asked me to change his name and the details of his life and history if I write about him, and I have.) Price is a charming man, articulate and well-read, and despite my initial uneasiness about calling him, I am enjoying our conversation. I had corresponded by e-mail with a number of wannabes, but had not managed to talk to any of them until now. The conversation has taken on an easy intellectual tone, more like a discussion between colleagues than an interview. Price is telling me about his efforts to get doctors to adopt some guidelines for deciding when a person with apotemnophilia should have surgery. I am tossing out ideas, trying out some of my thoughts, and I wonder aloud about a relationship between apotemnophilia and obsessive-compulsive disorder. I ask Price whether he feels that his desire is more like an obsession, a fantasy, or a wish. He says, "Well, it was definitely like an obsession. Until I cut my leg off, of course."

That brings me up short. I had been unaware that he had actually gone ahead with an amputation. "Ah," I say. I pause. Should I ask? I decide I should. "May I ask how you did it?" Price laughs. "It was kind of messy," he says. "I did it with a log splitter." He then explains, in a thoughtful, dispassionate manner, the details of his "accident" ten years ago—the research he had done on anesthesia and wound control, how he had driven himself to the emergency room after partially amputating his limb, the efforts of the hospital surgeons to reattach it. He lived with the reattached leg for six months, he said, until medical complications finally helped him persuade another surgeon to amputate it.

I met Price through an Internet discussion listserv called "amputee-by-choice," one of the larger lists. At first I had simply prowled through the archives and listened to the ongoing conversation. I found many of the archived messages very creepy. Here were people exchanging photographs of hands with missing fingers; speculating about black-market amputations in Russia; debating the merits of industrial accidents, gunshot wounds, self-inflicted gangrene, chainsaw slips, dry ice, and cigar cutters as means of getting rid of their limbs and digits. When I introduced myself to the active electronic group, however, the discussion abruptly stopped, like the conversation in a village pub when a stranger walks in. For several days only a handful of new messages were posted. But I had invited wannabes to get in touch with me individually, telling them that I was a university professor working on apotemnophilia, and over the next few days a dozen or so people responded. Some, like Price, were insightful and articulate. Some had become mental health professionals, in part as a way of trying to understand their desires. The few who had managed an amputation seemed (somewhat to my surprise) to have made peace with their desires. But others obviously needed help: they were obsessive, driven, consumed. Many seemed to have other psychiatric problems: clinical depression, obsessive-compulsive disorder, eating disorders, transvestism of a type that sounded anything but playful or transgressive. They did not trust psychiatrists. They did not want medication. They wanted to know if I could find them a surgeon. I felt like an ethnographer in a remote country, unfamiliar with the local customs, who the natives believe can help them. I began to understand how Robert Smith must have felt. I also began to wonder at the strength of a desire that would take people to such lengths.

By all accounts, the Internet has been revolutionary for wannabes. I can see why. It took me months to track down even a handful of scientific articles on the desire for amputation. It took about ten seconds to find dozens of Web sites devoted to the topic. Every one of the wannabes and devotees I have talked with about the Internet says that it has changed everything for them. "My palms were actually sweating the first time I typed 'amputee' into a search engine," one wannabe wrote to me. But the results were gratifying. "It was an epiphany," she wrote. When Krafft-Ebing was writing *Psychopathia Sexualis*, people with unusual desires could live their entire lives without knowing that there was anyone else in the world like them. Today all it takes is a computer terminal. On the Internet you can find a community to which you can listen or reveal yourself, and instant validation for your condition, whatever it may be. This same wannabe told me that she has never spoken about her desire for amputation with a friend, a family member, or a mental health professional, and that she never will. Yet she is a frequent anonymous participant on the wannabe discussion listserv.

"The Internet was, for me, a validation experience," writes a wannabe who is also a transsexual. She says she found herself thinking less about amputation after logging on, because her desire was no longer such a dark secret. "When one is afraid of discovery, I think one thinks rather more about the secret in order to guard against accidental revelation." She also points out that the Internet helped her get information on how to lose her legs. Another wannabe, a therapist, says that discovering the Internet was a mixed blessing. "There was a huge hole to be filled," she told me, and the Internet began to fill it. To discover that she was not alone was wonderful—but it also meant that a desire she had managed to push to the back of her mind now shoved its way to the front again. It occupied her conscious thoughts in a way that was uncomfortable. She says she knows wannabes who subscribe to as many as a dozen wannabe and devotee online mailing lists and spend hours every day wading through electronic messages.

The Gender-Identity Parallel

Even wannabes who describe their wish for amputations as a wish for completeness will often admit that there is a sexual undertone to the desire. "For me having one leg improves my own sexual image," one of my correspondents wrote. "It feels 'right,' the way I should always have been and for some reason in line with what I think my body ought to have been like." When I asked one prominent wannabe who also happens to be a psychologist if he experiences the wish to lose a limb as a matter of sex or a matter of identity, he disputed the very premise of the question. "You live sexuality," he told me. "I am a sexual being twenty-four hours a day." Even ordinary sexual desire is bound up with identity, as I was reminded by Michael First, a psychiatrist at Columbia University, who was the editor of the fourth edition of the American Psychiatric Association's *Diagnostic and Statistical Manual*. First is undertaking a study that will help determine whether apotemnophilia should be included in the fifth edition of the *DSM*. "Think of the fact that, in general, people tend to be more sexually attracted to members of their own racial group," he pointed out. What you are attracted to (or not attracted to) is part of who you are.

It is clear that for many wannabes, the sexual aspect of the desire is much less ambiguous than many wannabes and clinicians have publicly admitted. A man described seventeen years ago in the *American Journal of Psychotherapy* said that he first became aware of his attraction to amputees when he was eight years old. That was in the 1920s, when the fashion was for children to wear short pants. He remembered several boys who had wooden legs. "I became extremely aroused by it," he said. "Because such boys were not troubled by their mutilation and cheerfully, and with a certain ease, took part in all the street games, including football, I never felt any pity towards them." At first he nourished his desire by seeking out people with wooden legs, but as he grew older, the desire became self-sustaining. "It has been precisely in these last years that the desire has gotten stronger, so strong that I can no

longer control it but am completely controlled by it." By the time he finally saw a psychotherapist, he was consumed by the desire. Isolated and lonely, he spent some of his time hobbling around his house on crutches, pretending to be an amputee, fantasizing about photographs of war victims. He was convinced that his happiness depended on getting an amputation. He desperately wanted his body to match his self-image: "Just as a transsexual is not happy with his own body but longs to have the body of another sex, in the same way I am not happy with my present body, but long for a peg-leg." . . .

Ecological Niches

One of the novels that occasionally pop up on devotee and wannabe book lists is Katherine Dunn's *Geek Love* (1989), the story of a carnival family conceived through the ingenuity of Al and Lil Binewski. Lil, the family matriarch, has ingested pesticides, radioactive materials, and a variety of drugs in order to produce children who are special: Iphigenia and Electra, piano-playing conjoined twins; Olympia, the bald albino hunchback dwarf who narrates the story; Chick, who has telekinetic powers; and Arturo the Aqua Boy, who was born with flippers instead of arms and legs. Arty, the undisputed star of the carnival, swims and frolics in an aquarium and then preaches dark, enigmatic sermons to his assembled admirers. "If I had arms and legs and hair like everybody else, do you think I'd be happy? No! I would not!" he shouts to his audience. "Because then I'd worry did somebody love me! I'd have to look outside myself to find out what to think of myself!"

Arty's charisma eventually propels him into the leadership of an Arturan Cult, whose members tithe parts of their body in order to become more like him. His assistant, a rogue surgeon by the name of Dr. Phyllis, amputates the digits and limbs of enthusiastic Arturans. Off come toes and fingers, then hands, and feet, and finally, as converts approach ecstatic completeness, all four limbs in their entirety. "Can you be happy with the movies and the ads and the clothes in the stores and the doctors and the eyes as you walk down the street all telling you there is something *wrong* with you?" Arty asks a blubbering fat woman in the audience, like a preacher making an altar call. "No. You can't. You cannot be happy. Because, you poor darling baby, you *believe* them. . . ." Soon his caravan is trailed by thousands of armless and legless disciples, living in tents, begging for food, waiting patiently for another turn in the operating room with Dr. Phyllis.

Geek Love is an odd choice for a devotee or wannabe reading list. It is brutal in its mockery of amputee wannabes. Yet it makes sense of a darker side of American life that often goes unexplored in the mainstream media. The media generally treat the desire for body modification either as the well-worn terrain of fashion slaves and social strivers, who buy cosmetic surgery in an endless quest for beauty and perpetual youth, or as something bizarre and unexplainable, like genital mutilation or masochistic fetishes. *Geek Love* makes the desire for amputation plausible by setting it against the bland, cheery aesthetic of mainstream American beauty. *Geek Love* may mock amputee wannabes, but it does not mock them for their poor taste. The aesthetic sensibility of *Geek Love* comes straight out of a carnival sideshow. Its heroes are not "norms," as ordinary Americans are called in the book, but the freaks of the Binewski Carnival Fabulon. "We are masterpieces," Olympia says when asked if she would like to be a norm. "Why would I want to change us into assembly-line items? The only way you people can tell each other apart is by your clothes."

Geek Love may help us understand the cultural context that produces conditions like apotemnophilia. Why do certain psychopathologies arise, seemingly out of nowhere, in certain societies and during certain historical periods and then disappear just as suddenly? Why did young men in late-nineteenth-century France begin lapsing into a fugue state, wandering the continent with no memory of their past, coming to themselves months later in Moscow or Algiers with no idea how they got there? What was it about America in the 1970s and 1980s

that made it possible for thousands of Americans and their therapists to come to believe that two, ten, even dozens of personalities could be living in the same head? One does not have to imagine a cunning cult leader to envision alarming numbers of desperate people asking to have their limbs removed. One has only to imagine the right set of historical and cultural conditions.

So, at any rate, suggests the philosopher and historian of science Ian Hacking, who in a series of strikingly innovative books and articles has attempted to explain just how "transient mental illnesses" such as the fugue state and multiple-personality disorder arise. A transient mental illness is by no means an imaginary mental illness, though in what ways it is real (or "real," as the social constructionists would have it) is a matter for philosophical debate. A transient mental illness is a mental illness that is limited to a certain time and place. It finds an ecological niche, as Hacking puts it—an idea that helps to explain how it thrives. In the same way that the idea of an ecological niche helps to explain why the polar bear is adapted to the Arctic ecosystem, or the chigger to the South Carolina woods, Hacking's ecological niches help to explain the conditions that made it possible for multiple-personality disorder to flourish in late-twentieth-century America and the fugue state to flourish in nineteenth-century Bordeaux. If the niche disappears, the mental illness disappears along with it.

Hacking does not intend to rule out other kinds of causal mechanisms, such as traumatic events in childhood and neurobiological processes. His point is that a single causal mechanism isn't sufficient to explain psychiatric disorders, especially those contained within the boundaries of particular cultural contexts or historical periods. Even schizophrenia, which looks very much like a brain disease, has changed its form, outlines, and presentation from one culture or historical period to the next. The concept of a niche is a way to make sense of these changes. Hacking asks, what makes it possible, in a particular time and place, for this to be a way to be mad?

Hacking's books *Rewriting the Soul* (1995) and *Mad Travelers* (1998) are about "dissociative" disorders, or what used to be called hysteria. He has argued, I think very persuasively, that psychiatrists and other clinicians helped to create the epidemics of fugue in nineteenth-century Europe and multiple-personality disorder in late-twentieth-century America simply by the way they viewed the disorders—by the kinds of questions they asked patients, the treatments they used, the diagnostic categories available to them at the time, and the way these patients fit within those categories. He points out, for example, that the multiple-personality-disorder epidemic rode on the shoulders of a perceived epidemic of child abuse, which began to emerge in the 1960s and which was thought to be part of the cause of multiple-personality disorder. Multiple personalities were a result of childhood trauma; child abuse is a form of trauma; it seemed to make sense that if there were an epidemic of child abuse, we would see more and more multiples.

Crucial to the way this worked is what Hacking calls the "looping effect," by which he means how a classification affects the thing being classified. Unlike objects, people are conscious of the way they are classified, and they alter their behavior and self-conceptions in response to their classification. Look at the concept of "genius," Hacking says, and the way it affected the behavior of people in the Romantic period who thought of themselves as geniuses. Look also at the way in which their behavior in turn affected the concept of genius. This is a looping effect. In the 1970s, he argues, therapists started asking patients they thought might be multiples if they had been abused as children, and patients in therapy began remembering episodes of abuse (some of which may not have actually occurred). These memories reinforced the diagnosis of multiple-personality disorder, and once they were categorized as multiples, some patients began behaving as multiples are expected to behave. Not intentionally, of course, but the category "multiple-personality disorder" gave them a new way to be mad.

Contagious Desire

I am simplifying a very complex and subtle argument, but the basic idea should be clear. By regarding a phenomenon as a psychiatric diagnosis—treating it, reifying it in psychiatric diagnostic manuals, developing instruments to measure it, inventing scales to rate its severity, establishing ways to reimburse the costs of its treatment, encouraging pharmaceutical companies to search for effective drugs, directing patients to support groups, writing about possible causes in journals—psychiatrists may be unwittingly colluding with broader cultural forces to contribute to the spread of a mental disorder.

Suppose doctors started amputating the limbs of apotemnophiles. Would that contribute to the spread of the desire? Could we be faced with an epidemic of people wanting their limbs cut off? Most people would say, clearly not. Most people do not want their limbs cut off. It is a horrible thought. The fact that others are getting their limbs cut off is no more likely to make these people want to lose their own than state executions are to make people want to be executed. And if by some strange chance more people did ask to have their limbs amputated, that would be simply because more people with the desire were encouraged to "come out" rather than suffer in silence.

I'm not so sure. Clinicians and patients alike often suggest that apotemnophilia is like gender-identity disorder, and that amputation is like sex-reassignment surgery. Let us suppose they are right. Fifty years ago the suggestion that tens of thousands of people would someday want their genitals surgically altered so that they could change their sex would have been ludicrous. But it has happened. The question is why. One answer would have it that this is an ancient condition, that there have always been people who fall outside the traditional sex classifications, but that only during the past forty years or so have we developed the surgical and endocrinological tools to fix the problem.

But it is possible to imagine another story: that our cultural and historical conditions have not just revealed transsexuals but created them. That is, once "transsexual" and "gender-identity disorder" and "sex-reassignment surgery" became common linguistic currency, more people began conceptualizing and interpreting their experience in these terms. They began to make sense of their lives in a way that hadn't been available to them before, and to some degree they actually became the kinds of people described by these terms.

I don't want to take a stand on whether either of these accounts is right. It may be that neither is. It may be that there are elements of truth in both. But let us suppose that there is some truth to the idea that sex-reassignment surgery and diagnoses of gender-identity disorder have helped to create the growing number of cases we are seeing. Would this mean that there is no biological basis for gender-identity disorder? No. Would it mean that the term is a sham? Again, no. Would it mean that these people are faking their dissatisfaction with their sex? No. What it would mean is that certain social and structural conditions—diagnostic categories, medical clinics, reimbursement schedules, a common language to describe the experience, and, recently, a large body of academic work and transgender activism—have made this way of interpreting an experience not only possible but more likely.

Whether apotemnophilia (or, for that matter, gender-identity disorder) might be subject to the same kind of molding and shaping that Hacking describes is not clear. One therapist I spoke with, an amputee wannabe, believes that the desire for amputation, like multiple-personality disorder, is often related to childhood trauma. This is only one person's hypothesis, of course, and it may be wrong. But it is clear that sexual desire is malleable. It doesn't seem far-fetched to imagine that amputated limbs could come to be more widely seen as erotic, or that given the right set of social conditions, the desire for amputation could spread. For a thousand years Chinese mothers broke the bones in their daughters' feet and wrapped them in bandages, making the feet grow twisted and disfigured. To a modern Western eye, these feet look grotesquely deformed. But for centuries Chinese men found them erotic.

Ian Hacking uses the term "semantic contagion" to describe the way in which publicly identifying and describing a condition creates the means by which that condition spreads. He says it is always possible for people to reinterpret their past in light of a new conceptual category. And it is also possible for them to contemplate actions that they may not have contemplated before. When I was living in New Zealand, ten years ago, I had a conversation with Paul Mullen, who was then the chair of psychological medicine at the University of Otago, and who had told me that he was a member of a government committee whose job it was to decide whether pornographic materials should be allowed into the country. I bristled at the idea of censorship, and asked him how he could justify being a part of something like that. He just laughed and said that if I could see what his committee was banning, I would change my mind. His position was that some sexual acts would never even occur to a person in an entire lifetime of thinking about sex if not for seeing them pictured in these books. He went on to describe to me various alarming acts that, it was true, had never occurred to me. Mullen was of the opinion that people were better off never having conceptualized such acts, and in retrospect, I think he may have been right.

This is part of what Hacking is getting at, I think, when he talks about semantic contagion. The idea of having one's legs amputated might never even enter the minds of some people until it is suggested to them. Yet once it is suggested, and not just suggested but paired with imagery that a person's past may have primed him or her to appreciate, that act becomes possible. Give the wish for it a name and a treatment, link it to a set of related disorders, give it a medical explanation rooted in childhood memory, and you are on the way to setting up just the kind of conceptual category that makes it a treatable psychiatric disorder. An act has been redescribed to make it thinkable in a way it was not thinkable before. Elective amputation was once self-mutilation; now it is a treatment for a mental disorder. Toss this mixture into the vast fan of the Internet and it will be dispersed at speeds unimagined even a decade ago.

Michael First, the editor of the *Diagnostic and Statistical Manual*, is quite aware of this worry. When I asked him how the *DSM* task force decides what to include in the manual, he told me there were three criteria. One, a diagnosis must have "clinical relevance"— enough people must be suffering from the condition to warrant its inclusion. Thus more data must be gathered on apotemnophilia before a decision is made to include it in the next edition. Two, a new diagnostic category must not be covered by existing categories. This may turn out to be the catch for apotemnophilia, because if the data suggest that it is a paraphilia, it will be subsumed into that category. "People have paraphilias for all kinds of things," First says, "but we do not have separate categories for all of them."

Three, a new diagnostic category must be a legitimate "mental disorder." What counts as a disorder is hard to define and, in fact, varies from one age and society to the next. (Consider, for example, that homosexuality was defined as a mental disorder in the *DSM* until the 1970s.) One way *DSM-IV* marks off disorders from ordinary human variation is by saying that a condition is not a disorder unless it causes a person some sort of distress or disability.

However, the fuzziness around the borders of most mental disorders, along with the absence of certainty about their pathophysiological mechanisms, makes them notoriously likely to expand. A look at the history of psychiatry over the past forty years reveals startlingly rapid growth rates for a wide array of disorders—clinical depression, social phobia, obsessive-compulsive disorder, panic disorder, attention-deficit hyperactivity disorder, and body dysmorphic disorder, to mention only a few. In trying to pinpoint the causes for this expansion one could, depending on ideological bent, point to the marketing efforts of the pharmaceutical industry (more mental disorder equals more profits), the greater diagnostic skills of today's psychiatrists, a growing population of mentally disordered Americans, or a cultural tendency to look to psychiatry for explanations of what used to be called weakness, sin, unhappiness, perversity, crime, or deviance. But the fact is that none of these disorders could have expanded as they have unless they looked a lot like ordinary human variation at their edges. Mild social phobia looks a lot like extreme shyness, attention-deficit disorder can look a lot like garden-variety distractibility, and a lot of obsessive-compulsive behavior, as Peter Kramer told me, "verges on the normal." The lines between mental dysfunction and ordinary life are not as sharp as some psychiatrists like to pretend.

Which makes me wonder how sharply the lines around apotemnophilia can be drawn. The borders between pretenders, wannabes, and devotees do not look very solid. Many wannabes are also devotees or pretenders. A study published in 1983, which surveyed 195 customers of an agency selling pictures and stories about amputees, found that more than half had pretended to be amputees and more than 70 percent had fantasized about being amputees. Nor do the lines look very clear between "true" apotemnophiles (say, those for whom the desire is a fixed, long-term part of their identities) and those whose desire has other roots, such as an interest in extreme body modification. We also need to remember that even if a core group of people with true apotemnophilia could be identified, their diagnosis could come only from what they report to their psychiatrists. There is no objective test for apotemnophilia. People seeking amputation for other reasons—sexual gratification, for example, or a desire for extreme body modification— could easily learn what they need to say to doctors in order to get the surgery they want. Specialists working in gender-identity clinics were complaining of something similar with their patients as early as the mid-1970s. Intelligent, highly motivated patients were learning the symptoms of gender dysphoria and repeating them to clinicians in order to become candidates for sex-reassignment surgery.

The Elusiveness of 'Help'

I will confess that my opinions about amputation as a treatment have shifted since I began writing this piece. My initial thoughts were not unlike those of a magazine editor I approached about writing it, who replied, "Thanks. This is definitely the most revolting query I've seen for quite some time." Yet there is a simple, relentless logic to these people's requests for amputation. "I am suffering," they tell me. "I have nowhere else to turn." They realize that life as an amputee will not be easy. They understand the problems they will have with mobility, with work, with their social lives; they realize they will have to make countless adjustments just to get through the day. They are willing to pay their own way. Their bodies belong to them, they tell me. The choice should be theirs. What is worse: to live without a leg or to live with an obsession that controls your life? For at least some of them, the choice is clear—which is why they are talking about chain saws and shotguns and railroad tracks.

And to be honest, haven't surgeons made the human body fair game? You can pay a surgeon to suck fat from your thighs, lengthen your penis, augment your breasts, redesign your labia, even (if you are a performance artist) implant silicone horns in your forehead or split your tongue like a lizard's. Why not amputate a limb? At least Robert Smith's motivation was to relieve his patients' suffering.

It is exactly this history, however, that makes me worry about a surgical "cure" for apotemnophilia. Psychiatry and surgery have had an extraordinary and very often destructive collaboration over the past seventy-five years or so: clitoridectomy for excessive masturbation, cosmetic surgery as a treatment for an "inferiority complex," intersex surgery for infants born with ambiguous genitalia, and—most notorious—the frontal lobotomy. It is a collaboration with few unequivocal successes. Yet surgery continues to avoid the kind of ethical and regulatory oversight that has become routine for most areas of medicine. If the proposed cure for apotemnophilia were a new drug, it would have to go through a rigorous process of regulatory oversight. Investigators would be required to design controlled clinical trials, develop strict eligibility criteria, recruit

subjects, get the trials approved by the Institutional Review Board, collect vast amounts of data showing that the drug was safe and effective, and then submit their findings to the U.S. Food and Drug Administration. But this kind of oversight is not required for new, unorthodox surgical procedures. (Nor, for that matter, is it required for new psychotherapies.) New surgical procedures are treated not like experimental procedures but like "innovative therapies," for which ethical oversight is much less uniform.

The fact is that nobody really understands apotemnophilia. Nobody understands the pathophysiology; nobody knows whether there is an alternative to surgery; and nobody has any reliable data on how well surgery might work. Many people seeking amputations are desperate and vulnerable to exploitation. "I am in a constant state of inner rage," one wannabe wrote to me. "I am willing to take that risk of death to achieve the needed amputation. My life inside is just too hard to continue as is." These people need help, but when the therapy in question is irreversible and disabling, it is not at all clear what that help should be. Many wannabes are convinced that amputation is the only possible solution to their problems, yet they have never seen a psychiatrist or a psychologist, have never tried medication, have never read a scientific paper about their problems. More than a few of them have never even spoken face to face with another human being about their desires. All they have is the Internet, and their own troubled lives, and the place where those two things intersect. "I used to pretend as a child that my body was 'normal' which, to me, meant short, rounded thighs," one wannabe wrote to me in an e-mail. "As a Psychology major, I have analyzed and reanalyzed, and rereanalyzed just why I want this. I have no clear idea."

42

Women's Madness

Misogyny or Mental Illness?

Jane M. Ussher

The notion that mental illness is socially constructed rather than some objective pathology would surprise many, particularly those who subscribe to the medical model. This model asserts that mental disease is biologically based and physiologically determined, and it downplays the role of social forces. Social forces do, however, play an important role, predisposing some people to mental illness, insulating others, and at times acting in contradictory ways. Social forces also help shape perceptions of symptoms—which ones "count" as mental disease and under what conditions particular types of people will be bestowed the label "mad."

Drawing from the experiences of women, Ussher makes precisely this point. She argues that those who stray from proper feminine roles—who strike out on their own, behave autonomously, and violate gender-based conduct norms—are "positioned as mad." In reality, there is nothing ill about their behavior whatsoever. Quite the contrary, such conduct is entirely logical, and even praiseworthy. The quest for self-actualization is a basic human drive, so female resistance to constricting norms shows that it is alive and well. Patriarchy is to blame, a system that tells women to "know their place" or face the consequences. Diagnoses of depression, neuroses, and anxiety disorder emerge to pathologize their behavior; with labels come regulation, and with regulation comes control.

If there is any craziness, it is in the system itself, a system that stigmatizes behavior simply because it bucks prevailing expectations of acceptable "female" behavior. Enduring change can occur only if attributions of madness are exposed for what they are: ideological weapons geared to maintain the status quo.

Unless or until that happens, female deviance and mental illness will continue to be linked, resulting in psychological interventions geared to drug and counsel women into submission.

Madness and Misogyny: My Mother and Myself

When I was an adolescent my mother was mad. Because it was the 1970s she was deemed to be afflicted by her 'nerves.' Had it been 100 years ago, she would probably have been called 'hysterical' or 'neurasthenic.' Today, it might be 'post-natal depression.' Her particular madness manifested itself in what was termed depression. Her unhappiness, pain and fear resulted in withdrawal, apathy, tiredness and a sense of worthlessness. Sometimes she cried. Sometimes she was angry. Being a 'good mother,' a well-trained woman, as most of us are, she turned her anger in on herself, rather than outwards on her four children, all under twelve years old. She didn't eat a lot. She 'let herself go' by eschewing nice frocks and neatly curled hair. Her outward anger was less evident: no doubt we missed a lot, intent on pretending that everything was normal at home and that we were a happy family. As the unhappiness had no outlet in this world determined to deny women the right to their tears, to their torment, the anger was tightly controlled—stored up until it reached a breaking point, when cracked cups and saucers set aside specifically for this purpose would be taken out into the backyard and flung at the wall. We children loved it. Our mother was really potty. So we laughed, and felt relieved, because the broken cups were easier to deal with than the tears. The careful storing of any dropped and cracked cup for our mother's occasional smashing we could treat as a shared joke, a shared secret; some acknowledgement of her frustration and despair, but harmless. Sometimes at night she walked for hours, wearing out her frustration and her anger pounding the darkened pavements. Her absence from the house was never commented on, even when we feared she would not return.

Looking back now, I see it all as a blatant cry for help. A plea to be noticed, for someone to listen. But we four children, preoccupied with our own games and rivalries, were the only ones who heard. And we didn't really hear at all. We didn't want to.

When my mother tried to kill herself, I was told she was really mad. They put her in the local mental hospital, the one we joked about at school, taunting each other with cries that 'the white van has arrived to take you away.' Suddenly it wasn't very funny any more. They gave her ECT[1] which left her shaking and crying, and gave her a cocktail of drugs so that she forgot everything. She forgot her pain, her misery, her loneliness, the fears which kept her awake at night and which I can even now only imagine. But she forgot everything else. Sometimes she forgot our names, confusing us, calling each name in turn before reaching the right one. So she must have been mad. My father told me she was. Her nerves had given in. She was ill. And it was a secret. We weren't allowed to tell our friends, or our relatives and we didn't talk about it ourselves. I learnt the lesson of the stigma of madness early in life: shame, fear, guilt, perhaps for many people more debilitating than the symptoms called madness. So we feigned normality, and coped.

Nearly twenty years later all this seems a distant memory. My mother weaned herself off her debilitating drug dose and carried on living. She is no longer mad. She is happy, healthy and independent, having escaped from many of the bonds that tied her. But we never talk of this time. Perhaps the fear of the madness is still with us, the shame which we did not know until the secret was made, so that the word 'madness' was never spoken. Perhaps we fear it will happen to us. That it is 'in our genes.' That one day too our nerves will snap. That we will crack. That we will split in two, fall in a heap, face the terror head on. That this madness, now called depression, or schizophrenia, or neurosis, will afflict us, and we will lose control. Or perhaps it is a wider issue: that madness, although we joke about it and fear *real* contact with it, leaves us all with a sense of loss and a

sense of foreboding. For we recognize something of ourselves in the mad. And we don't know the answer to the question of madness, but turn away from it lest we find that the path which takes us there is one we are on ourselves.

For years I wanted to know: to know what was wrong, what to do, how to help. My inability to cure my mother in her earlier misery, to make her happy again, spurred me to seek solutions in an abstract, contained and academic way. Had the drugs and ECT been efficacious I might have turned to medicine, but the memories of those fearful days waiting for the slow recovery from the mind-numbing, body-breaking shocks created nothing but anger: an anger I learnt to direct outwards, not inwards, an anger which encouraged me to escape from the route so clearly laid out for me; to escape from hairdressing, shop work or an early marriage, and attempt to achieve the education which would be a passport to the world of the experts who I sometimes feared had made my mother *more* mad.

I studied psychology; this would be where I would find the answers. Nine years of undergraduate, postgraduate research and clinical psychology training equipped me with the academic armour with which to enter professional debates on the subject. But do I now have the answers? Unfortunately, I do not. My psychology gives me (or is designed to give me) a legitimate voice in the marketplace of the mad. It equips me with logical, well-researched explanations for madness. It gives me a myriad of labels with which to classify the different manifestations of madness, ranging from depression, anxiety, phobia, schizophrenia, to the more specific 'illnesses' such as post-traumatic stress disorder, premenstrual syndrome or post-natal depression. Symptoms—whether physical or psychological—can be grouped in neat clusters, and seen as different forms of madness, or 'mental illness' as the experts prefer, or *mental health problems* in our New Age of enlightenment. The mad can be scientifically classified—and then, supposedly, cured.

This allows me to argue that my knowledge and expertise are far greater than those who have only a loose (because untrained) understanding of the 'complex phenomenon' of madness in its many forms. I *know*; I can identify; and supposedly, I can cure. I am well trained, well rehearsed; I can give you the answers, quoting empirical research to substantiate my case. I am equipped with a whole barrage of theoretical explanations for madness, ranging from the behavioural, where absence of rewards in the environment or learned association makes us mad, to the cognitive, where it is our negative thoughts or irrational beliefs that create the problems. I can cite the psychoanalytic, where unconscious desires and childhood experiences create distress, or the social theories, where environmental deprivation and hardship are seen to cause ills. Or I can turn to the 'alternative' perspectives; to the cornucopia of newer theories advocated by experts desperate for recognition.

This knowledge gives me power. I can now use my hard-earned skills to treat other women (and men) deemed mad. Whether they are called anxious, depressed, phobic or stressed, I, as a professional clinical psychologist, can offer them an explanation for their misery, their despair. I can intervene in their pain, as the psychiatrist treating my mad, sad mother did all those years ago. As she is now happy, no longer throwing cups or hating herself, perhaps they were successful. Who knows whether *I* have been with the people I have tried to help? For I still don't know the answer. What I *do* know is that my mother was not mad, and that her anger, pain and despair were not unique to her. I know that women trapped in unhappy marriages, isolated, lonely, with young, demanding children, no money and no friends are often deemed mad. That to be a woman is often to be mad. If we stay inside our prescribed roles and routes as my mother did, or if we speak out, or move outside our designated paths we become mad. My mother may have been mad because she was adhering to the dictates of her feminine role, staying as wife and mother when she desperately wanted to flee. I can be called mad because I reject that same role. I am publicly called 'neurotic' or 'hysterical' by senior men at work if I speak out or criticize. It's a common

pattern. Women members of the British Parliament are continuously hectored and pathologized when they speak. Intelligent educated men still use the threat of the label of madness very cleverly, with no shame. It silences many of us. We are all in danger of being positioned as mad. Forming part of what it is to be a woman, it beckons us as a spectre in the shadows.

Madness is no more a simple set of symptoms or problems—an individual difficulty or illness experienced by each 'interesting case'—than any individual woman's history can be seen entirely independently of the history of *all* women. As we cannot hope to understand an individual woman without looking at the meaning of what it is to be 'woman' in a patriarchal society, so we cannot understand the pain and agony which makes up 'madness' without looking at the meaning of this very concept.

Psychology, or any expert profession, any academic discipline, does not have the answer, even if those who have invested years of their lives in learning and training would have it otherwise. I wish psychology *did* have the answer. I could then turn with confidence to those whom I was trained to help, and pronounce upon their problems, confidently offering the answer. But it is a utopian dream. Women are not mad merely because of our hormones, our genes, our faulty learning, our cognition or our unconscious desires. Our madness is not an illness; it is disguised as such by the legalistically worded classifications meted out to women. And why is it *women* who are mad? Why is it that it has *always* been women? [2] Is this madness actually the result of misogyny, as many feminists would claim, and are the symptoms not madness at all, but anger or outrage?

The vague unhappiness which I felt towards the apparent simplicity of the 'official' and legitimate theories for madness, the feelings of scepticism towards their certainty, was formalized and legitimated by my reading of the critical antipsychiatry and feminist literature which I devoured voraciously, and which opened my eyes. In this, the very concept of illness was questioned. Madness itself was deconstructed. Its social, political and historical roots were exposed.

In the antipsychiatry literature which blazed the trail for the madman [*sic*] as political dissident or as tortured artist in the late sixties and the early seventies, alternative explanations for the whole concept of madness were offered. The sickness was deemed to be within the system, either the family or society, not within the person. The mad were in reality protesting for the powerless. They were the ultimate scapegoats, burdened with the ills of society; categorized, castigated and separated from the rest of us, lest we see ourselves mirrored in their eyes.

The feminist critics, however, looked to misogyny. They looked to the oppression of women by men which has been taking place throughout the centuries, with the oppression of 'mad' women seen as just another form of misogynistic torture. In this view, misogyny makes women mad either through naming us as the 'Other',[3] through reinforcing the phallocentric discourse, or through depriving women of power, privilege and independence. Or misogyny causes us to be named as mad. It dismisses witches, wise women, suffragettes and battered women as mad. Labelling us mad silences our voices. We can be ignored. The rantings of a mad woman are irrelevant. Her anger is impotent.

So the psychological rhetoric filled me with knowledge, equipping me to work as a professional expert and to write as an authority on the subject of madness. The radically critical literature inspired me to question and criticize, to march and protest. The two perspectives seemed opposite and irreconcilable; contradictory. How could I practice as a clinical psychologist—as an 'expert' in madness—yet also be aware that the very concept of madness itself can be questioned; and that 'madness' serves to glorify and mystify the expert whilst dismissing the person deemed 'mad'? How could I live with the knowledge that women have been labeled and dismissed for centuries and that psychological theories and therapies, and the more invasive drug and ECT treatments still meted out to thousands, can all be seen as a means of control, comparable to other misogynistic means of controlling women such as Indian suttee, Chinese footbinding and clitoridectomy? How could I continue to practice when my head was filled with such knowledge, and especially with a realization of my own role as one of the oppressors, as the critics would describe all experts in the field of madness?

Yet I was also faced with the day-to-day reality of the misery of those deemed mad, and with the memories of my mother's madness, my childhood fear and my need to know. I knew that the despair, the anxiety, the desperate misery is far more than a label, more than a construction without firm basis in reality, far more than the voice of a tortured artist. For whilst the critiques are impassioned, thoughtprovoking, and inspirational, there seemed to be much left unexplained and unsaid. And what can we say, what can we do, if renouncing our professional mantles of power, we adopt the critical perspective? A theoretical deconstruction does not offer much, not even hope. A rousing rhetorical treatise may inspire, but what answer does it have? At least my training allowed me to give hope, to offer *some* answer. The fact that it might be the wrong one, or only a partial answer, I tried to ignore. The memory of the fearful child and the probably more fearful mother motivated me to seek the solution, to feel the need to offer *something*.

When I attempted to bring feminist theory into my clinical practice, it did not seem to fit. I worked with a woman who was referred by her GP for anxiety attacks and agoraphobia. As a well-trained clinical psychologist I initially worked with her to alleviate her symptoms, achieving a good measure of success. Yet in the therapy her marriage, and the lack of love, freedom or autonomy she was experiencing were what she really wanted to resolve. We spent hours discussing the implications of her relationship with a husband who would not allow her to have friends, to have work, to have a life; and who insisted on raising their son in a way which she could see was causing him to despise women. For at five years old he was ordering her around. Her husband would not engage in therapy, deriding her for making the suggestion. It was *she* who was ill. Over the course of our meetings, which were certainly as egalitarian and open as such things can possibly be, this woman became aware that her marriage was 'disastrous,' that she was leading a half life, and that it was not she who was mad. But she would or could not change it. She would not leave. He would not change. Was her realization of the misery of her situation and the fact that there were alternatives merely adding to her pain? Was I holding up to her an image of a different life which she felt she could not take? I wonder if I would have served her better by helping her with her anxiety symptoms and pronouncing her 'cured.'

It is much easier to split the two worlds, keeping feminism for the conference platform, orthodox psychology for the clinic. Many of those working with the mad carry on their professional lives, aware of the critiques, often rehearsing them on the conference platform, yet clinically practising within the traditional health professions at the same time: splitting the theory from the practice, reconciling the contradictions with the need to earn a living, and remembering the investment of time and energy in the long years of training. It is not easy to give it up.[4] But I did: I had to. I no longer practice as a clinical psychologist. The contradiction between the rhetoric of my chosen profession and the rhetoric of the critics, and particularly the feminists, could be split into different (and contradictory) parts of my life no longer. I could no longer bear the dual secrecy of hiding my criticisms from my psychology colleagues and my orthodox practice of clinical psychology from myself, or from feminists. This [article] is an attempt to unravel the contradictions in the conundrum which asks whether feminism or psychology (feminism or therapy, whether medical or psychological) has the answer for women. It explores the conflicts between the radical critiques of the so-called antipsychiatrists and the feminists, and those who, faced with the needs of women to receive some help, affirm the desperate pleas of women to be heard. To put the question simply: is women's madness the result of misogyny, as the feminists would say, or is it an illness, which can be cured?

Whilst my exploration . . .of the many accounts of women and of men, of academic, professional and lay persons, will open up the Pandora's box of academic and popular discourse that is madness as we know it, I have started with the personal. For all of us who write about madness bring our own baggage, our own perspectives, our own politics, our own pain. Many may pretend otherwise, but we cannot leave it behind us. The least we can do is make it evident. One of the tenets of a feminist perspective is the acknowledgement of the influence of our own subjectivity on our work, on our theories, research and accounts of the world.[5] We are not blank screens, rational and objective experts with no interests and no past. It is my past which prompted the question 'What is women's madness?' which prompted the search, and which provokes me to look beyond the explanations so readily and easily offered by the experts who say they *know*.

Women's Madness—Misogyny or Mental Illness?

Why Women?

One of the most common questions put to any feminist attempting to discuss women's experiences in a public forum is 'What about men?' Any talk I have ever given about the psychology of women, or about women's madness, has invariably provoked such a response. One retort is that men have long been the (often sole) focus of interest for psychologists, and that researchers or theoreticians who exclude *women* from their analysis are never taken to task on the matter; they never have to justify *their* exclusion of women. In fact, one could posit that psychology has developed as a singularly male enterprise, with men studying men and applying the findings to all of humanity, and thus it is time to redress the balance. But I usually manage to confine myself to a less confrontational analysis—actually answering the question—even though I find it lamentable that it is the one most frequently asked. The answer is that men are 'mad' too; that men need help too; but that often men's madness takes a different form in our society. It may have different roots. It certainly exists within a different framework from that of women's madness, within a different discourse: it has a different meaning. One of the easiest ways of illustrating this is the argument that if you compare the statistics on psychiatric admissions, and those on female depression, with the statistics on prison populations, and on male violence and criminality, the scales are evenly balanced. So men may be mad—but are likely to be positioned as bad. They are likely to manifest their discontent or deviancy as criminals. Whilst women are positioned within the psychiatric discourse, men are positioned within the criminal discourse. We are regulated differently. . . .

Notes

1. Electro convulsive therapy. See pp. 106–8, 151–3, for a discussion of this.
2. Men are diagnosed as mad, and receive psychiatric treatment, but it is women who have dominated in the psychiatric statistics for centuries, and women who are regulated through the discourse of madness. . . .
3. The concept of the 'Other' originates from Lacanian theory, where the woman is seen as always secondary in relation to the man within the symbolic order. He is the I and she is the not-I, the second sex.

4. Masson, J. M., 1989: *Against therapy*, Collins, London. This is one of the few psychoanalysts who has recognized the contradictions and publicly given up his practice, even if it has been suggested he was forced to do so by the psychoanalytic world which would not abide dissent (Malcolm, 1984). Many of the 'antipsychiatrists' continued to practice in traditional settings long after they had publicly castigated the very system which they were acting to support (Pilgrim 1990).
5. For example, see Blier, R., (ed.) 1988: *Feminist approaches to science*, Pergamon Press, New York, for accounts of feminist approaches to science, where the values of the researcher are made evident at the outset. See also Harding 1986.

References

Harding, J. 1986. Perspectives on gender and science, Falmer Press, Sussex.

Malcolm, J. 1984. In the Freud Archives. Flamingo: London.

Pilgrim, D. 1990. "Competing histories of madness," in Bentall, R. (ed.), Reconstructing Schizophrenia, Routledge, London.

43
Managing 'Crazy' Friends and Relatives

Accommodation Practices and Vernacular Treatments of Madness

Michael J. Lynch

All of us, at some point in our lives, have interacted with someone we consider to be a persistent source of trouble. These individuals embarrass us. They insist on always being right. They are sensitive to the smallest of insults. They engage in inappropriate behavior at the most inopportune times. They humiliate themselves and others, often without knowing it. Mental pathology is implicated in much of their conduct, but its management, rather than its source, is of more interest sociologically. Management hinges on our use of "accommodation practices," which Lynch explores here.

Such practices vary in form, content, and organization. Some involve the use of humor. Others rely on avoidance or manipulation. Still more hinge on deception and remedial covering. Common to all of them, however, is the attempt to construct normalcy out of an otherwise abnormal, "crazy" situation.

Lynch suggests that deinstitutionalized mental health care is likely to increase both the importance and salience of madness-accommodation practices. Greater numbers of unstable persons at large in the community require more such practices, more frequent use of them, in more situations. Such practices become mini-institutions in their own right, and effectively move social order down to the level of interaction. Though "the mad" may be integrated, it is a tenuous integration at best,

and their "illness" inevitably threatens to come to the surface at any moment.

Accommodation is nothing more than codependent behavior, and it may be every bit as "sick" as the behavior it tries to cover. Meaningful change can occur only if the "crazy person" is left to confront the mayhem he or she creates. Accommodation merely prolongs it, and no transformation will occur until the deviant is forced to hit bottom (perhaps not even then).

People are committed to mental hospitals after informal efforts to accommodate them in society fail. Studies report that spouses of prospective mental patients (Cumming and Cumming, 1957; Mayo *et al.*, 1971; Sampson *et al.*, 1962; Spitzer *et al.*, 1971; Yarrow *et al.*, 1955), co-workers (Lemert, 1962), and police officers (Bittner, 1967) claim that they contact psychiatric authorities only as a last resort, when informal methods of "care" are unavailable or are overwhelmed by the extremity of the person's disorder. There is widespread reluctance, especially in lower-class families (Hollingshead and Redlich, 1958:172–79; Myers and Roberts, 1959:213–20), to take a perspective on relational disorders which supports professional intervention and hospitalization. As a result, the population of potential mental patients is said to vastly outnumber the population of professionally treated patients (Srole *et al.*, 1962). Accommodating families can hide potential patients from official scrutiny by placing few demands upon them and allowing them to "exist as if in a one-person chronic ward, insulated from all but those in a highly tolerant household" (Freeman and Simmons, 1958:148).

Such observations suggest that a massive program of community care exists independently of formally established programs of inpatient and outpatient treatment. Countless numbers of undiagnosed, but troublesome, individuals, as well as an increasing number of diagnosed outpatients, are consigned by default to the informal care of family and community. Although the social characteristics of professionally administered mental health care institutions have been exhaustively analyzed, the practices that make up ordinary lay-operated "institutions" of care remain largely unexamined. In this study I call attention to such accommodation practices, elaborate upon previous descriptions of the practices, and present some conjectures on the social construction of the individual.

Accommodation practices are interactional techniques that people use to manage persons they view as persistent sources of trouble. Accommodation implies attempts to "live with" persistent and ineradicable troubles.[1] Previous studies mention a number of accommodation practices. Lemert (1962) describes how people exclude distrusted individuals from their organization's covert activities by employing methods of "spurious interaction." Such forms of interaction are:

> . . .distinguished by patronizing, evasion, "humoring," guiding conversation onto selected topics, under reaction, and silence, all calculated either to prevent intense interaction or to protect individual and group values by restricting access to them. When the interaction is between two or more persons in the individual's presence it is cued by a whole repertoire of subtle expressive signs which are meaningful only to them (1962:8).

Other methods for managing perceived "troublemakers" include: isolation and avoidance (Lemert, 1962; Sampson *et al.*, 1962), relieving an individual of ordinary responsibilities associated with their roles (Sampson *et al.*, 1962); hiding liquor bottles from a heavily drinking spouse (Jackson, 1954); and "babying" (Jackson, 1954).

Some studies (Yarrow *et al.*, 1955) treat accommodation practices as sources of delay in the recognition and treatment of mental illness; others (Goffman, 1961, 1969; Lemert, 1962) portray them as primary constituents of "illness." Whether the studies assume a realist or a societal reaction perspective on the nature of mental illness, they attempt to explain how persons become mental patients by reconstructing the social backgrounds of hospitalized patients. As Emerson and Messinger (1977:131) point

out, retrospective analyses of the "careers" of diagnosed mental patients presuppose a specific pathological outcome of the "prepatient's" biography. To avoid this problem, social scientists need to abandon retrospective methods and analyze contemporary situations where troublesome individuals are accommodated. Such people are not yet patients, and may never attain that status. Therefore, institutional records cannot be used to locate cases for study. An appropriate way to find them is to use vernacular accounts of madness or mental illness, and to document the patterns of accommodation that others use to control such troublesome people.

The Study

This study is an analysis of the results of an assignment which I gave to students in classes on the sociology of mental illness in 1981 and 1982. I instructed students to locate someone in a familiar social environment who was identified by others (and perhaps by themselves) as "crazy"; the subject need not appear "mentally ill," but need only be a *personal* and *persistent* source of trouble for others. The vast majority of the students had little trouble finding such subjects. I instructed them to interview persons who consistently dealt with the troublemaker in a living or work situation. The interviews were to focus on the practices used by others to "live with" the troublemaker from day to day. Students who were personally acquainted with the troublemaker were encouraged to refer to their own recollections and observations in addition to their interviews. They were instructed not to interview or otherwise disturb the troublemakers. Each student wrote a 5-7 page paper on accommodation practices with an appendix of notes from their interviews.

The Subjects

The persons the students interviewed described subjects who had already developed to an intermediate stage in the "natural history of trouble" (Emerson and Messinger, 1977). Few troublemakers carried formal designations of mental illness, but each was associated with recurrent organizational troubles. The troubles were defined non-relationally (Goffman, 1969); they were attributed to the personal agency of a troublemaker, and any possible mitigating factors were no longer considered pertinent. Although the students and their interviewees claimed a consensus on the fact that *something* was wrong with the troublemaker, just what was wrong was often a matter of speculation. Troublemakers' friends and acquaintances sometimes resorted to amateur psychologizing to account for the subjects' "problem," but often they expressed moral exasperation and disgust, without any mention of a possible "illness."

Students and those they interviewed used a rich variety of vernacular epithets for personal character types to identify their subjects. These included common insults, "crazy" terms used as insults, and a few straightforward "illness" designators. The following expressions illustrate different shadings in the ambiguity of the troublemakers' statuses as moral offenders and/or "sick" persons:

1. Commonplace vernacular terms for faults and faulted persons, without reference to insanity: "bullshitter," "bird" (as in "turkey"), "off the wall," "spiteful, nasty girl," "rude and argumentative," "an obnoxious pest," "catty," "space cadet," "chronic complainer," "frivolous and ridiculous," and nicknames such as "Ozone" and "The Deviant."

2. Vernacular cognates of madness which do not necessarily compel the serious connotation of illness: "crazy," "nuts," "bananas," "weird," "strange," "unpredictable," "highly emotional," "attention seeking and manipulative," "explosive, angry," and "sick."

3. Amateur uses of accounts associated with the helping professions: "paranoid," "developmentally disabled," "chemically imbalanced in the brain," "low self-esteem," "obsessed with food," and "alcoholic."

Except in a few cases when students reported a specific medical diagnosis, their accounts did not provide unique labels corresponding to stable categories of disorder. They did, however, point to a history of incidents supporting the conclusion that *something* was wrong with the person in question.

Some accounts emphasized that it was impossible to describe just what was wrong with the person. There was far more to the trouble than could be described by a few episodes: "disgusting eating habits," "he smells terrible," "he stands too close to people," "she asks you to repeat things over and over again," "she is so promiscuous that one of the fraternities has a song about fucking her!" Not all accounts were wholly negative or rejecting. At least some acquaintances whom students interviewed expressed some affection or attachment to troublemakers, or an obligation to maintain a minimal level of civility toward the person.

In the few cases where the troublemaker had a history of mental or neurological disorder, students reported that their informants used the illness to excuse incidents believed to be symptomatic of the disorder. Such special understandings did not entirely replace more hostile reactions, for many of the "symptoms" were also personal offenses:

> Margaret explained that she always attempts to start off calm when dealing with Joan and thinking of her as being a "lonely and sick woman," but that Joan "gets you so angry that it is difficult to stay level-headed and then I start screaming and have to leave." (Student report of an interview concerning a "senile" woman)

The students investigated a number of different organizational environments. Fraternities and sororities were most popular, followed by families (both nuclear and extended), dormitory residents, work groups, friendship cliques, athletic teams, and residents of apartment suites and local neighborhoods. One case dealt with a board and care home; another described a group of students on a retreat. Among the work groups observed were employees of a book store, a clothing store, a pharmacy, and a fast food restaurant. One noteworthy case involved a rock and roll band and its crew on a national tour. In each of these cases, membership in the group or organization provided the local basis of the troublemaker's existence. Membership furnished the context for day-to-day interactions with the troublemaker, and for accumulating an oral history of the troublemaker's antics. In the following discussion, I will use the term *members* to refer to all those who knew or related to the troublesome person through common membership in some organized group, network of relationship, acquaintance, or friendship.[2]

Because of the highly sensitive nature of the interactional circumstances which the students were investigating, I repeatedly asked them to respect the privacy of their subjects. They proved to be highly skilled at doing so, perhaps because they relied upon their own skills at performing accommodation practices to hide their inquiries from the troublemaker's attention.

I did not initially design the assignment in order to gather data for my own analysis. However, after reading the students' reports on their observations and interviews I found that despite their variability in descriptive and analytic quality and their obvious shortcomings as data, they described a diversity of accommodation practices, and suggested recurrent features of those practices which were not comprehensively treated in the literature. The information seemed worth reporting and students gave me permission to quote from their papers. I analyzed material from 32 of the student reports, each of which discussed a different case. In the remainder of this paper, all quotes not attributed to sources come from the students' papers.

I have organized accommodation practices under three thematic headings: (1) practices which *isolate* the troublemaker within the group; (2) practices which *manipulate* the troublemaker's behavior, perception, and understanding; and (3) practices which members use to influence how others react to the troublemaker. The first set of practices defines and limits the troublemaker's chances for interaction, expression, and feedback within the group. The second set directs the details of the troublemaker's actions and establishes the discrepant meanings of those actions for "self" and "other."

The third set includes attempts to make the troublemaker's public identity into a covert communal project.

Minimizing Contact With the Troublemaker

Avoiding and *ignoring* were the two accommodation practices mentioned most often by students. Both were methods for minimizing contact with the troublemaker, and had the effect of isolating the troublemaker within the organizational network. While both were negative methods of behavior control, attenuating the troublemaker's actual and possible occasions of interaction, they worked quite differently. Avoiding limited the gross *possibility* of interaction, while ignoring worked *within* ongoing occasions of interaction to limit the interactional *reality* of the encounter. Where avoiding created an absence of encounter, ignoring created a dim semblance to ordinary interaction.

Avoiding

In virtually every student's account, one or more of the members they interviewed mentioned that they actively avoided the troublemaker. Avoidance created an interactional vacuum around the troublemaker. Members managed to stay out of the way of the troublemaker without actually requesting or commanding the troublemaker to stay away from them. Methods of avoidance included individual and joint tactics such as "ducking into restrooms," "keeping a lookout for her at all times," and "hiding behind a newspaper or book."

Some members were better placed than others within the structure of the organization to avoid the troublemaker. In larger organizations like fraternities and sororities, persons could stake out positions which minimized contact with the troublemaker. In more intimate circles avoidance ran more of a risk of calling attention to the *absence* of usual interactional involvement. Avoidance *did* occur in such intimate groups as families (Sampson *et al.*, 1962), but only at the cost of threatening the very integrity of the group.

Ignoring/Not Taking Seriously

Ignoring differed from avoiding because it entailed at least some interaction, though of an attenuated and inauthentic kind. One account described conversations with the troublemaker as being "reduced to superficial 'hellos,' most of which are directed at her feet; there is an obvious lack of eye contact." Many accounts mentioned the superficiality of interactions with troublemakers. In some cases this was accomplished by what one student called "rehearsed and phony responses" to limit the openness of their conversations to a few stock sequences.[3]

Although ignoring entailed interaction, it was like avoidance in that it circumscribed the troublemaker's interactional possibilities. Where avoidance operated to limit, in a gross way, the intersection of pathways between troublemaker and other members, ignoring operated intensively to trivialize the troublemaker's apparent involvements in group activities.[4] Bids for positive notice were ignored, and had little effect on the troublemaker's position within the group.

Directly Managing the Troublemaker's Actions

Members used a number of more direct interventions to control and limit the troublemaker's behavior, including humoring, screening, taking over, orienting to local prospects of normality, and practical jokes and retaliations. While such methods had little hope of permanently modifying the behavior, they were used to curtail episodic disruptions by the troublemaker.

Humoring

Members often used the term humoring to describe attempts to manage the troublemaker by maintaining a veneer of agreement and geniality in the face of actions which would ordinarily evoke protest or disgust. For example, in the case of "an obnoxiously argumentative person," members offered superficial tokens of agreement in response to even the most outlandish pronouncements for the sake of avoiding more extreme disruptions.

Humoring was often made possible through insight into recurrent features of the troublemaker's behavior. Members recognized recurrent situations in ordinary interactions which triggered peculiar reactions by the troublemaker. They developed a heightened awareness of ordinary and seemingly innocuous details of interaction which could touch off an explosive reaction. One student described how her parents managed a "crazy aunt," who she said was prone to sudden and violent verbal assaults:

> My parents avoided discussing specific topics and persons that they knew distressed her. Whenever she began talking about an arousable [sic] event or person, my parents and her husband attempted to change the subject.[5]

Although members rationalized humoring as a way "to make it easy for everybody," they did not always find it easy to withhold their reactions to interactional offenses. A student wrote about her efforts to prepare her fiance for a first encounter with her grandmother, said to be suffering from senile dementia, Alzheimer type:

> I attempted to explain to him that he should not say anything controversial, agree with whatever she says, and generally stay quiet as much as possible. [He assured her that everything would be okay, but when he was confronted with the actual grandmother, the assurance proved quite fragile.] That encounter proved to be quite an experience for Charles—we left Grandma's house with Charles screaming back at her for his self-worth.

Other accounts mentioned the strain and difficulty of trying to humor troublemakers. They described an exceedingly fragile interactional situation which was prone to break down at any moment:

> You don't want to set him off, so you're very careful about what you do and say. You become tense trying to keep everything calm, and then something happens to screw it up anyway: The car won't start, or a light bulb blows. It's all my fault because I'm a rotten wife and mother.

Humoring often entailed obedience or deference to what members claimed (when not within earshot of the troublemaker) were outrageous or absurd demands:

> Everyone did what she asked in order to please her and not cause any bad scenes.

In some cases, members exerted special efforts or underwent severe inconvenience for the sake of a person they secretly despised. Not surprisingly, such efforts often, though not always, were exerted by persons over whom the troublemaker had formal authority. In one case the members of a crew traveling with a rock and roll band would set up the troublesome member's equipment before that of the others and set up daily meetings with him to discuss his "technical needs," while at the same time they believed it was foolish of him to demand such special attention. They described the special meetings and favors as a "bogus accommodation." In every case, whether correlated with formal divisions of authority or not, humoring contributed to the troublemaker's sense of interactional power over others.

Humoring always included a degree of duplicity in which members "kept a straight face" when interacting with the troublemaker or acted in complicity with the troublemaker's premises—premises which members otherwise discounted as delusional or absurd:

> We played along with her fantasy of a boyfriend, "John." We never said what a complete fool she was for waiting for him.

Commonly, members practiced *serial* duplicity by waiting until the troublemaker was out of earshot to display for one another's appreciation the "real" understanding they had previously suppressed:

> They pretend to know what she is talking about, they act as if they are interested . . .they make remarks when she is gone.

At other times they practiced *simultaneous* duplicity by showing interest and serious engagement to the troublemaker's face while expressing detachment and sarcasm to one another through furtive glances, gestures, and double entendres (Lemert, 1962:8).

> Those employees who she is not facing will make distorted faces and roll their eyes around to reaffirm the fact that she is a little slow. All the time this occurs Susan is totally oblivious to it, or at least she pretends to be.

In one fraternity, members devised a specific hand gesture (described as "wing flapping") which they displayed for one another when interacting with a troublemaker they called "the bird."

Members occasionally rationalized their duplicity by describing the troublemaker as a self-absorbed and "dense" person, whose lack of orientation to others provided ample opportunity for their play:

> People speak sarcastically to him, and Joe, so wrapped up in himself, believes what they are saying and hears only what he wants to hear.

Screening

Jackson (1954:572) reported that alcoholics' wives attempted to manage their husbands' heavy drinking by hiding or emptying liquor bottles in the house and curtailing their husbands' funds. One student described a similar practice used by friends of a person who they feared had suicidal tendencies. They systematically removed from the person's environment any objects that could be used to commit suicide.

Screening and monitoring of troublemakers' surroundings also occurred in the interactional realm. A few accounts mentioned attempts to monitor the moods of a troublemaker, and to screen the person's potential interactions on the basis of attributed mood. When one sorority's troublemaker was perceived to be especially volatile, members acted as her covert receptionists by turning away her visitors, explaining that she was not in or was ill. In this case members were concerned not only to control the potential actions of the individual, but also to conceal those actions from others, and by doing so to protect the collective "image" of their sorority from contamination.

Taking Over

A number of accounts mentioned efforts by members to do activities which ordinarily would be done by someone in the trouble-maker's social position. Like published accounts of cases in which husbands or mothers take over the household duties of a wife (Sampson *et al.*, 1962), the apartment mates of a troublemaker washed dishes and paid bills for her "as if she wasn't there." A circle of friends insisted on driving the automobile of a man they considered dangerously impulsive. Fraternity members gradually and unofficially took over the duties of their social chairman in fear of the consequences of his erratic actions and inappropriate attire. Taking over sometimes included such intimate personal functions as grooming and dressing, as when the spouse of a drunk diligently prepared her husband for necessary public appearances.

Orienting to Local Prospects of Normality

Yarrow *et al.* (1955) mention that wives of mental patients sustained efforts to live with their husbands by treating interludes between episodes as the beginnings of "recovery" rather than as periods of calm before the inevitable storms. By keeping tabs on the latest developments in the troublemaker's behavior, members were often able to determine when it was "safe" to treat the troublemaker as a "normal" person. This method was not always as unrealistic as one would be led to believe from Yarrow *et al.* (1955). Since most troublemakers were viewed as persons whose difficulties, though inherent, were intermittent, living with them required knowing what to expect in the immediate interactional future:

> I have observed the occasion when a friend at the fraternity house entered the television room and remained in the rear of the room, totally quiet, watching Danny, waiting for a signal telling him how to act. When Danny turned and spoke to him in a friendly, jovial manner, the young man enthusiastically pulled his chair up to sit next to Danny and began speaking freely.

Members described many troublemakers as persons with likeable and even admirable qualities, whose friendship was valued during their "good times." When a member anticipated an encounter with a trouble-maker, he or she wanted most of all to avoid touching off a "bad scene." The local culture of gossip surrounding a troublemaker tended to facilitate such an aim by providing a running file on the current state of his or her moods. By using the latest news members could decide when to avoid encounters and when they could approach the trouble-maker without undue wariness.

Practical Jokes and Retaliations

Although direct expressions of hostility toward troublemakers were rarely mentioned, it is possible that they occurred more frequently than was admitted. Practical jokes and other forms of retaliation were designed not to reveal their authors. The troublemaker would be "clued in" that *somebody* despised him or was otherwise "out to get" him, but he would be left to imagine just who it was. Some jokes were particularly cruel, and were aimed at the troublemaker's particular vulnerabilities. A member of a touring rock and roll band was known to have difficulty forming relationships with women:

> They would get girls to call his room and make dates they would never keep. Apparently, the spotlight operator was the author of a series of hot love letters of a mythical girl who was following Moog [a pseudonym for the troublemaker] from town to town and would soon appear in his bedroom. The crew must have been laughing their heads off for days. Moog was reading the letters out loud in the dressing room.

Influencing the Reaction to the Troublemaker

A group of practices, instead of focusing solely on the troublemaker's interactional behavior, attempted to control others' *reactions to* and *interpretations of* that behavior. These accommodations recognized that there could be serious consequences in the reactions of outsiders—non-members—to the troublemaker. Such practices included efforts by members to control the reactions of persons outside the group; and to control assessments not only of the individual troublemaker, but of the group as well. The responsibilities for, and social consequences of, the individual's behavior were thus adopted by members as a collective project.

Turning the Troublemaker Into a Notorious Character

In stories to outsiders as well as others in the group, members were sometimes able to turn the troublemaker into a fascinating and almost admirable character. A classic case was the fraternity "animal." Although litanies of crude, offensive, and assaultive actions were recounted, the character's antics were also portrayed with evident delight. Such descriptions incorporated elements of heroism, the prowess of the brawler, or the fearlessness and outrageousness of a prankster. In one case a student reported that the fraternity troublemaker, nicknamed "the deviant," was supported and encouraged by a minority faction who claimed to an outsider that he was merely "a little wild," and that nothing was wrong with him. This faction seemed unembarrassed by, and perhaps a bit proud of, the troublemaker's "animal" qualities that others might ascribe to the fraternity as well. The quasi-heroic or comical repute of the troublemaker did not overshadow many members' distaste for the disruptions, but it did constitute a supportive moral counterpoint.

Shadowing

In one instance a group of students living in a dorm arranged covertly to escort their troublemaker on his frequent trips to local bars. He had a reputation for drinking more than his capacity and then challenging all comers to fights. To inhibit such adventures members of the group volunteered to accompany him under various pretexts, and to quell any disputes he precipitated during the drinking sessions. In the case of the member of the rock and roll band, other members chaperoned him during interviews with media critics. When he said something potentially offensive, his chaperon attempted to turn his statement into a joke. Another account described efforts by a group to spy on a member who they believed was likely to do something rash or violent.

Advance Notices

As Lemert (1962) points out, members often build a legacy of apocryphal stories about their troublemaker. Stories told by one member to another about the troublemaker's latest antics provided a common source of entertainment, and perhaps solidarity. Some members admitted that they could not imagine what they would talk about with one another if not the troublemaker's behavior:

> The highlight of the day is hearing the latest story about Joanie.

Such gleeful renditions helped to prepare non-members for first encounters with the troublemaker.

A few students mentioned that the troublemakers they studied appeared normal or even charming during initial encounters, but that members soon warned them to be careful about getting involved with the person. Subsequent experience confirmed the warnings, although it was difficult to discern whether this was a result of their accuracy or of the wariness they engendered.

Members of a group that included a persistently troublesome character "apologized for him beforehand" to persons who shortly would be doing business with him. They also warned women he approached that he was "a jerk." In addition to preparing such persons for upcoming encounters, the apologies and warnings carried the tacit claim that "we're not like him." This mitigated any potential contamination of the group's moral reputation.

Hiding and Diluting the Troublemaker

Some fraternities and sororities institutionalized a "station" for hiding troublemakers during parties and teas where new members were recruited. Troublemakers were assigned out-of-the-way positions in social gatherings and, in some cases, were accompanied at all times by other members whose job it was to cut off the troublemaker's interaction with prospective members.

The methods used for hiding and diluting were especially artful when they included pretexts to conceal from the troublemakers that their role had been diminished. The troublemaker in the rock and roll band was said to embarrass other members with "distasteful ego tripping" on stage during public concerts. Such "ego trips" were characterized by loud and "awful" playing on his instrument and extravagant posturing in attempts to draw the audience's attention to himself. These displays were countered by the sound and light men in the crew.

> On those nights the sound man would turn up the monitors on stage so Moog sounded loud to himself and would turn down Moog in the [concert] hall and on the radio.

Simultaneously, the lighting director would "bathe him in darkness" by dimming the spotlights on him. These practices, in effect, technically created a delusional experience for the troublemaker. They produced a systematic distortion of his perception of the world and simultaneously diminished his public place in that world.

Covering For/Covering Up

Friends and intimates sometimes went to great lengths to smooth over the damages and insults done to others by the troublemaker. The husband of a "crazy woman" monitored his wife's offenses during her "episodes" and followed in the wake of the destruction with apologies and sometimes monetary reparations to offended neighbors. Similar efforts at restoring normality also occurred in immediate interactional contexts:

> Before she will even tell you her name, she is telling you how one day she was hitchhiking and was gang raped by the five men who picked her up. This caused so many problems for her that she ended up in a mental hospital and is now a lesbian. The look on people's faces is complete shock. . . . Those hearing this story for the first time will sit in shock as if in a catatonic stupor, with wide eyes and their mouths dropped open, absolutely speechless. Someone who has already heard this story will break the silence by continuing with the previous conversa-

tion, . . . putting it on extinction by ignoring it as if she never said anything.

Members sometimes conspired, ostensibly on behalf of the troublemaker, to prevent the relevant authorities from detecting the existence and extent of the troubles. One group of girls in a freshman dorm deliberately lied to hide the fact that one of their members was having great difficulty and, in their estimation, was potentially suicidal. When her parents asked how she was doing the students responded that she was doing "fine." Members tried to contain her problems and to create a "blockade" around any appearances of her problems that might attract the attentions of university authorities. Once underway, such coverups gained momentum, since the prospect of exposure increasingly threatened to make members culpable for not bringing the matter to the attention of remedial agents.

Discussion

A prevailing theme in the students' accounts of accommodation practices was the avoidance of confrontation. They described confrontation as potentially "unpleasant," to be avoided even when considerable damage and hardship had been suffered:

> When students' money began disappearing from their rooms, we had a group meeting to discuss our mode of intervention. Although we all believed Chris was responsible we did not confront her. Instead, we simply decided to make sure we locked our bedroom doors when not in our rooms.

In general, a number of reasons for avoiding confrontation were given, including the anticipation of denial by the troublemaker, fear that the troublemaker would create a "bad scene," and the belief that confrontation would make no difference in the long run.

Less direct methods were used to communicate the group's opinions to the troublemaker. Instead of telling the troublemaker in so many words, members employed a peculiar sort of gamesmanship. Systematic "leaks" were used to *barely* and *ambiguously* expose the duplicity and conspiracy, so that the troublemaker would realize something was going on, but would be unable or unwilling to accuse specific offenders. Duplicitous gestures or comments which operated *just* on the fringes of the troublemaker's awareness produced maximum impact.

The successful operation of these practices relied, in part, on the troublemaker's complicity in the conspiracy of silence:

Once I was in the room next door to her and the girls were imitating her. Two minutes later she walked in asking [us] to be quiet because she was trying to sleep. I thought I was going to die. Obviously Tammy realized what was going on as the walls are extremely thin; however, Tammy seems to be conspiring on the side of her "friends" to prevent any confrontation of the actual situation.

Hostilities were therefore expressed, and retaliations achieved, often with rather specific reference to the particular offenses and their presumed source. At the same time, they remained "submerged" in a peculiar way. They were not submerged in a psychological "unconscious," since both members and troublemakers were aware of what was going on. Instead, both members and troublemakers made every effort to assure that the trouble did not disturb the overtly normal interaction. "Business as usual" was preserved at the cost of keeping secret deep hostilities within the organization.

A few accounts did mention instances of explicit confrontation. However, members claimed that such confrontations did not alter troublemakers' subsequent behaviors; instead they resulted in misunderstandings or were received by troublemakers in a defensive or unresponsive way.

Efforts to remove troublemakers from organizations were rarely described, though members of the rock band eventually expelled their troublemaker after he hired a lawyer to redress his grievances against the group. In another case a fraternity "depledged" a new recruit who had not yet been fully initiated. In no other case was an established member removed, although numerous dramatic offenses were recounted and

widespread dislike for troublemakers was commonly reported.

Taken as a whole, accommodation practices reveal *the organizational construction of the normal individual*. The individual is relied upon both in commonsense reasoning and social theory as a source of compliance with the standards of the larger society. The normal individual successfully adapts to the constraints imposed by social structure. Troublemakers were viewed as persons who, for various reasons, could not be given full *responsibility* for maintaining normality. Instead, the burden of maintaining the individual's normal behavior and appearance was taken up by others. Troublemakers were not overtly sanctioned; instead, they were shaped and guided through the superficial performances of ordinary action. Their integration into society was not a cumulative mastery learned "from inside"; it was a constant project executed by others from the "outside."

Accommodation practices allow us to glimpse the project of the self as a practical struggle. A semblance of normal individuality for troublemakers was a carefully constructed artifact produced by members. When the responsibility for normality is assumed as an individual birthright, it appears inevitable that conformity or defiance proceeds "from inside" the individual, just as it appears in commonsense that gender is a natural inheritance. In the latter instance, a transsexual's unusual experience indicates the extent to which the ordinary behavior and appearance of being female is detachable from the individual's birthright, and can be explicated as a practical accomplishment (Garfinkel, 1967). Similarly, for the organizational colleagues of a troublemaker, the elements of normal individuality cannot be relied upon, but must be achieved through deliberate practice. Members together performed the work of minding the troublemaker's business, of guiding the troublemaker through normal interactional pathways, and of filling the responsibilities and appearances associated with the troublemaker's presence for others.[6]

Of course, such projects were less than successful; members complained of the undue burden, disruptions occurred despite their efforts, and the troublemaker was provided with a diminished self and a distorted reality. Perhaps all would have been better off had they "left the self inside where it belongs." Nevertheless, accommodation practices enable us to see the extent to which the division between self and other is permeable, and subject to negotiation and manipulation. We can see that individual responsibility for the conduct of affairs is separable from the actual performance of those affairs. Troublemakers were manipulated into a tenuous conformity by members who relied upon the fact that such conformity would be attributed to the individual's responsibility. The individual was thus reduced to the subject of an informal code of responsibility, separable from any substantive source of action (Goffman, 1969:357).

Implications

Previous research on accommodation practices in the societal reaction tradition has suggested that the individual symptoms of disorder can be explained in reference to social organization (Goffman, 1969; Lemert, 1962). I have not been concerned with how individual *disorder* is generated by social reaction. My interest instead has been to investigate how individual *normality* is socially constructed. This issue has both practical and theoretical consequences.

On a practical level, given the current institutional emphasis on the "community care" of mental disorders, it should be useful to know as much as possible about ordinary "institutions" of accommodation. The descriptive inventory provided in this study goes a small distance in that direction. Based on this study, it appears that accommodation practices are analogous, on a social level, to individual "defense mechanisms" (Henry, 1972:49). What remains to be determined is whether some of the practices are more effective than others; whether, like Freudian defense mechanisms, some can be viewed as pathological whereas others are relatively effective. It also remains to be seen whether accommodation practices can be improved by instruction, and operated in a humane and insightful fashion.

On a theoretical level, the analysis of accommodation practices enables us to consider the self as a social and normative construct as much as an internal province of operations. This is more than to say that the self is an *attribution* by others, since accommodation includes concrete actions to manipulate and maintain a semblance of normal selfhood on behalf of a troublemaker. In psychology and social-psychology, an inscrutable ego is normally required as a locus of operations for directing behavior and impression management (the latter by reacting to the reactions of others). Here we see both behavior and impression management being directed by overt and covert operations external to the individual. By implication, the individual's domain of action and responsibility is only provisionally established if it can be taken over by others.

Accommodation practices integrate the troublemaker into society, while requiring minimal initiative from the troublemaker. At the extreme, the troublemaker can be turned into a puppet whose behavior (especially in its more public consequences) is divorced from internal control. The individual is never altogether out of the picture, since at every turn individual responsibility is attributed. The puppet is given life (a life not of its making) through the conventional appearance of its overt actions. Instead of an ego projecting significant symbols outward, we find the surface of an individual being managed and shaped by communal activity, with or without the individual's knowledge and compliance. Whether this applies more generally than to the pathological circumstances described here remains to be established, but my research suggests that the individual self is a moral and attributional construct not to be confused with the theoretical requirements of social action.

Notes

1. The equally interesting topic of how patients accommodate to their own disorders (Critchley, 1971:290; O. Sacks 1974:227) is not included in this discussion of interactional practices.

2. Here the term *member* does not bear the more radical implication of "a mastery of natural language," defined in Garfinkel and Sacks (1970:350).

3. A topic needing further study is how members use greetings and other conversational "adjacency pairs" (Sacks, Schegloff, and Jefferson, 1974) to foreclose conversation with troublemakers at the earliest convenient point, but in such a way as not to call attention to their action as a snub.

4. See Wulbert (n.d.) for a poignant discussion of trivializing practices.

5. Jefferson and Lee (1980) characterize some of the detailed ways in which participants in ordinary conversations head off "troubles talk" and transform it to "business as usual." Such procedures are much more varied and intricate than can adequately be described by such phrases as "changing the subject."

6. My discussion of the social production of the individual is heavily indebted to Pollner and Wikler's (1981) treatment of that theme. Pollner and Wikler (1981) discuss a family's efforts to construct the appearance of normality for their (officially diagnosed) profoundly retarded daughter. Not only does *normality* become a communal project in these cases, *abnormality* becomes shared as well. One student in my research described an alcoholic's family as "three characters revolving around a central theme—alcoholism." The preoccupation with alcohol was shared along with the *denial* that the man's drinking was an official problem.

References

Bittner, Egon. 1967. "Police discretion in emergency apprehension of mentally ill persons." *Social Problems* 14(3):278–292.

Critchley, MacDonald. 1971. The Parietal Lobes. New York: Hafner Publishing Co.

Cumming, Elaine, and John Cumming. 1957. Closed Ranks. Cambridge, MA: Harvard University Press.

Emerson, Robert, and Sheldon Messinger. 1977. "The micro-politics of trouble." *Social Problems* 25(2):121–134.

Freeman, Howard, and Ozzie Simmons. 1958. "Mental patients in the community: Family settings and performance levels." *American Sociological Review* 23(2):147–154.

Garfinkel, Harold. 1967. Studies in Ethnomethodology. Englewood Cliffs, NJ: Prentice Hall.

Garfinkel, Harold, and Harvey Sacks. 1970. "Formal structures of practical actions." Pp. 337–366 in John McKinney and Edward Tiryakian (eds.), *Theoretical Sociology: Perspectives and Development*. New York: Appleton-Century Crofts.

Goffman, Erving. 1961. Asylums. Garden City, NY: Doubleday.

Goffman, Erving. 1969. "The insanity of place." *Psychiatry* 32(4):352–388.

Henry, Jules. 1972. Pathways to Madness. New York: Random House.

Hollingshead, August, and Frederick Redlich. 1958. Social Class and Mental Illness. New York: John Wiley and Sons.

Jackson, Joan. 1954. "The adjustment of the family to the crisis of alcoholism." *Quarterly Journal of Studies on Alcohol* 15(4):562–586.

Jefferson, Gail, and John Lee. 1980. "The analysis of conversations in which anxieties and troubles are expressed." Unpublished report for the Social Science Research Counsel, University of Manchester, England.

Lemert, Edwin. 1962. "Paranoia and the dynamics of exclusion." *Sociometry* 25(1):2–20.

Mayo, Clara, Ronald Havelock, and Diane Lear Simpson. 1971. "Attitudes towards mental illness among psychiatric patients and their wives." *Journal of Clinical Psychology* 27(1):128–132.

Myers, Jerome, and Bertram Roberts. 1959. Family and Class Dynamics. New York: John Wiley and Sons, Inc.

Pollner, Melvin, and Lynn Wikler. 1981. "The social construction of unreality: A case study of the practices of family sham and delusion." Unpublished paper, Department of Sociology, University of California, Los Angeles.

Sacks, Harvey, Emanuel Schegloff, and Gail Jefferson. 1974. "A simplest systematics for the organization of turn taking in conversation." *Language* 50(4):696–735.

Sacks, Oliver. 1974. Awakenings. New York: Doubleday.

Sampson, Harold, Sheldon Messinger, and Robert Towne. 1962. "Family processes and becoming a mental patient." *American Journal of Sociology* 68(1):88–98

Spitzer, Stephan, Patricia Morgan, and Robert Swanson. 1971. "Determinants of the psychiatric patient career: Family reaction patterns and social work intervention." *Social Service Review* 45(1):74–85.

Srole, Leo, Thomas Langer, Stanley Michael, Marvin Opler, and Thomas Rennie. 1962. Mental Health in the Metropolis: The Midtown Manhattan Study. New York: McGraw Hill.

Wulbert, Roland. —. "Second thoughts about commonplaces." Unpublished paper, Department of Sociology, Columbia University, (Circa, 1974).

Yarrow, Marian, Charlotte Schwartz, Harriet Murphy, and Leila Deasy. 1955. "The psychological meaning of mental illness in the family." *Journal of Social Issues* 11(4):12–24.

The author thanks Renee Anspach, David Davis, Robert Emerson, Harold Garfinkel, Richard Hilbert, James Holstein, Melvin Pollner, and Steven Vandewater for their comments. The exercise on accommodation practices which I used in this research was adapted from a similar exercise used by Robert Emerson and Melvin Pollner in their courses on the Sociology of Mental Illness at the University of California, Los Angeles. During part of this research I was supported by a fellowship from the National Institute of Mental Health Postdoctoral Training Program in Mental Health Evaluation Research, (# MH 14583). Correspondence to: School of Social Sciences, University of California, Irvine, CA.

44

The Suicidal Mind

Why Do We Kill Ourselves?

Edwin S. Shneidman

Psychological pain lies at the core of those who attempt or contemplate suicide. Shneidman has a word for it: psychache—the hurt, anguish, shame, fear, and loneliness that take over the mind and make life no longer worth living. Not everyone who experiences psychache becomes suicidal. Thresholds and tolerances vary from person to person; events that traumatize one person may be entirely manageable to another. Individuals also vary in their level of social supports, access to professional care, and economic resources. Protective influences, or their lack, can have a powerful influence in the etiology of suicide.

Conventional wisdom holds that suicide is an act of selfishness, the "easy way out" that severely harms the deceased person's loved ones. Losing a wife, husband, son, or daughter is an emotionally wrenching experience for anyone, but when it is perceived to be unnecessary and preventable, the pain is even more unbearable. Relatives of suicide victims commonly report feeling a sense of failure, as if they could have done something to "fix" the victim. Taking a more active role, however, typically is futile. Suicide is an intensely private act; many victims show no outward signs of distress before their final exit (not wishing to extend the burden onto someone else). The prospect of suicide also is liberating for many would-be victims, providing a promise of relief from chronic psychological pain. Telling others what you plan to do might jeopardize its availability as a solution.

Statistically speaking, females are more likely to attempt suicide than males, but males are more likely to be successful (their method of choice tends to be more lethal); whites are more at risk than blacks; the old are more susceptible than the young. In the United States,

31,000 suicides occur annually—the eighth leading cause of death; 5 million Americans report attempting suicide at some time in their lives (CBS News 2000). Some scholars suggest that these figures are actually conservative. The definition of suicide, they contend, is too restrictive and excludes all sorts of purposive behaviors that hasten an early death—from illegal drug use and drinking and driving to smoking, poor nutritional habits, and failure to exercise. Such behaviors, the argument goes, are just as self-destructive as putting a gun to one's head and pulling the trigger. The result is a lot longer in coming, but it is the same result nonetheless.

Shneidman focuses on the "truly" suicidal and offers the notion of psychache to conceptualize its occurrence. Vignettes and case studies are provided to explore the introspective process that precedes the final act of desperation.

Why Do We Kill Ourselves?

Suicide haunts our literature and our culture. It is the taboo subtext to our successes and our happiness. The reporting of a suicide of any public figure disturbs each of us. Amid our dreams of happiness and achievement lurk our nightmares of self-destruction. Who is not mindful of the potential self-defeating elements within our own personality? Each new day contains the threat of failure and assaults by others, but it is the threat of *self*-destruction that we are most afraid to touch, except in our secret moments or the hidden recesses of our minds. Yet suicide happens every day, and many people we know have had a relative or a friend who has committed suicide.

I got into suicide quite by accident. It was in 1949; I was 31. On that particular morning, I was in the subbasement, below the street level of the old Los Angeles Hall of Records, in the Coroner's vault, looking at file-folders of certified deaths. I had been asked by the Director of the Veterans Administration hospital where I worked as a clinical psychologist to prepare letters to be sent to two young widows whose husbands had committed suicide while they were still wards of the hospital. My intention that day was to look at the folders of the two men, make some notes, and get back to work.

The first folder contained something I had not seen before: a suicide note; the second folder did not. Who could stop at this point? I looked at several dozen folders. It seemed that every so often I would open a suicide folder and find a suicide note—about 1 in 15. I did a quick count of the number of the folders on one shelf and I estimated that I was in a room that contained at least a couple thousand suicide notes. It was a scientist's dream. Within the next few weeks I made photocopies of over 700 suicide notes and put them aside, without reading them, later to be compared in "blind," controlled studies with simulated suicide notes elicited from nonsuicidal people. Since that day, I have been intrigued by the topic of suicide and drawn to people who might be suicidal.

What is suicide anyway? How can we understand it and prevent it? This book has a definite point of view. Stripped down to its bones, my argument goes like this: In almost every case, suicide is caused by pain, a certain kind of pain—*psychological* pain, which I call *psychache (s ī k-ā k)*. Furthermore, this psychache stems from thwarted or distorted psychological *needs*. In other words, suicide is chiefly a drama in the mind. . . .

My statement about the root cause of suicide is an assertion that comes from my half-century of experience with suicidal individuals across the country. When I say that almost all suicide is caused by psychache, exactly how much suicide do I believe is so motivated? All?—not quite. Most?—certainly. Are there exceptions?—no doubt. Is this notion intended to apply equally to such events as hara-kiri, seppuku, suttee, or acts of suicidal terrorists?—no. I make no attempt to cover suicide in cultures different from our own Judeo-Christian tradition, explicitly not suicides in China or India or Islam, where special historical and cultural forces are sufficiently powerful that people are willing to die for them. This topic is a very complicated business. Some suicidal acts committed by people on what we call

"suicide missions" or who commit aberrant acts of terrorism are, when done by *our* side (in times of war), honored and rewarded by medals. Indeed, the Congressional Medal of Honor is awarded for brave actions that, by any normal calculations, would have resulted in death—and sometimes did. But wartime heroism and rare sacrificial suicides aside, this . . .is primarily intended for an American and European readership and is meant to address directly the state of the suicidal mind.

Even though I know that each suicidal death is a multifaceted event—that biological, biochemical, cultural, sociological, interpersonal, intrapsychic, logical, philosophical, conscious, and unconscious elements are always present—I retain the belief that, in the proper distillation of the event, its essential nature is *psychological.* That is, each suicidal drama occurs in the *mind* of a unique individual. An arboreal image may be useful: See the tree; that tree. There is the chemistry of the soil in which the tree lives. The tree exists in a socio-cultural climate. An individual's biochemical states, for example, are its roots, figuratively speaking. An individual's method of committing suicide, the details of the event, the contents of the suicide note, and so on, are the metaphoric branching limbs, the flawed fruit, and the camouflaging leaves. But the psychological component, the conscious choice of suicide as the seemingly best solution to a perceived problem, is the main trunk.

The implications of this psychological view are quite extensive. For one thing, it means that our best route to understanding suicide is not through the study of the structure of the brain, nor the study of social statistics, nor the study of mental diseases, but directly through the study of human emotions described in plain English, in the words of the suicidal person. The most important question to a potentially suicidal person is not an inquiry about family history or laboratory tests of blood or spinal fluid, but "Where do you hurt?" and "How can I help you?"

All of us know that life is sometimes pleasant, usually routine, and too often difficult.

This is as true today as it was in Caesar's time. The positive aspects of life include joy and happiness, contentment and well-being, success and comfort, good health and creative energy, love and reciprocal response—life's happy and exhilarating highways and byways.

Much of life is taken up by the routine, pedestrian, everyday, humdrum, habitual, and emotionally neutral stretches of life—life on automatic pilot, mindlessly cruising along.

And then there is pain and all of life's unhappy aspects: sorrow, shame, humiliation, fear, dread, defeat, anxiety. The dark side and dark moments.

When we experience these negative emotions in some heightened degree, psychological anguish and disturbance follow. We feel upset, disturbed, perturbed. Everyone has experienced emotional perturbation at one time or another, to some degree or another. Unfortunately, some of us live in a state of constant anguish. Anguish or disturbance or perturbation is caused by pain, sometimes physical pain, but more often psychological pain. Psychological pain is the basic ingredient of suicide. (But there's a lot more.) Suicide is never born out of exaltation or joy; it is a child of the negative emotions. But in order to begin to understand *suicide*, we need to think about what anguish means, as well as why people entertain thoughts of death, especially death as a way of stopping unbearable misery. Suicidal death, in other words, as an escape from pain. Perturbation and lethality are the bad parents of human self-destruction. Pain is Nature's great signal. Pain warns us; pain both mobilizes us and saps our strength; pain, by its very nature, makes us want to stop it or escape from it.

We can define *lethality* as the likelihood of an individual's being dead by his or her own hand in the near future. *Lethality* is a synonym for *suicidality*: How dangerous is this individual to himself or herself? The purpose of distinguishing these two terms (anguish and lethality) is not only a theoretical one, but a clinical and practical one. When dealing with a highly suicidal person, it is simply not effective to address the lethality directly (through confrontation or exhortation). We

can address thoughts about suicide by working with this person and asking why mental turmoil is leading to feelings of lethality. To defuse the situation, to mollify the kindled emotions, is the most effective course. In short, to do anything (within reason) to make that person less perturbed.

Practically every reader of these words has worried about suicide, directly or indirectly; has had moments of concern about a family member, a friend, or oneself. Our constant goal is prevention—but first must come understanding.

A basic rule for us to keep in mind is: We can reduce the lethality if we lessen the anguish, the perturbation. Suicidal individuals who are asked "Where do you hurt?" intuitively know that this is a question about their emotions and their lives, and they answer appropriately, not in biological terms, but with some literary or humanistic sophistication, in psychological terms. What I mean by this is to ask about the person's feelings, worries, and pain.

We can think of these concepts in another way: Perturbation is felt pain; lethality relates to the *idea* of death (nothingness, cessation) as the solution. By itself, mental anguish is not lethal. But lethality, when coupled with elevated perturbation, is a principal ingredient in self-inflicted death. Perturbation supplies the motivation for suicide; lethality is the fatal trigger.

Lethality—the idea that "I can stop this pain; I can kill myself"—is the unique essence of suicide. Anybody who has ever switched off an electric light deliberately to plunge a hideous room into darkness or, with equal deliberation, stopped the action of an annoying engine by turning the key to OFF, has, for that moment, been granted the swift satisfaction the suicidal person hungers for. After all, the suicidal person intends to stop the ongoing activities of *life*.

How is physical pain different from psychological anguish? For one thing, physical pain is not the kind of pain that is centrally involved in suicide. The wish for death by assisted suicide in a person suffering from AIDS or the early stages of Alzheimer's disease is related to the degradations and anxieties attendant to physical pain, rather than to just the physical pain itself, which can be controlled by appropriate doses of medicine.

It is hard to imagine a life without some occasional physical pain. We all know what pain feels like. The scraped knee, the accidental cut or bump, a hard hit on the head. What adults have not cried when they were babies? Many people experience rather intense, severe, even excruciating pain at one time or another, and survive with the memory of it.

Physical pain is a physical or somatic ache or hurt, proceeding from disease or bodily injury or dysfunction—a toothache, earache, stomachache; a cut, fracture, sprain, wound; gout, arthritis, cancer; an "ouch" experience. By pain, we mean physical pain.

There is a vast technical literature on physical pain. One contemporary survey book[1] contains hundreds of references to various kinds of pain: chronic pain, low back pain, phantom limb pain, intractable pain, among other topics. Most large hospitals have special clinics devoted to the management of pain. The control of physical pain is a major concern in the contemporary treatment of human suffering.

Here is an account of pain by a young man dying of AIDS:

I'm giving up. I want it to be over. I don't expect any miracle anymore. The swelling and the fevers just get me down. . . .And then I'd just like to go to sleep and die. I'm just tired. I woke up this morning. I was really frightened. I was saying, dear God, dear God, what am I going to do? Dear God, dear God, doesn't answer. . . .If there was a way I could end it now, I would do that.

This benighted young man's account of his swelling and fevers is an indirect way of his recounting his physical pain, but it is his fear, his psychological pain that haunts us most. . . .

My main purpose in discussing physical pain is to establish that it is *not* the kind of pain that is implicated in most suicide. Which leads us now to the kind of pain that *is* involved—namely, psychological pain, or psychache. . . .

Let me quote two verbatim accounts of psychological pain. The first is by Beatrice Bessen, a young woman who, as a student in my UCLA undergraduate course on Death and Suicide (which I taught for 20 years), volunteered to complete a Psychological Pain Survey. We had spoken privately and she assured me that she would not be distressed by doing it (and she had her therapist's approval). . . .

At the age of ten I woke up to the horrors of the world. I came out of my childhood innocence and dove head-first into the dark side of life. Recognizing that I was vulnerable to severe pain, and predicting my household was breaking up, I began to pull away from my family. By age 15 I was struggling with self-hate, not understanding what was happening to me. One day my boyfriend abruptly broke up with me. I had never felt such intense pain and I could not handle it. I was alone at home and ran desperately around, panicked over the flood of emotions that was travelling through my body. I ended up taking the kitchen knife into my room and cutting myself, slashes all along my arms. The physical pain let me pull my attention off the emotional agony and I just concentrated on not letting the blood spill over onto the carpet.

The second account is that of a young man written from his hospital bed after he had fortuitously survived a self-inflicted gunshot wound. We'll call him Castro Reyes. He had placed the barrel of a fully automatic pistol near the right side of his head meaning to blow his brains out, but in the tension of the moment he shot erratically and ended up shooting most of his face off. He could not speak, but he could, with effort, write. He was an unusual person: a Caribbean-American, a high school dropout, a scholar about certain aspects of European history, especially ancient Roman history. He was a genuine autodidact, a self-taught master, a young man who wrote polished English and had a command of spelling and grammar and a vocabulary that would have placed him among the top percentiles on most college verbal tests. The hospital staff where I saw him had him incorrectly pegged and treated him (I thought with some disdain) as though he were barely literate. Here, unchanged from his original scrawled text, are some of his penned words:

> There was no peace to be found. I had done all I could and was still sinking. I sat many hours seeking answers and all there was was a silent wind and no answers. The answer was clear. Die. I didn't sleep. The dreams were reality and reality dreams. My will to survive and succeed had been crushed and defeated. I was like a general alone on a battlefield being encroached upon by my enemy and its hordes: Fear, hate, self-depreciation, desolation. I felt I had to have the upper hand, to control my destiny, so I sought to die rather than surrender. Destiny and reality began to merge. Those around me were as shadows, bare apparitions, but I was not actually conscious of them, only aware of myself and my plight. Death swallowed me long before I pulled the trigger. I was locked within myself. The world through my eyes seemed to die with me. It was like I was to push the final button to end this world. I committed myself to the arms of Death. There comes a time when all things cease to shine, when the rays of hope are lost. I placed the gun to my head.

What these two people are talking about is psychological pain, or *psychache*. Psychache is the hurt, anguish, or ache that takes hold in the mind. It is intrinsically psychological—the pain of excessively felt shame, guilt, fear, anxiety, loneliness, angst, dread of growing old or of dying badly. When psychache occurs, its introspective reality is undeniable. Suicide happens when the psychache is deemed unbearable and death is actively sought to stop the unceasing flow of painful consciousness. Suicide is a tragic drama in the mind. . . .

Here are a half-dozen suicide notes from men and women; single, married, and separated; ages 24 to 74; death by gunshot, cutting, overdose, and hanging. They reflect the psychological pain of suicide.

Female, 45, married, overdose: "If I haven't the love I want so bad there is nothing left."

Female, 60, single, overdose: "I am tired of this emotional merry-go-round, so I'll get out of it by taking my life."

Female, 74, widowed, cut wrists: "I am powerless over my emotions. Life is unmanageable. I'm like a helpless 12-year-old."

Male, 24, married, hanging: "Dear Mary. I am writing these last lines to you because these are the last ones. I really thought that you and little Joe were going to come back into my life but you didn't. I know that you found someone else that is better than me. I hope the son of a bitch dies. I love you very much and Joe too. It hurts a lot that you and I didn't make it. I had a lot of dreams for all of us but they were only dreams. I always thought that dreams would come true but I guess not. I hope to go to heaven but in my case I'll probably go to hell. Please take care of little Joe because I love him with all my heart. Please don't tell him what happened. Tell him I went far away and will come back one of these days. Tell him you don't know when. Well, I guess that's it. Take care of yourself. PS. I know we could have made it but you didn't want to because you wanted to get fucked by someone else well you got it. I can't really say that I hate you or love you. You'll never know. Yours truly, Your husband, George."

Male, 31, separated, hanging: "Forgive me, for today I die. I just cannot live without you. I might as well be dead. Maybe there will be peace. I have this empty feeling inside me that is killing me. I just can't take it anymore. When you left me I died inside. I have to say, nothing left but the broken heart that is leading me into this. I cry to God to help me but he doesn't listen. There is nothing else for me to do."

Male, 49, married, gunshot wound to the head: "I sit alone. Now, at last, freedom from the mental torment I have been experiencing. This should come as no surprise. My eyes have spoken for a long, long, time of the distress I feel. The rejection, failures and frustrations overwhelm me. There is no way to pull myself out of this hell. Goodbye, love. Forgive me."

In all these notes there is unmistakable psychological pain. Suicide is the result of an interior dialogue. The mind scans its options; the topic of suicide comes up, the mind rejects it, scans again; there is suicide, it is rejected again, and then finally the mind accepts suicide as a solution, then plans it, and fixes it as the only answer. . . .

Each of us has an idiosyncratic disposition made up of psychological needs. Indeed, we can say that the relative weights we give these psychological needs is a window into our personality. It reflects what makes us tick. . . .

For practical purposes, most suicides tend to fall into one of five clusters of psychological needs. They reflect different kinds of psychological pain.

- Thwarted *love*, acceptance, and belonging—related to frustrated needs for succorance and affiliation.
- Fractured *control*, predictability, and arrangement—related to frustrated needs for achievement, autonomy, order, and understanding.
- Assaulted self-image and the avoidance of *shame*, defeat, humiliation, and disgrace—related to frustrated needs for

affiliation, defendance, and shame-avoidance.

- Ruptured key relationships and the attendant *grief* and bereftness—related to frustrated needs for affiliation and nurturance.
- Excessive *anger*, rage, and hostility—related to frustrated needs for dominance, aggression, and counteraction. . . .

Note

1. Ronald Melzack and Joel Katz, The McGill Pain Questionnaire: Appraisal and Current Status. In D. C. Turk and R. Melzack (eds.), Handbook of Pain Assessment. New York: Guilford Press, 1992, p. 156.

45

On Being Sane in Insane Places

David L. Rosenhan

The self does not exist apart from the society in which it operates. Self-image is entirely a function of how a person is perceived and treated by others (Cooley 1902). A person might be funny or smart or good-looking, but none of these qualities is possible or meaningful in the absence of communication with other people. Interaction makes attributions (social labels) possible, and attributions are then internalized to shape how and what a person thinks about himself or herself.

Attributions can, of course, be incorrect. Becker, in his classic study, Outsiders, suggested the intriguing possibility of "false accusation"—important in the context of deviance since people labeled deviant may actually not be deviant at all. Such labels are powerful, however, and can have just as profound an effect on subsequent behavior as any legitimately earned designation.

The principle of false accusation is critical to Rosenhan's study. Rosenhan, a psychologist, placed eight sane people in twelve different mental hospitals, "patients" who gained admission by virtue of reporting false symptoms during a diagnostic interview. After their admission, Rosenhan instructed his confederates to act completely normal, which was not difficult because there was nothing psychotic about any of them to begin with. Hospital staff, however, continued to treat them as if they were "mental," interpreting their behavior in ways consistent with the initial diagnosis: Everyday conflicts were defined as psychotic outbursts; unproductive boredom and fidgeting symbolized acute nervousness; note-taking was evidence of paranoia and pathology. Intriguingly, other "real" patients saw right through the researchers' charade, suspecting they were undercover in some capacity. Staff members, however, continued to treat them as psychotics, keeping some institutionalized for as long as 52 days.

Though all were eventually released, the staffs at the hospitals nevertheless retained the schizophrenic diagnostic label, insisting the "psuedopatients'" symptoms simply were in remission. Reality is what people perceive it to be, and perceptions drive actions. Rosenhan demonstrates the powerful implications of this axiom in the context of the social control of the mentally ill. As Rosenhan himself puts it, "the data speak to the massive role of labeling in psychiatric assessment. Having once been labeled schizophrenic, there is nothing the pseudopatient can do to overcome the tag."

If sanity and insanity exist, how shall we know them?

The question is neither capricious nor itself insane. However much we may be personally convinced that we can tell the normal from the abnormal, the evidence is simply not compelling. It is commonplace, for example, to read about murder trials wherein eminent psychiatrists for the defense are contradicted by equally eminent psychiatrists for the prosecution on the matter of the defendant's sanity. More generally, there are a great deal of conflicting data on the reliability, utility, and meaning of such terms as "sanity," "insanity," "mental illness," and "schizophrenia".[1] Finally, as early as 1934, Benedict suggested that normality and abnormality are not universal.[2] What is viewed as normal in one culture may be seen as quite aberrant in another. Thus, notions of normality and abnormality may not be quite as accurate as people believe they are.

To raise questions regarding normality and abnormality is in no way to question the fact that some behaviors are deviant or odd. Murder is deviant. So, too, are hallucinations. Nor does raising such questions deny the existence of the personal anguish that is often associated with "mental illness." Anxiety and depression exist. Psychological suffering exists. But normality and abnormality, sanity and insanity, and the diagnoses that flow from them may be less substantive than many believe them to be.

At its heart, the question of whether the sane can be distinguished from the insane (and whether degrees of insanity can be distinguished from each other) is a simple matter: Do the salient characteristics that lead to diagnoses reside in the patients themselves or in the environments and contexts in which observers find them? From Bleuler, through Kretchmer, through the formulators of the recently revised *Diagnostic and Statistical Manual* of the American Psychiatric Association, the belief has been strong that patients present symptoms, that those symptoms can be categorized, and, implicitly, that the sane are distinguishable from the insane. More recently, however, this belief has been questioned. Based in part on theoretical and anthropological considerations, but also on philosophical, legal, and therapeutic ones, the view has grown that psychological categorization of mental illness is useless at best and downright harmful, misleading, and pejorative at worst. Psychiatric diagnoses, in this view, are in the minds of the observers and are not valid summaries of characteristics displayed by the observed.[3-5]

Gains can be made in deciding which of these is more nearly accurate by getting normal people (that is, people who do not have, and have never suffered, symptoms of serious psychiatric disorders) admitted to psychiatric hospitals and then determining whether they were discovered to be sane and, if so, how. If the sanity of such pseudopatients were always detected, there would be prima facie evidence that a sane individual can be distinguished from the insane context in which he is found. Normality (and presumably abnormality) is distinct enough that it can be recognized wherever it occurs, for it is carried within the person. If, on the other hand, the sanity of the pseudopatients were never discovered, serious difficulties would arise for those who support traditional modes of psychiatric diagnosis. Given that the hospital staff was not incompetent, that the pseudopatient had been behaving as sanely as he had been outside of the hospital,

and that it had never been previously suggested that he belonged in a psychiatric hospital, such an unlikely outcome would support the view that psychiatric diagnosis betrays little about the patient but much about the environment in which an observer finds him.

This article describes such an experiment. Eight sane people gained secret admission to 12 different hospitals.[6] Their diagnostic experiences constitute the data of the first part of this article; the remainder is devoted to a description of their experiences in psychiatric institutions. Too few psychiatrists and psychologists, even those who have worked in such hospitals, know what the experience is like. They rarely talk about it with former patients, perhaps because they distrust information coming from the previously insane. Those who have worked in psychiatric hospitals are likely to have adapted so thoroughly to the settings that they are insensitive to the impact of that experience. And while there have been occasional reports of researchers who submitted themselves to psychiatric hospitalization,[7] these researchers have commonly remained in the hospitals for short periods of time, often with the knowledge of the hospital staff. It is difficult to know the extent to which they were treated like patients or like research colleagues. Nevertheless, their reports about the inside of the psychiatric hospital have been valuable. This article extends those efforts.

Pseudopatients and Their Settings

The eight pseudopatients were a varied group. One was a psychology graduate student in his twenties. The remaining seven were older and "established." Among them were three psychologists, a pediatrician, a psychiatrist, a painter, and a housewife. Three pseudopatients were women, five were men. All of them employed pseudonyms, lest their alleged diagnoses embarrass them later. Those who were in mental health professions alleged another occupation in order to avoid the special attentions that might be accorded by staff, as a matter of courtesy or caution, to ailing colleagues.[8]

With the exception of myself (I was the first pseudopatient and my presence was known to the hospital administrator and chief psychologist and, so far as I can tell, to them alone), the presence of pseudopatients and the nature of the research program was not known to the hospital staffs.[9]

The settings were similarly varied. In order to generalize the findings, admission into a variety of hospitals was sought. The 12 hospitals in the sample were located in five different states on the East and West Coasts. Some were old and shabby, some were quite new. Some were research-oriented, others not. Some had good staff-patient ratios, others were quite understaffed. Only one was a strictly private hospital. All of the others were supported by state or federal funds or, in one instance, by university funds.

After calling the hospital for an appointment, the pseudopatient arrived at the admissions office complaining that he had been hearing voices. Asked what the voices said, he replied that they were often unclear, but as far as he could tell they said "empty," "hollow," and "thud." The voices were unfamiliar and were of the same sex as the pseudopatient. The choice of these symptoms was occasioned by their apparent similarity to existential symptoms. Such symptoms are alleged to arise from painful concerns about the perceived meaninglessness of one's life. It is as if the hallucinating person were saying, "My life is empty and hollow." The choice of these symptoms was also determined by the *absence* of a single report of existential psychoses in the literature.

Beyond alleging the symptoms and falsifying name, vocation, and employment, no further alterations of person, history, or circumstances were made. The significant events of the pseudopatient's life history were presented as they had actually occurred. Relationships with parents and siblings, with spouse and children, with people at work and in school, consistent with the aforementioned exceptions, were described as they were or had been. Frustrations and upsets were described along with joys and satisfactions. These facts are important to remember. If anything, they strongly biased

the subsequent results in favor of detecting sanity, since none of their histories or current behaviors were seriously pathological in any way.

Immediately upon admission to the psychiatric ward, the pseudopatient ceased simulating *any* symptoms of abnormality. In some cases, there was a brief period of mild nervousness and anxiety, since none of the pseudopatients really believed that they would be admitted so easily. Indeed, their shared fear was that they would be immediately exposed as frauds and greatly embarrassed. Moreover, many of them had never visited a psychiatric ward; even those who had, nevertheless had some genuine fears about what might happen to them. Their nervousness, then, was quite appropriate to the novelty of the hospital setting, and it abated rapidly.

Apart from that short-lived nervousness, the pseudopatient behaved on the ward as he "normally" behaved. The pseudopatient spoke to patients and staff as he might ordinarily. Because there is uncommonly little to do on a psychiatric ward, he attempted to engage others in conversation. When asked by staff how he was feeling, he indicated that he was fine, that he no longer experienced symptoms. He responded to instructions from attendants, to calls for medication (which was not swallowed), and to dining-hall instructions. Beyond such activities as were available to him on the admissions ward, he spent his time writing down his observations about the ward, its patients, and the staff. Initially these notes were written "secretly," but as it soon became clear that no one much cared, they were subsequently written on standard tablets of paper in such public places as the dayroom. No secret was made of these activities.

The pseudopatient, very much as a true psychiatric patient, entered a hospital with no foreknowledge of when he would be discharged. Each was told that he would have to get out by his own devices, essentially by convincing the staff that he was sane. The psychological stresses associated with hospitalization were considerable, and all but one of the pseudopatients desired to be discharged almost immediately after being admitted. They were, therefore, motivated not only to behave sanely, but to be paragons of cooperation. That their behavior was in no way disruptive is confirmed by nursing reports, which have been obtained on most of the patients. These reports uniformly indicate that the patients were "friendly," "cooperative," and "exhibited no abnormal indications."

The Normal Are Not Detectably Sane

Despite their public "show" of sanity, the pseudopatients were never detected. Admitted, except in one case, with a diagnosis of schizophrenia,[10] each was discharged with a diagnosis of schizophrenia "in remission." The label "in remission" should in no way be dismissed as a formality, for at no time during any hospitalization had any question been raised about any pseudopatient's simulation. Nor are there any indications in the hospital records that the pseudopatient's status was suspect. Rather the evidence is strong that, once labeled schizophrenic, the pseudopatient was stuck with that label. If the pseudopatient was to be discharged, he must naturally be "in remission"; but he was not sane, nor, in the institution's view, had he ever been sane.

The uniform failure to recognize sanity cannot be attributed to the quality of the hospitals, for, although there were considerable variations among them, several are considered excellent. Nor can it be alleged that there was simply not enough time to observe the pseudopatients. Length of hospitalization ranged from 7 to 52 days, with an average of 19 days. The pseudopatients were not, in fact, carefully observed, but this failure clearly speaks more to traditions within psychiatric hospitals than to lack of opportunity.

Finally, it cannot be said that the failure to recognize the pseudopatients' sanity was due to the fact that they were not behaving sanely. While there was clearly some tension present in all of them, their daily visitors could detect no serious behavioral consequences—nor, indeed, could other patients. It was quite common for the patients to "detect" the pseudopatients' sanity. During the first three hospitalizations, when accurate counts were kept, 35 of a total of 118 patients on the admissions ward voiced their suspicions, some vigorously. "You're not crazy. You're a journalist, or a professor [referring to the continual note-taking]. You're checking up on the hospital." While most of the patients were reassured by the pseudopatient's insistence that he had been sick before he came in but was fine now, some continued to believe that the pseudopatient was sane throughout his hospitalization.[11] The fact that the patients often recognized normality when staff did not raises important questions.

Failure to detect sanity during the course of hospitalization may be due to the fact that physicians operate with a strong bias toward what statisticians call the type 2 error.[5] This is to say that physicians are more inclined to call a healthy person sick (a false positive, type 2) than a sick person healthy (a false negative, type 1). The reasons for this are not hard to find: It is clearly more dangerous to misdiagnose illness than health. Better to err on the side of caution, to suspect illness even among the healthy.

But what holds for medicine does not hold equally well for psychiatry. Medical illnesses, while unfortunate, are not commonly pejorative. Psychiatric diagnoses, on the contrary, carry with them personal, legal, and social stigmas.[12] It was therefore important to see whether the tendency toward diagnosing the sane insane could be reversed. The following experiment was arranged at a research and teaching hospital whose staff had heard these findings but doubted that such an error could occur in their hospital. The staff was informed that at some time during the following 3 months, one or more pseudopatients would attempt to be admitted into the psychiatric hospital. Each staff member was asked to rate each patient who presented himself at admissions or on the ward according to the likelihood that the patient was a pseudopatient. A 10-point scale was used, with a 1 and 2 reflecting high confidence that the patient was a pseudopatient.

Judgments were obtained on 193 patients who were admitted for psychiatric treatment. All staff who had sustained contact with or primary responsibility for the patient—attendants, nurses, psychiatrists, physicians, and psychologists—were asked to make judgments. Forty-one patients were alleged, with high confidence, to be pseudopatients by at least one member of the staff. Twenty-three were considered suspect by at least one psychiatrist. Nineteen were suspected by one psychiatrist *and* one other staff member. Actually, no genuine pseudopatient (at least from my group) presented himself during this period.

The experiment is instructive. It indicates that the tendency to designate sane people as insane can be reversed when the stakes (in this case, prestige and diagnostic acumen) are high. But what can be said of the 19 people who were suspected of being "sane" by one psychiatrist and another staff member? Were these people truly "sane," or was it rather the case that in the course of avoiding the type 2 error the staff tended to make more errors of the first sort—calling the crazy "sane"? There is no way of knowing. But one thing is certain: Any diagnostic process that lends itself so readily to massive errors of this sort cannot be a very reliable one.

The Stickiness of Psychodiagnostic Labels

Beyond the tendency to call the healthy sick—a tendency that accounts better for diagnostic behavior on admission than it does for such behavior after a lengthy period of exposure—the data speak to the massive role of labeling in psychiatric assessment. Having once been labeled schizophrenic, there is nothing the pseudopatient can do to overcome the tag. The tag profoundly colors others' perceptions of him and his behavior.

From one viewpoint, these data are hardly surprising, for it has long been known that elements are given meaning by the context in which they occur. Gestalt psychology made this point vigorously, and Asch[13] demonstrated that there are "central" personality traits (such as "warm" versus "cold") which are so powerful that they markedly color the meaning of other information in forming an impression of a given personality.[14] "In-

sane," "schizophrenic," "manic-depressive," and "crazy" are probably among the most powerful of such central traits. Once a person is designated abnormal, all of his other behaviors and characteristics are colored by that label. Indeed, that label is so powerful that many of the pseudopatients' normal behaviors were overlooked entirely or profoundly misinterpreted. Some examples may clarify this issue.

Earlier I indicated that there were no changes in the pseudopatient's personal history and current status beyond those of name, employment, and, where necessary, vocation. Otherwise, a veridical description of personal history and circumstances was offered. Those circumstances were not psychotic. How were they made consonant with the diagnosis of psychosis? Or were those diagnoses modified in such a way as to bring them into accord with the circumstances of the pseudopatient's life, as described by him?

As far as I can determine, diagnoses were in no way affected by the relative health of the circumstances of a pseudopatient's life. Rather, the reverse occurred: The perception of his circumstances was shaped entirely by the diagnosis. A clear example of such translation is found in the case of a pseudopatient who had had a close relationship with his mother but was rather remote from his father during his early childhood. During adolescence and beyond, however, his father became a close friend, while his relationship with his mother cooled. His present relationship with his wife was characteristically close and warm. Apart from occasional angry exchanges, friction was minimal. The children had rarely been spanked. Surely there is nothing especially pathological about such a history. Indeed, many readers may see a similar pattern in their own experiences, with no markedly deleterious consequences. Observe, however, how such a history was translated in the psychopathological context, this from the case summary prepared after the patient was discharged.

This white 39-year-old male . . .manifests a long history of considerable ambivalence in close relationships, which begins in early childhood. A warm relationship with his mother cools during his adolescence. A distant relationship to his father is described as becoming very intense. Affective stability is absent. His attempts to control emotionality with his wife and children are punctuated by angry outbursts and, in the case of the children, spankings. And while he says that he has several good friends, one senses considerable ambivalence embedded in those relationships also. . . .

The facts of the case were unintentionally distorted by the staff to achieve consistency with a popular theory of the dynamics of a schizophrenic reaction.[15] Nothing of an ambivalent nature had been described in relations with parents, spouse, or friends. To the extent that ambivalence could be inferred, it was probably not greater than is found in all human relationships. It is true the pseudopatient's relationships with his parents changed over time, but in the ordinary context that would hardly be remarkable—indeed, it might very well be expected. Clearly, the meaning ascribed to his verbalizations (that is, ambivalence, affective instability) was determined by the diagnosis: schizophrenia. An entirely different meaning would have been ascribed if it were known that the man was "normal."

All pseudopatients took extensive notes publicly. Under ordinary circumstances, such behavior would have raised questions in the minds of observers, as, in fact, it did among patients. Indeed, it seemed so certain that the notes would elicit suspicion that elaborate precautions were taken to remove them from the ward each day. But the precautions proved needless. The closest any staff member came to questioning these notes occurred when one pseudopatient asked his physician what kind of medication he was receiving and began to write down the response. "You needn't write it," he was told gently. "If you have trouble remembering, just ask me again."

If no questions were asked of the pseudopatients, how was their writing interpreted? Nursing records for three patients indicate that the writing was seen as an aspect of their pathological behavior. "Patient engages in writing behavior" was the daily nursing comment on one of the pseudopatients who was never questioned about his writing. Given that the patient is in the hospital, he must be psychologically disturbed. And given that he is a disturbed, continuous writing must be a behavioral manifestation of that disturbance, perhaps a subset of the compulsive behaviors that are sometimes correlated with schizophrenia.

One tacit characteristic of psychiatric diagnosis is that it locates the sources of aberration within the individual and only rarely within the complex of stimuli that surrounds him. Consequently, behaviors that are stimulated by the environment are commonly misattributed to the patient's disorder. For example, one kindly nurse found a pseudopatient pacing the long hospital corridors. "Nervous, Mr. X?" she asked. "No, bored," he said.

The notes kept by pseudopatients are full of patient behaviors that were misinterpreted by well-intentioned staff. Often enough, a patient would go "berserk" because he had, wittingly or unwittingly, been mistreated by, say, an attendant. A nurse coming upon the scene would rarely inquire even cursorily into the environmental stimuli of the patient's behavior. Rather, she assumed that his upset derived from his pathology, not from his present interactions with other staff members. Occasionally, the staff might assume that the patient's family (especially when they had recently visited) or other patients had stimulated the outburst. But never were the staff found to assume that one of themselves or the structure of the hospital had anything to do with a patient's behavior. One psychiatrist pointed to a group of patients who were sitting outside the cafeteria entrance half an hour before lunchtime. To a group of young residents he indicated that such behavior was characteristic of the oral-acquisitive nature of the syndrome. It seemed not to occur to him that there were very few things to anticipate in a psychiatric hospital besides eating.

A psychiatric label has a life and an influence of its own. Once the impression has been formed that the patient is schizophrenic, the expectation is that he will continue to be schizophrenic. When a sufficient amount of time has passed, during which the patient has done nothing bizarre, he is considered to be in remission and available for discharge. But the label endures beyond discharge, with the unconfirmed expectation that he will behave as a schizophrenic again. Such labels, conferred by mental health professionals, are as influential on the patient as they are on his relatives and friends, and it should not surprise anyone that the diagnosis acts on all of them as a self-fulfilling prophecy. Eventually, the patient himself accepts the diagnosis, with all of its surplus meanings and expectations, and behaves accordingly.[5]

The inferences to be made from these matters are quite simple. Much as Zigler and Phillips have demonstrated that there is enormous overlap in the symptoms presented by patients who have been variously diagnosed,[16] so there is enormous overlap in the behaviors of the sane and the insane. The sane are not "sane" all of the time. We lose our tempers "for no good reason." We are occasionally depressed or anxious, again for no good reason. And we may find it difficult to get along with one or another person—again for no reason that we can specify. Similarly, the insane are not always insane. Indeed, it was the impression of the pseudopatients while living with them that they were sane for long periods of time—that the bizarre behaviors upon which their diagnoses were allegedly predicated constituted only a small fraction of their total behavior. If it makes no sense to label ourselves permanently depressed on the basis of an occasional depression, then it takes better evidence than is presently available to label all patients insane or schizophrenic on the basis of bizarre behaviors or cognitions. It seems more useful, as Mischel[17] has pointed out, to limit our discussions to *behaviors*, the stimuli that provoke them, and their correlates.

It is not known why powerful impressions of personality traits, such as "crazy" or "insane," arise. Conceivably, when the origins of and stimuli that give rise to a behavior are remote or unknown, or when the behavior strikes us as immutable, trait labels regarding the *behavior* arise. When, on the other hand, the origins and stimuli are known and available, discourse is limited to the behavior itself. Thus, I may hallucinate because I am sleeping, or I may hallucinate because I have ingested a peculiar drug. These are termed sleep-induced hallucinations, or dreams, and drug-induced hallucinations, respectively. But when the stimuli to my hallucinations are unknown, that is called craziness, or schizophrenia—as if that inference were somehow as illuminating as the others.

The Experience of Psychiatric Hospitalization

The term "mental illness" is of recent origin. It was coined by people who were humane in their inclinations and who wanted very much to raise the station of (and the public's sympathies toward) the psychologically disturbed from that of witches and "crazies" to one that was akin to the physically ill. And they were at least partially successful, for the treatment of the mentally ill *has* improved considerably over the years. But while treatment has improved, it is doubtful that people really regard the mentally ill in the same way that they view the physically ill. A broken leg is something one recovers from, but mental illness allegedly endures forever.[18] A broken leg does not threaten the observer, but a crazy schizophrenic? There is by now a host of evidence that attitudes toward the mentally ill are characterized by fear, hostility, aloofness, suspicion, and dread.[19] The mentally ill are society's lepers.

That such attitudes infect the general population is perhaps not surprising, only upsetting. But that they affect the professionals—attendants, nurses, physicians, psychologists, and social workers—who treat and deal with the mentally ill is more disconcerting, both because such attitudes are self-evidently pernicious and because they are unwitting. Most mental health professionals would insist that they are sympathetic toward the mentally ill, that they are neither avoidant nor hostile. But it is more likely that an exquisite ambivalence characterizes their relations with psychiatric patients, such that their avowed impulses are only part of their entire attitude. Negative attitudes are there too and can easily be detected. Such attitudes should not surprise us. They are the natural offspring of the labels patients wear and the places in which they are found.

Consider the structure of the typical psychiatric hospital. Staff and patients are strictly segregated. Staff have their own living space, including their dining facilities, bathrooms, and assembly places. The glassed quarters that contain the professional staff, which the pseudopatients came to call "the cage," sit out on every dayroom. The staff emerge primarily for caretaking purposes—to give medication, to conduct a therapy or group meeting, to instruct or reprimand a patient. Otherwise, staff keep to themselves, almost as if the disorder that afflicts their charges is somehow catching.

So much is patient-staff segregation the rule that, for four public hospitals in which an attempt was made to measure the degree to which staff and patients mingle, it was necessary to use "time out of the staff cage" as the operational measure. While it was not the case that all time spent out of the cage was spent mingling with patients (attendants, for example, would occasionally emerge to watch television in the dayroom), it was the only way in which one could gather reliable data on time for measuring.

The average amount of time spent by attendants outside of the cage was 11.3 percent (range, 3 to 52 percent). This figure does not represent only time spent mingling with patients, but also includes time spent on such chores as folding laundry, supervising patients while they shave, directing ward clean-up, and sending patients to off-ward activities. It was the relatively rare attendant who spent time talking with patients or playing games with them. It proved impossible to obtain a "percent mingling time" for nurses, since the amount of time they spent out of the cage was too brief. Rather, we counted instances of emergence from the cage. On the average, daytime nurses emerged from the cage 11.5 times per shift, including instances when they left the ward entirely (range, 4 to 39 times). Late afternoon and

night nurses were even less available, emerging on the average 9.4 times per shift (range, 4 to 41 times). Data on early morning nurses, who arrived usually after midnight and departed at 8 a.m., are not available because patients were asleep during most of this period.

Physicians, especially psychiatrists, were even less available. They were rarely seen on the wards. Quite commonly, they would be seen only when they arrived and departed, with the remaining time being spent in their offices or in the cage. On the average, physicians emerged on the ward 6.7 times per day (range, 1 to 17 times). It proved difficult to make an accurate estimate in this regard, since physicians often maintained hours that allowed them to come and go at different times.

The hierarchical organization of the psychiatric hospital has been commented on before,[20] but the latent meaning of that kind of organization is worth noting again. Those with the most power have least to do with patients, and those with the least power are most involved with them. Recall, however, that the acquisition of role-appropriate behaviors occurs mainly through the observation of others, with the most powerful having the most influence. Consequently, it is understandable that attendants not only spend more time with patients than do any other members of the staff—that is required by their station in the hierarchy—but also, insofar as they learn from their superiors' behavior, spend as little time with patients as they can. Attendants are seen mainly in the cage, which is where the models, the action, and the power are.

I turn now to a different set of studies, these dealing with staff response to patient-initiated contact. It has long been known that the amount of time a person spends with you can be an index of your significance to him. If he initiates and maintains eye contact, there is reason to believe that he is considering your requests and needs. If he pauses to chat or actually stops and talks there is added reason to infer that he is individuating you. In four hospitals, the pseudopatient approached the staff member with a request which took the following form: "Pardon me, Mr. [or Dr. or Mrs.] X, could you tell me when I will be eligible for grounds privileges?" (or ". . .when I will be presented at the staff meeting?" or ". . .when I am likely to be discharged?"). While the content of the question varied according to the appropriateness of the target and the pseudopatient's (apparent) current needs, the form was always a courteous and relevant request for information. Care was taken never to approach a particular member of the staff more than once a day, lest the staff member become suspicious or irritated. In examining these data, remember that the behavior of the pseudopatients was neither bizarre nor disruptive. One could indeed engage in good conversation with them.

The data for these experiments are shown in Table 45.1 [not provided here], separately for physicians (column 1) and for nurses and attendants (column 2). Minor differences between these four institutions were overwhelmed by the degree to which staff avoided continuing contacts that patients had initiated. By far, their most common response consisted of either a brief response to the question, offered while they were "on the move" and with head averted, or no response at all.

The encounter frequently took the following bizarre form: (pseudopatient) "Pardon me, Dr. X. Could you tell me when I am eligible for grounds privileges?" (physician) "Good morning, Dave. How are you today?" (Moves off without waiting for a response.)

It is instructive to compare these data with data recently obtained at Stanford University. It has been alleged that large and eminent universities are characterized by faculty who are so busy that they have no time for students. For this comparison, a young lady approached individual faculty members who seemed to be walking purposefully to some meeting or teaching engagement and asked them the following six questions.

1. "Pardon me, could you direct me to Encina Hall?" (at the medical school: ". . .to the Clinical Research Center?").

2. "Do you know where Fish Annex is?" (there is no Fish Annex at Stanford).

3. "Do you teach here?"

4. "How does one apply for admission to the college?" (at the medical school: ". . .to the medical school?").

5. "Is it difficult to get in?"

6. "Is there financial aid?"

Without exception, as can be seen in Table 45.1 [not provided here], all of the questions were answered. No matter how rushed they were, all respondents not only maintained eye contact, but stopped to talk. Indeed, many of the respondents went out of their way to direct or take the questioner to the office she was seeking, to try to locate "Fish Annex," or to discuss with her the possibilities of being admitted to the university.

Similar data, also shown in Table 45.1 (columns 4, 5, and 6), were obtained in the hospital. Here too, the young lady came prepared with six questions. After the first question, however, she remarked to 18 of her respondents (column 4), "I'm looking for a psychiatrist," and to 15 others (column 5), "I'm looking for an internist." Ten other respondents received no inserted comment (column 6). The general degree of cooperative responses is considerably higher for these university groups than it was for pseudopatients in psychiatric hospitals. Even so, differences are apparent within the medical school setting. Once having indicated that she was looking for a psychiatrist, the degree of cooperation elicited was less than when she sought an internist.

Powerlessness and Depersonalization

Eye contact and verbal contact reflect concern and individuation; their absence, avoidance and depersonalization. The data I have presented do not do justice to the rich daily encounters that grew up around matters of depersonalization and avoidance. I have records of patients who were beaten by staff for the sin of having initiated verbal contact. During my own experience, for example, one patient was beaten in the presence of other patients for having approached an attendant and told him, "I like you." Occasionally, punishment meted out to patients for misdemeanors seemed so excessive that it could not be justified by the most radical interpretations of psychiatric canon. Nevertheless, they appeared to go unquestioned. Tempers were often short. A patient who had not heard a call for medication would be roundly excoriated, and the morning attendants would often wake patients with, "Come on, you m——-f——-s, out of bed!"

Neither anecdotal nor "hard" data can convey the overwhelming sense of powerlessness which invades the individual as he is continually exposed to the depersonalization of the psychiatric hospital. It hardly matters *which* psychiatric hospital—the excellent public ones and the very plush private hospital were better than the rural and shabby ones in this regard, but, again, the features that psychiatric hospitals had in common overwhelmed by far their apparent differences.

Powerlessness was evident everywhere. The patient is deprived of many of his legal rights by dint of his psychiatric commitment.[21] He is shorn of credibility by virtue of his psychiatric label. His freedom of movement is restricted. He cannot initiate contact with the staff, but may only respond to such overtures as they make. Personal privacy is minimal. Patient quarters and possessions can be entered and examined by any staff member, for whatever reason. His personal history and anguish is available to any staff member (often including the "gray lady" and "candy striper" volunteer) who chooses to read his folder, regardless of their therapeutic relationship to him. His personal hygiene and waste evacuation are often monitored. The water closets may have no doors.

At times, depersonalization reached such proportions that pseudopatients had the sense that they were invisible, or at least unworthy of account. Upon being admitted, I and other pseudopatients took the initial physical examinations in a semipublic room, where staff members went about their own business as if we were not there.

On the ward, attendants delivered verbal and occasionally serious physical abuse to patients in the presence of other observing patients, some of whom (the pseudopatients) were writing it all down. Abusive behavior, on the other hand, terminated quite abruptly when other staff members were known to be coming. Staff are credible witnesses. Patients are not.

A nurse unbuttoned her uniform to adjust her brassiere in the presence of an entire ward of viewing men. One did not have the sense that she was being seductive. Rather, she didn't notice us. A group of staff persons might point to a patient in the dayroom and discuss him animatedly, as if he were not there.

One illuminating instance of depersonalization and invisibility occurred with regard to medications. All told, the pseudopatients were administered nearly 2,100 pills, including Elavil, Stelazine, Compazine, and Thorazine, to name but a few. (That such a variety of medications should have been administered to patients presenting identical symptoms is itself worthy of note.) Only two were swallowed. The rest were either pocketed or deposited in the toilet. The pseudopatients were not alone in this. Although I have no precise records on how many patients rejected their medications, the pseudopatients frequently found the medications of other patients in the toilet before they deposited their own. As long as they were cooperative, their behavior and the pseudopatients' own in this matter, as in other important matters, went unnoticed throughout.

Reactions to such depersonalization among pseudopatients were intense. Although they had come to the hospital as participant observers and were fully aware that they did not "belong," they nevertheless found themselves caught up in and fighting the process of depersonalization. Some examples: A graduate student in psychology asked his wife to bring his textbooks to the hospital so he could "catch up on his homework"—this despite the elaborate precautions taken to conceal his professional association. The same student, who had trained for quite some time to get into the hospital, and who had looked forward to the experience, "remembered" some drag races that he had wanted to see on the weekend and insisted that he be discharged by that time. Another pseudopatient attempted a romance with a nurse. Subsequently, he informed the staff that he was applying for admission to graduate school in psychology and was very likely to be admitted, since a graduate professor was one of his regular hospital visitors. The same person began to engage in psychotherapy with other patients—all of this as a way of becoming a person in an impersonal environment.

The Sources of Depersonalization

What are the origins of depersonalization? I have already mentioned two. First are attitudes held by all of us toward the mentally ill—including those who treat them—attitudes characterized by fear, distrust, and horrible expectations on the one hand, and benevolent intentions on the other. Our ambivalence leads, in this instance as in others, to avoidance.

Second, and not entirely separate, the hierarchical structure of the psychiatric hospital facilitates depersonalization. Those who are at the top have least to do with patients, and their behavior inspires the rest of the staff. Average daily contact with psychiatrists, psychologists, residents, and physicians combined ranged from 3.9 to 25.1 minutes, with an overall mean of 6.8 (six pseudopatients over a total of 129 days of hospitalization). Included in this average are time spent in the admissions interview, ward meetings in the presence of a senior staff member, group and individual psychotherapy contacts, case presentation conferences, and discharge meetings. Clearly, patients do not spend much time in interpersonal contact with doctoral staff. And doctoral staff serve as models for nurses and attendants.

There are probably other sources. Psychiatric installations are presently in serious financial straits. Staff shortages are pervasive, staff time at a premium. Something has to give, and that something is patient contact. Yet, while financial stresses are realities, too much can be made of them. I have the impression that the psychological forces that result in depersonalization are much stronger than the fiscal ones and that the addition of more staff would not correspondingly improve patient care in this regard. The incidence of staff meetings and the enormous amount of record-keeping on patients, for example, have not been as substantially reduced as has patient contact. Priorities exist, even during hard times. Patient contact is not a significant priority in the traditional psychiatric hospital, and fiscal pressures do not account for this. Avoidance and depersonalization may.

Heavy reliance upon psychotropic medication tacitly contributes to depersonalization by convincing staff that treatment is indeed being conducted and that further patient contact may not be necessary. Even here, however, caution needs to be exercised in understanding the role of psychotropic drugs. If patients were powerful rather than powerless, if they were viewed as interesting individuals rather than diagnostic entities, if they were socially significant rather than social lepers, if their anguish truly and wholly compelled our sympathies and concerns, would we not *seek* contact with them, despite the availability of medications? Perhaps for the pleasure of it all?

The Consequences of Labeling and Depersonalization

Whenever the ratio of what is known to what needs to be known approaches zero, we tend to invent "knowledge" and assume that we understand more than we actually do. We seem unable to acknowledge that we simply don't know. The needs for diagnosis and remediation of behavioral and emotional problems are enormous. But rather than acknowledge that we are just embarking on understanding, we continue to label patients "schizophrenic," "manic-depressive," and "insane," as if in those words we had captured the essence of understanding. The facts of the matter are that we have known for a long time that diagnoses are often not useful or reliable, but we have nevertheless continued to use them. We now know that we cannot distinguish insanity from sanity. It is depressing to consider how that information will be used.

Not merely depressing, but frightening. How many people, one wonders, are sane but not recognized as such in our psychiatric institutions? How many have been needlessly stripped of their privileges of citizenship, from the right to vote and drive to that of handling their own accounts? How many have feigned insanity in order to avoid the criminal consequences of their behavior, and, conversely, how many would rather stand trial than live interminably in a psychiatric hospital—but are wrongly thought to be mentally ill? How many have been stigmatized by well-intentioned, but nevertheless erroneous, diagnoses? On the last point, recall again that a "type 2 error" in psychiatric diagnosis does not have the same consequences it does in medical diagnosis. A diagnosis of cancer that has been found to be in error is cause for celebration. But psychiatric diagnoses are rarely found to be in error. The label sticks, a mark of inadequacy forever.

Finally, how many patients might be "sane" outside the psychiatric hospital but seem insane in it—not because craziness resides in them, as it were, but because they are responding to a bizarre setting, one that may be unique to institutions which harbor nether people? Goffman[4] calls the process of socialization to such institutions "mortification"—an apt metaphor that includes the processes of depersonalization that have been described here. And while it is impossible to know whether the pseudopatients' responses to these processes are characteristic of all inmates—they were, after all, not real patients—it is difficult to believe that these processes of socialization to a psychiatric hospital provide useful attitudes or habits of response for living in the "real world."

Summary and Conclusions

It is clear that we cannot distinguish the sane from the insane in psychiatric hospitals. The hospital itself imposes a special environment in which the meanings of behavior can easily be misunderstood. The consequences to patients hospitalized in such an environment—the powerlessness, depersonalization, segregation, mortification, and self-labeling—seem undoubtedly counter-therapeutic.

I do not, even now, understand this problem well enough to perceive solutions. But two matters seem to have some promise. The first concerns the proliferation of community mental health facilities, of crisis intervention centers, of the human potential movement, and of behavior therapies that, for all of their own problems, tend to avoid psychiatric labels, to focus on specific problems and behaviors, and to retain the individual in a relatively non-perjorative environment. Clearly, to the extent that we refrain from sending the distressed to insane places, our impressions of them are less likely to be distorted. (The risk of distorted perceptions, it seems to me, is always present, since we are much more sensitive to an individual's behaviors and verbalizations than we are to the subtle contextual stimuli that often promote them. At issue here is a matter of magnitude. And, as I have shown, the magnitude of distortion is exceedingly high in the extreme context that is a psychiatric hospital.)

The second matter that might prove promising speaks to the need to increase the sensitivity of mental health workers and researchers to the *Catch-22* position of psychiatric patients. Simply reading materials in this area will be of help to some such workers and researchers. For others, directly experiencing the impact of psychiatric hospitalization will be of enormous use. Clearly, further research into the social psychology of such total institutions will both facilitate treatment and deepen understanding.

I and the other pseudopatients in the psychiatric setting had distinctly negative reactions. We do not pretend to describe the subjective experiences of true patients. Theirs may be different from ours, particularly with the passage of time and the necessary process of adaptation to one's environment. But we can and do speak to the relatively more objective indices of treatment within the hospital. It could be a mistake, and a very unfortunate one, to consider that what happened to us derived from malice or stupidity on the part of the staff. Quite the contrary, our overwhelming impression of them was of people who really cared, who were committed and who were uncommonly intelligent. Where they failed, as they sometimes did painfully, it would be more accurate to attribute those failures to the environment in which they, too, found themselves than to personal callousness. Their perceptions and behavior were controlled by the situation, rather than being motivated by a malicious disposition. In a more benign environment, one that was less attached to global diagnosis, their behaviors and judgments might have been more benign and effective.

Notes

1. P. Ash, J. *Abnorm. Soc. Psychol.* 44, 272 (1949), A. T. Beck, *Amer. J. Psychiat.* 119, 210 (1962), A. T. Boisen, *Psychiatry* 2, 233 (1938); N. Kreitman, *J. Ment. Sci.* 107, 876 (1961); N. Kreitman, P. Sainsbury, J. Morrisey, J. Towers, J. Scrivener, *ibid.*, p. 887, H. O. Schmitt and C. P. Fonda, *J. Abnorm. Soc. Psychol.* 52, 262 (1956); W. Seeman, *J. Nerv. Ment. Dis.* 118, 541 (1953). For an analysis of these artifacts and summaries of the disputes, see J. Zubin, *Annu. Rev. Psychol.* 18, 373 (1967); L. Phillips and J. G. Draguns, *ibid.* 22, 447 (1971).

2. R. Benedict, J. *Gen. Psychol.* 10, 59 (1934).

3. See in this regard H. Becker, *Outsiders: Studies in the Sociology of Deviance* (Free Press, New York, 1963); B. M. Braginsky, D. D. Braginsky, K. Ring, *Methods of Madness: The Mental Hospital as a Last Resort* (Holt, Rinehart & Winston, New York, 1969); G. M. Crocetti and P. V. Lemkau, *Amer. Sociol. Rev.* 30, 577 (1965); E. Goffman, *Behavior in Public Places* (Free Press, New York, 1964); R. D. Laing, *The Divided Self: A Study of Sanity and Madness* (Quadrangle, Chicago, 1960); D. L. Phillips, *Amer. Sociol. Rev.* 28, (1963); T. R. Sarbin, *Psychol. Today* 6, 18 (1972); E. Schur, *Amer. J. Sociol.* 75, 309 (1969); T. Szasz, *Law, Liberty and Psychiatry* (Macmillan, New York, 1963); *The Myth of Mental Illness: Foundations of a Theory of Mental Illness* (Hoeber-Harper, New York, 1963). For a critique of some of these views, see W. R. Gove, *Amer. Sociol. Rev.* 35, 873 (1970).

4. E. Goffman, *Asylums* (Doubleday, Garden City, N.Y., 1961).

5. T. J. Scheff, *Being Mentally Ill: A Sociological Theory* (Aldine, Chicago, 1966).

6. Data from a ninth pseudopatient are not incorporated in this report because, although his sanity went undetected, he falsified aspects of his personal history, including his marital status and parental relationships. His experimental behaviors therefore were not identical to those of the other pseudopatients.

7. A. Barry, *Bellevue Is a State of Mind* (Harcourt Brace Jovanovich, New York, 1971); I. Belknap, *Human Problems of a State Mental Hospital* (McGraw-Hill, New York, 1956); W. Caudill, F. C. Redlich, H. R. Gilmore, E. B. Brody, *Amer. J. Orthopsychiat.* 22, 314 (1952); A. R. Goldman, R. H. Bohr, T. A. Steinberg, *Prof. Psychol.* 1, 427 (1970); unauthored, *Roche Report* 1 (No. 13), 8 (1971).

8. Beyond the personal difficulties that the pseudopatient is likely to experience in the hospital, there are legal and social ones that, combined, require considerable attention before entry. For example, once admitted to a psychiatric institution, it is difficult, if not impossible, to be discharged on short notice, state law to the contrary notwithstanding. I was not sensitive to these difficulties at the outset of the project, nor to the personal and situational emergencies that can arise, but later a writ of habeas corpus was prepared for each of the entering pseudopatients and an attorney was kept "on call" during every hospitalization. I am grateful to John Kaplan and Robert Bartels for legal advice and assistance in these matters.

9. However distasteful such concealment is, it was a necessary first step to examining these questions. Without concealment, there would have been no way to know how valid these experiences were; nor was there any way of knowing whether whatever detections occurred were a tribute to the diagnostic acumen of the staff or to the hospital's rumor network. Obviously, since my concerns are general ones that cut across individual hospitals and staffs, I have respected their anonymity and have eliminated clues that might lead to the identification.

10. Interestingly, of the 12 admissions, 11 were diagnosed as schizophrenic and one, with the identical symptomatology, as manic-depressive psychosis. This diagnosis has a more favorable prognosis, and it was given by the only private hospital in our sample. On the relations between social class and psychiatric diagnosis, see A. B. Hollingshead and F. C. Redlich, *Social Class and Mental Illness: A Community Study* (Wiley, New York, 1958).

11. It is possible, of course, that patients have quite broad latitudes in diagnosis and therefore are inclined to call many people sane, even those whose behavior IS patently aberrant. However, although we have no hard

data on this matter, it was our distinct impression that this was not the case. In many instances, patients not only singled us out for attention, but came to imitate our behaviors and styles.

12. J. Cumming and E. Cumming, *Community Ment. Health* 1, 135 (1965); A. Farina and K. Ring, *J. Abnorm. Psychol.* 70, 47 (1965); H. E. Freeman and O. G. Simmons, *The Mental Patient Comes Home* (Wiley, New York, 1963); W. J. Johannsen, *Ment. Hygiene* 53, 218 (1969); A. S. Linsky, *Soc. Psychiat.* 5, 166 (1970).

13. S. E. Asch, *J. Abnorm. Soc. Psychol.* 41, 258 (1946); *Social Psychology* (Prentice Hall, New York,

14. See also I. N. Mensh and J. Wishner, *J. Personality* 16, 188 (1947); J. Wishner, *Psychol. Rev.* 67, 96 (1960); J. S. Bruner and R. Tagluri, in *Handbook of Social Psychology*, G. Lindzey, ed. (Addison-Wesley, Cambridge, Mass., 1954), vol. 2, pp. 634–654; J. S. Bruner, D. Shapiro, R. Tagiuri, in *Person Perception and Interpersonal Behavior*, R. Tagiuri and L. Petrullo, Eds. (Stanford Univ. Press, Stanford, Calif., 1958), pp. 277–288.

15. For an example of a similar self-fulfilling prophecy, in this instance dealing with the "central" trait of intelligence, see R. Rosenthal and L. Jacobson, *Pygmalion in the Classroom* (Holt, Rinehart & Winston, New York, 1968).

16. E. Zigler and L. Phillips, *J. Abnorm. Soc. Psychol.* 63, 69 (1961). See also R. K. Freudenberg and J. P. Robertson, *A.M.A. Arch. Neurol. Psychiatr.* 76, 14 (1956).

17. W. Mischel, *Personality and Assessment* (Wiley, New York, 1968).

18. The most recent and unfortunate instance of this tenet is that of Senator Thomas Eagleton.

19. T. R. Sarbin and J. C. Mancuso, *J. Clin. Consult. Psychol.* 35, 159 (1970); T. R. Sarbin, *ibid.* 31, 447 (1967); J. C. Nunnally, Jr., *Popular Conceptions of Mental Health* (Holt, Rinehart & Winston, New York, 1961).

20. A. H. Stanton and M. S. Schwartz, *The Mental Hospital: A Study of Institutional Participation in Psychiatric Illness and Treatment* (Basic, New York, 1954).

21. D. B. Wexler and S. E. Scoville, *Ariz. Law Rev.* 13, 1 (1971).

I thank W. Mischel, E. Orne, and M. S. Rosenhan for comments on an earlier draft of this manuscript.

Part IX

Stigma and Identity Management

Identity is generally defined as an individual's self-concept. Individual identity encompasses beliefs about who an actor is and how he or she is perceived and treated in social life. Although identities are often expressed by way of roles, identity as a concept is broader than role. Roles are expectations held about someone who occupies a position or social status; identity is a constellation of all of the roles an individual performs. Identity can be further divided into situated versus biographical. Situated identity is interactionally based and can assume any number of forms for an individual (soccer player, wife, theater-goer, construction worker). Biographical identity is grounded in demographic attributes such as historical lineage, gender, religion, race, nationality, and age (Biddle 1979; Dainton 1993; Hewitt 1979; McCall and Simmons 1978; Schlenker 1980; see also Jacobs 1996, 395).

The notion of "spoiled identity" is crucial to understanding deviant behavior. Spoiled identities are a function of stigma, attributes that are "deeply discrediting" (Goffman 1963, 3). Stigma results from gaps between virtual and actual social identities (Goffman 1963). Virtual identity is what an actor purports to be or wishes himself or herself to be; actual identity refers to who that person "really" is (in some physical, emotional, or biographical sense). Interactions between stigmatized persons and their "normal" counterparts define the former as "deviant, flawed, limited, spoiled, or generally unde-

sirable" (Jones et al. 1984, 4). Stigma, in other words, is a fundamentally relational concept (Levy 1993). To understand it, "a language of relationships, not attributes, is needed. An attribute that stigmatizes one type of possessor can confirm the usualness of another, and therefore is neither creditable nor discreditable as a thing in itself" (Goffman 1963, 3).

Attributes producing stigma are said to fall into three broad categories: abominations of the body, blemishes of individual character, and tribal stigma by race, nation, and religion (Goffman 1963). "A factor that cuts across these categories is whether these attributes are known or concealed from others" (Levy 1993, 227). The former refer to discredited stigma, the latter to discreditable. Related factors include the visibility of the attribute, previous knowledge others have about it, the stigma's obtrusiveness upon interaction, its perceived focus (that is, normals' perception of the things that stigmatized persons are disqualified from doing), its course or pattern of change over time, its origin and locus of responsibility, and its peril or imminence and degree of perceived danger (Jones et al. 1984).

Stigma has been a central concept in sociology since Goffman's (1963) seminal work. A diverse array of groups possessing some form of stigma have been extensively studied by researchers, including working class students in elite universities (Granfield 1991), animal experimenters (Arluke 1991), women

athletes (Blinde and Taub 1992), the involuntarily childless (Miall 1986), adoptive
parents (Miall 1987), divorcees (Gerstel
1987), adolescent parents (Bok 1978; Levy
and Thiel 1990), incest survivors (Green
1988), patients with chronic pain (Lennon
et al. 1989), older adults (Luken 1987), persons with Alzheimer's disease (Shifflet and
Blieszner 1988), persons with cancer
(Stahly 1988), the mentally retarded
(Baxter 1989), persons with chronic mental
illness (Goldin 1990), substance abusers
(Gomberg 1988), and the homeless (Cohen
1990).

Although, because they are stigmatized,
all of the groups mentioned in the preceding
paragraphs are considered socially marginal, they are of the "same culture as those
who stigmatize them and tend to hold the
same beliefs about identity as those who
stigmatize them" (Levy 1993, 228). The stigmatized people thus perceive themselves as
normal beings just like everyone else; it is
simply that their interactions constantly remind them of their "differentness." Shame
and embarrassment result when stigmatized
persons fail to measure up to prevailing normative expectations—feelings that can carry
over to the nonstigmatized, who, in turn, realize their own vulnerability. As Goffman observes, "The stigmatized and the normal are
part of each other; if one can prove vulnerable, it must be expected that the other can
too" (1963, 135). Indeed, normals often feel
ambivalent when interacting with the stigmatized, wanting to be friendly and helpful
on the one hand, yet exhibiting hostility and
rejection on the other (for an overview, see
Jones et al. 1984).

When researchers talk about presentation
of self and spoiled identity, they usually discuss it in terms of those who wish to make
their stigma as unobtrusive as possible (the
discredited) or those who wish to keep it hidden altogether (the discreditable). Appearances are central to both. Appearance symbolizes identity, and it has a regulatory
function over the responses of others (Stone
1977). Given that communication in public
is "overwhelmingly appearance dependent,
. . .communication between the unac-
quainted rests on symbolism, on individual

appearance, dress, and gesture" (Brooks
Gardner 1991, 251). Such interactions are
"embodied" (Goffman 1963)—salient to a
given moment. Since audiences largely base
assessments of situations on appearances,
stereotypes become an inescapable mechanism for passing judgment (Brooks Gardner
1991, 257).

Some researchers explore the management techniques that deviant actors use to
maintain secrecy about a discreditable attribute (Arluke 1991; Blinde and Taub 1992;
Goffman 1963). Others address the neutralization techniques that the stigmatized use
to contain social embarrassment once an attribute has somehow been exposed (Blum
1991; Granfield 1991; also see Goffman
1963). Exploration into stigma management
has focused on techniques of information
control (Goffman 1963)—passing and
disidentification, in particular. Passing refers to how deviants behave in nonstigmatizing ways without specifically claiming to
be nonstigmatized. Disidentification refers
to behaving in ways that indicate a
nonstigmatized (though false) identity. Both
tactics allow actors to "accomplish"
(Garfinkel 1967) a social situation without
drawing undue attention to a profoundly
negative attribute. Examination of embarrassment containment (that is, the handling
of negative affect once an attribute has been
exposed) has focused on the remedial use of
accounts—linguistic devices used to uphold
an idealized reputation, image, and character (Scott and Lyman 1968).

Broadly speaking, there are two types of
accounts: justifications and excuses. Justifications accept responsibility for some deviant act or status but deny that the act or status is wrongful; excuses deny responsibility
for deviance but recognize that deviance is
unseemly or untoward. Accounts are essentially deflection devices; they separate the
act from the person so that the former does
not reflect negatively on the latter. People inevitably want the approval and acceptance
of others, so even habitual rule-breakers will
frequently offer accounts to present their
bad conduct in the best possible light. Although retrospective in focus, accounts typically operate prospectively in the offender's

mind. If a person who contemplates deviance knows that he or she can explain it away later, deviant acts become much easier to commit. Whether deviants are consciously aware of choosing to act deviantly while relying on a later exculpatory account, or whether their accounts accurately reflect their *true* motives, are entirely different matters. As C. Wright Mills (1940) reminds us, the reasons people give for their actions are not themselves without reasons. These and other core concerns in deviant identities and their management are explored in this section. ✦

46
Anorexia Nervosa and Bulimia

The Development of Deviant Identities

Penelope A. McLorg

Diane E. Taub

The media-intensive society of the early twenty-first century has elevated the importance of physical attractiveness to new heights. Movies, television, and magazines bombard viewers with images of beauty and sexual allure. Billions of dollars are spent annually on products geared to enhance personal appearance. The implicit message of advertisements for everything from make-up and shampoo to clothes and cars is that these products will make one more desirable. In a culture obsessed with appearance, desirability has become something of an interpersonal Holy Grail.

The fixation on looks has had profound and troubling effects, marginalizing people who, in some form or fashion, do not measure up. More vexing, it has created entirely new standards of physical attractiveness that many find unattainable. Nowhere are these standards more exacting than in the realm of body weight. "Thin is in," and the consequences create special problems for women.

As socially constructed sex objects, women must conform to prevailing expectations about body weight or face "sanctions." Many justifiably fear, for example, that if they do not look a certain way, they will be unable to secure friends, boyfriends, family approval—or simply attention, which, in a media-intensive society, has become a commodity in and of itself. In some cases, the price of thinness is steep, culminating in full-blown eating disorders that are as emotionally harmful as they are physically dangerous.

Two disorders—anorexia nervosa and bulimia—have emerged with especially insidious effects. Anorexia is characterized by a combination of self-starvation and extreme exercise; bulimia involves binging on massive quantities of food (as many as 10,000 calories worth a day), which are then thrown up before digestion. Despite acute electrolyte imbalances, heart arrhythmias, and muscle loss, afflicted women feel they cannot stop. The specter of being "visually deviant" (overweight) is too much to handle, so their destructive habits continue.

Intriguingly, it is the obsession with conformity that lies at the core of most eating disorders. In this sense, anorexics and bulimics are "positive deviants," confirmed by the fact that most are model citizens in every way imaginable. They lead upstanding lives. They are excellent students and employees. They are popular and socially successful. They maintain strong ties to family and community.

Getting thin and staying that way becomes not only a lifestyle choice, it becomes a fixation. All other concerns are dismissed in favor of the exclusive focus on eating, exercise, and (for bulimics) vomiting. Admonitions by others to stop may actually make things worse, reinforcing the label of anorexic or bulimic in ways that lead to further role engulfment. This is secondary deviance at its worst, the amplification of norm-breaking by virtue of the social reaction of others. Putting an end to "deviant careers" of this sort is extraordinarily difficult; it is possible only with the understanding, empathy, and support of fellow sufferers. Self-help groups may be the only viable method for getting rid of the label and breaking the cycle, an application of differential association theory in reverse.

Introduction

Current appearance norms stipulate thinness for women and muscularity for men; these expectations, like any norms, entail rewards for compliance and negative sanctions for violations. Fear of being overweight—of being visually deviant—has led to a striving for thinness, especially among women. In the extreme, this avoidance of overweight engenders eating disorders, which themselves constitute deviance. Anorexia nervosa, or purposeful starvation, embodies visual as well as behavioral deviation; bulimia, binge eating followed by vomiting and/or laxative abuse, is primarily behaviorally deviant.

Besides a fear of fatness, anorexics and bulimics exhibit distorted body images. In anorexia nervosa, a 20–25 percent loss of initial body weight occurs, resulting from self-starvation alone or in combination with excessive exercising, occasional binge-eating, vomiting and/or laxative abuse. Bulimia denotes cyclical (daily, weekly, for example) binge-eating followed by vomiting or laxative abuse; weight is normal or close to normal (Humphries et al., 1982). Common physical manifestations of these eating disorders include menstrual cessation or irregularities and electrolyte imbalances; among behavioral traits are depression, obsessions/compulsions, and anxiety (Russell, 1979; Thompson and Schwartz, 1982).

Increasingly prevalent in the past two decades, anorexia nervosa and bulimia have emerged as major health and social problems. Termed an epidemic on college campuses (Brody, as quoted in Schur, 1984: 76), bulimia affects 13% of college students (Halmi et al., 1981). Less prevalent, anorexia nervosa was diagnosed in 0.6% of students utilizing a university health center (Stangler and Printz, 1980). However, the overall mortality rate of anorexia nervosa is 6% (Schwartz and Thompson, 1981) to 20% (Humphries et al., 1982); bulimia appears to be less life-threatening (Russell, 1979).

Particularly affecting certain demographic groups, eating disorders are most prevalent among young, white, affluent (upper-middle to upper class) women in modern, industrialized countries (Crisp, 1977; Willi and Grossman, 1983). Combining all of these risk factors (female sex, youth, high socioeconomic status, and residence in an industrialized country), prevalence of anorexia nervosa in upper class English girls' schools is reported at 1 in 100 (Crisp et al., 1976). The age of onset for anorexia nervosa is bimodal at 14.5 and 18 years (Humphries et al., 1982); the most frequent age of onset for bulimia is 18 (Russell, 1979).

Eating disorders have primarily been studied from psychological and medical perspectives.[1] Theories of etiology have generally fallen into three categories: the ego psychological (involving an impaired child-maternal environment); the family systems (implicating enmeshed, rigid families); and the endocrinological (involving a precipitating hormonal defect). Although relatively ignored in previous studies, the sociocultural components of anorexia nervosa and bulimia (the slimness norm and its agents of reinforcement, such as role models) have been postulated as accounting for the recent, dramatic increases in these disorders (Schwartz et al., 1982; Boskind-White, 1985).[2]

Medical and psychological approaches to anorexia nervosa and bulimia obscure the social facets of the disorders and neglect the individuals' own definitions of their situations. Among the social processes involved in the development of an eating disorder is the sequence of conforming behavior, primary deviance, and secondary deviance. Societal reaction is the critical mediator affecting the movement through the deviant career (Becker, 1973). Within a framework of labeling theory, this study focuses on the emergence of anorexic and bulimic identities, as well as on the consequences of being career deviants.

Methodology

Sampling and Procedures

Most research on eating disorders has utilized clinical subjects or non-clinical respondents completing questionnaires. Such studies can be criticized for simply counting and describing behaviors and/or neglecting the social construction of the disorders. Moreover, the work of clinicians is often limited by therapeutic orientation. Previous research may also have included individuals who were not in therapy on their own volition and who resisted admitting that they had an eating disorder.

Past studies thus disregard the intersubjective meanings respondents attach to their behavior and emphasize researchers' criteria for definition as anorexic or bulimic. In order to supplement these sampling and procedural designs, the present study utilizes participant observation of a group of self-defined anorexics and bulimics.[3] As the individuals had acknowledged their eating disorders, frank discussion and disclosure were facilitated.

Data are derived from a self-help group, BANISH, Bulimics/Anorexics In Self-Help, which met at a university in an urban center of the mid-South. Founded by one of the researchers (D.E.T.), BANISH was advertised in local newspapers as offering a group experience for individuals who were anorexic or bulimic. Despite the local advertisements, the campus location of the meetings may have selectively encouraged university students to attend. Nonetheless, in view of the modal age of onset and socioeconomic status of individuals with eating disorders, college students have been considered target populations (Crisp et al., 1977; Halmi et al., 1981).

The group's weekly two-hour meetings were observed for two years. During the course of this study, thirty individuals attended at least one of the meetings. Attendance at meetings was varied: ten individuals came nearly every Sunday; five attended approximately twice a month; and the remaining fifteen participated once a month or less frequently, often when their eating problems were "more severe" or "bizarre." The modal number of members at meetings was twelve. The diversity in attendance was to be expected in self-help groups of anorexics and bulimics:

> . . .most people's involvement will not be forever or even a long time. Most people get the support they need and drop out. Some take the time to help others after they themselves have been helped but even they may withdraw after a time. It is a natural and in many cases *necessary* process . . .(emphasis in original) (American Anorexia/Bulimia Association, 1983).

Modeled after Alcoholics Anonymous, BANISH allowed participants to discuss their backgrounds and experiences with others who empathized. For many members, the group constituted their only source of help; these respondents were reluctant to contact health professionals because of shame, embarrassment, or financial difficulties.

In addition to field notes from group meetings, records of other encounters with all members were maintained. Participants visited the office of one of the researchers (D.E.T.), called both researchers by phone, and invited them to their homes or out for a cup of coffee. Such interaction facilitated genuine communication and mutual trust. Even among the fifteen individuals who did not attend the meetings regularly, contact was maintained with ten members on a monthly basis.

Supplementing field notes were informal interviews with fifteen group members, lasting from two to four hours. Because they appeared to represent more extensive experience with eating disorders, these interviewees were chosen to amplify their comments about the labeling process, made during group meetings. Conducted near the end of the two-year observation period, the interviews focused on what the respondents thought antedated and maintained their eating disorders. In addition, participants described others' reactions to their behaviors as well as their own interpretations of these reactions. To protect the confidentiality of individuals quoted in the study, pseudonyms are employed.

Description of Members

The demographic composite of the sample typifies what has been found in other studies (Fox and James, 1976; Crisp, 1977; Herzog, 1982; Schlesier-Stropp, 1984). Group members' ages ranged from nineteen to thirty-six, with the modal age being twenty-one. The respondents were white, and all but one were female. The sole male and three of the females were anorexic; the remaining females were bulimic.[4]

Primarily composed of college students, the group included four non-students, three of whom had college degrees. Nearly all members derived from upper-middle or lower-upper class households. Eighteen students and two non-students were never-marrieds and uninvolved in serious relationships; two non-students were married (one with two children); two students were divorced (one with two children); and six students were involved in serious relationships. The duration of eating disorders ranged from three to fifteen years.

Conforming Behavior

In the backgrounds of most anorexics and bulimics, dieting figures prominently, beginning in the teen years (Crisp, 1977; Johnson et al., 1982; Lacey et al., 1986). As dieters, these individuals are conformist in their adherence to the cultural norms emphasizing thinness (Garner et al., 1980; Schwartz et al., 1982). In our society, slim bodies are regarded as the most worthy and attractive; overweight is viewed as physically and morally unhealthy—"obscene," "lazy," "slothful," and "gluttonous" (DeJong, 1980; Ritenbaugh, 1982; Schwartz et al., 1982).

Among the agents of socialization promoting the slimness norm is advertising. Female models in newspaper, magazine, and television advertisements are uniformly slender. In addition, product names and slogans exploit the thin orientation; examples include "Ultra Slim Lipstick," "Miller Lite," and "Virginia Slims." While retaining pressures toward thinness, an Ayds commercial attempts a compromise for those wanting to savor food: "Ayds . . .so you can taste, chew, and enjoy, while you lose weight." Appealing particularly to women, a nationwide fast-food restaurant chain offers low-calorie selections, so individuals can have a "license to eat." In the latter two examples, the notion of enjoying food is combined with the message to be slim. Food and restaurant advertisements overall convey the pleasures of eating, whereas advertisements for other products, such as fashions and diet aids, reinforce the idea that fatness is undesirable.

Emphasis on being slim affects everyone in our culture, but it influences women especially because of society's traditional emphasis on women's appearance. The slimness norm and its concomitant narrow beauty standards exacerbate the objectification of women (Schur, 1984). Women view themselves as visual entities and recognize that conforming to appearance expectations and "becoming attractive object[s] [are] role obligation[s]" (Laws, as quoted in Schur, 1984: 66). Demonstrating the beauty motivation behind dieting, a recent Nielsen survey indicated that of the 56 percent of all women aged 24 to 54 who dieted during the previous year, 76 percent did so for cosmetic, rather than health, reasons (Schwartz et al., 1982). For most female group members, dieting was viewed as a means of gaining attractiveness and appeal to the opposite sex. The male respondent, as well, indicated that "when I was fat, girls didn't look at me, but when I got thinner, I was suddenly popular."

In addition to responding to the specter of obesity, individuals who develop anorexia nervosa and bulimia are conformist in their strong commitment to other conventional norms and goals. They consistently excel at school and work (Russell, 1979; Bruch, 1981; Humphries et al., 1982), maintaining high aspirations in both areas (Theander, 1970; Lacey et al., 1986). Group members generally completed college-preparatory courses in high school, aware from an early age that they would strive for a college degree. Also, in college as well as high school, respondents joined honor societies and academic clubs.

Moreover, pre-anorexics and -bulimics display notable conventionality as "model children" (Humphries et al., 1982: 199), "the pride and joy" of their parents (Bruch, 1981: 215), accommodating themselves to the wishes of others. Parents of these individuals emphasize conformity and value achievement (Bruch, 1981). Respondents felt that perfect or near-perfect grades were expected of them; however, good grades were not rewarded by parents, because "A's" were common for these children. In addition, their parents suppressed conflicts, to preserve the image of the "all-American family" (Humphries et al., 1982). Group members reported that they seldom, if ever, heard their parents argue or raise their voices.

Also conformist in their affective ties, individuals who develop anorexia nervosa and bulimia are strongly, even excessively, attached to their parents. Respondents' families appeared close-knit, demonstrating palpable emotional ties. Several group members, for example, reported habitually calling home at prescribed times, whether or not they had any news. Such families have been termed "enmeshed" and "overprotective," displaying intense interaction and concern for members' welfare (Minuchin et al., 1978; Selvini-Palazzoli, 1978). These qualities could be viewed as marked conformity to the norm of familial closeness.[5]

Another element of notable conformity in the family milieu of preanorexics and bulimics concerns eating, body weight/shape, and exercising (Kalucy et al., 1977; Humphries et al., 1982). Respondents reported their fathers' preoccupation with exercising and their mothers' engrossment in food preparation. When group members dieted and lost weight, they received an extraordinary amount of approval. Among the family, body size became a matter of "friendly rivalry." One bulimic informant recalled that she, her mother, and her coed sister all strived to wear a size 5, regardless of their heights and body frames. Subsequent to this study, the researchers learned that both the mother and sister had become bulimic.

As pre-anorexics and -bulimics, group members thus exhibited marked conformity to cultural norms of thinness, achievement, compliance, and parental attachment. Their families reinforced their conformity by adherence to norms of family closeness and weight/body shape consciousness.

Primary Deviance

Even with familial encouragement, respondents, like nearly all dieters (Chennin, 1981), failed to maintain their lowered weights. Many cited their lack of willpower to eat only restricted foods. For the emerging anorexics and bulimics, extremes such as purposeful starvation or binging accompanied by vomiting and/or laxative abuse appeared as "obvious solutions" to the problem of retaining weight loss. Associated with these behaviors was a regained feeling of control in lives that had been disrupted by a major crisis. Group members' extreme weight-loss efforts operated as coping mechanisms for entering college, leaving home, or feeling rejected by the opposite sex.

The primary inducement for both eating adaptations was the drive for slimness: with slimness came more self-respect and a feeling of superiority over "unsuccessful dieters." Brian, for example, experienced a "power trip" upon consistent weight loss through starvation. Binges allowed the purging respondents to cope with stress through eating while maintaining a slim appearance. As former strict dieters, Teresa and Jennifer used binging/purging as an alternative to the constant self-denial of starvation. Acknowledging their parents' desires for them to be slim, most respondents still felt it was a conscious choice on their part to continue extreme weight-loss efforts. Being thin became the "most important thing" in their lives—their "greatest ambition."

In explaining the development of an anorexic or bulimic identity, Lemert's (1951; 1967) concept of primary deviance is salient. Primary deviance refers to a transitory period of norm violations which do not affect an individual's self-concept or performance of social roles. Although respondents were exhibiting anorexic or bulimic behavior, they did not consider themselves to be anorexic or bulimic.

At first, anorexics' significant others complimented their weight loss, expounding on their new "sleekness" and "good looks." Branch and Eurman (1980: 631) also found anorexics' families and friends describing them as "well-groomed," "neat," "fashionable," and "victorious." Not until the respondents approached emaciation did some parents or friends become concerned and withdraw their praise. Significant others also became increasingly aware of the anorexics' compulsive exercising, preoccupation with food preparation (but not consumption), and ritualistic eating patterns (such as cutting food into minute pieces and eating only certain foods at prescribed times).

For bulimics, friends or family members began to question how the respondents could eat such large amounts of food (often in excess of 10,000 calories a day) and stay slim. Significant others also noticed calluses across the bulimics' hands, which were caused by repeated inducement of vomiting. Several bulimics were "caught in the act," bent over commodes. Generally, friends and family required substantial evidence before believing that the respondents' binging or purging was no longer sporadic.

Secondary Deviance

Heightened awareness of group members' eating behavior ultimately led others to label the respondents "anorexic" or "bulimic." Respondents differed in their histories of being labeled and accepting the labels. Generally first termed anorexic by friends, family, or medical personnel, the anorexics initially vigorously denied the label. They felt they were not "anorexic enough," not skinny enough; Robin did not regard herself as having the "skeletal" appearance she associated with anorexia nervosa. These group members found it difficult to differentiate between socially approved modes of weight loss—eating less and exercising more—and the extremes of those behaviors. In fact, many of their activities—cheerleading, modeling, gymnastics, aerobics—reinforced their pursuit of thinness. Like other anorexics, Chris felt she was being "ultrahealthy," with "total control" over her body.

For several respondents, admitting they were anorexic followed the realization that their lives were disrupted by their eating disorder. Anorexics' inflexible eating patterns unsettled family meals and holiday gatherings. Their regimented lifestyle of compulsively scheduled activities—exercising, school, and meals—precluded any spontaneous social interactions. Realization of their adverse behaviors preceded the anorexics' acknowledgment of their subnormal body weight and size.

Contrasting with anorexics, the binge/purgers, when confronted, more readily admitted that they were bulimic and that their means of weight loss was "abnormal." Teresa, for example, knew "very well" that her bulimic behavior was "wrong and unhealthy," although "worth the physical risks." While the bulimics initially maintained that their purging was only a temporary weight-loss method, they eventually realized that their disorder represented a "loss of control." Although these respondents regretted the self-indulgence, "shame," and "wasted time," they acknowledged their growing dependence on binging/purging for weight management and stress regulation.

The application of anorexic or bulimic labels precipitated secondary deviance, wherein group members internalized these identities. Secondary deviance refers to norm violations which are a response to society's labeling: "secondary deviation . . .becomes a means of social defense, attack or adaptation to the overt and covert problems created by the societal reaction to primary deviance" (Lemert, 1967: 17). In contrast to primary deviance, secondary deviance is generally prolonged, alters the individual's self-concept, and affects the performance of his/her social roles.

As secondary deviants, respondents felt that their disorders "gave a purpose" to their lives. Nicole resisted attaining a normal weight because it was not "her"—she accepted her anorexic weight as her "true" weight. For Teresa, bulimia became a "companion"; and Julie felt "every aspect of her life," including time management and social activities, was affected by her bulimia. Group members' eating disorders became the salient element of their self-concepts, so that they related to familiar people and new acquaintances as anorexics or bulimics. For example, respondents regularly compared their body shapes and sizes with those of others. They also became sensitized to comments about their appearance, whether or not the remarks were made by someone aware of their eating disorder.

With their behavior increasingly attuned to their eating disorders, group members exhibited role engulfment (Schur, 1971). Through accepting anorexic or bulimic identities, individuals centered activities around their deviant role, downgrading other social roles. Their obligations as students, family members, and friends became subordinate to their eating and exercising rituals. Socializing, for example, was gradually curtailed because it interfered with compulsive exercising, binging, or purging.

Labeled anorexic or bulimic, respondents were ascribed a new status with a different set of role expectations. Regardless of other positions the individuals occupied, their deviant status, or master status (Hughes, 1958; Becker, 1973), was identified before all others. Among group members, Nicole, who was known as the "school's brain," became known as the "school's anorexic." No longer viewed as conforming model individuals, some respondents were termed "starving waifs" or "pigs."

Because of their identities as deviants, anorexics' and bulimics' interactions with others were altered. Group members' eating habits were scrutinized by friends and family and used as a "catch-all" for everything negative that happened to them. Respondents felt self-conscious around individuals who knew of their disorders; for example, Robin imagined people "watching and whispering" behind her. In addition, group members believed others expected them to "act" anorexic or bulimic. Friends of some anorexic group members never offered them food or drink, assuming continued disinterest on the respondents' part. While being hospitalized, Denise felt she had to prove to others she was not still vomiting, by keeping her bathroom door open. Other bulimics, who lived in dormitories, were hesitant to use the restroom for normal purposes lest several friends be huddling at the door, listening for vomiting. In general, individuals interacted with the respondents largely on the basis of their eating disorder; in doing so, they reinforced anorexic and bulimic behaviors.

Bulimic respondents, whose weight-loss behavior was not generally detectable from their appearance, tried earnestly to hide their bulimia by binging and purging in secret. Their main purpose in concealment was to avoid the negative consequences of being known as a bulimic. For these individuals, bulimia connoted a "cop-out": like "weak anorexics," bulimics pursued thinness but yielded to urges to eat. Respondents felt other people regarded bulimia as "gross" and had little sympathy for the sufferer. To avoid these stigmas or "spoiled identities," the bulimics shrouded their behaviors.

Distinguishing types of stigma, Goffman (1963) describes discredited (visible) stigmas and discreditable (invisible) stigmas. Bulimics, whose weight was approximately normal or even slightly elevated, harbored discreditable stigmas. Anorexics, on the other hand, suffered both discreditable and discredited stigmas—the latter due to their emaciated appearance. Certain anorexics were more reconciled than the bulimics to their stigmas: for Brian, the "stigma of anorexia was better than the stigma of being fat." Common to the stigmatized individuals was an inability to interact spontaneously with others. Respondents were constantly on guard against topics of eating and body size.

Both anorexics and bulimics were held responsible by others for their behavior and presumed able to "get out of it if they tried." Many anorexics reported being told to "just eat more," while bulimics were enjoined to simply "stop eating so much." Such appeals were made without regard for the complexities of the problem. Ostracized by certain friends and family members, anorexics and bulimics felt increasingly isolated. For respondents, the self-help group presented a non-threatening forum for discussing their disorders. Here, they found mutual understanding, empathy, and support. Many participants viewed BANISH as a haven from stigmatization by "others."

Group members, as secondary deviants, thus endured negative consequences, such as stigmatization, from being labeled. As they internalized the labels anorexic or bulimic, individuals' self-concepts were significantly influenced. When others interacted with the respondents on the basis of their eating disorders, anorexic or bulimic identities were encouraged. Moreover, group members' efforts to counteract the deviant labels were thwarted by their master statuses.

Discussion

Previous research on eating disorders has dwelt almost exclusively on medical and psychological facets. Although necessary for a comprehensive understanding of anorexia nervosa and bulimia, these approaches neglect the social processes involved. The phenomena of eating disorders transcend concrete disease entities and clinical diagnoses. Multifaceted and complex, anorexia nervosa and bulimia require a holistic research design, in which sociological insights must be included.

A limitation of medical/psychiatric studies, in particular, is researchers' use of a priori criteria in establishing salient variables. Rather than utilizing predetermined standards of inclusion, the present study allows respondents to construct their own reality. Concomitant to this innovative approach to eating disorders is the selection of a sample of self-admitted anorexics and bulimics. Individuals' perceptions of what it means to become anorexic or bulimic are explored. Although based on a small sample, findings can be used to guide researchers in other settings.

With only five to ten percent of reported cases appearing in males (Crisp, 1977; Stangler and Printz, 1980), eating disorders are primarily a women's aberrance. The deviance of anorexia nervosa and bulimia is rooted in the visual objectification of women and attendant slimness norm. Indeed, purposeful starvation and binging/purging reinforce the notion that "a society gets the deviance it deserves" (Schur, 1979: 71). As recently noted (Schur, 1984), the sociology of deviance has generally bypassed systematic studies of women's norm violations. Like male deviants, females endure label applications, internalizations, and fulfillments.

The social processes involved in developing anorexic or bulimic identities comprise the sequence of conforming behavior, primary deviance, and secondary deviance. With a background of exceptional adherence to conventional norms, especially the striving for thinness, respondents subsequently exhibit the primary deviance of starving or binging/purging. Societal reaction to these behaviors leads to secondary deviance, wherein respondents' self-concepts and master statuses become anorexic or bulimic. Within this framework of labeling theory, the persistence of eating disorders, as well as the effects of stigmatization, is elucidated.

Although during the course of this research some respondents alleviated their symptoms through psychiatric help or hospital treatment programs, no one was labeled "cured." An anorexic is considered recovered when weight is normal for two years; a bulimic is termed recovered after being symptom-free for one and one-half years (American Anorexia/Bulimia Association Newsletter, 1985). Thus deviance disavowal (Schur, 1971), or efforts after normalization to counteract the deviant labels, remains a topic for future exploration.

Notes

1. Although instructive, an integration of the medical, psychological, and sociocultural perspectives on eating disorders is beyond the scope of this paper.

2. Exceptions to the neglect of sociocultural factors are discussions of sex-role socialization in the development of eating disorders. Anorexics' girlish appearance has been interpreted as a rejection of femininity and womanhood (Orbach, 1979; Bruch, 1981; Orbach, 1985). In contrast, bulimics have been characterized as overconforming to traditional female sex roles (Boskind-Lodahl, 1976).

3. Although a group experience for self-defined bulimics has been reported (Boskind-Lodahl, 1976), the researcher, from the outset, focused on Gestalt and behaviorist techniques within a feminist orientation.

4. One explanation for fewer anorexics than bulimics in the sample is that, in the general population, anorexics are outnumbered by bulimics at 8 or 10 to 1 (Lawson, as reprinted in American Anorexia/Bulimia Association Newsletter, 1985: 1). The proportion of bulimics to anorexics in the sample is 6.5 to 1. In addition, compared to bulimics, anorexics may be less likely to attend a self-help group as they have a greater tendency to deny the existence of an eating problem (Humphries et al., 1982). However, the four anorexics in the present study were among the members who attended the meetings most often.

5. Interactions in the families of anorexics and bulimics might seem deviant in being inordinately close. However, in the larger societal context, the family members epitomize the norms of family cohesiveness. Perhaps unusual in their occurrence, these families are still within the realm of conformity. Humphries and colleagues (1982: 202) refer to the "highly enmeshed and protective" family as part of the "idealized family myth."

References

American Anorexia/Bulimia Association. 1983. Correspondence. April.

American Anorexia/Bulimia Association Newsletter. 1985. 8(3).

Becker, Howard S. 1973. Outsiders. New York: Free Press.

Boskind-Lodahl, Marlene. 1976. "Cinderella's stepsisters: A feminist perspective on anorexia nervosa and bulimia." *Signs, Journal of Women in Culture and Society* 2: 342–56.

Boskind-White, Marlene. 1985. "Bulimarexla: A sociocultural perspective." In S. W. Eimnett (ed.), *Theory and Treatment of Anorexia Nervosa and Bulimia: Biomedical, Sociocultural and Psychological Perspectives* (pp. 113–26). New York: Brunner/Mazel.

Branch, C. H. Hardin, and Linda J. Eurman. 1980. "Social attitudes toward patients with anorexia nervosa." *American Journal of Psychiatry* 137: 631–32.

Bruch, Hilde. 1981. "Developmental consideratlons of anorexia nervosa and obesity." *Canadian Journal of Psychiatry* 26:212–16.

Chennin, Kim. 1981. The Obsession: Reflections on the Tyranny of Slenderness. New York: Harper and Row.

Crisp, A. H. 1977. "The prevalence of anorexia nervosa and some of its associations in the general population." *Advances in Psychosomatic Medicine* 9: 38–47.

Crisp, A. H., R. L. Palmer, and R. S Kalucy 1976. "How common is anorexia nervosa? A prevalence study." *British Journal of psychiatry* 128:549–54.

DeJong, William. 1980. "The stigma of obesity: The consequences of naive assumptions concerning the causes of physical deviance." *Journal of Health and Social Behavior* 21: 75–87.

Fox, K. C., and N. McI. James. 1976. "Anorexia nervosa: A study of 44 strictly defined cases." *New Zealand Medical Journal* 84: 309–12.

Garner, David M., Paul E. Garfinkel, Donald Schwartz, and Michael Thompson. 1980. "Cultural expectations of thinness in women." *Psychological Reports* 47: 483–91.

Goffman, Erving. 1963. *Stigma*. Englewood Cliffs, NJ: Prentice Hall.

Halmi, Kathenne A., James R. Falk, and Estelle Schwartz. 1981. "Binge-eating and vomiting: A survey of a college population." *Psychological Medicine* 11:697–706.

Herzog, David B. 1982. "Bulimia: The secretive syndrome." *Psychosomatics* 23: 481–83.

Hughes, Everett C. 1958. *Men and Their Work*. New York: Free Press.

Humphries, Laurie L., Sylvia Wrobel, and H. Thomas Wiegert. 1982. "Anorexia nervosa." *American Family Physician* 26: 199–204.

Johnson, Craig L., Marilyn K. Stuckey, Linda D. Lewis, and Donald M. Schwartz. 1982. "Bulimia: A descriptive survey of 316 cases." *International Journal of Eating Disorders* 2(1): 3–16.

Kalucy, R. S., A. H. Crisp, and Britta Harding. 1977. "A study of 56 families with anorexia nervosa." *British Journal of Medical Psychology* 50: 381–95.

Lacey, Hubert J., Sian Coker, and S. A. Birtchnell. 1986. "Bulimia: Factors associated with its etiology and maintenance." *International Journal of Eating Disorders* 5: 475–87.

Lemert, Edwin M. 1951. *Social Pathology*. New York: McGraw-Hill.

———. 1967. *Human Deviance, Social Problems and Social Control*. Englewood Cliffs, NJ: Prentice Hall.

Minuchin, Salvador, Bernice L. Rosman, and Lester Baker. 1978. *Psychosomatic Families: Anorexia Nervosa in Context*. Cambridge, MA: Harvard University Press.

Orbach, Susie. 1979. *Fat Is a Feminist Issue*. New York: Berkeley.

———. 1985. "Visibility/invisibility: Social considerations in anorexia nervosa—a feminist perspective." In S. W. Emmett (ed.), *Theory and Treatment of Anorexia Nervosa and Bulimia: Biomedical, Sociocultural, and Psychological Perspectives* (pp. 127–38). New York: Brunner/Mazel.

Ritenbaugh, Cheryl. 1982. "Obesity as a culture-bound syndrome." *Culture, Medicine and Psychiatry* 6: 347–61.

Russell, Gerald. 1979. "Bulimia nervosa: An ominous variant of anorexia nervosa." *Psychological Medicine* 9: 429–48.

Schlesier-Stropp, Barbara. 1984. "Bulimia: A review of the literature." *Psychological Bulletin* 95: 247–57.

Schur, Edwin M. 1971. *Labeling Deviant Behavior.* New York: Harper and Row.

——. 1979. *Interpreting Deviance: A Sociological Introduction.* New York: Harper and Row.

——. 1984. *Labeling Women Deviant: Gender, Stigma, and Social Control.* New York: Random House.

Schwartz, Donald M., and Michael G. Thompson. 1981. "Do anoretics get well? Current research and future needs." *American Journal of Psychiatry* 138: 319–23.

Schwartz, Donald M., Michael G. Thompson, and Craig L. Johnson. 1982. "Anorexia nervosa and bulimia: The socio-cultural context." *International Journal of Eating Disorders* 1(3): 20–36.

Selvini-Palazzoli, Mara. 1978. *Self-Starvation: From Individual to Family Therapy in the Treatment of Anorexia Nervosa.* New York: Jason Aronson.

Stangler, Ronnie S., and Adolph M. Printz. 1980. "DSM-III: Psychiatric diagnosis in a university population." *American Journal of Psychiatry* 137: 937–40.

Theander, Sten. 1970. "Anorexia nervosa." *Acta Psychiatrica Scandinavica Supplement* 214: 24–31.

Thompson, Michael G., and Donald M. Schwartz. 1982. "Life adjustment of women with anorexia nervosa and anorexic-like behavior." *International Journal of Eating Disorders* 1(2): 47–60.

Willi, Jurg, and Samuel Grossman. 1983. "Epidemiology of anorexia nervosa in a defined region of Switzerland." *American Journal of Psychiatry* 140: 564–67.

47
Becoming a Shoplifter

The Seductions of Deviance

Jack Katz

Economic deviance—rule-breaking moti-vated by material reward—is often explained in terms of greed or need. This makes perfect sense. People who have money typically crave more; people with pressing fiscal deficits typi-cally want them removed as quickly as possi-ble. Yet even the most instrumental acts of eco-nomic deviance frequently have a strong ex-pressive component to them. Taking some-thing of value from someone else without their knowledge or consent is intrinsically reward-ing and can provide a high that rivals the most powerful of psychoactive drugs. The psychic benefits of economic deviance may even sur-pass the material rewards.

Katz explores these so-called "seductions of crime" and their influence on deviant identity formation (using shoplifters as a case study). Shoplifting, he contends, is a solitary offense but one rife with social and transactional over-tones; without the possibility of getting caught, there would be no motivation to steal. The of-fense becomes a dance with danger, and the thrill comes from successfully neutralizing the efforts of those with the power to detect and punish. Indeed, the items that shoplifters steal are often insignificant or worthless. The re-ward comes from "getting over," from stealing for stealing's sake. Katz offers an emotional perspective on deviance, one that underscores the motivating power of gamesmanship and personal challenge in its commission.

People are social creatures. Definitions of self are not possible in a social vacuum, and identities must be constructed and affirmed in a process of interaction. Most of the articles in this section center on the management and neutralization of discrediting information, in-formation that if exposed would spoil an oth-erwise conventional self-image. "Passing" is a central theme, with deviants sometimes tak-ing extraordinary measures to avoid negative attributions. Katz approaches from the oppo-site angle, exploring how ostensibly nondeviant individuals seize deviant opportu-nities to transcend labels.

Various property crimes share an appeal to young people, independent of material gain or esteem from peers. Vandalism defaces property without satisfying a desire for ac-quisition. During burglaries, young people sometimes break in and exit successfully but do not try to take anything. Youthful shop-lifting, especially by older youths, often is a solitary activity retained as a private mem-ory.[1] "Joyriding" captures a form of auto theft in which getting away with something in celebratory style is more important than keeping anything or getting anywhere in particular.

In upper-middle-class settings, material needs are often clearly insufficient to ac-count for the fleeting fascination with theft, as the account by one of my students illus-trates:

[82] I grew up in a neighborhood where at 13 everyone went to Israel, at 16 everyone got a car and after high school graduation we were all sent off to Europe for the summer....I was 14 and my neighbor was 16. He had just gotten a red Firebird for his birthday and we went driving around. We just happened to drive past the local pizza place and we saw the delivery boy getting into his car....We could see the pizza boxes in his back seat. When the pizza boy pulled into a high rise apart-ment complex, we were right behind him. All of a sudden, my neighbor said, "You know, it would be so easy to take a pizza!".....I looked at him, he looked at me, and without saying a word I was out of the door. . . .got a pizza and ran back....(As I remember, neither of us was hungry, but the pizza was the best we'd ever eaten.)

It is not the taste for pizza that leads to the crime; the crime makes the pizza tasty.

Qualitative accounts of *initial* experiences in property crime by the poorest ghetto youths also show an exciting attraction that cannot be explained by material necessity. John Allen, whose career as a stickup man living in a Washington, D.C., ghetto . . . recalled his first crime as stealing comic books from a junkyard truck: "we destroyed things and took a lot of junk—flashlights, telephones." These things only occasionally would be put to use; if they were retained at all, they would be kept more as souvenirs, items that had acquired value from the theft, than as items needed before and used after the theft.[2]

What are these wealthy and poor young property criminals trying to do? A common thread running through vandalism, joyriding, and shoplifting is that all are sneaky crimes that frequently thrill their practitioners. Thus I take as a phenomenon to be explained the commission of a nonviolent property crime as a sneaky thrill.

In addition to materials collected by others, my analysis is based on 122 self-reports of university students in my criminology courses.[3] Over one-half were instances of shoplifting, mostly female; about one-quarter described vandalism, almost all male; and the rest reported drug sales, nonmercenary housebreaking, and employee theft. In selecting quotations, I have emphasized reports of female shoplifters, largely because they were the most numerous and sensitively written.

The sneaky thrill is created when a person (1) tacitly generates the experience of being seduced to deviance, (2) reconquers her emotions in a concentration dedicated to the production of normal appearances, (3) and then appreciates the reverberating significance of her accomplishment in a euphoric thrill. After examining the process of constructing the phenomenon, I suggest that we rethink the relationships of age and social class to devious property crime.

Flirting With the Project

In the students' accounts there is a recurrent theme of items stolen and then quickly abandoned or soon forgotten. More generally, even when retained and used later, the booty somehow seems especially valuable while it is in the store, in the neighbor's house; or in the parent's pocketbook. To describe the changing nature of the object in the person's experience, we should say that once it is removed from the protected environment, the object quickly loses much of its charm.

During the initial stage of constructing a sneaky thrill, it is more accurate to say that the objective is to be taken or struck by an object than to take or strike out at it. In most of the accounts of shoplifting, the shoplifters enter with the idea of stealing but usually do not have a particular object in mind.[4] Indeed, shoplifters often make legitimate purchases during the same shopping excursions in which they steal. The entering mood is similar to that which often guides juveniles into the short journeys or sprees that result in pranks and vandalism.[5] Vandals and pranksters often play with conventional appearances; for example, when driving down local streets, they may issue friendly greetings one moment and collectively drop their pants ("moon") to shock the citizenry the next. The event begins with a markedly deviant air, the excitement of which is due partly to the understanding that the occurrence of theft or vandalism will be left to inspirational circumstance, creative perception, and innovative technique. Approaching a protected property with disingenuous designs, the person must be drawn to a particular object to steal or vandalize, in effect, inviting particular objects to seduce him or her. The would-be offender is not hysterical; he or she will not be governed by an overriding impulse that arises without any anticipation. But the experience is not simply utilitarian and practical; it is eminently magical.

Magical Environments

In several of the students' recountings of their thefts, the imputation of sensual power to the object is accomplished anthropomorphically. By endowing a thing with human sensibilities, one's reason can be overpowered by it. To the *Alice in Wonderland* quoted below, a necklace first enticed—"I found the one that outshone the rest and begged me to take it"—and then appeared to speak.

[15] There we were, in the most lucrative department Mervyn's had to offer two curious (but very mature) adolescent girls: the cosmetic and jewelry department. . . .We didn't enter the store planning to steal anything. In fact, I believe we had "given it up" a few weeks earlier; but once my eyes caught sight of the beautiful white and blue necklaces alongside the counter, a spark inside me was once again ignited. . . .Those exquisite puka necklaces were calling out to me, "Take me! Wear me! I can be yours!" All I needed to do was take them to make it a reality.

Another young shoplifter endowed her booty, also a necklace, with the sense of hearing. Against all reason, it took her; then, with a touch of fear, she tossed it aside in an attempt to exorcise the black magic and reduce it to a lifeless thing.

[56] I remember walking into the store and going directly to the jewelry stand. . . .This is very odd in itself, being that I am what I would consider a clothes person with little or no concern for accessories. . . .Once at home about 40–45 minutes after leaving the store, I looked at the necklace. I said "You could have gotten me in a lot of trouble" and I threw it in my jewelry box. I can't remember the first time I wore the necklace but I know it was a very long time before I put it on.

The pilferer's experience of seduction often takes off from an individualizing imputation. Customers typically enter stores, not to buy a thing they envisioned in its particularities but with generic needs in mind. A purchased item may not be grasped phenomenally as an individualized thing until it is grasped physically. Often, the particular ontology that a possession comes to exhibit—the charm of a favorite hat or an umbrella regarded as a treasure—will not exist while the item sits in a store with other like items; the item will come to have charm only after it has been incorporated into the purchaser's life—only when the brim is shaped to a characteristic angle or the umbrella becomes weathered. But the would-be thief manages to bring the particular charm of an object into existence before she possesses it. Seduction is experienced as an influence emanating from a particular necklace, compact, or chapstick, even though the particular object one is drawn to may not be distinguishable from numerous others near it.

In some accounts, the experience of seduction suggests a romantic encounter. Objects sometimes have the capacity to trigger "love at first sight."[6] Seduction is an elaborate process that begins with enticement and turns into compulsion. As a woman in her mid-thirties recalled:

A gold-plated compact that I had seen on a countertop kept playing on my mind. Heaven knows I didn't need it, and at $40 it was obviously overpriced. Still, there was something about the design that intrigued me. I went back to the counter and picked up the compact again. At that moment, I felt an overwhelming urge.[7]

Participant accounts often suggest the image of lovers catching each other's eyes across a crowded room and entering an illicit conspiracy. The student next quoted initially imagines herself in control and the object as passive—she is moving to put it in her possession; but at the end of her imagining, the object has the power to bring her pocket to life.

[67] I can see what I want to steal in plain sight, with no one in the aisle of my target. It would be so easy for me to get to the chapstick without attracting attention and simply place it in my pocket. . . .I'm not quite sure why I must have it, but I must. . . .

Some of the details that would make the deviant project hard or easy really are not up to the would-be shoplifter. In part the facility of the project is a matter of environmental arrangements for which she has no responsibility. While she is appreciating the object as a possible object of theft, she considers it at a particular angle. She will approach it from this side, with her back to that part of the scene, taking hold of it at just that part of its surface. In her experience that "It would be so easy," she is mobilizing herself to concentrate on the tangible details of the object. Thus the would-be shoplifter's sense of the facility of the project is constituted not as a feature of her "intent" or mental plan, but as a result of the position of the object in the store and the posture the object takes toward her.

To specify further how the would-be shoplifter endows the inanimate world with a real power to move her, we might consider why the initial stage of magical provocation is part of the project of sneaky thrills and not of other, equally fascinating, forms of deviance. Not all projects in deviance begin with the seductive sense, "It would be so easy." Indeed, some projects in deviance that are especially attractive to young people begin with an appreciation of the difficulties in becoming seduced to them. . . .

As the budding shoplifting project brings the object of deviance to life, the person and the object enter a conspiratorial relationship. "It would be so easy" contains a touch of surprise in the sudden awareness that no one else would notice. The tension of attraction/hesitation in moving toward the object is experienced within a broader awareness of how others are interpreting one's desires. For all *they* know, one's purposes are moral and the scene will remain mundane. The person's situational involvement in sneaky property crimes begins with a *sensual concentration on the boundary between the self as known from within and as seen from without. . . .*

The Reemergence of Practiced Reason

Independent of the would-be shoplifter's construction of a sense that she might get away with it are any number of contingencies that can terminate the process. For example, the sudden attentions of a clerk may trigger an intimidating awareness of the necessity to produce "normal appearances."[8]

At some point on the way toward all sneaky thrills, the person realizes that she must work to maintain a conventional, calm appearance up to and through the point of exit. The timing of this stage, relative to others in the process, is not constant. The tasks of constructing normal appearances may be confronted only after the act is complete; thus, during the last steps of an escape, vandals may self-consciously slacken their pace from a run to normal walking, and joyriders may slow down only when they finally abandon the stolen car.

In shoplifting, the person occasionally becomes fascinated with particular objects to steal only after appreciating an especially valuable resource for putting on normal appearances. In the following recollection of one of my students, the resource was a parent:

[19] I can clearly remember when we coaxed my mom into taking us shopping with the excuse that our summer trip was coming up & we just wanted to see what the stores had so we could plan on getting it later. We walked over to the section that we were interested in, making sure that we made ourselves seem "legitimate" by keeping my mom close & by showing her items that appealed to us. We thought "they won't suspect us, two girls in school uniforms with their mom, no way." As we carried on like this, playing this little game, "Oh, look how pretty, gee, I'll have to tell Dad about all these pretty things."

Eventually a necklace became irresistible.

Whichever comes first, the pull of the person toward the object to be stolen or the person's concentration on devices for deception, to enact the theft the person must bracket her appearance to set it off from her experience of her appearance, as this student's account shows:

[19] My shoplifting experiences go back to high school days when it was kind of an adventurous thing to do. My best friend & I couldn't walk into a store without getting that familiar grin on our faces. . . .Without uttering a word, we'd check out the place. . . .The whole process pretty much went about as if we were really "shopping" except in our minds the whole scene was different because of our paranoia & our knowledge of our real intentions.

Sensing a difference between what appears to be going on and what is "really" going on, the person focuses intently on normal interactional tasks. Everyday matters that have always been easily handled now rise to the level of explicit consciousness and seem subtle and complex. The thief asks herself, "How long does a normal customer spend at a particular counter?" "Do innocent customers look around to see if others are watching them?" "When customers leave a store, do they usually have their heads up or down?" The recognition that all these questions cannot possibly be answered correctly further stimulates self-consciousness. As one student expressed it,

> [19] Now, somehow no matter what the reality is, whether the salesperson is looking at you or not, the minute you walk in the store you feel as if it's written all over your face "Hi, I'm your daily shoplifter."

Unless the person achieves this second stage of appreciating the work involved—if she proceeds to shoplift with a relaxed sense of ease—she may get away in the end but not with the peculiar celebration of the sneaky thrill. Novice shoplifters, however, find it easy to accomplish the sense that they are faced with a prodigious amount of work. "Avoiding suspicion" is a challenge that seems to haunt the minute details of behavior with an endless series of questions—How fast should one walk? Do customers usually take items from one department to another without paying? and so on.

To construct normal appearances, the person must attempt a sociological analysis of the local interactional order. She employs folk theories to explain the contingencies of clerk-customer interactions and to guide the various practical tasks of the theft. On how to obscure the moment of illicit taking:

> [44] The jewelry counter at Nordstroms was the scene of the crime. . . .I proceeded to make myself look busy as I tried on several pairs of earrings. My philosophy was that the more busy you look the less conspicuous.

On where to hide the item:

> [15] Karen and I were inside the elevator now. As she was telling me to quickly put the necklace into my purse or bag, I did a strange thing. I knelt down, pulled up my pants leg, and slipped the necklace into

my sock! I remember insisting that my sock was the safest and smartest place to hide my treasure. I knew if I put it in an obvious place and was stopped, I'd be in serious trouble. Besides, packages belonging to young girls are usually subject to suspicion.

Some who shoplift clothes think it will fool the clerks if they take so many items into a dressing room that an observer could not easily keep count, as this student recalled:

> [5] We went into a clothing shop, selected about six garments a piece (to confuse the sales people), entered separate dressing rooms and stuffed one blouse each into our bags.

Others, like the following student, think it sufficiently strategic to take two identical garments in, cover one with the other, and emerge with only one visible:

> [46] We'd always take two of the same item & stuff one inside the other to make it seem like we only had one.

Many hit on the magician's sleight of hand, focusing the clerk's attentions on an item that subsequently will be returned to hide their possession of another.

> [56] [While being watched by a clerk] I was now holding the green necklace out in the open to give the impression that I was trying to decide whether to buy it or not. Finally, after about 2 minutes I put the green necklace back but I balled the brown necklace up in my right hand and placed my jacket over that hand.

In its dramatic structure, the experience of sneak theft has multiple emotional peaks as the thief is exposed to a series of challenges to maintaining a normal appearance. The length of the series varies with the individual and the type of theft, but, typically, there are several tests of the transparency of the thief's publicly visible self, as one student indicated:

> [122] I can recall a sneak theft at Penny's Dept. store very well. I was about 12 years old. . . .I found an eyeshadow kit. I could feel my heart pounding as I glanced around to make sure that others weren't watching. I quickly slipped the

eyeshadow in my purse and sighed heavily with relief when I realized that no one had seen. I nervously stepped out of the aisle and once again was relieved when I saw that there was no one around the corner waiting to catch me. I caught my friend's eye; she gave me a knowing glance and we walked to the next section in self satisfaction for having succeeded so far.

When the person devises the deviant project in advance, even entering the store normally may be an accomplishment. Having entered without arousing suspicion, the would-be shoplifter may relax slightly. Then tension mounts as she seizes the item. Dressing rooms provide an escape from the risk of detection, but only momentarily, as in this student's account:

[19] So, here we were, looking at things, walking around & each time getting closer to the dressing room. Finally we entered it & for once I remember feeling relieved for the first time since I'd walked into the store because I was away at last from those "piercing eyes" & I had the merchandise with me. At this point we broke into laughter. . . .We stuffed the items in our purses making sure that they had no security gadgets on them & then we thought to ourselves "well we're half way there." Then it hit me, how I was safe in the dressing room, no one could prove anything. I was still a "legitimate" shopper.

Then a salesperson may come up and, with an unsuspecting remark, raise the question of transparency to new heights:

[19] I remember coming out of the dressing room & the sales lady looking at me & asking me if I had found anything (probably concerned with only making her commission). I thought I would die.

Finally there is the drama of leaving the store:

[19] Walking out the door was always a big, big step. We knew that that's when people get busted as they step out & we just hoped & prayed that no one would run up to us & grab us or scream "hey you"! The whole time as we approached the exit I remember looking at it as a dark

tunnel & just wanting to run down it & disappear as I hung on to my "beloved purse."

Once they have hidden the booty and so long as they are in the store, the would-be-shoplifters must constantly decide to sustain their deviance. Thus, the multiple boundaries of exposure offer multiple proofs not only of their ability to get away with it but of their will toward immorality:

[5] We went into the restroom before we left and I remember telling Lori, "We can drop all this stuff in here and leave, or we can take it with us." Lori wanted to take everything, and as we neared the exit, I began to get very nervous.

Many of these shoplifters understand that clerks or store detectives may be watching them undercover, in preparation for arresting them at the exit door. They also believe that criminal culpability is only established when they leave with the stolen goods. As they understand it, they are not irretrievably committed to be thieves until they are on the other side of the exit; up to that point, they may replace the goods and instantly revert from a deviant to a morally unexceptional status. Were they to believe that they were criminally culpable as soon as they secreted the item, they would continue to face the interactional and emotional challenges of accomplishing deception. But because they think they are not committed legally until they are physically out of the store, they experience each practical challenge in covering up their deviance as an occasion to reaffirm their spiritual fortitude for being deviant. One student described the phenomenon this way:

[56] I guess I had been there so long that I started to look suspicious. I was holding a bright lime green necklace in my left hand and a brown Indian type necklace in my right. A lady, she must have been the store manager, was watching me. She was about 20 ft. away from me and on my left. I could feel her looking at me but I didn't look directly at her. . . .I remember actually visualizing myself putting back both the necklaces and walking out the store with pride and proving this bitch she was wrong and that I was smarter

than her, but I didn't. . . .I started out the store very slowly. I even smiled at the lady as I passed by the cash register. It was then that she started toward me and my mind said okay T. what are you going to do now. There was a table full of sweaters on sale near me and I could have easily drop the necklace on the table and continued out the door. I knew I could and I considered it but I wouldn't do it. I remember just holding the necklace tighter in my right hand. As she was coming toward me I even thought of dropping the necklace and running out the door but I continued in a slow pace even though the thought of them calling my mother if I was caught and what she would do to me was terribly frightening.

In addition to focusing on the practical components of producing a normal appearance, the would-be shoplifter struggles not to betray the difficulty of the project. This is the second layer of work—the work of appearing not to work at practicing normal appearances. The first layer of work is experienced as the emergence of a novel, analytical attention to behavioral detail; the second, as a struggle to remain in rational control, as the following statement by a student illustrates:

[19] You desperately try to cover it up by trying to remember how you've acted before but still you feel as if all eyes are on you! I think, that's the purpose of settling in one area & feeling everything & everyone out. It's an attempt to feel comfortable so that you don't appear obvious. Like maybe if I'm real cool & subtle about it & try on a few things but don't seem impressed w/ anything, I can just stroll out of here & no one will notice. . . .

Being Thrilled

Usually after the scene of risk is successfully exited, the third stage of the sneaky thrill is realized. This is the euphoria of being thrilled. In one form or another, there is a "Wow, I got away with it!" or an "It was so easy!" A necklace shoplifter stated:

[56] Once outside the door I thought Wow! I pulled it off, I faced danger and I pulled it off. I was smiling so much and I

felt at that moment like there was nothing I couldn't do.

After stealing candy with friends, another student recalled:

[87] Once we were out the door we knew we had been successful! We would run up the street . . .all be laughing and shouting, each one trying to tell just how he pulled it off and the details that would make each of us look like the bravest one.

The pizza thief noted:

[82] The feeling I got from taking the pizza, the thrill of getting something for nothing, knowing I got away with something I never thought I could, was wonderful. . . .I'm 21 now and my neighbor is 23. Every time we see each other, I remember and relive a little bit of that thrill. . . .

In a literal sense, the successful thieves were being thrilled: they shuddered or shook in elation, often to the rhythms of laughter. For many, whether successful or not, the experience of youthful shoplifting was profoundly moving, so moving that they could vividly recall minute details of the event years later. . . .

Notes

1. In her study of some 4,600 shoplifters arrested by detectives in a Chicago department store, Mary Cameron found that all the female shoplifters who were arrested at age 10 were shoplifting in groups, but 85 percent of the 19-year-olds who were arrested had been alone. She concluded that shoplifting becomes progressively more a solitary activity with age. See Mary Cameron, *The Booster and the Snitch* (New York: Free Press, 1964), pp. 102–3.

2. John Allen, *Assault with a Deadly Weapon*, ed. Dianne Hall Kelly and Philip Heymann (New York: McGraw-Hill, 1978), p. 13.

3. Bracketed numbers link quotes to cases in a data set, "Autobiographical Accounts of Property Offenses by Youths, UCLA, 1983–1984," no. 8950, Inter-university Consortium for Political Social Research, Ann Arbor, Michigan. The accounts were volunteered by students in three offerings of my criminology class during 1983 and 1984. Because of the age range of the students and because no time

limit was placed on the recollection, the events recounted cover acts by 7-year-olds and middle-aged office workers, with most falling within early adolescence.

4. Cameron (*Booster and Snitch*, p. 82) found that males and females shoplift in the same way as they shop. Males go in for particular items and commonly come out with just one new possession, which makes them harder to catch. Females more often "go shopping" when they shoplift, moving through the store to find items that will be especially appealing.

5. For an example of creative middle-class vandalism, see William J. Chambliss, "The Saints and the Roughnecks," *Society* 11 (November–December 1981): 24–31.

6. "Love-at-first-sight" consumer experiences may be a relatively recent phenomenon, or at least enhanced by the modern social structure of the department store. A student of shoplifting in England reports that "the post-Second World War invitation to shoppers to 'walk around without obligation' makes it very much easier for the shoplifter. Before this time it was never assumed that people entering a shop did not know what they wanted, or that they would leave without making a purchase, or would expect to be allowed to wander without supervision and intervention." D. P. Walsh, *Shoplifting* (London: Macmillan, 1978), p. 22. The supervision of a helpful attendant clerk not only makes sleight-of-hand more difficult, it interferes with the privacy that is so helpful in getting good romances started. Merchandisers' complaints about being burned by shoplifting usually neglect to mention their encouragement that consumers play with possessive passions.

7. L. B. Taylor, "Shoplifting: When Honest Ladies Steal," *Ladies Home Journal*, January 1982, pp. 88–89.

8. On the raising of normal appearances to a problematic level in the process of becoming deviant, see Matza, *Becoming Deviant*.

48
Stigma Management Through Participation in Sport and Physical Activity

Experiences of Male College Students With Physical Disabilities

Diane E. Taub

Elaine M. Blinde

Kimberly R. Greer

Most people take their physical health for granted. Walking, talking, dancing, going out, and a host of other activities come naturally and are taken for granted as features of human existence. It is only when one's ability to perform these activities is wrenched away that one realizes how important they really are. Things that used to be automatic become tortured and tedious. Other people treat individuals with disabilities differently, as if they were not "whole people"; being handicapped becomes a "master status" (Hughes 1945). They become frustrated and depressed. Exclusion and ostracization cause them to fundamentally reevaluate their place in society.

Physical disability is what Goffman called a "deeply discrediting attribute," an identity spoiler that comes to define one's very being, a characteristic that others dwell on to the exclu-

sion of everything else. It is perfectly understandable, then, that many disabled persons will do everything in their power to reorient social perceptions in ways that promote a more robust status, a status of health and vigor rather than illness and dysfunction. Participation in sport and athletic activity is one powerful method by which they do this.

For males of college age, proving physical prowess is particularly important, since they are judged against strict, often unforgiving standards of "acceptable masculinity." Athletic participation allows disabled men to transform a discrediting attribute into a positive source of valuation, resulting in positive reinforcement, enhanced self-esteem, and the respect of others. The cruel paradox is that, by buying into the notion that athletic participation and normalcy go hand-in-hand, disabled athletes reinforce the very norms that oppress them, norms that equate social value with being able-bodied. They accept the stigma of disability rather than question it.

Introduction

As a critical component of one's social identity, the body influences social interactions and perceptions of others (Cash, 1990; Shontz, 1990). Especially in Western cultures that promote ableism and beautyism, bodily configurations and physical attributes represent central defining dimensions of an individual (Cash, 1990; Hahn, 1984, 1988). An emphasis on physical prowess and "the body beautiful" can overshadow other personal attributes (Cash, 1990; Hahn, 1984).

Physical disability constitutes one of several socially defined categories of stigma, an attribute that is deeply discrediting (Goffman, 1963; Susman, 1994; Wang, 1992). Individuals with a physical disability fall outside the range of what is considered normative or ordinary, thus spoiling their social identity and complicating interactions with able-bodied persons (Goffman, 1963). When a physical disability becomes the defining feature of an individual, others often focus on the disability to the exclusion of relevant personal characteristics (Asch, 1984; Levitin, 1975). Even with increased mainstreaming and political lobbying, individuals with physical disabilities frequently experience various forms of devaluation and discrimination (Groch, 1994).

When disabilities are physical in nature, the body represents the mechanism through which the disability is manifest. Regardless of the context, type, or degree of physical disability, the disabled body is the focus of attention and the source that evokes a negative reaction (Gerschick & Miller, 1994, 1995; Shontz, 1990). Because this body is considered inferior, passive, and weak, it is viewed as atypical (Fine & Asch, 1988; Gerschick & Miller, 1994, 1995; Goffman, 1963). Assumed properties of a disabled body elicit a stigmatized response and illustrate a societal perception of "negative difference" (Susman, 1994, p. 15).

Qualities of a disabled body are thought to challenge notions of physical competence and to violate appearance norms (Hahn, 1988; Schur, 1984; Susman, 1994). Concerning physical competence, a disabled body is stigmatized because of its assumed lack of individual autonomy (Hahn, 1988) and condition of helplessness, passivity, and dependency (Elliott, Ziegler, Altman, & Scott, 1990; Fine & Asch, 1988; Gerschick & Miller, 1994, 1995). Everyday skills and competencies of individuals with physical disabilities also are questioned routinely (Higgins, 1980). Internalization of these assumptions by able-bodied others impairs social interactions and leads to a questioning of the legitimacy of the stigmatized (Elliott et al., 1990).

Along with challenging beliefs about physical competence, a disabled body violates conventional standards related to body build, physical attractiveness, and bodily expression (Hahn, 1988; Kaiser, Freeman, & Wingate, 1990; Shontz, 1990; Wendell, 1989). Such aspects of bodily appearance represent salient social stimuli that affect interactions (Cash, 1990; Shontz, 1990). Those individuals who depart from normative images of human physique and "fail to meet prescribed standards of physical attractiveness" are devalued and stigmatized (Hahn,

1988, p. 41). For people with physical disabilities, an atypical bodily appearance may reduce opportunities "that are open to others without hesitation" (Shontz, 1990, p. 157). Individuals with physical disabilities who also possess aspects of the prevailing standards of beauty are a source of ambivalence for the able-bodied community (Kaiser et al., 1990).

As the disabled body is the focal point of negative difference, the stigma of individuals with physical disabilities is often immediately perceivable. Possessing observable and devalued attributes, these individuals engender discredited stigma (Goffman, 1963). The particular form of stigma management utilized by persons with a discredited stigma consists of their attempts to control tension during social interactions. For example, one strategy to manage the stigmatizing effects associated with a physical disability is to compensate for the discrediting attribute (Elliott et al., 1990; Goffman, 1963). Compensation involves stigmatized individuals gaining proficiency in activities in which they are usually not included or expected to perform well (Elliott et al., 1990; Goffman, 1963).

One possible means to alter the image of a disabled body is through involvement in sport and physical activity (Pfuhl & Henry, 1993; Warren, 1980). For other stigmatized groups including black men and gay men, such participation may yield wider societal acceptance. In the black subculture, athletic prowess for black men elevates social status (Eitzen & Sage, 1993), whereas for gay men, sport involvement can lessen the stereotype of gay men as effeminate (Coakley, 1994). Sport and physical activity participation also may demonstrate that individuals with physical disabilities are more able and similar to able-bodied peers than stereotypes suggest (Nixon, 1984). This involvement can reaffirm ability rather than disability and serve as a means to affirm one's bodily competence (Asken, 1991).

The current study represents one aspect of a larger research project examining the sport and physical activity experiences of individuals with physical and sensory disabilities. Sport and physical activity is conceptualized as encompassing a broad spectrum, ranging from competitive and structured events (e.g., wheelchair basketball, road racing) to informal and unstructured physical fitness contexts (e.g., exercising, weight lifting, swimming). These activities include team and individual sports, as well as sport and physical activity that is done informally with friends or alone.

For this study, in-depth interviews were conducted with male college students with physical disabilities; responses related to managing a stigmatized identity emerged from discussions regarding positive and negative experiences associated with sport and physical activity. Given that a disabled body is assumed to violate norms of physical competence and bodily appearance, the purpose of this paper is to investigate how participation in this context may be one technique of stigma management for individuals with physical disabilities. The uniqueness of this research is that it explores how benefits of sport and physical activity involvement may be used as a means of compensating for a discrediting attribute.

Methods

Sampling Characteristics

Male college students with physical disabilities were recruited from both personal contacts and the Office of Disability Support Services (DSS) at a large Midwestern university in the U.S. Informational sign-up sheets posted at the DSS office were the primary recruiting device. Such convenience sampling is considered feasible when particular groups of people are difficult to access or when certain types of individuals are uncommon in the population (Maxwell, 1996).

The focus of this study was on permanent physical conditions that restrict movement and substantially limit one or more of the major life activities of an individual (Mayerson, 1991). Although people with physical disabilities differ in terms of their movement capabilities, they nevertheless are members of a group stigmatized because of their physical attributes. The sample included 24 male college students with a variety of physical disabilities, including para-

plegia ($n = 8$), quadriplegia ($n = 4$), cerebral palsy ($n = 4$), partial paralysis ($n = 3$), back injury ($n = 1$), spina bifida ($n = 1$), knee injury ($n = 1$), ankylosing spondylitis ($n = 1$), and osteogenesis imperfecta ($n = 1$). Nine individuals were born with a physical disability, whereas the other 15 students had acquired their disability. The length of time having an acquired disability averaged 11 years, ranging from 3 to 18 years.

Ages of respondents ranged from 20 to 51 years, with a mean age of 29. The sample was composed of 21 whites and three African-Americans. In addition, respondents had diverse participation patterns in sport and physical activity, ranging from limited (e.g., occasionally lifting weights) to frequent involvement (e.g., being a member of the university wheelchair basketball team). Their participation in sport and physical activity at the time of the study averaged two times per week. With the exclusion of wheelchair sports, involvement for these individuals primarily occurred in an integrated setting with the able-bodied.

Interview Protocol

As the focus of this research concerned the perceptions and lived experiences of male college students with physical disabilities, the interview method was selected as an appropriate data collection tool. Interview questions were derived from a review of the literature in the areas of stigma, physical disability, and sport, as well as from the responses of five pilot interviews conducted with male college students with physical disabilities. A variety of issues were addressed in the final interview schedule, including the life history of individuals' physical disability, relative importance of sport and physical activity in respondents' lives, degree of past and current involvement in sport and physical activity (e.g., type of activity, duration, frequency) as compared to other activities, personal outcomes of sport and physical activity, and self-perceptions of physical capabilities and body image.

Respondents also were asked about such issues as what they personally gain or lose from participation, how sport and physical activity makes them feel and what this involvement means to them, what they learn about themselves from this activity, and ways in which sport and physical activity might assist or hinder their interactions in other contexts. Other questions centered on how they view their bodies when engaged in sport and physical activity, and whether this perception differs from participation in non-physical activities (e.g., attending classes, working on a computer, and driving a vehicle). Individuals were asked how others react to their involvement in sport and physical activity, and how these reactions affect self-perceptions of their bodies. Physical, psychological, and social outcomes realized from their participation in sport and physical activity were examined.

To encourage individuals to fully discuss topics most salient to their lived experiences, interview questions were open-ended and techniques were utilized to promote clarification and elaboration of responses. For example, probes used by the interviewer included "please explain," "could you provide an example," "why do you think this," and "how did this make you feel." To facilitate fluid, uninterrupted discussions and accurate data gathering, interviews were tape-recorded. The interviews lasted between 60 and 90 minutes. Code numbers and pseudonyms were employed to ensure that responses were confidential.

Two graduate students individually conducted the interviews in a private campus office that was reserved for this research. Both interviewers had received extensive methodological training; each individual completed doctoral level methodology courses and was mentored in qualitative methods, including participation in pilot interviews, under the direction of the principal investigators.

Data Analysis

Verbatim transcriptions of the tape-recorded interviews were completed and examined for accuracy. Procedures for analyzing this data were modeled after those outlined by Bogdan and Biklen (1992). The investigators independently performed content analysis on the transcribed interviews to identify common themes, patterns, and concepts. Overall, this examination produced

consistency among the researchers. Upon completion of content analysis, mutually agreed-upon coding categories were identified. Coding categories were generated based on regularities in the data and reflected an array of responses. Two primary themes related to sport and physical activity as a form of stigma management were physical competence and enhanced bodily appearance. Secondary themes included physical skill, fit healthy body, muscular body, and liberated body. Summary sheets were developed for each secondary theme with relevant comments from the interviews transferred to their respective summary sheet. Because this research had a relatively small sample size, subgroup comparisons involving factors such as ethnicity, age, length of disability, participation patterns, and type of disability could not be examined in-depth.

Results

As the purpose of this paper is to explore how sport and physical activity lessens the devaluation of men with physical disabilities, the data analysis centered on the role of such participation in managing the stigma associated with a disabled body. Our focus was on the reasons individuals with physical disabilities believe sport and physical activity compensates for a discredited physical difference. Although involvement was generally viewed as positive, a few respondents did mention negative or disempowering aspects of their sport and physical activity. For example, trivialization of participation by onlookers, dependence on others to assist with their equipment, and awareness of physical limitations could detract from the overall benefits of involvement. However, such peripheral outcomes did not negate the principal findings that the vast majority of respondents perceived participation in sport and physical activity as a positive experience and as an effective avenue to manage the stigma concerning a disabled body.

From interview responses, two primary themes emerged that illustrate how sport and physical activity may compensate for a disabled body or exceed expectations associated with a physical disability. Responses from male college students with physical disabilities indicated that they believed such participation can facilitate (a) physical competence, and (b) enhanced bodily appearance.

Physical Competence

Individuals with physical disabilities are often stigmatized because of their presumed lack of physical competence. The able-bodied community frequently assumes that the bodies of individuals with physical disabilities are disabling and weak rather than enabling and healthy (Fine & Asch, 1988; Gerschick & Miller, 1994, 1995; Goffman, 1963). Two general areas of physical competence acquired through sport and physical activity were identified in the comments of respondents: (a) demonstration of physical skill, and (b) demonstration of a fit healthy body.

Demonstration of Physical Skill. One aspect of physical competence noted in the responses was the ability of sport and physical activity to provide opportunities for demonstrating a variety of physical skills. By displaying the body in an active manner, these individuals with physical disabilities believed they were countering stereotypes of their physical incompetence.

Throughout the interviews, it was evident respondents thought the able-bodied community doubted their physical capabilities and skills. Nearly all of these students mentioned that others assumed sport and physical activity was outside the physical domain of individuals with physical disabilities. For example, a respondent with cerebral palsy who has participated in bowling and volleyball commented, "The perception is that people who are handicapped can't do anything . . .there is a definite perception that people who are handicapped can't play sports because they are not physically fit enough." One individual with partial paralysis indicated that his goal for sport participation was to do "something they [able-bodied individuals] thought I could not do . . .to show that I as a handicapped person can do anything that a regular person can."

An individual with quadriplegia who plays basketball and tennis added that "people who have no knowledge of people with disabilities expect them to just kinda sit around." Another respondent who participates in tennis and plays on a wheelchair basketball team indicated that he likes "to show the world" that able-bodied persons are not the only ones who can participate in sport or who can say "Well, I've got a game, I gotta go."

Although nearly all respondents believed others doubted their physical ability, they thought sport and physical activity enhanced their movement capabilities. When asked what involvement in sport meant to him, an individual with congenital partial paralysis who swims and jet skis remarked:

> I think being engaged in some aspect of your body that you have control over, and where you can set new goals, new expectations for your body . . .counting up what your body can do I think is incredibly important for people with disabilities, because I think the whole society thing is well, since your body is different, you can't do it [sport].

Or, as another respondent who plays wheelchair basketball stated when asked how he views his body when engaged in sport, "The body just needs a little helping around, but it is still getting the job done." Commenting on attitudes of able-bodied individuals after they observed his participation in football and floor hockey, a student with osteogenesis imperfecta indicated that others "think I would be more limited than I am. They are more astounded that you can do it [sport]."

Approximately half of the respondents reported that individuals were amazed when they were able to demonstrate proficiency in sport skills. For example, one student who plays wheelchair basketball indicated that spectators are "in awe" of his participation, while an individual with congenital partial paralysis stated he "frequently amazed everyone else" with his involvement in scuba diving and swimming. Moreover, one respondent with paraplegia who has participated in snow skiing added that able-bodied observers are "surprised" at what he can do. While discussing his sport abilities, another individual with paraplegia remarked that he can catch a football better than people who are able-bodied. He further indicated that "I can be better than some people [in sport] regardless of whether I am in the chair or not."

Demonstration of a Fit Healthy Body. A second dimension of physical competence discussed in the interviews related to how respondents believed sport and physical activity facilitated development of a body that is healthy and physically fit. Through their participation, these individuals with physical disabilities felt they were challenging stereotypes of a disabled body as being sick and weak.

Comments of respondents indicated that nearly all of them were cognizant of negative attributes regarding health and fitness aspects of disabled bodies. For example, an individual with cerebral palsy stated, "A lot of people consider disability kind of synonymous with disease . . .by presenting ourselves as active, healthy, living, and contributing members of the society, we allow ourselves to break that stereotype." When asked what factors influence how he views his body, a respondent with paraplegia remarked:

A lot of people still tend to look at you as somehow frail or injured or helpless, things like this. I think that is really unfortunate because they [labels] may affect people and cause them to feel that way about themselves, and that is really sad.

Approximately half of these individuals mentioned that participation in sport and physical activity compensated for stereotypes associated with a disabled body by making their bodies appear healthier. Comments such as "Basketball made me much more healthier," "I'm a lot more healthier when I participate in sports," and "It [sport] is a way to stay healthy" were frequently given when discussing the effect of sport and physical activity. A 24-year-old respondent who had acquired quadriplegia 6 years ago stated that through his involvement in basketball and tennis, "[My body] looks much better than it did before [the disability] . . .much more healthy than I was before, definitely . . .I thought I looked frail before and I look much healthier." One individual with

paraplegia who has participated in wheelchair basketball indicated, "If you have a healthy body in society, you are gonna get around better especially if you are in a chair . . .sports is the big boost that makes me wanna better myself."

A benefit mentioned by approximately half of the respondents when discussing their involvement in sport and physical activity was fitness. Although commonly assumed to be outside the domain of individuals with physical disabilities (Coakley, 1994; Nixon, 1984), being in shape or being in good physical condition were often identified as desired outcomes of participation in sport and physical activity. Various components of physical fitness, including "endurance," "flexibility," "energy," and "strength" were noted in responses. For example, benefits such as "builds up my cardiovascular system," "keeps myself in good shape," and "gets my physical conditioning up" were frequently mentioned. One individual with paraplegia who has played basketball and softball stated, "I think I'm in a lot better shape than I would have . . .if I wasn't participating in sports. I would be a couch potato."

By being healthy and physically fit through sport and physical activity, nearly all respondents believed they were able to influence the attitudes of others toward them. For example, an individual with paraplegia described how he felt about the positive responses received from able-bodied spectators for his involvement in various sport activities. "[This reaction] makes me feel pretty good; I'm just showing them what I do. I'm doing something good for my body and I think that they see that." Moreover, during a discussion of how he thought his participation in activities such as scuba diving affected the perceptions of others, a student who had acquired partial paralysis revealed:

Especially since I'm so badly handicapped, I'm not supposed to be able to do any of these sporting activities. But I've got to keep myself in excellent shape, and I've got to be able to change everyone's opinions about the handicap view.

In summary, sport and physical activity furnished a context in which respondents believed they could defy or minimize stereotypes of their body as lacking physical skill and being physically unfit and unhealthy. This environment provided a unique opportunity for these individuals with physical disabilities to focus on their body and its capabilities. Involvement in sport and physical activity by individuals with physical disabilities may compensate for the negative physical difference associated with a disabled body. Respondents perceived that accentuating their physical competence can result in a disabled body that is less stigmatized and devalued.

Enhanced Bodily Appearance

The second theme emanating from interview comments related to how respondents thought sport and physical activity compensates for negative perceptions about the appearance of the disabled body. Individuals with physical disabilities are assumed to deviate from conventional standards of body build, physical attractiveness, and bodily expression (Hahn, 1988; Kaiser et al., 1990; Shontz, 1990; Wendell, 1989). Two aspects of appearance transformed through sport and physical activity were noted in the remarks of respondents: (a) demonstration of a muscular body, and (b) demonstration of a liberated body.

Demonstration of a Muscular Body. A disabled body may be viewed as atypical because of its physique and outward appearance. Respondents believed that as a result of assumed inactivity, the bodies of individuals with physical disabilities are commonly thought to lack muscularity and physical development. One bodily domain influenced by sport and physical activity related to the development of muscle definition.

Approximately half of the respondents voiced pride in "building up muscles," "becoming bigger," and "building myself up" through sport and physical activity. One individual with congenital partial paralysis reported that as a result of lifting weights, he was able to increase from a 36- to a 42-inch chest. Expressing pleasure at this improvement in his upper body, he commented that "I was building up areas of my body that I've never addressed before in that way, shape, or form." Another individual indicated that

through wheelchair basketball, "I've like noticed changes in my body, like my arms are getting more shape and more definition in them."

Participation in sport and physical activity enabled respondents to develop a physique they thought compensated for stereotypical assumptions about a disabled body. Individuals, especially those who use wheelchairs, discussed how able-bodied others were surprised at the muscular development of their bodies. For example, one respondent with paraplegia indicated that weight lifting helped his "body become more defined [and] more acceptable to people. [Others] want to see a nice, built body, and they'll say, 'he's strong, he's massive, he must work out all the time.'"

Demonstration of a Liberated Body. Respondents indicated another common assumption about individuals with physical disabilities is that their bodies depart from conventional standards of attractiveness and bodily expression. Sport and physical activity was perceived by these participants as one way to challenge the notion that their bodies are unattractive and unable to engage in movement of an expressive nature.

One dimension of a liberated body discussed by a few respondents was related to the issue of weight. While indicating awareness of a societal emphasis on an attractive bodily appearance, individuals often mentioned weight as one aspect of their bodies they felt they could transform. For example, when asked why they were involved in sport and physical activity, respondents frequently cited factors such as "want to lose weight" or "get thinner." While discussing his reason for sport participation, an individual with partial paralysis remarked:

> I feel I am too fat, too out of shape, getting flabby. I think that I am fat and out of shape. When I weight lift, I get thinner and I start to lose weight. When I lay off the weights, I see myself getting out of shape.

The topic of weight also was discussed when asked how sport and physical activity affected views of their bodies. For example, one individual with paraplegia who described himself as overweight thought that physical activity could help him achieve a socially desirable weight. Believing the appearance of his body was within his control, he described displeasure with being overweight: "[I am] a little angry . . .because I know I can work on my weight [through weight lifting]." Another individual with paraplegia discussed how perception of his body is influenced by sport participation:

> I want to be able to roll outside with a tank top on . . .and not have my stomach sticking out. If I was not doing sports I would probably . . .be a lot heavier and I . . .would not have the gumption to . . .really want to lose weight. . . .If I was not doing sports, I would be a fat tub of goo right now.

Further, through sport and physical activity, a few respondents thought that weight loss could affect impressions of able-bodied others about the physical attractiveness of individuals with physical disabilities. As a student with paraplegia stated, "[I] need to lose some weight and it's just all cosmetic . . .I feel that I'll look better, therefore people will like me more."

Sport and physical activity also provided these individuals with physical disabilities a context for demonstrating a liberated body by using their body in an unrestrained manner. Such participation can recast notions that a disabled body is unable to engage in expressive forms of movement. Through sport and physical activity, respondents found they could experience their bodies in a creative and graceful manner.

Nearly all individuals initiated discussions regarding the qualitative dimensions of their involvement in sport and physical activity. For one participant, wheelchair basketball was "a way to express myself," while another enjoyed the sensation of swimming because "when I'm in the water, I'm free of the wheelchair." Such experiences were discussed in reference to sport and physical activity being able to compensate for preconceived notions of a disabled body as rigid and void of refined movement.

Approximately half of the respondents thought the expressiveness of their body while participating in sport and physical activity affected their awareness of a physical self. As one individual commented, involvement in sport "completes the picture [by adding] a sense of the body self . . .to the mind self." In discussing what participation in sport meant to him, a respondent with congenital partial paralysis remarked:

> [Sport] may give them [individuals with physical disabilities] a self, a sense of their physical self as being beautiful and capable and natural. And I do not think many people with disabilities have that opportunity [or] are given that opportunity.

When asked how involvement in a variety of sport activities affected his body image, a student with congenital partial paralysis revealed, "Having engaged in sports has certainly changed my thinking and my body concept. I really do see my body as much more friendly."

In summary, these individuals with physical disabilities believed they experienced and displayed both a muscular and a liberated body through sport and physical activity. In contrast to nonphysical settings, this context provided a unique occasion in which respondents could more readily compensate for their stigma by altering the appearance of their body. Such participation may counter stereotypes of the disabled body as deviating from conventional standards of muscular body build, physical attractiveness, and bodily expression. Presenting the body through the domain of sport and physical activity can be one means by which the stigma of a disabled body may be managed.

Discussion

Being a participant in sport and physical activity represents a socially valued role that may allow individuals with physical disabilities to diminish the stigma of a physical disability (Goffman, 1963). Such involvement can serve to compensate for a discredited attribute in that stereotypes underlying the stigma of a disabled body are challenged (Elliott et al., 1990; Goffman, 1963). As participation in sport and physical activity is often unexpected for individuals with physical disabilities, their involvement may create an alternative impression of the disabled body. For example, such participation inverts notions of physical incompetence and negative appearance by highlighting physical skills and a liberated body.

While discussing personal outcomes of their involvement, respondents emphasize the importance of the participation experience itself rather than the type, intensity level, or formal nature of the physical activity. For these individuals, the opportunity to be involved in sport and physical activity is itself rewarding. Sport and physical activity generally is a privileged context for persons who are physically able and competent (Sage, 1990). Compared with nonphysical activity, sport and physical activity for individuals with physical disabilities transpires in a unique environment in which competence and appearance of their body can be altered.

Interview responses suggest that for men with physical disabilities, sport and physical activity is one domain especially conducive for the development and demonstration of masculine characteristics and qualities such as competitiveness, dominance, independence, and physical prowess (Messner, 1989, 1990a, 1992; Sage, 1990). For men with physical disabilities whose bodies are marginalized and stigmatized, attributes related to their manliness are routinely questioned (Gerschick & Miller, 1994, 1995). Being perceived by others as masculine is improbable for these individuals because of the incongruence between the expectations of hegemonic masculinity and the assumed incapabilities associated with physical disability (Gerschick & Miller, 1994, 1995). Compensation may be an especially important strategy for men with physical disabilities in challenging societal perceptions of a disabled body and in asserting claims of masculinity. The socialization of males to value sport involvement might partially explain why these men choose sport and physical activity as a context for stigma management.

Several comments from respondents indicate that individuals with physical disabilities internalize societal norms regarding both physical competence and bodily appearance. For example, acceptance of conventional standards of ableism and beautyism by respondents involves their equating physical skill and attractiveness with social desirability. Such normative internalization is common among members of socially marginalized groups (Miller, 1995; Wolf, 1986). Respondents seem unaware that they strive toward elitist standards of beauty and body image; their efforts are paradoxical as they identify with norms that are oppressive for individuals with physical disabilities.

To fully explore the dynamics of the role of sport and physical activity as a strategy of stigma management, additional research should be conducted. For example, it is important to examine the sport and physical activity experiences of women, and individuals of various age groups, with physical disabilities. Female participants may be doubly stigmatized in that they violate both the normative assumption of sport as a context for males and as a domain for the physically able. As sport is male-dominated and perpetuates notions of masculinity (Messner, 1989, 1990a, b, 1992; Sage, 1990), the outcomes of participation for women with physical disabilities can differ from the experiences of their male counterparts. Because women are not as socialized as men to value sport participation, women with physical disabilities might not readily choose physical activity as an avenue for stigma management. Further, as this study focuses on young adult to middle-aged individuals, future research should address outcomes of participation in sport and physical activity for both children and older adults with physical disabilities. Such investigations may refine understanding of the relationship between involvement in physical activity and stigma management.

Although self-perceptions of individuals with physical disabilities have real consequences for their personal behavior and social interactions, individuals without physical disabilities should be interviewed to assess their perceptions of respondents' involvement in sport and physical activity. Whereas respondents thought such participation may alter societal stereotypes of the disabled body, obtaining the beliefs of able-bodied others may provide further insights into whether they view individuals with physical disabilities differently following participation in sport and physical activity.

In conclusion, sport and physical activity is a context in which nearly all respondents believe they can manage the stigma associated with a disabled body. Through their involvement, individuals with physical disabilities may compensate or demonstrate an alternative image capable of diminishing the effect of a discrediting attribute. In particular, the assumed negative difference of their physical competence and bodily appearance can be transformed. Such modification does not negate the previously stigmatized self but provides an identity that may be perceived as more favorable. Even though respondents are not elite athletes, participation in activities ordinarily closed to them can provide opportunities to display a less stigmatized self. As sport and physical activity is unexpected among individuals with physical disabilities, compensation as a strategy of stigma management may result in a less spoiled identity.

References

Asch, A. 1984. "The experience of disability: A challenge for psychology." *American Psychologist*, 39, 529–536.

Asken, M. J. 1991. "The challenge of the physically challenged: Delivering sport psychology services to physically disabled athletes." *The Sport Psychologist*, 5, 370–381.

Bogdan, R. C., & Biklen, S. K. 1992. *Qualitative research for education* (2nd ed.). Boston: Allyn and Bacon.

Cash, T. F. 1990. "The psychology of physical appearance: Aesthetics, attributes, and images." In T. F. Cash and T. Pruzinsky (eds.), *Body images: Development, deviance, and change*. New York: The Guilford Press, pp. 51–79.

Coakley, J. J. 1994. *Sport in society: Issues and controversies* (5th ed.). St. Louis: Mosby.

Eitzen, D. S., & Sage, G. H. 1993. *Sociology of North American sport* (5th ed.). Madison, WI: Brown & Benchmark.

Elliott, G. C., Ziegler, H. L., Altman, B. M., & Scott, D. R. 1990. "Understanding stigma: Dimensions of deviance and coping." In C. D. Bryant (Ed.), *Deviant behavior*. New York: Hemisphere, pp. 423–443.

Fine, M., & Asch, A. 1988. "Disability beyond stigma: Social interaction, discrimination, and activism." *Journal of Social Issues*, 44: 3–21.

Gerschick, T. J., & Miller, A. S. 1994. "Gender identities at the crossroads of masculinity and physical disability." *Masculinities*, 2: 34–55.

Gerschick, T. J., & Miller, A. S. 1995. "Coming to terms: Masculinity and physical disability." In D. Sabo and D. F. Gordon (eds.), *Men's health and illness: Gender, power, and the body*. Thousands Oaks, CA: Sage, pp. 183–204.

Goffman, E. 1963. *Stigma: Notes on the management of spoiled identity*. Englewood Cliffs, NJ: Prentice Hall.

Groch, S. A. 1994. "Oppositional consciousness: Its manifestation and development. The case of people with disabilities." *Sociological Inquiry*, 64: 369–395.

Hahn, H. 1984. "Sports and the political movement of disabled persons: Examining nondisabled social values." *Arena Review*, 8: 1–15.

Hahn, H. 1988. "The politics of physical differences: Disability and discrimination." *Journal of Social Issues*, 44: 39–47.

Higgins, P. C. 1980. "Societal reaction and the physically disabled: Bringing the impairment back in." *Symbolic Interaction*, 3: 139–156.

Kaiser, S. B., Freeman, C. M., & Wingate, S. B. 1990. "Stigmata and negotiated outcomes: Management of appearance by persons with physical disabilities." In C. D. Bryant (ed.), *Deviant behavior*. New York: Hemisphere, pp. 444–464.

Levitin, T. E. 1975. "Deviants as active participants in the labeling process: The visibly handicapped." *Social Problems*, 22: 548–557.

Maxwell, J. A. 1996. *Qualitative research design: An interactive approach*. Thousand Oaks, CA: Sage.

Mayerson, A. 1991. "Title I—Employment provisions of the Americans With Disabilities Act." *Temple Law Review*, 64: 499–520.

Messner, M. 1989. "Masculinities and athletic careers." *Gender & Society*, 3: 71–88.

Messner, M. A. 1990a. "Boyhood, organized sports, and the construction of masculinities." *Journal of Contemporary Ethnography*, 18: 416–444.

Messner, M. A. 1990b. "Men studying masculinity: Some epistemological issues in sport sociology." *Sociology of Sport Journal*, 7: 136–153.

Messner, M. A. 1992. *Power at play: Sports and the problem of masculinity*. Boston: Beacon.

Miller, J. B. 1995. "Domination and subordination." In P. S. Rothenberg (ed.), *Race, class, and gender in the United States: An integrated study* (3rd ed.). New York: St. Martin's, pp. 57–64.

Nixon, H. L. II. 1984. "Handicapism and sport: New directions for sport sociology research." In N. Theberge and P. Donnelly (eds.), *Sport and the sociological imagination*. Fort Worth, TX: Texas Christian University Press, pp. 162–176.

Pfuhl, E. H., & Henry, S. 1993. *The deviance process* (3rd ed.). New York: Aldine de Gruyter.

Sage, G. H. 1990. *Power and ideology in American sport: A critical perspective*. Champaign, IL: Human Kinetics, 1990.

Schur, E. M. 1984. *Labeling women deviant: Gender, stigma, and social control*. New York: McGraw-Hill.

Shontz, F. C. 1990. "Body image and physical disability." In T. F. Cash and T. Pruzinsky (eds.), *Body images: Development, deviance, and change*. New York: The Guilford Press, pp. 149–169.

Susman, J. 1994. "Disability, stigma and deviance." *Social Science and Medicine*, 38: 15–22.

Wang, C. 1992. "Culture, meaning and disability: Injury prevention campaigns and the production of stigma." *Social Science and Medicine*, 35: 1093–1102.

Warren, C. A. B. 1980. "Destigmatization of identity: From deviant to charismatic." *Qualitative Sociology*, 3: 59–72.

Wendell, S. 1989. "Toward a feminist theory of disability." *Hypatia*, 4(2): 104–124.

Wolf, C. 1986. "Legitimation of oppression: Response and reflexivity." *Symbolic Interaction*, 9: 217–234.

This research was supported by a Southern Illinois University at Carbondale Special Research Grant to the first two authors. We appreciate the assistance of Becky Ahlgren and Lisa R. McClung in conducting and transcribing interviews.

49
Women Athletes as Falsely Accused Deviants

Managing the Lesbian Stigma

Elaine M. Blinde

Diane E. Taub

Female athletic participation has skyrocketed in recent years. Women young and old have discovered the thrills of competition and the adrenaline-pumping rush of heated games with zero-sum outcomes. In patriarchal societies, participation has its downside, however. To be athletic is to be masculine, and to be masculine is to risk the label of lesbian. Sport is not the "proper" domain of "ladies" and violates standards of appropriate gender-role conduct (though this has recently begun to change). How female athletes confront and resist this label is the explicit concern here.

Whether the athletes whom Blinde and Taub interviewed are indeed lesbian is not the issue (many claimed they were not). The presumption is all that matters, and it requires that those labeled respond. An array of impression management devices have evolved to this end. Some women thus portray a hyper-heterosexual identity in public settings. Others rely on excelling in nonsport areas (to generate alternative attributions). Still others attempt to conceal the fact that they are athletes.

The labeling process is powerful, and accused deviants must do everything in their power to fight it (lest they be stigmatized as outcasts). The irony is that in so doing, norm violators perpetuate the very power of the label they seek to fight. Female athletes fail to question the fundamental reason behind their deviant attribution, which strengthens the label's salience. Truly empowering stigma

management targets the source of the discreditation to defeat it. Obviously, this is a daunting task and largely beyond the scope of individual deviants to accomplish. As long as female athletic participation continues to rise at its current rate, however, its discrediting status may evaporate as a matter of course. As we all know, when enough people engage in some deviant activity, it stops being deviant.

Gender represents a powerful normative system that both evaluates and controls the behavior of men and women (Schur 1984). This system entails socially constructed conceptualizations of behavior intricately tied to societal perceptions of "masculinity" and "femininity" (Keller 1978).

Women occupy a unique position in this system of gender norms. Not only does it define appropriate and inappropriate behaviors, but the behaviors sanctioned for women are generally devalued in the broader society and often contribute to their subordination (Smith 1978). Women who engage in nontraditional gender behaviors capable of enhancing opportunities and self-actualization are subjected to various forms of social stigmatization (Schur 1984).

Widespread violation of gender norms by women constitutes a serious threat to the entire gender system. It is thus not surprising that women are stigmatized and labeled as deviant when their behaviors challenge traditional gender norms (Anderson 1988). As Schur (1984) suggests, stigmatization of behaviors not conforming to rigid gender role expectations reinforces women's overall subordination as it restricts women's roles and potential. Moreover, operating from a relatively disadvantaged position of power, women are more vulnerable to stigmatization (Anderson 1988). Stigmatization thus represents a means of social control as it preserves the traditional gender system. Fear of being labeled deviant keeps women "in their place" and reduces challenges to prevailing gender norms (Schur 1984). Not surprisingly, individuals who occupy positions of power or privilege, the "deviance-definers," benefit from continued subordination or suppression of the less powerful (Becker 1963).

Although all women experience devaluation and stigmatization by virtue of being female (Schur 1984), some women occupy roles or engage in behaviors that make them even more susceptible to deviant labeling. This labeling is particularly indicative of women who violate multiple categories of gender norms, including (1) presentation of self (e.g., emotions, nonverbal communication, appearance, speech), (2) marriage and maternity, (3) sexuality (e.g., sexual behavior/orientation), and (4) occupational choice (Schur 1984).

One group of women judged to violate multiple categories of gender norms and thus subjected to various forms of deviance labeling and stigmatization is athletes. Women athletes are frequently perceived to cross or extend the boundaries of socially constructed definitions of "femininity" (Theberge 1985; Willis 1982). In a culture that traditionally equates athleticism with masculinity, women who participate in sport are often viewed as masculine, unladylike, or manly (Willis 1982). Such descriptors imply that women athletes violate presentation of self and occupational gender norms (Schur 1984). Moreover, both the popular press and research literature have examined the assumed conflict between athleticism and femininity (Colker and Widom 1980; Griffin 1987; Hall 1988). This presumed incompatibility, along with equating sport and masculinity, results in a belief system linking women athletes with lesbianism (Lenskyj 1991). The lesbian label, representing a violation of sexuality norms (Schur 1984), is based on the idea that women who challenge traditional gender-role behavior cannot be "real" women (Lenskyj 1991).

The lesbian label as applied to women athletes is particularly significant given the assumed threat of lesbianism (as well as male homosexuality) to the prevailing gender system (Goodman 1977; Lenskyj 1991; Schur 1984). Stigmatization of lesbians is common as the phenomena of "heterosexual assumption" and "heterosexual privilege" ensure that lesbians realize they are indeed norm violators, deviants, and subjects of oppression

(Schur 1984; Wolfe 1988). Such stigmatization reflects contempt for those who stretch the boundaries of culturally defined gender roles.

Since the behavior of women athletes is often interpreted to challenge gender norms, they may be subject to various forms of devaluation and stigmatization. Although athleticism represents the initial discrediting attribute, its linkage with lesbianism magnifies the devaluation and stigmatization associated with female athletes. The present study examines the manner in which such forms of devaluation and stigmatization impact on women athletes and how they manage the lesbian label (and accompanying masculine image) attached to their sport participation. Not only has there been a paucity of research investigating the specific topic of the stigmatization of women athletes as lesbians, but the entire issue of the perceived presence of lesbianism in women's sport has been neglected (Griffin 1987).

Methodology

Sample

Athletic directors at seven large Division I universities were contacted to obtain names and addresses of all varsity women athletes for the purpose of telephone interviews. These universities represent a wide range of athletic conference affiliations and geographical regions. A larger number of universities than needed were contacted because of the projected low response rates; constraints both on time for compiling lists of athletes and utilization of athletes as research respondents were anticipated.

Three universities (two Midwestern and one Southern) provided names and addresses of all women athletes with at least one year of completed athletic eligibility who were participating in the school's sport programs during the 1990–1991 school year. All sport programs offered by the universities were represented. Varsity women athletes, rather than intramural or informal sport participants, were the focus of this study because of the salience of their athletic identities and their greater sport commitment. Four universities declined to participate due to time demands and institutional restrictions on athletes serving as research participants.

A final sample size between 20 and 30 was desired given its manageability for the projected interview length, yet sufficiently broad-based to depict a wide range of athletic experiences. An initial random sample of 48, equally selected from the three universities, was drawn to allow for potential nonrespondents.

Each athlete was mailed a letter explaining the importance and general purpose of the study. Because the interview schedule focused on topics other than lesbianism and since the lesbian issue was lodged in the broader area of stereotypes, the cover letter did not specifically mention the topic of lesbianism. Moreover, identifying the lesbian issue as a component of the interview could have influenced an athlete's decision to participate, thus leading to sample bias. Athletes were encouraged to return an informed consent form indicating their willingness to participate in a tape-recorded telephone interview. Based on this initial contact, 16 athletes returned informed consent forms.

To increase the sample to the originally desired size (20–30), 30 additional individuals were randomly drawn and equally selected from the three lists. An additional eight athletes agreed to participate, thus providing for a final sample of 24 (representing a distribution of 10–5–9 among the three universities).

These 24 athletes were currently participating in a variety of intercollegiate sports—basketball (5), track and field (4), volleyball (3), swimming (3), softball (3), tennis (2), diving (2), and gymnastics (2). With an average age of 20.2 years and predominantly white (92%), the sample consisted of 2 freshmen, 9 sophomores, 5 juniors, and 8 seniors. The majority (22) were receiving athletic scholarships.

Procedures

Two trained interviewers conducted in-depth and semi-structured tape-recorded telephone interviews that lasted 50–90 minutes. The interview schedule focused on several aspects of the intercollegiate sport experience, one of which related to societal perceptions of women's sport and female athletes. The lesbian topic usually surfaced in responses to questions regarding (1) positive and negative connotations associated with women's sport and female athletes, and (2) stereotypes associated with women athletes. In response to these two questions, 17 of the 24 athletes initiated discussion of the lesbian topic. When asked whether they were aware of the lesbian label being associated with women athletes, 6 of the 7 remaining athletes indicated strong familiarity with this association.

Further, several questions explored how athletes dealt with the lesbian label, for example, (1) why they felt women athletes are labeled lesbian, (2) which athletes or teams are most likely to be labeled, (3) who applies this label, (4) how this label affects athletes, and (5) the degree to which athletes discuss this topic among themselves. Questions were open-ended to allow athletes to discuss the most relevant aspects of their own experiences.

Data analysis of the verbatim transcriptions was an ongoing process as concepts and themes emerged throughout the interviews. Coding categories were constructed to represent the various concepts, themes, and patterns identified (Bogdan and Biklen 1982). A summary sheet was created for each concept or theme, and all relevant comments from the 24 interviews were included on the various summary sheets. For example, summary sheets depicted themes related to the lesbian label, including familiarity, rationale for existence, reaction, impact, and internalization. Summary sheets for each concept or theme were examined to identify both commonalities and variations in responses.

Overall, the design of the study allowed for the emergence of concepts from the data rather than imposing preconceived conceptual or theoretical frameworks on the interview protocol and data. Such an approach utilizes the voices of athletes to identify and develop emerging concepts and themes.

In analyzing and reporting the comments of athletes, the intent was not to construct a single profile characterizing the majority of respondents. Rather, realizing that athletes differ and that all comments are important, both similarities and variations in responses are explored.

Results and Discussion

Since athletes were highly aware that women in sport are labeled lesbian, the manner in which these athletes dealt with the lesbian label was examined. Although the study was not developed within a preexisting framework, data analysis revealed that the processes underlying athletes' responses paralleled concepts established by Becker (1963) and Goffman (1963).

This article focuses on Becker's (1963) construction of the "falsely accused deviant" and Goffman's (1963) conceptualization of "stigma management." Not only do these two concepts enhance our knowledge of the experiences of women athletes, but the athletes' experiences add further understanding and validation to the conceptualizations of the "falsely accused deviant" and "stigma management."

Falsely Accused Deviant

The vast majority of respondents thought that labeling women athletes lesbian (or at least questioning sexual preference) was quite common. One athlete referred to it as a "societal blanket covering all of collegiate female athletes."

Despite athletes' perception that the lesbian label is prevalent in women's sport and often indiscriminately applied to women athletes, it would be unreasonable to assume all women athletes are lesbian. Although our intent was not to ascertain the sexual orientation of respondents, it was clear that a large majority responded to questions as to suggest that they were not lesbians. For example, phrases like "lesbians don't bother me as long as they don't hit on me," "I have a boyfriend," "the label does not pertain to me," "I'm not really the person to ask about lesbianism because I don't really see enough of it," "people know how I am" (suggesting heterosexuality), or "it's not a problem I'm faced with" were common.

Another way athletes implied distance from lesbianism was through out-group

(e.g., "they" or "them") and in-group (e.g., "those of us who aren't" or "we joke about them") terminology. Even though women athletes as a whole frequently are viewed as the out-group in terms of social deviance, a secondary level of deviance exists within the athletic group. That is, within this deviant group, athletes use in-group and out-group terminology to distinguish between the nonlesbian and lesbian athlete.

Given this widespread disassociation from lesbianism, it was assumed that the majority of athletes interviewed were not lesbians. However, since the label is indiscriminately applied to women athletes, many are incorrectly labeled lesbian, typifying what Becker (1963) terms the "falsely accused deviant." One difficulty noted by Klemke and Tiedeman (1990) in the study of false accusations is documenting that accusations are indeed false. Relative to our research, the need of respondents to mislead interviewers should have been substantially reduced as the interviews were anonymous and conducted by strangers over the telephone.

The concept of the "falsely accused deviant" derives from Becker's (1963) original classification scheme of deviant behavior. Basic to Becker's typology are two factors: whether an individual (1) is a rule violator, and (2) has been labeled deviant. In contrast to the "pure deviant," correctly labeled a rule violator; the "conformist," correctly labeled a rule abider; and the "secret deviant," a rule violator not labeled as such, the "falsely accused deviant" is incorrectly labeled deviant (see Figure 49.1 [not provided here]).

Unfortunately, Becker (1963) does not systematically examine or discuss the "falsely accused deviant." In fact, this category of deviant is underresearched compared to the other three types. Neglect of the category exists despite its potential to enhance understanding of labeling, especially in terms of conditions and social processes involved in creating false conceptions of social reality (Klemke and Tiedeman 1990). Conceptualizations surrounding the "falsely accused deviant" are particularly useful in understanding why the lesbian label permeates women's sport.

Error-Types Underlying False Accusations. Klemke and Tiedeman (1990) identify four fundamental types of error underlying false accusations—pure, intentional, legitimatized, and victim-based. Interview responses of athletes suggest that each error-type helps account for labeling women athletes lesbian.

Pure error reflects unintended or accidental false accusation based on erroneous information (Klemke and Tiedeman 1990). A common example occurs when nondeviants are stigmatized because they associate with deviants. Some athletes indicated that they have gay or lesbian friends or teammates; interactions with known homosexuals lead outsiders to label athletes "guilty by association." For example, one athlete commented that members on certain teams are labeled lesbian "because the team is known to have homosexuals." In the case of women athletes, association with a known lesbian may result in "courtesy stigma" (Birenbaum 1970; Goffman 1963), a stigma conferred despite the absence of usual qualifying behavior. Sometimes public disclosure of lesbianism by a visible female athlete leads to courtesy stigma for all women in sport.

A second error-type, *intentional error*, occurs when the interests of others are enhanced by false labeling (Klemke and Tiedeman 1990). Two variations of this type of error may contribute to the lesbian labeling of women athletes. First, since traditional female gender norms emphasizing frailty, weakness, and dependency contribute to women's subordination (Schur 1984), the position of those with power in the larger society may be strengthened when women are discouraged from pursuing activities that challenge existing gender norms. As a mechanism to discourage women from seriously pursuing sport, the lesbian label enhances the position of those in control as it attempts to preserve sport as a bastion of male supremacy (Lenskyj 1986).

Second, indiscriminate usage of the lesbian label may vindictively aim to discredit or detract from the accomplishments of women athletes. When asked why they are labeled lesbians, women athletes sometimes indicated such a phenomenon. For example,

one respondent felt women athletes are a "threat to men since they can stand on their own feet." Others viewed labeling as a means to devalue women athletes or a "way to discredit successful women." Still another suggested that jealousy prompted the label as a means to "get back" at women athletes.

Representing a third error-type, *legitimatized error* employs criteria people feel are valid but in fact are not (Klemke and Tiedeman 1990). Such mistakes frequently arise when individuals rely on cultural belief systems without considering contrary evidence (Scheff 1964). Despite counter assertions, beliefs are maintained by the occasional identification of a woman athlete as lesbian. When well-known women athletes publicly disclose their lesbianism, these limited indicators grant inertia to stereotypes and perpetuate false labeling. The "societal blanket" mentioned by one athlete reflects a general cultural belief that women who seriously pursue sport are masculinized and thus lesbian. Athletes frequently mentioned that people do not attempt to "get to know them" as individuals, but rather assume that as athletes they must also be lesbian. Thus, their "master status" (Becker 1963) of lesbian overrides the athletic role.

In the fourth error-type, *victim-based*, the person receiving the label has actively and willingly sought to be labeled (Klemke and Tiedeman 1990; Pollak 1952). Although interview responses yield little evidence of such error-type, some women athletes felt others "ask for the label" given how they dress, walk, and conduct themselves. As one respondent stated, some women athletes just "play the part."

Societal Preconditions for False Accusation. Underlying these four error-types are general societal preconditions or organizational factors that increase the probability false accusations will occur (Klemke and Tiedeman 1990). Three factors in particular may account for why female athletes and women's sport, compared to other individuals and domains, are more often targets of lesbian accusations: (1) the growth of women's sport and its perceived threat to the male sport structure, (2) women athletes' lack of power and outsider status, and (3) stereotype adoption.

As the growth of women's sport challenges the male-controlled sport structure, attempts to devalue women's sport by dominant groups can be anticipated. Lenskyj (1986) argues that efforts to preserve sport as a stronghold of male supremacy positively relate to the movement of women into sport. The expansion of women's sport in the past 20 years (due in part to Title IX legislation promoting equal gender opportunity in educational institutions) has been perceived as a threat to men's sport, thus triggering an increased interest in preserving male sport (Blinde 1987). The generalization of the lesbian label to female athletes seeks to discredit and devalue women's sport and ultimately works to keep women "in their place" (Lenskyj 1986).

Second, since women as a group possess relatively little power in the large society, they are not only more likely to suffer false accusations but also be unable to challenge or disprove the label. In the sport context, women are generally not accorded the status and legitimacy granted males. As Klemke and Tiedeman (1990) suggest, targets of false accusations (including women athletes) are likely to possess limited power, outsider status, minimal organizational or societal backing, and little legitimacy. Conversely, individuals and groups who falsely label possess power, insider status, organizational or societal backing, and legitimacy. Support for this latter contention was found when athletes indicated that men, especially male athletes, were the most common group labeling women athletes lesbian.

Third, confounding this situation are longstanding stereotypes directed toward women who violate traditional gender norms. In the current example, the societal linkage of athleticism and masculinity increases the likelihood that women in sport will be the target of false charges of lesbianism.

Given the factors that lead to the indiscriminate stigmatization of women athletes, both lesbian and nonlesbian athletes adopt strategies to manage the lesbian stigma. As discussed in the following section, a variety of stigma management mechanisms are utilized by athletes to manage these labels.

Stigma Management

According to Goffman (1963), stigmas represent discrediting attributes that reflect a discrepancy between individuals' virtual (assumed) and actual (real) social identities. These attributes fall outside the range of what is considered ordinary or natural and generally "spoil" the social identity of the stigma possessor. Since the stigma taints and discredits the individual, attempts are generally undertaken to control and manage the discrediting attribute. The need for such management mechanisms is not necessarily limited to individuals who possess the discrediting attribute; stigma management is arguably the domain of the "falsely accused" as well.

As noted previously, sport participation (especially elite competition) is often considered outside the range of what is ordinary or normal for women. Moreover, given the widespread labeling of women athletes as lesbian and the corresponding stigmatization, women athletes must manage these discrediting attributes.

The particular strategy utilized to manage a stigma largely depends on the degree to which the attribute is visible or perceivable to others. Goffman (1963) distinguishes between individuals possessing attributes easily identifiable (i.e., discredited individuals) and not immediately perceivable (i.e., discreditable individuals). Techniques designed to manage the impact of these two types of attributes differ; the discredited individual manages tension while the discreditable manages information. Although the degree to which others can identify women as athletes varies, athletic status (and the accompanying lesbian label) is generally not immediately perceivable, thus resulting in a discreditable stigma. As Goffman (1963) suggests, such a stigma is associated with the control and management of information.

Concealment. One basic stigma management mechanism noted by athletes was concealment. As an information management technique to prevent association with the lesbian label, women athletes sometimes simply conceal information about their athleticism. Elliott, Ziegler, Altman, and Scott (1990) and Goffman (1963) identify several forms of concealment, including self-segregation, passing, and use of disidentifiers.

Common in the responses of athletes was *self-segregation,* a condition where the stigmatized interact primarily with those sharing a similar affliction or those considered "wise." Wise individuals are familiar and comfortable with the stigmatized but do not have the stigma (Goffman 1963). Athletes frequently indicated that most of their friends are athletes and interaction with the general student body is limited. This compressed social network reduces athletes' interactions with those most likely to react negatively toward their athletic participation. Such avoidance limits disruption in the pursuit of athletic goals (Elliott et al. 1990). Although the reason for self-segregation is not exclusively stigma management (e.g., some indicated they relate better to other athletes or that time prohibits developing friendships outside of sport), the comfortable, nonthreatening environment other athletes provide may enhance the prevalence of self-segregation. As one athlete indicated, those outside the women's sport community most commonly initiate the lesbian labeling.

Self-segregation, however, is not without its complications. As Adler and Adler (1987) suggest, self-segregation often isolates athletes both socially and culturally from the university student body. The protective environment of self-segregation is offset by the sometimes narrow and limited athletic subculture.

Since self-segregation is not always practical, women athletes also conceal their athletic identity by *passing.* As information management, passing involves controlling the disclosure of discrediting information about oneself to conceal the stigma entirely (Elliott et al. 1990). Several women described techniques they (or other athletes) use so others will not know they are athletes. For example, some simply withhold information about their athletic status in conversations with outsiders. Alternatively, one individual stated athletes sometimes "over-talk" the lesbian topic to disassociate the label from themselves.

Other athletes relied on what Goffman (1963) terms *disidentifiers* to separate themselves from things most stereotypically associated with lesbianism. For example, to contradict the masculine image identified with lesbianism, athletes sometimes consciously accentuated their femininity by wearing dresses, skirts, makeup, and earrings or by letting their hair grow. Others indicated that being seen with men or having a boyfriend is a common technique to reaffirm their heterosexuality. In a few instances this need to identify with men fosters more extreme behaviors including "hanging on men" in public or establishing a reputation as promiscuous with men. Some women athletes take care not to constantly be seen in public with groups of women; others were cautious about the nature of physical contact publicly displayed with women. In all cases, the athlete's presentation of self is consciously monitored or altered to conform to appropriate gender roles.

Although effective in controlling information, passing behaviors and disidentifiers can negatively affect individuals' psychological well-being, as well as alienate them from their personal identities (Goffman 1963). Goffman's work suggests that athletes who engage in passing may experience feelings of disloyalty and self-contempt as they disassociate themselves not only from their athletic identities but from qualities representing their personal essence.

In another form of disidentification, some athletes distanced themselves from athletes more seriously "contaminated" or stigmatized. This mechanism is accomplished through techniques such as making "rude comments" about a suspected lesbian teammate, establishing team cliques on the basis of sexual orientation, and being "very critical and mean" to lesbian teammates behind their backs.

Since the lesbian label is not equally applied to all athletes or teams, association with "certain" athletes increases the chance of stigmatization. In response to the question why women athletes are labeled lesbian, athletes identified three categories—appearance, personality characteristics, and nature of the sport activity.

Relative to appearance or externally identifiable characteristics, factors such as dress, hair style, body build, body posture/carriage, muscularity, and mannerisms were mentioned as underlying usage of the labels "dyke," "butch," or "lesbian." Athletes with personality characteristics such as being assertive, outgoing, strong, independent, aggressive, and hard-nosed are most likely to be labeled lesbian.

Regarding the nature of the sport activity, participants in team sports such as softball, basketball, and field hockey are more often recipients of the lesbian label. When asked why team sports are a more likely target, athletes indicated that such activities require more athleticism and strength, involve more physical contact, and are more commonly viewed as sports played by men. These qualities associated with team sports reflect traits socially defined as masculine (Bem 1974). Stigmatization of these team sports may discourage women from both engaging in "masculine sports" and participating in activities with potential to develop cooperation, teamwork, and solidarity among women (Lenskyj 1986). Self-distancing from those more seriously "contaminated," although effective for controlling information, may at the same time prevent women athletes from bonding together as a collective.

In a few instances athletes disassociate themselves from the lesbian label by publicly making fun of lesbian athletes or criticizing homosexuality. This disparaging behavior frequently occurs in the course of conversations with "outsiders" when the topic of women athletes is discussed. As Goffman (1963) suggests, a discreditable individual often finds it dangerous to refrain from joining in the vilification of one's own group. Such a strategy may protect the social identity of the individual athlete but impede the development and maintenance of the collective identity of women athletes.

When concealment is not possible, a stigmatized individual may adopt other stigma management strategies. Included are salience reduction through deflection and di-

rect confrontation through normalization (Elliott et al. 1990).

Deflection. Individuals may use deflection to reduce the importance or salience of a discrediting attribute. Representing the original source of stigmatization, the athlete role is publicly downplayed by athletes. Not only do women athletes use disidentifiers to distance themselves from this role, but they attempt to accentuate the significance of nonsport roles and attributes. It is thus important to many to be viewed as more than an athlete; efforts to demonstrate mastery in other areas (e.g., student role, social role) are common. For example, several athletes mentioned they want to do well in the classroom so that others will not identify them exclusively as athletes. Moreover, some athletes highlighted their social role by mentioning dating and party activities.

Normalization. In some situations it is difficult to reduce the visibility of the discrediting attribute (i.e., athletic status) when it is salient and relevant. This difficulty is particularly true of athletes who are visible on campus or the focus of media and where athletic status frequently impacts on the dynamics of social interaction. Rather than conceal or deflect, the individual has no choice but to directly confront the stigma. The ideal outcome for the athlete is a state of normalization where the discrediting attribute loses its stigmatizing capability. To accomplish normalization, strategies attempt to redefine the stigma and re-educate "normals" (Elliott et al. 1990). Although not widespread, redefinition efforts generally emphasize the positive characteristics or contributions of female athletes while re-education consists of athletes informing outsiders that lesbianism is not prevalent in women's sport or that sexual preference should be a non-issue.

Even though most respondents thought the lesbian label is unfairly applied to women athletes, attempts at normalization are difficult given their assumed violation of multiple gender norms. Although some athletes indicated the label did not bother them and that people could "think what they wanted," little evidence existed to suggest that the discrediting attribute of lesbian has lost its stigmatizing capability. Efforts to redefine or reeducate are generally futile since the vast majority of women athletes do not directly confront these labels, preferring to engage in other stigma coping strategies.

This refusal to confront the lesbian label resembles what Elliott and colleagues (1990) term capitulation. Even if false or inaccurate, the lesbian label assumes a master status for the individual (Becker 1963; Schur 1979) and becomes central to her identity and interactions. The stigmatized accept both the stereotypes placed upon them and the accompanying stigmatization. Athletes were generally not proactive in fighting the stereotypes; resistance to these stereotypes and labels usually emerges after a direct confrontation or challenge from an outsider. For example, one respondent stated "I am not an activist," while another indicated she "would not bring up the topic unless something negative was said."

Acceptance of the normative definition of deviance is often true of socially marginalized groups as they (1) rely on others for self-definition, (2) engage in self-hate, and (3) identify with the aggressor (Kitzinger 1987; Nobles 1973; Sarnoff 1951; Thomas 1971). Interestingly, several remarks from respondents demonstrate that women athletes accept and internalize societal stereotypes about themselves and incorporate these images into their identity accounts and personal interactions. For example, internalization of societal beliefs about appearance norms was evident in such comments as "I don't look like an athlete so I rarely am labeled a lesbian" and "I've never seen somebody that looks like a girl called a dyke or lesbian." One athlete dismissed lesbianism as a problem on her team since her "teammates were pretty." This same athlete implied, however, that lesbianism might be more prevalent on other teams since "most of the athletes on these teams looked like guys."

Self-hate was occasionally noted in responses as well. Although generally indicating the lesbian label angers them, athletes also mentioned that it makes them feel "unattractive" and "less desirable to men" and leads some to "always worry about how I look." Identification with aggressors was also evident in that some nonlesbian athletes engage in negative conversations that criticize or mock lesbian athletes.

Nevertheless, the presence of the deviant label does not necessarily garner negative outcomes (Elliott et al. 1990; Goffman 1963). As a few athletes' responses indicated, being labeled lesbian makes them stronger individuals and less dependent on what outsiders think of them. For example, learning to cope with the lesbian label helped one athlete "find confidence" in herself and encouraged another to learn more about homosexuality through reading and coursework. Moreover, some athletes claimed exposure to the issue of homosexuality makes them less judgmental and more accepting/respectful of dissimilar others.

Women athletes thus utilize a variety of stigma management techniques to control and manage information about their athleticism. This effort is somewhat paradoxical since most respondents were generally proud to be athletes and viewed their athletic experience as positive. The prevailing negative societal linkage of female athleticism with masculinity and lesbianism often overrides positive self-definitions of their athleticism.

Conclusion

This research examines ways the devaluation and stigmatization of women athletes impact on their social interactions and how they manage the lesbian label attached to their sport participation. Drawing upon Becker's (1963) construction of the "falsely accused deviant" and Goffman's (1963) conceptualization of "stigma management," the present analysis explicates both the social conditions and processes that facilitate false labeling, and stigma management strategies of women athletes. Although all respondents are deviant in that society views female athleticism in opposition to traditional gender norms (Schur 1984), indiscriminate application of the lesbian label to women athletes denotes many as falsely accused deviants.

In general, Klemke and Tiedeman's (1990) typology of error-types underlying false accusations (i.e., pure, intentional, legitima-tized, and victim-based) and discussion of societal conditions fostering false labeling (i.e., perceived threat, lack of power and out-sider status, and stereotype adoption) assist in understanding why false accusations are often directed at women athletes. Such fac-tors indicate that labeling is not a random process and that the study of false accusa-tion should focus on not only the falsely ac-cused but the false accusers as well (Klemke and Tiedeman 1990). As Klemke and Tiedeman (1990) argue, the "falsely accused deviant" is a conceptually rich category for analysis since it represents the quintessen-tial example of labeling and offers insight into the processes that generate false con-ceptions of social reality.

Responding to labels directed at women in sport, the athletes in this sample utilize a variety of stigma management techniques. These methods consist of concealment, in-cluding self-segregation, passing, and use of disidentifiers; deflection; and normaliza-tion. These strategies suggest that the falsely accused deviant reacts in a manner similar to the "pure deviant" (Becker 1963; Goffman 1963; Lemert 1972). Thus, stigma manage-ment is the domain of both the lesbian and nonlesbian athlete. Coping with a "spoiled identity," women athletes adopt various techniques to control and manage informa-tion about their athletic identities.

The role of labeling is undeniably central to understanding the experiences of women athletes forced to resort to stigma manage-ment strategies in the absence of deviant be-havior. Female athletes acquire the deviant label because more powerful groups impose their definition of morality on the athletic act (Erikson 1962; Kitsuse 1962). Critical in this labeling are the stigma-laden meanings female athleticism evokes and the processes by which these ideas are perceived and ap-plied. Such meanings are relayed to women reminding them of "their place" in the gen-der system (Henley and Freeman 1979).

Overall lack of power confounds the abil-ity of women athletes to actively challenge deviant labels. Not only do women in general lack power, but the discrediting attributes of athlete and lesbian diminish the power posi-tion of women athletes even further. Gen-erally lacking organizational backing and viewed as outsiders, women athletes, rather than actively challenge the stigma, rely on stigma management. This passivity not only has negative social and psychological out-comes for the athlete, but enhances the over-all power of the label itself. Since athletes re-sort to actions where silence and denial are central and internalization of deviant labels is frequent, the likelihood of resistance to these labels is significantly reduced.

References

Adler, Peter, and Patricia A. Adler. 1987. "Role Conflict and Identity Salience: College Athlet-ics and the Academic Role." *Social Science Journal* 24: 443–455.

Anderson, Margaret L. 1988. *Thinking About Women: Sociological Perspectives on Sex and Gender.* 2nd ed. New York: Macmillan.

Becker, Howard S. 1963. *Outsiders: Studies in the Sociology of Deviance.* New York: Free Press.

Bem, Sandra L. 1974. "The Measurement of Psy-chological Androgyny." *Journal of Consulting and Clinical Psychology* 42: 155–162.

Birenbaum, Arnold. 1970. "On Managing a Courtesy Stigma." *Journal of Health and So-cial Behavior* 11: 196–206.

Blinde, Elaine M. 1987. "Contrasting Models of Sport and the Intercollegiate Sport Experi-ence of Female Athletes." Ph.D. dissertation, Department of Physical Education, Univer-sity of Illinois, Urbana-Champaign.

Bogdan, Robert C., and Sari Knopp Biklen. 1982. *Qualitative Research for Education.* Boston: Allyn and Bacon.

Colker, Ruth, and Cathy S. Widom. 1980. "Corre-lates of Female Athletic Participation: Mascu-linity, Femininity, Self-Esteem, and Attitudes Toward Women." *Sex Roles* 6: 47–58

Elliott, Gregory C., Herbert L. Ziegler, Barbara M. Altman, and Deborah R. Scott. 1990. "Un-derstanding Stigma: Dimensions of Deviance and Coping." Pp. 423–443 in *Deviant Behav-ior,* edited by Clifton D. Bryant. New York: Hemisphere.

Erikson, Kai T. 1962. "Notes on the Sociology of Deviance." *Social Problems* 9: 307–314.

Goffman, Erving. 1963. *Stigma: Notes on the Management of Spoiled Identity.* Englewood Cliffs, NJ: Prentice Hall.

Goodman, Bernice. 1977. *The Lesbian: A Celebra-tion of Difference.* New York: Out and Out Books.

Griffin, Patricia S. 1987. "Homophobia, Lesbians, and Women's Sports: An Exploratory Analysis." Paper presented at the annual meetings of the American Psychological Association, New York.

Hall, M. Ann. 1988. "The Discourse of Gender and Sport: From Femininity to Feminism." *Sociology of Sport Journal* 5: 330–340.

Henley, Nancy, and Jo Freeman. 1979. "The Sexual Politics of Interpersonal Behavior." Pp. 391–401 in *Women: A Feminist Perspective*, edited by Jo Freeman. Palo Alto: Mayfield.

Keller, Evelyn F. 1978. "Gender and Science." *Psychoanalysis and Contemporary Thought* 1: 409–433.

Kitsuse, John I. 1962. "Societal Reaction to Deviant Behavior: Problems of Theory and Method." *Social Problems* 9: 247–256.

Kitzinger, Celia. 1987. *The Social Construction of Lesbianism*. London: Sage.

Klemke, Lloyd W., and Gary H. Tiedeman. 1990. "Toward an Understanding of False Accusation: The Pure Case of Deviant Labeling." Pp. 266–286 in *Deviant Behavior*, edited by Clifton D. Bryant. New York: Hemisphere.

Lemert, Edwin M. 1972. *Human Deviance, Social Problems, and Social Control*. 2nd ed. Englewood Cliffs, NJ: Prentice Hall.

Lenskyj, Helen. 1986. *Out of Bounds: Women, Sport and Sexuality*. Toronto: Women's Press.

———. 1991. "Combating Homophobia in Sport and Physical Education." *Sociology of Sport Journal* 8: 61–69.

Nobles, Wade W. 1973. "Psychological Research and the Black Self-Concept: A Critical Review." *Journal of Social Issues* 29: 11–31.

Pollak, Otto. 1952. "The Errors of Justice." *The Annals of the American Academy of Political and Social Science* 284: 115–123.

Sarnoff, Irving. 1951. "Identification with the Aggressor: Some Personality Correlates of Anti Semitism Among Jews." *Journal of Personality* 20: 199–218.

Scheff, Thomas J. 1964. "The Societal Reaction to Deviance: Ascriptive Elements in the Psychiatric Screening of Mental Patients in a Midwestern State." *Social Problems* 11: 401–413.

Schur, Edwin M. 1979. *Interpreting Deviance: A Sociological Introduction*. New York: Harper and Row.

———. 1984. *Labeling Women Deviant: Gender, Stigma, and Social Control*. New York: Random House.

Smith, Dorothy E. 1978. "A Peculiar Eclipsing: Women's Exclusion from Man's Culture." *Women's Studies International Quarterly* 1: 281–295.

Theberge, Nancy. 1985. "Toward a Feminist Alternative to Sport as a Male Preserve." *Quest* 37: 193–202.

Thomas, Charles W. 1971. *Boys No More*. Beverly Hills: Glencoe.

Willis, Paul. 1982. "Women in Sport in Ideology." Pp. 117–135 in *Sport, Culture and Ideology*, edited by Jennifer Hargreaves. London: Routledge and Kegan Paul.

Wolfe, Susan J. 1988. "The Rhetoric of Heterosexism." Pp. 199–224 in *Gender and Discourse: The Power of Talk*, vol. 30, edited by Alexandra Dundas Todd and Sue Fisher. Norwood, NJ: Ablex.

The authors thank two anonymous reviewers for their insightful and thorough comments.

50
Gay and Greek

The Identity Paradox of Gay Fraternities

King-To Yeung

Mindy Stombler

Deviance is a function of gaps between virtual and actual social identities, what Erving Goffman called stigma. Deviants typically seek to make the attribute that discredits them less glaring. There are a number of methods for doing this, from passing to disidentification to outright deception. Mainstreaming one's deviance, however—behaving in ways that make one's discrediting attribute more palatable—may be the most effective. To mainstream is to assimilate into the dominant culture but in ways that permit rule-breakers to maintain ties with their deviant world of choice. In so doing, offenders are able to "double-dip," enjoying the benefits of deviant subcultures while downplaying the defining nature of their stigmatization. Gay fraternities provide a case in point.

The fraternity is the quintessential heterosexual institution. It stands for everything that is macho—from homophobia and athletic prowess to alcohol abuse and the subjugation of women. Not surprisingly, fraternities have historically been no place for gay men. Yet some homosexuals have realized that the fraternity model can be co-opted—that is, harnessed for beneficial ends—and have used the institution as an arena for the collective expression of gay identity. Gay fraternities provide their members a resource for realizing wishes, desires, and preferences that would otherwise have to be kept hidden. They provide an institutional venue for the enactment of gay identity and a way to manage the oppressive heterosexual culture that exists on many college campuses. They allow members to engage in deviance under a rubric of institutional con-

formity, in essence hijacking the fraternity for their own subcultural ends.

Such activity is not without costs. Members of gay fraternities face considerable prejudice from straight fraternities and students at large precisely because they are "queer." It is not uncommon, for example, for the fraternities' campus advertisements to be destroyed and their property vandalized. This harassment may entice some members to be more covert, or "not as gay" as they might want to be, which contradicts the very reason for coming out—especially to form a fraternity. It also makes recruitment of additional members difficult. Regardless, gay fraternities represent a unique adaptation to stigma management, one that is as much organizational as interpersonal. Gay fraternities allow members to proclaim, celebrate, and affirm their homosexual identities even as they participate in what is arguably the epitome of "straight" institutions.

The concepts of identity construction, maintenance, and performance have been major areas of reflection for the gay community as members struggle to make sense of who they are in a society that defines them in negative terms (see e.g., Gamson 1995; Taylor and Whittier 1996; and Weeks 1977). The emergence and growth of the gay community was colored by how activists negotiated their sexual identities between the straight world and the gay world (Adam 1987; Altman 1982; D'Emilio 1983; Murray 1996; Warren 1974).[1] Debate between "assimilationists" and "liberationists," for instance, revealed a tension between legitimizing homosexuality in the straight world and creating autonomous space for lesbians and gay men (see Vaid 1995). Our research attempts to move beyond simple dichotomies such as assimilation/liberation; we seek to map out the complex and paradoxical processes of identity negotiation that allow groups both to emulate and to change the oppressive culture.

The development of a collective identity for the gay community is a social process. During the early period of community development, gay activists relied on the creation of a stable notion of gay identity for creating a sense of solidarity among members from a variety of social locations (Altman 1982; D'Emilio 1983; Hoffman 1968; Warren 1974). Through the construction of a coherent discourse and a unified knowledge of what it meant to be gay, members of the gay community could interact among homosexual "insiders" (Dank 1971; O'Mara 1997) and confidently confront heterosexual "outsiders" (Altman [1971] 1993; Fraser 1996; Seidman 1997). Using a binary opposition between homosexuality and heterosexuality, however, prevents theorists and activists from recognizing the inherent instability of gay identity as a social construction (Weeks 1995). Queer theorists, from a sociological perspective, recently targeted this problem and urged researchers to stress the centrality of sexual differences, projecting previously inaudible voices (Seidman 1996). Doing so potentially contributes to deconstructing a unified yet non-inclusive concept of gay identity that is characterized by terms and categories queer theorists view as oppressive (such as "lesbian," "gay," and "bisexual").

The opposition between "queers" and "gays" constitutes what Gamson (1995) referred to as the "queer dilemma," of choosing either a static gay identity or deconstructing all sexual identity. In other words, if activists use essentialized terms like "gay" or "lesbian" or "straight," as sexual identity categories, they can fight political battles for members of these categories. Yet in the process, minimally, identity-based activism marginalizes those not encompassed by the categories. However, if activists deconstruct the categories entirely, gay men, lesbians, and other "queer" individuals lose recognizable political voices for social change.

Thus, the logic of deconstructing a stable sexual identity for the purpose of inclusiveness seems incompatible with the political usefulness of a relatively stable notion of a gay identity. Gamson (1995:403) suggested that one way to begin resolving this dilemma is by recognizing that either logic operates within specific cultural and institutional configurations through which the dominant culture exerts oppression on the gay community. In essence, oppressions exist at multiple levels; activists must mobilize different organizational and cultural strategies to combat them. This calls for unpacking the layers of multiple identities and their social consequences that push and pull group members in different directions individually and collectively. Sexual identities and other social identities may be "washed away" by other, more salient, identities in specific situations (Brekhus 1996, 1998). This interplay among multiple identities can, in turn, produce the "paradoxes of identity" (Weeks 1995) referenced in regards to the queer dilemma (Gamson 1995).[2]

This paper responds to the call for a more dynamic view of sexual identity by analyzing how organizational structure, ideology, and member interaction impact sexual identities and their potential deconstruction. Although previous studies acknowledge institutional (Adam 1985; Foucault [1976] 1978; Gamson 1996; Greenberg 1988) and organizational impact (Esterberg 1997; O'Mara 1997; Wolf 1979) on the emergence of gay identity, few placed the paradoxes of identity at the center of analysis or situated the paradoxes within the dynamics of organizational structure and culture.[3] We contend that the paradoxes of identity, and the associated problems of presenting a unified identity, arise not only from the internal dynamics of the organizational practices and interactions among members of organizations, but also from the ways an organization is colored by its location in the gay and straight communities.

Our research will examine the tensions faced by a group of self-identified gay men as they sought both to emulate and change the oppressive majority culture. We examine how the collective identity of a particular organization, a gay fraternity, emerged as members negotiated their precarious location with one foot placed in one of the most traditionally heterosexist cultures in straight society, the college fraternity culture (Martin and Hummer 1989; Moffatt 1989; Stombler 1994) and the other placed in an oppositional gay culture. Current gay identity research tends to focus on identity construction as an act of activism against mainstream culture. By concentrating research efforts on this subset of the gay population, sociologists learn more about oppositional strategies than "mainstreaming" strategies in gaining legitimization from the dominant culture. Given the heterosexist nature of the traditional fraternity, this research juxtaposes how assimilation into and subversion of the dominant order can co-exist in paradoxical ways.

The national gay fraternity, Delta Lambda Phi (DLP)—consisting of sixteen chapters across the United States—served as a social alternative for gay college men. DLP modeled itself after traditional fraternities and retained the traditional features of brotherhood, rituals, and group hierarchical structure.[4] Its members shared straight fraternity goals such as involvement in campus social life, enhanced prestige on campus, networking opportunities and alumni connections, and, although not explicitly stated, achieving power over women and other men[5] (c.f. Martin and Hummer 1989; Sanday 1990; Stombler 1994; Stombler and Padavic 1997; Stombler and Martin 1994). Yet, based on our observations at the national convention and within the observed chapter and our interview and archival data, DLP rejected some traditional fraternity practices such as hazing, promoting single-race membership, encouraging sexual coercion, and enforcing individual conformity (Stombler, Wharton, and Yeung, 1997). We contend that DLP's choice to emulate the organizational structure of straight fraternities was not arbitrary, allowing DLP members to relate to both the gay and straight worlds. Using a fraternity model provided DLP members an opportunity to subvert the heterosexist fraternal tradition and potentially achieve legitimacy within the college campus community. A fraternity model that stressed brotherhood also allowed members to embrace and criticize aspects of the gay culture that they found unfulfilling. In both ways, adopting the fraternity model was a unique vehicle for members to restate what it meant to be gay and Greek. In doing so, however, DLP was faced with dilemmas that demanded that members choose between incompatible group strategies and ideologies. We will discuss not only how members constructed a collective identity within the gay fraternity, but also how the gay fraternity's placement, straddling both the gay and straight worlds, affected this development, creating a paradox of identity.[6]

Methods and Data

This paper is part of a larger research project on gay fraternities (Stombler, Wharton, and Yeung 1997). Data for the project came from 42 open-ended in-depth interviews, participant observation, official manuals, and archival data.

The project was divided into two phases. In the first phase Stombler conducted participant observation for a year in the mid-1990s in a DLP chapter-in-formation. She attended all fraternity chapter meetings, social events, rituals, and community service projects. In addition she conducted in-depth face-to-face interviews with fraternity members (all members volunteered to be interviewed). Stombler also attended the National Gay Fraternity Convention (Diva Las Vegas) where she observed interaction among members across the nation, interviewed members who responded to her research project announcement, and solicited additional interview volunteers for in-depth phone interviews.

In the second phase Yeung and Wharton joined the project and interviewed the previously recruited members from various chapters by telephone.[7] They also contacted chapter presidents and asked them for a list of additional interview volunteers. We also used the deviant cases sampling technique that involves seeking out respondents who are atypical to a setting such as straight or bisexual men in the case of the gay fraternity. Interviews—which were tape recorded and transcribed—averaged two hours. When the emergent concepts became "saturated" (Glaser and Strauss 1967), we ended the interview component of the project.[8]

Yeung and Wharton continued to conduct participant observation in the same chapter originally observed by Stombler until the chapter decided to seek official inactive status due to a shortage of active members. We then terminated the observation.

Archival data consisted of the official fraternity handbook, Internet web sites of the national and local chapters, newspaper articles, and magazine articles. As participant observation was conducted only in the Southwest, multi-regional archival data provided us with a picture of how chapters operated in a broader national context.

We used the grounded theory method to analyze these data (Charmaz 1983; Glaser and Strauss 1967; Martin and Turner 1986; Strauss and Corbin 1990, p. 994) and organized the findings around the emergent concepts generated using this method.

Constructing a Gay Identity

Gay organizations as communities of identity are self-reproducing (c.f., Melucci 1989) in two ways. First, the organization depends on a membership that includes individuals who identify themselves as gays or lesbians. This individual identification makes it possible for the organization to exist. Second, by participating in a gay organization, members are able to authenticate their sexual identity and reproduce the gay identity collectively. Gay identity is a point of entry for both the individual members and the organization to place sexual identity in the foreground while relegating other social identities to the background. In this section, we illustrate the dynamics of personal and collective reproduction of the gay identity by examining the ways DLP helped members to come out of the closet, bringing them into the gay community, and draw a collective boundary that challenged the traditional straight fraternity institution.

Coming Out and Moving Into the Gay World

Coming out of the closet represents the experience that gay men and lesbians have when first acknowledging their sexual orientation, identifying themselves as gay, acting on their sexual desire, disclosing this desire to others, and publicly entering the gay community (Dank 1971; Herdt 1992; Rhoads 1994; Troiden 1988). Some members of the gay fraternity reported that joining DLP marked their first coming out experience. In the observed chapter, many men used the fraternity rush event as their first function in the gay community. For instance, one member said he was so nervous that he was shaking during the rush party. Too scared to dress for the party in his dorm for fear of repercussions, he left in workout clothes and went to the mall where he purchased an outfit for the formal event and then changed into it before going to rush. The rush events often turned out to be the first time isolated gay college men met other gay men as a group.

For many members of DLP, the gay fraternity was the first site where they experienced their sexual identity in a structured form. The fraternity activities such as parties, rituals, and community service provided opportunities for new gay members to share their experiences and reaffirm their commonalities as members of the gay community:

> [During pledging] we have sort of a process where we go around and get signatures from all the active brothers and you talk about whatever. I went and talked with everyone about their coming out experience. . . .I feel like what brings us together is the experience of the fear of coming out. . . .I was so amazed that I was suddenly able to make connections with people who I had never felt like I could make them with before (B08).

DLP also used formal programming to explicitly bring forth the cultural aspect of gay sexual identity. For instance, one chapter held workshops on "how to do fabulous drag" and "how to deal with HIV-AIDS when it affects you or someone you love" (B07). Another chapter included the "essential gay history" in its coming out support program:

> There's a reason why [gay men] idolize Joan Crawford. There's a reason why they love Marilyn Monroe. . . .We teach gay history in the coming out group. Everybody is supposed to know the gay history [and is tested on it on fraternity pledge tests] (B22).

Besides transmitting a stock of knowledge about gayness, DLP also used cultural resources regarding gayness to bind its members, constructing a microcosm of the larger gay sub-cultural community. On movie nights, for instance, members often chose gay-theme movies such as "Jeffrey," or watched movies popular within gay culture:

> Instead of watching a regular old hit movie, [they] would seek out campy movies like "Breakfast at Tiffany's," "Mommy Dearest," and anything with Bette Davis [a gay icon] . . . [then, we went to the park] to play croquet and [it was] really campy. I'm like, "oh my god, my god, this is so gay, I love it!" (B30).

In another event, members played a game called "Gay Monopoly," which included "having discos instead of railroads, as well as locations and resorts popular among the gay community" (Hahn 1995). Through these events, members learned and created the cultural meaning of being gay.

Ultimately, DLP worked to redefine the meaning of being gay and helped members to recover from the fear, shame, or guilt they had experienced. Since the organization structured itself with an emphasis on brotherhood and mutual support among its members as a main goal (see below), the autonomy to become "who you are" found a structural support within the organization:

> One of our fraternity brothers was still in the closet. He didn't want to tell his family, but Pete [another brother] helped him along. He said, "Don't be ashamed of who you are. If your parents don't approve of you, fine, this is who you are." He told him, "You take it easy. Tell your parents individually or together, but you take it slowly. We'll work with you." He came out just fine even though his parents didn't approve of it at first. [His parents] kicked him out, but we found him a place to live (B27, observed chapter).

The secure environment that DLP fostered allowed members to identify, reaffirm, and celebrate their sexual identity as gay men, incorporating them into the larger gay community. These processes of identity formation were often grounded in group work and interaction within the organization. The processes of coming out as a group and as an individual were intertwined and reinforced one another:

> It's nice to belong to a group whose motto is "making your presence known" and to know that when you go out as a group, you are going out with the intention of letting people know you are there. You are not going to hide. It's very important to me when I came out to make people know. It was part of my battle to accept my sexuality and it is nice to be with a group of men. When we go out, we wear our shirts and you know we are there. You can't miss us (B32).

Group Boundaries in the Straight World

The extent to which members as individuals, and DLP as a group, could openly be out in the public, nonetheless varied according to DLP chapters' external social environments. The group boundary DLP established within the straight world was a contentious one, challenging the traditional fraternity institution on two levels. On one hand, the gay fraternity was striving to gain recognition within one of the most heterosexist institutions in American college life—the fraternity. On the other hand, DLP actively modified the traditional model by prohibiting hazing and other practices that were deemed "homophobic." At either level, DLP reconfigured its relations with the traditional institution by drawing a collective boundary that framed gayness as its core.

As a gay group, DLP demanded the right to enter the fraternity institution: "We feel if straight men can have the 'traditional' Greek experience, gay men should be able to have it as well" (DLP Web site). DLP's existence as an openly gay fraternity had the potential to "shock" the traditionally homophobic fraternity institution that encourages a "macho image" (Martin and Hummer 1989). Since the word fraternity "and the word gay are not usually associated" (B36) within this system, establishing a gay fraternity was particularly meaningful for campuses located in conservative regions:

> I think by virtue of calling ourselves the gay fraternity was making a statement nationally, especially down here. In San Francisco or Washington, D.C. or New York, gay fraternities might not be such a huge statement, but in the Bible belt, forming any kind of gay organization is making a statement (B21).

By coming out as a group, DLP demanded recognition: "It is making a statement to colleges and campuses saying, 'Hey, you need to recognize that you do have gay students; you have a large group of them'" (B09).

DLP also challenged the traditional fraternity model by prohibiting hazing. In official statements and group interaction, gay members claimed that hazing was unacceptable. This rejection reflected DLP's acknowledgment of oppression as part of the collective gay identity: "We feel that gays have been hazed enough by society" (DLP Web site). Unlike straight fraternities that have similar policies but often fail to follow them in practice (Nuwer 1990), DLP strictly followed the no-hazing policy, even at the local level. The gay fraternity also stood in contrast to traditional fraternities that solidify cohesion among members by stressing individual submission and obedience; by using physical coercion and humiliation, and by rejecting effeminacy or homosexuality.

By placing their identity as gay brothers in the foreground, and acknowledging themselves as part of an oppressed group, members of DLP also rejected the race, religion, and class homogeneity of the traditional fraternity system and collectively valued the importance of individuality and differences. One white member explained:

> I think we have experienced oppression for being gay. The whole idea of oppression or looking down or even separating yourself from another group whether it be ethnic religion, or otherwise wouldn't make any sense. If we are fighting for equality and all that sort of stuff for our gay selves then why would we inflict the same constraints or the same prejudice on anyone else? (B30).

While DLP encouraged diversity among its gay members, it also opened itself up to include straight and bisexual men, reflecting its inclusive agenda.[9] Embracing diversity could have been an organizational necessity since maintaining membership had indeed posed a major problem for the survival of some DLP chapters. The ideological aspect of DLP's encouragement of diversity, however, was equally important since this organizational ideology reflected an inversion of the historical exclusion of gay people from traditional fraternities (see Windmeyer and Freeman 1998). Both structural and ideological dynamics seemed to be working simultaneously to foster a diversified fraternity environment.

Many researchers describe traditional fraternities as organizations in which peer groups socially construct and reaffirm traditional gender relations and thus actively create gender inequality (Bryan 1987; Ehrhart and Sandler 1985; Garrett-Gooding and Senter 1987; Kalof and Cargill 1991; Martin and Hummer 1989; Sanday 1990; Stombler and Martin 1994; Stombler and Padavic 1997). Men in straight fraternities tend to define masculinity narrowly, emphasizing sexual conquest, competition, ability to consume alcohol, and a devaluing of the feminine (Martin and Hummer 1989; Moffatt 1989). Members of DLP did not embrace this narrow definition of masculinity. For example, gay members did not stigmatize effeminate behaviors; indeed, DLP members encouraged expressions of femininity. One member explained that "one thing in the gay fraternity that you don't see in the straight fraternities is that we don't have to play out our masculinity, you know, like prove our masculinity in certain ways" (B03). Members desiring to dress up in drag found the fraternity a safe place to practice "femaling" (Ekins 1997) and to express their individuality.

Embracing this gender fluidity and resisting hegemonic masculinity have been major components of gay identity (see Norton 1996). DLP's organizational events frequently structured (both intentionally and unintentionally) an arena for members to transgress gender boundaries. One member described how, at an initiation party, the "butch" members who had never thought of doing drag, attempted "border-crossing":

> The thing that sticks out the most from that evening is that we had what we call the Drag in the Bag Contest, which I think is unique to our chapter. . . .Without our knowledge, the little pledges got together all sorts of female and other paraphernalia . . .basically dress-up clothes, mostly female, but other things were in there also. You would see some of these really butch men dress up in drag and basically

just have a good time with it. They were taking pictures (B23).

Less frequently, members challenged gender boundaries outside the chapter and in public space. In one chapter, members organized an annual drag ball on campus that attracted a significant number of students. The ball gradually became a famous event on campus; one-year members estimated there were about 500 attendees.[10]

Through organizational ideology, formal rules, organizational practices, and interaction, DLP fostered a site where young men negotiated their sexual identity both internally and externally (c.f., O'Mara 1997). Individually, most brothers tended to view sexual identity as stable, something that one naturally acquires. DLP structured their organizational ideology in ways that promoted being gay as "who you are," while sharing the cultural resources of the gay community to assist members in this goal. Using gay culture as a cultural toolkit (Swidler 1986), DLP provided members a framework to structure their everyday existence as gay brothers. Collectively, DLP mirrored other gay organizations that construct a collective gay identity to transgress and to subvert (Gamson 1989). Resisting the homophobic traditional fraternity institution served to unify brothers as sexual dissenters from the legitimate model.

However, a paradox developed that concerned the individual gay identity of brothers, as well as the collective identity of DLP. DLP's desire for legitimate recognition within the traditional fraternity institution came into conflict with the very strategy it used to establish its group identity. Placing the gay identity in the background, or mainstreaming, risked antagonism from the gay world from which DLP often drew its support. Yet, by bringing gay identity to the foreground with the intention to transgress and subvert the current system, DLP risked losing the respectability and legitimacy they sought in the straight world.

The Paradox of Mainstreaming

The group goals of DLP were inconsistent; although attempting to contest the tradi-tional practices of straight fraternities, members also sought to construct a "normal," comparable fraternity image:

> We have a national [organization]; we have the same type of criteria that we all go through year after year. We're all men, and even though we are gay men, there's really not anything that really differentiates us from other men down the block in the other [straight] fraternities (B13).

Mainstreaming was thus a way for DLP to seek legitimacy in the straight world.[11] This process involved the fraternity seeking to build respectability and to emphasize sameness over difference vis-à-vis traditional fraternities. Downplaying differences to integrate into the mainstream was contradictory for an organization that was based on a gay membership. In order to reestablish what the fraternity thought was the appropriate image for gay men, primarily by defying stereotypes through desexualization and defeminization, DLP implicitly reaffirming the negative stereotypes imposed by the straight world. We will discuss these strategies to illustrate how DLP sought to downplay the gay identity in paradoxical ways.

Desexualizing

The gay fraternity was well aware of the misconceptions that members of the Greek system and the campus community had about gay men, in general, and DLP, specifically. Members found it particularly disturbing that outsiders associated being gay exclusively with sexual behavior. One member complained: "Here at the university they think we are the biggest sex club in the world. People have that viewpoint because you see gay and you see sex and that is all they think. We are not like that" (B27, observed chapter).

One way DLP members promoted the desexualizing goal (and group solidarity in case of failed relationships) was to formally discourage casual sex and in-group dating (especially between pledges and brothers whose relationships leaders defined as inherently unequal and therefore potentially exploitative). DLP was more tolerant of long-term monogamous relationships between brothers, especially considering that some brothers joined as couples. Even with a formal ban, some casual relationships and encounters did occur. We noted pledges interested in joining the fraternity to meet and date men, pledges dating brothers, brothers casually dating brothers, and rare incidences of open casual sex. Either way, intra-fraternity dating was more often a consequence of the men's proximity to one another than a characteristic of the fraternal form, and fraternity leaders explicitly discouraged it, promoting ideologies of familial relationships as opposed to sexual ones. Clearly by adopting the fraternal organizational form with its pseudo-familial kinship network of "brothers," and stressing the ideal of brotherhood over romance, DLP leaders made a strong statement against an overtly sexualized gay identity.

While DLP members did not always succeed in their desexualizing goal, their levels of sensitivity and reflexivity were reflected in how they dealt with problematic situations regarding the sexual image of DLP. During one gay pride event, a DLP chapter sold snow cones with "gay theme flavors" such as "lesbian lime." When "Gilbert's grapes"—referring to male genitals—appeared as a flavor, it triggered serious criticism from some members of the chapter:

I mean because children attend the event and some straight people attend the event, and to me, I am really quite tired of the sexual stereotype that straight people have of gays, and to me, I just thought that this strengthened the impression that other people have of us, and I think at a public event that there was no need to use that. . . .I don't want to belong to an organization that promotes or encourages sexual innuendo or the perception that straight people may have of us (B02).

This member successfully brought the issue to a vote where brothers decided their behavior was inappropriate and should be avoided in the future, thus reaffirming the desexualizing goal.

Public presentation of a non-sexualized image of DLP was paradoxical. It was impossible for DLP to address its own existence as a fraternity without also addressing the sexuality of its members. While desexualizing strategies presented DLP members as "normal" in the straight world, this strategy also interfered with another major goal, the celebration of sexual diversity. At the very least, we observed destigmatization of homosexuality only occurring in the backstage of fraternity interaction. For example, members welcomed private conversation and jokes packed with sexual innuendo (see Wharton 1998). Such a distinction between the public and private sphere reflected DLP's paradoxical efforts to establish both their identities as legitimized Greek members and as non-stigmatized gay males.

Defeminizing

Although some fraternity members enjoyed acting feminine within the private space of the fraternity, they were aware that, in order to gain acceptance on campus and in the general public, members could not act like "flaming queens." Feminine behavior was a concern for DLP and its public image, particularly in inter-fraternity functions:

The queeny guys sometimes don't want to tone it down, you know? It becomes really uncomfortable . . .to the more butch guys. I guess it's because [the butch guys] don't mind, but they don't want to be stereotyped as queeny. So when we're in public, it becomes a problem when the queeny guys just go off: "Girl Friend! Oh he's got a nice ass." And the straight-acting guys are like: "Uh-oh . . .let's, let's tone it down there. We don't want to draw too much attention to ourselves. We just like to keep a low profile" (B18).

In this instance, the concern over feminine behavior appeared to be an issue only for the "butch" members who felt uncomfortable with the "queens." Butch members perceived that acting "queeny" reinforced the stereotypes the straight population had about gay people. Indeed, straight-acting brothers often won such public controversy. When asked to "tone down" their queeniness, the queeny brothers usually complied.

By defining feminine behavior as inappropriate in public, many members co-opted the conventional prejudice that defined femininity as negative. In one chapter, the fraternity designed a specific program to ascribe gender-appropriate behavior. While the fraternity promoted tolerance of 'flaming' behavior, one member, nevertheless, admitted that tolerance of flaming behavior was bounded. "Flaming queens" were required to learn appropriate behavior from the chapter's "True Gentlemen Program" aimed at preparing members for the real world:

> [The program taught] what to do etiquette-wise when you are going out to dinner and when you are doing this or doing that. It is not appropriate in the business setting or in a meeting to turn around and snap your fingers and queen out. If we are in a social setting [i.e., within the chapter], you can do that all you want. It is just learning appropriateness (B09).

Prescribing and proscribing behaviors through member interaction and organizational practice also contradicted the group ideology of celebrating individuality that emphasized "being who you are." One member complained about this inconsistency:

> I got very aggravated at the brothers who, in a large group, act all butch and put others down for being nelly.[12] Then, in private, or when they get drunk, they turn into the biggest queens this side of Branson, Missouri (B10).

Concentrating on how straight people might react toward gay people through self-sanctioning, DLP shifted their group orientation from gay-focused to straight-referencing. The gay fraternity achieved this shift by clearly distinguishing between private space and the public sphere, thus splitting the public self from the private self (c.f. Goffman 1959) as described by the above brother. This split also resulted in different identity "markedness" (Brekhus 1996) according to the situation in which members were acting and interacting.

In the private fraternity space, the gay identity was salient both to the individual brothers and the fraternity as a collective. One brother explained that being feminine "was the standard pattern in the gay community, [such as] using feminine pronouns, and

even by [calling one another] feminine names. It's very normal" (B19). Described in the previous section, we also observed that the fraternity structured certain levels of gender fluidity, allowing members to pursue their individual preference of self-presentation.

In the public sphere, however, brothers often downplayed the stereotypical gay image, essentially reaffirming the negative connotation commonly attached to gay people.[13] Furthermore, by configuring a "normal" mainstream image, the gay fraternity restructured the gay identity at the collective level. Despite that essentially all of them were gay men, DLP used its group structure and group culture of brotherhood to reclaim their connection to the traditional fraternity institution in the hope of recognition. Rather than completely denying their gayness, members of DLP viewed mainstreaming as a way to reconstruct a new, more palatable gay image, if not a more realistic one. Yet DLP's decisions regarding how to operate in both the straight and gay worlds led to their public collective mainstreaming goal contradicting their private organizational goal of celebrating individuality, gay culture, and an uncompromised gay identity.

Gay Brotherhood: Creating an Alternative Gay Space

Just as mainstreaming strategies of the gay fraternity restated what it meant to be gay in the straight world, the formalization of a non-sexually defined brotherhood reshaped the meaning of membership in the larger gay community. Just as DLP utilized gay culture to challenge and modify the traditional fraternity model, it adopted the traditional fraternity ideal of brotherhood to create an alternative space in the gay community, attempting to improve a culture they found alienating and unfulfilling.

Despite their incorporation of aspects of the gay culture, many DLP members remained critical of aspects of the larger gay community. The founders of DLP recognized that while the larger gay community supported a plethora of clubs, most were either primarily motivated toward political or service goals or involved in "deviant" activities (Chapter Handbook). Current members of DLP also viewed the gay culture as oversexualized, filled with destructive behaviors, lacking depth, and too appearance-oriented. One member complained that:

A big part of the gay culture is the culture of sex and all the rituals that surround it—from the bar scene to social things....People are doing things that ostensibly are just fun and they are doing it because it is SO MUCH FUN. But if you think about it, there is really nothing all that fun about it; it is kind of self-destructive (B05).

Members also felt that the gay culture, as a whole, emphasized the "outside rather than the inside," because of its focus on appearance, youth, and power. Referring to Los Angeles, known as a gay hub, one member described a "pervasive superficiality":

"There is this competition to look like a model, to have the best looking [penis], the perfect body with all these muscles, a perfect looking face, clothes and cars, and all this stuff" (B12).

The members also judged the gay culture to be lacking cohesion:

Gay men are very alienated from each other. We go around; we walk around on the streets and see each other, but at the same time, there seems to be a lack of a real...there is just this lack of feeling that we are a community....There is a substantial amount of rejection of gay men toward each other (B21).

Other members found that gay men were too opinionated, that they tended to judge each other critically, and that they lacked trust toward one another and "put each other down a lot."

Drawing on the traditional fraternity model, the gay fraternity promoted a bond among its members using mythical ideals of brotherhood (see Clawson 1989; Clemens 1996). Brothers used shared symbols and rituals to foster a collective identity, creating a semblance of close relationships and connectedness:

We all go through the same ritual and education process. The common things that we all know are the same handshake; we all know the same signs; we know what letters stand for; we all wear the same letters. It is an opportunity to have something that links us and when we go out and see somebody and we talk about an event like the Night of Madness Party, everybody knows what a Night of Madness Party is. If they talk about the exam or learning the song or singing the song or doing the cheer, everybody knows it (B04).

Such shared experiences allowed strangers to identify as members; members described them as "amazing" and "unusual." One brother described his experience during the National Convention:

It was just amazing to me when I got there. I had never met any of them and they would just come up to me and say, "Hey, glad to see you!" Wow! I don't even know you....[It was a] very, very unusual experience for me. And I just got and felt really, really close to all these guys (B17).

The ideal of brotherhood conveys a sense of closeness and bonding among men who establish a quasi-familial relationship; it also entails mutual expectations and obligations such as trust and loyalty to the group (Martin and Hummer 1989). Through their group structure, DLP members actualized the ideals of true belonging, acceptance, and unconditional love in their daily interactions.[14] Members reported, for example, how they supported each other in personal crises. For instance, one member described how he received abundant financial and emotional support from other members when he experienced a financial crisis. He claimed this help was the most memorable incident in his fraternity life:

My brothers have been very financially helpful in the sense that if we were going out to dinner after a meeting, they'd say, "you wanna come along?" I'm like, "yeah, but I can't pay anything." And they're like, "don't worry about it; it's not a problem." So they were very understanding about my situation....They don't look down [on me] because some people could think of this as freeloading. But that's not it. We all are sort of looking out for each other and care for each other (B20).

Some members told how others who came from different backgrounds, had divergent political views, or had "extreme" personalities accepted each other and developed long-term friendships because, as one member put it, "in the end, brotherhood won out" (B24). The ideal of brotherhood was both a myth and an actual way for members to accomplish intimate relationships with one another.

Formalized rituals were particularly important for DLP members' expression of intimacy, especially for members who felt the need to get close to other gay men without the presence of any sexual connotations. Rituals such as the "warm fuzzy" helped achieve this goal:

> In our warm fuzzy exercise, we have a ball of yarn, or we have a warm, fuzzy pillow or something. And then one person starts and throws the pillow at somebody and gives that person a warm fuzzy. Like, "oh, thank you for helping me out, you're one of the nicest people I've seen." And that person has to throw it to somebody else in the fraternity. We did this like for two hours, until we're all like really comfortable and tired. It's all sappy, and then a box of Kleenex gets passed around. It's like, "hoo hoo [weeping sound] you're so wonderful to me." You know, a big drama, but it's great; it really pulls us all together (B18).

This organizational practice produced "emotion work" (Hochschild 1985) through which DLP members realized the ideal of brotherhood. Emotion work facilitated solidarity and allowed this non-conventional group to "create and legitimize new emotion norms that include expectations about how members should feel about themselves" (Taylor and Whittier 1996: 177). By fostering intimacy and emotional expression among gay men, the gay fraternity broke the conventional norms that detach masculinity from emotional expression for men in general (Cancian 1987) and for gay men in the particular clone culture (Blachford 1981; Levine 1998).[15] Thus, the brotherhood that DLP cultivated was both a brotherhood for

men and also uniquely "gay" in the sense that it was a direct response to the need of young, college, gay men who sought an alternative site for interaction and support. Using the traditional fraternity model, whose quasi-familial nature facilitated the desexualizing strategy that allowed DLP to both mainstream its image and redefine the meaning of gay male relationships in the gay world, helped DLP brothers address their dissatisfaction with the gay culture. Being gay and being brothers were two forms of collective identity that helped members of DLP connect themselves together in transcendental unity, downplaying all types of social differences. This collective identity also reflected the placement of the fraternity in two worlds, as it simultaneously emulated and resisted the straight world and reproduced and criticized the gay world.

Rejected by Both Worlds

Organizational logic of identity construction is, in part, a social consequence resulting from the configuration of oppression at both the institutional and cultural levels (Gamson 1995). The tension between identity construction, collective ideology and organizational structure in DLP becomes clearer when we situate the fraternity in both the gay world and the straight world. These two worlds, realistically inseparable, exerted different forces that DLP attempted either to resist or to accommodate, pulling and pushing the fraternity in directions of entering in or retreating from these worlds, and ultimately facing some level of rejection from both.

In the Straight World

The status of the gay fraternity within the traditional fraternity institution was precarious. While most straight fraternities did not publicly object to DLP's presence, most DLP chapters remained isolated from mainstream fraternities and prejudices against the gay fraternity on campus persisted. DLP members reported disturbances during gatherings and the destruction of their recruiting flyers. Some DLP chapters on conservative campuses continued to worry about the consequences of their visibility on campus. For instance, the observed chapter initially avoided joining the homecoming parade and also refused to have their photograph published in the school's yearbook, for fear of repercussions.

Even Inter-fraternity Council (IFC) affiliated chapters of DLP were conscious of their outsider status in the system. One member explained that other fraternities on campus regarded DLP as a "joke fraternity":

> They have IFC games during the homecoming week. And you know there are all these queens out there. . . .Of course we got our butts kicked most of the time, but we were still out there. We are like the joke fraternity. There have been a couple of members of our chapter who actually were in other [straight] fraternities, and they told us all about how they badmouthed us (B18).

Being tolerated by the legitimated institution does not necessarily mean full acceptance. Accommodation of and integration into an oppressive institution can be a limiting, if not paradoxical, strategy for groups that desire recognition in the mainstream culture (see Vaid 1995).

Although there were a few chapters that both immersed themselves in gay culture and functioned as full members of the Greek community on the IFC, most chapters had moved away from mainstreaming themselves as "just another fraternity for gay and progressive men" toward becoming gay organizations with autonomous existences. In 1996, DLP terminated its pursuit toward National Inter-fraternity Conference (NIC) membership, the national umbrella organization for college fraternities.[16] Rather than pursuing further rights to equal treatment in the straight world, giving up national recognition signified a retreat from the legitimated institution of traditional fraternities. Although not necessarily forgoing all mainstreaming strategies like desexualizing and defeminizing, this action represented a shift of collective identity and of group goals through time,[17] as one member elaborated:

> In the beginning we were very much interested in defining ourselves as a collegiate style fraternity. However, over the years, I think that through our maturing

of our members and our relationships and our real chapter experience, that is less important to us. In other words, being affiliated with a school is less important than to have our presence in the [gay] community (B04).

Giving up the pursuit of national recognition also signified a move back toward the gay-focused orientation: one brother recalled that "years ago the intention [of DLP] was to have another outlet for people who are discriminated against" (B02).

Mainstreaming strategies used by the gay fraternity were ways to encounter and negotiate the institutional oppression that was embedded in the traditional fraternity culture. Eliminating institutional oppression from the inside out placed DLP in a role that was inherently contradictory. The paradox of gay brotherhood, its simultaneous emulation of and dissension against its oppressor, remained contentious.

In the Gay World

The gay fraternity also related to the larger gay community in a contradictory way. Although DLP based its membership on gay identity, the gay community accused the fraternity of being "too Greek" because of its exclusionary practices in choosing members ("The boys of Delta Lambda Phi" 1993). Campus-based DLP chapters also found that other gay and lesbian campus organizations perceived DLP as a competitor, further dividing the already hard-to-find membership. "We tried to start chapters and have been squashed by resistance from the [student] gay groups," said one former chapter president (B31). These negative reactions from the gay community made members feel like outsiders from their "own kind." One member summed up:

> We are the outcasts. In reality, we offer a support group for the young gay male. However, in the eyes of many gay political leaders, we are discriminating because we do not allow [just] anyone in; you must be accepted. And of course, we're sexist in their eyes [referring to the exclusion of women] (B10).

Partly as a result of their criticism of and by the gay community, DLP ideologically separated itself in part from the gay culture. DLP failed to create strong links with other gay groups. Contacts with other organizations in the gay community were infrequent. Besides occasionally joining activities such as AIDS walks, Gay Pride Parades, voluntary work at AIDS hospices and supporting gay youth clubs, most of the time DLP chapters seemed concerned only with cultivating interpersonal relationships within their own organizations.

Emulating the fraternity model as an all-male social group further allowed DLP to see itself as an organization with a unique structure and not just as another gay organization. One brother told us that if the gay fraternity accepted women members, "it would not be brotherhood. It's not a fraternity at that point. It's a gay organization" (B13). As a relatively exclusive organization via its practice of excluding women, DLP conformed to the traditional fraternity model that prohibited out-group members' access to cultural resources (Clawson 1989; Wharton 1998). This exclusionary practice remained controversial, reflecting an identity dilemma of the fraternity as it negotiated its status in the gay world, a culture that, to a great extent, ideologically rejects sexism. However, as Levine (1998) argues, the gay movement has indeed opened a paradoxical channel for gay men to both emulate and parody oppressive institutions and culture. The possibility for gay men to reproduce a "straight" and sexist fraternity institution within a gay culture thus leads to the kind of "doubleness" (Levine 1998) that challenged similar gay organizations with contradictory identities such as gay Republicans.

Attempting to "take the best of both worlds" (B06) as one brother pointed out, DLP experienced some rejection from both. It became apparent in our analysis that the gay fraternity had turned its attention inward by constructing an alternative community for young gay men who sought to normalize their gay identity as men, just like all others, but who happened to be attracted to other men. The collective identity of DLP was shaped by both institutional oppression of the straight world and by DLP's dissatisfaction with the gay culture. Just as these two worlds are constantly changing, DLP will continue to renegotiate its collective identity, reconfigure its group ideology, and reform its organizational structure.

Conclusion

Group dynamics impact the construction, maintenance, and change of identity for individuals both personally and collectively. Focusing on the cultural and institutional embeddedness of identity construction, this paper suggests that people use multiple organizational strategies and cultural resources to make sense of their social locations. We argue that the process of identity construction and negotiation moves beyond choosing sides of dichotomies such as assimilation versus liberation, or between a totally deconstructed versus a reified notion of gay identity. Members of the gay fraternity used paradoxical strategies for identity construction as multiple social forces intersected with their self-understanding and performance of sexual identity.

By emulating the organizational structure and drawing upon cultural resources such as the ideal of brotherhood from traditional fraternities, members of DLP were able to formalize intimate relations between gay men, thus addressing their dissatisfaction with a gay culture they considered too alienating and too sexual. At the same time, the gay fraternity drew upon cultural resources from the gay world, realized in policies that prohibited hazing, celebrated diversity, and supported in-group actions like performing gender fluidity, in order to resist the institutional oppression of the traditional fraternity system.

Gay fraternity group strategies included a mix of contradictory elements that frequently placed its collective identity in question. Mainstreaming strategies and downplaying gayness in public space created a paradoxical situation, similar to closeting, that contradicted DLP's goal of "making our presence known." This assimilation strategy was clearly limiting for a group that sought recognition in both the college and gay communities. In addition to the mainstream straight fraternity institution, the cultural configuration of the larger gay community shaped the way DLP organized its boundaries. Arguing for an alternative space that valued non-sexual intimacy, members' support of a men-only ideology based on the fraternity model also came into conflict with a gay culture that, to a great extent, advocates gender inclusivity. DLP thus operated in relative isolation compared to other gay organizations in the gay community and other fraternities in the collegiate Greek system. Consequently, DLP failed to become a full member of either world.

At the theoretical level, gay fraternity strategies for dealing with its paradoxical identity shed light on debates on the nature of collective identity. The tendency for sociologists either to reify or completely abandon the notion of identity (see Epstein 1996; Seidman 1996) can be mitigated by understanding how gay fraternity members simultaneously constructed their collective identity while destabilizing the social location in which they anchored it, as evidenced by the statement we presented earlier: "We're all men; even though we're gay men there's not anything that differentiates us from other men down the block in the other fraternities" (B13). DLP's emphasis on constructing a relatively stable gay identity within their private gay space led to their less salient presentation of gayness in public space.

Multiple social identities submerge and reemerge according to cultural and institutional configuration, organizational structure and group ideology. The special organizational arrangement of the gay fraternity, marking the distinction between private fraternity space and public spheres for group presentation, suggested that identities operated at different levels of salience or "markedness" (Brekhus 1996, 1998). While certain identities were placed at the foreground, others retreated to the background. Identity markedness in DLP varied according to institutional and cultural embeddedness, and according to the organizational practices by which brothers, as active agents, made sense of their social world, allowing us to avoid either a deconstructionist or an essentialist approach to social identity construction and change (c.f. Hostetler and Herdt 1998).

Like other social identities, the paradox of sexual identity as a "necessary fiction" (Weeks 1995) helps theorists see both the social origin and the social consequences of collective identity. We invite further exploration of how an organization's unique location in our system of oppression affects group structure, ideology, and member interaction. Such exploration should compare the gay fraternity to other groups potentially facing paradoxes of identity such as lesbian sororities, gay Republicans, gay religious fundamentalists, and African-American fraternities.

Notes

1. The term "the gay community" refers to "an idea, as well as a group of people...who have a sense of oneness" (Warren 1974:13). While we focus on gay men, the community also consists of lesbians, bisexuals, transsexuals, and others who participate in "sexual dissent" (see Duggan and Hunter 1995). By "sexual identities" we are simply referring to the way people classify and present themselves as gay, straight, bisexual, transsexual, or transgendered. Individuals can also construct their sexual identity independently from attraction, desire, sexual practices, and other dimensions of their sexuality (see Schwartz and Rutter 1998; Laumann, et al. 1994).

2. This approach is also compatible with Epstein's (1996) description of "queering" that moves toward bridging the gap between identity politics and deconstructionism by redefining "queening" as balancing both sides of the queer dilemma. For Epstein, queening is an analytic strategy to "maintain identity and difference in productive tension by guarding against reification of identity without completely abandoning investigation of identity formation" (Epstein 1996:156).

3. Gamson's (1996) study of New York gay and lesbian film festival organizations comes closest to our analysis by focusing on the way collective identities changed over time, based on organizational response to institutional changes (such as the lesbian and gay market economy). While not excluding a discussion on change, our paper focuses on the paradoxical process that simultaneously constructed and deconstructed a collective identity through organizational structure and culture.

4. While DLP modeled itself after the traditional college fraternity, only one chapter had a fraternity house.

5. See Wharton and Stombler (1999) for a discussion of DLP's reproduction of hegemonic masculinity.

6. By "paradox" we mean something with seemingly contradictory qualities in reference both to being gay and to being involved in a fraternity (where masculinity has traditionally been defined hegemonically as not-gay and not female) and to claiming simultaneous oppositional and mainstream identities. This understanding of the paradoxical nature of sexual identity is closer to that of Weeks (1995).

7. The respondents either signed consent forms ensuring confidentiality or gave their verbal consent to participating. We use a number system in this paper m identify individual members (e.g. "B23").

8. Saturation refers to the point in the process of data collection and analysis where incidents of a particular category become repetitive and additional data no longer elaborate upon the meaning of the category (Charmaz 1983).

9. However, most DLP members did not really believe that any straight person would want to join a gay fraternity. From our investigation, we could only locate one straight brother throughout the nation. Prior to joining DLP, this straight brother was already friends with some DLP brothers. He found no problem assimilating into the fraternity. In fact, the fraternity treated him as an "endangered species," granting certain special treatment to accommodate his heterosexuality (Wharton 1998).

10. While members challenged some aspects of hegemonic masculinity, others remained intact. The policy of women's exclusion revealed contradiction and inconsistency in DLP's group ideology. Furthermore, members often described women in stereotypical sexist terms. Thus, by conforming to the traditional men-only fraternity membership policy, DLP reproduced a core element of hegemonic masculinity (see Wharton and Stombler 1999).

11. DLP's group strategies were similar to the early Homophile movement in the pre-Stonewall era when activists engaged in mainstreaming to "normalize" the gay identity by establishing respectability in the public sphere (D'Emilio 1983). But unlike the early Homophiles, the post-Stonewall cul-

tural and institutional configuration no longer provided DLP an environment in which the fraternity could seek normalization without also addressing itself as a transgressive "agent." The strategic use of public and private presentation, which we will discuss below, was a reflection of this dilemma.

12. According to DiLallo (1994), "nelly" refers to gay men being effeminate.

13. This public/private distinction was far from an intentional group goal for DLP. Downplaying the gay identity in the public was a consequence and potentially a reconciliation of DLP's contradictory attempts at both legitimization and transgression.

14. Although the ideal of brotherhood served as a cohesive agent to group solidarity, it did not guarantee cohesion, by any means. We observed and members reported many situations where brotherhood failed. Internal conflict was sometimes resolved by group rituals where brothers sat together and talked frankly about their interpersonal and organizational grievances. Members had mixed reactions when describing the effectiveness of this ritual since at times conflict was exacerbated as a result or continued to exist after the ritual exposed it.

15. According to Levine's (1998) ethnographic study, the gay clone culture, which emerged in the 1970s and gradually retreated in the mid-1980s, was a subset of the gay culture that parodied the presentational style of heterosexual working class men—a tough macho image—and favored anonymous sexual relations as a way of displaying "real" masculinity.

16. DLP members claim they were "well received" and even treated "like celebrities" when they attended the NIC convention. While some brothers were interested in pursuing membership, others saw the requirements as "limiting" since, for example, they required a certain number of men per chapter, prohibited non-student active fraternity members, and limited men from retaining membership in more than one fraternity (some DLP members continued to be members of straight fraternities). At DLP's national convention, the membership voted against petitioning the NIC for membership. Membership in the NIC, on many campuses, is a requirement for a local chapter's membership in their campus Interfraternity Council.

17. Although we noted that DLP had gradually withdrawn from seeking legitimization in straight fraternity circles, mainstreaming strategies remained central to DLP because such tactics helped the fraternity restate what it meant to be gay in the gay world as well.

References

Adam, Barry D. 1985. "Structural foundations of the gay world." *Comparative Studies in Society and History* 27(4):658–670.

——. 1987. *The Rise of a Gay and Lesbian Movement*. Boston: G. K. Hail.

Altman, Dennis. [1971]. *Homosexual: Oppression and Liberation*. New York: New York University Press. 1993

Altman, Dennis. 1982. *The Homosexualization of America, The Americanization of the Homosexual*. New York: St. Martin's.

Blachford, Gregg. 1981. "Male dominance and the gay world." In *The Making of the Modern Homosexual*, ed. Kenneth Plummer, 184–210. Totowa, NJ: Barnes & Noble.

Brekhus, Wayne. 1996. "Social marking and the mental coloring of identity: Sexual identity construction and maintenance in the United States." *Sociological Forum* 11(3):497–522.

——. 1998. "A sociology of the unmarked: Redirecting our focus." *Sociological Theory* 16(1):34–51.

Bryan, William A. 1987. "Contemporary fraternity and sorority issues." In *Fraternities and Sororities on the Contemporary College Campus*, eds. R. B. Winston, Jr., W. R. Nettles III, and J. H. Opper, Jr., 37–56. *New Directions for Student Services* 40 (Winter) San Francisco: Jossey-Bass.

Cancian, Francesca M. 1987. *Love in America: Gender and Self-Development*. Cambridge, UK: Cambridge University Press.

Chapter Handbook Delta Lambda Phi. (archival data).

Charmaz, Kathy. 1983. "The grounded theory method: An explication and interpretation." In *Contemporary Field Research*, ed. R. Emerson, 109–126. Boston: Little Brown.

Clawson, Mary Ann. 1989. *Constructing Brotherhood: Class. Gender, and Fraternalism*. Princeton, NJ: Princeton University Press.

Clemens, Elisabeth S. 1996. "Organizational form as frame: Collective identity and political strategy in the American Labor Movement. 1880–1920." In *Comparative Perspectives on Social Movements: Political Opportunities, Mobilizing Structures, and Cultural Framings*, eds. Doug McAdam, John D. McCarthy, and Mayer N. Zald, 205–226. Cambridge, MA: Cambridge University Press.

Dank, Barry M. 1971. "Coming out in the gay world." *Psychiatry* 34(2):180–197.

D'Emilio, John. 1983. *Sexual Politics, Sexual Communities: The Making of a Homosexual Minority in the United States, 1940–1970*. Chicago: University of Chicago Press.

DiLallo, Kevin. 1994. *The Unofficial Gay Manual: Living the Lifestyle (or at Least Appearing To)*. New York: Doubleday.

DLP Web site http://members.aol.com/dlpalpha/faq.html (archival data).

Duggan, Lisa, and Nan D. Hunter, (eds.) 1995. *Sex Wars: Sexual Dissent and Political Culture*. New York: Routledge.

Ehrhart, Julie D., and Bernice R. Sandler. 1985. *Campus Gang Rape: Party Game?* Washington, DC: Association for American Colleges.

Ekins, Richard. 1997. *Male Femaling: A Grounded Theory Approach to Cross-Dressing and Sex-Changing*. London: Routledge.

Epstein, Steven. 1996. "A queer encounter: Sociology and the study of sexuality." In *Queer Theory/Sociology*, ed. Steven Seidman, 145–167. Cambridge, MA: Blackwell.

Esterberg, Kristin G. 1997. *Lesbian and Bisexual Identities: Constructing Communities, Constructing Selves*. Philadelphia: Temple University Press.

Foucault, Michel. [1976]. *The History of Sexuality*, Vol. I: Introduction, translated by Robert Hurley. New York: 1978 Vintage Books.

Fraser, Michael R. 1996. "Identity and representation as challenges to social movement theory: A case study of Queer Nation." In *Mainstream(s) and Margins: Cultural Politics in the 90s*, eds. Michael Morgan and Susan Leggett, 32–44. Westport, CT: Greenwood Press.

Gamson, Joshua. 1989. "Silence, death, and the invisible enemy: AIDS activism and social movement 'newness.'" *Social Problems* 36(4):351–367.

——. 1995. "Must identity movements self-destruct? A queer dilemma." *Social Problems* 42(3):390–407.

——. 1996. "The organizational shaping of collective identity: The case of lesbian and gay film festivals in New York." *Sociological Forum* 11(2):231–261.

Garrett-Gooding, J., and Robert Senter, Jr. 1987. "Attitudes and acts of aggression on a university campus." *Sociological Inquiry* 57:348–372.

Glaser, Barney, and Anselm Strauss. 1967. *The Discovery of Grounded Theory*. Chicago: Aldine.

Goffman, Erving. 1959. *The Presentation of Self in Everyday Life*. Garden City, NY: Doubleday.

Greenberg, David F. 1988. *The Construction of Homosexuality*. Chicago: University of Chicago Press.

Hahn, Shannon. 1995. "Gay frat first in U.S. to get house." *The Minnesota Daily*, October 24 (archival data).

Herdt, Gilbert. 1992. "Coming out as a rite of passage: A Chicago study." In *Gay Culture in America: Essays from the Field*, ed. Gilbert Herdt, 29–67. Boston: Beacon Press.

Hochschild, Arlie Russell. 1985. *The Managed Heart: Commercialization of Human Feeling*. Berkeley: University of California Press.

Hoffman, Martin. 1968. *The Gay World: Male Homosexuality and the Social Creation of Evil*. New York: Basic Books.

Hostetler, Andrew, and Gilbert H. Herdt. 1998. "Culture, sexual lifeways, and developmental subjectivities: Rethinking sexual taxonomies." *Social Research* 65(2):249–290.

Kalof, Linda, and Timothy Cargill. 1991. "Fraternity and sorority membership and gender dominance attitudes." *Sex Roles* 25:417–423.

Laumann, Edward O., John H. Gagnon, Robert T. Michael, and Stuart Michaels. 1994. *The Social Organization of Sexuality: Sexual Practices in the United States*. Chicago: University of Chicago Press.

Levine, Martin R. 1998. *Gay Macho: The Life and Death of the Homosexual Clone*. New York: New York University Press.

Martin, Patricia Yancey, and Robert A. Hummer. 1989. "Fraternities and rape on campus." *Gender and Society* 3(4):457–473.

Martin, Patricia Yancey, and Barry A. Turner. 1986. "Grounded theory and organizational research." *Journal of Applied Behavioral Science* 22(2):141–157.

Melucci, Alberto. 1989. *Nomads of the Present: Social Movements and Individual Needs in Contemporary Society*. London: Century Hutchinson.

Moffatt, Michael. 1989. *Coming of Age in New Jersey: College and American Culture*. New Brunswick: Rutgers University Press.

Murray, Stephen O. 1996. *American Gay*. Chicago: University of Chicago Press.

Norton, Rictor. 1996. *The Myth of the Modern Homosexual: Queer History and the Search for Cultural Unity*. London: Cassell.

Nuwer, Hank. 1990. *Broken Pledges: The Deadly Rite of Hazing*. Atlanta: Longstreet Press.

O'Mara, Kathleen. 1997. "Historicising outsiders on campus: The reproduction of lesbian and gay insiders." *Journal of Gender Studies* 6(1):17–31.

Rhoads, Robert A. 1994. *Coming Out in College: The Struggle for a Queer Identity*. Westport, CT: Bergin and Garvey.

Sanday, Peggy Reeves. 1990. *Fraternity Gang Rape: Sex, Brotherhood, and Privilege on Campus*. New York: New York University Press.

Seidman, Steven. 1996. "Introduction." In *Queer Theory/Sociology*, ed. Steven Seidman, 1–29. Cambridge, MA: Blackwell.

——. 1997. *Difference Troubles: Queering Social Theory and Sexual Politics*. Cambridge, UK: Cambridge University Press.

Schwartz. Pepper, and Virginia Elisabeth Rutter. 1998. *The Gender of Sexuality*. Thousand Oaks, CA: Pine Forge Press.

Stombler, Mindy. 1994. "'Buddies' or 'slutties': The collective sexual reputation of fraternity little sisters." *Gender and Society* 8(3):293–296.

Stombler, Mindy, and Irene Padavic. 1997. "Sister acts: Resisting men's domination in black and white fraternity little sister programs." *Social Problems* 44(2):257–275.

Stombler, Mindy, and Patricia Yancey Martin. 1994. "Bringing women in, keeping women down: Fraternity 'little sister' organizations." *Journal of Contemporary Ethnography*, 23(2):150–184.

Stombler, Mindy, Renee Wharton, and King-To Yeung. 1997. "A house with no closets: Exploring the structure of and dynamics within gay fraternities." Paper presented at the Annual Meeting of the Society for the Study of Social Problems, Toronto. (August 10).

Strauss, Anselm, and Juliet Corbin. 1990. *Basics of Qualitative Research: Grounded Theory Procedures and Techniques*. Newbury Park, CA: Sage.

——. 1994. "Grounded theory methodology: An overview." In *Handbook of Qualitative Research*, eds. Norman K. Denzin and Yvonna S. Lincoln, 273–287. Thousand Oaks, CA: Sage.

Swidler, Ann. 1986. "Culture in action: Symbols and strategies." *American Sociological Review* 51:273–286.

Taylor, Verta, and Nancy E. Whittier. 1996. "Analytical approaches to social movement culture: The culture of the Women's Movement." In *Social Movements and Culture. Social Movements, Protest, and Contention*, Vol. 4, eds. Hank Johnston and Bert Klandermans, 163–187. Minneapolis, MN: University of Minnesota Press.

"The Boys of Delta Lambda Phi." 1993. *Washington Post*, F, 1:2 (November 28) (archival data).

Troiden, Richard R. 1988. *Gay and Lesbian Identity: A Sociological Analysis*. Dix Hills, NY: General Hall.

Vaid, Urvashi. 1995. *Virtual Equality: The Mainstreaming of Gay/Lesbian Liberation*. New York: Doubleday

Warren, Carol A. B. 1974. *Identity and Community in the Gay World*. New York: John Wiley and Sons.

Webster's New Collegiate Dictionary. 1980. Springfield, MA: G. and C. Merriam Company.

Weeks, Jeffrey. 1977. *Coming Out: Homosexual Politics in Britain, from the Nineteenth Century to the Present*. London: Quartet Books.

———. 1995. *Invented Moralities: Sexual Values in an Age of Uncertainty*. New York: Columbia University Press.

Wharton, Renee. 1998. *Hegemonic Masculinity in Gay Fraternities: Reproduction or Resistance?* Master's Thesis. Lubbock, TX: Texas Tech University.

Wharton, Renee, and Mindy Stombler. 1999. "Making men in gay fraternities: Reproducing and resisting hegemonic masculinity." Unpublished manuscript. Texas Tech University.

Windmeyer, Shane L., and Pamela W. Freeman. 1998. *Out on Fraternity Row: Personal Accounts of Being Gay in a College Fraternity*. New York: Alyson Books.

Wolf, Deborah Goleman. 1979. *The Lesbian Community*. Berkeley, CA: University of California Press.

The authors value the insightful comments of Joshua Gamson, Steven Seidman, Mary Ann Clawson, and an anonymous reviewer, who played an integral role in shaping the theoretical framework of this article: Irene Padavic; Charles W. Peek; Debra Street; Marc Steinberg; Xiao-Hui Xin; and the graduate student Social Problems Seminar at UC Irvine. We thank research team member, Renee Wharton, for collaborating on data collection and analysis. We are indebted to the members of Delta Lambda Phi for their openness. cooperation, and commitment to the larger project. Small grants for this research were provided by the Institute for University Research; the Office of Research Services; the College of Arts and Sciences; and the Department of Sociology, Anthropology, and Social Work at Texas Tech. Direct correspondence to: Mindy Stombler, Department of Sociology, Texas Tech University, Lubbock, TX 79409–1012.

51
Return to Sender

Reintegrative Stigma-Management Strategies of Ex-Psychiatric Patients

Nancy J. Herman

Mental illness is typically not something that goes away quickly and easily. For many, it is a life-long affliction that even major therapeutic advances will not mitigate. In days gone by, the truly intractable were separated from the rest of society, warehoused in large, impersonal asylums, and maintained there in relative obscurity (but reasonable comfort), often for the rest of their lives. With the 1970s and 80s came massive deinstitutionalization, and with deinstitutionalization came a wholesale transfer of mental patients into communities. In the real world, "ex-mentals," as they were called, faced multiple and pressing problems. Most came down to how they could manage information about a profoundly deviant status in ways that permitted some semblance of reintegration into the conventional world.

Exposure of one's stigmatizing status is fraught with problems, especially soon after release and especially when it involves people one does not know or trust. Tactics of information control and concealment have to be developed accordingly. Disclosing sensitive information, wittingly or unwittingly, can be more than a faux pas; it can profoundly and permanently undermine friendship networks and social capital. The concealment process is both challenging and unpredictable, so ex-patients have to be in a constant state of alert.

With time comes trust, and with trust comes the social support necessary to disclose, albeit selectively, one's stigma. Disclosures can be therapeutic or preventive, but both are on the patients' own terms. Patients craft the disclosure, deciding when and how to make it and how to embellish it in ways that

reflect less negatively on their essential character. Some patients take an additional step by trying to normalize their illness, proving through action that they are just as "regular" as the next person. Normalization is risky and does not always work, but the rewards (e.g., social, interpersonal) can be sweet when it does.

Like other researchers working in the field of discreditability, Herman explores how deviant individuals manage impressions and control information in ways that permit social reintegration. Implicit in such efforts is the deviants' abiding desire to be just like everyone else. Of course, some deviants will move beyond normalization to question the very label that has been foisted upon them. They become activists, aiming to fundamentally redefine what is deviant and why; in this sense, being "mental" becomes not something to hide but something to celebrate.

Although scholars have addressed the exit phase of deviant careers (see Adler and Adler 1983; Faupel 1991; Frazier 1976; Glassner et al. 1983; Harris 1973; Inciardi 1975; Irwin 1970; Luckenbill and Best 1981; Meisenhelder 1977; Ray 1961), the issue of reintegrating deviants into society has received little sociological attention. So too has little attention been given to the wide array of factors affecting role exit and reintegration.

Brown (1991) focussed on the reintegration of deviants who became "professional ex-s," individuals who capitalized on their deviant identity and status by moving into therapeutic counseling careers. Similarly, Braithwaite (1989) studied the effects of shaming individuals into role exit. Only a few studies (Chambliss 1984; Shover 1983, 1985; Snodgrass 1982) centered on the lives of ex-deviants in order to document their postdeviant worlds. These studies focused on the effects of former (prior) attributes, activities, or processing on their subsequent lives. Another notable exception is Adler (1992), who conducted a follow-up study of upper-level drug dealers and smugglers and the factors affecting reintegration into society. She found that individuals returned to the mainstream due to certain structural factors and when trafficking was no longer considered enjoyable but anxiety-provoking. Moreover, Adler documented the problems that ex-traffickers faced in attempting to secure or return to mainstream, legitimate, occupational realms and the career-based factors that aided or inhibited reintegration....

Setting and Method

. . .I initially conducted informal interviews with each of the ex-patients in coffee shops, their homes, in malls, or at their places of work. The interviews lasted from 3 to 5.5 hours. These interviews not only provided me with a wealth of information about the social worlds of ex-patients, but many subjects invited me to subsequently attend and participate with them in various social settings, including self-help group meetings, activist group meetings and protest marches, and therapy sessions. In addition, I frequently met with ex-patients during coffee and lunch breaks where they worked and was able to observe them interacting with co-workers. I ate lunches and dinners in their homes (as they did in mine) and watched them interacting with family members, friends, and neighbors. Each Wednesday afternoon, I met a group of 6 ex-patients at a local donut shop where they would discuss the problems they were facing "on the outside" and collectively search for possible remedy. . . .

Mental Illness and Strategies of Information Management

Some studies on the discreditable (Edgerton 1967; Humphreys 1972; Ponse 1976) have suggested that individuals either disclose their attribute to others *or* make attempts to actively conceal such information about their selves. Other studies (Bell and Weinberg 1978; Miall 1986; Schneider and Conrad 1980; Veevers 1980) have suggested that being a "secret deviant" is far more complex than either choosing to disclose or not disclose one's "failing." These studies suggest that individuals *selectively* conceal such

information about themselves at certain times, in certain situations, with certain individuals, and freely disclose the same information at other times, in other situations, with other individuals. Concealment and disclosure, then, are contingent on a "complex interaction of one's learned perceptions of the stigma [of their attribute], actual 'test' experiences with others before or after disclosure, and the nature of the particular relationship involved" (Schneider and Conrad 1980, 39).

The complex reality of how individuals selectively conceal and disclose information was evident in the case of nonchronic ex-psychiatric patients. Examination of their posthospital worlds revealed that many ex-patients not only faced economic hardships, had problems coping in the community, and experienced adverse side-effects from their "meds"[1] but also their perception of mental illness as a potentially stigmatizing attribute presented severe problems in their lives. Many lived their lives in states of emotional turmoil, afraid and frustrated—deciding who to tell or not tell, when to tell and when not to tell, and how to tell. Joan, a 56-year-old waitress, aptly summed it up for most nonchronics:

> It's a very difficult thing. It's not easy to distinguish the good ones from the bad ones. . . .You've gotta figure out who you can tell about your illness and who you better not tell. It is a tremendous stress and strain that you have to live with 24 hours a day!

Ex-psychiatric patients learned how, with whom, and under which circumstances to disclose or conceal their discreditable aspects of self, largely through a process of trial and error, committing numerous faux pas along the way. Frank, a 60-year-old factory worker, spoke of the number of mistakes he made in his "management work":

> I was released over 2 years now. And since then, I've developed an ulcer trying to figure out how to deal with my "sickness"— that is, how or whether others could handle it or not. I screwed up things a few times when I told a couple of guys on the bowling team. I made a mistake and

thought that they were my buddies and would accept it.

In fact, even if no faux pas were committed, there was no guarantee that others would accept proffered meanings and definitions of self. As Charlie, a 29-year-old graduate student hospitalized on three occasions, remarked,

> I'm not a stupid person. I learned how to handle effectively the negative aspects of my sickness—I mean how others view it. I've been doing OK now since my discharge, but still, each time I'm entering a new situation, I get anxious. I'm not always 100% sure of whether to tell or not to—especially in the case of dating relationships. Even if you've had success in telling certain types of people, there's always the chance—and it happens more than you think—that people will just not "buy" what you're trying so desperately to "sell" them.

Nearly 80% of the nonchronics in this study engaged in some form of information control about their illnesses and past hospitalizations. Specifically, the stratagems adopted and employed by the ex-patients resemble those observed in other deviant groups (see Davis 1961; Hewitt and Stokes 1978; Levitin 1975; Miall 1986; Schneider and Conrad 1980): selective concealment, therapeutic disclosure, preventive disclosure, and political activism—stratagems adopted by ex-patients in their effort to lessen or avoid the stigma potential of mental illness, elevate self-esteem, renegotiate societal conceptions of mental illness as a discreditable attribute, and alter deviant identities.

Selective Concealment

Selective concealment can be defined as the selective withholding or disclosure of information about the self perceived as discreditable in cases where secrecy is the major stratagem for handling information about an attribute. Especially during the time period directly following their psychiatric treatment, the majority of nonchronics had a marked desire to conceal such information about their selves from all others.

Decisions about disclosure and concealment were made on the basis of their perceptions of others, that is, whether they were "safe others" or "risky others." So too were decisions based on prior, negative experiences with "certain types" of others. Speaking of her classification of others into "trustworthy" and "untrustworthy" others, Dawina, a 46-year-old secretary institutionalized on seven occasions, said,

> It's like this. There are two types of people out there: "trustworthy" ones—the people who will be understanding and supportive—and "untrustworthy" ones. Out of all of my friends and relations and even the people I work with at the company, I only decided to tell my friend Sue.

Moreover, there was a hierarchical pattern of selective disclosure based on the individual's perceived degree of closeness and the ex-patient's revealing his or her discreditable attribute. In general, such information was most frequently revealed to family members, followed by close friends, and then acquaintances—a pattern also reflected in the literature on epileptics (Schneider and Conrad 1980) and involuntary childless women (Miall 1986). As Sarah, a 36-year-old mother of two, put it,

> When I was discharged, I didn't automatically hide from everyone the fact that I was hospitalized for a nervous breakdown again. But I didn't go and tell everyone either. I phoned and told my relatives in "Logenport," and I confided in two of my close, good friends here in town.

Further, selective disclosures to normal others were frequently made to test reactions. Similar to Schneider and Conrad's (1980) epileptics, the continued disclosure of ex-patients' mental illness was contingent upon responses they received to previous disclosures. Rudy, a 39-year-old hospitalized on ten occasions, stated,

> You learn through trial and error. When I was let out back in 1976, I was still naive, you know. I decided to tell a few people. Boy was that a mistake. They acted as if I had AIDS. Nobody wanted anything further to do with me. . . .Since then, I've

pretty much dummied up and not told anyone!

In those cases where concealment was the dominant strategy of information management, ex-patients usually disclosed only to one or two individuals. As Simon, a 25-year-old ex-patient, aptly expressed,

> I decided from the moment that my treatment ended I would tell as few people as possible about my stay in the psychiatric hospital. I figured that it would be for the best to "keep it under a lid" for the most part. So, to this day, I've only confided in my friend Paul and a neighbor who had a similar illness awhile back.

The employment of concealment as a stratagem of information management took the following forms: avoidance of selected "normals," redirection of conversations, withdrawal, the use of disidentifiers, and the avoidance of stigma symbols. Speaking on his efforts to redirect conversations, Mark, a 34-year-old nonchronic, explained,

> Look, you've got to remain on your toes at all times. More often than not, somebody brings up the topic about my past and starts probing around. Sometimes these people won't let up. . . .I use the tactic where I change the subject [or] answer their question with a question. . . .I try to manipulate the conversation so it works out in my favor.

For still others, concealment of their discreditable attribute was achieved through withdrawal. Over two-thirds of the ex-patients in this study engaged in withdrawal as a form of concealment, especially during the early months following discharge. Speaking of his use of this technique, Harry, a college junior, remarked,

> Sometimes when I'm at a party or some type of gathering with a number of people, I just remain pretty reticent. I don't participate too much in the conversations. . . .I'm really unsure how much to tell other people. For the most part, I just keep pretty quiet and remain a wallflower. People may think I'm shy or stuck-up, but I'd rather deal with that than with the consequences of others finding out that I'm a mental patient.

A third technique employed by over one-third of the ex-patients to conceal their discreditable aspects from others involved the use of disidentifiers (Goffman 1963, 44). That is, ex-patients used misleading physical or verbal symbols in an effort to prevent normal others from discovering their "failing." Similar to homosexuals (Carrier 1976; Delph 1978), unwed parents (Christensen 1953; Pfuhl 1978), and lesbians (Ponse 1976), who frequently made use of disidentifiers in their management work, nonchronic ex-patients also employed such techniques. Specifically, disidentifiers took the form of making jokes about psychiatric patients when in the presence of "normal" others and participating in protests *against* the integration of ex-patients into the community. Mike, a 26-year-old recently released after three hospitalizations, remarked (with some remorse) on his use of this tactic:

> They wanted to use this house down the street for a group home for discharged patients. All the neighbors on the street were up in arms over it. It didn't upset me personally, but the neighbors made up this petition, and to protect myself, I not only signed it but I also went door-to-door convincing other neighbors to sign it and "keep those mentals out." . . .I felt sort of bad afterwards, but what else could I do?

In a similar vein, Morgan, a 49-year-old history professor, explained how his joke telling aided in the concealment of his attribute:

> I conceal this information about myself—my psychiatric past—by frequently telling jokes about mental patients to my colleagues in the elevator, and sometimes even [in] my lectures and in everyday conversation. It's really a great ploy to use. People may think the jokes are in bad taste, but at the very least, it helps me to keep secret my illness.

A final form of concealing information on the part of ex-patients was through the avoidance of stigma symbols (Goffman 1963, 43)—signs that would bring into the forefront or disclose individuals' discreditable attribute. It is interesting to note that the data presented here on nonchronics and their avoidance of stigma symbols supports observations made of other deviant groups—for example, transsexuals (Bogdan 1974; Kando 1973) and unwed fathers (Pfuhl 1978). Among the 146 ex-patients studied, over two-thirds avoided contact with such stigma symbols as other ex-mental patients with whom they had become friends while institutionalized as well as self-help groups for ex-patients. They also avoided frequenting drop-in centers, attending dances and bingos for ex-patients, and, in general, placing themselves where other "patients and ex-patients hung out." For still others, avoidance of stigma symbols entailed not attending posthospital therapy sessions. Margarette, a stocky middle-aged female of German descent, explained her avoidance of postdischarge therapy sessions in the following manner:

> After I was released, my psychiatrist asked that I made appointments and see him every 2 weeks for follow-up maintenance treatments. But I never did go because I didn't want someone to see me going into the psychiatric department of "Meadowbrook Hospital" and sitting in the waiting room of the "Nut Wing." Two of my nosy neighbors are employed at that hospital and I just couldn't take the chance of them seeing me there one day.

In sum, as a strategy of information management, selective concealment of their attribute and past hospitalizations was done to protect themselves from the perceived negative consequences that might result from the revelation of their illness—an "offensive tactical maneuver" through which ex-patients attempted (although often unsuccessfully) to mitigate the stigma potential of mental illness on their daily lives. Notably, employing concealment as a strategy of information management was a *temporal* process. The majority of ex-patients employed this strategy primarily during the first 8 months following their discharge. During this time, in particular, they expressed feelings of anxiety, fear, and trepidation. However, as time passed, ex-patients began to test reactions, encountered both positive and negative responses from certain "normals," and their strong initial desires for secrecy were replaced by alternative strategies.

Therapeutic Disclosures

Therapeutic disclosure can be defined as the selective disclosure of a discreditable attribute to certain "trusted," "empathetic" supportive others in an effort to renegotiate personal perceptions of the stigma of "failing."

Similar to Miall's (1986) study on involuntary childless women and Schneider and Conrad's (1980) study on epileptics, 36% of the ex-patients felt that discussing their mental illnesses and past hospitalizations, getting it off their chests in a cathartic fashion, functioned to alleviate much of the burden of their loads. Attesting to the cathartic function disclosing served, Vincent, a 29-year-old ex-patient, remarked,

> Finally, letting it all out, after so many secrets, lies, it was so therapeutic for me. Keeping something like this all bottled up inside is self-destructive. When I came clean, this great burden was lifted from me!

Therapeutic disclosure was most often carried out with family members, close friends, and with other ex-psychiatric patients—individuals "sharing the same fate." Ida, a 52-year-old, discussing the circumstances surrounding her disclosure to a neighbor who had also been hospitalized in a psychiatric facility at one time, said,

> At first, I was apprehensive to talk about it. But keeping it inside of you all bottled up is no good either. One day, I walked down the street to a neighbor of mine and she invited me in to have tea. I knew what had happened to her years ago (her deceased husband confided in my husband). I let out all my anxieties and fears to her that afternoon. . . .I told her everything and she was so sympathetic. . . .She knew exactly what I was going through. Once I let it all out, I felt so much better.

Even in cases where ex-patients disclosed to individuals who turned out to be unsympathetic and unsupportive, some considered this therapeutic:

When I came out of hiding and told people about my sickness, not everyone embraced me. A lot of people are shocked and just tense up. Some just stare. . . .A few never call you after that time or make up excuses not to meet with you. . . .But I don't care, because overall, telling made me feel better.

Just as therapeutic disclosure functioned to relieve ex-patients' anxieties and frustrations, it also allowed for the renegotiation of personal perceptions of mental illness as a discreditable attribute. Speaking of the manner by which she came to redefine mental illness in her own mind as a less stigmatizing attribute, Edith explained,

When I finally opened up and started talking about it, it really wasn't so bad after all. My Uncle John was very supportive and helped me to put my mind at rest, to realize that having mental illness isn't so bad—it's not like having cancer. He told me that thousands of people go into the hospital each year for psychiatric treatment and probably every third person I meet has had treatment. . . . After much talking, I no longer think of myself as less human, but more normally. . . .Having mental illness isn't the blight I thought it was.

In short, ex-patients employed therapeutic disclosure to relieve feelings of frustration and anxiety, to elevate their self-esteem, and to renegotiate (in their own minds) personal perceptions of mental illness as stigmatizing.

Preventive Disclosure

Preventive disclosure can be described as the selective disclosure to "normals" of a discreditable attribute in an effort to influence others' actions and/or perceptions about the ex-patient or about mental illness in general (see Miall 1986; Schneider and Conrad 1980). Preventive disclosure of their mental illness and past hospitalizations occurred in situations where ex-patients anticipated future rejection by "normal" others. To minimize the pain of subsequent rejection, 34% of the sample decided that the best strategy to employ with certain people was preventive disclosure *early* in their relationships. As Hector, a 40-year-old janitor, stated,

I figured out that, for me, it is best to inform people right off the bat about my mental illness. Why? Because you don't waste a lot of time developing relationships and then are rejected later. That hurts too much. Tell them early, and if they can't deal with it and run away, you don't get hurt as much!

Preventive disclosure, then, represented a way that ex-patients attempted to prevent a drop in their status at a later date or as a way of testing acquaintances in an effort to establish friendship boundaries.

Just as nonchronics used preventive disclosure to avoid future stigma and rejection, so too did they employ this strategy to influence normals' attitudes about themselves and about mental illness in general. Specifically, ex-patients used the following devices: medical disclaimers (see Hewitt and Stokes 1978; Miall 1986; Schneider and Conrad 1980), deception/coaching (see Goffman 1963; Miall 1986; Schneider and Conrad 1980), education (see Schneider and Conrad 1980), and normalization (see Cogswell 1967; Davis 1961,1963; Levitin 1975; McCaghy 1968; Scott 1969).

Medical Disclaimers

Similar to Schneider and Conrad's (1980) epileptics and Miall's (1986) involuntary childless women, 52% of the ex-patients frequently used medical disclaimers in their management work—"blameless, beyond-my-control medical interpretation(s)" developed to "reduce the risk that more morally disreputable interpretations might be applied by naive others" discovering their failing (Schneider and Conrad 1980, 41). Such interpretations were often used by ex-patients to evoke sympathy from others and to ensure that they would be treated in a charitable manner. As Dick, an unemployed laborer, put it,

When I tell people about my hospitalization in a psychiatric hospital, I immediately emphasize that the problem isn't anything I did—it's a biological one. I didn't ask to get sick—it was just plain biology, or my genes that fucked me up. I try to tell people in a nice way so that they see mental illness just like other diseases—you know, cancer or the mumps. It's not my parents' fault or my own. . . .I just tell them, "Don't blame me, blame my genes!"

In a similar vein, Anna, a 29-year-old waitress, explained her use of medical disclaimers:

Talking about it is quite tricky. When I tell them about it, I'm careful to emphasize that the three times I was admitted was due to a biochemical imbalance—something that millions of people get. I couldn't do anything to help myself—I ate properly, didn't drink or screw around. It's not something I deserved. When you give people the facts and do it in a clinical fashion, you can sway many of them to sympathize with you.

Further, 11 ex-patients revealed their mental illness and past hospitalizations as a side effect of another medical problem or disease, such as childbirth, stroke, or heart disease, thereby legitimizing what otherwise might be considered a potentially stigmatizing condition. As Rebecca, a 36-year-old ex-patient, confessed,

I have had heart problems since birth. I was a very sick baby. I've had four operations since that time, and I've been on all kinds of medications. The stress of dealing with such an illness led to my depression and subsequent breakdowns . . . .When my friends hear about mental illness in this light, they are very empathetic.

Whereas Sue spoke of her successes in influencing others' perceptions about her attribute and mental illness in general, Lenny lamented about his failure with the same strategy:

Life's not easy for ex-nuts, you know. I tried telling two of my drinking buddies about my schizophrenia problem one night at the bar. I thought if I told 'em it's a "disease" like having a heart problem that they would understand and pat me on the butt and say it didn't matter to them and that I was OK. Shit, it didn't work out like I planned—they flipped out on me. Sid couldn't handle it at all and just let out of there in a hurry. Jack stayed around me

for about 20 minutes and then made some excuse and left.

In sum, through the use of medical disclaimers, ex-patients hoped to elevate their self-esteem and to renegotiate personal perceptions of mental illness as a nonstigmatizing attribute.

Deception/Coaching

Deception differed from strategies of concealment in that with the former, ex-patients readily disclosed their illness and past hospitalizations but explicitly distorted the conditions or circumstances surrounding it. Similar to Miall's (1986) involuntary childless women and Schneider and Conrad's (1980) epileptics, about one-third of the ex-patients employed deceptive practices developed with the assistance of coaches. Coaches included parents, close friends, spouses, and other ex-patients sharing the same stigma. Coaches actively provided ex-patients with practical suggestions on how to disclose their attribute in the least stigmatizing manner and present themselves in a favorable light. Maureen, a 32-year-old ex-patient, explained her "coaching sessions" with relatives:

My parents and grandma really helped me out in terms of what I should say or tell others. They were so afraid I'd be hurt that they advised me what to tell my schoolmates [and] the manager at Wooldo where I got hired. We had numerous practice exercises where we'd role-play and I'd rehearse what I would say to others. . . .After a while I became quite convincing.

Moreover, it is interesting to note that about one quarter of the ex-patients employed deceptive practices together with medical disclaimers. As Benjamin, a 62-year-old ex-patient, aptly expressed,

To survive in this cruel, cold world, you've got to be sneaky. I mean, that you've got to try to win people over to your side. Whoever you decide to tell about your illness, you've got to make it clear that you had nothing to do with getting sick—nobody can place blame on anyone. . . .And you've got to color the truth about how you ended up in the hospital by telling heart-sob stories to get people sympathetic to you. You never tell them the whole truth or they'll shun you like the plague!

Education

A third form of preventive disclosure used by ex-patients to influence others' perceptions of them and their ideas about mental illness was education. Similar to Schneider and Conrad's (1980) epileptics and Miall's (1986) involuntary childless women who revealed their attribute in an effort to educate others, 28% of the ex-patients revealed for the same educational purposes. Marge, a 39-year-old ex-patient, speaking on her efforts to educate friends and neighbors, stated,

> I have this urge inside of me to teach people out there, to let them know that they've been misinformed about mental illness and mental patients. We're not the way the media has portrayed us. That's why people are afraid of us. I feel very strongly that someone has to tell people the truth [and] . . .give them the facts. . . .And when they hear it, they're amazed sometimes and begin to treat me without apprehension. . . .Each time I make a breakthrough, I think more highly of myself too.

Ex-patients did not automatically attempt to educate everyone they encountered but, rather, based on subjective typification of normals, made value judgments about whom to "educate." Brenda, speaking on this matter, explained,

> You just can't go ahead and tell everyone. You ponder who it is, what are the circumstances, and whether you think that they can be educated about it. There are some people that these efforts would be fatal and fruitless. Others, however, you deem as a potential, and these are the people you work with.

Whereas education proved successful for some ex-patients in their management activities with certain individuals, others found it less successful. Jim, recalling one disastrous experience with a former poker buddy, said,

> I really thought he would learn something from my discussion of the facts. I really misjudged Fred. I thought him to be an open-minded kind of guy but per-

haps just naive, so I sat him down one afternoon and made him my personal "mission." I laid out my past and then talked to him about all the kinds of mental illnesses that are out there. He reacted terrible. All his biases came out, and he told me that all those people should be locked up and the key thrown away—that they were a danger to society. He was probably thinking the same thing about me too!

Following Goffman (1963), medical disclaimers, deception/coaching, and education are forms of "disclosure etiquette"— they are formulas for revealing a stigmatizing attribute "in a matter of fact way, supporting the assumption that those present are above such concerns while preventing them from trapping themselves into showing that they are not" (p. 101).

Normalization

A final form of preventive disclosure employed by ex-psychiatric patients to manage stigma was normalization. This concept is drawn from Davis's (1963) study on children with polio and is akin to deviance disavowal (see Davis 1961). Normalization is a strategy that individuals use to deny that their behavior or attribute is deviant—it "seeks to render normal and morally acceptable that which has heretofore been regarded as abnormal and immoral" (Pfuhl 1986, 163). Similar to observations made on pedophiles (McCaghy 1968), the obese (Millman 1980), the visible handicapped (Levitin 1975), and paraplegics (Cogswell 1967), about one-quarter of the ex-psychiatric patients I studied also employed this same strategy. Such persons were firmly committed to societal conceptions of normalcy and were aware that according to these standards they were disqualified—they would never "measure up." Yet ex-patients made active attempts at rationalizing and downplaying the stigma attached to their failing. So, for example, they participated in a full round of normal activities and aspired to normal attainments. They participated in amateur theater groups, played competitive sports such as hockey and tennis, enrolled in college, and so on. Ex-patients whose stigma could be considered "discreditable," that is, not readily or visibly apparent to others, would disclose such information for preventive reasons, thereby rendering them "discredited" in the eyes of others. They would then attempt to negotiate with normals for preferred images, attitudes, roles, and nondeviant conceptions of self and for definitions of mental illness as less stigmatizing. Discussing his use of this technique, "Weird Old" Larry, a 59-year-old ex-patient, stated,

> The third time I got out [of the hospital], I tried to fit right in. I told some of my buddies and a couple of others about my sickness. It was easier to get it out in the open. But what I tried to show 'em was that I could do the same things they could, some of them even better. I beat them at pool, at darts, [and] I could outdrink them. I was holding down two jobs—one at the gas station and [the other] at K-Mart. I tried to show them I was normal. I was cured! The key to success is being up front and making them believe you're just as normal as them. . . .You can really change how they see and treat you.

If successfully carried out, this avowal normalized relations between ex-patients and others.

This is not to imply, however, that the strategy of normalization worked for all patients in all situations. Similar to Millman's (1980) overweight females who were accepted in certain roles but treated as deviant in others, many ex-patients expressed similar problems. Frederick, speaking on this problem with respect to co-workers, said,

> It's really tragic, you know. When I told the other people at work that I was a manic-depressive but was treated and released, I emphasized that I was completely normal in every way . . .but they only accepted me normally part of the time, like when we were in the office. . . .But they never really accepted me as their friend, as one of "the boys," and they never invited me over to dinner with their wife and family—they still saw me as an ex-crazy, not as an equal to be worthy of being invited to dinner or playing with their kids.

It is interesting to note that just as ex-patients whose attribute was discreditable employed the strategy of normalization, so too did other ex-patients with discrediting attributes (conditions *visibly apparent* or *known* to others) employ this same technique. Explaining how medication side effects rendered him discredited and how he attempted to reduce the stigma of mental illness through normalization, Ross said,

> Taking all that dope [they] dish out makes my hands tremble. Look at my shaking legs, too. I never used to have these twitches in my face either, but that's just the side effects, a bonus you get. It really fucks things up, though. If I wanted to hide my illness, I couldn't—everyone just looks at me and knows. . . .So, what I do is to try to get people's attention and get them to see my positive side—that I can be quite normal, you know. I emphasize all the things that I can do!

In short, by presenting themselves as normals, ex-patients hoped to elicit positive responses from others whose reactions were deemed important. From a social psychological perspective, others accepted and reinforced a nondeviant image of self through this process of negotiation, allowing ex-patients to achieve more positive, nondeviant identities.

In many cases, ex-psychiatric patients progressed from one strategy to another as they managed information about themselves. Specifically, they moved from a strategy of initial selective concealment to disclosure for therapeutic and preventive reasons. According to the ex-patients, such a progression was linked to their increased adjustment to their attribute as well as the result of positive responses from others to the revelation of their mental illness.

Political Activism

Just as ex-psychiatric patients developed and employed a number of individualized forms of information management to deal with the stigma potential of mental illness, enhance self-images, and alter deviant identities, they also employed one collective management strategy[2] to achieve the same ends, namely, joining and participating in ex-mental patient activist groups (see

Anspach 1979). Such groups, with their goal of self-affirmation, represent what Kitsuse (1980) terms "tertiary deviation"—referring to the deviant's "conformation, assessment, and rejection of the negative identity embedded in secondary deviation, and the transformation of that identity into a positive and viable self-conception" (p. 9).

Political activism served a threefold function for ex-patients: (a) it repudiated standards of normalcy (standards to which they could not measure up) and the deviant labels placed on these individuals; (b) it provided them with a new, positive, nondeviant identity, enhanced their self-respect, and afforded ex-patients a new sense of purpose; and (c) it served to propagate this new, positive image of ex-mental patient to individuals, groups, and organizations in society. The payoff from political activism was, then, both personal as well as social.

Similar to such activist groups as the Gay Liberation Front, the Disabled in Action, the Gray Panthers, or the radical feminist movement, ex-mental patient activists rejected prevailing societal values of normalcy through participation in their groups. They repudiated the deviant identities, roles, and statuses placed on them. Moreover, these individuals flatly rejected the stigma associated with their identities. Steve, a 51-year-old electrician, aptly summed it up for most ex-patient activists when he stated,

> The whole way society had conceived of right and wrong, normal and abnormal is all wrong. They somehow have made us believe that to be mentally ill is to be *ashamed* of something—that these people are to be feared, that they are to blame for their sickness. Well I don't accept this vein anymore.

After repudiating prevailing cultural values and deviant identities, ex-patient activists collectively redefined themselves in a more positive, nondeviant light according to their *own* newly constructed set of standards. Speaking of her having embraced a new nondeviant identity, Susan, a 39-year-old ex-patient who recently returned to teaching school, said,

> I no longer agree to accept what society says is normal and what is not. It's been so unfair to psychiatric patients. Who are they to say, just because we don't conform, that we're rejects of humanity? . . .The labels they've given us are degrading and make us feel sick . . .[and] have a negative connotation to them. . . .So, we've gotten together and liberated ourselves. We've thrown away the old labels and negative images of self-worth, and we give ourselves new labels and images of self-worth—as human beings who should be treated with decency and respect.

In contrast to other ex-patients who employed various individual management strategies to deal with what they perceived to be their *own personal* problems—personal failings—ex-patient activists saw their problems not as personal failings or potentially stigmatizing attributes but as *societal* problems. To the extent that ex-patients viewed their situations in this manner, it allowed them to develop more positive self-images. Speaking of this process as one of "stigma conversion," Humphreys (1972) stated,

> In converting his stigma, the oppressed person does not merely exchange his social marginality for political marginality. . . .Rather, he emerges from a stigmatized cocoon as a transformed creature, one characterized by the spreading of political wings. At some point in the process, the politicized "deviant" gains a new identity, an heroic self-image as crusader in a political cause. (P. 142)

Sally, a neophyte activist, placed the "blame" on society for her deviant self-image:

> It's not any of our faults that we ended up the way we did. I felt guilty for a long time. . . .I crouched away, feeling that I had something that made me "different" from everyone else, a pock on my life. . . .But I learned at the activist meetings that none of it was my fault. It was all society's fault—they're the one who can't deal with anything that is different. Now I realize that having mental illness is nothing to be ashamed of—it's nothing to hide. I'm now proud of who . . .and what I am!

Just as political activism, as contrasted with other adaptive responses to stigma, sought, in repudiating the dominant value system, to provide ex-patients with positive, nondeviant statuses, so too did it attempt to propagate this new positive, normal image of ex-psychiatric patient to others in society. Thus, through such activities as rallies, demonstrations, protest marches, attendance at conferences on human rights for patients, lobbyist activities directed toward politicians and the medical profession, and the production of newsletters, ex-patient activists sought to promote social change. Specifically, they sought to counter or remove the stigma associated with their "differentness" and present society with an image of former psychiatric patients as human beings capable of self-determination and political action. Abe, the president of the activist group, aptly summed up the aim of political activism during a speech to the selected political figures, media personnel, and "upstanding" citizens:

> Simply put, we're tired of being pushed around. We reject everything society says about us because it's just not accurate. We reject the type of treatment we get . . .both in the hospital . . .and out. We don't like the meaning of the words [people] use to describe us—"mentals" and "nuts." We see ourselves differently, just as good and worthy as everybody out there. In our newsletter, we're trying to get across the idea that we're not the stereotypical mental patient you see in the movies. We're real people who want to be treated equally under the Charter of Rights. We're not sitting back now—we're fighting back!

In sum, then, through participation in political activist groups, many ex-patients internalized an ideology that repudiated societal values and conventional standards of normalcy, rejected their deviant identities and statuses, adopted more positive, nondeviant identities, and attempted to alter society's stereotypical perceptions about mental patients and mental illness in general.

Discussion: Becoming an 'Ex-Crazy'—Role Exit and Reintegration

With the exception of a few studies (Adler 1992; Chambliss 1984; Shover 1985; Snodgrass 1982), little systematic attention has been given to individuals' postdeviant careers. Centering on the lived experiences and accounts of 264 ex-psychiatric patients, this article has dealt with the key elements and dimensions of their exit process and their (albeit problematic) social reintegration. More generally, my research has attempted to make a contribution to the existing literature on deviant careers, the perception of stigmatizing attributes, stigma management strategies, and the reintegration of deviants.

When psychiatric patients are discharged from the institutions or psychiatric wards of general hospitals, their problems[3] are far from over. In fact, numerous problems lie ahead for such persons in their efforts to return to a conventional life. As Erikson (1966), Ebaugh (1988), and others have noted in their studies on role exit and the reintegration of deviants into society, there exist virtually no formal rights of passage to mark the ex-deviant's passage out of deviant identities and roles. Whereas society has developed and employed various "degradation ceremonies" (Garfinkel 1956) marking the passage of individuals from "normal" to "deviant" identities and statuses, there are no such comparable ceremonies to re-instate the "transformed" or "ex-deviant." My findings suggest that ex-patients realized not only that no such ritualistic ceremonies existed to "transform them back" but also that they possessed a stigma that severely impeded such a transformation of self and endangered their future participation in society. In response to their undesirable posthospital social situations, nonchronic ex-psychiatric patients employed five strategies, which if successfully carried out, lessened or mitigated the stigma of their failing, enhanced self-esteem, aided self-transformation, and also allowed for renegotiation of societal conceptions of mental illness as a discreditable attribute. Strategies of stigma management have important consequences for social identities. Ebaugh (1984), in her study of nuns leaving the convent, spoke of the process of becoming an "ex-" in terms of the concepts of "role exit" and "self-transformation." Specifically, she asserted that "ex" roles represent a unique sociological phenomenon in that definitions of self and societal expectations are shaped and often determined by a previous identity. That is, on the one hand, individuals are fighting to leave behind their *old* identities, statuses, and roles, while, on the other hand, others are continually taking those into account when interacting with them. Ebaugh (1984) further pointed out that there are some "ex" roles in our society that are fairly well-defined, such as ex-president, but what we are seeing in society today is an increasing number of "ex" roles for which there are few well-defined normative expectations. In these situations, the "ex's" themselves have to create role definitions as they play out their lives. Supporting others' (Ebaugh 1984; Glassner et al. 1983; Irwin 1970; Meisenhelder 1977; Shover 1983) documentations of role-exiting experiences that portrayed individuals' attempts to shake off their old roles and create new roles designed to reformulate societal expectations of their selves, I discovered a similar process operating with respect to discharged nonchronic patients. In their process of self-transformation, former patients struggled to cast off their deviant identities and roles largely due to their perception of mental illness as a stigmatizing attribute. As Goffman (1963) stated, "The stigmatized individual tends to hold the same beliefs about identity that we do. His deepest feeling about what he is may be his sense of being a 'normal person,' a human being like anyone else, a person, therefore, who deserves a fair break. What is desired by the individual is what can be called acceptance" (p. 78). The creation of a new identity of "ex-crazy" or "ex-mental patient," a positive, nondeviant, nonstigmatizing identity, arose then through an ongoing process of negotiations with normals in a bid for "acceptance." In particular, ex-patients were successful in transforming their deviant aspects of self when (or if)[4] (a) they began to think of themselves in terms of current, nondeviant

roles and began to project such an image to others and (b) others began to relate to them in terms of those *new* roles. . . .

Notes

1. See Herman (1986) for a detailed discussion of such other posthospital problems.
2. Following Lyman's (1970) typology on deviant voluntary associations, ex-mental patient political activist groups represent an "instrumental-alienative" type of association. It is interesting to note that chronic ex-patients also employed one collective form of stigma management; specifically, they formed and participated in deviant subcultures (see Herman 1987).
3. For a detailed discussion of their problems as pre- and inpatients, see Herman (1986).
4. It is important to reiterate that transforming deviant identities is extremely difficult and complex. The implementation of the various strategies discussed in this article in no way guaranteed success. Many times, ex-patients were unsure about when to use them, in which situations, with whom, and so forth. Even if they were used correctly, there was no guarantee that others would react in a positive manner, that is, that they would accept proffered meanings and definitions.

References

Adler, Patricia. 1992. "The 'post' phase of deviant careers: Reintegrating drug traffickers." *Deviant Behavior* 13:103–26.

Adler, Patricia, and Peter Adler. 1983. "Shifts and oscillations in deviant careers: The case of upper-level drug dealers and smugglers." *Social Problems* 31:195–207.

Anspach, Renee. 1979. "From stigma to identity politics: Political activism among the physically disabled and former mental patients." *Social Science and Medicine* 13A:765–73.

Bar-Levav, Reuven. 1976. "The stigma of seeing a psychiatrist." *American Journal of Psychotherapy* 30:473–82.

Bartell, Gilbert D. 1971. *Group sex: A scientist's eye witness report on the American way of swinging.* New York: Wyden.

Becker, H. S. 1963. *Outsiders: Studies in the sociology of deviance.* New York: Free Press.

Bell, Alan, and Martin S. Weinberg. 1978. *Homosexualities: A study of diversity among men and women.* New York: Simon & Schuster.

Berger, P., and T. Luckmann. 1966. *The social construction of reality.* New York: Doubleday.

Bogdan, Robert. 1974. *Being different: The autobiography of Jane Fry.* New York: Wiley.

Bord, Richard James. 1970. "Rejection of the mentally ill: Continuities and further developments." *Social Problems* 18: 490–512.

Braithwaite, John. 1989. *Crime, shame and reintegration.* Cambridge: Cambridge University Press.

Brown, J. David. 1991. "The professional ex-: An alternative for exiting the deviant career." *Sociological Quarterly* 32: 219–30.

Carrier, J. M. 1976. "Family attitudes and Mexican male homosexuality." *Urban Life* 50: 359–75.

Chambliss, William J. 1984. *Harry King: A professional thief's journey.* New York: Wiley.

Cheadle, A. J., H. Freeman, and J. Korer. 1978. "Chronic schizophrenic patients in the community." *British Journal of Psychiatry* 132: 221–27.

Christensen, Harold T. 1953. "Studies in child spacing: Premarital pregnancy as measured by the spacing of the first birth from marriage." *American Sociological Review* 18: 53–59.

Clausen, John. 1981. "Stigma and mental disorder: Phenomena and terminology." *Psychiatry* 44 (4): 287–96.

Cochrane, R., and K. Nieradzik. 1985. "Public attitudes towards mental illness—The effects of behavior, roles, and psychiatric labels." *International Journal of Psychiatry* 31 (1): 23–33.

Cogswell, B. 1967. "Rehabilitation of the paraplegic: Processes of socialization." *Sociological Inquiry* 37:11–26.

D'Arcy, Carl, and Joan Brockman. 1977. "Public rejection of the ex-mental patient: Are attitudes changing?" *Canadian Review of Sociology and Anthropology* 14 (1): 68–80.

Davis, Fred. 1961. "Deviance disavowal: The management of strained interaction by the visibly handicapped." *Social Problems* 9: 120–32.

——. 1963. *Passage through crisis: Polio victims and their families.* Indianapolis: Bobbs-Merrill.

Delph, E. 1978. *The silent community: Public homosexual encounters.* Beverly Hills, CA: Sage.

Doll, W., Edward Thompson, Jr., and Mark Lefton. 1976. "Beneath acceptance: Dimensions of family affect towards former mental patients." *Social Science and Medicine* 10 (6): 307–13.

Ebaugh, Helen Rose Fuchs. 1984. "Leaving the convent: Role exit and self-transfomation." In *The existential self in society,* edited by J. A. Kotarba and A. Fontana, 156–76. Chicago: University of Chicago Press.

——. 1988. *Becoming an ex: The process of role exit.* Chicago: University of Chicago Press.

Edgerton, Robert. 1967. *The cloak of competence: Stigma in the lives of the mentally retarded.* Berkeley: University of California Press.

Erikson, Kai T. 1966. *Wayward puritans.* New York: Wiley.

Estroff, Sue E. 1981. *Making it crazy: An ethnography of psychiatric clients in an American community.* Berkeley: University of California Press.

Farina, Amerigo, and Kenneth Ring. 1965. "The influence of perceived mental illness on interpersonal relations." *Journal of Abnormal Psychology* 70: 47–51.

Faupel, Charles E. 1991. *Shooting dope: Career patterns of hard-to-reach heroin users.* Gainesville: University of Florida Press.

Frazier, Charles. 1976. *Theoretical approaches to deviance.* Columbus, OH: Charles Merrill.

Freeman, H. D., and O. G. Simmons. 1961. "Feelings of stigma among relatives of former mental patients." *Social Problems* 8: 312–21.

Garfinkel, Harold. 1956. "Conditions of successful degradation ceremonies." *American Journal of Sociology* 61: 420–24.

Glassner, Barry, Margret Ksander, Bruce Berg, and Bruce D. Johnson. 1983. "A note on the deterrent effect of juvenile vs. adult jurisdiction." *Social Problems* 31: 219–21.

Goffman, Erving. 1961. *Asylums.* New York: Doubleday.

——. 1963. *Stigma.* Englewood Cliffs, NJ: Prentice Hall.

Goldmeir, J., M. Shore, and F. Mannino. 1977. "Cooperative apartments: New programs in community mental health." *Health and Social Work* 2 (1): 120–40.

Harris, Mervyn. 1973. *The dillyboys.* Rockville, MD: New Perspectives.

Herman, Nancy J. 1981. "The making of a mental patient: An ethnographic study of the processes and consequences of institutionalization upon self-images and identities." Master's thesis, McMaster University, Hamilton, Ontario, Canada.

——. 1986. "Crazies in the community: An ethnographic study of ex-psychiatric clients in Canadian society—Stigma, management strategies and identity transformation." Ph.D. diss., McMaster University, Hamilton, Ontario, Canada.

——. 1987. "'Mixed nutters and looney tuners': The emergence, development, nature and functions of two informal, deviant subcultures of chronic, ex-psychiatric patients." *Deviant Behavior* 8: 235–58.

Hewitt, J., and R. Stokes. 1978. "Disclaimers." In *Symbolic interactionism*, edited by L. Manis and B. N. Meltzer, 308–19. Boston: Allyn & Bacon.

Humphreys, Laud. 1972. *Out of the closets: The sociology of homosexual liberation*. Englewood Cliffs, NJ: Prentice Hall.

Inciardi, James. 1975. *Careers in crime*. Chicago: Rand McNally.

Irwin, John. 1970. *The felon*. Englewood Cliffs, NJ: Prentice Hall.

Kando, T. 1973. *Sex change: The achievement of gender identity among feminized transsexuals*. Springfield, IL: Charles C Thomas.

Kitsuse, John. 1980. "Presidential address." *Society for the Study of Social Problems* 9: 1–13.

Kreisman, D. E., and V. D. Joy. 1974. "Family responses to the mental illness of a relative: A review of the literature." *Schizophrenia Bulletin* 1 (10): 34–57.

Lamb, J., and V. Goertzel. 1977. "The long-term patient in the era of community treatment." *Archives of General Psychiatry* 34: 679–82.

Lamy, Richard E. 1966. "Social consequences of mental illness." *Journal of Abnormal Psychology* 70: 47–51.

Lefton, Mark, S. Angrist, S. Dinitz, and B. Pasamanick. 1962. "Social class, expectations and performance of mental patients." *American Journal of Sociology* 68: 79–87.

Levitin, T. 1975. "Deviants as active participants in the labeling process: The case of the visibly handicapped." *Social Problems* 22: 548–57.

Lorber, J. 1967. "Deviance as performance: The case of illness." *Social Problems* 14: 302–10.

Luckenbill, David F., and Joel Best. 1981. "Careers in deviance and respectability: The analogy's limitations." *Social Problems* 29: 197–206.

Lyman, Stanford M. 1970. *The Asian in the West*. Reno/Las Vegas, NV: Western Studies Center, Desert Research Institute.

McCaghy, Charles H. 1968. "Drinking and deviance disavowal: The case of child molesters." *Social Problems* 16: 43–49.

Meisenhelder, Thomas. 1977. "An exploratory study of exiting from criminal careers." *Criminology* 15: 319–34.

Miall, Charlene E. 1984. "Women and involuntary childlessness: Perceptions of stigma associated with infertility and adoption." Ph.D. diss., York University, Toronto, Canada.

———. 1986. "The stigma of involuntary childlessness." *Social Problems* 33 (4): 268–82.

Miller, Dorothy, and Wm. Dawson. 1965. "Effects of stigma on reemployment of ex-mental patients." *Mental Hygiene* 49: 281–87.

Millman, Marcia. 1980. *Such a pretty face*. New York: Norton.

Nunnally, J. 1961. *Popular conceptions of mental health*. New York: Holt, Rinehart & Winston.

Pfuhl, Erdwin H., Jr. 1978. "The unwed father: A 'nondeviant' rule breaker." *Sociological Quarterly* 19: 113–28.

———. 1986. *The deviance process*. 2d ed. Belmont, CA: Wadsworth.

Ponse, Barbara. 1976. "Secrecy in the lesbian world." *Urban Life* 5: 313–38.

Rabinowitz, Jonathon. 1982. "Shared ethnicity as a correlate of acceptance of the formerly hospitalized mentally ill." *Journal of Sociology and Social Welfare* 9: 534–40.

Ray, Marsh. 1961. "The cycle of abstinence and relapse among heroin addicts." *Social Problems* 9: 132–40.

Reynolds, David K., and Norman Farberow. 1977. *Endangered hope: Experiences in psychiatric aftercare facilities*. Berkeley: University of California Press.

Robins, L. 1980. "Alcoholism and labeling theory." In *The labeling of deviance*, edited by W. Gove, 34–47, 2d ed. Beverly Hills, CA: Sage.

Sagarin, E., and R. Kelly. 1980. "Sexual deviance and labeling perspectives." In *The labeling of deviance*, edited by W. Gove, 347–79, 2d ed. Beverly Hills, CA: Sage.

Scheff, Thomas. 1975. *Labelling madness*. Englewood Cliffs, NJ: Prentice Hall.

———. 1984. *Being mentally ill: A sociological theory*. 2d ed. Chicago: Aldine.

Schneider, J., and R. Conrad. 1980. "In the closet with illness: Epilepsy, stigma potential and information control." *Social Problems* 28: 32–44.

Schur, Edwin. 1979. *Interpreting deviance: A sociological introduction*. New York: Harper & Row.

Scott, Robert. 1969. "The socialization of blind children." In *Handbook of socialization theory and research*, edited by D. Goslin. Chicago: Rand McNally.

Segal, S. P., J. Baumohl, and E. W. Moyles. 1980. "Neighborhood types and community reaction to the mentally ill: A paradox of intensity." *Journal of Health and Social Behavior* 21: 345–59.

Shover, Neil. 1983. "The later stages of ordinary property offenders' careers." *Social Problems* 31: 208–18.

——. 1985. *Aging criminals.* Beverly Hills, CA: Sage.

Snodgrass, John. 1982. "The jack-roller at seventy: A fifty-year follow-up study." Lexington, MA: Lexington.

Taylor, S. Martin, Michael Dear, and G. Hall. 1979. "Attitudes toward the mentally ill and reactions to mental health facilities." *Social Science and Medicine* 13D: 281–90.

Thoits, Peggy. 1985. "Self-labelling processes in mental illness: The role of emotional deviance." *American Journal of Sociology* 91: 221–49.

Thomas, W. I. 1931. *The unadjusted girl.* Boston: Little, Brown.

Trute, B., and A. Loewen. 1978. "Public attitudes toward the mentally ill as a function of prior personal experience." *Social Psychiatry* 13: 79–84.

Veevers, Jean. 1980. *Childless by choice.* Toronto: Butterworths.

Webber, Avery, and James D. Orcutt. 1982. "Employers' reaction to racial and psychiatric stigmata: A field experiment." Paper presented at the 31st Annual Meeting of the Society for the Study of Social Problems, San Francisco.

Whatley, C. D. 1959. "Social attitudes toward discharged mental patients." *Social Problems* 6: 313–20.

I wish to thank the Social Sciences and Humanities Research Council of Canada for their generous support of this long-term research endeavor. In addition, I wish to thank Larry T. Reynolds and Bernard N. Meltzer for their helpful comments and suggestions on earlier drafts of this article.

52
Leaving Deviance

The Case of Upper-Level Drug Dealers and Smugglers

Patricia A. Adler

Peter Adler

Deviance has often been discussed in career terms—the process by which involvement starts, escalates, plateaus, and declines. The career metaphor, however, may be a bit misplaced; it implies a consistency of purpose, stability, linearity, and definable trajectory, which many deviant careers simply do not have. In the pithy words of Gottfredson and Hirschi (1986), most deviant careers "start at the bottom and proceed nowhere." Yet the career metaphor is useful for understanding how individuals learn and apply deviant norms in real-life settings and circumstances. As a heuristic tool, it also is helpful for exploring the relationships that deviants have with one another, the forms of social organization that emerge, and how these forms evolve into networks with definable microstructures.

Participation in deviant careers waxes and wanes, ebbs and flows, and changes substantively depending on context and circumstance. Entry into a deviant career does not usually mean continuation, or continuation in any stable sense. Deviance "oscillates" more than anything else—moving back and forth, up and around, and side to side in an uncertain fashion that is difficult to predict. Accounting for the nonlinearity of deviant careers is one of the most important tasks any sociologist can undertake.

Successful transition out of a deviant lifestyle requires a stake in conformity, ties to conventional others, and opportunities for reintegration. Even with such resources, reintegration will not happen unless or until the deviant recognizes that his or her life is no longer manageable. Such recognition requires sensi-

tivity, awareness, and a willingness to do things differently—qualities in short supply for many rule-breakers, especially serious ones. The point is that deviants usually cannot be convinced to change because it is in their best interest or because they will derive long-term benefits or because it is the "right thing to do" (Jacobs 2000, 144). Enduring transformation requires a hard and sober look at one's existence and the realization that it must be changed. The Adlers explore these and other issues, paying particular attention to the evolution of deviant careers and their mid- and longer-term consequences.

The upper echelons of the marijuana and cocaine trade constitute a world which has never before been researched and analyzed by sociologists. Importing and distributing tons of marijuana and kilos of cocaine at a time, successful operators can earn upwards of a half million dollars per year. Their traffic in these so-called "soft"[1] drugs constitutes a potentially lucrative occupation, yet few participants manage to accumulate any substantial sums of money, and most people envision their involvement in drug trafficking as only temporary. In this study we focus on the career paths followed by members of one upper-level drug dealing and smuggling community. We discuss the various modes of entry into trafficking at these upper levels, contrasting these with entry into middle- and low-level trafficking. We then describe the pattern of shifts and oscillations these dealers and smugglers experience. Once they reach the top rungs of their occupation, they begin periodically quitting and re-entering the field, often changing their degree and type of involvement upon their return. Their careers, therefore, offer insights into the problems involved in leaving deviance. . . .

We gained entry to Southwest County's upper-level drug community largely by accident. We had become friendly with a group of our neighbors who turned out be heavily involved in smuggling marijuana. Opportunistically (Riemer, 1977), we seized the chance to gather data on this unexplored activity. Using key informants who helped us gain the trust of other members of the community, we drew upon snowball sampling techniques (Biernacki and Waldorf, 1981) and a combination of overt and covert roles to widen our network of contacts. We supplemented intensive participant-observation, between 1974 and 1980,[2] with unstructured, taped interviews. Throughout, we employed extensive measures to cross-check the reliability of our data, whenever possible (Douglas, 1976). In all, we were able to closely observe 65 dealers and smugglers as well as numerous other drug world members, including dealers' "old ladies" (girlfriends or wives), friends, and family members. . . .

Shifts and Oscillations

. . .[D]espite the gratifications which dealers and smugglers originally derived from the easy money, material comfort, freedom, prestige, and power associated with their careers, 90 percent of those we observed decided, at some point, to quit the business. This stemmed, in part, from their initial perceptions of the career as temporary ("Hell, nobody wants to be a drug dealer all their life"). Adding to these early intentions was a process of rapid aging in the career: dealers and smugglers became increasingly aware of the restrictions and sacrifices their occupations required and tired of living the fugitive life. They thought about, talked about, and in many cases took steps toward getting out of the drug business. But as with entering, disengaging from drug trafficking was rarely an abrupt act (Lieb and Olson, 1976: 364). Instead, it more often resembled a series of transitions, or oscillations,[3] out of and back into the business. For once out of the drug world, dealers and smugglers were rarely successful in making it in the legitimate world because they failed to cut down on their extravagant lifestyle and drug consumption. Many abandoned their efforts to reform and returned to deviance, sometimes picking up where they left off and other times shifting to a new mode of operating. For example, some shifted from dealing cocaine to dealing marijuana, some dropped to a lower level of dealing, and others shifted

their role within the same group of traffickers. This series of phase-outs and re-entries, combined with career shifts, endured for years, dominating the pattern of their remaining involvement with the business. But it also represented the method by which many eventually broke away from drug trafficking, for each phase-out had the potential to be an individual's final departure.

Aging in the Career

Once recruited and established in the drug world, dealers and smugglers entered into a middle phase of aging in the career. This phase was characterized by a progressive loss of enchantment with their occupation. While novice dealers and smugglers found that participation in the drug world brought them thrills and status, the novelty gradually faded. Initial feelings of exhilaration and awe began to dull as individuals became increasingly jaded. This was the result of both an extended exposure to the mundane, everyday business aspects of drug trafficking and to an exorbitant consumption of drugs (especially cocaine). One smuggler described how he eventually came to feel:

> It was fun, those three or four years. I never worried about money or anything. But after awhile it got real boring. There was no feeling or emotion or anything about it. I wasn't even hardly relating to my old lady anymore. Everything was just one big rush.

This frenzy of overstimulation and resulting exhaustion hastened the process of "burnout" which nearly all individuals experienced. As dealers and smugglers aged in the career they became more sensitized to the extreme risks they faced. Cases of friends and associates who were arrested, imprisoned, or killed began to mount. Many individuals became convinced that continued drug trafficking would inevitably lead to arrest ("It's only a matter of time before you get caught"). While dealers and smugglers generally repressed their awareness of danger, treating it as a taken-for-granted part of their daily existence, periodic crises shattered their casual attitudes, evoking strong feelings of fear. They temporarily intensified security precautions and retreated into near isolation until they felt the "heat" was off.

As a result of these accumulating "scares," dealers and smugglers increasingly integrated feelings of "paranoia"[4] into their everyday lives. One dealer talked about his feelings of paranoia:

> You're always on the line. You don't lead a normal life. You're always looking over your shoulder, wondering who's at the door, having to hide everything. You learn to look behind you so well you could probably bend over and look up your ass. That's paranoia. It's a really scary, hard feeling. That's what makes you get out.

Drug world members also grew progressively weary of their exclusion from the legitimate world and the deceptions they had to manage to sustain that separation. Initially, this separation was surrounded by an alluring mystique. But as they aged in the career, this mystique became replaced by the reality of everyday boundary maintenance and the feeling of being an "expatriated citizen within one's own country." One smuggler who was contemplating quitting described the effects of this separation:

> I'm so sick of looking over my shoulder, having to sit in my house and worry about one of my non-drug world friends stopping in when I'm doing business. Do you know how awful that is? It's like leading a double life. It's ridiculous. That's what makes it not worth it. It'll be a lot less money [to quit], but a lot less pressure.

Thus, while the drug world was somewhat restricted, it was not an encapsulated community, and dealers' and smugglers' continuous involvement with the straight world made the temptation to adhere to normative standards and "go straight" omnipresent. With the occupation's novelty worn off and the "fast life" taken-for-granted, most dealers and smugglers felt that the occupation no longer resembled their early impressions of it. Once they reached the upper levels of the occupation, their experience began to change. Eventually, the rewards of trafficking no longer seemed to justify the strain and risk involved. It was at this point that the straight world's formerly dull ambiance became transformed (at least in theory) into a potential haven.

Phasing Out

Three factors inhibited dealers and smugglers from leaving the drug world. Primary among these factors were the hedonistic and materialistic satisfactions the drug world provided. Once accustomed to earning vast quantities of money quickly and easily, individuals found it exceedingly difficult to return to the income scale of the straight world. They also were reluctant to abandon the pleasure of the "fast life" and its accompanying drugs, casual sex, and power. Second, dealers and smugglers identified with, and developed a commitment to, the occupation of drug trafficking (Adler and Adler, 1982). Their self-images were tied to that role and could not be easily disengaged. The years invested in their careers (learning the trade, forming connections, building reputations) strengthened their involvement with both the occupation and the drug community. And since their relationships were social as well as business, friendship ties bound individuals to dealing. As one dealer in the midst of struggling to phase-out explained:

> The biggest threat to me is to get caught up sitting around the house with friends that are into dealing. I'm trying to stay away from them, change my habits.

Third, dealers and smugglers hesitated to voluntarily quit the field because of the difficulty involved in finding another way to earn a living. Their years spent in illicit activity made it unlikely for any legitimate organizations to hire them. This narrowed their occupational choices considerably, leaving self-employment as one of the few remaining avenues open.

Dealers and smugglers who tried to leave the drug world generally fell into one of four patterns.[5] The first and most frequent pattern was to postpone quitting until after they could execute one last "big deal." While the intention was sincere, individuals who chose this route rarely succeeded; the "big deal" too often remained elusive. One marijuana smuggler offered a variation of this theme:

My plan is to make a quarter of a million dollars in four months during the prime smuggling season and get the hell out of the business.

A second pattern we observed was individuals who planned to change immediately, but never did. They announced they were quitting, yet their outward actions never varied. One dealer described his involvement with this syndrome:

When I wake up I'll say, "Hey, I'm going to quit this cycle and just run my other business." But when you're dealing you constantly have people dropping by ounces and asking, "Can you move this?" What's your first response? Always, "Sure, for a toot."

In the third pattern of phasing-out, individuals actually suspended their dealing and smuggling activities, but did not replace them with an alternative source of income. Such withdrawals were usually spontaneous and prompted by exhaustion, the influence of a person from outside the drug world, or problems with the police or other associates. These kinds of phase-outs usually lasted only until the individual's money ran out, as one dealer explained:

I got into legal trouble with the FBI a while back and I was forced to quit dealing. Everybody just cut me off completely, and I saw the danger in continuing, myself. But my high-class tastes never dwindled. Before I knew it I was in hock over $30,000. Even though I was hot, I was forced to get back into dealing to relieve some of my debts.

In the fourth pattern of phasing out, dealers and smugglers tried to move into another line of work. Alternative occupations included: (1) those they had previously pursued; (2) front businesses maintained on the side while dealing or smuggling; and (3) new occupations altogether. While some people accomplished this transition successfully, there were problems inherent in all three alternatives.

1. Most people who tried resuming their former occupations found that these had changed too much while they were away. In addition, they themselves had

changed: they enjoyed the self-directed freedom and spontaneity associated with dealing and smuggling, and were unwilling to relinquish it.

2. Those who turned to their legitimate front business often found that these businesses were unable to support them. Designed to launder rather than earn money, most of these ventures were retail outlets with a heavy cash flow (restaurants, movie theaters, automobile dealerships, small stores) that had become accustomed to operating under a continuous subsidy from illegal funds. Once their drug funding was cut off they could not survive for long.

3. Many dealers and smugglers utilized the skills and connections they had developed in the drug business to create a new occupation. They exchanged their illegal commodity for a legal one and went into import/export, manufacturing, wholesaling, or retailing other merchandise. For some, the decision to prepare a legitimate career for their future retirement from the drug world followed an unsuccessful attempt to phase-out into a "front" business. One husband-and-wife dealing team explained how these legitimate side businesses differed from front businesses:

We always had a little legitimate "scam" [scheme] going, like mail-order shirts, wallets, jewelry, and the kids were always involved in that. We made a little bit of money on them. Their main purpose was for a cover. But [this business] was different; right from the start this was going to be a legal thing to push us out of the drug business.

About 10 percent of the dealers and smugglers we observed began tapering off their drug world involvement gradually, transferring their time and money into a selected legitimate endeavor. They did not try to quit drug trafficking altogether until they felt confident that their legitimate business could support them. Like spontaneous phase-outs, many of these planned withdrawals into legitimate endeavors failed to generate enough money to keep individuals from being lured into the drug world.

In addition to voluntary phase-outs caused by burnout, about 40 percent of the Southwest County dealers and smugglers we observed experienced a "bustout" at some point in their careers.[6] Forced withdrawals from dealing or smuggling were usually sudden and motivated by external factors, either financial, legal, or reputational. Financial bustouts generally occurred when dealers or smugglers were either "burned" or "ripped-off" by others, leaving them in too much debt to rebuild their base of operation. Legal bustouts followed arrest and possibly incarceration: arrested individuals were so "hot" that few of their former associates would deal with them. Reputational bustouts occurred when individuals "burned" or "ripped-off" others (regardless of whether they intended to do so) and were banned from business by their former circle of associates. One smuggler gave his opinion on the pervasive nature of forced phase-outs:

> Some people are smart enough to get out of it because they realize, physically, they have to. Others realize, monetarily, that they want to get out of this world before this world gets them. Those are the lucky ones. Then there are the ones who have to get out because they're hot or someone else close to them is so hot that they'd better get out. But in the end when you get out of it, nobody gets out of it out of free choice; you do it because you have to.

Death, of course, was the ultimate bustout. Some pilots met this fate because of the dangerous routes they navigated (hugging mountains, treetops, other aircrafts) and the sometimes ill-maintained and overloaded planes they flew. However, despite much talk of violence, few Southwest County drug traffickers died at the hands of fellow dealers.

Re-Entry

Phasing-out of the drug world was more often than not temporary. For many dealers and smugglers, it represented but another stage of their drug careers (although this may not have been their original intention), to be followed by a period of reinvolvement.

Depending on the individual's perspective, re-entry into the drug world could be viewed as either a comeback (from a forced withdrawal) or a relapse (from a voluntary withdrawal).

Most people forced out of drug trafficking were anxious to return. The decision to phase-out was never theirs, and the desire to get back into dealing or smuggling was based on many of the same reasons which drew them into the field originally. Coming back from financial, legal, and reputational bustouts was possible but difficult and was not always successfully accomplished. They had to re-establish contacts, rebuild their organization and fronting arrangements, and raise the operating capital to resume dealing. More difficult was the problem of overcoming the circumstances surrounding their departure. Once smugglers and dealers resumed operating, they often found their former colleagues suspicious of them. One frustrated dealer described the effects of his prison experience:

> When I first got out of the joint [jail], none of my old friends would have anything to do with me. Finally, one guy who had been my partner told me it was because everyone was suspicious of my getting out early and thought I made a deal [with police to inform on his colleagues].

Dealers and smugglers who returned from bustouts were thus informally subjected to a trial period in which they had to re-establish their trustworthiness and reliability before they could once again move in the drug world with ease.

Re-entry from voluntary withdrawal involved a more difficult decision making process, but was easier to implement. The factors enticing individuals to re-enter the drug world were not the same as those which motivated their original entry. As we noted above, experienced dealers and smugglers often privately weighed their reasons for wanting to quit and wanting to stay in. Once they left, their images of and hopes for the straight world failed to materialize. They could not make the shift to the norms, values, and lifestyle of the straight society and could not earn a living within it. Thus, dealers and smugglers decided to reenter the drug business for basic reasons: the material perquisites, the hedonistic gratifications, the social ties, and the fact that they had nowhere else to go.

Once this decision was made, the actual process of re-entry was relatively easy. One dealer described how the door back into dealing remained open for those who left voluntarily:

> I still see my dealer friends, I can still buy grams from them when I want to. It's the respect they have for me because I stepped out of it without being busted or burning someone. I'm coming out with a good reputation, and even though the scene is a whirlwind—people moving up, moving down, in, out—if I didn't see anybody for a year I could call them up and get right back in that day.

People who relapsed thus had little problem obtaining fronts, re-establishing their reputations, or readjusting to the scene.

Career Shifts

Dealers and smugglers who re-entered the drug world, whether from a voluntary or forced phase-out, did not always return to the same level of transacting or commodity which characterized their previous style of operation. Many individuals underwent a "career shift" (Luckenbill and Best, 1981) and became involved in some new segment of the drug world. These shifts were sometimes lateral, as when a member of a smuggling crew took on a new specialization, switching from piloting to operating a stash house, for example. One dealer described how he utilized friendship networks upon his re-entry to shift from cocaine to marijuana trafficking:

> Before, when I was dealing cocaine, I was too caught up in using the drug and people around me were starting to go under from getting into "base" [another form of cocaine]. That's why I got out. But now I think I've got myself together and even though I'm dealing again I'm staying away from coke. I've switched over to dealing grass. It's a whole different circle of people. I got into it through a close friend I used to know before, but I never did business with him because he did grass and I did coke.

Vertical shifts moved operators to different levels. For example, one former smuggler returned and began dealing; another top-level marijuana dealer came back to find that the smugglers he knew had disappeared and he was forced to buy in smaller quantities from other dealers.

Another type of shift relocated drug traffickers in different styles of operation. One dealer described how, after being arrested, he tightened his security measures:

> I just had to cut back after I went through those changes. Hell, I'm not getting any younger and the idea of going to prison bothers me a lot more than it did 10 years ago. The risks are no longer worth it when I can have a comfortable income with less risk. So I only sell to four people now. I don't care if they buy a pound or a gram.

A former smuggler who sold his operation and lost all his money during phase-out returned as a consultant to the industry, selling his expertise to those with new money and fresh manpower:

> What I've been doing lately is setting up deals for people. I've got foolproof plans for smuggling cocaine up here from Colombia; I tell them how to modify their airplanes to add on extra fuel tanks and to fit in more weed, coke, or whatever they bring up. Then I set them up with refueling points all up and down Central America, tell them how to bring it up here, what points to come in at, and what kind of receiving unit to use. Then they do it all and I get 10 percent of what they make.

Re-entry did not always involve a shift to a new niche, however. Some dealers and smugglers returned to the same circle of associates, trafficking activity, and commodity they worked with prior to their departure. Thus, drug dealers' careers often peaked early and then displayed a variety of shifts, from lateral mobility, to decline, to holding fairly steady.

A final alternative involved neither completely leaving nor remaining within the deviant world. Many individuals straddled the deviant and respectable worlds forever by continuing to dabble in drug trafficking. As a result of their experiences in the drug world they developed a deviant self-identity and a deviant *modus operandi*. They might not have wanted to bear the social and legal burden of full-time deviant work but neither were they willing to assume the perceived confines and limitations of the straight world. They therefore moved into the entrepreneurial realm, where their daily activities involved some kind of hustling or "wheeling and dealing" in an assortment of legitimate, quasi-legitimate, and deviant ventures, and where they could be their own boss. This enabled them to retain certain elements of the deviant lifestyle, and to socialize on the fringes of the drug community. For these individuals, drug dealing shifted from a primary occupation to a sideline, though they never abandoned it altogether.

Leaving Drug Trafficking

This career pattern of oscillation into and out of active drug trafficking makes it difficult to speak of leaving drug trafficking in the sense of final retirement. Clearly, some people succeeded in voluntarily retiring. Of these, a few managed to prepare a post-deviant career for themselves by transferring their drug money into a legitimate enterprise. A larger group was forced out of dealing and either didn't or couldn't return; the bustouts were sufficiently damaging that they never attempted re-entry, or they abandoned efforts after a series of unsuccessful attempts. But there was no way of structurally determining in advance whether an exit from the business would be temporary or permanent. The vacillations in dealers' intentions were compounded by the complexity of operating successfully in the drug world. For many, then, no phase-out could ever be definitely assessed as permanent. As long as individuals had skills, knowledge, and connections to deal they retained the potential to re-enter the occupation at any time. Leaving drug trafficking may thus be a relative phenomenon, characterized by a trailing-off process where spurts of involvement appear with decreasing frequency and intensity.

Summary

Drug dealing and smuggling careers are temporary and fraught with multiple attempts at retirement. Veteran drug traffickers quit their occupation because of the ambivalent feelings they develop toward their deviant life. As they age in the career their experience changes, shifting from a work life that is exhilarating and free to one that becomes increasingly dangerous and confining. But just as their deviant careers are temporary, so too are their retirements. Potential recruits are lured into the drug business by materialism, hedonism, glamor, and excitement. Established dealers are lured away from the deviant life and back into the mainstream by the attractions of security and social ease. Retired dealers and smugglers are lured back in by their expertise, and by their ability to make money quickly and easily. People who have been exposed to the upper levels of drug trafficking therefore find it extremely difficult to quit their deviant occupation permanently. This stems, in part, from their difficulty in moving from the illegitimate to the legitimate business sector. Even more significant is the affinity they form for their deviant values and lifestyle. Thus few, if any, of our subjects were successful in leaving deviance entirely. What dealers and smugglers intend, at the time, to be a permanent withdrawal from drug trafficking can be seen in retrospect as a pervasive occupational pattern of midcareer shifts and oscillations. More research is needed into the complex process of how people get out of deviance and enter the world of legitimate work.

Notes

1. The term "soft" drugs generally refers to marijuana, cocaine, and such psychedelics as LSD and mescaline (Carey 1968). In this paper, we do not address trafficking in psychedelics because, since they are manufactured in the United States, they are neither imported nor distributed by the group we studied.

2. We continued to conduct follow-up interviews with key informants through 1983.

3. While other studies of drug dealing have also noted that participants did not maintain an uninterrupted stream of career involvement

(Blum *et al.*, 1972; Carey, 1968; Lieb and Olson, 1976; Waldorf *et al.*, 1977), none have isolated or described the oscillating nature of this pattern.

4. In the dealers' vernacular, this term is not used in the clinical sense of an individual psychopathology rooted in early childhood traumas. Instead, it resembles Lemert's (1962) more sociological definition which focuses on such behavioral dynamics as suspicion, hostility, aggressiveness, and even delusion. Not only Lemert, but also Waldorf *et al.* (1977) and Wedow (1979) assert that feelings of paranoia can have a sound basis in reality, and are therefore comprehended and even empathized with others.

5. At this point, a limitation to our data must be noted. Many of the dealers and smugglers we observed simply "disappeared" from the scene and were never heard from again. We therefore have no way of knowing if they phased-out (voluntarily or involuntarily), shifted to another scene, or were killed in some remote place. We cannot, therefore, estimate the numbers of people who left the Southwest County drug scene via each of the routes discussed here.

6. It is impossible to determine the exact percentage of people falling into the different phase-out categories: due to oscillation, people could experience several types and thus appear in multiple categories.

References

Adler, Patricia A., and Peter Adler. 1982. "Criminal commitment among drug dealers." *Deviant Behavior* 3: 117–135.

Anonymous. 1969. "On selling marijuana." In Erich Goode (ed.), *Marijuana* (pp. 92–102). New York: Atherton.

Atkyus, Robert L., and Gerhard J. Hanneman. 1974. "Illicit drug distribution and dealer communication behavior." *Journal of Health and Social Behavior* 15 (March): 36–43.

Biernacki, Patrick, and Dan Waldorf. 1981. "Snowball sampling." *Sociological Methods and Research* 10(2): 141–163.

Blum, Richard H., and Associates. 1972. *The Dream Sellers*. San Francisco: Jossey-Bass.

Carey, James T. 1968. *The College Drug Scene*. Englewood Cliffs, NJ: Prentice Hall.

Douglas, Jack D. 1976. *Investigative Social Research*. Beverly Hills, CA: Sage.

Goode, Erich. 1970. *The Marijuana Smokers*. New York: Basic.

Langer, John. 1977. "Drug entrepreneurs and dealing culture." *Social Problems* 24(3): 377–385.

Lemert, Edwin. 1962. "Paranoia and the dynamics of exclusion." *Sociometry* 25 (March): 2–20.

Lieb, John, and Sheldon Olson. 1976. "Prestige, paranoia, and profit: On becoming a dealer of illicit drugs in a university community." *Journal of Drug Issues* 6 (Fall): 356–369.

Luckenbill, David F., and Joel Best. 1981. "Careers in deviance and respectability: The analogy's limitations." *Social Problems* 29(2): 197–206.

Mouledoux, James. 1972. "Ideological aspects of drug dealership." In Ken Westhues (ed.), *Society's Shadow: Studies in the Sociology of Countercultures* (pp. 110–122). Toronto: McGraw-Hill, Ryerson.

Riemer, Jeffrey W. 1977. "Varieties of opportunistic research." *Urban Life* 5(4): 467–477.

Waldorf, Dan, Sheila Murphy, Craig Reinarman, and Bridget Joyce. 1977. *Doing Coke: An Ethnography of Cocaine Users and Sellers*. Washington, DC: Drug Abuse Council.

Wedow, Suzanne. 1979. "Feeling paranoid: The organization of an ideology." *Urban Life* 8(1): 72–93.

From *Social Problems*, vol. 31, no. 2, December 1983, excerpts taken out of pp. 195–207. Copyright © 1983 by The Society for the Study of Social Problems. Reprinted by permission. ✦

Part X

Deviance and Social Control [1]

The quest to explain social order is as old as sociology itself. No system can survive, or survive for long, in the absence of social order. Conventional wisdom holds that order is not possible without cohesion and that there can be no cohesion without social control. Social control refers broadly to "all of the human practices and arrangements that contribute to social [stability] and . . .influence people to conform" (Black 1993, 4). Social control can be implicit or explicit, individualistic or institutional, informal or formal. Styles of control vary, from repressive and compensatory to conciliatory and therapeutic. The end goal, however, is invariably the same: to neutralize deviance, settle conflict, and restore reciprocity. Social stability depends on the efficient resolution of emergent grievances (see Black 1983; Horwitz 1990; Gouldner 1960).

Control and deviance have a dynamic, symbiotic relationship. Each adapts to the other in a continuous cycle of evolution. Initiatives to clamp down on deviants may work for a while, but deviants invariably respond in ways that keep the deviance alive. Control agents adapt, deviants adapt in turn, and the cycle takes on a self-perpetuating quality (Ryan 1994).

Law obviously represents social control at its most advanced. Legal systems tend to evolve in complex societies, where diverse, heterogeneous populations require official methods of deviance detection and conflict resolution. An intricate matrix of enforcers, adjudicators, arbitrators, and mediators develops to absorb disputes that cannot otherwise be settled. It is traditionally thought that the bulk of social control is legalistic in nature: Someone is victimized by a crime and he or she calls the police to resolve the conflict. This account assumes that access to the law is democratic, but it is not. Victims who themselves are involved in crime, for example, cannot be "victims" and thus have no formal recourse. To right perceived wrongs, they must take the law into their own hands. Retaliation becomes a modal response.

Reprisal is by no means limited to criminal victims. Self-help flourishes among *law-abiding* citizens and "most of it involves ordinary [people] who seemingly view their conduct as a perfectly legitimate exercise of social control" (Black 1993, 36). Indeed, the bulk of social control is meted out informally, and many of these actions are, paradoxically, *criminal* in nature. Robbery, murder, theft, arson, vandalism, and even rape are common moralistic responses designed to "right" past wrongs (Black 1983). Such moralism should not be surprising, especially in light of the existing criminal justice system, a system based on deterrence yet whose deterrent power is weak. The vast majority of offenses go undetected or are not acted upon by police. Temporal gaps between detection, arrest, and conviction mean that an offense can go unpunished for a long time. Bungled prosecutions some-times result in the guilty going free. As confidence in the system wanes and skepticism rises, citizens increasingly feel the need to take matters into their own hands. Retaliation becomes the only way to bring the swiftness, certainty, and severity of punishment back into deterrence.

Policymakers have attempted an end run around this problem by raising the severity of punishments and by extending punishments to previously unsanctioned behavior, but scare tactics intended to legislate conformity are doomed to fail. Certainty of punishment, not its severity, is the key to deterrence, and the certainty remains quite low (see Tittle 1980). Self-help emerges as the most logical, or available, response for many.

Street justice is particularly salient in worlds where formal social control is thoroughly distrusted. This distrust exists in many urban communities around the country, where the police represent an alien force with hostile intentions, are seen as corrupt and arbitrary, are perceived to use discretion for sinister ends, and are defined as adversaries to be avoided at all costs (see also Anderson 1999; Sherman 1993). The war mentality held by many urban police departments fuels pernicious tactics that amplify social disorganization and erode informal social controls (Miller 1996, 2, 102). Use of such tactics, in turn, helps to create a "jungle" atmosphere that prompts ordinary people to develop their own brutal brand of vigilantism. Even if outside authorities were useful and available, they feel that it is not necessarily wise to enlist them. Powerful conduct norms militate against reliance on "the man." Status and security come only by taking care of one's own business (Anderson 1999, 307–308).

As more advanced techniques of social control penetrate more deeply into all spheres of social life, however, the need for informal justice may decline as a matter of course. This is precisely what seems to be happening. Some scholars suggest that we have entered a new culture of surveillance, where technology is being applied to detect ever-increasing forms of rule-breaking in ever-greater numbers of settings. Central to this burgeoning culture is the rise of "intelligence armamentaria" (Miller 1996, 103)—video cameras, listening and tracking devices, computer monitoring, profiling, checkpoints, drug testing, and the like—all designed to identify more deviance and more deviants in more places. Through such devices, social control becomes not so much hierarchical as capillary, extending totally yet unobtrusively to the remotest corners of social systems, providing a painless way to monitor the maximum number of people with maximum efficiency (Staples 1997). The surveillance culture is part and parcel of the widespread decentralization and democratization of social control that some believe will eventuate in a Big Brother type of state (Marx 1988); many claim we have already reached it. Insofar as surveillance societies also become totalitarian ones, the availability of law will penetrate all areas of social life. When this happens, citizens increasingly rely on and are encouraged by the state to use its "coercive apparatus" to redress their grievances. Snitching becomes commonplace, making each person dangerous (to others) yet vulnerable (to others) at the same time. What results is a "war of all against all" within a highly regulated framework of the state (Black 1993, 45, n. 21). Total social control may bring lasting security, but the price is steep—so steep that many citizens may fear the consequences of paying it. The line between formal and informal social control may become irreversibly blurred in the process.

Endnotes

1. Parts of this section were adapted from *Robbing Drug Dealers: Violence Beyond the Law*, Bruce A. Jacobs, Aldine de Gruyter, 2000. ✦

53
Driving While Black

Elijah Anderson

The mission of the police is to serve and protect—to maintain public order and enforce society's laws in a fair and impartial manner. The police are supposed to symbolize everything that is right, just, and good in society. Officers are moral beacons, shining examples of what people can do by giving their lives to public service. At one time, police work was among the most honorable and highest-status vocations anyone could hope to get into. Things have since changed.

The image of black motorist Rodney King being beaten by four white Los Angeles police officers is forever emblazoned in the minds of many Americans, an incident that (ultimately) sparked a race riot which enveloped much of Los Angeles and which transfixed millions of television viewers across the country. Police brutality, corruption, and racism are now common staples on the evening news. For racial minorities, and blacks in particular, unfair treatment is all too common, triggering fundamental distrust of and contempt for authority. Many perceive the police to be an alien force with hostile intentions, who use discretion arbitrarily and for nefarious ends. Police are seen as adversaries one wants to avoid—predators with a badge (see Jacobs 2000, 131).

Most white Americans take their freedom of movement for granted, going where they want, how they want, when they want. Black citizens, and black males in particular, cannot say the same. Defined as "suspicious," "dangerous," and "threatening," their conduct is scrutinized in ways never applied to white men. Many are routinely stopped, interrogated, and frisked simply because they are black and male and because some officer suspects they are up to no good. Conditions have become so bad in some places that a new acronym has penetrated the public discourse—DWB, or "driving while black." Some state legislatures now require police departments to document the racial status of all people stopped and detained to prove they are enforcing the law in an unbiased manner. Police officers seen to be biased are punished.

Perhaps the most pernicious aspect of differential enforcement is the possibility that law-abiding, upstanding citizens can be ensnared by the justice system through no fault of their own. We know from labeling theory that the behavior of social control agents plays a defining role in the development of deviant careers and that falsely accused deviants are just as susceptible to secondary deviation as their accurately identified counterparts. Although police often claim that they are just doing their jobs and that aggressive stop-and-search tactics are necessary to prevent the streets from being overrun by criminals, the antagonism that such tactics create undermines truly effective social control, and it may trigger rule-breaking where none existed before.

The Police and the Black Male

The police, in the Village-Northton as elsewhere, represent society's formal, legitimate means of social control.[1] Their role includes protecting law-abiding citizens from those who are not law-abiding, by preventing crime and by apprehending likely criminals. Precisely how the police fulfill the public's expectations is strongly related to how they view the neighborhood and the people who live there. On the streets, color-coding often works to confuse race, age, class, gender, incivility, and criminality, and it expresses itself most concretely in the person of the anonymous black male. In doing their job, the police often become willing parties to this general color-coding of the public environment, and related distinctions, particularly those of skin color and gender, come to convey definite meanings. Although such coding may make the work of the police more manageable, it may also fit well with

493

their own presuppositions regarding race and class relations, thus shaping officers' perceptions of crime "in the city." Moreover, the anonymous black male is usually an ambiguous figure who arouses the utmost caution and is generally considered dangerous until he proves he is not. . . .

There are some who charge . . .that the police are primarily agents of the middle class who are working to make the area more hospitable to middle-class people at the expense of the lower classes. It is obvious that the police assume whites in the community are at least middle class and are trustworthy on the streets. Hence the police may be seen primarily as protecting "law-abiding" middle-class whites against anonymous "criminal" black males.

To be white is to be seen by the police—at least superficially—as an ally, eligible for consideration and for much more deferential treatment than that accorded blacks in general. This attitude may be grounded in the backgrounds of the police themselves. Many have grown up in Eastern City's "ethnic" neighborhoods.[2] They may serve what they perceive as their own class and neighborhood interests, which often translates as keeping blacks "in their place"—away from neighborhoods that are socially defined as "white." In trying to do their job, the police appear to engage in an informal policy of monitoring young black men as a means of controlling crime, and often they seem to go beyond the bounds of duty. The following field note shows what pressures and racism young black men in the Village may endure at the hands of the police:

- At 8:30 on a Thursday evening in June I saw a police car stopped on a side street near the Village. Beside the car stood a policeman with a young black man. I pulled up behind the police car and waited to see what would happen. When the policeman released the young man, I got out of my car and asked the youth for an interview.

   "So what did he say to you when they stopped you? What was the problem?" I asked. "I was just coming around the corner, and he stopped me, asked me what was my name, and all that. And what I had in my bag. And where I was coming from. Where I lived, you know, all the basic stuff, I guess. Then he searched me down and, you know, asked me who were the supposedly tough guys around here? That's about it. I couldn't tell him who they are. How do I know? Other gang members could, but I'm not from a gang, you know. But he tried to put me in a gang, though." "How old are you?" I asked. "I'm seventeen, I'll be eighteen next month." "Did he give any reason for stoppin' you?" "No, he didn't. He just wanted my address, where I lived, where I was comin' from, that kind of thing. I don't have no police record or nothin'. I guess he stopped me on principle, 'cause I'm black." "How does that make you feel?" I asked. "Well, it doesn't bother me too much, you know, as long as I know that I hadn't done nothin', but I guess it just happens around here. They just stop young black guys and ask 'em questions, you know. What can you do?"

On the streets late at night, the average young black man is suspicious of others he encounters, and he is particularly wary of the police. If he is dressed in the uniform of the "gangster," such as a black leather jacket, sneakers, and a "gangster cap," if he is carrying a radio or a suspicious bag (which may be confiscated), or if he is moving too fast or too slow, the police may stop him. As part of the routine, they search him and make him sit in the police car while they run a check to see whether there is a "detainer" on him. If there is nothing, he is allowed to go on his way. After this ordeal the youth is often left afraid, sometimes shaking, and uncertain about the area he had previously taken for granted. He is upset in part because he is painfully aware of how close he has come to being in "big trouble." He knows of other youths who have gotten into a "world of trouble" simply by being on the streets at the wrong time or when the police were pursuing a criminal. In these circumstances, particularly at night, it is relatively easy for one black man to be mistaken for another. Over the years, while walking through the neighborhood I have on occasion been stopped and questioned by police chasing a mugger, but after explaining myself I was released.

Many youths, however, have reason to fear such mistaken identity or harassment, since they might be jailed, if only for a short time, and would have to post bail money and pay legal fees to extricate themselves from the mess (Anderson 1986). When law-abiding blacks are ensnared by the criminal justice system, the scenario may proceed as follows. A young man is arbitrarily stopped by the police and questioned. If he cannot effectively negotiate with the officer(s) he may be accused of a crime and arrested. To resolve this situation he needs financial resources, which for him are in short supply. If he does not have money for an attorney, which often happens, he is left to a public defender who may be more interested in going along with the court system than in fighting for a poor black person. Without legal support, he may well wind up "doing time" even if he is innocent of the charges brought against him. The next time he is stopped for questioning he will have a record, which will make detention all the more likely.

Because the young black man is aware of many cases when an "innocent" black person was wrongly accused and detained, he develops an "attitude" toward the police. The street word for police is "the man," signifying a certain machismo, power, and authority. He becomes concerned when he notices "the man" in the community or when the police focus on him because he is outside his own neighborhood. The youth knows, or soon finds out, that he exists in a legally precarious state. Hence he is motivated to avoid the police, and his public life becomes severely circumscribed.

To obtain fair treatment when confronted by the police, the young man may wage a campaign for social regard so intense that at times it borders on obsequiousness. As one streetwise black youth said: "If you show a cop that you nice and not a smartass, they be nice to you. They talk to you like the man you are. You gonna get ignorant like a little kid, they gonna get ignorant with you." Young black males often are particularly deferential toward the police even when they are completely within their rights and have done nothing wrong. Most often this is not out of blind acceptance or respect for the "law," but

because they know the police can cause them hardship. When confronted or arrested, they adopt a particular style of behavior to get on the policeman's good side. Some simply "go limp" or politely ask, "What seems to be the trouble, officer?" This pose requires a deference that is in sharp contrast with the youths' more usual image, but many seem to take it in stride or not even to realize it. Because they are concerned primarily with staying out of trouble, and because they perceive the police as arbitrary in their use of power, many defer in an equally arbitrary way. Because of these pressures, however, black youths tend to be especially mindful of the police and, when they are around, to watch their own behavior in public. Many have come to expect harassment and are inured to it; they simply tolerate it as part of living in the Village-Northton.

After a certain age, say twenty-three or twenty-four, a black man may no longer be stopped so often, but he continues to be the object of police scrutiny. As one twenty-seven-year-old black college graduate speculated:

- *I think they see me with my little bag with papers in it. They see me with penny loafers on. I have a tie on, some days. They don't stop me so much now. See, it depends on the circumstances. If somethin' goes down, and they hear that the guy had on a big black coat, I may be the one. But when I was younger, they could just stop me, carte blanche, any old time. Name taken, searched, and this went on endlessly. From the time I was about twelve until I was sixteen or seventeen, endlessly, endlessly. And I come from a lower middle-class black neighborhood, OK, that borders a white neighborhood. One neighborhood is all black, and one is all white. OK, just because we were so close to that neighborhood, we were stopped endlessly. And it happened even more when we went up into a suburban community. When we would ride up and out to the suburbs, we were stopped every time we did it.*

  If it happened today, now that I'm older, I would really be upset. In the old days when I was younger, I didn't know any better. You just expected it, you knew it was, gonna happen. Cops would come up, "What you doin', where you comin' from?" Say things to you. They might even call you nigger.

Such scrutiny and harassment by local police makes black youths see them as a problem to get beyond, to deal with, and their attempts affect their overall behavior. To avoid encounters with the man, some streetwise young men camouflage themselves, giving up the urban uniform and emblems that identify them as "legitimate" objects of police attention. They may adopt a more conventional presentation of self, wearing chinos, sweat suits, and generally more conservative dress. Some youths have been known to "ditch" a favorite jacket if they see others wearing one like it, because wearing it increases their chances of being mistaken for someone else who may have committed a crime.

But such strategies do not always work over the long run and must be constantly modified. For instance, because so many young ghetto blacks have begun to wear Fila and Adidas sweat suits as status symbols, such dress has become incorporated into the public image generally associated with young black males. These athletic suits, particularly the more expensive and colorful ones, along with high-priced sneakers, have become the leisure dress of successful drug dealers, and other youths will often mimic their wardrobe to "go for bad" in the quest for local esteem. Hence what was once a "square" mark of distinction approximating the conventions the wider culture has been adopted by a neighborhood group devalued by that same culture. As we saw earlier, the young black male enjoys a certain power over fashion: whatever the collective peer group embraces can become "hip" in a manner the wider society may not desire (see Goffman 1963). These same styles then attract the attention of the agents of social control.

The Identification Card

Law-abiding black people, particularly those of the middle class, set out to approxi-mate middle-class whites in styles of self-presentation in public, including dress and bearing. Such middle-class emblems, often viewed as "square," are not usually embraced by young working-class blacks. Instead, their connections with and claims on the institutions of the wider society seem to be symbolized by the identification card. The common identification card associates its holder with a firm, a corporation, a school, a union, or some other institution of substance and influence. Such a card, particularly from a prominent establishment, puts the police and others on notice that the youth is "somebody," thus creating an important distinction between a black man who can claim a connection with the wider society and one who is summarily judged as "deviant." Although blacks who are established in the middle class might take such cards for granted, many lower-class blacks, who continue to find it necessary to campaign for civil rights denied them because of skin color, believe that carrying an identification card brings them better treatment than is meted out to their less fortunate brothers and sisters. For them this link to the wider society, though often tenuous, is psychically and socially important. The young college graduate continues:

- *I know [how] I used to feel when I was enrolled in college last year, when I had an ID card. I used to hear stories about the blacks getting stopped over by the dental school, people having trouble sometimes. I would see that all the time. Young black male being stopped by the police. Young black male in handcuffs. But I knew that because I had that ID card I would not be mistaken for just somebody snatching a pocketbook, or just somebody being where maybe I wasn't expected to be. See, even though I was intimidated by the campus police—I mean, the first time I walked into the security office to get my ID they all gave me the double take to see if I was somebody they were looking for. See, after I got the card, I was like, well, they can think that now, but I have this [ID card]. Like, see, late at night when I be walking around, and the cops be checking me out, giving me the looks, you know. I mean, I know guys, students, who were getting stopped all the time, sometimes by the same officer, even though they had the ID. And even they would say, "Hey, I got the ID, so why was I stopped?"*

The cardholder may believe he can no longer be treated summarily by the police, that he is no longer likely to be taken as a "no count," to be prejudicially confused with that class of blacks "who are always causing trouble on the trolley." Furthermore, there is a firm belief that if the police stop a person who has a card, they cannot "do away with him without somebody coming to his defense." This concern should not be underestimated. Young black men trade stories about mistreatment at the hands of the police; a common one involves policemen who transport youths into rival gang territories and release them, telling them to get home the best way they can. From the youth's perspective, the card signifies a certain status in circumstances where little recognition was formerly available. . . .

Notes

1. See Rubinstein (1973); Wilson (1968); Fogelson (1977); Reiss (1971); Bittner (1967); Banton (1964).
2. For an illuminating typology of police work that draws a distinction between "fraternal" and "professional" codes of behavior, see Wilson (1968).

References

Anderson, Elijah. 1986. "Of old heads and young boys: Notes on the urban black experience." Unpublished paper commissioned by the National Research Council, Committee on the Status of Black Americans.

Banton, Michael. 1964. *The Policeman and the Community*. New York: Basic Books.

Bittner, Egon. 1967. "The Police on Skid Row." *American Sociological Review* 32:699–715.

Fogeslon, Robert. 1977. *Big City Police*. Cambridge: Harvard University Press.

Goffman, Erving. 1963. *Behavior in Public Places*. New York: Free Press.

Reiss, Albert. 1971. *The Police and the Public*. New Haven: Yale University Press.

Rubenstein, Jonathan. 1973. *City Police*. New York: Farrar, Strauss, and Giroux.

Wilson, James Q. 1968. "The police and the delinquent in two cities." In *Controlling Delinquents*. Stanton Wheeler, ed. New York: John Wiley.

54

Life on Death Row

Robert Johnson

Few issues spark more controversy than the death penalty. Supporters contend that capital punishment is appropriate retribution for heinous behavior. Opponents argue that the death sentence is tantamount to state-sanctioned murder—cruel and unusual punishment that has no deterrent effect. Some critics go so far as to suggest that capital punishment may actually promote more crime by implying that lethal aggression is an acceptable solution to one's problems. Homicide rates provide partial support for this so-called "brutalization hypothesis"; states with the death penalty historically report more murders per capita than states without it.

The turn of the twenty-first century witnessed what some claim to be the beginnings of a profound shift in death penalty policy. Governor George Ryan of Illinois instituted a temporary moratorium after learning that several condemned men had been falsely accused or had received inadequate counsel. DNA evidence uncovered by a Northwestern University journalism professor exonerated yet more inmates on death row. Texas death row inmate Gary Graham orchestrated a media-intensive eleventh-hour campaign to get his execution stayed. Although he was ultimately unsuccessful, his efforts and similar ones helped to push death penalty policy to the forefront of American political consciousness.

This selection focuses on the actual experiences of death row inmates in lockup—how they cope with the unremitting loneliness, physical deprivation, emotional desperation, and disabling depression that accompanies the knowledge that their fate has been permanently and irrevocably sealed. Johnson calls death row an assault on humanity itself, where one's only companion is fear and where death can actually be a reprieve. All the while, inmates communicate a facade of courage, convincing themselves and others that they can handle the sentence and be "a man" to the very end.

Death row is social control at its maximum. Social control subsumes all manner of forms and styles, from repressive and penal to restitutive and compensatory (Black 1983). The premise for penal control is first and foremost reprisal, or "payback." Indeed, the notion that penitentiaries exist for rehabilitation is dubious at best; in reality, many inmates behave far worse after getting out of prison than they did going in (assuming they do get out). Whether capital punishment, in the broad scheme of things, is immoral is a subjective matter open to debate. Many do wonder, however, whether governments who use lethal force can do so without being hypocrites, and without promoting more violent behavior in the process.

Death row assaults the senses with the sights and sounds—and sometimes the smells—of death. "Don't tell me about the Valley of the Shadow of Death," says Mumia Abu-Jamal, a prisoner on Pennsylvania's death row. "I live there."[1] He lives there alone with the image of death giving substance to his world. All condemned prisoners do. Death row reeks with the threat of death. For the condemned, death gives meaning and purpose to every facet of his world defining:

- *place*—the prisoners live on death row; typically spend their final hours in the death house, confined to a death cell; they meet their fate in the death chamber;

- *process*—time on death row is called dead time; life on death row is known as a living death; the final hours of confinement are called a deathwatch, which usually unfolds in the death house, while the prisoner is confined in the death cell, awaiting the reading of the death warrant, which occurs on the threshold of the death chamber;

- *people*—the team that carries out the execution is the death team or deathwatch team or simply the execution team; those on whom the team labors are of course condemned to death; and, finally,

- *outcome*—death by execution, by whatever means necessary as defined by the jurisdiction in question.

Death constrains death row; death row constrains those condemned to die. Condemned captives-cum-corpses suffer an existence rather than a way of life—they are the living dead until the execution team can "get them dead," to paraphrase one prison warden. That such an existence brings psychological devastation in its wake hardly requires elaboration.

Donald Cabana, a former warden with considerable experience working with the condemned, tells us that death row "is a place that exacts a toll in human destruction."[2] Any death row. All death rows. Always. And a heavy toll, at that. Charlie Jones, warden at Alabama's Atmore Prison, concurs. Jones, like Cabana, has run a solitary-confinement type death row and has overseen a number of executions. He states bluntly that death row reforms, ultimately, are cosmetic, even though he takes a legitimate pride in reforms he has personally instituted in Alabama. "I don't give a damn what you give him," he states uncompromisingly, "you've done some damage" by the sheer fact of confining the prisoner under sentence of death.[3] That damage affects the keeper and the kept, Cabana and Jones agree, although each acknowledges that the heavier burden by far falls upon the condemned. In this chapter we examine this damage by turning our attention first to the prisoners, later to the staff. . . .

With only rare exceptions, condemned prisoners are demoralized by their bleak confinement and defeated by the awesome prospect of death by execution. Worn down in small and almost imperceptible ways, they gradually but inexorably become less than fully human. At the end, the prisoners are helpless pawns of the modern execution drill. They give in, give up, and submit; yielding themselves to the execution team and the machinery of death.

The reforms examined in the preceding chapter do nothing to reduce the dehumanization experienced by condemned prisoners. In no instance in even the most extensively reformed death row are condemned prisoners prepared in any way for the ordeal they must face. And as executions occur with increasing frequency, a trend that has gathered considerable momentum in recent years, there is every reason to believe that conditions of confinement on death rows will continue to become more restrictive. I noted . . .that a return to a standard regime of solitary confinement was a real possibility. Oklahoma's H-Unit . . .stands as a monument to this troubling trend.

Deathwatch regimes remain as they have been throughout this century, retaining vestiges of confinement practices from centuries gone by. No death row reforms undertaken to date affect the deathwatch, the period that culminates death row confinement and ends in the execution of the prisoner. . . .This period continues to be one of virtually unmitigated solitary confinement under conditions of total security. As we shall see, the stress of life under sentence of death reaches its zenith during the deathwatch.

Living on Death Row: The Psychology of Human Warehousing

The bleak quality of life on all death rows, reformed and unreformed, reflects their common goal: human storage. This goal dictates that condemned prisoners be treated essentially as bodies kept alive to be killed. This concern for preserving the body without regard for the quality of life reaches an extreme in suicide prevention efforts that amount to treating the person like a piece of meat.

Philip Brasfield, for example, reported that a suicidal prisoner on death row in Texas, where Brasfield himself was also confined while under sentence of death, was

placed in a straightjacket that was left open at the back to secure him to a bare mattress on the bunk. In addition, handcuffs were placed on his wrists. A crash helmet much like a motorcyclist would wear, was placed on his head and there he lay for weeks, helpless, alone, and drugged. The care and feeding he received was from the inmate porters. At times, he'd call for assistance for over an hour before a guard would open the door and untie him so he could urinate.[4]

Similar procedures apply to inmates whose mental health problems present trouble. On the reformed death row I studied . . .an inmate testified to these procedures:

Should any individual with psychiatric problems present a problem [to staff], his cell will be stripped of all belongings (including clothing and hygiene items), and he is subject to be chained to the cell's bare steel bunk. This has happened to me, personally, and I have seen the same happen to other men.

Yet another example of preserving the body but ignoring the person was related to me by Alvin Bronstein of the American Civil Liberties Union's (ACLU's) National Prison Project. One of his condemned clients required triple-bypass heart surgery but refused treatment. Officials allegedly urged the prisoner to undergo surgery so he could be alive for his execution, at one point asking Bronstein to argue their case with his reluctant client. Bronstein declined. The prisoner subsequently died of a heart attack.[5]

Daily procedures on death row embody the storage premise quite explicitly. "Neat and efficient," in the words of social scientists Jackson and Christian, these procedures are tellingly described in terms that objectify the prisoners. For instance, Jackson and Christian tell us that

death row inmates get showers one at a time. The noun takes a verb form: "I'm going to shower the row now," the guard says. "I'm opening one row cell 13 to shower Jones." One is "being showered" rather than "taking a shower." The option is the guards', always. The same thing happens with recreation; it becomes a verb: "I'm going to recreate group three now," the guard says, meaning he will let one-quarter of the men on the row out of their cells and into the small dayroom.[6]

The immediate result of such efficient storage arrangements is a radical reduction in the prisoner's privacy. Indeed, prisoners typically claim that on death row one has no privacy at all. In the words of Caryl Chessman, who spent twelve years on San Quentin's death row before his execution in 1962:

You have no privacy. Day and night, you're watched closely. Having claimed it, the state is jealous of your life. Every possible safeguard is taken to prevent you from cheating the executioner—by digging, cutting, or assaulting your way to stolen freedom; by self-destruction; by fleeing to the world of the insane. You've come to the wrong place if curious eyes and the probing beams of flashlights make you uneasy.[7]

A present-day death row prisoner seconded Chessman's observations, reminding us that nothing essential has changed on the row:

They read your mail. Take a visit, they're standing over your shoulder. They know everything you're saying. You shower and they're watching you. At night they're shining flashlights in your cell. You never have a free moment.[8]

Regular prisoners are permitted to develop an informal society and, to some extent at least, police themselves.[9] But the margin for failures of control on death row is exceedingly narrow. The prisoners are watched closely—though not continuously, as in the death house—and without apology.[10]

Held powerless on death row, condemned prisoners also come to feel powerless—that is, alone and vulnerable. Many—as many as seven out of every ten[11]—deteriorate in measurable ways. All are to some degree weakened and demoralized. Those condemned prisoners who reach the deathwatch . . .are subjected to constant surveillance and experience complete loss of privacy. Made susceptible by their death row confinement, they collapse under the substantial pressure of the deathwatch. In the final analysis, they are reduced to dehumanized objects that are mere pawns in the modern execution process.

Powerlessness

Close confinement combined with almost constant surveillance renders death row inmates powerless to alter or influence their daily existence in any meaningful way. Their lives are monotonous and lonely, and they are predictably bored, tense, and depressed. Chronic irritability and periodic lapses in personal control can leave prisoners feeling alienated from themselves. The prisoner comes to see himself as essentially a stranger in a strange land.[12] Powerlessness and its emotional sequelae, established in the *Harries* case as key factors in the cruelty of Tennessee's death row . . .affect prisoners on all death rows. The reason is straightforward: All death rows are, at bottom, sterile, eventless, oppressive environments that demoralize their inhabitants as a direct function of the setting's emphasis on custodial repression.

Death rows offer deadening, unchanging routines as a central feature of existence. On Louisiana's death row, at Angola Prison, "The occasional callouts, and mealtimes, are the only contact a condemned prisoner has with other inmates. The dominant activity of death row is shower time."[13] Most of the prisoner's time is spent in the cell, vegetating before a TV set or leaning against the cell bars wielding a peeper in a strained effort to glimpse another human face. "Men in isolated cells often grow weary of talking to walls, windows and bars. A human face, even if viewed through a makeshift mirror, adds meaning to a destitute existence."[14]

The isolated life on death row produces, in many inmates, a kind of self-imposed retreat from others. Many prisoners even refrain from outdoor exercise, the only chance they get to shake off the isolation of their cells and speak directly with other inmates. A death row security officer at Angola tells us that "Death row inmates don't go out on the yard too regular. They have the privilege but they don't take advantage of it. I talk to them and try to get them to go out, to get a little fresh air and sunshine, but they seldom do."[15] These prisoners add self-imposed isolation to the state-imposed isolation of the death row regime, consigning themselves to a life

that is, in the view of one death row inmate on San Quentin's death row, a kind of nightmare version of the movie *Groundhog Day*, a comedy in which Bill Murray's character, Phil, lives the same day over and over again. The movie is funny and even insightful; Phil uses his redundant existence to perfect his coping skills, land the woman of his choice, and go on to become a better person. The story line as applied to death row is quite different. There, each day is a redundant experience of failure and rejection—of being powerless to effect change, cut off from supportive human contact, vulnerable to others in a world where people want you dead. Each day the condemned are a little more dead—more like passive objects and less like autonomous beings—than the day before. The inmate who compared life on death row to the Murray movie had, for a time, a column that others would put on the Internet for him. His Internet pseudonym: Dead Man Talking.

The experience of powerlessness—of being an object imbedded in a routine—is magnified on solitary-confinement death rows, in which warehousing for death takes its most blatant, unvarnished form. The barren dimensions of the condemned prisoners' lives on such death rows are evident in the empty diversions they employ to occupy their time. In the prisoners' words:

- I've got so bored at times, I used to hook cockroaches together, sort of like they was a team of mules, to drag a matchbox around on the floor to pass time. I mean that may sound weird to you or somebody else, and it might be. Matter of fact I just flushed a little frog down the shit jack the other day that I had back there [in my cell]. It came up through the shit jack. I kept him back there a couple of weeks and I kicked roaches and things to feed him. Just any little old thing. . . .To more or less keep your mind off the damned chair and the things that you're seeing around you. Anything to occupy your mind.

- I got a big dictionary. I look in there and I read—just look at words, I can't even pronounce the words I be looking at, you know, but I read the meaning to them. I like doing stuff like that. It's hard to stay at that thing, you get sleepy—without moving—you can't stay up but an hour at a time, you have to lay back down. I can't seem to settle down in my cell. Like, I spend 23 1/2 hours in there and I can't ever come to peace with myself. It irritates me all the time.[16]

Long hours in the cell are a source of psychological pressure and emotional turmoil. All prisoners experience some pressure; for some, the experience is almost disabling. For example:

I sit in that cell, you know, and it seems like I'm just ready to scream or go crazy or something. And you know, the pressure, it builds up, and it feels like everything is—you're sitting there and things start, you know, not hearing things, things start to coming in your mind. You start to remember certain events that happened, bad things. It just gets to a person. I sit up at night, you know. You just sit there, and it seems like you're going to go crazy You've got three walls around you and bars in front of you, and you start looking around, you know, and it seems like things are closing in on you. Like last night, when I sit in there and everything's real quiet, things, just a buzzing noise gets to going in my ears. And I sit there, and I consciously think, "Am I going to go crazy?" And the buzzing gets louder; and you sit there and you want to scream and tell somebody to stop it. And most of the time you get up—if I start making some noise in my cell, it will slack off. And it sounds stupid, I know, but it happens. . . .[S]ometimes I wonder if I don't get it stopped, I'm going crazy or something. And you know, maybe tonight when I lay down it's not going to break when I get up and try to make some noise.[17]

Against the suffocating vacuum of the cell, a chance to place a simple order at the commissary can be an exhilarating, liberating experience—a small freedom so sweet it accentuates the bitter constraints that envelop one's life on death row.

They have one day which is a store day. That one day actually is to these people on death row like Christmas and all they actually get is cigarettes and candy or cookies, and that's actually become to be a thing like Christmas. I've surveyed it from watching the guys and everybody gets excited and they are actually more happy on Tuesday when they get that little package. But you see this is actually what we have been reduced to as far as being men, trying to be a man, finally enjoying a little thing like a cookie. To me it's actually absurd, this actually affects me to that point and there is no way out of it, there is no way to rebel against it.[18]

Prisoners on reformed death rows generally have more autonomy than those on solitary-confinement death rows. (I say generally because reformed death rows go through periodic lockdowns, during which the prisoners are kept in solitary confinement as punishment. On the reformed death row I studied, one such lockdown lasted a full five months.) These prisoners normally have the company of their dayroom companions to fall back on, and this can, no doubt, be a source of comfort, giving them a sense of a more normal and at least minimally autonomous daily life. Contact with other prisoners, however, can be a double-edged sword. One's fellows can be a source of pressure, harassment, and sometimes violent victimization, all of which add to feelings of helplessness. As a case in point, on our reformed death row a man was brutally attacked by a fellow prisoner in the dayroom. The victim was paralyzed for life.

Even congenial conversations in dayrooms (for those on reformed death rows) or with men in neighboring cells (for those in solitary confinement) offer only limited opportunities for autonomous action or emotional support. Eventually, one says and does all that one can say and do in the compressed world that is death row. One's social life, as it were, becomes numbingly redundant and oppressive in its own right. It is worth recalling that Sartre's notion of hell was of being confined for eternity with people one despises. For many prisoners, perhaps especially on reformed death rows, the fact that they have "no exit" from other condemned prisoners may make their confinement a kind of hell. It is, in my view, entirely fitting that a wide-ranging anthology of writings from death row goes by the title, *Welcome to Hell*.[19]

The enduring difficulty is that on death row—any death row—everything remains the same. "It's continuously having the same walls, the same bars, the same papers, the same books," said one condemned prisoner. "Nothing changes. Only the outside, the light. We have day and we have night, we have day and then we have night." People become fixtures, as unchanging as the schedule. A paradoxical dependence is bred; routines come to hold in check the very resentments they produce. "If something changes, it's like a shock to you," observed one inmate. "You'll hear them yelling and screaming and everything else."[20] With the inevitable return of routine, the inmates retreat once more into the familiar, however impoverished it may be.

Loneliness

Though familiar, the routine on death row offers little real comfort—to the prisoners, that is. For the staff, routine can become an end in itself, a means of distancing themselves from the prisoners. Too often, the staff become insensitive to the human tragedies unfolding among the condemned; they seem unwilling or unable to offer meaningful support. "Caring," observed one group of researchers studying death row officers, "is simply not part of the job."[21] "Nobody is going to help you," confirmed an inmate. "Nobody is going to give you a kind word. Nobody is going to ask you, 'How's it going, how's your day? Is everything coming out okay?' You're totally ignored." Nor do other prison officials fill the emotional void. Like the occasional citizen's groups that tour death rows, "they just look in the cage and they go away."[22] Though these are almost surely overstatements on the part of the inmates—some officers and officials say they care, and try to show it—they indicate widely and firmly held perceptions of the social reality on death row. Almost to a man, condemned prisoners feel abandoned by the prison staff, denied simple human compassion, treated "as if already dead."[23]

Feeling abandoned by the prison staff often goes hand in hand with feeling abandoned by the world. The custodial regime not only insulates guards from prisoners, it also isolates prisoners from the moral and social community of the outside world. Inmates suffer "a symbolic isolation that comes from living with the fact that 12 members of your community have determined that you are a worthless person who should no longer be permitted to exist." Prisoners may feel "so isolated that it is nearly impossible to share a religion with those on the outside." As time passes and they gradually exhaust their appeals, prisoners may feel further removed from the world of the living. One reason is that fewer people are apt to write or visit in support of a lost (or losing) cause.[24] Another is that failed appeals mark progressive stages in the killing and dying process, "pull[ing] layers of legal legitimacy over a corpse that hasn't quit moving and complaining yet."[25]

Their isolation on death row contributes to the weakening and often the dissolution of the prisoners' relationships with their loved ones. In one condemned man's words, "While most people rely on their families for their major source of support, it is not at all uncommon for this resource to be unavailable to death row prisoners."[26] One reflection of this sad fact is an empty visiting room. "On the death row visiting day," Jackson and Christian tell us, "the room is usually empty. It is rare for even two death row inmates to get a visit at the same time."[27]

Visits are a precious but rare—and precarious—commodity in the eyes of the condemned. Visits are not matters of right but rather privileges that can be—and, in fact, regularly are—suspended at the discretion of prison officials.[28] Officials discourage visits through a variety of restrictive rules and regulations. For example, visits can take place only on certain days and for limited periods of time. This creates logistical problems for the prisoners' loved ones. And though no physical contact is allowed during typical visits, the staff nevertheless carefully monitor all visits. What is worse, after all visits, inmates are shackled and subjected to thorough body searches, even when the visits involved no physical contact. For some prisoners, the pain and humiliation engendered by such treatment outweigh the pleasure of the visit. One prisoner could barely suppress his rage when describing his experience with visits:

> Your people come to this place. You go down and you sit down for an hour or whatever you stayed and you get your mind away from this place. And just as soon as you come in after having enjoyed yourself for a little bit, just as soon as you get up from out there and walk in here, they strip you, look up your asshole and in your mouth and strip search you and handcuff you behind your back and drag you back up that hall. Well, you see, they just broke your whole fucking visit. You would have been better off, in a way, if you'd just stayed in your cell and if you could have slept through that hour. . . .I mean that's the kind of attitude that leaves you with after they fuck with you. Knowing your people drove and went through all this trouble to come see you, to give you an hour or something. Then they have taken the fucking time to figure out a way to fuck it up for you.[29]

Condemned prisoners tend to see the death row regime as a calculated and gratuitous assault on their humanity. For them, the physical setting is punitively spartan; rules and regulations are means to inflict pain.[30] The intrusive procedures associated with visits do much to fuel the prisoners' angry perception that their keepers mean them harm.

Aside from humiliating searches, the rules regulating visits with condemned prisoners make these encounters strained and potentially divisive. Visiting arrangements for Florida's condemned, under which visitors are continuously observed, have been found to impede the flow of information and emotional support between families and condemned prisoners, "thereby sustaining rather than alleviating feelings of isolation and uncertainty."[31] The visiting routine on Alabama's death row frustrates any attempt at congenial conversation. The visiting situation in Alabama, as I stated after observing visits there firsthand, is more akin to a wake than to a supportive family gathering.

> The priorities on [Alabama's] death row seem almost unforgivable in regard to visits. The routine surrounding visits might be compared with the preparations for a funeral. Noncontact visits, in particular, seem peculiarly reminiscent of the viewing at a wake. The inmate sits alone in an enclosed chamber, neatly dressed and carefully groomed, almost as if on display for his loved ones. The need to shout across the barrier separating the inmate and his visitors precludes intimate conversation and results in awkward interludes of silence. Visitors speak as much among themselves as with their prisoner; they appear nervous and out of place. The prisoners, too, seem ill at ease.[32]

It is hard to be natural when yelling to loved ones or when officers are looking over your shoulder, perhaps eavesdropping as well. In turn, truncated conversations and awkward interludes of silence can leave people feeling confused and lonely: What did she *really* mean by this pause or that phrase? The prisoner, on returning to his cell, is left to wonder. And worry.

As a general rule, states Abu-Jamal, the condemned prisoner in Pennsylvania, visits on death row "are an exercise in humiliation." These demoralizing visits are, moreover, experienced by many inmates as an *intentional* effort to destroy the human relationships that sustain condemned prisoners. "In Pennsylvania, as in many other death states, noncontact visits are the rule. It is not just a security rule; it is a policy and structure that attempts to sever emotional connection by denying physical connection between the visitor and the inmate."[33] The empty existence on death row may, in any case, render prisoners mute during visits. They and their loved ones live in utterly different worlds, with little or no common ground to draw on to sustain communication (though more accommodating visiting conditions would certainly improve matters). After years of noncontact visits and, for many inmates, ultimately, no visits at all, the result is that "Prisoners are as isolated psychologically as they are temporally and spatially. By state action, they become 'dead' to those who know and love them, and therefore dead to themselves. For who are people, but for their relations and relationships?"[34] Unrewarding visits thus reflect and reinforce the prisoners' basic sense of alienation from the world of the living. As a result, most condemned prisoners describe themselves as abandoned by the free world and left to their own devices to endure their confinement.[35]

Vulnerability

Held powerless under conditions of indifference and neglect, prisoners tend to resent their guards, who are the nearest at hand to blame for their helpless and lonely state. Prisoners also come to feel vulnerable to harm by their keepers. Alone and defenseless when in their cells, living at all times in harsh and deprived conditions, convenient objects of contempt, condemned prisoners feel vulnerable to abuse from their keepers. Condemned prisoners are usually held in the most secluded quarters of the prison—a condition that, absent effective supervision of the guard force, invites, indeed almost authorizes, abuse. Their stark vulnerability may be apparent from the moment prisoners set foot on death row. One prisoner put the matter like this:

The biggest fear is when you walk onto this place. I've seen one man walk out there and he stood right there and he broke down and cried. I've seen more come in here and live three days and start praying. I've seen them come in here and cuss the day they was born because of fear. I've seen grown men come in here and get down and pray like kids. And cry.[36]

Condemned prisoners see death row as a law unto itself, one based on the premise "Might makes right." As one prisoner observed, "They can do anything they want to you. Who's going to stop them?" Power, many say, emanates from the butt end of the baton or billy club that is often standard equipment for death row officers. This weapon, sometimes tellingly called an axe handle by the prisoners, functions as both a symbol of violence and an instrument of social control. As one prisoner observed:

You have to more or less watch what you say to these guys because if they want to get you back, they could easily do that. You're on your way out to the yard, the guy could say as soon as you get out of the center—around that little bend—where the rest of the guys couldn't see you, they could easily claim "well, he turned around and hit me," "he turned around and I thought he was attacking me," or "he pushed me." And one whack with one of those axe handles up against your head, if you're not going to be dead, you're going to be insane for the rest of your life. And then you're not going to be able to help no one. . . .I am really afraid of that. I'm trying to hold on to my own common sense, you know, because I feel that is one of the main factors that I do have that is still mine. My knowledge that I can think and my ability to learn and do my own research on my own case. I feel that if I got hit with one of those sticks, I wouldn't have that much sense. So, I live in constant fear of that actually all the time."[37]

In a curious throwback to an earlier—and more primitive—era in penology, San Quentin's death row features guards armed with machine guns patrolling the catwalks and the outdoor recreation area. To my knowledge, San Quentin is unique in this regard; no other prison in the United States features armed officers within the prison's perimeter. San Quentin's death row, intimidating even to hardened convicts, is housed in Eastblock, a cell block that has been described by one condemned prisoner as "cavernous, dark, loud and smelly." Keepers and kept, we learn, move about in hazy, "subdued light" that is "filtered by dirt and grime on the windows" of the exterior walls, adding an element of almost surreal gloom. Cells are small and cramped, bare and uninviting. Life outside these tiny habitats always brings with it a tangible presumption of risk. "All the Guards that are not on the gunrails are required to wear bullet proof vests; in case there is an incident where shots are fired, they will have protection."[38] Condemned prisoners at San Quentin have access to outside recreation, but they must undergo strip-searches to get there and then must contend with the danger posed by their fellow inmates as well as that posed by armed officers, who shoot into the enclosed recreation area with some regularity in efforts to control prisoner behavior.

> The first time I went to the yard, a few days after I arrived in Eastblock, I was walking around the yard to get my bearings and to check out my environment a bit. As I made a few circuits around the compound, I noticed the concrete had a lot of holes in it. Later, I was leaning against the wall talking with one of the guys and I commented on the poor workmanship of the concrete. The guy looked at me as if I was drooling on myself. He snickered and said, "That's not poor workmanship, it's because of poor marksmanship." It turns out that all the chips I had noticed were from the bullets fired into the yard during altercations. It was at that point that I began to wonder if I really wanted to hang out in a place where part of the exercise program was dodging bullets.[39]

The yard on San Quentin's death row also provides an unimpeded view of the death house, which for some inmates is frightening and depressing, and reason enough to stay in one's cell.

> I think that what finally made up my mind for me is the "Chimney." Everyday that I went to the yard, I would end up leaning against the wall. As I leaned there, I could watch what was going on around me. At the end of the row of yard compounds is where the Gas Chamber is located. Sticking out of the roof of the Chamber is a huge green pipe, used to vent the poison gas after an execution is carried out. I would catch myself staring at this pipe everyday and wondering if that pipe would someday be venting the poison gas used to execute me. It was soon after this that I decided that I didn't really want to hang out in the yard any longer.[40]

The self-isolation of prisoners on death row, then, may plausibly feature elements of retreat into the comfort of routine as well as retreat from the threat of danger that lurks outside the cell door. Yet the cell can provide but a limited sanctuary, since it is policed by officers, who can enter at will, bringing the threat of violence with them. At San Quentin, at least, the vulnerability of prisoners in cells is highlighted when officers on catwalks shoot onto the tiers to maintain order, with some bullets and debris making their way into the cells. This may not happen often, but from my own visits to San Quentin's death row I know that it does happen, and that it is a source of fear among the prisoners.

Abuse, including violence, may be implicitly if unintentionally authorized in the training of many death row officers. Colin Turnball's research revealed that death row officers' training emphasized "combat duty" and made "no attempt to help the guard approach the extremely difficult task of maintaining appropriate human relations [with condemned prisoners]."[41] This surely applies to the armed officers at San Quentin, if not indeed to their colleagues in bullet proof vests patrolling the tiers. The profound suspiciousness of the officers on the reformed death row I studied, a suspiciousness demanded by their superior officer, promoted a combat mentality among many of these officers. Cabana, when he was warden at Parchman Prison in Mississippi, praised the custodial skills of officers, particularly those on death row, who looked for threat in even such innocent-sounding activities as Bible study.[42] Informal socialization on the job, moreover, is apt to alert the guards of any death row to the potential dangers of their work, reinforcing the apparent value of a cold and even pugnacious stance with the inmates. One prisoner put this matter plainly:

> They got us one sorry motherfucker right here and that's the only way I know how to put it. One of the most sorriest motherfuckers right here that could be working in a penitentiary. Now he comes to work and sits his ass down right up there, and sits there and tries to figure out a way to fuck somebody back there on death row. And he's the one that shows the others how to do us. . . .It's just like father teach son—that's their routine. When a guard comes here, instead of giving him [formal] training and everything and teach him how he should cope with these things in prison and stuff, they bring him right up here, put him under one of the worst sons-of-bitches there is

here. Then father teach son. Then it's just a very short period of time until they have built up this attitude and they look at you the same way he does. . . .Now I been in down here since way back. So a whole lot about the outside, I don't know nothing about it. But about these sons-of-bitches, I do. And that's why I say, when a guy come into here and he say, "Well, there goes a good guard." Shit. It won't be three days before he's just as sorry as the next motherfucker.[43]

One can readily imagine the threat posed by a "sorry motherfucker" with a gun, as in the unique and troubling case offered by San Quentin.

Many condemned prisoners believe that their keepers, with or without provocation, would resort to violence.[44] Indeed, some prisoners' fear of violence from their keepers merges with their fear of execution. One prisoner, visibly afraid, had this to say:

> When you're on death row and you're laying down in your cell and you hear a door cracking, you'll think of where it comes from. When you hear it crack. And when you hear the keys and everything, when something like this happens, the keys come through here: I'm up. I'm up because you don't know when it's going to take place. The courts give you an execution date, that's true. But you don't know what's going to take place between then and your execution date. You don't know when you're going to be moved around to the silent cell over here. That's right down the hall, what they call a waiting cell. You don't know when you're going to be moved down there. And this keeps you jumpy, and it keeps you nervous, and it keeps you scared.[45]

Such fear, which borders at times on raw panic, may be more prevalent among condemned prisoners than one would imagine. It bespeaks the profound vulnerability these prisoners feel, and the deep distrust they have for their keepers

Coping and the Crucible of Deterioration

Many condemned prisoners describe death row as a human pressure cooker. Ten-

sion is pervasive, pernicious, and, in varying degrees, disabling. Symptoms of depression and lifelessness are common. Deterioration in some form affects many, if not most, death row prisoners at various points in their confinement. "The main thing," said one condemned prisoner, "is the mental pressure: you're always depressed. But I think another main thing is the physical deterioration of the body. You sit up there and you just feel yourself getting weaker, you know? Your back hurts, ya know? You're sick a lot—cold and low blood. You lose your energy."[46] The threat of deterioration can be a source of considerable anxiety, leading prisoners to question their capacity to maintain their psychological equilibrium. "I'm already walking on a hairline of being sane and insane," observed one prisoner, "I could fall either way at any time."[47]

Some prisoners do in fact become psychiatric casualties of death row. I was able to study one such man who had, in the brutally frank words of a fellow prisoner, "done cold left himself." Our exchange on this man's history of deterioration went as follows:

> When I first come down here, he talked good, he could carry on a good conversation, he could talk real good. We used to talk to each other, you know. But it's got to where now sometimes at night he would be sitting down there in his cell and he'd tear up pieces of cloth all night long, tear his mattress all night long, get at the bar and yell out "Mama, Mama," continuously at the top of his lungs. And you can't sleep with that there going on. Yell out other people's names and so forth. I think, I think he needs help, a lot more than what he's getting up there.

> *Do you think it's a psychiatric condition now?*
> I think it's worked into that, yeah. Because every time somebody mentions the chair—every time someone mentions this thing in here, walking around it or anything, he flies off the handle.[48]

Few inmates were supportive of this man, who had become an irritant. Others resented him because they thought he was faking mental illness. A few taunted him, at least until his symptoms made it apparent that he was profoundly disturbed.

Anytime someone mentions the electric chair, he gets real uptight?

Yeah, he gets uptight. One of the inmates will joke with him about it, or say something to him in a way, I call it smart cracking, just to see if he's going to do it again. Which isn't right, but they do it. They yell at him; they say something like, "Hey, he's the first to go" and a bunch of other stuff that they make up and say to him. This'll trigger him off. I mean, it would trigger me off.

Do you think they want to trigger him off?

They do sometimes. But they got to where, I don't know, that's been about a year or something ago, and he hasn't got out of it yet. They've quit joking as far as, you know, reving him up. But he hasn't got better. It's just with him, it's just a thing that's with him and he does, he needs, he needs help, I mean, you know, a doctor's help.[49]

By the time I interviewed this man (for an earlier book), he impressed me as being "only a shell of a person." I caught him in a lucid period, one of few. He'd been transferred to the local jail in his hometown to pursue legal matters, and the respite from death row gave him a second wind, one long enough at least to report on his psychological demise. Here is our exchange.

This place here just caves in on you. The same thing every day, that just stacks up on top of you, ya know what I mean? So I got out from under it, ya know what I mean? Like a brand new life, man. Like I just came in yesterday I feel relaxed a lot more now, and I can hold a better conversation with you because of the time I spent in court. . . .

But before I started going to court and things, my mind just flips out on me. . . .I done flipped out three or four times in different tiers, you know? My mind just right up and leave me. I didn't expect the thing to happen. And everything just, you know, how you just go. I can't explain it and everything that has taken place, but I just flipped out.

This happens from out of nowhere?

Just out of nowhere. Just flipped out . . .I stayed up for weeks at a time. I don't know why, I just couldn't go to sleep. . . . I'd be depressed and lost. Like the officers would come by and they'd talk to me, some of them, and say I was lost, man, say "it was like you was in another world, man" ya know? I say, "yeah, that's the way I felt, like I was in another world." I felt sometimes for weeks at a time that I wasn't even here.[50]

During his weeks of mental absence, this prisoner would hear voices that would tell him to set fire to his cell. He would stop eating. He would hold loud conversations with himself and with his neighbors, some of whom would tease and taunt him out of frustration. The only thing missing from his life was help, from professionals or peers.

I do not know what has become of this clearly disturbed prisoner. The subjects of that book—and this one—were given anonymity, so I never connected the names of persons with the interviews I conducted. It is possible that this man has been executed. Mentally ill people like him have been put to death in the past and continue to be today.[51] We may expect more such executions over the coming years. Mentally ill prisoners are particularly vulnerable to environmental pressures, pressures that are growing worse on death rows across our nation as the pace of executions picks up. Marginally adjusted prisoners will see their coping deficits shade into psychoses; psychotics will see their mental disorders reach extreme states of distress.[52] All the while, the other death row prisoners will see in these tragic human breakdowns living reminders of what the future may well hold for them as their execution dates inexorably draw near.

A Living Death

The cumulative impact of death row, as noted by the court in the *Harries* case, is an "overall sense of defeat."[53] The sources of this defeat emanate from the various conditions of confinement we have reviewed. In the words of Rideau and Wikberg, both inmates at Angola Prison and authors of noted essays on that prison's death row, the typical condemned prisoner's experiences can be summed up as follows:

Frustration gnaws at his gut. Loneliness embraces him daily, driving him deeper into a world of nothingness. Fear—a constant, never-changing fear—eats away at his sanity. Two years ago, three years ago, today, tomorrow—the same, all the same; there is no inkling that the torture will end. Hope has become merely a flickering candle whose light pales quickly before the all-engulfing feeling of devastation.[54]

Abu-Jamal, an African American, draws attention to the role of racism on death row. He gives the stark example of differential conditions available for recreation, a key outlet for death row prisoners. "The cages were for the blacks on death row. The open yards were for the whites on the row." In his view, this could be no accident. "The blacks, due to racist insensitivity and sheer hatred, were condemned to awaiting death in indignity. The event provided an excellent view, in microcosm, of the mentality of the criminal system of injustice, suffused by the toxin of racism."[55] Evidence from other sources indicates that racism may be a factor in some of the uglier encounters between staff and inmates on death row. As one inmate observed just after his arrival on death row, "I was looking at the chair and they said, 'Bring him on in here.' They showed me the chair and they said, 'Yeah, we are going to sit your ass in there.' You know, they were calling me nigger and shit. They were asking why I did what I done and did I want to die . . ."[56]

The cumulative destructiveness of death row for minority prisoners Abu-Jamal expressed this way:

Mix in solitary confinement, around-the-clock lock-in, no-contact visits no prison jobs, no educational programs by which to grow, psychiatric "treatment" facilities designed only to drug you into a coma; ladle in hostile, overtly racist prison guards and staff; add the weight of the falling away of family ties, and you have all the fixings for a stressful psychic stew designed to deteriorate, to erode one's humanity—designed, that is, by the state, with full knowledge of its effects.[57]

Research on life under sentence of death has not systematically explored the role of rac-

ism in shaping the experiences of African-American inmates on death row, though the problem of racism in our society and in our prisons, not to mention in the administration of the death penalty in times past and today, is well known.

Putting aside any unique problems that may be borne by black prisoners, the literature on the subject of reactions to death row confinement draws attention to a pervasive and profoundly human problem of hopelessness. In one prisoner's words:

You can hear its empty sound in the clanging of the steel doors, in the rattle of chains, in the body searches, in the lack of privacy, in the night sounds of death row, and you can see it in the eyes of the guards who never really look at you, but are always watching to see that you do not commit suicide.[58]

The "normal" reaction in such an environment, observed the noted psychiatrist Seymour Halleck, who testified as an expert in the *Harries* case, features depression and lethargy.[59] (Harries himself showed signs of psychological deterioration that a number of experts attributed to the conditions of his confinement on death row, an attribution supported by a body of empirical research and accepted by the court.[60]) Prisoners of other death rows bear out his observation, describing death row as a "living death" and themselves as the "living dead." As one prisoner poignantly observed, "You need love and it ain't there. It leaves you empty inside, dead inside. Really, you just stop caring."[61]

Death row prisoners, to restate Halleck's point, give up on life as we normally know it. They exist rather than live. That existence, however, can be deceptive to outside observers, even to correctional officers and officials on the scene. For on a social level, death row prisoners, and, to a lesser extent, their keepers, create a make-believe world premised on denying the reality of the death penalty. Prisoners talk tough and act cool, posturing even within the cells that cage them, desperate to deceive themselves and those around them.

An intriguing example is provided by reactions to the passing of the old year and the coming of the new, which is accompanied by

New Year's Eve celebrations on at least some death rows; celebrations that are not entirely unlike those taking place outside the prison. One inmate found humor in the situation.

> I am always amused on New Year's Eve. At the stroke of midnight, a lot of guys will start cheering and whistling. I could never figure out why. There is a cartoon that I am reminded of whenever the guys start cheering. It's called "Mr. Boffo." A regular theme of "Mr. Boffo" is something called, "People [Unc]lear On The Concept." Whenever I hear the cheering, I think to myself, here is the essence of people not clear on the concept. Since time is something that we all have very little of (on Death Row) I think that to cheer the passing of time is one of those bizarre ironies that are common in a situation like this.[62]

Cheering the *passing* of time on death row is one thing; still being alive is a kind of victory. It would be an equally bizarre irony if the death row inmates cheered the *coming* of a new year, as most New Year's revelers do. This, too, would be an example of people unclear on the concept, because the new year does not bring a fresh start for condemned prisoners so much as it brings them closer to death. In either case, any form of New Year's celebration gives a profoundly misleading image of death row to the outside world. People who conclude from such celebrations that life is carefree or easy on death row are, to echo the sentiments of our inmate, "unclear on the concept," not unlike those who once thought that the singing of field slaves was an expression of contentment with their lot in life.[63]

Humor is used by death row prisoners to bolster a facade of manliness, as well as to distract attention from inner doubts and turmoil. The prisoner who found humor in the curious cheerfulness of condemned men on New Year's Eve may thereby find some relief from his own anxieties about his impending mortality; the revelers almost certainly get some relief from inner turmoil through their celebration, especially if they are able to secure "home-brew"—homemade alcohol—to ring in the New Year. In both instances we see denial, and denial is a psychological

gambit that always comes home to roost. As one prisoner of a solitary-confinement death row put it:

> The row ain't serious; it's a lot of funny things happening on the row. Everybody seeing who can be the funniest, you know. So, I contribute in that there, too. I figure if I contribute in that, that will keep me going halfway. But I figure now when things really get hard and everybody stops joking, that's when you are going to see about ten people just bug out from the jump. All of us are going to bug out sooner or later.[64]

Things "get hard," to complete the prisoner's point, when someone is executed—as happens these days with increasing regularity. These executions would seem to be both the logical and the psychological culmination of death row confinement.

Notes

1. M. Abu-Jamal, *Live From Death Row* (Reading, Mass.: Addison-Wesley, 1995).

2. D. A. Cabana, *Death at Midnight: The Confession of an Executioner* (Boston: Northeastern University Press, 1996), 148.

3. Quoted in G. E. Goldhammer, *Dead End* (Brunswick, Me.: Biddle Publishing Company, 1994), 108.

4. P. Brasfield with J. M. Elliot, *Deathman Pass Me By: Two Years on Death Row* (San Bernardino: Borgo Press, 1983), 91–92.

5. A. Bronstein, personal communication.

6. B. Jackson and D. Christian, *Death Row* (Boston: Beacon Press, 1980), 14.

7. C. Chessman, "Trial by Ordeal," in *Death Row: An Affirmation of Life*, ed. S. Levine (New York: Ballantine, 1972), 4.

8. Jackson and Christian (n. 6), 94.

9. See G. Sykes, *The Society of Captives* (New York: Atheneum, 1966); J. Irwin, *Prisons in Turmoil* (Boston: Little, Brown, 1980); and R. Johnson, *Hard Time: Understanding and Reforming the Prison*, 2nd ed. (Belmont: Wadsworth, 1996).

10. For an insightful discussion of privacy and incarceration, see B. Schwartz, "Deprivation of Privacy as a 'Functional Prerequisite': The Case of the Prison," *Journal of Criminal Law and Criminology* 63 (1972): 235–236.

11. I and Professor Stanley Brodsky of the University of Alabama independently found 70 percent of Alabama's condemned prisoners to be showing signs of deterioration. My finding, based on content analysis of interviews, was that "7 of every 10 prisoners diagnosed themselves as suffering physical, mental or emotional deterioration in what was typically portrayed as the interpersonal vacuum constituting the human environment of death row." See R. Johnson, "Life Under Sentence of Death," in *The Pains of Imprisonment*, ed. R. Johnson and H. Toch (Prospect Heights, Ill.: Waveland Press, 1988), 132. Brodsky found a 70 percent deterioration rate for this same population using objective personality tests. Brodsky's results are reported in depositions pertaining to Jacobs v. Dutton, No. 78–309H et al. (S.D. Ala., 1979).

Other studies have described the problem of deterioration as common among condemned prisoners but have not provided statistics on the prevalence of symptoms. See R. Johnson, *Condemned to Die: Life Under Sentence of Death* (Prospect Heights, Ill: Waveland Press, 1989) (Chapter 6 contains a fuller ethnographic description of deterioration among Alabama's condemned than that found in the article cited above); Jackson and Christian (n. 6), 174–189 (examining Texas's death row); L. West, "Psychiatric Reflections on the Death Penalty," *American Journal of Orthopsychiatry* 45 (1975): 689–700 (covering death row prisoners generally); H. Bluestone and C. L. McGahee, "Reaction to Extreme Stress: Impending Death by Execution," *American Journal of Psychiatry* 119 (1962): 393–396 (covering death row prisoners at Sing Sing); and J. Gallemore and J. Panton, "Inmate Responses to Lengthy Death Row Confinement," *American Journal of Psychiatry* 129 (1972):167–172 (covering death row prisoners in North Carolina). In 1968, Congress heard testimony on the problem of deterioration among the condemned. See U.S. Congress, Senate Committee on the Judiciary, *To Abolish the Death Penalty: Hearings before the Subcommittee on Criminal Laws and Procedures*, 90th Cong., 2nd sess., March 20 and 21 and July 2, 1968, S. 1760.

12. C. M. Lambrix, "The Isolation of Death Row," in *Facing the Death Penalty: Essays on a Cruel and Unusual Punishment*, ed. M. L. Radelet (Philadelphia: Temple University Press, 1989), 199.

13. W. Rideau and R. Wikberg, *Life Sentences: Rage and Survival Behind Bars* (New York: Times Books, 1992), 264.

14. Ibid., 265.

15. Ibid., 270.

16. Johnson, *Condemned to Die* (n. 11), 48.

17. Ibid., 49.

18. Ibid., 51.

19. J. Amens, ed., *Welcome to Hell: Letters and Writings from Death Row* (Boston: Northeastern University Press, 1997).

20. Jackson and Christian (n. 6), 232, 226.

21. M. L. Radelet, M. Vandiver, and F. Berardo, "Families, Prisons, and Men with Death Sentences: The Human Impact of Structured Uncertainty," *Journal of Family Issues* 4 (4): 596 (December 1983). For many regular prison guards, caring, expressed as a concern for delivering human services and thereby ameliorating the stresses of confinement, is a central feature of their work. See H. Toch, "Is a Correctional Officer, by Any Other Name, a 'Screw'?" *Criminal Justice Review* 3 (1978): 19–35; R. Johnson and J. Ponce, "The Complete Correctional Officer: Human Service and the Human Environment of Prison," *Criminal Justice and Behavior* 8 (3): 343–373 (1981); L. Lombardo, *Guards Imprisoned: Correctional Officers at Work*, 2nd ed. (Cincinnati: Anderson, 1989); and Johnson, *Hard Time* (n.9), Chap. 8.

22. Jackson and Christian (n. 6), 90, 19.

23. Brasfield with Elliot (n. 4), 80.

24. Lambrix (n. 12), 198, 200, 200.

25. Jackson and Christian (n. 6), 31. See also Lambrix (n. 12).

26. Lambrix (n. 12), 199.

27. Jackson and Christian (n. 6), 15. See also Johnson, *Condemned to Die* (n. 11); Radelet, Vandiver, and Berardo (n. 21); and B. Eshelman, *Death Row Chaplain* (New York: Signet Books, 1972).

28. M. Vandiver, "Coping with Death: Families of the Terminally Ill, Homicide Victims and Condemned Prisoners," in *Facing the Death Penalty: Essays on a Cruel and Unusual Punishment*, ed. M. L. Radelet (Philadelphia: Temple University Press, 1989), 133.

29. Johnson, *Condemned to Die* (n. 11), 54.

30. Ibid., 50.

31. Radelet, Vandiver, and Berardo (n. 21), 605.

32. Johnson, *Condemned to Die* (n. 11), 115.

33. Abu-Jamal (n. 1), 9, 11.

34. Ibid., 9, 11.

35. Johnson, *Condemned to Die* (n. 11), Chap. 1; Radelet, Vandiver, and Berardo (n. 21); and Jackson and Christian (n. 6), 100–109.

36. Jackson and Christian (n. 6), 78.

37. Johnson, *Condemned to Die* (n. 11), 70–71, 71.

38. "Dead Man Talking," the Internet, http://www.monkey.hooked.net/monkey/M/Hut/deadman/deadman.html, col. 4.

39. Ibid., col. 5.

40. Ibid., col. 5.

41. C. Turnball, "Death by Decree: An Anthropological Approach to Capital Punishment," *Natural History* 87 (1978): 54.

42. Cabana notes that Connie Evans asked to meet with another condemned prisoner for an informal Bible study session as Evans's execution drew near. Cabana was "reminded by an ever diligent security supervisor that it could be part of a plan to escape or create a disturbance of some kind . . ." Cabana viewed the admonition as "appropriate and appreciated," though he "chose to grant Evans his request." Cabana (n. 2), 178.

43. Johnson, *Condemned to Die* (n. 11), 65.

44. Ibid., Chap. 4.

45. Ibid., 74.

46. Ibid., 103.

47. Ibid., 106.

48. Ibid., 106–107.

49. Ibid., 107.

50. Ibid., 106–109.

51. K. S. Miller and M. L. Radelet, *Executing the Mentally Ill* (Newbury Park, Calif.: Sage,1993), 73 and generally. This is a thoughtful and moving work on the plight of the mentally ill condemned prisoner. For a heartbreaking account of the travails of daily life for mentally ill prisoners, as seen by the prisoners themselves, see H. Toch, *Mosaic of Despair: Human Breakdowns in Prison* (Washington, D.C.: American Psychological Association Press, 1992), esp. Chap. 4.

52. If the psychotic prisoners are properly diagnosed, they will be determined to be incompetent to be executed because they do not understand the punishment they face; they will then be transferred to a hospital for the criminally insane and subjected to treatment the object of which will be to render them competent to be executed. See Miller and Radelet (n. 51).

53. *Groseclose v. Dutton*, 609 F. Supp. 1432 (D.C. Tenn. 1985), 1436.

54. Rideau and Wikberg (n. 13), 263.

55. Abu-Jamal (n. 1), 34.

56. Johnson, *Condemned to Die* (n. 11), 83; see also page 136 for a discussion of racism and larger societal and criminal issues as seen by black death row prisoners.

57. Abu-Jamal (n. 55), 29–30.

58. J. M. Giarratano, "The Pains of Life," in *Facing the Death Penalty: Essays on a Cruel and Unusual Punishment*, ed. M. L. Radelet (Philadelphia: Temple University Press, 1989), 195.

59. *Groseclose* (n. 53), 1436.

60. See n. 11.

61. Johnson, *Condemned to Die* (n. 11), and Jackson and Christian (n. 6).

62. "Dead Man Talking," (n. 38), col. 9.

63. "I have often been utterly astonished . . . to find persons who could speak of the singing, among slaves, as evidence of their contentment and happiness. It is impossible to conceive of a greater mistake. Slaves sing most when they are most unhappy." F. Douglass, *Narrative of the Life of Frederick Douglass: An American Slave, Written by Himself* (New York: Penguin, 1968). It may well be that condemned prisoners joke most when they are most unhappy on death row.

64. Johnson, *Condemned to Die* (n. 11), 112, 96.

55
Race, Class, and Gender in Female Sentencing

An Ethnographic Perspective

Jody Miller

universal. They vary greatly, depending on a host of mediating factors. Poor black female offenders, for instance, are often perceived to be an entirely different breed of deviant than their affluent white counterparts and are treated by the system accordingly.

Labeling and radical theorists tell us that deviance of the powerless tends to be sanctioned much more severely than deviance of the powerful and that prejudices extend well beyond the construction of rule-breaking and into its regulation and control. The intersection of race, gender, and class denote an instance of "triple disadvantage," leading to greater scrutiny and steeper punishment when female minority deviance is detected.

The notion that discretion lies at the heart of the administration of justice would strike many as surprising. After all, legislators make laws and the police and courts exist to enforce those laws equally and without prejudice. Everyone, we are told, is treated the same—regardless of age, gender, race, or social class. In practice, nothing could be further from the truth.

Decades of sociological research have established the existence of systematic bias in the criminal justice system, and the prejudicial treatment of female offenders is especially pronounced. Controlling for type of offense, scholars have shown that females are sentenced more harshly than males, that more girls than boys are placed in diversion programs for non-criminal conduct, and that girls placed in detention centers typically stay there longer than their male counterparts. Feminist scholars contend that this differential treatment is deeply rooted in patriarchal conceptions of "acceptable femininity," so females who violate gender role expectations will be singled out for especially punitive treatment. Male deviance, by contrast, is normal, natural, and expected—an attribute of its "masculinity."

Miller explores how gender interacts with race and social class to affect the sentencing decisions of juvenile justice officials. Until recent years, feminist researchers explored gender as a "universal" construct, excluding other variables with which it might combine to influence juridical outcomes. As Miller reminds us, however, conceptions of femininity are not

While feminist researchers have extensively documented gender bias within the field of criminology (Cain, 1989b; Campbell 1981; Chesney-Lind, 1977, 1978, 1988; Daly and Chesney-Lind, 1988; Gelsthorpe and Morris, 1990; Leonard, 1982; Smart, 1976, 1977), we have rarely examined our own theories and research for biases related to race, class and ethnicity. Instead, feminist scholarship about gender and criminal justice has tended to examine gender discrimination extracted from its race and class contexts. Only recently have debates among feminist criminologists expanded to include critiques of our own universalizing tendencies (Daly, 1991; Hudson, 1989, 1990; Klein, 1991; Rice, 1990).

The goals of the current research are to examine the ways that race and class shape the treatment of delinquent girls, and in doing so, to contribute to a theoretical alternative to unitary explanations of gender discrimination—one which recognizes the interconnected dynamics of race, class, age, sexuality and gender. To do so, I will examine investigation reports written to provide judges with recommendations for deciding upon girls' dispositions. Specifically, I will provide a detailed analysis of the discursive frameworks drawn upon to describe delinquent girls and to justify the court's decisions about their handling. The handling of delinquent girls is based not just on their actions, but also on their ways of being in the world. I will reveal how the interpretive frameworks used by juvenile court officials are shaped by hegemonic understandings of race, class, gender, sexuality and generation.

The most widely accepted theoretical framework used by feminists to explain the treatment of girls within the juvenile justice system is the thesis of judicial paternalism. According to this perspective, female offenders are treated more severely than male offenders at all levels of the juvenile justice system. This is a consequence of two factors. First, it is theorized that female criminals are treated harshly in order to punish them for violating normative gender expectations (Armstrong, 1977; Cain, 1989b; Figueria-McDonough, 1985; Mann, 1979; Parisi, 1982). Second, it is argued that punitiveness is a consequence of attempts to protect girls "from 'temptation' and their own sexuality." (Chesney-Lind, 1977: 128, 1978, 1988; Chesney-Lind and Sheldon, 1992).

A large number of studies have documented the existence of gender discrimination within the juvenile justice system (Alder, 1984; Cain, 1989a, 1989b; Canter, 1982: 388; Chesney-Lind, 1977, 1978, 1988; Chesney-Lind and Shelden, 1992; Figueira-McDonough, 1985: 279–280; Gelsthorpe, 1986, 1989; Gelsthorpe and Morris, 1990; Hudson, 1989, 1990; Kersten, 1989; Krohn, et al., 1983; Mann, 1979, 1984; Sarri, 1976; Visher, 1983, but see Teilmann and Landry, 1981). Discriminatory treatment has been reported in varying degrees at all levels of the system: police arrest and diversion decisions, police decisions to forward cases to court, adjudication and disposition decisions, and treatment received within placement facilities. Often these findings are drawn upon to offer support for the judicial paternalism thesis.

However, the notion of "paternalism" as an explanatory tool for the treatment of females is race and class bound (Collins, 1990; Davis, 1981; Rice, 1990; Smith and Stewart, 1983; White, 1985; Woodward, 1988). In the United States, protection has been extended to middle class and white women, to the exclusion of poor and working class women and women of color. Judicial paternalism may contribute to our understanding of the types of discriminatory treatment faced by middle-class white status offenders. However, it provides limited theoretical usefulness for explaining the variations in girls' treatment by race and class.

While it is sometimes mentioned in passing in their analyses (Chesney-Lind and Shelden, 1992; Gelsthorpe, 1989), there has been little attempt by researchers to analyze in depth the impact of race and class on the types of treatment girls face within the juvenile justice system. This is despite the fact that much research within the field of criminology reveals the existence of widespread racial and class bias within the criminal and juvenile justice systems (Bondavalli and Bondavalli, 1981: 55–56; Chesney-Lind and Shelden, 1992; Dannefer and Schutt, 1982; Empey and Stafford, 1991; Feyerherm, 1981; Krisberg, et al., 1986; Krohn, et al., 1980 Laub and McDermott, 1985; Quinney, 1974; Rice, 1990; Sarri, 1983; Scott, 1982; Visher, 1983; although for contradictory findings, see Empey and Stafford, 1991: 315). These studies reveal that the investigation of gender discrimination divorced from the contexts of discrimination based on race and class is problematic, and provides a limited picture of the true and complex dynamics of girls' experiences within the juvenile justice system.

Method

Data for this project were gathered from the case files of girls on probation in an area office of the Los Angeles County Probation Department. The area office was chosen because it was a racially mixed region within the county, with significant populations of whites, Latino/a, and African Americans, and therefore provides a useful means of comparative analysis. Approximately 200 girls were on probation in the region when the investigation began in May 1992. For the current research, I stratified the population of girls by race, then randomly selected 30 case files for close content analysis: these included 10 African-American girls, 10 Latina girls and 10 white girls.[1] . . .

Generational Dynamics

Parental Authority

The creation of the juvenile justice system was grounded in the development of the doctrine of *parens patriae* and the construction of the delinquent child as in need of protection and guidance (Chesney-Lind, 1978; Chesney-Lind and Shelden, 1992; Empey and Stafford, 1991; Mann, 1984). According to Platt, "[m]any of the child savers' reforms were aimed at imposing sanctions on conduct unbecoming youth and disqualifying youth from the benefit of adult privileges." (in Chesney-Lind, 1978: 172). This concern with the control and development of children's morality led to a commitment by the court to uphold parental authority. This commitment remains, and many girls find entry into the juvenile justice system through complaints initiated by their parents (Chesney-Lind, 1982, 1988; Chesney-Lind and Shelden, 1992; Hudson, 1989, 1990; Teilmann and Landry, 1981).

Not surprisingly, probation officers often discussed girls within the investigation reports by examining their relationships to their parents, particularly in terms of their willingness to accept both parental and adult authority. To begin with, hierarchical relationships between adults and juveniles were emphasized in the reports by consistently referring to the individual in question as "minor" or "the minor" rather than by name. In addition, parents were not referred to throughout by name, but were categorized as "the father" or "the mother." This treatment was consistent within all of the investigative reports. Likewise, the investigating officers did not call themselves by name, but, in the context of the reports were "this officer." These linguistic constructs functioned to diminish the individuality of girls, as well as the parents and probation officers, and highlight and mark the girls' lack of full adulthood, while reinforcing the power relations of adults over them.

Girls were spoken of harshly in the case files when they challenged these generational power relations. One way some girls challenged this relationship was by not accepting the definition of the situation offered by their parents, probation officer, or other authority figure. Tonia,[2] for example, was an upper-middle income African-American girl arrested for shoplifting. The probation officer, mother and a counselor attempted to situate her shoplifting in a framework of emotional problems requiring counseling. Tonia rejected this definition, and as a result, the probation officer concluded, "minor denies that there is a problem. She has very little insight into her own behavior." Likewise, another probation officer expressed concern about Amber, an African-American girl, because she "refused all help" from the adults around her.

More frequently, girls were criticized for what was seen as more direct defiance of parental authority. Marsha, a middle-income white girl, was arrested after a fight with her mother. According to the investigative report, when "the minor became belligerent towards her . . . the victim felt that the minor was beyond her control and she was taken into custody. . . ." Later in the report, the probation officer continued: "the minor acted in a defiant and disobedient manner toward the mother. . . . Minor refuses to adhere to any parental instructions and has had absolutely no concept to the seriousness of her behavior. . . . [She] flat out refuses her mother's control." As a result, part of the probation officers' concept of their role was to help restore parental authority.

For example, Dora, an upper-middle-income Latina, was arrested after taking her parents' car without permission. While the offense was not deemed serious, the probation officer recommended formal probation because "she seems to be having difficulties in following the directions of her mother and may be beyond her control." The definition of juveniles as "beyond parental control" was frequently called upon to justify official intervention, as in Dora's case, where it was used to "provide her mother with a certain amount of support and guidance in helping to control her." This goal of restoring parental authority sometimes came as a result of explicitly rejecting the girl's definition of her relationship with her parents.

Finally, girls were critiqued for attempting to exert their adulthood. Diana, a middle-income African-American girl, was harshly described by the probation officer because she was perceived as "insistent upon having her way at all costs. She shows no respect to her mother and does nothing [she] does not want to do." According to the probation officer, Diana "talks to her mother as a peer. She responds to the probation officer in much the same manner." As a result, the probation officer stated, "This is the consummate spoiled brat. One who has decided she is running her own world." Diana's attempt to exert her adulthood by interacting with adults without proper deference was used to justify the recommendation that she receive counseling. At the end of the report, the officer softened, but remained paternalistic in recommending that "[t]he minor is not lost, she just needs a lot of help."

Diana's case was not unique, instead there was a tendency to view early adulthood negatively. Amber, for example, was critiqued because "she thinks she is grown." And Vanessa, an African-American AFDC recipient, was described as a "young [lady] with a desire to grow up fast and be on [her] own." The probation officer recommended that "minor needs to become involved in a counseling program so that she can explore the problems of growing up into adulthood in a more mature fashion."

Class, Gender, and Parental Accountability

While girls from all class and racial classifications were expected to respect parental authority, many files secondarily assessed the competence of parents, labeling some more fit than others. These labels tended to emerge in specific class contexts. Probation officers' constructions of parental abilities and responsibilities revealed greater approval of middle-class mothers, parents who were married and living together and fathers who took the initiative to be interviewed. Disapproval of the family environment tended to be expressed more harshly against working-class and single parents. Because the majority of parents interviewed at the probation department were mothers, these constructs were most frequently levied at mothers.

In fact, it was not assumed that fathers had a responsibility to be interviewed for the probation report. Fathers' absences from the investigation interview were never commented on in the probation reports, but mothers' absences were perceived as indicative of family problems, for example, one probation officer "suspected" that Leanne, a working-class Latina, had "serious problem in the home," in part because of "the *failure* of the mother to attend the interview..." [my emphasis]. No such expectations of fathers' behavior emerged. All of the fathers who came for interviews with investigating officers were described positively as parents. For example, Maria's father, a working-class Latino, was described as "making an honest effort to provide effective parental supervision." According to the probation officer, he "appears to be a concerned parent who has had difficulty controlling minor's behavior both in and outside the home." However, he "feels capable of controlling minor's behavior with probation assistance."

Harsher language was used to describe Rochelle's mother, an African-American woman receiving AFDC to support her family. She was described as "cooperative . . . but this officer's impression was that mother had little in the way of parenting skills and has allowed her daughter to become a school dropout, which contributed to her involvement in a delinquent act." In this instance, in contrast to Maria's, Rochelle is not just out of her mother's control, but her mother is conceived as partially responsible for this by having *allowed* her inappropriate behavior. Likewise, Becky's participation in school vandalism was explained by the probation officer as stemming in part from emotional problems, but there was implicit mother-blaming in the officer's discussion of her mother, a white AFDC recipient who had a number of children and a husband with a long term illness: "It is believed that this situation rendered the mother relatively non-nurturing, if ever she was, and it is highly unlikely that minor or anyone else in the family was ever aware or able to express the frustrations created by unfulfilled needs."

Middle-class parents tended not to be held responsible for their children's behavior in the ways that working-class and poor parents were. Vickie's mother, a middle-class Latina, "impressed the probation officer as being a caring and supportive parent." Similarly, while Rochelle and Becky's mothers had been implicitly held accountable for their daughter's behaviors, Linda's middle-class Latino parents were not held responsible for her assault on another girl:

> The minor seems impulsive and she had been having some problems getting along at home and in school. The reasons for these problems are not really known as she has a united family, but apparently she had the need to feel more important that was satisfied by her negative associations and behavior.

This notion of the traditional middle-class nuclear family was common. Something about being middle class and/or dual parent provided many families with an air of legitimacy that allowed them to escape discursive frameworks which held them accountable for their children's actions. Tonia's upper-middle-income African-American parents "have provided her with a stable home and financial security that she has taken for granted." Similarly, Susan's family was described as an all-American white middle-class family: "The minor comes from a united family and they appear interested and concerned in her welfare." In general then, working-class parents, especially mothers, were held accountable for their children's involvement in delinquent activities, while middle-class parents were perceived as having provided their children with "the good life," which their children refused or were unable to accept.

Sexuality, Pregnancy, and Motherhood

Much of the research on the treatment of girls within the juvenile justice system focuses on the treatment of female status offenders, because their handling often provides the clearest examples of the system's preoccupation with the protection and control of juvenile morality, particularly the sexual morality of girls (Chesney-Lind, 1977, 1978; Hudson, 1989, 1990; Sarri, 1976). In addition, evidence on the impact of deinstitutionalization and diversion programs point to a continued preoccupation

with the "morality" of delinquent girls (Alder, 1984; Chesney-Lind, 1988; Chesney-Lind and Shelden, 1992).

Interestingly, this was not an issue dwelt upon for very many of the girls in the current investigation. This may be due to the fact that these were girls on probation for criminal offenses rather than status offenses, and may also be reflective of the more punitive approach to delinquency that has shaped juvenile justice in the last decade (Krisberg, et al., 1986). Nevertheless, the handful of girls who probation officers discussed in terms of their sexual experiences and/or maternity are worth investigation for what they reveal about normative standards of morality and definitions of appropriate motherhood. In all, there were four cases in which sexuality, pregnancy and/or motherhood constituted the framework in which probation officers discussed girls. They included two African-American girls, both of whose families were in higher-income brackets (one $20,000 to $45,000; one over $45,000), one white girl whose family was on AFDC, and one lower income/non-AFDC Latina.

The first case involved Angela, a middle-income African-American girl, arrested for bringing a gun to school. According to the report, Angela was threatened by a female classmate who claimed that Angela had let the girl's brother and two other boys fondle her. The girl was physically larger than Angela and according to Angela, "there were all sorts of rumors of what I did. I was going to scare her. . . .The deans are afraid of the kids and you have to take it up on [sic] yourself when there are problems." Angela's mother agreed with her daughter that "the school has very poor control of students" and felt this was why her daughter "overreacted" and brought a gun to school. While Angela and her mother situated the event in terms of her daughter's personal safety in the school environment, the probation officer resituated the event with a focus on Angela's alleged sexual behavior:

> The initial incident . . .involved the allegation that the minor had allowed other boys to fondle her inappropriately. Minor claims these are just rumors. Counseling should focus on this area and on the minor's ability to maintain social relation-

ships at school. . . .Given the aggravating circumstances surrounding the present offense it is felt that the minor should go home under a stayed placement order rather than straight home on probation.

Two issues are significant in the probation officer's framing of events. First, the minor was not believed. Her testimony that the girl who threatened her was spreading rumors was discounted, and instead was seen as further evidence that she needed treatment to uncover the underlying causes of her sexual behavior and her denial of its existence. Second, the probation officer was placing a value judgment on Angela's alleged sexual behavior, labeling it "inappropriate" and recommending that her disposition be more severe as a result.[3] The "aggravating circumstances" surrounding the offense were not that the school environment was not safe, but that the minor was allegedly sexually active; and as a result, this was used as evidence of her need to receive "appropriate counseling."

Angela's case was unique in the manner that she was framed sexually. Three other girls were framed by probation officers in related ways, but in reference to pregnancy and motherhood rather than specifically sexuality. Stacy, an upper-middle-income African-American girl, and Heather, a white AFDC recipient, both were framed by probation officers in terms of the need to protect their "unborn children." Heather was arrested for shoplifting, and was pregnant at the time of the investigation. Although it was her first arrest and she was nearly of age, the probation officer chose to recommend a more restrictive treatment than is often recommended under such circumstances, in order to monitor the "safety" of Heather's fetus:

Probation officer feels that minor is too irresponsible to be expected to function adequately on an informal probation program and it is felt that formal probation services will be required to monitor subject's future behavior if only for her unborn child's benefit.

Similarly, Stacy was pregnant at the time of her arrest. Her parents were divorced, and her father, who was wealthy, accused her of having an adult boyfriend and of using drugs. Both Stacy and her mother, who was lower income, denied that she was using drugs. The probation officer believed the father rather than Stacy and her mother, and concluded:

The minor is pregnant and possibly involved with drugs. . . .[She] should be committed to the California Youth Authority (CYA) where they have a unit for pregnant girls. They would be able to provide for the safety of the fetus within this minor. She would not be able to use drugs during her pregnancy.

Further, the probation officer stated: "She has made irresponsible decisions about boyfriends and pregnancy. The minor is in need of counseling." While the probation officer had no evidence of drug abuse, she recommended the harshest sentence available for juvenile offenders because of her perception that the fetus needed protection. In both Stacy's and Heather's cases, the social control imposed upon them was more intense specifically because they were pregnant. The sanctions recommended by the probation officers were less about their delinquent acts than about the desire to monitor their pregnancies, "unborn babies," and motherhood.

In a similar case, Sylvia, a lower-income Latina girl was framed by the probation officer in very negative terms due in part to the probation officer's perception of her as a bad mother. Arrested for a stolen vehicle charge, "the minor has set a pattern of living on the streets generally abandoning her child to associate with car thieves." It was stressed several times in the report that she had "left her child," who remained in the care of Sylvia's mother. According to the probation officer, Sylvia "generally rationalized her socially deviant behavior...[and] failed to acknowledge the seriousness of her actions. . . ." It is significant that the only minor who was described as deviant in any of the reports I investigated was one whose "deviance" was clearly linked to being a bad mother and abandoning her child.

These four cases point to the fact that, for at least some girls, sexuality, pregnancy and motherhood are drawn upon to wield greater social control over their lives. The interesting question that remains, however, is why this treatment was the exception rather than the rule, particularly given the fact that these were not the only girls who were sexually active and/or mothers. In the following section, I will explore the more frequent discursive frameworks drawn upon to construct delinquent girls.

Race, Class, and the Construction of Female Delinquency

Premise of Individualized Causation

Within the investigation reports, there was a consistent discursive pattern among probation officers of emphasizing individualized causes of girls' delinquent behaviors, removed from their social contexts and wider social, political or economic causes. Officers did not attempt to search for answers to the question of why girls committed offenses beyond the individuals' emotional health, family dynamics or peer group influences. Evidence of the wider social influences on delinquent activities, particularly among African-American girls, was frequently deemed unimportant or incorrect, and girls' behaviors were resituated in a discursive framework emphasizing individualized solutions. Girls who attempted to call upon wider social influences to explain their behavior faced harsher interpretations of their behavior and attitudes because they were perceived as not taking responsibility for their actions.

Amber was an African-American girl whose family received AFDC. Involved in a fight with a school official, she was put in a choke-hold that she and her mother both claimed left her "foaming at the mouth." As a result, she became "very loud and aggressive . . .extremely uncooperative and violent," shouting threats and obscenities at school officials and the officers who arrested her. While the minor framed her behavior in terms of the outrage caused by her treatment by school personnel the probation officer and school officials deemed her anger an inappropriate way of responding, and even argued that it might be a sign of mental illness. While admitting that one-on-one, she "was pleasant, cooperative, and promised to do

better," the probation officer argued that Amber didn't act "as a normal person would" when she was angry:

> Minor has severe problems controlling her emotions when upset. Whether this is indicative of severe mental disorder or simply immaturity and rage, is not known. . . .she needs to have a psychological evaluation. . . .A counseling program . . .coupled with a psychological evaluation should help minor gain insight into her self and her behavior.

Gloria's experience provided the most vivid example of the lengths to which probation officers would go in order to reinscribe juveniles' behavior as an individual trouble. A lower-income African-American girl Gloria was arrested after taking a gun to school. According to the minor, she "had been threatened and told she would be 'jumped' after school by . . .gang members" and therefore borrowed the gun to protect herself. She had "told the assistant principal . . .about the threats against her" and explained that "she would not have taken the gun to school if they, the school had taken care of the problem she had reported to them."

Gloria was placed in a violent school environment, and attempted to protect herself by brandishing a weapon. Rather than examine the dangerous environment she was expected to survive in, the probation officer deemed her response not just inappropriate but indicative of deeper mental health problems: "Due to threats against the minor, she feels she was justified in bringing a loaded gun to school. This type of thinking concerns this officer and feels the minor needs and would benefit from a program of counseling." This case reveals the lengths juvenile justice officers will go to in ignoring the social causes of delinquent acts.

Roots of Delinquent Behavior

The most striking difference in the framing of delinquent girls by race was in the discursive constructs used to describe the roots of their delinquent activities. African-American girls' behavior was sometimes pathologized as seen above in Amber's (and to a certain extent Gloria's) case; it was also framed in terms of inappropriate "lifestyle" choices. On the other hand, white girls' delinquent acts were frequently described as resulting from their being "easily influenced" by "negative peer influences," or, less frequently, as a result of "abandonment issues" having to do with their relationships with their fathers. Significantly, these discursive constructs were not used in *any* of the analyses of African-American girls. Latina girls were framed using both those constructs typically used to describe African-American girls, and those used to describe white girls.

Janice, an African-American AFDC recipient, was arrested after she lied to the police "in order to protect her brother." In making recommendations to the judge, the probation officer stated: "She needs to participate in counseling so that she can explore her current lifestyle and set positive goals for her future." These discursive constructs—"positive goals" and "lifestyle"—seem to function as codes for class expectations. In a more blatant example, Diana, a middle-income African-American girl was harshly criticized for failing to assimilate into a middle-class lifestyle when provided with the opportunity. According to the probation officer, Diana resented her mother for divorcing her father. However, the officer was very critical of Diana's feelings, and her criticism was steeped in class-based value judgments:

> [Minor] knows that when her mother and father were together the family was on welfare and living in the inner city. In the process of *lifting her family up*, the mother has found that she is not at all in touch with minor's stated desires, which seem to be to return to the *insidious place* they left [my emphases].

In both Diana's and Janice's cases, social class was reflected in the probation officers' recommendations. For Diana, non-conformity to proper class and age positions (see above) were at the heart of the sanctions the probation officer recommended. Diana was defined as "manipulative" and "self-centered," and the officer stated that "the minor needs to delve into why she finds it necessary to behave as she does." The probation officer pathologized her behavior, rather than examining what values or relationships her

mother may have left behind in the "inner city" that Diana might legitimately choose not to abandon.

Like Diana, Tonia, an African-American girl, was judged harshly for rejecting the upper-middle class expectations that came with her family's position: "Minor is spoiled and immature. She lives for the moment and is not goal-oriented." According to Tonia's mother, she "gravitates toward losers." However, the twist in Tonia's case, which was not found in the descriptions of lower-income African-American girls, but was found consistently among white and Latina girls of all income levels, was the label "self-destructive" rather than having negative "lifestyle" choices. In being framed as "self-destructive," she was in need of help and protection. On the other hand, girls with poor "lifestyle" choices were framed instead as deviant, as when Leanne, a lower-income Latina, was described as "devoid of values" for her participation in a gang.

Except for the label "self-destructive," even Tonia was not afforded the explanations frequently drawn upon to describe white girls' actions. In contrast to the above examples, the delinquent acts of a number of white girls were framed in ways that emphasized their vulnerability to the "corrupting" influences of others, or their fragility as a result of emotional problems. In these cases, the girls weren't delinquent because of some "badness" within them, but from some weakness or from external sources. Becky, an AFDC recipient arrested for vandalism, was described as having a difficult time "withstand[ing] the negative influence" of her peers. In addition, the probation officer theorized that Becky had "an unhealthy blocking of feelings and growing rage." As a result, the officer concluded:

> It is very doubtful that she would commit this type of offense of society again but probation officer believes that she is very capable of becoming self-destructive without intense therapy. This destruction might begin as simply as failing her classes but would then progress into poor, destructive relationships and any negative activity that might result from those relationships.

In addition to negative peer influences and self-destructive tendencies, several white girls were described as also having low self-images. Nowhere did such a construct appear to describe African-American girls. Cathy, a lower-income white girl, was characterized as "easily influenced by others." She has "a tendency to pick the wrong kind of friends, but she does not seem to be delinquently sophisticated." As a result, the probation officer recommended that "participation in counseling might help her develop a more positive self-image and ability to think for herself." Cathy's behavior was not characterized as originating from her own delinquent proclivities, but rather from those of negative peers.

Similarly, Marsha, a middle-income white girl "does not appear inordinately delinquent . . .[but] can best be described as a teenager unable to set limits for herself. . . .Minor has low self-esteem and has continually reinvolved herself with less than positive peers." Her need for help was framed as stemming from "low-esteem" rather than from lifestyle choices; the discourse drawn upon described her as influenced by negative peers, rather than being inherently delinquent herself. Likewise, Karen was a middle-income white girl arrested for shoplifting. While Leanne was described as "devoid of values" for her gang involvement (see above), Karen's gang involvement was framed as a consequence of "family dysfunction":

> Although in a relative sense, this is not a serious offense, there are numerous severe problems in this minor's life which need ongoing supervision. Her stepfather is an alcoholic and her mother is an enabler. . . .Minor denies that she is self-destructing by her ongoing truancy, gang associations et cetera. . . .Minor must become involved in some type of self-help group to deal with her feelings regarding her alcoholic stepfather, her natural father's abandonment of her and her anger towards her mother for her own codependency.

Interestingly, Latina girls were framed in ways that paralleled those found in the descriptions of both African-American and white girls. Some Latina girls were characterized by drawing upon paternalistic discursive constructs similar to those describing white girls, as "self-destructive," having a "negative self-image," and "negative peers." For example, of Dora, the probation officer said, "[a]lthough this offense should not be taken lightly, it appears as though she may have been acting from emotions rather than in a delinquent manner." Other Latina girls were framed in more punitive ways (see Leanne and Sylvia above).

This dichotomized treatment of Latina girls may be related to probation officers' interpretations of gender norms in Latino culture. Perhaps girls who violate gender norms by participating in offenses deemed particularly masculine (in the above cases, car theft, burglary and gang membership) face harsher treatment than Latina girls who commit offenses perceived as feminine, or commit offenses as a result of their involvement with a boyfriend. These findings point to the need for further investigation of the treatment of delinquents from Latino communities, an area of research that is currently lacking (Bondavalli and Bondavalli, 1981: 551; Empey and Stafford, 1991).

Discussion

Unitary analyses of gender discrimination, based on comparisons between the treatment of delinquent boys and girls, miss the intersecting dimensions of race, class, age and gender. Through detailed content analyses of investigation reports, I have attempted to explore the variations and nuances which exist in the construction of delinquent girls. While the analysis in this paper was based on a relatively small number of cases, it reveals many complexities in the discursive construction of female delinquency. The interpretive frameworks used by juvenile court officials are shaped, not simply by assumptions about gender, but by hegemonic understandings of race, class and generational power relations as well. . . .

[C]ultural stereotypes about women and girls differently depict girls by race and class, and may be drawn upon by probation officers, consciously or unconsciously, in their attempts to analyze the "needs" of the girls they interview and report on. Cultural stereotypes of white females depict them as "tender, warm, quiet and gentle" while depicting African-American females as "aggressive, rebellious, rude and loud" (Smith and Stewart, 1983: 2). Likewise, popular images of Latina women present them as submissive and dependent, a counterpart to Latino men's machismo (Sanchez, 1990; Zinn, 1982). It is likely that girls' treatment is partially rooted in these stereotypes. . . .

Notes

1. While I had hoped to include Asian girls in my comparative analysis, I could only locate six girls on active probation in the area. Of these, two had unique extenuating circumstances which would make them problematic to use for the analysis. This left only four girls, which I did not feel provided enough cases for inclusion in the sample.

2. Names used throughout this paper are fictitious.

3. Suitable placement orders are not technically defined as more "severe." They are recommended for those juveniles who are believed to have emotional problems which contribute to their delinquent behavior, for which "treatment" in a placement facility can "help" them. However, in that they are taken out of the home (in Angela's case a stayed placement was recommended, not removing her from the home immediately but leaving the probation officer the power to do so at a later date), it is a disposition that involves greater intervention on the juvenile's life than probation does, and in that sense is more severe.

References

Alder, Christine. 1984. "Gender Bias in Juvenile Diversion." *Crime & Delinquency,* 30(3): 400–414.

Armstrong, Gail. 1977. "Females under the Law-Protected but Unequal." *Crime & Delinquency,* 14(1): 61–76.

Baca Zinn, Maxine. 1982. "Mexican-American Women in the Social Sciences." *Signs,* 8(2): 259–272.

Bondavalli, Bonnie J. and Bruno Bondavalli. 1981. "Spanish-Speaking People and the North American Criminal Justice System," in R. L. McNeely and Carl E. Pope, eds. *Race,*

Crime and Criminal Justice. Beverly Hills: Sage Press.

Cain, Maureen, ed. 1989a. *Growing Up Good. Policing the Behavior of Girls in Europe.* London: Sage Publications.

——. 1989b. "Feminists Transgress Criminology." In Maureen Cain, ed. *Growing Up Good. Policing the Behavior of Girls in Europe.* London: Sage Publications.

Campbell, Anne. 1981. *Girl Delinquents.* New York: St. Martins Press.

Canter, Rachelle J. 1982. "Sex Differences in Self-Report Delinquency." *Criminology,* 20: 373–393.

Chesney-Lind, Meda. 1977. "Judicial Paternalism and the Female Status Offender: Training Women to Know Their Place." *Crime & Delinquency* 23: 121–130.

——. 1978. "Young Women in the Arms of the Law." In Lee H. Bowker, ed. *Women, Crime and the Criminal Justice System.* Lexington, Massachusetts: Lexington Books.

——. 1988. "Girls and Status Offenses: Is Juvenile Justice Still Sexist?" *Criminal Justice Abstracts* 20(1): 144–65.

——. and Randall G. Sheldon. 1992. *Girls, Delinquency and Juvenile Justice.* Pacific Grove, California: Brooks/Cole Publishing Company.

Collins, Patricia Hill. 1990. *Black Feminist Thought.* Boston: Unwin Hyman.

Davis, Angela Y. 1981. *Women, Race & Class.* New York: Vintage Books.

DeFleur, Lois B. 1975. "Biasing Influences on Drug Arrest Records: Implications for Deviance Research." *American Sociological Review.* 40: 88–103.

Daly, Kathleen. 1991. "Impact of Feminist Theory on Studies of Law and Crime." Paper presented at the American Society of Criminology annual meeting.

Daly, Kathleen and Meda Chesney-Lind. 1988. "Feminism and Criminology." *Justice Quarterly* 5(4): 497–538.

Dannefer, Dale and Russell K Schutt. 1982. "Race and Juvenile Justice Processing in Court and Police Agencies." *American Journal of Sociology,* 87: 1113–1132.

Empey, LaMar T. and Mark C. Stafford. 1991. *American Delinquency: Its Meaning & Construction.* Belmont, California: Wadsworth Publishing Company.

Feyerherm, William. 1981. "Juvenile Court Dispositions of Status Offenders: An Analysis of Case Decisions" in R. L. McNeely and Carl E. Pope, eds. *Race, Crime and Criminal Justice.* Beverly Hills: Sage Press.

Figueira-McDonough, Josephina. 1985. "Are Girls Different? Gender Discrepancies Between Delinquent Behavior and Control." *Child Welfare*, 64: 273–289.

Garfinkel, Harold. 1967. *Studies in Ethnomethodology*. Englewood Cliffs, New Jersey: Prentice Hall.

Gelsthorpe, Loraine. 1986. "Towards a Skeptical Look at Sexism." *International Journal of the Sociology of Law*, 14: 125–152.

——. 1989. *Sexism and the Female Offender: An Organizational Analysis*. Aldershot, England: Gower.

——. and Allison Morris, eds. 1990. *Feminist Perspectives in Criminology*. Milton Keynes/Philadelphia: Open University Press.

Hudson, Annie. 1990. "Elusive subjects: Researching Young Women in Trouble." In Loraine Gelsthorpe and Allison Morris, eds. *Feminist Perspectives in Criminology*. Milton Keynes/Philadelphia: Open University Press.

Hudson, Barbara. 1989. "Justice or Welfare? A Comparison of Recent Developments in the English and French Juvenile Justice Systems." Pp. 96–113 in *Growing Up Good: Policing the Behaviour of Girls in Europe*, Maureen Cain, ed. London: Sage.

Kersten, Joachim. 1989. "The Institutional Control of Girls and Boys: An Attempt at a Gender-Specific Approach." In Maureen Cain, ed. *Growing Up Good: Policing the Behavior of Girls in Europe*. London: Sage Publications.

Klein, Dorie. 1991. "Dilemmas of Diversity for Feminist Criminology." Paper presented at the American Society of Criminology annual meeting.

Krisberg, Barry, Ira M. Schwartz, Paul Litsky, and James Austin. 1986. "The Watershed of Juvenile Justice Reform." *Crime & Delinquency*, 32: 5–38.

Krohn, Marvin, Ronald Akers, Marcia Radosevich, and Lonn Lanza-Kaduce. 1980. "Social Status and Deviance: Class Context of School, Social Status, and Delinquent Behavior." *Criminology*, 18: 303–318.

——. James P. Curry, and Shirley Nelson-Kilger. 1983. "Is Chivalry Dead?" *Criminology*, 21: 417–439.

Laub, John H. and M. Joan McDermott. 1985. "An Analysis of Serious Crime by Young Black Women." *Criminology*, 23: 31–98.

Leonard, Eileen. 1982. *Women, Crime and Society: A Critique of Theoretical Criminology*. New York: Longman.

Mann, Coramae Richey. 1979. "Making Jail the Hard Way: Law and the Female Offender." *Corrections Today*, 41: 35–41.

Mann, Coramae Richey. 1984. *Female Crime and Delinquency*. University of Alabama: University of Alabama Press.

Parisi Nicolette. 1982. "Are Females Treated Differently? A Review of the Theories and Evidence on Sentencing and Parole Decisions." In Nicole Rafter and Elizabeth Anne Stanko, eds. *Judge, Lawyer, Victim, Thief: Woman, Gender Roles and Criminal Justice*. Boston: Northeastern University Press.

Quinney, Richard. 1974. *Critique of Legal Order: Crime Control in Capitalist Society*. Boston: Little, Brown and Company.

Rice, Marcia. 1990. "Challenging Orthodoxies in Feminist Theory: A Black Feminist Critique." In Loraine Gelsthorpe and Allison Morris, eds. *Feminist Perspectives in Criminology*. Milton Keynes/Philadelphia: Open University Press.

Sarri, Rosemary. 1976. "Juvenile Law: How It Penalizes Females." In Laura Crites, ed. *The Female Offender*. Lexington, Massachusetts: Lexington Books.

——. 1983. "Gender Issues in Juvenile Justice." *Crime and Delinquency*, 29: 381–397.

Smart, Carol. 1976. *Women, Crime and Criminology: A Feminist Critique*. London: Routledge & Kegan Paul.

——. 1977. "Criminological Theory: Its Ideology and Implications Concerning Women." *British Journal of Sociology*, 28(1): 89–100.

Smith, Althea and Abigail J. Stewart. 1983. "Approaches to Studying Racism and Sexism in Black Women's Lives." *Journal of Social Issues*, 39(3): 1–15.

Teilmann, Katherine S. and Pierre H. Landry, Jr. 1981. "Gender Bias in Juvenile Justice." *Journal of Research in Crime and Delinquency*, 18: 47–80.

Visher, Christy A. 1983. "Gender, Police Arrest Decisions, and Notions of Chivalry." *Criminology* 21: 5–28.

White, Deborah Gray. 1985. *Aren't I a Woman?* New York: W. W. Norton & Company.

Woodward, Carolyn. 1988. "Real Women and the Cult of True Womanhood." In Jo Whitehorse Cochran, Donna Langston, and Carolyn Woodward, eds. *Changing Our Power: An Introduction to Women's Studies*. Dubuque, Iowa: Kendall/Hunt Publishing Company.

From *Legality and Illegality: Semiotics, Postmodernism, and Law*, edited by W. Richard Janikowski and Dragan Milovanic. Copyright © 1995. Adapted with permission from Peter Lang Publishing, Inc. For editorial reasons, the title of this selection has been modified from the original. ✦

56
Surveillance and Reputation in America

Steven L. Nock

In olden times, social control was easy. Communities were small and cohesive. Population density was low. Life was based on tradition and custom. Everybody knew everybody else. Rule-breaking was infrequent, relatively innocuous, and easily detected. Punishments were swift yet judicious, after which offenders were brought back into the fold. The prospect of chronic future law-breaking was thereby short-circuited.

With population growth and geographic mobility came profound changes in family structure. People began to strike off on their own at younger and younger ages, undermining the stabilizing influence of family. People chose city life, with its impersonal and anonymous relations with strangers. No one really "knew" anybody anymore. Trust ceased to exist. If trust is the necessary and sufficient condition for social order, how is order possible in its absence?

Steven Nock suggests that the answer lies in the creation and application of surveillance, specifically, credentials and ordeals. A credential is something that announces one's status; an ordeal is something that proves it. Common credentials are driver's licenses, credit cards, and educational certificates. Typical ordeals involve tests of some sort, tests that prove people are what they say they are (e.g., lie-detector tests, drug tests, and integrity tests). Both are ways to keep tabs on people and are artifacts of societies that can no longer take people at their word. Surveillance is the cost of living in an anonymous, impersonal, and private social world; surveillance, in other words, is the cost of privacy.

Credentials and ordeals become increasingly intrusive as societies become more and more private (as Nock argues, privacy leads to more surveillance and, paradoxically, less privacy). Recent advances in genetic and biochemical identification are illustrative. The completion of the Human Genome Project (a genetic map of every human cell) provides the ability to assess the biological roots of all human conduct. If deviant *conduct results from physiological abnormalities and these abnormalities are objectively knowable, "it becomes possible both to explain past actions* and *to predict future ones* scientifically. Reputation thereby becomes (or appears to become) scientifically predictive of [forthcoming] behaviors" (Nock 1993, 113). Individual civil liberties are increasingly imperiled as governments, insurance companies, and employers gain access to and use this information for their own purposes. A cultural atmosphere is created where only absolute conformity is acceptable.

Introduction

How, in an anonymous society of strangers, is trust produced? How do people transact business, extend or receive credit, select their doctors, or hire employees when the parties to such exchanges do not know one another? How can people board airplanes, buses, and taxicabs driven by total strangers confident that their safety is not in jeopardy?

More generally, how is it possible to depend on or believe in other people when we have never met them? We trust those who, we believe, accept and abide by the same moral rules we do; people who are known to *conform* to those standards we hold as important. Those who refuse to play by those rules or those we are not sure about are not so likely to be trusted. We suspect them. We doubt their word.

In this [article] I will argue that historically, increasing numbers of strangers produced greater and more pervasive personal privacy. Modern Americans enjoy vastly more privacy than did their forebears because ever and ever larger numbers of strangers in our lives are legitimately denied access to our personal affairs. Changes in familial living arrangements are largely responsible for these trends. Privacy, however, makes it difficult to form reliable opinions of one another. Legitimately shielded from other's regular scrutiny, we are thereby more immune to the routine monitoring that once formed the basis of our individual reputations. Reputation, I will argue, is a necessary and basic component of the trust that lies at the heart of social order. To establish and maintain reputations in the face of privacy, social mechanisms of *surveillance* have been elaborated or developed. In particular, various forms of credentials and modern ordeals produce reputations that are widely accessible, impersonal, and portable from one location to another. *A society of strangers is one of immense personal privacy. Surveillance is the cost of that privacy.*

Trust and the ability to take others at their word are basic ingredients in social order. If we never knew who to trust, could never be sure that what we were told was true, or that promises made would be promises kept, there would be little to bind us together or make groups cohesive. A collection of soloists who pursued their individualistic ends without respect to conventional standards and moral obligations would amount to little more than a random grouping of people. Such a group would not constitute an organization or society. Trust, in short, lies at the base of any cohesive collectivity. Therefore, the extent to which trust among people is possible determines, in part, the degree of solidarity to be found in any society.

In their ordinary day-to-day lives, people frequently organize their behaviors by reference to their own and others' reputations. A reputation is a shared, or collective, perception about a person. It is the product of innumerable contacts among and between people. Through our dealings with others, an image is developed of the degree to which we do or do not conform to the standards that matter to them. Those who enjoy a "good" reputation are thought to accept and abide by those standards—perhaps even demonstrating extraordinary conformity to them.

The highly respected civic leader is one who has shown a willingness or desire to accept selflessly the burdens of duty to others. In so doing, such a person has conformed to a value shared by members of the community. That person will be trusted. His word is believed; his promise accepted.

If we try to imagine a society without reputations, of anonymous strangers, it is a frightening image. Among those we know, much of our behavior is governed by reputation. We know to distrust the well-known scoundrel as surely as we believe a priest. *Reputation is a mantle worn with clear consequences for others' behaviors.* Deserved or not, a bad reputation marks someone as an outsider—beyond the ordinary boundaries of our own moral community. Strangers, however, present us with a dilemma not encountered when dealing with a person who enjoys a good or bad reputation.

When someone has no reputation, that person is a stranger. We don't trust strangers as much as people whose reputations are known. Strangers are suspect and must demonstrate that they can be trusted—that they respect and abide by the same rules we do—before they will be embraced as members of any group. Strangers must *earn* other peoples' trust. To do that, they must somehow earn a good reputation.

No matter how difficult it may be to earn a good reputation, the problem for a person with a *bad* reputation is usually much worse. A bad reputation marks someone as an outsider—as someone who might not respect the important standards of a group or community. Just as a good reputation opens doors, a bad reputation closes them. And just as one must earn a good reputation, so too, a bad reputation must be earned.

Conformity to group standards is necessary to earn a good reputation. A bad reputation is usually the product of having been shamed. And there are powerful incentives to avoid shame because once shamed, there are few ways to absolve the bad reputation. One must either renounce the group doing the shaming, or redefine the self in accordance with the group standards, that is, one must either leave or change one's ways. Given what is required to undo a bad reputation, and given the consequences of having one, we may assume that there is powerful incentive to avoid earning one. Shame, or the threat of it, in other words, is a form of social control; a collective method of enforcing conformity or punishing deviance.

So long as people know one another, good and bad reputations guide much of their social life. But what about complex societies where very few people are known; where the overwhelming majority of other people are strangers? How, in such a society, can we know whether to trust the strangers we deal with on a regular day-to-day basis? *How can we trust the people we see but do not know; those who live near us, who work near us, who must sometimes be counted on to help us?* That is the question I address. . . .

The answer to this question is that complex societies have produced impersonal arrangements that establish or maintain individual reputations—both good and bad. These reputations, unlike that of the civic leader in the small community, are easily transportable. They do not depend on a particular locale or group. They follow us as we move and they are accessible when they are needed. They can be altered, or created, in a matter of minutes. Reputations, in short, have become portable in our times just like other forms of capital ("human," or otherwise).

There are two methods used to establish or maintain reputations among modern strangers; *credentials* and *ordeals*. Together these constitute the two elementary forms of overt *surveillance*. Surveillance of this sort (overt) is directed, primarily or solely, at reputations. And although credentials and ordeals may be useful for other purposes, their role in establishing reputations is the most important use.

Before going into detail about surveillance, it will help to consider the proposed reason for it—*strangers*. My argument states that it is the presence of strangers that calls forth surveillance. I will argue that recent decades have been periods of significant and rapid growth in both the numbers of strangers and in both types of overt surveillance.

What does it mean to say there has been a growth in the number of strangers? We may assume that so long as there have been large societies there have been many people who were not known to one another. I argue, however, that there are more strangers now than in the past, primarily as a result of changes in our living arrangements.

Historically individuals have been given opportunities to openly demonstrate their willingness to abide by the rules; in open congregational "relations" (confessions required for admission to the church), through ordinary and regular contacts with public officials (constables or "tithingmen" who were charged with monitoring the coming and going of members of a community's households), and many other public forums. But more than any other traditional source of reputation, the family has been the most important. As sociologists would say, the family is the source of a person's *ascriptive status*; one's initial location in society. The child born two centuries ago to a laborer began life with a name and social position. That position reflected the general appraisal of the father in the community—his reputation and social standing. Traditional family government relied on patriarchs to enforce community standards. Prior to the establishment of an official civic police force (middle nineteenth century) his was the dominant authority, and, if shared, was shared with a representative of a church. For most of our history a person was known, first, by his or her family name. The family "name" served as a reputation among those familiar with one another.

The most notorious criminals frequently are described by the media as "loners," unknown by neighbors and unconnected to family. When deviance of virtually any sort is discovered, we look for its causes in the deviant's family situation because the family has served as the dominant form of social control in all societies. Embedded within their parents' or their own families, individuals are subject to many demands not made on people who live alone. By custom and law, the head of the household has been held accountable for the actions of all members of the family. Husbands have been required to settle the debts of their wives just as parents have been required to compensate others for the wrongful actions of their children. But family members have also been held accountable for the actions of the patriarch. In nineteenth century America, wives and children were held legally accountable for the unsettled debts of the head of the household.

The methods by which families control the behaviors of their members are diverse. To summarize these, sociologists refer to socialization—the process by which we learn the ways of a social group so that we can function within it. Socialization is a concept that summarizes the learning of numerous skills and motives that result in conformity (Elkin and Handel, 1984:4). The irreducible minimum requirement for socialization is another person; interaction is the core around which all theories of socialization are based. But what is it about interaction that produces conformity?

Supervision, or surveillance, is one unremarkable element that explains a vast amount of conformity in any society. Supervision establishes reputations. I hope to show that as traditional methods of family supervision decline, institutional methods of surveillance arise that serve the same social control functions. It is the relationship between trends in familial living arrangements and trends in surveillance that occupies the core of this book.

For the past 50 years in America, growing numbers of individuals have, for one reason or another, formed independent, nonfamily living arrangements. Several demographic trends have contributed to this outcome. Among the elderly, differential male/female life expectancy (females outlive males) combined with age heterogamy in marriage (husbands are typically 2 to 3 years older than their wives) result in significant numbers of widows who maintain their own homes after their husbands die. Thirty-six percent of all women 65 to 74 are widowed; 9 percent of men are (U.S. Bureau of the Census,1991a, Table 1 [not shown]). Among middle-aged (35 to 45 years old) individuals, high rates of marital disruption produce separate households (usually temporary) for the formerly married (32 percent of women this age are known to have been divorced)

(U.S.Bureau of the Census, 1990, Table A [not shown]).

Another trend of even greater significance has produced solitary living arrangements among Americans. There is now a new and historically unique stage of the life course that intervenes between that of adolescence (when children live at home with their parents) and adulthood (when grown children establish their own families). Beginning in the 1960s, large numbers of youths began to leave their parents' home to establish independent households. Although an historic anomaly, so commonplace has the practice become that it is now considered routine or unexceptional. One in four males and one in five females 20 to 29 do not live in any form of family arrangement (U.S. Bureau of the Census, 1991a, Table 2 [not shown]). Though seemingly unremarkable as a stage in the life course of youth, it is quite remarkable in its consequences for our society.

For a period of several years, large numbers of young Americans live independently of their parents' families while not yet having established their own families. Lacking clearly defined and accepted standards of conduct, people who occupy this stage enjoy immense freedoms and privacies. No longer viewed as adolescents, and legally beyond the age of majority—legally "adults"—young people who live outside of any family setting constitute an entirely new social category in our society. Like any group of solitary individuals, this group of young people, whom I call the "emancipated," pose significant problems for social order.

Emancipation is a release from restraint or influence. When young men or women leave the parental home and strike out alone, they are freed from certain immediate influences over their behaviors. They are no longer subject to the direct parental supervision that was undoubtedly a part of their lives. Their comings and goings are less likely to be noticed. The rhythms of their daily routines are now hidden from parents' scrutiny. It is hard to know to what extent such emancipation might alter behaviors. But it is certainly reasonable to presume that greater freedom is one reason for seeking emancipation; young adults on their own are relatively immune from routine monitoring and that is a reason they are on their own.

Be it parent or spouse, the presence of intimate others in the home is a source of restraint on behaviors. The source of that restraint may be the sense of moral commitment that grows in conjugal relationships, the normative obligation to obey the wishes of parents, or the sense of responsibility that arises in dependent relationships. But it may also be little more than the scrutiny and supervision of others—a consequence of knowing that one's actions will be seen and evaluated.

There is nothing new about these observations. Family living has historically been required (by law or custom) of those who wished to participate fully in the social life of their communities. So when large numbers of people live otherwise, we are left to ponder whether something has been lost. Are the emancipated excluded from some measure of participation in social life? Is collective life less "orderly" by virtue of the presence of the emancipated? Is deviance more likely in a society where many people do not live with relatives? Is emancipation a problem for traditional methods of social control? I do not hope to address all such questions, though I believe each warrants scholarly research. There are many types of nonfamily living: divorced, widowed, never-married. My primary concern is with the implications of independent living among the never married— of emancipation—for methods of sustaining social order and trust.

Emancipation has very obvious implications for the cohesiveness that binds us together as a society. The freedoms and privacies that accompany emancipation are direct evidence of ambiguous or unknown reputations. The privacy gained by living alone is the consequence of immunity from supervision. People who are not subject to direct scrutiny are also free from direct influence. *Those we do not watch, we do not know*. To restate this obvious point, the emancipated are less likely to have reputations. If reputations are the basis for trust, and trust a basis for social order, then the emancipated pose a problem. If we cannot know whether our neighbor or co-worker abides by the same rules we do, how can we trust them? If no one is watching over them, why should they rein in their deviant impulses? What makes them conform? Indeed, are people free from direct supervision as likely to obey the rules? That is the unanswered question that makes trusting them so problematic. . . .

Privacy grows as the number of strangers grows. And since strangers do not have reputations, there will be more surveillance when there are more strangers. *Privacy is one consequence, or cost, of growing numbers of strangers. Surveillance is one consequence, or cost, of privacy.*

The proposition that privacy is more widespread than it was in the past deserves greater elaboration. Modern data storage and retrieval systems arouse justifiable concerns over privacy and the possibility that it is threatened. The ability to computerize individual biographies (or portions of them) makes the storage and use of such information less costly and vastly more efficient than were parish records or more informal systems of record-keeping. However, the *ability* to store, access, and use biographical information is not the main factor in the expansion or restriction of privacy. Privacy results from the legitimate denial of *access* to one's actions or records. Privacy is defined by the socially-recognized legitimate right to restrict others from observing or knowing about one's actions.

To know whether Americans enjoy more or less privacy today than their ancestors did, one would have to determine whether there has been an increase or a decrease in the range of behaviors and circumstances legitimately defined as beyond the scrutiny of uninvited others. In the course of a typical day, are modern Americans better able to escape the watchful eyes of others than their grandparents were? Are there more opportunities to seclude oneself behind closed doors than there once were? Are more areas of life legitimately viewed as beyond others' scrutiny? I have already argued that the answer to these questions is yes. . . .

Notable technological changes have contributed to greater privacy. Modern conveniences such as the telephone, television, washer, dryer, air conditioner, and VCR make it less necessary for individuals to leave their homes to venture into public. Televisions, radios, and videotape machines produce entertainment that is enjoyed behind closed doors. Washers and dryers mean that people no longer hang their laundry out to dry and make fewer trips to commercial laundries. Air conditioning reduces the need to sit on the front porch, visit public lakes, swimming pools, or parks. Telephones reduce the need to visit others in person (Popenoe, 1985).

New methods of information-gathering and dissemination by employers, creditors, and governments that strike many as worrisome, are not necessarily violations of privacy. These developments have occurred in the name of objectives that are widely regarded as legitimate: freedom of the press, the protection of public order, the prevention of subversion, and administrative efficiency. Each has been generally accepted as reasonable and useful. Almost all depend on voluntary self-disclosure (the completion of credit, insurance or drivers license, or employment forms, for example). Disclosure of such information is not a violation of privacy unless it is given to parties to whom an individual does not want it made available. . . .

Privacy grows as the number of strangers grows. Strangers are those whose reputations we cannot know, not solely those people who are isolated from one another. Two people who have never met, and who never will, certainly are strangers to each other. But it is our diminished *ability* to know about others that has led to an increase in the prevalence of strangers. The same forces that Shils credits for having increased our privacy may be seen as having increased our ability to restrict others' scrutiny of our af-fairs. By enforcing our autonomy (or privacy), we safeguard our reputations. We may, if we choose, elect to remain strangers to many others; that is what our privacy permits, and is one reason it is desired. That is also one reason for the increase in surveillance.

Overt surveillance consists of credentials and ordeals. Each is a means by which the basis for trust may be established. . . .A credential is something that gives a person access to credit or confidence. Credentials may certify many things: competence, completion of a course of study, membership in formal or voluntary associations, or credit-worthiness. . . .[A]n ordeal [is] a ritual that determines whether an individual is telling the truth. It always begins with a presumption of guilt. . . .Commonplace examples of ordeals include drug tests, lie-detector tests, [and integrity tests]. . . .

References

Elkin, Frederick and Gerald Handel 1984. *The child and society: The process of socialization,* 4th ed. New York: Random House.

U.S. Bureau of the Census. 1990. Studies in household and family formation. CPR, Series P-23; No. 169. Washington, D.C.: U.S. Government Printing Office.

U.S. Bureau of the Census. 1991a. Marital status and living arrangements: March, 1990. CPR, Series P-20; No. 450. Washington, D.C.: U.S. Government Printing Office.

57

Everyday Surveillance

Vigilance and Visibility in Postmodern Life

William G. Staples

It has been said that the voyeuristic impulse is a fundamental part of the human psyche. How many of us can claim to have never peered in a window, stolen a furtive glance, or leered at salacious photos to satisfy some prurient curiosity? People like to watch other people. They like to see them at their most intimate moments. They like to see them fight and disagree. They like to judge them without having to be judged back.

Within the last five years, hundreds of Internet sites have popped up for precisely this purpose, offering a bird's eye view of everything from public squares to women's dorm rooms. Each week, tens of millions of people tune in to programs like "The Real World," "Temptation Island," and "Survivor" to secure their own voyeuristic rush. As societies become more complex, populous, and anonymous, the need for human contact manifests itself in intriguing ways. Voyeur TV may be one consequence.

Surveillance is part and parcel of voyeurism, and the exploding availability of cheap, effective methods for watching people has made surveillance easier than ever before. Historically, surveillance was the exclusive domain of government spies, undercover police, and private investigators. No longer. A multibillion dollar "spy shop" industry has created all manner of gizmos, widgets, and gadgets and has made them inexpensive and accessible to anyone with a suspicion, a grudge, and a few hundred dollars. In most states, spying on people without their knowledge or consent is completely legal, as long as both the spy and the target are private citizens

and no trespassing laws have been broken in the process.

Staples suggests that we are rapidly approaching the total surveillance society ominously depicted in George Orwell's 1984, where telescreens (surveillance cameras) occupy every corner, sophisticated monitoring techniques determine when a person is thinking something she or he should not be, and snitches fill the streets. Americans, too, are being watched like never before. Surveillance penetrates every aspect of life—from cameras to electronic bugs to computer monitoring to credit card tracking to DNA testing: such sources reveal deviance of the most personal sort in the most intimate places, including that which afflicts the very cells of the body itself. Staples suggests that the diffusion of surveillance out from traditional nodes of social control (e.g., the criminal justice system, the family) has created a community of corrections, where everyone is an offender, or potential offender, who deserves to be scrutinized. The more sophisticated the monitoring system, the more deviance is likely to be detected, creating standards of conformity that real people simply cannot attain.

> Throughout the U.S., thousands of criminals are placed under "house arrest," their movements monitored electronically by a transmitter attached to their ankle. In many states, criminal defendants and judges carry out proceedings on video monitors. In Arizona, a "welfare" mother has a court-ordered contraceptive device surgically implanted in her arm. In New York, a high-tech courtroom collects a myriad of information about a single defendant that is kept in an electronic file folder. Most "clients" in community corrections programs are subjected to random drug and alcohol testing.

At the same time:

> Sixty-seven percent of major U.S. employers engage in some form of electronic monitoring of workers. In New York City, more than two thousand private surveillance cameras are taping citizens on public streets. In California, every citizen wishing to be issued a driver's license must have their thumbprint computer scanned. In Massachusetts, a company

tracks the Web surfing habits of more than thirty million Internet users. Nearly 90 percent of U.S. manufacturers are testing workers for drugs.

The preceding examples illustrate a blurring distinction between the practices of the official justice system and the everyday lives of ordinary people. How are we to understand these developments? Are they simply "advances" in our struggle against illegal, deviant, or "troublesome" behavior, or do they signal the rise of what might be called a "culture of surveillance"? What kind of society has produced these practices, and why do we appear so willing to adopt them? . . .

The techniques I have in mind range along a continuum. They begin with the "soft," seemingly benign and relatively inconspicuous forms of monitoring such as those used in the very bookstore where I sat with my friend. In that business, as in thousands across the United States, a security system monitored our interaction with video cameras, while the store's spatial arrangement was designed for optimal surveillance of customers and employees alike. Computerized checkout stations kept track of inventory, calculated store performance figures, assessed the credit worthiness of patrons through remote data banks, collected personal information about customers so they could be targeted for marketing campaigns, monitored the log-on and log-off times of employees, and calculated the average number of customers those employees processed per hour. All this was accomplished "behind the scenes" as it were, without disruption to the manufactured ambiance of soft leather chairs, melodic Muzak, and the sound and smell of cappuccino making.

At the "hard" end of the spectrum are the more obtrusive and confrontational practices that often begin with the assumption of guilt and are designed to uncover the "truth," to test an individual's character, and, more generally, to make people consciously aware that they are indeed being watched and monitored. Of course, this element was also evident at the corporate bookstore I visited with

my friend, as they had "tagged" all the merchandise so that both of us could be electronically "frisked" as we walked through the sensor gates at the exit. These are what I call "surveillance ceremonies." They include random drug and alcohol testing, the use of lie detectors, pre-employment integrity tests, and "sobriety checkpoints" in the streets. They also include the practices of electronically monitored "house arrest," adolescent curfews, and the use of metal detectors.

Between these soft and hard types of social control lies a vast array of techniques and technologies—exercised on and by people both inside and outside the justice system—that are designed to watch our bodies, to regulate and monitor our activities, habits, and movements, and, ultimately, to shape or change our behavior. These procedures are often undertaken in the name of law and order, public safety, the protection of private property, or simply "sound business practice"; other procedures are initiated for an individual's "own good" or benefit. But no matter what the stated motivation, the intent of social control is to mold, shape, and modify actions and behaviors.[1] . . .

. . .[A]s new forms of social control are localized in everyday life, they are capable of bringing wide-ranging populations, not just the official "deviant," under their watchful gaze. As I indicated earlier, trust is becoming a rare commodity in our culture. The notion of "innocent until proven guilty" seems like a cliche these days, when people are apt to be subjected to disciplinary rituals and surveillance ceremonies simply because statistics indicate that they have the potential for being offenders (for example the police tactic known as "racial profiling" as a justification for stopping motorists). Data generated through surveillance techniques produce "types" or whole classes of individuals who are deemed "at risk" for behavior, whether any one particular individual has engaged in such behavior or not. These data, of course, are then used to justify even closer surveillance and scrutiny of this group, thereby increasing the likelihood of uncovering more offenses; and so it goes. In the context of these changes, social control becomes more about predicting and preventing deviance—always assuming that it will, indeed, happen—rather than responding to a violation after it has occurred.[2] Therefore, when put in place, ritualistic monitoring and surveillance ceremonies often blur the distinction between the official "deviant" and the "likely" or even "possible" offender. Indeed, what separates the convicted felon, the college athlete, or the discount store cashier if each is subjected to random drug screening? One consequence of this blurring is that we may be witnessing a historical shift from the specific punishment of the individual deviant to the generalized surveillance of us all. . . .

. . .[L]et us consider an incident that took place recently in my hometown. In this case, a school bus driver was accused of physically restraining an unruly child. The driver was fired, and many debates took place in the local newspaper about the child's behavior on the bus, the reported good reputation of the driver, and about the way school district administrators (mis)handled the case. It was clear that no one trusted anyone's account of what had actually transpired on the bus that day. A few months later there was an announcement that each of the district's fleet of new buses would be equipped with a video camera "black box." The bus company claimed that, on any given day, just three video cameras would be rotated among all the district's buses and that, given the design of the boxes, neither the students nor the drivers would know when their bus was equipped with a camera. The bus company's manager stated that the use of the cameras would "help to improve student discipline" as well as ensure that the drivers follow "proper procedures."

Now, the principle behind the rotating camera is not new; it originates with a design by Jeremy Bentham dating from 1791 called the Panopticon, a central guard tower inside a prison or reformatory. The tower was designed in such a way that prisoners were never quite sure whether a guard was present or not and would have to assume that they were being watched. The inmates, in effect, watched themselves, internalizing, if you will, the watchful gaze of the keeper. It

was a simple, even elegant, solution to the problem of disciplining people in an enclosed space—a dilemma brought about with the birth of the asylum, the modern "solution" to criminal behavior, madness, poverty, and the like. The evolution of this idea two hundred years later—and applied in a postmodern context—produces a flexible design, routinely applied in the everyday life of schoolchildren and their adult supervisors, none of whom apparently are trusted to act responsibly. Inexpensive video technology—and our willingness to define schoolchildren's behavior on a bus as being so problematic that it warrants "objective" surveillance rather than personal monitoring—makes the use of this new form of social control possible. . . .

Let us consider another contemporary example. I find it remarkable how quickly people will agree to give up their constitutional right to freedom of movement in order to stop what some claim to be rampant drunk-driving behavior. We accept this, despite the evidence that so-called "sobriety checkpoints" apprehend very few excessive drinkers.[3] Supporters of these bodily based surveillance ceremonies contend that "if you have nothing to hide, you have nothing to fear." Yet we know from experience that unbridled police powers are likely to present a serious challenge to individual liberties. Obviously, even one person injured or killed by a drunk driver is a tragedy, but it might be argued that creating a police state to thwart the behavior could be an even greater catastrophe. As Supreme Court Justice John Paul Stevens declared in his dissenting opinion on the legality of such roadblocks, "Unfortunately the Court is transfixed by the wrong symbol—the illusory prospect of punishing countless intoxicated motorists—when it should keep its eyes on the road plainly marked by the Constitution."[4] Why not focus our efforts on education and safety programs (funded by the businesses that profit from the sale of alcohol)?

Next, consider the proliferation of metal detectors and bodily searches, not simply at airports but also in schools, courthouses, dance clubs, and the like, to thwart the possession of weapons. (Ironically, at the same time, a majority of states has passed laws that *permit* people to carry concealed weapons.) Rather than seriously confront the issue of the widespread availability of guns in our society (in this case, a "right" that is arguably not protected under the Constitution's Second Amendment concerning a "well regulated Militia," and not permitted in any other "developed" country), we subject all citizens to this kind of daily surveillance and monitoring.[5] This, it seems, may be the most fundamental question raised by this book: Are we, in our attempts to preserve our freedom and security, entrapping ourselves in our own solutions? . . .

As I have noted in this chapter, postmodern surveillance practices have four characteristics:

1. They are increasingly technology-based, methodical, automatic, and sometimes anonymously applied, and they usually generate a permanent record as evidence.

2. Many new techniques target and treat the body as an object that can be watched, assessed, and manipulated.

3. The new techniques are often local, operating in our everyday lives.

4. Local or not, they manage to bring wide-ranging populations, not just the official "deviant," under scrutiny. . . .

Notes

1. The term *social control* has a long history in sociology. See Jack Gibbs, *Norms, Deviance, and Social Control: Conceptual Matters* (New York: Elsevier, 1981); Stanley Cohen and Andrew Scull, *Social Control and the State* (New York: St. Martin's Press, 1983); and Donald Black, *The Social Structure of Right and Wrong* (New York: Academic Press, 1999).

2. This perspective is rooted in recent "neo-liberal" models of managing the "risk society" where, as Ericson puts it, "deviance gives way to risk as the concept for the understanding of how dangers are both identified and responded to technologically. The concern is less with the labeling of deviants as outsiders,

and more on developing a knowledge of everyone to ascertain and manage their place in society." This perspective strikes me as positively frightening. See Richard V. Ericson's review of an earlier edition of *Policing the Risk Society*.

3. Some contend that in no other area of the law is the Fourth Amendment being eroded as it is in the case of "sobriety checkpoints." In Kansas City, police stopped nearly 10,000 cars at checkpoints in 1998 and arrested 449 persons for driving under the influence of alcohol, a 4.5 percent rate. This seems to be typical nationally. "Sobriety checkpoints: Police stops may deter drunken driving. Some consider them illegal," *Kansas City Star,* 31 August 1997, 1(A).

4. The U.S. Supreme Court has upheld the constitutionality of sobriety checkpoints but established specific guidelines for their use. Police are required to give notification of a checkpoint, and they cannot detain motorists for an unreasonable amount of time. The court has also indicated that an arrest rate of less than 5 percent would raise questions of whether there is a legitimate government interest in the procedure. . . . "Excerpts from Supreme Court Decision." *New York Times,* 15 June 1990, 11(A).

5. This country is awash in so many guns that they have been declared a public health hazard. In 1997, more than 35,000 Americans died by gunfire. (By comparison, handguns were used to murder 2 people in New Zealand, 15 in Japan, 30 in Great Britain, and 106 in Canada.) Guns kept in the home for self-protection are forty-three times more likely to kill someone in the home than to kill in self-defense. More than twice as many women are shot and killed by their husbands or lovers than by strangers. And for every "justifiable homicide" where a citizen used a gun in defense, 131 lives were ended in firearm murders, suicides, and unintentional shootings. See http://www.handguncontrol.org [accessed 6 June 2000].

References for Article Introductions and Section Introductions

Adler, Patricia A. 1985. *Wheeling and Dealing.* New York: Columbia University Press.

Agar, Michael. 1973. *Ripping and Running: A Formal Ethnography of Urban Heroin Addicts.* New York: Seminar Press.

Anderson, Elijah. 1999. *Code of the Street.* New York: Norton.

Arluke, Arnold. 1991. "Going into the closet with science: Information control among animal experimenters." *Journal of Contemporary Ethnography* 20:306–330.

Baxter, Christine. 1989. "Investgating stigma as stress in social interactions of parents." *Journal of Mental Deficiency Research* 33:455–466.

Becker, Howard S. 1963. *Outsiders: Studies in the Sociology of Deviance.* New York: Free Press.

Beirne, Piers, and James Messerschmidt. 1991. *Criminology.* Fort Worth, TX: Harcourt Brace.

Bell, C. and H. Newby. 1972. *Community Studies.* New York: Praeger.

Bernard, Jesse. 1982. *The Future of Marriage,* Second Edition. New Haven, Conn.: Yale University Press.

Biddle, Bruce J. 1979. *Role Theory: Expectations, Identities, and Behaviors.* San Diego, CA: Academic Press.

Bishop, Donna M. 1984. "Legal and extralegal barriers to delinquency: A panel analysis." *Criminology* 22:403–419.

Black, Donald. 1983. "Crime as social control." *American Sociological Review* 48:34–45.

——. 1993. *The Social Structure of Right and Wrong.* San Diego, CA: Academic Press.

Blinde, Elaine M., and Diane E. Taub. 1992. "Women athletes as falsely accused deviants: Managing the lesbian stigma." *The Sociological Quarterly* 33:521–533.

Blum, Nancy. 1991. "The management of stigma by Alzheimer's caregivers." *Journal of Contemporary Ethnography* 20:263–284.

Blumstein, Alfred. 1995. "Youth violence, guns, and the illicit drug industry." *Journal of Criminal Law and Criminology* 86:10–36.

Bok, Sissela. 1978. *Lying: Moral Choice in Public and Private Life.* New York: Pantheon.

Bourgois, Philippe. 1995. *In Search of Respect: Selling Crack in El Barrio.* Cambridge: Cambridge University Press.

Boxer, Sarah. 2000. "Truth or lies? In sex surveys, you never know." July 22, retrieved at http://nytimes,qpass.com/qpass-arc...s+!db!+!doc!+10+wAAA+sex%20studies

Brooks Gardner, Carol. 1991. "Stigma and the public self: Notes on communication, self and others." *Journal of Contemporary Ethnography* 20:251–262.

Brown, Stephen E., Finn-Aage Esbensen, and Gilbert Geis. 1996. *Criminology: Explaining Crime and Its Context.* Cincinnati: Anderson.

Brownmiller, Susan. 1975. *Against Our Will: Men, Women, and Rape.* New York: Simon and Schuster.

Bureau of Justice Statistics (BJS). 1993. U.S. Department of Justice, Criminal Victmization in the United States. Washington, D.C.: U.S. Government Printing Office.

CBS News. 2000. "CBS This Morning," October 4.

Chesney-Lind, M. and R. G. Sheldon. 1992. *Girls' Delinquency and Juvenile Justice.* Pacific Grove, CA: Brooks/Cole.

Cleckley, Hervey. 1988. *The Mask of Sanity.* New York: Emily S. Cleckley.

Cohen, Neal L. 1990. "Stigma is in the eye of the beholder: A hospital outreach program for treating homeless mentally ill people." *Bulletin of the Menniger Clinic* 255–258.

Conklin, John. 1977. *Illegal but Not Criminal.* Englewood Cliffs, NJ: Prentice Hall.

Cooley, Charles H. 1902. *Human Nature and Social Order.* New York: Scribner's.

Cullen, Francis, William J. Maakestad, and Gary Cavender. 1987. *Corporate Crime Under Attack.* Cincinnati: Anderson.

Curran, Daniel J., and Claire M. Renzetti. 1994. *Theories of Crime.* Boston: Allyn and Bacon.

Curtis, Richard. 1999. "The ethnographic approach to studying drug crime." In *Looking at Crime From the Street Level: Plenary Papers of the 1999 Conference on Criminal Justice Research and Evaluation: Enhancing Policy and Practice Through Research,* volume 1, Washington, D.C.: National Institute of Justice.

Dainton, Marianne. 1993. "The myths and misconceptions of the stepmother identity: Descriptions and prescriptions for identity management." *Family Relations* 42:93–98.

Davis, Kingsley. 1966. "Sexual behavior." Pp. 354–372 in Robert K. Merton and Robert Nisbet, eds., *Contemporary Social Problems,* 2nd ed. New York: Harcourt, Brace, and World.

Denzin, Norman K. 1995. *The Cinematic Society.* London: Sage.

Dorn, N., and K. Murji. 1992. "Low level drug enforcement." *International Journal of the Sociology of Law* 20:159–171.

Dorn, N., and Nigel South. 1990. "Drug markets and law enforcement." *British Journal of Criminology* 30:171–188.

Dowie, Mark. 1977. "Pinto madness." *Mother Jones* September/October 2–13.

Drug Enforcement Agency. 1997. *Changing Dynamics of the U.S. Cocaine Trade.* Washington, D.C.: U.S. Department of Justice.

Dunlap, Eloise, Bruce D. Johnson, and Lisa Maher. 1995. "Female crack sellers in New York City: Who they are and what they do." Unpublished paper.

Durkheim, Emile. 1938. *The Rules of Sociological Method.* New York: The Free Press.

——. 1951. *Suicide, a Study in Sociology.* Translated by J.A. Spaulding and G. Simpson, edited with an introduction by G. Simpson. Reprint, Glencoe, NY: The Free Press.

Edgerton, Robert B. 1972. "Violence in East African tribe societies." Pp. 159–170 in *Collective Violence* edited by James F. Short, Jr., and Marvin E. Wolfgang. Chicago: Aldine Press.

Eysenck, H. 1977. *Crime and Personality.* London: Routledge and Kegan Paul.

Federal Bureau of Ivestigation (FBI). 1996. *Uniform Crime Reports.* Washington, D.C.: USGPO.

Fleisher, Mark S. 1995. *Beggars and Thieves.* Madison: University of Wisconsin Press.

Freud, S. 1943. "Femininity." Pp. 80–92 in *Women and the Politics of Culture* edited by M. W. Zak and P. A. Motts. New York: Longman.

Garfinkel, Harold. 1967. *Studies in Ethnomethodology.* Englewood Cliffs, NJ: Prentice Hall.

Gerstel, Naomi. 1987. "Divorce and stigma." *Social Problems* 34:172–186.

Glassner, Barry. 1999. *The Culture of Fear.* New York: Basic Books.

Goffman, Erving. 1963. *Stigma: Notes on the Management of Spoiled Identity.* Englewood Cliffs, NJ: Prentice Hall.

Goldin, Carol S. 1990. "Stigma, biomedical efficacy, and institutional control." *Social Science and Medicine* 30:895–900.

Golub, Andrew, and Bruce D. Johnson. 1999. "Cohort changes in illegal drug use among arrestees in Manhattan: From the heroin injection generation to the blunts generation." *Substance Use and Misuse* 34:1733–1763.

Gomberg, Edith L. 1988. "Alcoholic women in treatment: The question of stigma and age." *Alcohol and Alcoholism* 23:507–514.

Goode, Erich. 1997. *Deviant Behavior,* Fifth Edition. Upper Saddle River, NJ: Prentice Hall.

Gottfredson, Michael, and Travis Hirschi. 1986. "The true value of Lambda would appear to be zero: An essay on career criminals, criminal careers, selective incapacitation, cohort studies, and related topics." *Criminology* 24:213–234.

Gouldner, Alvin W. 1960. "The norm of reciprocity: A preliminary statement." *American Sociological Review* 25:161–178.

Granfield, Robert. 1991. "Making it by faking it: Working-class students in an elite academic environment." *Journal of Contemporary Ethnography* 20:331–351.

Green, David. 1988. "Resisting the stigma of incest: An experiment in personal construct psychotherapy." *Journal of Adolescence* 11:299–308.

Hagan, John, and Bill McCarthy. 1997. *Mean Streets: Youth Crime and Homelessness.* New York: Cambridge University Press.

Hamid, Ansley. 1998. *Drugs in America.* Gaithersburg, MD: Aspen.

Harris, Paul. 2000. "The Paul Harris Show," Broadcast on KTRS, AM 550.

Heimer, Carol A. 1988. "Social structure, psychology, and the estimation of risk." *Annual Review of Sociology* 14:491–519.

Henslin, James M. 1972. "Studying deviance in four settings: Research experiences with cabbies, suicides, drug users, and abortionees." In *Research on Deviance* edited by J. Douglas. New York: Random House.

Hewitt, John P. 1979. *Self and Society,* Second Edition. Boston: Allyn and Bacon.

Hirschi, Travis. 1969. *Causes of Delinquency.* Berkeley, CA: University of California Press.

Horwitz, Allan V. 1990. *The Logic of Social Control.* New York: Plenum Press.

Hughes, Everett C. 1945. "Dilemmas and contradictions of status." *American Journal of Sociology* 50:353–359.

Inciardi, James A., Ruth Horowitz, and Anne E. Pottieger. 1993. *Street Kids, Street Drugs, Street Crime.* Belmont, CA.: Wadsworth.

Irwin, John. 1972. "Participant observation of criminals." In *Research on Deviance*, edited by J. Douglas. New York: Random House.

Jacobs, Bruce A. 1996. "Cognitive bridges: The case of high school undercover officers." *The Sociological Quarterly* 37:391–412.

———. 1999. *Dealing Crack: The Social World of Streetcorner Selling*. Boston: Northeastern University Press.

———. 2000. *Robbing Drug Dealers: Violence Beyond the Law*. New York: Aldine de Gruyter.

Jacobs, Bruce A., and Jody Miller. 1998. "Crack dealing, gender, and arrest avoidance." *Social Problems* 45:550–569.

Jacobs, Bruce A., and Richard Wright. 1999. "Stick-up, street culture, and offender motivation." *Criminology* 37:149–173.

Jacobs, Bruce A., Volkan Topalli, and Richard Wright. 2000. "Managing retaliation: Drug robbery and informal sanction threats." *Criminology* 38:171–198.

Johnson, Bruce D., Eloise Dunlap, Kathleen Boyle, and Bruce Jacobs. 1997. "Natural transitions in crack distribution/abuse." Prepared for NIDA, New York: NDRI.

Jones, Enrico E., A. Farina, A. H. Hastorf, H. Markus, D. T. Miller, and R. A. Scott. 1984. *Social Stigma: The Psychology of Marked Relationships*. New York: W. H. Freeman.

Katz, Jack. 1988. *Seductions of Crime: Moral and Sensual Attractions in Doing Evil*. New York: Basic Books.

Klassen, Albert D., Colin J. Williams, and Eugene E. Levitt. 1989. *Sex and Morality in the U.S.* Middletown, CT: Wesleyan University Press.

Langer, E. J. 1975. "The illusion of control." *Journal of Personality and Social Psychology* 32:311–328.

Laub, John H. 1997. "Patterns of criminal victimization in the United States." Pp. 9–26 in *Victims of Crime*, Second Edition, edited by A. Lurigiou, W. Skogan, and R. Davis. Newbury Park, CA: Sage.

Lemert, Edwin. 1967. *Human Deviance, Social Problems, and Social Control*. Englewood Cliffs, NJ: Prentice Hall.

Lennon, Mary C., B. G. Link, J. J. Marbach, and B. P. Dohrenwend. 1989. "The stigma of chronic facial pain and its impact on social relationships." *Social Problems* 36:117–134.

Levy, Alan J. 1993. "Stigma management: A new clinical service." *Families in Society* April:226–231.

Levy, Alan J., and K. S. Thiel. 1990. "Adolescent fathers—absent or ignored?" TEC Networks Newsletter of the Charles Stewart Mott Foundation March:2–3.

Lex, Barbara W. 1990. "Narcotics addicts' hustling strategies: Creation and manipulation of ambiguity." *Journal of Contemporary Ethnography* 18:388–415.

Llewellyn, Karl N., and E. Adamson Hoebel. 1941. "The Cheyene way: Conflict and case law in primitive jurisprudence." Norman: University of Oklahoma Press.

Luckenbill, David. 1981. "Generating compliance: The case of robbery." *Urban Life* 10:25–46.

Luken, Paul C. 1987. "Social identity in later life: A situational approach to understanding old age stigma." *International Journal of Aging and Human Development* 25:177–193.

Maher, Lisa, and David Dixon. 1999. "Policing and public health: Law enforcement and harm minimization in a street-level drug market." *British Journal of Criminology* 39:488–512.

Marx, Gary T. 1981. "Ironies of social control: Authorities as contributors to deviance through escalation, nonenforcement, and covert facilitation." *Social Problems* 28:221–246.

———. 1988. *Undercover: Police Surveillance in America*. Berkeley, CA: University of California Press.

McCall, George J. and Jerry L. Simmons. 1978. *Identities and Interactions*. New York: Free Press.

McCarthy, Bill and John Hagan. 1995. "Getting into street crime: The structure and process of criminal embeddedness." *Social Science Research* 24:63–95.

McWilliams, Peter. 1996. *Ain't Nobody's Business If You Do: The Absurdity of Consensual Crimes in Our Free Country*. Los Angeles: Prelude Press.

Meier, Robert F., and Gilbert Geis. 1997. *Victimless Crime?* Los Angeles: Roxbury.

Merton, Robert K. 1938. "Social structure and anomie." *American Sociological Review* 3:672–682.

Messner, Steven F., and Richard Rosenfeld. 1994. *Crime and the American Dream*. Belmont, CA: Wadsworth.

Miall, Charlene E. 1986. "The stigma of involuntary childlessness." *Social Problems* 33:268–282.

———. 1987. "The stigma of adoptive parent status: Perceptions of community attitudes toward adoption and the experience of informal sanctioning." *Family Relations* 36:34–39.

Miller, Jerome G. 1996. *Search and Destroy: African-American Males in the Criminal Justice*

System. Cambridge: Cambridge University Press.

Miller, Walter B. 1958. "Lower class culture as a generating milieu of gang delinquency." *Journal of Social Issues* 14:5–19.

Mills, C. Wright. 1940. "Situated actions and the vocabulary of motive." *American Sociological Review* 6:904–913.

Neuman, William L. 1999. *Social Research Methods: Qualitative and Quantitative Approaches*, Fourth Edition. Boston: Allyn and Bacon.

Nock, Steven L. 1993. *The Costs of Privacy*. New York: Aldine de Gruyter.

Pfohl, Stephen J. 1985. *Images of Deviance and Social Control*. New York: McGraw-Hill.

Polk, Kenneth. 1993. "Observations on stranger homicide." *Journal of Criminal Justice* 21:573–582.

Polsky, Ned. 1967. *Hustlers, Beats, and Others*. Chicago: Aldine.

Reiman, Jeffrey H. 1990. *The Rich Get Richer and the Poor Get Prison: Ideology, Class, and Criminal Justice*, Third Edition. New York: Macmillan.

Reiss, Albert J., and Albert D. Biderman. 1980. *Data Sources on White-Collar Law-Breaking*. Washington, D.C.: U.S. Department of Justice, National Institute of Justice.

Rengert, George F. 1996. *The Geography of Illegal Drugs*. Boulder, CO: Westview.

Ryan, Kevin. 1994. "Technicians and interpreters in moral crusades: The case of the drug courier profile." *Deviant Behavior* 15:217–240.

Schlenker, Barry R. 1980. *Impression Management: The Self-Concept, Social Identity, and Interpersonal Relations*. Monterey, CA: Brooks/Cole.

Schur, Edwin H. 1965. *Crimes Without Victims: Deviant Behavior and Public Policy*. Englewood Cliffs, NJ: Prentice Hall.

Scott, Marvin B., and Stanford M. Lyman. 1968. "Accounts." *American Sociological Review* 33:46–62.

Sellin, Thorsten. 1938. *Culture Conflict and Crime*. New York: Social Science Research Council.

Shapiro, Joseph P. 1994. "Straight talk about gays." *U.S. News and World Report*, July 5:47.

Sherman, Lawrence. 1993. "Defiance, deterrence, and irrelevance: A theory of the criminal sanction." *Journal of Research in Crime and Delinquency* 30:445–473.

Shifflet, Peggy A., and Rosemary Blieszner. 1988. "Stigma and Alzheimer's disease: Behavioral consequences for support groups." *Journal of Applied Gerontology* 7:147–160.

Siegel, Ronald K. 1989. *Intoxication: Life in Pursuit of Artificial Paradise*. New York: Dutton.

Skolnick, Jerome H. 1966. *Justice Without Trial*. New York: John Wiley and Sons.

Sluka, Jeffrey A. 1990. "Participant observation in violent social contexts." *Human Organization* 49:109–128.

Spreen, Marius. 1992. "Rare populations, hidden populations, and link-tracing designs: What and why?" *Bulletin de Methodologie Sociologique* 6:34–58.

Stahly, G. B. 1988. "Psychosocial aspects of the stigma of cancer: An overview." *Journal of Psychosocial Oncology* 6:3–27.

Stansell, C. 1982. "Women, children, and the uses of the streets: Class and gender conflict in New York City, 1850–1860." *Feminist Studies* 2:309–335.

Staples, William G. 1997. *The Culture of Surveillance*. New York: St. Martin's Press.

Steffensmeier, Darrell J., and Robert Terry. 1986. "Institutional sexism in the underworld: A view from the inside." *Sociological Inquiry* 56:304–323.

Steinmetz, Susan. 1977–1978. "The battered husband syndrome." *Victimology* 2(3–4):499–509.

Stone, Gregory P. 1977. "Personal acts." *Symbolic Interaction* 1:2–19.

Sutherland, Edwin. 1937. *The Professional Thief*. Chicago: University of Chicago Press.

Sutherland, Edwin, and Donald Cressey. 1970. *Criminology*, Eighth Edition. Philadelphia: Lippincott.

Sykes, Gresham, and David Matza. 1957. "Techniques of neutralization: A theory of delinquency." *American Sociological Review* 22:667–670.

Szasz, Thomas. 1985. *Ceremonial Chemistry*. New York: Learning Publications.

Tannenbaum, F. 1938. *Crime and the Community*. Boston: Ginn and Company.

Tedeschi, James T., and Richard B. Felson. 1994. *Violence, Aggression, and Coercive Actions*. Washington, D.C.: American Psychological Association.

Tittle, Charles R. 1980. *Sanctions and Social Deviance: The Question of Deterrence*. New York: Praeger.

Tittle, Charles R., and Raymond Paternoster. 2000. *Social Deviance and Crime: An Organizational and Theoretical Approach*. Los Angeles: Roxbury.

Watters, J. K., and Patrick Biernacki. 1989. "Targeted sampling: Options for the study of hidden populations." *Social Problems* 36:416–430.

Wolfgang, Marvin E. 1958. *Patterns in Criminal Homicide*. Philadelphia: University of Pennsylvania Press.

Wolfgang, Marvin E., and Franco Ferracuti. 1967. *The Subculture of Violence*. London: Social Science Paperbacks.

Yochelson, Samuel and Stanton E. Samenow. 1976. *The Criminal Personality: A Profile for Change*. Vol. 1. Northvale, NJ: Jason Aronson. ✦

Relevant Internet Sites

Sexual Assault

National Coalition Against Sexual Assault http://ncasa.org

Rape, Abuse and Incest National Network (RAINN) http://www.rainn.org

Assault Prevention Information Network http://galaxy.einet.net/galaxy/Community/Safety/AssaultPrevention/apin/APINintro.html

Sexual Assault Information Page http://www.cs.utk.edu/~bartley/saInforPage.html

Rape Victim Advocates http://www.lib.uchicago.edu/~loakleaf/RVA.html

Sexual Assault Crisis Center http://www.cs.utk.edu

Sexual Assault Throughout the U.S.: Risk Factors and Prevention Tactics http://rivervision.com/safe/ar.html

Date Rape http://www.aaets.org/arts/art13.htm

National Clearinghouse on Marital & Date Rape http://members.aol.com/ncmdr

Resource Guide on Marital Rape http://www.wellesley.edu/WCW/projects/mrape.html

Family Violence and Sexual Assault Institute http://www.fvsai.org

Homosexuality and Bisexuality

Homosexual Information Center http://mentalhealth.about.com/library/h/orgs/bl0736.htm?iam=dpile&terms=homosexuality

Sexual Orientation and Homosexuality: Answers to Commonly Asked Questions Provided by the American Psychological Association http://www.apa.org/pubinfo/orient.html

Homosexuality: Common Questions & Statements http://hcqsa.virtualave.net

Homosexuality and Bisexuality http://www.religioustolerance.org/homosexu.htm

Bisexual Resource Center http://www.biresource.org

Bisexual Issues Listing of Internet Resources Devoted to Bisexuality http://sexuality.about.com/cs/bisexuality/index.htm?iam=dpile&terms=bisexuality

Prostitution

Effects of Prostitution http://www.feminista.com/v1n5/depasquale.html

Historical Overview of Sex Work http://votech.about.com/library/weekly/aa071400b.htm?iam=dpile&terms=%22sex+work%22

Prostitution Research Education Website http://www.prostitutionresearch.com

C.O.Y.O.T.E. (a prostitute advocacy group) http://www.freedomusa.org/coyotela/index.html

Network of Sex Work Projects. International Organization Advocating for Sex Workers' Rights http://www.walnet.org/csis/groups/nswp/index.html

Promise (organization offering support services and support to women who have chosen to get out of prostitution) http://www.sirius.com/~promise

National Task Force on Prostitution http://www.bayswan.org/NTFP.html

Prostitutes Education Network http://www.bayswan.org/penet.html

Prostitution & Male Supremacy (speech by Andrea Dworkin) http://www.igc.org/Womensnet/dworkin/MichLawJournalI.html

Women's Human Rights Resources—Prostitution—Index http://www.law-lib.utoronto.ca/Diana/prost/prost.htm

Nevada Legal Prostitution FAQ Providing Positive and Helpful Information on All Forms of Human Sexuality http://www.sexuality.org/l/workers/nevada.html

Yahoo! Society and Culture Sexuality Sex Work http://dir.yahoo.com/Society_and_Culture/Sexuality/Sex_Work/Prostitution

The World Sex Guide—Researching Prostitution Around the World http://www.worldsexguide.org

The Rights of Exotic Dancers http://www.bayswan.org/EDAindex.html

Drugs, Alcohol, and Tobacco

National Institute on Drug Abuse http://www.nida.nih.gov

BJS Statistics on Drugs and Crime http://www.ojp.usdoj.gov/bjs/drugs.htm

Office of National Drug Control Policy http://www.whitehousedrugpolicy.gov

Drug Enforcement Administration http://www.usdoj.gov/dea/index.htm

Bureau of Justice Statistics' Drug and Crime Page http://www.ojp.gov/bjs/drugs.html

Center for Substance Abuse Research http://www.bsos.umd.edu/cesar/cesar.html

Justice Information Center: Drugs and Crime http://www.ncjrs.org/drgshome.html

NORML: National Organization for the Reform of Marijuana Laws http://www.norml.org

Marijuana Policy Project http://www.mpp.org

The Lindesmith Center Presents: Marijuana Myths, Marijuana Facts http://www.marijuanafacts.org

The Cato Institute http://www.cato.org

Constructive Information on Illegal Drug Abuse http://www.druguse.com

Partnership for a Drug-Free America http://www.drugfreeamerica.org

National Council on Alcoholism and Drug Dependence, Inc. (NCADD)—Home Page http://www.ncadd.org

National Clearinghouse for Alcohol and Drug Information http://www.health.org/aboutn/html

Higher Education Center for Alcohol and Other Drug Prevention http://www.edc.org

Binge Drinking: Harvard School of Public Health College Alcohol Study http://www.hsph.harvard.edu

Drinking: A Student's Guide http://www.glness.com

College Drinking Crackdown http://alcoholism.about.com/library/weekly/aa102898.htm?iam=dpile&terms=alcohol+drinking

NIDA Research Report (on nicotine) http://www.nida.nih.gov

World Smoking News Service http://www.worldsmoking.com

Cigarettes and Addiction http://www.cctc.ca/ncth/docs/faq/faq-addiction.html

American Cancer Society http://www.cancer.org

American Heart Association http://americanheart.org

Mental Illness

National Alliance for the Mentally Ill Home Page http://www.nami.org

Mental Health InfoSource http://www.mhsource.com

Mental Health Information http://www.mentalhealth.com

National Mental Health Screening Programs Home Page http://www.nmisp.org

"Reversing the Stigma of Mental Illness" with Otto Wahl, PhD http://webmd.lycos.com/content/article/1707.50041

National Science Foundation Guide to Severe Mental Illness http://www.nsf.org

Suicide

National Institute of Mental Health—Suicide Research Consortium http://www.nimh.nih.gov/research/suicide.htm

Suicide Prevention Skills and Workshops http://www.suicideassessment.com

Suicide—Information About Suicide http://www.umm.drkoop.com

suicide@rochford.org—Information and Education http://www.rochford.org/suicide

Suicide Information and Education Center (SIEC)—Suicide Prevention, Research http://www.siec.ca

Suicide on the Internet http://mentalhealth.about.com/library/weekly/ aa101397.htm?iam=dpile& terms=%2Bsuicide

Suicide—Causes http://depression.about.com/cs/suicidecauses/index.htm?iam=dpile&terms=%2 Bsuicide

White-Collar and Organized Crime

National White Collar Crime http://www.iir.com/nwccc.htm

Financial Crimes Enforcement Network http://www.ustreas.gov/treasury/bureaus/fincen/fincen.html

National Fraud Information Center http://www.nfic.inter.net

Electronic Crime http://police.sas.ab.ca/prl/elect.html

The National White Collar Crime Center http://www.cybercrime.org—National White Collar Crime Center, Fairmont W.V.

White Collar and Organized Crime http://talkjustice.com/files/ch10link.html

White Collar Crime Statistics http://crime.about.com/cs/statisticsindex.htm?iam=dpile&terms= white+collar+crime

International Organized Crime http://www.afpc.org/issues/crime.html

Organized Crime Site http://organizedcrime.about.com/index.htm?iam=dpile&terms=orga-nized+crime

Organized Crime Statistics http://www.crime.org

Crimes of Persuasion: Computer Crime http://www.crimes-of-persuasion.com

Cybercrime http://www.usdoj.gov/criminal/cybercrime/index.html

Infowar: Corporate Hacking http://netsecurity.about.com/library/weekly/aa012599.htm?iam=dpile& terms=%22computer+crime%22

Department of Justice Computer Crime and Intellectual Property Section http://www.usdoj.gov/criminal/ cybercrime

Physical Disabilities and Eating Disorders

World Association of Persons With Disabilities http://www.wapd.org

Disabilities: Physical or General http://www.kidsource.com/kidsource/pages/dis.physical.html

National Association of the Physically Handicapped http://mentalhealth.about.com/library/h/orgs/ bl0259.htm?iam=dpile&terms=physical+disabilities

Links to Sites on Physical Disabilities http://www.kwa.on.ca/w_Int/kwaasrpd.html

Directory of Resources for Persons With Physical Disabilities http://www.co.arlington.va.us/dhs/aging/ physdir.html

Anorexia Nervosa and Eating Disorders http://www.anad.org

Anorexia Nervosa & Bulimia Association, Home Page http://www.ams.queensu.ca/anab

Eating Disorders: Anorexia and Bulimia http://www.pacific-attitude.com

Anorexia Nervosa and Related Eating Disorders http://www.anred.com

Racial Profiling

American Civil Liberties Union—Manual on Fighting Police Abuse http://www.aclu.org/library/fighting_ police_abuse.html

Racial Profiling Stories http://dir.yahoo.com/society_and_culture/issues_and_causes/race_relations http://dir.yahoo.com/society_and_culture/cultures_and_groups/people_of_color/racial_profiling http://fullcoverage.yahoo.com/full_coverage/us/racial_profiling

Gender and the Law

Women and Justice http://www.mcgill.pvt.k12.al.us/jerryd/cm/gender.htm
http://www.udayton.edu/-gender/
http://dir.yahoo.com/society_and_culture/cultures_and_groups/women/law
National Center for Women and Policing http://www.feminist.org/police/ncwp.html

Prison

NIC Publication: Supermax Prisons http://www.nicic.org
Prison-Related Publications http://prisonactivist.org/pubs
Prisoner Activist Resource Center http://www.prisonactivist.org
Supermaximum Security Prisons http://www.hrw.org/about/initiatives/supermax.html
U.S. News Online: Capturing Life Behind Bars (photo essay) U.S.News & World Report http://www.usnews.com
Bureau of Prisons Content Information http://www.bop.gov/rframe.html
Prison Information Links http://www.soci.niu.edu/~critcrim/prisons/prisons.html
Federal Bureau of Prisons Homepage http://www.bop.gov

Death Row

Death Penalty Links http://www.derechos.org
Death Row http://www.deathrowbook.com
Victims of Death Row Inmates http://www.murdervictims.com
Death Penalty Information Center http://www.essential.org/dpic
National Coalition to Abolish the Death Penalty http://www.ncadp.org
Pro Death Penalty.com http://www.prodeathpenalty.com
Justice: Denied: Publication Devoted to the Wrongly Convicted http://library.thinkquest.org/2760/homep.html
Death Row: Annual Publication of Death Row Inmates http://www.editionnine.deathrowbook.com/deathrow.html

Surveillance

Privacy Times http://www.privacytimes.com
The Privacy Page http://www.privacy.org
ACLU and Cyberliberties http://www.aclu.org/issues/cyber/hmcl.html
ACLU—Cyber-Liberties, Big Brother In the Wires http://www.aclu.org/issues/cyber/wiretap_brother.html
Everyday Surveillance http://www.urc.ukans.edu

Violence

Citizens Against Violent Crime http://www.webserve.com/iandi/org/cave
Guns Laws in the United States http://www.cnn.com/specials/1998/schools/gun.control
Justice Information Center http://www.ncjrs.org
Bureau of Justice Statistics (firearms and crime statistics) http://www.ojp.usdog.gov.bjs/guns.htm

Domestic Violence

ABA Commission on Domestic Violence http://www.abanet.org/domviol/cdv.html
Violence Against Women Office, U.S. Department of Justice http://www.usdoj.gov/vawo
Contemporary Headlines http://dir.yahoo.com/society_and_culture/crime/crimes/domestic_violence

Domestic Violence Information Center http://www.feminist.org/other/dv/dvhome.html
Men Against Domestic Violence http://www.silcom.com/~paladin/madv
National Organization of Women http://www.now.org
Office for Victims of Crime, U.S. Dept. of Justice http://www.ojp.usdoj.gov/ovc
Abused Men Association http://www.abusedmen.org
Victim Services Domestic Violence Shelter Tour http://www.dvsheltertour.org
National Victim Center http://www.nvc.org

Street Gangs

Gangs in Schools http://eric-web.tc.columbia.edu/digests/dig99.html
National Youth Gang Center http://www.iir.com/nygc/nygc.html
Gangs in Los Angeles County (history of Crips and Bloods; links to related sites) http://www-bcf.usc.edu
The Economics of Street Gangs http://www.ncpa.org/pi/crime/july98b.html
Juvenile Street Gang, Intelligence and Consultation http://www.ibfletch.tripod.com
Juvenile Gangs and Crime (internet sites covering juvenile gangs and juvenile crime) http://law.about.com/
cs/juvenilegangs/index.htm?iam=dpile&terms=street+gangs
Street Gang Intelligence Manual http://pimall.com/nais/bk.gang.html
Street Gang Dynamics http://www.gangwar.com
American Street Gangs http://www.pressenter.com/~dpedersn
Office of Juvenile Justice and Delinquency Prevention http://www.ncjrs.org/ojjhome.html

Hate Crime

National Center for Victims of Crime, Summary of Hate-Crime Statistics http://www.ncvc.org/special/
hatec.html
FBI—Uniform Crime Reports—Hate Crime Statistics 1995 http://www.fbi.gov/ucr/hatecm.html
Hate Crimes Research Network http://www.irn.pdx.edu/~blazakr/hcrn.html
Hate Crimes Today: American Psychological Association http://www.apa.org/pubinfo/hate
Stop the Hate http://www.stopthehate.org
Fighting Hate Across the Nation http://www.civilrights.org/lcef/hat.html
Combat-Hate.org http://www.combat-hate.org
Hate Crimes Prevention Act http://www.hrcusa.org
Hate Crime Initiatives—The White House Conference on Hate Crimes http://www.ojp.usdoj.gov

About the Contributors

Barry D. Adam is University Professor of Sociology at the University of Windsor, and author of *The Survival of Domination, The Rise of a Gay and Lesbian Movement, Experiencing HIV,* and coeditor of *The Global Emergence* and *Gay and Lesbian Politics.* He has also published articles on new social movement theory, on gay and lesbian issues, and on social aspects of AIDS. Website: http://www.cs.uwindsor.ca/users/a/adam.

Patricia A. Adler is Professor of Sociology at the University of Colorado. She is author of *Wheeling and Dealing,* a study of high-level drug smugglers. She has also served as co-editor of the *Journal of Contemporary Ethnography.*

Peter Adler is Professor of Sociology at the University of Denver. He is coauthor (with wife Patricia) of *Backboards and Blackboards,* an ethnography of college athletes. In the past, he has coedited the *Journal of Contemporary Ethnography.*

Robert Agnew is Professor of Sociology at Emory University in Atlanta. He has authored or coauthored several important books and articles on juvenile delinquency. He is perhaps best known for his general strain theory of crime, a fusion of psychology and sociology.

Elijah Anderson is the Charles and William L. Day Professor of the Social Sciences and Professor of Sociology at the University of Pennsylvania. He has written numerous books on urban life, including *Streetwise, Code of the Street,* and *A Place on the Corner.*

Phyllis L. Baker is an Associate Professor of Sociology and Women's Studies and the Associate Dean of the College of Social and Behavioral Sciences at the University of Northern Iowa. She received her Ph.D. in sociology from the University of California at San Diego. She has published a book *Bored and Busy at Work* and several articles in which she studies marginalized groups of women.

Howard S. Becker recently served as Professor of Sociology and Ethnomusicology at the University of Washington. He has authored a number of important and groundbreaking books, including *Outsiders, The Other Side, Boys in White,* and *Writing for Social Scientists.*

Elaine M. Blinde is Professor of Physical Education and Sociology at Southern Illinois University at Carbondale. Her research focuses on identity management as it relates to sport. Gender is a major concern in her work.

John Braithwaite is Professional Fellow of Law at the Australian National University, located in Canberra, Australia. He is best known for his groundbreaking book, *Crime, Shame, and Reintegration,* a contemporary extension of labeling theory.

Amy Carson, at the time this selection was written, was affiliated with the University of Iowa and served as part of a research consortium designed to better understand substance abuse treatment.

Donald R. Cressey was Professor of Sociology at the University of California, Santa Barbara. An award-winning scholar, he authored numerous books and articles, including *Principles of Criminology* with Edwin H. Sutherland. He died in 1987.

Kathleen Daly is a Professor in the School of Justice Administration at Griffith University in Queensland, Australia. She has authored or coauthored numerous books and articles on gender and crime. She is considered a leading scholar in feminist criminology.

Scott H. Decker is Professor of Criminology and Criminal Justice at the University of Missouri-St. Louis. He has authored or coauthored numerous books and articles on street crime and crime control policy. He is currently working on a project involving qualitative interviews with convicted drug runners.

Lawrence H. Diller, M.D., practices in Walnut Creek, California. He has previously published work in the *Family Therapy Networker* and the *Hastings Center Report.*

Keith F. Durkin is a Research Fellow and Assistant Professor of Sociology at Ohio Northern University. His current research interests are the relationship between technological innovation and deviant behavior, as well as binge drinking by college students. He has contributed papers to *Deviant Behavior, Federal Probation,* the *Encyclopedia of Criminology and Deviant Behavior,* the *Journal of Alcohol and Drug Education,* and the *College Student Journal.*

Carl Elliott is Associate Professor of Pediatrics and Philosophy at the University of Minnesota, and the author of *A Philosophical Disease: Bioethics, Culture and Identity* (Routledge 1999). He is also the editor of *Slow Cures and Bad Philosophers: Essays on Wittgenstein, Medicine and Bioethics* (Duke 2001) and co-editor with John Lantos of *The Last Physician: Walker Percy and the Moral Life of Medicine* (Duke 1999).

Carolyn Ellis teaches in the areas of Communication and Sociology at the University of South Florida. Professor Ellis is author of *Final Negotiations: A Story of Love, Loss, and Chronic Illness.*

Kai T. Erikson was Professor of Sociology and American Studies at Yale University. In the past, he served as president of the American Sociological Association. He is the author of several important books, including *Wayward Puritans.*

John H. Gagnon was Professor of Sociology at SUNY-Stony Brook at the time this selection was published. He has authored or coauthored several books and articles on the topic of sexuality and has done groundbreaking work on the concept of "sexual scripts."

Gilbert Geis is Professor Emeritus of Social Ecology at the University of California at Irvine. He is past-president of the American Society of Criminology and winner of that organization's Sutherland Award, its highest honor.

Barry Glassner is Professor of Sociology at the University of Southern California. He has authored numerous books, including *Career Crash* and *Bodies.* His work has been featured in many national news publications, including the *New York Times* and the *Chicago Tribune.* He has been a guest on ABC News' "Nightline," NBC's "The Today Show," and CNN's "Headline News." His new book is *The Culture of Fear,* an examination of the media's role in shaping perceptions of deviance and social problems.

Michael Gottfredson recently joined the faculty of the University of California, Irvine. He is a Professor in the Criminology, Law, and Society Department. He also serves as Executive Vice Chancellor for the University. Author of numerous books and articles, he is perhaps most famous for *A General Theory of Crime* coauthored with Travis Hirschi.

Kimberly R. Greer is an Assistant Professor in the Department of Sociology and Corrections at Minnesota State University. Her teaching and research interests include the sociology of emotions, gender responsive programming, adolescent and adult female offenders, and restorative justice.

Frank E. Hagan is a Professor in the Graduate Program, Administration of Justice, at Mercyhurst College. He has authored or coauthored numerous books and articles on crime and deviance.

Nancy J. Herman has published extensively on the sociology of mental illness, focusing on, among other things, the subcultures and day-to-day activities of ex-psychiatric patients.

Travis Hirschi is Regents Professor Emeritus at the University of Arizona. He is past-president of the American Society of Criminology and a recipient of that organization's Sutherland Award, its highest honor. He has written numerous books on crime and delinquency, including his groundbreaking *Causes of Delinquency.*

Robert A. Hummer teaches sociology at the University of Texas at Austin. Professor Hummer conducts research in a number of areas, including population studies.

Jennifer Hunt has published in the area of policing and gender. Previous articles appear in *Symbolic Interaction* and *Human Organization,* among other outlets.

Bruce A. Jacobs is Associate Professor of Criminology and Criminal Justice at the University of Missouri-St. Louis. He is author of *Robbing Drug Dealers: Violence Beyond the Law* and *Dealing Crack: The Social World of Streetcorner Selling*.

Robert Johnson is Professor of Justice, Law, and Society in the School of Public Affairs at American University in Washington, D.C. He is author of *Culture and Crisis in Confinement* and *Hard Time: Understanding and Reforming the Prison*, among others. He is past winner of the American University Award for Outstanding Scholarship and the American University Teacher/Scholar of the Year Award.

Ann Jones is author of *Next Time She'll Be Dead: Battering and How to Stop It*. At the time her book was written, she was affiliated with Mount Holyoke College.

Jack Katz is Professor of Sociology at the University of California, Los Angeles. He has published numerous and important studies on deviance, including his provocative book, *Seductions of Crime*.

John H. Laub is Professor of Criminology and Criminal Justice at the University of Maryland. He is coauthor of *Crime in the Making* (with Robert Sampson), a provocative book about how and why deviant behavior changes across the life course.

Edward O. Laumann is the George Herbert Mead Distinguished Service Professor in the Department of Sociology at the University of Chicago. He has served as Chair of the Department of Sociology, Dean of the Social Sciences Division, and provost of the University of Chicago. He has written numerous books and articles and is considered one of the nation's foremost experts on human sexuality. In 1990, he was named a fellow of the American Association for the Advancement of Science.

Jack Levin is Professor of Sociology and Criminal Justice at Northeastern University in Boston. He has published extensively on a wide variety of crime- and deviance-related issues and is a noted expert and contact for various national media organizations.

Michael J. Lynch is Professor of Criminology at the University of South Florida. He has published extensively in the field of radical criminology, focusing on how power shapes the form and content of law and social control.

Patricia Yancey Martin is an endowed Professor at Florida State University in Tallahassee. Her research focuses principally on gender issues, with a particular emphasis on rape.

Amos D. Martinez is Program Administrator for the Mental Health Licensing Section, Division of Registrations, in the Colorado Department of Regulatory Agencies. He received his Ph.D. in public administration at the University of Colorado.

David Matza received his Bachelor's degree in 1953 from the City of New York College. In addition, he received his Master's and Doctorate degrees from Princeton. Presently, Matza is a Professor Emeritus at the University of California's Department of Sociology.

Jack McDevitt is Professor of Criminal Justice at Northeastern University in Boston. He is an expert on hate crimes. He is currently doing research on racial profiling.

Penelope A. McLorg conducts research in the area of biological anthropology. At the time she coauthored this selection, she was a Ph.D. candidate in Anthropology at Southern Illinois University, Carbondale.

Robert F. Meier is Professor of Criminal Justice at the University of Nebraska, Omaha. He has served as associate editor for numerous scientific journals, including the *American Sociological Review* and *Criminology*. He recently coauthored *Victimless Crimes?* with Gilbert Geis.

Steven F. Messner is Professor of Sociology and Chair of the Department of Sociology at the University of Albany, State University of New York. He has published widely on the social sources of crime and violence in all of the major journals in criminology and sociology. He also is coauthor of *Crime and the American Dream* (3rd ed., Wadsworth 2000) with Richard Rosenfeld.

Robert T. Michael is Dean of the Harris Graduate School of Public Policy Studies at the University of Chicago and also the Eliakim Hastings Moore Distinguished Professor there. He previously served as Director of the National Opinion Research Center.

Stuart Michaels served as Project Manager of the National Health and Social Life Survey (NHSLS) and, at the time this selection was published, was a researcher at the University of Chicago.

Jody Miller is Assistant Professor of Criminology and Criminal Justice at the University of Missouri-St. Louis. She is author of the recently published book *One of the Guys: Girls, Gangs, and Gender.* She is currently working on a book about sex tourism and prostitution in Sri Lanka.

Heather Montgomery received her Ph.D. in social anthropology from Cambridge University. She is a research fellow at the Norweigan Center for Child Research at the University of Trondheim, Norway.

Daniel Patrick Moynihan is former Senator from New York and currently a Senior Scholar at the Woodrow Wilson Center in Washington, D.C.

Steven L. Nock is Associate Professor of Sociology at the University of Virginia. He is author of *The Sociology of the Family* and co-author (with Paul Kingston) of *The Sociology of Public Issues.*

R. Kim Oates, M.D., is Professor of Pediatrics and Child Health at the University of Sydney, Australia, and Chairman of the Division of Medicine at The New Children's Hospital. He has authored or coauthored several books in the field of child abuse and pediatrics.

Mark R. Pogrebin is Professor of Criminal Justice and Director of the Criminal Justice Program in the Graduate School of Public Affairs at the University of Colorado. He received his Ph.D. in social science at the University of Iowa.

Eric D. Poole is Professor of Criminal Justice and former Associate Dean and Dean of the Graduate School of Public Affairs at the University of Colorado. He received his Ph.D. in sociology at Washington State University.

Carol Rambo Ronai teaches at the University of Memphis. Professor Ronai's research specializations include gender and qualitative methods. She is a noted expert on the social world of strip-dancing.

Richard Rosenfeld is Professor and Chair of the Department of Criminology and Criminal Justice at the University of Missouri-St. Louis. He has authored or coauthored numerous important studies, including *Crime and the American Dream* (with Steven Messner). He is one of the nation's foremost experts on homicide, focusing on the macrolevel sociological variables that drive rates up and down across cultures.

David L. Rosenhan is a Professor of Psychology and Law at Stanford University. Along with Martin Seligman, he has written *Abnormal Psychology* and *Abnormality* and has written 80 research papers.

Earl Rubington is a Professor of Sociology at Northeastern University in Boston. He has published in the field of deviance and is coauthor of *Deviance: The Interactionist Perspective* with Martin S. Weinberg.

Robert J. Sampson is Lucy Flowers Professor of Sociology at the University of Chicago. He coauthored *Crime in the Making* with John Laub and has written several important articles on social disorganization and deviance in the life course. His recent work appears in the *American Sociological Review* and the *American Journal of Sociology.*

E. Glenn Schellenberg is an Associate Professor in the Department of Psychology at the University of Toronto. Most of his research is on music cognition. Website: http://www.erin.utoronto.ca/~w3psygs.

Alan Sears teaches sociology at the University of Windsor. He is the coauthor (with Barry Adam) of the book *Experiencing HIV: Personal, Family and Work Relations.* He also writes about the changing welfare state.

Edwin S. Shneidman is Professor of Thanatology Emeritus at the University of California, Los Angeles. He is author of *The Suicidal Mind,* published by Oxford University Press.

David R. Simon is Professor of Administration of Justice at San Jose State University. He has authored or coauthored numerous books and articles and is a noted expert on white-collar deviance and social problems.

William G. Staples is Professor and Chair of the Sociology Department at the University of Kansas. He received his Ph.D. from the University of Southern California. He is author of *Castles of Our Conscience* and *Everyday Surveillance*.

Bonnie Steinbock is Professor of Philosophy at the University at Albany, State University of New York. She is author of *Life Before Birth* and has published widely on the topic of biomedical ethics.

Gene Stephens is a professor in the College of Criminal Justice at the University of South Carolina. He also is editor of *The Police Futurists* and is a contributing editor on topics in criminal justice for *The Futurist*.

Mindy Stombler received her B.S. from the University of Florida and both her M.S. and Ph.D. from Florida State University. In 1995, she accepted a position at Texas Tech University, where she teaches both graduate and undergraduate courses and is actively involved in the Faculty Senate, AAUP, and the Women's Studies Council. She also advises the new Sociology Club.

Edwin H. Sutherland (1883–1950) is one of the most famous and respected of all American criminologists. He is author of several important and groundbreaking books, including *Criminology and The Professional Fence*. He is generally regarded as one of the founders of modern American criminology. The American Society of Criminology awards its highest scholarly honor each year in his name, the Edwin H. Sutherland Award.

Gresham Sykes was Professor of Sociology at the University of Virginia until 1994. He is most famous for his drift theory of delinquency, published in 1957 with David Matza.

Diane E. Taub is Associate Professor of Sociology at Southern Illinois University, Carbondale. She is an expert on the study of stigma management, with a particular focus on eating disorders and physical disabilities.

E. Fuller Torrey, M.D., has authored or coauthored numerous books on the topic of mental health, including *The Death of Psychiatry, Schizophrenia and Civilization,* and *Surviving Schizophrenia: A Manual for Families, Consumers, and Providers.*

Jane M. Ussher was a lecturer at Sussex University at the time this selection was published. She has written other books, including *Psychology of the Female Body* and *Gender Issues in Clinical Psychology.*

Barrik Van Winkle was educated and trained at the University of Chicago. He has held numerous teaching and research positions throughout the United States, most recently at Pitzer college. He is currently a systems analyst with Academic Computing at the University of Texas at Austin.

Ann Colston Wentz is a physician who specializes in women's health issues. ✦